T0325013

Handbook of Research on Heterogeneous Next Generation Networking:
Innovations and Platforms

Stavros A. Kotsopoulos
University of Patras, Greece

Konstantinos G. Ioannou
University of Patras, Greece

INFORMATION SCIENCE REFERENCE
Hershey · New York

Director of Editorial Content:	Kristin Klinger
Director of Production:	Jennifer Neidig
Managing Editor:	Jamie Snavely
Managing Development Editor:	Kristin M. Roth
Assistant Managing Editor:	Carole Coulson
Typesetter:	Chris Hrobak
Editorial Assistant:	Rebecca Beistline
Cover Design:	Lisa Tosheff
Printed at:	Yurchak Printing Inc.

Published in the United States of America by
Information Science Reference (an imprint of IGI Global)
701 E. Chocolate Avenue, Suite 200
Hershey PA 17033
Tel: 717-533-8845
Fax: 717-533-8661
E-mail: cust@igi-global.com
Web site: http://www.igi-global.com

and in the United Kingdom by
Information Science Reference (an imprint of IGI Global)
3 Henrietta Street
Covent Garden
London WC2E 8LU
Tel: 44 20 7240 0856
Fax: 44 20 7379 0609
Web site: http://www.eurospanbookstore.com

Copyright © 2009 by IGI Global. All rights reserved. No part of this publication may be reproduced, stored or distributed in any form or by any means, electronic or mechanical, including photocopying, without written permission from the publisher.

Product or company names used in this set are for identification purposes only. Inclusion of the names of the products or companies does not indicate a claim of ownership by IGI Global of the trademark or registered trademark.

Library of Congress Cataloging-in-Publication Data

Handbook of research on heterogeneous next generation networking : innovations and platforms / Stavros Kotsopoulos and Konstantinos Ioannou, editors.

    p. cm.

  Includes bibliographical references and index.

  Summary: "This book presents state-of-the-art research, developments, and integration activities in combined platforms of heterogeneous wireless networks"--Provided by publisher.

  ISBN 978-1-60566-108-7 (hardcover) -- ISBN 978-1-60566-109-4 (ebook)

  1. Wireless communication systems. 2. Heterogeneous computing. 3. Computer networks. I. Kotsopoulos, Stavros, 1952- II. Ioannou, Konstantinos, 1975-

  TK5103.2.H3368 2009

  004'.35--dc22

                        2008016294

British Cataloguing in Publication Data
A Cataloguing in Publication record for this book is available from the British Library.

All work contributed to this book is original material. The views expressed in this book are those of the authors, but not necessarily of the publisher.

If a library purchased a print copy of this publication, please go to http://www.igi-global.com/agreement for information on activating the library's complimentary electronic access to this publication.

Editorial Advisory Board

Konstantinos Anagnostou
Technological Educational Institute of Lamia, Greece

Garmpis Aristogiannis
Technological Educational Institution of Messolonghi, Greece

John Fasoulas
Aristotle University of Thessaloniki, Greece

Spiros Fotopoulos
University of Patras, Greece

Eyh Karavatselou
University of Patras, Greece

Michael Kotzakoulakis
Michael Development Defense & Homeland Security, INFO-QUEST , Greece

Michael Koukias
University of Patras, Greece

Theodoros Latsos
Technological Educational Institute of Lamia, Greece

Athina A. Lazakidou
Universirty of Piraeus, Greece

Georgios Oikonomou
University of Patras, Greece

Zafeiris Pantelis
HELETEL Hellenic Electronic Communications, Greece

Kyprianos Papadimitriou
Technical University of Crete, Greece

Konstantinos M. Siassiakos
Universirty of Piraeus, Greece

Euripides Sotiriades
Technical University of Crete, Greece

Peter Stavroulakis
Technical University of Crete, Greece

Vasileios Stylianakis
University of Patras, Greece

Stathis Vagenas
Hellenic Airforce Academy Research Department of Hellenic Airforce, Greece

List of Contributors

Table of Contents

Section I
Core and Multiple Access Networks

Detailed Table of Contents

Section I
Core and Multiple Access Networks

Chapter I
Dzmitry Kliazovich, DIT - University of Trento, Italy
Michael Devetsikiotis, North Carolina State University, USA
Fabrizio Granelli, DIT - University of Trento, Italy

This chapter highlights the past accomplishments and promising research trends of the important topic of cross-layering in the creation of future wireless communication networks. A detailed survey of the state-of-the-art of the cross-layering is given and formal methods in the design are presented in order to provide high performance, mobility support, high resource utilization, and QoS in wireless networks.

Chapter II
Dimitris Toumpakaris, University of Patras, Greece
Jungwon Lee, Marvell Semiconductor Inc., USA

This chapter introduces the cross-layer scheduling and resource allocation for single-hop wireless systems. The necessity of these entities is analyzed by giving an approach to the characteristic of variability of the networks (i.e. the case of varying channel in a system where the transmitter and the receiver are fixed). The case of power and delay-efficient scheduling over fading Gaussian channels are examined. Moreover the cross-layer scheduling and resource allocation among many users in cellular networks, for fading multiple access and broadcast channels, for CDMA and ODMA wireless systems and multiple antenna systems are presented.

Chapter III
Prashant Pillai, University of Bradford, UK
Yim Fun Hu, University of Bradford, UK

This chapter describes the MSEC-AAA framework that allows Network Providers to authenticate and authorise users requesting multicast data, to restrict multicast content access to only authenticated users, to monitor the different multicast sessions accessed by end users and to enable flat-rate or usage based charging mechanisms to be implemented. The authors review the existing Multicast Security Mechanisms (i.e. IGAP, Gothic Multicast Architecture, L2/L3 Authentication before Join and the IETF Multicast Security Architecture). In addition they concentrate on the AAA for Multicast (i.e. the IGMPx Service Access Control Mechanism and the extension to the MSEC Architecture to support AAA). Finally, by an implemented OPNET simulation model corresponding results are taken for Test Case 1: All users input the correct credentials, Test Case 2: One user inputs the wrong credentials and the verification of the accounting mechanisms for Multicast Communications.

This chapter presents in detail the Wavelength-division multiplexing (WDM) technologies (such as Dense WDM and coarse WDM) and their recent applications in optical networks. The authors investigate the parameters affecting the increment of the bit rate in a TDM system and the methods for increasing the number of optical carriers. Moreover, they present the WDM technologies, the fundamentals of DWDM and describe the mechanism of the fiber optic transmission by explaining the entities of light sources and detectors, optical amplifiers, Multiplexers – Demultiplexers, Optical Add/Drop multiplexers and DWDM Interfaces.

This chapter addresses the main issues relating to the hybrid fiber radio technology and points out the key factors for its exploitation in current and next generation broadband networks. The performed analysis by the authors is focused on the RoF technology by examining the involved RoF architectures and deployments (RoF Techniques for Generation and Distribution of Electrical Signals, Intensity Modulation Direct Detection (IM-DD), Remote Heterodyne Detection (RHD), RoF Optical Components). Moreover the RoF Architectures and Link Deployments are examined. Their work end by giving RoF applications for NGNs and in addition they present a short demonstration on basic RoF operations.

This chapter presents the basic characteristics of the HASP-related technology. The multi-beam adaptive antenna array is a basic component of the system's RF payload. Via this array, many cellular patterns on the ground can be implemented and dynamically adjusted according to the specific telecommunication needs. Serving high-speed mobile routers requires reliable DOA estimation techniques. The author investigates the parameters affecting the coverage planning, the capacity and interference issues, the call admission control, the performed handover operational procedures and the involved network layer issues. Finally, the TCP performance issue is analyzed. It is concluded that in the transport layer, multi-cast protocols that take into account the on-board proxy functionalities of the HASPs can offer enhanced packet error rate performance.

Section II
Service Control and Quality of Service

Chapter VII

Dimitrios K. Lymberopoulos, University of Patras, Greece

This chapter is focused on the framework that is employed globally by the standardization organizations, as well as by the telecommunication operators and the third party providers, for the creation, deployment and execution of services. The author analyses the present status of the telecommunication services (i.e. additional services created by the telecom carriers and operators, bundled services offered by different telecom providers and by co-operating telecom and third party providers). Moreover, describes in detail the implementation of services using conventional networks and protocols. The need for converged services and infrastructures are given by focusing on the demanded functionality in NGNs. Finally, an NGN service architecture is described by concentrating on the features of NGN services, The major trends in development of NGN services, the presence / telepresence service [Salinas], and the home management services.

Chapter VIII

Konstantinos S. Kotsopoulos, University of Bradford, UK
Pouwan Lei, University of Bradford, UK
Yim Fun Hu, University of Bradford, UK

The Management architecture for NGNs according to the ITU-T M.3060 recommendation is presented in this chapter. Four architectural views are described, giving more emphasis on the functional architectural view of the management plane. Moreover, the Service Oriented Architecture (SOA) concept is introduced as well as the Web Service paradigm, in order to illustrate the benefits of that technology, which is the enabler of the SOA philosophy. The authors of this chapter describe in detail the NGN architecture by focusing on the evolution of the management plane. Moreover, a generic scenario using FCAPS functional sets is provided in order to show how the management functions can be applied. This scenario is an information flow diagram for network traffic control, which describes how a number of fully automated, generic management roles work together in an integrated fashion to perform a business purpose. Finally, the SOA is analyzed by considering issues relating to managing the NGNs and expose the challenges of managing NGN using SOA.

Chapter IX

Ioannis Papapanagiotou, North Carolina State University, USA
Georgios S. Paschos, VTT Digitalo, Finland

The authors of this chapter discuss and analyze three main subjects that arise within the Wireless Next Generation Networks philosophy. Mobility issues, such as the battery depletion and roaming tend to become major problems in the convergence towards 4G Networks. Quality of Service cannot be guaranteed since small and large scale fading, path loss and shadowing make the wireless channel unpredictable and thus there is no guarantee for the correct reception of the packets. The power management issue and the handovering in both WLANs and WMANs are explained. Finally, cooperative solutions and optimization focused on the heterogeneous Handover (i.e. handovers across different technology networks preformed in multiradio client platforms) are analyzed. It is noted that this type of handover is the key element of Next Generation Networks.

Chapter X

Panagiotis Kasimatis, Nokia Siemens Networks GmbH, Germany
Dimitra Varla, Ericsson Hellas S.A., Greece

This chapter refers to the most important IMS network components and describes their functionality in the integrated network. IMS is the core of Fixed-Mobile Convergence. It supports interoperability among different networks, access-awareness, security, quality of service, simple deployment of innovative and convenient multimedia services. Finally, IMS introduces the Internet to the Telecoms, combining the unique advantages of the telecom industry with an evolutional application world. The authors describe the evolution path towards the IP convergence by focusing on the functions, interfaces and the key protocols in the IMS. Finally, typical test procedures for performance evaluation of Quality of Service (QoS) in current and upcoming telecom systems are given.

The authors of this chapter present the fundamentals of positioning in various NGN network platforms. The positioning issue in the wireless networks (cellular, ad hoc and sensors) is one of the most important topics and is analyzed in detail. Fundamental positioning methods are similar regardless of network platform. The difference usually lies in positioning accuracy. This is caused by technical parameters of the particular application platform. Moreover, experiments related to positioning accuracy increase in cellular and ad hoc (sensor) networks have been performed. The authors discuss on the sources of positioning error and on the measures of positioning accuracy. Finally, simulation results are compared to corresponding theoretical results.

The authors of this chapter strongly believe that NGNs can become a key differentiator in the rapidly integrated communication industry, as long as three key imperatives for profit are met: to deliver a distinctive value to the customer, to use NGN in order to create a defensible differentiation and avoid the building of another "me too" proposition, and to provide compelling products, that are simple and intuitive to use. Actually, the authors seek to assess whether an integrated bundled network can itself become the gateway for the efficient delivery of multimedia applications and services. The Resource-Based View (RBV) theory is deployed and it is shown how Fixed-Mobile Convergence has fallen short of offering the much anticipated competitive advantage, given that it has failed to fulfil any of the pre-conditions.

Section III
The Terminal Equipment and Channel Characterization

This chapter presents the reconfigurable techniques applied to two important receiver techniques, namely, channel decoding and equalisation. It is shown that reconfigurability is a desirable feature towards the implementation of energy efficient receivers without performance sacrifices. The authors discuss on the efficient 3G turbo decoder in indoor/low range outdoor environment and on UMTS data flow issues. In the following, simulation results based on specific implemented algorithms are presented demonstrating how receiver reconfigurability is a promising method to achieve complexity/delay efficient receivers while maintaining prescribed quality of service (QoS) constraints.

Regarding equalisation, it has been shown that the equaliser length is a parameter difficult to set a priori since it heavily depends on the instantaneous channel impulse response and operating SNR. Finally, a reconfigurable structure (segmented equaliser) and a length-controlling algorithm are proposed that show the ability issues to adjust the equaliser length in an efficient way in response to changes in the channel impulse response or SNR level.

This chapter presents the current status and novel research directions in the framework of array systems. The authors analyze the MIMO techniques and the architectures for narrowband antenna arrays, the digital beamforming. The transceiver front-ends based on non linear antennas arrays are also presented. It is shown that due to their advantages over single antenna systems, they provide a capability for new applications that require large bandwidths while maintaining a high quality of service (QoS), and facilitate the coexistence of heterogeneous wireless networks.

By taking into account that the de facto wireless nature of NGNs mandates the development of efficient radio channel simulation techniques in order to rapidly and cost-effectively design and develop NGWNs, this chapter is focused on small scale fading and presents the most popular small scale fading modeling and simulation techniques for the mobile radio channel. Some popular simulation models are presented and classified, while a short discussion took place for each type of technique. Furthermore, two channel simulation tools (one statistical and one deterministic) are proposed and results are presented.

The author of this chapter investigates composite stochastic models, in which the diffuse component arises from three dimensional (3-D) multipath scattering. This case appears in dense scattering environments, in which the a category of physical or technical obstacles cause an arrival of multipath power in the elevation plane, besides that arriving in the azimuth one. Two existing types of composite models are considered. The first is a modified Loo model, where a line of sight (LOS) component, besides the diffuse one, with lognormally distributed amplitude, exists and the second is an extended Suzuki model where the process for the diffuse scattering component is multiplied by a lognormal one. The most important metrics of each model are presented, according to the stated assumptions of each one. An efficient deterministic simulation scheme is derived, which implements both models on a digital computer. Finally a curve fitting of the level crossing rate (LCR) to real world data, drawn from channel measurements, demonstrates the flexibility and the usefulness of each model.

This chapter presents a primary interested in the characterization of radio links between the transmitter and the receiver antennae. The channel is described in terms of path loss, shadowing and multipath fading. More specifically, we presented the free-space model in order to study the path loss and we referred to empirical models that offer a better description of the path loss. The shadowing component is investigated by means of the lognormal distribution and in parallel an attention is given for the description of multipath fading. The author illustrates the various categories of fading channels using appropriate parameters. Narrowband and wideband fading channels are basically these categories and include other subcategories. In the case of narrowband fading, it is quoted a significant number of statistical models. Finally, a new small-scale model is proposed and investigated in depth offering besides its novelty an application in order to achieve a better comprehension of the theory.

Section IV
Multiple Applications

Chapter XVIII

Fotis C. Kitsios, Technical University of Crete, Greece
Spyros P. Angelopoulos, Technical University of Crete, Greece
John Zannetopoulos, Hellenic Ministry of the Interior, Greece

The objective of this chapter is an in depth overview of the current status of e-government phenomenon. E-government is considered to be one of the key contributors to the development of an information society. However, the application of information and communication technologies, and especially the use of heterogeneous next generation networks in e-government should not be considered as an end in itself.

Chapter XIX

Spyros P. Angelopoulos, Technical University of Crete, Greece
Fotis C. Kitsios, Technical University of Crete, Greece
Eduard Babulak, Fairleigh Dickinson University, Canada

The authors of this chapter present their own vision on future automated environment via information cyberspace for the year 2015. The integration of automated environments and intelligent cyberspaces in light of applied robotics, logistics, smart devices, smart antennas and intelligent systems are suggested. The pervasive computing is analyzed and the issues concerning the context, e-commerce via ubiquitous internet and future home 2015 are also analyzed.

Chapter XX

Fotis C. Kitsios, Technical University of Crete, Greece
Panagiotis Tzortzatos, Technical University of Crete, Greece
Constantin Zopounidis, Technical University of Crete, Greece

This chapter provides a detailed study in order to investigate the factors that have impact on the success and failure in creating new services. The authors, analyze the nature of industry, they give the economical sizes of mainer telecommunication companies and finally provide the results from an exploratory research by analyzing a conceptual model and the four primary domains of service provider strategies.

The authors of this chapter combine the properties of different communication networks (internet, mobile and GPS) developing a marketplace model where geographically static and moving members are able to make trade transactions via auctions. More specifically, it modifies a previously proposed Internet auction model to support mobile auctions and conduct them on the basis of location-sensitive information. The model integrates location-awareness.

This chapter analyzes a set of concepts, middleware and tools, which enables people to compose UbiComp applications by combining the services offered by artifacts and infrastructure. The design of GAS-OS allows the integration of several communication protocol components, making the middleware protocol independent. Moreover, the requirements that Ubiquitous Computing systems have from wireless networks and how Heterogeneous Next Generation Networks (HNGN) can be used to support GAS compatible applications are investigated.

The authors of this chapter analyze the trends of future applications in the sector of transportation. Special attention should be given to the design parameters of such systems. The NGNs characterized by the heterogeneity of the involved wireless networks and also of the restrictions in the frequency spectra. In this case, a dynamic channel management scheme suitable to support efficiently the communication services in ubiquitous communications infrastructures for future transportation technologies is analyzed and implemented. Finally, simulation results show that the outcome performance is improved by taking into account restrictions of the instant offered traffic load.

Foreword

Networking is young. Many of us, with only a touch of grey in our hair, can easily remember the days before the World-Wide-Web, when looking up an obscure fact meant a trip to the library. We remember the infancy of email, back when we might send an email to a research colleague, but certainly not to our parents. Home networking was totally unnecessary, since the single terminal at my home connected quite nicely to the university's computer via a 1200 baud modem over a normal telephone line.

Now, scarcely a generation later, an inexpensive home network connects my laptop, computers, and digital television recorder. It is inconceivable that I would go on a trip without my laptop, and I expect Internet access in my hotel room along with the television and telephone (which I am far less likely to use). As I wait in line at the grocery store, I will probably check my email on my cell phone. I expect to be connected, to be networked, wherever I go.

As networking enters the next generation, there are a multitude of challenges. The Internet Protocol (IP), for better or worse, is firmly in place. Telecommunication providers are competing to gain market share by expanding their networks to provide data, video, and voice, while providing some guarantee of performance and quality of service. Cellular networks must co-exist with local broadband networks such as WiFi yet interact with satellite networks. Governments and businesses are struggling to adapt to this new information infrastructure.

This handbook identifies key issues that networks face as they enter the next generation and highlights promising technologies. The first section focuses on the shared core network and multiple access networks, examining modeling, security, performance, and delivery methods. The next section more deeply examines the service layer, emphasizing service control and quality of service — key components necessary for the integration of data, video, and voice. That section is complemented by the third section, which examines the terminal / antenna systems that will be necessary and their channel characteristics.

The final section is particularly far-reaching, considering the societal impact of these next-generation networks. What role does information technology play in the development of e-government? What will supplant my primitive home network a decade from now? How will the telecommunications industry change? How will the network consider my location to better support e-commerce? Do we have any hope of answering these questions in some unified framework?

Dr. Robert A. Walker
Kent State University, Computer Science Department
233 Math & Computer Science Building, Kent OH 24242 USA
Email: walker@cs.kent.edu

Considering its genesis, applications of telecommunications and networking have evolved over a rather extensive period. From the humble beginnings of the telegraph in the 1840's, this evolution continues at an ever-increasing pace. Advancements like the telephone in 1876, wireless telecommunication in the 1880's, and transatlantic wireless communication at the start of the twentieth century have planted the seed for a vision of instant, seamless global communication. The integration of voice, data, and image created the emergence of new media. With this new media came new opportunities in commerce, governance, and social networking. This handbook offers a comprehensive snapshot of the state of this new media, the technology behind it, the applications afforded by it, and the challenges to the direction in which it is currently headed.

It is difficult to predict the ultimate goal of next generation networks, or even the next 'big thing.' Current thinking suggests its direction will be some hybrid of wired and wireless networking, will facilitate new, more tightly integrated applications, and likely move us closer to perpetual real-time global telecommunications involving ultra-portable multimedia appliances. Today we see the application of some of these appliances, but with convergence comes both new opportunities and challenges. Privacy, for example, is a current issue that continues to be threatened by smart, ubiquitous networking.

When Netscape 1.0 was released in 1994, the Internet became an overnight success, as they say, 100 years in the making. Internet traffic grew exponentially in days, and phrases like 'in Internet time' offer a reflection of the increased speed with which applications and development continue to progress. Today's trends, such as Web 2.0, illustrate the continued growth of applications unimagined a very short time ago.

With such applications comes a need for ubiquitous, perpetual wireless network technologies. This handbook discusses these technologies from a series of perspectives. It starts by looking at new and emerging models to increase interoperability of multiple network architectures, moving from past goals of rapid application development to current demands for network performance. New applications will demand greater bandwidth for more devices seeking multicast capabilities. With market penetration of cellular telephones approaching half the world's population and applications on network devices rapidly converging, these are important issues. Service providers will be challenged to offer new types of service at faster speed to increasing numbers of consumers. The 'always connected lifestyle' described in the book poses daunting performance and provision challenges for next generation networks. What these connections will offer in terms of business, government, and personal lifestyle remains to be seen. One can only conclude from perusing a timeline of developments in the technology, and applications of that technology, that change will continue with a voracious appetite for new bandwidth, network appliances, and corresponding services.

This book offers a comprehensive view of new technologies, applications, and directions for next generation networks. As the Chinese curse is said to state: 'May you live in interesting times'. We do. The book discusses forthcoming challenges and issues, and offers a broad snapshot of the state and directions of wireless networking in 2008. It will be intriguing to follow the next ten years of network developments, and then to look back to this manuscript to see exactly how close our visions proved to be. If anything, I expect we will have underestimated the magnitude and complexity of the changes ahead, bold as our predictions may be. I hope you find the material in this book as comprehensive, compelling and exciting as I do.

Drew Parker, PhD, I.S.P.
Associate Professor, Information Technology
Faculty of Business Administration, Simon Fraser University
8888 University Drive, Burnaby, British Columbia, Canada   V5A1S6
Email: drew@sfu.ca

Drew Parker, *B.Comm., MBA (Calgary), PhD (Western Ontario) is an associate professor of information technology in the Faculty of Business Administration at Simon Fraser University in British Columbia, Canada. He holds the Canadian 'Information Systems Professional' designation, and is the founding member of the Management Information Systems area at Simon Fraser University. Drew teaches and publishes on Internet-related topics, focusing on networked human-computer interfaces and systems development theory and methodology. He has taught internationally face to face, online, and in hybrid applications, and has served as a director and advisor for several Internet-based businesses.*

Preface

The Heterogeneous Next Generation Networks (H-NGNs) can be defined as networks which adopt different access technologies having packet-based architecture, supporting the provision of existing and emerging broadband services through an open and converged communications infrastructure (ITU-T definition). The convergence refers to the integration of the appropriate technical operational procedures based on advanced communication and computing functionalities for supporting voice, data, video and multimedia services on a seamless basis over various wireless telecom infrastructures and platforms. The advantage of the application of these networks is bringing forward a series of innovative opportunities but also a greater array of challenges, touching upon competition, interconnection agreements and new business models. The last few years, several worldwide scientific research teams in Universities, Institutes and R&D Manufacturers have started the try to combine the heterogeneous wireless systems under the same framework.

According to the All-IP convergence issue, the last years, the involved scientists in the wireless telecommunication science, are focused on the research, development and integration of Heterogeneous Wireless Networking platforms in order to both converge the existing technology and to deliver to the users multimedia services of high intrinsic and perceived Quality of Service (QoS). Actually, this integration refers to the evolution aspects from "one network – one service" to "one network – many services". In this case, the philosophy of the combined heterogeneous wireless networking is one of the main technical features that are needed in order to develop new technologies suitable to support the demands of the Next Generation Networks (NGNs). It is noted that the researchers of the unified heterogeneous wireless networking platforms are committed to use the Internet Protocol (IP) as a core network by taking into account for each case the interoperability issues of the involved wireless networks (i.e: cellular networks, terrestrial and satellite broadcast networks, High Altitude Stratospheric Platforms and broadband access networks [WiFi, WiMAX]). Soft and hard handovering, location based techniques, stochastic channel characterization and mobility management become the main research focal point. In addition, there is a need for the multimode – multiband portable units to be transparent (seamless and inter-system roaming) to the involved heterogeneous wireless technologies of the telecom platform and also to co-op with the corresponding involved system's complexity and the dynamics from the operational procedures point of view, of the NGNs. Due to the multimedia services, the possible packet loss could be a severe problem that reduces the end-to-end QoS. In this case, special strategies should be adopted in order to force the information through different and optimal heterogeneous wireless network platform's routes by sensing the existing network's under service traffic load, the local signal level of the user's unit due to the possible occurred fading phenomena and the occurred possible Doppler drift due to the speed of motion of the user. Finally, macro-mobility and micro-mobility become very important research issue to the demanded convergence of the IP technology with the entities of the heterogeneous wireless network platform.

Based, on the advances in the heterogeneous network convergence issues that is characterized as the next major challenge in the evolution of the telecom industry, the present handbook contains a number of original and review contributions which direct the leading key technologies and technical issues in the next shortcoming years. From the technical point of view, the emphasis of the content of this work is focused on the NGN functions: the shared core network that contains the involved issues of the control and transport layer, the multiple access networks, the service layer, the terminal equipment, the multiple applications and the wireless channel characterization.

The scope of this handbook is to provide to the readers in detail the appropriate technical knowledge about NGNs with contributions received by known research teams. The reader should have a good background on telecommunication engineering.

The received technical studies are grouped into four (4) sections. A brief overall section synopsis for preliminary orientation is given in the following:

Section I deals with both the shared core network and the multiple access networks. The entities that are discussed here are: cross-layer design approaches and solutions, scheduling procedures under fading environments, security mechanisms and their inadequacies and finally, multiple access technologies comprising the heterogeneous networking environment. It is noted that the shared core network is the new converged network that has to be designed in such a way to carry voice, data, video and multimedia over the same physical network and by adopting appropriate protocol schemes. From the operator's point of view, there will be the ability for reducing the network elements and the maintenance costs. The used access technology will allow higher bandwidth demands to support telecom services and from the operator's point of view this depends on their existing infrastructure.

Dzmitry Kliazovich, Michael Devetsikiotis and Fabrizio Granelli give a detailed survey of the state-of-the-art and future directions in the usage of formal methods for cross-layer modeling and optimization of wireless networks. The cross-layer scheduling and resource allocation for wireless systems and an overview of some of the approaches and proposed algorithms are presented by Dimitris Toumpakaris and Jungwon Lee. The comparison of some of the existing security mechanisms and their inadequacies for providing efficient multicast security are analyzed by Prashant Pillai and Yim Fun Hu. Dense and coarse wavelength division multiplexing and their recent applications in optical networks are described by Nikos Merlemis and Dimitrios Zevgolis. The overview of Radio-over-Fiber technology, as an emerging infrastructure for next generation and fiber-based wireless access broadband networking are presented by Sotiris Karabetsos, Spiros Mikroulis and Athanase Nassiopoulos. Finally, Konstantinos Birkos analyzes the main technological aspects of the High Altitude Startospheric Platforms and their usage to increase the overall system's capacity under certain traffic and SNR levels by performing optimum handovering procedures.

In **Section II**, the service layer, service control and the quality of service (QoS) issues are presented. In the next generation era of the networks convergence of media information and the communication technology with the appropriate involved computing technology will lead to new wide scenarios os services having dynamic bandwidth issues. The service delivery wiil depend upon requested QoS classes. The service will allow: rapidness in the creation by using the appropriate software and control tools, mobility issues, management techniques, interoperability, security mechanisms, location-based techniques, QoS mechanisms and billing.

Dimitrios Lymberopoulos presents and analyzes the nowadays status and the fundamentals of the conventional and converged bundled and value added services, and then depicts their transformation in distributed NGNs services. The complexity and the arising problems in the NGN management plane and the introduction of a new framework that will solve many problems that operators face today, are analyzed by Konstantinos Kotsopoulos, Pouwan Lei and Yim Fun Hu. A thorough investigation of the QoS, energy conservation and mobility in 802.11 and 802.16 standards is presented by Ioannis Papapanagiotou and Georgios Paschos. The various applied mobile system architectures, showing the evolution path towards the IP convergence issue with the introduction of the IP Multimedia Subsystem (IMS) is described by Panagiotis Kasimatis and Dimitra Varla. The important issue of mobile positioning in wireless heterogeneous next generation networks is analyzed by Peter Brida, Peter Cepel and Jan Duha. Finally, Antony Ioannidis and Jiorgis Kritsiotakis seek to assess whether an integrated bundled network can itself become the gateway for the efficient delivery of multimedia applications and services. Applying, the Resource – based View theory on the recent developments in the fixed mobile convergence space, the performed analysis concurs with industry-wide skepticism and provides guidelines for the fulfillment of the NGN promise.

Section III presents the technical equipment and the wireless channel issues. It is expected that the terminal equipment in the NGNs philosophy will be capable to support multiple types of access transport functions on a simultaneous basis. This means from one hand that converged operational and communication procedures should be implemented and from the other hand new techniques in the receiver front-end should be developed. In this case diversity techniques and smart antennae will be used to receive signals in problematic geographic areas where strong fading phenomena exist. Moreover, the user equipment should enable interface adaptation to vary user requirements, including the convergence service for connection with commonly provided user interface and service platform.

Modern and future wireless communication systems such as UMTS and beyond 3G systems (B3G) are expected to support very high data rates to/from mobile users. This issue, poses important challenges on the handset design as these should be able to attain an acceptable operating bit error rate (BER) while employing a limited set of resources (i.e. low complexity, low power) and often, with tight processing delay constraints. According to the analysis of Costas Chaikalis and Felip Riera – Palou, simulation results are given demonstrating how receiver reconfigurability is a promising method to achieve complexity/delay efficient receivers while maintaining prescribed quality of service (QoS) constraints.

Multi-antenna systems incorporating smart antenna techniques present numerous advantages compared to their single antenna counterparts including capacity and range, by exploring spatial diversity. The current status and novel research directions in the framework of such array systems are presented by Apostolos Georgiadis and Carles Fernandez Prades. Furthermore, the application of nonlinear antenna arrays in the design of novel RF/microwave front-ends, that present compact, low cost and energy efficient solutions for smart antenna array applications is demonstrated.

Small-scale fading strongly affects the performance of a radio link; therefore radio channel simulation tools and models are broadly being used in order to evaluate the impact of fading. Furthermore, channel simulation tools and models are considered to be of utmost importance for efficient design and development of new products and services for Next Generation (Wireless) networks (NGNs and NGWNs). A description of the most popular and broadly accepted mobile radio channel models and simulation techniques are given by Stelios Mitilineos, Christos Capsalis and Stelios Thomopoulos, mainly with respect to small-scale fading.

The composite stochastic models, in which the diffuse component arises from three dimensional (3-D) multipath scattering are investigated by Petros Karadimas. That case occurs especially in dense scattering environments, in which the tall obstacles cause an arrival of multipath power in the elevation plane, besides that arriving in the azimuth one. Also the multipath components are assumed to arrive at the mobile receiver in specific angular sectors in the azimuth receiver's plane. The last is physically justified by multipath power blocking due to the channel obstacles (shadow fading), or/and lack of scattering objects at specific angular directions, or/and directional antennas utilization.

As a consequence of the growing interest in wireless communications systems, much effort is being devoted to the channel characterization and modelling. This is obvious since the performance depends fundamentally on the channels under consideration, so a communication system design must be preceded by the study of channel characteristics. Anastasios Papazafeiropoulos analyzes the propagation environment in which a wireless system operates. His work is focused on the characterization of radio links between the transmitter and the receiver antennae that will be modelled by randomly time-variant linear systems.

Section IV is devoted to the area of applications. The vision of "one network – many services and applications" depicts the necessity to access the appropriate technology on a neutral basis. Vertical integration of business models remain on the top of the interest area. This will lead to the evolution of the existing regulatory framework. E-government is a phenomenon of our times. E-business is becoming vital on both the private sector and the governmental Institutions. The use of Information and Communication Technology in order to change the structures and processes of government organizations is an attempt to allow the exchange of information with citizens, business and other arms of government for improving the efficiency, convenience and better accessibility of public services. The analysis performed by Fotis Kitsios, Spyros Angelopoulos and Giannis Zanetopoulos lead to answers to a number of arising questions during the implementation of the aforementioned application. In addition, Spyros Angelopoulos, Fotis Kitsios and Eduard Babulac present the current state-of-the-art in the world of telecommunications and Internet technologies, new technological trends in the Internet and automation industries, e-manufacturing, Ubiquity, convergence and the concept of the fully-automated future house. In order to survive in the marketplace, service organizations need to make the most of all of their resources in order to introduce new services to market ahead of the competition. The service innovation management issues are presented by Fotis Kitsios, Panagiotis Tzortzakos and Constantin Zopounidis. In the following, Dimitrios Emiris and Charis Marentakis analyze and match the properties of heterogeneous wireless networks and set the framework for the development of Reverse

M-auction based Marketplaces operating in a location sensitive contact with application in the freight transport market where potential suppliers are able to place bids for Less-Than-Truckload shipments. Achilles Kameas uses Gadgetware Architectural Style and presents a set of concepts, middleware and tools which enables engineers to compose Ubicomp applications by combining the services offered by artifacts and infrastructure. Finally, Ioannis Fraimis, Eduard Babulac, Konstantinos Ioannou and Athanasios Ioannou present a channel management scheme for a mobile communication system that supports services in Ubiquitous communications infrastructures for future transportation technologies and applications.

Stavros A. Kotsopoulos
Wireless Telecommunications Laboratory,
Dept. of Electrical and Computer Engineering,
University of Patras

&

Konstantinos G. Ioannou
Wireless Telecommunications Laboratory,
Dept. of Electrical and Computer Engineering,
University of Patras

June 2008

Acknowledgment

We would like to thank Mr. Angelos Koulos for acting as a technical editor—consultant and reviewing the work.

Finally, we would like to express our sincere thanks to our wives Aleka and Elina for their support and encouragement to edit the present handbook.

Section I
Core and Multiple Access Networks

Chapter I
Formal Methods in Cross Layer Modeling and Optimization of Wireless Networks:
State of the Art and Future Directions

Dzmitry Kliazovich
DIT - University of Trento, Italy

Michael Devetsikiotis
North Carolina State University, USA

Fabrizio Granelli
DIT - University of Trento, Italy

ABSTRACT

The layering principle has been long identified as a way to increase the interoperability and to improve the design of telecommunication protocols, where each layer offers services to adjacent upper layers and requires functionalities from adjacent lower ones. In the past, layering has enabled fast development of interoperable systems, but at the same time limited the performance of the overall architecture, due to the lack of coordination among layers. This issue is particularly relevant for wireless networks, where the very physical nature of the transmission medium introduces several performance limitations for protocols designed for wired networks. To overcome these limitations, a modification of the layering paradigm has been proposed, namely, cross-layer design, or "cross-layering." Several cross-layering approaches have been proposed in the literature so far. Nevertheless, little formal characterization of the cross-layer interaction among different levels of the protocol stack is available yet. A clear need exists for identifying approaches able to analyze and provide quantitative guidelines for the design of cross-layer solutions, and, more importantly, to decide, in each case, whether cross-layering represents an effective solution or not. This chapter provides a detailed survey of the state-of-the-art and future directions in the usage of formal methods for cross-layer modeling and optimization of wireless networks. The text starts by detailing the principles of layered (ISO/OSI and TCP/IP) protocol stacks as well as the cross-layer paradigm. An overview of the architectures of existing and perspective wireless networks is presented along with an analysis of the potential limitations deriving from the layering approach and detailed description of possible optimization solutions enabled by cross-layer design. Subsequent sections are devoted to the issues of modeling and optimization of wireless networks. The remaining

Copyright © 2009, IGI Global, distributing in print or electronic forms without written permission of IGI Global is prohibited.

sections cover performance optimization as well as architecture optimization (specifically in terms of signaling). The chapter ends with a summary and outlines about future directions of research on the topic.

INTRODUCTION

ISO/OSI and TCP/IP Protocol Stacks Principles

Currently, design of network architectures is based on the layering principle, which provides an attractive tool for designing interoperable systems for fast deployment and efficient implementation.

ISO/OSI model (Jain, 1993) was developed to support standardization of network architectures using the layered model. The main concepts motivating layering are the following:

- Each layer performs a subset of the required communication functions
- Each layer relies on the next lower layer to perform more primitive functions
- Each layer provides services to the next higher layer
- Changes in one layer should not require changes in other layers

Such concepts were used to define a reference protocol stack of seven layers, going from the physical layer (concerned with transmission of an unstructured stream of bits over a communication channel) up to the application layer (providing access to the OSI environment).

Services between adjacent layers expressed in terms of primitives and parameters:

- Primitives, which specify function to be performed (4 primitives are defined: REQUEST, INDICATION, RESPONSE, CONFIRMATION)
- Parameters, to pass data and control information

A protocol at a given layer is implemented by a (software, firmware, or hardware) entity, which communicates with other entities (on other networked systems) implementing the same protocol by Protocol Data Units (PDUs). A PDU is built by payload (data addressed or generated by an entity at a higher adjacent layer) and header (which contains protocol information). PDU format as well as service definition is specified by the protocol at a given level of the stack.

The same concepts are at the basis of the de-facto standard protocol stack on the Internet, namely the TCP/IP protocol stack (Murhammer & Murphy, 1998).

The main advantage deriving from the layering paradigm is the modularity in protocol design, which enables interoperability and improved design of communication protocols. Moreover, a protocol within a given layer is described in terms of functionalities it offers, while implementation details and internal parameters are hidden to the remainder layers (the so-called "information-hiding" property).

The Cross-Layering Paradigm

Standardization of layered protocol stacks has enabled fast development of interoperable systems, but at the same time limited the performance of the overall architecture, due to the lack of coordination among layers. This issue is particularly relevant for wireless networks, where the very physical nature of the transmission medium introduces several performance limitations (including time-varying behavior, limited bandwidth, severe interference and propagation environments). As a consequence, the performance of higher layer protocols (e.g., TCP/IP), historically designed for wired networks, is severely limited.

To overcome such limitations, a modification of the layering paradigm has been proposed, namely, *cross-layer design*, or "cross-layering." The core idea is to maintain the functionalities associated to the original layers but to allow coordination, interaction and joint optimization of protocols crossing different layers.

Several cross-layering approaches have been proposed in the literature so far (Toumpis & Goldsmith, 2003; Pollin, Bougard, & Lenoir, 2003; Chen, Low, & Doyle, 2005; Lin & Shroff, 2005).

In general, on the basis of available works on the topic, two approaches to cross-layering can be defined:

- **Weak cross-layering:** Enables interaction among entities at different layers of the protocol stack; it thus represents a generalization of the adjacency interaction concept of the layering paradigm to include "non-adjacent" interactions.
- **Strong cross-layering:** Enables joint design of the algorithms implemented within any entity at any level of the protocol stack; in this case, individual features related to the different layers can be lost due to the cross-layering optimization. Potentially, strong cross-layer design may provide higher performance at the expense of narrowing the possible deployment scenarios and increasing cost and complexity.

An alternative notation is "evolutionary approach" for the "weak cross-layering" and "revolutionary approach" for the "strong cross-layering" (Aune, 2004)

Nevertheless, no formal characterization of the cross-layer interaction among different levels of the protocol stack is available yet, with the exception of (Vadde & Syrotiuk, 2004), where the impact of different layers is studied in order to optimize service delivery in mobile ad-hoc networks, and (Hui & Devetsikiotis, 2006), where the authors introduced a metamodeling approach to study cross-layer scheduling in wireless local area networks.

A clear need is thus emerging for identifying approaches able to analyze and provide guidelines for the design of cross-layer solutions, and, even more important, to decide whether cross-layering represents an effective solution or not.

In this scenario, it should be underlined, the authors partially share some of the insights provided in (Kawada & Kumar, 2005), where it is clearly evidenced that cross-layering has advantages as well as limitations that should be properly considered against the more common layering approach. In particular, higher and tighter integration among layers could generate unexpected or unforeseen results in terms of overall system behavior.

In addition, a relevant related issue which is not currently addressed in the literature is control signaling, as cross-layer design implies coordination and information exchange within a single protocol stack (possibly through proper interfaces) or even across links or networks. Given its importance, a section at the end of chapter is devoted to an analysis of candidate schemes to fulfill the crucial task of signaling in cross-layer architectures.

OVERVIEW OF WIRELESS NETWORKS

Existing Architectures

In the following paragraphs, a brief classification of wireless networks is provided, based on the target coverage area.

Wireless Wide Area Network (WWAN). WWANs offer connections through broad geographical areas with the use of multiple antenna sites (cells). Current WWANs are primarily based on second generation (2G) cellular technologies such as GSM and CDMA (Lee, 2005). The third generation (3G) cellular networks were envisioned to replace 2G technologies, but suffered from the enormous costs for spectrum licenses as well as difficulties in identifying proper killer applications. Currently 3G technologies correspond to a smaller slice of the overall cellular market than 2G, with a high penetration evidenced in Asia Pacific and North America regions (Portio Market Research, 2007).

Wireless Metropolitan Area Network (WMAN). WMANs represent a good alternative to optical fiber technologies which enable commutations between multiple locations within a metropolitan area. The key wireless technology considered for WMANs is based on IEEE 802.16 standard (IEEE Std. 802.16, 2001), which is also referred as Worldwide Interoperability for Microwave Access (WiMAX). Initially, WiMAX technology was designed as a metropolitan backbone for interconnection of smaller networks or fixed individual users requiring broadband access. This is often referred to as Fixed WiMAX and corresponds to IEEE 802.16 finally approved in 2004. Then, Mobile WiMAX has been developed – an air interface modification aimed more at end-users, rather than small networks, providing the support for nomadic mobility. Mobile WiMAX is based on IEEE 802.16e standard amendment (IEEE Std. 802.16e, 2005) approved in 2005.

Wireless Local Area Network (WLAN). WLAN technologies provide connectivity to the end-user terminal devices covering a small geographic area, like corporate or campus building. The IEEE 802.11 (IEEE Std. 802.11, 1999), commonly known as WiFi, became the de facto standard for WLAN networking. While the original WiFi specification approved in 1997 aimed at 1 or 2 Mb/s at the physical layer, later physical air interface modifications increased the transmission rate: 802.11a (1999) for up to 54 Mb/s in 5GHz band, 802.11b (1999) for up to 11 Mb/s in 2.4 GHz band, 802.11g (2003) of up to 54 Mb/s in 2.4 GHz band, and 802.11n (expected in 2008) for up to 250 Mb/s in both 5GHz and 2.4 GHz bands. In WiFi, mobile stations establish connections to wireless access points which serve as a bridge between the radio link and a wired backbone network. As an option, in case mobile stations are located within the transmission range of each other and no network backbone access is required, an ad hoc network may be created.

Wireless Personal Area Network (WPAN). WPANs are designed to connect user devices located within personal communication range which is typically considered of up to 10 meters from a person. Bluetooth (Mc-Dermott-Wells, 2005) is a leading industry standard for WPANs. Nowadays, WPANs are supported by mobile phones, PDAs, laptops and other wireless devices. Nevertheless, the main application for Bluetooth remains wireless headset connection.

A promising technology in the WPAN scenario is based on Ultra-wideband (UWB) radio communications (Fontana, 2004), potentially able to provide 1Gb/s links over short range. UWB PAN is specified in IEEE 802.15.4a standard (De Nardis & Di Benedetto, 2007) completed in March 2007.

Performance Metrics for Optimization

Nowadays, most of the leading wireless technologies are widely deployed at the last mile – connecting end-user to the core of the network, and follow infrastructure network organization, where wireless links are mostly used to connect end user equipment to the base station which in turn provides connectivity to the fixed network.

Indeed, last mile is the most critical issue in today's network architectures. The characteristics of the last mile links often determine the performance of the overall network representing the actual capacity bottleneck on the entire path from the data source to the destination and influencing the characteristics of traffic patterns flowing through the network.

In particular, wireless networks suffer from several performance limitations, in some cases related to excessive burden deriving from the layering paradigm employed for the TCP/IP protocol stack design. In fact, TCP/IP originally designed for wired links (characterized by high bandwidth, low delay, low packet loss probability - high reliability, static routing, and no mobility) performs poorly in wireless domain (Balakrishnan, Padmanabhan, Seshan, & Katz, 1997; Xylomenos, Polyzos, Mahonen, & Saaranen, 2001)

The main reasons for poor performance are in the very nature of wireless technologies and come from the advances their enable:

Mobility. One of the main advances offered by wireless networks corresponds to user terminal mobility which allows network access from different locations while maintaining uninterrupted service. However, mobility - an essential requirement for network provisioning on anytime, anywhere basis — comes at a price.

While most of the existing wireless technologies evolve into a converged All-IP network (Newman, 2004) the underlying TCP/IP protocol stack reference model (Murhammer & Murphy, 1998) designed for the fixed Internet does not allow smooth adaptation for the mobility mainly due to its layering model (Chan & Ramjee, 2002; Alfredsson, Brunstrom, & Sternad, 2006).

Traditionally, mobility management solutions resided within a single layer, with a logical division into network (layer-3) layer solutions and link (layer-2) layer solutions (Henderson, 2003). However, the decision for which layers should be involved in order to provide efficient mobility support represents a hot discussion topic (Eddy, 2006; Le, Fu, & Hogrefe, 2006). What becomes clear is that the solutions implemented at different layers are more complementary to each other rather than alternative. While some layers appear to handle mobility better than others, it becomes clear that mobility support cannot be implemented within a single layer in an efficient way, and thus requires cross-layer awareness and cooperation as proposed in (Le, Fu, & Hogref, 2006).

Similar conclusion is currently driving the design of next generation cellular network followed by 3GPP group which identifies cross-layering as the approach able to reduce handoff (handover) latency (3GPP, TR 25.913) fitting the requirements of many streaming, interactive, and VoIP applications.

Typical solutions aims at handoff latency reduction such as (Wu, Cheng, Huang, & Ma, 2001) and (El Malki, 2007) suggest notifying the network layer even before the handoff is completed at the link layer. This allows network layer to initiate and perform several handoff procedures in parallel.

The differentiation into pre-handoff and post-handoff link layer messages is implemented by Tseng et al. in (Tseng, Yen, Chang, & Hsu, 2005). These messages are used along with cross-layer network topology information. The topology information includes logical and physical location of neighboring access points, the association between them, and location and movement direction of the mobile node, and used primarily to reduce probing delay and improve routing of redirected traffic.

In (Hsieh, Zhou, & Seneviratne, 2003), the authors propose S-MIP (Seamless Mobile IP) architecture aimed at handling seamless handoff for Mobile IP. The main intelligence is added with an introduction of Decision Engine (DE) which makes handoff decisions for its network domain justified on the basis of the global view of nodes connection states and their movement patterns (which allow a certain degree of prediction).

Data transfer performance in wireless networks suffers from several performance limitations such as limited capacity, high propagation delay, static routing, and high error rate. High bit error rates (BERs), which vary from 10^{-3} up to 10^{-1} for wireless links while staying between 10^{-8} to 10^{-6} for wired channels, has high impact on data transfer performance using TCP protocol, which supports the vast majority of Internet connections (Miller, Thompson, & Wilder, 1997; Fraleigh, Moon, Lyles, Cotton, Khan, Moll, Rockell, Seely, & Diot, 2003). In general, such error rates greatly degrade the performance of TCP due to the additive increase multiplicative decrease (AIMD) congestion control, which treats all losses as congestion losses and thus underestimates the actual capacity provided by the network. Moreover, the conducted research revealed that it is not always possible to compensate undesirable characteristics optimizing bit error rate at the physical, link layers or producing transport protocol adaptation to high error rates if done separately (Granelli, Kliazovich, & da Fonseca, 2005). However, interlayer communication, wireless medium awareness, and joined optimization are envisioned as essential components in the field of potential solutions.

Most of them aimed at data transfer improvement in wireless networks are based on either tight interaction between the link and physical layers, or implement techniques enabling TCP layer awareness of the wireless link it operates on. For example, the collided packets may not be discarded immediately but stored in memory and then combined with future retransmissions triggered at the link layer for the purpose of joint packet decoding (Tsatsanis, Zhang, & Banerjee, 2000). This technique, defined as network-assisted diversity multiple access (NDMA), exploits diversity of network resources leading to throughput performance benefits coming at the expense of increased receiver complexity.

The techniques bringing awareness of the physical medium into TCP are typically implemented using different explicit notification techniques. One of the first proposals in this category presented in (Ramakrishnan, Floyd, & Black, 2001) is Explicit Congestion Notification (ECN). It reserves a specific bit inside the IP header which brings indication of network congestion back from a router to the sender node. This allows TCP sender to justify its congestion control actions differentiating between congestion and link error related losses. The functionality of other explicit notification schemes is similar to ECN. In this way, in Explicit Bad State Notification (EBSN) (Bikram, Bakshi, Krishna, Vaidya, & Pradhan, 1997) the sender is notified by the remote host of the bad state experienced on the link in order to reset retransmission timeouts, while in Explicit Rate Change Notification (ERCN) (Wang & Lee, 2005) is allowed to control TCP outgoing rate while accommodating delay-sensitive traffic needs. In (Sarolahti, Allman, & Floyd, 2007) Sarolahti et al. proposed explicit signaling algorithm allowing network routers to increase TCP startup performance over high-speed network paths.

Having the core algorithms controlling TCP functionality such as congestion control and error recovery implemented at the sender node turns the design of optimization algorithms towards explicit notification solutions which usually demonstrate considerable performance advantages. However, the main drawback for such solutions is the requirement for the modification of TCP sender code traditionally implemented inside the operating system kernel, making the deployment of these schemes difficult on the wide scale. This drawback opens the possibility for receiver-side-only modifications or cross-layer schemes limiting protocol stack modification to below IP layer that can be implemented at the driver level or inside the interface card.

One of such schemes called ARQ proxy is presented in (Kliazovich, Granelli, Redana, & Riato, 2007; Kliazovich, Ben Halima, & Granelli, 2007). It aims at overhead reduction deriving from the multilayer ARQ employed at the link and transport layers. To this aim, it introduces ARQ proxy at the base station and ARQ client at the mobile node agents which substitute the transmission of the TCP ACK packet with a short link layer request sent over the radio link. As a result, ARQ proxy releases radio link resources required for TCP ACK packet transmission - which can be used by other transmitting stations.

Energy efficiency. A mobile terminal equipment relies on battery power, which imposes the requirement for energy efficient operation in order to increase the device lifetime. Traditionally, power efficient design attempted to increase capacity of the battery and decrease the amount of energy consumed by the terminal. However, physical design limitations of battery power units and high energy consumption of wireless interfaces position the main challenge of energy efficient communications into the system management domain. The main focus is devoted into joined optimization of the entire protocol stack increasing the "sleep mode" duration for terminal transceiver – the mode with power consumption of at least an order to magnitude lower with the respect to terminal transmitting or receiving modes (Feeney & Nilsson, 2001), at the same moment operating a tradeoff with efficiency of network communications such as connectivity, data routing, scheduling, and others.

Current cellular networks include power efficient design implemented across several protocol layers. These techniques include proper modulation chosen at the physical layer, channel dependant scheduling, cross-layer resource allocation schemes (Jiang, Zhuang, & Shen, 2005), emitting power control, smart management of idle and sleep modes – all involve tight cooperation between the mobile node and the base station, which is performed at different layers of the protocol stack (Lee, 2005). This fact positions cellular networks among the leaders of energy efficient technologies, with a typical battery life for the mobile terminal of several days.

In WiFi networks, similar optimization steps are being proposed, like Feeney et al. (Feeney & Nilsson, 2001) suggest facing the problem of energy efficiency jointly at the link and network layers, or Singh et al. (Singh, Woo, & Raghavendra, 1998) pave the way for power-aware routing proposals by defining routing metrics which include terminal and transmission power awareness.

The problem of maintaining network connectivity with terminals spending most of the time in "sleep" mode is proposed to be solved with prediction of movements in (Dong & Yau, 2005) which involves cooperation between layers 1-3.

At the transport layer, the study shows that most of the widely used TCP modifications nowadays do not satisfy all the requirements in an energy constrained network environment (Zorzi & Rao, 2001). This requires the energy efficiency to become a part of TCP protocol design. Such a design approach is followed by Ci et al. in TCP Quick Timeout (TCP-QT) proposal (Ci, Turner, & Sharif, 2003). TCP-QT aims at increasing the "sleep" mode duration by introducing a link layer feedback triggering fast retransmission before retransmission timeout occurrence.

While most of the previously mentioned solutions require cross-layer interactions between two or at most three layers the authors of (Eberle, Bougard, Pollin, & Catthoor, 2005) present a complete methodology for the design of cross-layer solutions aimed at energy efficient communications, including definition of the scenario, performance-cost modeling, simulation, analysis of dependency and other which provide systematic exploration, problem partitioning and defining the cross-layer interactions that are required for optimal energy efficiency of the system.

Quality of Service (QoS). One of the first approaches for QoS provisioning, IntServ (Braden, Clark, & Shenker, 1994), was based on the idea of reservation of network resources through the entire path. The fact that IntServ required support from all network routers on the path, and it did not scale to large networks due to the requirement to maintain large number of reservations is overcame in DiffServ approach (Kilkki, 1999) which still requires support from network routers but instead of circuit-like reservation over entire network path it operates on packet basis. In DiffServ, each packet is marked with QoS requirements by the ordinator which are typically satisfied by using multi-queue processing techniques at network routers favoring higher priority. The QoS requirements are specified via Type of Service (TOS) field of the IPv4 header. However, despite of the introduction of TOS fields since IPv4 was developed (RFC 791, 1981), most of the Internet routers do not handle it. The DiffServ, being a network layer solution, provides good level of performance in wired network. However, additional medium-dependant techniques are required in the wireless domain.

The most widely considered QoS solution for wireless networks is in combination of layer-3 approaches aimed at QoS support on a network-wide scale with layer-2 approaches providing QoS at the wireless link connecting mobile users to the network core. This approach is realized in WiFi networks in IEEE 802.11e amendment (IEEE Std. 802.11e, 2005), and WiMAX networks (IEEE Std. 802.16e, 2005).

In (Firoiu, Le Boudec, Towsley, & Zhang, 2002), Firoiu et al. provide a comprehensive survey of available QoS mechanisms from technical as well as from the business perspective, demonstrating that no complete QoS solution can be performed within a single protocol layer. In (Zhu, Li, Chlamtac, & Prabhakaran, 2004), the authors motivate the need for cross-layer interactions for QoS provisioning in mobile networks in order to avoid duplicating signaling efforts.

QoS provisioning and reduced energy consumption represents a challenging issue in battery equipped mobile terminals. Generally, ensuring better QoS leads to an increase in energy consumption – the result of longer waiting times. Solutions to this problem typically involve power-aware scheduling and QoS provisioning (Chen, Lv, & Zheng, 2004; Kozat, Koutsopoulos, & Tassiulas, 2006; Zhou, McKinley, & Sadjadi, 2004; Huang, & Letaief, 2007) involving tight cooperation between physical and link layers with QoS requirements specified and controlled at the application layer.

Another type of cooperation could involve transport, link and physical layers, the example of which is presented in (Narula-Tam, Macdonald, Modiano, & Servi, 2004). This scheme implements dynamic resource allocation strategy synchronizing bandwidth allocation requests with TCP window evolution.

In (Tian, Bose, Law, & Xiao, 2005), the authors propose CLA-QOS approach, which involves cooperation between application, network, and link layers of the protocol stack. The application layer at the destination monitors level of QoS constraints satisfaction in terms of packet loss ratio and feeds it back to the source node, letting the latter to adapt traffic class. The network layer is evolved into end-to-end delay measurement of network paths, which is provided to the link layer scheduler performing traffic differentiation according to the urgency factor.

Table 1 presents a summary of the characteristics of the main wireless network standards, aimed at underlining the common features and similarities among them and outlining the level of cross-layer design penetration. The table underlines the existence of a tradeoff between mobility, data transfer performance, energy consumption, and quality of service. One of such examples is presented in (Zhou, McKinley, & Sadjadi, 2004) where authors balance between QoS and energy efficiency. However, the general trend shows that network performance and functionalities are closely related with the level of penetration of cross-layer techniques into the design of different wireless systems.

MODELING OF CROSS-LAYER INTERACTIONS

This section provides and overview of modeling techniques that can be employed to analyze cross-layer interactions, in order to outline the current scenario and possible future approaches.

Need for Formal, Quantitative Modeling

The cross-layer approach to system design derives from enabling *interaction* among protocols operating at different layers of the protocol stack in order to provide improvement in terms of some performance metric.

Quantifying the effect of these interactions is very important in order to be able to systematically relate such interactions to system outcomes and be able to quantify the decision to take such interactions into account – using a cost-benefit analysis, so that the benefits outweigh the cost of additional complexity and "layer violation". This aspect has been generally neglected in the area of wireless networks, where the discussion has been mostly qualitative or architectural, assuming the more the cross-layer interactions, the better the performance.

Indeed, more generally, a crucial issue is to identify methodologies to systematically analyze and provide systematic *guidelines* for the design of cross-layer solutions, and, even more important, to decide beforehand whether cross-layering represents an effective solution or not. However, little or no formal characterization of the cross-layer interaction among different levels of the protocol stack is available yet.

This chapter, and this section in particular, aim at providing an overview of potential frameworks that can provide suitable tools for the systematic, quantitative modeling of cross-layer interactions. As is correctly pointed out in (Kawada, & Kumar, 2005), there is a need for a "holistic" approach to understanding and utilizing cross-

Table 1. Characteristics of leading wireless technologies

Technology	Mobility	Data transfer performance		Energy consumption/ battery life	Quality of Service	Cross-Layer Design Penetration
		Physical rate	Spectrum efficiency			
Wireless Personal Area Network (WPAN)						
Bluetooth (2.0)	Direct communication	Up to 2.1 Mb/s	2 bit/s/Hz	Hours	High (dedicated channels)	Low
UWB		675 Mb/s	1.35 bit/s/Hz		n/a	
Wireless Local Area Network (WLAN)						
802.11b	Nomadic subnet roaming	11 Mbps	0.55	Hours	Low (Best effort or 802.11e if employed)	Low
802.11a/g		54 Mbps	2.7			
802.11n		250 Mbps	7.22			
Wireless Metropolitan Area Network (WMAN)						
Fixed WiMAX (802.16-2004)	Fixed	10 Mb/s (max up to 70 Mb/s)	3.75 bit/s/Hz	n/a	Normal (4 traffic classes, but not supported for network wide connections)	Medium
Mobile WiMAX (802.16e-2005)	Pedestrian Mobility	2-3 Mb/s (max up to 15 Mb/s)	2 bit/s/Hz	Hours		
Wireless Wide Area Network (WWAN)						
2G (GSM)	Seamless global roaming	9.6 – 57.6 Kb/s	0.52 bit/s/Hz	Days	High (dedicated channels, voice over data priority)	High
3G (UMTS)		384 Kb/s (mobile) 2Mb/s (stationary)	Up to 2.88 bit/s/Hz			
3G LTE		100 Mb/s	5 bit/s/Hz			

layering. The subject of systematic study of cross-layering from a "system theoretic" point of view and the closest available to a holistic view, is found in the work of Law and Doyle, for example (Chiang, Low, Calderbank, & Doyle, 2007). The authors follow a top-down approach to set "holistic" objectives as opposed to the wide-spread "bottom up" and "ad hoc" identification and usage of cross-layer formulations on a case by case empirical basis.

Doyle's "NUM" methodology allows the formulation of systematic cross-layering as a "decomposition" of an optimization problem, and thus begins to address the important issues of modularity versus optimality, also other tradeoffs including signaling and locality.

An issue still remaining is **how** to accomplish or guide this decomposition, which is somehow assumed by Doyle/Low. Other than some mention to "graph theory" we have not seen much else in order to address this. Therefore, we describe here and instantiate the need and some proposed ways to quantify interactions, allowing eventually the grander formulation as a decomposed optimization problem, but with quantifiable parameters, factors and effects.

System Design Issues

Utility

Network design is based on goals to achieve suitable performance levels to support the specific applications the network is aimed at.

The "raw" performance metrics e_i will typically be incorporated into utility functions U(e) that express better how valuable the performance metric is to the system owner or user. Examples include functions of the system throughput, overall delay or jitter, and system capacity (number of possible subscribers or streams). The utility function can have several forms and shapes (see for example, Scott Shenker's categories and diagrams for real time, elastic and other types (Shenker, 1995). The exact functional form of the utility and resulting objective function are less important than their *curvature* (often convex to denote a certain "saturation") and their ability to preserve a *relative* ordering of the engineering alternatives, to enable ultimate design decisions.

In some cases, a "negative" version of the utility or a *penalty* function may instead be available with the model; this can be a function quantifying the degree of dissatisfaction resulting from a performance metric being under or over a desirable level or "service level agreement" (SLA).

Prices

In such a formal economic model, the controllable parameters (factors or resources) will also likely to have assigned to them actual (literal) or virtual prices, say \$$a$ per unit of design parameter D X and \$$b$ per unit of T Y in the aforementioned case study, resulting in an overall monetary (or virtual) cost for each design pair (*TX, DY*):

P(X, Y) = $aX + bY$

The function P(X, Y) can also be non-linear, accounting for volume discounts or other saturation effects.

System Optimization

Based on the utility and pricing model, the overall system design would then be affected by optimal design considerations, including

- Performance/utility targets (e.g., U(e) > u)
- Resource constraints (e.g., $D < d$, $T < t$)
- Performance/utility maximization (e.g., max U(e))
- Max-min and fairness performance targets
- Service level agreement satisfaction via penalty function minimization

Analytical, numerical or simulation-based methods could be used to achieve the design goals, either up front (i.e., parameter optimization), or on-line (i.e., optimal control).

In the cross layer model that we have been considering, all such approaches would be utilizing the cross layer partial derivatives described previously, calculated, approximated or simulated, only now obtained for the requisite utility function U(e), or the composite "net" function U($e(D,T)$) – P(D,T).

Design Guidelines

Results achieved during the system optimization phase can then be employed to define guidelines for system design. More in detail, by employing the proposed framework, it is possible to select:

- The (near-)optimal operating point of the system (direct consequence of the optimization process);
- The proper cross-layer interactions to enable (based on sensitivity of the system with respect to specific design or operating parameter values);
- The appropriate signaling architecture to employ (allowing the designer to identify the set of parameters and measurements to use).

Cross-Layer Modeling Techniques

System modeling should be based on mathematical analysis (e.g., Markov analysis, queueing or numerical approximations). However, closed form mathematical expressions are often unattainable for real systems, reinforcing the need for the use of *empirical* methods that include testing, emulation and computer simulation.

This section provides a survey about existing modeling techniques that can be applied to analyze cross-layer interactions.

Meta-modeling, Response Surface Modeling and sensitivity analysis using simulated or actual laboratory testing results.

Quantifying the Cross-Layer Interactions

Independent of the actual modeling approach employed, cross layer interactions can be quantified by defining factors (*parameters*) and effects (*measurements*) across layers, in a way that is common in system science and operations research. In such framework, a wireless system is assumed to be characterized by vectors of "factors" (controllable parameters), across all the layers:

$$\overline{p}^{TOT} = \left[\overline{p}^1 \mid \overline{p}^2 \mid ... \mid \overline{p}^7 \right]$$

and by performance metrics ("effects") across all the layers:

$$e_i = f_i \left(\overline{p}^{TOT} \right), i = 1, ..., I$$

The sensitivity of the system response and the interactions among factors, within and across layers, can then be captured naturally by use of partial derivatives of the output with respect to the various parameters and their combinations:

$$\frac{\partial f_k}{\partial p_i^j} \text{ and } \frac{\partial^2 f_k}{\partial p_i^j \partial p_l^m}$$

at least over a "grid" of interesting coordinates, where p_i^j is the i-th parameter at layer j. Using such quantitative tools, one can then (near) optimize the performance e_i with respect to a subset of p^{TOT} under general constraints by using steepest ascent, stochastic approximation, ridge analysis, stationary points, etc. (Box & Draper, 1987; Kleijnen, 1998). Alternatively, one may wish to make *local* steps or decisions at a given operating point, in the context of game-theoretic or other economic-driven adjustments. Or one may wish to dynamically control the response f_k over time (optimal control). We provide some discussion in the following sections.

The function $f_k()$ can be analytically calculated or empirically estimated, and possibly approximated by a linear or higher order function, depending on degree of approximation desired and the tractability of the particular system.

Based on the level of interaction (for example, normalized sensitivity combined with statistical or numerical accuracy), one can subsequently assign varying degrees of "weak" versus "strong" cross layer interactions and identify to what degree a performance metric f_k needs to be jointly maximized with respect to e_{i_1} and e_{i_2}, with i_1 and i_2 in different layers. And, consistent with previous sections, if layers i_1 and i_2 are adjacent, the degree of cross layer interaction can be categorized differently from the case where i_1 and i_2 are further apart in the layer stack.

The quantitative degree of cross-layer interaction and sensitivity will also guide one to a decision of whether to actually take a specific interaction into account or not, since cross layer designs have implicit disadvantages in terms of cost and complexity.

ECLSA: Experimental Cross-Layer Sensitivity Analysis

When the function $f_k()$ cannot be analytically calculated, which is quite common, the system designers utilize empirical methods, including emulation, laboratory testing and computer simulation. These methods provide statistical estimates of f_k which are used instead of the "actual" response values. In a cross-layer design setting we advocate the estimation of the partial derivatives discussed in the previous section, which amounts to performing systematic cross-layer sensitivity analysis with respect to p_i^j, the i-th parameter at layer j. This can be done via several methods (see (Rubinstein & Melamed, 1998) and numerous references therein):

a.   "Naïve" estimation of gradients and Hessians via finite-difference approximations $\Delta f_k / \Delta p_i^j$, also called "crude Monte Carlo" (CMC) techniques.

b.   By use of Infinitesimal Perturbation Analysis, IPA, which is related to the interchange of the expectation and the differentiation operators.

c.   By use of accelerated sensitivity analysis via simulation. Such techniques are referred to as "modern simulation" techniques and are variations of the Score Function (SF) method.

d.   Gradient estimation combined with optimization, via stochastic approximation and via non-gradient methods like Simulated Annealing (see (Devetsikiotis & Townsend, 1993) and references therein).

A family of relevant composite approaches combine some of the methods (a)-(d) with *variance reduction*, making use of the technique of *Importance Sampling* (IS). Such techniques are valuable when the performance metrics targeted involve rare events and high variance estimates. IS is a variance reduction method that modifies the sampling distribution utilized in order to induce an increased frequency of the relevant "important events" and subsequently uses a weight function (equivalent to a likelihood ratio) to make the estimates statistically unbiased (Heidelberger, 1995).

The Fast Importance Sampling based Traffic Engineering (FISTE) approach proposed in (Zhang, Huang, & Devetsikiotis, 2006) extrapolates the end-to-end probability of traffic overflow on a network path, as a function of the mean rates of the traffic flows entering the network. When FISTE is combined with a heuristic search algorithm such as Simulated Annealing, we can estimate the required reductions in those mean rates so that multiple end-to-end overflow requirements are satisfied in a network. We believe FISTE has great potential in cross-layer settings as well.

CLRSM: Cross-Layer Response Surface Modeling

a   Response Surface Methodology

Response surface methodology (RSM), first introduced by Box and Wilson (Box & Wilson, 1951), is a set of statistical and mathematical techniques that can be used to find optimal settings of parameters (usually called "factors") that minimize or maximize the objective function (also called the "response"). RSM can also be applied to stochastic simulation models, treating the system being evaluated as a black box (Donohue, Houck, & Myers, 1995).

Using RSM, first one uses a series of experiments (in the lab or by simulation) to estimate the approximate local shape of the response, called the "response surface". This is done by "fitting" first or higher-order polynomial (and other) models to the responses estimated by the experiments (see for example our (Granelli, Kliazovich, Hui, & Devetsikiotis, 2007).

This general modeling framework fits very well the formal cross-layer multi-parameter model of interactions that we introduced previously, for the typical real system cases where a closed-form performance function is not available. In these cases, we advocate its use as a formal "cross-layer response surface modeling" approach, CLRSM for short. Specifically, in this case, one locally estimates cross-layer sensitivities such as:

$$\frac{\partial f_k}{\partial p_i^j} \text{ and } \frac{\partial^2 f_k}{\partial p_i^j \partial p_l^m}$$

via CLRSM, i.e., experimental estimation of f_k w.r.t. to parameters p_i^j *across the layers*, and thus constructing a cross-layer response surface. Subsequently, optimization can also be performed by moving along the steepest decent direction on the cross-layer response surface. Case studies were performed with validating experiments in (Hui & Devetsikiotis, in press; Granelli, Kliazovich, Hui , & Devetsikiotis, 2007).

b.   Importance Sampling Accelerated Cross-Layer Response Surface Modeling

Fast and accurate performance evaluation can help not only in understanding the behavior of the system during development (i.e., cross-layer design), but also in capacity planning and operational tuning during deployment (i.e., cross-layer *control*). However, the efficiency of the overall procedure becomes particularly important when dealing with performance measures such as probabilities of overload, outage probabilities or packet loss ratios that may be *very small* when the system is designed well.

For this we propose to combine powerful variance reduction techniques such as Importance Sampling (Heidelberger, 1995; Hsu & Devetsikiotis, in press) briefly mentioned previously, with the CLRSM approach, into an automatic cross-layer framework that can be used to optimize system performance indicators in an on-line or off-line fashion. For optimization, we advocate the use of CLRSM for its simplicity and its ability to describe the cross-layer behavior of a system in a whole *neighborhood* of cross layer parameter values. And simultaneously, in order to efficiently obtain the response data for different parameter settings, a reusable Importance Sampling (IS) simulation or testing method can be applied. We described this novel method based on a combined Response Surface and Importance Sampling (RS-IS) framework in (Hsu & Devetsikiotis, 2007) and we illustrated its usefulness via simulated examples that minimize total cost in an example of a capacity planning problem.

IS-based methods are often used to accelerate the evaluation at the settings where performance measures such as unavailability probabilities correspond to *rare* events. In practice, even when the targets to be evaluated are not rare, IS-based methods can still be used to reduce the variance of the simulation or testing. Moreover, since the sampling procedure in a CLRSM step usually requires simulation/testing within a local neighborhood, we suggest that the same IS trace can even be reused to further decrease the simulation time. In the proposed CLRSM-IS framework, we can also add an *m*-out-of-*k* reuse strategy, which was verified in the simulation examples to vastly reduce the simulation time while still retain very accurate results (Hsu & Devetsikiotis, 2007).

Game Theoretic Approaches

Game theory (Fudenberg & Tirole, 1991) is a formal tool to describe and analyze interactive decision situations. It represent an analytical framework to predict the outcome of complex interactions among individual rational entities, where rationality is represented by adherence to a strategy based on perceived or measured results.

In the framework of the game theory, a model is called "game" and decision makers are "players". Players play the game by selecting a single action from a set of feasible actions. The outcome of the game depends from the choices of all players, where the interaction among players is represented by their influence on the resulting outcome. Each player is able to evaluate the outcome of the game through a "utility" function.

Normal form representation of a game is given by $G = \langle N, A, \{u_i\}\rangle$, where N is the set of players, A_i is the action set for player i and $\{u_i\}$ is the set of utility functions that each player wishes to maximize. For every player i, the utility function is a function of the action chosen by player i, a_i, and the actions chosen by all the other players in the game, denoted by a_{-i}.

Analysis of the interactions among the players and estimation of the outcome of the game are performed by studying the evolution of the game in terms of dynamic or steady-state conditions.

Currently, no works are available in the literature related to the usage of dynamic approaches to analyze communication networks, while some exist on the identification of steady-state conditions. In this latter framework, the analysis is usually oriented to the identification of Nash Equilibria and / or Pareto Optimal outcomes.

A Nash equilibrium is defined as a set of actions that corresponds to the best mutual response: for each player, the selected action represents the best response to the actions of all other players. Nash equilibria are a consistent prediction of the outcome of a game.

An outcome is Pareto optimal if there is no other outcome that makes every player at least as well off while making at least one player better off.

Considering its definition, game theory can be considered a suitable analytical tool to model different scenarios of interaction among protocols and entities in a communication network. In the context of wireless networks, game theory seem to have the potential to address modeling issues ranging from protocols at different layers to nodes in an ad-hoc network.

A relevant survey on the application of game theory to analyze wireless ad-hoc networks is represented by (Srivastava et al., 2005).

More in general, game theory is envisioned to provide novel tools to model and optimize wireless networks, addressing issues related to distributed power control, medium access control, multi-hop wireless networks, and cognitive networks.

Considerations

Modeling cross-layer interactions still represents an open problem. However, as shown in the previous sections, some interesting frameworks are available or being studied that seem to provide useful steps towards a complete characterization of such crucial aspect in communication networks.

The following table provides a brief summary of the reviewed techniques with the aim of helping the reader to identify the differences and applicability of each one. The reader should note that the table is not intended to represent all available approaches, but rather to find a suitable classification of the examined frameworks.

However, not many works aim at providing a unified and suitable method to model cross-layering interactions are currently available in the literature. In this scenario, the key issue is represented by proper characterization and modeling of the complex interactions among the layers of the protocol stack, where each protocol has a different goal and employs different measurements.

Promising approaches that could provide interesting steps forward in modeling of cross-layer interactions are:

- Approaches based on "quantifying" cross-layer interactions, where the complexity is tackled through the employment of simulation- or measurement-based schemes;
- Approaches based on game theory, where such novel tool can be employed to express different goals at each layer and to capture the interaction among protocols.

CROSS-LAYER OPTIMIZATIONS AND SIGNALING

This section of the chapter aims at providing an overview of available cross-layer solutions designed to overcome limitations of standard TCP/IP protocol reference model in wireless networking: mobility, data transfer perfor-

Table 2.

Method	Based on	Complexity	Degree of Information	Works online / offline
ECLSA	Experiments	Medium	Sensitivity to parameters	Offline
CLRSM	Experimental / simulation data	High	Performance vs. design parameters	Offline
Game Theory	Interaction models	Low	Steady-state performance	Online/Offline

mance, energy efficiency, and quality of service. Then, different cross-layer signaling architectures are presented and analyzed through the comparison of their core characteristics. Finally, an overview of current standardization activities followed by guidance to cross-layer design concludes the section.

Cross-Layer Signaling Architectures

An availability of large variety of optimization solutions requiring information exchange between two or more layers of the protocol stack raises an important issue concerning implementation of different cross-layer solutions inside TCP/IP protocol reference model, their coexistence and interoperability, requiring the availability of a common cross-layer signaling model (Srivastava & Motani, 2005). This model defines the implementation principles for the protocol stack entities implementing cross-layer functionalities and provides a standardized way for ease of introduction of cross-layer mechanism inside the protocol stack.

In (Raisinghani & Iyer, 2006), Raisinghani et al. define the goals the cross-layer signaling model should follow. They aim at rapid prototyping, portability, and efficient implementation of the cross-layer entities while maintaining minimum impact on TCP/IP modularity.

In this framework, several cross-layer signaling architectures have been proposed by the research community. While the following paragraphs will provide an overview and comparison between the most relevant solutions, it is important to note that research on the topic is far from being complete. In fact, up to now, just of few of cross-layer signaling proposals were prototyped and none of them is included into current operating systems.

Interlayer signaling pipe. One of the first approaches used for implementation of cross-layer signaling is revealed by Wang et al. (Wang & Abu-Rgheff, 2003) as *interlayer signaling pipe*, which allows propagation of signaling messages layer-to-layer along with packet data flow inside the protocol stack in bottom-up or top-down manner. An important property of this signaling method is that signaling information propagates along with the data flow inside the protocol stack and can be associated with a particular packet incoming or outgoing from the protocol stack.

Two methods are considered for encapsulation of signaling information and its propagation along the protocol stack from one layer to another: packet headers or packet structures.

- *Packet headers* can be used as interlayer message carriers. In this case, signaling information included into an optional portion of IPv6 header (Deering & Hinden, 1998), follow packet processing path and can be accessed by any subsequent layer. One of the main shortcomings of packet headers is in the limitation of signaling to the direction of the packet flow, making it not suitable for cross-layer schemes which require instant communication with the layers located on the opposite direction. Another drawback of packet headers method is in the associated protocol stack processing overhead, which can be reduced with packet structures method.
- *Packet structures.* In this method, signaling information is inserted into a specific section of the packet structure. Whenever a packet is generated by the protocol stack or successfully received from the network interface, a corresponding packet structure is allocated. This structure includes all the packet related information such as protocol headers and application data as well as internal protocol stack information such as network interface id, socket descriptor, configuration parameters and other.

Consequently, cross-layer signaling information added to the packet structure is fully consistent with packet header signaling method but with reduced processing. Moreover, employment of packet structures does not violate existing functionality of separate layers of the protocol stack. In case the cross-layer signaling is not implemented at a certain layer, this layer simply does not fill / modify the corresponding parts of the packet structure and does not access cross-layer parameters provided by the other layers. Another advantage of packet structure method is that standardization is not required, since the implementation could vary between different solutions.

Direct Interlayer Communication proposed in (Wang & Abu-Rgheff, 2003) aims at improvement of interlayer signaling pipe method by introducing signaling shortcuts performed out of band. In this way, the proposed Cross-Layer Signaling Shortcuts (CLASS) approach allows non-neighboring layers of the protocol stack to exchange messages, without processing at every adjacent layer, thus allowing fast signaling information delivery to the destination layer. Along with reduced protocol stack processing overhead, CLASS messages are not related to data packets and thus the approach can be used for bidirectional signaling. Nevertheless, the absence of this association is twofold since many cross-layer optimization approaches operate on per-packet basis, i.e. delivering cross-layer information associated with a specific packet traveling inside the protocol stack.

One of the core signaling protocols considered in direct interlayer communication is Internet Control Message Protocol (ICMP) (Postel, 1981; Conta & Deering, 1998). Generation of ICMP messages is not constrained by a specific protocol layer and can be performed at any layer of the protocol stack. However, signaling with ICMP messages involves operation with heavy protocol headers (IP and ICMP), checksum calculation, and other procedures which increase processing overhead. This motivates a "lightweight" version of signaling protocol CLASS (Wang & Abu-Rgheff, 2003) which uses only destination layer identification, type of event, and related to the event data fields.

However, despite the advantages of direct communication between protocol layers and standardized way of signaling, ICMP-based approach is mostly limited by request-response action - while more complicated event-based signaling should be adapted. To this aim, a mechanism which uses *callback functions* can be employed. This mechanism allows a given protocol layer to register a specific procedure (callback function) with another protocol layer, whose execution is triggered by a specific event at that layer.

Central Cross-layer Plane implemented in parallel to the protocol stack is probably the most widely proposed cross-layer signaling architecture. In (Chen, Shah, & Nahrstedt, 2002), the authors propose a shared database that can be accessed by all layers for obtaining parameters provided by other layers and providing the values of their internal parameters to other layers. This database is an example of passive Central Cross-Layer Plane design: it assists in information exchange between layers but does not implement any active control functions such as tuning internal parameters of the protocol layers.

Similar approach is presented by the authors of (El Defrawy, El Zarki, & Khairy, 2006), which introduces a Central Cross-layer Plane called Cross-layer Server able to communicate with protocols at different layers by means of Clients. This interface is bidirectional, allowing Cross-layer server to perform active optimization controlling internal to the layer parameters.

Another approach, called ECLAIR, proposed by Raisinghani et al. in (Raisinghani & Iyer, 2006) is probably the most detailed from the implementation point of view. ECLAIR implements optimizing subsystem plane, which communicates with the protocol stack by means of cross-layer interfaces called tuning layers. Each tuning layer exports a set of API functions allowing read/write access to the internal protocol control and data structures. These API can be used by protocol optimizers which are the building blocks of the optimizing subsystem plane. This makes the optimizing system a central point for coordination of cross-layer protocol optimizers in order to avoid loops and other conflicts.

Similar goals are pursued by Chang et al. (Chang, Gaydadjiev, & Vassiliadis, 2007) with another architecture falling into Central Cross-Layer Plane category. It assumes simultaneous operation of multiple cross-layer optimization approaches located at different layers of the protocol stack and aims at coordination of shared data access, avoiding dependency loops, as well as reduction of the overhead associated with cross-layer signaling. To this aim, an Interaction Control Middleware plane is introduced to provide coordination among all the registered cross-layer optimizers implemented in different layers. The main difference of this cross-layer architecture proposal with other proposals of this category is that signaling information propagates along the protocol stack with regular data packets - making it a unique combination of Central Control Plane and interlayer signaling pipe approaches.

Network-wide Cross-Layer Signaling. Most of the proposals aim at defining cross-layer signaling between different layers belonging to the protocol stack of a single node. However, several optimization proposals exist which perform cross-layer optimization based on the information obtained from the protocol layers of different network nodes. This corresponds to network-wide propagation of cross-layer signaling information, which adds another degree of freedom in how cross-layer signaling can be performed.

Among the methods overviewed, packet headers and ICMP messages can be considered as good candidates. Their advantages, underlined in the single-node protocol stack scenario, become more significant for network-wide communication. For example, the way of encapsulating cross-layer signaling data into optional fields of the protocol headers almost does not produce any additional overhead and keeps an association of signaling

Figure 1. Cross-layer signaling architectures

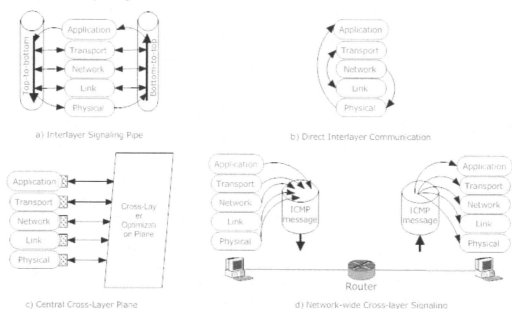

information with a specific packet. However, this method limits propagation of signaling information to packet paths in the network. For that reason, it is desirable to combine packet headers signaling with ICMP messages, which are well suited for explicit communication between network nodes.

One of the early examples of cross-network cross-layering is the Explicit Congestion Notification (ECN) presented in (Ramakrishnan, Floyd, & Black, 2001). It realizes in-band signaling approach by marking in-transit TCP data packet with congestion notification bit. However, due to the limitation of signaling propagation to the packet paths this notification need to propagate to the receiver first, which echoes it back in the TCP ACK packet outgoing to the sender node. This unnecessary signaling loop can be avoided with explicit ICMP packets signaling. However, it requires traffic generation capabilities form network routers and it consume bandwidth resources.

An example of adaptation of Central Cross-Layer Plane-like architecture to the cross-network cross-layer signaling is presented in (Kim, 2001). The paper suggests the use of a network service which collects parameters related the wireless channel located at the link and physical layers, and then provides them to adaptive mobile applications.

A unique combination of local and network-wide cross-layer signaling approaches called Cross-Talk is presented in (Winter, Schiller, Nikaein, & Bonnet, 2006). CrossTalk architecture consists of two cross-layer optimization planes. One is responsible for organization of cross-layer information exchange between protocol layers of the local protocol stack and their coordination. Another plane is responsible for network-wide coordination: it aggregates cross-layer information provided by the local plane and serves as an interface for cross-layer signaling over the network. Most of the signaling is performed in-band using packet headers method, making it accessible not only at the end host but at the network routers as well. Cross-layer information received from the network is aggregated and then can be considered for optimization of local protocol stack operation based on the global network conditions.

Main problems associated to deployment of cross-layer signaling over the network, also pointed in (Sarolahti & Floyd, 2007), include security issues, problems with non-conformant routers, and processing efficiency. Security considerations require the design of proper protective mechanism avoiding protocol attacks attempted by non-friendly network nodes by providing incorrect cross-layer information in order to trigger certain behavior. The second problem addresses misbehavior of network routers. It is pointed out that, in 70% of the cases, IP packets with unknown options are dropped in the network or by the receiver protocol stack. Finally, the problem with

Table 3. Comparison of the cross-layer signaling methods

Cross-layer signaling method	Scope	Propagation latency	Communication overhead	Processing overhead	Direction of signaling	Requires standardization
Interlayer signaling pipe						
Packet headers	Local	Medium	High	Medium	Path dependant	√
Packet structures	Local	Medium	High	Medium	Path dependant	×
Direct interlayer communications						
ICMP messages	Local	Low	Medium	High	Path independent	√
Callback functions	Local	Low	Low	Low	Path independent	×
Central cross-layer plane	Local	Low	Low	Low	Path independent	×
Network-wide Cross-layer Signaling						
Packet headers	Local/Network-wide	High	Low	Medium	Path dependant	√
ICMP messages	Local/Network-wide	High	High	High	Path independent	√

processing efficiency is related to the additional costs of the routers' hardware associated with cross-layer information processing. While it is not an issue for the low-speed links, it becomes relevant for high speeds where most of the routers perform simple decrement of the TTL field in order to maintain high packet processing speed.

A comparison of different cross-layer signaling methods through the comparison of their essential design and deployment characteristics is presented in Table 3. Such features include:

• *Scope* defines cross-layer approach operation boundaries. Solutions which limit their operation to a single protocol stack are more flexible in the choice of signaling techniques: they can use internal protocol stack techniques such as packet structures or callback functions, thus avoiding processing related overhead and the need for standardization effort.

• *Propagation latency* parameter describes the delay associated with signaling message delivery. It becomes essential for signaling performed across the network, where the delay corresponds to the delay of communication links and time messages spend in router buffers. For local signaling methods, the delay is usually several orders of magnitude lower than for network-wide cross-layering. However, signaling using interlayer signaling pipe method is slower than direct interlayer communications due to layer-by-layer processing. Moreover, interlayer signaling pipe can only afford asynchronous reaction to the event occurred, while direct communication allows instantaneous reaction.

• *Communication overhead* parameter is more essential for network-wide communication and describes the amount of network resources needed for signaling. Encapsulation of signaling information into packets headers does not require any additional network resources in case reserved fields are used, or corresponds to just minor increase in case optional packet header fields are involved. On the contrary, ICMP messages require a dedicated effort for their delivery from the network, consuming considerable amount of network resources – including also protocol (ICMP and IP headers) overhead. The communication overhead for local signaling corresponds to the amount of operations (CPU cycles) required to deliver the message from one layer to another. This parameter is different from processing overhead, which includes message encapsulation and processing. The highest communication overhead for local communications is associated with interlayer signaling pipe due to subsequent processing at several protocol layers before message delivery.

- *Processing overhead* is the amount of processing power required for message creation, encapsulation, extraction, and analysis. Medium processing effort is required for signaling messages transmitted using packet headers and packet structures inside the protocol stack (mainly needed for allocation of memory and data copy procedures). Higher processing overhead is required for ICMP message creation, which involves execution of ICMP and IP layer functions of the protocol stack. For network-wide signaling, the overhead of packet headers method is medium. The procedures at the end nodes are similar to packet headers signaling performed locally, while no additional effort associated with signaling information delivery is taken. This is due to the fact that signaling information is encapsulated into the regular data packet and is being delivered along with it.

- *Direction of signaling* is an important characteristic which defines the applicability of the signaling approach to the chosen cross-layer optimization scheme. The schemes which do not rely on regular traffic flow (or out-of-band) signaling are packet path independent, providing a faster reaction to an event. This reaction can be preformed also in synchronous way, while packet path dependant signaling provides only asynchronous reaction. The speed and flexibility of path independent signaling comes at the expense of the additional communication resources. Nevertheless, path independence cannot be only considered as an advantage: many cross-layer optimization algorithms require signaling information associated with a specific packet transmitted through the network - making path dependant signaling more attractive in such cases. In order to implement packet association in non-path dependant approaches, a unique identification or a copy of the packet associated with the transmitted signaling information should be attached to the message. A good example of this technique is "Time Exceeded" ICMP message sent by a router for a packet dropped due to expired TTL, which includes IP header and part of data of this packet.

- *Requires standardization* parameter specifies whether standardization effort is needed for the cross-layer signaling method which is considered to fully support effective deployment. Standardization is required for signaling performed over the network while standardization of network protocols which are used solely inside the protocol stack of the single node is still desirable but can be avoided. This positions internal protocol signaling methods based on packet structures or callback function be less dependent on standardization bodies and thus more flexible for the deployment form the implementation point of view as well as time wise.

The comparison among different optimization approaches should not be seen as an attempt to select the best signaling scheme to serve as an implementation basis for future cross-layer optimization solutions. On the contrary, the comparison demonstrates that no scheme is able to achieve absolute leadership in all the evaluated criteria. This fact suggests using a combination of several signaling schemes based on the specific cross-layer solution and target optimization goals.

In case of cross-layer optimization of a local protocol stack, Central Cross-Layer Plane methodology as well as Direct Interlayer Communication using callback functions seems to be appropriate, unless the optimization algorithm requires signaling of information associated with a particular packet. In such case, Interlayer Signaling Pipe using packet structures method would provide relevant performance advantages.

In case of network-wide cross-layer optimization, it is suggested to use packet headers for the transmission of periodic, delay tolerant, or information associated with particular packets. ICMP headers should be used if instant feedback is needed and size of signaling message along with associated overhead is relatively small, and avoided otherwise in order to reduce consumption of network resources.

In addition, it is necessary to evaluate the tradeoff between optimization gains and introduced signaling overhead, especially in case the proposed cross-layer optimization solution implements network-wide signaling.

Cross-Layer Standardization Activities

Nowadays, with wireless technologies driving evolution of networking, cross-layer design is envisioned as a proper solution for extending traditional TCP/IP reference model into new boundaries and overcoming its design limitations. However, this goal requires paradigm shifts by relaxing the restrictions of OSI/ISO layered model and allowing a broader view and interdependence between the layers. In (Srivastava & Motani, 2005), the authors identify the broadcast nature of the wireless link as opposed to the point-to-point nature of wired links to be the fundamental reason for limitation of the layered structure in such scenario. Furthermore, in (Stine, 2006), the author define cross-layering as the only option for design of Mobile Ad Hoc Networks (MANETs) along with presenting standardization proposal comprised of four parts: MANET subnetwork layer and interfaces, a heterogeneous routing protocol, hierarchical addressing schemes, and cross-layer signaling mechanisms.

While standardization process of unified framework for cross-layer design proposals or new protocol stack architectures employing cross-layer interactions is still far away, the amount of standardization proposals involving cross-layer techniques within standardization bodies is constantly increasing becoming on track in different IETF working groups. A good example of recently submitted RFC proposal to include transport-layer considerations for explicit cross-layer indications is presented in (Sarolahti & Floyd, 2007).

CONCLUSION

Cross-layering represents a promising design paradigm to provide high performance, mobility support, high resource utilization, and QoS in wireless networks. Its deployment does not represent a completely novel breakthrough in the framework of wireless communications, as cross-layer design is already successfully employed in specific communication systems – such as 3G and upcoming 3G LTE cellular networks.

In this framework, some interesting approaches are available to bridge the gap between theory and practice, aiming at defining suitable formal methods to support cross-layer solutions. However, no methods are available to address a generic yet effective model for cross-layer paradigm, and therefore the way is yet open to a "unifying theory" of cross-layer design.

The chapter contributed to such ongoing discussion by:

- Systematically defining relevant cross-layer performance metrics, and relating them to current wireless technologies.
- Describing a framework for the quantification of the sensitivity and optimization of such performance metrics with respect to design and operating parameters *across the layers*.
- Establishing some important guidelines for the implementation of cross-layer schemes by use of signaling architectures.

REFERENCES

3GPP, TR 25.913. *Requirements for Evolved UTRA and Evolved UTRAN.* www.3gpp.org.

Alfredsson, S., Brunstrom, A., & Sternad, M. (2006). Transport Protocol Performance over 4G Links: Emulator Methodology and Results. *International Symposium on Wireless Communication Systems ISWCS*, Valencia, Spain.

Aune, F. (2004). Cross-Layer Design Tutorial. *Norwegian University of Science and Technology, Dept. of Electronics and Telecommunications*: Trondheim, Norway.

Balakrishnan, H., Padmanabhan, V. N., Seshan, S., & Katz, R. H. (1997). A comparison of mechanisms for improving TCP performance over wireless links. *IEEE/ACM Transactions on Networking*, 5(6), 756 – 769.

Bikram, S., Bakshi, B., Krishna, P., Vaidya, N. H., & Pradhan, D. K. (1997). Improving Performance of TCP over Wireless Networks. *International Conference on Distributed Computing Systems*.

Box, G. E. P., & Draper, N. R. (1987). *Empirical Model Building and Response Surfaces*. New York, NY, USA: John Wiley & Sons, Inc.

Box, G., & Wilson, K. (1951). On The Experimental Attainment of Optimum Conditions. *Journal of Royal Statistical Society*, 13(1), 1-38.

Braden, R., Clark, D., & Shenker, S. (1994). Integrated Services in the Internet Architecture: an Overview. *RFC 1633*.

C.-C. Tseng, L.-H. Yen, H.-H. Chang, & K.-C. Hsu, (2005). Topology-aided cross-layer fast handoff designs for IEEE 802.11/mobile IP environments. *IEEE Communications Magazine*, 43(12), 156 – 163.

Chan, M. C., & Ramjee, R. (2002). TCP/IP performance over 3G wireless links with rate and delay variation. *ACM International Conference on Mobile Computing and Networking*, 71 – 82.

Chang, Z., Gaydadjiev, G. N., & Vassiliadis, S. (2007). Infrastructure for Cross-Layer Designs Interaction. *The 16th IEEE International Conference on Computer Communications and Networks (IC3N)*, Honolulu, Hawaii USA.

Chen, J., Lv, T., & Zheng, H. (2004). Cross-layer design for QoS wireless communications. *Proceedings of the 2004 International Symposium on Circuits and Systems (ISCAS)*, 217 – 220.

Chen, K., Shah, S. H., & Nahrstedt, K. (2002). Cross-Layer Design for Data Accessibility in Mobile Ad hoc Networks. *Wireless Personal Communications, Special Issue on Multimedia Network Protocols and Enabling Radio Technologies*, 21, 49-75, Kluwer Academic Publishers.

Chen, L., Low, S.H., & Doyle, J.C. (2005). Joint Congestion Control and Media Access Control Design for Ad Hoc Wireless Networks. *Proc. INFOCOM 2005*.

Chiang, M., Low, S. H., Calderbank, A. R., & Doyle, J. C. (2007). Layering as Optimization Decomposition: A Mathematical Theory of Network Architectures. *Proceedings of the IEEE*, 95(1), 255 – 312.

Ci, S., Turner, S. W., & Sharif, H. (2003). An energy-efficient TCP quick timeout scheme for wireless LANs. *IEEE International Performance, Computing, and Communications Conference*, 193 – 197.

Conta, A., & Deering, S. (1998). *Internet Control Message Protocol (ICMPv6) for the Internet Protocol Version 6 (IPv6) Specification*. RFC 2463.

De Nardis, L., & Di Benedetto, M.-G. (2007). Overview of the IEEE 802.15.4/4a standards for low data rate Wireless Personal Data Networks. *4th Workshop on Positioning, Navigation and Communication*, 285 – 289.

Deering, S., & Hinden, R. (1998). *Internet Protocol, Version 6 (IPv6) Specification*. RFC 2460.

Deguang Le, Xiaoming Fu, & Hogref, D. (2006). A review of mobility support paradigms for the internet. *IEEE Communications Surveys & Tutorials*, 8(1), 38 – 51.

Devetsikiotis, M., & Townsend, J. K. (1993). Statistical Optimization of Dynamic Importance Sampling Parameters for Efficient Simulation of Communication Networks. *IEEE/ACM Transactions on Networking*, 1(3), 293 – 305.

Dong, Y, & Yau, D. K. Y., (2005). Adaptive Sleep Scheduling for Energy-efficient Movement-predicted Wireless Communication. *Proceedings of the 13TH IEEE International Conference on Network Protocols (ICNP)*, 391 – 400.

Donohue, J., Houck, E., & Myers, R. (1995). Simulation Designs for the Estimation of Response Surface Gradients in the Presenced of Model Misspecification. *Management Science*, 41(2), 244-262.

Eberle, W., Bougard, B., Pollin, S., & Catthoor, F. (2005). From myth to methodology: cross-layer design for energy-efficient wireless communication. *Design Automation Conference*.

Eddy, W. M. (2006). At What Layer Does Mobility Belong? *IEEE Communications Magazine,* 42(10), 155-159.

El Defrawy, K. M., El Zarki, M. S., & Khairy, M. M. (2006). Proposal for a cross-layer coordination framework for next generation wireless systems. *ACM International Conference On Communications And Mobile Computing*, 141 – 146.

El Malki, K., (2007). Low-Latency Handoffs in Mobile IPv4. RFC 4881.

Feeney, L. M., & Nilsson, M. (2001). Investigating the energy consumption of a wireless network interface in an ad hoc networking environment. *Twentieth Annual Joint Conference of the IEEE Computer and Communications Societies (INFOCOM)*, 3, 1548 – 1557.

Firoiu, V., Le Boudec, J.-Y., Towsley, D., & Zhang, Z.-L. (2002). Theories and models for Internet quality of service. *IEEE Proceedings*, 90(9), 1565 – 1591.

Fontana, R. J. (2004). Recent System Applications of Short-Pulse Ultra-Wideband (UWB) Technology (Invited Paper). *IEEE Microwave Theory & Tech.*, 52(9), 2087-2104.

Fraleigh, C., Moon, S., Lyles, B., Cotton, C., Khan, M., Moll, D., Rockell, R., Seely, T., & Diot, S.C. (2003). Packet-level traffic measurements from the Sprint IP backbone. *IEEE Network*, 17(6), 6 – 16.

Fudenberg, D., & Tirole, J. (1991). *Game Theory*, The MIT Press.

Granelli, F., Kliazovich, D., & da Fonseca, N. L. S. (2005). Performance Limitations of IEEE 802.11 Networks and Potential Enhancements. In Yang Xiao (ed) & Yi Pan (ed), *Wireless LANs and Bluetooth*, Hardbound: Nova Science Publishers.

Granelli, F., Kliazovich, D., Hui, J., & Devetsikiotis, M. (2007). Performance Optimization of Single-Cell Voice over WiFi Communications Using Quantitative Cross-Layering Analysis. *In Proceedings of ITC 20*, Ottawa, Canada.

Heidelberger, P., (1995). Fast simulation of rare events in queuing and reliability models. *ACM Transactions on Modeling and Computer Simulation (TOMACS)*, 5(1), 43 – 85.

Henderson, T. R. (2003). Host Mobility for IP Networks: A Comparison, *IEEE Network*, Nov. 2003, pp. 18–26

Hsieh, R., Zhou, Z. G., & Seneviratne, A. (2003). S-MIP: a seamless handoff architecture for mobile IP. *Twenty-Second Annual Joint Conference of the IEEE Computer and Communications Societies*, 3, 1774 – 1784.

Hsu, C.-C., & Devetsikiotis, M. (in press). An Adaptive Approach to Accelerated Evaluation of Highly Reliable Systems. *ACM Transactions on Modeling and Computer Simulation.*

Hsu, C-C., & Devetsikiotis, M. (2007). A Framework for Automatic Software Performance Evaluation and Optimization Using Response Surface Methodology and Importance Sampling. *In Proceedings of the 40th Annual Simulation Symposium*, Norfolk.

Huang, W. L., & Letaief, K. B. (2007). Cross-Layer Scheduling and Power Control Combined With Adaptive Modulation for Wireless Ad Hoc Networks. *IEEE Transactions on Communications*, 55(4), 728 – 739.

Hui, J. & Devetsikiotis, M. (2006).Metamodeling of Wi-Fi Performance. *Proc. IEEE ICC 2006*: Istanbul, Turkey.

Hui, J., & Devetsikiotis, M. (in press). A Metamodeling Framework for Wi-Fi Performance Evaluation. *IEEE Transactions on Wireless Communications.*

IEEE Std. 802.11 (1999). IEEE Standards for Information Technology -- Telecommunications and Information Exchange between Systems -- Local and Metropolitan Area Network -- Specific Requirements - Part 11: Wireless LAN Medium Access Control (MAC) and Physical Layer (PHY) Specifications. *IEEE Press.*

IEEE Std. 802.11e (2005). *Local and metropolitan area networks - Specific requirements Part 11: Wireless LAN Medium Access Control (MAC) and Physical Layer (PHY) specifications Amendment 8: Medium Access Control (MAC) Quality of Service Enhancements*, IEEE Press.

IEEE Std. 802.16 (2001). IEEE Standard for Local and Metropolitan Area Networks, part 16, Air Interface for Fixed Broadband Wireless Access Systems. *IEEE Press*.

Jain, B., & Agrawala, A. (1993). *Open Systems Interconnection*. New York: McGraw-Hill.

Jiang, H., Zhuang, W., & Shen, X., (2005). Cross-layer design for resource allocation in 3G wireless networks and beyond. *IEEE Communications Magazine*, 43(12), 120 -126.

Kawada, V., & Kumar, P. R. (2005). A Cautionary Perspective on Cross-Layer Design. *IEEE Wireless Communications*, 12(1), 3-11.

Kilkki, K. (1999). *Differentiated Services for the Internet*. Indianapolis, IN, USA: Macmillan Technical Publishing.

Kim, B.-J. (2001). A network service providing wireless channel information for adaptive mobile applications: I: Proposal. *IEEE International Conference on Communications (ICC)*, 1345 – 1351.

Kleijnen, J. P. C., (1998). *Experimental design for sensitivity analysis, optimization, and validation of simulation models*.

Kliazovich, D., Ben Halima, N., & Granelli, F., (2007). Cross-Layer Error Recovery Optimization in WiFi Networks. *Tyrrhenian International Workshop on Digital Communication (TIWDC)*, Ischia island, Naples, Italy.

Kliazovich, D., Granelli, F., Redana, S., & Riato, N. (2007). Cross-Layer Error Control Optimization in 3G LTE. *IEEE Global Communications Conference (GLOBECOM)*, Washington, DC, U.S.A.

Kozat, U. C., Koutsopoulos, I., & Tassiulas, L. (2006). Cross-Layer Design for Power Efficiency and QoS Provisioning in Multi-Hop Wireless Networks. *IEEE Transactions on Wireless Communications*, 5(11), 3306 – 3315.

Lee, W. C. Y. (2005). Wireless and Cellular Communications. 3 edition, McGraw-Hill Professional.

Lin, X., & Shroff, N.B. (2005). The Impact of Imperfect Scheduling on Cross Layer Rate Control in Wireless Networks. *Proc. INFOCOM 2005*.

McDermott-Wells, P. (2005). What is Bluetooth? *IEEE Potentials*, 23(5), 33- 35.

Miller, G. J., Thompson, K., & Wilder, R. (1997). Wide-area Internet traffic patterns and characteristics. *IEEE Network*, 11(6), 10 – 23.

Murhammer, M. W. & Murphy, E. (1998). *TCP/IP: Tutorial and Technical Overview*. Upper Saddle River, NJ: Prentice-Hall.

Narula-Tam, A., Macdonald, T., Modiano, E., & Servi, L. (2004). A dynamic resource allocation strategy for satellite communications. *IEEE Military Communications Conference (MILCOM)*, 1415 – 1421.

Newman, P. (2004). In search of the all-IP mobile network. *IEEE Communications Magazine*, 42(12), s3- s8.

Pentikousis, K. (2000). TCP in Wired-Cum-Wireless Environments. *IEEE Communications Surveys*, 3(4), 2-14.

Pollin, S., Bougard, B., & Lenoir, G. (2003). Cross-Layer Exploration of Link Adaptation in Wireless LANs with TCP Traffic. *Proc. IEEE Benelux Chapter on Communications and Vehicular Technology*.

Portio Market Research (2007). Worldwide Mobile Market Statistics 2007. *Portio Market Research*.

Postel, J. (1981). *Internet Control Message Protocol*. RFC 792.

Raisinghani, V. T., & Iyer, S. (2006). Cross Layer Feedback Architecture for Mobile Device Protocol Stacks. *IEEE Communications Magazine*, 44(1), 85 – 92.

Ramakrishnan, K., Floyd, S., & Black, D. (2001). The Addition of Explicit Congestion Notification (ECN) to IP. *RFC 3168*.

RFC 791 (1981). Internet Protocol.

Rubinstein, R. Y., & Melamed, B. (1998). *Modern Simulation and Modeling.* New York, NY, USA: John Wiley & Sons, Inc.

Sarolahti, P., & Floyd, S. (2007). *Cross-layer Indications for Transport Protocols.* Internet draft draft-sarolahti-tsvwg-crosslayer-00.txt.

Sarolahti, P., Allman, M., & Floyd, S. (2007). Determining an Appropriate Sending Rate Over an Underutilized Network Path. *Computer Networks Special Issue on Protocols for Fast, Long-Distance Networks*, 51(7).

Shenker, S. (1995). Fundamental Design Issues for the Future Internet. *IEEE Journal of Selected Areas in Communication*, 13(7), 1176-1188.

Singh, S., Woo, M., & Raghavendra, C. S. (1998). Power-aware routing in mobile ad hoc networks. *Proceedings of the 4th annual ACM/IEEE international conference on Mobile computing and networking*, 181 – 190.

Srivastava, V., & Motani, M. (2005). Cross-layer design: a survey and the road ahead. *IEEE Communications Magazine*, 43(12), 112 – 119.

Srivastava, V., Neel, J., MacKenzie, A. B.. Menon, R., DaSilva, L.A., Hicks, J.E., Reed, J.H., Gilles, R.P. (2005). Using Game Theory to Analyze Wireless Ad Hoc Networks. *IEEE Communications Surveys & Tutorials*, 7(4), 46-56.

Stine, J. A. (2006). Cross-Layer Design of MANETs: The Only Option. *Military Communications Conference*, 1-7.

Tian, H., Bose, S. K., Law, C. L., & Xiao, W. (2005). CLA-QOS: A Cross-Layer QoS Provisioning Approach for Mobile Ad-hoc Networks. *TENCON*, 1 – 6.

Toumpis, S., & Goldsmith, A. J., (2003). Capacity Regions for Wireless Ad Hoc Networks. *IEEE Transactions on Wireless Communications*, 2(4), 746-748.

Tsatsanis, M., Zhang, R., & Banerjee, S. (2000). Network-assisted diversity for random access wireless networks. *IEEE Transactions on Signal Processing*, 48(3), 702–711.

Vadde, K. K., & Syrotiuk, V. R. (2004). Factor Interaction on Service Delivery in Mobile Ad Hoc Networks. *IEEE Journal on Selected Areas In Communications (JSAC)*, 22(7), 1335-1346.

Wang, L.-C., & Lee, C.-H. (2005). A TCP-physical cross-layer congestion control mechanism for the multirate WCDMA system using explicit rate change notification. *International Conference on Advanced Information Networking and Applications*, 2, 449 – 452.

Wang, Q., & Abu-Rgheff, M. A. (2003). Cross-layer signaling for next-generation wireless systems. *IEEE Wireless Communications and Networking (WCNC)*, 1084 – 1089.

Winter, R., Schiller, J. H., Nikaein, N., & Bonnet, C. (2006). CrossTalk: cross-layer decision support based on global knowledge. *IEEE Communications Magazine*, 44(1), 93 – 99.

Wu, J. C.-S., Cheng, C.-W., Huang, N.-F., & Ma, G.-K. (2001). Intelligent Handoff for Mobile Wireless Internet. *ACM/Kluwer Mobile Networks and Applications (MONET)*, 6(1), 69 – 79.

Xylomenos, G., Polyzos, G. C., Mahonen, P., & Saaranen, M. (2001). TCP performance issues over wireless links. *IEEE Communications Magazine*, 39(4), 52 – 58.

Zhang, B., Huang, C., & Devetsikiotis, M. (2006). Simulated Annealing Based Bandwidth Reservation for QoS Routing. *In proceedings of IEEE ICC 2006*, Istanbul.

Zhou, Z., McKinley, P. K., & Sadjadi, S. M. (2004). On quality-of-service and energy consumption tradeoffs in FEC-encoded audio streaming. *IEEE International Workshop on Quality of Service*, 161 – 170.

Zhu, H., Li, M., Chlamtac, I., & Prabhakaran, B. (2004). A survey of quality of service in IEEE 802.11 networks. *IEEE Wireless Communications*, 11(4), 6 – 14.

Zorzi, M., & Rao, R. R. (2001). Energy efficiency of TCP in a local wireless environment. *Mobile Networks and Applications*, 6(3), 265 – 278.

KEY TERMS

Energy Efficiency: Amount of work or energy released by the process to the quantity of work or energy used as an input to run the process.

Heterogeneity: The fact or state of being dissimilar.

Network Architecture: The organization of computer and communications systems which supports communication and co-operation between them.

Network Complexity: Is the number of nodes and alternate routes, number of communication mediums and protocols running in the network.

Network Path: A sequence of network node the data is routed through while following from data source to the destination.

TCP/IP (Transmission Control Protocol / Internet Protocol): A collection of Internet communication protocols between two computers. The TCP protocol is responsible reliable data delivery between applications, while IP protocol is responsible for data delivery between two network nodes.

Wireless Communication: The transfer of information over a distance without the use of electrical conductors.

Chapter II
Cross–Layer Resource Allocation and Scheduling for Wireless Systems

Dimitris Toumpakaris
University of Patras, Greece

Jungwon Lee
Marvell Semiconductor Inc., USA

ABSTRACT

This chapter presents an introduction to cross-layer scheduling and resource allocation for wireless systems and an overview of some of the approaches and proposed algorithms. The use of scheduling is motivated by first considering the fading Gaussian channel. Then, the focus shifts to scheduling and resource allocation for cellular systems. Existing approaches for the uplink and the downlink are discussed, as well as research results relating to the fading Multiple Access and the fading Broadcast Channel. Schemes for OFDMA and CDMA systems as well as systems using multiple antenna transmission are also presented. It is hoped that this survey will affirm the improvement in performance that can be achieved by use of cross-layer approaches in the design of Next-Generation Networks.

INTRODUCTION

Next-Generation Networks will be expected to deliver high data rates to a large number of different users in diverse environments. Moreover, they should be able to accommodate different user needs in terms of Quality of Service (QoS) and, in the same time, guarantee fairness. As the networks expand, energy efficiency will also be required, especially for wireless systems where battery life and radiation levels are major concerns. In order to meet successfully these demands, improved and new system designs are being developed. The designs encompass all system aspects, from smaller, faster and more energy-efficient circuits to sophisticated applications allowing seamless user connectivity and mobility.

Copyright © 2009, IGI Global, distributing in print or electronic forms without written permission of IGI Global is prohibited.

Traditionally, system design has been greatly facilitated by following a layered approach where each layer of the network is designed and optimized separately. As an example, the link layer can be optimized by viewing the physical layer as a bit pipe with given capacity and bit-error rate. Historically, systems have greatly benefited from this level of abstraction. However, this view is suboptimal. In order for future networks to achieve the required performance gains and exploit the available resources to the fullest possible extent, more than one layer should be considered jointly when designing the system and when making scheduling and resource allocation decisions. In many cases the attained performance gains (and the associated financial revenue) may justify the increased complexity in the system design and implementation.

This survey focuses on cross-layer resource allocation and scheduling policies for cellular wireless systems. As will be described in the following, these policies consider not only the channel condition (state), but also some utility function that depends, in general, on QoS and fairness criteria. Moreover, because user traffic appears randomly, in order to guarantee stability and increase the achievable rates, the number of bits (or packets) waiting for transmission in the user or node queues often needs to be taken into account. Unlike earlier approaches, the physical layer does not decide on the rate and the modulation scheme independently. Rather, a cross-layer controller schedules users that are allowed to transmit during a given interval and allocates the usage of the resources of the channel at the physical layer based on the traffic needs of higher layers. In general, the controller also implements scheduling, allocation and routing policies at higher layers. However, the focus of this survey is on joint physical and link/network layer adaptation.

Several reviews on cross-layer resource allocation and scheduling have appeared recently, an evidence of the increased research interest in the area. In (Lin, Shroff & Srikant, 2006) a survey of policies for both single-hop and multiple-hop networks is given. For single-hop networks it is assumed that only one user can transmit (or receive) at any given time. While this is generally true in systems using time division and the model can also apply to frequency and code division with appropriate changes, from an information-theoretic point of view it may be optimal to transmit to more than one user simultaneously. In (Berry & Yeh, 2004) the authors focus on techniques for fading multiple access (MAC) and fading broadcast (BC) channels and examine policies that allocate a vector of powers and rates to more than one users, in general. Finally, (Chiang et al., 2007) reviews the current status of the "layering as optimization decomposition" effort to develop a mathematical framework for future networks where an appropriate vertical layer topology is first defined, and each layer is then optimized horizontally.

The aim of the present survey is to provide the reasons and the motivation for the use of cross-layer techniques in Next-Generation Networks, and to give a brief overview of some interesting results that have been obtained from the current research in the area. Therefore, for the details on each particular scenario and policy, the reader is encouraged to consult the references that are provided at the end of this chapter. First, it is explained why the particular nature of the wireless channel creates a need for cross-layer policies if one wants to exploit efficiently the available resources. Cross-layer scheduling is first motivated using the fading Gaussian channel paradigm where the tradeoff between the transmit energy and the packet delay is discussed. Next, a summary of the cross-layer framework and major results for multiple user channels is given assuming orthogonal multiplexing. A transition is then made to the more general case where users are allowed to transmit simultaneously in the uplink and the Base Station is allowed to transmit simultaneously to more than one user in the downlink. The survey concludes with a review of some cross-layer policies for OFDMA and CDMA, as well as a brief discussion on cross-layer scheduling and resource allocation for multiple antenna systems. It should be mentioned that this chapter focuses exclusively on single-hop cellular networks and does not deal with the very interesting problem of cross-layer design for multi-hop networks and the associated issues (such as joint congestion control and routing).

CROSS-LAYER SCHEDULING AND RESOURCE ALLOCATION: A NECESSITY AND AN OPPORTUNITY FOR FUTURE WIRELESS SYSTEMS.

Although wireless systems share many common characteristics and are based on the same principles as other communications systems (such as wire-line, optical, and magnetic) their special nature also calls for modified and/or new design approaches. One important characteristic of wireless systems is their *variability*. This refers to the varying channel in a system where the transmitter and the receiver are fixed (e.g. a WiFi connection where the Mobile Station is not moving), but also to the topology of the system that may be changing. The changes in topology may occur because of receiver or transmitter mobility, or both. Moreover, the number of users sharing the wireless medium may be changing, the most familiar example being that of a cellular network where users initiate and complete calls continuously. This last example also touches on another very important aspect of wireless communications, *i.e.*, *medium sharing*. While medium sharing examples can also be found in other systems (such as Ethernet), it could be argued that in wireless systems medium sharing is ubiquitous and is encountered in its most general form since users may be distributed in the three-dimensional space, they may be moving, and communication may be taking place through a channel subject to attenuation, noise, shadowing and fading.

Traditionally, channel variation was viewed as an annoyance, and diversity techniques were developed to average its effect on transmission. In part, this was also convenient for complexity reasons, since it simplified system design. However, as processing speeds increase and user requirements in terms of data rates and Quality of Service (QoS) become more stringent, channel variations can be seen in a favorable light. More specifically, several opportunistic approaches have been proposed where a user transmits at higher rates when the channel condition is favorable and may even abstain from transmitting if the channel gain is small. This way, multiuser diversity can be exploited. This is the strategy that is followed in the downlink of CDMA2000 1xEV-DO (IS-856) where the Base Station transmits to only one user with fixed power and adapts the rate based on the current channel condition (Tse & Viswanath, 2005). This is a simple example of a cross-layer strategy where the physical layer is not viewed as a bit pipe with constant average data rate. In general, a controller schedules use of the physical layer by different users depending on some allocation strategy. In addition to improving the achievable rate, this approach can satisfy other criteria, too, such as delay constraints and limits on energy consumption.

The sharing of the wireless medium and the change in topology creates interdependencies among users and complicates the interaction between different layers of a wireless system. Users cannot be viewed in isolation. Therefore, when a new service request is placed, the decision whether to honor it and which system resources to allocate should take many factors into account. As an example, latest-generation wireless systems employ Orthogonal Frequency Division Multiple Access (OFDMA) in the physical layer. Even if there are enough remaining resources to admit a user in a cell, the inter-cell interference that will be generated will affect users of neighboring cells. The impact on the physical layer and, consequently, on upper layers, has to be considered in an efficient system design.

An additional factor that complicates scheduling and resource allocation is the randomness of the arriving traffic (Gallager, 1985). In realistic systems, the assumption that a user always has data to send (what is frequently referred to as the *infinite-backlogged* case) does not usually hold. Instead, traffic arrives according to an external arrival process. In a point-to-point link this does not affect modeling since all traffic corresponds to a single user and no other user can take advantage of idle periods. Either the data rate will be sufficient to accommodate the user needs or queue overflow will occur. In a Multiple Access Channel (MAC) where many users request communication with a Base Station, such as the uplink of a cellular system, the traffic characteristics of the users are important in determining how the channel will be used. The MAC capacity region provided by Information Theory is not by itself sufficient for the modeling of the system and a combination of Queuing Theory and Information Theory is needed (Telatar & Gallager, 1995). The questions that are asked here is what rates can be achieved, and how (with which policies). This has led to the notions of the capacity region of a policy, and the network capacity region, *i.e.*, the closure of the set of all arrival user rates that can be stably supported by a network when all possible scheduling, routing and resource allocation policies are considered (Georgiadis, Neely & Tassiulas, 2006). The policies can have perfect knowledge of the entire network and of its traffic including the future. Hence, the network capacity region is an upper bound for the capacity region of each policy. The network capacity region depends on specific assumptions on the traffic arrival statistics and on the physical and access layer parameters of the system; it is not a capacity region in the information-theoretic sense.

A related notion is *throughput optimality*. A scheduling scheme is throughput optimal if it guarantees system stability, meaning that all individual queues of the network are stable. Good scheduling schemes achieve large capacity regions (in some cases as large as the network capacity region) and are, at the same time, throughput optimal. Nevertheless, even throughput optimality cannot guarantee the *fairness* of a policy in terms of delay or other requirements. Throughput optimality and fairness issues are some of the topics that are discussed in this survey.

In analogy to the MAC, use of cross-layer optimization also benefits the downlink of a wireless cellular system that constitutes a fading Broadcast Channel (BC). In a BC, the Base Station needs to schedule its transmissions to the users in order to satisfy QoS, fairness and rate criteria. Moreover, it is desired that the policy capacity region be as close as possible to the network capacity region. Although the objectives are similar with the MAC, because of the differences between the two channel models, the results from the MAC do not always extend to the BC in a straightforward way. In fact, it can be argued that, for the time being, less is known on cross-layer scheduling and resource allocation for fading BC channels compared to fading MAC.

While the fading MAC and the fading BC capacity regions represent the ultimate limits in achievable rates in the uplink and downlink, respectively, transmitting close to capacity is very complicated and still a distant goal given the technology and the processing power that is presently available. Current implementations employ sub-optimal approaches, the most widespread being CDMA and OFDMA. It is expected that the latter will dominate the physical layer implementations of commercial WLAN and WMAN systems in the near future. Therefore, scheduling and resource allocation for CDMA and OFDMA is of particular importance in order to improve the performance of Next-Generation Networks. Scheduling and resource allocation in CDMA consists of deciding which users to transmit to (and receive from), selecting the modulation, the coding scheme, the number of codes used and the transmission power. For OFDMA, in addition to the scheduling of users, the controller determines the assignment of subcarriers to the users, the coding and modulation scheme, and the transmitted power. Latest wireless systems also employ multiple antenna transmission (in the form of MISO, SIMO or MIMO) in order to improve the reliability and/or increase the data rates. Scheduling and resource allocation for multi-antenna systems is another active area of research that is briefly mentioned in this chapter (Viswanathan & Kumaran, 2005).

POWER- AND DELAY-EFFICIENT SCHEDULING OVER FADING GAUSSIAN CHANNELS

Although the full structure of a wireless cellular system is captured by the fading Multiple Access Channel (for the uplink) and the fading Broadcast Channel (for the downlink), in many cases the fading Gaussian channel can model satisfactorily the link between a Base Station (BS) and a Mobile Station (MS) once it has been established. Moreover, fading Gaussian channels are good models for several point-to-point links. One can get useful insights on the benefits of cross-layer in the simpler setting of Gaussian fading before moving on to the more complex cases of the fading MAC and the fading BC.

Consider transmission through a fading Gaussian channel as shown in Fig. 1. Since, by definition, the channel is dedicated to one pair of users, there is no contention for usage of the channel. However, because of fading, the data rate that the user can transmit depends on the instantaneous value of the channel taps and on the power that he is willing to use. From an information-theoretic point of view, if the transmitter knows the channel gain and has a given average power budget P he should perform energy waterfilling in time (Goldsmith & Varaiya, 1997). This way the transmitting user exploits opportunistically the peaks of the channel in order to achieve the best possible rate given his power budget. Depending on the power budget and the channel statistics the user may not transmit during some intervals where the channel is bad. It has been shown that rate gains with respect to flat power allocation increase as the signal-to-noise ratio (SNR) decreases. For high SNR the gains with respect to flat power allocation vanish. From a network point of view, opportunistic transmission on the fading channel has two implications: First, the upper layers can only view the physical layer as a bit pipe if the time window is large enough to average the variations of the channel and the transmitted rate and power. Second, as the SNR decreases the average transmission delay increases, since the transmitter will wait more, on the average, for a favorable channel. In a practical scenario, action needs to be taken if the delays become unacceptably large. The transmission rate can be increased (and therefore packets of the queue can be pushed to the channel) by increasing the transmission power. Obviously, this, in turn, will result in an increase of the overall average power. Cross-layer techniques attempt to achieve good delay-power tradeoffs.

The scheduler used for transmission over a Gaussian fading channel has the following objective: Find a power allocation policy $P = P(h,q)$ that allocates power using Channel State Information (CSI) h and Queue State Information (QSI) q and minimizes the average power subject to the delay not exceeding a value D_{max}. Alternatively,

Figure 1. Power adaptation for transmission through a fading Gaussian channel

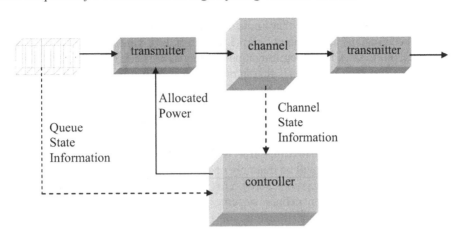

the dual objective of minimizing the average delay subject to the average power not exceeding P_{max} is considered. The delay constraint can either be a single transmission deadline where D_{max} is the same for all packets, or an individual delay constraint, different for each packet (Chen, Neely & Mittra 2007). When the constraint is a single transmission deadline D_{max} it has been shown that the average power is a strictly decreasing and convex function of D_{max}. This simplifies the scheduler complexity that can be solved using dynamic programming techniques (Berry & Gallager, 2002). When no delay can be tolerated, channel inversion needs to be performed in order to empty the queue at the end of each scheduling period. The average power will depend on the fading statistics. For Rayleigh fading the channel inversion scheme leads to infinite average power even for regular traffic. Hence, some outage probability should be tolerated and the scheduler would need to abstain for transmitting occasionally.

Another approach to scheduling is to find the optimal solution assuming full knowledge of all channel gains. This is frequently referred to as *offline scheduling*, since scheduling cannot be performed real-time (causally) because the future gains are not available at the transmitter. After finding the optimal offline scheduler, the intuition provided by the solution is used to develop heuristic online methods. This methodology was used in (Uysal-Biyikoglu, El-Gamal & Brabhakar, 2002) to develop an algorithm named Look-ahead Waterfilling (LW). LW sets a target transmission rate that is not constant, but depends on the size of the queue backlog. Based on this target rate, power is allocated according to waterfilling in time. It was shown that the performance of the LW algorithm is close to that of the offline optimal scheduler. Compared to waterfilling without using information on the queue size, LW reduces the average energy and the variance of the packet delay. The price to be paid is an increase in the average delay, which is one more manifestation of the aforementioned energy vs. delay tradeoff in fading Gaussian channels.

CROSS-LAYER SCHEDULING AND RESOURCE ALLOCATION AMONG MANY USERS IN CELLULAR NETWORKS

Having motivated the use of cross-layer techniques by considering the fading Gaussian channel, the focus is now shifted to multiple users with the uplink and downlink of a cellular system in mind. As explained previously, in a wireless system, variability and medium sharing create interdependencies across the users and the different layers of the system (Lin, Shroff & Srikant, 2006). Cross-layer optimization attempts to determine joint resource allocation and user scheduling policies. The goal of the policies is two-fold: First, ensure that system requirements, such as data rate, fairness, energy consumption, and delay constraints are met. Second, while exploiting the available system resources to the fullest possible extent, ensure stability of the network. Arguably, the problem is very complex and, in some cases, simplified approaches need to be followed. A common approach is to incorporate the allocation of resources across multiple layers in a unified optimization framework. In some cases the framework may have a layered structure that limits the degree of cross-layer coupling, therefore facilitating the development of scheduling and allocation policies (Lin, Shroff & Srikant, 2006). For a recent effort in this area see (Chiang et al., 2007). As expected, optimization techniques are heavily used in cross-layer scheduling. An additional difficulty in wireless networks is that in many occasions the problem to be solved is non-convex which means that additional tools, such as combinatorial optimization, stochastic stability, graph theory, and large deviations theory may need to be used.

Since this survey focuses mostly on the cellular paradigm, the framework presented here relates mainly to scheduling for single-hop networks. Details on the framework for joint congestion control and scheduling for multi-hop wireless networks can be found in (Lin, Shroff & Srikant, 2006) and in (Georgiadis, Neely & Tassiulas, 2006). Also, a fundamental assumption will be that only one transmission can occur at a given time, frequency or code slot, *i.e.,* orthogonal multiplexing is considered. This is not optimal from a theoretic-information point of view, but it corresponds to the way current cellular systems operate. Cross-layer scheduling and link adaptation for the MAC and the BC using simultaneous transmission is considered later in this chapter.

As explained in the previous section, because of the burstiness of traffic and the varying nature of a wireless system, the design of latest-generation systems favors opportunistic scheduling where the resources of a system are offered to the users that can make the best use of them. This design philosophy is different from earlier systems where variability was viewed as a nuisance, and an effort was made to treat all users equally once they were admitted in the system. Obviously, although opportunistic scheduling makes it possible to better exploit the system resources by using favorable channel states rather than averaging and leads to gains in the sum of the data rates over a scheduling period, it creates the potential for unfairness in the system. Therefore, the controller needs to be designed appropriately in order to guarantee fairness criteria such as: fairness in time (a user can communicate for at least a given amount of time over each period); minimum guaranteed data rate over a period, proportional fairness (increasing the relative rate of one user does not decrease the relative aggregate rate of other users by a larger amount); or more generalized functions and combinations of the aforementioned. In the same time, the scheduling policy needs to be throughput optimal, *i.e.,* guarantee stability of the network. In the following, a brief outline of results is presented for the *infinite backlog* case where it is considered that there are always data to transmit in all user queues, and the *finite backlog* case where the queue lengths vary depending on an external arrival process and the rate assigned by the controller. More details can be found in (Lin, Shroff & Srikant, 2006).

Consider a cellular system downlink (without loss of generality) and N users to whom a Base Station wishes to send data, as shown in Fig. 2. The Base Station has a dedicated queue for each user. Time is slotted. The infinite-backlogged case is considered first, where there are always data waiting to be sent in a user queue. Each user can receive data from the Base Station at rate r_i during the scheduling slot under consideration. The BS can only transmit to one user during one slot. Let $U_i(r_i)$ be the *utility function* associated with sending data rate r_i to user x_i. The utility function expresses the value of providing user x_i with data r_i. U_i is a very general function and depends, in general, not only on user i but also on the entire system, since sending data to user i may adversely affect other users as well as the overall fairness of the scheduler. The scheduler has full knowledge of the parameters affecting U_i, including Channel State Information (CSI). Finally, it is assumed that the channel varies according to a stationary stochastic process. Another model considers that the channel conditions are created by an adversary that creates worst-case conditions. More details on scheduling in the presence of an adversary can be found in (Andrews, 2005). During each scheduling period the controller determines the index i of the user that is selected for transmission using a scheduling policy Q that is a function of all the $U_i(r_i)$: $i = Q(U_1(r_1), U_1(r_2), ..., U_N(r_N))$ among the set of possible policies P. Then, data are transmitted to user i with rate r_i.

One approach to scheduling and resource allocation is to maximize the average sum utility of the N users subject to fairness constraints, and can be formulated as follows

$$\max_{Q \in \mathbf{Q}} \sum_{i=1}^{N} \mathrm{E}[U_i(r_i)]$$

subject to $\mathbf{F}(Q) \succ \mathbf{0}$

Figure 2. Downlink of a cellular system

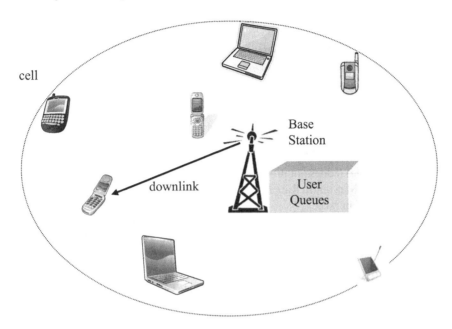

where Q is the selected policy, $\mathbf{Q}$ is the set of all stationary scheduling policies and $\mathbf{F}(Q)$ is a vector containing the fairness constraints for each user. The solution to the previous problem involves solving a non-convex problem, in general. However, for some of the problems (such as when $\mathbf{F}$ is a time fairness constraint dictating a minimum guaranteed transmission time to each user), the optimal policy has the form

$$Q^* = \arg\max_i \{\beta_i\},$$

where β_i is obtained using a stochastic approximation algorithm (Lin, Shroff & Srikant, 2006). Other related problems have solutions of the form

$$Q^* = \arg\max_i \{\alpha_i U_i(r_i) + \beta_i\}.$$

It has been shown that when the objective is proportional fairness, maximization of

$$\sum_{i=1}^{N} \log E[(r_i)]$$

should be performed. This results in the Proportional Fair scheduling algorithm (Tse & Viswanath, 2005) that has been used in several systems, including IS-856 (CDMA2000). At each scheduling period, the decision on which user to transmit to is based on the following rule:

$$Q^* = \arg\max_i \left\{ \frac{r_i(t)}{T_i(t)} \right\},$$

where $T_i(t)$ denote average throughputs that are updated with an exponentially weighted low-pass filter:

$$T_k(t+1) = \begin{cases} (1-\tau)T_k(t) + \tau\, r_k(t) & \text{if } k = Q^* \\ (1-\tau)T_k(t) & \text{otherwise} \end{cases}$$

for a constant τ. The intuition behind the algorithm is the following: The user that is scheduled to transmit is the one whose achievable rate is the best compared to his average. This way, even users with low rates will get to transmit if they encounter a channel state that is much more favorable compared to their average case. Although with the proportional fair scheduling algorithm every user gets the opportunity to transmit (else the argument of $\log R_i$ would be equal to 0 for some i) it does not provide any guarantees on the minimum rate. A variation called Proportional Fair with Minimum/Maximum Rate Constraints (Andrews, 2005) guarantees that the rate of each user stays within pre-determined bounds.

Up to this point, an infinite backlog was considered. In practice, users may not always have data to send. Hence, for the finite backlog case, it is essential that scheduling algorithms guarantee stability. Consider the simple example of a system with two users with arrival rates λ_1 and λ_2, respectively. Without loss of generality, assume that $\lambda_1 < \lambda_2$. If the channel gain for both users is the same, *i.e.*, $|h_1| = |h_2|$, and a fairness constraint is imposed that requires that both users transmit for the same amount of time, user 1 may remain idle for part of his transmission slot, while, in the same time, the Base Station may not be able to transmit all data destined for user 2. In practical scenarios this will lead to the queue corresponding to user 2 becoming unbounded and the network becoming unstable. Therefore, in realistic wireless systems, throughput optimal scheduling policies, i.e., policies that ensure stability of the network are required. Moreover, it is desired that these policies operate close to the capacity region of the network so that the gains from opportunistic transmission be harnessed. In fact, it has been shown that Proportional Fair scheduling is unstable in the finite backlog case (Andrews, 2005).

In a landmark paper on scheduling and resource allocation (Tassiulas & Ephremides, 1993), the authors demonstrated that throughput optimality can be achieved using a Max-Weight algorithm that takes into account the queue length of each user

$$Q^* = \arg\max_i \{q_i r_i\}.$$

In retrospect, the reason why Proportional Fair scheduling may become unstable is because the queue lengths of each user are not taken into account. Therefore, the queue of a user with large arrival rate and relatively bad channel may become unstable even if the user gets a fair share of channel use time. It is interesting to note that knowledge of the arrival rate of each user is not required for the Max-Weight (MW) policy (Georgiadis, Neely & Tassiulas, 2006). Another characteristic of MW is that, with the exception of the symmetric case of queues with equal arrival and connectivity statistics, it does not guarantee delay fairness. Consider again a system with two users, the arrival rate of user 1 being much lower than that of user 2 ($\lambda_1 \ll \lambda_2$). Also, assume that the BS can offer a much smaller rate to user 1 than to user 2 ($r_1 \ll r_2$). Therefore, user 1 may need to wait for a long time before $q_1 r_1$ becomes larger than $q_2 r_2$ resulting in the scheduler allowing him to transmit, and the policy is, consequently, unfair to users with smaller rates. Moreover, favoring the user with the higher rate creates asymmetry in the system that may lead to inefficient utilization of the resources (Georgiadis, Neely & Tassiulas, 2006). To address fairness, one approach that has been proposed is to schedule according to

$$Q^* = \arg\max_i \{a_i d_i r_i\},$$

where d_i is the delay of the first packet of the queue of user i and α_i is a constant. Other metrics have also been suggested where the weight of each queue is not a linear function of the delay (Lin, Shroff & Srikant, 2006).

CROSS-LAYER SCHEDULING AND RESOURCE ALLOCATION FOR FADING MULTIPLE ACCESS AND BROADCAST CHANNELS

Fading MAC

The uplink of a cellular system corresponds to the information-theoretic fading Multiple Access Channel (fading MAC). The capacity of the Gaussian MAC is given by the set of all non-negative vectors $\mathbf{r} = (r_1, r_2, ..., r_N)$ that satisfy

$$\sum_{i \in S} r_i \leq W \log \left(1 + \frac{\sum_{i \in S} |h_i| p_i}{N_0 W} \right)$$

for all sets $S \subseteq \{1, 2, ..., N\}$, W is the used bandwidth, $|h_i|^2$ are the channel gains and N_0 the single-sided noise power spectral density. The Base Station then uses Successive Interference Cancellation (SIC) (Tse & Viswanath, 2005) to decode each user. Current uplink implementations use suboptimal encoding schemes for communication through the MAC channel, the main reason being complexity. Although in CDMA systems users transmit simultaneously, they also are suboptimal, since for the decoding of each user all other users are treated as noise. In a fading MAC channel the situation becomes more complicated compared to AWGN. In the symmetric case where all users have the same channel statistics the sum capacity is achieved by scheduling transmission of only the user with the largest channel gain during each slot (orthogonal multiple access). However, the sum capacity criterion may not be fair in the asymmetric case where users have different average channel energy. In the latter case, it turns out that orthogonal multiple access is suboptimal compared to simultaneous transmission and SIC. The rates and the powers need to be adapted dynamically as a function of the network topology and the channel (Tse & Viswanath, 2005).

The information-theoretic capacity of fading MAC channels is defined the closure of all rate vectors that can be achieved long-term if the channel is averaged in a sufficient time period. However, as mentioned before, this view implies regular traffic patterns from all users. In cellular networks, traffic arrives randomly. Even if the rates of the users averaged over a sufficiently long period of time are inside the capacity region of the fading MAC, this does not necessarily mean that transmission with these rates can be achieved. Similar to the cases of the fading Gaussian channel and the uplink where only one user is allowed to transmit at any given time, the reason for this is the burstiness of the traffic. Since user data arrive randomly, it is possible that during some scheduling periods the volume of the data to be transmitted exceeds the capacity of the channel. Therefore, the need arises for scheduling and resource allocation algorithms for the fading MAC channel. Again, the scheduler needs to consider not only the Channel State Information of each user (as required by information theory in order for the capacity to be achieved) but also the Queue State Information (QSI) before making a decision on which users should be allowed to transmit to the Base Station, their power level, the coding scheme to be employed and the resulting data rate. In practical systems, additional constraints, such as a limit on peak power, may also need to be taken into account.

Note that, for the fading MAC, the scheduler output consists of more than one quantities, in general, in contrast with the model used up to this point, where it was considered that the decision taken by the scheduler was which user will be allowed transmit at a given period and the rate was pre-determined by the available user power (orthogonal multiple access). One approach to scheduling (Berry & Yeh, 2004) is the following: First determine a *power allocation policy* that is a function of the channel states and the queue states and satisfies the peak and average power constraints. Then, find the *rate allocation policy* based on the chosen power allocations. Both power and rate allocation consist of a vector $\mathbf{p}$ and $\mathbf{r}$, respectively.

In a practical system with external arrivals, the scheduling policy should be stable. One of the most elegant results for the fading MAC channel is that the network capacity region coincides with the information-theoretic capacity region under power control (Yeh & Cohen, 2003). Therefore, as long as the average rates of the users are inside the fading MAC information-theoretic capacity region, a power-and-rate allocation policy exists that guarantees stability. Conversely, the network becomes unstable if the rate vector is outside the information-theoretic capacity region. (Yeh & Cohen, 2004) have derived a throughput optimal policy for the fading MAC proving that the information-theoretic capacity of a fading MAC can actually be achieved by scheduling even if the rates of the users are not known (the complexity and other idealized assumptions such as perfect CSI notwithstanding). The policy is based on the following criterion: Given the queue sizes q_i find a power and rate allocation (**p**, **r**) that maximizes $\Sigma \alpha_i q_i r_i$, subject to **r** belonging to the fading MAC information-theoretic capacity region and satisfying the peak power constraints (if any). The α_i are constants denoting the priority (utility) of each user. For the maximization of the weighted rates the solution of (Tse & Hanly, 1998) for the fading MAC can be used.

As aforementioned, instead of jointly determining the vector (**p**, **r**), the scheduler can be simplified by first determining a power allocation policy followed by rate allocation. For some scenarios (such as the symmetric case where all channels experience fading with the same statistics and all utility functions are the same) the power allocation policy can be determined easily. Given a power allocation policy the optimal rate allocation for the fading MAC satisfies the so-called longest weighted queue highest possible rate principle (LWQHPR) and has a closed-form solution (Berry & Yeh, 2004). In summary, the solution consists of ordering the user in decreasing order of their queue sizes and performing superposition coding using the given power allocation.

As explained previously, throughput optimality of an allocation policy does not guarantee delay fairness. In fact, delay fairness for fading MAC scheduling policies is still an open problem (Berry & Yeh, 2004). In some cases, delay-optimal policies have been derived. More specifically, for fading MAC channels where the fading is symmetric, *i.e.*, each user "sees" the same fading distribution with the same average channel gain power, the following policy has been shown to be delay-optimal in the sense that it minimizes the average delay of packets: Allocate power using a symmetric power allocation policy that only considers the channel state of each user and is such that the allocated power does not depend on the index of the user, but only on the channel. Given the power allocation, find the rate allocation **r** that maximizes $\Sigma q_i r_i$ (note that $\alpha_i=1$ which means that all queues are weighted equally). A delay-optimal power and rate allocation policy for the general fading MAC channel has not been obtained to this date, to the best of the authors' knowledge.

Fading BC

A wireless system downlink is an example of a Broadcast Channel (BC). Similar to the uplink, in general, more than one Mobile Stations request to receive data from a Base Station. The information-theoretic capacity region of the BC and the coding scheme that achieves it are different than the MAC, and, consequently, the power and rate allocations for cross-layer also need to be modified. However, the goal here is again the same: Find the network capacity region, compare it to the information-theoretic capacity, obtain throughput optimal policies, if they exist, and, finally, determine if and how delay optimality can be achieved. Interestingly, some of the results for the BC are similar to those for the MAC despite the different information-theoretic capacity regions.

In a BC, the Base Station sends different information to each Mobile Station. The information-theoretic capacity of the AWGN BC is given by the set of rate vectors that satisfy

$$r_i \leq W \log\left(1 + \frac{\alpha_i |h_i|^2 P}{N_0 W + \sum_{j>i} \alpha_j |h_j|^2 P}\right),$$

where P is the available power at the Base Station, the users are ordered by increasing channel gain and the α_i are nonnegative and sum to 1. Again, in contrast to current wireless systems designs, the optimal solution, in general, is to transmit to more than one user simultaneously using superposition coding. Each Mobile Station performs SIC in order to recover the information signal destined for him. In the process, he also decodes information of the users with worse SNR than his. For networks with random traffic, the scheduler needs to decide how much power to allocate to each user (the value of α_j), a decision that also has an impact on the sequence of superposition coding and SIC. The decision is based on CSI and QSI.

Similar to the fading MAC, the network capacity region of the fading BC coincides with the information-theoretic region. Moreover, throughput optimal power and rate allocation methods exist for the BC. One method consists of using methods that maximize $\Sigma\alpha_i q_i r_i$, in analogy with the MAC case.

Regarding delay optimal scheduling and resource allocation for the BC, little progress has been made to date and no delay optimal methods are known to exist even for a given power control policy (Barry & Yeh 2004). Recently, it was observed that if the allocated rates for the users of a BC are proportional to their queue lengths, delay fairness can be achieved when the traffic of different users is asymmetric. Moreover, the average delay is decreased with respect to the case when LWQHPR policies are used. This scheduling policy, often referred to as Queue Proportional Scheduling (QPS) (Seong, Narasimhan & Cioffi, 2006) is the solution of a Geometric Program and has been shown to be throughput optimal. Although it is intuitively plausible that QPS is delay-optimal, no proof exists to this date.

CROSS-LAYER SCHEDULING AND RESOURCE ALLOCATION FOR CDMA AND OFDMA WIRELESS SYSTEMS

Research on cross-layer scheduling and resource allocation strategies for the fading MAC and the fading BC tries to establish the limits of performance of wireless networks. However, and despite their increasing degree of sophistication, current implementations of wireless systems are suboptimal compared to the physical layer encoding schemes that achieve the information-theoretic capacity. Therefore, it is interesting to study scheduling and resource allocation in the context of the two most widespread multiple access technologies, namely Code Division Multiple Access (CDMA) and Orthogonal Frequency Division Multiple Access (OFDMA).

In OFDMA systems, a combination of time and frequency division is used. More specifically, users share subcarriers of OFDM symbols belonging to frames, each frame comprising more than one OFDM symbol. Hence, the scheduling problem consists of determining which users should be allowed to transmit in a given frame, whereas the resource allocation problem deals with allocating the available subcarriers to the users, choosing the power with which each user should transmit in each subcarrier, as well as dictating the modulation and coding scheme to be employed. One important consideration in OFDMA systems is inter-cell interference. Because of the small bandwidth occupied by each subcarrier (in contrast to CDMA) the system needs to employ a rotation scheme for the subcarriers of each cell so that the inter-cell interference to a given user be randomized (Tse & Viswanath, 2005). Therefore, ideally, the system should take into account the needs of all users, including those of neighboring cells. Clearly, this is a complicated problem.

If the inter-cell interference is considered to be random (because of a good underlying rotation scheme), for the scheduling and resource allocation problem it can be assumed that only Gaussian noise is present in each subcarrier (due to the thermal noise and the randomized inter-cell interference). When the channel estimates are not perfect, a self-noise term can also be included. In (Agrawal et al., 2006) a scheduling and resource allocation scheme for the downlink of an OFDMA system was proposed that uses a gradient-based scheduling framework. This consists of selecting the rate vector that has the maximum projection onto the gradient of a system utility function. An optimization problem of the form

$$\mathbf{r}^{*} = \max_{r \in R}\{\nabla U(\mathbf{W})^{T}\mathbf{r}\}$$

is solved, where $U(\mathbf{W}) = \Sigma U_i(W_i)$ is an increasing concave utility function of W_i, the throughput of the user i averaged over time, and R is the set of vectors belonging to the feasible rate region which, in turn, depends on average and peak power constraints. Different expressions can be used for U_i. In general, the problem can be viewed as a maximization of a weighted sum of rates, where the weights vary in time and depend on the average throughput of each user, fairness criteria and QoS requirements. The rate vector depends on the number of subcarriers that are allocated to each user and the amount of transmit power in each subcarrier. Moreover, users are allowed to time-share a subcarrier in the sense that during one frame (consisting of multiple OFDM symbols) a given user may transmit on the subcarrier during some OFDM symbols, followed by another user and so on.

With these assumptions, and if the channel state is known by the scheduler for all users and tones with a known estimation error, it is shown that scheduling and resource allocation can be formulated as a convex problem, which means that the controller can perform scheduling and resource allocation using convex program solvers. The output of the scheduler at each period is the indices x_{ij} indicating the (time) portion of the frame during which user i can transmit on subcarrier j and the powers p_{ij} with which transmission should occur. Therefore, assuming that inter-cell interference is sufficiently random for the assumptions to hold and that a good choice of the weights is made, scheduling and resource allocation in OFDMA is a tractable problem.

A recent approach to OFDMA scheduling and power allocation includes the effect of inter-cell interference (Koutsopoulos & Tassiulas, 2006). Two heuristic scheduling and resource allocation algorithms are developed, a vertical one considering each subcarrier separately across different cells, and a horizontal scheme based on waterfilling across the subcarriers in each cell. The vertical algorithm is shown to perform better. However, the algorithm does not guarantee fairness in rate allocation, an issue that remains to be addressed.

Similar approaches can be applied to CDMA systems. Again, the downlink case is mentioned here as an example. The approach can also be applied to the uplink with the appropriate changes in the parameters. The difference compared to OFDMA is that the transmitter sends data to all users simultaneously. Therefore, resource allocation consists of choosing the modulation and coding scheme, the number of spreading codes and the transmit power. In (Agrawal, Subramanian, & Berry, 2007) a scheduling and resource allocation policy is proposed that employs a gradient-based framework, in analogy to the gradient-based OFDMA approach. The capacity region is parameterized by the number of spreading codes n_i and the power p_i assigned to each user i. The parameters correspond to a physical layer operating point and are subject to a constraint on the number of used codes and to an average power constraint. Moreover, it is assumed that all spreading codes are mutually orthogonal. Interestingly, the authors show that additional constraints, such as peak power, maximum rate (overall and per code) and maximum SINR (overall and per code) can be formulated as per user power constraints that are input to the scheduler. When the constraint is a limit on the SINR or on the rate per code, the optimization problem turns out to be convex, leading to a simplification of the scheduler.

MULTIPLE ANTENNA SYSTEMS

Transmission using multiple antennas at the transmitter, at the receiver or both is becoming increasingly prevalent in latest-generation wireless systems, the reason being the spatial diversity and the additional degrees of freedom (in the case of MIMO) that are achieved. The challenge here is how to reduce the correlation among different paths as much as possible in order to improve the system performance. Moreover, even if the system can be modeled with satisfactory accuracy, the SIMO, MISO and MIMO systems are more complicated than their SISO counterparts. As an example, the coding scheme that achieves the information-theoretic capacity region of the Gaussian BC when the Base Station employs more than one antenna was not known until very recently (Weingarten, Steinberg & Shamai, 2006).

As expected, cross-layer scheduling and resource allocation algorithms for MIMO systems have not been as extensively studied as their SISO counterparts. MIMO technology is being introduced gradually in wireless systems and it can be argued that the deployment of full-blown MIMO systems is still some years away. Therefore, from a practical point of view, it makes more sense to focus on cross-layer for existing topologies. Moreover, from the researchers' aspect, understanding the behavior of cross-layer is easier in systems whose physical layers issues have been solidly understood.

An intermediate step on the way to MIMO scheduling and resource allocation is the MISO paradigm where a Base Station with Multiple Antennas communicates with single-antenna Mobile users. This scenario is also very realistic since use of multiple antennas at the Base Station is becoming increasingly prevalent because the cost and space constraints are less stringent compared to the Mobile Station side. For example, IEEE802.16e-based systems include the option of using Alamouti's space-time code, (or other space-time codes when more than two transmit antennas are employed). Another interesting scenario where the MISO model can be applied is when a Mobile Station establishes simultaneous connections with more than one Base Stations.

In (Viswanathan & Kumaran, 2005) the authors consider the simplified downlink problem where the Base Station transmits to many users simultaneously using beamforming techniques. In contrast to the optimal solution for the BC that employs joint (dirty paper) coding for the users, separate coding is considered. It is shown that, in some very special cases (such as when the SNR of all users is the same and the users are mutually orthogonal), the strategy of encoding separately is optimal. As it turns out, unlike the SISO BC, where in the symmetric case the Base Station only transmits to the best user, in the MISO case it may be better to simultaneously transmit to more than one Mobile Stations. A scheduling and resource allocation algorithm is derived whose goal is to minimize the average delay across all users. Infinite queues and perfect channel estimation are assumed. The output of the algorithm is the set of user indices to whom the Base Station will transmit as well as the power allocation across the users. It is shown that transmitting to multiple users provides capacity gains as long as the angle spread of propagation at the Base Station is small compared to the beam widths.

In addition to the increased complexity of multiple antenna systems, it should be kept in mind that satisfying the assumptions made in the derivation of cross-layer schemes may be more challenging, since information from more links, user queues and, possibly, cells needs to be collected by the controller. The increasing popularity of multiple antenna systems and the interesting issues associated with scheduling and resource allocation will very likely result in significant research activity in the future.

CONCLUDING REMARKS

This chapter provided an overview of cross-layer scheduling and resource allocation for single-hop wireless systems. The treatment of the subject was far from being exhaustive, the purpose being to introduce this research area, motivate its use in Next-Generation Networks and refer to some of the interesting ideas and approaches that have appeared recently. Although cross-layer optimization is a relatively new topic, some algorithms have already been applied to commercial systems. The challenges in the future will be to address the complexities associated with the application of cross-layer techniques to the increasingly sophisticated wireless networks and to design efficient schemes that will exploit the available resources to the best possible extent. It is expected that cross-layer optimization for multi-hop and, possibly, heterogeneous networks will also be of particular importance.

REFERENCES

Agrawal, R., Berry, R., Huang, J., & Subramanian, V. (2006). Optimal scheduling for OFDMA systems. In *Fortieth Asilomar Conference on Signals, Systems and Computers* (pp. 1347-1351). IEEE.

Agrawal, A., Subramanian, V., & Berry, R. (2007). Joint scheduling and resource allocation in CDMA systems. Retrieved September 8, 2007, from http://www.ece.northwestern.edu/~rberry/opt.pdf

Andrews, M. (2005). A survey of scheduling theory in wireless data networks. In *Proc. of the 2005 IMA summer workshop on wireless communications.*

Berry, R. A., & Gallager, R. G. (2002). Communication over fading channels with delay constraints, *IEEE Transactions on Information Theory,* 48(5), 1135-1149.

Berry, R. A., & Yeh , E. M. (2004). Cross-layer wireless resource allocation, *IEEE Signal Processing Magazine,* 21(5), 59-68.

Chen, W., Neely M. J., & Mittra, U. (2007). Energy Efficient Scheduling with Individual Packet Delay Constraints: Offline and Online Results, In *Proc. IEEE INFOCOM 2003. Twenty-Sixth Annual Joint Conference of the IEEE Computer and Communications Societies: Vol. 1.* (pp. 1136-1144), IEEE.

Chiang, M., Low, S. H., Calderbank, A. R., & Doyle, J. C., Layering as optimization decomposition: a mathematical theory of network architectures, *Proceedings of the IEEE*, 95(1), 255-312.

Gallager, R. G. (1985). A perspective on multiaccess channels, *IEEE Transactions on Information Theory,* 31(2), 124-142.

Georgiadis, L., Neely, M. J., & Tassiulas, L. (2006). *Resource allocation and cross-layer control in wireless networks*. Now.

Goldsmith, A., & Varaiya, P (1997). Capacity of fading channels with channel side information, *IEEE Transactions on Information Theory*, 43(6), 1986-1992.

Goyal, M., Kumar, A., & Sharma, V. (2003). Power constrained and delay optimal policies for scheduling transmission over a fading channel. In *Proc. IEEE INFOCOM 2003. Twenty-Second Annual Joint Conference of the IEEE Computer and Communications Societies: Vol. 1.* (pp. 311-320), IEEE.

Koutsopoulos, I., & Tassiulas, L. (2006). Cross-layer adaptive techniques for throughput enhancement in wireless OFDM-based networks, *IEEE/ACM Transactions on Networking*, 14(5), 1056-2006.

Lin, X., Shroff, N. B., & Srikant, R. (2006). A tutorial on cross-layer optimization in wireless networks, *IEEE Journal on Selected Areas in Communications*, 24(8), 1452-1463.

Seong, K., Narasimhan, R., & Cioffi, J. M. (2006). Queue proportional scheduling via geometric programming in fading broadcast channels, *IEEE Journal on Selected Areas in Communications*, 24(8), 1593-1602.

Tassiulas, L., & Ephremides, A. (1993). Dynamic server allocation to parallel queues with randomly varying connectivity, *IEEE Transactions on Information Theory*, 39(2), 466-478.

Telatar, I. E., & Gallager, R. G. (1995). Combining queuing theory with information theory for multi-access, *IEEE Journal on Selected Areas in Communications* ,13(6), 963-969.

Tse, D., & Viswanath, P (2005). *Fundamentals of wireless communication*, Cambridge University Press.

Tse, D., & Hanly, S. (1998). Multi-access fading channels: Part I and Part II, *IEEE Transactions on Information Theory*, 44(7), 2796–2831.

Uysal-Biyikoglu, E., El-Gamal, A., & Prabhakar, B. (2002). Adaptive transmission of variable-rate data over a fading channel for energy efficiency. In *Proc. Global Telecommunications Conference (GLOBECOM): Vol. 1.* (pp. 97-101), IEEE.

Viswanathan, H., & Kumaran, K. (2005). Rate scheduling in multiple antenna downlink wireless systems, IEEE Transactions on Communications, 53(4), 645-655.

Weingarten, H., Steinberg, Y., & Shamai, S (2006). The capacity region of the Gaussian Multiple-Input Multiple-Output Broadcast Channel, *IEEE Transactions on Information Theory,* 52(9), 3936-3964.

Yeh, E. M., & Berry, R (2005). Throughput optimal control of cooperative relay networks. In Proc. *International Symposium on Information Theory (ISIT).* pp.1206-1210. IEEE.

E. Yeh and A. Cohen, (2004) "Information theory, queuing, and resource allocation in multi-user fading communications," in *Proc. Conf. Information Sciences and Systems*, Princeton, NJ, 2004, pp. 1396–1401.

Yeh, E. M., & Cohen, S. A. (2003). "Throughput and delay optimal resource allocation in multiaccess fading channels," in *Proc. Int. Symp. Information Theory*, Yokohama, Japan, 2003, p. 245.

KEY TERMS

Broadcast Channel (BC): A channel comprising a user x_0 wishing to send (in general different) information to users x_i i=1,...,N through a shared medium resulting to each user receiving the signal emitted by x_0 (in general through a different channel).

Channel State Information (CSI): Information on the state of the channel, namely channel gain and/or channel phase. Used by the controller for scheduling and resource allocation.

Information-Theoretic Capacity Region: The closure of the set of all achievable rates in a channel as found from Information Theory (*i.e.*, the supremium of the mutual information). Assumes regular traffic (or traffic averaged for a sufficiently long time so that burstiness is eliminated).

Multiple Access Channel (MAC): A channel of N users x_i i=1,...,N wishing to send information to a user x_0 though a shared medium resulting to superposition of the signals that x_0 receives from each user.

Network Capacity Region: The closure of the set of all arrival user rates that can be stably supported by a network when all possible scheduling, routing and resource allocation policies are considered. This includes knowledge of future states. The network capacity region cannot exceed the information-theoretic capacity region.

Queue State Information (QSI): Information on the queue corresponding to a user. The state may correspond to the queue length, the delay of the packet at the head of the queue, or to more general quantities such as individual packet priorities.

Throughput Optimality: The property that characterizes a scheduling scheme that guarantees system stability (stability of all individual queues of the network).

Chapter III
An AAA Framework for IP Multicast Communication in Next Generation Networks

Prashant Pillai
University of Bradford, UK

Yim Fun Hu
University of Bradford, UK

ABSTRACT

IP multicast mechanisms provide efficient bandwidth consumption and distribution of high volume contents such as audio/video streaming, audio/video-on-demand and file sharing to multiple users. To commercially deploy multicast services in next generation networks it is important for Network Providers (NPs) to be able to control user access to the multicast content and to be able to account the multicast usage. This chapter compares some of the existing security mechanisms and highlights their inadequacies for providing efficient multicast security. The chapter then describes an AAA framework for IP multicast, which combines the IETF MSEC architecture with efficient AAA techniques to provide secure multicast content and to enable NPs to authenticate, authorise and provide efficient access control of end users requesting multicast content. This AAA framework also supports both post-paid and pre-paid accounting of users and allows the monitoring of session information like session duration and data volume for each multicast session.

INTRODUCTION

When an end user wants to access multicast content, he or she needs to send an Internet Group Management Protocol (IGMP) (Cain, 2002) *Join* message to its next hop router. Upon receiving the request, this router uses a multicast protocol such as Protocol Independent Multicast (PIM) (Estrin, 1998) for setting up a distribution tree so that the multicast data can be routed from the source to the receiver. As stated by Cain (2002), joining a multicast group is an "unprivileged operation", or in other words, in standard multicast operation, any end user (i.e. host device) is allowed to join any multicast group and gain access to multicast traffic without authentica-

Copyright © 2009, IGI Global, distributing in print or electronic forms without written permission of IGI Global is prohibited.

tion. This implies that there is not a single mechanism defined to restrict access of the multicast traffic only to an authenticated and authorised set of users, or to inhibit un-authenticated users gaining access to multicast traffic, which are meant only for a specific user group. Hence NPs cannot limit or control the access to the multicast content making it impossible to account the users for their multicast service usages. In addition, these protocols do not enable the sender i.e. the Content Provider (CP) to know who is accessing the multicast data at any given time. Hence the sender cannot account users for the multicast usage, leading to an unclear business model for both the NP and the CP (Savola, 2005).

The traditional method of providing any form of accounting for multicast services is to associate it with security. In this mechanism, the multicast content is encrypted by the CP before transmission and the users who require access to this content have to request the security keys from the CP to decrypt the transmitted content. The CP may then charge these users to disclose the security keys to them. Though this provides a simple method in which the CP may charge users accessing the multicast content, it is merely a method to charge users once for providing the keys. This method does not provide the flexibility offered by standard Authentication, Authorisation and Accounting (AAA) protocols to allow access control by the NP, nor does it provide time and/or volume based pre-paid and post-paid charging. The Group Security Association and Key Management Protocol (GSAKMP) (Harney, 2006) and the Group Domain of Interpretation (GDOI) (Baugher, 2003) multicast security protocols based on the multicast security architecture (Baugher, 2005) defined by Internet Engineering Task Force (IETF) Multicast Security (MSEC) working group also use this traditional method for securing the multicast traffic. The biggest drawback with such a mechanism is that only the CP has the ability to control and charge the users. In a distributed architecture, the NP to which the user may be connected, has no control on the multicast usage and hence cannot charge the user for their network usage, making IP multicast service provision unattractive to the NP for commercial deployment. Since the NP has no control, a malicious user may send an IGMP *Join* message to join any multicast group with the intention to launch a Denial-of-Service attack.

AAA protocols such as RADIUS (Rigney, 2000) and Diameter (Calhoun, 2002) are being used very successfully and efficiently to ensure revenue generation for unicast by controlling the access to network resources. Similar AAA functionalities are also required for multicast services. Accounting multicast usage is most important for revenue generation in commercial networks. Hence it is required that the NP should be able to authenticate and authorise the user requesting access to the multicast content, measure the duration and volume of all multicast sessions and finally bill the user. In addition the multicast distribution trees should only be setup for authenticated users to prevent any denial-of-service attacks. This would prevent un-necessary network bandwidth consumption with data requested by an unauthenticated user.

Existing Multicast Security Mechanisms

The following sub-sections of the chapter describe some of the possible security architectures for securing multicast services by using existing multicast and security protocols.

IGAP

The Internet Group membership Authentication Protocol (IGAP) (Hayashi, 2003) (Hayashi, 2004) is based on the IGMP v2 protocol and is used for authentication of the join request sent by the multicast receiver to the first hop router. The protocol proposes to modify the IGMP v2 packet to include user specific information which can be used for authentication and accounting.

The procedure for user authentication using the IGAP protocol is shown in Figure 1where the user device initiates multicast access by sending an IGAP *Join* request to the IGAP router. This IGAP *Join* request consists of the group address of the multicast groups that the user is interested to receive data from and the user credentials, i.e. the username and password. If the Challenge-Response authentication mechanism is used, the process of requesting a *ChallengeID* and a subsequent response is added. On receiving this IGAP *Join* request, the IGAP router sends a RADIUS *Access-Request* to the backend RADIUS enabled AAA server. A Diameter enabled backend server may also be used. The AAA server can then authenticate the user and can then check the user profile to authorise the access request for the multicast content. If the user is a valid user and has the rights to

Figure 1. Access control procedure using IGAP

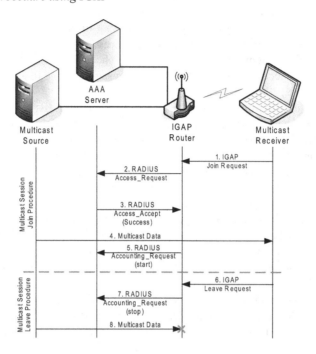

get access to the multicast data, then the AAA server returns a RADIUS *Access-Accept* message to the IGAP router. On the other hand if the user is not a valid user, or if the user is a valid user but the user profile does not authorise the access to multicast data then the AAA server sends back the RADIUS *Access Reject* message to the IGAP Router. When the IGAP router receives the RADIUS *Access-Accept* message, it starts forwarding the multicast traffic to the user. The IGAP Router then sends a RADIUS *Accounting-Request* message to start accounting for the usage.

When the user decides to stop the multicast session, the receiver sends an IGAP *Leave* message. The IGAP router then sends a RADIUS *Accounting-Request* to the AAA server to stop the accounting for the session. This message contains the total time for the session and the data volume transferred for the session. Hence both time and volume based accounting can be performed.

Some of the major drawbacks of this mechanism are as follows:

• The IGAP protocol is based on IGMP v2 when IGMP v3 has already become a standard.
• The transferring of passwords in clear text using the Password Authentication Protocol (PAP) mechanism (Llyod, 1992) is highly insecure. Any other receiver can easily use this to learn the credentials of the users.
• The Challenge Handshake Authentication Protocol (CHAP) authentication mechanism (Llyod, 1992) is weak against offline dictionary attacks. Also CHAP requires new messages for requests and responses to be defined.
• It proposes to extend IGMP to support authentication. This is not extensible since IGMP itself is not an authentication protocol and does not support several mechanisms in the same way as the Extensible Authentication Protocol (EAP) (Aboba, 2004) framework does. Currently, there is support for only two authentication mechanisms (PAP and CHAP).
• The method is also highly susceptible to Man-in-the-middle attacks and replay attacks. In man-in-the-middle attacks, an attacker may intercept the authentication messages between the user and the authenticator, act-

ing as the authenticator towards the user and acting as the user towards the authenticator. In such a way it would be able to intercept and retrieve the user security credentials. In replay attacks valid authentication messages are recorded and replayed at a later time.

- Only simple user credentials like usernames and password or challenges can be used. There is no support for carrying other credentials like digital certificates.

Gothic Multicast Architecture

The Gothic architecture (Judge, 2002) aims to provide multicast group access control by controlling the ability of hosts to join the multicast group and also provide anycast server group access control by controlling the ability of the hosts to advertise themselves for the anycast addresses. The Gothic architecture proposes a group member authorisation system that is responsible for authentication and authorisation of hosts before they access any multicast content. This system consists of three main entities: the Host (H) who is trying access multicast content, the router (R) and the Access Control Server (ACS) which performs the authentication and authorisation. The Gothic architecture uses the Public-Key Infrastructure (PKI) and hence does not use any standard AAA protocols like RADIUS and Diameter.

The procedure for access control in the Gothic architecture is shown in Figure 2. As the Gothic architecture uses PKI, the Host and the ACS both have public keys denoted by K_{+H} and K_{+ACS} respectively and also have corresponding private keys denoted by K_{-H} and K_{+-ACS} (Judge, 2002). $CERT_{K_{+x}}$ denotes the certificate containing the public-key K_{+x} issued by a trusted authority. These certificates are used as digital signatures for the messages. All messages signed by digital signatures are denoted as $[message]_{K_{-x}}$, where K_{-x} is the private key used for the signature.

As shown in Figure 2, the Host initiates the procedure by sending the request for authorisation (AR) to the ACS. This request consists of the multicast Group ID (GID) of the group that the host wants to join and the host's public key certificate.

Hence, $AR = \left[GID, CERT_{K_{+H}} \right] K_{-H}$

The ACS now authenticates the host and then checks the group policy to determine if the host has access rights to join the requested group (Judge, 2002). The Authorisation Acknowledgement (AA) is sent back from the ACS

Figure 2. Access control procedure in gothic architecture

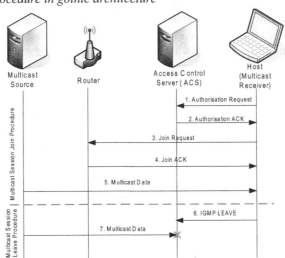

to the host informing the outcome of the authentication and authorisation. If the authentication and authorisation is successful, then this acknowledgement consists of the host's IP address, the host's distinguished name, the multicast group address, the expiry time and the public-key certificate of the ACS.

$$\text{Hence, } AA = \left[IP_H, DN_H, GID, T_{\exp}, CERT_{K_{+ACS}} \right] K_{-ACS}$$

On receiving the successful authorisation acknowledgement, the host sends an IGMP *Join* request to the router. This request contains the authorisation acknowledgement. The router would check the validity of the acknowledgement by verifying the ACS's signature, checking the expiry time and verifying the sender of the acknowledgement (This is done by comparing the IP address in the acknowledgment and the IP address of the host who sent join request).

Hence the Gothic architecture provides a means for authenticating and authorisation of the hosts and provides access control for multicast services. There are several issues in the procedure and the architecture that does not make it a very suitable approach as outlined below:

- In this architecture, the user directly sends authorisation requests to the ACS server. It is not very feasible to let user have direct access to the ACS, especially because the ACS would have access to all the user and group policy databases. It would be very easy for an attacker/hacker to target this ACS.
- The IGMP membership reports have to be modified to be able to carry the authorisation acknowledgement.
- One of the main problems in the architecture is the extra processing that needs to be done by the router. The router needs to process the authorisation acknowledgement inside the join request to perform access control. For this the router would need to understand PKI and would need to also have some means of getting keys of the ACS. As the router needs to process the acknowledgements, it is susceptible to Denial-of-Service Attacks (Ueno, 2005), where an adversary may send a large number of join requests for different multicast groups with invalid acknowledgments. The router would have to perform time consuming PKI processing for each of these messages and in-turn may not be able to provide service to legitimate users.
- Standard protocols like RADIUS and Diameter cannot be used in this architecture. New protocols/messages have to be defined especially for the interactions between the host and the ACS.
- Another major problem is that the sender plays no role in access control. The sender would not know who is receiving the data and would not be able to also keep track of the usage by different users.

L2/L3 Authentication before Join

Another possible architecture to provide AAA for multicast services is to perform Layer 2/Layer 3 authentication for users connecting to the NP. The message sequence charts for this architecture is shown in Figure 3. When the user wants to connect to the NP, it initiates the Layer 2 authentication mechanism. The figure shows a 802.1x enabled WLAN laptop as the multicast receiver, which initiates the EAP authentication mechanism by sending the *EAPoW Start* message. The 802.1x enabled router sends an EAP *Request* message, requesting the identity of the user. The EAP *Reply* message contains the user information i.e. the username. The 802.1x enabled router is connected to a backend RADIUS (or Diameter) AAA server. The router then extracts the user information from the EAP message and would put it in a RADIUS *Access-Request* message, which is sent to the RADIUS server. If the Challenge-Response authentication mechanism is used, the process of requesting a *ChallengeID* and replying is added. The AAA server can then authenticate the user. If the user is a valid user of the network then the AAA server returns a RADIUS *Access-Accept* message to the router. On the other hand if the user is not a valid user then the AAA server would return back the RADIUS *Access-Reject* message to the 802.1x Router. When the 802.1x enabled router receives the RADIUS *Access-Accept* message, it sends an EAP *Success* message to the WLAN laptop to inform the user of the successful outcome of the authentication. An optional message EAPOW *Key* is used for key exchange if Wired Equivalent Privacy (WEP) (Gast, 2005) is used. After the authentication process, the user sends an IGMP *Join* message requesting the access to the multicast content. When the user decides to stop the multicast session, the receiver sends an IGMP *Leave* message.

One of the main issues with this mechanism is that it can only be used to provide network access control, that is this authentication procedure takes place at the time the user connects to the network and the access to the network resources is controlled. Hence the user is authenticated before they can access any services. In other words, this authentication is not for any particular service (unicast or multicast) but for network access only. Such a mechanism is only feasible where all valid users of the network have the rights to access any services including the multicast services. Such a network can only use flat-rate pricing plans for unicast and multicast services. The user is billed for the total time he/she was connected to the network, or for the total volume of data (unicast and multicast).

Another main issue in this method is the support for accounting procedure. As this procedure provides user authentication for network access and not for any particular service, as shown in Figure 3, the accounting is started as soon as the user authentication finishes when the user connects to the network and stops when the user leaves the network. It is important to note that the user has to explicitly inform the network of his/her intention to leave the network; otherwise the accounting would not stop. Instead of accounting for the duration the user is connected to the network, it may also be required to account for the duration of a particular service. This would be essential when flat-rate pricing plans are not used and services may be charged differently.

Figure 3. Access control procedure using L2/L3 authentication

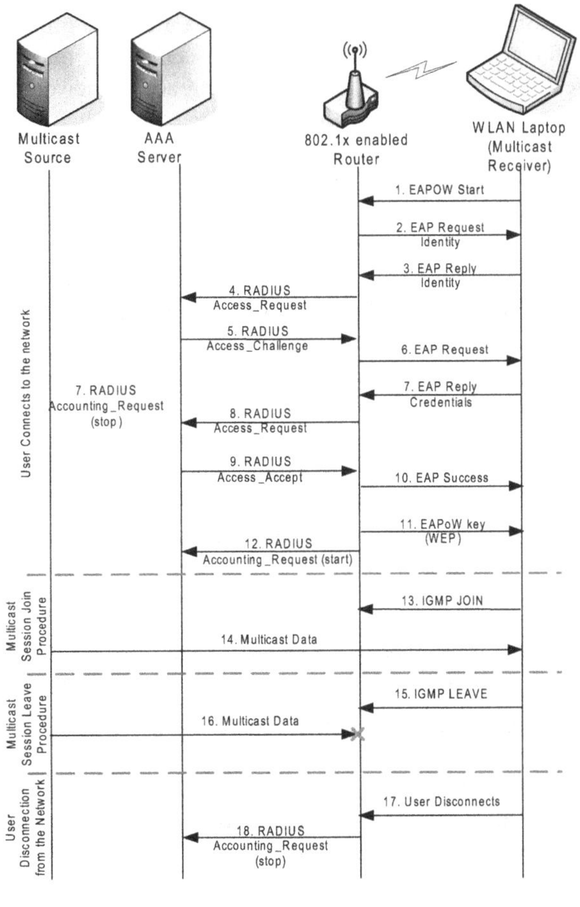

Figure 4. IETF MSEC group security achitecture

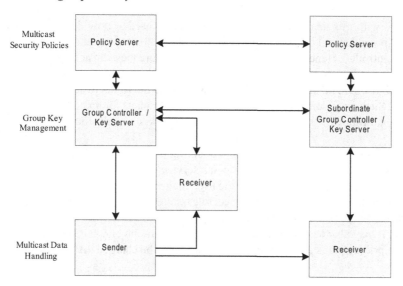

IETF Multicast Security Architecture

The IETF Multicast Security (MSEC) working group has defined a multicast group security architecture (Hardjono, 2004) that provides a reference framework for providing security for multicast services. This reference framework is shown in Figure 4. The different entities of the reference framework are:

- **Policy Server:** The policy server defines all the security policies for the particular multicast group
- **Group Controller/Key Server (GC/KS):** The GC/KS is responsible for the issuance and management of the different cryptographic keys used by a multicast group and for performing user authentication and authorization checks.
- **Subordinate GC/KS (S-GC/KS):** In a distributed architecture, the S-GC/KS shall perform the key management and user authentication functionalities within its domain to provide extensive scalability.
- **Senders:** Entities that send data to the multicast group.
- **Receivers:** Entities that send their credentials to the GC/KS for authentication to join the multicast group to receive the multicast content.

The multicast data is encrypted using the multicast extension for IPSec Protocol (Weis, 2006) at the sender's end before transmission. The GC/KS authenticates the user and sends the security keys that can be used for the decryption of the received traffic at the receiver's end to recover the multicast content. The following three protocols have been defined by the working group by which users can request to join a multicast group and the keys can be sent to the authenticated users:

- Multimedia Keying (MIKEY) (Arkko, 2004)
- Group Domain of Interpretation (GDOI) (Baugher, 2003)
- Group Security Association and Key Management Protocol (GSAKMP) (Harney, 2006)

While the multicast security architecture has several advantages including support for access control, protection of the multicast traffic by encryption, support for efficient re-keying mechanisms, the following disadvantages make it unsuitable for direct use in our network scenarios:

- There is a lack of support of standard AAA protocols that may have already been used by NPs for their unicast service provision. The NPs may prefer to extend their existing infrastructure to deliver multicast services rather than to deploy a new infrastructure for these services.
- The biggest disadvantage of this architecture is that all protocols defined by the working group that are used for carrying user credentials, authentication and security keys, has no link to the IGMP *Join* request that the user device needs to send to the router. This is because the authentication process is merely for the provision of the security keys and not for the network resources. Hence even if a user does not have the security keys for any multicast group, this does not stop the user to send an IGMP *Join* to his next hop router. This will setup the multicast distribution tree and the multicast data would be forwarded to the user. Though the receiver would not be able to decrypt the encrypted multicast content, it will still receive the data traffic. This can give rise to Denial-of-Service attacks, where an adversary can send several IGMP *Join* messages to such multicast groups. Even though the data is encrypted, distribution trees will be setup for all the multicast groups, and data from all these groups is sent unnecessarily to the rogue user. This may be a big issue where the bandwidth is limited and expensive like multicast over satellite.

AAA for Multicast

This section described a new multicast AAA framework that provides receiver access control, and authentication of end user together with pre-paid and post-paid accounting for multicast services. Before going into details of the proposed framework, the steps in providing efficient AAA functionalities for multicast services are summarised as follows:

- An end user sends a request to join a multicast group.
- This should trigger the authentication procedure, to authenticate and authorise this user.
- If the user is successfully authenticated and authorised to receive the content, then the multicast traffic should be forwarded to the user.
- If the user is not successfully authenticated and authorised to receive the content, then there should be a mechanism to restrict their access to the multicast traffic.
- The duration and the data volume of the multicast sessions for all the authenticated users shall be recorded to provide efficient usage-based charging.

Keeping in mind the above mentioned steps and the security requirements defined in the previous chapter, it can be seen that an efficient AAA framework for multicast services should contain the following functional blocks:

- **Access control mechanism:** The access control mechanism should provide the following functionalities:
  - It should initiate an authentication procedure when a user sends a request to join a multicast group.
  - It should be able to provide a means to restrict access to multicast traffic only to authenticated users.
- **Authentication mechanism:** The authentication mechanism should provide the following functionalities:
  - It should be able to provide a mechanism to authenticate the end user.
  - It should support the authentication by a back end AAA server.
  - It should support proxy authentication for distributed networks.
- **Accounting mechanism:** The accounting mechanism should provide the following functionalities:
  - It should be able to provide a mechanism to measure the amount of traffic and the time duration of the different multicast sessions for all users.
  - It should calculate the charges for multicast services. This may be either fixed charge or usage based charged according to the adopted business model

Figure 5. Components of IGMPx access control mechanism

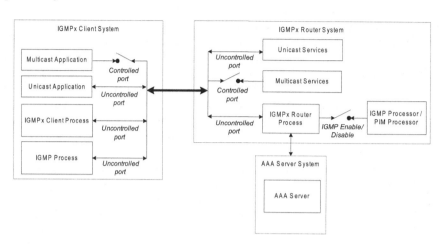

IGMPx Service Access Control Mechanism

The IGMPx (Pillai, 2007) mechanism is a port-based service access control mechanism specifically designed for multicast services. It provides the means of authenticating and authorising end user devices directly attached to a Designated Router (DR) and of preventing access to multicast services on a port at which the authentication procedure fails. When an end user device requests to join any multicast group by sending an IGMP membership report to the DR, service access control for the multicast group is achieved by the DR enforcing end user authentication. Based on the authentication result, the DR can determine whether the user is authorised to access the multicast content on that controlled port. As shown in Figure 5, the IGMPx service based access control architecture for multicast is made up of the following three component systems:

- **IGMPx Client System:** This is the end user device requesting to gain access to multicast services.
- **IGMPx Router System:** This is the Designated Router (DR) that controls multicast service access.
- **AAA Server System:** This is the backend AAA server responsible for authenticating and authorising the end user.

The following different sub-components are present in the IGMPx Client System:

- **Multicast Application:** This is the multicast application running on the end-user device that needs to join a multicast group.
- **Unicast Application:** This is the unicast application running on the end-user device.
- **IGMPx Client Process:** This is the IGMPx process running on the end user device that responds to the authentication request sent by the IGMPx Router Process in the IGMPx Router System. It supports different authentication mechanisms/algorithms and takes part in the authentication procedure.
- **IGMP Processor:** This is the IGMP process in the IP layer of the end user device that sends an IGMP membership request to join a multicast group when instructed by the multicast application.

The following different sub-components are present in the IGMPx Router System:

- **IGMP Processor:** This is the IGMP process in the IP layer that processes the received IGMP packets from the IGMPx Router Process and then instructs the PIM process to set up the multicast distribution tree towards the multicast source.

- **IP Unicast Service:** This is the unicast services provided by the system. No access control is provided for these services.
- **IP Multicast Service:** This is responsible for forwarding the multicast traffic to end user devices that are interested and are authorised to receive the content.
- **IGMPx Router Process:** This is the IGMPx process running on the router that performs access control and initiates the authentication procedure when it received an IGMP *Join* request from an end user device.

This IGMPx system architecture can be extended to provide access control mechanism for multiple user devices connected to the IGMPx Router System. Each IGMPx Client Systems is connected to a corresponding IGMPx Router System via a dedicated physical port. Access control is provided only for the corresponding port. The following steps are carried out in the access control procedure using IGMPx:

- **Step 1—Multicast group join:** In the beginning all the controlled ports present in both the IGMPx Client System and the IGMPx Router System and the IGMP Enable/Disable switch are in the unauthorised state. When the user starts the multicast application it instructs the IGMP process to initiate a join. The IGMP process sends an IGMP membership report to the IGMPx Router System requesting to join a multicast group. This IGMP membership report would be received and processed by the IGMPx Router Process.
- **Step 2—User authentication triggering:** On receiving the IGMP membership report, the IGMPx Router Process extracts the source IP address and the multicast group address. As it sees that this is a join request, the IGMPx Router Process triggers the authentication procedure of the end user. The IGMPx Router Process stores the received IGMP membership report that would be processed later if the user is successfully authenticated.
- **Step 3—User authentication procedure:** In this step the user presents its credentials to the IGMPx Router Process, which forwards it to the backend AAA server for authentication. EAPoL is used to carry these messages between the IGMPx Client Process and the IGMPx Router Process, while Diameter Protocol is used between the IGMPx Router Process and the AAA Server. The IGMPx Router Process acts as a "passthrough", forwarding the EAP messages back and forth between the IGMPx Client System and the AAA Server System. The IGMPx access control mechanism does not mandate any particular authentication mechanism. As it uses EAP, it supports all the different authentication mechanisms supported by EAP like MD5, PAP, CHAP, TLS, TTLS, etc.
- **Step 4—Multicast service activation procedure at the router:** On receiving authentication success message from the AAA server the IGMPx Router Process knows that user has been successfully authenticated and is also authorised to access the multicast group. It activates the IGMP Enable/Disable switch and forwards the IGMP membership report to the IGMP processor in the IP layer for processing. The IGMP processor then instructs the PIM process to set up the multicast distribution tree. The controlled port connected to the Multicast Services is finally activated to allow multicast traffic flow. If the authentication fails then the IGMP Enable/Disable Switch will not be activated and the stored IGMP membership report is destroyed. In this case, the controlled port will remain unauthorised and hence no multicast traffic can be sent on this port.
- **Step 5—Multicast service activation procedure at the client system:** Upon successful authentication, the IGMPx Router Process forwards the Authentication Success message to the IGMPx Client Process. This authorises the controlled port in the IGMPx Client System so that the multicast application can now receive the multicast content. For a failed authentication the controlled port in the IGMPx Client System will remain unauthorised, baring the multicast application from receiving multicast content.
- **Step 6—Multicast group leave initiation:** When the end user wishes to stop receiving the multicast content, an IGMP membership report is sent requesting to leave the specified Multicast Group. On receiving this leave request the IGMPx Router Process deactivates the IGMP Enable/Disable switch and also sets the controlled port connected to the multicast services to 'unauthorised', stopping multicast traffic from the specified multicast group to be sent on this port.

Figure 6. Multicast security framework for different administrative domains

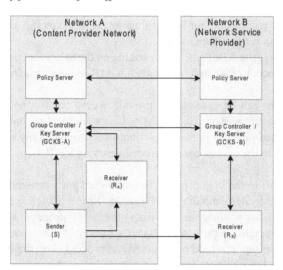

Extension to the MSEC Architecture to Support AAA

The shortcomings of the multicast group security architecture proposed by the IETF MSEC Working Group were described in Section 3.4. To overcome these shortcomings and interwork with AAA mechanisms, two main modifications are needed to the architecture:

i)   Support for distributed architecture where group members are present in different administrative domains.

ii)   Interworking with the AAA and IGMPx service access control mechanism.

Distributed MSEC Architecture Under Different Administrative Domains

The IETF multicast security reference framework when used in a distributed environment (Hardjono, 2004) is shown in Figure 4. The main rationale to support such a distributed system was to provide a scalable solution for

Figure 7. Multicast group security associations

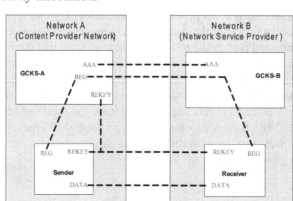

large groups across wide geographic regions of the Internet. Hence large number of users accessing a particular content could be divided into smaller groups, with each of these groups having its own Group Controller/Key Server (GCKS). The different GCKSs interact with each other to securely pass the security keys and policies that would be used by the individual GCKS for providing access control and authentication of the users and for key management within its group. It is also stated in RFC3740 that in such a scenario, each member of the multicast group interacts with the primary GCKS entity (i.e. the 'nearest' GCKS entity).

One weakness of this architecture is that it does not consider the fact that the different group members may actually be present in different administrative domains as shown in Figure 6, where the sender S and receiver R_A is in Network A, which is a Content Provider Network (CPN), and receiver R_B is in Network B, which is a Network Service Provider (NSP). If the standard IETF multicast security architecture is followed, then the GCKS-A provides the policies and the keys to GCKS-B which can then authenticate and control the access of all the group members that connect to network B. As these two networks are in different administrative domains, sharing of such user information may not be possible. In other words, it is highly unlikely that Network A would want to provide the user credentials of all the group members to Network B. Also in this mechanism Network A would not be able to know how many users from Network B actually request access to the multicast content. The CPN knows the user credentials for all valid group members which are used for granting the user access to the multicast content provided by the CPN. It is envisaged that the CPN would not want to pass these to any NSP. In other words, the CPN is responsible for authenticating the user's access to the multicast content. In order to support an efficient distributed multicast security framework, the GCKS present in the NSP should act as a proxy to the GCKS present in the CPN. In this case, when a group member in Network B sends a request to join the multicast group to GCKS-B, this request is forwarded to GCKS-A. Only Network A has the credentials to authenticate the user for access to the multicast content, and hence is responsible for authenticating this request from the receiver.

The group security associations for the proposed multicast architecture across multiple administrative domains are shown in Figure 7. The proposed group security associations consist of the Registration SA (REG SA), the Re-key SA (REKEY SA) and the Data Security SA (DATA SA) and the AAA SA. In addition to the REG SA, the REKEY SA and the DATA SA, which were defined by the IETF MSEC Working Group by Hardjono (2005), a new SA called the Authentication-Authorisation-Accounting (AAA) SA is proposed between the different GCKS in the different domains. The four categories of the SA's are:

- **Registration SA (REG SA):** It is a separate unicast SA between the main GCKS (in the CPN) and the group members (i.e. senders or receivers) present in the different administrative domains. For group members that are not present in the same administrative domain as the source, this REG SA passes through the proxy GCKS (in the NSP) to the main GCKS (in the CPN).
- **Data Security SA (DATA SA):** It is a multicast SA between each multicast source and the group receivers across all the administrative domains. This SA is used to secure the actual multicast data/content sent by the source and hence is shared by all the receivers of the data for correct decryption of the data.
- **Re-Key SA (REKEY SA):** It is a single unidirectional multicast SA between the main GCKS in the CPN and the group members present in the different administrative domains. This REKEY SA will be used to protect any Re-key messages carrying the new DATA SA.
- **AAA SA (AAA SA):** It is a separate unicast SA between the main GCKS (present in the CPN) and the proxy GCKS (present in the NSP). This SA is used to transfer user information/credentials, policies and security keys between these two GCKS. Diameter protocol is used for communication between the main GCKS and the proxy GCKS. Hence this AAA SA is essentially the IPSec or TLS tunnel (mandatory in Diameter) between these entities.

Support for Network Access Control

The IETF MSEC Working Group has defined registration protocols like GDOI, and GSAKMP for setting up a REG SA. However, these protocols are application layer protocols and are independent of the IGMP *Join* messages. These protocols were designed only to provide an authentication mechanism to securely distribute the security keys to the authenticated user and not to control network access. Hence the registration protocol used in the proposed architecture has to be triggered by an IGMP *Join* message. The solution to provide network access control by making use of the GDOI and GSAKMP protocols is to define a new EAP application method to carry these registration protocols between the user and the proxy GCKS. Figure 8 shows how GSAKMP can be carried by EAP over LAN between the user device and the Network Access Server (NAS) and then carried by EAP over Diameter between the NAS and the GCKS. When the user sends an IGMP *join* message requesting access to the multicast content, the NAS running the proposed IGMPx authentication mechanism has its ports in the unauthorised state and hence initiates the user authentication procedure by sending an EAP message. On receiving this message, the user starts the GSAKMP procedure by sending the GSAKMP *Request_to_Join* message which would be encapsulated in the data field of the EAP message. The Diameter EAP Application (Eronen, 2005) is used for carrying these EAP messages (with the encapsulated GSAKMP messages) from the NAS to the proxy GCKS and then further to the main GCKS. On completion of the GSAKMP procedure, the main GCKS sends a *Diameter-EAP-Answer* message with the *ResultCode* AVP set to *Success*. Hence the NAS knows that the authentication procedure is successful and will then authorise the corresponding ports.

While this mechanism is acceptable for carrying the GSAKMP protocol messages from the user to the GCKS where no underlying SA is needed, it is not feasible for carrying GDOI messages. RFC3547 states that GDOI is a "phase 2" protocol which must be protected by a "phase 1" protocol that provides a mechanism for peer authentication and then provides confidentiality and message integrity for the GDOI messages. The Internet Keying Exchange (IKE) Protocol (Harkins, 1998) is used as the phase 1 protocol for securing the subsequent

Figure 8. GSAKMP over EAP and Diameter

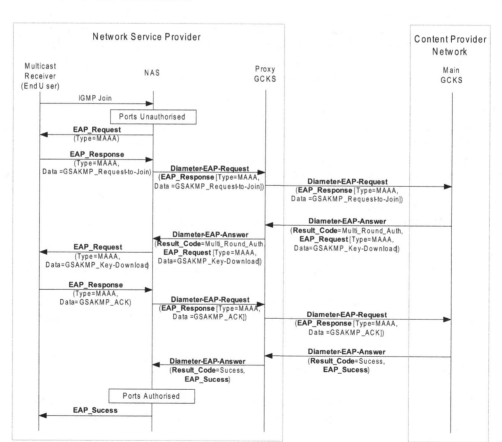

GDOI messages. Hence a mechanism is required to provide mutual authentication and session key derivation that can be used for protecting the GDOI messages between the user and the main GCKS. The solution proposed for this is to use an EAP method that can be used for peer authentication and security SA setup before GDOI is transmitted over EAP. As shown in Figure 9, when the user sends an IGMP *Join* message requesting access to the multicast content, the NAS initiates a mutual authentication procedure whereby the user device and the proxy GCKS can mutually authenticate each other. After successful authentication, a Security Association (SA) is setup between the user and the proxy GCKS (i.e. a secret security key is derived). This SA is used for securing the GDOI messages.

Figure 9. GDOI over EAP tunnel

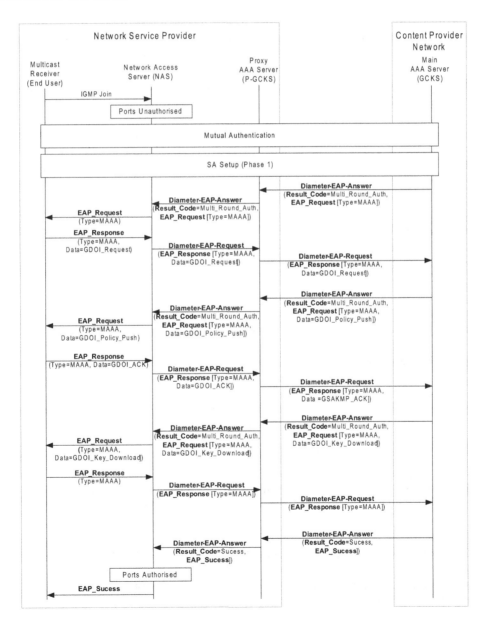

As the proposed Multicast AAA Framework is a generic framework, no single mechanism to perform this procedure of mutual authentication and SA setup is mandated. There are several different EAP methods currently being investigated by the IETF Point-to-Point Protocol Extension (pppext) Working Group, the IETF Extensible Authentication Protocol (eap) Working Group and the IETF EAP Method Updates (emu) Working Group that can be used for this purpose. Some of the examples are:

- **EAP-PSK:** The EAP PSK (Bersani, 2007) method provides mutual authentication and session key derivation using a pre-shared key and not certificates. It relies on a single cryptographic primitive, AES-128. The pre-shared key may be derived from the password. The master session key derived may be used to secure the GDOI messages
- **EAP-PAE:** EAP Password Authenticated Exchange (PAE) (Clancy, 2006) is designed for authentication using a shared key and makes use of two separate sub-protocols, PAX_STD and PAX_SEC. PAX_STD is a simple, lightweight protocol for mutual authentication using a shared key, supporting authenticated data exchange. PAX_SEC complements PAX_STD by providing support for shared-key provisioning and identity protection using a server-side public key.
- **EAP-SAKE:** EAP method for Shared-secret Authentication and Key Establishment (SAKE) (Vanderveen, 2006) supports mutual authentication of the client and the server and session key derivation based on a static pre-shared secret data. EAP-SAKE is based on the Bellare-Rogaway mutual authentication mechanism. The session key derived can be used to protect the GDOI messages.
- **EAP-TLS:** The EAP-TLS method (Aboba, 1999) is based on the Transport Layer Security (TLS) protocol (Dierks, 1999) and provides mechanisms for mutual authentication using digital certificates and mechanism for dynamic session key establishment. EAP-TLS uses the concepts of Public Keying Infrastructure (PKI). The derived session key can be used to protect the GDOI messages.
- **EAP-GPSK:** EAP Generalised Pre-shared key (GPSK) method (Clancy, 2007) is a lightweight shared-key authentication protocol that supports mutual authentication of the user and the server and the key derivation. EAP-GPSK exhibits low computational overheads as it does not make use of any public key cryptography, but instead fully relies on symmetric cryptography.
- **EAP-SKL:** EAP-SKL (Otto, 2005) relies on the cryptographic protocol Secure Key Exchange Mechanism protocol (SKEME) (Krawczyk, 1996). It provides mutual authentication and key derivation based on a pre-shared secret.

MSEC-AAA Framework for Multicast Services

A user who wants to access any multicast content has the following two sets of security credentials:

- **Network Access Identifier (NAI):** The NAI is known by the NSPand is used for granting access to any network resources. In other words it is the username used by the user for connecting to the NSPto gain network services.
- **Service Access Identifier (SAI):** The SAI is known by the CPN and is used for providing access to the multicast content. In other words it is the username used by the user for requesting access to the multicast content provided by the CPN.

Figure 10 shows the procedure of a MSEC-AAA framework for multicast services across networks under different administrative domains. The sequence of the AAA procedure can be categorised into the following three phases:

- **Authentication by NSP:** This phase is performed when the end user requests to join any multicast group. This phase involves the authentication and authorisation of the user (identified by the NAI) by the NSP. The NSP may have different levels of memberships, where certain members may not be allowed to access any multicast services. The NSP may also want to control the number of multicast groups that a user may be allowed to join at any given time.

Figure 10. MSEC-AAA framework for multicast in distributed networks

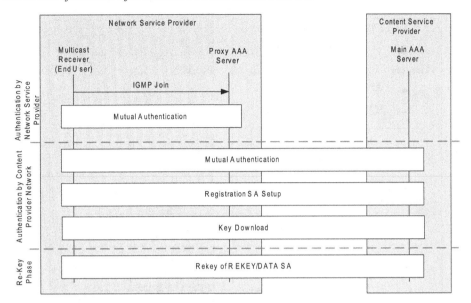

- **Authentication by CPN:** Once the NSP has authenticated and authorised the user, the CPN authenticates the user (identified by the SAI) and then sets up the REG SA. Then the security keys are sent to the user under the protection of the REG SA. This phase marks the end of the AAA functionalities.
- **Re-key Phase:** This phase involves the re-key mechanism used for sending the new REKEY SA or DATA SA to the user whenever the corresponding security keys are changed. This is not a requirement for the AAA framework but is an integral part of the IETF MSEC architecture. Hence support for such a re-key mechanism is mandatory.

EAP Multicast-AAA Method

This section describes the new proposed EAP method defined for the proposed MSEC-AAA architecture. This method is called the EAP Multicast-AAA (EAP MAAA) method. The different messages and the packet format of this EAP MAAA method is described in detail in this section. This EAP method is used for carrying the GDOI and GSAKMP messages and for also providing a key download and re-key facilities when GDOI or GSAKMP is not used.

EAP MAAA Messages

Figure 11 shows the message sequence chart for the new EAP MAAA method for providing AAA functionalities for multicast services. First the Network Service Provider authenticates the user based on the NAI and then the Content Provider Network authenticates the user based on the SAI. After this the Content Provider Network sends the REKEY SA and the DATA SA. For the two mutual authentication and Registration SA setup steps, the EAP MAAA method does not mandate any particular mechanism but provides the mechanism to carry other EAP methods and GSAKMP and GDOI protocol messages. Hence for the mutual authentication step between the user and the AAA Server in Network Service Provider, an EAP method like GPSK, PSK, SAKE SKL, etc. may be used. On the other hand for the mutual authentication and Registration SA Setup procedure between the user and the Content Provider Network, the three scenarios, namely GSAKMP over EAP, GDOI over EAP and

Figure 11. EAP MAAA message sequence chart

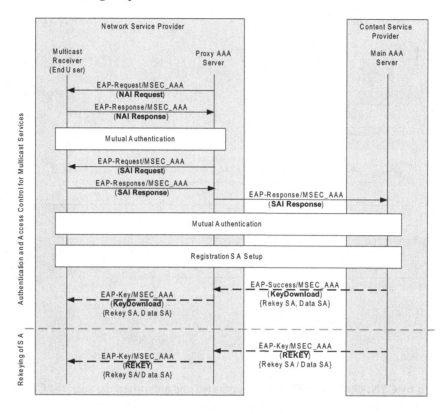

all EAP can be used. To support an all EAP mechanism, Key download and Re-key messages have also been defined. The messages in the new proposed EAP MAAA method are:

- **NAI Request:** This message is sent to the user requesting the NAI.
- **NAI Response:** This message is sent by the user and it is used for carrying the NAI.
- **SAI Request:** This message is sent to the user requesting the SAI.
- **SAI Response:** This message is sent by the user and it is used for carrying the SAI.
- **Protocol_over_EAP:** This message is used for carrying messages of other protocols like GDOI or GSAKMP or other EAP methods within an EAP MAAA packet.
- **Start MSEC:** In all the standard EAP methods, the authentication procedure begins from the user end, when the user sends his/her identity to the server. However, in the case of the GDOI and GSAKMP the mechanism starts from the server end, where the *Start_MSEC* message is used by the server for informing the user to initiate the MSEC protocol (GDOI or GSAKMP) over EAP. If the user device is capable of performing either GDOI or GSAKMP, then it will use the GCKS preferred protocol.
- **Key Download:** This message is used for carrying the REKEY SA and the DATA SA from the GCKS to the user.
- **Rekey:** This message is used for sending the new REKEY SA and/or DATA SA to the user when an all EAP mechanism is used.

EAP MAAA Packet Header

Figure 12 shows the packet header of the EAP MAAA method. The EAP MAAA header consists of the following fields:

Figure 12. EAP MAAA packet header

Figure 13. Flags field of the EAP MAAA packet header

- **Code:** The code specifies the type of the EAP message. It is set to 1 for EAP Request, 2 for EAP Response, 3 for EAP Success and 4 for EAP Failure.
- **Identifier:** This identifier is used for matching the requests and the responses.
- **Length:** This denotes the total length of the packet including the header also.
- **Type:** The Type identifies the EAP Method Type, here it is the proposed EAP MAAA method.
- **Flags:** Figure 13 shows the Flags field in the EAP MAAA packet header. The following flags are defined:
    - **Sub-Type:** The sub-type is the first 3 bits of the Flags field. It is used to denote the type of the MAAA message. It is set to 0 for the NAI Request message, 1 for the NAI Response Message, 2 for the SAI Request message, 3 for the SAI Response message, 4 for the Protocol_over_EAP message, 5 for the Start MSEC message, 6 for the Key Download message and 7 for the Re-key messages.
    - **S:** The start bit *'S'* is used to indicate the start of fragment.
    - **M:** The *'M'* bit is set to indicate the presence of more fragments.
- *Next Payload:* The next payload field is 3 bits in size and is used to denote the type of protocol message being carried by the EAP MAAA packet. It is set to 0 when no other protocol messages are carried in the EAP MAAA packet. It is set to 1 when it is used to carry GDOI messages, 2 when it is used to carry GSAKMP messages, 3 when it is used to carry PSK messages, 4 when it is used to carry GPSK messages, 5 when it is used to carry SAKE messages, 6 when it is used to carry MD5 messages, 7 when it is used to carry CHAP messages. Other values after 7 may be assigned for other EAP methods that may be supported in the future.
- **Payload:** This is the data carried by the EAP MAAA packet.

Fragmentation Support

The EAP MAAA messages provide the mechanism to carry other protocols like GSAKMP and GDOI. While the MTU for an EAP packet is 1024 Bytes, GSAKMP and GDOI messages are usually of the order of a few Kbytes. Hence support for fragmentation of the messages is mandatory. The 'S' and 'M' flag bits are used for this purpose. The 'S' bit is set on the first fragment, and the 'M' bit is set if there are more fragments. Hence for the first fragment both the 'S' and 'M' bits are set to 1. The subsequent fragments have the 'S' bit set to 0 and the 'M' bit set to 1, and finally the last fragment has both the 'S' bit and 'M' bit set to 0. For messages that do not require any fragmentation and fit in a single EAP MAAA packet, the 'S' bit is set to 1 and the 'M' bit is set to 0.

Figure 14. Simulation system architecture

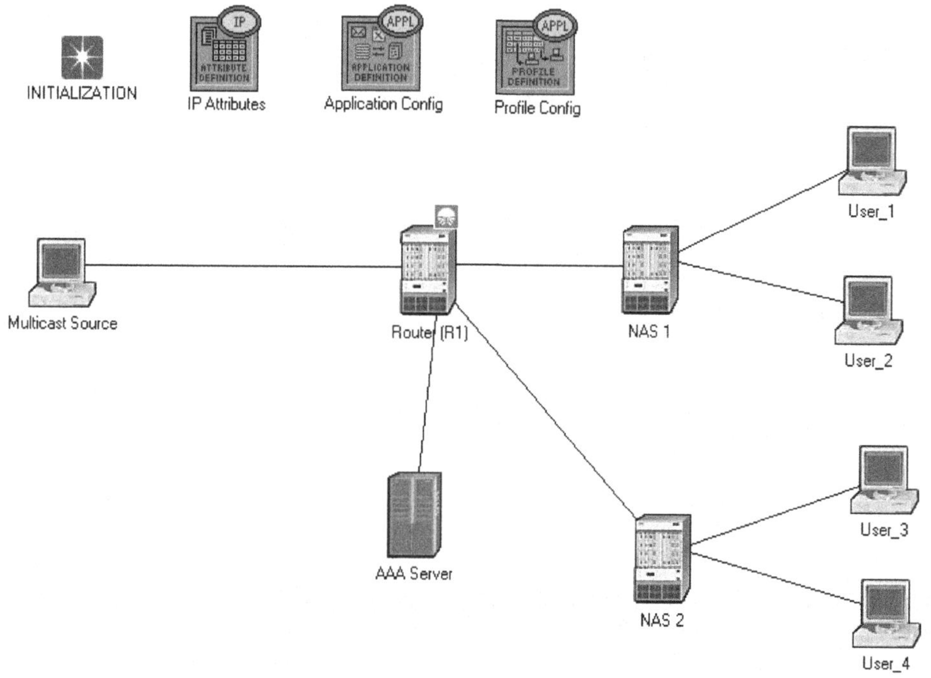

Simulation Results

An OPNET model was built to verify the working of the MSEC-AAA framework. The simulation system architecture is shown in Figure 14. It consists of User 1 and User 2 connected to NAS 1, and User 3 and User 4 connected to NAS 2. Both the NASs are IGMPx enabled routers and also act as Diameter clients and EAP peers. A Diameter based AAA server is also present which runs the Diameter-EAP Application. Hence when the users send EAP messages to the NAS and the AP, these are encapsulated in Diameter messages and forwarded to the AAA server. The multicast source and the backend AAA server are both connected to Router R1. The video conferencing application begins at 400 seconds and runs till 1300 seconds. User 1 joins the multicast group at 150 seconds and leaves the group at 900 seconds, User 2 joins the group at 175 seconds and leave at 1200 seconds, User 3 joins the multicast group at 200 seconds and leaves at 1200 seconds and User 4 joins at 225 seconds and leaves at 1000 seconds.

Test Case 1: All Users Input the Correct Credentials

The following results are expected for this case:

- At the application layer, a single copy of the video conference application is sent by the multicast source.
- All the four users start receiving the video conferencing application traffic from 400 seconds. User 1, User 2, User 3 and User 4 will stop receiving the traffic at 900 seconds, 1200 seconds, 1200 seconds and 1000 seconds respectively.
- Two IGMP messages from each user, one for joining and one for leaving the multicast group will be generated.

Figure 15. Results for Test Case 1

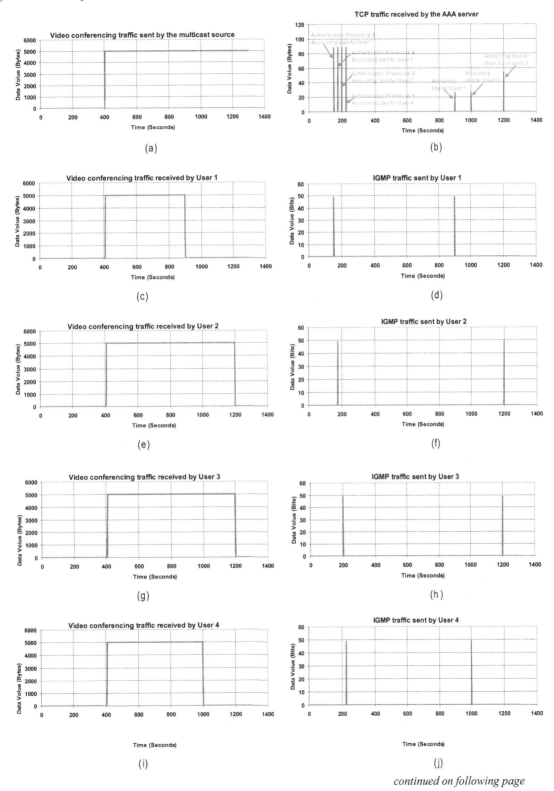

continued on following page

Figure 15 conitinued

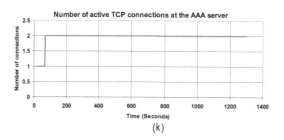

(k)

- At the TCP level, eight sets of transactions between the NAS and the AAA server are expected. One set (for each user) for the authentication procedure and accounting initiation triggered by the IGMP *Join* message and a second (also for each user) set for accounting-stop triggered by the IGMP *Leave* message.

Figure 15 (a) to (k) reflects the expected results and hence the correct operations of IGMPx is verified. All the users send the IGMP *Join* and *Leave* messages as expected, and receive the multicast traffic accordingly. As seen in Graph (k) there are two active TCP connections for the AAA server. This is because the TCP connection between the NAS and the AAA server is setup at 20 seconds and the TCP connection between the WLAN AP and the AAA server is setup at 70 seconds.

Test Case 2: One User Inputs the Wrong Credentials

The expected results for this case will be the same as the previous case with the difference that User 3, who inputs the wrong credentials, does not receive the multicast traffic and no Diameter *accounting-stop* message is sent when this User 3 sends an IGMP *Leave* message. Figure 16 (a) to (j) confirms the expected results.

Verification of the Accounting Mechanisms for Multicast Communications

Both post-paid and pre-paid accounting is supported by the MSEC-AAA framework. While for post-paid accounting, the user session information is recorded at the end of the multicast session, for pre-paid accounting, real-time checks with the user account is performed.

Post-Paid Accounting for Multicast Services

The MSEC-AAA framework can be used to provide post-paid accounting of the users for the multicast services accessed by them. The simulation scenario discussed in the previous section uses the post-paid accounting mechanism. For post-paid accounting, the session duration and data volumes are all collected by the NAS. When a user wants to leave a multicast group, it sends an IGMP *Leave* message to the NAS. The NAS then sends a Diameter *accounting-stop* message containing all these session information to the AAA server. The billing system then takes all this information and can apply different pricing plans to generate suitable bills for charging the users for the multicast services accessed by them.

Pre-Paid Accounting for Multicast Services

In pre-paid accounting, the user account is checked at the beginning to see that the user has enough credits in his account to access the service. Small quotas are allocated to users when they successfully authenticate. When the user has used up the quota, a Diameter *accounting-interim-update* message is sent to the AAA server requesting more quotas. Two cases are simulated for verification of the pre-paid accounting mechanism:

- **Test Case 1:** When the user have enough credits in his/her account to access the service till the end of the multicast session.

Figure 16. Results for Test Case 2

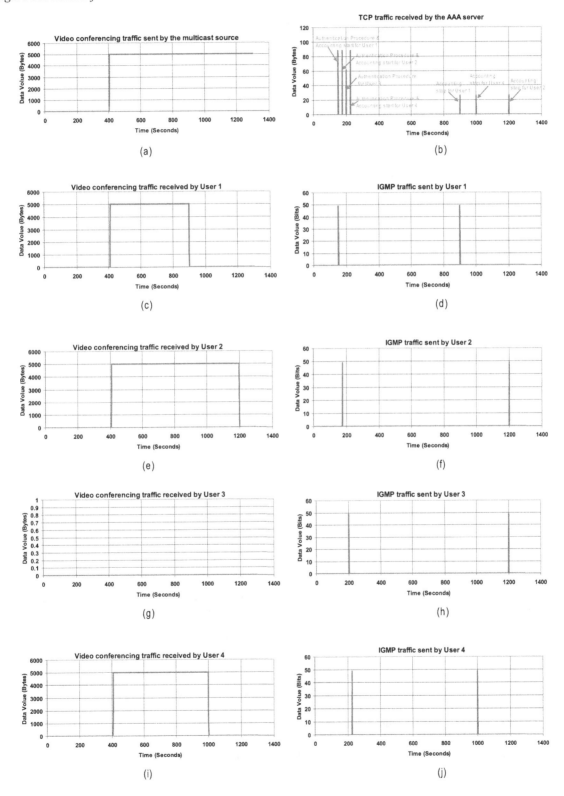

Figure 17. Results for Test Case 1

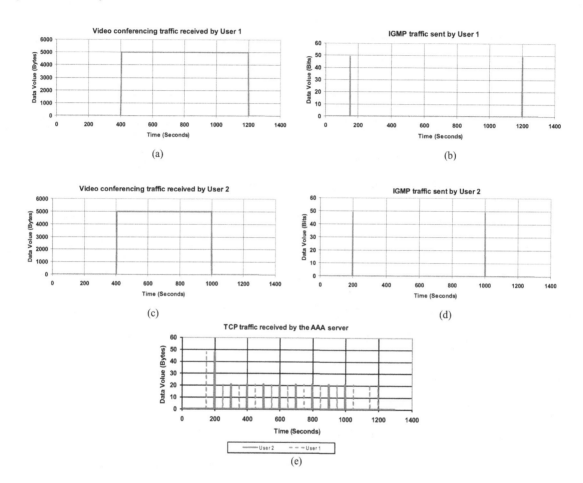

- **Test Case 2:** When the user does not have enough credits in his/her account to access the service till the end of the multicast session.

To simulate both these cases and to verify the working of the pre-paid accounting mechanism for multicast communications, the same simulation architecture is used but with two wired users only. User 1 joins the group at 150 seconds and leaves the group at 1200 seconds. User 2 joins the group at 200 seconds and leaves the group at 1000 seconds. The interim update interval is 100 seconds.

a) Test Case 1

In this test case both the users have enough credits to receive the traffic till the end of the session at 1200 seconds. Figure 17 (b) and (d) shows that User 1 and User 2 send an IGMP *Join* and *Leave* messages at the expected times. Graph (a) and (c) show that as expected both users start receiving the multicast traffic at 400 seconds, but while User 1 sops receiving at 1200 seconds, User 2 stops receiving at 1000 seconds. Graph (e) shows the Diameter messages received by the AAA server. The graphs shows the messages sent for both the users. It can be seen that for both users, periodic Diameter *accounting-interim-update* messages (with 100 seconds interval time) are sent to the AAA server.

Figure 18. Results for Test Case 2

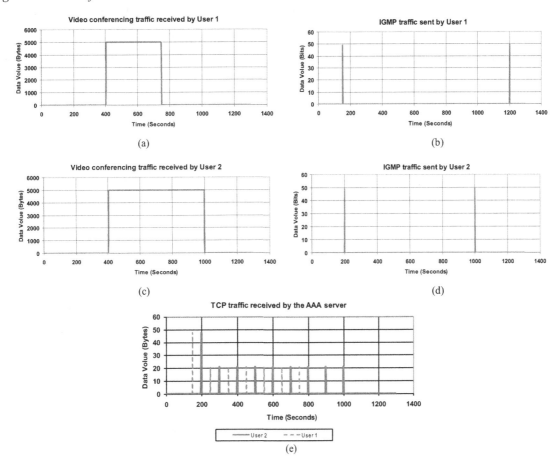

b)   Test Case 2

In this test case User 1 does not have enough credits to receive the traffic till the end of the session at 1200 seconds, i.e. User 1 has enough money in his/her account to only run 350 seconds on the requested multicast service. The expected results are the same as the previous test case, with the only difference that User 1 stops receiving the multicast traffic when it runs out of quotas. Figure 18 (a) to (e) confirms the expected results.

CONCLUSION

This chapter described the MSEC-AAA framework that allows Network Providers to authenticate and authorise users requesting multicast data, to restrict multicast content access to only authenticated users, to monitor the different multicast sessions accessed by end users and to enable flat-rate or usage based charging mechanisms to be implemented.

The MSEC-AAA framework includes the new IGMPx port-based service access control mechanism that provides the means of initiating user authentication and authorisation when the user requests to join a multicast group and of preventing access to the multicast services by unauthenticated users. In the MSEC-AAA framework the GCKS in the Network Provider domain acts as a proxy to the GCKS present in the Content Provider domain. This allows the Network Provider to forward the authentication requests to the Content Provider who can authenticate the user. Hence the Network Provider and Content Provider under different administrative domains are not required to share any security information and can authenticate users individually. The MSEC-AAA Framework also protects the Network from any Denial-of-Service attacks since the distribution trees are only created for authenticated users. Both post-paid and pre-paid accounting is supported by the MSEC-AAA framework.

REFERENCES

Aboba and D. Somin (1999). PPP EAP TLS Authentication Protocol, IETF RFC 2716.

B. Aboba, L. J. Blunk, J. R. Vollbrecht, J. C. and H. Levkowetz (2004). Extensible Authentication Protocol (EAP), IETF RFC 3748.

J. Arkko, E. Carrara, F. Lindholm, M. Naslund and K. Norrman (2004). MIKEY: Multimedia Internet Keying, IETF RFC3830.

M. Baugher, B. Weis, T. Hardjono, H. Harney (2003). The Group Domain of Interpretation, IETF RFC3547.

M. Baugher, R. Canetti, L. R. Dondeti, F. Lindholm, "Multicast Security (MSEC) Group Key Management Architecture", IETF RFC4046, April 2005.

F. Bersani and H. Tschofenig (2007), "The EAP-PSK Protocol: A Pre-Shared Key Extensible Authentication Protocol (EAP) Method", IETF RFC 4764.

B. Cain, S. Deering, I. Kouvelas, B. Fenner and A. Thyagarajan (2002). Internet Group Managemet Protocol, Version 3, IETF RFC2236.

P. R. Calhoun, J. Loughney, J. Arkko, E. Guttman and G. Zorn (2002). Diameter Base Protocol", IETF RFC 3588.

T. C. Clancy and W. Arbaugh (2006). Extensible Authentication Protocol (EAP) Password Authenticated Exchange, IETF RFC 4746.

T. C. Clancy and H. Tschofenig (2007). EAP Generalised Pre-Shared Key (EAP-GPSK), work in progress, draft-ietf-emu-eap-gpsk-02.txt.

T. Dierks and C. Allen (1999). The TLS Protocol: Version 1.0, IETF RFC 2246.

P. Eronen, T. Hiller and G. Zorn (2005). Diameter Extensible Authentication Protocol (EAP) Application, IETF RFC 4072.

D. Estrin, D. Farinacci, A. Helmy, D. Thaler, S. Deering, M. Handley, V. Jacobson, C. Liu, P. Sharma and L. Wei (1998). Protocol Independent Multicast-Sparse Mode (PIM-SM): Protocol Specifications, IETF RFC 2362.

M. Gast (2005). 802.11 Wireless Networks: The Definitive Guide, O-Reilly Publishing.

T. Hardjono and B. Weis (2004). The Multicast Group Security Architecture, IETF RFC3740.

Dan Harkins and Dave Carrel (1998). The Internet Key Exchange (IKE), IETF RFC 2409.

H. Harney, U. Meth, A. Colegrove and G. Gross (2006). GSAKMP: Group secure Association Key Management Protocol", IETF RFC 4535.

T. Hayashi, D. Andou, H. He, W. Tawbi, and T. Niki (2003). Internet Group Membership Authentication Protocol, Internet Draft (expired), draft-hayashi-igap-03.txt.

T. Hayashi, A. Tanabe, D. Andou, K. Izutsu, H. Satou, H. He and W. Tawbi (2004). IGAP: Secure group management protocol for multicast content delivery network, in the proceedings of the 2004 Joint Conference of the 10th Asia Pacific Conference on Communications and the 5th International Symposium on Multi-Dimensional Mobile Communications, Volume 2, pages: 626-630.

P. Judge and M. Ammar (2002). Gothic: A Group Access Control Architecture for Secure Multicast and Anycast, in the proceedings of IEEE 21st Annual Joint Conference of the IEEE Computer and Communications Societies, INFOCOM 2002, Volume: 3, pages: 1547-1556.

H. Krawczyk (1996). SKEME: A versatile secure key exchange mechanism for Internet, in the Proceedings of the 1996 IEEE Symposium on Network and Distributed Systems Security, pages: 114-127.

B. Llyod and W. A. Simpson (1992). PPP Authentication Protocol, IETF RFC 1334

T. Otto (2005). The EAP SKL Protocol, work in progress, draft-otto-eap-skl-0.2.txt.

P. Pillai and Y. F. Hu (2007). An AAA Framework for commercial deployment of IP Multicast, submitted to IEEE Communications Magazine.

C. Rigney, A. C. Rubens, W. A. Simpson and S. Willens (2000). Remote Authentication for Dial In User Service (RADIUS), IETF RFC2865.

P. Savola (2005). Multicast: is it ever going to take off?, 22nd NORDUnet Networking Conference, Svalbard. http://www. nordunet2005.no/index.html.

H. Ueno, H. Suzuki, N. Ishikawa and O. Takahashi (2005). A Receiver Authentication and Group Key Delivery Protocol for Secure Multicast, IEICE Transaction on Communications, Volume E88-B, number 3, pages: 1139-1148.

M. Vanderveen and H. Soliman (2006), "Extensible Authentication Protocol method for Shared secret Authentication and Key Establishment (EAP-SAKE)", IETF RFC 4763

B. Weis, G. Gross and D. Ingjatic (2006). Multicast Extensions to the Security Architecture for the Internet Protocol, work in progress, draft-ietf-msec-IPSec-extensions-04.txt.

KEY TERMS

AAA: Authentication, Authorisation and Accounting.

ACS: Access Control Server.

CHAP: Challenge handshake Authentication Protocol.

CP: Content Provider.

DR: Designated Router.

EAP: Extensible Authentication Protocol.

EAPoL: EAP over LAN.

GCKS: Group Controller and Key Server.

GDOI: Group Domain of Interpretation.

GSAKMP: Group Security Association and Key Management Protocol.

IETF: Internet Engineering Task Force.

IGAP: Internet Group membership Authentication Protocol.

IGMP: Internet Group Management Protocol.

MSEC: Multicast Security.

NAS: Network Access Server.

OPNET: Optimised Network Engineering tool.

PAE: Password Authenticated Exchange.

PAP: Password Authentication Protocol.

PIM: Protocol Independent Multicast.

RADIUS: Remote Authentication for Dial-in User Service.

SAKE: Shared-secret Authentication and Key Establishment.

TLS: Transport Layer Security.

TTLS: Tunnelled Transport Layer Security.

WLAN: Wireless Local Area Network.

Chapter IV
Wavelength Division Multiplexing Technologies and their Applications

N. Merlemis
Technological Educational Institute—TEI of Athens, Greece

D. Zevgolis
Hellenic Open University, Patras, Greece

ABSTRACT

This chapter is an introduction of the Wavelength-division multiplexing (WDM) technologies (such as Dense WDM and coarse WDM) and their recent applications in optical networks. WDM is used to multiplex multiple optical carrier signals on a single optical fibre by using different wavelengths of laser light to carry different signals. This allows for a multiplication in available bandwidth and, in addition, makes possible to perform bidirectional communications over one strand of fibre. We present the optical components used in WDM and review some of the most important applications of the technology.

Introduction to Multiplexing Technologies

The explosion in demand for network bandwidth today, forces long-haul service providers to move away from Time Division Multiplexing (TDM) based systems, which were optimized for voice but now, prove to be costly and inefficient. In addition, the explosive growth of data traffic (due mainly to the rapid growth of Internet applications based on the Internet Protocol IP) is followed at the same time with higher complexity of the nature of the traffic itself. Traffic carried on a backbone can originate as circuit based (TDM voice and fax), packet based (IP), or cell based (Asynchronous Transfer Mode ATM and Frame Relay) and at the same time delay sensitive data, such as voice over IP and streaming video are also becoming increasingly important.

In order to handle the dramatically increasing capacity while constraining costs, carriers have two options:

a.   Install new fibre
b.   Increase the effective bandwidth of existing fibre.

Copyright © 2009, IGI Global, distributing in print or electronic forms without written permission of IGI Global is prohibited.

Laying new fibre to expand existing networks is a rather costly solution (most of the cost is the cost of permits and construction rather than the fibre itself). Increasing the effective capacity of existing fibre can be accomplished either by increasing the bit rate of existing systems or by increasing the number of wavelengths of light transmitted in a fibre.

Increase the Bit Rate in a TDM system

Time Division Multiplexing (TDM) was invented as a way of maximizing the amount of voice traffic that could be carried over a medium. In the old telephone network each telephone call required its own physical link which makes the network to be expensive and unscalable. With the invention of multiplexing, it is possible to have more than one telephone on a single physical link. TDM increases the capacity of the transmission link by slicing time into smaller intervals (slots) so that the data from multiple telecommunicating entities can be carried on the same link, with each entity making use of one time slot (Figure 1).

Each entity is serviced in a cyclical way, thus making this method fair but inefficient, since each time slot is reserved even when there is no data to send. This problem is mitigated by the use of statistical multiplexing used in Asynchronous Transfer Mode (ATM), although there are practical limits to the speed that can be achieved, due to the fast electronics required for segmentation and reassembly of ATM cells.

Using TDM, data can be transmitted at 2.5 Gbps (OC-48), at 10 Gbps (OC-192) and more recently at speeds of 40 Gbps (OC-768). However, technical issues such as increase of chromatic dispersion in higher speed, the effect of nonlinear phenomena due to the greater transmission power required at the higher bit rates and polarization mode dispersion restrict the applicability of this approach.

Optical transmission of TDM data is covered by standards adopted by the telecommunications industry such as the Synchronous Optical Network (SONET) or Synchronous Digital Hierarchy (SDH), where SONET is used in North America and SDH elsewhere. SONET/SDH standards specify the parameters in order to take a number of n bit streams of a bit rate equal to b, to multiplex them, to optically modulate the signal and to send it into the fibre using a light emitting device with a final bit rate equal to b × n. For example traffic arriving from four places at 2.5 Gbps rate will go into the fibre as a single stream at 10 Gbps.

Increase the Number of Optical Carriers (Light Wavelengths)

In this approach, a number of wavelengths are combined onto a single fibre. This multiplexing method is called Wavelength Division Multiplexing (WDM). In this method it is possible to combine even 128 or 160 wavelengths on a single fibre, thus increasing the effective capacity of existing fibre plant by the same factor without having to lay new fibre (Figure 2).

Figure 1. TDM with three input links. The output link is divided in three time slots and data from each input link make successive use of first, second and third time slot

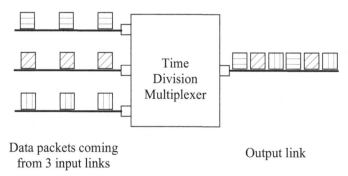

Data packets coming
from 3 input links

Output link

Figure 2. WDM with three input links. Data is carried on a different wavelength (λ1, λ2, λ3) in every input link (fibre). The multiplexer combines all wavelengths onto a single output fibre. Each optical signal is transmitted independently and at the same time through the fibre.

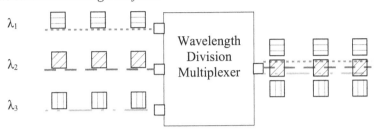

The signals are demultiplexed at the receiving end and similar to TDM, the resulting capacity is an aggregate of the input signals. However in the case of WDM each input optical signal is independent meaning that each channel has its own dedicated bandwidth and all signals arrive at the same time. In contradiction, in TDM each signal is being broken up and carried in time slots (Figre 1). WDM makes use of single mode fibres to carry light of different wavelengths (this should not be confused with multimode transmission, where a single wavelength is used and light is emitted into the fibre at different angles).

As a conclusion, bandwidth-hungry applications and the explosive growth of the Internet have exceeded the limits of traditional TDM, such as SONET which takes synchronous and asynchronous signals and multiplexes them to a single higher bit rate for transmission at a single wavelength over fibre. In this way source signals may have to be converted from electrical to optical or from optical to electrical and back to optical before being multiplexed. With the technology of WDM, multiple optical signals can be mapped to different wavelengths which are multiplexed over a single fibre (WDM can carry in this way multiple protocols).

Fibre Optic Transmission

The technology of fibre optic transmission began to advance rapidly in the second half of the twentieth century with their use in applications in industry and medicine (fiberscope), such as in laparoscopic surgery. The next important step in the development of fibre optics was to find a light source that would be sufficiently powerful, has a narrow band and divergence. The light-emitting diode (LED) and especially the laser diode proved capable of meeting these requirements. From the first lasers invented in the 1960s, the development of solid state lasers and especially of the semiconductor lasers were proved to be the most important light sources widely used in fibre optics transmission today.

Due to the much higher frequency of light compared to the highest radio frequencies, light has information carrying capacity 4 orders of magnitude higher. In addition fibre optics transmission technologies have the ability to carry signals over long distances with low error rates, immunity to electrical interference, security, and light weight compared to copper wires. Disadvantages such as the loss of signal strength, or attenuation in the first applications of glass fibres in the 1960s were overcome in 1970s by Corning with the introduction of communication-grade fibres. With attenuation less than 20 dB/km, this purified glass fibre exceeded the threshold for making fibre optics a viable technology for telecommunications.

Transmission at 45 Mbps for multimode fibres (DS3 speed as standardized first by AT&T) was soon overcame with the introduction of single-mode fibres that were capable of transmission rates 10 times that speed in larger distances (32 km). Further developments in fibre optics were succeeded with the use of light radiation with wavelengths in selected regions (windows) of the optical spectrum where optical attenuation is low. The earliest systems used a first window in silica based optical fibre around 850 nm, with a second window (S band) at 1310 nm soon proved to be superior because of its lower attenuation, followed by a third window (C band) at 1550 nm with an even lower loss and a fourth window (L band) near 1625 nm under development today (Figure 3).

Figure 3. Spectrum of the electromagnetic radiation close to the wavelengths used for optical transmission in optical fibres. The four windows (bands) of low attenuation are shown in the infrared region of the spectrum.

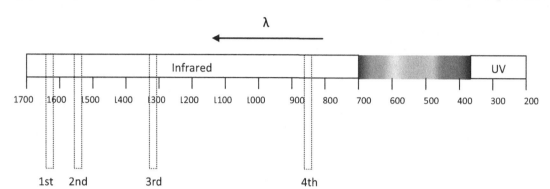

WDM Technologies

The concept was first published in 1970, and by the end of the decade WDM was demonstrated in the laboratory. The first systems combined only two optical signals. Modern systems can handle up to 160 signals and can thus expand a basic 10 Gbit/s fibre system to a theoretical total capacity of over 1.6 Tbit/s over a single fibre pair. Most WDM systems need single mode optical fibre to operate (core diameter of 9 μm).

WDM systems are divided to coarse and dense WDM, depending on the wavelength pattern selected. Conventional WDM systems provide up to 16 channels in the 3rd transmission window (C-band) of silica fibres around 1550 nm with a channel spacing of 100 GHz. Coarse WDM (CWDM) uses the entire wavelength band between second and third transmission window (1310/1550 nm respectively) and increased channel spacing to allow less sophisticated and thus cheaper transceiver designs. Recently, ITU has standardized a 20 nanometre channel spacing grid for use with CWDM, using the wavelengths between 1310 nm and 1610 nm. For CWDM, in contrast to the other systems, wideband optical amplification is not available since the signals are not spaced appropriately for amplification by erbium doped fibre amplifiers (EDFAs), thus limiting the optical transmission to a few tens of kilometres (which is suitable for metropolitan networks). CWDM is commonly used for data-rates up to 4.25 Gbps.

Dense WDM (DWDM) uses the 3rd transmission window (C-band) of silica fibres around 1550 nm but with less channel spacing (50 GHz or even 25 GHz) thus allowing more parallel optical channels (from 64 to 160). This wavelength band is suitable for the use of erbium doped fibre amplifiers, which are effective for wavelengths between approximately 1525 nm - 1565 nm (C band), or 1570 nm - 1610 nm (L band). EDFAs, originally developed to replace SONET/SDH optical-electrical-optical (OEO) regenerators, can amplify any optical signal in their operating range, regardless of the modulated bit rate and if enough pump energy is available, EDFAs can amplify as many optical signals as can be multiplexed into its amplification band. Therefore a single-channel optical fibre link can be upgraded in bit rate simply by replacing equipment at the ends of the link, while retaining the existing amplifiers along a long haul route. DWDM is commonly used for data rates around 10Gbps.

Fundamentals of DWDM

A simple DWDM schematic for four optical channels is shown in Figure 4. Each optical channel occupies its own wavelength.

The system performs the following main functions:

Figure 4. DWDM schematic for four optical channels (four wavelengths that appear as different colours and line patterns in the schematic). A multiplexer and a demultiplexed are used to combine and separate the channels respectively

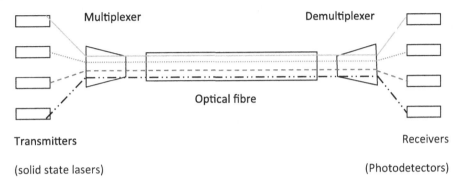

- Generation of the optical signals. The source is a solid-state laser that must provide stable light within a specific narrow bandwidth that carries the digital data, modulated as an analog signal.
- Multiplexing the signals. The different wavelengths are multiplexed (using an optical multiplexer) into a single optical fibre. Wavelength converting transponders are used to receive and convert the input optical signals of the client-layer (SONET/SDH signals for example) into electrical signal and to retransmit the signal using a 1550 nm band laser. One wavelength converting transponder is needed for every wavelength signal of the 1550 nm band. There is some inherent loss associated with multiplexing and demultiplexing. This loss is dependent upon the number of channels but can be mitigated with optical amplifiers, which boost all the wavelengths at once without electrical conversion (fore example EDFAs).
- Transmission of the signals through the fibre. The effects of crosstalk and optical signal degradation or loss must be considered and should be minimized by controlling parameters such as channel spacing, wavelength tolerance, and laser power. Over a transmission link, the signal may need to be optically amplified. An intermediate Optical Add-Drop (OAD) multiplexer can be used to amplify the multi-wavelength signal that may have traversed up to 140 km or more before reaching the remote site and also to remove and drop localy several signals out of the multi-wavelength optical signal.
- Demultiplexing the received signals. The multi-wavelength optical signal is separated back into individual optical signals which are transmitted on separate fibres for client-layer systems (such as SONET/SDH) to detect.
- Detection of the demultiplexed optical signals (using appropriate photodetectors).

In order for a DWDM system to operate, it needs some essential components that can be classified as follows:

- On the transmitting side, lasers with precise, stable wavelengths.
- On the link, optical fibre that exhibits low loss and transmission performance in the relevant wavelength spectra, in addition to flat-gain optical amplifiers to boost the signal on longer spans.
- On the receive side, photodetectors and optical demultiplexers using thin film filters or diffractive elements.
- Optical add/drop multiplexers and optical cross-connect components.
- Wavelength converting transponders in order to translate the transmit wavelength of a client signal into one of the DWDM system's internal wavelengths in the 1550-nm band.

Optical Fibres

Optical fibres are composed of fine threads of glass in layers, called the core and cladding. The light is transmitted with a velocity of about two-thirds the velocity of light in vacuum (depending on the refractive index of the fibre). The transmission of light through an optical fibre can be explained using the principle of total internal reflection (this is an oversimplification of the underlying physics covering the propagation of light in an optical fibre), where 100 percent of light beam that strikes a surface is reflected and there is no refraction of the beam.

A light beam is subject to total internal reflection when the following conditions are met:

1. Beam passes from a more optically dense (greater index of refraction) to a less optically dense material. The material's refractive index is $n=c/c_0$, where c is the velocity of light in the material and c_0 is the velocity of light in vacuum.
2. The incident angle of the light beam is less than a critical angle for which light stops being refracted (the incident angle measured from the surface).

Total internal reflection exists in a fibre due to the higher refractive index of the core than the cladding and thus the beam that strikes the surface between core and cladding with angle less than the critical angle is totally reflected. Figure 5 shows the phenomenon in the case of two beams, one that is totally reflected and a second one that does not meet the critical angle requirement and is refracted.

The core and the cladding of an optical fibre are consisted of highly pure solid glass (silica) that is mixed with specific elements (dopants), to adjust their refractive indices. The critical angle requirement is met by controlling the angle at which the light is injected into the fibre. Two or more layers of protective coating around the cladding ensure that the glass can be handled without damage.

There are two general categories of optical fibres: multimode fibres and single mode fibres:

Multimode fibre, the first type of fibre to be commercialized, has a larger core than single mode fibre. In multimode fibres light can be transmitted in numerous modes (different light rays in a simplified view as shown in Figure 6). In a step index optical fibre (core has a uniform refractive index that changes suddenly in the interface between core and cladding), different modes travel different distances to arrive at their destinations, thus arriving at different times at the end of the fibre (as shown in Figure 6). This phenomenon is called modal dispersion

Figure 5. Total internal reflection of a beam (1st beam) that fulfils the critical angle requirements (θ less than a critical angle). The 2nd beam is refracted into the cladding. The core has higher refractive index than the cladding (n2>n1)

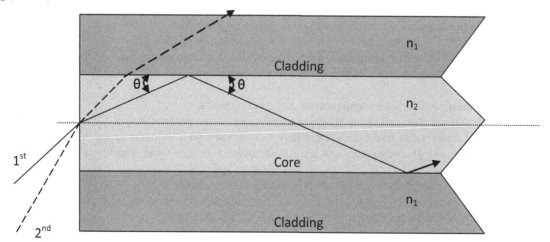

Figure 6. Multimode fibre with propagation of different modes. Note that the condition for total internal reflection is not met for light rays with incident angle outside the acceptance cone of the fibre

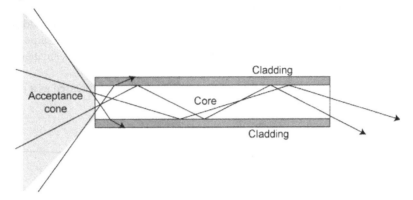

and results in poor signal quality at the receiving end of the fibre and ultimately limits the transmission distance, thus multimode fibres are suitable for wide area applications. This effect can be compensated by using graded-index fibres, where the refractive index of the core is graded (gradually decreases from the center of the core outward). Higher refraction at the center of the core leads to slower propagation for the light rays (modes) that are propagating near the center compared to those that pass far from the center, thus all the rays can reach the end of the fibre at about the same time and reduce the modal dispersion.

Single mode fibre, has a core of much smaller diameter that allows the propagation of only one mode of light through the core. As a result modal dispersion is greatly reduced and the fidelity of the signal is better retained over longer distances. Consequently single mode fibres have a higher bandwidth capacity than multimode fibres, have lower intrinsic loss and are preferred for longer distance and higher bandwidth applications such as DWDM.

Transmission of light signal in optical fibres presents several challenges such us:

- Attenuation of signal strength, as the signal propagates through the fibre.
- Chromatic dispersion - spreading of light pulses as they propagate through the fibre
- Nonlinear effects due to the interaction of light with the fibre material, resulting in changes of the propagating light wave and interactions between different light waves.

Attenuation in an optical fibre is caused primarily by scattering and absorption of light, and by extrinsic factors, including stress from the manufacturing process, the environment, and physical bending. The most common form of scattering, Rayleigh scattering, is caused by small variations in the density of glass as it cools in the manufacturing process. Rayleigh scattering affects short wavelengths more than long wavelengths and limits the use of wavelengths below 800 nm.

Absorption of light is caused due to the impurities in the glass and any atomic defects in the glass. These impurities absorb photons and reduce the optical power of the light transmitted. While Rayleigh scattering is important at shorter wavelengths, intrinsic absorption is an issue at longer wavelengths and increases dramatically above 1700 nm. In some new fibre types, water absorption (introduced in the fibre at the manufacturing process) is possible to be eliminated. Attenuation in optical fibres depends on the length of the fibre and the wavelength of the light transmitted (optical amplifiers should be used in order to amplify the signal after a certain length of the fibre).

The main disadvantage of the multimode optical fibers is their limited bandwidth due to **mode dispersion** phenomena. This effect has the following interpretation: different (hundreds or thousands) angles of light incidence follow different modes of propagation inside the fiber and travel under different routes covering unequal distances. Consequently the form of the output signal will have a different profile from the input pulse. As the angle of incidence increase, so does the number of different modes grow up drastically. In such multimode fibers the dispersion effect disfeatures the output signal, see Figure 6.

In order to limit the dispersion effect, we use optical fibers with cores made from material with a graded-index distribution. In this case the index of refraction is changed gradually between core and cladding, thus, light beams travelling in different routes will have different speeds and all of them will meet at the same time at the exit point. The monomode fibers balance out the dispersion completely. Their core diameter is smaller than 10μm and only one mode propagates within it.

The core refractive index as a function of the radius r can generally be expressed as a power-law function

$$n(r) = n_{co}\sqrt{1 - 2\Delta \cdot \left(\frac{r}{r_{co}}\right)^g} \quad 0 \leq r \leq r_{co}$$

$$n(r) = n_{cl} \quad r \geq r_{co},$$

where r_{co} is the core radius,

$$|\Delta| = \frac{n_{co} - n_{cl}}{n_{co}}$$

and g is the profile exponent lying in the range $1-\infty$. With $g=\infty$ the step-index profile is also included. For $g=2$ the modal dispersion is minimum and thus the delays between the modes are approximately the same.

The common types of optical fibres are based on the graded-index and the step-index profile. Despite these, there are other types of optical fibres as the birefringent **polarization mode fibres** and more recently the **photonic crystal fibres** based on non-linear effects. The polarisation-mode fibres (PMD) are optical fibres in which the polarisation planes of the light waves launched into them are maintained during propagation with little or no cross-coupling of optical power between the polarisation modes. The attainment of polarisation is increasingly important in modern telecommunication systems, as the technological society demands higher bandwidth and more complex optical networks. The photonic-crystal fibres (PCF) constitute a new class of optical fibres based on the properties of photonic crystals. Because of their ability to confine light in hollow cores, the PCFs are interesting candidates for telecommunication applications, new laser systems and smart devices for sensitive gas sensors.

Light Sources (LED, Lasers)

The light sources used in optical transmission are carefully selected since their characteristics are often a strong limiting factor in the final performance of the optical link. Light emitting devices must be compact, monochromatic, stable, long-lasting and have a reasonable cost. Light Emitting Diodes (LEDs) and laser diodes, or semiconductor lasers are often used as light sources in optical communications. LEDs are relatively slow devices (suitable for use at speeds of less than 1 Gbps), have a relatively wide spectral width and divergence, but are inexpensive and are often used with multimode fibres. On the other hand, semiconductor lasers have better performance characteristics and are used for optical transmission in single mode fibres.

The LED is thus formed by doping thin layers on the surface of a crystal wafer, one above the other, in a way such that an n-type region and a p-type region are formed, resulting in a p-n diode. When this structure is forward biased, holes and electrons can be found in the same region and their recombination leads to spontaneous emission. In other words the electron may reoccupy the energy state of the hole, which leads to the emission of a photon with energy equal to the energy difference (recombination energy) of the two states involved.

Laser action can be obtained if an electron and a hole that coexist in the same area are forced to be recombined by a nearby photon (that exists due to spontaneous emission) with energy equal to the recombination energy. This process is called stimulated emission and generates another photon of the same frequency, travelling in the same direction, with the same polarization and phase as the first photon. This phenomenon can lead to gain of the optical wave and lasing, if the gain region is surrounded with an optical cavity (usually a Fabry-Perot resonator) to form a semiconductor laser.

Optical communications require that lasers have precise wavelength, narrow spectrum width, sufficient power, and control of chirp (change of frequency over time). Semiconductor lasers satisfy the first three requirements. Chirp can become a limiting factor at high bit rates (above 10 Gbps) if the modulation of the laser is made internally (direct modulated lasers), while external modulation is better performing.

Two types of semiconductor lasers are widely used in WDM:

- Monolithic Fabry-Perot lasers (where a Fabry-Perot resonator is used for wavelength selection and amplification of the laser signal))
- Distributed Feedback Lasers (DFB).

Table 1. The ITU standard G.692

Frequency (THz)	Wavelength (nm)	Frequency (THz)	Wavelength (nm)
196.1	1528.77	193.8	1546.92
196.0	1529.55	193.7	1547.72
195.9	1530.33	193.6	1548.52
195.8	1531.12	193.5	1549.32
195.7	1531.9	193.4	1550.12
195.6	1532.68	193.3	1550.92
195.5	1533.47	193.2	1551.72
195.4	1534.25	193.1	1552.52
195.3	1535.04	193.0	1553.33
195.2	1535.82	192.9	1554.13
195.1	1536.61	192.8	1554.94
195.0	1537.4	192.7	1555.75
194.9	1538.19	192.6	1556.56
194.8	1538.98	192.5	1557.36
194.7	1539.77	192.4	1558.17
194.6	1540.56	192.3	1558.98
194.5	1541.35	192.2	1559.79
194.4	1542.14	192.1	1560.61
194.3	1542.94	192.0	1561.42
194.2	1543.73	191.9	1562.23
194.1	1544.53	191.8	1563.05
194.0	1545.32	191.7	1563.86
193.9	1546.12		

The latter type is particularly well suited for DWDM applications, as it emits a nearly monochromatic light, is capable of high speeds, has a better signal-to-noise ratio, and has superior linearity. In DFB lasers a diffraction grating is etched close to the p-n junction of the diode in order to stabilize and select the lasing wavelength. The grating leaves only a single wavelength to be fed back to the gain region and to be amplified, thus provides the feedback that is required for lasing at the specific wavelength. The DFB laser has a stable wavelength that is set during manufacturing (in the region around 1310 nm, and from 1520 to 1565 nm) by the pitch of the grating, and can be tuned slightly with temperature. The latter wavelength range is compatible with EDFAs. Table 1 shows the International Telecommunication Union (ITU) standard G.692 that defines a laser grid based on 100 GHz (0.1 THz) wavelength spacing for point-to-point WDM systems.

Narrow spectrum tuneable lasers are also available and wider spectrum tuneable lasers that will lead to dynamically switched optical networks are under development.

Light Detectors (Photodetectors)

Photodetectors are used on the receive end in order to convert the optical signals transmitted at different wavelengths on the fibre to the original electrical signals. This is done after the demultiplexing of the optical multi-wavelength signal of a WDM system, since photodetectors are by nature wideband devices (meaning that they can not selectively detect specific wavelengths).

Two types of photodetectors are widely deployed, the positive intrinsic negative (PIN) photodiode and the avalanche photodiode (APD). PIN photodiodes is similar to a LED device that works in the reverse, that is, light is absorbed rather than emitted, and each photon is converted to an electron. On the other hand, APDs provide gain through an amplification process, which means that each absorbed photon releases many electrons. This is achieved by applying a high reverse bias voltage which is great enough to accelerate the previously generated photoelectrons to the point that they can ionize atoms in the material and increase rapidly the number of the electrons that become part of the process.

Advantages of PIN photodiodes are the low cost and good reliability, but APDs have higher detection sensitivity and accuracy. In addition to the higher cost of the APDs they can also have very high electrical current requirements and they are temperature sensitive devices.

Optical Amplifiers

As already mentioned, signal attenuation is a limiting factor to how long a fibre segment can propagate a signal with integrity before it has to be regenerated. Signal amplification was traditionally accomplished by optical to electrical conversion, regeneration of the signal and conversion back to optical. This procedure requires a repeater for every signal transmitted. Optical Amplifiers (OA) has made it possible to amplify all the wavelengths at once and without optical-electrical-optical conversion. Besides their application in optical link amplification, OAs can be also used to boost signal power after multiplexing or before demultiplexing.

A key technology for optical amplification over long distances is the Doped Fibre Amplifiers (DFA). In general, DFAs are optical amplifiers which use a doped optical fibre as a gain medium to amplify an optical signal. The principle of operation is similar to that of fibre lasers. A pump laser is used to excite the doping ions in the fibre into a higher energy level from where they can decay, via stimulated emission of a new photon at the signal wavelength entering the amplifier, back to a lower energy level. As this process continues down the fibre, the signal grows stronger, thus leading to amplification of the weak signal while it is propagating through the fibre. The signal to be amplified and the pump laser necessary for the excitation of the active medium (doped fibre) are multiplexed into the fibre.

In a DFA, the efficiency of light amplification can be reduced by two additional decay mechanisms that compete with stimulated emission. First, the excited ions can also decay spontaneously (spontaneous emission) and second they can decay through nonradiative processes involving interactions with phonons of the glass matrix.

The most common example of DFA is the Erbium Doped Fibre Amplifier (EDFA). In this case, the core of a silica fibre is doped with trivalent Erbium ions (Er^{+3}), which can be efficiently pumped with a laser at 980 nm or at 1480 nm and exhibits gain at the 1,550 nm region, which is perfectly suited for optical transmission in DWDM systems. Both of the two bands developed in the third transmission window (the Conventional (C-band) from approximately 1525 nm - 1565 nm, and the Long (L-band) from approximately 1570 nm to 1610 nm) can be amplified by EDFAs, but it is normal to use two different amplifiers, each optimized for one of the bands.

Gain, gain flatness (same gain for all wavelengths), noise level, and output power are key parameters in the operation of optical amplifiers. Flat gain is a key parameter because all signals must be amplified uniformly. Since signal gain of an EDFA is inherently wavelength dependent, gain flattening filters can be used to correct the problem, often built into modern EDFAs. Low noise is also an important parameter because noise is amplified along with the signal. In a single fibre link the signal-to-noise ratio is an ultimate limiting factor that determines the length of the link, since amplification of noise limits the number of amplifiers that can be used. Regeneration of the signal is necessary for long links (600 to 1000 km), since optical amplifiers merely amplifies the signals and do not perform the 3R functions (reshape, retime, retransmit).

Multiplexers – Demultiplexers

Multiplexing is the technique used to combine the different input signals over a single fibre, while demultiplexing is necessary at the receiving end of the link in order to separate out the components of the light so that they can be discreetly detected. Multiplexers take the optical signals from different fibres and converges them into one beam. Demultiplexers separate the received beam into its wavelength components and couple them onto individual fibres. Different wavelength signals must be separated at the receiving end, because photodetectors are inherently broadband devices that cannot selectively detect a single wavelength.

Multiplexers and demultiplexers can be either passive (based on prisms, diffraction gratings, or filters) or active in design (combining passive devices with tunable filters). The primary challenges in these devices are to minimize cross-talk (how well the channels are separated) and maximize channel separation (making easier to distinguish each wavelength).

Several techniques can be used for multiplexing or demultiplexing. For example the refraction properties of a prism can be used in a simple arrangement, for demultiplexing a parallel beam of polychromatic (multi-wavelength) light that impinges on a prism surface. Different wavelengths are refracted into different angles and the output light (separated wavelengths) is focused by a lens onto different fibres. The same components can be used in reverse to multiplex different wavelengths onto one fibre.

Another technique includes the application of a diffraction grating. The different wavelength components of a multi-wavelength light beam that impinges on a diffraction grating are diffracted at a different angle and therefore to a different point in space (due to diffraction and optical interference). As in the case of the prim, a lens is used to focus these wavelengths onto individual fibres.

Diffraction of light is also used in the case of the Array waveguide gratings (AWG). In this case an array of curved-channel waveguides or a bundle of optical fibers with a fixed difference in the path length between adjacent channels is used. Cavities are placed at the input and the output of the waveguide. The light is diffracted as it enters into the input cavity and then propagates and enters into the waveguide array. The constant optical path difference of each waveguide introduces a phase change on the light passing through. Finally light diffracted from the output of each waveguide, propagates in the space of the output cavity and interferes constructively at different spatial positions for each wavelength, where it gets refocused onto an array of output fibres.

A different technology uses multilayer interference filters. Again interference effects permits only one wavelength to be transmitted through each filter while all other wavelengths are reflected. By cascading these filters it is possible to demultiplex a multi-wavelength signal.

Optical Add/Drop Multiplexers

It is often desirable to be able to insert or remove one or more wavelengths at some point along the span of a WDM link. This function is achieved using Optical add/drop multiplexers (OADMs)."Add" and "drop" here refer to the capability of the multiplexer to add one or more new wavelength channels to an existing multi-wavelength WDM signal, or to drop (remove) one or more wavelengths and route them to another network path. An OADM may be considered to be a specific type of optical cross-connect. Rather than combining or separating all wavelengths, the OADMs can selectively remove or add wavelength channels. OADMs differ from SONET ADM, since only optical wavelengths are added or dropped and there is no optical to electrical signal conversion.

A traditional OADM consists of three stages: an optical demultiplexer, an optical multiplexer and a method of reconfiguring the paths between them and a set of ports for adding and dropping signals. Optical signal from an input fibre are demultiplexed and the separate wavelengths are guided (either using a fibre patch panel or by optical switches) onto drop ports (to drop the selected wavelength) or to the optical multiplexer. The optical multiplexer multiplexes the wavelengths that are set to continue on with those from the add ports, onto a single output fibre.

There are two general types of OADMs. The fixed OADMs are physically configured to add or/and drop specific predetermined wavelengths. The reconfigurable OADMs (ROADMs) and capable of dynamically selecting which wavelengths are added and dropped (by using remotely reconfigurable optical switches).

There are several technologies for the realization of an OADM, such as thin film filters, fibre Bragg gratings with optical circulators, free space grating devices and integrated planar Arrayed Waveguide Gratings (for demultiplexing and multiplexing). Techniques for switching or reconfiguration functions range from the manual fibre patch panel to a variety of switching technologies such as MEMS (Microelectromechanical systems).

DWDM Interfaces

DWDM systems can support optical interfaces to standard SONET/SDH client devices (for example OC-48c/STM-16c interface operating at the 1310 nm wavelength), or other interfaces important in metropolitan or access networks such as Ethernet or Fibre Channel. Incoming optical signals are converted by transponders into the precise ITU-standard wavelengths to be multiplexed.

A transponder is used to convert the client optical signal to an electrical signal and performs the 3R functions (reshape, retime, retransmit). This electrical signal is then used to drive the WDM laser and it is converted back to an optical signal. Each transponder converts its client's signal to a slightly different wavelength, which is then optically multiplexed with other wavelengths and fed onto the optical fibre. The reverse process takes place in the end site of the link, where the wavelengths are demultiplexed and fed to individual transponders, which convert the signal to electrical and drive a standard interface to the client.

A simplified scheme describing the process is shown in Figure 7.

The process includes the following steps:

- The transponder accepts input in the form of standard single-mode or multimode laser, which can originate from different physical media and have different protocols and traffic types.
- The wavelength of each input signal is mapped to a DWDM wavelength.
- DWDM wavelengths from each transponder interface and direct optical signals to the multiplexer are multiplexed into a single optical signal and transmitted onto the fibre.

Figure 7. Schematic of a DWDM unidirectional system

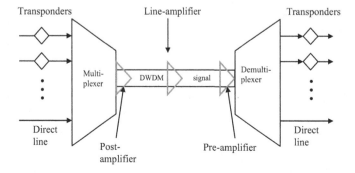

- A post-amplifier.
- Optical amplifiers can be used along the fibre link as needed (optional).
- A pre-amplifier can be used to boost the optical signal before it enters the end system.
- The incoming DWDM signal is demultiplexed into individual wavelengths.
- Each wavelength is mapped to the required output type (for example, OC-48 single-mode fibre) and sent out through the client interface of the transponder.

REFERENCES

G. P. Agrawal, Fiber-Optic Communication Systems, 3rd , Wiley, New York, 2002.

W. Daum, J. Krauser, P. Zamzow, O. Ziemann, Polymer optical fibers for data communication, Springer-Verlag Berlin Heidelberg 2002.

I. P. Kaminow and, T. Li, Eds., Optical Fiber Telecommunications, Vols. III-A, III-B (1997), IV-A and IV-B (2002), Academic Press, San Diego.

Stamatios V. Kartalopoulos DWDM: Networks, Devices, and Technology, Wiley-IEEE Press, 2002.

R. Ramaswamiand, K. N. Sivarajan, Optical Networks, 2nd, Morgan Kaufmann, San Francisco, 2002.

Jun Zheng, Hussein T. Mouftah, Optical WDM Networks: Concepts and Design Principles, Wiley-IEEE Press, 2004.

KEY TERMS

Doped Fibre Amplifiers: Similar to: "optical amplifiers", "light amplification". Associated in the manuscript with: "optical amplification for optical transmission"

Optical Add/Drop Multiplexer: Similar to: "multiplexing devices", "multiplexer", "optical cross-connect". Associated in the manuscript with: "multiplexing techniques in wavelength division multiplexing systems"

Photodiode: Similar to: "light detection techniques". Associated in the manuscript with: "conversion of optical signal to electrical signal"

Semiconductor Laser: Associated in the manuscript with: "semiconductor lasers for optical communications", "Distributed Feedback lasers", "Fabry-Perot lasers"

Time Division Multiplexing: Multiplexing technique. Associated in the manuscript with: "Multiplexing technologies in optical fibres"

Total Internal Reflection: Similar to: "light waveguiding". Associated in the manuscript with: "transmission of light onto optical fibres"

Wavelength Division Multiplexing: Associated in the manuscript with: "Multiplexing technologies in optical fibres"

Chapter V
Radio over Fiber for Broadband Communications:
A Promising Technology for Next Generation Networks

Sotiris Karabetsos
Technological Educational Institution of Athens, Greece

Spiros Mikroulis
Technological Educational Institution of Athens, Greece

Athanase Nassiopoulos
Technological Educational Institution of Athens, Greece

ABSTRACT

The high capacity offered by the optical fiber, combined with the mobility and the flexibility of wireless access, either fixed or not, provides an efficient approach to alleviating the requirements posed by the envisaged provision of any-service, anytime and anywhere, next generation communication networks. The objective of this chapter is to present an overview of Radio-over-Fiber technology, as an emerging infrastructure for next generation, fiber-based, wireless access broadband networking. In particular, the fundamental concept of Radio-over-Fiber technology is reviewed and the partial components comprising it are discussed. Furthermore, the associated architectures are depicted and a short literature survey of trends and applications is considered.

INTRODUCTION

Nowadays, it is well acknowledged that there has been a tremendous growth in communication technologies spanning from mobile telephony and wireless networks, to high definition television and satellite communications. Additionally, a great number of standards has been developed, setting the requirements and the specifications for this rapid expansion (ITU, 2002; IEEE, 1999; ETSI, 2001; IEEE, 2004). Despite this fact, there is an increased necessity for integration or, otherwise, collaboration of heterogeneous technologies, especially for mobile and wire-

Copyright © 2009, IGI Global, distributing in print or electronic forms without written permission of IGI Global is prohibited.

Figure 1. The Mobile/Wireless communications landscape in terms of data rates, frequency bands and the most common applications

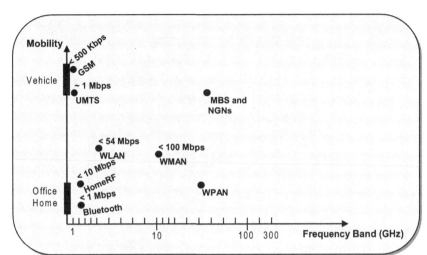

less communications, into a universal backbone network being capable of providing mobile, broadband, reliable and ever-present services to end users. In other words, this rapid expansion is characterized by the ever increasing requirement for faster and mobile communications with enhanced Quality of Service (QoS). Next generation networks (NGNs) should have the ability to offer mobile multimedia (video, audio and Internet) services to end users, anytime and anywhere (Kim, 2003; Agrawal, 2004; Arroyo-Fernandez, 2003; Arroyo-Fernandez, 2004).

The issues of mobility and multimedia services are strictly connected with the development of wireless broadband networks and network access technologies. An overview of the development of past, current and future wireless communication systems is depicted in Figure 1. Compared to cable networks, broadband wireless networks offer not only user mobility, but also reduced installation and maintenance cost. On the other hand, cable access is still superior in terms of high-speed data delivery. Therefore, the potential of accomplishing similar capacities in wireless networks is of great interest. However, the development of advanced wireless broadband networks, being able to efficiently handle (in terms of NGN services) radio frequency (RF) signals at the mm-wave bands, entails many inherent difficulties that cannot be solved straightforwardly through mainstream microwave technology. In this new communication scenery, Radio-over-Fiber (RoF) technology has an augmented potential to be adopted as an emerging infrastructure for broadband, high-speed mobile/wireless communications.

RoF TECHNOLOGY

The move towards high capacity wireless networks entails the exploitation of higher frequency bands than those utilized at present. In order to achieve similar capacity to cable networks, a shift to mm-wave signals is expected to be essential (2 to 60GHz and beyond). However, several critical issues have to be accounted for the effective deployment of wireless communication systems at these bands. For instance, by shifting towards higher frequencies, the propagation loss, either for uplink or downlink, becomes very high and coverage is severely limited. Additionally, current topologies of wireless systems rely on point-to-point (and point-to-multipoint) transmission of RF signals from a central/control station (CS) to several base stations (BS), where a re-transmission to end users occurs. This process has an increased cost for infrastructure equipment, since the necessary number of required BSs increases, and offers limited system granularity in view of millimetre wave bands utilization for micro-cellular and pico-cellular provision for high capacity mobile communications. Therefore, in order to

Figure 2. The RoF concept: (a) Centralized processing of mm-wave signals and distribution via optical fiber to several base stations, where RF transmission/reception is utilized, (b) a typical RoF link between a control/central station and a base station

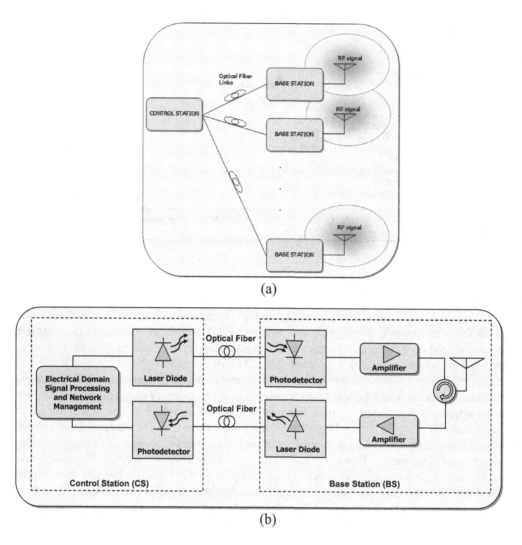

overcome these inherent difficulties, a centralised processing of RF signals that would lead to a simplified base station structure and an effective frequency re-use scheme would be advantageous and cost effective.

Radio-over-Fiber (RoF) or Hybrid Fibre-Radio (HFR) or Fiber-based wireless (Fi-Wi) technology is the process of modulating the RF electrical signal on an optical carrier and its distribution through a fiber or a fiber network. In a broader sense, RoF belongs to the Microwave-Photonics technology, an area which exploits the merging of photonic, microwave and wireless technologies (Lee, 2007; Seeds, 2006). It is apparent that the exploitation of fiber technology, in the context of broadband wireless networks, enables for ultra high bandwidth availability, which in turn leads to augmented capacity. The fundamental idea and advantage behind Radio-over-Fiber systems is the centralized concept of central stations that consequently lead to the minimization of the required baseband and RF signal processing in base stations or remote antenna units (RAUs). The central stations are connected to base stations via optical fibers, making the latter simple, flexible and cost-effective. For example, in WLANs the CS could be the central headend site while the BS could be the radio access point (RAP). The centralised concept of RoF and the general block diagram of a RoF link are illustrated in Figure 2.

In a typical RoF link deployment, the baseband data signal is generated at the CS and is up-converted to an RF signal that modulates an optical source. The most common type of modulation can be either direct or external. The optical signal is then distributed via fiber to the BS site, where it is converted back to electrical signal by a photodetector and fed to the (remote) antenna for transmission to end users. In the reverse situation, the end user signals are captured by the BS antenna and transmitted to the CS through fiber following the same procedure.

Using the aforementioned deployment, we see that all complex task concerning either the RF functionality or the signal processing and network aware issues, are transferred to the CS site, making the entire procedure completely centralised. Moreover, the BS needs to perform only simplified functionality, namely electrical to optical conversion (E/O), optical to electrical conversion (O/E), amplification and RF transmission/reception. This is highly beneficial since it allows for small size, compact and cost effective deployment of BSs. Due to this straightforward kind of arrangement, RoF technology has a great prospective to support high speed wireless access, having scalable and enhanced coverage through small cell (micro/pico cellular) sizes enabling for efficient re-use of frequencies, supported by a large number of BSs.

In summary, the exploitation of RoF technology for mobile/wireless broadband communications offers the following advantages (Al-Raweshidy, 2002; Lee, 2007; Way, 1993):

* Better coverage and high capacity via the distributed BS configuration and the utilization of fiber as a low loss, large bandwidth and electromagnetic interference (EMI) free transmission medium.
* Simplified design and cost effective deployment of BSs.
* Centralized upgrading, adaptation and dynamic configuration of radio resources.
* Increased reliability and decreased maintenance costs.
* Support for future broadband applications, multimedia services and next generation networks.
* Low power remote antenna units (RAU) and scalable distances between CS and BSs.
* Ability for transparency not only to modulation schemes but also to radio interface formats that consequently lead to the support of multiple and different services using the same infrastructure.

In addition, several research efforts have depicted that the consolidation of RoF technology in microcell or picocell network design, can significantly contribute to the efficient exploitation of the mm-wave band and to achieve higher capacities than mainstream wireless networks (Noel, 1997; Ogawa, 1992).

In contrast, RoF technology implies some limitations that should be properly compensated for a successful deployment in high speed multi-service wireless networks. Since RoF is by nature an analogue link capable of transmitting either RF or intermediate frequency (IF) and baseband signals (BB), certain demands on the linearity as well as the dynamic range of the optical link have to be conformed. The most limiting restrictions concern the nonlinear behaviour of the optical modulator, which leads to harmonic and intermodulation distortion, the loss and noise due to E/O and O/E conversion (i.e. relative intensity noise (RIN)), the frequency response of the optical modulator and the optical fiber dispersion in the case of using other than monomode optical fiber (Ackerman, 2001; Cox, 2006; Pinter, 2005; Fernando, 2006 IEEE). These factors are described in more detail in the following section of this chapter.

RoF COMPONENTS ARCHITECTURES AND DEPLOYMENTS

The deployment scheme of a RoF system is characterized by the methods utilized in generating and transmitting the microwave signals. In general, these methods can be discriminated in three categories, based on their distinct functionality. The first one concerns the approach by which the light source is being modulated. The second category deals with the format of the electrical signal, while the third manages the exploitation of the available bandwidth. Every method appears with some advantages and disadvantages and the corresponding choice depends on the specific characteristics of the wireless application (Kitayama, 2000; Novak, 2007). This section synoptically describes both the main components and the fundamental techniques related to the deployment of hybrid fiber radio systems.

Figure 3. Schematic representation of an intensity modulation—Direct Detection (IM-DD) link

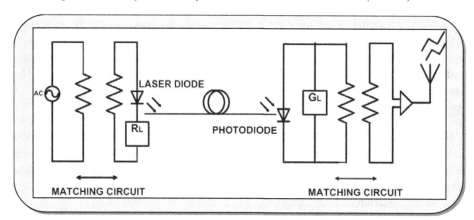

RoF Techniques for Generation and Distribution of Electrical Signals

The generation and distribution of microwave signal via optical fibers implies the following techniques:

a.   Intensity Modulation Direct Detection
    i.   Direct Modulation
    ii. External Modulation
b.   Remote heterodyning

Intensity Modulation Direct Detection (IM-DD)

Among several techniques for distributing and generating radio-frequency (RF) signals, the Intensity Modulation – Direct Detection (IM-DD) is the most usable (Cox, 1997). In this method the intensity of the light source is directly modulated with the RF signal and a photodetector is used for direct detection in order to recover it prior to amplification and transmission to the wireless channel (see Figure 3). A directly modulated optical source (laser) or an external modulator can be utilized, respectively. In the former approach the RF signal is directly applied to modulate the laser's current, while in the latter case the laser operates in continuous wave (CW) mode and the RF signal is applied in an external modulator, as for example, a Mach-Zehnder Modulator (MZM).

The directly modulated approach is the simplest, cost-effective solution at frequencies up to approximately 10 GHz, limited by the laser's resonance frequency (Stephens, 1987). The aforementioned restriction occurs due to the limited availability of commercially lasers with cut-off frequencies above 10GHz. Moreover, an additional impairment occurs due to the change in the laser current which also causes a variation to the laser's optical frequency (chirping) resulting in superimposed frequency modulation (Olesen, 1982).

The external modulation approach (see Figure 4), which is a solution for frequencies above 10 GHz, suffers from distortion due to the intrinsic nonlinearity of the modulators, high power consumption, and complexity. External modulation can be performed using three different devices:

1.   Electro-optical
2.   Electroabsorption
3.   Interferometric modulators

The most commonly used device in the external modulation approach is the Mach-Zehnder interferometric modulator in Lithium Niobate $LiNbO_3$. The modulation mechanism is the linear electrooptic effect, with a small

Figure 4. Schematic representation of an external modulation scheme employing a Mach-Zehnder interferometer

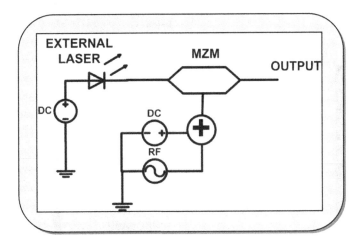

dependence on wavelength and temperature and with frequency response in the order of 100GHz (Cox, 2006). Commercially available versions of such MZM modulators have passed the Telcordia qualification, which includes 10 000 h of operation at 85 C (Maack, 1999).

Remote Heterodyne Detection (RHD)

Remote heterodyne detection is based on the principle of coherent mixing in the photodiode in order to recover the RF signal. The resulting photocurrent on the photodiode will be proportional to the square of the sum of the optical fields. Instead of the field terms, the photodiode current can approximately be expressed as a function of the optical power signals as (Ng'oma, 2005):

$$i(t) \approx 2R\sqrt{P_1(t)P_2(t)} \cos\left[\left\{ \omega_1(t) - \omega_2(t) \right\} \cdot t + \varphi_1(t) - \varphi_2(t) \right],$$ (1)

where R is the responsivity of the photodetector, P_1(t) and P_2(t) are the optical power signals with frequencies, ω_1 and ω_2 and phases φ_1 and φ_2 respectively.

RHD is an approach for generation of high frequencies, limited only by the photodetector's bandwidth. Moreover, RHD yields higher power and signal to noise ratio (SNR). This is due to the summation of both mixed optical power signals in the generated signal. Moreover, RHD technology offers in RoF systems functionalities such as modulation and frequency conversion in addition to transparency (Gliese, 1998).

A major drawback of RHD, as it is the case in all coherent techniques, is the induced variation of the frequency of the generated carriers due to laser's phase (frequency) noise. Phase noise is responsible for the finite spectral linewidth of laser diodes and vise versa. Thus, extra care has to be taken to reduce the spectral linewidth of lasers, which in turns increases the complexity of the transmitter.

RoF Optical Components

Laser Transmitters

The performance of RoF systems depends critically on the choice of the laser. There are three main types of lasers (Wake, 2004) which can be used in the specific application:

Figure 5. Schematic representation of a DFB laser

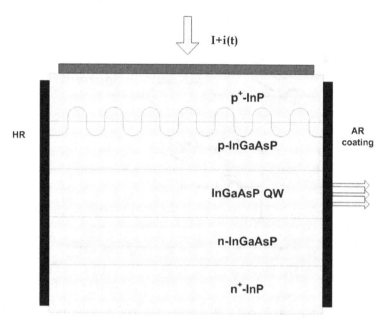

1. Fabry-Perot (F-P) lasers
2. Distributed Feedback (DFB) lasers
3. Vertical-Cavity Surface Emitting Laser (VCSEL)

In Fabry-Perot (F-P) lasers, feedback occurs from the active medium's reflective facets which are fabricated with cleaving. The emission wavelengths of such a device are calculated as:

$$\lambda_m = \frac{2nL}{m},$$ (2)

where L is defined as the physical length of the cavity, n is the material's effective refractive index, and m is an integer. In practice, typical Fabry-Perot edge-emitting lasers need a minimum cavity length in order to have efficient gain, so the number of longitudinal modes cannot be limited. Multimode emission from F-P lasers is the most important deterioration due to the respective increase of the relative intensity noise (RIN), which restricts significantly the intensity modulation performance of such a device.

The performance of optical communication systems is strongly affected by the RIN, which is known to be a critical factor in determining the signal to noise ratio (SNR). The spectral density of the RIN increases at the laser's resonance frequency. Moreover, in F-P lasers, multimode emission results in enhanced low frequency RIN. This enhanced low-frequency RIN is attributed to the asymmetric nonlinear gain due to the carrier density pulsation (CDP) effect. Although this noise enhancement is at a relatively low frequency, it degrades significantly the system's SNR due to beating effect with the modulation signal (Lu, 1996; Lau 1988).

Distributed Feedback (DFB) lasers are the proper light sources for analog transmission, operating both at 1300 and 1550 nm carrier frequencies, due to their spectral purity, enabling thus low relative intensity noise (RIN) values. In DFB lasers, feedback takes place continuously all over the active waveguide length. This coupling occurs due to the periodical spatial refractive index variation and consequent gain modulation (see Figure 5).

Figure 6: Schematic representation of a high speed DFB laser utilizing integrated optical feedback section (From Radziunas, M., Glitzky, A., Bandelow, U., Wolfrum, M., Troppenz, U., Kreissl, J., & Rehbein, W., "Improving the modulation bandwidth in semiconductor lasers by passive feedback" IEEE J. Selected Topics in Quantum Electronics, 13(1), 2007. With permission. © 2007 IEEE).

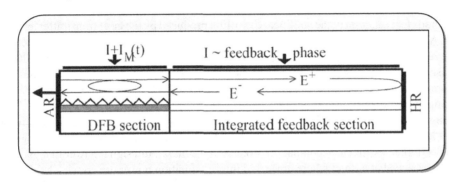

DFB laser spectral purity outcomes due to the fact that the oscillation frequency of the modes is determined by the Bragg condition. Typical values of side-mode suppression ratio (SMSR) are in the order of 40dB. However, due to their intrinsic and extrinsic nonlinearity, they inherently have a serious problem of induced distortion. The most important nonlinear factors are (Watanabe, 1996); spatial-hole burning (SHB), leakage current, nonlinear interaction of carriers and photons, gain compression, nonlinear I-V characteristics in a p-n heterojunction, and power dependent absorption.

The SHB takes place due to nonuniform photon distribution along the laser cavity, which depends on both the coupling coefficient and the grating phase at laser facets, and can be eliminated by proper device design. The leakage current, which flows out of an active layer, also causes the degradation of the L-I linearity. The distortion induced by the leakage current becomes dominant at a high-power operation, because the leakage current increases in high-bias condition, irrespective of the modulation frequency.

The most important nonlinear factor is the intrinsic nonlinear interaction between carriers and photons, which drastically increases the harmonic or intermodulation distortion as the modulation frequency approaches the laser's resonance frequency. Today, there are a few concepts trying to increase the carrier-photon resonance frequency, leading in an increment of the optical bandwidth (today up to 10GHz for typical commercially available devices). The resonance frequency can be directly extracted through a measurement of the RIN's spectral peak. The relationship between the 3dB bandwidth and the resonance frequency, f_R is given by (Lu, 1995):

$$BW = \sqrt{1 + \sqrt{2}} f_R,$$ (3)

One of the proposed techniques in order to increase the resonance frequency is based on the optimization of the laser design and composition (Akram, 2004). Moreover, Multi-Quantum Well (MQW) DFB lasers enable high differential gain values, thus increasing significantly the laser's resonance frequency. Another promising approach relies on injection locking techniques by utilization of optical feedback leading to optical bandwidth up to 40GHz (Radziunas, 2007; Troppenz, 2006). This technique is based on a passive feedback laser (PFL) technique (Fig. 6) inducing a photon-photon (PP) resonance at a frequency in the order of 40GHz and at the same time suppressing the usually observed electron-photon (EP) resonance. However, such devices are available only in research labs and typical commercially packed devices enable resonance frequencies about few GHz (Smyth, 2004).

In a subcarrier multiplexed system, the intrinsic nonlinearity of the laser transmitter leads to the generation of intermodulation distortions, which increase significantly the noise level at the receiver (Tonguz, 1996). The total power due to third order intermodulation distortion at the central channel in the receiver can be calculated as:

$$P_{IMD3} = \frac{3(N^2 - 2N + 1)}{8} \left(\frac{I_0^2 a_3^2 m_0^6}{2} \right), \tag{4}$$

where m_0 is the modulation index, and I_0 is the current at the photodiode and N is an integer corresponding to the number of channels.

Several methods for reduction of the nonlinear distortion produced by the laser transmitter have been proposed up to this time. A feedforward compensation scheme has been proposed (Fock, 1992) for nonlinear distortion and intensity noise reduction, while predistortion approaches have been investigated in (Roselli, 2003; Moon 2006), and external laser injection by (Smyth, 2004; Lee, 2006). Predistortion compensation techniques compensate the transmitter's nonlinearity by inducing an inverse transfer characteristic to the original, resulting in an overall system operating almost linearly.

When the signal power increases, intermodulation power enlarges due to the respective raise of the nonlinearity. Thus, at low signal power levels dynamic range is limited by the noise, while at high signal power levels dynamic range is limited by the intermodulation products. The maximum signal power that gives the maximum dynamic range is reached at a point where noise and intermodulation power are equal. The difference between signal and noise/intermodulation product is defined as the spurious free dynamic range (SFDR) (Al-Raweshidy, 2002) which is the most important quality measure for a laser to be employed in analog (RoF) systems.

Up to now, DFB lasers in cooled packages have been developed with SFDR around 120 dBHz$^{2/3}$ (Wake, 2004). Moreover, highly linear uncooled InGaAsP DFB lasers have been reported with SFDR >100 dBHz$^{2/3}$ at 25C and SFDR >90 dBHz$^{2/3}$ at 85C (Hartmann, 2004), while typical wireless systems require SFDR in the order of 90dB Hz$^{2/3}$ or more.

The DFB laser performance characteristics and the induced nonlinear impairments can be accurately described by the rate equations that govern the electron-photon interaction within the laser cavity. With the rate equations the DFB laser's nonlinearity can be adequately described also taking into account for static and dynamic limitations (i.e. memory effect) (Al-Raweshidy, 2002). The variation of the electric field E and the injected electron concentration n are:

$$\frac{dE}{dt} = \tfrac{1}{2}(1 + i\alpha) \left[G - \frac{1}{\tau_p} \right] E + F(t), \tag{5}$$

$$\frac{dn}{dt} = \frac{I}{eV} - \frac{n}{\tau_s} - G|E|^2, \tag{6}$$

where V is the volume of the active region, G is the modal gain,

$$G = A(1 - s|E|^2), \tag{7}$$

s is the self gain suppression coefficient and A is the linear gain coefficient given by,

$$A = v_g g(n - n_0), \tag{8}$$

where g is the differential gain coefficient, n_0 is the carrier concentration at transparency, τ_p is the photon lifetime, e is the electron charge, τ_s is the carrier lifetime, v_g is the group velocity, and α is the linewidth enhancement factor. Equations (5) – (8) can be used to simulate the DFB laser operation. In the rate equations, usual Langevin noise source is represented by the term F(t) in Eq. 1.

The laser diodes that have been already discussed are edge-emitting devices, characterized by the significant length of the active medium. Another type of laser, which can be used as a transmitter in RoF systems, is vertical-cavity surface emitting laser (VCSEL). The origin of the terms vertical-cavity are due to the fact that the light travels at right angles to the active region. The small size of the resonant cavity enables single mode emission from these devices and the fabrication of the mirror layers with single step growth makes these devices promising candidates for high-scale integration. Moreover, VCSELs can be designed in order to have a symmetrical beam profile and they can be more efficiently focused into the fiber, yielding thus high coupling efficiencies. VCSELs enable coupling efficiency in the order of 85%, while edge emitting lasers enable much less coupling efficiency, which is in the order of 30-50% (Yee, 2006), requiring thus more complicated optics.

On the contrary, typical commercially available VCSELs operate in 850/650nm, where high propagation loss, high chromatic dispersion and multi-transverse mode propagation exists for typical glass optical fibers, (GOF). However, prototype VCSELs at 1550 nm with a modulation frequency response up to 40 GHz have been recently reported (Chrostowski, 2004). Prototype VCSELs at 850nm with SFDR up to 100 dBHz$^{2/3}$ (Carlsson, 2001; Carlsson, 2004) and commercially available with SFDR >90 dBHz$^{2/3}$ (Wake, 2004) have been also reported.

A major advantage of VCSEL's technology is that they can be properly used with multimode fiber (MMF). Especially VCSELs are also excellent candidates for high-speed, low cost optical networks employing plastic optical fiber (POF) (for more details see also the section regarding Optical Fibers).

Optical Fibers

When a wave is coupled into an optical fiber a number of modes exist depending on the refractive index, the size of the fiber, and the angle of incidence. For appropriate values of the aforementioned parameters, single mode operation can be achieved, eliminating thus multi-mode pulse broadening occurring due to the modal dispersion effect. Silica (SiO_2)-based single mode fibers (SMF) enable optimum performance and diminished pulse spreading. Typical core diameter for SMF can be in the range of 5 to 10 μm. Dispersion in SMF occurs due to the wavelength dependent refractive index and thus pulse broadening diminishes for relatively small fiber lengths, as it is the case of typical RoF systems. On the contrary, SMF are expensive and fragile turning thus the market needs towards multi-mode fibers (MMF). Additionally, more than 99.5% of all fibers deployed in the U.S. are multi-mode fibers (Kurt, 2006).

Silica-based MMF are cheap, easy to install and to handle. Apart from the chromatic dispersion that also exists in SMF, modal dispersion is the most important impairment in MMF. Typical core diameter for MMF can be 50 or 62.5 μm. There are mainly two types of multimode fibers: step index and graded-core index (Hecht, 2002). The latter is developed for canceling most of the pulse spreading with gradually changing the core index of the fiber according to a profile, the most popular one being the α-profile (Gloge, 1973). However, accurate alignment using a ferrule in the connector is a significant restriction for both SMF and MMF for low cost installation.

In recent years poly methyl methacrylate (PMMA) plastic optical fiber (POF) has emerged as a powerful candidate for very low cost optical links operating around 650nm, where standard POF exhibits minimum optical attenuation (in the order of 100dB/km (Kaino, 1984). POF relaxes installation requirements compared to glass optical fibers (GOF) due to the very large diameter and mechanical resilience to stresses and installation, and wide range of possible applications. Following this, Gb optical transmitter technologies in 650nm window are required in order to satisfy typical consumer applications. However, conventional red lasers already used in other applications (i.e. DVD) have a high noise figure and require high operating power. For these high-speed applications, VCSELs with emission wavelengths in the range of 650nm to 690nm have been proposed, designed and fabricated (Hung, 2007). As an example, a bandwidth of more than 3GHz has been achieved with a VCSEL operating at bias currents of less than 10mA.

However, the most serious impairments of the POF are its reduced bandwidth, which is limited by modal dispersion, and its high attenuation. Improved modulation techniques, as for example Optical Frequency Multiplication (OFM), have been employed in order to overcome the modal dispersion induced limitations (Koonen, 2007). The feasibility of the technique has been demonstrated on a system level delivering 100 Mb/s at a carrier frequencies of 17 GHz over a propagation distance of 100m graded index (GI)-POF.

Graded-index (GI) POF can reach up to three-times higher bandwidth-length product (BLP) and lower modal dispersion. In GI-POF the core's refractive index decreases as a function of the radius. Moreover, an appropriate performance for application in high speed optical networks can be achieved, utilizing perfluorinated (PF) amorphous polymer-based GI-POF (PF-GI-POF) (Koike, 1997; Yoshihara, 1998). In PF-GI-POF typical attenuation is in the order of 40dB/km even in the near infrared region. Moreover, PF-GI-POF has smaller material dispersion than GOF or PMMA POFs, enabling bandwidth up to 10GHz km (Ishigure, 2000).

Photodetectors

The role of an optical receiver is to convert the optical signal to electrical signal, thus recovering the original microwave carrier transmitted in a RoF system. The elementary component of the receiver is a photodetector, based on typical semiconductor materials. Different types of photodetectors include p-i-n photodiodes and avalanche photodiodes (APDs) based on Si or InGaAs, depending on the required operating wavelength. The relationship between the generated photocurrent and the incident optical power is defined as:

$$I_p = \Re P_{in},$$ (9)

where $\Re$ is the responsivity in units [A/W]. For laboratory calculations, it is more convenient to measure the voltage that appears in a resistor, so we define the generated electrical voltage as:

$$V_p = G p_{in}$$ (10)

where G is the conversion gain in units [V/W]. The conversion gain and the responsivity are related with eq. 11:

$$G = \Re R_L / 2,$$ (11)

An important parameter for a photodetector is the noise equivalent power (NEP), which is defined as the minimum inserted optical power per unit bandwidth required to produce an SNR value of one (Agrawal, 1997). The sensitivity is then dependent on both the NEP and the signal's bandwidth as:

$$P_m = NEP \sqrt{BW},$$ (12)

From equation 12, it is extracted that the receiver's sensitivity can be significantly improved by using an electrical band-pass filter. Typical values of NEP are in the range of 1-10 pW/Hz$^{1/2}$ (Agrawal, 1997).

In addition, the performance of an optical receiver depends on the SNR. Noise in photodetectors occurs due to two fundamental physical mechanisms, which produce shot noise and thermal noise. The domination of each mechanism strongly depends on the incident optical power. In the low power regime thermal noise dominates, while in the high power range shot noise makes the most significant contribution. For links, where optical power levels at the receiver are high, as it is the case in short-haul RoF based networks, shot noise dominates. Hence, a priority has been given to techniques that reduce the total average received optical power at the receiver while at the same time both the SFDR and linearity have to be kept at high levels (Darcie, 2006).

Commercially available photodetectors are much more linear than typical laser diodes, so little distortion is added to a RoF system by the photodiode (Al-Raweshidy, 2002). Nonlinearity can be a problem in the case of very high power (i.e. 5- 10mW or greater), as for example in CATV links.

As an example, operational characteristics for a typical InGaAs-based APD are: operating wavelength 1550 nm, a responsivity in the order of 0.6 A/W, and a 3 dB bandwidth of 25 GHz or greater.

Figure 7. Radio over Fiber link schemes, (a) RF-over-Fiber, (b) IF-over-Fiber, and (c) BB-over-Fiber

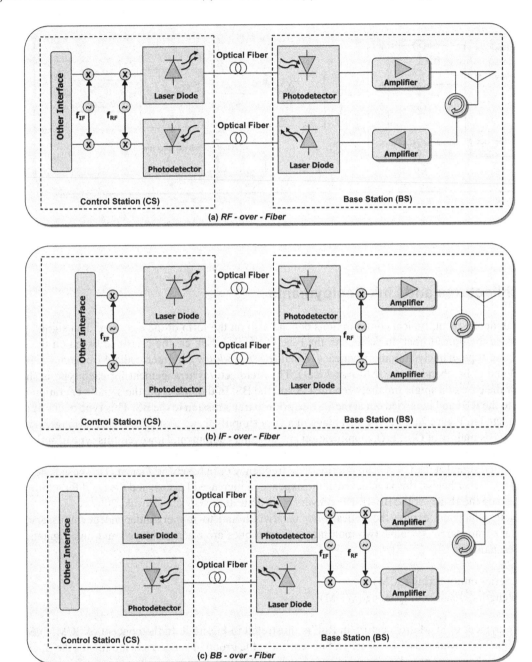

Figure 8: Sub-carrier multiplexing in RoF links. Independent data services on different RF carriers are transmitted via the same optical fiber to the BSs.

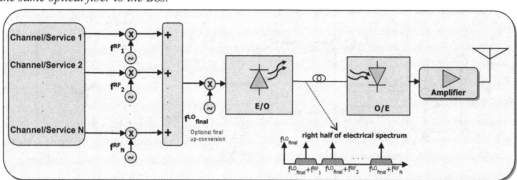

RoF Architectures and Link Deployments

In a RoF link deployment, typical configurations depend also on the form of the electrical data signal, prior to distribution via the optical fiber. In particular, the type of the RoF link can be classified based on the signal's frequency band type, namely, a) radio frequency signal (*RF-over-Fiber*), b) intermediate frequency signal (*IF-over-Fiber*) and c) baseband signal (*BB-over-Fiber*). The architectural arrangement for each type is shown in Figure 7, for the case of a single link between the CS and the BS. In the first type, the signal generation and up-conversion to the RF band is carried out at the CS site prior to transmission to the BS. This type of configuration, which is depicted in Figure 7(a), has the advantage of a very simplified and cost effective BS arrangement, since the latter consists mainly of O/E, E/O, amplification and antenna equipment. However, this type of link is prone to fiber dispersion and phase noise. The performance penalty due to the fiber dispersion effect is severely limited if the transmitted signal at the CS is in an intermediate frequency or in baseband format. This case is depicted in figures 7(b),(c). Nevertheless, this is achieved at the expense of increased BS cost and the need for additional BS equipment, since the IF-RF or the BB-IF-RF conversion is done at the BS site (Novak, 2007).

In order to effectively exploit the optical fiber bandwidth and to support independent multi-service and radio-interface transparent systems, two multiplexing techniques are often employed and investigated in RoF architectures, namely:

- Sub-carrier multiplexing (SCM)
- Wavelength division multiplexing (WDM)

The employment of SCM architecture in RoF is illustrated in Figure 8. In the concept of SCM, every individual RF signal is considered as a subcarrier. Subsequently, the group of subcarriers modulates the final optical carrier, which is then transmitted via optical fiber at each BS. Optical carrier modulation is performed according to the techniques already described. It is apparent that each subcarrier, which occupies a specific frequency band, constitutes an autonomous communication channel that might involve either digital or analogue data. In SCM technique, different modulation schemes per subcarrier can be employed. Moreover, SCM configuration offers relaxation of synchronization requirement (Hui, 2002; Tonguz, 1996). Additionally, the SCM scheme allows for the integration of multiple services, since it offers flexibility due to the transparency of every subcarrier on the modulation format. However, it is susceptible to non-linear and noise effects (Yuen, 2005).

In WDM, each radio carrier (or subcarrier) is allocated to a designated optical channel (wavelength) and the group of these channels is transmitted to its destination via optical fiber. In WDM-RoF systems an optical channel corresponds to a BS or a RAU. Next, the BS has to demultiplex and transmit its signal to end-users through

Figure 9. General architecture of WDM-RoF, (a) WDM-RoF network, (b) Distribution of independent services via WDM-RoF

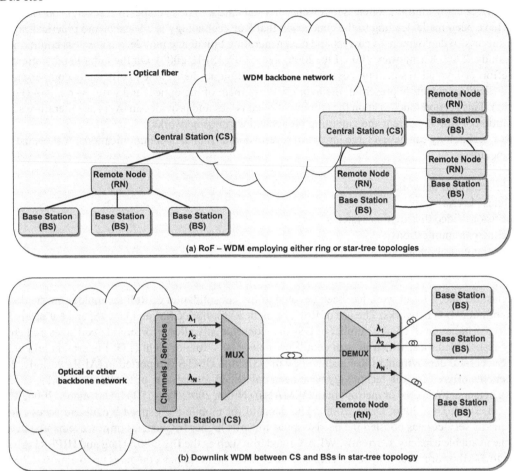

a wireless link. The opposite procedure occurs when the BS has to receive, multiplex and transmit the end-user signals to the CS. In this way, a fiber-based backbone network is developed, that interconnects the CS to all BSs. Consequently, an efficient, easily manageable and upgradeable point-to-multipoint network topology is achieved. The general overview of the architecture for a WDM-RoF system is illustrated in Figure 9. Recently, the utilization of dense wavelength division multiplexing (DWDM) combined with single-side-band (SSB) modulation has been addressed for broadband wireless RoF systems, since it offers the ability to exploit a large number of optical channels which is necessary in view of next generation (wireless) services requiring many BSs. More details on the deployments of WDM-RoF systems can be found in (Kitayama, 2002; Lin, 2005; Nakasyotani, 2006; Bakaul, 2006).

RoF APPLICATIONS IN THE PROSPECT OF NEXT GENERATION NETWORKS

A large part of academic and industrial research effort, along with the available literature on the development of hybrid fiber radio technology, is devoted to the potential and the suitability of RoF technology in view of upcoming and already existing wireless communication standards. In particular, the resourceful exploitation of

RoF capabilities in terms of not only ultrahigh bandwidth and architectural flexibility, but also independency and transparency in the baseband to RF modulation scheme, is of great interest due to the ability of transmitting multiple services using multiple wireless (or even cable) standards. In this perspective, several contributions and proposals have been made, leading to the conclusion that RoF technology is a feasible and practical infrastructure for a successful deployment of current and next generation broadband mobile and wireless communications (Al-Raweshidy, 2002; Kurniawan, 2006; Liu, 2006; Lee, 2007; IEEE, 2007). On the other hand, a great deal of research effort is devoted to signal processing issues and techniques being able to efficiently compensate on the inherent difficulties currently present in the hybrid environment of the optical and wireless domain (Fernando, 2006 ACM). This section touches upon the aforementioned issues and provides an overview literature survey on the exploration of RoF in current and emerging broadband wireless networks.

The RoF technology can have a large impact in several domains of data communications. A short list of these domains includes:

- Mobile/Cellular networks
- Wireless LANs
- Television/Video distribution systems
- Satellite communications
- Vehicular communications
- Next generation Mixed Optical and Wireless access networks

In the last decade, a lot of work has been devoted to the consolidation of RoF technology in the domain of mobile communication networks. The use of RoF is beneficial for both GSM and UMTS, since it offers flexible and effective installation of a large number of BSs that consequently allows for smaller cell sizes and enhanced frequency re-use scenarios, which in turn entail low power BSs, line of sight (LOS) operation and enhanced capacity. Successful deployment of RoF technology in GSM and UMTS is reported in (Al-Raweshidy, 2002).

The benefits offered by RoF technology have been envisaged for the case of wireless networks, either local (WLANs), personal (WPANs) or metropolitan (WMANs) (Niiho, 2006; Tang, 2004; Hartmann, 2004; Mitchell, 2004; Ismail, 2004; Das, 2006; Dang, 2005). The demand for mobile high-speed broadband access networks and multimedia services has boosted the need to move towards higher frequencies (mm-wave bands) in order to increase the available capacity. Currently, WLAN standards such as the IEEE 802.11a/g and HIPERLAN/2 offer speeds up to 54Mbps or more, while emerging ones (e.g. IEEE 802.11n) push the rates up to almost 720Mbps, at the 2.4GHz and 5GHz bands. In addition, towards the transition to the 4G era, where the terms all-IP, anytime and anywhere, broadband services dominate, the IEEE 802.16 standard (or most commonly the Wireless MAN or WiMAX technology) along with other, similar or not, technologies such as UMTS, ultra wideband (UWB) communications and many more, are tailored to push the accessible frequency bands beyond 60GHz. In this context, RoF technology offers large benefits in terms of high capacity and micro- and pico-cellular coverage for indoor or last mile access to these networks. Although there is no extensive literature concerning a thorough experimentation on the performance of RoF on these standards, recent publications address in detail the feasibility of using RoF to transfer this kind of signals in a successful, efficient and cost-effective way (Mitchell, 2004; Ismail, 2004; Das, 2007; Crisp, 2007). Currently, a European funded research project, named *ISIS (InfraStructures for Broadband Access in wireless/photonics and Integration of Strenghts in Europe)*, aims, among other targets, to extensively evaluate the adequacy of RoF in supporting and delivering the most dominant current and emerging wireless communication standards. Experimental assessment has shown that carefully designed RoF systems are able to cope with these standards (*www.ist-isis.org*). Similar projects on Radio over Fiber research are, UROOF (Ultra Wideband Radio over Optical Fiber, http://www.ist-uroof.org), Gandalf (http://www.ist-gandalf.org), and BONE (Building the Future Optical Network in Europe, http://www.ict-bone.eu). Furthermore, another point of interest is the integration of mobile (cellular) communications and WLANs and, in extend, the simultaneous transmission of multiple services over the same backbone fiber-based network (Yuen, 2005).

In the perspective of 3G and 4G communications, the most dominant modulation schemes are wideband code division multiple access (WCDMA) and orthogonal frequency division multiple access (OFDMA). So, it is of great importance to evaluate the sufficiency of RoF links regarding the requirements set up by the standards utilizing these schemes. The most important factors that greatly influence the overall performance of RoF links can be listed as:

- Estimation and equalization of both the time varying wireless channel and the non-linear optical channel. Nonlinearity in the optical channel is present due to both light source (eg. laser) and the optical fiber. In addition, modal dispersion (similar to the wireless channel) is also present when MMF (GOF or POF) fibers are used (Hartmann, 2004; Kurt, 2006; Fernando, 2006 ACM).
- The link's noise profile. Inherent noise sources are present due to both optical and electrical domain. The relative intensity noise (RIN) is of major concern as well, since recently it was shown that RIN depends on not only the optical power, but also on the modulation index (Fernando, 2006 IEEE; Fernando, 2006 ACM).

An analysis of the considered factors for the design of an efficient RoF link for IM/DD, in the framework of next generation multimedia services, is summarized in (Fernando, 2006 ACM). Furthermore, sophisticated signal processing techniques, either in optical or electrical domain, have been developed to powerfully compensate the previous issues. These include OFM for efficient generation of microwave signal over MMF (Ng'oma, 2005; Larrode, 2006), the exploitation of the OFDM's cyclic prefix in WLAN transmission via MMF (Kurt, 2006) and compensation of both optical and electrical channels (Pinter, 2005), to name but a few.

Moreover, there are numerous reports in available literature relative to the potential, the employment and the performance of RoF in non standardized high speed network applications (Hirata, 2002; Hirata, 2003). Another very interesting application of RoF technology is in the area of television provision in CATV networks and in the last mile (interactive) video distribution systems (Maeda, 2005; Tzeng, 2006; Chung, 2007; Cvijetic, 2007).

The RoF infrastructure has also been successfully employed in the field of vehicular technology. Deployment examples for the case of road-to-vehicle and broadband Internet access in train environment are described in (Park, 2000; Sato, 2005) and (Lanoo, 2007) respectively.

Additionally, RoF is productively implied in the field of satellite communications, where RoF links are utilized for the interconnection and control between satellite earth stations and control centers.

Ultimately, the role of RoF is to enhance and simplify the necessary infrastructure in the broader area of fiber-to-the-home (FTTH) and fiber-to-the-antenna (FTTA) or, otherwise stated, to support the momentum towards the seamless integration of super broadband optical and wireless networks (Koonen, 2006; Liu, 2006; Shen, 2007; Jia, 2007; Chang, 2007; IEEE, 2007).

A SHORT DEMONSTRATION ON BASIC ROF NONLINEARITY ISSUES: AN ILLUSTRATIVE EXAMPLE

This section provides an introductory demonstration on both the characterization of the laser transmitter and the impact of its nonlinear behavior for the case of an IM/DD RoF link, employing orthogonal frequency division multiplexing (OFDM). In this example, a typical RoF system utilizing a few km of single-mode fibre (SMF) is assumed, ensuring high bandwidth and low-distortion and transparency throughout the simulations. Moreover, since commercially available photodetectors are much more linear than typical laser diodes, little distortion is added to the system by the photodiode. Therefore, the response of the photodiode is assumed to be constant over the studied frequency range.

The laser transmitter behavior is partially described by the dynamic amplitude-frequency response. The dynamic amplitude response of a DFB laser transmitter as a function of the operating frequency is depicted in Figure 10, at a constant value of the RF current amplitude (I_0=5mA). This result is calculated utilizing the rate equation model described in the respective section. A significant nonlinear amplitude behaviour emerges at an operating frequency in the order of the laser's resonance frequency, (~6GHz), or greater. This effect would be a significant drawback for broadband multi-service signals at the receiver (Rx) using ordinary linear processing techniques since the response does not exhibits a uniform performance.

Figure 10. Amplitude response of a typical DFB laser

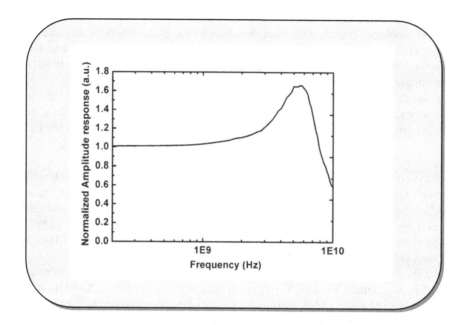

In addition, a strong indicator of the laser's performance is its dynamic Light–Current (L-I) characteristics (Figure 11). The L-I characteristics are obtained by numerically solving the rate equations using as an input excitation a triangular pulse at frequencies of 2.4 and 5.8 GHz, respectively. The reason for using pulse excitation is to evaluate the dynamic transfer characteristics, which are strongly dependent on the operating frequency, while static L-I curves can be used as a diagnostic tool only for frequencies less than 5 times the laser's resonance frequency (Lu, 1996). As it can be clearly observed the degradation of the L-I curve linearity is strongly enhanced in the case of 5.8 GHz.

It is very interesting to study the potential effect of the DFB laser's intrinsic nonlinearity on an orthogonal frequency division multiplexing (OFDM) scheme. OFDM is already a mainstream technology in broadband communications and has been adopted in various technologies and international standards. Figure 12 presents the calculated spectra using the already mentioned DFB laser's model for 5mA and 20mA current amplitudes and 5.8 GHz RF carrier (Mikroulis, 2007). For illustrative purposes a special OFDM symbol comprising of 16 adjacent unmodulated subcarriers, 32 zero valued subcarriers followed by 16 adjacent unmodulated subcarriers has been considered. Using this arrangement, intermodulation products can be clearly observed from the calculated OFDM spectra. As it can be seen, strong intermodulation products appear only for the case of high current amplitude (high RF signal power) due to the limited nonlinearity at low current amplitude (low RF signal power). These products would be a significant impairment degrading significantly the SNR of a corresponding system, depicting the necessity for carefully designed RoF links.

CONCLUDING REMARKS

In this chapter, we have addressed the main issues relating to the hybrid fiber radio technology and we have pointed out the key factors for its exploitation in current and next generation broadband networks. Moreover, we have not only depicted the advantages of RoF utilization, but also identified the optimization challenges

Figure 11. Dynamic Light-Current (L-I) characteristics for the DFB laser

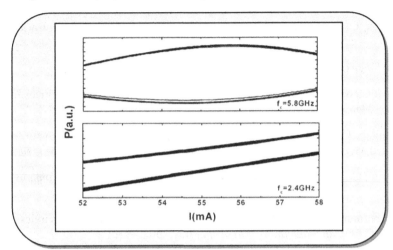

Figure 12. Intermodulation effect due to DFB laser's intrinsic nonlinearity in an orthogonal frequency division multiplexing (OFDM) scheme

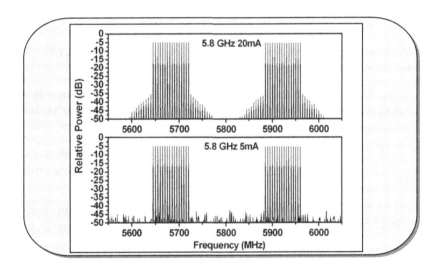

regarding its wide scale deployment. In addition, the ongoing world-wide research effort on the convergence of the optical and wireless access networks clearly indicates that the adoption of RoF as an infrastructure scheme, capable of providing micro/pico cellular coverage and supporting multiple data services in an efficient and cost-effective manner, is feasible. In conclusion, RoF is an interdisciplinary and very challenging area of research and development, aiming at efficiently integrating and combining the fields of radio and optical communications for fiber-based wireless access. This objective is expected to have a large impact towards the development of next generation networks of enhanced mobility and ultra high capacity.

REFERENCES

Ackerman, E. I., & Cox, C. H. (2001). RF Fiber-Optic Link Performance. *IEEE Microwave*, December 2001, 50-58.

Agrawal G. P. (1997). *Fiber Optic communication systems*. NY. Wiley.

Agrawal, P., Chuah, M. C., & Zander, J. (2004). Multimedia Multicast/Broadcast Services in 3G/4G Networks. *IEEE Communications Magazine*, February 2004.

Akram, M. N., Silfvenious, C., Kjeborn, O., and Schatz, R. (2004). Design optimization of InGaAsP-InGaAlAs 1.55 strain-compensated MQW lasers for direct modulation applications. *Semicond. Sci. Technol.*, 19, 615-625.

Al-Raweshidy, H. & Komaki, S. (2002). *Radio over Fiber Technologies for Mobile Communications Networks*. Artech House.

Arroyo-Fernandez B., Fernandes, J., & Prasad R. (2003). Composite Reconfigurable Wireless Networks: The EU R&D Path Toward 4G. *IEEE Communications Magazine*, July 2003, Part I.

Arroyo-Fernandez, B., Fernandes, J. & Prasad R. (2004). Composite Reconfigurable Wireless Networks: The EU R&D Path Toward 4G. *IEEE Communications Magazine*, May 2004, Part II.

Bakaul, M. (2006). *Technologies for DWDM Millimetre-Wave Fibre-Radio Networks*. Doctoral Dissertation, University of Melbourne, Australia.

Carlsson C., et al. (2001). High Performance Microwave Link Using a Multimode VCSEL and a High-Bandwidth Multimode Fiber. *IEEE International Topical Meeting on Microwave Photonics (pp. 81-84)*. IEEE

Carlsson, C., Larsson, A., & Alping, A. (2004). RF Transmission Over Multimode Fibers Using VCSELs - Comparing Standard and High-Bandwidth Multimode Fibers. *IEEE J. Lightwave Technology.*, 22, 1694-1702.

Chang, G.-K., Yu, J., & Jia, Z. (2007). Architectures and Enabling Technologies for Super-Broadband Radio-over-Fiber Optical Wireless Access Networks. *IEEE International Topical Meeting on Microwave Photonics (pp. 24-28)*. IEEE.

Chrostowski, L., Zhao, X., Chang-Hasnain, C., Shau, R., & Amann, M. (2004). Very high resonance frequency (>40 GHz) optical injection-locked 1.55 μm VCSELs. *IEEE International Topical Meeting on Microwave Photonics (pp. 255–258)*. IEEE.

Chung, H. S., Chang, S. H., Park, J. D., Chu, M.-J. & Kwangjoon, K. (2007). Transmission of Multiple HD-TV Signals Over a Wired/Wireless Line Millimeter Wave Link With 60 GHz. *IEEE J. Lightwave Technology*, 25(11).

Cox, C. H. III, Ackerman, E. I., Betts, G. E., & Prince, J. L. (2006). Limits on the Performance of RF-Over-Fiber Links and Their Impact on Device Design. *IEEE Trans. Microwave Theory Techniques.* 54, 906- 920.

Cox, C., Ackerman, E., Helkey, R., & Betts, G. E. (1997). Techniques and performance of intensity-modulation direct-detection analogue optical links. *IEEE Trans. Microwave Theory Techniques.* 45(8), 1375–1383.

Crisp, J., Li, S., Watts, A., Penty, R.V., & White H. Ian. (2007). Uplink and Downlink Coverage Improvements of 802.11g Signals Using a Distributed Antenna Network. *IEEE J. Lightwave Technology*, 25(11).

Cvijetic, N., Wilson, S. G., & Zarubica, R. (2007). Performance Evaluation of a Novel Converged Architecture for Digital-Video Transmission Over Optical Wireless Channels. . *IEEE J. Lightwave Technology*, 25(11).

Dang, B. L., & Niemegeers, I. (2005). Analysis of IEEE 802.11 in radio over fiber home networks. *Proc. 30th IEEE Conf. LCN*, pp. 744–747.

Darcie, T. E., & Driessen, P. F. (2006). Class-AB Techniques for High-Dynamic-Range Microwave-Photonic Links. *IEEE Photon. Technol. Let.* 18(8), 929-931.

Das, A., Mjeku, M., Nkansah, A., & Gomes, N. J. (2007). Effects on IEEE 802.11 MAC Throughput in Wireless LAN Over Fiber Systems. *IEEE J. Lightwave Technology*, 25(11), 3321-3328.

Das, A., Nkansah, A., Gomes, N. J., Garcia, I. J., Batchelor, J., & Wake, D. (2006). Design of low-cost multimode fiber fed indoor wireless networks. *IEEE Trans. Microw. Theory Tech.*, 54(8), 3426–3432.

ETSI EN300-744 v1.2.1, Digital Video Broadcasting (DVB): Framing Structure, channel coding and modulation for digital terrestrial television, ETSI 1999-01.

Fernando, X. (2006). Improved Expression for Intensity Noise in Multimedia over Fiber Networks. *International Conference on Industrial and Information Systems ICIIS 2006 (pp. 425-429). IEEE.*

Fernando, X., (2006). Radio over Fiber in Multimedia Access Networks. *International Conference on Access Networks (AccessNets'06). ACM.*

Fock, L., Kwan, A., & Tucker R. S. (1992). Reduction of semiconductor laser intensity noise by feedforward compensation: experiment and theory. *IEEE J. Lightwave Technology*, 10, 1919–1925.

Gliese, U., Norskov, T., Norskov, S., & Sturkjaer, T. E. (1998). Multifunctional fiber-optic microwave links based on remote-heterodyne detection. *IEEE Trans. Microw. Theory Tech.*, 46, 458- 468.

Gloge, D., & Marcatili, E. A. J. (1973). Multimode theory of graded-core fibers. *Bell Systems Tech. J.*, Nov. 1973, 1563-1578.

Hartmann, P., Penty, R.V., White, I.H., Seeds, A.J., (2004). Dual Service Wireless LAN antenna-remoting system using uncooled directly modulated DFB Laser diodes. *CLEO 2004.*

Hartmann, P., Qian, X., Penty, R. V., & White, I. H. (2004). Broadband multimode fibre (MMF) based IEEE 802.11a/b/g WLAN distribution system. *IEEE Int. Top. Meeting Microw. Photon. (pp. 173–176)*, IEEE.

Hecht, J. (2002). *Understanding Fiber Optics.* Prentice Hall.

Hirata, A., Harada, M., & Nagatsuma, T. (2003). 120-GHz Wireless Link Using Photonic Techniques for Generation, Modulation, and Emission of Millimeter-Wave Signals. *IEEE J. Lightwave Technology*, 21(10), 2145-2153.

Hirata, A., Minotani, T., & Nagatsuma, T. (2002) .Millimeter-Wave Photonics for 10 Gbit/s Wireless Links. *LEOS 2002, vol.2, (pp. 477 – 478)*. LEOS.

Hui, R., Zhu, B., Huang, R., Allen, C.T. , Demarest, K.R., & Richards, D. (2002). Subcarrier multiplexing for high-speed optical transmission. *IEEE J. Lightwave Technol*ogy., 20, 417–427.

Hung, V. W., Mc Garvey B., et al. (2007). Red VCSEL Transceivers for Gigabit Data Transmission over Plastic Optical Fibre. *16th international conference on plastic optical fibers, Italy, 2007.*

IEEE 802.16.2. (2004). Recommended Practice for Local and metropolitan area networks. Coexistence of Fixed Broadband Wireless Access Systems. *IEEE Computer Society & IEEE Microwave Theory and Techniques Society*, March 2004.

IEEE Std 802.11a-1999. (1999). Part 11: Wireless LAN Medium Access Control (MAC) and Physical Layer (PHY) specifications: High Speed Physical Layer in the 5GHz Band. *IEEE.*

IEEE, (2007). Special Section on Convergence of Optical and Wireless Access Networks. *IEEE J. Lightwave Technology,* 25(11).

Ishigure T., Koike Y., & Fleming J. W. (2000). Optimum Index Profile of the Perfluorinated Polymer-Based GI Polymer Optical Fiber and Its Dispersion Properties. *IEEE J. Lightwave Technology*, 18, 178-184.

Ismail, T., Liu, C. P., & Seeds, A. J. (2004). Uncooled directly modulated high dynamic range source for IEEE802.11a wireless over fibre LAN applications. *Optical Fibre Communications 2004 (OFC 2004).*

ITU, "World Telecommunication Development Report 2002: Reinventing Telecoms", March 2002 (available online:http://www.itu.int/itud/ict/publications/).

Jia, Z., Yu, J., Chowdhury, A., Ellinas, G., & Chang, G.-K. (2007). Simultaneous Generation of Independent Wired and Wireless Services Using a Single Modulator in Millimeter-Wave-Band Radio-Over-Fiber Systems. *IEEE Photonics Technology Letters.* 19(20), 1691-1693.

Kaino T., Fujiki M., & Jinguji K., (1984). Preparation of plastic optical fibers. *Rev. Electron. Commun. Lab.*, 32, 478–488.

Kim, Y., Jeong, B. J., Chung, J., Hwang, C-S., Ryu, J. S., Kim, K-H., & Kim Y. K., (2003). Beyond 3G: Vision, Requirements, and Enabling Technologies. *IEEE Communications Magazine*, March, pp. 120 – 124.

Kitayama, K. (2000). Architectural Considerations of Fiber-Radio Millimeter-Wave Wireless Access Systems. *Fiber and Integrated Optics*, 19(2), 167-186.

Kitayama, K., Kuri, T., Onohara, K., Kamisaka, T., & Murashima, K. (2002). Dispersion effects of FBG filter and optical SSB filtering in DWDM millimeter-wave fiber-radio systems. *IEEE J. Lightwave Technology.*, 20(8), 1397–1407.

Koike Y. & Ishigure T., (1997). *Progress of low-loss GI polymer optical fiber from visible to 1.5-mm wavelength.* 23rd European Conf. Opt. Commun. (ECOC), vol. 1, Edinburgh, Scotland. pp. 59–62.

Koonen, A. M. J., Ng'oma A., et al., (2007). *In-house broadband wireless service delivery using radio over fibre.* 16th international conference on plastic optical fibers, Italy, 2007.

Koonen, T. (2006). Fiber to the home/fiber to the premises: What, where and when?" *Proc. IEEE*, 94(5), 911–934.

Kurniawan, T., Nirmalathas, A., Lim, C., Novak, D., & Waterhouse, R. (2006). Performance analysis of optimized millimeter-wave fiber radio system, *IEEE Transactions on Microwave Theory and Technique*, 54. 921-928.

Kurt, T., Abbas Yongacoglu, A., & Chouinard, J-Y. (2006). OFDM and Externally Modulated Multi-mode Fibers in Radio over Fiber Systems. *IEEE Trans. On Wireless Communications*, 5(10), 2669-2674.

Lannoo, B., Colle, D., Pickavet, M., & Demeester, P. (2007). Radio-over-Fiber-Based Solution to Provide Broadband Internet Access to Train Passengers. *IEEE Communications Magazine*, February 2007, 56-62.

Larrodé M. G., Koonen, A. M. J. & Vegas Olmos, J. J. (2006). Overcoming Modal Bandwidth Limitation in Radio-over-Multimode Fiber Links. *IEEE Photonics Technology Letters.* 18(22), pp. 2428-2430.

Lau, K. Y., & Blauvelt, H. (1988). Effect of low-frequency intensity noise on high frequency direct modulation of semiconductor injection lasers. *Appl. Phys. Lett.*, 52, 694-696.

Lee, Chi H. (Ed.). (2007). *Microwave Photonics.* CRC Press.

Lee, S. H., & Kang, J. M. (2006). Linearization of DFB Laser Diode by External Light-Injected Cross-Gain Modulation for Radio-Over-Fiber Link. *IEEE Photon. Technol. Let.*, 18(14), 1545-1547.

Lin, Wen-Piao. (2005). Wavelength Division Multiplexed Millimeter Waveband Radio-on-Fiber System Using Continuum Light Source. *IEEE J. Lightwave Technology*, 23(9), 2610–2621.

Liu, C. P., Ismail, T., & Seeds, A. J. (2006). Broadband access using wireless-over-fibre technologies. *BT Technology Journal*, 24(3), 130-143.

Lu, H., Makino, T., & Li, G. P., (1995). Dynamic properties of partly gain-coupled 1.55-μm DFB lasers. *IEEE J. Quant. Electron.*, 31, 1443-1450.

Lu, X., Su, C. B., Lauer, R. B., Meslener, G. J., & Ulbricht L. W. (1996). Analysis of relative intensity noise in semiconductor lasers and its effect on subcarrier multiplexed Lightwave systems. *IEEE J. Lightwave Technology*, 12, 1159-1165.

Maack D., (1999). Reliability of lithium niobate Mach Zehnder modulators for digital optical fiber telecommunication systems. *SPIE Crit. Rev.*, vol. CR 73, 197–230.

Maeda, M., Nakatogawa, T., & Oyamada, K. (2005) Optical fiber transmission technologies for digital terrestrial broadcasting signals. *IEICE Trans. Commun*, E88-B(5), 1853–1860.

Mikroulis, S., Karabetsos, S., Pikasis, E. & Nassiopoulos A. (2008). Performance Evaluation of a Radio over Fiber (RoF) System Subject to the Transmitter's Limitations for Application in Broadband Networks. IEEE Transactions on Consumer Electronics, 54(2), 437 - 443.

Mitchell J. E., (2004). Performance of OFDM at 5.8 GHz using radio over fibre link. *Electronics Letters*, 40(21).

Moon, H., & Sedaghat R. (2006). FPGA-Based adaptive digital predistortion for radio-over-fiber links. *Microprocessors and Microsystems*, 30, 145–154.

Nakasyotani, T., Toda, H., Kuri, & Kitayama, K. (2006). Wavelength Division Multiplexed Millimeter Waveband Radio-on-Fiber System Using Continuum Light Source. *IEEE J. Lightwave Technology.*, 24(1), 404–410.

Ng'oma, A. (2005). *Radio-over-Fibre Technology for Broadband Wireless Communication Systems.* Doctoral Dissertation, Eindhoven University of Technology, Netherlands.

Niiho, T., Nakaso, M., Masuda, K., Sasai, H., Utsumi, K., & Masaru, Fuse M. (2006). Transmission Performance of Multichannel Wireless LAN System Based on Radio Over-Fiber Techniques. *IEEE Transactions on Microwave Theory and Techniques*, 54(2), 980-989.

Noel, L., Wake, D., Moodie, D. G., Marcenac, D. D., Westbrook, L. D., & Nesset D. (1997). Novel techniques for high capacity 60-GHz fiber-radio transmission system. *IEEE Trans. Microwave Theory and Techniques*, 45(8), 1416–1423.

Novak, D., Nirmalathas, A., Lim, C., Waterhouse, R., Bakaul, M., & Kurniawan, T. (2007). Hybrid Fiber Radio – Concepts and Prospects. In Chi H. Lee (Ed.), *Microwave Photonics (pp. 157-183).* CRC Press.

Ogawa, H., Polifko, D., & Banba S. (1992). Millimeter-wave fiber optics systems for personal radio communication. *IEEE Trans. Microwave Theory and Techniques*, 40, 2285–2292.

Olesen, H. & Jacobsen, G. (1982). A theoretical and experimental analysis of laser fields and power spectra. *IEEE J. Quant. Electron.*, 18, 2069- 2080.

Park, Y.-H., Okada, M., & Komaki, S. (2000). The Performance of Fiber-Radio Road Vehicle Communication System with Macro-Diversity. *Wireless Personal Communications*, 14, 125-132.

Pinter, Z. S., & Fernando, N. X. (2005). Fiber-Wireless Solution for Broadband Multimedia Access. *IEEE Canadian Review*, First Quarter 2005, 6-9.

Radziunas M., Glitzky, A., Bandelow, U., Wolfrum, M., Troppenz, U., Kreissl, J., Rehbein, W. (2007). Improving the modulation bandwidth in semiconductor lasers by passive feedback. *IEEE J. Selected Topics in Quantum Electronics*, 13(1), 136-142.

Roselli, L., Borgioni ,V., Zepparelli, F., Ambrosi, F., Comez, M., Faccin, P., & Casini A. (2003). Analog Laser Predistortion for Multiservice Radio-Over-Fiber Systems. *IEEE J. Lightwave Technology*, 21(5).

Sato, K., Fujise, M., Shimizu, S. & Nishi, S. (2005). Millimeter-Wave High-Speed Spot Communication System Using Radio-over-Fiber Technology. *IEICE Trans. Electron.*, E88-C(10), 1932-1938.

Seeds, A. J. & Williams K. J. (2006). Microwave Photonics. *IEEE J. Lightwave Technology*, 24(12), 4628 – 4641.

Shen, G., Tucker, R. S., & Chae, C.-J. (2007). Fixed Mobile Convergence Architectures for Broadband Access: Integration of EPON and WiMAX. *IEEE Communications Magazine*, August 2007. 44-50.

Smyth, F., Kaszubowska, A., Barry, L.P. (2004). Overcoming laser diode nonlinearity issues in multi-channel radio-over-fiber systems. *Optics Communications*, 217–225.

Stephens, W. E. & Joseph T. R. (1987). System characteristics of direct modulated and externally modulated RF fiberoptic links. *IEEE J. Lightwave Technology*, LT-5, 380- 387.

Tang, P. K., Ling Chuen Ong, Alphones A., Luo, B., & Fujise, M. (2004). PER and EVM Measurements of a Radio-Over-Fiber Network for Cellular and WLAN System Applications. *IEEE J. Lightwave Technology,* 22(11), 2370-2376.

Tonguz, O. K., & Jung H. (1996). Personal communication access networks using subcarrier multiplexed optical links. *IEEE J. Lightwave Technology*, 14, 1400-1409.

Troppenz, U., Kreissl J., Rehbein W., Bornholdt C., Gaertner T., Radziunas M., Glitzky A., Bandelow U., Wolfrum M. (2006). *'40 Gb/s directly modulated InGaAsP passive feedback DFB laser'*, European Conference on Optical Communications (ECOC) Proc. Ser., paper Th 4.5.5.

Tzeng, S.-J. (2006). CATV/Radio-on-Fiber transport system based on direct modulation. *Optics Communications*, 259, 127-132.

Wake D., Webster M., Wimpenny G., Beacham K.and Crawford L. (2004). *Radio over fiber for mobile communications*. IEEE Conference on Microwave Photonics, invited paper.

Watanabe, H., Aoyagi, T., Takemoto, A., Omura, B. (1996). 1.3-μm strained MQW-DFB Lasers with extremely low intermodulation distortion for high-speed analog transmission. *IEEE J. Quant. Electron*, 32(6), 1015-1023.

Way, W. I. (1993). Optical fiber-based microcellular systems: An overview. *IEICE Trans. Commun.*, E76–B(9), 1091–1102.

Yee, M. L., Luo, B., Ong, L. C., Zhou, M. T., Shao, Z., Fujise, M. (2006). *Performance and noise analysis of VCSEL RoF using spherical ended multimode fiber coupling.* 6th international conference on ITS telecommunications.

Yoshihara N. (1998). *Low-loss, high-bandwidth fluorinated POF for visible to 1.3-mm wavelength.* Optic. Fiber Commun. Conf. (OFC'98), San Jose, CA, Feb. 1998, Paper ThM4.

Yuen, R., & Fernando, X. N., (2005). Analysis of Sub-Carrier Multiplexed Radio Over Fiber Link for the Simultaneous Support of WLAN and WCDMA Systems. *Wireless Personal Communications.* 33,1-20.

KEY TERMS

Base Station (BS): In Radio over Fiber topology, the Base Station is every individual access point to the underlying network, acting as the radio interface for the user and the optical interface for the network. The BS is also referred to as Remote Station or Remote Antenna Unit.

Central Station (CS): In Radio over Fiber, the Central Station is responsible for the generation and distribution of mm-wave signals and the general management of a group of Base Stations. The CS is connected to each BS through optical fiber. The CS is also known as Central Site or Control Station.

Code Division Multiple Access (CDMA): A spread spectrum modulation technique and multiple access scheme as well, where each user or terminal is assigned a different (spreading) codeword.

Intensity Modulation / Direct Detection (IM/DD): A modulation scheme where the intensity of an optical source is modulated by the RF or mm-wave signal. Demodulation is achieved through direct detection of the optical carrier and conversion using a photodetector.

Orthogonal Frequency Division Multiple Access (OFDMA): Is an extension of OFDM for the case of multiuser systems for an efficient utilization of the spectrum resources. For example, OFDMA can be used as a multiple access scheme where groups of the subcarriers are allocated to different users.

Relative Intensity Noise (RIN): Intrinsic noise of a Laser diode due to spontaneous emission and relaxation oscillation.

Sub-Carrier Multiplexing (SCM): A multiplexing scheme where each individual baseband signal is allocated to a different RF subcarrier.

Spurious Free Dynamic Range (SFDR): It refers to the dynamic range achieved up to the point where the signal power causes the intermodulation products to reach the noise power level or the noise floor.

Wavelength Division Multiplexing (WDM): A multiplexing scheme where each individual mm-wave signal or any information signal is assigned to a different wavelength optical source.

Chapter VI
High Altitude Stratospheric Platforms (HASPs)

Konstantinos Birkos

University of Patras, Greece

ABSTRACT

High Altitude Stratospheric Platforms (HASPs) have gained much of attention from the scientific society and the communication industry in the recent years. Their use in the Next Generation Networks can offer enhanced coverage and facilitate the implementation of several heterogeneous wireless networks schemes. In this chapter, the main aspects of the HASP-related technology are presented. Emphasis is given in the ways the intrinsic characteristics of these platforms can be used effectively in order to compensate for the disadvantages of both the existing terrestrial and satellite solutions. Antennas and coverage planning, capacity and interference, call admission control, handover, mobility management, networking and TCP/IP performance are the main issues addressed. The provided mathematical tools and the state-of-the-art techniques presented here, can be useful to engineers interested in designing and evaluating performance of HASP-aided hybrid networks.

INTRODUCTION

Ubiquitous coverage and integration of different technologies are key characteristics of the Next Generation Networks. High quality wireless services will aim to subscribers of different types, either fixed or mobile, in remote or highly-density areas, with different propagation characteristics and different bandwidth, delay and jitter demands, depending on the type of service. The terrestrial cellular network is a good candidate as a base for the deployment of a platform offering a greater variety of services than the traditional voice/data/video services currently offered by the 3G cellular systems. Nevertheless, the extended high-cost terrestrial infrastructure in terms of base stations and the multipath phenomena especially in urban areas are issues that cannot be neglected. As for the satellite solutions, they suffer from increased delay, huge cost of development and low capacity. Dealing with the so-called 'last mile' problem, i.e. reliable delivery of information between the access point and the end-user, is a matter of concern. High Altitude Stratospheric Platforms (HASPs) seem to be telecommunication components that can alleviate these limitations and be part of effective heterogeneous architectures. HASPs are unmanned airships that fly on the stratosphere at altitudes between 17 and 22 kilometers and offer wireless coverage in areas on the ground.(Djuknic, Friedenfelds & Okunev, 1997) They are equipped with multi-beam smart adaptive antenna arrays that can illuminate certain areas with a variety of ways. They are also known as

Copyright © 2009, IGI Global, distributing in print or electronic forms without written permission of IGI Global is prohibited.

High Altitude Platforms (HAPs), High Altitude Aeronautical Platforms (HAAPs) and High Altitude Long Endurance (HALE) platforms. In order to achieve easier integration, HASPs can be based on existing communication standards with some modifications suitable for their operational environment. (Grace et al., 2005)

The use of HASPs is characterized by several advantages. HASPs can replace or fill the gaps in existing ground infrastructures, especially in remote areas with deficient or corrupted base stations. Compared with the terrestrial systems, HASPs offer mainly Line-of-Sight (LOS) links, thus they perform better in terms of propagation and rain attenuation, offering large capacity at the same time. The capacity offered from HASPs is significantly larger in comparison with the satellite systems. They also offer better link budget and lower delay than satellites. In addition, developing and putting in service a stratospheric platform is a more cost effective solution than developing a satellite. The reason is that less sophisticated equipment is used and no launch is required. HASPs are environmentally friendly owing to the use of alternative power resources like fuel-cells and solar power. (Tozer, 2000)

Several applications can be supported by a HASP-aided wireless system. Broadband Wireless Access (BWA), 3G and beyond, navigation/localization, military communications, surveillance and emergency applications are the most important of them. (Tozer & Grace, 2001; Avangina, Dovis, Ghiglione & Mulassano, 2002; Dovis, Lo Presti & Mulassano, 2005) In general, HASPs are not foreseen as stand-alone platforms but as parts of integrated schemes in a NGN environment. (Faletti, Laddomada, Mondin & Sellone, 2006) They can cooperate with the terrestrial cellular networks and with the GEO satellites. They can also form constellations of multiple HASPs using inter-HASP links. (Figure 1) Flexibility is one of the most important features that make HASP technology a strong candidate in future generation wireless networks. A HASP-based network can be connected with other public or private networks via gateway stations. According to where switching takes place, two implementations are possible: bent-pipe platform with on-ground switching and on-board switching. In the multi-platform scenario, HASPs may be interconnected either via ground stations or via inter-platform links. Interworking with other networks includes loose and tight interworking. In loose interworking the HASP is used complementarily to other access networks and it is more independent as there are no common network elements. In tight interworking a HASP is the sub-part of other networks. (Kandus, Svigelj &Mohorcic, 2005) Although existing techniques and methodologies of wireless communications can be applied in HASPs, there are some intrinsic characteristics that engineers should take into account as they can increase performance and flexibility. In the following sections, the main aspects of the HASP-related technology are presented along with effective solutions in several domains.

COVERAGE PLANNING AND ANTENNAS

HASP can carry communicational payload able to produce several cellular patterns on the ground. (Thornton, Grace, Spillard, Konefal & Tozer, 2001) Actually, HASPs can be considered as very low orbit satellites or very tall cellular masts. Consequently, many elements of the satellite theory are applicable. The geometrical characteristics given in this section are necessary for coverage planning and choosing the appropriate antenna configuration. El-Jabu and Steele (2001) have conducted a thorough study that is summarized next. The maximum area that can be theoretically covered by a satellite is given by

$$S = 2p R_e W \tag{1}$$

where R_e is the radius of the earth and W is the depth from the earth's surface. Considering a system of Cartesian coordinates on the same plane with the HASP and the earth's diameter, the distance from the platform to point (x, y) is

$$d = \sqrt{x^2 + (h + R_e - y)^2} \tag{2}$$

where h is the platform's nadir height. The arc describing the distance from the point (x, y) to the reference point $(R_e, 0)$ on the earth surface just below the platform is

Figure 1 - Synergic integration of GEO satellite, multiple HASPs and terrestrial cellular networks for the provision of BWA services

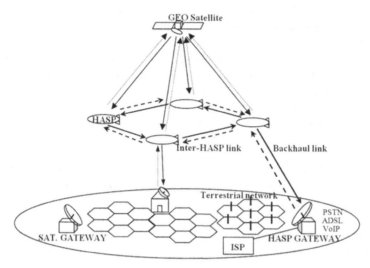

$$l = R_e \tan^{-1} \frac{\sqrt{R_e^2 + y^2}}{y} \tag{3}$$

The angle from bore-sight from which the platform sees a terminal in point (x, y) is

$$a = \tan^{-1} \frac{\sqrt{R_e^2 - y^2}}{h + R_e - y} \tag{4}$$

The actual coverage area, assuming that point (x, y) determines the edge of coverage, is

$$S_c = 2\pi R_e (R_e - y) \tag{5}$$

A multi-beam antenna on the HASP will provide LOS links to ground stations and/or direct links to fixed or mobile terminals on the ground. Moreover, the chosen antenna has to be able to produce several cellular spot beams that can be dynamically adjusted according to the specified capacity and frequency reuse needs, so cells of different radius have to be available. Another feature is the steering ability of beams. Each beam has to be steered independently in order to support the network's capacity-on-demand. A related application will be the provision of broadband internet access to high-speed moving subscribers, i.e. in high-speed trains. The HASP's steerable beam can constantly follow the train and provide link to the on-board moving router, via which passengers can have internet access. There are several approaches for the used antennas such as circular arrays, planar arrays and arrays of aperture antennas. Beam-forming is going to be a significant issue, with digital beam-forming techniques being the most appropriate for the system's needs. Next it is shown how a planar array can be used for the desired formulation of cells.

Consider a rectangular or planar array that consists of N and M elements along the x and y coordinates respectively. According to the array theory, a planar array can be seen as an array of linear arrays and having in mind the multiplication rule, the overall array factor can be estimated as,

$$|F_{ik}(\theta,\phi)| = C_{ik} \left| \frac{\sin\left[\frac{\pi N d_x}{\lambda}\left\{\sin\theta\cos\varphi - \sin\theta_i\cos\varphi_k\right\}\right]}{\sin\left[\frac{\pi d_x}{\lambda}\left\{\sin\theta\cos\varphi - \sin\theta_i\cos\varphi_k\right\}\right]} \right| \cdot$$

$$\left| \frac{\sin\left[\frac{\pi M d_y}{\lambda}\left\{\sin\theta\sin\varphi - \sin\theta_i\sin\varphi_k\right\}\right]}{\sin\left[\frac{\pi d_x}{\lambda}\left\{\sin\theta\sin\varphi - \sin\theta_i\sin\varphi_k\right\}\right]} \right| \tag{6}$$

The elevation plane half-power beam-width can be approximated by,

$$BW_\theta = \frac{1}{\cos\theta_i\sqrt{\theta_{x0}^{-2}\cos^2\varphi_k + \theta_{y0}^{-2}\sin^2\varphi_k}} \tag{7}$$

and the azimuth plane half-power beam-width by

$$BW_\varphi = \frac{1}{\sqrt{\theta_{x0}^{-2}\sin^2\varphi_k + \theta_{y0}^{-2}\cos^2\varphi_k}} \tag{8}$$

It is easy to examine the formulation of cells by deriving the equation corresponding to the footprint of the half-power beam-width on the ground. For our calculations, it is convenient to define a new system of coordinates that describes the plane that is perpendicular to the elevation angle of the center of the produced cell. Then, the equation is,

$$y = \pm h\tan\varphi_h\cos\theta_i\left(1 + \frac{x}{h}\tan\theta_i\right)\sqrt{1 - \left(\frac{1}{\tan\theta_h}\right)^2\left\{\frac{\frac{x}{h} - \tan\theta_i}{1 + \frac{x}{h}\tan\theta_i}\right\}^2} \tag{9}$$

where $\varphi_h = BW_\varphi/2$ and $\theta_h = BW_\theta/2$. (Figure 2) It is useful to derive an expression of the received downlink Signal-to-Interference Ratio (SIR) of a mobile terminal on the ground. Assuming J interfering beams and after interference analysis it is proved that,

$$SIR = \frac{G_T(\theta_\alpha,\varphi_\alpha)}{\sum_{j=1}^{J}G_{Ij}(\theta_\alpha,\varphi_\alpha)} \tag{10}$$

where

Figure 2. The formation of the cell pattern on the ground

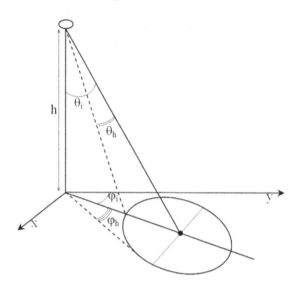

$$G_T(\theta_\alpha,\phi_\alpha) = C^2 \left| \frac{\sin\left[\frac{\pi N}{2}\left\{\sin\theta_\alpha\cos\varphi_\alpha - \sin\theta_g\cos\varphi_g\right\}\right]}{\sin\left[\frac{\pi}{2}\left\{\sin\theta_\alpha\cos\varphi_\alpha - \sin\theta_g\cos\varphi_g\right\}\right]} \right|^2 \cdot$$

$$\left| \frac{\sin\left[\frac{\pi N}{2}\left\{\sin\theta_\alpha\sin\varphi_\alpha - \sin\theta_g\sin\varphi_g\right\}\right]}{\sin\left[\frac{\pi}{2}\left\{\sin\theta_\alpha\sin\varphi_\alpha - \sin\theta_g\sin\varphi_g\right\}\right]} \right|^2 \tag{11}$$

$$G_I(\theta_\alpha,\phi_\alpha) = C^2 \left| \frac{\sin\left[\frac{\pi N}{2}\left\{\sin\theta_\alpha\cos\varphi_\alpha - \sin\theta_c\cos\varphi_c\right\}\right]}{\sin\left[\frac{\pi}{2}\left\{\sin\theta_\alpha\cos\varphi_\alpha - \sin\theta_c\cos\varphi_c\right\}\right]} \right|^2 \cdot$$

$$\left| \frac{\sin\left[\frac{\pi N}{\lambda}\left\{\sin\theta_\alpha\sin\varphi_\alpha - \sin\theta_c\sin\varphi_c\right\}\right]}{\sin\left[\frac{\pi}{2}\left\{\sin\theta_\alpha\sin\varphi_\alpha - \sin\theta_c\sin\varphi_c\right\}\right]} \right|^2 \tag{12}$$

In the last formulas, it is considered that the mobile terminal is located in the point $(\theta_\alpha, \varphi_\alpha)$, the serving beam is directed towards the point (θ_g, φ_g) and the interfering beam is directed towards the point (θ_c, φ_c). Also, a square array and equal maximum gains for all beams are assumed. An interesting observation is that, because of the LOS nature of the architecture, the SIR levels in a HASP system are mainly determined by the on-board antenna and the users' position on the ground. As a result, effective speed and direction adaptive techniques stem from this feature, as we will see later.

In the presented analysis, the amplitude and phase errors of the radiators where neglected. In order to have a more precise estimation of the Side Lobe Levels (SLL) and for the interference analysis to be more accurate, these errors need to be included.

The amplitude radiated by the n-th element of the array is given by (Ku et al., 2002)

$$A_n = A_n^0 \varepsilon_n = A_n^0 \rho_n e^{i\phi_n} \tag{13}$$

where ρ_n and φ_n are the amplitude and phase errors respectively. In the θ-plane, the statistical evaluation of the average radiated power for N independent pattern realizations is calculated by,

$$P_{av}(\theta) = \frac{1}{N}\sum_{i=1}^{N}\left|E_i(\theta)\right|^2 \tag{14}$$

The average fluctuation of power is then,

$$P_d(\theta) = \sqrt{\frac{1}{N}\sum_{i=1}^{N}(P_{av}(\theta) - \left|E_i(\theta)\right|^2)^2} \tag{15}$$

and the upper sidelobe envelope is determined by

$$P_{up}(\theta) = P_{av}(\theta) + P_d(\theta) \tag{16}$$

One of the main problems arising from the formation of spot-beams, is that their footprint on the ground changes with the distance. More distant cells have an elliptic shape instead of the ideal circular one. To compensate for this drawback, asymmetric beams have been proposed. Combining an aperture antenna with a lens as a secondary aperture can lead to the desired pattern. The far-field pattern of a corrugated horn as a primary feed is given by (Thornton, 2004),

$$F_p(\theta) = (1+\cos\theta)\int_{r=0}^{r_1} J_0\left[kr\sin\theta\right]J_0\left[2.405\frac{r}{r_1}\right]\exp\left(-j\frac{kr^2}{R}\right)\frac{r}{r_1}dr \tag{17}$$

while the aperture field distribution of the lens is,

$$A(r) = \sqrt{\frac{(n\cos\theta-1)^3}{f^2(n-1)^2(n-\cos\theta)}}F_p(\theta) \tag{18}$$

where r_1 is the horn aperture radius, n is the lens refractive index, r is the normalized aperture radius, R is the horn aperture flare radius, f is the focal length and k is the wave number. In order to produce the asymmetric beam, we need to broaden the beamwidth in one plane while leaving the other unaltered. This is done by modifying the aperture phase distribution by applying a phase shift across the x axis. Now, the new lens field aperture distribution is multiplied by exp(-jkβ). The β factor can be derived by several functions, like cubic polynomials.

$$\beta = \alpha\left|x\right| + b\left|x\right|^2 + c\left|x\right|^3 \tag{19}$$

The selection of the a, b and c constants actually determines whether a poor or good fit to the target curve is going to be achieved. Simulations have proved that this implementation yields quite satisfactory results.

The main problem in cellular coverage from HASP using aperture antennas is that increased directivity results in excessive power roll-off at the cell's edge and in high SLL, whereas reduced directivity makes considerably high amounts of power falling out of the cell area. Therefore, maximizing directivity at the cell edges is an important design issue. If we approximate the antenna main lobe by a cosine function raised to a power n (which is the case in aperture antennas of medium and high directivity) the problem of optimizing directivity can be significantly simplified. More specifically (Thornton, Grace, Capstick & Tozer, 2003)

$$D = D_{max} (\cos\theta)^n \tag{20}$$

where

$$D_{max} = \frac{32\log 2}{\theta_{3dB}^2 + \varphi_{3dB}^2} \tag{21}$$

Under the assumption of circularly symmetric cells

$$\theta_{3dB} = 2\arccos(\sqrt[n]{0.5}) \tag{22}$$

Hence, the directivity maximization problem can be reduced to a single value problem (n) by setting $\theta=\theta_{edge}$. Applying these results, the directivity seen at (x, y) is,

$$D = D_{max} \left[\cos(\theta_\alpha \cos\varphi_\alpha)\right]^{n_\theta} \left[\cos(\theta_\alpha \sin\varphi_\alpha)\right]^{n_\varphi} \tag{23}$$

In cell planning, certain directivity related goals can be met by adjusting the values of the n_θ and n_φ parameters.

As mentioned before, an important application of HASPs is providing communication links to moving trains by means of smart antenna arrays. Hence, direction-of-arrival (DOA) estimation is required along with estimation of the number of trains present. Several techniques have been developed for this purpose. These techniques are based on the statistical estimation of the spatial correlation matrix which is defined as (White & Zakharov, 2007),

$$\mathbf{R} = \frac{1}{S}\sum_{s=1}^{S} \mathbf{r}(s)\mathbf{r}^H(s) \tag{24}$$

where $(.)^H$ is the conjugate transposition, S is the number of snapshots per measurement interval and $\mathbf{r}(s)$ is the vector of samples at the s-th snapshot.

$$\mathbf{r}(s) = \mathbf{V}diag\left[\rho_1(s),...\rho_n(s)\right]\mathbf{p}(s) + \Lambda\mathbf{n}(s) \tag{25}$$

where $\mathbf{V}$ is the matrix containing the steering vectors associated with each train, ρ_i is the received signal power from the train i, $\mathbf{p}$ is a set of QPSK symbols from the trains, Λ is the noise power and $\mathbf{n}$ is a set of complex additive white Gaussian noise samples. The steering vector of the n-th train is

$$\mathbf{v}_n = \left[u_n(1),...,u_n(M)\right]^T \tag{26}$$

$$u_n\left((m_y-1)\sqrt{M} + m_x\right) = e^{jm_x w_x(n)}e^{jm_y w_y(n)} \tag{27}$$

$$\omega_x(n) = \frac{2\pi}{\lambda}d\sin\theta_n\cos\varphi_n \tag{28}$$

$$\omega_y(n) = \frac{2\pi}{\lambda}d\sin\theta_n\sin\varphi_n \tag{29}$$

In the formulas m_x, m_y are the element indices along the x, y axes of the array, d is the distance between two successive elements and λ is the wavelength. Estimating the DOA pair (θ,φ) is the target of a DOA estimation problem. Following the Barlett's method, the DOA pair is estimated according to the formulas,

$$\hat{\mathbf{v}} = \arg\max_{\mathbf{v}} \left(\hat{P} \right) \tag{30}$$

$$\hat{P}(\theta,\varphi) = \mathbf{v}^H \mathbf{R} \mathbf{v} \tag{31}$$

The method performs faster if the scanning area is reduced. Another method, the polynomial-based DOA estimation, characterized by reduced scanning requirements, uses a polynomial expression C(z):

$$\hat{P}(z) = \frac{1}{C(z)} \tag{32}$$

$$z = e^{j\omega}, \quad \omega = \frac{2\pi}{\lambda} d \sin\gamma \tag{33}$$

where γ is the angle between the DOA and the normal to a linear array. Now peaks in P(z) correspond to the roots of C(z). The methodology for the computation of the polynomial coefficients of C(z) is based on eigen values decomposition.

CAPACITY AND INTERFERENCE

Future generation multimedia applications demand increased capacity, so millimeter wave band is a necessity in the case of HASP. HASPs have a unique advantage over other wireless platforms. Their position in the stratosphere results in better link budget compared to satellites while their link lengths are characterized by less rain attenuation compared to terrestrials systems. Efficient spectrum reuse will be crucial for the provision of bandwidth-demanding services.

The main idea is to take advantage of some specific characteristics of the HASP-based architecture and apply proper techniques aiming to maximize spectral efficiency. By exploiting highly directive user antennas, frequency reuse can become feasible even in adjacent cells, as relevant studies have proved. This fact allows spatial discrimination between the HASP in the sky, allowing users in different cells sharing the same spectrum. Although it is not practical for mobile users to carry highly directional antennas, it is applicable for fixed or mobile routers on the ground which in turn can serve the mobile users. Furthermore, this feature can be applied in moving vehicles, such as military, police, public transport etc.

In the first examined scenario, a constellation of HASP serves a common area on the ground, without cellular splitting. The area is covered by a single beam from each platform. Each terminal user can communicate with only one platform at a time (main HASP) by pointing it with its directive antenna. Thus, the main source of interference is the power radiated by the other HASPs which is received via the user antenna's side lobes. The main factor that determines capacity and spectral efficiency is the Carrier-to –Interference-plus-Noise-Ratio (CINR). In this case, following the analysis introduced by Grace, Thornton, Chen, White and Tozer (2005), the CINR is given by,

$$CINR = \frac{T_m G_m(\varphi_m)}{N_F + \sum_{j \in \mathrm{N}, j \neq m} T_j G_j(\varphi_j) G_U(\theta_{m,j})} \tag{34}$$

where m indicates the main HASP, j indicates the interfering HASPs, T is the transmission factor related with the transmitted power and free space losses, $G_m(\varphi_m)$ is the gain of the main HASP at an angle φ_m from boresight, $G_j(\varphi_j)$ is the gain of the interfering HASP at an angle φ_j from boresight and $G_U(\theta_{m,j})$ is the user antenna gain at an angle $\theta_{m,j}$ between the main and the interfering HASP. When referring to boresight, we mean the straight line pointing from the platform to the center of coverage. (Figure 3) The link length from the user located at the point $(x_u, y_u, 0)$ to a HASP j located at the point (x_j, y_j, h) is calculated by

$$l_j = \sqrt{(x_j - x_u)^2 + (y_i - y_u)^2 + h^2} \tag{35}$$

The angle between any two HASPs as seen by a user is

$$\theta_{a,b} = \arccos\left(\frac{l_a^2 + l_b^2 - l_{ab}^2}{2l_a l_b}\right) \tag{36}$$

where l_a, l_b are the distances from the user to HASPs a and b respectively and l_{ab} is the distance between the two HASPs. The simplified antenna model,

$$G_U(\theta_{ab}) = G_{U\max} \max\left[(\cos\theta_{ab})^n, s_f\right] \tag{37}$$

can be used, where $G_{U\max}$ is the maximum or boresight gain of the user antenna and s_f is a notionally flat sidelobe floor. The CINR levels are directly related to bandwidth efficiency according to the Shannon equation

$$\eta \sim \log_2(1 + CINR) \tag{38}$$

Having in mind that at the same point on the ground N users can be served with the same bandwidth resources, pointing at N different HASPs, the most important measure of the system's performance is the aggregate bandwidth efficiency,

$$\eta_{agg} \sim \sum_{j \in N} \log_2(1 + CINR_j) \tag{39}$$

Although the Shannon equation can be used as an abstract measure, more accurate results require the exact modulation and coding schemes to be considered, especially in time-varying CINR conditions.

Figure 3. Interference geometry in multiple-HASPs coverage

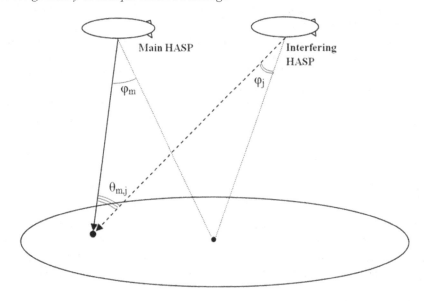

In a multi-cellular environment covered by a cluster of HASPs, the interference analysis presented before has to be modified. In this case, the spot beams of the interfering HASPs are not the only sources of interference. A designer has also to include the interfering power from the antennas of the main HASP illuminating the other cells than the cell in which the user is located. In addition, the antennas of the interfering platforms illuminating these cells produce more interference. All these considerations are summarized in the following formula, describing the CINR in a multi-cellular HASP-based environment,

$$CINR = \frac{P_m(\varphi_m)}{N_F + \sum_{k=1}^{K-1} P_{m,k}(\varphi_k) + \sum_{j \in N, j \neq m} \sum_{k=1}^{K} P_{j,k}(\varphi_{j,k}) A_U(\theta_{j,m})} \tag{40}$$

where K denotes the number of cells in the covered area, P_m is the received power from the main HASP, $P_{m,k}$ is the received power from the main HASP's transmitters charged with illuminating the other K-1 cells and $P_{j,k}$ is the received power from the j-th interfering HASP illuminating k-th cell. (Figure 4) Therefore, the second term of the denominator expresses the interference produced by the main HASP due to cellular-idea-based coverage, while the third term expresses the interference produced by the interfering HASPs.

Simulations have verified the effectiveness of the idea of sharing the same frequency resources by the constellation of platforms. Acceptable levels of interference are achieved in case a user is served by a single HASP of the constellation constantly. Nevertheless, inter-HASP handover to the platform from which the strongest signal is received enhances performance and uniformity of coverage. (Birkos, Chrysikos & Kotsopoulos, 2007) There are two key optimization factors that have not been addressed yet: the minimum angular separation and the minimum link length ratio of the receivers and the interferers. Although there do not exist any analytical tools that include these parameters, their role is important in the CINR on the ground. Further optimization of downlink capacity in packet-based communications can be achieved by means of adaptive modulation schemes and queuing strategies. (Pearce & Grace, 2003)

HASP can be used to provide WCDMA coverage along with other applications. Estimating both the reverse and forward capacity is of great significance. In this case, the previously described frequency reuse feature cannot be applied because of the omni-directional user antennas and a single platform produces the cellular spot beams. Hong, Ku, Park, Ahn and Jang (2005) have developed mathematical formulas for the calculation of the HASP/CDMA capacity. The capacity of a CDMA system is given by

Figure 4. Interference geometry in multiple-HASPs-multiple-cells coverage

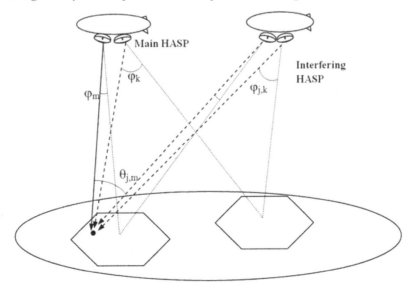

$$N = \frac{1}{v}\left(\frac{W/R}{E_b/N_t} - N_0' \right) + 1$$

(41)

where v is the signal activity factor, W is the total bandwidth, R is the information bit-rate, E_b is the energy per bit, N_t is the noise spectral density and

$$N_0' = \frac{N_0 W}{S}$$

(42)

where N_0 is the ground noise power density and S is the received signal power at the base station. The intra-cell interference power is expressed by

$$I_{intra} = v(N-1)S$$

(43)

$$I_{interj} = vS \int_0^{2\pi} \int_0^D \left(\frac{l_{ij}}{l_{0,ij}} \right)^\mu \frac{\varepsilon_{0,ij}}{\varepsilon_{ij}} \frac{G(\psi_{0,ij})}{G(\psi_{ij})} \frac{N}{\pi D^2} r_{ij} dr_{ij} d\theta_{ij}$$

(44)

where $\varepsilon_{0,ij}$ and ε_{ij} are the shadowing factors of the main and interfering paths respectively and $G(\psi_{0,ij})$ and $G(\psi_{ij})$ are the corresponding gains. Indices i and j denote the i-th mobile interfered by the j-th base station. In the examined system, the main source of interference is from the on-board base-stations serving the co-channel cells. The key element that characterizes CDMA over HASP is that the base stations are located close to each other and the signal traverses almost the same path, subjected to approximately the same shadowing. Under this observation, the interference produced by users in the j-th interfering cell is expressed by

$$I_{interj} = vNS \int_0^{2\pi} \int_0^D \frac{G(\psi_{0,ij})}{G(\psi_{ij})} \frac{1}{\pi D^2} r_{ij} dr_{ij} d\theta_{ij}$$

(45)

The total inter-cell interference is

$$I_{inter} = \sum_{j=1}^J I_j$$

(46)

The formula that gives the reverse link capacity of a HASP-based CDMA system is

$$N = \left[\frac{1}{v}\left(\frac{W/R}{E_b/N_t} - N_0' \right) + 1 \right] F_{ur}$$

(47)

where F_{ur} is the reverse link frequency reuse efficiency defined by

$$F_{ur} = \frac{1}{1 + \sum_{j=1}^J \int_0^{2\pi} \int_0^D \frac{G(\psi_{0,ij})}{G(\psi_{ij})} \frac{1}{\pi D^2} r_{ij} dr_{ij} d\theta_{ij}}$$

(48)

Now we will proceed in the estimation of the forward link capacity. The received power at the i-th mobile from the j-th base station is

$$P_r(r_{ij}\theta_{ij}) = P_{req}\, f(r_{ij},\theta_{ij})G(\psi_{ij})\varepsilon_{ij}l_{ij}^{-\mu} \tag{49}$$

where P_{req} is the required signal power and f is the function of power control applied by the base station. The total transmitted power is

$$P_T = \frac{N}{\pi D^2}\int_0^{2\pi}\int_0^D P_{req}\, f(r_{ij},\theta_{ij})r_{ij}dr_{ij}d\theta_{ij} \tag{50}$$

According to these derivations, the intra-cell interference and the inter-cell interference are, respectively,

$$I_{intra} = \nu\,(P_T G(\psi_{ij})\varepsilon_{ij}l_{ij}^{-\mu} - P_T(r_{ij}\theta_{ij})) \tag{51}$$

$$I_{inter} = \nu\sum_{j=1}^{J}P_T G(\psi_{ij})\,\varepsilon_{ij}l_{ij}^{-\mu} \tag{52}$$

Then, the forward link frequency reuse efficiency becomes,

$$F_{uf} = \frac{\pi D^2 f(r_{ij},\theta_{ij})}{\sum_{j=1}^{J}\dfrac{G(\psi_{0,ij})}{G(\psi_{ij})}\int_0^{2\pi}\int_0^D f(r_{ij},\theta_{ij})r_{ij}dr_{ij}d\theta_{ij}} \tag{53}$$

If optimum power control is considered, each user receives the same amount of power regardless of its position. In this case, the frequency reuse efficiency is,

$$F_{uf} = \frac{\pi D^2}{\sum_{j=1}^{Q}\int_0^{2\pi}\int_0^D r_{ij}dr_{ij}d\theta_{ij}} \tag{54}$$

CALL ADMISSION CONTROL

The fact that all the on-board base stations in a HASP share the same limited amount of power, creates the need for centralized downlink call admission control (CAC) with dynamic power management aiming to respond to the traffic demands of the different cells on the ground. The conventional method of allocating fixed amounts of power to individual base stations is not the optimum solution. The basic idea behind the CAC schemes in a terrestrial network, is that a call is blocked if admitting the call causes at least one of the base stations to exceed its individual maximum available power. On the contrary, in a HASP-based UMTS system, a call is blocked if a power allocation among the base stations satisfying certain interference criteria cannot be found.

Assuming that there are Q active mobile terminals served by the HASP and if p_i is the transmitted power allocated to mobile i, the we denote the **p** vector as (Foo, Lim & Tafazolli, 2002)

$$\mathbf{p} = [p_1,...,p_Q] \tag{55}$$

For the signal to be received correctly, a certain SIR threshold must be satisfied. If k and l indicate the cells to which mobile terminals i and j belong, then this condition, for a specific terminal, is expressed as,

$$\gamma_i = \frac{g_{ik}p_i}{\sum_{\substack{j=1\\j\neq i}}^{Q}g_{ij}p_j + n_i} \geq \gamma_i^t \tag{56}$$

To expand the formula for all the terminals, we have to define

$$h_{ij} = \begin{cases} \gamma_i^t \dfrac{g_{il}}{g_{ik}}, i \neq j \\ 0, i = j \end{cases} \tag{57}$$

$$\eta_i = \gamma_i^t \dfrac{n_i}{g_{ik}} \tag{58}$$

Thus, the corresponding inequality is written as

$$(\mathbf{I} - \mathbf{H})\mathbf{p} = \eta \tag{59}$$

Apart from this inequality, a feasible power vector **p** must not exceed the maximum available downlink power of the platform. This limitation is expressed by,

$$\begin{cases} \mathbf{p} \geq \mathbf{0} : \gamma_i \geq \gamma_i^{\;t} \forall i \\ 0 \leq \sum_{i=1}^{Q} p_i \leq P_{PF}^t \end{cases} \tag{60}$$

where P_{PF}^t is the total available power of the platform which is dynamically distributed among the cells. For a terrestrial system, this condition is,

$$\begin{cases} \mathbf{p} \geq \mathbf{0} : \gamma_i \geq \gamma_i^{\;t} \forall i \\ 0 \leq P_k \leq P_k^t \end{cases} \tag{61}$$

where P_k is the total output power of base station k. It is obvious that since each terrestrial base station poses its own power limitations in the formation of the problem, there is no much freedom in the derivation of an optimum solution. Because of the fact that the HASP-based system has the advantage of allocating power among the on-board base stations according to a centralized CAC policy, it is characterized by enhanced flexibility. Therefore, there is the possibility of finding a power allocation that cannot be realized in a terrestrial system or, in other words, a call that is blocked in the terrestrial system, may not be blocked in the HASP environment since there is greater possibility to find a power vector **p** that meets the SIR and maximum power requirements. This results in lower blocking and dropping probability and better Grade of Service (GoS) performance. It is useful to point out that in order to achieve the same levels of GoS between the two systems, the total power required by applying the technique proposed previously is significantly lower than the total power required by the terrestrial base stations.

Call dropping, i.e. forced call termination, is more objectionable in mobile cellular networks than call blocking. Offering low levels of dropping probability would be easier if there was a mechanism able to predict users' mobility, thus allowing the base station controllers to reserve channel or bandwidth resources in the cells which the mobile user is likely to move towards. This would guarantee QoS and could support the effectiveness of a NGN. The implementation of these techniques is simpler in HASP-based cellular networks because all spot beams originate from the same platform and the produced interference is highly predictable and so is the pilot channels signal power received by the mobile users on the ground. By constantly monitoring the energy per chip to interference power density ratio of the Common Pilot Channel (CPICH) E_c/I_0 of the serving cell/spot beam and the neighboring cells, the base station controller can estimate the direction and speed of the mobile users. In fact, what is estimated is not the exact direction and speed in space, but to which cell and how soon the subscriber is more likely to move in the next time samples. After all necessary data is collected, the controller can dynamically adjust the call admission thresholds to ensure that there will be available resources for the handoff procedure.

Under the assumption that fast fading can be averaged out due to its short correlation length, the differences between the E_c/I_0 of different cells values are the differences in antenna gains. We define the difference between the E_c/I_0 of the i-th's mobile terminal serving base station and the E_c/I_0 of the strongest neighboring base station (Foo & Lim, 2005)

$$\varepsilon_i = \left(\frac{E_c}{I_0}\right)_{s,i} - \left(\frac{E_c}{I_0}\right)_{n,i} \tag{62}$$

and the rate of change

$$\hat{\varepsilon} \equiv \frac{\Delta\varepsilon_i}{\Delta t} = \frac{\varepsilon_i(t) - \varepsilon_i(t+\tau)}{\tau} \tag{63}$$

where τ is the sampling period. The rate of change indicates how fast the mobile terminal is moving towards a neighboring base station. We note that $\varepsilon_i(t)$ is proportional to the difference between the normalized antenna gain levels of the serving and the strongest neighboring base station, according to the angles the terminal is seen by these base stations. Given the fact that the radiation patterns of the antennas and the minimum and maximum speeds of the subscribers are known, the parameters ε_{min}, ε_{max} can be extracted. Let J_u be the set of mobile terminals having BS_u as the neighboring station which the higher value of E_c/I_0 is received from. Let M_u be the number of mobiles that satisfies the equation,

$$\hat{\varepsilon}_{i\in J_u} > \beta\hat{\varepsilon}_{max} \tag{64}$$

where $0<\beta<1$ is a design parameter. The size of the M_u of a cell defines the likeliness of moving users from neighboring cells to enter its area. The main strategy behind the applied CAC scheme is dynamically adjusting the call admission threshold in each cell according to the number of handoff calls it is predicted to receive. This feature is implemented by adding a margin to the call admission threshold depending on the expected arriving subscribers. The new SIR threshold becomes,

$$\gamma^t_{n,uNEW} = \gamma^t_{n,u} + \Delta\gamma_u \tag{65}$$

where the margin added is defined as

$$\Delta\gamma_u = \frac{M_u}{M_{max}}\Delta\gamma_{max} \tag{66}$$

where $M_{max} = max(M_1,\ldots,M_U)$ and $\Delta\gamma_{max}$ is the maximum SIR margin. From the equations given previously it is derived that cells expecting more users to enter their service area, adopt higher threshold configuration for new calls. In fact, there is a trade-off between new and handoff calls with emphasis on the latter. The impact of this technique is a significant reduction in dropping probability with minimum increase in blocking probability. In this procedure, the values assigned to the design parameters described play an important role.

In modern WCDMA systems, traffic is characterized by different bit rates and BER requirements, apart from the best effort services. Bit rates are related to the spreading gain factor according to the formula (Abrardo, Benelli & Sennati, 2001)

$$R_j = \frac{W}{S_j} \tag{67}$$

where R_j is the bit rate of the j-th uplink connection, W is the system bandwidth and S_j is the corresponding spreading gain factor. Similarly, the normalized bit rate is

$$r_j = \frac{1}{S_j} \tag{68}$$

In an effective radio resource management strategy, different traffic classes must be considered. We denote N_C the number of classes, $C_{m,k}$ the set of mobile terminals belonging to class k and being served by base station m, $B_m = C_{m,Nc-1}$ the set of best-effort mobile terminals connected to base station m, $B = B_1 \cup B_2 \cup ... \cup B_{Nbs}$ the set of best-effort terminals in the system, where N_{bs} is the number o base stations, Θ the set of possible rate vectors defined by the available spreading codes and ρ_k the minimum transmission rate required by class k. The problem of maximizing the system throughput can be transformed to assigning the maximum available bit rates to BET mobile terminals. Then the problem is mathematically expressed as finding the vector **r** such that,

$$\mathbf{r} = \arg\max_{r\in\Theta} \sum_{j\in B} r_j = \arg\max_{r\in\Theta} \sum_{j\in B} \frac{\gamma_j}{\left(E_b / I_C\right)_j} \tag{69}$$

$$r_j = \rho_k \forall j \in C_k \tag{70}$$

and also SIR and maximum available power constraints are met. In order for local fairness to be guaranteed, all BET terminals served by the same base station must transmit at the same rate. Consequently, the following constraint has to be added to the formation of the problem.

$$r_j = r_l \forall j,l, j \neq l \in B_m, 1 \leq m \leq N_A \tag{71}$$

The solution to the problem demands the maximization of a non-linear function of a set of variables subject to some linear constraints. A simplified method of rate assignment that could provide local fairness is therefore more convenient. The simplified approach, based on the idea of the ideal cellular system, yields in the following equation

$$\left(\frac{E_b}{I_C + N_0}\right)_B \rho_I(m) = \frac{a_B}{N_{m,0} + \sum_{l=2}^{N_c(m)-2} N_{m,l} a_{m,l}} \tag{72}$$

where $\rho_I(m)$ is the normalized bit rate assigned to mobile terminals served by base station m, a_B is the normalized received signal power for best effort mobile terminals, $N_{m,l}$ is the number of l-class terminals served by base station m and $\alpha_{m,l}$ is the corresponding normalized received signal power.

HANDOVER

The performance of CDMA systems is affected by the non-uniformity of traffic. To alleviate this disadvantage, it has been proposed to dynamically adjust the soft handoff thresholds according to the downlink output power of the base station. This is called adaptive soft handover algorithm and the main difference of a HASP-based cellular environment when compared to the terrestrial case is the theoretical possibility of each of the on-board base stations to be assigned the maximum output power of the platform. A description of the conventional soft handover algorithm follows. Each mobile terminal is characterized by the active and the monitored set. The active set consists of the cells that have an assigned link to the mobile. The monitored set consists of the cells that do not belong to the active set. If the E_C/I_0 of a cell of the monitored set has been measured greater than a certain threshold T_add for a period of time ΔT, the cell is added to the active set provided that the active set is not full. If there are more than one strong monitored cells, then they are added to the active set according to the magnitude of the E_C/I_0. The add threshold is given by

$$T\_add = Best\_AS\_Ss - \delta_{add} \tag{73}$$

where Best_AS_Ss is the strongest average received E_C/I_0 and δ_{add} is the add margin. The strongest cell in the monitored set is denoted Best_Cand_Ss. A cell is removed from the active set if the corresponding average E_C/I_0 has been measured lower than a drop therhold T_drop for a time period ΔT. Therefore

$$T\_add = Best\_AS\_Ss - \delta_{drop} \tag{74}$$

In case the active set is full, if the E_c/I_0 of the Best_Cand_Ss is greater than the replace threshold T_rep for a period ΔT, the Worst_AS_Ss, i.e. the cell in the active set with the poorest performance, is replaced by the Best_Cand_Ss.

$$T\_rep = Worst\_AS\_Ss - \delta_{rep} \tag{75}$$

According to the softer handover algorithm, developed by Lim, Foo and Tafazolli (2002), the add and drop margins of the mobile terminals are dynamically adjusted according to the loading conditions of their serving base stations. Adjustment is implemented by adding a margin adaption factor δ_{AF} to the existing margins. This factor is given by,

$$\delta_{AF}^{j} = \alpha \left(\frac{P_{BS}^{j}}{P_{BS}^{th}} \right) + \delta_{AF}^{min} \tag{76}$$

$$a = \delta_{AF}^{max} - \delta_{AF}^{min} \tag{77}$$

P_{BS}^{j} is the output power of the base station j. P_{BS}^{j} is a threshold above which the margin adaption factor remains fixed. P_{BS}^{j}, δ_{AF}^{max} and δ_{AF}^{min} are design parameters. The algorithm checks the current platform downlink power P_{PF}. If it exceeds a certain percentage of the maximum available platform power, the add and drop margins will be adjusted appropriately. If P_{PF} is below this threshold, the conventional softer handover algorithm is applied. This procedure is described as,

$$\delta_{add,adapt}^{j} = \begin{cases} \delta_{add} + \delta_{AF}^{j} & for \ 0 \le P_{BS}^{j} \le P_{BS}^{th} \\ \delta_{add} + \delta_{AF}^{max} & for \ P_{BS}^{th} \le P_{BS}^{j} \le P_{BS}^{max} \end{cases}, P_{PF} > \beta \ P_{PF}^{max} \tag{78}$$

$$\delta_{add,adapt}^{j} = \delta_{add}, P_{PF} \le \beta \ P_{PF}^{max} \tag{79}$$

An equivalent procedure is applied in the adjustment of the dropping margins:

$$\delta_{drop,adapt}^{j} = \begin{cases} \delta_{drop} + \delta_{AF}^{j} & for \ 0 \le P_{BS}^{j} \le P_{BS}^{th} \\ \delta_{drop} + \delta_{AF}^{max} & for \ P_{BS}^{th} \le P_{BS}^{j} \le P_{BS}^{max} \end{cases}, P_{PF} > \beta \ P_{PF}^{max} \tag{80}$$

$$\delta_{drop,adapt}^{j} = \delta_{drop}, P_{PF} \le \beta \ P_{PF}^{max} \tag{81}$$

The adaptive softer handover algorithm allows a more loaded cell to handover mobile terminals to the neighboring less loaded cells more easily. At the same time, it makes handover to loaded cells more difficult. It aims at balancing the traffic load among the cells in the area of coverage. The algorithm leads in good blocking and dropping probability performance. By assigning the appropriate values to β and P_{BS}^{th} a tradeoff between resource utilization and QoS is established.

The inter-cell handover between cells produced by a HASP system was previously described. As HASPs are more likely to be used in hybrid systems, offering heterogeneous wireless access to the mobile subscribers in a NGN environment, it is important for inter-system handover techniques to be applied. The most important scenario includes HASP-aided cellular UMTS systems. The provision of high data rates wireless services will lead in small-radius cell coverage. The role of HASPs is providing macrocellular coverage in order to bridge the islands of microcells. It is evident that three basic handoff procedures coexist in this application: (a) soft handover between microcells of the terrestrial systems, (b) soft handover between macrocells of the HASP system and (c) hard handover between terrestrial microcells and HASP macrocells. HASPs will be charged with serving high-speed moving subscribers while the terrestrial cellular system will serve mostly low-speed moving subscribers.

The usefulness of this concept it is explained by the fact that a fast moving terminal passes through several micro-cells, thus multiple inter-cell handovers are needed. This results in increased call dropping probability. Another reason is that when a fast moving terminal leaves a micro-cell-covered area needs extra wireless access network resources. In ubiquitous coverage environments, these resources are provided by the HASP.

A mobile served by the HASP macrocells is handed over the terrestrial microcells if its speed is measured lower than the speed threshold v_{th} and at the same time the received $(E_C/I_0)_{micro}$ by a microcell is measured greater than the $(E_C/I_0)_{macro}$ received by the currently serving macrocell plus a hysteresis margin ΔH^{macro} for a period of time ΔT. Any inter-macro-cell handover attempts that are in progress are terminated. It has to be clarified that despite the fact that the previous conditions may be fulfilled, the inter-system handover will not take place if assigning radio resources to the incoming mobile terminal reduces the minimum E_C/I_0 received by the other terminals below an acceptable threshold.

There are two cases in which a mobile terminal served by a terrestrial microcell is handed over a HASP macrocell. At first, the handover takes place if the mobile's speed is measured higher than the speed threshold v_{th}, regardless of the $(E_C/I_0)_{macro}$ value. Secondly, mobile served by the terrestrial microcells is handed over the HASP macrocells if its speed is measured lower than the speed threshold v_{th} and at the same time the received $(E_C/I_0)_{macro}$ by a macrocell is measured greater than the $(E_C/I_0)_{micro}$ received by the currently serving microcell plus a hysteresis margin ΔH^{micro} for a period of time ΔT.

Following the basic idea of the adaptive softer handover algorithm described previously, the hysteresis margins can be dynamically adjusted.

The algorithm that handles handoff of users served by the HASP-macrocellular layer dynamically adjusts the hysteresis margins of the terminals according to the loading condition of the HASP. The following formulas describe the adjustment procedure (Lim, Foo & Tafazolli, 2005),

$$\delta_{PF} = \alpha^{macro} \left(\frac{P_{PF}}{P_{PF}^{\max}} \right) + \delta_{PF}^{\min} \tag{82}$$

$$a^{macro} = \delta_{PF}^{\max} - \delta_{PF}^{\min}, \quad \delta_{PF}^{\min} = -\delta_{PF}^{\max} \tag{83}$$

$$\Delta H_{adapt}^{macro} = \Delta H^{macro} - \delta_{PF} \quad \text{for} \quad 0 \leq P_{PF} \leq P_{PF}^{\max} \tag{84}$$

where $\delta_{PF}^{\min}$ and $\delta_{PF}^{\min}$ are the minimum and maximum loading factors of the platform respectively, P_{PF} is the current platform downlink output power, $P_{PF}^{\max}$ is the maximum platform output power, ΔH^{macro} is the fixed hysteresis margin of the users served by the macrocells and ΔH_{adapt}^{macro} is the corresponding adjusted margin.

For the UMTS-microcellular layer there are two proposed algorithms that can be applied to control inter-system handover. According to the first algorithm, the hysteresis margins are adjusted as (Lim et al., 2005)

$$\delta_{BS}^{microj} = \alpha_1^{micro} \left(\frac{P_{BS}^{microj}}{P_{BS}^{\max}} \right) + \delta_{BS}^{\min} \tag{85}$$

$$a_1^{micro} = \delta_{BS}^{\max} - \delta_{BS}^{\min}, \quad \delta_{BS}^{\min} = -\delta_{BS}^{\max} \tag{86}$$

$$\Delta H_{adapt}^{microj} = \Delta H^{micro} - \delta_{BS}^{microj} \quad \text{for} \quad 0 \leq P_{BS}^{macroj} \leq P_{BS}^{\max} \tag{87}$$

where δ_{BS}^{microj} is the loading factor of the base station of the j-th microcell, $\delta_{BS}^{\min}$ and $\delta_{BS}^{\max}$ are the minimum and maximum base station loading factors respectively, P_{BS}^{microj} is the current downlink output power of the j-th base station, $P_{BS}^{\max}$ is the maximum base station output power, ΔH^{micro} is the fixed hysteresis margin and $\Delta H_{adapt}^{microj}$ is the dynamically adjusted hysteresis margin.

The second algorithm compares the loading condition of the UMTS and HASP layers before the adjustment of the hysteresis margin. If the loading condition of the serving microcell is worse than the loading condition of the HASP, the adjustment is a function of the output power of the serving base station. On the contrary, if the loading condition of the serving microcell is better than the loading condition of the HASP, the adjustment is a function of the output power of the HASP. The algorithm is mathematically expressed by (Lim et al., 2005)

If $\dfrac{P_{BS}^{microj}}{P_{BS}^{\max}} \geq \dfrac{P_{PF}}{P_{PF}^{\max}}$

$$\Delta H_{adapt}^{microj} = \begin{cases} \Delta H^{micro} - \delta_{BS}^{microj}, & \beta^{micro} P_{BS}^{\max} \leq P_{BS}^{macroj} \leq P_{BS}^{\max} \\ \Delta H^{micro}, & \text{otherwise} \end{cases} \tag{88}$$

else

$$\Delta H_{adapt}^{microj} = \begin{cases} \Delta H^{micro} + \delta_{PF}, & \beta^{macro} P_{PF}^{\max} \leq P_{PF} \leq P_{PF}^{\max} \\ \Delta H^{micro}, & \text{otherwise} \end{cases} \tag{89}$$

where β^{micro} and β^{macro} are the minimum loading factors of the microcell and the platform respectively. P_{PF} and $P_{PF}^{\max}$ are the current downlink output power of the platform and the maximum platform output power respectively. The last algorithm achieves a more balanced loading between the terrestrial layer and the HASP layer because it is based on the loading condition of both layers.

Another type of handover is inter-HASP handover. In a multiple-HASP-based system, inter-HASP handover is a necessary operation related with the user's mobility and/or the quality of coverage. Especially when directive antennas are used by the end-users, dynamic algorithms that choose the desirable platform according to the instantaneous traffic conditions can be applied. Fairness in terms of blocking and dropping probability is achieved if new users are directed to less congested platforms. Moreover, the stringent requirements for connections with high-speed moving terminals can be met if dynamic allocation is combined with a proper priority strategy. (Birkos & Kotsopoulos, 2007)

NETWORK LAYER ISSUES

Users' mobility has a deep impact on the effectiveness of routing in modern wireless networks. HASP-based networks are also affected, since they include backhaul links and inter-platform links apart from user-to-HASP links. It is evident that efficient solutions are required for the provision of reliable ubiquitous IP wireless access. The most widely accepted solution for mobility management is Mobile IP (MIP) which can be deployed in HASP networks. In MIP, a mobile node has two addresses: a permanent home address and a temporary Care-of-Address (CoA) associated with the network the mobile node is visiting. Two network components are invoked: the home agent that stores information about mobiles that belong to its network and the foreign agent that stores information about mobiles visiting its network. A node that wants to communicate with the mobile node sends the packets using the mobile's home address. The home agent receives the packets and forwards them to the foreign agent using the mobile's CoA via tunneling. The foreign agent receives the packets, removes the tunneling-related IP headers and delivers the packets to the mobile nodes. In the reverse procedure, the mobile node sends the packets directly to the corresponding node through the foreign agent. (Javenski, 2003)

In a HASP-aided system, mobile routers exist along with mobile terminals. An example of mobile router is a router placed on public transportation vehicles such as trains that provides wireless IP access to the mobile terminals of the customers. The principles of the MIP can be applied to mobile network routing with some modifications. The home agent intercepts all packets for an entire network domain and forwards them to the mobile router.

The MIP approach suffers from the triangular problem. Hence, route optimization is required. In HASP networks mobile routers would most likely stay within the platform's coverage area. Due to this characteristic, better placement of the mobile router's home agent can compensate for the triangular problem to some degree. The most usual location of the home agent is in the fixed network in the company's headquarters. After the vehicle leaves its base it is mainly covered by the HASP. Having this in mind, one can correctly assume that it is inefficient to route traffic through the home network since during a course, traffic deviates from the optimal paths. HASP backhaul links and inter-HASP links are additionally penalized. Therefore, placing the home agent on the HASP seems a more effective solution. Nevertheless, new issues arise from this concept. Direct mobile router-to-HASP links are not always available due to tunnels and several obstacles. In this case, users are served by terrestrial wireless networks such as WLANs. But supposing the home agent is placed on the platform, packets will have to travel through the HASP backhaul link and then down again to the currently serving fixed network. Placing the home agent in the HASP ground station is a possible solution to this effect. In general, the proper choice of the home agent placement depends on several parameters like the HASP visibility and the congestion of the backhaul links. (Vilhar & Novak, 2005)

Multi-layered networking will be a substantial NGN feature. Hybrid HASP-satellite architectures are very promising solutions towards the integration of wireless networks and they could handle the 'last mile' problem with high data rate services. (Cianca et al., 2005) Consequently, multi-layered routing is important and affects the overall system's performance. The examined scenario consists of a satellite and cluster of HASPs serving the same area. The satellite offers wide area coverage, producing an umbrella cell overlapping the coverage area of each platform. User terminals are dual-mode, i.e. they can communicate with both the HASP and the satellite layer. The satellite is controlled by the Satellite Master Control Station (SMCS) while each HASP is controlled by the HASP Master Control Station (HMCS). A HASP Gateway (HGTW) exists for each platform and there is also a Satellite Gateway (SGTW). If source user and destination user are in the same HSP coverage area the communication is established through the serving platform via the corresponding HMCS. If the two end users are in different HASP coverage areas both the HGTW and the SGTW are involved. The optimal path via which communication is established between two terminals can be chosen according to the available link capacity, the number of hops from source to destination and the end-to-end delay. Finding the optimal path is actually a linear programming problem. The description of the problem is (Pace & Aloi, 2007):

$$\begin{cases} \min z \\ z = \max_{i,j} \left(\dfrac{f_{ij}}{C} \right) \end{cases} \tag{90}$$

with the constraints

$$\sum_j V_{ij} U_{ij} \le N_i \forall i \tag{91}$$

$$U_{ij} = U_{ji} \forall i,j \tag{92}$$

$$f_{ij} = \sum_m \sum_n X_{ij}^{mn} \forall i,j \tag{93}$$

$$f_{ij} \le C V_{ij} U_{ij} \forall i,j \tag{94}$$

$$\sum_j X_{ji}^{mn} - \sum_j X_{ij}^{mn} = \begin{cases} T^{\min} &, i=m \\ -T^{\min} &, i=n \\ 0 & \text{otherwise} \end{cases} \forall i,m,n \tag{95}$$

$$X_{ij}^{mn} \geq 0 \quad \forall i,j,m,n \tag{96}$$

$$U_{ij} \in \{0,1\} \quad \forall i,j \tag{97}$$

where N is the number of HASPs, N_i is the maximum link amount for the i-th HASP, C is the HASP link capacity, T^{ij} is the offered traffic requirement from HASP i to HASP j, V_{ij} is the visibility between the HASP I and the HASP j, U_{ij} is the link connectivity between HASP i and HASP j, X_{ij}^{mn} is the traffic of link (i,j) due to source-destination pair (m,n) and f_{ij} is the total traffic of link (i,j). This problem is practically impossible to be solved and the computation time increases exponentially with the number of nodes. Thus, a heuristic approach is a more practical way. The proposed algorithm takes into consideration the regularity of the HASP coverage and the hot-spot of the paths, i.e. the most congested inter-HASP link (IHL) in the path. At first, the algorithm finds the set of minimum-hop paths (shortest paths) between the source user and the destination user provided that their end-to-end delay is lower than the satellite link delay. Then, the maximum-usage cost for every path in the set is found and the path characterized by the minimum maximum-usage cost is selected in order the most congested hot-spot not to be used. In case there is no such path available or the path delay is higher than the satellite link delay, the new connection is not admitted over the HASP layer and the CAC procedure will be performed over the satellite layer. The evaluation of point to point delay is performed according to the relations

$$\Delta T = T_{UP-DOWN} + T_{IHLs} + \sum_{i=1}^{N+1} T_{proc}(i) + \sum_{i=1}^{N+1} T_{queue}(i) \tag{98}$$

$$T_{IHLs} = \sum_{i=1}^{N} L_{IHL}(i)/c \tag{99}$$

where T_{UP_DOWN} is the uplink and downlink propagation delay, T_{IHLs} is the aggregate propagation delay through the N steps of the HASP constellation, $L_{IHL}(i)$ is the length of the link I, c is the speed of light, T_{proc} is the processing delay of the link i and T_{queue} is the queuing delay of the link i. The heuristic multi-layered routing algorithm is formulated by the following expressions:

$$\begin{cases} \min z \\ z = C(P_{S \rightarrow D}) \end{cases} \tag{100}$$

$$C(P) = \sum_{l \in P} C_l \tag{101}$$

$$C_l = \frac{1}{vacancy(l)} \tag{102}$$

C_l denotes the cost of each link, the vacancy parameter corresponds to the number of available channels over the j-th link, P_{S-D} denotes the path from the source HASP to the destination HASP and C(P) denotes the cost of the path P, i.e. the sum of the link costs that belong to path P. The algorithm focuses on avoiding any critical bottleneck link that could limit the overall performance of the system and guarantees that the traffic is distributed as evenly as possible among the links. Its computational simplicity equals the simplicity of the Dijkstra's algorithm. The difference is that while the Dijkstra's algorithm chooses the minimum cost paths, the heuristic inter-HASP/satellite algorithm chooses paths that do not create non-uniformities in the links. As a result, it balances the traffic load over the HASPs constellation.

TCP PERFORMANCE

Under the concept of the provision of ubiquitous wireless internet access in a NGN environment, HASPs can cover large areas serving numerous fixed and mobile end users. Different Internet Service Providers (ISPs) will be connected to the HASP via earth stations and they will share the same bandwidth resources. To respond to the user requests, each earth station forwards the packets through the HASP channel in competition with other earth stations. Therefore, bandwidth allocation algorithms are a necessity. In addition, to compensate for packet corruption, a possible error correction scheme to be used is the Forward Error Correction (FEC). Each earth station can dynamically adjust the amount of redundancy bits, according to the channel condition. The redundancy bits decrease the available bandwidth for data transfer and the real bandwidth of the z-th earth station is given by (Bisio & Marchese, 2006),

$$C_z^{real} = \beta_z C_z, \quad \beta_z \in [0,1], \quad \beta_z \in \mathbb{R} \tag{103}$$

Each earth station has a single buffer that handles TCP traffic from all the ISP sources connected to this station. The aim of the bandwidth allocator is to split the total available bandwidth to the earth stations. The problem is defined as

$$\mathbf{C}^{opt} = \left\{ C_0^{opt}, ..., C_z^{opt}, ...C_{Z-1}^{opt} \right\} = \arg\min_{\mathbf{C}} \left[\mathbf{F}(\mathbf{C}) \right] \tag{104}$$

$$\sum_{z=0}^{Z-1} C_z = C_{tot} \tag{105}$$

where Z-1 is the number of earth stations, C_z is the capacity allocated to the z-th station, $\mathbf{C}^{opt}$ is the optimal vector of capacities, C_{tot} is the total capacity and $\mathbf{F}$ is the performance vector.

$$\mathbf{F}(\mathbf{C}) = \left\{ f_0(C_0), ... f_{Z-1}(C_{Z-1}) \right\} \tag{106}$$

The performance function f_z is the average packet loss probability which is a function of C_z, β_z and the number of active sources N_z.

$$f_z(C_z) = \mathop{E}_{\beta_z} \left[P_{loss}^z (C_z, N_z, \beta_z) \right] \tag{107}$$

The defined problem is a multi-objective programming problem. Its optimal solution is a Pareto optimal point. In practice, the performance functions compete one another and a variation in capacity enhancing the performance of an earth station implies performance deterioration of at least another station.

Several allocation methodologies can be applied in order to provide solutions to the problem and they were examined by Bisio and Marchese (2006). The fixed bandwidth allocation determined by

$$C_z = \frac{C_{tot}}{Z}, \quad \forall z \in [0, Z-1] \tag{108}$$

is not efficient as it does not respond to traffic and channel condition variations. A heuristic approach suggests that the bandwidth allocated to an earth station should be a weighted portion of the total bandwidth available for TCP traffic. The weights are proportional to the amount of traffic of each station. Therefore,

$$C_z = k_z C_{tot}, \quad k_z = \frac{N_z}{\beta_z} \left(\sum_{j=0}^{Z-1} \frac{N_j}{\beta_j} \right)^{-1}, \quad \sum_{j=0}^{Z-1} k_z = 1 \tag{109}$$

Another solution is based on minimizing the sum of the single performance functions. More specifically:

$$J(\mathbf{C}) = \sum_{z=0}^{Z-1} f_z(C_z) \tag{110}$$

$$\mathbf{C}^{opt} = \arg \min_{\mathbf{C}} J(\mathbf{C}) \tag{111}$$

The fourth option is the Nash Bargain solution which uses utility functions. A possible utility function is

$$U_z(C_z, N_z, \beta_z) = \frac{1}{\underset{\beta_z}{E} \left[P_{loss}^z (C_z, N_z, \beta_z) \right]} \tag{112}$$

and the formulation of the problem is

$$J_{NBS}(\mathbf{C}) = \prod_{z=0}^{Z-1} U_z(C_z, N_z, \beta_z) \tag{113}$$

$$\mathbf{C}_{NBS}^{opt} = \arg \max_{\mathbf{C}} J_{NBS}(\mathbf{C}) \tag{114}$$

An equivalent expression is

$$J_{NBS}(\mathbf{C}) = \sum_{z=0}^{Z-1} \ln \left[U_z(C_z, N_z, \beta_z) \right] \tag{115}$$

$$\mathbf{C}_{NBS}^{opt} = \arg \max_{\mathbf{C}} J_{NBS}(\mathbf{C}) \tag{116}$$

Notice that contrary to the previous approaches, the Bargain Nash approach is a maximization problem. The last method, called Minimum Distance Method, bases the allocation decision on the ideal solution. The ideal performance vector is

$$\mathbf{F}^{id}(\mathbf{C}^{id}) = \left\{ f_0^{id}(C_0^{id}), ..., f_{Z-1}^{id}(C_{Z-1}^{id}) \right\} \tag{117}$$

$$f_z^{id}(C_z^{id}) = \min_{C_z} \left\{ \underset{\beta_z}{E} \left[P_{loss}^z (C_z, N_z, \beta_z) \right] \right\} \tag{118}$$

The solution to the problem is given by the equation

$$\mathbf{C}_{MD}^{opt} = \arg \min_{\mathbf{C}} \left(\left\| \mathbf{F}(\mathbf{C}) - \mathbf{F}^{id}(\mathbf{C}^{id}) \right\|_2 \right)^2 \tag{119}$$

The Minimum Distance method minimizes the distance between the performance vector and the ideal solution.

Invoking HASPs in TCP traffic delivering can be advantageous in heterogeneous networks. Satellite internet has a major disadvantage: Typically, in the forward direction, the satellite transmits the packets directly to the end-users whereas the reverse channel includes a fixed cable infrastructure connected with the satellite gateway. This asymmetric configuration reduces the maximum throughput but it is adopted because of the availability of low cost receivers. Even if symmetric configuration is applied, providing that more complex terminals are used, the problematic nature of the user-to-satellite channel significantly limits TCP performance. When a HASP is placed between the satellite and the user as an intermediate component, both forward and return channel go through the platform. The satellite-earth link is split in two parts and less expensive terminal equipment is required in comparison with the Return Channel via Satellite (RCS) case. (Cianca, De Luise, De Sanctis, Ruggieri & Prasad, 2004) The most important feature is that the error recovery mechanisms are more effective in the user-to-HASP link owing to the lower transmission delay. Thus, enhanced throughput is observed. TCP splitting offers the possibility of introducing intermediate agents performing some actions on behalf of the end-points to the benefit of performance. It is an idea stemmed from the so-called Performance Enhancing Proxy Techniques. The TCP-related problems can be isolated by dividing the connection into two sub-connections: a sub-connection characterized by transmission errors but short Round Trip Time (RTT) and a sub-connection characterized by long RTT but relatively error free. This is an example of how integration can improve performance and alleviate intrinsic architectural drawbacks of existing wireless systems. (Duca, Carrozzo & Roseti, 2007)

Effective multicast protocols have been developed taking advantage of the on-board proxy functionalities of the HASPs. A short description of the protocol proposed by Alocci, Berioli, Celandroni, Giambene and Karapantazis (2007) is given next. The protocol consists of six states. The end-user enters the first state when he receives the first packets of a group of data packets or the first packets of a set of redundancy packets for a previous group of data packets (FEC is assumed). A timer waiting_for_data_HASP is set. In the second state the end-user checks if it is possible to decode the received group of packets. If so, it enters state 3. While being in state 3, if a new group of packets arrives, the user switches into state 1. If the received group of packets cannot be decoded, the user switches into state 4. In this state, the timer timer_nack is computed and set for sending the NACK corresponding to the number of missed packets. The interval for sending NACKs is divided in slots of fixed duration that are organized in groups. There are k groups named sub-intervals. A user that misses h packets sends a NACK in one of the slots of the sub-interval R_h. The sub-interval R_0 is used for sending NACKs in case packet retransmissions for a previous group of packets have not permitted packet recovery. If the timer_nack times out, the user switches into state 5. In state 5, a NACK is sent and timer_ncf is started. Its length is greater than the maximum RTT between the HASP and the end-users plus the packet processing, transmission and propagation times. If timer_ncf times out, the user switches into state 4, otherwise it switches into state 6. A user can enter state 6 either via state 5 or via state 4 if a NACK confirmation is received before timer_nack expires. In state 6, a timer_redata initiates according to the redundancy packets that have to be sent to the end-user. If timer_redata expires, switching into state 4 takes place. If redundancy data is received on-time, the user switches into state 1.

The main feature of this protocol is that it prioritizes the NACKs related to the end-users having lost the greater number of packets in a transmission group. It yields a performance close to the theoretical upper bound in terms of bandwidth efficiency and packet error rate.

CONCLUSION

In this chapter, the basic characteristics of the HASP-related technology were presented. The multi-beam adaptive antenna array is a basic component of the system's RF payload. Via this array, many cellular patterns on the ground can be implemented and dynamically adjusted according to the specific telecommunication needs. Serving high-speed mobile routers requires reliable DOA estimation techniques. The coexistence of multiple HASPs in the same environment produces interference which can be computed and analyzed with the aid of the tools provided in the chapter. The level of interference affects the system's performance in terms of bit error rate and capacity. The intrinsic characteristics of a HASP-based system give engineers the possibility to implement effective call admission control schemes based on the prediction of the speed and direction of the mobile users. Handover is another important issue addressed. Adaptive soft handover schemes suitable for HASPs have been developed and it has been shown that they offer reduced blocking and dropping probability. In the network layer, the home agent placement on-board or in the HASP gateway can determine the effectiveness of the mobility management. Furthermore, within the scope of the synergic integration of different wireless communication networks, multi-layered routing algorithms have been proposed. The terrestrial, HASP and GEO satellite systems can cooperate to facilitate the provision of ubiquitous coverage and resolve the 'last mile' problem. In the transport layer, multi-cast protocols that take into account the on-board proxy functionalities of the HASPs can offer enhanced packet error rate performance. In conclusion, HASPs are strong candidates as communicational components in NGNs and they can be integrated into existing wireless networks in terms of infrastructure as well as in terms of services.

REFERENCES

Abrardo, A., Benelli, G., & Sennati, D. (2001). Centralized radio resource management strategies with heterogeneous traffics in HAPS WCDMA cellular systems. *IEEE Vehicular Technology Conference, 2*, 640-644

Alocci, I., Berioli, M., Celandroni, N., Giambene, G., & Karapantazis, S. (2007). Proposal of a reliable multicast protocol in a HAP-satellite architecture. *IEEE Vehicular Technology Conference*, 1380-1384.

Avangina, D., Dovis, F., Ghiglione, A., & Mulassano, P., (2002). Wireless networks based on high-altitude platforms for the provision of integrated navigation/communication services. *IEEE Communications Magazine, 40*(2), 119-125.

Birkos, K., Chrysikos, T., & Kotsopoulos, S. (2007). An inter-HAP handover scheme over a worst case fading scenario. *Proceedings of the 7th European Conference of young research and science workers (TRANSCOM 2007), 3*, 19-22.

Birkos, K., & Kotsopoulos, S. (2007, May). On the intrinsic quality of service performance issues of a new proposed multiple-HAPs based system architecture. *Paper presented at the World Wireless Congress*, San Francisco, CA.

Bisio, I., & Marchese, M., (2006). Study and performance evaluation of bandwidth controls over high altitude platforms. *11th IEEE Symposium on Computers and Communications.*

Cianca, E., De Luise, A., De Sanctis, M., Ruggieri, M., & Prasad, R. (2004). TCP/IP performance over satellite and HAP integrated systems. *Proceedings of IEEE Aerospace Conference*, 2, 1209-1216.

Cianca, E., Prasad, R., De Sanctis, M., De Luise, A., Antonini, M., Teotino, D. et al. (2005). Integrated satellite-HAP systems. *IEEE Communications Magazine*, 43(12), 33-39.

Djuknic, G., Freidenfelds, J., & Okunev, Y. (1997). Establishing wireless communications services via high-altitude aeronautical platforms: a concept whose time has come?. *IEEE Communications Magazine*, 35(9), 128-135.

Dovis, F., Lo Presti, L., & Mulassano, P. (2005). Support infrastructures based on high altitude platforms for navigation satellite systems. *IEEE Wireless Communications Magazine*, 12(5), 106-112.

Duca, E., Carrozzo, V., & Roseti, C. (2007). Performance evaluation of a hybrid satellite network based on high-altitude-platforms. *IEEE Aerospace Conference*, 1-12.

El-Jabu, B., & Steele, R. (2001). Cellular communications using aerial platforms. *IEEE Transactions on Vehicular Technology*, 50(3), 686-700.

Falletti, E., Laddomada, M., Mondin, M., & Sellone, F. (2006). Integrated services from high-altitude platforms: a flexible communication system. *IEEE Communications Magazine*, 44(2), 85-94.

Foo, Y. C., & Lim, W. L. (2005). Speed and direction adaptive call admission control for high altitude platform station (HAPS) UMTS. *IEEE Military Communications Conference*, 4, 2182-2188.

Foo, Y. C., Lim, W. L., & Tafazolli, R. (2002). Centralized downlink call admission control for high altitude platform station UMTS with onboard power resource sharing. *IEEE Vehicular Technology Conference*, 1, 549-553.

Grace, D., Capstick, M. H., Mohorcic, M., Horwath, J., Bobbio, M., & Fitch, M. (2005). Integrating users into the wider broadband network via high altitude platforms. *IEEE Wireless Communications*, 12(5), 98-105.

Grace, D., Thornton, J., Chen, G., White, G. P., & Tozer, T. C. (2005). Improving the system capacity of broadband services using multiple high-altitude platforms. *IEEE Transactions on Wireless Communications*, 4(2), 700-709.

Hong, T. C., Ku, B. J., Park, J. M., Ahn, D., & Jang, Y. (2005). Capacity of the WCDMA system using high altitude platform stations. *International Journal of Wireless Information Networks*, 13(1), 5-17.

Janevski, T. (2003). *Traffic analysis and design of wireless IP networks*. Boston: Artech House

Kandus, G., Svigelj, A., & Mohorcic, M. (2005). Telecommunication network over high altitude platforms. *7th International Conference on Telecommunications in Modern Satellite, Cable and Broadcasting Services*, 2, 344-347.

Ku, B. J., Ahn, D. S., Lee, S. P., Shishlov, A. V., Reutov, A. S., Ganin, S. A. et al. (2002). Radiation pattern of multibeam array antenna with digital beamforming for stratospheric communication **system:** statistical simulation. *ETRI Journal*, 24(3), 197-204.

Lim, W. L., Foo, Y. C., & Tafazolli, R. (2002). Adaptive softer handover algorithm for high altitude platform station UMTS with onboard power resource sharing. *5th International Symposium on Wireless Personal Multimedia Communications*, 1, 52-56.

Lim, W. L., Foo, Y. C., & Tafazolli, R. (2005). Inter-system handover algorithms for HAPS and tower–based overlay UMTS. *5th International Conference on Information, Communications and Signal Processing*, 419-424.

Pace, P., & Aloi, G. (2007). Multilayered architecture supporting efficient HAP-satellite routing. *IEEE Vehicular Technology Conference*, 1360-1364.

Pearce, D. A., & Grace, D. (2003). Optimizing the downlink capacity of broadband fixed wireless access systems for packet-based communications. *IEEE International Conference on Communications*, 3, 2149-2153.

Thornton, J. (2004). A low sidelobe asymmetric beam antenna for high altitude platform communications. *IEEE Microwave and Wireless Components Letter*s, 14(2), 59-61.

Thornton, J., Grace, D., Capstick, M. H., & Tozer, T. C. (2003). Optimizing an array of antennas for cellular coverage from a high altitude platform. *IEEE Transactions on Wireless Communications*, 2(3), 484-492.

Thornton, J., Grace, D., Spillard, C., Konefal, T., & Tozer, T. C. (2001). Broadband communications from a high-altitude platform: the European HeliNet program. *Electronics and Communication Engineering Journal*, 13(3), 138-144.

Tozer, T. C. (2000). High altitude platforms: The future for communications?, http://www.skylarc.com/HAPs-mainpres2000/HAPSmainpres.pdf.

Tozer, T. C., & Grace, D. (2001). High-altitude platforms for wireless communications. *Electronics and Communication Engineering Journal*, 13(3), 127-137.

Vilhar, A., & Novak, R. (2005). Home agent placement optimization for HAP-based network mobility. *2nd International Symposium on Wireless Communication Systems*, 873-877.

White, G. P., & Zakharov, Y. V. (2007). Data communications to trains from high-altitude platforms. *IEEE Transactions on Vehicular Technology*, 56(4), 2253-2266.

KEY TERMS

DOA (Direction of Arrival) Estimation: A set of techniques used to predict the most possible trajectory of a mobile terminal. The estimation results are used for enhanced radio resource reservation.

Frequency Reuse Efficiency: A measure of the effectiveness of the radio resource utilization in a cellular network.

HASP Gateway (HGTW): A gateway that interconnects a HASP-based network with other telecommunication infrastructures or networks.

HASP Master Control Station (HMCS): A ground station that controls the functionality of a HASP and deals with offered services, network management, dynamic cell planning and power control issues.

High Altitude Stratospheric Platforms (HASPs): Airships or aircrafts that fly on the stratosphere and carry communicational payload for the provision of broadband wireless services.

Margin Adaption Factor: A factor that is added in the add and drop margins of the handoff procedure in order to dynamically respond to the loading conditions of the base stations and reduce the call dropping probability.

TCP Splitting: The practice of using intermediate agents between two end users in order to enhance the TCP performance. A HASP can be the intermediate agent in a hybrid HASP/Satellite network.

Section II
Service Control and Quality of Service

Chapter VII
Test Template for Data Mining Publications

Dimitrios K. Lymberopoulos
University of Patras, Greece

ABSTRACT

The Next Generation Network (NGN) is a very complex environment, where various parties (network operators, services and application providers, integrators, etc.) necessarily cooperate on the provision of advanced converged services. This chapter presents the current status and fundamentals of conventional, converged and bundled value-added services, and then depicts their transformation into distributed NGN services. The characteristics of NGN services are considered with respect to the architecture of the NGN service stratum and the enterprise framework, both standardized by the International Telecommunications Union (ITU). Finally, the implementation and deployment of interoperable NGN services through open interfaces are considered in conjunction with market trends and the standardization efforts of several international organizations or other independent initiatives, forums, alliances, etc.

INTRODUCTION

Next Generation Networks (NGNs) create a homogeneous communication environment providing the ability to interconnect different transport technologies using fixed and wireless, as well as circuit-switched and packet-switched infrastructure. The NGNs integrate broadband fixed and mobile technologies, enabling users to communicate using broadband services regardless of whether they are using a terminal in a fixed location or if they are on the move.

However, the key promise lies in the context of services that might be offered on an NGN service platform. NGNs allow the reusability of existing resources, e.g. software components of existing services, and the rapid and efficient integration of these resources within new services. Hence, they provide the ability to design, implement and deploy innovative and lucrative services. For these reasons, network operators and service providers see NGNs providing a new revenue stream from potentially expanded service offerings. Therefore, it is important to explain how converged NGN technologies and solutions lead to efficient service creation.

This chapter analyses the state of the art for supporting converged and value-added telecommunication services in NGNs. In order to familiarize the reader with research and development trends in telecommunication services, firstly the current status of service provision upon existing wired and wireless telecommunication infrastructures

Copyright © 2009, IGI Global, distributing in print or electronic forms without written permission of IGI Global is prohibited.

is described. It sketches out the philosophy of binding, deploying and supporting different telecommunication services and capabilities via the access network, either by individual telecom providers (network providers and operators) or by cooperating telecom and third party providers.

There follows a discussion of the current paradigm shift to converged telecommunications services, as well as all operational and structural primitives formulating these services. Subsequently, on the basis of the converged services, there is an analysis of the architecture and functionality of the NGN services stratum, as specified by the International Telecommunications Union (ITU) and other international standardization organizations, initiatives, alliances, forums, etc.

Moreover, there is an analysis of the NGN enterprise framework, which is well defined by the ITU and which allows the development of both core services by the underlying transport infrastructure providers and value-added transport-agnostic services by independent third party providers.

This chapter also discusses several standardization results concerning the design and implementation of open interfaces that guarantee the seamless and interoperable operation of services designed and deployed by different developers. Finally, it sketches major trends in developing NGN services, and considers two characteristic examples, namely the presence / telepresence service and the home management service.

THE CURRENT STATUS OF TELECOMMUNICATION SERVICES

Covering the communication needs of subscribers continues to be the main business activity in the field of telecommunications. Yet, across the globe, fixed and mobile communications are nearing saturation point, a fact that reduces potential profit margins of carriers and operators whose simultaneous aim is to increase subscriber numbers.

As a result, in recent years telecommunication organizations have focussed on increasing the average revenue per user, rather than the number of subscribers, by introducing new telecommunication services that offer much more than standard voice services. These services are based on the interaction of sound, video and text with unrestricted access to the multimedia, information systems and relevant services, thus providing subscribers with greatly enhanced control over their interactions with the wider world.

These additional services are end-to-end services that operate through dedicated servers and add value to the access network. They are reported as premium pricing services, as their providers have the ability to apply individual deployment and charging policy (premium charging - PRMC) per service, irrespective of the policies applied to the underlying networking infrastructure employed.

The introduction of additional services to fixed and mobile access networks has impelled the providers of the networking infrastructure to provide additional connectivity (premium connectivity) in order to guarantee the required augmented quality per service.

From the point of view of the market, the providers of the additional services cooperate in order to package different premium services offered to the customers as product (bundled service). There follows an analysis of the most important ways in which such additional and bundled services are created and promoted.

Additional Services Created by Telecom Carriers and Operators

With the wide spread of legacy-fixed digital networks (e.g. PSDN, ISDN, GSM) and mobile networks, their operators have independently developed and promoted various additional telecommunications services in addition to the existing standard voice services.

These services mainly exploit the bearer capabilities of the signalling protocols (e.g. SS7) which are employed by the installed legacy telecommunications nodes. They are provided via additional node equipment, mainly special servers, and via special capabilities of the terminals. From an architectural point of view, the total equipment of the additional services comprises an upper (dedicated purpose) network with respect to the existing underlying fixed and mobile legacy networks. The Intelligent Network (IN) best represents these networks. Examples of additional IN services provided by the telecom carriers and operators are:

- *Telephone number portability*, providing the capability to transfer existing fixed-lines and mobile numbers assigned by a network carrier and reassign them to another carrier.
- *Private-number plans*, with numbers remaining unpublished in directories.
- *Abbreviated numbering*
- *Prepaid calling*, allowing the telephone user to be independent of the network operators by buying services in advance in the form of prepaid telephone cards. The value of the card is reduced accordingly depending on the duration and fee of the connection. Prepaid cards are offered by most fixed-line and mobile operators around the world.
- *Account card calling*, allowing the owners of credit or debit cards to use them as an alternative payment method to cash when making calls.
- *Universal personal number (UPN)*. The user always has a specific call number that is independent from the number of the appliance on which the user is called each time. A subscribers registry (database) is employed, which is maintained by the service provider, where the user tele-registers the new telephone number to which his calls are to be addressed.
- *Toll free call,* or green number service, providing the subscriber with the ability to call a special call number (e.g. 800) to which the cost of the call will be charged. The service provider has the ability to apply various charging policies accordingly to the amount of calls, the operational cost of the employed trunk between the called party and the network node, etc.
- *Call screening*, providing an evaluation of telephone call characteristics before each conversation.
- *Televoting*, providing a cost-effective method for opinion polling using the telephone.
- *Creation of virtual private network (VPN)*. VPNs are networks tunneled through other networks; they are accessible to closed groups of users and implemented for a specific purpose. VPNs provide secure communication over insecure networks (e.g. Internet), a defined performance level and certain privileges for users.
- *Centrex service*, providing public fixed and mobile network subscribers with PBX capabilities such as call transfer, call divert, three party conference, ring back, last number redial, call pick up, reminder, call waiting, call divert, non-dialed connection, etc.
- *Mass-calling service*
- *Seamless MMS message access* from abroad.

The aforementioned optimized services can easily handle many millions of transactions per hour with low investment. The main objective of each telecom operator is to launch additional services in the market that will be used by a large number of users, and so produce essential revenues based exclusively on the volume or of usage charging. These services are known as "*killer*" services. In mobile networks, the Short Message Service (SMS) is globally characterized as a killer service.

Bundled Services Offered by Different Telecom Providers

This category includes discrete services offered via the same end user (subscriber) access network. In the early deployment stage, each such service was offered and maintained by an independent provider. This meant customized contract and billing per service and user. For example, in the case of a residence, the telephony provider would offer the voice service, while the cable network provider would offer the cable television service.

During the next deployment stage, the wide diffusion of Internet has led different providers of Internet, fixed and mobile broadband networks to collaborate in order to bind more than one service into a single commercial package. This is due to the catholic nature of the Internet that includes: a) a global addressing/numbering scheme, where the assignment and the analysis of addresses is performed by domain servers, and b) diverse applications, such as electronic mail, file transport and the World Wide Web .

The package is provided to broadband subscribers through aggregate contract and billing, with each included service functioning independently of the rest and with its own qualitative and administrative characteristics guaranteed. In the global telecommunications market up to now, the packages launched constitute combinations of: a) two broadband services, which are the high speed access to the Internet and the distribution of television signals (analogue and digital), and b) one narrowband fixed or mobile telephony service.

The simplest case is the double-play service, where the subscriber selects one broadband and telephony service. For example, in the residential market, if the provider is a fixed telephony operator, subscribers receive high speed Internet access and telephony services via a mainly ADSL-type access network. If the provider is a cable television operator, subscribers receive high speed Internet and television signal distribution services via broadband coaxial cables and special MODEMS. On the other hand, if the provider is a mobile operator, subscribers receive high speed Internet access and telephony services.

A more complex case is the triple-play service, where the subscriber selects Internet, telephony and cable television services through a mainly VDSL-type broadband access wired line. Standardisation and promotion of the triple play service constitute the framework of various worldwide forums, such as the Triple Play Alliance (www.triple-play-alliance.com).

The transmission of the triple-play service both wire and mobile broadband access networks has led to the quadruple-play service. This service offers enormous dynamics and competitive advantages to its providers, because it facilitates the mobility of users and the unification of user access networks, e.g. using WiMax and JEEE 802.16 technology.

The integrated triple and quadruple-play services are commonly referred as multiplay services.

The establishment of the aforementioned services/products does not simply signal a further technological development; it has changed the essence of the providers since, for example, the cable television (pay TV) providers and the network providers operate as telecommunications operators (TELCOs). It has also motivated different service and network providers to collaborate closely. Substantially, it has marked the beginning of the convergence of the three basic telecommunication networks (fixed, mobile and Internet).

Bundled Services Offered by Cooperating Telecom and Third Party Providers

The increasing competition among multiplay service providers has led to the creation of more complex relationships with their own subscribers. Their relationship is no longer based in bundling and pricing the basic three services (voice, video and Internet) or in providing access networks. New opportunities have arisen for packaging, transporting and distributing various types of multimedia content, in the form of value-added telecommunications services.

The value-added services are end-to-end services that function via special content management servers and are generally independent of the structure and characteristics of the underlying broadband telecommunication infrastructure. Their provider can be either any telecommunication carrier and operator or any other independent third party provider using the infrastructure of one or more telecommunication carriers in order to interlink its own servers and users.

The portfolio of value-added services includes new types of communication, productivity, usefulness and entertainment services. These services can also be extended to satisfy fully the broadband communication needs of each subscriber, and generally to provide **value-added in the subscribers themselves.** The third party providers that mainly provide these services are primarily commercial bodies that focus on concrete market segments, such as health, education, trade, entertainment, transports, mass briefing, sports, culture, tourism, etc

Value-added services belong to the on-demand unicast services that use the streaming data transmission mode. Examples of such services are video-on-demand (VoD) services, distribution of television signal (IPTV), messaging service, telecollaboration, tele-education, telemedicine, gaming, audio services, etc. In streaming services, each final user has individual flows of application data and proprietary usage patterns. Note that conventional networks are unable to provide such types of patterns directly.

A sub-category of value-added services includes the basic multicast and broadcast services for video, voice, data and Internet elements. However, the competition and differentiation of providers is focused on unicast services, since multicast and broadcast services are already considered to be primary commodities.

Implementation of Services Using Conventional Networks and Protocols

Legacy telecommunications networks, such as ISDN, PSDN, IP, Internet, mobile, wireless, etc., have the capability of supporting the sum of the aforementioned additional and value-added services. Modeling and realization of these services are based on the consolidated paradigm of *vertical telecommunications services standardization*, which has yielded an architectural structure of services that is known as *stovepipe* or *silo* architecture.

According to the rules of silo architecture, each service is structured by a concrete number of telecommunications protocols that are ordered vertically in levels, a structure known as the *protocols stack*. The number of levels, as well as the type of protocols that realize operations of each level, are determined by concrete models. For example, the Open Systems Interconnection (OSI) model includes seven levels, while the TCP/IP model has five levels. The precise specification of the architectural structure of each telecommunication service **constitutes privilege** of a concrete standardization organism (e.g. ITU, ETSI, ANSI, IEEE, IETF, etc.) or a specialized industrial forum.

Silo services are usually provided as commercial products tightly related to a concrete internetworking scheme, switching mode and type of terminal equipment, as well as the standardization followed. Generally, due to rapid technological development, silo services have a small life cycle. Hence, the main criteria for their implementation focus upon facility, local optimization, and low short-term development and deployment costs. Any factor that could decrease the performance, expand the production time or increase the cost is systematically isolated from the silo service stack. Moreover, all required contributory or secondary operations (e.g. billing, management, safety, etc) are consolidated in the main service operations, implemented in such a way that it is almost impossible for them to be shared with other products or services that run concurrently or share the same communication equipment or network infrastructure.

It is obvious that above a network infrastructure (telephone, mobile, leased line, radio transmission, etc) there are many different services, such as different and non-cooperative stacks of protocols. Therefore, although vertical protocol implementation can produce a killer service, it is nearly impossible for the developed resources and faculties of this killer service to be reused for the implementation of a new service. On the contrary, most contributory operations have to be developed from the beginning and integrated individually into the new service.

The inherent weaknesses of silo architecture, emerging on a wide scale in both standards and products, constitute a permanent threat to the telecommunications business; this is known as *silo syndrome*. From the perspective of developers, this syndrome results in a number of problems, such as high investment costs in case of parallel deployment of multiple silo products, high integration costs, etc. On the other hand, the lack of unified standards across service domains has produced various problems for service providers. For example, the establishment of new services requires much data to be replicated (e.g. subscriber information that appears in databases) and many functions to be duplicated. Moreover, the deployment of any service requires its functional entities to be integrated with the underlying network infrastructure from scratch. In any case, sharing features across services requires knowledge of their own operations and management facilities as well as a detailed knowledge of the network, resulting in significant cost for the service providers.

Silo syndrome has led to the deployment of many high cost non-standard implementations which, despite sharing the same features, are provided to subscribers with completely incompatible interfaces and operational capabilities.

THE NEED FOR CONVERGED SERVICES AND INFRASTRUCTURES

The weaknesses of silo architecture have caused great concern and frustration among service providers and network operators over the architecture of next bearer and premium services, as well as the next bundle of value-added telecommunication services.

In 1995, in the Y.100 series of recommendations, the International Telecommunication Union — Telecommunication Standardization Sector (ITU-T) launched the Global Information Infrastructure (GII) standards. The GII describes a common vision of future networks and services with the goal of preparing for the emerging information age. To be precise, it describes the provision of various services by a variety of service providers through a variety of network technologies from different industry sectors. GII is considered to be a simple enterprise model with identified interfaces, roles (business activities) and players (an organization that undertakes roles). ITU considers the GII to be the infrastructure facilitating the development, implementation and interoperability of existing and future information services and applications. The GII reference model specifies interactive, broadcast and other multimedia delivery mechanisms coupled with capabilities for individuals to share, use and manage information, anytime and anywhere, with security and privacy protection, and at levels of acceptable cost and quality. The ITU-T (Rec. Y.120/Annex A) has described same example scenarios based on the GII reference model.

Hence, in the world of service standards, there has been a paradigm shift from standardizing silo services to standardizing service components. These components are variously referred to as service building blocks, service enablers or service capabilities.

Each service component is an independent and reusable niche service targeted at a specific niche market, which concerns a specialized user group or supports a specific communication capability. Aggregating various service components, it is able to build differentiated bearer, end-to-end or value-added services. However, for niche services, avoiding the silo syndrome means seamless integration into the aggregate service, centralized management, and network (fixed, mobile, wireless, IP, Internet) agnostic operation.

Thereafter, the target is the creation of a communication environment allowing the proliferation of niche services rather than searching for the next killer services. This environment is based on generalized standard service components and development tool-kits that facilitate shorter development cycles and reduce the need for product integration and deployment. For this reason, it is expected that there will be a large number of such niche services, generating considerable revenue for developers and providers, mainly through economies of scale.

The service component paradigm is the impetus for the implementation of converged fixed and mobile communication services, as well as value-added services provided by third party providers or through the Internet. Converged services should be seamless and consistent across network domains. They should guarantee a seamless federation of interconnected communications capabilities providing users' interoperability; such capabilities concern, for example, incorporating circuit and packet switches, and line-fed and wireless connectionless or connection oriented infrastructures.

Moreover, a converged service may be executed above group collaborating schemes (client-server, pear-to-pear or mixed) handling diverse signaling and data transfer protocols, multimedia data formats, and end user device capabilities.

Nevertheless, the converged services should have unrestricted and practically unlimited application areas. They should include applications concerning health (e.g. telemedicine, home care), education (e.g. distance learning, tele-training,), culture (e.g. electronic museums), city information services, electronic commerce, intelligent transports, electronic libraries, nomadicity (continuity of access in space and time), etc. However, their modeling and authoring need to focus on the essential characteristics of the service, which are related to the targets and objectives of the application domains, the habits and capabilities of users, and the required gradation of the quality of service (QoS) offered. On the other hand, a deep understanding or operational knowledge of the underlying heterogeneous networks, protocols, end-user devices or customer or regulator-driven requirements is not necessary. It is noted that accurate QoS specification and assignment of its management capabilities at service level constitute the key success factor for any converged service.

The GII concept for establishing converged services in global communications has forced standardization organizations, even the competitive ones (e.g. ITU and IETF), and industrial forums to collaborate and to agree on homogeneous communication and information standards. This collaboration has reinforced the establishment of a new universal model for future networks, known as Next Generation Networks (NGNs). NGNs are also standardized by ITU-T in the Y.2000 series of recommendations, and differ from their conventional counterparts in both architecture and services. Figure 1 shows the paradigm shift from conventional network and silo services to those of NGNs.

NGN architecture constitutes of two layers (strata), one for transport and one for services, as opposed to the existing OSI and TCP/IP multilayered models. The transport stratum accepts Internet Protocol (IP) packet-based high-bandwidth core transmission (e.g. WDM and DWDM technologies, optical cross-connects), last mile transmission (e.g. DSL, fiber to the home (FTTH), passive optical networks, etc), and packet-based switching (e.g. ATM, MPLS,), as the only universal future communication technologies.

Figure 1. Comparison of NGN and conventional networks (OKI, 2007)

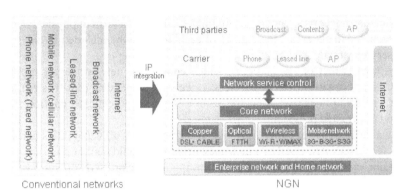

NGNs support the provision of all kinds of services (e.g., multimedia, data, video, telephony) with convergence of their control and management functions. Service functions are separated from transport functions and their provision is decoupled from networks. All types of communication services have to be supported and these services have their own evolution independent of network infrastructure. However, these features rely on a wide range of transfer characteristics, such as real and non-real-time, low to high bit rates, QoS differentiation, point-to-point, multicast, broadcast, conversational, conference, etc. Generalized mobility and nomadicity are also strongly featured by NGNs.

By definition, an NGN is an enhanced IP-based packet network, since it introduces needs that were not originally envisaged when the first generation of packet networks was designed. It allows telecommunication services to make use of multiple broadband QoS-enabled transport technologies in which service-related functions are independent from underlying transport-related technologies. An NGN is also based on the existing *universal nature* of the Internet infrastructure including a global addressing plan, address assignment and resolution by domain name servers, and a number of killer applications such as World Wide Web , email and file transfer. The Internet has not been integrated into this NGN architecture because designers envision a separate Internet coexisting alongside NGNs.

SERVICES FUNCTIONALITY IN NGNS

The service stratum enhances unlimited access for users to various services of their choice through competing networking infrastructure and service providers. The NGN includes processing and storage resources on which services and applications can run (services' platforms), or databases for application content storage.

The service providers organize services' platforms that provide the user with services such as voice services (including telephone service), data services (including but not limited to Web -based services) and video services (including movies and TV programmes and other streaming applications), or some theme combination (e.g., multimedia services such as video telephony and gaming). Each such service may be the seamless integration of diverse niche services. ITU-T (Rec. Y.2011) considers the service to be: a) a stratum involving a complex set of geographically distributed services' platforms or in the simple case just the service functions in two end-user sites, and b) supporting generalized mobility that guarantees consistent and ubiquitous provision of services to users.

The NGN service stratum also includes the service control and management functions for supported mediated and non-mediated services, as well as functions supporting its interconnection with external applications and services as well as end-users' domains.

The ITU-T (Y.2000 series of Rec.) specifies the NGN functional architecture (Figure 2), where the NGN is decomposed into sets of functional control and management entities, each providing a unique function. Relationships and the connection between two non-overlapping function entities are conceptually identified in terms of reference points. The reference points specify, in a logical abstract level, the information exchanged between this pair of functions, and may not correspond to certain implementation in form of physical interfaces. The total function entities are organized in six areas; the entities of each area may be included in one service stratum or distributed over more service strata.

The first functional area is that of *Applications*, which consists of network/server providers themselves (trusted providers) and inferior organizations or partners, as well as independent (not-trusted) service providers. The functions of the service stratum enablers take the responsibility to authenticate, control, and filter access to resources of inferior and not-trusted providers.

The second functional area is that of *Other Networks* ,which supports all capabilities and features (e.g. IN) of the legacy networks (e.g. ISDN, IN, PSDN). The legacy networks should neither stunt the evolution of NGN architecture (e.g. in session management) nor cause any limiting impacts on NGN operations.

The third functional area is that of the *End-User,* which consists of a diversity of end-user networks that may be connected to the NGN access network through diverse end-user interfaces. The terminal equipment of the end-user may employ fixed, mobile or wireless connectivity protocols.

The fourth area is that of *Service Control Functions*, handling the invocation of services by end-users. The main functions of this area perform resource control, end user registration and authorization and, at service level, mutual authentication between the service and end user. Specific functions perform the control of media resources, such as specialized resources and gateways at the service-signaling level. Other functions of this area form date service user profiles in the service stratum. These profiles are functional databases with combined user information and other control data, which may be specified and developed as cooperating databases with distributed functionalities throughout the NGN. Network Attachment Control Function (NACF) and Resource and Admission Control Functions (RACF), both constituting the transport control functions, as well as the Service Control Functions, may be distributed and instantiated over different NGN provider domains.

The fifth area includes *Application Support Functions* and *Service Support Functions*. This area cooperates with *Service Control Functions* to provide the other areas with registration, gateway, authentication, authorization and other similar functions, as well as all the NGN services they request. Specifically, this area offers the *Applications* area certain service-enabling resources and capabilities (e.g. presence, charging function, security schemes, location information, etc) of the underlying transport stratum.

The sixth area is the *Management Functions* area, providing fundamental NGN management capabilities governing the quality, security, and reliability of NGN services. The service stratum includes fault, accounting, configuration, performance and security management functions. These functions also concern end-user operations taking place either prior to or following a service invocation.

Moreover, theThe NGN functional architecture specifies network interfaces which allow functional entities of the six NGN areas to exchange information with function entities of user and service provider domains, or with other NGNs and IP multimedia networks.

The *Applications* area interacts with both service and transport NGN stratums through the Applications Network Interface (ANI). ANI is a channel offering capabilities and resources between NGNs and applications and ensuring the received functions and capabilities are agnostic with respect to the underlying NGN infrastructure. Through API, the NGN has to provide an open service interface that should be network agnostic, in order to ensure that third-party service providers can efficiently access the network capabilities.

The *Application Support* Functions and *Service Support Functions* and the *Service Control Functions* areas provide reference points for *End-User* and *Other Network* functional areas through the User Network Interface (UNI) and strata through the Network - Network Interface (NNI), respectively. The UNI, NNI and ANI are general NGN reference points that can be mapped to specific physical interfaces depending on the particular physical implementations.

Figure 2. NGN architecture overview (ITU-T Y.2012, 2006)

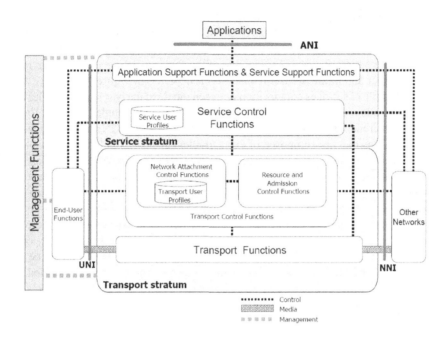

ENTERPRISE FRAMEWORK FOR NGNS

The NGN service stratum is an all encompassing and consistent service layer. From a business perspective, it is a *value-creation environment* in which operators can differentiate their offering from that of their competitors. It also allows them to extend their value chain and implement new business models. To achieve this, operators require more sophisticated business-to-business interfaces, improved assurance of interoperability and internationally available open standards that are network independent.

The ITU has defined an enterprise model that distinguishes six (6) basic roles of general commercial and technical importance assigned to an individual, a household with multiple end users, or a small or large business with multiple end users, and five (5) different service providers (Figure 3):

- *Retailing service provider* determining the user profile and the total after sales service level agreement (SLA). This role provides the contact point for the consumer to arrange for - and the service provider to offer - services that employ communication services as the delivery mechanism
- *Integrating service provider* creating unique new service offerings from services provided by other roles.
- *Service control provider* handling call, session, location, registration, presence and other control services.
- *Value-added service provider* handling dedicated purpose (e.g. e-commerce, e-health, etc) and content delivery value-added services.
- *Core, access and transit transport provider* handling underlying network connectivity. This delivers the communication services that transport information, which may be either control or resources plane information.

Within a business function, one or more roles can be integrated, and different business functions can be partitioned into business domains. This solid business framework is known as the third party service delivery model and facilitates operators to create genuine revenue streams and engage in business-to-business relationships with third-party developers and application service providers. Per converged service, the aforementioned roles define specific technical relationships among the interconnected functional entities of the resources, control and management plane. This will result in third party service providers offering next generation value-added converged services such as audio/video conferencing, integrated browsing, Virtual Private Networks (VPNs), Internet call waiting and messaging services. An example of the services delivery chain from telecom operator to third-party service provider and finally to user (consumer) is depicted in Figure 4.

Figure 5 depicts an example of services composition between the third party service provider and the network operator of Figure 4; each node represents a service. The service provider includes complex Video on Demand (VoD), Streamed Audio Conferencing (AC) and Shared Whiteboarding (SWB) NGN services. Each complex service is composed of simple services that are composed of even simpler (generic, stable and re-usable) services. The simple services are re-usable software sub-components (e.g. implementing a simple authentication mechanism) that encapsulate service-independent logic. The even simpler services encompass independent logic processes for session or call control, service management and connection control in the network operator's domain.

The ITU enterprise model defines a specific logical reference point between the business domains. A different number of reference points is selected according to the implementation aspects of the enterprise model. The seamless integration of simple services (a simple service set may constitute the functionality of a role) and the transport (network) agnostic character of converged services requires the reference points to be implemented as open interfaces. The example in Figure 6 depicts a five domain business model, the value-added (third party and integrating) service provider, the network connectivity (transport) provider, the broker and the customer (service user), as well as the logical reference points (APIs) between the domains.

As a consequence of the aforementioned business model, the general NGN technical architecture of Figure 2 should be depicted as a multi-layer operational (service delivery) architecture, usually referred to as a Service Delivery Platform (SDP). In this architecture, the NGN Distributed Processing Environment (DPE) operates as a separate layer that uncouples the network intelligence from physical network elements. Thus, an upper separate layer is used to distribute intelligence to the most suitable locations in the network. For example, network intelligence could reside on specific functions (e.g., service control points, intelligent peripherals, and services nodes in an AIN environment), or on edge devices close to the consumer. Hence, the service/session control is separated from the underlying transport elements and included in the intelligence layer. This allows operators and carriers to employ transport elements independent of control elements. Moreover, it allows the clean separation between access, service and communications session control types, and for each control type to be decomposed into several micro-control elements. Hence, each service is developed independently of the type of transport used.

An approach to the service delivery NGN architecture including four vertical layers is depicted in Figure 7. The relationships between layers are based on Service Level Agreements (SLAs), which are predefined policies for resource manipulation. In this architecture, the domain of the third party provider is included in the upper (fourth) insecure layer (referred to as the Application Layer). This layer must include a) the value-added services and applications, b) a service creation environment, and c) certain interfaces and service specific logic to manipulate elements in the operator's domain via the open interfaces. These interfaces are implemented by means of open yet secure network Application Programming Interfaces (APIs) and new middleware development tools.

On the other hand, the operator's secure domain is represented by three layers. The third layer handles the inherent NGN's intelligence regarding (service, generic call and connection) control and service management. This layer enables the operator to deliver services from many sources, for example integrating Internet-type third-party applications with a full set of the network services (e.g. call control, messaging, location, and billing) available in today's wired, wireless and data networks.

The second layer composes the Distributed Processing Environment (DPE) based on middleware such as CORBA, enabling the call and connection resources in the service intelligence layer to access and control physical resources in the network resource layer. The lower layer includes the networking capabilities of the operator.

Figure 3. NGN roles defined by ITU ((ITU-T Y.2012, 2006)

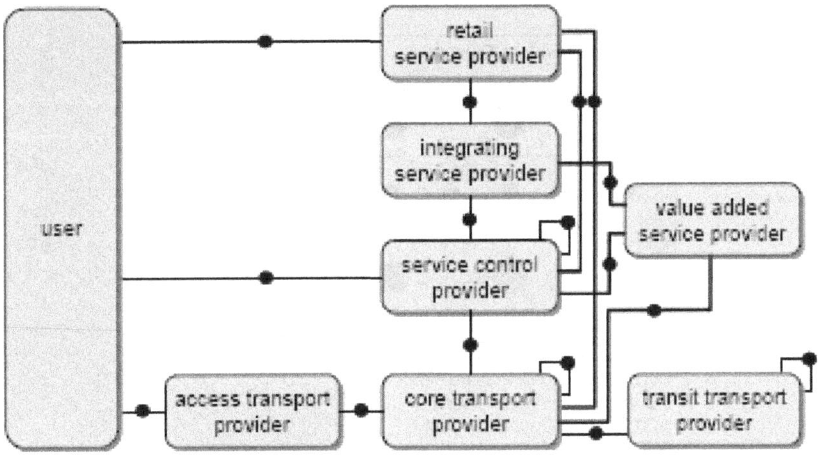

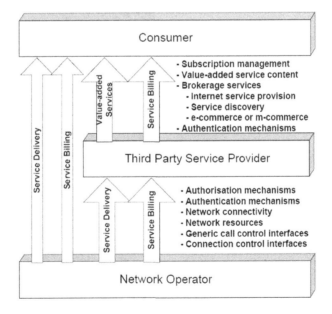

Figure 4. Example of third party delivery model (Nana, 2001)

THE STANDARDIZATION OF NGN APIS

APIs provide standards-based interfaces that are network technology independent, easy to use value-added service interfaces that allow applications to access core network functionality. APIs make the telecom functionality residing in the network accessible to a large developer community. Accordingly, rapid services are set to evolve, ranging from premium rate information and messaging services, m-commerce applications, location-based application, click-to-dial and third party call control services up to advanced enterprise portal services.

Figure 5. Example of service composition between service provider and NGN operator (Nana, 2002)

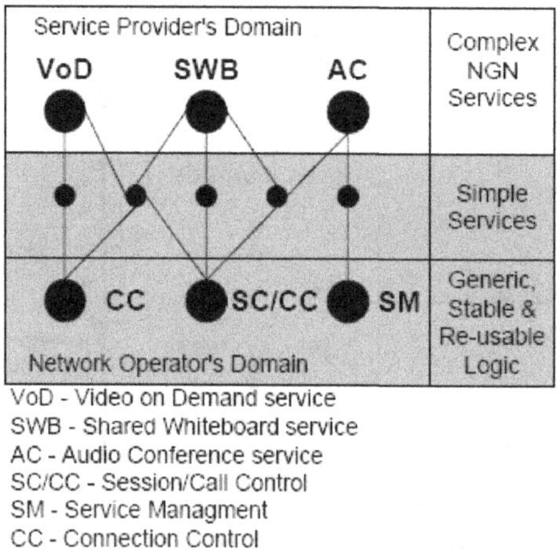

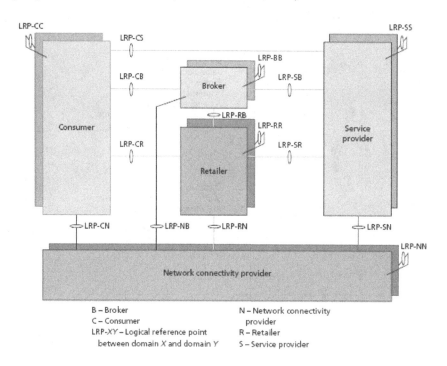

Figure 6. Example of an NGN business model (John-Luc Bakker, 2000)

The European Telecommunications Standards Institute (ETSI), the Parlay Group and the 3rd Generation Partnership Project (3GPP) have collaborated and jointly defined a series of APIs that are included in the Open Service Access (OSA) standards. OSA describes how services are included in the architecture of 3rd generation mobile telecommunication networks or the UMTS. The Parlay/OSA specifications define APIs but do not specify ways of implementating them. The OSA specifications are also extended to provide Parlay Web Services, and Parlay-X Web Services, which integrate Web Services with the telecom networks and preserve the operator's ability to ensure quality of service and network reliability.

Figure 7. The multi-layer operational NGN architecture (Nana, 2001)

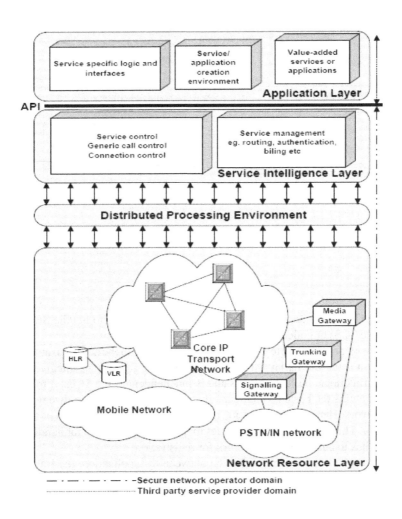

The implementation of OSA/APIs adds a new network element to the operational NGN architecture of Figure 7, referred to as Parlay Gateway (Figure 8). This gateway is located between telecom capabilities (the lower three layers of Figure 7) and applications capabilities (the upper layer of Figure 7). The Parlay Gateway is provided by vendors either as a stand-alone module (e.g., the Ericsson NRG, AePONA Causeway, HERIT Parlay/Parlay X Gateway), or it is embedded in an IN Service Control Point (e.g. the Telcordia OSP).

The Parlay Gateway includes both a set (an array) of Service interfaces or Service Capability Feature (SCF) interfaces and a framework interface.

The SCFs offer applications total network functionality, which includes call control, user interaction, messaging, location, and data connectivity, via abstract interfaces. Each SFC concerns a specific network service and provides the mechanism by which any applications can access underlying network capabilities that are handled by the specific service. Hence an application can use similar capabilities of different nodes. For example: a) a location service via both a home location register (HLR) and a gateway mobile location center (GMLC), or b) a call control service via several customized applications for mobile network enhanced logic (CAMEL), or c) a message transfer service via a Short Message Service (SMS) and the wireless application protocol (WAP). Usu-

Figure 8. Parlay/OSA architecture (Adel Al-Hezmi, 2003)

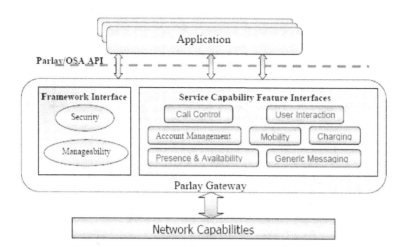

ally, SCFs run on Service Capability Servers (SCSs), allowing applications to handle SCFs that are spread (or distributed) across multiple SCSs or collocated on a single SCS transparently.

The OSA/APIs framework provides the telecom network operator with the ability to authenticate applications and prevent any application using the Parlay API from affecting the security or integrity of the network. It is composed of a number of functional building blocks and is independent of the SCFs. It mediates between SCSs and applications, and it contains the basic mechanisms that enable applications to discover and use the service capabilities within the network. Hence, the application needs to know only the location of the service factory and the features it is looking for. The framework also provides management functions for handling fault and overload situations; each new SCF has to contact the framework for registration.

The OSA/API standard specifies the communication between the application, the framework and the SCFs. On the other hand, it does not specify the communication between any application and its users.

When an application requests a specific service provided by the network, it contacts the framework that first discovers all SCFs (collocated into the same network or distributed over different networks) that serve this service and need to be accessed. Subsequently, the framework performs the appropriate authorization and authentication control in order to identify the application and to verify if this application is allowed to use the requested SCFs. The conditions under which any application is allowed to use any SCF are configured in the framework.

Following the verification process, the application selects the appropriate implementations of the required SCFs that satisfy its requirements (using information from the Service Capability Servers). The conditions under which the application may use any SCF are sent by the framework to the SCS, which creates an instance per SCF. In this step, the application is able to use all the accessed SCF implementations.

The OSA/API specifications are structured in fifteen parts and included in the ES 202 195 standard. The OSA/API is defined using Unified Modelling Language (UML) and is technology independent. The OSA specification provides detailed documentation describing the interfaces that developers must implement. The specifications themselves provide sequence and class diagrams, state transition diagrams and more for the API calls they describe.

The Parlay standards do not include specifications for the implementation of the OSA/APIs and the underlying service components. Implementing an OSA/API is a structured process that is generally characterized by consequent but interrelated steps. First, the requirements definition is performed using cases to explain the key principles. Following this, a generic Information Model is defined, which describes the draft version of API and the classes, attributes and operations of information crossing the interfaces of this API. Finally, the targeted middleware protocol (e.g. Common Object Request Broker Architecture – CORBA, Common Object Model - COM, and Java Remote Rethod Invocation – JRMI) is chosen. Each protocol uses an Interface Definition Language (IDL) to specify the API and the supported middleware services. The language prescribes the information typing and exchange between client and server programs, as well as ensuring interoperability among distributed but cooperating functional entities (hardware and software). The middleware also supplies the application developer with the framework of a set of common services (e.g, tools) that can be used as a foundation (for example, naming, events, and security). These tools make the application developer more productive when developing in a distributed environment.

THE NEXT GENERATION SERVICE ARCHITECTURE

Features of NGN Services

The presence of NGNs has put the individual end-user at the centre of service provisioning. Hence, the communications world has moved from the conventional network-centric view to a new customer-centric (or I-centric) view. The new applications and services should be tailored to the real needs of users and in a full network-agnostic manner. That means shaping the user's communication system on the basis of his individual communication preferences, contexts, spaces and ambient information; the preferences are provided by personalization and the ambient information by ambient awareness. In some cases, a reference model is required to describe personalization, ambient awareness and adaptability. Hence, service providers should have the flexibility to focus on micro-marketing, as opposed to mass-marketing.

The creation of a service with the aforementioned characteristics requires in-depth study of user behavior so that the author of the service may deduce realistic behaviour patterns (creation of a user profile). Hence, more *personal intelligence* is distributed throughout the network, and *intelligent agents* can sense the presence of these patterns and perform specific functions on behalf of them. On the other hand, user interfaces should shield users from the complexity of information gathering, displaying, processing, customization and transportation. The user interfaces should also establish an *intelligent information management environment*, giving the user the ability to manipulate the entire communication and processing overheads both efficiently and stably.

The specification of rules for constructing NGN services can be found at the centre of the research and standardization activity of several international bodies. The Wireless Word Research Forum (WWRF) has formulated the I-centric communications environment. The WWRF (Working Group 2) has specified a reference model focusing on I-centric communications to support at least three major service capabilities (personalization, ambient awareness, and adaptability) (Figure 9).

The reference model introduces a user communication space where the user interacts with defined contexts and objects. The underlying service platform constitutes a communication system that is based on individual communication spaces, contexts, preferences, and ambient information. The IP-based communication subsystem links the different objects in the communication spaces even if the user roams between different core or access networks (wired or wireless). Hence, a connection in the IP-based communication subsystem might use different physical connections in the underlying networks. The devices and communication end systems provide the physical end system infrastructure that supports all other layers. The ambient awareness, personalization, and adaptability features affect all layers and have to be vertically provided to all layers.

The reference model also takes into account generic service elements implementing common functionalities on all layers. Each element can be seen as a *service component* from which complex services can be assembled and executed dynamically.

The Fixed-Mobile Convergence Alliance (FMCA) encourages greater industry collaboration between operators and vendors so as to accelerate the development of new products and services. The FMCA has introduced Convergence Application Scenarios aimed at urging third party developers and handset manufactures to jointly create and deliver innovative converged services. FMCA considers these scenarios will deduce a core set of applications (mainly by handset vendors) that should stimulate great convergence opportunities. The major FMCA scenarios concern:

Figure 9. The WWRF reference model for I-centric communications

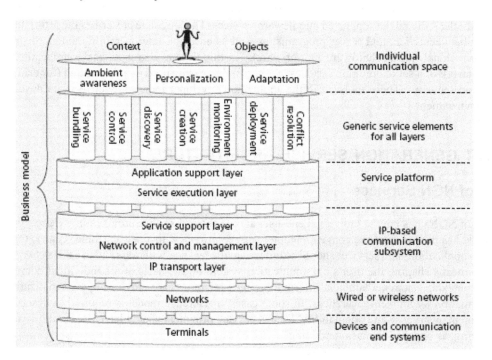

- Converged personal contacts with a central network address book.
- Secure access to user personal multimedia content (stored at home and/or in the network) from any device.
- Voice and multimedia call with data sharing.
- Combinatorial services, such as including voice, integrated messaging (e-mail, SMS/MMS, or IM) and file sharing, through different connections and during the same communication session.
- Electronic program guides for remote programming and access of personal or network-based multimedia recorders (e.g. personal video recorders – PVR)
- Automation control of home-based functions (e.g. temperature, access, etc) and monitoring conditions within the home (e.g. burglar alarm, home CCTV, etc).
- Convergent call control for automatic diversion or handling of calls based on user information (e.g. calendar) or external events (e.g. weather).
- Multimodal services that mix voice and data sessions performed either simultaneously or sequentially.

FMCA also identifies relevant standardization efforts that are considered key convergence enablers and provides some foresight into the expected convergence application requirements common to telecom operators. These requirements concern the APIs provided to application developers, the functionality provided by the hardware platform, the embedded applications provided by handset vendors and the network protocols supported by the device.

The Home Gateway Initiative (HGI) boosts the availability of home communication services to residential broadband customers by means of a detailed list of requirements for the Home Gateway. HGI and FMCA are jointly composing detailed technical documents that will provide telecom operator guidance for the convergence of services, networks and devices in the broadband home.

The Major Trends in Development of NGN Services

The NGNs enable the creation of a wide range of services and applications. The following sections give a brief description of several services that would appear to represent the major trends in service design, implementation and usage, and which also seem to be important drivers in the NGN environment. These trends range from the basic voice and data services to more advanced virtual reality creation services [Odtr01/88].

In respect to the existing voice and data services, the NGNs do not intend to duplicate all these services as they are, but to use their most important features (e.g. Call Forwarding, Multi Party Calling, Call Waiting) required by the existing regulations, and, furthermore, to introduce new features (e.g., personalized connectivity through individualized call admission control, and dynamic bandwidth-on-demand and bandwidth management).

The Presence/Telepresence Service [Salinas]

The presence service provides access to dynamic information (called presence information) about a user or an abstract entity such as a computer service. IETF has defined the presence information within the Internet models of Presence and Instant Messaging. Due to this fact, presence service may not be considered a standalone service but a complementary (and sometimes mandatory) service offered by many real-time (or quasi real-time) communication services (one-to-one or one-to-several). Nowadays, there are several applications using the presence service, such as telephone directories (yellow pages), Push-to-talk over Cellular (PoC) 2G and 3G networks, Internet instant messaging, etc. These applications can be classified as presence-enabled and presence-enhanced applications (Figure 10) or presence-based information channels, as well as person-to-person, content-to-person or corporate applications. Salinas has dealt with presence architectures in different environments and has studied how these could be integrated to enable network convergence.

On the other hand, telepresence allows a person to feel as if they were present, to give the appearance that they were present, or to have an effect, at a location other than their true location. The existing real-time multimedia services, which allow multiple parties (distributed around different geographical locations) to interact using voice, video, and/or data, constitute conventional telepresence services (e.g. videoconference service). These services assist users to converse with each other while displaying visual information, and to organize collaborative/groupworking schemes.

NGN telepresence services will enhance user experiences of realism while communicating. For example, on a mass basis, video conferencing could replace or augment the basic voice service (telephony). The aim of the unified presence service is to acquire and share information (from/to all members of a cooperating group) concerning the availability of all members for communication purposes at anytime, anyplace and on any device. The telepresence services constitute significant core network functionality, which is used in the design and development of selected education, telemedicine and other value-added applications by third part party providers. Further value can be added to telepresence applications by:

- Augmenting services handling additional information (e.g. attached files with jointly undertaken work during a telepresence meeting) that could allow telepresence to surpass real face-to-face communication.
- Adding three-dimensional aspects to the imaging capabilities enhancing the telepresence experience (e.g. business applications enabling users to sit down to a virtual meeting and hold real-time discussions while viewing other users on three-dimensional monitors).
- Creating virtual reality and tele-immersion environments, which apart from the obvious entertainment applications are important in telemedicine and teletraining (e.g. flight simulators to train pilots) or in assisting designers in industry.

The Home Management Services

Networking and intelligence in-home capabilities have deduced several service categories. One category concerns the management of home digital appliances and energy and security systems; another concerns access control

Figure 10. Presence-enhanced phone book [Nokia Oyj]

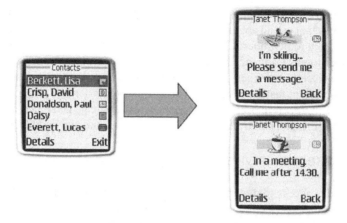

to the broadband Internet and content delivery services. Remote monitoring services allow the surveillance of rooms (e.g. parents watch their children while they are at work) and external home space. Last but not least, access services to the entertainment audio/video streams and media content compose one of the largest residential markets. The audio services handle mainly personalized channel-based distribution of radio station programmes with the same quality of service as current broadcast radio services. The video services are IPTV services handling multiple IPTV channels that are simultaneously accessed by different home users from various devices in the home. The video content access service handles access to IPTV–PVR/DVR–Home Network Storage to view a previously recorded movie; the movie may be recorded on a storage device (e.g. Set Top Box - STB) but it can be viewed on any TV or video display device that is connected to the home network. The media content access service handles access to the home media server that stores photos, videos and other family information. The media content can be accessed by different devices located in or outside the home.

CONCLUSION

With regard to their current status in the global telecommunications market, telecom carriers and operators are facing critical challenges in delivering a wide spectrum of services and applications to their customers. The appearance of NGNs has led to the introduction of new technologies and a multitude of new innovative multimedia applications. It is obvious that all players in the future telecommunications and multimedia market have acquired an efficient and powerful field for the integration and validation of new ideas and the creation of products of high added value.

This chapter has focused on the framework that is employed globally by the standardization organizations, as well as by the telecommunication operators and third party providers, for the creation, deployment and execution of services. It highlights the benefits of adopting NGNs with respect to existing ITU standards and those of other organizations.

In conclusion, the NGN service platforms facilitate the provisioning of advanced added value services, which span heterogeneous core/access fixed or mobile networks. Further work is needed by all players to familiarize themselves with the new telecommunications paradigm, and subsequently analyze migration strategies from existing architectures (such as IN) towards NGN platforms in greater depth.

REFERENCES

Adel Al-Hezmi (2003). 'Design and Implementation of an OSA/Parlaycompliant Interactive Multimedia Response Unit for Mobile All-IP Networks', Thesis, Technische Universität Berlin.

Bakker John-Luc, McGoogan Judith R., Opdyke William F., and Panken Frans (July–September 2000). 'Rapid Development and Delivery of Converged Services Using APIs', Bell Labs Technical Journal.

Fixed-Mobile Convergence Alliance (2006). 'FMCA Convergence Application Scenarios', Release 1.0.

Home Gateway Initiative (2006). 'Home Gateway Technical Requirements: Release 1', Version 1.0.

ITU-T Recommendation Y.120/Annex A (Feb 1999.). 'Global information infrastructure scenario methodology – Example of use'.

ITU-T Recommendation Y.2001 (Dec., 2004) 'General overview of NGN'.

ITU-T Recommendation Y.2011 (Oct., 2004). 'General principles and reference model for NGNs'.

ITU-T Recommendation Y.2012 (Sept., 2006). 'Functional requirements and architecture of the NGNs of Release-1', .

ITU-T Recommendation Y.2013 (Dec., 2006). 'Converged services framework functional requirements and architecture'.

Nana P., Mohapi S. and Hanrahan H (2002). 'Re-usable service components based on the Parlay API and TINA for the Next Generation Network', Proceedings of SATNAC.

Nana, P., Mohapi, S. and Hanrahan, H., (2001). 'An API based representation of TINA's Service Session Manager (SSM) for use in Next Generation Networks (NGNs).' Proceedings of SATNAC.

Nokia, Oyj (April 30, 2003). Presence Application Development Guide, Version 1.0, Forum Nokia.

Office of the Director of Telecommunications Regulation (ODTR) (2001). 'Next Generation Networks', Odtr01/88, Irish Life Centre, Dublin.

OKI, 'Next Generation Solutions.' Retrieved from http://www.oki.com/en/NGN/#difference

Parlay Group, 'Parlay and Next Generation Networks.' White Paper, May 2005.

Salinas, Arturo (2006). 'Advantages and disadvantages of using presence service', Helsinki University of Technology, TKK T-110.5190 Seminar on Internetworking, -05-4/5.

Wireless World Research Forum (2003). 'I-centric Communications – Basic Terminology', Version 1.0, Working Group 2: Service Architectures for the Wireless World, Whitepaper.

KEY TERMS

3GPP: 3rd Generation Partnership Project.

ADSL: Asymmetric Digital Subscriber Line.

ANSI: American National Standards Institute.

ANI: Applications Network Interface.

API: Application Programming Interface.

ARPU: Average Revenue per User.

CORBA: Common Object Request Broker Architecture.

DCOM: Distributed Component Object Model.

DPE: Distributed Processing Environment.

ETSI: European Telecommunications Standards Institute.

FMCA: Fixed-Mobile Convergence Alliance.

GII: Global Information Infrastructure.

GSM: Global System for Mobile communications.

HGI: Home Gateway Initiative.

IDL: Interface Definition Language.

IEEE: Institute of Electrical and Electronics Engineers.

IETF: Internet Engineering Task Force.

IN: Intelligent Network.

IP: Internet Protocol.

ISDN: Integrated Services Digital Network.

ITU: International Telecommunication Union.

NACF: Network Attachment Control Function.

NGN: Next Generation Networks.

NNI: Network Network Interface.

OSI: Open System Interconnection.

QoS: Quality of Service.

OSA: Open Service Access.

PRMC: Premium Charging.

PSTN: Public Switched Telephone Network.

RACF: Resource and Admission Control Functions.

SLA: Service Level Agreement.

SMS: Short Message Service.

SS7: Signaling System No.7.

SWB: Shared Whiteboarding.

TELCO: Telecommunications Operators.

UNI: User Network Interface.

UML: Unified Modelling Language.

UMTS: Universal Mobile Telecommunications System.

UPN: Universal Personal Number.

VDSL: Very high Speed Digital Subscriber Line.

VoD: Video on Demand.

VPN: Virtual Private Network.

WAP: Wireless Application Protocol.

WDM: Wavelength Division Multiplexing.

WiMax: Worldwide Interoperability of Microwave Access.

WWRF: Wireless Word Research Forum.

W3C: World Wide Web Consortium.

XML: Extensible Markup Language.

Chapter VIII
The Adoption of Service–Oriented Architecture (SOA) in Managing Next Generation Networks (NGNs)

Konstantinos S. Kotsopoulos
University of Bradford, UK

Pouwan Lei
University of Bradford, UK

Yim Fun Hu
University of Bradford, UK

ABSTRACT

Next Generation Networks (NGNs) will accommodate heterogeneous architectures that need to be managed in order to provide services with high QoS to the users. The complexity of NGNs will give new challenges to network operators and service providers. The aim of this chapter is to present the complexity and the problems in the NGN management plane and to introduce a new framework that will solve many problems that operators face today. This chapter is separated in two parts. The first part presents the management architecture for NGNs according to ITU-T M.3060 recommendation. The second part introduces the concept of the Service Oriented Architecture (SOA) for managing the Next Generation Networks.

INTRODUCTION

Over the last few years, many network operators have put into practise network upgrade plans to implement Next Generation Networks (NGNs). The desire for mobility and the rapid expansion of multimedia, digital traffic, and converged services are driving the need for networks that are packet-based, able to provide all kind of services that are available in any place, at any time, and on any device. NGNs are based on a new set of technologies that will transform the way that we communicate today, and will revolutionise the way that services will be delivered

Copyright © 2009, IGI Global, distributing in print or electronic forms without written permission of IGI Global is prohibited.

in the future. In NGNs, applications and services, such as voice data and video, are separated from the underlying transport and will be organized into packets and delivered on an integrated IP network. The network architectures, services, and traffic pattern in NGNs will radically differ from existing circuit-switched and IP-based networks. Furthermore, the need for global roaming across different networks (mobile, wireless cellular networks, satellite or fixed-LAN) couple with the increasing number of users and terminals require the redesign of the existing architectures right from the infrastructure physical layer to the top business process layer.

One of the most challenging tasks for network operators and service providers is the management of NGNs. NGNs will accommodate different architectures and will provide services with different QoS to end users. The International Telecommunication Union (ITU) is the leading standardisation body in the telecommunication sector. ITU-T M.3060 recommendation (ITU-T M.3060, 2006) proposes the management requirements for managing NGNs to support business processes and the management requirements of network operators and service providers to plan, provision, install, maintain, operate and administer NGN resources and services.

The NGN Architecture

The ITU defines the term Next-Generation Network (NGN) in Recommendation Y.2001 (ITU-T Y.2001, 2004) as a packet-based network able to provide telecommunication services and able to make use of multiple broadband, QoS-enabled transport technologies and in which service-related functions are independent from underlying transport-related technologies. It offers unrestricted access for users to different service providers. It supports generalized mobility, which will allow consistent and ubiquitous provision of services to users.

The NGN architecture, as it is recommended by the ITU, is divided into two independent functional stratums: the Service stratum and the Transport stratum as shown in Figure 1. By separating the Transport stratum from the Service stratum, the system provides flexibility in several aspects. One of the benefits is the installation independency. This means that the equipment used on stratum is independent of the equipment that is used on other stratum, allowing flexible deployment scenarios to meet the capacity requirements of each component. New services can be deployed to the service stratum (i.e. session-based services and non-session services) while the transport equipment remains unchanged. Another benefit of that separation is the migration independency. The transport elements can be upgraded or replaced with new technologies without changing service provisioning facilities. A common Transport stratum could be used by different retail sections of the same provider group. This modularity is a unique feature of the NGN architecture (Morita, 2007).

The NGN Service stratum provides functions that control and manage network services in order to enable end-users services and applications. The services can be voice, data or video applications. In more detail, these functions provide session-based services such as IP telephony, video chatting and videoconferencing and non session-based services such as video streaming and broadcasting. In addition, the Service stratum functions provide all the network functionality associated with existing Public Switched Telephone Network/Integrated Services Digital Network (PSTN/ISDN) services (Knightson, 2005). The Transport stratum provides functions that transfer data between peer entities and functions that control and manage transport resources in order to carry these data among terminating entities. The data could be user, control and/or management information data. In addition, the Transport stratum is responsible to provide end-to-end QoS, which is a desirable feature of the NGN. IP is recognized as the most promising transport technology for NGNs. Thus, the IP provides IP connectivity for end-user equipment outside a NGN, as well as controllers and enablers that reside on servers inside a NGN.

THE EVOLUTION OF THE MANAGEMENT PLANE

The layers of the NGN Framework are concerned with systems that provide communication between users or enhance applications such as transmission, switching, resource and service control, content hosting and distribution, and value-adding applications. These are control and user plane operations. The management plane encompasses all concerns with the operation of facilities and services, and business relationships with customers, partners and suppliers. It captures the behind-the-scenes operations that are required to enable service to be delivered.

Figure 1. The NGN architecture (ITU-T M.3060, 2006)

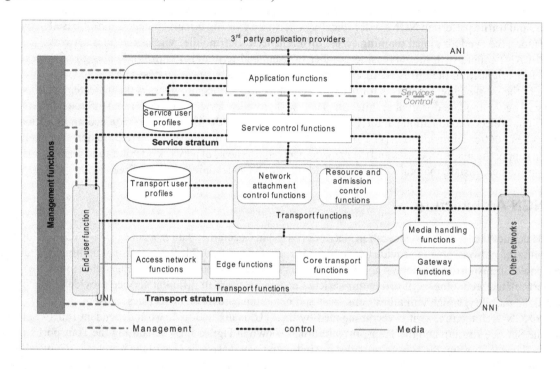

These operations are captured in two terms: Operations Support Systems (OSS) and Business Support Systems (BSS). The OSS provides a set of processes that a network operator requires to monitor, control and analyse the network. Moreover, the OSS includes processes that are required to manage and control faults, and perform functions that involve interactions with customers. Operations Support includes the historical term *network management* which means to control and manage the network elements. A Business Support System (BSS) provides processes that a service provider requires to conduct relationships with external stakeholders including customers, partners and suppliers. The boundary between Operations Support and Business Support is indistinct. Business Support functions are the customer-oriented subset of Operations Support. Business Support processes, for example, taking an order from a customer for a new service must flow into the Operations Support processes to configure the resources necessary to deliver the service. Support Systems are therefore often described as OSS/BSS systems (Hanrahan, 2007).

Network management has evolved from a simple manager-agent model to complex OSS and BSS systems (Hanrahan, 2007). Various standards are involved in this evolution. These models are: Open Systems Interconnection (OSI) network management model, the Internet management model, the Telecommunications Management Network (TMN), and the Telemanagement Forum (TMF) initiatives. The objectives and nature of management systems have changed during this evolution. Figure 2 illustrates three typical stages in the evolution of OSS/BSS.

At the first stage of the OSS/BSS, the OSI and IETF network management models utilize a simple manager-agent model, together with protocol-based communication between the manager and the managing entity, called agent. The network element that is managed is represented by a defined set of information that forms a part of a larger structure called the Management Information Base (MIB). This tight coupling of manager-agent architecture has the following problems (Zhang, 2006, Kreger, 2005):

- Due to the lack of cooperation between network management systems it is hard to implement advanced management functions.

Figure 2. Stages of OSS/BSS evolution (Hanrahan, 2007)

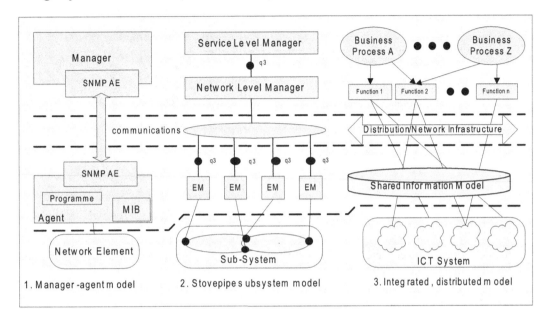

- Multiple network management interfaces bring heavy burden and apply more complexity to different network management systems.
- The integration of different network management systems to fulfill the constantly evolving business requirements is difficult to implement.

At the second stage, operators are required to manage sub-systems within their networks, for example SDH transmission systems, a set of TDM switches or a Signaling System No. 7 (SS7) network. The management systems are focused on elements and how they function as a system. For example, the SDH standards developed an architecture and information models that can represent end-to-end connections and their components. With a network-wide management view, the services that are offered on the network require management. Hence, managing systems require extra layers; for example a service layer to manage specific services and a network layer to co-ordinate the control of elements. Another example is the leased line service provisioning that would require allocation of SDH resources to support the required bandwidth. Such management systems are essentially stovepipe or silo systems with little co-operation between systems.

The third stage in Figure 2 illustrates several developments. Management information needs to be sharable across management applications, in order to support integrated management. The structure of managing systems allows the separation between the generic functions and the business processes they support. Functionality is modular and higher level processes orchestrate its use. The system has become large and inherently distributed and proper distribution support exists. The NGN management plane should be implemented as an integrated, distributed model allowing the separation between the generic functions and the business processes. In addition, the ITU-T M.3060 recommendation (ITU-T M.3060, 2006) specifies that the management plane should use the Service-Orientation paradigm.

NGN Management Architecture Overview

The ITU-T M.3060 recommendation (ITU-T M.3060, 2006) defines the framework for NGN management in terms of four basic architectural views: Business process view, Management functional view, Management Informational view and Management physical view. Each of these views gives a different perspective into the management plane. This management framework consists of functions that give the ability to manage the NGN in

Figure 3. NGN management architecture (ITU-T M.3060, 2006)

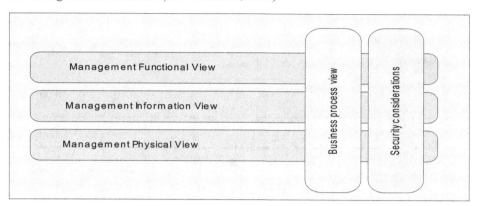

order to provide services with expected quality, security and reliability. Figure 3 illustrates the four architectural views of the NGN management architecture.

Business Process View

The business process view is based on the enhanced Telecom Operations Map (eTOM) model which is specified in the ITU-T recommendation M.3050 series (ITU-T M.3050, 2007). eTOM provides a reference framework for categorizing the service provider's business processes. The business processes are organized as multi-level matrix with horizontal (functional) and vertical (flat-through) process groupings. In the horizontal process groupings, process elements are grouped according to reference accomplished functionalities (e.g. Market and Product and Customer management, Service management, etc.) and in vertical process groupings, process elements are grouped within End-To-End processes (e.g. Fulfilment, Assurance, etc.) accomplished by the Service Provider enterprise. In addition, it provides basic mappings between business processes and management function sets. Figure 4 illustrates the eTOM business process framework.

Management Functional view

The functional view of the NGN management is a structural and generic framework of the management functionality. The functional view provides the functions that need to be achieved in the management implementation. The management functional view consists of management functions. A management function is the smallest part of a business process or management service as perceived by the user of the process or service (ITU-T M.3060, 2006). In Figure 5 the different types of management function block can be seen.

- **Operations Systems Function block (OSF).** Operations Systems Function (OSF) block represents all the processes that are associated with the management of the NGN. The purpose of management in this context is to monitor/coordinate and/or control the resources to be provided by the network in order to meet the quality objectives. The OSF gets the management information, such as alarm status of the managed entity, directing the managed entities to take appropriate corrective functions (e.g. requesting a performance test), and performing the required information processing activities on the retrieved information (e.g. correlating alarms in order to determine the cause). Due to the separation of the NGN Service stratum from the NGN Transport stratum (ITU-T Y.2011, 2004), the OSF is decomposed into service functions, transport functions and common functions. In more detail, the OSF is decomposed into the Service Management Function (SMF), Service Resource Management Function (SRMF) and Transport Resource Management Function (TRMF). The TRMF can be further decomposed into Transport Element Management Function (TEMF) and

Figure 4. eTOM Business process framework (ITU-T M.3050, 2007)

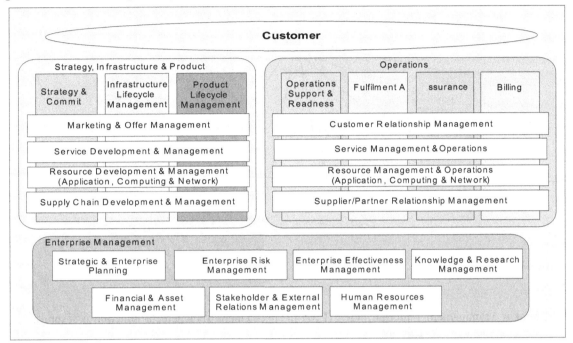

Transport Network Management Function (TNMF). Similarly the SRMF can be further decomposed into Service Element Management Function (SEMF) and Service Network Management Function (SNMF).

- **Service Management Function block (SMF).** The SMF provides service instance management (ITU-T M.3060, 2006). More specifically, it is dedicated to provide management of service life cycles, management of contractual aspects of the Service Level Agreements (SLAs), management associated with customers and their subscribed service profiles. In addition, it provides management of service and network resources necessary for service enabling activation including connectivity, bandwidth and QoS requirements.
- **Service Resource Management Function block (SRMF).** The SRMF provides logical service infrastructure management including network resources and mechanisms for supporting subscription and controlling access to services, managing service applications and data. Moreover, it provides rooting and billing services to end users, actions of the end-user on their profiles, subscriber data and user profile database.
- **Transport Resource Management Function block (TRMF).** TRMF is a functional block that provides the realization of the requested connectivity, network topology, geographical information and logical addresses. Furthermore, TRMF provides management of the network resources (e.g., admission control configuration, QoS mechanisms), provision of network to service correlation and connectivity across multiple networks.
- **Network Management Function block (NMF).** The Network Management Function block manages a network by coordinating activity across the network and supports the network demands made by the resource management function. NMF is responsible for the technical performance of the network. It can identify the resources that are available in the network, how they are organized and geographically allocated and how they can be controlled.
  The NMF has five principal roles:
  - control and coordinate the network view of all network elements
  - provision, modify network capabilities for the support of service to customers
  - maintain the statistical and log data about the network and interact with the resource management
  - Manage the relationships (e.g., connectivity) between NEFs
  - Maintaining the network capabilities

Figure 5. Management function blocks (ITU-T M.3060, 2006)

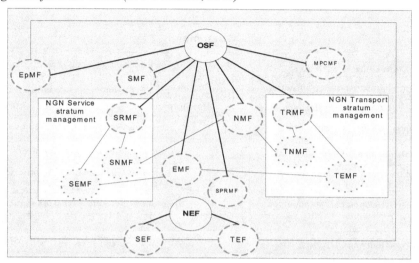

- **Element Management Function block (EMF).** The Element Management Function is responsible for managing the network elements.
  The EMF has three principal roles:
  - ○ Maintain statistical, log and other data concerning the control of the elements
  - ○ Control and coordinate a subset of network elements on an individual NEF basis
  - ○ Control and coordinate a subset of network elements on collective basis

  If the EMF is located in the Service stratum of the NGN then it is called Service Element Management Function (SEMF), whereas if it is located in the Transport stratum is called Transport Element Management Function (TEMF).

- **Supplier/Partner Relationship Management Function block (SPRMF).** The SPRMF provides the communication with the suppliers and partners for importing external transport or service resources for use by the enterprise. SPRMF is not concerned with the management of the NGN strata directly.
- **Market, Product and Customer Management Function block (MPCMF).** The MPCMF is responsible for creating, managing, and maintaining service provider products. It includes operational processes such as management of the customer interface, ordering, problem handling, SLA management and billing.
- **Enterprise Management Function block (EpMF).** The EpMF is a function block that is responsible for the basic business processes that are essential to run and manage any business. These processes contain the security and fraud management, disaster recovery, quality management and IT planning and architecture.
- **Network Element Function block (NEF), Service Element Function block (SEF) and Transport Element Function block (TEF).** The SEF provides telecommunication and support functions which are required by the Service stratum of the NGN to be managed, whilst the TEF provides the same functions for managing the Transport stratum. The Network Element Function block is a functional block with properties of both an SEF and TEF.

Management Layers within the Management Functionality

Management of the NGNs is very complex to implement. It is easier to deal with this complexity by decomposing the management functionality into logical layers. The Logical Layer Architecture (LLA) organizes the functions

Figure 6. NGN management logical architecture (ITU-T M.3060, 2006)

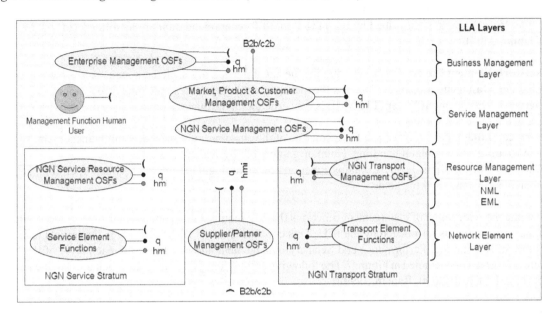

into groups which are called logical layers. Each layer deals with particular aspects of management functions. Figure 6 illustrates the logical layer architecture.

The management functionality is grouped into the following logical layers:

- **Enterprise management:** Enterprise management layer is responsible for the basic processes and functions that are required for managing any large business.
- **Market, product, and customer management:** The main purpose of this layer is to provide a common functionality for order management of Service Provider's products and to administer and mange functionality that uses information from the Service Management Layer. In addition, it manages the instances of Product Objects during their whole lifecycle and handles the dialog with customers through a well-defined business interface.
- **NGN service management:** This layer is responsible for managing the delivery and assurance of services to end-users according to the customer's expectation.
- Resource Management: This layer deals with the management of the logical service and transport infrastructures. The Resource Management is divided into two categories:
  - **Service resource management:** Deals with the management of the NGN Service stratum.
  - **Transport resource management:** Deals with the management of the NGN Transport stratum.
- **Service and transport element management:** A specialization of Network Element Function (NEF) representing the telecommunication service and transport functions
- **Supplier and partner relationship management:** Deals with the supplier's and partner's communication for importing external transport or service resources that the enterprise will use.

Management Hierarchy Reference Model

In a broader categorization, the management logical architecture could be separated into five hierarchical layers as it is described in the ITU-T M.3010 recommendation (ITU-T M.3010, 2000). The ITU-T M.3010 gives a well established categorization of management layers. These layers range from lower layers that involve managing details of individual pieces of network equipment, to higher layers that are closer to the running of the business that the network supports. Figure 7 illustrates these layers in a pyramid form and can be linked together with the management logical layer architecture of the NGN.

The five logical layers as described by the ITU-T M.3010 recommendation are as follows (ITU-T M.3010, 2000; Clemm, 2007):

- **Network Element Layer:** This layer contains the agent portion of the element manager.
- **Element Management Layer:** Contains the management entity for a single managed element.
- **Network Management Layer**: The NML is concerned with the management of an entire network consisting of a number of elements.
- **Service Management Layer:** The SML consists of the customer interface, account management, service provisioning and complaint handling. No management of physical entities takes place.
- **Business Management layer:** Contains functions for planning, agreements between operators, setting, implementing and tracking goals.

To handle the wide range of management functions that are required in an operational support environment, a second categorization is introduced by the ITU. This concept is called FCAPS which is the initials for Fault, Configuration, Accounting, Performance and Security management and is deployed in each layer of the NGN management framework depicted in Figure 7. The following subsection gives a detailed explanation of the FCAPS concept (ITU-T M.3010, 2000; Raman, 1999):

Fault Management

Fault management functional area addresses ongoing maintenance functions when the network is configured and services are offered to the customers. These functions allow a management system to monitor for failure events and requests tests to be performed in order to isolate these faults. The functions of fault management can be seen as follows:

- **Reliability, availability, and survivability (RAS):** The reliability, availability, and survivability group includes functions such as service, network, and network element outage reporting.
- **Alarm surveillance:** Alarm surveillance functions provide network fault event analysis, alarm reporting, alarm correlation. In addition, it provides filtering and Failure event detection and reporting.

Figure 7. The logical layers redefined with FCAPS

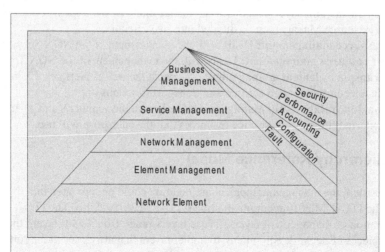

- **Fault localization:** Fault localization functions take action when the fault has been detected. Those functions include verification of parameters and connectivity. Fault localization at the network and network element levels, and Running diagnostics for gathering additional information in order to determine where the fault has been occurred.
- **Fault correction:** Fault correction functions are performed in order to provide scheduling and dispatch administration of repair forces, management of repair process, network element fault correction and automatic restoration. Testing functions can be performed in two ways: A management system may report a specific test to be performed and the network element reports the results. With the second way, access to test or monitor points are requested by the management system. Test tones are applied and the analysis of the data is performed by the management system.
- **Testing:** The testing functions include circuit selection, test correlation and fault location, test access configuration, test circuit configuration and test access path management.
- **Trouble administration:** Trouble administration used in order to exchange trouble reports, monitoring the status of the trouble reports. The functions include trouble report status change notification trouble report policy, trouble information query and trouble ticket administration.

Performance Management

Performance management is used in order to monitor the performance of the entire network. The collected data can be used to correct potential degradation of the resources so that the quality of service promised to the customer can be maintained. The function sets that provide performance management are listed as follows:

- **Performance quality assurance:** Is used by the service provider in order to establish the quality measures. The function sets provide QoS performance goal setting, subscriber service quality criteria and network performance assessment.
- **Performance monitoring:** For collecting data on monitored parameters such as severely error seconds, unavailable time, number of retransmitted packets and compare them against predefined thresholds. By continuously monitoring these parameters, degradation in the performance of the resources can be identified and corrected as a result preventing service outages. The function sets in the performance monitoring include: data aggregation and trending, traffic status, traffic performance monitoring and performance monitoring data accumulation.
- **Performance control:** These functional sets are responsible for controlling the routing traffic and setting thresholds for the parameters for which data are being collected.
- **Performance analysis:** Is used in order to analyse the data, characterize the performance of the entity and determine the changes and enhancements required. These activities are related to the business level abstraction. For example, traffic forecasting, traffic exception analysis, and network performance characterization.

Configuration Management

Configuration management functions are used for planning the network so that it can meet the desired capacity measures, to install the network equipments, to provisioning them in setting up circuits. The configuration's management categorization can be seen as follows:

- **Network planning and engineering:** Are functions that are involved with activities such as demand forecasting, product line budget, routing design and building the infrastructure. Examples of these functions are: scheduling and dispatch administration of the installation force function set, loading software into the network entities and software administration function set. Many of these functions support installing telecommunication equipments (hardware and software) that form the network.
- **Installation:** Installation functions are used in order to perform testing before providing it to the customer.

- **Service planning and negotiation:** These functions are focused on the business level functions such as service feature definition function set, external relations (legal, regulators, stockholders, public relations) and customer need identification.
- **Provisioning:** Provisioning functions include access route determination, leased circuit route determination, network connection management, inter-exchange circuit design and network element configuration.
- **Status and control:** This function group includes functions such as priority service policy, network element status and control, transport network status and notification of state changes by the network elements.

Accounting Management

The accounting management is responsible for collecting the information that concern the usage of the services and billing. The function groups can be seen as follows:

- **Usage measurement:** The usage measurement allows a management system to set up various triggers in order to collect the usage of various resources providing the service. In addition it retrieves the collected information either as individual usage record or as summarized on the basis of a customer/service/product. The usage measurement has similarities with the data collection of the performance monitoring. The main difference is that in performance monitoring the triggers are time based (i.e. the data are collected every 10 minutes) whereas in usage measurement the triggers can be both time based and event based. Some of the functions that are included in the usage measurements are: usage aggregation, usage surveillance, administration of usage data collection, network usage correlation, usage generation and usage validation.
- **Tariffing/pricing:** Tariffing/Pricing functions addresses policies for tariffing, assignment of charges for the various services.
- **Collections and finance:** The collection and finance category consist of functions that administer customer accounts, inform customers of balances, payment dates, and receiving payments.
- **Enterprise control:** These functions are in general applicable for any enterprise. These functions are involved with activities that the network and service providers organizations perform to manage the finances of the organization.

Security Management

The aim of security management is to provide functions in order to control access to network resources according to some well-defined policy so that unauthorized personnel cannot access the network (Clemm, 2007). The functions of security management areas are as follows:

- **Prevention:** Prevention functions define various measures to prevent intrusions. For example physical access security, personnel risk analysis and security screening. Intrusions may still occur even with the best prevention.
- **Detection:** Detection functions are required in order to investigate breach of security. These functions include customer usage pattern analysis, investigation of theft of services and network security alarm.
- **Containment and recovery:** Containment and recovery functions identify how to limit the damage incurred as well as to recover from them. Examples of these functions are: service intrusion recovery, severing external connections, administration of network revocation list and protected storage of business data.
- **Security administration:** These functions are used in order to set policies for access to management information about the network, analyse audit trails and alarms, and plan security measures. In addition, these functions are used to administer parameters to support security services; for example authentication, access permission and encryption.

Example of Using the FCAPS Functional Sets

A generic scenario is provided in order to show how the management functions can be applied. This scenario is an information flow diagram for network traffic control, which describes how a number of fully automated, generic management roles work together in an integrated fashion to perform a business purpose. The purpose of this scenario, depicted in Figure 8, is to make rapid changes in network routing patterns in order to minimize the loss of traffic in the event of an unexpected loss of switching or transport capacity or unusual changes in the amount or distribution of offered load (ITU-T M.3400, 2000). The first interaction (interaction 1) is used to set up the network traffic control process. A scenario triggered by an extraordinary situation starts with the report of an overload by interaction 2. The arrows with the numbers show the sequence of the interaction in the flow diagram. The interactions in this scenario use the FCAPS management functional sets. More specifically this network traffic control scenario uses the Performance, Configuration and Fault management functions in order to be implemented.

Management Informational View

The management of a telecommunications environment is an information processing application. In order to effectively manage complex networks and support network operator/service provider business processes, it is necessary to exchange management information between management applications, implemented in multiple managing, and managed systems. Thus, telecommunication management is a distributed application. The Management Informational view is an object-oriented or service-oriented approach which allows the Open Systems Interconnection management principles to be applied in the NGN context. A network information model is a uniform, consistent and rigorous method for describing the resources in a network, including their attribute types, events, actions and behaviors. The network information model is generic to ensure that a wide range of network resources can be modeled. ITU-T Recommendation M.3100 (ITU-T M.3100, 2005) defines a generic network information model for TMN, following the approach of the OSI management model. Physical resources are represented by managed objects, registered on appropriate branches of the object identifier tree. Definitions are inherited from the OSI management information definitions.

Figure 8. Network Traffic control

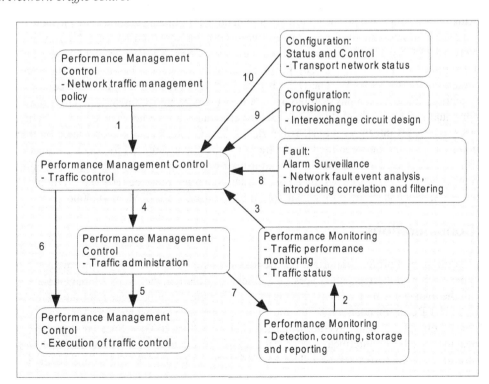

Figure 9. NGN Physical view (ITU-T M.3060, 2006)

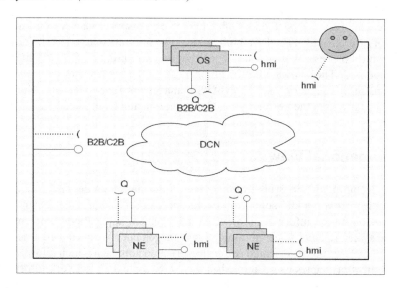

Management Physical View

The management physical view, as defined by the ITU-T M.3060 (ITU-T M.3060, 2006), consists of physical blocks and communication interfaces. A physical block is an architectural concept representing a realization of one or more function blocks. Actually, a physical block can be a hardware system, a software application, or a combination of the two. A communication interface is an architectural concept enabling interoperable interconnection at reference points between physical blocks by realizing the reference points.

Figure 9 illustrates a simplified physical view for a management implementation. The physical blocks in the management physical view contain the Operations Systems (OS), the Network Elements (NE) and the Data Communication Network (DCN). The OS is a system that performs OSFs. The NE consists of telecommunication equipment and support equipment or any item or groups of items considered belonging to the telecommunications environment that performs NEFs. The DCN is a support service that provides the capability to establish paths for information flow between physical blocks in a management environment. The DCN may consist of a number of individual sub-networks of different types, interconnected together. The communication interfaces are: Q interfaces, B2B/C2B interfaces and HMI interfaces. The Q interface is characterized by that portion of the information model shared between the OS and those management elements to which it directly interfaces. The B2B/C2B interface is used to interconnect two administrative domains or to interconnect a compliant environment with other networks or systems. Finally, the Human Machine Interface (HMI) is an interface applied at HMI reference point, which is exposed for consumption by the users (ITU-T M.3060, 2006).

Security Considerations

Security has the mission to protect important business assets against different types of threats. Assets can be of different types such as buildings, employees, machines, information, etc. NGN Management is specifically concerned with the management of security aspects of the NGN and with the security of the NGN Management infrastructure. ITU-T Recommendations X.805 and M.3016.x series are considered for securing the NGN management infrastructure. ITU-T X.805 recommendation (ITU-T X.805, 2003) defines concepts and components intended to provide reusable countermeasures across multiple layers of the infrastructure, including transport and service stratum. The M.3016.x series (ITU-T M.3016.0, 2005) focuses on end-to-end security, both in the case where management traffic is separate from user traffic and when they are mixed together. To overcome the complexity of securing the NGN infrastructure, including its management plane, there is a need to automate the application of various security services, mechanisms, and tools by using operation systems to automate the process.

SERVICE-ORIENTED ARCHITECTURE (SOA)

The ITU-T Recommendation M.3060 specifies the Service-Oriented Architecture (SOA) as a software architecture of services, policies, practices and frameworks in which components can be reused and repurposed rapidly in order to achieve shared and new functionality. This enables rapid and economical implementation in response to new requirements, ensuring that services respond to perceived user needs (ITU-T M.3060, 2006; Erl, 2004). SOA is an ideal paradigm to integrate heterogeneous environments due to the loose coupling encouraged by services. The heterogeneity in an environment refers to the incompatibility that exists in term of hardware, interfaces, operating systems, communication protocols, format and data (Hegering, 1999). In addition, in an SOA environment, individual units of logic can exist autonomously but in a way that they are not isolated from each other. Units of logic are still required to follow a set of principles that allow them to evolve independently, whilst still maintaining a sufficient amount of commonality and standardization. From the SOA perspective, these units of logic are known as services. One of the architectural principles behind the management architecture for NGNs is that of being a Service-Oriented Architecture (SOA), (ITU-T M.3060, 2006; Erl, 2006).

The most general principles of the term 'service' in SOA are:

- Service is a view of a resource (e.g., a software asset, business, a hard disk), anything that provides some capability. Implementation details are hidden behind the service interface.
- The communication among services is based on messages. The structure of the message and the schema, or form, of its contents is defined by the interface.
- Services are stateless. This means that all the information needed by a service to perform its function is encapsulated in the messages used to communicate with it.

Services discover and communicate with each other using the publish, find, bind (Erl, 2006) paradigm. A service publishes its interface definition to the network, a service consumer finds the definition and by using the information in the definition, is able to bind (resolve the address and send messages), to the service. An important aspect of SOA is the just-in-time integration of applications facilitated by these three operations. In other words, the interface definition, which describes the form of messaging combined with facilities for publishing and discovering it, enables late-binding between entities to create dynamic aggregations of services.

The Evolution of Systems Architecture

The evolution of SOA is represented in the following figure (Figure 10). Before 1980 the architectural platforms consisted monolithic mainframe systems that empowered organizations with appropriate computational resources. These environments had bulky mainframe back-ends and they were serving thin clients. Until the mid 90's the platforms were based on the two-tier client-server architecture. This concept introduced the fat client who had intelligence, thus allowed the logic and the processing duties to be performed on individual workstations. A new architecture that introduced in the mid 90's, was the multi-tier client-server architecture. This network centric architecture broke the monolithic client executable into components. The distributed application logic among multiple components (some residing on the client others on servers) reduced the deployment problems by centralizing a greater amount of the logic on servers. Additionally, the Remote Procedure Call (RPC) technology was introduced, such as CORBA and DCOM which allowed for remote communication between components residing on the client workstations and servers. The Service Oriented Architecture is not a new concept (Erl, 2004). It took all best practices from previous architectures and is the next evolutionary step in computing environment. SOA has gained popularity due to the wide use of web services. It is the first step to the realization of dynamically reconfigurable architectures.

Figure 10. The evolution of systems architecture

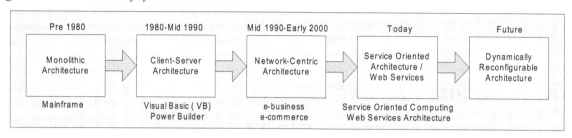

Principles of SOA

There are no official sets of service-orientation principles, but there are common principles mostly related to service orientation (Erl, 2006). These common principles are related to reuse, service contract, loose coupling, service abstraction, composability, autonomy, statelessness and discoverability. In more detail:

Service reusability: Services are designed in order to provide potential reuse. Service-orientation encourages reuse in all services, even if there is no immediate requirement for reuse. This principle facilitates all form of reuse, including inter-application interoperability, composition, and the creation of utility services. Due to the fact that a service is a collection of related operations, it is thus the logic encapsulated by the individual operations that must be considered reusable in order to warrant representation as a reusable service.

Services are sharing a formal contract: In order to enable services interact with each other; they need to share a formal contract that describes each service and defines the terms of information exchange. Services adhere to a communication agreement, as defined collectively by one or more service description documents. These contracts give a formal definition of:

- The service endpoint
- Each service operation
- Rules and characteristics of the service and its operations
- Every input and output messages supported by each operation

Services are loosely coupled: Services need to be designed in a way that they would be able to interact with each other without the tight and cross-service dependencies. A service obtains knowledge of another service while still remains independent of that service.

Services represent an abstraction of the underlying logic: Service hides its logic from the "outside world" and the only part that is visible is what it is exposed via the service contract. This abstraction allows services to act as black boxes, hiding the underlying logic.

Services are composable: A collection of services could form other services. A service can represent any range of logic from various types of sources, including other services. As a result the logic can be represented at different levels of granularity and could promote the creation of abstraction layers as well as reusability.

Services are autonomous: A service should have a high level of control over its underlying runtime environment. It should be managed within its own environment, and be able to support a high degree of reliability and performance.

Services are stateless: Services should minimize resource consumption by deferring the management of state information, when necessary. A service that maintains state it is also likely to reduce reusability, as it is then likely to impose a certain process or functional dependency on the service.

Services are discoverable: A service should allow its underlying logic to be discovered, accessed and understood by new potential service requestors. Thus, services need to be naturally discoverable.

SOA Underlying Technologies

The technology that enables service-oriented implementations is the Web Services technology. Web services are interfaces describing a collection of operations that can access the network through standardized XML messages. Web services use a standard, formal XML notion (its service description) which covers all the details needed to interact with the service, including transport protocols, message formats and location. Services can be independent from the software or hardware platform on which they are implemented and they are independent from the programming language in which they are written. This happens due to the fact that the interface hides the implementation details of the service. Hiding the implementation details allow Web Services-based to be loosely coupled, with cross-technology implementations. Web Services perform a specific task or a set of tasks/operations. They can be used independently or with other Web Services to complete a business transaction or a complex aggregation (Kreger, 2001). Web Services provide a way of communication among applications running on different operating systems, written in different programming languages and using different technologies whilst using the internet as their transport.

The Web Service Model

The basic Web Service model is based on interactions among three roles:

- Service provider
- Service registry
- Service requestor

The Web Services involve three different interactions. Those interactions using the publish, find, and bind paradigm. The service provider hosts a network-accessible software module (an implementation of a Web service). The service provider publishes the service description (WSDL) for the Web service to a service registry (UDDI). The service requestor retrieves the service description by using the find operation from the service registry. Then it uses this service description in order to interact with the service provider by using the bind operation. Due to the fact that the roles of the service provider and the service requestor are logical constructs, service can display characteristics of both. Figure 11 demonstrates the basic Web service model and the interaction between its components (Gottschalk, 2002).

Roles and Operations in Web Services Architecture

- **Service provider:** The Service provider is the platform that hosts access to the service, and the applications that deliver the service capabilities. Furthermore, the service provider is the owner of the service.
- **Service requestor:** The service requestor is the application that invokes and initiates an interaction with a service. Its role can be played by a browser driven by a person or a program without a user interface (i.e. another Web service). From a business point of view, the service requestor is the business that requires certain functions to be satisfied.
- **Service registry:** It is a searchable registry that facilitates the Service providers to publish their service descriptions. The Service requestors are able to discover services by obtaining binding information (in service descriptions) provided by the registry. For service requestors that are statically bound, the service registry is optional, due to the fact that service provider can send the service description directly to service requestors. Similarly, a service description (WSDL) can be obtained by service requestors from other sources except for a service registry (i.e., a FTP site, local file, Advertisement and Discovery of Services (ADS) or a Web site).

Figure 11. Find, bind and execute paradigm

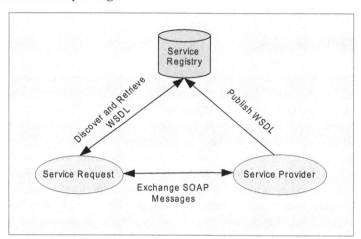

There are three behaviors that must take place in order an application to take advantage of Web Services. These behaviors are (Kreger, 2001):

- **Publish:** A service description, in order to be accessible to the service requestor needs to be published. The place that service requestor is published can vary depending on the application's requirements.
- **Find:** The service requestor retrieves a service description directly or queries the service registry for the type of service required. The find operation can be involved in two different lifecycle stages for the service requestor: the first stage of the find operation's involvement is at the design time in order to retrieve the service's interface description for program development, and the second stage is at runtime in order to retrieve the service's binding and location description for invocation.
- **Bind:** Finally, a service needs to be invoked. Using the bind operation, the service requestor initiates an interaction with the service at runtime using the binding details in the service description to locate, contact and invoke the service.

Web Services Technologies

The following section will introduce the technologies of Web Services. XML, SOAP, WSDL and UDDI are the technologies that allow the creation of Web Services and are the underlying technologies that will enable the Service-Orientated implementations.

Extensible Markup Language (XML)

The XML is a World Wide Web Consortium's (W3C) recommended (W3C XML, 2006) general-purpose, simple, flexible and text format markup language for creating special-purpose markup languages, able to describe many different kinds of data. To put it another way, XML is a method of exchanging information between applications in documents that simultaneously identifies the data fields and contains the data in those fields. XML documents have been widespread accepted due to their ability to define documents or schemas for application domains. The easy readability of XML documents by humans has also aided acceptance. The main purpose of XML is to facilitate data sharing across different systems, particularly systems that are connected via the Internet. Languages that are based on XML (i.e., RDF/XML, SVG, RSS, XHTML and Atom) are defined in a formal way, enabling programs to modify and validate documents in these languages without previous knowledge of their particular form.

Simple Object Access Protocol (SOAP)

The communication between services in the SOA concept is message-based, and it should be standardized so that all services can use the same format and transport protocol. SOAP is the standard transport protocol for messages processed by Web services (Bih, 2005). This protocol exchanges XML-based messages over a computer network, normally using HTTP. SOAP is an XML-based protocol that exchange information in a decentralized, distributed environment. It consists of three parts:

- **Envelope:** It defines the framework for describing a message contains and how to process it
- **A set of encoding rules:** The encoding rules are used in order to express the instances of application-defined data types
- A convention for representing Remote Procedure Calls (RPC) and responses.

SOAP forms the foundation layer of the Web services stack, providing a basic messaging framework that abstract layers can build on. Remote Procedure Call (RPC) is the most common type of messaging patterns in SOAP, where the network node A (i.e., client) sends a request message to the network node B (i.e., server), and the network node B immediately sends a response message to the network node A. From a network transport perspective, using the SOAP over HTTP gives the ability to the SOAP messages not to filtered by the network firewalls whereas, using other distributed protocols like DCOM or GIOP/IIOP are normally filtered by firewalls (W3C SOAP, 2007).

Web Services Description Language (WSDL)

WSDL is one of the essential parts of the SOA framework for service description. The service description provides the key ingredient to establishing a consistently loosely coupled form of communication between services implemented as Web Services. For this purpose, description documents are required to accompany any service wanting to act as an ultimate receiver. The primary service description document is the WSDL definition. WSDL is an XML-based format that describes network services as a set of endpoints operating on messages containing either procedure-oriented or document-oriented information. The messages and operations are described abstractly, and then bound to a concrete network protocol and message format to define an endpoint. Related concrete endpoints are combined into abstract endpoints (services). WSDL is extensible to allow description of endpoints and their messages regardless of the message formats or network protocols are used to communicate. The typical bindings with WSDL are SOAP, HTTP GET/POST, and MIME (W3C WSDL, 2001).

Universal Description, Discovery and Integration (UDDI)

UDDI is a registry, where Web services can be registered and it describes the programming interfaces for publishing, retrieving, and managing information about services. Actually, UDDI itself consists of Web services. The UDDI specification identifies services that support the description and discovers:

- The Web services they make available
- Businesses, organizations, and other Web services providers
- Technical interfaces that be used to access and manage those services.

UDDI is based on established industry standards, like HTTP, XML, XML Schema (XSD), SOAP and WSDL (OASIS, 2004).

SOA in Managing the NGNs

Next Generation Network is a very dynamic environment. Services will continuously need to be activated and deactivated in the service stratum. Devices will be added, removed and change configuration in the Transport stratum; therefore, managing NGN will be a challenging task. True NGN might be considered as one network, but it is by far the most complex of all. Its management has to deal with multiple vendors, multiple applications, multiple physical devices from data and voice networks, multiple databases, and multiple service layers (infrastructure plane, control plane, service plane). Any management solution for NGN must be architected in a way that it can scale to manage the current and future NGNs. This scalability challenge is a requirement for flexibility so that the solution can be rapidly adapted to support new services and technologies in the future without the need for long term and complex upgrades. SOA can improve the scalability factor. Furthermore, it can provide more adaptable solutions for dynamic scaling up and offers consistent performance. SOA-based architecture facilitates loose coupling and "plugability" of new interfaces. As a result, it provides extensibility and flexibility. By adopting the SOA philosophy, the vital management operations can be applied as services (i.e retrieving the status of a device, controlling it, changing its configuration settings and provisioning). Services are software components with formally defined, message-based, request-response interfaces and the logic behind those interfaces is hidden from the users. By using the SOA approach, programming an agent or a management application is a much easier job, due to the fact that services are highly reusable and management functionality is exposed via consistent interfaces. A service may provide both simple and complex functionality. For instance, a simple service could return the temperature settings or the fan speed of a device. A complex service could perform complex diagnostics requiring the correlation of information from multiple sensors and internal event logs. Services are able to cooperate with each other, and more sophisticated services can be formed by layering atop lower-level services. For example, by choosing appropriate services from a services library, a vendor can provide management agents for an entire range of routers, from low-end to high-end. SOA services can build management applications, proxy agents and management agents. The type of client application that must be used is not dictated by SOA; therefore, Web, Graphical User Interface (GUI), or fully automated applications requiring no human involvement can be used. These client applications usually invoke services remotely via management protocols. Advanced SOA implementations offer excessive flexibility and automation. Agents can load new services and protocol adapters without the need to shut down or reboot computers. Figure 12 shows an example of using the SOA to converge the heterogeneity of the different entities in a management system. All the FCAPS functionalities as well as the different OSS could be implemented as one OSS providing a fully integrated customer oriented service control.

Challenges of Managing NGN Using SOA

The role of SOA in the NGN management plane is to break the management architecture into services. The management functionality will be described and exposed as services. These services can then be composed in a loosely-coupled form which will contain management functionality. Moreover, the services will be well-defined, self-contained resources and will be using open standard interfaces to communicate with each other across the heterogeneous network. In order to implement a robust and agile network management system for NGNs the design of the functional entities will be the most critical part of this implementation. Another challenging factor for the SOA adoption is the complexity of managing the information that is exchanged between services. Due to the fact that the management architecture will consist of multiple services, where services will exchange messages in order to perform specific tasks, the management system will generate many unnecessary messages. As a result, managing and providing information on how services are interacting with each other efficiently is a very complicate task.

CONCLUSION

NGNs essentially deliver convergence between the traditional world of public switched telephone networks, and the new world of data networks. One of the most critical factors that will be a challenge for network operators and service providers is the Management of the NGNs. The aim of NGN Management plane is to facilitate the effective interconnection between various types of Operations Systems (OSs) and NGN resources for the exchange of management information, using an agreed architecture with standardized interfaces including protocols and messages. One of the architectural principles behind the management architecture for NGNs is being Service-Oriented.

Figure 12. Network and Service management implementation

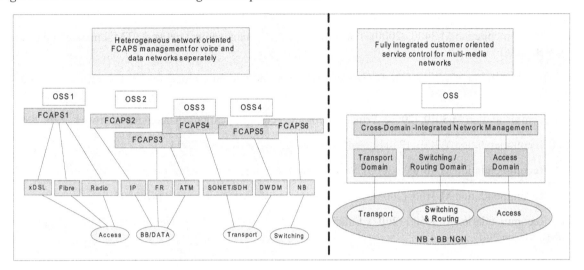

This chapter has presented the Management architecture for NGNs according to the ITU-T M.3060 recommendation. In addition, the four basic architectural views were described, giving more emphasis on the functional architectural view of the management plane. Moreover, in this chapter, the Service Oriented Architecture concept was introduced as well as the Web Service paradigm, in order to illustrate the benefits of that technology, which is the enabler of the SOA philosophy. Architectures using the Service-Orientation principles could deliver agility, scalability, reusability, flexibility and automation in distributed heterogeneous environments. SOA uses open standard principles and facilitates loose coupling and "plugability" of new interfaces. By adopting the SOA philosophy for the NGN management plane many problems that the network operators and service providers face today will be solved.

REFERENCES

Bih, J. (2005) Deploy XML-based network management approach, Potentials IEEE, Volume 24, Issue 4, Oct.-Nov. 2005 Pages: 26 – 31.

Clemm, A., (2007). Network Management Fundamentals: A guide to understanding how network management technology really works, Cisco Press, 2007.

Erl, T. (2004). Service-Oriented Architecture: A Field Guide to Integrating XML and Web Services, Prentice Hall, 2004.

Erl, T., (2006). Service-Oriented Architecture: Concepts, Technology, and Design, Prentice Hall, 2006.

Gottschalk, K., Graham, S., Kreger, H., Snell, J. (2002). Introduction to Web Services Architecture, IBM Systems Journal, Vol41, No2, 2002.

Hanrahan, H. (2007). Network Convergence: Services, Applications, Transport and Operation Support, Willey & Sons, ltd, 2007.

Hegering, HG, Abeck, S., Neumair, B. (1999). Integrated Management of Networked Systems: Concepts, Architectures, and Their Operational Application. Morgan Kaufmann, 1999.

ITU-T Recommendation M.3060/Y.2401, (2006). Principles for the Management of Next Generation Networks, March 2006.

ITU-T Recommendation M.3400, (2000). Telecommunications management network: TMN management functions, Feb. 2000.

ITU-T Recommendation Y.2011, (2004). General principles and reference model for Next Generation Networks, Oct. 2004.

ITU Recommendation M.3010, (2000). Principles for a telecommunications management network, Feb. 2000.

ITU-T Recommendation Y.2001, (2004). General overview of NGN, Dec. 2004.

ITU-T Recommendation M.3016.0. (2005). Security for the management plane: Overview, May 2005.

ITU-T Recommendation M.3100. (2005). Generic network information model, April 2005.

ITU-T Recommendation M.3050.1 (2007). Enhance Telecom Operations Map: The Business Process Framework (eTOM), March 2007.

ITU-T Recommendation X.805, (2003). Security architecture for systems providing end-to-end communications, Oct. 2003.

Kreger, H. et al. (2005). Management Using Web Services: A Proposed Architecture and Roadmap, tech report, IBM, Hewlett-Packard, and Computers Assoc., June 2005.

Knightson, K., Morita, N., Towle, T. (2005). NGN Architecture: General Principles, Functional Architecture, and Implementation. IEEE Communication Magazine, Oct. 2005.

Kreger, H. (2001). Web Services Conceptual Architecture (WSCA 1.0), IBM Software Group, May 2001.

Morita, N., Imanaka, H. (2007). Introduction to the Functional Architecture of NGN. IEICE Trans. Commun., VOL.E90-B, no.5, May 2007.

OASIS, (2004). Introduction to UDDI: Important features and Functional Concepts, Organization for the Advancement of Structured Information Standards (OASIS), White Paper, Oct. 2004.

Raman, G. L., (1999). Fundamentals of Telecommunications Network Management, IEEE Press, 1999.

World Wide Web Consortium Recommendation (W3C), (2001). Web Service Description Language (WSDL) 1.1, March. 2001. http://www.w3.org/TR/wsdl

World Wide Web Consortium Recommendation (W3C), (2007). Simple Object Access Protocol (SOAP) version 1.2 Part 1: Messaging Framework (Second Edition), April 2007. http://www.w3.org/TR/soap12-part1/

World Wide Web Consortium Recommendation (W3C), (2006). Extensible Markup Language (XML) 1.0 (fourth edition), Sep. 2006. http://www.w3.org/TR/REC-xml

Zhang, Y., Qui, X., Meng, L. (2006). A Web services-based dynamically cooperative network management architecture. IEEE Conference in Communications and Networking, Oct. 2006.

KEY TERMS

BSS: Business Support System.

CORBA: Common Object Request Broker Architecture.

DCOM: Distributed Component Object Model.

eTOM: Enhanced Telecom Operations Map.

GIOP: General Inter-Orb Protocol.

GUI: Graphical User Interface.

HTTP: Hypertext Transfer Protocol.

IETF: Internet Engineering Task Force.

IIOP: Internet Inter-Orb Protocol.

IP: Internet Protocol.

ISDN: Integrated Services Digital Network.

ITU: International Telecommunication Union.

LAN: Local Area Network.

LLA: Logical Layer Architecture.

MIB: Management Information Base.

NGN: Next Generation Networks.

OSI: Open System Interconnection.

OS: Operations System.

QoS: Quality of Service.

OSS: Operations Support System.

PSTN: Public Switched Telephone Network.

RDF: Resource Description Framework.

RPC: Remote Procedure Call.

RSS: Really Simple Syndication.

SDH: Synchronous Digital Hierarchy.

SOA: Service Oriented Architecture.

SOAP: Simple Object Access Protocol.

SS7: Signaling System No.7.

SVG: Scalable Vector Graphics.

TDM: Time Division Multiplexing.

TMF: Telemanagement Forum.

TMN: Telecommunication Management Network.

UDDI: Universal Description Discovery and Integration.

WSDL: Web Services Description Language.

W3C: World Wide Web Consortium.

XML: Extensible Markup Language.

Chapter IX
A Case Study on the QoS, Energy Consumption and Mobility of WLANs and WMANs

Ioannis Papapanagiotou
North Carolina State University, USA

Georgios S. Paschos
VTT Digitalo, Finland

ABSTRACT

The present chapter contains a thorough investigation of Quality of Service, Energy Conservation and mobility in 802.11 and 802.16 standards. Interest on these two technologies arises from the fact that they are designed to cooperate offering wireless access capabilities in Next Generation Networks (NGNs). Under NGN Wireless architectures, key challenges must be taken into account: (a) Broadband technologies are based on QoS Enabled Telecommunication Services; (b) Mobile devices are battery limited. In fact, how to prolong the life time of a mobile device and minimize power usage is a very important design issue; (c) Wireless operation means that the user is expected to roam freely, which must also be taken into account. The dependability of NGN operation is obviously depended on these three features.

INTRODUCTION

Two very important features of the Wireless Next Generation Networks (Wireless NGNs) are the energy consumption and the mobility of terminals. Energy consumption constrains the infinite bandwidth-roaming space of a wireless terminal and therefore it requires a careful power saving strategy every time that a communication endpoint needs to reside to battery life. On the other hand, the term mobility has been used to describe many different aspects of a wireless network like the movement of the wireless nodes (cellular networks mostly), the ability to transfer network layer settings (like mobile IP) and the handover theory. This chapter is dedicated to study of power saving mechanisms, Quality of Service (QoS) and handover mechanisms in modern wireless networks in view of the forthcoming Wireless NGNs. These mechanisms are necessary to combat the problems that arise from mobile wireless communication and make this capability efficient, transparent and above all possible.

Copyright © 2009, IGI Global, distributing in print or electronic forms without written permission of IGI Global is prohibited.

Introduction to Power Management

The transfer of information is associated with energy consumption even from the principles of Physics. The amount of energy per bit required in a specific communication depends casually on the modulation scheme, on the interference and Noise levels and several other transmission issues and techniques. Taking the above into account the following symbols are introduced:, a terminal requires on average a P_T power level to communicate sending information via the wireless transmitter and P_R to receive information from it. Moreover, when the transmitter is idle (in other words in a state waiting for an information arrival), it also utilizes P_I power on the average. Even when the transceiver is set off, the wireless terminal will still consume energy which is signified by the average P_S level. It is straight-forward that for an average transceiver it holds $P_T > P_R > P_I > P_S$. If the terminal occupies the energy state **k** for a time duration T_K in every hypothetical transmission circle, the average power consumption per transmission cycle will be the following sum $\Sigma T_K P_K$. A power saving mechanism is an effort to minimize this sum using either a transmission technique or a network algorithm. The generalization of power saving strategies of a specific Network is usually referred to as the Power Management feature of a Wireless Network.

There are three different categories of Power Saving schemes:

• **Physical Layer (Layer-1) Power Saving Schemes.**

On the Physical Layer, the effort is focused on improving the transmission techniques so as to lower bit-error rate (BER) using a fixed Signal-to-Noise ratio (SNR) or equivalently conserve power by transmitting the same amount of information with lower power levels. In this context, the aim is to minimize P_T, and sometimes P_R levels while maintaining the same performance. This can be achieved with novel modulation, coding and multiple access techniques, by using multiple channels and different kind of antennas, or even transmission concepts as the use of relay nodes or optimal power control and power allocation, (Tourki, 2007; Han 2002).

• **Medium Access Control Layer (Layer-2) Power Saving Schemes.**

On the Medium Access Control (MAC) Layer, power levels are assumed fixed, as the underlying Physical Layer dictates. The aim here is to minimize T_T and T_R and maximize T_I and T_S while the efficiency of communications is maintained and the packet transfer is not delayed. These MAC Layer approaches oftenly correspond to a centralized scenario where the central base station schedules the transmissions accordingly and more rarely to distributed scenarios where the effects of turning off the transceiver are much more destructive for the network performance, (Salkitzis, 1998; Xiao, 2005).

• **Network Layer (Layer-3) Power Saving Schemes.**

Network Layer perspective is much more distributed in its essence. The network is considered as a graph and weights are assigned per graph edge indicating the link cost in terms of power consumption. In this case, the flow of information is monitored and the optimal route is discovered for maintaining low energy consumption. Another possibility is to categorize nodes in different clusters and devise clustering algorithms that for a given amount of information transactions the consumed energy per node is minimized or evenly shared in a fair way. This case of Power Saving Schemes applies more to the case of Mobile Ad hoc Networks (MANETs) and Wireless Sensor Networks (WSNs), (Kawadia, 2003; Bandyopadhyay, 2003).

Power Management at the MAC Layer has been already introduced in GSM networks (2G), (Redl, 1995). When the GSM mobile station (MS) is not in the process of an ongoing connection with the base station, it switches off the transceiver for a fixed period of 1/8sec in order to save energy. Had it not been for this basic Power Saving Scheme, the mobile battery would be consumed ten times faster when the phone is not active! In this case, the power saving mechanism is simplified by the nature of the GSM networks and the fact that it is used only in non-activity regions and for fixed intervals. In modern Wireless Networks, these mechanisms are utilized in more complex situations where centralized control is not so evident and the terminal saves power even when an ongoing connection is active. In any case, it is then obvious that an optimal Power Saving Mechanism is required if the terminal is expected to go mobile and rely on its battery life. This is true both for cellular mobile networks and for MANETs. Such a mechanism must promote the following merits:

- The Link Layer power consumption must be minimum while,
- Packets are not lost,
- The delay of connection setup is kept relatively low,
- The node availability does not damage the network functionality,

This chapter focuses on the MAC Layer Power Saving Schemes which are currently deployed for Wireless Access and are expected to be the basis of the NGNs. In the first section, power saving mechanisms for Wireless Local Area Networks (WLANs) are studied, and more specifically the IEEE 802.11e standard extension, which defines a new method to deliver the frames buffered at the Acess Point (AP) while the station is in Power Save (PS) Mode, the Automatic Power Save Delivery (APSD). APSD is very useful in Voice over IP (VoIP) applications where the data rates are roughly the same in both directions. The AP can choose between the standard Power Save Mode and the APSD mode. In APSD mode, two types of Service Periods are defined: a) the unscheduled-APSD (U-APSD) and b) the scheduled-APSD (S-APSD). However the Wi-Fi Alliance has started certification of the Wi-Fi multimedia extensions (WMM™) and the WMM Power Save™ which include the distributed type of access, EDCA and EDCA plus U-APSD functionality.

In the section of Wireless Metropolitan Area Networks (WMANs), the IEEE 802.16e (IEEE 802.16, 2006), deploys a mapping between QoS classes and energy consumption mechanisms by providing different types of Power Saving Classes. More specifically, a MS has two operation modes, namely awake mode and sleep mode. Only in the awake mode can a MS transmit/receive data. However special care should be taken into account due to the bursty traffic characteristics of various applications such as WEB browsing. In order to use energy more efficiently, the MS can be absent from the serving BS in sleep mode during the pre-negotiated period which is composed of sleep and listening windows.

Introduction to Handover Theory

In a multiaccess system it is often expected that a user should switch from one type of resource to another depending on the conditions. In cellular networks, switching from one frequency channel to another due to mobility is termed handover or handoff. The term handover can be extended to cover many different scenarios of altering the resource provider. The traditional meaning of the term, however, refers to an intra-system inter-cell switch when the quality offered from the target cell is better than that offered from the source cell. Interest features regarding handovers namely are the handover criteria, the handover effects, the soft handover and the several effects the handover has to the network.

The following categories of handover are usually met in wireless cellular networks:

- Inter or Intra cell handover, depending on whether the handover occurs inside a cell or binding two cells,
- Inter or Intra system handover, depending on whether the user switches between two systems,
- System-initiated or User-initiated handover, depending on the initiator of the switching,
- Hierarchical handover, when the user switches between different categories of cells (umbrella cell, micro to pico cell handover),
- Hard, Soft or Softer handover, depending on how many uplink and downlink connections the user maintains during the process,
- Vertical or Horizontal handover, depending on switching between different radio technologies.

The handover criteria also depend upon the handover case. In the simple scenario, monitoring the signal strength or the SNR is enough. The actual hop is made after a decision rule regarding a comparison of the two signals and or the use of a threshold. In interference-limited networks (as CDMA), the Signal to Interference Ratio (SIR) can be used instead. In system-initiated handovers, the criterion can be relative to user mobility or to the congestion of the two cells. In case of a soft handover, maximum throughput and less amount of interference might be the criterion, while in vertical handovers even user preference or application types can be decisive. Nevertheless, the choice of the handover criterion is important to prevent quality drops and the phenomenon of repeated handovers (called ping-pong phenomenon).

In terms of Quality of Service, handover mechanisms are of critical importance since a failure can cause a drop of a connection. User feedback has shown that the user-perceived quality of a dropped connection is of dramatic importance and usually this particularity is usually carefully treated by network operators. For this reason, handover mechanisms are very important for the NGNs. In the section of the WLANs, the procedures taking place in mobile scenarios with multiple BSSs, is described based on the 802.11r standard. In the context of WMANs, the 802.11e standard is explained and state of the art solutions are presented.

WIRELESS LOCAL AREA NETWORKS (WLANS)

Wireless Local Area Networks, have been widely deployed nowadays, playing a complementary access role to cellular networks in 3rd Generation Partnership Project (3GPP, 2005) by providing low cost broadband internet access. One of the major goals in such technologies is to introduce mobility so as to extend the location constrains.

The general role of Wi-Fi in Next Generation Networks can be summarized in:

- Major cities have already installed Wi-Fi networks.
- Until 2004, 30 - 80% of cellular calls initiated in Wi-Fi operating areas
- The total shipments of Wi-Fi products to North American Market for On-Site Industrial Monitoring and Control Applications in 2004 was in $150.5 Million (33.6% of all wireless tech.) and is expected to rise up to 409$ Million (41.4% of all wireless tech.) in the end of 2007

This widespread application of Wi-Fi networks together with their versatility in connecting mobile computers is expected to cause their adoption as one of the cooperating Wireless technologies for NGNs.

Power Save Mode

IEEE 802.11(IEEE 802.11, 1999) has proposed a specific type of Power Save Mechanism (PSM), so as to save quick depletion of mobile station batteries. Such mechanisms tend to power down the transceiver. Thus when the

Figure 1. Data rate of various dot11 technologies

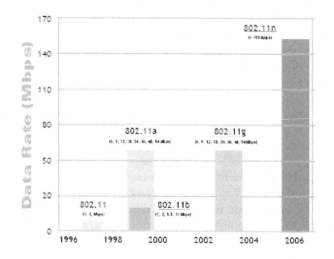

Mobile STA physical interface is off, the station is said to be in *sleeping* or *dozing*. On the contrary when it is on, it is said to be *awake* or *active*. The general functioning is called *Power-Saving Mode* (PS).

- **Awake**: STA is fully powered
- **Doze**: STA is not able to transmit or receive and consumes very low power

Vendor Example Cases:
Orinocco WLAN cards: TxPower=1.400mW, RxPower=900mW Idle=700mW and DozeMode=60mW
Cisco AIR-PCM350:   TxPower=1.875mW, RxPower=1.300mW, Idle=1080mW and
                        DozeMode=45mW

Power Management in BSS

In BSS WiFi networks, that is networks that use Access Points (AP), the power saving mechanism can achieve the highest performance. If the STA is in Power Save Mode (PSM) then the AP shall not arbitrarily transmit MSDUs, but buffer them and transmit them in designated times. However the AP shall also announce periodically which stations have frames in the AP buffer. Such an announcement is made in a Traffic Indication Map (TIM), which shall be included within all beacons generated by the AP (Beacon Intervals are usually 100ms). Stations power up their transmitter to transmit polling frames, when they are informed that there is a reason to be ON. One of the key parameters in this mechanism is the Listening Interval, which is the number of Beacon periods for which the STA may choose to sleep. Bigger Listening Intervals (LI) mean that the buffer occupancy increases and consequently the delay, but the battery is depleted with a lower rate. If the STA fails to check for any buffered frames after the LI, the frames are discarded without notification (Cast, 1999).

The TIM shall indentify the STAs for which traffic is pending and buffered in the AP. This information is coded in *partial virtual bitmap*. Additionally the TIM contains an indication whether the broadcast/multicast traffic is pending. For identifying the independent STAs, each one has an Association (ID) code. When the AP wants to broadcast a packet the SID is set to 0, otherwise SID is set to the corresponding value of the unicast recipient.

The STAs request the delivery of their buffered frames at the AP by sending a power-save poll (PS-Poll). After that, the AP sends a single buffered frame to the STA or responds with an acknowledgement. If nothing of these happen, then the STA retries the sequence by transmitting another PS-Poll frame. On the contrary, if PS-Poll

Figure 2. Power management with AP presence (IEEE 802.11, 1999)

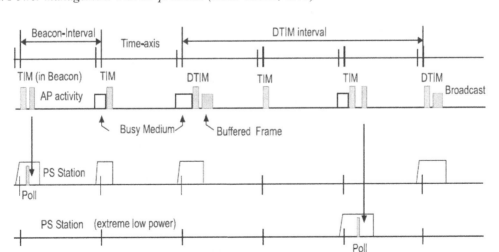

Example: DTIM at every 3 TIM intervals

frames are received from the AP they are ignored until the frame is either successfully delivered, or presumed failed due to the maximum number of retries exceeded. Another case is when more than one packet is buffered in a sequence (possibly after fragmentation) for the same STA. In such an occasion in the frame control field, the More Data bit is set to 1 (IEEE 802.11, 1999; Cast, 1999). This ensures that the buffer of the AP empties.

In PSM there is also another TIM type called DTIM. After a DTIM, the AP shall send out the buffered broadcast/multicast frames using normal transmission rules, before transmitting any unicast frames. TIM is transmitted in every beacon, whereas DTIM is transmitted in every beacon after a DTIM period. In Figure 2 from (IEEE 802.11, 1999) the Infrastructure power management operation is shown.

Power Management in IBSS

In Ad-hoc mode, power management becomes complex and inefficient. In such distributed networks the STAs use Announcement (or adhoc) Traffic Indication Messages (ATIMs), to preempt other stations from sleeping. So when a STA wants to transmit data to another one, the data are buffered to the transmitter STA and an ATIM frame is send as notification to keep the receiver awake for a window, specified as *ATIM Window*. In this window only Beacon or ATIM frames are transmitted. ATIM transmission times are randomized, after a Beacon frame is either transmitted or received by the STA, using the backoff procedure with the contention window equal to aCWmin. Direct ATIMs shall be acknowledged, but if they do not, the STA executes the Backoff procedure for retransmission of the ATIM.

If a STA receives a directed ATIM frame during the ATIM Window, it shall acknowledge the directed ATIM and stay awake for the entire beacon interval waiting for the announced frame to be received. If a STA does not receive an ATIM, it may enter the Doze state at the end of the ATIM Window. Some cases exist where multiple ATIMS can be transmitted to multiple receivers and a station that has received an ATIM can receive more than one MSDU from the transmitting station.

Transmission of frames, after an acknowledged ATIM or broadcast/multicast MDSUs that have been announced with an ATIM, shall be done using the DCF access procedure as specified in (IEEE 802.11, 1999).

IEEE 802.11e, Quality of Service and Extended Power Provisioning

Heterogeneous multimedia applications require advance editing over the standard to provide specific QoS characteristics, and combination with Power Saving Mechanisms.

Figure 3. IEEE 802.11e MAC protocol Enhancement. Voice has smaller interframe space than data thus accessing the channel faster

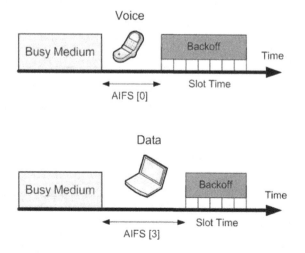

The IEEE 802.11e standard (IEEE 802.11e, 2005) revises the former IEEE 802.11 by proposing Quality of Service (QoS) enhancements for LAN applications. To accomplish such QoS needs of multimedia applications, the new standard proposes enhanced access methods summarized in the Hybrid Coordination Function (HCF). Similarly to the legacy dot11, there exist two access methods: the HCF Controlled Access Method (HCCA), based on a polling mechanism controlled by the Hydrid Coordinator (HC), located in the QAP, and the Enhanced Distributed Access Method (EDCA), which is a contention based access method. Both of them are extension of the legacies DCF and PCF from the 802.11. The deference between these two access methods is that distributed EDCA, offers *prioritized* QoS, whereas HCCA offers *parameterized* QoS. In the standard, QoS support is done through differentiation of packets, using different priorities and maps them to eight Traffic Classes and these respectively to four ACs, that are buffered in separate queues both in the AP and in the QoS enhanced stations (QSTAs). This way, Voice and Video applications retain access to the channel in a more reliable way than e-mail and other Best Effort applications. These are depicted in Table 1

IEEE 802.11e introduces also a new feature called TxOP. TxOP (Transmit Opportunity) is a bounded interval in which the QSTA can send as many frames as possible. If the frames are too large to be included in a single TxOP, then they are fragmented according to the TxOP limit. Such a mechanism reduces the problem of low rate stations gaining an inordinate amount of channel time.

Levels of services are provided through different assignments of the AC parameters: AIFS, CW and TxOP limits.

EDCA

EDCA mechanism functions in a distributed manner. It is specified for both IBSS and BSS networks. The EDCA functions as DCF (CSMA/CA) with a backoff algorithm, but it also offers QoS, by providing higher access probability to delay sensitive applications such as VoIP and Video. These applications tend to take higher portion of the bandwidth, whilst having less delay. The concept behind this is that e-mail and HTTP transactions are not delay sensitive. For example no problem exists if an e-mail is received some seconds later than it is scheduled. Whereas in VoIP applications (G.711) if the delay is higher than 200ms, there is a significant degradation in the quality of speech (ITU-T G.711, 1998). In order to differentiate the access timing the following parameters are defined in the standard.

Table 1. Differentiation of access mechanism according to the application

Priority	UP (Same as 802.1D user Priority)	Application	Access Category	Initial Contention Window (CWmin)	Maximum Contention Window (CWmax)	Arbitrary Interframe Space (AIFS)
LOW	0 AC_BK	Backround	AC0	31	1023	SIFS+7
	1 AC_BK	Backround				
	2 AC_BE	Best Effort	AC1	31	1023	SIFS+3
	3 AC_BE	Best Effort				
	4 AC_VI	Video	AC2	15	31	SIFS+2
	5 AC_VI	Video				
	6 AC_VO	Voice (VoIP)	AC3	7	15	SIFS+2
HIGH	7 AC_VO	Voice (VoIP)				

AC_VO: *Highest priority category, assigned to voice calls*
AC_VI: *Allows video to be transported with priority over data applications, but not voice packets*
AC_BE: *For traffic from applications that have relaxed QoS requirements; e.g. Web browsing and e-mail*
AC_BK: *Lowest priority category; examples would include file downloads and print jobs*

EDCA in Summary

- The Arbitration Interframe Space (AIFS) provides good prioritization, if there are not any DCF stations.
- Adjustment of backoff value can lead to fluctuations on waiting backoff delay and collisions (collision tend to affect VoIP applications relatively a lot).
- In the presence of legacy DCF stations, reduction of backoff values can lead to better differentiation.
- Low priority classes get congested relatively fast, without admission control, and tend to affect higher classes.
- Admission Control is an optional feature for IEEE 802.11e EDCA, but is needed to provide higher QoS.

HCCA

HCCA inherits some of the characteristics of PCF, such as providing polled access to the wireless medium. QoS polling can take place during CP and scheduling of packets is based on admitted TSPECs. Thus any CP can be interrupted by a CFP. Such method is called Controlled Access Phase (CAP) and is used whenever a QAP wants to send a frame to a station, or receive a frame from a station, in a contention free manner. In such CFP the QAP controls the medium whereas in the CP all stations function as in EDCA.

In HCCA, Traffic Classes (TC) and Traffic Streams (TS) are also defined. The scheduling mechanism is not included in the standard except from some basic characteristics. Such as the QSTAs give info about the queue lengths of each TC, and then the HC can give priority to QSTAs that have more packets in QAPs queues according to the scheduling mechanism. During CP, the HC allows QSTAs to send data by sending CF-Poll frames.

Implementation of 802.11e HCCA requires significantly increases in memory, than their predecessor. This is because the queues from two (Broadcast/Multicast - Unicast) are increased to 6 (Broadcast/Multicast – Unicast – 4 ACs). Moreover complexity is increased, due to the fact that a central coordinator is needed.

However the great advantage of HCCA to EDCA is that the QoS can be configured with great precision. Additionally the complexity of upgrading a STA to QSTA, which functions under HCCA, is not significant since polling mechanism should be implemented in the QSTA and scheduler and queuing mechanism in the QAP.

HCCA in Summary

- Polled access is ideal for high density voice applications, because it guarantees specific delay thresholds and lower ACs do not affect higher ones.
- Scheduling and Admission Control can be performed more effectively, thus providing guaranteed reservation.
- Collisions from Intercell interference (neighbor QAPs) affect the QoS.

Interframe Spaces

Analyzing the whole CSMA/CA with QoS features is outside the scope of this chapter. We will introduce some specific changes over in Interframe Spaces that are made in the enhanced standard. In (IEEE 802.11, 1999) and IEEE 802.11e, the time interval between frames is called IFS. In (IEEE 802.11e, 2005) a new priority level for access to the wireless media is introduced and is differentiated according to the AC. It is called Arbitration inteframe space (AIFS) and provides a type of prioritization when trying to access the channel after the end of the Backoff Slots. Different IFS are independent of the STA bit rate, but IFS timings are gaps on the medium fixed for each PHY.

Automatic Power Save Delivery (APSD)

IEEE 802.11 introduces some additional features to the legacy dot11 MAC protocol. Some of these are APSD, Block Acknowledgements (BA), No ACK, and DLS. The major of these optional characteristics is the APSD,

Figure 4. IFS Differentiation and backoff (IEEE 802.11e, 2005)

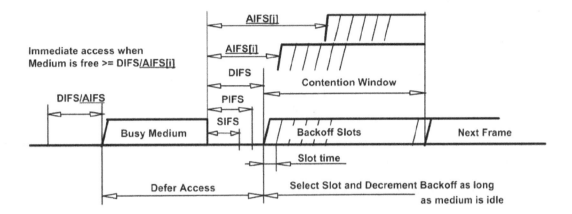

which is an enhanced Power Save Mode. The rest of the characteristics will not be analyzed explicitly, since they are out of the scope of the chapter.

Due to the fact that APSD is optional, the QAPs that are capable of supporting power save delivery, signal this capability through the use of the APSD subfield in the Capability Information Field in Beacon, Probe Response, and (Re)-Association Response management frames. Thus the QAP can select the method for the delivery of the buffered frames between standard PSM and APSD.

The reason for specifying a new Power Save Mechanism in IEEE 802.11e, is that devices need to guarantee QoS requirements for delay-sensitive applications like multimedia streaming, while aiming to reduce the power consumption of mobile stations in the same time. One of the drawbacks of standard PSM is the dependency between data frames MAC downlink delay and the listen interval. Especially for delay prone applications, some listen intervals can result in high downlink delays (X. Perez-Costa, 2006; X. Perez-Costa, 2007).

In APSD there exist two different modes. On one hand, *Unscheduled APSD (U-APSD)* is a distributed mechanism, where QSTAs decide by their own when to wake to receive packets from the AP or other QSTAs. U-APSD operates together with EDCA (*Wi-Fi™ Alliance* is certifying the *WMM Power Save™*(Wi-Fi Alliance) based on U-APSD). On the other hand, *Scheduled APSD (S-APSD)* is the centralized mechanism where the QAP determines a schedule for the station to awake and receive the frames that are buffered for it.

In both cases the Service Period (SP) is said to be the time in which the QSTA is awake, receiving frames from the QAP. The SP ends with the frame End of Service Period Flag Set (EOSP).

Unscheduled APSD (U-APSD)

The main idea of U-APSD is similar to PSM. The AP buffers some frames when the QSTA is in doze mode and transmits them using the EDCA mechanism. The main difference is that now the QSTA generates some indications, called *triggers*, when it is awake. The QAP then transmits the buffered data, which had been stored when the QSTA was in doze mode, while the station is awake. Thus when the QAP receives the trigger, an *unscheduled SP* begins and ends when the QSTA receives a QoS Data or QoS Null frame indicating the End of Service (EOSP). In this period, the AC delivering the data frames is called *delivery-enabled*. However it is straightforward that before accepting the data frames, the AC should have been *trigger-enabled*, which means that it must have sent an indication that it is awake for a SP.

In U-APSD, the role of QoS Null Frames is similar to PS-Polls in PSM. However such frames can be transmitted by the QSTA occasionally, when the QSTA is delivering but not transmitting. This creates a great advantage over PSM, because most of the applications usually do not congest the uplink, but rather the downlink (similarly to the performance of ADSL). The number of frames that are sent in an unscheduled SP is limited to the maximum service period length. (Field contained in the QoS Info Field). However if there exist more frames buffered to the AP, then the More Data (MD) bit is sent to 1 to indicate that more data are scheduled for a delivery-enabled AC. (X. Perez-Costa, 2006)

U-APSD/EDCA Advantages Over PSM/DCF

1. Fully supports the enhanced Quality of Service features implemented in IEEE 802.11e.
2. Minimizes the delay, since the QSTAs decide when to send triggers, and make their ACs trigger-enabled, whereas in PSM it should wait for the Listen Interval (Dependency of MAC downlink delay and Listen Intervals).
3. Maximum SP Length let the QSTA receive up to a number of frames, without the need to transmit PS-Poll after each frame.

Scheduled APSD (S-APSD)

The respective for the centralized type of transmission is the S-APSD. In this type of Energy Conservation the QAP schedules the instants when each QSTA shall wake to receive frames buffered at the QAP. Since HCF provides both access methods (EDCA and HCCA) the QSTA transmits a request frame, called ADDTS (add traffic stream), to the QAP with the APSD and Schedule Subfields of the TS Info Field element both set to 1. The QAP then decides, if it will serve the request and responds in the Schedule Element the *Service Start Time* (SST) and the *Service Interval* (SI). Both these variables specify the scheduling of the delivery of each traffic stream to the QSTAs but also the doze/awake time.

Two basic rules exist when the QAP wants to update the service schedule. The new SST shall not exceed the beginning of the previous SP by more than the defined minimum and maximum service times. The QSTA can also update the service schedule by deleting its existing traffic specification in some other messages. (X. Perez-Costa, 2007).

S-APSD/HCCA Advantages Over PSM/PCF

1. Fully supports the enhanced Quality of Service features implemented in IEEE 802.11e.
2. The QAP does not need to transmit a PS-Poll after each frame, but receive multiple packets without any signaling frame
3. Less signaling frames cause less collisions in CP periods in which they are transmitted. Thus higher QoS and greater sleep intervals can be achieved.

Handover and Fast BSS Transitions

The massive use of the Wireless Local Area Networks (WLANs) has resulted in an urgent need for handover support. Users tend to move at multiple speeds and location, while requiring continuous services without degradation of QoS. However, in the first generation WiFi networks, insufficient handover mechanisms led to high delays and disruption of connectivity (A.Mishra, 2003). Enhancements, such as those introduced in (IEEE 802.11e, 2005; IEEE 802.11i, 2004), tend to make the handover process more complicated.

Except from the handover process, security was also a major problem to the first Wi-Fi devices. Thus, IEEE taskgroup decided to study some new security enhancements offered in IEEE 802.11i (IEEE 802.11i, 2004). The goal was to correct some weaknesses in the original security mechanism (especially after the easy decryption of WEP). Features such as stronger encryption, authentication and key management method to guarantee data and system security are introduced.

In the following subsection we are going to analyze the homogeneous case of handovers within a WLAN environment. In such a case, the complete set of a handover process is split in two parts. The first one is the intelligent recognition of the wireless medium condition, the QoS features and other relative characteristics, that are related to the decision of handover. The second one is the Fast procedure of the Handover itself. (A.Mishra, 2003) makes this division of the handover in IEEE 802.11 networks by proposing two discrete mechanisms *Discovery* and *Reauthentication.*

Seamless Basic Service Set (BSS) transitions in 802.11 WLANs can be performed with IEEE 802.11k and 802.11r amendments. The IEEE 802.11k (IEEE 802.11/D7.0, 2003) amendment provides information to discover the best available access point. Whereas IEEE 802.11r (IEEE 802.11r/D6.0, 2006) defines the mechanism for secure and fast transitions between access points within the same Extended Service Set (ESS). It also incorporates the latest security enhancements provided in dot11i and QoS ones introduced in dot11e as described in the previous section.

In order to explain the handover process we will divide the handover process in three parts (than two as in (A.Mishra, 2003; S.Pack, 2007). First will be the *Decision*, then the *Discovery* and then the *Association and Reauthentication.*

Decision

In order to make a handover, either the STA or the AP must decide, under some circumstances, that it is time to do it. In the following, the decision of making Wi-Fi roaming is based on:

- *Signal Degradation*; as the STA is moving away from the AP, it must roam to another AP with higher receiving signal strength. Roaming can be also be done when part of the AP cell experiences high interference, noise or path loss, that generally degrade the SNR.
- *Load Balancing*; if the load increases in high values, it is better to roam to another AP, in order to increase the overall throughput of the network.
- *Quality of Service*; if the initial QoS specifications (TSPECs), which are initial negotiated cannot be accomplished, handover is required to another AP which can offer better services to multimedia applications.

Discovery

After making the decision for roaming, the STA must find the correct candidate. IEEE 802.11k (IEEE 802.11k/ D7.0, 2003) enables smart roaming within the Wi-Fi network. The STA uses the IEEE 802.11k neighbor report, that is provided by the current AP, to find other candidate APs in the vicinity. After examining the above reasons for handover, the STA selects the AP capable of providing the best throughput and adequate QoS.

It is interesting to know the mechanism that is required, in the MAC layer, for finding the best candidate. This function is called scanning. In the 802.11 standard, two types of scans exist: passive and active. In the passive scan, the STA listens to the wireless medium for beacon frames. In the Beacon frames timing and advertising information are included. Once such information is decoded, the STA can decide which AP is suitable for association. On the contrary, in the active scanning mode, the STA is transmitting probe request frames and the AP is responsible to receive them. In such a case the STA scans all the channels, and can select the next AP to associate.

Association and Authentication

When the decision and scanning has been done, the STA must associate with the new AP, and re-authenticate. Association is the procedure to establish a logical connection between a new STA and an AP. Practically, in the authentication the AP either accepts or rejects the identity of the new STA. This is done, because the AP might not be able to fulfill the requirements (SNR/QoS) of the new STA.

The reason for adding the Decision part, in the handover concept is that the legacy 802.11 assumed a handover only when there was signal (or SNR) degradation. However lately with the new IEEE 802.11r [13] things have changed since QoS and Security play a substantial role to the handover process. 802.11i and 802.11e standards introduce additional overhead and complexity, during the re-authentication process due to management frame exchanges. This is particularly true since the IEEE 802.1X (IEEE 802.1X, 2004) port-based network access control mechanism (Security method for Authentication, Authorization and Accounting using the most common

RADIUS) to authenticate STAs was introduced, which adds significant latencies to complete the communication to the authentication server. Such latencies affect multimedia applications, especially VoWLAN. Thus 802.11r was formulated to minimize latencies during the BSS transition.

Leaving out the security enhancements in the 802.11r, a QSTA may request QoS resources at the time of association, thus control messages are exchanged prior to data transfer. Another advantage is that it is possible to inform the QSTA if the QAP can support the requested QoS resources.

The first stage of a handover with Fast BSS transition, is that the STA informs the QAP that a FT is going to be used. The QSTA examines if the QAP is FT-enabled by scanning the beacons. If the AP accepts the STA, then open authentication is performed. The second stage is the re-association, which includes any resource allocation requests plus a message integrity check (MIC) to authenticate the request.

In conclusion, the homogeneous handover process for Wi-Fi networks is relatively complex, because it correlates handover with security and QoS through a new mechanism.

WIRELESS METROPOLITAN AREA NETWORKS (WMANS)

Quality of Service in 802.16 Networks

WiMAX scheduler is expected to occupy many laboratories and R&D departments of several Telecommunication providers in the near future. This section has as a goal to provide a complete description of the possible features that every Telco could control to enhance the performance of its WiMAX devices.

The standard provides four features to enhance its support for QoS: Fragmentation, Concatenation, Contention and Piggyback. In addition, for differentiation among the data streams, IEEE 802.16 provides four scheduling service flows which represent the data handling mechanisms supported by the MAC scheduler for data transport on each type of connection. The standard offers details of the SSs request upstream minislot functionality and the expected behavior of the BS upstream scheduler.

Scheduling Service Flows

- **Unsolicited Grant Service Flows (UGS):** This service flow is designed to support Real time data streams, where fixed data packets are generated on periodic basis, such as TDM voice and T1/E1. QoS for these applications is provided through unsolicited data grants which are issued at periodic intervals. The advantage of this service flow is that it eliminates the overhead and latency of the SS to send request for transmission. In UGS, the SS is prohibited from using any contention and piggyback requests, and the BS does not provide any unicast request opportunities. To ensure the ability of the UGS service flow to support delay prone applications, four key service parameters are included: Unsolicited Grant Size, Grants per Interval, Nominal Grant Interval and Tolerated Grant Jitter.
- **Real-Time Polling Service Flows (rtPS):** This service flow is designed to support similar data streams to UGS case, but with variable size data packets, such as MPEG video and VoIP with Silence suppression. This flow type offers periodic unicast request opportunities, which meet the flow's real-time needs and allow the SS to specify the size of the desired grants. As in UGS contention and piggyback request are prohibited to be sent. In this service flow the key parameters are Nominal Polling Interval, Tolerated Poll Jitter and Minimum Reserved Traffic Rate.
- **Non Real-Time Polling Service Flows (nrtPS):** nrtPS is designed to support non-real-time service flows that require variable size data grants on a regular basis, but using more spaced intervals than rtPS. This service flow can support bandwidth to data streams under heavily saturation condition, due to its polling feature. The BS provides SS the opportunity to request bandwidth using unicast and contention period. In addition piggyback request opportunities are also available. The key service parameters are: Nominal Polling Interval, Minimum Reserved Traffic Rate and Traffic Priority (a range 0-7).
- **Best Effort Service Flows (BE):** BE supports any other traffic without significant quality constrains such as HTTP. All available mechanisms of the protocol for transmission requests are available. This service flow

uses only contention request opportunities and unicast request opportunities. The key service parameters are: Minimum Reserved Traffic Rate and Traffic Priority (a range 0-7).

QoS Features

The scheduler is in charge of controlling the common uplink bandwidth as well as distributing resources to flows for maintain quality. The QoS features provided by the scheduler are expected to be the only amendments to the protocol allowed, and therefore the most possible to be custom-tailored by the client Telco according to each needs.

Piggybacking is used as a request for additional bandwidth sent together with a data transmission. The key advantage of this approach is that piggybacking obviates contention. Concatenation is used in the MAC protocol to send more than a frame during a transmission opportunity so as to reduce packet overhead. In the following we investigate concatenation combined with fragmentation and prove that both give an improvement to throughput and provide a better use of resources. The third feature that can be sometimes managed is the backoff window of the exponential backoff algorithm part of the contention period of the BE service flow. We investigate the performance of the network by differentiating the values of the Backoff Window.

The last but not least parameter which can be modified, from the interface of each WiMAX device, by the Telecommunication providers, is the Traffic Priorities of the BE service flow. Each Telco can provide an alternative to low bandwidth DSL lines by specifying the Traffic Priority to each client. It is proved by simulation that higher Traffic Priorities can provide better delay performance and thus accomplish the specified Service Level Agreements (SLAs) of each connection. (G. S. Paschos, 2006)

Sleep Mode Operation in the Enhanced 802.16e

The IEEE 802.16e standards for mobility (IEEE 802.16e, 2006) define a detailed process of power saving with view to application in the complex environment of WMANs. QoS dominates even sleep mode operation by dictating the division of power saving mechanism in three classes; class type 1 for data applications, class type 2 for isochronous transmissions like UGS QoS class applications and class type 3 for management operation and multicast connections.

According to the standards, the IEEE 802.16e terminal can be in awake mode when it is available for transmitting and receiving packets, or otherwise in sleep mode when it totally disappears from the network by switching off the transceiver. When in sleep mode, the terminal alternates between periods of availability and unavailability, called listen window and sleep window respectively.

In the rest of the section, a description of each sleep mode class is given and finally they are all combined in the hybrid case.

Figure 5. QoS architecture in 802.16.

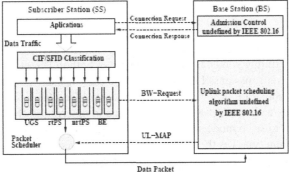

Table 2.

Service Flow	Definition	Applications
UGS	Real time data streams with fixed size data packets issued at periodic intervals	T1/E1, VoIP without silence suppression.
rtPS	Real time data streams with variable size data packets issued at periodic intervals	MPEG video, VoIP with Silence suppression
nrtPS	Delay Tolerant data streams with variable size data packets issued at periodic intervals	FTP, Telnet
BE	Delay Tolerant data streams, background traffic or any either application without significant QoS constrains	HTTP, E-mail

Sleep Mode Class Type 1

This class is assigned to all flows that operate under the QoS classes Best Effort (BE) and non-Real time Variable Rate (NRT-VR). The standard describes an exponential algorithm for sleep windows, starting from the *initial-sleep window* and growing up to *final-sleep window*.

When the activity of a flow is over, the Mobile Service Station (MSS) sends a message to the Base Station (BS) called MOB-SLP-REQ in which negotiation information is included regarding the initial and final sleep windows as well as other relative parameters. The BS then replies with a MOB-SLP-RSP message indicating whether it allows for a sleep mode period. By making this contract with the BS, the MSS has agreed that it will be available at the conclusive listening periods (calculated by the above information). As regards this specific flow and the BS, the MSS can be totally absent for the rest time. In practice, this is subject to the rest of the flows.

The process goes on like expected. After the first sleep window, the MSS receives a MOB-TRF-IND message for incoming traffic waiting at the BS. If there is neither outgoing traffic nor ingoing, then the sleep window is doubled and the process goes on until the *final-sleep window* is reached. After that point, the sleep window remains constant. In between the increasing or stable sleeping windows, listening windows are always constant and usually equal to three frames. Take notice, that even if the MSS happens to switch the transceiver on for another flow, the previous flow retains its own sleep mode state.

The reason hiding under this strange growing sleep strategy, is the fact that under this pattern, sleep mode can be efficiently used for two distinct scenarios. At first, sleeping can be very energy-efficient for long vacation periods, when the MSS has no activity, thanks to the *final-sleep window*. Secondly, sleeping can be utilized even in operational cases in between transmissions. In the latter case, the small *initial-sleep window* can greatly reduce the delay caused by sleeping.

Sleep Mode Class Type 2

In case of isochronous transmissions like the UGS class of IEEE 802.16 networks, sleeping can be extremely efficient. Since the transmission timing is precalculated and known both to BS and MSS, it is easy to schedule sleeping periods between these transmissions. This, in fact, is the case in sleep mode class type 2.

Any UGS or Real-time Variable Rate (RT-VR) flow can request a sleep mode with a MOB-SLP-REQ message. Naturally, the BS responds with a MOB-SLP-RSP message to determine whether it agrees or not. Upon confirmation, the MSS switches to sleep mode with fixed listen and sleep windows. Apart from the fixed sleep windows, the great difference from type 1 is the fact that the MSS is expected to transmit and receive data during the listening windows. This enables the isochronous flows to request a sleep mode at all times. However, it is clear that each separate flow should always have its own sleep mode process.

Sleep Mode Class Type 3

Finally, there exist another sleep mode class (type 3), which is utilized for a one-time sleep. The parameter used here is simply the *final-sleep window* borrowed from type 1. After this sleeping period the user is automatically transitioned to the awake mode. This type of sleep mode is used for multicast flows when the sleep mode can be even initiated by the BS. Every vacation period of multicast downlink can be exploited with a new unsolicited call for sleep mode from the BS. The same messages with above are used for exchanging sleep mode information. This type of sleep mode can also be used for network management and Periodic Ranging purposes.

Sleep Mode: The Hybrid Operation

Up to now, it is evident that each flow has its own sleep mode process. But, what is finally the actual sleeping periods? It seems that sleeping windows are not so important as listening windows. The MSS has made a complex contract with the BS which describes the moments that MSS has to be available for each flow (that is the AND of all listen windows). That enables the MSS to calculate locally all the periods that all flows happily coincide to be at sleep window and find the actual sleeping windows. These are the true periods that the terminal is allowed to be unavailable and therefore the only periods that it can really switch the radio off.

Homogeneous Handover Procedures in the Enhanced 802.16e

The rapid growth in the demand for high data rate, in the Next Generation Wireless Networks, while allowing the capability of moving, have created a need for roaming among cells. Recently the IEEE 802.16e (IEEE 802.16e) has been developed, supporting Mobile Service Stations (MSSs) moving at vehicular speeds. The handover is an important process and is defined by the migration of a MS between air-interfaces belonging to different BSs. By such a function, the network has a target to provide continuity of services, when MSs are travelling in the boundaries of two or more BSs.

The standard defines three basic types of handover: Hard Handover (HHO), Macro Diversity Handover (MDHO) and Fast Base Station Switching (FBSSS). Since the standard is based on OFDMA, an MSS basically conducts hard handover and the other two are optional. In this part of the chapter we are going to divide the handover process in two phases: a) pre-registration and b) actual handover. In the first phase, messages are exchanged, which include actual handover requests and a list of possible target BSs. In the second phase Signal Strength of neighbor BSs are measured so as to facilitate the handover decision.

The handover process may be used in the following situations

- When the MS moves and (due to signal fading, interference levels, etc.) needs to change the BS to which it is connected in order to provide a higher signal quality.
- When the MS can be serviced with higher QoS at another BS.

Hard Handover

The hard handover or else called break-before-make handover is the major handover mechanism in IEEE 802.16. In this type the MS communicates each time with just one BS. This means that there is always a short period, in which, the MS is not connected to any BS. Although hard-handover is very simple, the main target is to diminish this short period, because it creates latency in multimedia applications. The basic steps are:

Network Topology Acquisition

To be able to perform a handover, the MS must acquire information about the network topology. This is done either with network topology advertisements or by scanning the neighbor BSs.

A BS shall broadcast information about the network topology using the MOB_NBR-ADV message. This message provides channel information for neighboring BSs. Whereas the BS obtains that information over the backbone.

Figure 6. Hybrid mode operation (IEEE 802.16e, 2006)

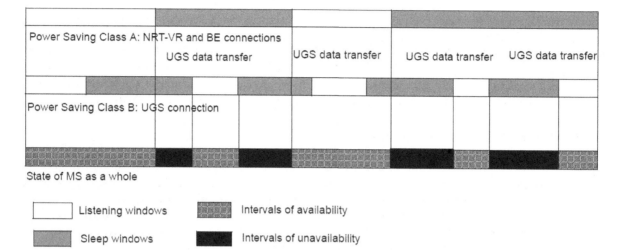

In the standard there is also a scanning interval, which is an allocated time by the BS to the MS for scanning and monitoring suitability the neighbor BSs as HO targets. The MS can also request a group of scanning intervals using the MOB-SCN-REQ message. The reason for allocating or requesting scanning intervals, is that during the scanning the BS must buffer the incoming data for the MS. The MS can terminate the scanning by sending one or more MPDUs to the BS. Then the BS regards the scanning period ended and returns to normal operation. To reduce the overhead due to many scanning request the MS can ask for a group of scanning intervals.

An optional feature in the scanning is the association procedure. The function of Association is to enable the MS to acquire and record ranging parameters and service availability information for the purpose of proper selection of HO target (or potential future handover). Three types of associations exist: a) Scan/Association without coordination b) Association with Coordination and c) Network Assisted Association Reporting

HO Process

The main HO process includes six stages which are:

a. **Cell reselection:** The stage in which the MS acquires information about neighbor BSs, by decoding MOB_NBR-ADV message (may request scanning intervals, sleep intervals, or possibly range neighbor BSs)

b. **HO Decision and Initiation:** A handover begins with a decision either from the MS or the serving BS. The one who requests the Handover sends MOB_MSHO-REQ/MOB_BSHO-REQ message.

c. **Synchronization to Target BS downlink:** For the complete communication the MS must synchronize to downlink transmission of Target BS and obtain UL and DL transmission parameters. If the MS has already received MOB_NBR-ADV message then the process can be shortened. Whereas if the BS had received HO notification from the serving BS over the backbone, then the target BS may allocate a non-contention-based initial Ranging Opportunities.

d. **Ranging:** It is the procedure where the MS receives the correct transmission parameters e.g. time offset and power level. The two cases here are the MS can conduct either Initial Ranging or the Target BS Handover Ranging. In this part of Handover the Authentication and Establishment phase is done. Similarly to the previous case, some parts of the ranging process can be omitted, if information has been passed to the Target BS from the Backbone.

e.   **Termination of MS context:** It is the final step of the handover in which all the connections to the serving BS, and context associated with (e.g. info in the queues, counters, timers etc) are terminated.

f.   **HO Cancellation:** An MS can cancel the handover after the transmission of MOB_HO-IND message.

Macro Diversity Handover (MDHO) and Fast BS Switching (FBSS)

In this type of HO the MS can listen or transmit to several BSs at the same time. MDHO is also called soft handover. Both the MDHO and FBSS can be enabled or disabled in the REG-REQ/RSP message exchange. The MS will perform diversity combining on the signals received from the BSs and the BSs will in turn perform diversity combining to get the uplink PDUs. The following stages, for the MS, are defined in the standard:

- **MDHO Decision:** An MDHO can start with either MOB-MSHO-REQ or MOB_BSHO-REQ. The decision is taken, for the MS to receive/transmit from/to multiple BSs at the same time.
- **FBSS HO Decision:** A FBSS HO can start with the same messages. The decision is taken for an MS to receive/transmit from/to the Anchor BS that may change within the Diversity Set.
- **Diversity Set* Selection/Update:** An MS can scan the neighbor BS and select BSs that are suitable to be included to the Diversity Set
- **Anchor BS* Selection/Update:** An MS is required to continuously monitor the signal strength of the BSs that are included in the Diversity S9et.
  ○ Diversity Set contains the list of active BSs to the MS.
  ○ Anchor BS is defined as the BS where the MS is registered, synchronized, performs ranging and monitors the DL for control information. Both definitions are applicable to MDHO and FBSS HO.

COOPERATIVE SOLUTIONS AND OPTIMIZATION

Heterogeneous Handover means handovers across different technology networks, and is preformed in multiradio client platforms. Such type of handover is the key element of Next Generation Networks. The major part of standardization of such a concept is left upon the emerging IEEE 802.21 standard (IEEE 802.21, 2005).

IEEE 802.21

The initial thinking was based on developing a common standard across 802 media, and defining media independent information to enable mobile devices to detect and select networks effectively. In addition it defines the way to transport information and data across these heterogeneous technologies (802.3, 802.11, 802.16, Cellular). The key benefits of such an operation is optimum network selection, seamless roaming to maintain data connections and lower power operation for multi-radio devices. Figure 7 depicts the functioning of 802.21.

In the backhaul of the network there is Media Independent Information Service, which contains information about all networks from single radio. Such information can help with Network Discovery and Selection leading to more effective Handover decisions.

The events that can trigger such a handover are divided in three parts: a) State Change Events (Link Up/ Link Down/Parameters Change), b) Predictive Events (Link Going Down) and c) Network Initiated Events (Load Balancing/Operator Preferences). Thus IEEE 802.21 has the advantage of offering Co-operative Handover Decision Making, making it the best candidate for Wireless Next Generation Networks.

Cellular Assisted Heterogeneous Networking (CAHN)

CAHN (M. Danzeisen, 2003) is an approach for managing mobile nodes in a heterogeneous environment. The main part of CAHN is based on GSM/GPRS, but has as a target to interconnect heterogeneous networks with different characteristics such as AAA, power consumption, coverage and bit rates. A cellular network like GSM

Figure 7. IEEE 802.21 multi-radio functioning

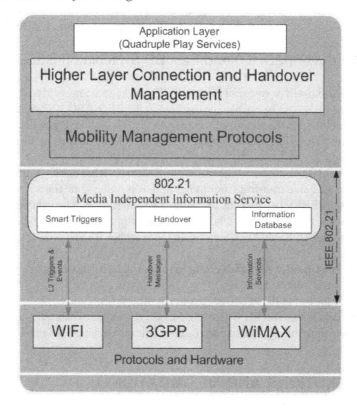

is applied for the signaling plane, which is provided by a cellular operator. CAHN makes use of the Mobile Subscriber Integrated Services Digital Network Number (MSISDN) to identify users rather than IP, MAC or other addressing schemes. All the authentication and identification is done through the MSISDN. However when a join request for a session arrives the devices can scan the available technologies such as WLAN, Bluetooth, WiMAX etc. and setup a connection through a desired medium. The great advantage is that signaling is separate on a low power, always connected, interface whereas high bandwidth interface, which consume more power, are not continuously activated. So CAHN is cooperative solution for low consumption heterogeneous handover

CONCLUSION

In the above chapter three main subjects that arise with the Wireless Next Generation Networks have been studied. Mobility issues, such as the battery depletion and roaming tend to become major problems in the convergence towards 4G Networks. Quality of Service cannot be guaranteed since small and large scale fading, path loss and shadowing make the wireless channel unpredictable and thus there is no guarantee for the correct reception of the packets.

It is readily seen that compliment multiradio systems, that support both WiMAX and WiFi networks will be implemented in most mobile handheld devices. The problem, that such technologies solve, is the inadequacy of the cellular technologies to provide high-speed and reliable wireless access (internet access). Thus they can extend the capabilities of wireless networks, to include both the transmission of Voice and data and in addition to converge to the new era of all-IP networks.

For this we have investigated and presented the solutions of all these problems with a cooperative solution when multiple Wireless Access Technologies are implemented in one device. All these multiple access technologies, cooperating with other ones such as iBurst, HIPERMAN, UMB, UMTS Revision 8 (LTE) and WiBRO will be the core of all the Wireless Next Generation Networks.

REFERENCES

3GPP, (2005). Technical Specification Group Services and System Aspects; 3GPP System to Wireless Local Area Networks (WLAN) Interworking; System Description (Release 6), 3GPP TS 23.234 v.6.6.0.

ITU-T G.711, (1998). Pulse Code Modulation (PCM) of voice parameters.

Bandyopadhyay, S., Coyle, E. J. (April, 2003). An Energy Efficient Hierarchical Clustering Algorithm for Wireless Sensor Networks. *IEEE Infocom 2003*.

Bangolea, S., Bell, C., Qi, E. (2006). Performance Study of Fast BSS Transition using IEEE 802.11r. *International Conference on Communications and Mobile Computing 2006*, (pp. 737-742), Vancouver, British Columbia, Canada.

Cast, Mathew (1999). 802.11 Wireless Networks, The definitive Guide, O'reilly.

Danzeisen, M., Rodellar, D., Braun, T., Winiker, S. (Oct., 2003). Heterogeneous Networking Establishment assisted by cellular operators. *The 5th IFIP TC6 International Conference on MWCN 2003*, Singapore.

Han, Z., Himsoon, T., Siriwongpairat, W. P., Liu, K. J. R. Power Control with Cooperative Diversity over Multisuser OFDM Networks: Who helps whom and how to cooperate, *White papers,* University of Maryland.

Han, Z., Liu, K. J. R. (2002) Adaptive coding for joint power control and beamforming over wireless networks, *SPIE Advanced Signal Processing Algorithms, Architectures and Implementations XII*, Dec.

IEEE 802.16e, (Feb., 2006). Air Interface for Fixed and Mobile Broadband Wireless Access Systems – Amendments for Physical and Medium Access Control Layers for Combined Fixed and Mobile Operation in Licensed Bands, IEEE Standard.

IEEE 802.21, (May, 2005). Handover and interoperability between heterogeneous network types including both 802 and non 802 networks.

IEEE Std. 802.1X, (2004). IEEE Standard for Port-Based Network Access Control.

IEEE 802.11, (Aug., 1999). Wireless LAN Medium Access Control (MAC) and Physical Layer (PHY) specifications", IEEE Standard, .

IEEE 802.11k/D7.0, (2003). Wireless LAN Medium Access Control (MAC) and Physical Layer (PHY) specifications: Specification for Radio Resource Measurement. IEEE 802.11k Workgroup

IEEE 802.11r/D6.0, (2004). Wireless LAN Medium Access Control (MAC) and Physical Layer (PHY) specifications: Fast Roaming/Fast BSS Transition, IEEE 802.11r Workgroup.

IEEE 802.11i, (July, 2004). Wireless LAN Medium Access Control (MAC) and Physical Layer (PHY) specifications: Medium Access Control (MAC) Security Enhancements, IEEE 802.11i Workgroup, .

IEEE 802.11e, (July, 2005). Wireless LAN Medium Access Control (MAC) and Physical Layer (PHY) specifications: Medium Access Control (MAC) Enhancements for Quality of Service (QoS), IEEE 802.11e Workgroup.

Kawadia, V., Kumar, P. R. (2003). Power Control and Clustering in Ad Hoc Networks. *IEEE Infocom 2003*, April.

Mishra, M. Shin, W. Arbaugh, (2003). An empirical analysis of the IEEE 802.11 MAC layer Handoff Process, *ACM SIGCOMM Computer Communications Review*, vol. 33, no. 2, (pp. 93-102).

Pack, S., Choi, J., Kwon, T. and Choi, Y. (2007). Fast Handoff Support in IEEE 802.11 Wireless, *appeared in IEEE Communication Surveys and Tutorials*. (S.Pack, 2007).

Paschos, G.S. Papapanagiotou, I., Argyropoulos C.G., and Kotsopoulos, S.A. (September, 2006). A Heuristic Strategy for IEEE 802.16 WiMAX scheduler for Quality of Service. *FITCE 2006*. Athens, Greece.

Perez-Costa, X. and Camps-Mur, D. (2006). AU-APSD: Adaptive IEEE 802.11e Unscheduled Automatic Power Save Deliver. *IEEE International Conference (ICC) 2006*, Vol.5. (pp. 2020-2027). Istanbul, Turkey.

Perez-Costa, X., Camps-Mur, D., Palau, J. Rebolleda, D. and Akbarzadeh, S. (April, 2007). Overlapping Aware Scheduled Automatic Power Save Delivery Algorithm. *European Wireless,* Paris, France.

Redl, S., Weber, M. K., Oliphant, M. (1995). An Introduction to GSM. Artech House, Mar.

Salkintzis, A.K. and Chamaz, C. , (1998). An in-band power saving protocol for mobile data networks, *IEEE Transactions on Communications*, vol. 46, (pp. 1194-1205).

Tourki, K., Gesbert, D., Deneire, L. (2007). Cooperative Diversity using per-user Power Control in the multiuser MAC channel, *IEEE International Symposium on Information Theory,* Nice, France, Jun.

Wi-Fi Alliance. Retrieved from www.wi-fi.com

Xiao, Y. (2005). Energy Saving Mechanism in the IEEE 802.16e Wireless MAN", *IEEE Communication Letters*, Vol. 9, No. 7.

KEY TERMS

ADDTS: Add Traffic Stream.

AIFS: Arbitrary Interframe Space.

AP: Access Point.

APSD: Automatic Power Save Delivery.

ATIM: Announcement (or Adhoc) Traffic Indication Message.

BE: Best Effort.

BK: Backround.

BS: Base Station.

BSS: Basic Service Set.

CAHN: Cellular Assisted Heterogeneous Networking.

CAP: Controlled Access Phase.

CP: Collision Period.

CFP: Collision Free Period.

CW: Contention Window.

CSMA/CA: Carrier Sense Multiple Access/Collision Avoidance.

CWmax: Contention Window Maximum.

CWmin: Contention Window Minimum.

DCF: Distributed Coordination Function.

DL: Downlink.

DIFS: Distributed Interframe Space.

DSL: Digital Subscriber Line.

DTIM: Distributed Traffic Indication Message.

EDCA: Enhanced Distributed Coordination Access.

EOSP: End of Service Period.

FBSS: Fast BS switching.

HO: Handover.

HCCA: Hydrid Coordination Access Method.

HCF: Hydrid Coordination Function.

HTTP: Hypertext Transfer Protocol (World Wide Web protocol).

IBSS: Independent Basic Service Set.

IP: Internet Protocol.

ISDN: Integrated Services Digital Network.

LI: Listening Interval.

MAC: Medium Access Control.

MDL: More Data.

MDHO: Macro Diversity Handover.

MS: Mobile Station.

MSDU: MAC Service Data Unit.

MSISDN: Mobile Subscriber ISDN.

PCF: Point Coordination Function.

PIFS: Priority Interframe Space.

PSM: Power Save Mechanism.

PS-Poll: Power Save Poll.

QAP: Quality Enhanced AP.

QoS: Quality of Service.

QSTA: Quality Enhanced STA.

RADIUS: Remote Access Dial-In User Service.

SS: Service Station.

SIFS: Short Interframe Space.

STA: Station.

S-APSD: Scheduled APSD.

TC: Traffic Classes.

TIM: Traffic Indication Map.

TS: Traffic Streams.

TxOP: Transmission Opportunity.

U-APSD: Unscheduled APSD.

UL: Uplink.

VoIP: Voice over IP.

VoWLAN: Voice over WLAN.

WEP: Wire Equivalent Protocol.

WLAN: Wireless Local Area Network.

Wi-Fi: Wireless Fidelity.

Chapter X
Mobile Telecom System Architectures—IMS an Evolution Path Towards IP Convergence

Panagiotis Kasimatis
Nokia Siemens Networks GmbH, Germany

Dimitra Varla
Ericsson Hellas S.A., Greece

ABSTRACT

This chapter deals with the description of the various applied Mobile System Architectures, showing the evolution path towards the IP Convergence issue, with the introduction of the IP Multimedia Subsystem. It contains the most important networks entities of the different Mobile Networks Systems and their integration to the IMS. Being the core of the Fixed-Mobile Converge, IMS' operation, functionality and interoperability with the other Telecom platforms are analyzed. Furthermore, aiming in a cost effective high QoS solution, typical performance evaluation strategies of the network manufacturers are described. Its scope is to give an overview of the existing architectures, their network components, their characteristics and their differences, while also show how nearly all traditional Telecom networks can be converged, with the use of the IMS, to an all-IP network, where various applications can be accessed by heterogeneous network platforms.

INTRODUCTION

Across the years, man's need to communicate with each other has resulted to the development of many heterogeneous telecom systems and network architectures. The beginning has been done with the implementation of basic analogue fixed networks, which across the years became digital and more complex, also with the addition of new IP based technologies like VoIP and xDSL.

However, the increasing need for mobility deployed the mobile cellular telephone systems. With the GSM standard of 2nd Generation, only voice based services could be offered to the clients. But soon, the increasing

Copyright © 2009, IGI Global, distributing in print or electronic forms without written permission of IGI Global is prohibited.

necessity for new data services, which required a broader bandwidth and data transmission rate overcoming the emerged problems and restrictions, has resulted to the research, development and introduction of new modulation and channel management techniques, as well as new improved systems and network architectures.

Therefore, with the introduction of the 2G+ (or 2.5 Generation), a packet data oriented technology, called General Packet Radio Service (GPRS), has been integrated as an overlay architecture to the existing circuit switched one of the GSM. New Core Network entities, like Serving GPRS Support Node (SGSN) and Gateway GPRS Support Node (GGSN), have been introduced, as well as new data radio transmission techniques like HSCSD (High Speed Circuit Switched Data) and EDGE/EGPRS (Enhanced Data rates for GSM evolution).

The introduction of 3rd Generation, based on the UMTS 3GPP release 99 standard, has considerably increased the offered data transmission rate and was then able to offer new exciting data demanding services like streaming video, supporting QoS R99 attributes. Also here new modulation and protocol improvement techniques like High-Speed Packet Access (HSPA) are being developed. The UMTS standard introduced new entities at its UMTS Terrestrial Radio Access Network (UTRAN), like the Node B and the Radio Network Controller (RNC).

A UMTS network comprises integrated elements for both Circuit and Packet Switched area, interworking with existing mobile networks, while also supporting high bit rate with negotiated QoS. In UMTS release 4, the transport bearer and bearer control in the CS core network are separated and ATM (AAL2) or IP can be used as data transport bearer also in the CS domain.

In UMTS release 5, improved modulation techniques like High Speed Downlink Packet Access (HSDPA) are adopted, while the IP Multimedia Subsystem (IMS), based on the Session Initiation Protocol (SIP), is introduced aiming in unifying heterogeneous fixed and wireless networking platforms. The IP Convergence issue that arises, has been developed to the idea of the Fixed Mobile Convergence (FMC)

IMS—A STANDARDIZED NEXT GENERATION NETWORK ARCHITECTURE FOR FIXED/MOBILE CONVERGENCE

Mobile Telecom System Architectures—The IP Convergence Issue

Initial Generation Concept of the Cellular Telecom Systems

Initially radio communication was based on simple single cell analogue systems. After the early 80ties introduction to mass market, digital systems were soon adopted. It is not only the architectural technology but also the transmitted information and data rate that characterize the different generations. To be more precisely, the widely applied and used generations till the present time can be summarized in the following:

- **1st Generation (1G):** Transmission of analogue Information
- **2nd Generation (2G):** Analogue systems give their place to digital ones and Transmission of digital Information is adopted.
  - Implementation based on the GSM Standard aiming mainly on voice services.
- **2nd+ Generation (2G+):** Implementation based on combined Voice and Packet Technology. Introduction of the GPRS.
  - IN Intelligent Networks Services and Data Services with higher Transmission Rate.
- **3rd Generation (3G):** Based on the UMTS Standard.
  - Applications for simultaneously Voice, Picture, Video and Data Transmission

Evolution of the Data Transmission Techniques

As aforementioned, the need for higher Transmission Rate has played a significant role to the evolution of Radio Communications through the years. One issue that arose was the high costs of the technical equipment and therefore the need to re-use the existing one also in new architectures. In order that to be achieved successfully but also smoothly, new modulation and transmission techniques were developed such as:

- **HSCSD (High Speed Circuit Switched Data):**
  - ° Circuit Switched data service for applications demanding higher bandwidth. Enhancement of the GSM Standard in order that higher Data Transmission Rate to be achieved.
  - ° Technically it is about a combination of many neighboring Time-Slots in one logical connection. With the combination of 1-8 timeslots per subscriber, a maximum of 14.4 Kbit/s per timeslot instead of 9.6Kbit/s is achieved.
  - ° Practically its Maximum is 4x14,4, that is to say up to 57,6 Kbit/s
  - ° No new network elements, only SW modifications are needed.
- **EDGE/EGPRS (Enhanced Data rates for GSM evolution):**
  - ° Increase of the Data Rate in the GSM Networks via the use of different modulation procedure.
  - ° Able to realize up to 69.2Kbit/s.
  - ° With the introduction of EDGE, the already existing GPRS and HSCSD systems are enhanced to the E-GPRS (Enhanced GPRS) and ECSD (Enhanced Circuit Switched Data) respectively.
  - ° EDGE is like GPRS. It comprises only a low cost enhancement of the GSM/GPRS Systems, in terms of software updates and component change, which can be installed at the already existing GPRS Networks.
  - ° Only modification to the modulation method is needed.
- **GPRS (General Packet Radio Service):**
  - ° It characterizes the 2.5 Generation, being an enhancement of the GSM Systems with the addition of a packet-oriented technology.
  - ° 1-8 timeslots per subscriber is possible. Maximum bit rate per timeslot up to 21.4Kbit/s.
  - ° New network elements and protocol architecture. Prerequisite for UMTS.

Generally, the concept of the GPRS technology that differs from the already existing one of the GSM includes the following:

- Packet Switched Technology
- Resource Optimization
- Transfer Rate up to 171.2Kbit/s
- Direct Connection to PDNs
- Billing based on the Data Volume
- SMS: more than 160 Characters
- Support of QoS

On the other hand on the 3G side, the advantages of the UMTS Concept have resulted later to the adoption of the UMTS standard, which comprises characteristics such as:

- CDMA Coding Method (W-CDMA)
- UMTS supports both Circuit und Packet Switched Modes
- Applications with simultaneously Voice, Picture, Video and Data Transfer
- Supports high bit-rate with negotiable QoS, especially for asymmetric Traffic
- Support of QoS R99

As also in the case of GPRS, new techniques are developed in order that higher Data Rate to be achieved. Therefore, improved Modulation Schemes with enhanced Protocols are being applied under the general name of High-Speed Packet Access (HSPA). HSPA consists of:

- High-Speed Downlink Packet Access (HSDPA) which delivers improved Down-link Services up to theoretically 14.4Mbits/s. For the time being a bit-rate only up to 3.6Mbit/s is available with maximum Up-link up to 384 Kbit/s.
- High-Speed Uplink Packet Access (HSUPA) which delivers improved Up-link Services up to theoretically 5.76Mbits/s. For the time being no Mobile Phone with this technology is available.

Figure 1. Data rate evolution across the system architectures

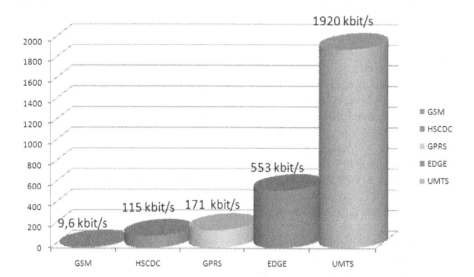

- High Speed OFDM Packet Access (HSOPA) which is still under development. It scopes to a maximum of 100Mbps Data Rate on the Down-link side and 50Mbps on the UP-link side. Completely new and different Air Interface System and incompatible with W-CDMA.

Overview of the System Architectures of the Mobile Networks

Every Mobile Network (GSM/GPRS/UMTS) consists of two main architectural parts:

- The Core Network (CN) in which the transmission of signals between the different Nodes and Platforms of the Mobile Network takes place.
- The Radio Access Network (RAN) in which the Transmission of signals between a Mobile Antenna and the Mobile Phones takes place.

In both of them, two Switching capabilities are used in terms of the available Services. Moreover, Circuit Switching is mainly used for Voice Services, where the Packet Switching for Packet (Data) Services.

2G/2.5G/2.75 (EDGE) GSM-GPRS—3GPP Release 99 Architecture

The Radio Access Network (RAN) is an important part of a mobile network. It comprises the air interface, coupled with those components controlling the networking between the Mobile Equipment, the Base Stations and the Core Network. It is can be either a GRAN or a GERAN:

- **GRAN:** Abbreviation of the GSM Access Network.
    - It consists of Base Transceiver Stations (BTS) and Base Station Controllers (BSC), which together are called Base Station Subsystem (BSS).
- **GERAN:** Abbreviation of the GSM EDGE Access Network.
    - It connects the Base Stations (Ater and Abis Interfaces) and the BSC (Base Station Controllers)
    - A GERAN Network without EDGE is a GRAN. Therefore their concept is quite identical

The Core Network is the other very important part of the mobile networks. It is actually the central part, the "heart" of a mobile network. It can be divided into two categories:

- **NSS (Network Switching Subsystem) or GSM core network.**
  - It performs the Switching tasks and controls the communication between the Mobile Phones and the Public Switched Telephone Network (PSTN).
  - Circuit-Switched Core Network, for traditional GSM Services like voice calls, SMS and Circuit Switched Data calls.
- **GPRS Core Network.**
  - Central part of the GPRS Systems, which also offer support for WCDMA based 3G Networks.
  - It is an Overlay Architecture on the GSM Core.
  - It provides Mobility Management, Session Management and Transport for Internet Protocol (IP) packet services in GSM and WCDMA networks
  - It offers Packet-Switched Data Services.
  - It provides Mobile Phones with access to Services like WAP, MMS and Internet-Access.

GSM Public Land Mobile Network (PLMN)

With the term Cell is stated the area that a BSS serves, which in general means the Antenna area of a Base Station (BS). Each BSS consists of a Base Station Controller (BSC) that controls one or more Base Transceiver Stations (BTS).

The BSS of a Radio Access Network is connected with the NSS, thus the Core Network, and both of them consist the whole PLMN. A typical GSM PLMN and its interfaces can be presented as seen in Figure 2.

2.5G GSM - GPRS Network Architecture

With the evolution of the 2.5G and the introduction of the GPRS in the mobile networks, new important entities were needed. These entities and their functionality can be generally summarized in the following:

Figure 2. GSM system architecture

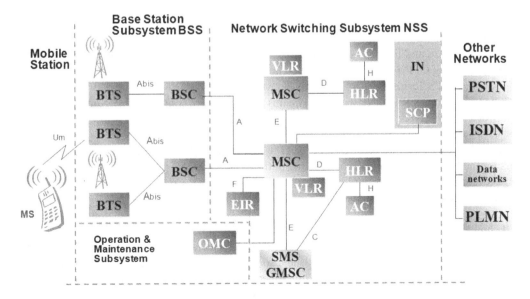

Figure 3. GSM—GPRS system architecture

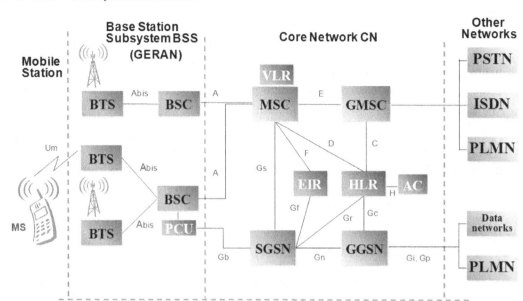

- **SGSN:** Mobility management functions, paging, security functions, routing functions e.t.c.
- **GGSN:** Routing function, interworking with PDNs, collection of charging information.
- **PCU:** Management of GPRS channels, organization of packet transfer uplink and downlink.
- **CCU:** Channel Coding, Radio channel measurements.

Therefore, even though the architecture of a 2.5G Network seems quite similar to the 2G one, it comprises new nodes and interfaces, mainly concerning and contributing to the packet transfer side. A general aspect of such a network is presented in Figure 3.

3G Mobile Networks—UMTS

The idea and the implementation of the Core Network of a 3G UMTS Mobile Network seem quite similar to the GPRS. Only the Database and the connections (ATM) are changed. That is because the UMTS Core Network was based on the existing GPRS one. However, differences arise in the Radio Access Network of UMTS, which is called UTRAN (UMTS Terrestrial Radio Access Network).

UTRAN consists of many Radio Network Subsystems (RNS) that are connected with each other but also with the Core Network. Respectively to the BTSs and BSCs of GERAN, UTRAN includes the entities of:

- **RNC (Radio Network Controller):** Supervises the Radio connections of the UMTS Network, handles the Codes for the WCDMA Channels, contributing in the Service control (power control) and the Handovers. One RNC controls many Cells, typically three or six.
- **Node B:** It is the Base Station of the UMTS and it is controlled by the RNCs.

Figure 4 shows a typical 3GPP Rel. 99 GSM - GPRS - UMTS implementation:

Even though that offered bandwidth of the mobile networks keeps increasing, it is a fact that several problems, that can even block the originating or ongoing calls and so affecting the Quality of Service, still exist. Extended researches have been made by scientists in proposing, for example, improved call admission techniques, scoping to an improved QoS for the mobile network operators and consequently for the end users (Panoutsopoulos, I.,

Figure 4. Overview of an integrated mobile network Rel. 99

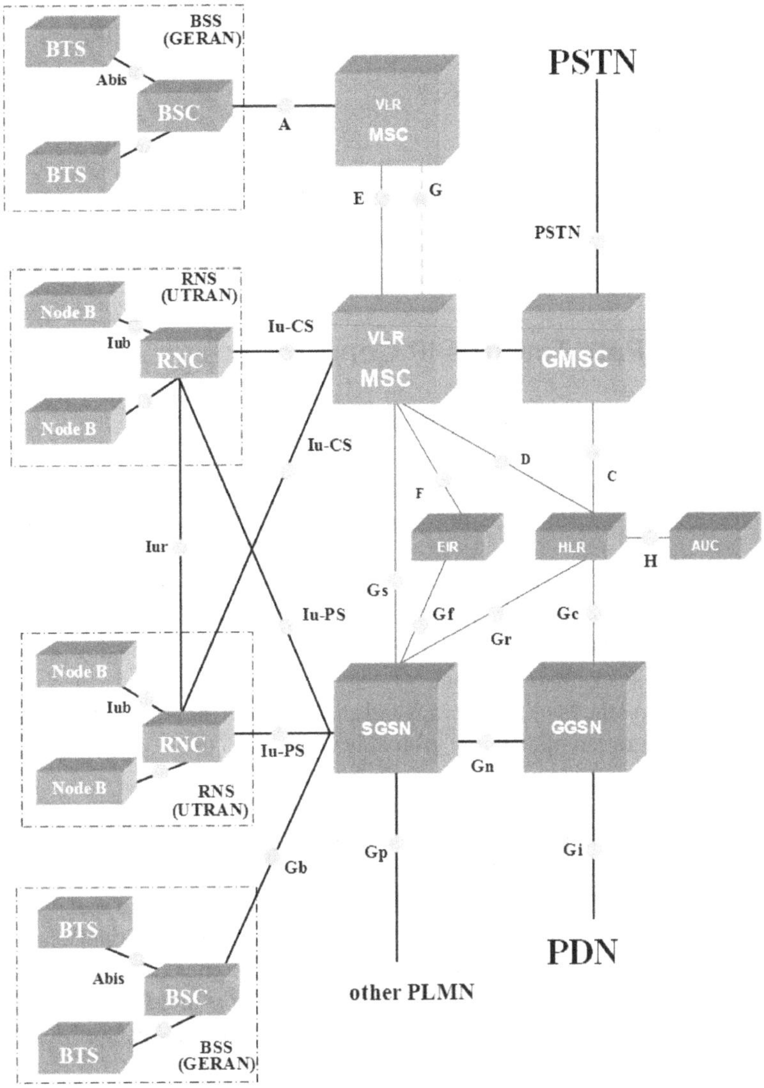

Kotsopoulos, S. and Tountopoulos, V., 2002, July). However, since the introduction of 3GPP Release 4, mobile networks go one step further and extended capabilities appear, affecting in the end also the end user.

The most important changes between 3GPP R99 and R4 are:

- Separation of the Transport Bearer and the Control Bearer at the CS Core Network
- Introduction of new interfaces at the CS Core Network
- ATM (AAL2) or IP can be used for Data Transmission at the CS
- Multimedia Services at the CS
- Real-Time Handover Application at the PS
- Gb over IP
- IPv6 Optional

3G UMTS 3GPP Release 5 Architecture & IP Multimedia Subsystem (IMS)

The most important features of the 3GPP Rel. 5 can be summarized in the following:

* HSDPA: High Speed Downlink Packet Access
* CAMEL Phase 4
* IPv6 mandatory
* Introduction of the IP Multimedia Subsystem (IMS) and use of SIP

A more extensive analysis of the 3GPP Release 5/6/7 and consequently of IMS, towards the Next Generation Networks scope of Fixed – Mobile IP Convergence (FMC), follows.

IMS — The Evolution Path Towards IP Convergence

FMC & IMS — 3GPP Releases 5/6/7

A Next Generation Network (NGN) supports the convergence of heterogeneous IP based Telecom Networks like Fixed, Mobile Networks e.t.c. A general aspect of NGN can be shown further in Figure 10. Its System Architecture consists of:

* **Media Gateways:** They physically connect the different Networks, taking also care of the Information Transmission, as what it concerns the Format and Data Conversion. From analog or digital switched-circuit form (PSTN, SS7) to the packet-based IP one.
* **Softswitches:** They control the Media Gateways and also establish the connections at the Networks' borders enabling the correct integration of different protocols within the NGN.

The IP Multimedia Subsystem (IMS) is a standardized NGN architecture for an Internet media-service capability defined by the European Telecommunications Standards Institute (ETSI) and the 3rd Generation Partnership Project (3GPP).

IMS is the heart of FMC. It is based on Session Initiation Protocol (SIP) and specified at 3GPP Rel.5/6/7. It provides all the signaling procedures which are mandatory for the integration of the Packet Switched Networks. Therefore, it unifies and connects under one platform different technologies like 2G/3G (GPRS, UMTS), xDSL, WLAN, WiMAX, fixed IP telephony, Circuit Switched PLMN networks and PSTN (Figure 6). Moreover, it offers various characteristic Peer-to-Peer Multimedia Services like Presence, Instant Messaging (IM), Call and Video Conference e.t.c.

A distinction between the transport part of the network and the services that run on top of it is taking place in NGNs, and consequently also in IMS. Therefore, whenever a new service, is to be defined, that is realized at the service layer without considering the transport layer.

IMS first appeared in 3GPP Release 5, when SIP-based multimedia services were added. Support for the legacy networks (GSM, GPRS) was also provided. The 3GPP Release 6 introduced interworking with WLAN and 3GPP Release 7 added the support of access via fixed networks, by working together with TISPAN, Release R1.1.

FMC supports a way of Subscription that allows Roaming and Handover of nomadic Subscribers under all integrated Networks. It consists of (Figure 7):

* IMS (IP Multimedia Subsystem)
* Application Servers
* Variable Telecom Networks and IP Elements:
  * Mobile Networks (GERAN, UTRAN und GPRS/UMTS PS core networks, CS PLMN)
  * Fixed TDM
  * VoIP Networks
  * xDSL

- ○ WLAN
- ○ WiMAX
- ○ PSTN/CS Gateways

Figure 7 shows various IMS terminals attaching to the network using a radio link, a WLAN or an ADSL line. There are also terminals that can access the IMS services by any network, such as Personal Digital Assistants (PDAs) and personal computers.

According to the specifications, the IMS architecture comprises of functions, instead of nodes, linked by standardized interfaces. There are multiple ways to implement the IMS, by combining two functions into a single node, that means a single physical entity, or splitting a single function into two or more nodes.

Figure 5. Overview of an integrated mobile network Rel. 4

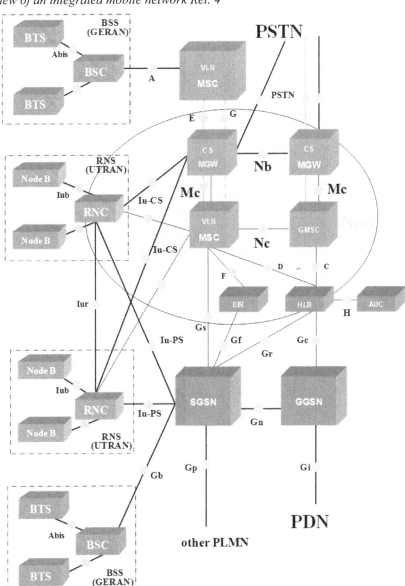

Figure 6. The concept of IMS

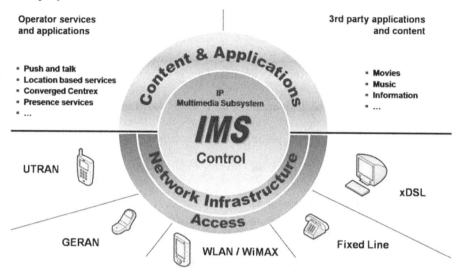

Figure 7. Overview of IMS architecture

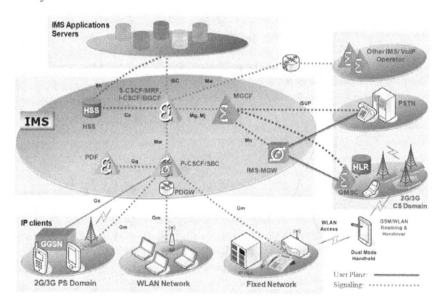

Figure 7 includes the main functions of an IMS network. These are:

- One or more user databases, called Home Subscriber Servers (HSSs) and Subscriber Location Functions (SLFs)
- One or more SIP servers, known as Call Session Control Functions (CSCFs)
- One or more Application Servers (ASs)
- One or more Media Resource Functions (MRFs), further divided into Media Resource Function Controllers (MRFC) and Media Resource Function Processors (MRFP)

- One or more Breakout Gateway Control Functions (BGCFs)
- One or more PSTN gateways, each one divided into a Signaling Gateway (SGW), a Media Gateway Controller Function (MGCF) and an Media Gateway (MGW).

Note that Figure 7 does not include charging collector functions.

Why IMS?

Nowadays, this question usually employs the attention of operators, either mobile or fixed. The answer has many options, in general though, the main benefit is a large variety of innovative multimedia services that are implemented using open standards and can be provided to users of multiple access networks. Moreover, IMS introduces a new telecom model without revoking the legacy networks.

Convergence: Service Layer

An essential benefit of IMS is that it enables convergence in access network, application and service layer. As the service is concerned, IMS architecture provides a number of common functions. These are for instance authentication, presence, provisioning, operation and management, and charging.

IMS provides functions that can be reused by all services in the network. This is due to the horizontal structure according to which IMS network is implemented. Traditional networks use separate implementations of each layer according to the provided service and consist of replicated entities across the network. This kind of network structure is high-cost and inflexible in maintenance.

In IMS networks, many functions are served by common entities. This capability has important impact on the cost of operators' investment in deployment and maintenance of the network functions, offers reliability as the functionality is already used and proven and provides additionally flexibility in the development of new applications and their insertion in the system.

Convergence: Application Layer

IMS architecture provides convergence in application layer as well. Common services, such as presence, push-to-talk, video and telephony, are provided in the fixed, mobile and converged networks separately or at the same time. The same services (presence, group-list) are used whether the subscriber is connected by a mobile device or a personal computer. For example, if a contact in the buddy list goes offline, this change is known by any device where the user is logged on.

Convergence: Access Network

The integration of different access networks is an important benefit of the IMS architecture. As aforementioned, an IMS terminal is able to use the services provided by IMS connecting in a GPRS mobile network or a wireless network or even a VoIP fixed network. The implementation includes also gateways that connect the PSTN and PLMN world with the new IP-based network, concluding to an all-IP convergence. This implies a comfortable way of communication for the end-user, as he/she can be connected any time everywhere, by even a single device, and provides additionally mobility and roaming services that secures the continuity of this communication.

Apart from the mobility issue, the integration of access networks is significant for QoS reasons. There are different requirements for every provided service, such as high bandwidth, low latency etc. This means that services can be provided with the proper quality if the core function is aware of the different capabilities of the access networks. In this way, IMS leads to a true FMC.

Authentication

In the traditional networks, the authentication process could take place many times after the initial user connection to the network, depending on the service the subscriber needs to use. In IMS networks, the authentication process is simpler. The log-on is followed by the user authentication, which is handled by the Call Session Control Function (CSCF) and Home Subscription Server (HSS), and enables the subscriber to access all the IMS services that he/she is authorized to use. When the user requests an application, the Application Server (AS) is informed that the user identity has been checked and so a re-authentication is not necessary.

One-Number – One Bill – One Provider

The convergence of services and access provides the possibility of one number and one common bill. The subscriber can connect to IMS with the same number through different access networks or locations. This enables pricing flexibility, like different tariff according to the location (home, office, elsewhere). Furthermore, as the charging function is common, no matter which access network the user is connected to, it is possible to have one bill for all services. This implies also that all communication services of the user can be supplied by a single provider, which leads to a long-term relationship between the operator and the customer and to a reduction of the churn rate.

Service Development and Delivery

IMS services are hosted on multiple Application Servers. This means that the same infrastructure can be used for new services, so the main focus is on the development of the actual application and not on its introduction in the system, as all the required functions, like authentication and charging are already implemented in the network, due to its horizontal architecture.

Hence, the IMS architecture makes potential services more transparent and guarantees small Operating Expenditures (OPEX) and Capital Expenditures (CAPEX) while it minimizes the business risks and time-to-market.

FUNCTIONAL DESCRIPTION OF IMS NETWORK FUNCTIONS AND INTERFACES

Home Subscriber Server

The *Home Subscriber Server (HSS)* is a database that stores the subscription information of all users in the IMS domain. It stores the User Profiles of all IMS subscribers. These profiles include the subscriber's identity information (e.g. IMSI, IMPI, MSISDN etc.), Service Provisioning information (e.g. Filter criteria), the address of S-CSCF which is assigned to the user and charging information (e.g. SGSN-ID, GCID etc).

Referring to an example user, it could have one user profile for business use and another for private use. These user profiles have different Public Identities and can include different IMS Services.

In case more than one HSS are installed, if for example the number of users in the domain exceeds the capacity of one HSS, a *Subscriber Location Function (SLF)* is deployed and stores the address of the HSS that serves a user.

Both HSS and SLF interface with I-CSCF, S-CSCF and SIP Application Server using Diameter, as shown in Figure 7.

The integration of IMS in a mobile or IT network means usually that the HSS interworks with the HLR of the legacy network so that both databases are synchronized.

Figure 8. Fixed – Mobile Networks: The traditional way

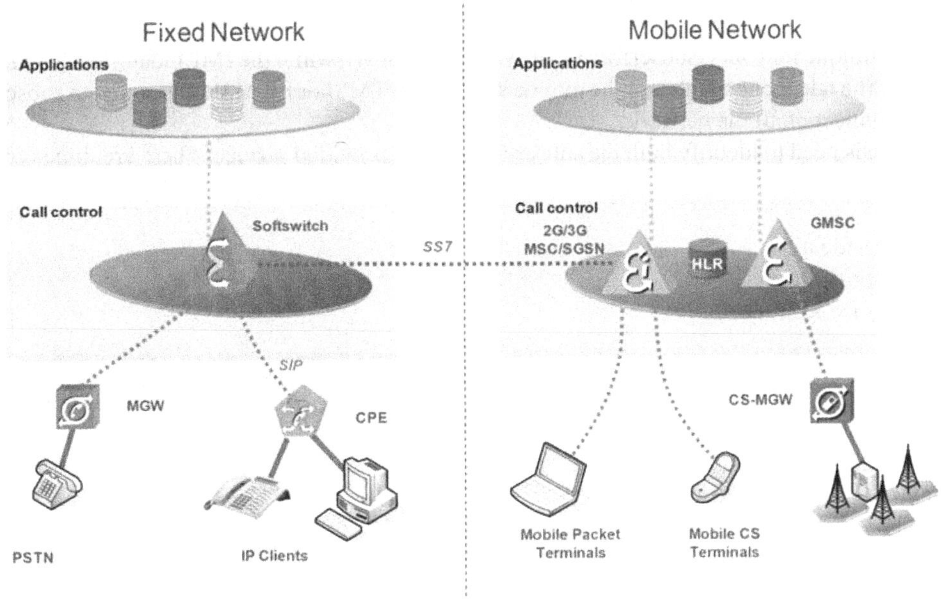

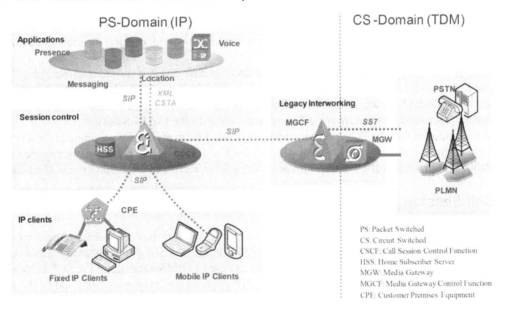

Figure 9. Fixed – Mobile Networks. The IMS based way

User Identities

In the mobile networks, the following identities are used:

- International Mobile Subscriber Identity (IMSI)
- Temporary Mobile Subscriber Identity (TMSI) or Packet TMSI (P-TMSI)

- International Mobile Equipment Identity (IMEI)
- Mobile Subscriber ISDN Number (MSISDN)

The IMSI is unique for every Subscriber Identity Module (SIM), while the IMEI identifies the mobile device. The MSISDN is the telephone number of the mobile subscriber. TMSI or P-TMSI is assigned to subscriber during its successful connection to the network.

In IMS, there is need to identify both the subscriber and the provided service. There are three types of identities:

- Public User Identity
- Private User Identity
- Public Service Identity

An IMS user is attributed with one or more Public User Identities and also carries a Private User Identity. The Public User Identity is either a SIP URI or a TEL URI. The SIP URI has typically the following form:

sip:first.last@operator.com

while TEL URI is like

tel:+1-234-555-0123

The Public User Identity is to IMS what MSISDN is to the mobile networks.

The Private User Identity is similar to IMSI and stored in the smart card as IMSI is stored in SIM. It has the form of a Network Access Identifier (NAI): username@operator.com. Although the Public User Identity is used for SIP signaling forwarding, the Private User Identity is used for subscription identification and authentication purposes.

According to 3GPP Release 5 specifications, an IMS user can have one Private and multiple Public User Identities assigned. Release 6 introduces the possibility to have more than one Public User Identities that are related to different Private User Identities. This allows a Public User Identity to be used by two IMS terminals with two different Private User Identities that means different smart cards in the two IMS devices.

Release 6 introduced also the Public Service Identity (PSI). This is an identity attributed to a service hosted in an Application Server. It may have the form of a SIP URI or a TEL URI. The PSI is not assigned to an IMS user like Public and Private User Identities. Furthermore, it is not related to a specific Private User Identity.

Proxy Call Session Control Function

The Proxy Call Session Control Function (P-CSCF) is a SIP Proxy and the first contact point for IMS clients and thus the IMS network element to which the IMS clients address the SIP signaling traffic. The P-CSCF may be located either in the home or in the visited network; in case of GPRS access, the P-CSCF is located in the same network as GGSN. The P-CSCF receives all the SIP requests and responses from and to the IMS users and forwards them accordingly. During the registration of the IMS subscriber, a single P-CSCF is assigned and communicates with it.

The main role of P-CSCF is security and signaling compression. At first, it establishes IPsec associations with the IMS subscriber providing also integrity check that means detection of changes in the content of the message during its transmission. Since the IMS user is authenticated, P-CSCF declares the user's identity to the rest IMS elements so that reauthentication is not necessary later, in generation of charging records for example.

In addition, P-CSCF compresses and decompresses the SIP messages that receives and sends to the IMS user in order to reduce the time of transmission on the air interface, using SigComp. The IMS clients use respective compressors and de-compressors of the SIP messages.

The P-CSCF also generates charging information that is sent to the Charging Collector Function (CCF), located in the same domain.

The P-CSCF may include a Policy Decision Function (PDF) which allocates the media plane resources and authorizes Quality of Service (QoS). PDF is either embedded in the P-CSCF or implemented as a stand-alone unit.

The P-CSCF also provides Lawful Interception and Emergency Services support.

Interrogating Call Session Control Function

The Interrogating Call Session Control Function (I-CSCF) is a SIP proxy which is listed in the DNS list of a domain and handles its incoming SIP traffic. Firstly, it determines the S-CSCF with which the IMS subscriber should register. This is the result of a query to HSS on a Diameter interface which responds whether the user is allowed to register in the network and the address of the corresponding S-CSCF. Then the I-CSCF contacts the S-CSCF with the register and forwards the SIP messages to that function.

The I-CSCF, up to Release 6, may include the THIG (Topology Hiding Inter-network Gateway) functionality which concerns the encryption of any information in SIP messages that depict the topology of the domain, for example the name of DNS, the number of servers etc. From Release7, this functionality is removed from I-CSCF; it is embedded in the IBCF (Interconnection Control Border Function) which is a gateway to external networks, providing NAT and firewall functions.

Serving Call Session Control Function

The Serving Call Session Control Function (S-CSCF) is the central node of IMS. It is a SIP server responsible mainly for the authentication of IMS user and session control.

The Authentication

As described previously, the I-CSCF contacts the HSS to retrieve the address of the S-CSCF that is responsible for the IMS user. Then I-CSCF forwards the request of the user to be registered in the domain to the corresponding S-CSCF. The latter sends a request for an authentication vector to the HSS. This vector includes authentication data, including RAND, AUTN, and XRES. The S-CSCF sends a SIP message to the I-CSCF that contains RAND and AUTN. The I-CSCF forwards this message to the P-CSCF and this sends the message to the IMS user.

The user checks AUTN and calculates the RES. Then the IMS user sends a SIP message to the P-CSCF including RES. This message is forwarded to the I-CSCF and after the HSS query, to the responsible S-CSCF. The S-CSCF compares the received RES with the XRES; if they are identical, the user is authenticated. The S-CSCF informs the HSS for the successful authentication and also the IMS user through I-CSCF and P-CSCF.

In addition to the authentication, the S-CSCF communicates with the HSS to inform it that this is the S-CSCF assigned to the IMS user during its registration. They interface also in case the S-CSCF retrieves the user profile from the HSS. This user profile holds the user's filter criteria which are triggers relative to specific Application Servers (AS). All SIP messages that the IMS user sends, reach the S-CSCF and they are relayed to one or more AS in a row, according to the evaluation of the messages in reference to the triggers. These AS are responsible for the service provision.

Since all SIP messages traverse the S-CSCF, this is able to block the establishment of sessions which the user is not authorized to, in order to apply the policy of the network operator.

Another functionality of the S-CSCF is the Number Translation Service which is provided when the IMS user dials a telephone number instead of a Uniform Resource Identifier (URI).

The S-CSCF also maintains counters for the user's sessions and provides billing information to the charging function.

A network, as in case of the other CSCFs, usually comprises more than one S-CSCF in the interest if scalability and redundancy. The S-CSCF is always located in the home network.

Application Server

The Application Server (AS) hosts and executes all the IMS applications and services. It can be dedicated to a single application or provide several services. It is also possible to combine services from many AS in order to provide a unified application to the end-user. For example, an IMS user can combine presence and video calling simultaneously although these services are hosted in different AS.

An AS can operate in one of the following mode, depending on the service it provides, the SIP proxy mode, the SIP User Agent (UA) mode and the SIP Back-to-Back User Agent (B2BUA) mode. It interfaces the S-CSCF with SIP and the HSS, when located in the home network, with Diameter. The AS communicates with the HSS in order to get information that is required in the operation of the call, as for example the presence of the called subscriber, the caller/called party's preferences, the current credit of the subscribers etc. Examples of AS are the Presence AS, the Instant Messaging AS and the Voice Mail AS.

Media Resource Function (MRF)

The Media Resource Function (MRF) provides media processing in the home network.

The MRF is divided into the Media Resource Function Controller (MRFC), controlling the signaling plane and the Media Resource Function Processor (MRFP), processing the media plane. The MRFC is a SIP User Agent which interfaces the S-CSCF with SIP and the MRFP with H.248/Megaco. The MRFC gets instructions from the AS to manage the media stream handled by the Media Server and controls the resources in the MRFP. The MRFP supports all the media-related functions, for example playing and mixing audio for conference calls, converting codecs or making media analysis and generating statistics.

Breakout Gateway Control Function (BGCF)

The Breakout Gateway Control Function (BGCF) is a SIP server which is used only in sessions where the calling party is a subscriber in the CS network, such as in the PSTN or PLMN. It routes the telephony sessions, based on the telephone number, to a Media Gateway Control Function (MGCF) which selects a Media Gateway (MG) or to a BGCF in another operator's network.

Media Gateway Control Function (MGCF)

The Media Gateway Control Function (MGCF) performs the protocol translation between SIP and the signaling protocol that is used in the CS network, for example the ISUP. In addition, it controls a Media Gateway (MG) which performs the translation between RTP and the media format provided by the CS network and also media transcoding of voice and video if necessary. The MGCF interfaces the CSCF with SIP, the control plane of PSTN/PLMN with ISUP and the MG with H.248 protocol.

Figure 10 shows the interfaces of the MGCF and MGs with the nodes of a Next Generation Network.

Signaling Gateway (SG)

The Signaling Gateway (SG) interacts with the MGCF and the switch of the CS network (PSTN, PLMN). It performs lower layer protocol translation; it converts the lower MTP into SCTP for the communication of a PSTN network for instance with the MGCF. In other words, it transforms the ISUP over MTP to ISUP over SCTP and vice versa.

Charging

Charging is the collection of accounting tickets for the purpose of billing. The accounting tickets provide information about the type and the length of the sessions that an IMS subscriber establishes and also for the media traffic during the sessions.

According to the 3GPP specifications, the IMS provides two charging modes, the offline and the online mode. Offline charging is used for subscribers who pay periodically, every month for instance and online charging or credit-based charging is typically applied in case of prepaid services. The accounting tickets in IMS are transferred on the Diameter-based interfaces Rf and Ro.

Offline Charging

All the SIP nodes (P-CSCF, I-CSCF, S-CSCF, BGCF, MRFC, MGCF, AS), excluding HSS and SLF, send accounting tickets to the Charging Collector Function (CCF) over the Diameter-based Rf interface. The CCF collects the accounting information and generates Charging Data Records (CDRs), in a standardized format, which is sent to the Billing System (BS) over the Bi interface. Regarding the GPRS access, the accounting information is sent by SGSN and GGSN to the Charging Gateway Function (CGF) over Ga interface. The CGF relays CDRs to the BS over Bp interface. The Bi and Bp interfaces are typically based on File Transfer Protocol (FTP).

In 3GPP Release 6 the CCF is replaced by the Charging Data Function (CDF). The accounting information is transferred from the IMS nodes to CDF over Rf interface; the CDRs are sent by the CDF to the CGF over Ga interface and the CGF forwards them to the BS.

Online Charging

Online or credit-based charging as often called is used for the real time check of subscriber's credit. If the subscriber runs out of credit, services are not further accessible and the session is terminated.

The online charging is implemented over the Ro Diameter-based interface which provides communication between the Application Servers and the MRFC towards the Event Charging Function (ECF). Additionally, the S-CSCF interfaces the Session Charging Function (SCF) which is similar to a SIP application server over the ISC interface. The SCF informs the S-CSCF in case of lack of credit to invoke the termination of current session.

KEY PROTOCOLS IN IMS

Session Initiation Protocol (SIP)

SIP is the main signaling protocol in an IMS network. It was developed by the IETF and selected by 3GPP Release 5 as a standard for IMS.

SIP is an application layer protocol in the OSI model. It is used in the establishment, modification and termination of multimedia sessions over IP networks. These sessions may refer to delivery of media such as video, voice and chat; the media transport is handled separately.

SIP is a transaction based (using Requests and Responses), Peer-to-Peer Protocol that has a client-server architecture. SIP messages are encoded in ASCII text format which means that as a text-based protocol, it enables debugging and extension of the provided services in the IMS network. In addition, it works end-to-end and supports mobility management, session setup, session management and the flexibility to dynamically add or remove participants to a multimedia session. These capabilities of SIP are the main reasons why it was selected by 3GPP to serve the IMS network.

Diameter

Diameter is the Authentication, Authorization and Accounting (AAA) protocol in the IMS networks. It is an evolution of RADIUS which is widely used on the internet as an AAA protocol. In comparison with RADIUS, Diameter has improved proxy, session control, and security. Furthermore, it uses Transmission Control Protocol (TCP) or Stream Control Transmission Protocol (SCTP) and not UDP as transport.

Diameter comprises a base protocol and the Diameter Applications. The Diameter Applications are customizations or extensions to Diameter and provide particular applications.

Figure 10. Interfaces of the MGCF and MGs in a next generation network

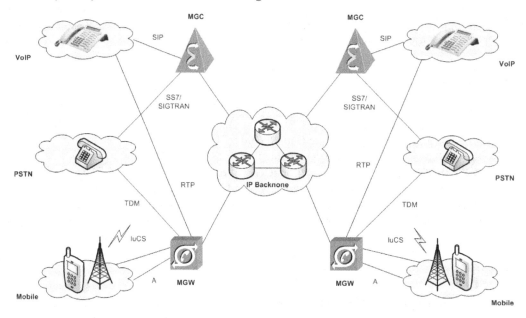

Diameter is used in many interfaces in the IMS network. However, different applications may be used on each one. For example, a Diameter application serves the authentication of IMS users and another one provides credit control for accounting purposes.

H.248

H.248 is a media control protocol. It was developed by ITU-T and IETF and is also called the MEdia GAteway COntrol (MEGACO) protocol.

H.248 is used between media control functions and nodes in the media plane. For instance, it is used for the communication between the Media Gateway Control Function (MGCF) and Media Gateways or between the Media Resource Function Controller (MRFC) and the Media Resource Function Processor (MRFP).

Real-Time Transport Protocol (RTP), Real-Time Transport Control Protocol (RTCP)

RTP and RTCP were developed by IETF. RTP is used in the media (audio and video) transmission while RTCP is used to control QoS.

Typical Test Procedures for Performance Evaluation of Quality of Service (Qos) in Current and Upcoming Telecom Systems

The offered QoS by the network is always a big issue in the telecoms industry. High level quality, comprising speed, accuracy and dependability experienced by the user is essential. Due to new and increasing IP based multimedia services, the possible packet loss could pose a severe problem reducing the end-to-end QoS. Therefore, the quality of promising possibilities of the Next Generation Networks has become mandatory. Moreover, special strategies in System Test Engineering under Load and Stress conditions are necessary to be adopted in order to guarantee a high quality of the offered services to the operators and the end users.

Quality of Service Evaluation in Legacy Networks

In general, the QoS of a telecom system is guaranteed after various tests in laboratory on specific parts of the network, using real or simulated equipment.

In the PS mobile area, System Tests are performed, also under Load and Stress conditions to ensure the five nines reliability, the downtime (min/year) and the Mean Time Between Failures (MTBF), according to the related specifications. The tests include simulation of the estimated maximum traffic that would be performed in the field. The QoS is evaluated by measurements of the probability of signaling procedure errors, packet drop rate and probability of corrupted, duplicated or miss-routed packets. For that purpose various counters are used: on the SGSN and GGSN that give statistics about the number of dropped, misrouted or corrupted packets, on the Base Station Subsystems (BSS) and Radio Network Subsystems (RNS) emulators that give statistics and decoding of the sent and received from the node signaling messages and data, on the routers that are connected between the network entities and also on the protocol monitoring equipment. In this way, signaling error rate, packet error rate and delay are calculated and afterwards compared with the recommended values by the related specifications (e.g. 3GPP, ITU-T).

In the VoIP area, the QoS is evaluated based on measurements of end–to–end delay, comprising processing delay, propagation delay and queuing delay, jitter and packet loss. These parameters are measured or calculated using external tools, for example Ethereal/Etherpeek and also counters on the IP routers.

Concerning the voice over PCM area, the QoS is translated into end–to–end perceived speech quality. This is evaluated by the use of tools that calculate the jitter, delay, attenuation, background noise, signal to noise ratio (SNR) and the mean opinion score (MOS) of speech samples over the PCM line. Opera, by Opticom, is such a tool that uses the Perceptual Evaluation of Speech Quality (PESQ) standard of ITU-T.

Quality of Service Evaluation Example – Laboratory Tests in Mobile PS Core Network

During testing of QoS in a mobile PS network, there are phases, from the functional testing to an end-to-end test performed with real equipment. The latter is usually carried out in conditions of load and stress, which means that a high number of subscribers are attached on the node and perform traffic that may stress the system to the limits. There are two kinds of test procedures that are followed, the short duration, which may include overload tests, security tests, or even error cases (e.g. erroneous message flows), and the long duration tests which may include a stable traffic that runs on the system for a couple of days. The purpose on both cases is to evaluate the performance of the network and its stability, after measurements on control and user plane also.

A long duration test usually simulates the mean traffic running on a real network. After the run, there are specific parameters that have to be checked in order to evaluate the performance and the probable errors.

A major aspect in the evaluation of the run is the stability of traffic during the test period, which in the example that follows is assumed as one night. Figure 11 shows the traffic in mErlang that ran on SGSN over the night. On the left the attachment of the subscribers is shown and also the gradual increase of the traffic. On the right, the decrease on the curve implies that an amount of the subscribers stop producing traffic.

In this example, at about 9 o'clock, there is a slight decline of the traffic, which may be caused by an error on any entity in the network, or even an error from the BSS/RNS side. In order to investigate the error, appropriate statistics have to be retrieved from all the nodes of the network, starting from the SGSN. There are also alarms notifications generated by the SGSN which can be useful in the evaluation of the run.

Then, the next step is the evaluation of the performance counters taken by the SGSN. There are statistical information about the signaling procedures and the data as well. In the specifications, there are some limits about the signaling errors (e.g. attach, routing area updates, pdp context activations, deactivations, modifications etc) and about the user plane (e.g. packet drop probability, duplicated packet probability, miss-routed or corrupted packet probability) that must be taken into consideration. In the evaluation of the error or of the performance in general, the signaling and packet error rates are calculated by the combination of the statistics retrieved by the SGSN, the GGSN (see Figure 13), the BSS and RNS and also by the Ethernet switches that may be located

Figure 11. Overnight traffic in mErlang

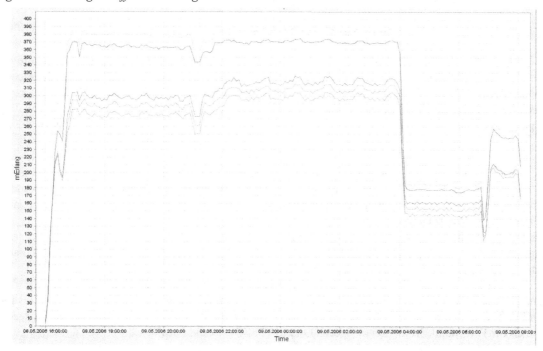

Figure 12. Overnight traffic in mErlang

Scanner ID	Scanner Name	Value Total	Value Hour	Value Second	Long Text	Duration / sec
					meanNbrOfPmmInmsc	58.500
406 sgsn3gGMMAF		4.978			meanNbrOfPmmConnected	58.500
407 sgsn3gSM		2.899.167	178.410	49,56	attActPdpContext	58.500
407 sgsn3gSM		5	0	0,00	succActPDPContextHighPriority	58.500
407 sgsn3gSM		2.899.154	178.409	49,56	succActPDPContextLowPriority	58.500
407 sgsn3gSM		2.899.167	178.410	49,56	attActPdpContextDyn	58.500
407 sgsn3gSM		2.899.159	178.409	49,56	succActPdpContextDyn	58.500
407 sgsn3gSM		7.950			meanActPDPContextLowPriority	58.500
407 sgsn3gSM		8.224.572	506.127	140,59	attDeactPdpContextMs	58.500
407 sgsn3gSM		8.224.569	506.127	140,59	succDeactPdpContextMs	58.500
407 sgsn3gSM		522.718	32.167	8,94	nbrOfActPDPContextLowPriority	58.500
407 sgsn3gSM		295.638	18.193	5,05	nbrActivePdpPerSgsn	58.500
407 sgsn3gSM		4.501			meanActivePdpPerSgsn	58.500
407 sgsn3gSM		15	0	0,00	attDeactPdpContextSgsn	58.500
407 sgsn3gSM		15	0	0,00	succDeactPdpContextSgsn	58.500
407 sgsn3gSM		644.647	39.670	11,02	attUpdPdpContextSgsn	58.500
407 sgsn3gSM		644.647	39.670	11,02	succUpdPdpContextSgsn	58.500
407 sgsn3gSM		50	3	0,00	attModPdpContextSgsn	58.500
407 sgsn3gSM		50	3	0,00	succModPdpContextSgsn	58.500
407 sgsn3gSM		644.597	39.667	11,02	attModPdpContextMs	58.500
407 sgsn3gSM		644.596	39.667	11,02	succModPdpContextMs	58.500
407 sgsn3gSM		435.497.018	26.799.816	7.444,39	totalPdpContextDuration	58.500
412 sgsnGMMAF		16.641	1.024	0,28	attInsertSubDataHlrUpdLoc	58.500
412 sgsnGMMAF		16.641	1.024	0,28	attUpdateGprsLocationHlr	58.500
412 sgsnGMMAF		16.641	1.024	0,28	succUpdateGprsLocationHlr	58.500
412 sgsnGMMAF		50	3	0,00	attCancelLocHlrSgsnChg	58.500
412 sgsnGMMAF		899.729	55.367	15,38	attReqAuthSetsHlrV3	58.500
412 sgsnGMMAF		899.729	55.367	15,38	succReqAuthSetsHlrV3	58.500
412 sgsnGMMAF		1.968.177	121.118	33,64	attMapMtForwardSms	58.500
412 sgsnGMMAF		1.915.643	117.885	32,75	succMapMtForwardSms	58.500
412 sgsnGMMAF		50	3	0,00	attContextRequestFromPsgsn	58.500
412 sgsnGMMAF		50	3	0,00	succContextRequestFromPsgsn	58.500
413 ra3gGMMAF		2.369.320	145.804	40,50	succGprsAttach	58.500
413 ra3gGMMAF		34.655.420	2.132.641	592,40	attIntraSgsnRaUpdate	58.500
413 ra3gGMMAF		34.655.340	2.132.636	592,40	succIntraSgsnRaUpdate	58.500
413 ra3gGMMAF		1.403.572	86.373	23,99	attGprsDetachMs	58.500
413 ra3gGMMAF		50	3	0,00	attInterSgsnRaUpdate	58.500
413 ra3gGMMAF		50	3	0,00	succInterSgsnRaUpdate	58.500
413 ra3gGMMAF		949.172	58.410	16,23	attCombiDetachMS	58.500
418 sgsn3gSecurity		865.999	53.292	14,80	attAuthProcsSgsnUsim	58.500
418 sgsn3gSecurity		865.999	53.292	14,80	succAuthProcsSgsnUsim	58.500
418 sgsn3gSecurity		50	3	0,00	attContextRequestToPsgsn	58.500
418 sgsn3gSecurity		50	3	0,00	succContextRequestToPsgsn	58.500

Figure 13. Overnight statistics

```
SUP720#execute-on all-mwams all show gprs access-point statistics 1
----------- Slot 7/CPU 1, show gprs access-point statistics 1------------
ERROR: Invalid option. Use ? for help.

----------- Slot 7/CPU 2, show gprs access-point statistics 1------------
        PDP activation intiated by MS:                  2454280
        Successful PDP activation intiated by MS:       2454280
        Dynamic PDP activation initiated by MS:         926541
        Successful dynamic activation initiated by MS:  926541
        PDP deactivation initiated by MS:               2454272
        Successful PDP deactivation initiated by MS:    2454273
        Network initiated PDP activation:               0
        Successful network initiated PDP activation:    0
        PDP deactivation initiated by GGSN:             0
        Successful PDP deactivation initiated by GGSN:  0
        active PDP:                                     7
        upstream data volume in octets:                 74865848800
        downstream data volume in octets:               320899807680
        upstream packet count:                          615095201
        downstream packet count:                        615087275
        DHCP address requests sent by GGSN:             0
        DHCP address requests successful:               0
        DHCP address release sent by GGSN:              0


----------- Slot 7/CPU 3, show gprs access-point statistics 1------------
        PDP activation intiated by MS:                  2452668
        Successful PDP activation intiated by MS:       2452668
        Dynamic PDP activation initiated by MS:         926118
        Successful dynamic activation initiated by MS:  926118
        PDP deactivation initiated by MS:               2452663
        Successful PDP deactivation initiated by MS:    2452663
        Network initiated PDP activation:               0
        Successful network initiated PDP activation:    0
        PDP deactivation initiated by GGSN:             0
        Successful PDP deactivation initiated by GGSN:  0
        active PDP:                                     5
        upstream data volume in octets:                 74688081792
        downstream data volume in octets:               320142509712
        upstream packet count:                          613646449
        downstream packet count:                        613638465
        DHCP address requests sent by GGSN:             0
        DHCP address requests successful:               0
        DHCP address release sent by GGSN:              0


----------- Slot 7/CPU 4, show gprs access-point statistics 1------------
        PDP activation intiated by MS:                  2454981
        Successful PDP activation intiated by MS:       2454981
        Dynamic PDP activation initiated by MS:         926522
        Successful dynamic activation initiated by MS:  926522
        PDP deactivation initiated by MS:               2454978
        Successful PDP deactivation initiated by MS:    2454978
        Network initiated PDP activation:               0
        Successful network initiated PDP activation:    0
        PDP deactivation initiated by GGSN:             0
        Successful PDP deactivation initiated by GGSN:  0
        active PDP:                                     3
        upstream data volume in octets:                 74951983488
        downstream data volume in octets:               321284981720
        upstream packet count:                          615842750
        downstream packet count:                        615834862
        DHCP address requests sent by GGSN:             0
        DHCP address requests successful:               0
        DHCP address release sent by GGSN:              0


----------- Slot 7/CPU 5, show gprs access-point statistics 1------------
```

between the nodes. Figure 12 shows a view of the counters taken by the SGSN that include the information about the control plane of the traffic.

There is also another source of statistics in the network. This is the monitoring equipment which could be connected between two entities and screen the interface. For instance, a monitoring device can be connected with the BSS on the one side and the SGSN on the other side in order to process the traffic running on Gb interface. With "process" it is implied that the device shows graphically the monitored traffic on a screen and also takes statistics of the events which take place on that interface (see Figure 7). These statistics are analyzed and compared with the counters of the nodes. In this way, the packet loss or errors and also the signaling faults can be calculated and evaluated.

The procedure described previously is an example of the laboratory tests performed in order to ensure the quality of service of a Mobile PS node. In the Next Generation Networks, there are respective test procedures that check the security, the end-to-end data delivery, the policy, the charging and the rest signaling processes. The final purpose is the same; the operator should be able to offer real-time and non-real time services in the users' expected quality while maintaining the stability of the system. The introduction of IMS makes this goal

Figure 14. Statistics of agilent technologies monitoring equipment

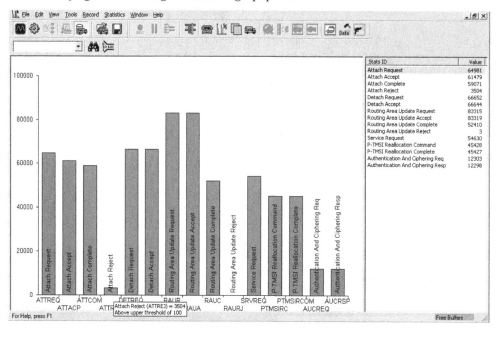

even more important, since all traditional telecom networks are converged and controlled by a single function. Hence, the high quality of service is mandatory and provides the basis for the further evolution of Next Generation Networks to a breakthrough in services and applications.

CONCLUSION

The need for communication is a strong motive that has leaded to a significant cultural and technological progress over the centuries. Nowadays, the communication revolves around the sharing of everyday life experience, anywhere, anytime, on any device and network. The Fixed-Mobile Convergence scheme implements an all-IP network where anyone can be connected from heterogeneous networks and access a wide variety of multimedia applications. This chapter describes the structure, the operation and a sample test procedure for the control of Quality of Service in the Mobile Networks, and also their descendant, IMS. The chapter refers to the most important IMS network components and describes their functionality in the integrated network.

IMS is the core of Fixed-Mobile Convergence. It supports interoperability among different networks, access-awareness, security, quality of service, simple deployment of innovative and convenient multimedia services. Finally, IMS introduces the Internet to the Telecoms, combining the unique advantages of the telecom industry with an evolutional application world.

REFERENCES

3rd Generation Partnership Project. (2002, September). Network Architecture (Release 1999). TS 23.002.

3rd Generation Partnership Project. (2003, June). Network Architecture (Release 4). TS 23.002.

3rd Generation Partnership Project. (2003, December). Network Architecture (Release 6). TS 23.002.

Bannister, J., Wiley InterScience (Online Service), & John Wiley & Sons (2004). *Convergence Technologies for 3G Networks IP, UMTS, EGPRS and ATM.* (1st ed ed.) Chichester: John Wiley Sons Ltd.

Camarillo, G. & Garcia-Martin, M. A. (2006). The 3G IP multimedia subsystem (IMS) merging the Internet and the cellular worlds. (2nd ed ed.) Chichester: Wiley.

Camarillo, G., Kauppinen, T., Kuparinen, M. and Ivars, I. M. (2007, March). Towards an Innovation Oriented IP Multimedia Subsystem, IEEE Communications Magazine.

Chakraborty, S., Peisa, J., Frankkila, T. and P. Synnergren. (2007). IMS Multimedia Telephony over Cellular Systems, JohnWiley & Sons.

Ericsson. (2005, April). Evolution towards converged services and networks, White Paper.

Ericsson. (2007, March). Introduction to IMS, White Paper.

Koukal, M., Bestak, R. (2006, June). Architecture of IP Multimedia Subsystem. IEEE, 48th International Symposium ELMAR, Zadar, Croatia

Lin, Y. B. & Ebooks Corporation (2005). *Wireless and Mobile All-IP Networks.* Hoboken: John Wiley & Sons, Inc.

May, P. (2005). Application Services in an IP Multimedia Subsystem (IMS) Network, Data Connection Limited, White Paper.

Nexus Telecom, Neeser, F. (2005, May). Testing Media Gateways to Enable Convergence, White Paper.

Panoutsopoulos, I., Kotsopoulos, S. and Tountopoulos, V. (2002, July). Handover and New Call Admission Policy Optimization in G3G Systems", Journal on Wireless Networks, Vol.8, No.4, pp.381-389.

Tektronix. (2002, June). UMTS Technology Seminars, June 2002

Siemens. (2006, April). Fixed Mobile Convergence (FMC) Based on IMS. For Mobile Network Operators.

Vrdoljak, M., Vrdoljak, S. I. and Skugor, G. (2000, February). Fixed-Mobile Convergence Strategy: Technologies and Market Opportunities, IEEE Communications Magazine.

KEY TERMS

3GPP: Third Generation Partnership Project .

AAA: Authentication, Authorization and Accounting.

AC: Authentication Center.

BGCF: Breakout Gateway Control Function.

BS: Base Station.

BSC: Base Station Controller.

BSS: Base Station Subsystem.

BTS: Base Transceiver Station.

CAMEL: Customised Applications for Mobile networks Enhanced Logic.

CCU: Channel Control Unit.

CDMA2000: Code Division Multiple Access.

CN: Core Network.

CSCF: Call Session Control Function.

ECSD: Enhanced Circuit Switched Data.

EDGE: Enhanced Data rates for GSM Evolution.

EGPRS: Enhanced GPRS.

EIR: Equipment Identity Register.

ETSI: European Telecommunications Standards Institute.

FMC: Fixed – Mobile Convergence.

FW: Fire Wall.

GERAN: GSM EDGE Access Network.

GGSN: Gateway GPRS Support Node.

GMSC: Gateway MSC.

GPRS: General Packet Radio Service.

GRAN: GSM Access Network.

GSM: Global System for Mobile communications.

GSTN: General Switched Telephony Network.

HLR: Home Location Register.

HSCSD: High Speed Circuit Switched Data.

HSDPA: High-Speed Downlink Packet Access.

HSOPA: High Speed OFDM Packet Access.

HSPA: High-Speed Packet Access.

HSUPA: High-Speed Uplink Packet Access.

HSS: Home Subscriber Server.

I-CSCF: Interrogating-CSCF.

IETF: Internet Engineering Task Force.

IMS: IP Multimedia Subsystem.

IN: Intelligent Networks.

IP: Internet Protocol.

ISC: IMS Service Control.

ISUP: ISDN User Part.

MGCF: Media Gateway Control Function.

MGW: Media Gateway.

MRF: Media Resource Function.

MRFC: Media Resource Function Controller.

MRFP: Media Resource Function Processor.

MSC: Mobile Switching Center.

NAT: Network Address Translation.

NSS: Network Switching Subsystem.

O&M: Operation and Maintenance.

OFDM: Orthogonal Frequency-Division Multiplexing.

OMC: Operations and Maintenance Center.

P-CSCF: Proxy-CSCF.

PCU: Packet Control Unit.

PDN: Public Data Networks.

PoC: Push to talk over Cellular.

PLMN: Public Land Mobile Network.

PSTN: Public Switched Telephony Network.

QoS: Quality of Service.

RAN: Radio Access Network.

RNC: Radio Network Controller.

RNS: Radio Network Subsystem.

RTP: Real-time Transport Protocol.

S-CSCF: Serving-CSCF.

SCTP: Stream Control Transmission Protocol.

SGSN: Serving GPRS Support Node.

SIP: Session Initiation Protocol.

SMS: Short Message Service.

SLF: Subscriber Location Function.

TCP: Transmission Control Protocol.

TISPAN: Technical committee within ETSI for Next Generation Networks.

TDM: Time Division Multiplexing.

UDP: User Datagram Protocol.

UMTS: Universal Mobile Telecommunications System.

UTRAN: UMTS Terrestrial Radio Access Network.

VLR: Visitor Location Register.

VoIP: Voice over IP.

WCDMA: Wideband Code Division Multiple Access.

WiFi: Wireless Fidelity.

WiMAX: Worldwide interoperability for Microwave Access.

WLAN: Wireless Local Area Network.

Chapter XI
Mobile Positioning in Next Generation Networks

Peter Brida
University of Zilina, Slovakia

Peter Cepel
Siemens PSE s.r.o., Zilina, Slovakia

Jan Duha
University of Zilina, Slovakia

ABSTRACT

This chapter deals with mobile positioning in wireless heterogeneous next generation networks. Positioning process is analyzed and the chapter gives an overview of the basic positioning principles and methods that can be used in various NGN platforms. The main focus is given on cellular, ad hoc and sensor networks. Fundamental positioning methods are similar regardless of network platform. The difference usually lies in positioning accuracy. This is caused by technical parameters of the particular application platform. The end of the chapter deals with positioning experiments. The main purpose of authors is simple explanation of fundamental positioning principles for various NGN network platforms.

INTRODUCTION

Mobile positioning is a broad topic that has received considerable attention from the research community over the past few decades. There is increasing interest towards positioning technologies and Location Based Services (LBS), but the utilization of mobile positioning in emergency situations and LBS are not alone. The mobile device position information will play an important role in radio resource management algorithms. Positioning in wireless ad hoc and sensor networks is important in term of routing algorithms and effective communication between particular network elements. Application of ad hoc networks is not only in security services but also in location based applications. Ability to define mobile device position depends on accurate positioning data achieving. This information is used to calculate the mobile device position. The data capturing is realized by measuring

Copyright © 2009, IGI Global, distributing in print or electronic forms without written permission of IGI Global is prohibited.

particular parameters of the radio signal. Measurements relate either explicitly or implicitly the mobile device position to the position of reference devices or to the specific behavior of the mobile device and its surrounding environment. Each measurement defines a line of position and the mobile device lies on this line. The mobile device position can be calculated by the intersection computation of measured lines of position.

Mobility of the mobile devices is high and there is usually no restriction regarding the mobile device environment. It is necessary to differentiate indoor and outdoor positioning environment and to choose correct positioning technology on the base of corresponding environment. The most accurate positioning results can be obtained by means of GNSS based positioning, but this system is applicable only in outdoor environment. Indoor environment requires the different positioning technologies, e.g. cellular, ad hoc, sensor or RFID positioning.

Generally, we can say that the application of positioning system needs to take into consideration two basic factors: the positioning accuracy and deployment costs. These factors may be opposite, but they are important for successful positioning based solution.

POSITIONING IN WIRELESS NETWORKS

The concept of positioning is not limited just to the geographic representation of physical location with sets of coordinates (latitude, longitude, and altitude). It is also applicable to symbolic location in a non-geographic sense, such as location in time or in a virtual information space, such as a data structure or the graph of a network.

Common to all notions of location is the concept that the individual locations are all relative to each other, meaning that they depend on a predefined frame of reference. This leads to a differentiation of the relative and absolute positioning (Tseng, Huang & Kuo, 2005).

If position information is used in reference to a geographic map or a global time reference, the context information can be extended. An absolute position is given with respect to an inertial system and a reference point in the inertial system. On the other side, a relative position can only be given with respect to other points resolving the distances and the geometric configuration, e.g., the topology.

When talking about physical location in the traditional way, points are usually viewed as three-dimensional coordinates $[x; y; z]$ in a Cartesian reference coordinate system.

Usually, $[x; y; z]$ coordinates by themselves are not meaningful for context-aware system services and the other information needs to be associated with this position information. In these cases, it is important to introduce the fourth dimension – time. If a time dimension is introduced, we are able to specify where and when a certain event took place resulting in sets of $[x; y; z; t]$ for each position information. The four-dimensional fix can be used to put subsequent events into a context frame.

Positioning Methods Classification

There are numerous methods that can be considered for implementation in wireless position location systems. We will discuss the most often used methods. It is possible to define many criterions for separation of the particular methods.

One viewpoint of examining positioning methods is to consider where the position measurements are made and where the position information is used for position estimation. There are two basic positioning groups: mobile based positioning and network based positioning.

In a mobile based positioning (self positioning in (Drane, 1998) or mobile centric in (Klukas, 1997)) method the receiver (localized mobile device) makes the appropriate signal measurements from geographically distributed transmitters (reference devices, e.g., base stations, reference nodes). These measurements are used to determine receiver location. Computing operations are done in mobile device, e.g. Mobile Station (MS). The best known mobile based positioning system is Global Positioning System (GPS). MS knows its position, and the applications collocated with the MS can use this information to make position based decisions. This position information can be also sent to another system, e.g., monitoring centre.

In a network based positioning (remote positioning or network centric) method, receivers (reference devices) at one or more locations measure a signal originating from the positioned device. These measurements are communicated to a central site where they are combined to give an estimate of the mobile device location. This position information can be used at the central site or sent to another system (application), which require the location of given mobile device.

The hybrid positioning method is combination of previously mentioned methods. It is possible to send position measurements from mobile device to a network or vice versa. For example, the necessary measurements can be done in the mobile device and measured results are sent to the network part. The position is estimated in the network part. It is also known as a mobile assisted positioning.

The next criterion for positioning method classification is complexity of the real network implementation. The implementation complexity of particular methods is not same. The majority of methods require the changes either in network part or in mobile device part. Such methods can be classified into three categories. Either the positioning method will require a modification in the existing mobile devices or the method can be designed in such a way that all the modifications take place at the network (reference devices, e.g., base stations or the switching center) with no modifications in the existing mobile devices. The last possibility is that the modifications are done on the both parts.

Another classification is based on the measurement principle (Laitinen et al., 2001). The measurement principle of each method belongs to one of three categories: multilateral, unilateral and bilateral method. In multilateral methods, several reference devices make simultaneous (or almost simultaneous) measurements. Multilateral measurement principle leads to network based positioning. Unilateral means that the mobile device measures signals, which are sent by several reference devices. This category leads to mobile based or mobile assisted implementation. For bilateral methods multiple measurements are not needed: either mobile device measures signal from a single reference device or reference device measures signal from mobile device. This does not exclude any of the three implementation categories. Multilateral methods require co-ordination of simultaneous measurements at multiple sites. Unilateral methods are generally better for capacity and signaling load. Bilateral methods are optimal for rural coverage since only one reference device is involved (Laitinen et al., 2001).

Positioning methods can be also divided into two basic categories: range based and range free (Jayashree, Arumugam, Anusha & Hariny, 2006). The range based methods are based on the indirect measurements of distance or angle between sensors. The important thing to note is that the indirect measurements always have errors and individual measurements are not independent of each other. These measurements are strongly influenced by the surrounding environment and transmission system.

The devices in some systems (e.g., wireless sensor networks) have the hardware limitations. To overcome the limitations of the range based positioning methods, many range free solutions have been proposed. These solutions estimate the location of mobile devices (sensors, nodes or mobile stations) either by exploiting the radio connectivity information among neighboring mobile devices, or by exploiting the sensing capabilities of the mobile devices. Therefore the range free positioning solutions are cost-effective alternative to more expensive range based approaches.

Due to the distinct characteristics of these two approaches, we categorize the range free positioning methods into: reference device based methods and reference device free methods. For the first method, the presence of devices, that have knowledge about their location, is assumed in the network. And the second method requires no special sensor nodes for positioning.

Positioning Process

Positioning process generally consists of three components (Tseng et al., 2005):

- Identification and data exchange.
- Measurement and data acquisition.
- Computation to derive location.

Simplified positioning process is shown in the following figure (Figure 1). Initiation of the process is based on the positioning request. The request is originated by location oriented application. The next step of the positioning process is to collect (measure) data that are used for position estimation. Calculating algorithm defines mobile device position estimation. The location information is forwarded to the target unit (e.g., localization server), that is handling and evaluating this information. In the case of emergency safety service (E911), the server sends the information to the most appropriate Public Safety Answering Point (PSAP). Server can also send the position information to a third-party service provider, mobile Internet portal or even back to the mobile device (SnapTrack, 2003).

Positioning Requirements

It is necessary to use at least three reference devices to resolve positioning ambiguities in the two-dimensional space. Moreover, in a case of three-dimensional space, at least four reference devices are required to use. Increasing number of reference devices usually means more accurate position estimation (Brida, Cepel & Duha, 2006).

Before we will discuss particular positioning methods, we define basic requirements of the positioning system:

- Maximum possible accuracy of the system.
- Faster positioning method to minimize time of location process.
- Location process should not be too difficult for the system operation.
- Privacy protection, possibility to disable positioning in a case of assault.
- Possibility to determine the position of various mobile devices at once.
- Possibility to locate all the mobile devices without any restrictions.

CELLULAR POSITIONING

Mobile services have reached mass-market status over the past decade. LBS are very interesting and it is expected that this kind of services will have substantial market share in the future. Therefore the field of mobile positioning has attracted in recent years. Initially, mobile positioning was seen as advantageous for system management purposes. Knowing the accurate locations of mobile stations may assist the system in effective resources allocation. However, the focus of mobile station positioning has shifted from system needs to human needs. The excellent example is mobile station positioning in an emergency situation. Other applications also exist, e.g., fleet management, tracking of stolen vehicles as well as important persons carrying cellular telephones. The number of proposed services depends on positioning accuracy and that is the reason of increased attention in this area. Installation of GPS modules within mobile handset is also becoming popular. Anyway, this solution increases the mobile handset cost.

The most of cellular positioning methods present the range based group. Various methods for the mobile station positioning in cellular networks have been developed. Note that there is no method suitable for every location based application. Basic positioning methods in the GSM networks have been introduced in the ETSI (2002a,b,c)

Figure 1. Positioning process

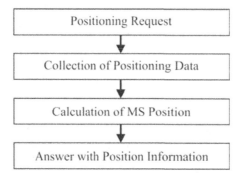

specifications. Positioning methods for UMTS network have been introduced in (ETSI, 2006). Basic positioning principles are similar for every network but the names of proposed methods can be different.

Main classification of positioning methods is possible on the basis of measured parameter used for positioning:

- Cell identification.
- Received signal strength.
- Time of arrival.
- Angle of arrival.

The reference device represents Base Station (BS) and mobile device represents Mobile Station (MS) in the following part (cellular positioning). At first, it is necessary to define the basic parameters for mathematical explanation. For simplification we consider the location in a two-dimensional (2-D) plane. Let the true position of MS is $[x_s; y_s]^T$, the computed MS location is $[x; y]^T$ and the position of the ith BS is expressed by $[x_i; y_i]^T$, $i = 1,2,...,N$; where N is the number of BSs. The positioning errors in mathematic formulations are not considered.

Cell Identification

The Cell IDentification (Cell ID) method operates in all cellular networks. This method is also known as Cell of Origin (CoO) based positioning. It is the simplest, cheapest and easiest way to describe the general location of a mobile station. It is a network based positioning method and requires identification of the BS which serves the located MS. Each BS is associated with unique cell ID and the BS coordinates must be known. If this information is available, the Cell ID identifies MS location as the BS location and forwards this information to the next processing. Two major approaches are used to determine the location of the MS when Cell ID is known. Position of the MS is determined either as a BS location coordinate or as a center coordinate of the cell coverage area (Krievs, 2002). The first option is more applicable for the cells deployed with omnidirectional antennas. It is often used in a case of rural areas. The second option is more suitable for cells deployed with sector antennas.

A wide range of enhancements for the basic Cell ID method has been developed. Further cell area reducing by using sector antennas is a typical strategy used to improve accuracy (see Figure 3). The other enhancements mainly include Cell ID + RSCP (Received Signal Code Power) method (Zhu & Zhu, 2000) and Cell ID + RTT (Round Trip Time) method. These methods have emerged from Cell ID + TA (Timing Advance) method that had been developed for GSM (Silventoinen & Rantalainen, 1996; Spirito & Mattiolli, 1999).

In the case of TA in GSM network is resolution approximately 550 m. This resolution is caused by bit duration (3.69 µs). Due to larger bandwidth and relatively short chip duration in the UMTS network (0.26 µs) is RTT measurement accuracy significantly higher. Theoretically can be mobile-to-base station distance (based on a single RTT measurement) estimated with an accuracy of 36 m (Borkowski & Lempiäinen, 2006). However the accuracy of estimates is reduced by multipath propagation in practical implementation.

Important advantage of this method is availability without any changes to networks or MSs. Location based services can be offered without extra costs. Since the MS can be anywhere in the cell, the accuracy of this method depends on the cell size. The accuracy can be very poor in a lot of cases, because the maximum radius of cell can be up to 35 km. Third generation network accuracy is higher because of the smaller cell dimensions. Advantage of this method is also that no calculations are needed to obtain location information.

Positioning is generally more accurate in urban areas with a dense network of small cells comparing to rural areas with a small number of BSs. Ultimately, the diversity of the cell size and density makes the accuracy of this technology inconsistent. Thus, Cell ID method is fast and suitable for applications requiring high capacity and poor accuracy.

Received Signal Strength Based Method

Methods based on Received Signal Strength (RSS) are one of the oldest positioning methods. Transmitted signal between transmitting BS and receiving MS is attenuated and this phenomenon is utilized by means of RSS

Figure 2. Positioning in a 2-D plane

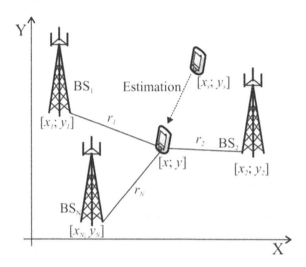

Figure 3. Cell identification based positioning - Cell ID

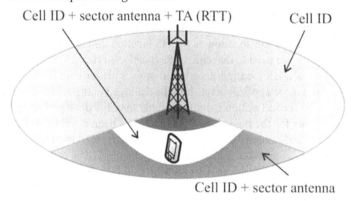

method. Basic principle of this method lies in signal strength measuring. Measurement can be realized either at the MS (measuring the signals propagating from several BSs) or at the several BSs (measuring the signal strength of the MS). Therefore the method can be realized as mobile based or network based positioning. The received signal level (*RxLev*) measurements are then converted to distances between MS and particular BSs. Each *RxLev* measurement will provide a circle, centered at the corresponding BS. The distance between MS and BS represent circle radius i.e. MS lies on the circle. The MS location can be calculated by the intersection computation of circles of known radius by using a calculation algorithm (e.g. geometric or statistical approach). For two dimensional positioning it is necessary to use at least three BSs in order to resolve ambiguities arising from multiple crossings of the lines of position (see Figure 4).

It is possible to describe RSS method by following formula, describing signal level dependency versus distance between transmitter and receiver (Willassen, 1998)

$$\Delta P(dB) = 10\alpha \log\left(\frac{f}{c}\right) - 10\beta \log(4\pi d),$$

(1)

Figure 4. Circle triangulation

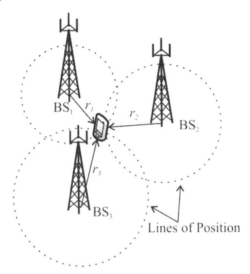

Figure 5. Example of the signal strength map (omnidirectional and sector antenna)

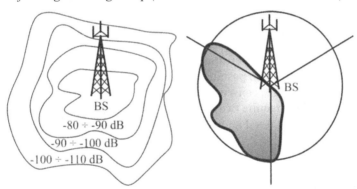

where ΔP is the difference between transmitted and received signal level, f is the carrier frequency [Hz], d is the distance in meters, c is the light speed [m/s], constant α means frequency factor and β describes terrain properties.

Large number of mathematical models describes behavior of a signal propagating in a particular environment. Every kind of environment is described with a typical model e.g. open area, rural area, urban and suburban area, indoor area, etc. The Hata model is the most known path loss model (Hata & Nagatsu, 1980). Positioning accuracy is increasing in case that the correct model is used.

The most serious reason of positioning error is the measurement ambiguity. It is possible to obtain the same signal strength in the different positions (see Figure 5).

Compared with most other location solutions, RSS positioning method does not require expensive base station equipment. There is faster deployment speed, and covers current and legacy MSs making it a low-cost solution for emerging location based services across the world.

Time Based Methods

Distance between MS and BS in the time based methods can be indirectly determined by means of propagation delay. There are several solutions based on the measuring of time. All of these solutions lead to circle or hyperbolic multilateral that will be briefly described.

The basic time based method is called Time of Arrival (ToA). In the ToA method is the distance between MS and BS measured by specifying the one way propagation time of a signal traveling from BS to MS. Measurement can be realized either at the MS or at the several BSs. In this case, the line of position is circle centered at the BS and MS must lie over there. By using at least three BSs we resolve ambiguities, and MS position is given by intersection of mentioned circles (see Figure 4).

The measured ToA in i^{th} BS can be expressed

$$t_i = r_i / c = \sqrt{(x_i - x)^2 + (y_i - y)^2} / c, \tag{2}$$

r_i is measured or computed distance between MS and i^{th} BS, $[x_i; y_i]$ is location of ith BS, $[x; y]$ is computed MS position (unknown) and c is speed of light. If we are using three BSs, we will get a system of three equations. Calculation of this system results in the intersection point that represents coordinates of estimated position. But this is ideal case and the real situation is slightly different. Intersection point is usually not a single point but the plane where the MS should be situated. This situation will be more precisely described later.

ToA measurements can be performed either at the BSs or at the MS. However, this requires very accurate timing reference at the MS that needs to be synchronized with the BS clock. If the BSs and MS are fully synchronized, ToA measurement is directly related to the BS - MS distance. Clearly, this solution is very difficult to achieve.

ToA measurements can be used only in a differential manner if the network is not synchronized (e.g. GSM network). Time of arrival differences are used for positioning and this method is called Time Difference of Arrival (TDoA). Time difference between two BSs is a constant and defines the line of position. This provides a hyperbola with foci at the BSs. Two lines of position require two hyperbolas i.e. we need three BSs. The intersection of the two hyperbolas then estimates the position (see Figure 6). The TDoA method is called hyperbolic trilateration.

The final hyperbola formula is defined:

$$(t_i - t_j)c = r_i - r_j = R_{ij} = \sqrt{(x_i - x)^2 + (y_i - y)^2} - \sqrt{(x_j - x)^2 + (y_j - y)^2}, \tag{3}$$

Figure 6. Hyperbolic triangulation

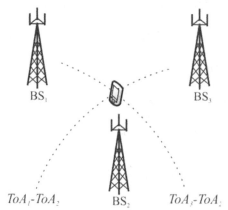

$ToA_1\text{-}ToA_2$ BS$_2$ $ToA_3\text{-}ToA_2$

where c is the signal propagation speed, R_{ij} is the range difference distance between the ith and j^{th} base station, r_i is the distance between the ith base station and the MS, and r_j is the distance between the jth BS and the MS. Finally, $(t_i - t_j)$ is the estimated *TDoA* between the ith and j^{th} base station. Computation of the MS coordinates in the two-dimensional space needs at least three BSs (Aatique, 1997; Rappaport, Reed & Woerner, 1996). This defines the set of nonlinear hyperbolic equations whose solution gives the estimated position by means of calculating interception point of the hyperbolas.

Time based methods rely on accurate estimates of the *ToAs* or *TDoAs* from the signals received at several BSs or at the MS. Several approaches have been developed for estimation of these important parameters, e.g. (Goud, Sesay & Fattouche, 1991; Mizusawa, 1996). The methods can be realized as network or mobile based positioning. In this case, the network based positioning method has two drawbacks compared to mobile based positioning: it is only possible to perform the measurements in dedicated mode and there may be capacity problems due to multilateral measurement principle. The advantage is that the network based implementation does not require modification of MS.

It is necessary to note that time based methods require new network components, called Location Measurement Unit (LMU). These measuring units can be either integrated in the BSs or they can be placed independently.

Many authors declared that the positioning accuracy of time based methods is higher in comparison with different location methods. Positioning accuracy depends on the number of LMU units that will be used for MS position specification. Increasing number of LMU units results in higher accuracy.

Very important issue that influences positioning accuracy lies in conditions of propagation and environment (e.g. Non Line of Sight environment - NLoS). Reducing the influence of NLoS environment is described in following articles (Jakobsson, Swindlehurst & Stoica, 1998; Knapp & Carter, 1976; Najar & Vidal, 2001; Venkatraman, Caffery & Heung-Ryeol, 2004).

Various modifications of time based methods are known. The modifications depend on the kind of network, realization etc. We briefly list most important modified time based methods: Enhanced Observed Time Differences (EoTD), Observed Time Difference of Arrival (OTDoA), Idle Period Downlink (IPDL), Advanced Forward Link Trilateration (AFLT), Enhanced Forward Link Trilateration (EFLT).

Angle of Arrival Method

Angle of Arrival (AoA) positioning method estimates the MS position by measuring the arrival angles of a signal from MS at several BSs. It is illustrated in Figure 7, where the user location is determined as the point of intersection of minimal two straight lines drawn from the BSs. Angles θ_1, θ_2 and θ_3 in the Figure 7 refer to *AoA* estimates of a signal transmitted by the MS and received at BSs. The AoA estimates are obviously with respect to some reference direction. The position estimate is then the intersection of the bearings from the two cell sites. The information from each BS is sent to the location server, where it is analyzed and used to generate coordinates of MS. The AoA method can determine uniquely a two-dimension location point.

Scattering near and around the MS and BS will alter the measured *AoA* (Caffery, 2000). It is seen that AoA method needs Line of Sight (LoS) propagation conditions between the MS and the BSs to obtain correct position estimates. Reflected signal can be used for positioning in the absence of a LoS signal component but it may not be coming from the direction of the MS. Additionally, if a LoS component is present, multipath will still cause a huge problem with the angle measurements. The utilization of the method is not suitable in dense urban areas where line of sight to minimal two BSs is seldom present. However, the AoA method could be used in rural and suburban areas where the attainable accuracy is better. An advantage in mentioned environments of the AoA method is that it is able to locate a MS by means of two BSs.

The accuracy of the method also diminishes with increasing distance between the MS and BS due to fundamental limitations of the devices used to measure the arrival angles as well as changing scattering characteristics. Achieved accuracy depends on the number of available measurements, geometry of BSs around the MS and multipath propagation.

A major barrier to implement the AoA method in existing GSM networks is that it can be realized only by means of antenna array. It means that the actual BS antennas have to be replaced by antenna array. It would be very expensive to build an overlay of AoA sensors to existing cellular network. In 3G systems *AoA* measurements

Figure 7. Positioning with angle of arrival measurements

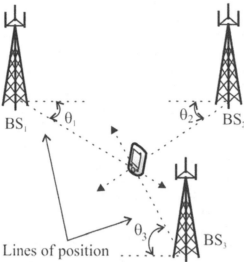

may become available without separate hardware if adaptive BS antennas (arrays) will be widely deployed. This method belongs to the network based positioning methods since it is difficult to place antenna array in a MS and that's the reason why the *AoA* measurements are done exclusively at the BS.

In addition to financial issues, AoA method may have a capacity problem. Multilateral measurement principle (measurement at several BSs) requires the co-ordination of almost simultaneous measurements at several BS sites, and it is difficult to serve a large number of users.

Fingerprinting Method

The main problem of range based methods lies in the accuracy of estimation the distance between MS and BS. This phenomenon is mostly caused by negative radio channel propagation conditions (multipath propagation, delay spread...). The results of various authors show that the suitable way to suppress this effect is correlation method. This method is called fingerprinting method, pattern matching or database correlation method. The collected signal characteristics are called *fingerprints*, due to similarity to the fingerprint comparison in forensics.

We can generally divide this method into two main phases. The aim of the first phase (so-called offline phase) is to create radio map of the particular area. Radio map is the database of points with the strictly defined position. Every point has the various signal characteristics information from several BSs (signal strengths, propagation times, pulse responses or angles). The entire area is covered by a grid of points. Every person has unique fingerprints and also every point from database contains unique combination of the signal characteristic from some BSs.

MS positioning is realized in the second phase (online phase). MS will create a sample measured vector of signal characteristics from different reference devices (e.g. BSs). This vector is compared with the information about every radio map point (fingerprint). The aim is to find fingerprint that is most similar to the measured vector. Particular fingerprint can be specified as position estimation.

There is large number of algorithms dedicated to the final location estimation from the points in database. The most common algorithm used to estimate the location is Euclidean algorithm. It computes the Euclidean distance between the measured signal characteristics vector and each fingerprint in the database and then the coordinates associated with the fingerprint that provides the smallest Euclidean distance is returned as the estimate of the position. This process cannot be realized in the MS due to computational complexity. That's why is this method mobile assisted.

The advantage of a fingerprinting positioning method is that it allows determining the location very accurately as all the signal propagation oddities can be taken into account. However, the more details are learned, the

Figure 8. Fingerprints from RxLev

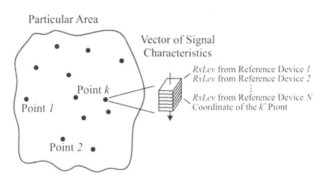

more vulnerable is this radio map to changes in the environment, such as construction of new buildings, weather conditions, moving furniture (indoor positioning) or even people and cars moving inside or outside the buildings. The important factor is that these characteristics are consistent in time, e.g. a medium-weak signal from a given source at a given location is likely to be similar tomorrow and next week.

The most frequent signal characteristic in the fingerprinting positioning is the received signal strength (see Figure 8). The main reason to use this parameter is that no additional hardware is required for its implementation to existing networks.

Performance of the fingerprint method with *RxLev* is better in areas with significant multipath propagation. Due to the big demanding effort during radio signal strength collection from the concerned area to realize a fingerprint database, predicted *RxLev* data of the area are rather used. For this reason is utilized a predictive algorithm. Possible predictive algorithms include *k*-Nearest Neighbors, Support Vector Machines, Neural Networks, or other machine learning algorithms for supervised learning (Brunato & Battiti, 2005; Hearst, 1998; Mitchell, 1997).

Fingerprinting method can be used with different network platforms (e.g., cellular, 802.11), with different types of input data and for different environment (urban, rural or indoor).

Assisted Global Navigation Satellite System

Assisted Global Navigation Satellite System (AGNSS) is a positioning technology that is presently used for mobile device positioning in wireless networks. AGNSS is probably the best solution to meet the accuracy requirements for LBS (e.g. emergency services E911 in USA and E112 in EU).

AGNSS compensates for the major faults of satellite (GNSS) and cellular (GSM/UMTS) positioning. A purely cellular based technology does not provide sufficient accuracy, and pure GNSS solutions suffer from long delays before position delivery (typically several minutes).

The principle of AGNSS consists of coupling satellite positioning and communication networks and sending assistance data to the receiver integrated in the mobile station to improve its performance. AGNSS principle is shown in Figure 9.

A Wide Area Reference Network (WARN) consists of reference GNSS receivers that are deployed geographically over the coverage area of the wireless network. The WARN collects the broadcast navigation message from the GNSS satellites and provides it to the AGNSS server for caching.

A location request of given MS is sent to the AGNSS server, when a location oriented application requires MS location. The AGNSS server calculates the GNSS assistance data. Location of the BS is used as the approximate MS location and this information is sent to the MS. Particular MS realize necessary location measurements and the information is either processed or sent to the AGNSS server (in order to realize the next processing). The last step depends on operation mode of AGNSS.

There are two different primary modes of operation for AGNSS, namely mobile based and mobile assisted mode. In mobile based AGNSS mode, the MS requests assistance data from the AGNSS server. The obtained

Figure 9. Assisted GNSS principle

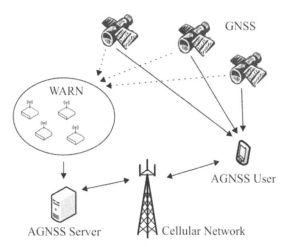

information is used to lock onto the satellites in view and calculate the position of the MS. In mobile assisted AGNSS, the MS requests assistance data from the AGNSS server and it is only used to lock onto the GNSS satellites. GNSS measurements are sent to the AGNSS server for the position calculation. The AGNSS server is also a mobile location server determining the location of mobile stations within a cellular network. The AGNSS server provides assistance data to the AGNSS cellular mobile station through the air in a case of contact with BS.

Assistance data can include the ephemeris, reference time, ionosphere model, UTC model, real time integrity and acquisition assistance (Harper, 2006). Acquisition assistance data provides the GNSS mobile station with information that allows faster and more reliable GNSS signals detection. This is done by means of providing information about direction of the signals. A size of assistance data depends on operation mode.

There are several advantages of performing the mobile assisted AGNSS mode. Quantity of transmitted information is smaller and the position calculation is centralized. It means that any software problem can be fixed in one place (server) instead of huge amount of MSs (Harper, Nicholson, Mumford & Poon, 2004).

Described positioning technology provides higher accuracy in comparison with cellular positioning methods. AGNSS offers very short latency to get a position compared to standard GNSS. Satellite data transfer is much faster than standard GNSS itself, i.e. low Time To First Fix (TTFF) parameter. Very low power consumption means optimized use of handset battery. The next advantage is increased sensitivity, i.e. increased availability of the location based service, particularly in dense urban and indoor environments.

This section has been dedicated to the general principles of AGNSS technology. It is well known that the AGNSS method at present needs participation of GPS. Another suitable needed satellite system is European Geostationary Navigation Overlay Service (EGNOS), Wide Area Augmentation System (WAAS), Multi-Functional Satellite Augmentation System (MSAS), GLObal NAvigation Satellite System (GLONASS) and Galileo in the future.

Different location based applications requires different conditions. The way to meet these requirements lies in hybrid positioning methods that combine several methods described previously to provide position estimates with better accuracy, reliability and coverage for different environments (indoor, outdoor, urban and rural). The drawbacks of hybrid methods are usually greater processing requirements and increased network costs. Usually the costs using a hybrid method (i.e. involving two techniques) will be as high as using two separate solutions (Laitinen et al. 2001).

There are various papers presenting combinations of particular positioning methods, e.g. in (Laitinen et al., 2001) is presented combination OTDoA + AoA and AoA + RTT. Hybrid methods TOA + RSS and TDOA + RSS are shown in (Catovic & Sahinoglu, 2004).

POSITIONING IN WIRELESS AD HOC AND SENSOR NETWORKS

Positioning in ad hoc and sensor wireless networks plays a major role in the development of geographic aware routing and multicasting protocols that result in new more efficient ways for routing data in multihop networks that span large geographic regions.

Localized mobile device is usually called node. A node with known coordinates is called a Reference Node (RN) (anchor). Otherwise, it is referred to as Blindfolded Node (BN), since it does not know own location.

Ad hoc network positioning is specific. It is given by network properties and hardware limitations of network devices. The capabilities of individual nodes are very limited and nodes are often powered by batteries only. To conserve energy, collaboration between nodes is required and communication between nodes should be minimized. To achieve these goals nodes in wireless ad hoc and sensor networks need to determine a device's context. Since each node has limited power, it is necessary to determine the location of individual sensor nodes without relying on external infrastructure (base stations, satellites, etc.) (Bachrach & Taylor, 2005). Therefore the positioning in these networks should meet following criteria:

- Self positioning (positioning does not depend on global infrastructure).
- Robust (tolerant of node failures and range errors).
- Energy efficient (requires little computation and, especially, communication).

In this section several of many approaches suitable for wireless ad hoc and sensor networks will be discussed. A lot of ad hoc networks and especially sensor networks use range free positioning methods. The main reasons for exploitation of these methods lies in hardware realization, penetration of nodes and low expenses for the positioning system implementation.

DV—Hop Algorithm

This approach was named DV - hop in (Niculescu & Nath, 2001), and Hop - TERRAIN in (Savarese, Rabay & Langendoen, 2002). It is the most basic algorithm, and it consists of three phases. First, it employs a classic distance vector exchange so that all nodes in the network determine distances to the reference nodes (in hops). In the second phase, the hop counts are converted into distances. This conversion consists of multiplying the hop count by an average hop distance. The average hop distance between them is derived in following way. When a reference node infers the position of another reference node, it computes the distance between them and this distance is divided by the number of hops. The average hop distance as correction is flooded into the network. When an arbitrary blindfolded node received the correction, it may then have estimate distances to three or more reference nodes, in meters, which can be used to perform the trilateration to estimate its own location.

DV—hop works well in dense and regular topologies, but for sparse or irregular networks the accuracy degrades to the radio range (Savarese et al., 2002).

DV —Distance Algorithm

This method is also known as Sum-dist (Bachrach & Taylor, 2005). It is similar to previous method with the difference that distance between neighbouring nodes is presented in meters instead of hops. The simplest solution for determining the distance to the reference node is simply adding the ranges encountered at each hop during the network flood. As a metric, the distance vector algorithm is now using the cumulative traveling distance (in meters). Each receiving node adds the measured range to the path length and forwards the message. The propagation range may be measured either by means of received signal strength or by time of arrival. The final result is that each node will have stored the position and minimum path length to at least flood limit reference nodes.

Described method is more precise than DV - hop method, because not all hops have the same size, but, on the other hand it is sensitive to measurement errors.

Figure 10. DV - hop algorithm

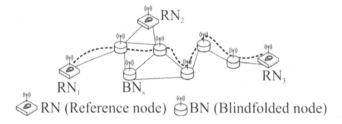

RN (Reference node)   BN (Blindfolded node)

"Euclidean" Propagation Algorithm

Niculescu & Nath (2001) have been proposed different method for determining distance between blindfolded and reference node. Proposed method is based on the local geometry of the nodes around a reference node and it is called Euclidean propagation algorithm. The principle will be briefly described by means of Figure 11. At least two nodes (BN_1 and BN_2) are required to determine distance between blindfolded node BN_X and reference node RN. It is necessary to know distances to the reference node and mutual distance between BN_1 and BN_2. Thus, with the known distances c, d, and e, there are two possible values (r_1 and r_2) for the distance of the node to the reference node. The details of described method can be found in (Niculescu & Nath, 2001).

The advantage of this method is that it provides better accuracy under certain conditions, and there is no correction to be deployed later (Bachrach, & Taylor, 2005). If a blindfolded node finds out the distance from three reference nodes, it is possible to find the own position by means of trilateration.

Other methods based on DV algorithm were proposed (DV - Coordinate, DV - Bearing and DV - Radial) in (Niculescu & Nath, 2003a,b). These algorithms are proposed for utilization in Ad hoc Positioning System (APS).

Proximity Based Positioning

Proximity based positioning also belongs to the group of range free positioning. Positioning using proximity measurements is popular, when low cost takes precedence in priority over accuracy. Since, messages necessarily pass between neighbors, there is no additional bandwidth required to proximity. Proximity measurements simply report whether or not two nodes are 'connected' or 'in-range'. However, the term 'in-range' may mislead readers to believe that proximity is purely a function of geometry - whether or not two nodes are separated by less than a particular distance. In fact, proximity is determined by whether or not a receiver can demodulate and decode a packet sent by a transmitter (Patwari & Alfred, 2003). The proximity based positioning has been used by numerous researchers for positioning in ad hoc and wireless sensor networks with different titles (Doherty, Pister & El Ghaoui, 2001; Nagpal, Shrobe & Bachrach, 2003; Niculescu & Nath, 2001; Sundaram & Ramanathan, 2002). We will use the CoMmon Proximity (CMP). The estimated location is determined on the basis of the closest node location, i.e. the blindfolded node has same location coordinates as the closest node

$$[x\_cmp_{est}; y\_cmp_{est}] = [x_{closest-device}; y_{closest-device}].$$

(4)

The positioning accuracy depends on reference nodes density.

There are various methods to improve basic proximity method, e.g. centroid proximity that has been proposed in (Bulusu, Heidemann & Estrin, 2000). In the case of CeNtroid Proximity (CNP), the position of blindfolded node is calculated as mean value of coordinates N of the closest reference nodes, which are in range. It is defined by the centroid of these reference nodes (see following equation and Figure 12).

$$[x\_cnp_{est}; y\_cnp_{est}] = \left[\frac{1}{N} \sum_{i=1}^{N} x_i ; \frac{1}{N} \sum_{i=1}^{N} y_i \right]. \tag{5}$$

Positioning accuracy depends on separation distance between two or more adjacent reference points and the transmission range of these reference points. The number and location of reference nodes also influence accuracy (Brida, Duha & Krasnovsky, 2007).

It is possible to increase centroid proximity accuracy by means of weighting data entering centroid proximity. This is so-called WEighted Proximity (WEP) (Brida et al., 2007). Proposed algorithm results from centroid proximity, but the each input part (particular coordinates of nodes) is individually weighted. The fundamental of WEP is increased influence of closer reference nodes at the expense of further nodes. The mean value of coordinates obtained after the weighting gives the WEP estimate. The main benefit of the WEP algorithm is the accuracy gain by combining information contributed from multiple inputs. Figure 13 shows overview of the WEP algorithm in order to combine N reference nodes (input parts).

The position estimate is computed from the N nearest reference nodes, where $[x_j; y_j]^T j = 1,2,\ldots,N$ is vector of their coordinates. Then, the WEP estimate $[x\_wep_{est}; y\_wep_{est}]^T$ is written as:

$$[x\_wep_{est}; y\_wep_{est}] = \left[\sum_{i=1}^{N} x_i.w_i.\left(\sum_{i=1}^{N} w_i \right)^{-1} ; \sum_{i=1}^{N} y_i.w_i.\left(\sum_{i=1}^{N} w_i \right)^{-1} \right]. \tag{6}$$

where $[w_i]^T i = 1,2,\ldots,N$ are input weights.

Approximate Point in Triangulation Test

Approximate Point in Triangulation test (APIT) is an area based range free positioning method (He et al., 2003). This method leads to the specification of area with blindfolded node. It assumes that a small number of reference nodes know its location (obtained via GPS or some other mechanism). APIT determines position estimation by isolating the environment into triangular regions between reference nodes as shown in Figure 14. Triangle is bounded with the three reference nodes placed in the corners. Theoretical method used to reduce the possible area with a target blindfolded node is called Point In Triangulation test (PIT) (He et al.). A node's presence inside or outside of these triangular regions allows a node to reduce the potential position area.

Utilization of the different combinations of reference nodes can reduce the size of estimated area with a blindfolded node. Finally, APIT calculates the center of gravity of the triangles intersection to determine the node estimated position.

Several positioning methods for wireless ad hoc and sensor networks were investigated. Each method means different compromise solution in term of accuracy, signaling complexity, coverage and the isotropy of the network. There is a lot of positioning methods, developed by many authors. The main target of this publication was to show basic examples of the positioning methods and not to describe every one proposed method. In fact a lot of methods are modification of the basic methods.

Radio Frequency Identification

Radio Frequency IDentification (RFID) is an automatic identification method, mainly proposed to replace bar code identification. RFID can be also used as localization technique based on trilateration measurements of a user in relation to reference devices. It relies on storing and remote retrieving data using devices called RFID tags or transponders. Typical RFID systems consist of transponders (called tags) with antennas and readers. Long range RFID tags can be placed at known locations and a mobile device that carries a reader can retrieve the tag information (e.g. the 3-D coordinates of the tag). Position of the mobile device can be determined by network of

Figure 11. Determining distance using Euclidean

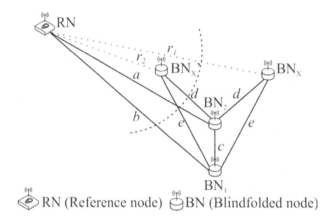

Figure 12. Centroid proximity

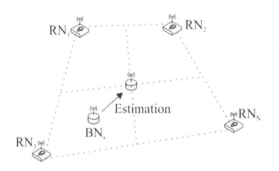

the tags. The read range depends on the type of tag (active or passive). Long range tags are usually active tags with own power supply. Possible reading range of long range tag is up to 100 m. To achieve a higher positioning accuracy for location determination, the read range can be limited by reducing the sensitivity in the reader.

The most important differentiation criteria for RFID systems are the operating frequency, physical coupling method and range of the system. RFID systems are able to operate at the frequencies, ranging from 135 kHz to 5.8 GHz. Electric, magnetic and electromagnetic fields are used for the physical coupling. Finally, the achievable range of the system varies from a few millimeters till 15 m (Finkenzeller, 2003).

RFID technique or integration of GPS, RFID and other wireless positioning technologies can be used as effective positioning infrastructure for indoor and outdoor applications. In addition to the common applications (e.g. goods inventory monitoring etc.) location based solution for logistics and supply chain management by integrating GPS and RFID can be realized.

There are three main factors that affect positioning accuracy. Accuracy of every method depends on the precise information necessary for positioning (e.g., *AoA, ToA, TDoA, RxLev*). Another important factor lies in processing by means of calculation algorithms. Environment characteristics (indoor, urban, rural area etc.) also affect positioning accuracy.

It is necessary to choose suitable network platform (cellular, ad hoc, RFID etc.) for mobile device positioning in the NGN architecture. Zigbee, Bluetooth, WiFi and RFID technology seems to be the most useful solution in the case of indoor area. GNSS systems should be used in outdoor area and dense city areas will probably use combination of GNSS systems and cellular technologies.

Every one presented network technology (platform) and positioning method has positive and negative properties. It is not easy to clearly define the best positioning method. On the base of various comparisons and scientific

Figure 13. Overview of the WEP algorithm

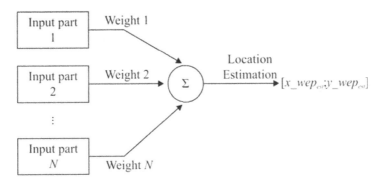

studies we can conclude that GNSS based positioning solutions achieve the highest accuracy. Very accurate positioning results in all network platforms can be obtained by time base methods. Angle of Arrival method can achieve the high accuracy if the smart antenna technology has been applied. Other methods are more dependent on the environment and network platform. Received signal strength method is less accurate comparing to previous examples. It is the most often used indoor positioning method at present. The main advantage lies in a simple realization. The proximity based methods and Cell ID method have the same advantage. They don't need significant costs for realization. In general, enhanced positioning accuracy increases costs for its realization.

Finally, the main criterions to choose appropriate positioning method are required positioning accuracy and implementation costs. Therefore it is suitable to implement positioning methods that can be realized with existing network and mobile device equipment e.g. cellular positioning (Deligiannis & Kotsopoulos, 2007).

MEASURES OF POSITIONING ACCURACY

To evaluate the performance of a positioning method, several benchmarks have been proposed. The most commonly used measure of positioning accuracy is the comparison of the Mean Square Error (MSE) of the position estimation with Cramér-Rao Lower Bound (CRLB). The Root Mean Square Error (RMSE) can also be used as a measure of positioning accuracy, is calculated as the square root of the MSE

$$RMSE = \sqrt{MSE} = \left(x - x_s\right)^2 + \left(y - y_s\right)^2, \tag{7}$$

where $[x; y]$ are estimated coordinates and $[x_s; y_s]$ are known true coordinates of MS.

CRLB bound is a classical result from statistics that gives a lower bound on the error covariance matrix for an unbiased estimate of an estimated parameter (Savvides & Srivastava, 2004). It is inverse matrix of the Fisher information matrix. Detailed information can be found in (Van Trees, 2001).

A simple measure of the positioning accuracy is Circular Error Probability (CEP). The CEP is a measure of the uncertainty in location estimator relative to its mean. For a 2D system, the CEP is defined as the radius of a circle which contains the given number of the random vector realizations with the mean as its center.

If the position location estimator is unbiased, CEP is a measure of uncertainty relative to the true transmitter position. If the estimator is biased and bound by bias B, then with a probability of one-half, a particular estimate is within a distance B + CEP from the true transmitter position. Figure 16 illustrates the 2-D geometrical relations.

The effect of reference devices geometric configuration (BSs and reference nodes) on the accuracy of the position estimation is measured by Geometric Dilution Of Precision (GDOP). There is a simple relationship between GDOP and CEP measures

Figure 14. APIT method

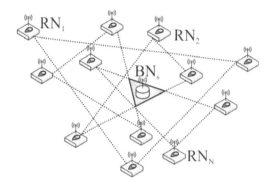

$$CEP \cong \left(0,75\sigma_v\right)GDOP, \tag{8}$$

where σ_v denotes fundamental ranging error. GDOP is useful criterion for selecting the set of reference devices to minimize positioning error.

SOURCES OF POSITIONING ERROR

There are various sources of positioning error. Typical source of error is the limited accuracy of devices used to measure basic parameters dedicated to position finding (signal strength, angle of arrival, time of arrival). The highest impact on positioning accuracy is presented by radio channel. Character of radio channel is stochastic. Density and the distribution of the reference stations (BSs and reference nodes) is also important issue that influences positioning accuracy. It is necessary to think about it during the process of network infrastructure planning.

Following section describes basic factors that can be considered as sources of positioning errors.

- **Multipath Propagation.** Multipath propagation is phenomenon that results in radio signals' reaching the receiving antenna by two or more paths. Combination of the multipath signals cause phenomenon so-called fading. Received multiple signals make it difficult to accurately determine the signal strength, angle of arrival and time of arrival. In radio signal strength measurements, multipath fading and shadowing causes up to $30 \div 40$ dB variation over distances on the order of half a wavelength. Furthermore, scattering near the receiver will affect AoA measurements. In time based methods, conventional delay estimators based on correlation are influenced by the presence of multipath fading, which results in a shift in the peak of the correlation (Savvides & Srivastava, 2004).

- **Non line of sight propagation.** NLoS propagation describes the scenario where the direct path between the source and receiver is blocked. Accuracy of every positioning method is influenced by this phenomenon. NLoS environment presence affects the AoA method when the *AoA* from a longer path is much different from the true *AoA*. Additionally, in time based methods, the NLoS path can be much longer than the direct path. It means that the measured time of arrival is significantly higher and the result is that the computed distance between reference and localized mobile device is bigger in comparison with the real distance.

- **Multiple-Access Interference.** All cellular networks suffer from co-channel interference. Especially, in CDMA systems in which high-power users may mask the low-power users due to near-far effects. It can also be a problem in ad hoc and sensor networks if nodes share the same frequency band. The biggest influence of this effect is in a case of time based methods.

Figure 15. RFID

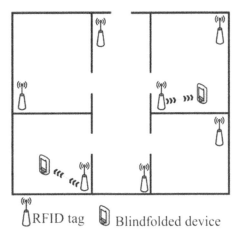

RFID tag   Blindfolded device

Each of mentioned impairments must be taken into consideration in order to achieve accurate location in wireless systems. We did not cover sources of error that arise from hardware limitations.

There are many research groups specialized in the application of various algorithms dedicated to suppress influence of positioning error sources (Venkatraman, Caffery & Heung-Ryeol, 2004; Wang, Wang & O'Dea, 2003).

POSITIONING RESULTS

Following chapter will introduce some experiments regarding positioning in various wireless networks. The main objective of scientists working on positioning is accuracy increase. There are several methods to increase positioning accuracy and very interesting principle lies in modification of standard calculation algorithms. We were realizing this possibility. We will introduce two examples of particular method performance increase by means of algorithm improvement.

Positioning Results in Cellular Networks

Positioning accuracy has been increased by means of solution, proposed in (Brida, Cepel & Duha, 2006). This solution lies in modified calculation algorithm. This modification was applied on the RSS method and the activity of this new method can be simply verified in real GSM network. Basic principle of RSS method was previously described and we will focus on the algorithm description.

In general, two approaches can be used on the basis of signal strength measurements for MS location searching (Caffery, 2000). The straightforward approach is to use a geometric interpretation of the measurements and to compute the intersection of the lines of position (in this case it means circles). The second approach is statistical approach. Achieved results will be compared with the basic geometric algorithm and standard Least Squares (LS) method.

Geometric algorithm

The function of suggested Geometric Algorithm (GA) is estimation of the MS location point (with the highest probability).

The circles are intersected in one point and MS location is uniquely defined in ideal case. We can't assume this solution in real environment. There are three relevant intersections, but the algorithm has to calculate one point. Figure 17 shows two possible situations arisen from intersection circles calculation.

Figure 16. The geometry of CEP

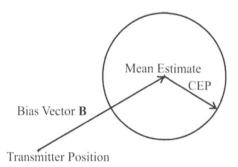

Figure 17. Existing and nonexistent intersection of all three circles

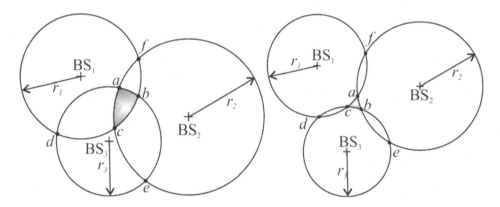

After calculating intersections between couple of circles, following coordinates of intersections are acquired:

$$I = [x_j ; y_j], j = 1,2,...,2q.$$ (9)

It is necessary to choose relevant points from these intersections (10), because not all points from previous step are appropriate for final point calculation (MS location).

$$I_{RELEVANT} = [x_j ; y_j], j = 1,2,...,q.$$ (10)

The mean of these q - relevant intersection points is defined as the coordinates of MS position estimate. It is calculated as:

$$x = \frac{1}{q} \sum_{l=1}^{q} x_l, \; y = \frac{1}{q} \sum_{l=1}^{q} y_l, \; l = 1,2,...,K$$ (11)

where q is the number of BSs and K is the number of relevant intersections.

Figure 18. Adaptive geometric algorithm process

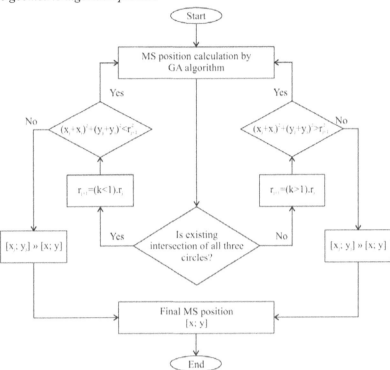

Adaptive Geometric Algorithm

The nature of Adaptive Geometric Algorithm (AGA) results from basic geometric algorithm. Coordinates of MS position are calculated by means of GA during the first iteration. In the next iterations is an area surrounded by relevant intersections reduced (see Figure 17, points *a, b, c*).

The reduction of area is done by decreasing (increasing) circle radiuses. The values of circle radiuses are multiplied by factor *k*, i.e. all the circles are reduced (enlarged) proportionally. Factor *k* can be either less than one or bigger than one. It depends on arisen situation (Figure 17). This process continues until the target area is found. When the intersection area (highlighted) is the smallest, it is denoted as target area. The same calculation as GA algorithm is made, but now is used a potentially much more reduced area. Figure 18 shows AGA process.

AGA algorithm is proposed for using in a case of three BSs. Following example is presented. In case of use *n* BSs for positioning are selected the *n* nearest BSs to the MS. If the distance between BS and MS is bigger, error of estimated distance (according to propagation model) is also bigger (See Figure 19). For example the error 1 dBm causes different distance error at the estimation of distance between MS and BS. Figure 19 demonstrates the fact that the decreasing value of *RxLev* means increasing of the distance error. Therefore the using more BSs for positioning does not bring accuracy increase. In the case of using three BSs for positioning, the accuracy should be the highest and the error should be the lowest. This observation has more important impact in the environment with larger cells (rural area). This fact has been confirmed by using basic GA algorithm (Brida, Cepel & Duha, 2006).

Simulation environment

In this section, we introduce the proposed system and RSS measurement model. We assume the system model as following:

Figure 19. RxLev versus distance between MS and BS

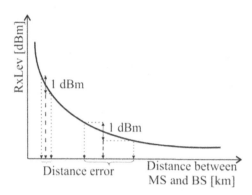

Figure 20. Configuration of cells arrangement

Figure 21. RSS measurement model

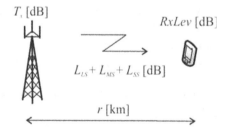

- The number of BSs is N.
- Signals from N - BSs are measured at MS.
- Received signal strength from each BS is independent to each other.

Simulations are done in two cases. In the first case we assume urban environment. In second case we assume rural environment. Service area consists of 7 cells as shown in Figure 20. All cells in the system are deployed with omnidirectional antennas. The cell radius (r_c) is 1 km for urban and 5 km for rural environment.

For each environment is used proper Hata's model. In urban environment we consider NLoS propagation and LoS propagation is considered in rural environment.

Figure 21 shows measurement model for RSS based mobile positioning.

$$RxLev = T_x - (L_{LS} + L_{MS} + L_{SS}), \tag{12}$$

where $RxLev$ is received signal strength and T_x is transmitted signal strength. Following parameters influence signal attenuation:

- L_{LS}: signal degradation, caused by large-scale propagation.
- L_{MS}: signal degradation, caused by medium-scale propagation.
- L_{SS}: signal degradation, caused by small-scale propagation.

All of the parameters are in [dB].

It is easy to define distance between MS and BS from $RxLev$ measurement at the MS from i^{th} BS.

Simulation parameters for each environment are shown in the Table 1. Signal fading is decomposed into two parts - long-term fading (path loss and shadowing) and short-term fading. The cell radius is different for both environments (urban r_c = 1 km, rural r_c = 5 km). For urban environment MS moves randomly (according to Gaussian distribution N(0,1)) in the area $-2km \leq x_s, y_s \leq 2km$ and for rural environment in the area $-10km \leq x_s, y_s \leq 10km$.

Simulations are performed from three till seven transmitters. In case of decreased number of transmitters, we prefer transmitters with higher signal strength. All results were based on 5000 independent runs.

Performance of AGA algorithm is compared with GA and LS algorithm (Wang et al., 2003). The results provide detailed analysis of accuracy in terms of circular error probability as a function of the number of BSs used for positioning. We will focus on 50 % probability (marked CEP50). The results are compared and numerically expressed in the Table 2.

On the basis of obtained results it is possible to note, that the increasing number of BSs used for position calculation reach lower accuracy. This effect was explained previouslyf. According to obtained results, the performance of the proposed AGA algorithm is better in comparison to GA and LS algorithm.

The results obtained in rural environment are similar to the urban results with the difference in error scale. The best results have been achieved in rural and urban environment with AGA algorithm. The worst results have been achieved with standard LS algorithm. The method works more accurately in urban environment. This is mainly caused by shortest distance between BSs. The distance between BSs is more important fact as a signal fading.

Previous part deals with simulation results. The validity of the results was verified in the real network. Practical experiment has been also realized in urban and rural environment in the surrounding of University of Zilina (Slovakia) (Brida, Cepel, Duha & Vestenicky, under review). Measurements have been stationary, i.e. there was no movement in 5 seconds during the measurement. The number of realized measurements in each environment is 500. True MS coordinates were measured by GPS receiver. The final position (RSS positioning) was expressed in WGS84 coordinate system, because of easier comparison with result from GPS receiver.

Obtained results (CEP vs. BSs number) are shown in Table 3. The availability [%] represents probability of using data from a given number of base stations. The data from seven BSs were always available, but it is not always possible to use these data for the position calculation. Different situation has occurred in the case of more sectors from the same BS. Sector with the highest $RxLev$ is used for the position calculation in this case. We assume that the chosen sector has direct contact with MS (comparing to other sectors).

We verified a simple and efficient positioning algorithm using $RxLev$ measurement proposed in (Brida, Cepel & Duha, 2006). According to the results, performance of the AGA algorithm is better in comparison to the conventional algorithms. Therefore an implementation of AGA algorithm increase accuracy of RSS based positioning. Real experiments confirmed the results that have been achieved by means of simulations. Complete overview of the measurements and results is presented in (Brida, Cepel, Duha & Vestenicky, under review).

Implementation of AGA algorithm in the positioning methods using circular lines of position (e.g. ToA) may also bring accuracy increase. The accuracy of RSS method is smaller in comparison with the time based methods, but it is satisfactory for the purposes of commercial location based services. On the other hand the initial implementation costs for the time based positioning are higher comparing to the RSS based positioning.

Table 1. Parameters of particular environments and distributions used for description

Environment	Urban		Rural	
Fading	Shadowing	Short - term	Shadowing	Short - term
Distribution	Normal	Rayleigh	Normal	Ricean
σ [dB]	6	7	3	2
μ [dB]	0	-3	0	-1
k	-----	-----	-----	10

Table 2. CEP vs. Number of Base Stations and environment (Simulation results)

BSs No.	Urban			Rural		
	CEP50 [km]			CEP50 [km]		
	GA	AGA	LS	GA	AGA	LS
3	0.1383	0.0935	0.1538	0.468	0.3548	0.7345
4	0.3777	-----	0.3975	0.9548	-----	0.8662
5	0.4441	-----	0.6266	1.2391	-----	1.4648
6	0.5275	-----	0.69	1.4756	-----	2.0894
7	0.5705	-----	0.6789	1.8192	-----	2.7085

Table 3. CEP vs. number of base stations and environment (real experiment results)

BSs No.	Urban				Rural			
	Availability [%]	CEP50 [km]			Availability [%]	CEP50 [km]		
		GA	AGA	LS		GA	AGA	LS
3	100	0.2679	0.1972	0.3126	100	0.9782	0.7503	1.4567
4	100	0.4684	-----	0.305	100	1.254	-----	2.4568
5	92.7	0.4716	-----	0.4156	82.7	1.9713	-----	3.4687
6	24.6	0.5036	-----	0.5984	74.6	2.541	-----	4.5483
7	3.9	0.648	-----	0.6785	29.4	3.9725	-----	4.9783

Positioning Results in Ad hoc Networks

Following part will demonstrate influence of the basic algorithm modification on the accuracy of Proximity based positioning. This method is often used in ad hoc or sensor networks. Basic principle of this method was previously described and we will focus on the achieved results.

Simulation Environment

Specifically, consider a network of m reference and n blindfolded nodes. The relative location problem corresponds to the estimation of blindfolded node coordinates. For simplicity, we consider the location in 2-D plane. Let $[x_i; y_i]^T$

$i = 1,2,...,m$ are coordinates of reference devices and $[x_j; y_j]^T$ $j = 1,2,...,n$ are coordinates of blindfolded nodes.

Simulations are realized for one propagation environment. All devices are situated in a square 10x10m. Reference nodes positions are simulated in two cases.

Reference nodes can lie in expressly defined points in the first case. These nodes are forming raster with equally defined spacing. Raster spacing depends on the number of reference nodes used in simulation. We can also assume randomly situated reference nodes (according to Gaussian distribution N(0,1)). A thousand trials have been performed.

In each trial, the locations of reference nodes and blindfolded node are generated at first. In the next step, *RxLev* are calculated between each reference nodes and blindfolded node on the base of following equation

$$RxLev_{i,j} \text{ (dBm)} = P_0 \text{(dBm)} - 10.n_p.\log(d_{i,j}/d_0), \tag{13}$$

where $RxLev_{i,j}$ is measured received signal strength at node j transmitted by node i (in dBm), P_0 is the received signal strength at the reference distance d_0. Typically $d_0 = 1$ m, and P_0 is calculated by the free space path loss formula (Tseng et al., 2005). The path loss exponent n_p is a function of the environment. Currently we are using $n_p = 2$ (free space). Consequently is done proximity measurement.

The proximity measurement S is determined by the measured signal. $S_{i,j}$ is obtained from $RxLev_{i,j}$ and it is equal to 1 if devices i and j are in range, and it is 0 if not. It is necessary to clearly define transition from status "in range" to "out of range". Therefore, we define a threshold. If the received signal strength ($RxLev_{i,j}$) at j device transmitted by i device is higher as defined threshold then i device is assumed to be in range of the j device. Thus,

$$S_{i,j} = \begin{cases} 1, & RxLev_{i,j} \geq RxLev_T \\ 0, & RxLev_{i,j} < RxLev_T \end{cases}. \tag{14}$$

A reference node that does not fulfill the threshold condition is rejected. Finally, the location coordinates of blindfolded node are determined by the remaining reference nodes.

Presented numerical simulations compare the performance of various solutions of proximity based methods - common (CMP), centroid (CNP) and weighted proximity (WEP).

The simulations are realized for each allocation of reference nodes according to the following criterions:

- Influence of reference nodes allocation on the location accuracy.
- Optimization of the reference nodes number used for location estimation.
- Influence of the number all reference nodes used in simulation of all proximity based methods.

Influence of different weights (used for particular input data) on location accuracy is examined in (Brida et al., 2007). Only the three closest reference nodes are weighted with the weight {6-3-1} in our experiments (regarding results in (Brida et al.)). We compare the influence of reference nodes allocation on location accuracy just for $m = 10$ (the number of reference nodes). The results in a case of increased number of reference nodes are very similar.

Figure 22 shows the dependence of positioning error versus N (the number of reference nodes used for calculation of CNP and WEP position estimation). We can see two different situations in this figure. On the left side is introduced simulation in a case that the reference nodes form raster with equally defined spacing. The case of randomly allocated reference nodes is introduced on the right. Naturally, the change of N does not impact on accuracy of common proximity (dotted line). The results of CNP and WEP are similar. The number of reference nodes used for estimation calculation plays important role in positioning accuracy. The minimal error is interesting for us. The results confirm the fact, that weighted proximity achieves the minimal positioning error in comparison with other proximity based methods. Minimal positioning error in the first case was achieved while using four reference devices. The situation is different in the second case (randomly allocated reference nodes). In general, we can say that the accuracy decreases with a growing number of reference nodes used for CNP and

Figure 22. RMSE versus N for different allocation of reference nodes

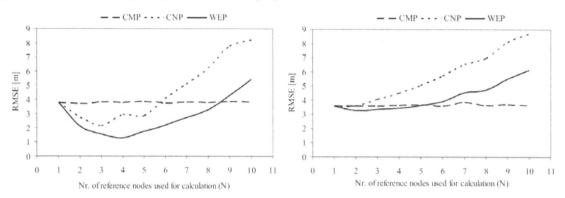

Figure 23. RMSE versus the number of reference nodes

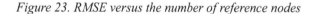

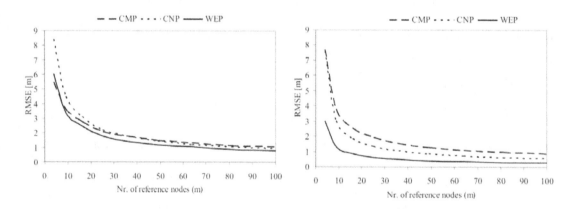

WEP calculation (except $N = 2$). The differences are smaller in comparison with the first case, but WEP is still the most accurate technique.

Figure 23 shows the dependence of RMSE versus the number of reference nodes m. On a basis of the obtained results we conclude that the WEP achieves more accurate results comparing to centroid and common proximity in both cases. The RMSE is an exponential function of the number of reference devices m. A growing number of reference devices mean increasing of the RMSE.

The situation of reference nodes lying in raster is only theoretical and the second case (random nodes allocation) is more similar to reality. Naturally, the positioning in the first case is much more accurate in comparison to random allocation of the reference devices. We can say that the reference nodes are optimally allocated in the first case. Hence, it is necessary to consider about allocation of nodes in process of implementation of wireless ad hoc and sensor networks.

CONCLUSION

In this chapter we presented the fundamentals of positioning in various NGN network platforms. We discussed the fundamental information about positioning, positioning process and major positioning methods. A few positioning experiments related to positioning accuracy increase in cellular and ad hoc (sensor) networks has been presented at the end of the chapter.

REFERENCES

Aatique, M. (1997). *Evaluation of TDOA techniques for position location in CDMA systems*. Unpublished master's thesis, Faculty of the Virginia Polytechnic Institute and State University, Virginia.

Bachrach, J., & Taylor, C. (2005). Localization in sensor networks. In I. Stojmenović (Ed.), *Handbook of sensor networks: algorithms and architectures* (pp. 277-310). New Jersey, Hoboken: John Wiley & Sons, Inc.

Borkowski, J., & Lempiäinen, J. (2006). Practical network-based techniques for mobile positioning in UMTS. *EURASIP Journal on Applied Signal Processing*, doi:10.1155/ASP/2006/12930, 1-15.

Brida, P., Cepel, P., & Duha, J. (2006). A novel adaptive algorithm for RSS positioning in GSM networks. In *CSNDSP 2006 PROCEEDINGS*: (pp. 748-751). Greece: University of Patras.

Brida, P., Cepel, P., Duha, J. & Vestenicky, M. (under review). An experimental evaluation of AGA algorithm performance for RSS positioning in GSM networks. Manuscript submitted for publication.

Brida, P., Duha, J., & Krasnovsky, M. (2007). On the accuracy of weighted proximity based localization in wireless sensor networks. In *Proccedings of the 12th IFIP Internacional Conference on Personal Wireless Communications*: (pp. 423-432). Czech Republic: Prague.

Brunato, M., & Battiti, R. (2005). Statistical learning theory for location fingerprinting in wireless LANs. *Computer Networks and ISDN Systems*, 47(6), 825-845.

Bulusu, N., Heidemann, J., & Estrin, D. (2000). GPS-less low cost outdoor localization for very small devices. *IEEE Personal Communications*, 7(5), 28-34.

Caffery, J. J., Jr. (2000). *Wireless location in CDMA cellular radio systems* (1st ed.). Massachusetts: Kluwer Academic Publishers.

Catovic, A. & Sahinoglu, Z. (2004). Hybrid TOA/RSS and TDOA/RSS location estimation schemes for short-range wireless networks. *Bechtel Telecommunication Technical Journal*, 2(2), 77-84.

Deligiannis, N. & Kotsopoulos, S. (2007). Mobile positioning based on existing signalling messaging in GSM Networks. In Proceedings of 3rd International Mobile Multimedia Communications Conference (MSAN). 27-29 August 2007, Greece: Nafpaktos.

Doherty, L., Pister, K. S. J., & El Ghaoui, L. (2001). Convex position estimation in wireless sensor networks. In *Proceedings IEEE of Infocom 2001, Vol. 3*, (pp. 1655-1663). USA: Anchorage.

Drane, C. (1998). Positioning GSM telephones. *IEEE Communications Magazine*, 36(4), 46-59.

ETSI (2002a). TS 101 528: *Location Services (LCS); Broadcast network assistance for Enhanced Observed Time Difference (E-OTD) and Global Positioning System (GPS) positioning methods*; version 8.4.1.

ETSI (2002b). TS 101 529: *Location Services (LCS); Serving Mobile Location Centre - Serving Mobile Location Centre (SMLC - SMLC)*; version 8.1.1.

ETSI (2002c). TS 101 724: *Location Services (LCS); Functional description*, 3GPP TS 03.71, version 8.7.0.

ETSI (2006). TS 125 302: *Universal Mobile Telecommunications System (UMTS); Services provided by the physical layer* (3GPP TS 25.302 version 7.1.0).

Finkenzeller, K. (2003). *RFID handbook: Fundamentals and applications in contactless smart cards and identification* (2nd ed.). West Sussex: John Wiley & Sons, Ltd.

Goud, P., Sesay, A., & Fattouche, M. (1991). A spread spectrum radiolocation technique and its application to cellular radio. In *IEEE Pacific Rim Conference on Communications, Computers and Signal Processing: Vol. 2.* (pp. 661-664). Canada: Victoria.

Harper, N. (2006). Using Assisted-GNSS to locate handsets in wireless networks. *Coordinates,* 2(12), 24-27.

Harper, N., Nicholson, P., Mumford, P., & Poon, E. (2004). Process for improving GPS acquisition assistance data and server-side location determination for cellular networks. *Journal of Global Positioning Systems*, 3(1-2), 133-142.

Hata, M., & Nagatsu, T. (1980). Mobile location using signal strength measurements in a cellular system. *IEEE Transaction on Vehicular Technology*, 29(2), 245-252.

He, T., Huang, C., Blum, B. M., Stankovic, J. A., & Abdelzaher, T. (2003). Range-free localization schemes in large scale sensor networks. In *Proceedings of the 9th Annual International Conference on Mobile Computing and Networking (Mobicom)*: (pp. 81-95). USA: San Diego.

Hearst, M. A. (1998). Support Vector Machines. *IEEE Intelligent Systems*, 13(4), 18-28.

Jakobsson, A., Swindlehurst, A. L., & Stoica, P. (1998). Subspace-based estimation of time delays and doppler shifts. *IEEE Transactions on Acoustics, Speech and Signal Processing*, 46(9), 2472-2483.

Jayashree, L. S., Arumugam, S., Anusha, M., & Hariny, A. B. (2006). On the accuracy of centroid based multi-lateration procedure for location discovery in wireless sensor networks, In *Proceedings of Wireless and Optical Communications Networks.* 11-13 April 2006, India: Bangalore.

Klukas, R. (1997). *A superresolution based cellular positioning system using GPS time synchronization.* Unpublished doctoral dissertation, University of Calgary, Calgary, Alberta, Canada.

Knapp, C. H., & Carter, G. C. (1976). The generalized correlation method for estimation of time delay. *IEEE Transactions on Acoustics, Speech and Signal Processing*, 24(4), 320-327.

Krievs, R. (2002). Using fading to improve accuracy of Cell ID based mobile positioning algorithms: Analysis of special cases. In *Scientific Proceedings of Baltic Electronic Conference (BEC)*. Estonia: Tallinn.

Laitinen, H., Ahonen, S., Kyriazakos, S., Lähteenmäki, J., Menolascino, R., & Parkkila, S. (2001, November). *Cellular Location Technology* (Project: Cellular network optimisation based on mobile location). Cello Consortium.

Mitchell, T. (1997). *Machine learning* (1st ed.). USA: McGraw-Hill Higher Education.

Mizusawa, G. A. (1996). *Performance of hyperbolic position location techniques for code division multiple access.* Unpublished master's thesis, Faculty of the Virginia Polytechnic Institute and State University, Blacksburg, Virginia.

Nagpal, R., Shrobe, H., & Bachrach, J. (2003). Organizing a global coordinate system from local information on an ad hoc sensor network. In *Proceedings of the 2nd International Workshop on Information Processing In Sensor Networks.* April, 2003, USA: Palo Alto.

Najar, M., & Vidal, J. (2001). Kalman tracking based on TDOA for UMTS mobile location. In *Proceedings of IEEE PIMRC, Vol. 1.* (pp. 45-49). USA: San Diego.

Niculescu, D., & Nath, B. (2001). Ad hoc positioning system (APS). In *Proceedings of IEEE GLOBECOM 2001: Vol. 5.* (pp. 2926–2931). USA: San Antonio.

Niculescu, D., & Nath, B. (2003a). Ad hoc positioning system (APS) using AoA. In *Proceedings of IEEE INFO-COM 2003: Vol. 3.* (pp. 1734-1743). USA: San Francisco.

Niculescu, D., & Nath, B. (2003b). DV based positioning in ad hoc networks. *Telecommunication Systems,* 22(1-4), 267–280.

Patwari, N., & Alfred O. Hero III (2003). Using proximity and quantized RSS for sensor localization in wireless networks. In *Proceedings of WSNA'03*, (pp. 20-29). USA: San Diego.

Rappaport, T. S., Reed, J., & Woerner, B. (1996). Position location using wireless communications on highways of the future. *IEEE Communication Magazine*, 34(10), 33-41.

Savarese, C. Rabay, J., & Langendoen, K. (2002). Robust positioning algorithms for distributed ad-hoc wireless sensor networks. In *Proceedings of the USENIX Technical Annual Conference*, (pp. 317-328). California: Monterey.

Savvides, A., & Srivastava, M. B. (2004). Location discovery. In S. Basagni, M. Conti, S. Giordano & I. Stojmenović (Eds.), *Mobile ad hoc networking* (pp. 231-254). Hoboken, New Jersey: IEEE Press and John Wiley & Sons, Inc.

Silventoinen, M. I., & Rantalainen, T. (1996). Mobile station emergency locating in GSM. In *Proceedings of IEEE ICPWC '96,* (pp. 232-238). India: New Delhi.

SnapTrack (2003). SnapTrack's Wireless Assisted GPS™ (A-GPS) Solution Provides the Industry's Best Location System. Whitepaper from *SnapTrack, A QUALCOMM Company*.

Spirito, M. A., & Mattiolli, A. G. (1999). Preliminary experimental results of a GSM mobile phones positioning system based on timing advance. In *Proceedings of the 50th IEEE Vehicular Technology Conference, Vol. 4.* (pp. 2072-2076). The Netherlands: Amsterdam.

Sundaram, N., & Ramanathan, P. (2002). Connectivity based location estimation scheme for wireless ad hoc networks. In *Proceedings of IEEE Globecom 2002, Vol. 1*, (pp. 143-147). Taiwan: Taipei.

Tseng, Y. C., Huang, C. F., & Kuo, S. P. (2005). Positioning and Location Tracking in Wireless Sensor Networks. In M. Ilyas & I. Mahgoub (Eds.), *Handbook of sensor networks: compact wireless and wired sensing systems*. Florida, Boca Raton: CRC Press LLC.

Van Trees, H. L. (2001). *Detection estimation and modulation theory, Part 1* (republished in paperback). NY: John Wiley & Sons, Inc.

Venkatraman, S., Caffery, J. Jr., & Heung-Ryeol, Y. (2004). A novel ToA location algorithm using LoS range estimation for NLoS environments. *IEEE Transactions on Vehicular Technology*, 53(5), 1515-1524.

Wang, X., Wang, Z., & O'Dea, B. (2003). A TOA-based location algorithm reducing the errors due to non-line-of-sight (NLOS) propagation. *IEEE Transactions on Vehicular Technology,* 52(1), 112 - 116.

Willassen, S. Y. (1998). A method for implementing Mobile Station Location in GSM. Retrieved September 16, 2005, from http://www.willassen.no/msl/node1.html.

Zhu, L., & Zhu, J. (2000). Signal-strength-based cellular location using dynamic window-width and double-averaging algorithm. In *Proceedings of the 52nd IEEE Vehicular Technology Conference, Vol. 6,* (pp. 2992-2997). USA: Boston.

KEY TERMS

Ad Hoc Network Positioning: Localization of mobile device (node) in ad hoc networks. Position estimation of mobile device is result of ad hoc networks positioning.

Adaptive Geometric Algorithm (AGA): The function of AGA is mobile device location estimation. The AGA is improvement of basic geometric algorithm. The AGA provides more accurate results compare with geometric algorithm.

Cellular Positioning: Localization of mobile devices in cellular networks. Position estimation of mobile device is result of cellular positioning.

Geometric Algorithm (GA): The function of Geometric Algorithm (GA) is mobile device location estimation (with the highest probability) by means of calculation of lines of position intersection. The triangulation is used for calculation of the intersection.

Mobile Based Positioning: A localized mobile device makes the appropriate signal measurements from geographically distributed reference devices, (e.g., base stations, reference nodes). These measurements are used to determine mobile device location. Computing operations are done in mobile device, e.g. Mobile Station (MS).

Network Based Positioning: Reference devices at one or more locations measure a signal originating from the localized device. These measurements are communicated to a central site where they are combined to give an estimate of the mobile device location. This position information can be used at the central site or sent to another system (application), which requires the location of given mobile device.

Positioning Requirements: Basic requirements of a positioning system. These should be fulfilled for satisfied positioning. For example, the requirements include: maximum possible accuracy of the system; privacy protection, possibility to disable positioning in a case of assault.

Range Based Positioning: The form of positioning it is based on the indirect measurements of distance or angle between sensors. The important thing to note is that the indirect measurements always have errors and individual measurements are not independent of each other. These measurements are strongly influenced by the surrounding environment and transmission system.

Range Free Positioning: Category of positioning methods, which estimate the location of mobile devices (sensors, nodes or mobile stations) either by exploiting the radio connectivity information among neighboring mobile devices, or by exploiting the sensing capabilities of the mobile devices. The range free positioning methods are cost-effective solutions.

Weighted Proximity Positioning (WEP): This modified positioning method increases proximity accuracy by means of weighting data entering centroid proximity. The fundamental of WEP is increased influence of closer reference nodes at the expense of further nodes. WEP belongs to the group of range free positioning. Positioning using proximity measurements is popular, when low cost takes precedence in priority over accuracy.

Chapter XII
Converged Networks and Seamless Mobility:
Lessons from Experience

Anthony Ioannidis
Athens University of Economics and Business, Greece

Jiorgis Kritsotakis
Hellenic American University, Greece

ABSTRACT

Convergence in the communication industry is a reality – networks are being integrated, digital devices are being unified, and organizations seeking to take advantage of the breadth of opportunities are moving into neighboring industries. These ground-shifting changes have precipitated the emergence of what has come to be known as the Next Generation Network (NGN). Bridging the fixed and mobile divide, that enables the "always connected lifestyle", where all electronic equipment can be connected to each other in a seamless manner, and users access a wide range of services free of any time, location, and device constraints, stands out as the most notable manifestation of an NGN proposition. This is also known as the Fixed Mobile Convergence (FMC). Given the general confusion and uncertainty that characterizes the rapidly integrated communications industry, this paper seeks to assess whether an integrated bundled network can itself become the gateway for the efficient delivery of multimedia applications and services. Applying the Resource Based View (RBV) theory, on the recent developments in the FMC space, this paper concurs with industry-wide skepticism and provides guidelines for the fulfillment of the NGN promise.

HISTORICAL CONTEXT

According to what has come to be known as the Telecommunications Old Paradigm, the telecommunications industry rested on three structuring principles: first, protected franchise. Domestically incumbent telecommunications operators enjoyed steady revenue flows stemming from the exploitation of their own (mainly monopoly controlled) networks (see Table 1).

The second structuring principle was quarantined Operators. Public Telecommunications Operators (PTOs) were restricted from the conduct of any affairs outside their pre-determined sphere of control and as such, were

Copyright © 2009, IGI Global, distributing in print or electronic forms without written permission of IGI Global is prohibited.

Table 1. International competitive regimes (selective) (Owen, 1991:53)

Country	Local	National	International
USA	Limited	Yes	Yes
Japan	Yes	Yes	Yes
UK	Yes	Yes	Yes
Germany	No	No	No
France	No	No	No
Other EU	No	No	No

further barred from exporting their experience and influence into adjacent and more competitive markets. The third structuring principle was what the industry referred to as the "*cradle to grave*" regulation. Based on a bilateral framework (see Figure 1), prices, terms, and conditions of the PTOs service had to be sold to the regulators before they could be sold to the customers.

Technologically, under the old paradigm, PTOs by and large operated within an industry that consisted of three layers (see Figure 2).

In the first layer of the old paradigm, switches, transmission systems, and customer terminals were produced and were combined to form the telecom networks.

Within the natural monopoly hypothesis that underpinned most of the PTOs, the equipment layer was less regulated. The production of telecommunications equipment varied in its organization. On the most liberalized end of the scale, there was a pattern of vertical integration. On the less liberalized end, PTOs of smaller countries were less integrated in their operations. For most of them, equipment was procured from a handful of globally competing suppliers. The middle ground was covered by industrialized nations, whose domestic markets were sufficiently large to cover their equipment needs (see Figure 3). It is not surprising that from the 1950s and onwards, most of the technological developments occurred in this layer.

In the second layer, although individual countries did vary significantly, they all shared a common underpinning technology. Namely, dedicated circuits that connected the sender to the information recipient or to the circuit-switched networks. It wasn't until the 1970s that the first commercial packet switched data network (PSDN) made a shy appearance and slowly started to change the nature of the products and services offered. Under the old paradigm and towards its later years, the main services (Layer 3) that monopoly network operators offered and pretty much defined the industry, were to a large extent confined into voice, fax, and enhanced services (i.e., toll free numbers).

Shifting Sands: Emerging Paradigm

The liberalization of the European telecommunications industry was a gradual process that begun in 1984 and underwent four phases:

- Preparation for harmonization (Green Paper publication)
- Transition from monopoly to phased competition (White Paper on the single market and competition rules)
- Implementation of asymmetric regulation (imposition of restrictions to the former monopolies and a directive for opening up access to their networks)
- Application of EU-wide competition law (regulatory framework for electronic communications network)

Next to the politically driven institutional reforms, a quiet yet rapid 'convergence' started to take place and radically reshaped the global telecommunications field. The term itself is an *ex post* construct which aims to

Figure 1. Bilateral framework

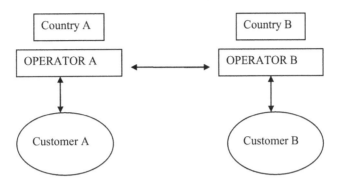

Figure 2. Layers of the old paradigm

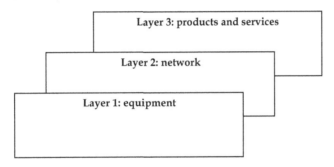

Figure 3. Degree of PTO integration

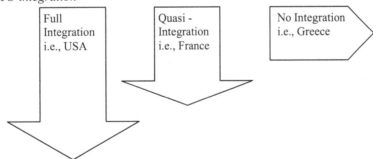

describe developments that are both parallel and sequential, as well as recursive. Although convergence eludes precise definition, the 1997 European Union's Green Paper describes it as:

The ability of different network platforms to carry essentially similar kinds of services or The coming together of consumer devices such as the telephone, television and the personal computer.

The manifested convergence reflected the summation of intended and unintended consequences of actions that stemmed from two disembedding mechanisms that Giddens (1991) refers to as: *symbolic,* and *expert.* The former, in the shape of open networks, and the latter, in the form of the required segregation between the state and

Figure 4. Levels of convergence

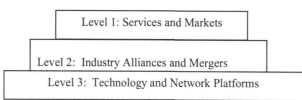

its assets. In more detail, convergence seemed to occur on three levels: Network platforms, involved industries, and emerged services and markets. Developments which, in more ways than one, were understood as influencing each other (see Figure 4).

Level 1: Technological Platform Convergence and the Fuse Agent

One of the first areas where convergence began to show was through the interconnectivity among all four layers of the telecommunication networks that were originally designed to carry different types of information separately. To clarify, let us provide a short description of each of those layers.

- **Layer 1:** Corresponds to the prerequisites for the establishment of the following layers and primarily relates to the assigned frequencies, space segments, rights of way, etc.
- **Layer 2:** Corresponds to the physical elements required for the transmission of information and mainly pertains to cables and radio emission base stations.
- **Layer 3:** Extends to cover the equipment for coding and transmitting the information. This layer relates to the transmission equipment, multiplexers, compression/decompression modules, etc.
- **Layer 4:** Relates to all the equipment that allows point to point communication through the previously mentioned networks. It encompasses all the systems for the switching, signaling, and configuration of the network.

The fuse agent that facilitated the emergence of this interconnectivity was the process of digitization. Although the digitization of the telecommunications infrastructure had been rather slow, its acceleration during the last two decades of the 20th century marked a watershed. The instrumental role in the successful transition of telecommunications from analogue to digital was credited to fiber optic cables. As digitization steadily progressed and more and more fiber was installed, the global network infrastructure changed in three ways. First, the drastic reduction in the number of faults per line allowed the increase of network reliability and enabled the uninterrupted transfer of voice and data. Second, networks enjoyed a dramatic increase in their available capacity. This facilitated the installation of more lines, generated higher rates of penetration, and altogether heralded the possibilities for the easier transfer of larger chunks of datasets. Third, and most important, this also increased the networks' reliability, speed, and capacity, enabling them to be transformed into communication platforms which could transfer voice, text, image, and video.

Level 2: Industry Convergence

The combination of the platform convergence and the gradual liberalization of telecommunications markets began to bring together players from neighboring industries. New relations began to emerge between localities distant, both in terms of space (country of origin) as well as industry (field of expertise). One manifestation of this was the massive wave of mergers and alliances that have reshaped and continue to drastically alter the markets worldwide. Mega-mergers between reflexive telecom operators, computer groups, media and entertainment conglomerates, and information providers were inevitable. Such ventures represented a wide spectrum of transactions and, on

Figure 5. Trajectory of industry change (McGahan, 2004:3)

Core assets / Core activities	Threatened	Not Threatened
Threatened	**Radical Change** *Everything is up in the air.* Examples: makers of landline telephone handsets, overnight letter-delivery carriers, and travel agencies	**Creative Change** *The industry is constantly redeveloping assets and resources.* Examples: the motion picture industry, sports team ownership, and investment banking
Not Threatened	**Intermediating Change** *Relationships are fragile.* Examples: automobile dealerships, investment brokerages, and auction houses	**Progressive Change** *Companies implement incremental testing and adapt to feedback.* Examples: online auctions, commercial airlines, and long-haul trucking

the whole, fall under two types of strategies: Integration and diversification. Companies that followed integration strategies were usually involved in intra-industry (sometimes cross-border) types of alliances and acquisitions. Consolidation, risk sharing, market share defense or just growth were the main drivers. In the US for example, as early as 1996, immediately following the Telecommunications Act a merger between Bell Atlantic and Nynex, two large American regional telephone companies occurred. Similarly, in Europe some years later, several alliances, such as the foundation of the FreeMove Alliance or Starmap have begun to re-write the script. Companies that implement diversification strategies are mainly looking at cross-industry alliances, as they seek to expand into the higher value segments. T-Mobile for example, joined forces with Google and developed new ways of browsing the Web via mobile handsets. BskyB formed an alliance with Vodafone, the mobile service provider, in order to jointly develop an entertainment channel available through the Vodafone network. In the words of Nortel Europe's CEO, *"the industry had become a big bed...."*

Level 3: Service Convergence

As the boundaries of the telecommunications, computing, and broadcasting sectors were significantly stretched to foster their hybrid arrangement, the last and perhaps more readily recognizable level of convergence emerged. Namely, the coming together of the user devices that make up the fifth layer of infrastructure, which is the user application layer. The examples are numerous. Already by the mid 1990s, the industry saw the emergence of mobile telephones that could provide internet access and by now, mobile devices can stream television, download MP3s, synchronize with office software, and much more.

In conclusion, firms in what have traditionally been known to be part of the wider telecommunications sector are midway through a trajectory of what McGahan (2004) refers to as radical change. According to McGahan, when industries undergo radical change, both the core assets and the core activities are under threat (see Figure 5).

NEXT GENERATION NETWORKS (NGNS): THE FUTURE IS NOW

In light of these changes, a growing number of major telecommunications operators, internet service providers, and non-traditional communications industry players, such as cable operators, utilities/power companies, and wireless companies have been making plans for NGN and have established test-beds for their equipment and services for the future deployment of NGN. The obvious shift towards the NGN will definitely impact not only the business models of ICT service providers and manufacturers, but also the way a business is carried out in many other sectors and the way private communications are conducted. The NGN is expected to facilitate e-commerce and e-business more effectively than the existing PSTN and will make it possible to offer more flexible and customized services for customers (OECD, 2005).

There is no single accepted definition of NGN. Usually, these definitions are quite broad, such as those provided by organizations like the European Telecommunications Standards Institute (ETSI) and ITU-T. ITU-T describes NGN as a packet-based network able to provide services including telecommunications services, and has the ability to use multiple broadband, quality of service enabled transport technologies, and in which service-related functions are independent from the underlying transport-related technologies (ITU, 2004). NGN not only covers network characteristics but also service characteristics which provide new opportunities to network operators, service providers, communications manufacturers, and users.

There are three major driving forces for deploying NGNs:

First, there are structural changes in the telecommunications markets. During the last decade, the telecommunications market has undergone significant structural and regulatory change. Competition has increased significantly both in traditional PSTN markets and through other services such as cellular mobile services and cable. Incumbent telecommunications operators have been privatized, unbundling has been required in several countries to varying degrees, and new services have emerged. These developments have resulted in a decline in the traditional sources of revenue in the voice market. The main threat for PSTN operators is the shift of revenue and communications volumes to other service providers.

Second, there are changes in services and user needs. With the rapid diffusion of broadband internet services, network service providers have identified growing customer needs for more flexible broadband multimedia services, which cannot be accommodated by the current PSTN network. The increasing problem of the current PSTN network is the limited interworking capacity in a heterogeneous network environment. The innovative developments in Voice Over Internet Protocol (VoIP), cellular, wireless, and digital TV services added pressure for telecommunications operators to accommodate the increasing needs of customers by embracing the efficiencies of packet-switched multi-service networks. Together with broadband internet, the widespread use of VoIP has acted as a catalyst to stimulate the development of NGNs and also place pressure on prices offered by PSTN service providers.

Third, there is technological evolution. The technological developments in the area of Internet Protocol (IP), digitalization, increase in computer power and memory, and optics, allow for a combination of voice and multimedia traffic over networks. In addition, the quality of service and call control technology for IP has improved noticeably. These technological developments have allowed for the provision of internet access, including email and VoIP, using the cable facilities.

As early as 2000, Crimi suggested that certain types of services would become the drivers in the NGN environment, in terms of how much profit margins they are likely to generate and how pervasive they will be, namely:

- **Voice telephony:** NGNs will need to support various existing voice telephony services, such as call waiting, call forwarding, three-way calling, various Advanced Intelligent Network (AIN) features, and various Centrex features. NGNs do not attempt to duplicate each and every traditional voice telephony service currently offered. They rather attempt to support only a small portion of these traditional services, with an initial focus on the most marketable features as well those features required from a regulatory perspective.
- **Data connectivity services:** Allows for the real-time establishment of connectivity between endpoints, along with the various value-added features, such as bandwidth-on-demand.
- **Multimedia services:** Allows multiple parties to interact using voice, video, and data. This not only allows customers to converse with each other while displaying visual information, but also allows for collaborative computing and groupware.

Figure 6. The CTP solution (Ovum, 2004:3)

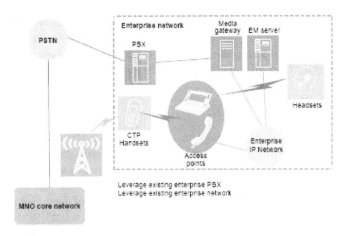

- **Virtual private networks (VPNs):** Voice VPNs improve the interlocation networking capabilities of businesses by allowing large, geographically dispersed organizations to combine their existing private networks with portions of the PSTN, thus providing customers with uniform dialing capabilities. Data VPNs, on the other hand, provide added security and networking features, which allow customers to use a shared IP network as a VPN.
- **Public network computing:** Provides public network-based computing services for businesses and consumers, such as generic processing and storage capabilities, business applications (e.g., enterprise resource planning), and consumer applications.
- **Unified messaging:** Supports the delivery of voice mail, email, fax mail, and pages through common interfaces, thus allowing users to access and be notified of various message types, independent of the means of access.
- **Information brokering:** Involves advertising, finding and providing information to match consumers with providers.
- **E-Commerce:** Allows consumers to purchase goods and services electronically over the network (e.g., home banking, home shopping, business-to-business applications).
- **Call Center Services:** Allows customers to place a call to a call center agent by clicking on a Web page.
- Interactive gaming, home manager (e.g., control of home security or entertainment systems, energy systems), and Distributed Virtual Reality (e.g., technological representations of real-world events, people, places, experiences, in which the participants in and providers of the virtual experience are physically distributed).

NGNS: THE CASE OF FIXED-MOBILE CONVERGENCE (FMC)

FMC Wider Convergence Context

Historically, services have to some extent been defined by the networks that carry them. However, the transition to digitization and the arrival of deregulation has directly contributed to the breaking of the barriers that existed between media platforms, services, and industries. Although the body of literature that addresses these developments in the wider communications sector is still evolving, this rapid transformation is universally referred to as "convergence."

Convergence, of course, means different things to different people. Scholars have approached it from different angles. Some academics define convergence as a process of technological integration (Danowski and Choi, 1998;

Fidler, 1997; Pavlik, 1998). Others define it as the destruction of regulatory boundaries between different sectors of an economy (Kang & Johansson, 2000). In summary, according to Chon et al. (2003), convergence can be seen from three perspectives: (a) the consolidation through industry alliances and mergers, (b) the combination of technology and network platforms, and (c) the integration between services and markets. Among them, convergence through cross-industry mergers and acquisitions leads not to the horizontal expansion of market share but to the cooperation among companies from different sectors, or the expansion of companies into unrelated industries.

Towards an FMC Definition

With the rapid unbundling of available services from networks, the barriers between fixed and mobile telephony have begun to blur, making the distinction between wireline and wireless services redundant and FMC a reality. But what is FMC and which were the main precipitating drivers behind its arrival?

FMC, while still in its formative stages, is an effort to provide users with "the best of both worlds." Namely, through the use of a single hybrid device, consumers will be offered all of the convenience and features of a cellular phone but with a fixed line cost and the quality and reliability of a fixed line. For example, when a user is at home, with the use of the hybrid device that will communicate with an installed

Wi-Fi hub, the call made will be routed via the fixed network on fixed line prices and fixed line call quality and reliability. As the user walks outside of his/her home, through the use of the same hybrid device, the call will be seamlessly routed to the GSM or any other mobile network.

Fixed Mobile Convergence is not a 21st century phenomenon. Its evolution can be traced back to the early nineties and BT's abortive efforts to enter the market with the "OnePhone" proposition. The key drivers behind FMC's inevitable revival are four:

- **Fixed mobile substitution:** voice minutes continue to move away from fixed networks to mobile. In the US, for example, 36% of local and 60% of long distance calls are now being made through mobile networks.
- **Changing consumer patterns:** the "always connected lifestyle" is becoming the norm and consumers around the Western world take for granted that seamless connectivity will be guaranteed at home, at work, on the road, and during leisure time.
- Ever-increasing pressure on fixed line operators to identify new revenue sources and simultaneously prevent further subscriber leakage.
- Significant technological breakthroughs and standards adoption: Indicatively, we can mention Wi-Fi-VoIP, mobile handsets able to seamlessly handle call transferring over different networks.

Figure 7. The UMA solution (Ovum, 2004:4)

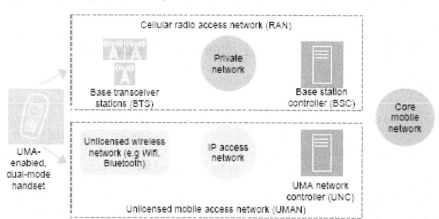

FMC Standards

The FMC proposition is currently supported by two alternative short-rage technologies: Cordless Telephony Profile (CTP) and Unlicensed Mobile Access (UMA). CTP, is a profile defined within the Bluetooth specification, by the Bluetooth Special Interest Group. CTP allows a Bluetooth-enabled cell phone to be used as a cordless telephone when it is within range of a Bluetooth CTP access point. CTP is thus a way of adding limited mobility – cordless-ness – to the fixed network. It is currently deployed to a limited number of manufacturers and operators as an interim solution, primarily due to its ability to be attached to existing networks (see Figure 6).

Although superficially similar to the CTP, UMA is actually very different. For a start, while CTP is limited to the Bluetooth air interface technology, UMA is an 'air interface agnostic' specification, which can be used in conjunction with Bluetooth, Wi-Fi, or even as yet undefined access technologies. The specification has been developed by a group of manufacturers, with limited input from some operators, notably BT (see Figure 7).

Despite the similarities between the two alternatives, there is a clear strategic difference between them – the CTP technology avoids the mobile network and provides a limited amount of mobility on the fixed network. The UMA on the contrary, is a technology that can enable the extending of the mobile network into the building, allowing both the call and the subscriber to remain under the control of the mobile network.

FMC: Selected Offers

As mobile and fixed operators are trying to capitalize on the opportunities, FMC propositions are mushrooming around the world (see Table 2).

However, as evident in Table 2, distinctions need to be made between the different propositions. According to a study by the Yankee Group (2004), FMC takes many forms (see Figure 8).

- On its most basic level, FMC relates to what is called packaging convergence. Here, the two previously separate products of mobile and fixed telephony are packaged or bundled together in terms of a single provider, single bill, or single point of contact for the consumer.
- Building on the organizational and marketing bundling that has been achieved via packaging, a feature-based convergence connects the two through the provision of a number of enhanced services. Without changing anything on the network, operators can now offer services like a single voice mailbox for the consumer.
- Product convergence is achieved when the distinct product boundaries are removed and there is one product capable of delivering a service that would otherwise have been delivered by two separate entities. The emergence of the unified/hybrid Motorola KRZR device is one such example. Here, the subscriber can enjoy the functionality of making calls via fixed and mobile networks while using a single device.
- Ultimately, FMC will be able to deliver a seamless user experience across multiple locations, devices, and types of use. This will allow the ubiquitous "sliding" between different networks and devices while services will retain the already set customization profile of the end user.

Table 2. Selected FMC offers

Country	Operator	FMC Offer
UK	BT – Fusion	One stop shop: one handset, one number, one bill – seamless transition
South Korea	Korea Telecom – DU	Single dual mode handset but without Seamless Network Handover
USA	Verizon	Automatic forwarding of incoming calls from mobile to fixed when cell phone is in the cradle at home
France	FT – Unifie	A virtual network between the company PBX extensions and cell phones with a private numbering plan and discounted tariffs

In summary, the current industry momentum allows us to experience FMC across multiple levels (see Table 3).

RESOURCE-BASED VIEW (RBV) THEORY

The Resource-Based View of the firm (RBV) stands as a key theoretical perspective that management scholars deploy in order to suggest and explain how firms build and sustain a competitive advantage. Barney (1991) notably offers one of the most detailed explanations of the resource-based perspective. His central theoretical claim is that "organizational resources that are valuable, rare, difficult to imitate, and non-substitutable" can result in the creation of a sustained competitive advantage. According to Barney, organizational resources can vary from raw materials, brands, products, and management processes to organizational structures, strategies, and people. For Barney, competitive advantage will be created when a resource, or a combination of resources fulfils the four requirements outlined by the RBV theory:

- **Valuable:** Allow the firm to exploit opportunities or neutralize threats in its external environment
- **Rare:** Possessed by few, if any, current and potential competitors
- **Costly to imitate:** When other firms either cannot obtain them or must obtain them at a much higher cost
- **Non-substitutable:** The firm must be organized appropriately to obtain the full benefits of the resources in order to realize a competitive advantage

Table 3. The FMC consumer experience (Yankee Group 2004:4)

Level of Convergence	Suite of FMC Proposition Enhancements
Packaging	• One-stop shopping with single bill and cost analysis for all services • Simplified pricing
Feature	• One address book available from any device • Single voice mailbox
Product	• Common devices with a common set of user interfaces and services • Service security and privacy
Seamless	• Seamless roaming/ handover between Wi-Fi, WiMAX, GSM, 3G, 4G • Office applications, multi-media & web available from any device, anywhere at best speed • Guaranteed coverage and Quality of Service across networks/devices

Figure 8. FMC propositions (Yankee Group 2004:1)

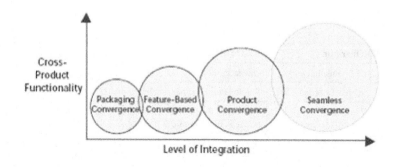

Assuming that firms are amalgamations of heterogeneous and mobile resources, the RBV provides a viable alternative to the dominant Porterian view that identifies the external environment as being the key proponent in the creation and maintenance of a competitive advantage. With the focus of managers and scholars pinned on internal resources, the RBV has succeeded in informing many debates in the strategy field.

Some theorists have looked at the more fundamental contribution of resources to sustainable advantage for single-business firms and examined how or why resources contribute to the advantage of one firm over another in a particular product/market (e.g., Barney, 1991; Conner, 1991; Powell, 1992).

Arguments have been advanced further by looking at particular types of resources, such as information technology (Mata, Fuerst, & Barney, 1995; Powell, 1997), strategic planning (Michalisin et al., 1997), organizational alignment (Powell, 1992), human resources management (Flood, Smith, & Derfus, 1996; Lado & Wilson, 1994), and top management skills (Castanias & Helfat, 1991). Moreover, the number of proponents that have elevated the RBV from the status of "view" to "theory" has enhanced its visibility and also suggests widespread acceptance (e.g., Barney, 1996)

A summary of the main research programs that have been rooted in the RBV theory can be found in Table 4.

THE BT FUSION CASE

The launch of BT Fusion was a landmark point in the organization's efforts to differentiate from the competition and actively seek to defend the eroding core of its consumer business. While BT initially did not extensively promote the service to its users, the partnership with a key high street retailer openly indicated its commitment to grow the business and further the penetration of the Fusion service. (For the chronology of events see Figure 9.)

For all their efforts however, the take up has remained limited and the number of subscribers low, ranging from 40,000 to 50,000 across the 68 million mobile subscribers of the UK market. Using the RBV lens, we will attempt to provide an explanation as to why the rate of penetration has been so limited. In previous parts of this

Table 4. Research programs in strategic management

Research Topic	Research Program	Representative Authors
Strategy concepts	1. Alternative Frameworks 2. Agency theory 3. Theory of the firm 4. Innovations and advantage 5. Organizational learning	Barney (1991) Sherer, Rogovsky, & Wright (1998) Barney (1996); Conner (1991) Bates & Flynn (1995) Grant (1996)
Strategic management processes	Behavioral models and culture; culture/resource selection	Fiol (1991)
Board of directors	Top management teams	Flood, Smith, & Derfus (1996)
General management roles in strategy management	Managerial action and prescriptions	Marino (1996)
Strategy formulation	Competitive strategy and building competitiveness	Black & Boal (1994)
Environmental analysis	Environment and resource relationships	Fahy (1996)
Strategy implementation and evaluation	Industry structure/knowledge	Lado & Wilson (1994)
Formal planning systems	Strategic assets and planning	Michalisin, Smith, & Kline (1997); Powell (1992a)
Strategic control	Strategic information support systems	Mata, Fuerst, & Barney (1995)

Figure 9. BT Fusion—chronology of events (Ovum, 2006:5)

paper, we explained that firms can capture and sustain an advantage over their competitors if four conditions/requirements are satisfied. To recap, we said that a competitive advantage will be formulated when the resources that are deployed are Valuable (allowing the firm to exploit opportunities or neutralize threats in its external environment); Rare (possessed by few, if any, current and potential competitors); Costly to imitate (when other firms either cannot obtain them or must obtain them at a much higher cost) and Non-substitutable (the firm must be organized appropriately to obtain the full benefits of the resources in order to realize a competitive advantage).

When applying the RBV lens over the BT Fusion case, it emerges that the lack of apparent success can be attributed to the fact that none of the aforementioned preconditions of the framework were being met. Allow us to examine each one separately.

Valuable: While few will doubt the resourcefulness of NGN and the FMC proposition, the inherent complexity (at least in user perception) that has not been neutralized ultimately cancels out BT's efforts to exploit the technology. While most players in the FMC space will openly recognize the significance of common standards and user-friendly technologies as key elements of quicker service take up, the reality seems to suggest otherwise. Leading industry commentators have openly asked for operators to "get on with it" and the BT case is echoing the previous statement. On a micro level, next to technological glitches, usage problems continue to provide alarming insights as to the necessity to provide the user with a pain-free service experience. Indicatively, we can mention the following:

- How complex it is to install an FMC solution is a technology-related question that operators have not properly addressed. With consumer threshold at a low, installation may not be as easy as initially stated.
- How wide is the range of devices available to the final user?
- How long is the battery life (WiFi has an impact on power consumption, standby is the main issue rather than talk time) of the chosen device?

Rare: Perhaps of all the four RBV preconditions, rareness is the "Achilles heel" of the FMC proposition. With potentially many operators launching a wide variety of FMC propositions, added complexity is introduced to the mind of the final user. As recent reports from telecom consultancies suggest, BT's Fusion is a member of the rapidly crowded FMC market populated by many constituents:

- Integrated operators with a fixed arm
- Fixed only through Mobile Virtual Network Operators (MVNOs)
- Integrated broadband and mobile players
- Mobile only (through virtual deals)
- Completely virtual players that wholesale all the elements (retail brands, for instance)

With so many options available, buyers find it difficult to differentiate between BT Fusion and other competing offers, rendering the proposition anything but rare.

Costly to imitate: With so many options available to the final user, it is almost self evident that the cost to imitate has failed to raise the protective barrier that Fusion required in order to build a take up for its service. The proliferation of technologies that underpin the product offers, the competing standards, different support requirements, and multiple operator dependent devices all point towards a cluttered market with low barriers to entry.

Non-Substitutable: With regards to issues of substitutability, the BT Fusion case openly illustrates both the lack and the subsequent necessity for organizational clarity. Attracting and retaining customers in the face of intense competitive pressure and low barriers to entry requires integrated market approaches. BT's ill-defined converged segmentation reflects a poorly aligned organization towards serving the highly fragmented end-user needs. Different organizational cultures, competing organizational structures and most importantly non-integrated market analytics, all result in organizational inability to execute the defined strategy.

LESSONS LEARNED FOR RAPID NGN ADOPTION

The aforementioned analysis highlights the following three lessons:

Lesson 1: Commercialization

With regards to issues of commercialization, the FMC experiment can provide valuable lessons for NGN service adoption across countries. Perhaps the most critical success factor is the ability of the different operators to master the marketing of their product/service.

- Starting with the obvious, the FMC case illustrates the necessity for meaningful market gauging and a well-defined value proposition. Operators, so far, have been incapable of distinguishing benefits for the consumer and enterprise segments, allowing their offers to remain a story largely about reduced tariffs.
- With potentially lots of operators launching a wide variety of FMC propositions, added complexity is introduced to the mind of the final user. As recent reports from telecom consultancies suggest, the FMC market is rapidly becoming very crowded.
- The cost of devices is also important.
  - Currently FMC devices are mid range, but we know that some chipset manufacturers (for example, TI) have aggressive strategies to bring down the ~~build of~~ cost in the medium term
  - For FMC to penetrate less-developed markets, there will need to be lower cost devices

Lesson 2: Regulation

In the midst of competitor overcrowding, the role of regulation is critical to the development of the FMC market.

- Recent European experience suggests that we should avoid the communication of mixed signals. Potentially, like the UK case, regulators can use the FMC in order to increase competition in the market (for example, they may mandate MVNO access for broadband players to offer FMC services). When, however, regulators question the ability of incumbents to launch (Italian market), an additional factor for slower take up is indicated and must be avoided.
- In addition to the aforementioned, regulators must also consider, the impact of an all-IP network on issues of interconnection and numbering, in an effort to avoid increased complexity around the service.

Lesson 3: Technology and Devices

While most players in the FMC space will openly recognize the significance of common standards and user friendly technologies as key elements of quicker service take up, the reality seems to suggest otherwise. Leading industry commentators have openly asked for operators to "get on with it" and our case is echoing the aforementioned statement. On a macro level, FMC is held back by the proliferation of technologies that underpin the product offering. Competing standards, different support requirements, and operator dependent devices all contribute to the cluttering of the market.

On a micro level, current FMC usage problems continue to provide valuable insights as to the necessity to provide the user with a pain-free service experience.

CONCLUSION

In order to take advantage of the arrival of NGN's companies, we will be required to do more than just rely on the technological developments. As our analysis of the BT Fusion case has indicated, simply relying on a new technology is hardly a differentiator. Having deployed the RBV theory, we have shown how FMC has fallen short of offering the much anticipated competitive advantage, given that it has failed to fulfil any of the pre-conditions. So, where does this leave us? Should we be led to believe that since NGN technologies are available to most industry players, then by definition, differentiation will remain an elusive gamble? The short answer to this is no. The authors strongly believe that NGNs can become a key differentiator in the rapidly integrated communication industry, as long as three key imperatives for profit are met:

- Deliver a distinctive value to the customer. This means providing customers access to their information in a seamless fashion across devices and platforms. It also means that firms will be able to offer unique content and desired applications, not just technologies. Last but not least, services must be attractively priced, in order to overcome the expected switching cost/barrier that most consumers are confronted by.
- Use NGN in order to create a defensible differentiation and avoid the building of another "me too" proposition. This will require the most dominant players to actively leverage scale and reach, and in effect lower the cost of operation and invest the savings in building differentiated skills and relationships.
- Provide compelling products, that are simple and intuitive to use. Consumers are looking for ease of use, plug and play solutions that will have a minimum disruptive effect on prior experiences with similar products.

In summary, the arrival of NGNs is a real opportunity for both consumers and industry alike. It may take some years for its applications to take off and it may face considerable obstacles along the way. However, players must realize that an integrated bundled network is difficult in itself to become the key driver that will allow profitable differentiation.

REFERENCES

Barney, J.B. (1991). Firm resources and sustained competitive advantage. *Journal of Management*, 17:99-120.

Barney, J.B. (1996). The resource-based theory of the firm. *Organizational Science*, 7:469.

Bates, K.A., & Flynn, J.E. (1995). Innovation history and competitive advantage: A resource-based view analysis of manufacturing technology innovations. *Academy of Management Best Papers Proceedings*: 235-239.

Black, J.A., & Boal, K.B. (1994). Strategic resources: Traits configurations and paths to sustainable competitive advantage. *Strategic Management Journal*, 15 (Summer Special Issue):131-148.

Castanias, R.P., & Helfat, C.E. (1991). Managerial resources and rents. *Journal of Management*, 17:155-171.

Chon, B.S., Choi, J.H., Barnett, G.A., Danowski, J.A., & Joo, S.H. (2003). A structural analysis of media convergence: cross industry mergers and acquisitions in the information industries. *Journal of Media Economics* 16(3): 141-157.

Conner, K.R. (1991). A historical comparison of resource-based theory and five schools of thought within industrial organization economics. Do we have a new theory of the firm? *Journal of Management*, 17: 121-154.

Crimi, J.C. (2000) *Next Generation Network (NGN) Services*. A White Paper. Telcordia Technologies.

Danowski, J.A., & Choi, J.H. (1998). Convergence in the information industries: Telecommunications, broadcasting and data processing 1981-1996, in H. Sawhney &

G.A. Barnett (Eds), *Progress in Communication Sciences* (Vol 15: 125-150) Stamford, CT: Ablex.

Fahy, J. (1996). Competitive advantage in international services: A resource-based view. *International Studies in Management and Organization*, 26 (2):24-37

Fidler, R. (1997). *Mediamorphosis: Understanding New Media*. Thousand Oaks, CA: Pine Forge Press.

Fiol, C.M. (1991). Managing culture as a competitive resource: An identity-based view of sustainable competitive advantage. *Journal of Management*, 17: 191-211.

Forrester Research. June (2006), *European Mobile Landscape*

Flood, P.C., Smith, K.A., & Derfus, P. (1996). Guest Editors' introduction –*Top management teams: A neglected topic in strategic human resource management*. Ibar, 17: 1-17.

Giddens, A. (1991) *Modernity and Self-Identity: Self and Society in the Late Modern Age*. Stanford University Press: California.

Grant, R.M. (1996). Prospering in dynamically-competitive environments: Organizational capability as knowledge integration. *Organizational Science*, 7:375-387.

Green Paper 1997, *On the Convergence of the Telecommunications, Media and Information Technology Sectors, and the Implications for Regulation*.

ITU, *NGN 2004 Project Description*, version 3, February 2004.

Kang, N. & Johansson, S. (2000) Cross-border mergers and acquisitions: Their role in industrial globalisation. *STI Working Papers No 2000/1.*

Lado, A.A., & Wilson, M.C. (1994). Human Resource Systems and sustained competitive advantage: a competency-based perspective. *Academy of Managment Review*, 19:699-727.

OECD Directory for Science, Technology, and Industry, Working Party on Telecommunication and Information Services Policies, *Next Generation Network Development in OECD Countries*, January 2005.

Marino, K.E. (1996). Developing consensus on firm competencies and capabilities. *Academy of Management Executive*: 10(3):40-51.

Marshall, P., Barrabee, L., & Griffin, K. (2004). *Divergent Approach to Fixed/Mobile Convergence*. The Yankee Group.

Mata, F.J., Fuerst, W.L., & Barney, J.B. (1995). Information technology and sustained competitive advantage: A resource-based analysis. *MIS Quarterly*, 19:487-505.

McGahan, A. (2004) How Industries Change, *Harvard Business Review*, *82*(10):98-106.

Michalisn, M.D., Smith, R.D., & Kline, D.M. (1997). In search of strategic assets. *International Journal of Organizational Analysis*, 5:360-387.

OECD 1998. *Content as a new growth industry*

Owen, G.M.W. (1991) Competing for the Global Telecommunications Market. *Long Range Planning,* 54(21):52-56.

Pavlik, J.V. (1998) *New Media Technology: Cultural and Commercial Perspectives*. Boston: Allyn & Bacon.

Pawsey, C. (2004) *FMC: Explaining CTP and UMA*, Ovum.

Pawsey, C. (2006) *BT Fusion - The FMC Story so far*, Ovum.

Powell, T.C. (1992). Strategic Planning as competitive advantage. *Strategic Management Journal*, 13: 551-558.

Powell, T.C. (1997). Information technology as competitive advantage: The role of human, business and technology resources. *Strategic Management Journal*, 18:375-405.

Sherer, P.D., Rogovsky, N., & Wright, N. (1998). What drives employment relationships in taxicab organizations? Linking agency to firm capabilities and strategic opportunities. *Organizational Science*, 9:34-48.

KEY TERMS

Competitive Advantage: It is the distinct way a business or firm is positioned in the market in order to obtain an advantage over competitors, which means an ability to maintain sustained levels of profitability above the industry average.

Cordless Telephony Profile (CTP): It is a profile defined within the Bluetooth specification, by the Bluetooth Special Interest Group. CTP allows a Bluetooth-enabled cell phone to be used as a cordless telephone when it is within range of a Bluetooth CTP access point. CTP is thus a way of adding limited mobility – cordlessness – to the fixed network. It is currently deployed to a limited number of manufacturers and operators as an interim solution, primarily due to its ability to be attached to existing networks.

Fixed-Mobile Convergence (FMC): It is the term used to describe a wide range of mobile services that converge elements of fixed communications infrastructure to complement the core mobile service.

ICT: Information & Communications Technology.

ITU: International Telecommunication Union.

Resource-Based View (RBV): It argues that firms possess resources, a subset of which enable them to achieve competitive advantage, and a subset of those that lead to superior long-term performance. Resources that are valuable and rare can lead to the creation of competitive advantage. That advantage can be sustained over longer time periods to the extent that the firm is able to protect against resource imitation, transfer, or substitution. In general, empirical studies using the theory have strongly supported the resource-based view.

Next Generation Network (NGN): It is a packet-based network able to provide services including Telecommunication Services and able to make use of multiple broadband, QoS-enabled transport technologies and in which service-related functions are independent from underlying transport-related technologies. It offers unrestricted access by users to different service providers. It supports generalized mobility which will allow consistent and ubiquitous provision of services to users.

PSTN: Public Service Telecommunications Network.

PTO: Public Telecommunications Operator.

Strategy: It is a planned course of action undertaken to achieve the goals and objectives of an organization. The term was originally used in the context of warfare to describe the overall planning of a campaign as opposed to tactics, which enable the achievement of specific short-term objectives.

Unlicensed Mobile Access (UMA): While CTP is limited to the Bluetooth air interface technology, UMA is an 'air interface agnostic' specification, which can be used in conjunction with Bluetooth, Wi-Fi, or even as yet undefined access technologies. The specification has been developed by a group of manufacturers, with limited input from some operators.

Section III
The Terminal Equipment and Channel Characterization

Chapter XIII
Efficient Receiver Implementation for Mobile Applications

Costas Chaikalis
TEI of Larissa, Greece

Felip Riera-Palou
University of the Balearic Islands, Spain

ABSTRACT

Modern and future wireless communication systems such as UMTS and beyond 3G systems (B3G) are expected to support very high data rates to/from mobile users. This poses important challenges on the handset design as they should be able to attain an acceptable operating bit error rate (BER) while employing a limited set of resources (i.e. low complexity, low power) and often, with tight processing delay constraints. In this chapter we study how channel decoding and equalisation, two widely used mechanisms to combat the deleterious channel effects, can be made adaptable in accordance to the instantaneous operating environment. Simulation results are given demonstrating how receiver reconfigurability is a promising method to achieve complexity/delay efficient receivers while maintaining prescribed quality of service (QoS) constraints.

INTRODUCTION

Channel coding and equalisation are two widely used techniques to counteract the distortion and noise introduced by the channel. While channel coding is useful when the incoming data is uncorrelated, that is, there is no inter-symbol interference (ISI), equalisation is effective in those cases where the channel correlates the transmitted symbols introducing ISI. In this chapter the reconfigurability potential of these two subsystems is explored in detail. In the first part of this chapter an efficient 3G turbo decoder implementation is discussed, whereas in the second part we present a B3G efficient equaliser implementation. Although both mechanisms are studied here separately, as mentioned at the end of the chapter, these two functions are indeed complementary and therefore, a receiver could be designed exploiting a combined equaliser-decoder reconfigurable structure.

Copyright © 2009, IGI Global, distributing in print or electronic forms without written permission of IGI Global is prohibited.

EFFICIENT 3G TURBO DECODER IN INDOOR/LOW RANGE OUTDOOR ENVIRONMENT

Turbo Codes

Turbo codes (Berrou, 1996) represent a powerful channel coding technique. Universal Mobile Telecommunications System (UMTS) belongs to the third generation (3G) of mobile communication systems. Turbo codes have been incorporated as a channel coding scheme in UMTS for data rates higher or equal to 28.8 kbps (Holma, 2000). They also provide high coding gains in flat fading channels with the use of outer block interleaving (Woodard, 2000; Hall, 1998). Soft-input/soft-output (SISO) decoder is part of a turbo decoder and two candidate algorithms to be used in a SISO decoder are soft output Viterbi algorithm (SOVA) and log maximum a-posteriori (log-MAP) algorithm (Woodard, 2000; Robertson, 1995; Hagenauer, 1989; Pietrobon, 1998).

Dynamic reconfiguration in cellular networks is a popular topic in published literature (Kotsopoulos, 1991; Kotsopoulos, 1992), while different propagation (mobile channel) issues, tested by experimental procedures, have been presented in Bouzouki (2001), Ioannou (2004) and Kitsios (2005). A reconfigurable turbo decoder can be derived according to the common operations of the two algorithms, optimal in terms of performance and latency (Chaikalis, 2003; Chaikalis, 2004; Chaikalis, in press). We consider just SOVA and log-MAP and not other turbo decoding algorithms like max-log-MAP or MAP, because SOVA is better in terms of delay, while log-MAP is better in terms of performance (Woodard, 2000; Robertson, 1995).

UMTS Data Flow

A transport channel transfers data over radio interface from Medium Access Control sub-layer of layer 2 to physical layer and is characterized by its transport format set, which consists of different transport formats. They must have the same type of channel coding and time transmission interval (TTI), while the transport block set or data frame size can vary. The transport block set determines the number of input bits to the channel encoder and can be transmitted every TTI, with possible values for TTI of 10, 20, 40 and 80 msec (Holma, 2000; 3GPP TS 25.201, 2002). After channel coding, outer block interleaving is performed, and since the frame duration in UMTS is 10 msec, the number of columns of the outer block interleaver can be 1, 2, 4 or 8, depending on TTI value. Therefore, the TTI values and the number of columns of the outer block interleaver are interrelated. Furthermore, every transport channel is assigned a radio access bearer with a particular data rate, which provides the transfer of the service through the radio network. A mobile terminal may use several parallel transport channels simultaneously, each having its own characteristics (transport format set).

UMTS radio interface transfers multiple applications. Parameters like bit error rate (BER) performance and delay are assigned to these applications. Four different service traffic classes are defined: conversational, streaming, interactive and background. For real-time conversational and streaming classes BER has to be less than 10^{-3}, while for non-real time interactive and background classes BER has to be less than 10^{-5}. The maximum acceptable delay for conversational class is 80 msec, for streaming it is 250 msec, for interactive it is 1 sec, while for background it is higher than 10 sec (Holma, 2000; 3GPP TS 25.201, 2002).

Channel

The discrete representation of flat Rayleigh fading channel is given by the following equation:

$$y_k = a_k \cdot x_k + n_k \tag{1}$$

where k is an integer symbol index, x_k is a binary phase shift keying (BPSK) symbol amplitude (± 1), n_k is a Gaussian random variable and y_k is a noisy received symbol. The fading amplitude a_k is a sample from a correlated Gaussian random process with zero mean and is generated using the Sum of Sines or Jakes model, which is described in Jakes (1974). This model is based on summing 9 sinusoids whose frequencies are chosen as samples of the Doppler spectrum. The properties of Jakes model are further analysed in Patzold (1998).

Simulation Parameters and Scenarios

For the simulation model a carrier frequency $f_c = 2$ GHz is considered. It is also assumed that 1000000 bits are transmitted and grouped into frames whose length k_f must be ≥ 40 and ≤ 5114, according to UMTS specifications (Holma, 2000; 3GPP TS 25.212, 2002). For a particular transport channel, every TTI the data with the characteristics specified in a transport format of the transport channel (k_f bits), is turbo encoded (constraint length $K = 4$ and rate $r_c = 1/3$) at the transmitter. Furthermore, each time instant it is assumed that the two recursive systematic convolutional encoders of the turbo encoder start encoding from all-zero state. After turbo coding and block interleaving using the UMTS parameters, the bits are BPSK modulated and transmitted through the mobile channel. At the receiver, outer block deinterleaving and turbo decoding is performed. The received values are not quantized which means that floating point arithmetic is used. The receiver is also assumed to have exact estimates of the fading amplitudes (perfect channel estimation without side information), while 8 iterations are used in the turbo decoder.

SOVA and log-MAP algorithms share common operations which have been addressed in Chaikalis (2003) and Chaikalis (2004). These common operations form a turbo decoder which can be reconfigured and choose the suitable turbo decoding algorithm for different applications (reconfigurable SOVA/log-MAP turbo decoder). In Chaikalis (2003) and Chaikalis (2004) is also shown that in a reconfigurable SOVA/log-MAP turbo decoder scaling of the extrinsic information is possible with a common scaling factor, which is constant and independent of signal-to-noise ratio for additive white Gaussian noise (AWGN) channels. In Chaikalis (in press) it is shown that in the case of a flat Rayleigh fading channel for a reconfigurable SOVA/log-MAP decoder a common scaling factor with value 0.7 is the optimal choice.

Table 1 illustrates 8 different UMTS dedicated transport channels with different transport format sets, which represent different implementation scenarios of the reconfigurable turbo decoder. The transport format set for each transport channel consists of different example transport formats and also of dynamic and semi-static parts. The semi-static part (turbo encoder parameters, TTI) is the same for all transport formats of the transport format set, while the dynamic part (frame size) differs (Holma, 2000; 3GPP TS 25.201, 2002; 3GPP TR 25.944, 2001). Moreover, as published simulation results have shown (Woodard, 2000; Hall, 1998), in flat Rayleigh fading channels data rate, outer block interleaving (thus TTI) and signal-to-noise ratio (SNR) greatly affect BER performance: for each scenario of Table 1 these three parameters differ considering also the examples presented in 3GPP TR 25.944 (2001).

According to Holma (2000) and 3GPP TS 25.201 (2002), three different operating environments are specified in UMTS:

- Rural outdoor operating environment with maximum supported mobile terminal speed 500 km/h and maximum data rate of 144 kbps. Here, it has to be mentioned that a speed of 500 km/h corresponds to high speed vehicles (e.g. trains). More typical value for this environment is 300 km/h.
- Urban or suburban outdoor operating environment with maximum supported mobile speed 120 km/h and maximum data rate of 384 kbps.
- Indoor or low range outdoor operating environment with maximum supported mobile speed 10 km/h and maximum data rate of 2 Mbps.

In Chaikalis (in press) the approach is similar, but we considered the first two operating environments: a terminal speed of 300 km/h for a rural outdoor environment and a terminal speed of 100 km/h for an urban/suburban outdoor environment. Here, we focus on the last operating environment and we choose a low terminal speed of 4 km/h. This means that the maximum data rate of 2 Mbps can be considered. A terminal speed of 4 km/h is a typical common value and it is important to be explored: represents walking human speed. In other words, each implementation scenario of the reconfigurable decoder of Table 1 is applied to indoor or low range outdoor operating environment. Moreover, similarly to Chaikalis (2003), Chaikalis (2004) and Chaikalis (in press), for the calculation of total maximum delay per frame for SOVA and log-MAP we use the following equations assuming a pipeline turbo decoder architecture and a processor that runs at the same rate for both SOVA and log-MAP:

Total max delay using SOVA: $t_d = 2 \times TTI + \left(\dfrac{k_f}{R_b} \times N \right)$ (2)

Total max delay using log-MAP: $t_d = 2 \times TTI + \left(\dfrac{k_f}{R_b} \times N \times 2.8 \right)$ (3)

where t_d is the total delay, k_f is the frame size, R_b is the data rate of the radio bearer assigned to the transport channel and N is the number of turbo decoder iterations. In these equations the higher complexity of log-MAP compared to SOVA (2.8 times) is also considered.

Simulation Results Analysis

The suitable decoding algorithm for each scenario is chosen according to performance and delay. Therefore, for each scenario of Table 1 all four service classes are applied to determine the quality of service profile parameters for different applications. Delay is calculated for each algorithm using equations (2) and (3), while the simulated BER for each scenario is given in the following subsection together with a brief analysis of the results. Particularly, Table 2 shows quality of service for the different frame lengths of scenarios 1, 2, 3, while Tables 3 and 4 present quality of service for scenarios 4, 5 and 6, 7, respectively. Finally, Table 5 presents quality of service for scenario 8.

Scenario 1

The simulated BER for this scenario is shown in Figure 1 assuming a symbol rate R_s of 86.4 Kbaud, normalised fade rate $f_d T_s = 0.000085$ with Doppler frequency $f_d = 7.407$ Hz. Two frame lengths are considered in this scenario: 576 and 1152 bits, as Table 2 illustrates.

Conversational Service Class

At a SNR of 32 dB, the conversational class cannot be considered for this scenario because even though the BER criterion is satisfied, latency is too high for all frame lengths for either SOVA or log-MAP.

Table 1. Implementation scenarios

Transport channel type	Transport format set				Data rate R_b (kbps)	SNR (dB)	Scenario
	Dynamic part	Semi-static part					
	Transport block set or frame sizes (bits)	Turbo encoder parameters		TTI (msec)			
		K	Code rate				
Dedicated channel	576, 1152	4	1/3	40	28.8	32	1
	576, 1152, 1728, 2304	4	1/3	40	57.6	30	2
	336, 672, 1008, 1344	4	1/3	20	64	30	3
	336, 672, 1344, 2688	4	1/3	20	128	30	4
	336, 672, 1344, 2688, 3024	4	1/3	20	144	28	5
	168, 336, 672, 1344, 2016, 2688, 3360, 4032	4	1/3	20	384	28	6
	2560	4	1/3	40	64	30	7
	336, 1344, 2688, 4032, 4704	4	1/3	40	2000	40	8

Table 2. Quality of service and proposed decoding algorithm for scenarios 1, 2 and 3 of Table 1

		Frame size (bits)	t_d using SOVA (msec)	t_d using log-MAP (msec)	Max latency (msec)	Log-MAP BER	SOVA BER	BER range	Proposed decoding algorithm
Scenario 1	**Conv. class**	576	240	528	80	0.000472	0.000523	$<10^{-3}$	Cannot be applied
		1152	400	976	80	0	0	$<10^{-3}$	
	Streaming class	576	240	528	250	0.000472	0.000523	$<10^{-3}$	SOVA
		1152	400	976	250	0	0	$<10^{-3}$	Cannot be applied
	Non-real time classes	576	240	528	Up to 1 sec interactive, >10 sec background	0.000472	0.000523	$<10^{-5}$	Cannot be applied
		1152	400	976		0	0	$<10^{-5}$	Log-MAP or SOVA
Scenario 2	**Conv. class**	576	160	304	80	0.001836	0.002096	$<10^{-3}$	Cannot be applied
		1152	240	528	80	0.000988	0.001036	$<10^{-3}$	
		1728	320	752	80	0.000582	0.000634	$<10^{-3}$	
		2304	400	976	80	0	0	$<10^{-3}$	
	Streaming class	576	160	304	250	0.001836	0.002096	$<10^{-3}$	Cannot be applied
		1152	240	528	250	0.000988	0.001036	$<10^{-3}$	
		1728	320	752	250	0.000582	0.000634	$<10^{-3}$	
		2304	400	976	250	0	0	$<10^{-3}$	
	Non-real time classes	576	160	304	Up to 1 sec interactive, >10 sec background	0.001836	0.002096	$<10^{-5}$	Cannot be applied
		1152	240	528		0.000988	0.001036	$<10^{-5}$	
		1728	320	752		0.000582	0.000634	$<10^{-5}$	
		2304	400	976		0	0	$<10^{-5}$	Log-MAP or SOVA
Scenario 3	**Conv. class**	336	82	157.6	80	0.003485	0.003888	$<10^{-3}$	Cannot be applied
		672	124	275.2	80	0.00146	0.00183	$<10^{-3}$	
		1008	166	392.8	80	0.000779	0.000984	$<10^{-3}$	
		1344	208	510.4	80	0.000519	0.000538	$<10^{-3}$	
	Streaming class	336	82	157.6	250	0.003485	0.003888	$<10^{-3}$	Cannot be applied
		672	124	275.2	250	0.00146	0.00183	$<10^{-3}$	
		1008	166	392.8	250	0.000779	0.000984	$<10^{-3}$	SOVA
		1344	208	510.4	250	0.000519	0.000538	$<10^{-3}$	SOVA
	Non-real time classes	336	82	157.6	Up to 1 sec interactive, >10 sec background	0.003485	0.003888	$<10^{-5}$	Cannot be applied
		672	124	275.2		0.00146	0.00183	$<10^{-5}$	
		1008	166	392.8		0.000779	0.000984	$<10^{-5}$	
		1344	208	510.4		0.000519	0.000538	$<10^{-5}$	

Table 3. Quality of service and proposed decoding algorithm for scenarios 4 and 5 of Table 1

		Frame size (bits)	t_d using SOVA (msec)	t_d using log-MAP (msec)	Max latency (msec)	Log-MAP BER	SOVA BER	BER range	Proposed decoding algorithm
Scenario 4	Conv. class	336	61	98.8	80	0.003465	0.004047	$<10^{-3}$	Cannot be applied
		672	82	157.6	80	0.001584	0.001713	$<10^{-3}$	
		1344	124	275.2	80	0.000796	0.000934	$<10^{-3}$	
		2688	208	510.4	80	0	0	$<10^{-3}$	
	Strea ming class	336	61	98.8	250	0.003465	0.004047	$<10^{-3}$	Cannot be applied
		672	82	157.6	250	0.001584	0.001713	$<10^{-3}$	
		1344	124	275.2	250	0.000796	0.000934	$<10^{-3}$	SOVA
		2688	208	510.4	250	0	0	$<10^{-3}$	SOVA
	Non-real time classes	336	61	98.8	Up to 1 sec interactive, >10 sec background	0.003465	0.004047	$<10^{-5}$	Cannot be applied
		672	82	157.6		0.001584	0.001713	$<10^{-5}$	
		1344	124	275.2		0.000796	0.000934	$<10^{-5}$	
		2688	208	510.4		0	0	$<10^{-5}$	Log-MAP or SOVA
Scenario 5	Conv. class	336	58.6	92.26	80	0.005771	0.006268	$<10^{-3}$	Cannot be applied
		672	77.3	144.5	80	0.003005	0.003287	$<10^{-3}$	
		1344	114.6	249.06	80	0.000704	0.0010007	$<10^{-3}$	
		2688	189.3	458.13	80	0	3.091e-05	$<10^{-3}$	
		3024	208	510.4	80	0	0	$<10^{-3}$	
	Strea ming class	336	58.6	92.26	250	0.005771	0.006268	$<10^{-3}$	Cannot be applied
		672	77.3	144.5	250	0.003005	0.003287	$<10^{-3}$	
		1344	114.6	249.06	250	0.000704	0.0010007	$<10^{-3}$	Log-MAP
		2688	189.3	458.13	250	0	3.091e-05	$<10^{-3}$	SOVA
		3024	208	510.4	250	0	0	$<10^{-3}$	SOVA
	Non-real time classes	336	58.6	92.26	Up to 1 sec interactive, >10 sec background	0.005771	0.006268	$<10^{-5}$	Cannot be applied
		672	77.3	144.5		0.003005	0.003287	$<10^{-5}$	
		1344	114.6	249.06		0.000704	0.0010007	$<10^{-5}$	
		2688	189.3	458.13		0	3.091e-05	$<10^{-5}$	Log-MAP
		3024	208	510.4		0	0	$<10^{-5}$	Log-MAP or SOVA

Streaming Service Class

For this class only a frame length of 576 bits can be applied. In this case SOVA satisfies both requirements, while log-MAP exceeds the maximum acceptable delay limit. For a frame of 1152 bits delay for SOVA and log-MAP is too high to achieve the limit for this class.

Interactive/background Service Classes

For a frame length of 576 bits neither algorithm can be used because of the low BER criterion, while both requirements are achieved from both algorithms for a frame length of 1152 bits. Thus, a 576 bit frame service can not be applied, whereas in an 1152 bit frame service either SOVA or log-MAP can be used.

Scenario 2

The simulated BER results for this scenario are shown in Figure 2 assuming a symbol rate R_s of 172.8 Kbaud, normalised fade rate $f_d T_s = 0.000042$ and a SNR of 30 dB.

Conversational Service Class

According to Table 2, for this class the 4 different frame lengths cannot be applied because of the tight delay limit (80 msec).

Streaming Service Class

Similarly, as illustrated in Table 2, the 4 frame lengths are not applicable. Particularly, for frame lengths of 576 and 1152 bits SOVA satisfies the delay criterion, but does not satisfy BER criterion. On the other hand, the use of log-MAP gives unacceptable delay. For frame lengths of 1728 and 2304 bits although BER is satisfied from both algorithms, maximum acceptable delay is exceeded.

Figure 1. BER vs E_b / N_0 for scenario 1

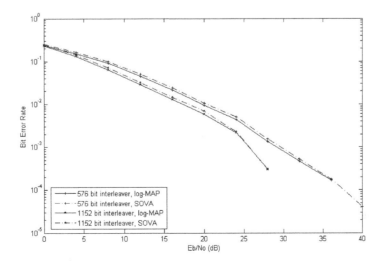

Table 4. Quality of service and proposed decoding algorithm for scenarios 6 and 7 of Table 1

		Frame size (bits)	t_d using SOVA (msec)	t_d using log-MAP (msec)	Max latency (msec)	Log-MAP BER	SOVA BER	BER range	Proposed decoding algorithm
Scenario 6	Conv. class	168	43.5	49.8	80	0.0073	0.008	<10⁻³	Cannot be applied
		336	47	59.6	80	0.0065	0.007	<10⁻³	
		672	54	79.2	80	0.0051	0.0062	<10⁻³	
		1344	68	118.4	80	0.0022	0.0028	<10⁻³	
		2016	82	157.6	80	0.000654	0.001307	<10⁻³	
		2688	96	196.8	80	0	0	<10⁻³	
		3360	110	236	80	0	0	<10⁻³	
		4032	124	275.2	80	0	0	<10⁻³	
	Streaming class	168	43.5	49.8	250	0.0073	0.008	<10⁻³	Cannot be applied
		336	47	59.6	250	0.0065	0.007	<10⁻³	
		672	54	79.2	250	0.0051	0.0062	<10⁻³	
		1344	68	118.4	250	0.0022	0.0028	<10⁻³	
		2016	82	157.6	250	0.000654	0.001307	<10⁻³	Log-MAP
		2688	96	196.8	250	0	0	<10⁻³	Log-MAP or SOVA
		3360	110	236	250	0	0	<10⁻³	Log-MAP or SOVA
		4032	124	275.2	250	0	0	<10⁻³	SOVA
	Non-real time classes	168	43.5	49.8	Up to 1 sec interactive, >10 sec background	0.0073	0.008	<10⁻⁵	Cannot be applied
		336	47	59.6		0.0065	0.007	<10⁻⁵	
		672	54	79.2		0.0051	0.0062	<10⁻⁵	
		1344	68	118.4		0.0022	0.0028	<10⁻⁵	
		2016	82	157.6		0.000654	0.001307	<10⁻⁵	
		2688	96	196.8		0	0	<10⁻⁵	Log-MAP or SOVA
		3360	110	236		0	0	<10⁻⁵	Log-MAP or SOVA
		4032	124	275.2		0	0	<10⁻⁵	Log-MAP or SOVA
Scenario 7	Conv. class	2560	400	976	80	0	0	<10⁻³	Cannot be applied
	Streaming class	2560	400	976	250	0	0	<10⁻³	Cannot be applied
	Non-real time classes	2560	400	976	Up to 1 sec interactive, >10 sec background	0	0	<10⁻⁵	Log-MAP or SOVA

Figure 2. BER vs E_b/N_0 for scenario 2

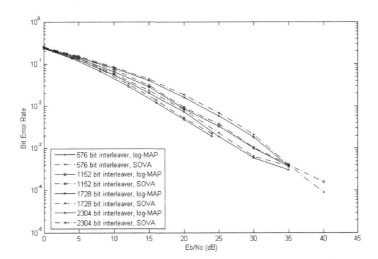

Figure 3. BER vs E_b/N_0 for scenario 3

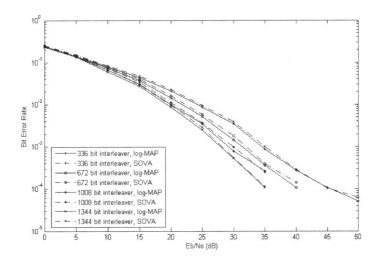

Interactive/Background Service Classes

For these service classes it is well-known that BER must be low and latency limits are not very strict. Thus, the first 3 frame lengths cannot be applied due to not acceptable BER. For a frame length of 2304 bits the 2 criteria are achieved by both decoding algorithms: either SOVA or log-MAP can be used.

Scenario 3

Figure 3 presents the simulation results for this scenario using the following parameters: R_s = 192 Kbaud, $f_d T_s$ = 0.000038 and a SNR of 30 dB.

Table 5. Quality of service and proposed decoding algorithm for scenario 8 of Table 1

		Frame size (bits)	t_d using SOVA (msec)	t_d using log-MAP (msec)	Max latency (msec)	Log-MAP BER	SOVA BER	BER range	Proposed decoding algorithm
Scenario 8	Conv. class	336	81.34	83.76	80	0.001815	0.0019574	$<10^{-3}$	Cannot be applied
		1344	85.37	95.05	80	0.001414	0.0016548	$<10^{-3}$	
		2688	90.75	110.1	80	9.97e-07	9.97e-07	$<10^{-3}$	
		4032	96.12	125.1	80	0	0	$<10^{-3}$	
		4704	98.81	132.68	80	0	0	$<10^{-3}$	
	Streaming class	336	81.34	83.76	250	0.001815	0.0019574	$<10^{-3}$	Cannot be applied
		1344	85.37	95.05	250	0.001414	0.0016548	$<10^{-3}$	
		2688	90.75	110.1	250	9.97e-07	9.97e-07	$<10^{-3}$	Log-MAP or SOVA
		4032	96.12	125.1	250	0	0	$<10^{-3}$	Log-MAP or SOVA
		4704	98.81	132.68	250	0	0	$<10^{-3}$	Log-MAP or SOVA
	Non-real time classes	336	81.34	83.76	Up to 1 sec interactive, >10 sec background	0.001815	0.0019574	$<10^{-5}$	Cannot be applied
		1344	85.37	95.05		0.001414	0.0016548	$<10^{-5}$	
		2688	90.75	110.1		9.97e-07	9.97e-07	$<10^{-5}$	Log-MAP or SOVA
		4032	96.12	125.1		0	0	$<10^{-5}$	Log-MAP or SOVA
		4704	98.81	132.68		0	0	$<10^{-5}$	Log-MAP or SOVA

Conversational Service Class

According to the analysis of Table 2, the 4 frame lengths give too high delay. Thus, their application is not possible for SOVA or log-MAP.

Streaming Service Class

The analysis of Table 2 clearly shows that for all frame lengths SOVA satisfies the delay limit of 250 msec at 30 dB. On the other hand the BER limit is not achieved for the small frames of 336 and 672 bits. Thus, SOVA can be used for frames of 1008 and 1344 bits. For log-MAP and frames of 672, 1008, 1344 bits the delay limit cannot be achieved. For a small frame of 336 bits the delay limit is achieved, but the BER limit is not achieved.

Interactive/Background Service Classes

For these non-real time service classes and for all 4 frames the achieved BER is lower than the acceptable limit. Therefore, although the delay limit is achieved the 4 frames can not be applied.

Figure 4. BER vs E_b/N_0 for scenario 4

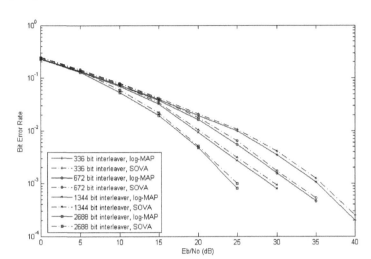

Scenario 4

Figure 4 presents the simulated BER for this scenario using the following parameters: R_s = 384 Kbaud, $f_d T_s$ = 0.000019 with f_d = 185.1 Hz and a SNR of 30 dB.

Conversational Service Class

Again, for this class the 4 frames cannot be applied because of high delay. For a frame of 336 bits although delay is acceptable for SOVA, BER criterion is not satisfied. According to Table 3 it is obvious that this service scenario is not possible to be implemented.

Streaming Service Class

The analysis of Table 3 clearly shows that for all frame lengths SOVA satisfies the delay limit of 250 msec at 30 dB. On the other hand the BER limit is not achieved for the small frames of 336 and 672 bits. Thus, SOVA is the proposed turbo decoding algorithm for frames of 1344 and 2688 bits. For log-MAP and frames of 1344, 2688 bits the delay limit cannot be achieved. For small frames of 336 and 672 bits the delay limit is achieved, but the BER limit is not achieved.

Interactive/Background Service Classes

According to Table 3, for these classes and for the first 3 frames the achieved BER is lower than the acceptable limit. Therefore, although the delay limit is achieved these frames can not be applied. On the other hand, for a frame of 2688 bits the 2 parameters (BER, delay) are satisfied by both algorithms.

Scenario 5

For Figure 5 the following parameters are assumed: Rs = 432 Kbaud, $f_d T_s$ = 0.000017 and a SNR of 28 dB. Figure 5 shows BER performance for the 5 different frame lengths specified in Table 1 for this scenario.

Figure 5. BER vs E_b / N_0 for scenario 5

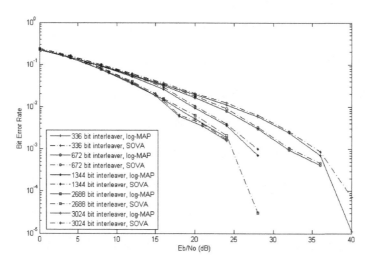

Conversational Service Class

For this class (Table 3) for all 5 frames the delay criterion is too low to be achieved from both algorithms. There is an exception for the small frames of 336 and 672 bits, where the delay criterion is achieved for SOVA but BER criterion is not. It is obvious that the constraints of the 2 parameters cannot be achieved by both algorithms.

Streaming Service Class

The analysis of Table 3 identifies 3 cases:

- Small frames of 336 and 672 bits. Here, the delay limit is achieved, but the BER limit is not for SOVA and log-MAP. This means that these frames cannot be implemented.
- Medium frame of 1152 bits. Here, the delay limit is achieved by both algorithms. Log-MAP is the proposed choice because it can achieve the BER limit as well. SOVA cannot achieve the BER limit. Thus, log-MAP represents the proposed algorithm.
- Large frames of 2688 and 3024 bits. Here, SOVA is the algorithm that can be implemented. The reason is the following: BER limit is achievable by both algorithms, whereas delay limit is achieved only by SOVA.

Interactive/Background Service Classes

According to Table 3, the delay limit is achieved by both SOVA and log-MAP for all frames. Furthermore, for the first 3 frames the BER limit is not achieved, but for 2688 bits frame it is achieved only by log-MAP. In this case log-MAP is proposed. For a frame of 3024 bits the limits of the 2 parameters are achieved by both algorithms.

Scenario 6

Figure 6 illustrates the simulated BER of the different frame lengths for this scenario using the following parameters: Rs =1152 Kbaud $f_d T_s$ = 0.000064, and a SNR of 28 dB.

Figure 6. BER vs E_b/N_0 for scenario 6

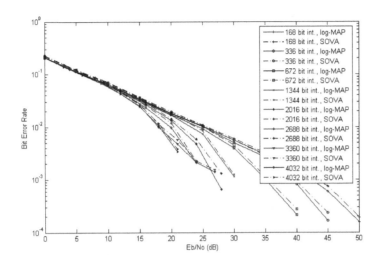

Conversational Service Class

For this class (Table 4) for the first 3 frames although delay criterion is satisfied, BER criterion is not satisfied. For the next 4 frames either BER, or delay limits are not achieved for SOVA and log-MAP. Thus, this service class is not possible to be implemented for all frames.

Streaming Service Class

The analysis of Table 4 identifies 4 cases:

- Frames of 168, 336, 672 and 1344 bits. Here, the delay limit is achieved, but the BER limit is not achieved for SOVA and log-MAP. This means that these frames cannot be implemented.
- Frame of 2016 bits. Here, the delay limit is achieved by both algorithms. Log-MAP is the proposed choice because it can achieve the BER limit as well, while SOVA cannot achieve the BER limit. Thus, log-MAP represents the proposed algorithm.
- Frames of 2688 and 3360 bits. Here, SOVA and log-MAP achieve both limits. Therefore, both algorithms can be used.
- Frame of 4032 bits. Here, SOVA is the algorithm that can be implemented. The reason is the following: BER limit is achievable by both algorithms, whereas log-MAP gives unacceptable delay.

Interactive/Background Service Classes

According to Table 4, the delay limit is achieved by both SOVA and log-MAP for all frames. Furthermore, for the first 5 frames the BER limit is not achieved. Thus, they cannot be implemented. For frames of 2688, 3360 and 4032 bits the limits of the 2 parameters are achieved by both algorithms.

Scenario 7

In Figure 7 BER performance for the different frame lengths for this scenario can be seen using the following parameters: R_s = 192 Kbaud, $f_d T_s$ = 0.000038 and a SNR of 30 dB.

Figure 7. BER vs E_b / N_0 for scenario 7

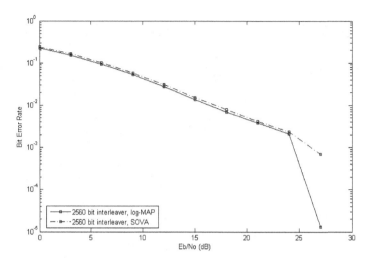

Conversational/Streaming Service Classes

The analysis of Table 4 clearly shows that the frame of 2560 bits gives unacceptable delay for both real time classes and both decoding algorithms. Therefore, they cannot be implemented.

Interactive/background service classes

For non-real time classes both limits are achieved by both algorithms, which mean that they are both suitable for this application.

Scenario 8

Figure 8 presents BER performance of the different frame lengths for this scenario using the following parameters: R_s = 6000 Kbaud, $f_d T_s$ = 0.0000012 and a SNR of 40 dB.

Conversational Service Class

For all 5 frames the calculated delay, according to Table 5, is too high. Thus, this scenario cannot be implemented for this service class.

Streaming Service Class

Here, delay criterion is achieved by both algorithms and for all frames. Furthermore, for frames of 336 and 1344 bits the BER limit is not achievable by the 2 algorithms. This means that these 2 frames cannot be implemented. On the other hand, for frames of 2688, 4032 and 4704 bits the 2 criteria are satisfied by both algorithms: they are equally suitable.

Figure 8. BER vs E_b/N_0 for scenario 8

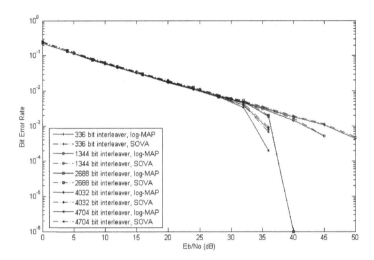

Interactive/Background Service Classes

From Table 5 it can be seen that the analysis is similar to the previous section: the first 2 frames cannot be established, whereas for the last 3 frames either SOVA or log-MAP can be used.

RECONFIGURABLE EQUALISERS

Multipath Propagation

In all previous sections it has been assumed that the channel did not introduce any intersymbol interference (ISI). This model is accurate when representing a scenario where there is line-of-sight between transmitter and receiver and all the energy of a given transmitted symbol reaches the receiver before the next symbol is transmitted. In many practical wireless scenarios, the propagation of the signal is subject to reflection, diffraction and scattering from objects in the environment (Rappaport, 1996). All these propagating mechanisms make the transmitted signal arrive at the receiver via multiple paths resulting in a phenomenon called multipath propagation which will often cause ISI. Moreover, as a mobile user or some of the objects in his surroundings move, the multipath profile changes, causing fluctuations in the received signal's amplitude or phase, giving rise to what is called multipath fading (Bello, 1963). Multipath propagation and fading pose important limitations on the transmission of information over the mobile channel.

The type of degradation introduced by the channel is largely dominated by the relation between the symbol period T_s (e.g. inverse of the transmission symbol rate) and the maximum channel delay spread T_m which is a measure of the channel time dispersion (Sklar, 2001). When $T_m < T_s$, all the received multipath components arrive within the symbol period. In this case, the channel is said to be frequency non-selective. This condition means that there is no interference between successively transmitted symbols. Nevertheless, some degradation occurs as the different components may add up destructively and cause a drop in the received SNR giving rise to the so called Rayleigh flat fading channel. In order to compensate this effect, and similarly to the AWGN case, some form of diversity or channel coding should be used. If $T_m > T_s$, neighbouring symbols interfere with each other causing ISI which usually leads to a considerable increase in BER. In the frequency domain, the existence of ISI

Figure 9. Generic system inversion problem with upper words indicating how it applies to channel equalisation

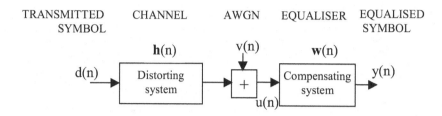

implies that not all spectral components of the transmitted signal are subject to the same transmission (complex) gain, that is, some components might be amplified while others are attenuated and phase relations may not be preserved. Consequently, we refer to this environment as a frequency-selective channel. There are basically two methods to combat frequency selectivity: 1) **Equalisation** (Lucky, 1965) is a receiver technique which tries to invert the distortion introduced by the channel thus restoring the originally transmitted signal. 2) **Multicarrier systems** (Cimini, 1985) deal with frequency-selective channels by splitting the available frequency band into parallel non-frequency selective channels operating at a lower symbol rate. Since each of the parallel channels does not distort the transmitted signal, the use of complex equalisation procedures is avoided. Owing to its spectral efficiency and low complexity implementation, Orthogonal frequency division multiplexing (OFDM), is the most commonly employed technique to implement multicarrier systems. While second and third generation mobile systems (e.g. GSM, IS-54, UMTS) rely on single-carrier equalisation-based architectures, indoor wireless networks (e.g. IEEE802.11x, HIPERLAN) are based on multicarrier principles. As for the future, the *multicarrier vs single-carrier* debate seems far from settled and there are proposals which integrate both approaches depending on the link direction (uplink or downlink) (Martin, 2005; Falconer 2002; WINNER project). For the rest of this chapter, we will focus on an arbitrary single carrier equalisation scenario.

Basic Equalisation Concepts

As mentioned, equalisation tries to revert the channel effects in an attempt to recover the originally transmitted signal and can therefore be seen as a particular case of the general class of Inversion problems (Haykin, 1996). Figure 9 depicts a basic setup for the channel equalisation scenario.

Over the years many different techniques have been proposed addressing the design of equalising mechanisms (see (Qureshi, 1985) for a comprehensive review). A possible way to classify the most important types of equalisers is shown in Table 6. An important design factor is whether channel state information (CSI) is available at the receiver. If this is the case, the coefficients of a finite impulse response filter (FIR) with or without a feedback section can be computed resulting in the linear equaliser (Direct LE) or decision feedback equaliser (Direct DFE), respectively. The coefficients are calculated by minimising some error cost function. A common measure is the mean square error (MSE) whose minimising coefficients can be found by means of the Wiener-Hopf equation (Haykin, 1996). Using the notation given in Fig. 9, the Wiener-Hopf solution, $\mathbf{w}_{opt}$, is given by:

Table 6. Equaliser classification

	Linear	Non-linear
CSI available at receiver	Direct LE	Direct DFE Viterbi equaliser
CSI not available at receiver	Adaptive LE	Adaptive DFE

$$\mathbf{w}_{opt} = \mathbf{R}^{-1}\mathbf{p} \tag{4}$$

where $\mathbf{R}=E[\mathbf{u}(n)\mathbf{u}(n)^T]$ is the autocorrelation matrix of the equaliser input vector $\mathbf{u}(n)$ consisting of all consecutive samples in the equalising filter at instant n, and $\mathbf{p}$ is the crosscorrelation between the desired output and the input vector, $\mathbf{p}=E[\mathbf{u}(n)d(n)]$. The desired data, d(n), is usually available in the form of a training sequence known at the receiver.

Alternatively, optimum detections on the transmitted bits can be made using the Viterbi algorithm (Forney, 1973) which chooses the most likely symbol sequence that has been transmitted given the available CSI. Usually, the CSI is considered to be static during the transmission of a whole packet and therefore, the computation of the LE or DFE filter coefficients needs to be done only once per packet (i.e. if the channel is static over the packet, so is the corresponding equaliser). If the channel is unknown (no CSI available) or it changes over the duration of a packet, the LE or DFE filters should be made adaptive to cope with the dynamics of the channel. In this case, an adaptive algorithm is required to drive the coefficients towards their optimum values for each transmitted symbol. Usually, a training sequence of symbols is transmitted preceding the transmission of real data. The receiver can then use these symbols to get an estimate of the channel impulse response, compute the equaliser coefficients or, in the case of adaptive equalisers, begin the adaptation of the filters.

We note that in either case, with or without CSI, the equaliser can also be classified as linear, that is the case of the LE, or non-linear when using a DFE or a Viterbi equaliser. For the rest of this chapter our focus will be on the adaptive LE/DFE which constitute the most appropriate solution for rapidly varying environments such as those found in 3G communications while at the same time, keeping the computational complexity low. Concluding this section, it should be mentioned that adaptive equalisation, although traditionally used in TDMA-based systems such as GSM or IS-54, it has also recently found its way into CDMA-based systems like UMTS (Hooli, 2002). In CDMA systems, the equaliser typically operates at chip level and its mission is to restore the spreading code orthogonality among the different users which is typically lost due to the multipath propagation.

Adaptive Equaliser Structures and Algorithms

As it has been mentioned in the previous section, an adaptive equaliser consists of two components: the filtering structure on one hand and the adaptive algorithm controlling the filter coefficients on the other hand. We first describe the two most common structures while later techniques on how to update their coefficients are covered.

Linear Equaliser

The adaptive linear equaliser (Lucky, 1965), depicted in Fig. 10, just consists of a finite impulse response (FIR) filter which is then followed by the threshold detector. The filter weights in Fig. 10, denoted by w_i, are the coefficients to be set to minimise the ISI whereas T denotes the symbol period. Following the notation of Fig. 9, let us denote by H(f) the Discrete Fourier transform of the distorting system (e.g. $H(f)=DFT[\mathbf{h}(n)]$) which will typically include the pulse shaping filter at the transmitter, the wireless channel and the matched filter just preceding the equaliser at the receiver. It can be shown that under the assumption of an infinite length LE, the frequency domain Wiener-Hopf solution leading to the minimum mean square error (MMSE) filter coefficients are given by:

$$W(f) = \frac{1}{H(f)+N_0} \tag{5}$$

where N_0 represents the noise power spectral density. The frequency response of a finite length LE with its coefficients computed using the Wiener-Hopf equation will result in an approximation of (5). The frequency domain representation of the combined system-equaliser is then given by:

$$Y(f) = W(f)H(f) = \frac{H(f)}{H(f)+N_0}. \tag{6}$$

Figure 10. Linear equaliser

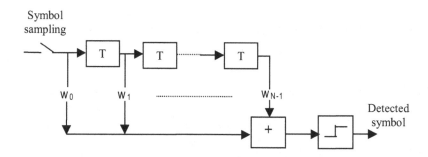

Equation (6) shows that, in the event of very low noise level (N_0 close to zero), $Y(f)=1$, which means that the overall system barely distorts the transmitted signal. The main advantages of linear equalisers are their simplicity, their tolerance to changing phase channels (going from minimum to maximum phase) and their immunity to decision errors. This last point will be better understood when the LE is compared with decision feedback equaliser (DFE). The main drawback of LE, as it can be deducted from (6), is its sensitivity to noise level which in some situations can render the equaliser completely useless.

Decision Feedback Equaliser

To overcome some of the problems associated with the LE, the decision feedback equaliser was proposed in 1975 in (Austin, 1975). The idea behind DFE is that once a symbol has been detected, and since the symbol is already known, its postcursor interference can be perfectly cancelled. The precursor ISI is handled with a conventional linear equaliser. Figure 11 shows the structure of a DFE. It has two FIR filters; one is a feedforward filter (FFF) which acts as a LE (coefficients given by w_i), and the other one is a feedback filter (FBF) which performs the postcursor cancellation (coefficients given by b_i). The inputs to the FFF are the samples coming out of the matched filter whereas the inputs to the FBF are the previously detected symbols. It is important to recognise that the DFE is a non-linear structure because of the symbol detection used to form the inputs to the FBF. This significantly complicates any theoretical analysis of the performance of the DFE.

The greatest advantage of DFE over LE is the avoidance, in great measure, of any noise enhancement. This is explained by the observation that the FBF works on noise-free samples. As a consequence, the MMSE-DFE achieves a much lower MSE value than the corresponding MMSE-LE when the channel is heavily distorted (i.e. has a spectral null) as it will not raise the noise floor when compensating spectral gaps. Its biggest drawback is the phenomenon called error propagation arising when incorrect decisions are made at the output of the FFF and these are then feedback through the FBF increasing the probability of error of the following symbols.

Adaptive Algorithms

Over the years many different algorithms have been proposed to adjust the coefficients of an adaptive filter (see (Haykin, 1996) for a comprehensive review). Here, we focus on the least mean squares (LMS) algorithm which is the most widely used adaptive scheme due to its simplicity and robustness. It was originally proposed in (Widrow, 1960) and since then a huge number of variants and applications have appeared in the technical literature.

The LMS algorithm is derived from a general technique known as steepest descent (SD), which is often used in optimisation problems. The SD algorithm finds the minimum MSE (MMSE) point by computing the gradient vector of the MSE, that is, the direction of maximum MSE increase, and then updating the coefficients one step in the opposite direction (maximum MSE decrease). By iterating this basic procedure, the filter weights will converge to the values producing the MMSE. The algorithm is given by the equations:

$$\nabla \mathbf{MSE}(n) = -2\,\mathbf{p} + 2\,\mathbf{R}\,\mathbf{w}(n) \quad \text{Gradient computation} \tag{7}$$

$$\mathbf{w}(n+1) = \mathbf{w}(n) - \mu \nabla \mathbf{MSE}(n) \quad \text{Filter update} \tag{8}$$

In the above equations, $\nabla \mathbf{MSE}(n)$ denotes the gradient vector of the MSE, $\mathbf{R}$ is the autocorrelation matrix of input data, $\mathbf{p}$ is the cross-correlation vector between the desired and observed data and $\mathbf{w}$ is the filter weights vector. All these vectors have length equal to the filter order (N). The parameter μ is an arbitrary step size that defines the amount of correction applied to the filter weights. From a practical point of view, the SD algorithm has one important problem: typically, $\mathbf{R}$ and $\mathbf{p}$ are unknown in real situations, and therefore the exact gradient of equation (7) cannot be computed.

Fortunately, an estimation of the gradient vector can be computed from the available data. This estimated gradient, $\hat{\nabla}\mathbf{MSE}(n)$, is given by (Haykin, 1996):

$$\hat{\nabla}\mathbf{MSE}(n) = -2\mathbf{u}(n)d(n) + 2\mathbf{u}(n)\mathbf{u}^{T}(n)\hat{\mathbf{w}}(n) \tag{9}$$

where d(n) is the desired output value. We use a different notation for the filter weights, $\hat{\mathbf{w}}(n)$, to emphasise that they are computed using an estimated (noisy) gradient.

Using this estimated gradient vector, rather than the exact one in equation (8), the LMS algorithm is given by the following pair of equations:

$$e(n) = d(n) - \hat{\mathbf{w}}^{T}(n)\mathbf{u}(n) \tag{10}$$

$$\hat{\mathbf{w}}(n+1) = \hat{\mathbf{w}}(n) + \mu\,\mathbf{u}(n)e(n) \tag{11}$$

A few points are important to mention regarding the LMS equations: firstly, the use of an approximation for the gradient implies that the equaliser coefficients do not converge to the Wiener solution (e.g. minimum MSE) but to an approximation and, therefore, the LE will not attain the MMSE level. The difference between the MMSE and the attained MSE level by LMS is called the excess MSE (EMSE). Secondly, the desired data symbol, d(n), during the equaliser adaptation is usually obtained in the form of a training sequence during the equaliser filter adaptation. Once the coefficients have converged, and to allow some tracking capability, the LMS adaptation can

Figure 11. Decision feedback equaliser

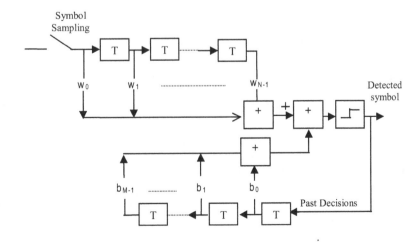

still operate using the detected symbols as the desired ones. Finally, notice that the complexity of the algorithm given by equations (10) and (11) is only O(2N) where N is the order of the filter.

The main advantages of the LMS algorithm are its low computational complexity, ease of implementation and generally good performance. Its main drawback is the slow convergence it exhibits when the channel to be equalised is severely frequency selective. Fast converging algorithms such as the recursive least squares (RLS) algorithm (Haykin, 1996) are available although at the cost of a higher computational complexity and/or numerical stability issues.

The Need for Reconfigurability

Given a known channel impulse response with N taps and a given signal-to-noise ratio level, there are no rules predicting how many taps will be needed, in either an LE or a DFE, to achieve an irreducible MMSE level. One possible solution to this problem is to set the equaliser length, M, to a very large number of taps, typically several times N. Since mobile systems have to operate in a wide range of scenarios, the equaliser length would need to be set in accordance with the longest channel that could be encountered. This approach presents two problems. First, in many cases the equaliser will be over-dimensioned as a much shorter equaliser would achieve an almost identical MMSE level. The computational waste provoked by system overdimensioning might be a concern in systems with restricted power consumption such as mobile terminals. Second, although increasing the equaliser length will never result in an increase in the MMSE level, it may very well cause an increase in the overall MSE level due to the EMSE introduced if an adaptive algorithm such as the LMS is used.

As a motivating example, Figures 12-13 show the channel impulse and frequency (magnitude) response for two different channels. Channel 1 is a representative realisation of a typical urban scenario according to the COST207 channel model whereas Channel 2, extracted from (Proakis, 1995), is a classical example of a bad channel because of a deep frequency null.

The next two figures (Figs. 14 and 15) show the computed MMSE (stars) for an LE obtained by solving the Wiener-Hopf equation for a wide range of equaliser lengths for the Channel models 1 and 2 under different E/No conditions. The steady-state MSE values attained when using the LMS algorithm are also shown on the figures (circles). The curves in Figs. 14 and 15 help to identify what would be the optimum lengths for both channels at different E/No levels. We note that by optimum is meant the smallest length that achieves the minimum MMSE level in each curve. Clearly this optimum varies from curve to curve. It is also important to recognize that increasing the equaliser length does not necessarily imply better performance (i.e. lower MSE). In fact, it can be seen that when using the LMS algorithm, not only the computational complexity is unnecessarily increased, but performance is degraded.

Since a mobile receiver has to be able to deal with these two, and many more, types of channels/scenarios, and as it has been shown in Figs. 14 and 15 different equaliser lengths are required, it seems logic to pursue the idea of a reconfigurable equaliser able to change its length according to the operating conditions.

SEGMENTED LINEAR EQUALISER

Starting from the basic idea of a typical linear equaliser as depicted in Fig. 10, we now introduce the idea of segmented LE, first proposed in (Riera-Palou, 2001) generated by partitioning the original M-tap FIR equalising filter into K smaller and concatenated P-tap subfilters where M=KP. Figure 16 illustrates this idea.

Having decomposed the original filter into K segments, it is now possible to compute the output of each subfilter separately at any given instant. Connecting serially the adders of each segment to the following one, the output of one segment corresponds to the accumulated filtering operation up to that segment.

Notice that provided KP=M, the output of the last segment of the segmented equaliser gives the same results as the output of a conventional M-tap FIR filter. Comparing the structure of Fig. 16 with the one from an ordinary filter, the segmented filter needs K-1 extra adders. Later on it will be shown that combining this structure with the algorithm presented in the next subsection only requires of one extra adder.

Figure 12. Impulse response (upper plot) and magnitude frequency response (lower plot). Channel model 1

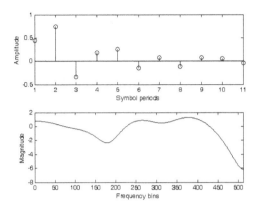

Figure 13. Impulse response (upper plot) and magnitude frequency response (lower plot). Channel model 2.

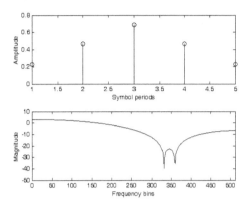

Figure 14. MMSE/LMS Steady State MSE comparison for different length equalisers. Channel model 1.

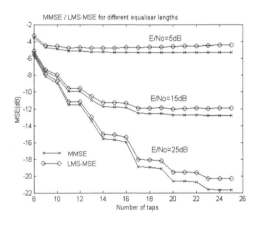

Figure 15. MMSE/LMS Steady State MSE comparison for different length equalisers. Channel model 2.

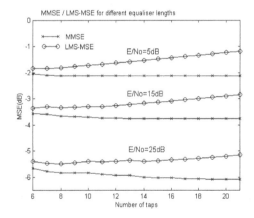

Any other properties the original equaliser may have, such as linearity, are preserved when it is converted into a segmented structure. Basically what this new structure allows is to "monitor" how the filtering operation is progressing.

Figure 17 shows how segmented filters can be used in a linear equaliser. From this graph it is clear that each segment produces a partially equalised output. Ideally, each successive segment should improve the equalisation process making its output closer to the detected bit than the previous segment's output, in this case $e_0(n) \geq e_1(n) \geq \cdots \geq e_{K-1}(n)$. In practice it may happen, as has been shown through Figs. 14 and 15, that the last segments/taps may even increase the error level. However with the partitioned architecture it is possible to detect when this happens and do something about it.

The segmented equaliser structure does not offer any significant benefit over the conventional linear equaliser unless there is some means to modify the equaliser length dynamically. The structure depicted in Fig. 16 has the potential to increase or decrease the number of taps used in the equalisation process, however there is still the

Figure 16. *Structure of a segmented FIR filter*

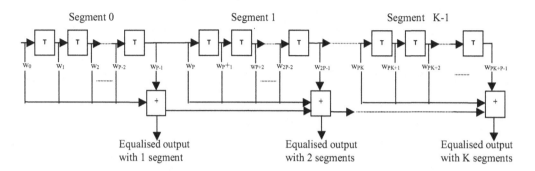

Figure 17. Segmented linear equaliser

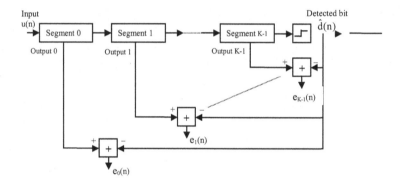

question of what criterion to follow in order to reconfigure the filter in an efficient manner. The length-adjustment algorithm should have two properties:

- It must only use the information available to the equaliser subsystem, that is, no external information should be required (such as noise level, Doppler spread).
- It should be easy to compute. There is no point in using criteria that require lot of computations, as then the benefits of reducing the number of taps might be lost.

The criterion proposed here is a finite-window least-squares function which we call the accumulated squared error (ASE) and is defined as:

$$\text{ASE}(n) = \sum_{i=0}^{n} \beta^{n-i} |d(n) - y(n)|^2 = \sum_{i=0}^{n} \beta^{n-i} e(n)^2 \tag{12}$$

where $\beta < 1$ is a forgetting factor used to emphasise recent data in the window over older data. Note that the ASE(n) and instantaneous MSE(n), assuming ergodicity and reasonably large n, are related by:

$$MSE(n) = \frac{ASE(n)}{n} \qquad (13)$$

Looking again at Fig. 17, it is clear that a distinctive $ASE_i(n)$ value can be computed for every segment, using the different error signal $e_i(n)$ available at every segment's output. In this way the measures $ASE_0(n)$, $ASE_1(n), \ldots ASE_{K-1}(n)$ are obtained.

It is now possible to state an algorithm that dynamically updates the length of the equaliser. Suppose that at any given moment an equaliser made of K segments of P taps/segment is only using the first L segments with L $\leq$ K, the rest of the segments (K-L) have their taps set to zero and they are not being updated. At every iteration, the $ASE_L(n)$ and $ASE_{L-1}(n)$ are being computed and the following decision algorithm is executed:

$$ASE_{L-1}(n) = \sum_{i=0}^{n} \beta^{n-i} |d(n) - y_{L-1}(n)|^2 \qquad (14)$$

$$ASE_L(n) = \sum_{i=0}^{n} \beta^{n-i} |d(n) - y_L(n)|^2 \qquad (15)$$

If $ASE_L(n) \; \alpha_{up} \; ASE_{L-1}(n) \quad \rightarrow \quad$ Add one segment (P extra taps) $\qquad (16)$

If $ASE_L(n) \; \alpha_{dw} \; ASE_{L-1}(n) \quad \rightarrow \quad$ Remove one segment (P less taps) $\qquad (17)$

with $0 < \alpha_{up}, \alpha_{dw} \leq 1$ and $\alpha_{up} \leq \alpha_{dw}, \beta \leq 1$.

Algorithm 1: Equaliser length control.

This algorithm can be translated into plain words as: if an equaliser with L segments performs significantly better than one with L-1 segments then add another segment. If an equaliser with L segments performs similarly to one with L-1 segments remove the last segment. The function of the variables α_{up} and α_{dw} is to determine the amount of improvement or worsening necessary to force the equaliser to expand or contract, so they control the sensitivity of the equaliser to change length. The simple heuristic of Algorithm 1 limits the number of segments to those that really make a significant contribution in the equalisation process. Notice that this algorithm satisfies the qualities sought: it only relies on information available to the equalising subsystem (only uses the different $e_i(n)$), and its computational complexity is low, requiring only four products and four additions per iteration. Also important is the fact that with the given algorithm only the performance of the last two segments is monitored, therefore only one extra adder is required.

Figure 18. Variable E/No profile

Figure 19. Equaliser length evolution with different variable-length equalisers (LMS).

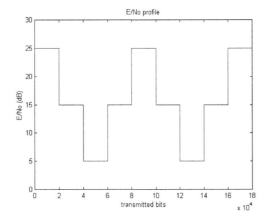

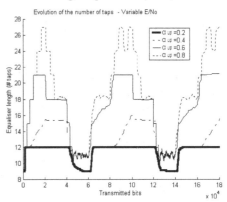

In order to demonstrate the effectiveness of the proposed length adaptation algorithm, a first set of simulations are now presented corresponding to a system where there are sudden variations in the E/No level. For these simulations, and without loss of generality, BPSK modulation was used. The system is assumed to operate in the environment given by Channel model 1. The abrupt changes in SNR can come from different physical phenomena such as sudden shadowing of the signal by an object, for example, a big building. Also in the context of CDMA systems, the signal from other users can be roughly modelled as AWGN (Wilson, 1993). In this case, the switching on and off of users in the system will provoke abrupt variations in the E/No level.

The E/No profile used in this set of simulations is shown in Fig. 18. As can be seen in the figure, the E/No level oscillates between 5 dB and 25 dB in steps of 10 dB at regular instants (every 20,000 samples). This profile helps to highlight how the variable-length equaliser confronts these variations.

The length evolution for different α_{up} values is shown in Fig. 19. There are several points worth noting in this figure. First and mainly, the equaliser length tracks the E/No profile, expanding when the noise level is low and contracting when it is high. Contrasting the data in Fig. 19 with that of Fig. 14, it can be concluded that Algorithm 1 successfully adjusts the equaliser length to the most appropriate value under the different E/No conditions. Secondly, different values of α_{up} offer different levels of performance. Clearly low α_{up} values, which tend to make the equaliser very short, will not be used as their performance is very limited, however the designer may choose to use a value in the range [0.6 .. 0.9] taking into account the computational power available.

A second illustrative example to demonstrate the advantageous performance of the variable-length equaliser consists of scenarios where abrupt changes in the channel profile take place. In mobile/cellular systems such changes are very common and might be caused, for example, by the handover from one base station to another or by some sudden change such as going from an outdoor to an indoor environment.

In the results presented here the channel impulse response corresponds initially to Channel model 1, then switches to Channel model 2 and later on goes back to Channel model 1. For the simulations in this section, the length was set to 180,000 bits, with the switching instants fixed at 60,000 bits (1st change) and 120,000 bits (2nd change). The E/No has been set to 35 dB. The E/No is made deliberately very high in order to "isolate" the behaviour of the equaliser in front of a channel profile change as it has been seen that the E/No level also influences the response of the variable-length equaliser. In this set of simulations the MSE has also been windowed as otherwise the whole curve would be dominated by the largest MSE level achieved.

As it can be appreciated initially the equaliser expands up to 30 or 33 taps (depending on the α_{up} used), which as inferred from Fig. 6, is a reasonable value give the large Es/No level and rather benign channel profile . When the channel changes to Channel model 2, the equaliser immediately detects that fewer taps are needed to attain the irreducible MSE level and shrinks to 18 taps. Finally when the channel goes back to channel model 1, it expands again up to 30 or 33 taps.

Both examples, varying Es/No profile and abrupt channel changes scenarios, demonstrate that the reconfigurable LE is effective in adjusting the equaliser length in response to changes in the environment. We conclude this section by mentioning that an enhanced algorithm for controlling the variable-length equaliser has recently appeared in (Wei, 2007). This new algorithm automatically tunes the parameters controlling the length adjustment, avoiding in this way the trial and error tuning of the algorithm variables (e.g. α_{up}, α_{dw}, M, P,...).

APPLICATIONS OF VARIABLE-LENGTH EQUALISERS

The idea underpinning variable-length linear equalisation can also be exploited in other receiver architectures. An important structure also suitable for variable length equalisation is the DFE. Typically, DFEs consist of a short length feed forward filter (FFF) to minimise the precursor interference and a long feedback filter (FBF) combating the postcursor interference. The reason the feedback filter is usually much longer than the FFF is because wireless channels tend to be close to minimum-phase, that is, their profile normally consist of a few strong paths at the beginning of the response followed by many low energy paths (very much like Channel model 1 introduced earlier). Since the FFF is nevertheless kept short, there is no need to have its length adjusted. In contrast, the number of postcursors in the channel varies widely depending on the environment and consequently, it is useful to adjust the length of the FBF. A detailed study of the DFE with a variable-length feedback section

Figure 20. Equaliser length evolution for different variable-length equalisers (LMS). Abrupt channel change: 1-2-1. E/No=35 dB

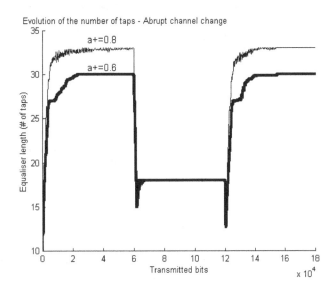

first appeared in (Riera-Palou, 2002). More recently, (Li, 2006) proposed the use of a modified variable-length FBF in conjunction with frequency domain FFF in the context of 4G systems.

Another interesting application of variable-length equalisers results from the combination with reconfigurable decoding schemes such as those presented in the first part of this chapter. Channel (or error correction) coding and equalisation are somehow "orthogonal" in their functioning. While error correction coding requires of an AWGN channel for its correct functioning, equalisers (as shown in Figs. 14 and 15) cannot do much when the environment is dominated by noise. This suggests that a reconfigurable receiver able to dynamically distribute the available computational resources between the equaliser and the channel decoder according to the instantaneous channel conditions would outperform the independent operation of both subsystems.

DISCUSSION AND CONCLUSION

In this chapter we have presented reconfigurable techniques applied to two important receiver techniques, namely, channel decoding and equalisation. It has been shown that reconfigurability is a desirable feature towards the implementation of energy efficient receivers without performance sacrifices.

Particularly for channel coding function and for a UMTS turbo decoder, SOVA and log-MAP correspond to the main decoding algorithms. Considering performance and complexity or delay, SOVA is the best choice in terms of complexity, while log-MAP is the best choice in terms of performance. The similarities in the data-flow of the two algorithms support the idea of a reconfigurable SOVA/log-MAP turbo decoder (Chaikalis, 2003; Chaikalis, 2004). Moreover, according to Woodard (2000) at low terminal speeds BER is worse than at higher terminal speeds. For UMTS some applications require the lowest possible delay, while for others the lowest possible performance is sufficient. Having in mind the results of Chaikalis (in press) it is observed that at rural and urban/suburban outdoor operating environments more frames can be established compared to indoor/low range outdoor environment. Thus, for indoor/low range outdoor environment there are many applications which cannot be established. Particularly, our analysis for indoor/low range outdoor environment shows that:

- For all implementation scenarios real time conversational class cannot be established. Obviously, the reason is the low terminal speed considered, which gives high BER. In Chaikalis (in press) for urban/suburban environment, this class can be applied to medium sized frames and high data rates, whereas in rural outdoor operating environment this class can be applied to small frames and low or medium data rates.
- For real time streaming class the proposed algorithm choice depends on data rate. For low data rates all frames cannot be applied, except for small frames where SOVA is optimal. For medium data rates (64 kbps, 128 kbps) small frames cannot be applied, while for medium-sized frames SOVA is proposed. For 144 kbps again SOVA is proposed for larger frames, while for medium-sized frames log-MAP is optimal. For high data rates (384 kbps) small frames cannot be considered, for medium frames log-MAP is proposed, while for large frames SOVA is proposed. For the other frame lengths either algorithm is proposed. For very high data rates (2 Mbps) small frames cannot be established: for the other frames either SOVA or log-MAP can be used. On the other hand, in Chaikalis (in press) for streaming class applications urban/suburban and rural outdoor operating environments SOVA is optimal for the scenarios that can be established. It is remarkable that, similarly to Chaikalis (in press), as data rate increases more and larger frames can be applied.
- For non-real time applications performance is the priority and delay requirements are looser. We observe that for all scenarios small frames cannot be applied due to tight BER. For larger frames both algorithms are equally suitable. Furthermore, for medium data rates and medium frames log-MAP is the proposed algorithm choice. In Chaikalis (in press) for urban/suburban outdoor environment the conclusions are similar. In Chaikalis (in press) but for rural outdoor environment log-MAP is optimum for the small frames, whereas SOVA and log-MAP are equally suitable for larger frames.

Regarding equalisation, it has been shown that the equaliser length is a parameter difficult to set a priori since it heavily depends on the instantaneous channel impulse response and operating SNR. Since equaliser length is an important parameter trading off performance and computational complexity, it is interesting to be able to dynamically change the equaliser length. A reconfigurable structure (segmented equaliser) and a length-controlling algorithm have been proposed which have been shown to be able to adjust the equaliser length in an efficient way in response to changes in the channel impulse response or SNR level.

REFERENCES

3GPP TS 25.212 V3.9.0. (2002). *Multiplexing and channel coding (FDD)*, Release 1999.

3GPP TR 25.944 V3.5.0. (2001). *Channel coding and multiplexing examples*, Release 1999.

3GPP TS 25.201 V3.3.0. (2002). *Physical layer-General description*, Release 1999.

Austin, A. (1967). *Decision-Feedback Equalisation for Digital Communication over Dispersive Channels*, M.I.T. Res. Lab Electron., Tech. Rep. 461.

Bello, P.A. (1963). *Characterization of Randomly Time-Variant Linear Channels*, IEEE Transactions on Communication Systems, Vol. CS-11.

Berrou, C., & Glavieux, A. (1996). *Near optimum error correcting coding and decoding: Turbo codes*. IEEE Transactions on Communications, Vol. 44, No. 10, 1261-1271.

Bouzouki, S., Kotsopoulos, S., Karagiannidis, G., Hasomeris, K., & Lymberopoulos, D. (2001). *On optimal cell planning case study for a DCS 1800 System*, International Journal of Communication Systems. Vol. 14, No. 9, 857-870.

Chaikalis, C. (2003). *Reconfigurable structures for turbo codes in 3G mobile radio transceivers*, PhD thesis, School of Engineering Design and Technology, University of Bradford, UK.

Chaikalis, C. (in press). *Implementation of a reconfigurable turbo decoder in 3GPP for flat Rayleigh fading*. Elsevier Digital Signal Processing Journal.

Chaikalis, C., & Noras, J. M. (2004). *Reconfigurable turbo decoding for 3G applications*. Elsevier Signal Processing Journal, Vol. 84, No. 10, 1957-1972.

Cimini, L.J. (1985). *Analysis and Simulation of a Digital Mobile Channel Using Orthogonal Frequency Division Multiplexing*. IEEE Transactions on Communications, Vol. COM-33, No. 7.

Falconer, D., Ariyavisitakul, S., Benyamin-Seeyar, A., & Eldson, B. (2002). *Frequency-Domain Equalisation for Single-Carrier Broadband Wireless Systems*. IEEE Communications Magazine, Vol. 2002, No. 4.

Forney, G.D. (1973). *The Viterbi algorithm*. Proceedings of the IEEE Vol. 61, No. 3.

Hagenauer, J., & Hoher, P. (1989). *A Viterbi algorithm with soft outputs and its applications*, IEEE GLOBECOM '89, Dallas, USA, 1680-1686.

Hall, E., & Wilson, S. (1998). *Design and analysis of turbo codes on Rayleigh fading channels*. IEEE Journal on Selected Areas in Communications, Vol. 16, No. 2, 160-174.

Haykin, S. (1996). *Adaptive Filter Theory, 3rd Edition*, Prentice Hall, Upper Saddle River (US).

Holma, H., & Toskala, A. (2000). *WCDMA for UMTS: Radio Access for Third Generation Mobile Communications*, J.Wiley.

Hooli K., Juntti M., Heikkilä M.J., Komulainen P., Latva-aho M., & Lilleberg J. (2002). *Chip-Level Channel Equalisation in WCDMA Downlink*. Eurasip Journal on Applied Signal Processing, Vol. 2002, No. 8.

Ioannou, K., Panoutsopoulos, I., Koubias, S., & Kotsopoulos, S. (2004). *A new Dynamic Channel Management Scheme to Increase the Performance Index of Cellular Networks*. IEE Electronics Letters, Vol. 40, No. 12, 744-746.

Jakes, W. C. (1974). *Microwave Mobile Communications*, J. Wiley & Sons, New York.

Kitsios, F., (2005), *Innovation Management in New Service Development*, PhD dissertation, Technical University of Crete.

Kotsopoulos, S., & Lymberopoulos, D. (1991). *A new Medical Data Management Concept in a Hybrid Cellular Mobile Radio Communication Network*, IEEE GLOBECOM'91, Phoenix, USA, 674-680.

Kotsopoulos, S., & Lymberopoulos, D. (1992). *Communication protocols and on-board processor for a new national scale private mobile radio service*, IEEE International Conference on Selected Topics in Wireless Communications, Vancouver, Canada.

Li, Y., Wei, X., Cruickshank, D.G.M. & McLaughlin, S. (2006). *Hybrid DFE with variable length feedback filter*. IEE Proceedings, Vol. 154, No. 1.

Lucky, R.W. (1965). *Automatic Equalisation for Digital Communication*. The Bell System Technical Journal, Vol. 44, No. 4.

Martin, R.K., & Johnson, C.R. (2005). *Adaptive Equalisation: Transitioning from Single-carrier to Multicarrier Systems*. IEEE Signal Processing Magazine.

Patzold, M., Killat, U., Laue, F., & Li, Y. (1998). *On the statistical properties of deterministic simulation models for mobile fading channels*. IEEE Transactions on Vehicular Technology, Vol. 47, No. 1, 254-269.

Pietrobon, S. (1998). *Implementation and performance of a turbo/MAP decoder*. International Journal of Satellite Communications, Vol. 16, No. 1, 23-46.

Proakis, J.G. (1995). *Digital Communications, 3rd Edition*, McGraw-Hill, New York (US).

Qureshi, S.U.H. (1985). *Adaptive Equalisation*, Proceedings of the IEEE, Vol. 73, No. 9.

Rappaport, T.S. (1996). *Wireless Communications Principles and Practice*, Prentice Hall, Upper Saddle River (US).

Riera-Palou, F. (2002). *Reconfigurable structures for Direct Equalisation in Mobile Receivers*, PhD thesis, University of Bradford. Available on-line at http://dmi.uib.es/~friera/phdthesis .

Riera-Palou, F., Noras J.M., & Cruickshank, D.G.M. (2001). *Linear equalisers with dynamic and automatic length selection.* IEE Electronics Letters, Vol. 37, No. 25.

Robertson, P., Villebrun, E., & Hoeher, P. (1995). *A comparison of optimal and sub-optimal MAP decoding algorithms operating in the log domain*, IEEE ICC'95, Seattle, USA, 1009-1013.

Sklar, B. (2001). *Digital Communications: Fundamentals and Applications, 2ⁿᵈ Edition*, Prentice Hall PTR, Upper Saddle River (NJ, US).

Wei, X., Cruickshank, D.G.M., Mulgrey, B., & Riera-Palou, F. (2007). *A Unified Approach to Dynamic Length Algorithms for Adaptive Equalisers.* IEEE Transactions on Signal Processing, Vol. 55, No. 3.

Widrow, B., & Hoff, M.E. (1960). *Adaptive Switching Circuits*, IRE WESCON Convention Record, Pt. 4.

Wilson, S.K., & Cioffi, J.M. (1993). *Equalisation Techniques for Direct Sequence Code-Division Multiple Access Systems in Multipath Channels*, IEEE International Symposium on Information Theory, San Antonio (US).

WINNER project. Information available at https://www.ist-winner.org/

Woodard, J., & Hanzo, L. (2000). *Comparative study of turbo decoding techniques: An overview.* IEEE Transactions on Vehicular Technology, Vol. 49, No. 6, 2208-2233.

KEY TERMS

Adaptive Algorithm: Algorithm used to drive the coefficients of an adaptive filter (such as an adaptive equaliser) to a set of values minimising some prescribed error function.

Adaptive Equaliser: Digital equaliser whose coefficients can vary in response to variations of the channel.

Equaliser: In the communications literature, an equaliser is a filter (fixed or adaptive) used at the receiver to compensate the channel effects.

Least Mean Squares (LMS): A computationally simple yet powerful adaptive algorithm based on gradient descent.

Log Maximum A Posteriori (log-MAP): A simplified powerful version of well known MAP algorithm, which is used for turbo decoding and is based on a posteriori probabilities.

Reconfigurable Equaliser: Equaliser whose structural properties like for example its length, can vary in response to changes in the environment conditions.

Reconfigurable Turbo Decoder: Turbo decoder whose structural properties like for example its decoding algorithm, can vary according to the required quality of service.

Soft Output Viterbi Algorithm (SOVA): A modified version of well known Viterbi algorithm, which is used for turbo decoding. Generally is less powerful than log-MAP, but less complex.

Turbo Decoder: In the communications literature a turbo decoder represents an iterative procedure used at the receiver to compensate the channel effects.

Universal Mobile Telecommunications Standard (UMTS): A high data rate 3G mobile communications standard already available in market.

Chapter XIV
Novel Multi–Antenna and Smart Antenna Techniques for Next Generation Wireless Communication Networks

Apostolos Georgiadis
Centre Tecnològic de Telecomunicacions de Catalunya (CTTC), Spain

Carles Fernández Prades
Parc Mediterrani de la Tecnologia (PMT), Spain

ABSTRACT

Multi-antenna systems incorporating smart antenna techniques present numerous advantages compared to their single antenna counterparts including increased capacity and range, by exploring spatial diversity. The current status and novel research directions in the framework of such array systems are presented. Furthermore, the application of nonlinear antenna arrays in the design of novel RF/microwave front-ends, that present compact, low cost and energy efficient solutions for smart antenna array applications is demonstrated. In this manner, the advantages of such systems in terms of their application within next generation networks are highlighted both from the point of view of digital signal processing techniques, as well as alternative analog radio front-end architectures.

INTRODUCTION

Research efforts on next generation wireless communication networks focus on the integration of coexisting heterogeneous types of networks, while providing an increasing number of applications and services, which, in turn, require a high quality of service (QoS). On the other hand, there is an increasing demand for energy efficiency and low cost solutions.

Multi-antenna systems offer higher speed and range compared to single antenna systems, by exploring spatial diversity. Smart antenna techniques applied in multiple antenna systems have a significant impact on the efficient use of the spectrum, the minimization of the cost of establishing new wireless networks, the enhancement of the

Copyright © 2009, IGI Global, distributing in print or electronic forms without written permission of IGI Global is prohibited.

quality of service, and the realization of re-configurable, robust and transparent operation across multi-technology wireless networks.

This chapter provides an overview on novel research directions in the framework of such antenna arrays. First, the capability of increasing the capacity of traditional mobile communication links by placing multiple antennas at the receiver and at the transmitter (MIMO systems) is demonstrated. Second, multi-antenna architectures are presented, analyzing the various advantages, disadvantages, as well as challenges that have to be addressed by implementing the transmitter and receiver functions in the digital domain versus the analog domain. The use of digital signal processing techniques applied in beam-forming and adaptive beam-forming methodologies is then presented. Finally, an introduction to nonlinear antenna arrays is provided, followed by a demonstration of their potential application as novel analog front-ends with beam-forming capabilities within the framework of smart antenna arrays.

MIMO TECHNIQUES

The recent introduction of multi-antenna "multiple-input multiple-output" (MIMO) techniques in terrestrial mobile communications has received a lot of interest in the past decade (Figure 1). The possibility to boost the capacity of traditional mobile communication links by placing multiple antennas at the receiver and at the transmitter has spurred a considerable volume of research. Nowadays, MIMO architectures are fairly well studied and understood, up to the point that MIMO techniques are currently being introduced in multiple mobile communication standards. For example, the IEEE 802.11n extension to the IEEE 802.11 standard for wireless LAN (WiFi) (http://standards.ieee.org/getieee802/802.11.html) supports MIMO links up to 4 by 4 (4 spatial streams), space-time block coding techniques and rates up to 600 Mbps over a 40 MHz bandwidth. Another example is given by the IEEE 802.16e amendment to the 802.16 standard for wireless MAN (WiMAX) (http://standards.ieee.org/getieee802/802.16.html), which also provides support for MIMO operation with beamforming, space-time coding, and spatial multiplexing. In the following, we present the fundamental advantages and trade-offs of this kind of systems.

Multiplexing Gain

A narrowband time-invariant wireless channel with N_t transmit and N_r receive antennas is described by an N_r by N_t deterministic matrix **H**. What are the key properties of **H** that determine how much spatial multiplexing it can support? We answer this question by looking at the capacity of the channel.

The observation obtained at one channel access assuming a time-invariant channel model can be mathematically described at a particular channel access by

$$\mathbf{y} = \mathbf{H}\mathbf{x} + \mathbf{w} \tag{1}$$

where $\mathbf{x} \in \mathbf{C}^{N_t}$, $\mathbf{y} \in \mathbf{C}^{N_r}$, $\mathbf{w} : CN(\mathbf{0}, N_o \mathbf{I}_{Nr})$ respectively denote the transmitted signals at the N_t transmit antennas, the corresponding N_r received signals and an additive spatially white Gaussian noise respectively. The channel matrix $\mathbf{H} \in C^{N_r \times N_t}$ is initially assumed to be deterministic, constant at all times.

Figure 1. A new file has been sent for this figure

Tx   MIMO CHANNEL   Rx

Assuming that the receiver has perfect knowledge of the channel matrix (usually referred to as channel state information, CSI), the instantaneous capacity of an N_t x N_r MIMO channel **H** with AWGN is given in Telatar (1999):

$$C = \max_{tr(\mathbf{Q})<P} \log_2 \det\left(\mathbf{I_{N_r}} + \frac{1}{N_o} \mathbf{HQH^H} \right) \quad \text{bps/Hz} \tag{2}$$

where **Q** is the covariance matrix of **x** and P is the total power of the transmitter. If the transmitter does not have access to CSI, uniform power allocation seems to be the most reasonable transmit strategy, resulting in the following capacity expression

$$C_{UPA} = \log_2 \det\left(\mathbf{I_{N_r}} + \frac{SNR}{N_t} \mathbf{HH^H} \right) = \sum_{i=1}^{\min(N_r,N_t)} \log_2\left(1+\frac{SNR}{N_t}\lambda_i \right) \tag{3}$$

where we have used the following singular value decomposition of the channel matrix

$$\mathbf{H} = \sum_{i=1}^{N_{\min}} \sqrt{\lambda_i}\mathbf{u}_i\mathbf{v}_i^H \tag{4}$$

where $\sqrt{\lambda_i}$ denote the singular values of the channel matrix **H**, N_{min}=min(N_t, N_r) and $\mathbf{u}_i$ and $\mathbf{v}_i$ are the left/right singular vectors respectively. We can observe that capacity is obtained as if we decomposed the vector channel into a set of parallel, independent scalar Gaussian sub-channels. This shows the multiplexing capabilities of MIMO communications.

At moderate and high SNR, the capacity is approximately equal (up to an additive constant) to $N_{min} \log_2 SNR$ bps/Hz, so that it increases linearly with min(N_t, N_r). This exemplifies the fact that, for the same transmitted power, the transmission rate can be much higher than in conventional single-input single-output systems. A possible method for exploiting the rate advantage of MIMO architectures is to multiplex different information streams in the spatial domain. This is the basic principle behind the V-BLAST transmission technique (Foschini, 1998), which proposes to send independent information streams through each of the transmit antennas. This architecture tries to mimic the structure of the ergodic capacity expression at high SNR in (3).

When there is CSI at the transmitter (CSIT), the optimal strategy consists in transmitting several parallel streams according to the singular value decomposition of the MIMO channel in (4) so that each of the parallel communications takes place simultaneously through a different pair of singular vectors acting as beamformers at the transmitter and the receiver (each of the parallel streams travels through a different "eigenmode"). In this case, the transmitter can allocate different amounts of power in the different eigenmodes according to a water-filling strategy (Telatar, 1999). The following capacity results

$$C_{CSIT} = k\log_2\left[\lambda_G\left(\frac{P}{k}+\lambda_H^{-1} \right) \right] \tag{5}$$

where λ_G and λ_H denote the geometric and harmonic means of the k largest eigenvalues, where k is the number of activated eigenmodes in the water-filling power allocation technique. Note that while the maximal channel entropy is desirable for both capacities in (3) and (5) (i.e. maximal eigenvalue geometric mean), the inverse of the harmonic mean also contributes to increase capacity if there is channel information at the transmitter. Also note that, when a strong line-of-sight (LOS) is present, the channel matrix **H** becomes rank one, and only one of the singular values becomes different from zero. This means that all the power is going to be allocated in the direction indicated by the eigenmode that is associated to the positive eigenvalue. Thus, the beamforming solution will be optimal in terms of capacity whenever there is LOS and CSIT.

In mobile communications, it is common practice to assume that the channel behaves according to a block fading model. This means that the channel is constant during the transmission of a particular block of information, but behaves randomly and independently from one block to the next. Under this model, the mutual information in (2) is a random quantity, because it depends on the channel matrix (which is in turn drawn from a random process at each channel access) and the capacity of the MIMO channel in the Shannon sense is identically zero. Indeed, no matter how high we choose the transmit signal power, there is always a non-zero probability that the transmitted codeword will not be properly decoded due to the instantaneous channel fading. Hence, instead of the traditional capacity measures, MIMO fading channels are more properly described by two other quantities related to the mutual information: the ergodic capacity, defined as the mean mutual information (average over the channel statistics), and the outage capacity, defined as the minimum mutual information that is at least with a certain probability.

Diversity and Beamforming Gain

The use of multiple antennas in radio communication links has traditionally been regarded as an efficient means to counteract fading and exploit spatial diversity at either the transmitter or the receiver. Spatial diversity is generated by sampling the spatial domain using different antennas. Assuming that the antennas are located sufficiently separated from one another and that the scenario presents a certain degree of variability, the channel seen from each of the receive antennas will be sufficiently different from one another to guarantee that any deep fades on one of the channels can be compensated by using the signals coming from the other links. Exactly the same reasoning applies to transmit diversity, where modified copies of the same signal are transmitted from different antennas. If these transmit antennas are well separated in the spatial domain and the scenario presents some degree of variability, the transmit path from each one of them to a particular receive antenna will behave according to an essentially independent pattern. Therefore, any deep fades in one of the links can be overcome using the information coming from the other antennas.

In formal terms, the diversity order is defined as the slope of logarithm of the symbol error rate as a function of the logarithm of the received signal to noise ratio (SNR) for a fixed transmit power as this last quantity grows without bound. It is well known that some applications must work on the low SNR region, for which the mathematical definition of diversity is not fully operative. In any case, the diversity advantage will indicate the robustness of the system against individual fading losses in particular paths between transmit and receive antennas.

One of the main differences between transmit and receive diversity phenomena, is the fact that channel state information (CSI) is usually available at the receivers, *CSIR*, but not at the transmitters. This leads to a fundamental limitation with regard to the method for exploiting the inherent degrees of freedom that diversity offers. Indeed, whereas received diversity can easily be exploited by coherently combining the signals at each receive antenna, transmit diversity under unknown CSI needs to be exploited using more sophisticated techniques that make use of both spatial and time domains, and which are usually referred to as space-time codes. In this type of techniques, the information is coded in both the spatial and the time domain. By adding redundancy across these two dimensions, the system becomes more robust against particular fading nulls in individual links at the transmit side. To illustrate this, consider a system with two transmit antennas and one receive antenna, and denote by h_1 and h_2 the channel response between the first and second transmit antenna respectively and the receive one (we consider the case where the channels are real-valued). Consider the transmission of two symbols during two channel accesses. In particular, imagine that the system transmits two different real valued symbols through the first antenna $[s_1, s_2]$ whereas the second antenna transmits $[-s_2, s_1]$. The received signal is usually processed by applying a matched filter in the space-time domain. The instantaneous bit error rate under a BPSK transmission is given by

$$P_e|_{h_1,h_2} = \frac{1}{2} erfc\left(\sqrt{\left(h_1^2 + h_2^2\right)\frac{P}{\sigma^2}} \right)$$

(6)

where P is the total transmitted power and σ^2 denotes the noise power at the receiver. Now, averaging over the channel statistics, and assuming that they are independent, identically distributed according to a Gaussian law with zero mean and variance σ_h^2, the mean bit error rate takes the form

$$P_e = \left(\frac{1-\mu}{2}\right)^2 (2-\mu), \quad \mu = \sqrt{\frac{\overline{SNR}_R}{1+\overline{SNR}_R}}, \quad \overline{SNR}_R = \sigma_h^2 \frac{P}{\sigma^2} \tag{7}$$

so that, at high values of the signal to noise ratio

$$P_e \approx 3 \left(\frac{1}{4\overline{SNR}_R}\right)^2 \tag{8}$$

which decays as the square of the signal to noise ratio, showing a diversity order of two.

For low SNR scenario, Space-Time Trellis Codes are known to have better bit error rate performance complexity than Space-Time Block Codes, the penalty will be a higher decoding complexity. Space-Time techniques do not require CSIT but only CSIR, and complexity at reception is in fact one of the aspects that help to decide among different space-time coding choices.

When there is CSIT, other transceiver structures are motivated. In the most generic setting, the transmitted signal is obtained by a three step linear transformation: a composition of a rotation, a scaling operation, followed by another rotation. Payaró (2005) considered transmitter designs, both for deterministic and for *statistical CSIT*, taking also into account the crucial aspect of *imperfect channel* knowledge at the transmitter, which leads to the so-called robust MIMO transmission. Pascual (2005 and 2006) provides schemes for the LOS case. An interesting aspect is that when average BER is the target and statistical CSIT is available the performance finally depends again on the geometric and harmonic mean as in the case of capacity. See the work of Lagunas (2006) for further details.

At this point, the question naturally arises as to whether it is possible to simultaneously achieve the rate and diversity advantage of a particular MIMO channel. The answer is negative, as it can be already perceived from the basic transmit architectures presented so far. Indeed, the fundamental trade-off between the diversity and multiplexing capabilities of MIMO fading channels was established by Viswanath (2002) and Shin (2003). It turns out that, assuming that the transmission block length is sufficiently high, the maximum diversity gain d given an integer multiplexing gain $0 \le r \le \min (N_t, N_r)$, is upper bounded by

$$d \le (N_t - r)(N_r - r) \tag{9}$$

For non-integer multiplexing gains, the bound is extended by piecewise linear joining the aforementioned integer points. Note that the maximum diversity gain $N_t \times N_r$ is only achieved at a zero rate advantage, whereas the maximum rate advantage of $\min(N_t, N_r)$ is achieved when there is no diversity gain in the system.

Most of the MIMO architectures taken into account so far rely on some degree of channel knowledge. Quite usually, the CSI is assumed to be known at the receiver, where a channel estimation process can be performed during the training period in which the transmitter sends a training sequence. In fact, the channel response can be acquired by the receivers themselves, or by an external calibration network. Recent investigations have shown that the assumption of spatially colored noise leads to algorithms that are robust to coherent multipath and interferences with a reasonable computational effort (Seco, 2005; Fernández 2006).

In any case, multi-antenna algorithms need to be aware of the potential errors in the CSI, which may be caused by either the channel estimation procedure itself, or by the feedback procedure that makes this information available at the transmitter. In these situations, robust MIMO techniques are good alternatives to more classical MIMO architectures, in the sense that they take into account these errors in the CSI.

ARCHITECTURES FOR NARROWBAND ANTENNA ARRAYS

There are two technical approaches to steerable antennas: mechanically moved dishes and electronically steerable antenna arrays. In the case of dishes, the source/target tracking is performed by means of a mechanical engine, i.e., the antenna is physically moved to point the desired direction. This solution implies high mechanical complexity and consequently high maintenance costs. In addition, this kind of antenna does not provide any capability of spatial processing, for instance by nulling the reception of other unwanted signals or adaptive processing, and hence they have limited interference rejection.

On the other hand, antenna arrays are pointed electronically: while the antenna remains physically immobile, the underlying signal processing steers the radiation pattern to the desired direction. Moreover, they provide interesting capabilities of autonomous tracking and adaptive nulling. An array of sensors has the potential for improving the overall transmission performance in environments with several sources of interference, clutter, multipath propagation or low signal-to-noise ratio.

Three approaches might be considered in the architecture of antenna array beamforming: digital, analog and a mixed strategy. Performance in terms of computational cost, estimation accuracy, hardware complexity and availability of commercial off-the-shelf (COTS) devices should be analyzed:

- In an analog architecture, weights combining the signal of each antenna are implemented by means of attenuators and phase shifters. A set of different weights needs to be implemented for each source/target to be tracked (Figure 2a).
- In digital beamforming, signal of each antenna is processed digitally. In this case, the weights are simply complex multipliers which are implemented in programmable devices such as FPGAs (Figure 2b).

Figure 2. Block diagram of a) an analog array architecture, b) a fully digital antenna array

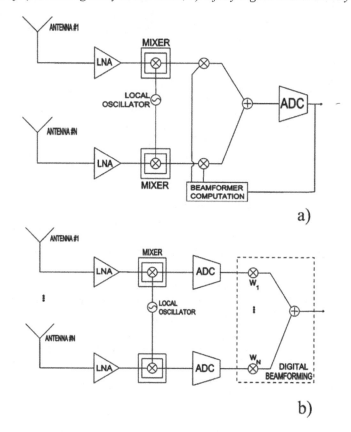

- In the mixed analog/digital strategy, the antenna elements are grouped in subarrays. Each subarray implements a delay-and-sum beamforming with only phase shifters. In case of transmitters, signals are digitally weighted and then converted to the analog domain, feeding the subarrays. In case of receiver architectures, the outputs are downconverted and digitized, leading to a digital beamforming stage where nulling capabilities and other advanced processing can be performed.

All three strategies imply advantages and disadvantages. In the pure analog technology, only a frequency shift per antenna array is needed, because all the beamformings are performed at the radio-frequency (RF) stage. Computational cost is reduced compared to the digital strategy because the weights are implemented physically with attenuators and phase shifters, and there is no need of complex multiplications. On the other hand, the dynamic range for attenuation and phase shifting is quite limited; current technology is in the order of five bits of resolution for both. Every tracked source or target needs a complete set of attenuators and phase shifters and additional hardware such as directional couplers for each antenna, resulting in an increased hardware complexity. This complexity is mitigated in the mixed strategy, because only phase shifters are needed. In both cases, a calibration system is also envisaged in order to maintain a time reference between all channels. Miscalibration is a main source of beamforming malfunction, so it should be mitigated by some controlling and monitoring system.

Digital beamforming at the receiver implies a frequency conversion for each antenna, and the corresponding digitation. The computational load increases as the huge amount of collected data needs to be processed in near real-time. Problems such as miscalibration or hardware misadjustment are reduced, since all the processing is done digitally. This strategy allows a great flexibility in the design and is able to mitigate effects such as multipath or interferences. Even several beamforming methods can be implemented, and then select the best suited in a given environment. This is a software-based solution, implying an upgradeable capability, in contrast to the analog version.

Currently, technology is mature enough (in terms of computational power, availability of suitable D/A and A/D converters, well-known up/downconversion methods and cost of such devices) to implement the digital strategy, overcoming several potential sources of malfunction due to hardware variability. Moreover, allows more complex and robust beamforming algorithms than the analog approach. Digital beamforming is a rapidly developing technology, being most advanced approach to antenna array radiation pattern control. When implemented at the array element level, digital beamforming enables full utilization of the maximum number of degrees of freedom in the array. This can lead to significant improvements in beamforming of simultaneous multiple independent beams, adaptive pattern nulling and space-time adaptive processing, compared to traditional analog array control techniques. Because of its flexibility, digital beamforming may find use in a wide range of phased array antenna applications.

Digital array receivers include, but are not limited to, the following features: RF receiver front-end for RF-to-IF or RF-to-baseband demodulation, analog-to-digital converters (ADC) for bandpass or baseband sampling, and digital finite impulse response (FIR) filtering for decomposition of sampled signals into in-phase and quadrature (I/Q) components. Digital beamforming receiver technology requires all of these core digital receiving capabilities, plus many others which are essential for digital control and optimization of phased array antenna patterns. These include, but are not limited to the following:

- FIR digital filtering for digital beamforming receiver channel equalization to enable wideband array-level channel-to-channel calibration,
- Use of either digital sub-banding schemes such as multi-rate digital filtering or implementation of fractional sample digital time delays, to enable wideband beamforming and adaptive nulling,
- A high degree of built-in programmability for implementation of advanced algorithms for beamforming, channel filtering and sub-banding,
- Module-level digital self-registration capabilities with respect to the system-level distribution and temporal aligning of digital clock and synchronisation signals, coherent phasing of RF local oscillator (LO) signals, and array channel calibration RF pilot tones, and

- Module-level self-assessment capabilities that monitor the overall in-situ performance of the digital beamforming receiver array channel. In order to ensure the proper working of the beamforming, the amplitude and phase reference of each antenna must be kept; and this is indeed the main risk in this approach.

Accurate alignment of channels would require high precision hardware components and consequently a high economic cost. Thus, there is a need of a calibration system. A calibration must be performed to match the phase and amplitude of the different hardware channels. The calibration must also track variations in time due to temperature, humidity or frequency, and also to be transparent and have no or a small noticeable effect on the normal operation of the adaptive array antenna. Depending on the calibration method used, there will be a limited resolution in the calibration process and the residual calibration error will degrade the performance.

DIGITAL BEAMFORMING

This section will focus on the ability of antenna arrays to filter signals in a space-time field by exploiting their spatial characteristics. Since the angles of arrival can be estimated (or a priori known, as in satellite-based navigation applications), it makes sense to spatially filter the incoming signals such that a signal from a particular angle, or set of angles, is amplified by a constructive combination while noise and signals from other angles are rejected by destructive interference. The spatial filter which performs such combination is commonly referred to as *beamformer*.

Beamforming with antenna arrays is a technique that consists of several antennas which outputs are controlled in phase and gain, i.e., multiplied by complex weights, in order to achieve a gain pattern that can be manipulated electronically. Then, all the weighted signals are combined to obtain a single output. Considering an N-element array, these mentioned weights can be stacked in a complex-valued vector, $\mathbf{w} \subset \mathbf{C}^{N\times 1}$ the signal samples received by each antenna can be arranged in a matrix $\mathbf{X} \subset \mathbf{C}^{N\times K}$ (where K is the number of samples) and the output signal of the beamformer can be computed as $\mathbf{y} = \mathbf{w}^H \mathbf{X}$. The weighting vector $\mathbf{w}$, also known as *beamvector*, can be designed following several criteria, usually exploiting the spatial filtering provided by antenna arrays. If the design of the beamvector takes into account the received signals stored in matrix $\mathbf{X}$, we speak about *adaptive* beamforming. Classical references on this field are the works of Monzingo (1980), Van Veen (1988) and Van Trees (2002), just to name a few of the vast literature available.

In order to illustrate the concept of beamforming, we will describe three examples using the following notation:

$$\mathbf{x} = \mathbf{As} + \mathbf{n} \tag{10}$$

where $\mathbf{x} \in \mathbf{C}^{N\times 1}$ is a vector containing the signal received by each one of the N antennas, matrix $\mathbf{A} \in \mathbf{C}^{N\times M}$ contains in its columns the spatial signature of each one of the M impinging signals, $\mathbf{s} \in \mathbf{C}^{M\times 1}$ is a vector containing these signals and $\mathbf{n} \in \mathbf{C}^{N\times 1}$ is the noise term. If we collect a set of K samples, the resulting equation can be arranged in a matrix form as

$$\mathbf{X} = \mathbf{AS} + \mathbf{N} \tag{11}$$

where $\mathbf{x} \in \mathbf{C}^{N\times K}$, $\mathbf{S} \in \mathbf{C}^{M\times K}$ and $\mathbf{N} \in \mathbf{C}^{N\times K}$.

Minimum Variance Beamformer

The classical Minimum Variance Beamformer (MVB) (Capon, 1967; Appelbaum, 1976; Wax, 1996), also known as Capon beamformer, consists on minimizing the total output power while forcing the beamformer to always point to the desired direction or directions, centred around a known frequency. This has the effect of preserving the desired signals while minimising contributions to the output due to other interfering signals, multipath and noise arriving from directions other than the directions of interest. Considering the signal model expressed in (11), the MVB can be stated as

$$\hat{\mathbf{w}}_{MVB} = \arg\min_{\mathbf{w}} \left[E\left\{\left|\mathbf{w}^H\mathbf{X}\right|^2\right\} = E\left\{\mathbf{w}^H\mathbf{X}\mathbf{X}^H\mathbf{w}\right\} = \mathbf{w}^H\hat{\mathbf{R}}_{XX}\mathbf{w} \right] \tag{12}$$

subject to $\quad \mathbf{w}^H\mathbf{A} = \mathbf{1}_{1\times M}$

where $\hat{\mathbf{R}}_{XX}$ is the estimation of the data autocorrelation matrix. Applying the Lagrange multipliers method, the MVB results in

$$\hat{\mathbf{w}}_{MVB} = \hat{\mathbf{R}}_{XX}^{-1}\mathbf{A}\left(\mathbf{A}^H\hat{\mathbf{R}}_{XX}^{-1}\mathbf{A}\right)^{-1}\mathbf{1}_{1\times M} \tag{13}$$

Equation (13) implies $M<N$ linear constraints on $\mathbf{w}$, and each linear constraint uses one degree of freedom in the beamvector. Therefore, with M constraints there are $N-M$ degrees of freedom available for minimising variance. Other possibilities for choosing the constraint matrix (and the corresponding response vector) could be the derivative or the eigenvector constraint approaches.

It is worthwhile to notice that the constraints are assumed to be linearly independent, and thus $\mathbf{A}$ has rank M. This implies that the directions of interest must be different between them, and a small angular separation between desired sources can produce numerical instability on the solution.

The performance of the MVB is often analyzed in terms of the signal-to-interference-plus-noise ratio (SINR), which is affected by many parameters such as the signal-to-noise ratio (SNR), the interference-to-noise ratio (INR), the signal-to-interference ratio (SIR), the angular separation between the desired signal and the interference, the array size and shape, the presence of steering vectors errors, the correlation between the signal and the interference or the finite sample size. An extensive analysis of performance of the MVB is provided in Wax (1996), giving the idea that the algorithm tries to combine destructively the impinging undesired signals in order to minimize their contribution to the beamformer output power.

Temporal Reference Beamformer

Another classical approach to beamforming is based on the minimization of the mean square error, understanding error as the mismatch between the actual output signal and a reference signal. In this case, the temporal diversity is exploited provided that the signal waveform is a priori known. If spatial signatures are not taken into account, the temporal reference can be expressed as $\mathbf{S}$ and this criterion can be written as

$$\hat{\mathbf{w}}_{TE} = \arg\min_{\mathbf{w}} E\left\{\left|\mathbf{w}^H\mathbf{X} - \mathbf{S}\right|^2\right\} \tag{14}$$

A straightforward gradient computation leads to

$$\hat{\mathbf{w}}_{TE} = \hat{\mathbf{R}}_{XX}^{-1}\hat{\mathbf{R}}_{XS} \tag{15}$$

where $\hat{\mathbf{R}}_{XX}$ is defined as aforementioned, and $\hat{\mathbf{R}}_{XS} = \frac{1}{K}\mathbf{X}\mathbf{S}^H$. The behavior of the temporal reference beamforming tends to combine constructively all the impinging signals in order to increase the contribution of the desired signals in the beamformer output.

Hybrid Space-Time Beamformer

In some applications the temporal reference is not completely known but parameterized by some values of interest, by instance synchronisation parameters. By contrast, the steering matrix could be a priori known or estimated, providing a valuable reference for the system. Both spatial and temporal diversities can be combined leading to an approach known as hybrid beamforming (Seco, 2005). The derivation of the multiple hybrid beamformer (MHB) is as follows.

The mean square error (MSE) between the output of a beamformer with weights $\mathbf{w}$ and a temporal reference signal $\mathbf{S}$ is

$$J_1(\mathbf{w},\mathbf{p}) = \frac{1}{K}\left\|\mathbf{w}^H\mathbf{X} - \mathbf{S}(\mathbf{p})\right\|^2 \tag{16}$$

In this case, the temporal reference is not completely known but parameterised by a vector $\mathbf{p}$. In order to take advantage of the knowledge of the steering matrix $\mathbf{A}$, a spatial constraint is imposed to force the beamformers to always point the desired signals. The criterion of combining temporal and spatial information could be stated as follows (Fernandez, 2006):

$$\hat{\mathbf{w}}_{HB} = \hat{\mathbf{R}}_{XX}^{-1}\hat{\mathbf{R}}_{XS} + \hat{\mathbf{R}}_{XX}^{-1}\mathbf{A}\left(\mathbf{A}^H\hat{\mathbf{R}}_{XX}^{-1}\mathbf{A}\right)^{-1}\left(\mathbf{1} - \mathbf{A}^H\hat{\mathbf{R}}_{XX}^{-1}\hat{\mathbf{R}}_{XS}\right) \tag{17}$$

where $\mathbf{1}$ is a 1 x M vector with all ones. This result indicates that the beamformer is a linear combination of two previously known results. On the one hand, $\hat{\mathbf{w}}_{TE} = \hat{\mathbf{R}}_{XX}^{-1}\hat{\mathbf{R}}_{XS}$ is the result of the MSE criterion taking into account only the temporal reference, as shown in equation (15). On the other hand, the second term in (17) is a linear combination of the columns of $\hat{\mathbf{R}}_{XX}^{-1}\mathbf{A}\left(\mathbf{A}^H\hat{\mathbf{R}}_{XX}^{-1}\mathbf{A}\right)^{-1}$, each column being a MVB pointing to the direction given by one column of $\mathbf{A}$. These two terms in (17) show a different behavior against multipath: while $\hat{\mathbf{w}}_{TE}$ tries to combine constructively the desired signal with the other replicas in order to increase the SINR, $\hat{\mathbf{w}}_{MVB}$ combines destructively such signals to minimize the output signal power. The presented hybrid beamformer combines these two behaviors in order to mitigate multipath and interferences.

Robust Beamforming

Uncertainties in the steering matrix due to hardware maladjustments cause a dramatic loss in performance. Pointing errors can arise from several sources. Errors in the array attitude determination appear to have a greater impact in DOA estimation, specially when considering a mobile array and the attitude has to be constantly measured. These errors are ascribable to the Inertial Measurement Unit (IMU) used; a low-cost Micro Electro Mechanical System (MEMS) has a typical accuracy of about ± 5 degrees and a drift rate of 3 degrees/hour. Even with a high-accuracy IMU, pointing errors due to an array miscalibration could not be dismissible at all, provided that array systems are known to be quite sensitive to mismatches between the presumed and the actual DOA.

Robustness in adaptive beamforming was presented in Cox (1987), where a quadratic inequality constraint on the array gain was used to mitigate spatially white noise. When only linear constraints are considered, performance degradation arises because errors in the assumed steering vector of the desired signal break orthogonality to the noise subspace of the array covariance matrix. A correction of the steering vector to make it orthogonal is proposed by Youn (1994), achieving interference mitigation in presence of array imperfection. Other projection methods used to modify the steering vector are discussed in Feldman (1994 and 1996), also coping with sample covariance error in sample matrix inversion (SMI) processing.

The application of convex optimization to robust beamforming was introduced by Lebret (1997). An implementation devoted to the Global Positioning System (GPS) based on a MVB, minimising the array output power while guaranteeing that the gain in the direction of the source (in this case, the corresponding satellite) is greater than unity for all values in an uncertainty ellipsoid, is described in Lorenz (2005). Second order cone programming, applied to the worst-case performance optimization can be found in Vorobyov (2003). General-rank signal models are handled in Shahbazpanahi (2003), where the robustness is achieved by means of an explicit modelling of uncertainties in the desired signal array response and data covariance matrix as well as worst-case performance optimization, obtaining a closed-form solution with reasonable computational complexity, since it is based on the principal eigenvector computation of a diagonal-loaded matrix. Finally, Gershman (2003) provides an overview of recent trends in robust adaptive beamforming.

TRANSCEIVER FRONT-ENDS BASED ON NONLINEAR ANTENNA ARRAYS

Nonlinear antenna arrays based on active integrated antennas (AIAs) have a number of advantages due to their compact size, low cost, light weight and energy efficiency. As a result they have been extensively considered in the design of novel RF/microwave front-ends. An AIA consists of a passive radiating element and an active circuit, integrated in the same substrate (Lin, 1994; Qian, 1998; Chang, 2002; Navarro, 1996). One may distinguish between transmitter and receiver configurations of AIAs, however it is more practical to classify them depending on their nonlinear functionality into oscillator, amplifier, and frequency conversion AIAs (Lin, 1994).

In oscillator AIAs, a radiating element, such as a patch antenna, acts both as a load and a resonator to an active element properly biased to provide a negative resistance necessary to produce an oscillation. An oscillator AIA is typically used in transmitter configurations (Lin, 1994; Qian, 1998; Chang, 2002; Navarro, 1996).

In frequency conversion applications, the AIA is used as a mixer or multiplier, in both receiving and transmitting applications. Moreover, the active device maybe biased to operate as a self-oscillating mixer (SOM) providing the functionality of both an oscillator and mixer at the same time (Lin, 1994; Qian, 1998; Chang, 2002; Navarro, 1996).

Finally, in an amplifier configuration the radiating element is integrated to the input or the output of an active device biased to operate as an amplifier. As a result one obtains a low noise amplifier (LNA) receiving AIA or a medium to high power transmitting AIA respectively. The active device may also be used to match the impedance of the antenna to a significantly lower frequency than its resonance frequency, thus reducing its size and allowing for compact implementations at low frequency applications (UHF or VHF) (Chang, 2002).

Oscillator and SOM AIAs can be injection locked to each other forming AIA arrays that have found numerous applications in power combining, phased array and retro-directive array applications (Lin, 1994; Qian, 1998; Chang, 2002; Navarro, 1996). In such arrays, the various oscillator elements oscillate at the same frequency and their relative phases can be electronically set, for example by controlling their free-running (uncoupled) frequencies. The relative phases of the radiating AIAs ultimately define the main beam direction of the array and, generally, the shape of the radiation pattern. Retro-directive arrays have the special property that radiate an incoming wave to its source without the need for signal processing in order to derive the direction of arrival. Various coupling network configurations have been investigated from unilateral to bilateral coupling (Lin, 1994; Qian, 1998; Chang, 2002; Navarro, 1996), and from wideband to narrow-band coupling networks (Lynch, 2001), allowing for different methods to control the phase of the elements.

The progress in recent years in nonlinear simulation techniques has led to more accurate design and optimization methods for nonlinear dynamical systems. Complicated circuits containing a large number of state variables and time-delays can now be efficiently analyzed using nonlinear analysis tools, leading to accurate design methodologies for nonlinear circuits such as oscillators (Kundert, 1990; Giannini, 2004). These nonlinear simulation tools can be combined with EM simulation in order to analyze radiating structures and nonlinear antennas (Rizzoli, 2004; Georgiadis, 2006). Still, large arrays present a challenge to the designer as a number of approximations need to be used to reduce the simulation time. Such are, describing function models, and macro-models for non-linear elements (Kurokawa, 1969; Kurokawa, 1973; Vanassche, 2003; Lai, 2004), along with infinite array approximations (Pogorzelski, 2003).

In the following sections, the application of oscillator and mixer arrays of AIAs in smart antenna beam forming applications will be presented. Applications related to narrow-band communication systems will be described.

Basic Characteristics and Methods of Analysis

In a coupled oscillator array, the various AIAs are synchronized with the help of a coupling mechanism. The underlying principle for the synchronization is that of injection locking. According to the theory of injection locking, when a signal of sufficient power and frequency close to that of the free-running frequency of an oscillator is injected to one of its nodes, the oscillator is forced to oscillate at the injection frequency with a fixed phase difference compared to that of the injection signal. Among the first to study the locking phenomena in oscillators was Adler (1946). He provided a differential equation that governs the phase difference ϕ between the free-running oscillator and the injection source:

$$\frac{d\varphi}{dt} = -\sqrt{\frac{P_{inj}}{P_o}} \frac{\omega_o}{2Q} \sin(\varphi) + \Delta \omega_o \tag{18}$$

where P_{inj} is the injection signal power, P the free-running oscillator power, Q the loaded quality factor of the oscillator, ω_o the free-running oscillator frequency and, $\omega = \omega_o + \Delta\omega_o$ the injection frequency. When locking is achieved, the steady state solution phase difference ϕ_o, defined by $d\phi/dt = 0$ is,

$$\sin(\varphi_o) = 2Q \sqrt{\frac{P_o}{P_{inj}}} \frac{\Delta\omega_o}{\omega_o} \tag{19}$$

One can see that the phase shift between the oscillators depends on their frequency difference, their power ratio and the injected oscillator Q. The locking bandwidth corresponds to the maximum frequency difference between the injection signal and the oscillator, which is given by $\left|\sin(\varphi_o)\right| = 1$.

One may also conclude from (19) that there exist up to two solutions for every injection signal power, oscillator power, and frequency values. In nonlinear systems, in addition to determining the existence of a steady state solution, one has to examine their stability. This is commonly done by perturbing the steady state solution. Setting $\phi = \phi_o + \delta\phi$ in (18) one obtains to first order,

$$\frac{d\delta\varphi}{dt} = -\sqrt{\frac{P_{inj}}{P_o}} \frac{\omega_o}{2Q} \cos(\varphi_o) \, \delta\varphi \tag{20}$$

As a result, the perturbation $\delta\phi$ will eventually decay to zero for $\cos(\phi_o) > 0$, defining the stable solutions as $\left|\phi_o\right| \leq \pi/2$.

Using a more rigorous mathematical representation, a nonlinear dynamical system such as an oscillator is described by a number of state variables that satisfy a nonlinear differential equation:

$$\dot{\mathbf{v}} = \mathbf{g}(\mathbf{v}, \mathbf{v}_{inj}, \boldsymbol{\mu}) \tag{21}$$

In (21), $\mathbf{v}$ is a vector of the oscillator state variables, $\mathbf{v}_{inj}$ is the injection signal vector and, $\boldsymbol{\mu}$ is a vector of parameters controlling the free running frequency of each oscillator. Most commonly, the Van der Pol cubic nonlinearity model for the oscillator is used in $\mathbf{g}$ (Endo, 1976; York, 1994; Heath, 2004). Considering an almost sinusoidal oscillation by ignoring higher harmonics as low power, the state variables $v_j(t)$ can be written as

$$v_j(t) = V_j(t) \cos(\omega t + \theta_j(t)) \tag{22}$$

where $V_j(t)$ and $\theta_j(t)$ are assumed to be slowly varying functions of time t. Then, one may employ the method of multiple time scales and averaging (Jordan, 1999) to derive a system of first order differential equations for the oscillator amplitude and phase. This methodology, originally applied in oscillator injection locking by Kurokawa (1969,1973), has been extensively used in the study of oscillators and oscillator arrays (Endo, 1976; York, 1994; Heath, 2004; Vanassche, 2003). Defining $\mathbf{x}(t) = \begin{bmatrix} \mathbf{V}(t) & \boldsymbol{\theta}(t) \end{bmatrix}^T$, $\mathbf{x}_{inj}(t) = \begin{bmatrix} \mathbf{V}_{inj}(t) & \boldsymbol{\theta}_{inj}(t) \end{bmatrix}^T$, one obtains the following equation for the oscillator dynamics:

$$\dot{\mathbf{x}} = \mathbf{f}(\mathbf{x}, \mathbf{x}_{inj}, \boldsymbol{\mu}) \tag{23}$$

where the superscript T denotes the transpose operation.

In AIA oscillator arrays, a coupling network is used to help synchronize the oscillators that compose the array. In its simplest form, radiation coupling alone is used to achieve phase locking of the various elements (Kykkotis, 1998). Usually resistive loaded transmission line coupling networks are employed in the literature (Stephan,

1986; Liao, 1993; Nogi, 1993; Auckland, 1997). However, other types of networks have also been considered and studied, such as narrowband networks (Lynch, 2001), and unilateral coupling networks employing amplifiers (Deal, 1997). Assuming an array of N oscillators and letting $\mathbf{X} = \begin{bmatrix} \mathbf{x}_1^T & \mathbf{x}_2^T & \dots & \mathbf{x}_N^T \end{bmatrix}^T$, one has

$$\dot{\mathbf{X}} = \mathbf{H}(\mathbf{X}, \mathbf{X}_{inj}, \boldsymbol{\mu}) = \mathbf{F}(\mathbf{X}, \mathbf{X}_{inj}, \boldsymbol{\mu}) + \mathbf{L}(\mathbf{X}) \tag{24}$$

where $\mathbf{X}_{inj}$ is a vector of injection signals $\mathbf{x}_{inj}$. $\mathbf{L}$ is a linear operator that describes the coupling networks. Operator $\mathbf{F}$ contains the actions of the nonlinear operators $\mathbf{f}$ associated with each oscillator element. The steady state solutions $\mathbf{X}_o$ of (24) are found by setting $\dot{\mathbf{X}} = \mathbf{0}$:

$$\mathbf{H}(\mathbf{X}_o, \mathbf{X}_{inj}, \boldsymbol{\mu}) = \mathbf{F}(\mathbf{X}_o, \mathbf{X}_{inj}, \boldsymbol{\mu}) + \mathbf{L}(\mathbf{X}_o) = \mathbf{0} \tag{25}$$

They correspond to oscillating solutions of common frequency ω. The solution of (25) can be obtained using standard nonlinear algebraic-equation solving algorithms, such as Newton-Raphson (Kundert, 1990; Giannini, 2004).

In the case of weak coupling where $\mathbf{L}(\mathbf{X}) \ll \mathbf{F}(\mathbf{X}, \mathbf{X}_{inj}, \boldsymbol{\mu})$, one may assume that the steady state $\mathbf{X} = \mathbf{X}_o + \delta\mathbf{X} = (\mathbf{X}_u + \Delta\mathbf{X}) + \delta\mathbf{X}$ is only a first order perturbation of the free-running (uncoupled) steady state $\mathbf{X}_u$, given by $\mathbf{F}(\mathbf{X}_u, \mathbf{X}_{inj}, \boldsymbol{\mu}) = \mathbf{0}$, thus obtaining a linear approximation to the array steady state (Georgiadis, 2006)

$$\mathbf{H}_L(\mathbf{X}_u + \Delta\mathbf{X}, \mathbf{X}_{inj}, \boldsymbol{\mu}) = \mathbf{DF}(\mathbf{X}_u, \mathbf{X}_{inj}, \boldsymbol{\mu})\Delta\mathbf{X} + \mathbf{L}(\mathbf{X}_u + \Delta\mathbf{X}) = \mathbf{0} \tag{26}$$

where $\mathbf{DF}(\mathbf{X}, \mathbf{X}_{inj}) = d\mathbf{F}(\mathbf{X}, \mathbf{X}_{inj})/d\mathbf{X}$. The stability of the solutions is evaluated by considering a perturbation $\mathbf{X} = \mathbf{X}_o + \delta\mathbf{X} = (\mathbf{X}_u + \Delta\mathbf{X}) + \delta\mathbf{X}$ leading to

$$\dot{\delta\mathbf{X}} = \mathbf{DH}(\mathbf{X}_o, \mathbf{X}_{inj}, \boldsymbol{\mu})\delta\mathbf{X} \tag{27}$$

where $\mathbf{DH}$ is the Jacobian matrix $\mathbf{DH}(\mathbf{X}_o, \mathbf{X}_{inj}, \boldsymbol{\mu}) = d\mathbf{F}(\mathbf{X}_o, \mathbf{X}_{inj}, \boldsymbol{\mu})/d\mathbf{X} + d\mathbf{L}(\mathbf{X}_o)/d\mathbf{X}$.

Phased Array Operation of Coupled Oscillator Arrays (COAs)

In phased array applications the beam is steered by controlling the phases of the array elements. In the case of a uniform linear array (ULA), a constant phase shift θ among successive elements results in a main beam steering at an angle ψ from broadside (Balanis, 2005) (Figure 3):

$$\theta = -kd \sin(\psi) \tag{28}$$

where k is the wavenumber and d is the distance of the elements. More elaborate beam patterns can be synthesized by controlling both the amplitude and phase of the array elements (Balanis, 2005).

In Stephan (1986), the nonlinear properties of AIA oscillator arrays were used to synthesize constant phase shift distributions among the array elements. As shown in Figure 4a, when a linear array is injected at both ends with two signals of a certain phase difference, a constant phase shift distribution is generated among the array elements. In Liao (1993), it was proved that the desired constant phase shift distribution maybe synthesized by detuning by equal amount and opposite sign the free-running frequency of the array edge elements. In a linear array this means that only 2 elements need to be tuned (Figure 4b), whereas an M x N planar array requires tuning of 2(M+N-2) elements (Pogorzelski, 2001). Alternative methods for electronic scanning of coupled oscillator arrays have also been presented in the literature (Heath, 2004).

Due to the nonlinear nature of oscillator arrays, for every desired phase distribution among the array elements, it is necessary to determine both whether it exists and furthermore, whether it is stable. The maximum stable constant phase difference that can be generated depends greatly on the coupling network, and, also, on the

Figure 3. Uniform linear array (ULA) ($V_1 = V_2 = ... V_N$)

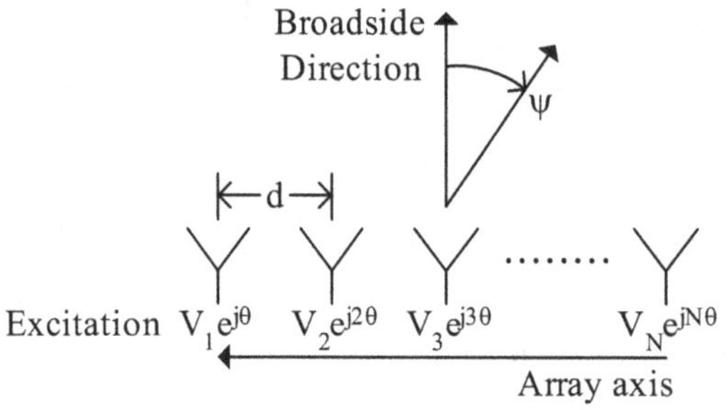

Figure 4. COA configurations. a) constant phase shift distribution generated by injection locking the array edge elements to phase shifted versions of an external signal. b) constant phase shift distribution generated by tuning the free-running frequency of the edge elements. c) arbitrary phase distributions generated by tuning the free-running frequency of all elements. Effect of radiation coupling is mitigated by introducing loading networks at the edge elements. Modulation introduced through injection locking to an external signal

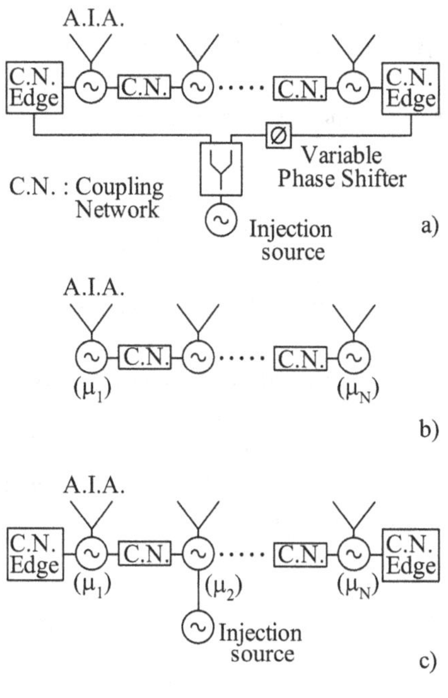

nonlinear properties of the oscillating elements (Endo, 1976; York, 1994; Heath, 2004). It is common to employ resistive loaded transmission line coupling networks (York, 1994) due to their broadband nature and manufacturing simplicity. There have also been reported methods that extend the maximum phase shift range for example by employing unilateral coupling (Deal, 1997; Heath, 2004) or by harmonic radiation (Alexanian, 1995; Sanagi, 2006; Georgiadis, 2007).

In studying coupled oscillator arrays, it is usually assumed that radiation coupling among the elements is significantly less than coupling through the coupling network and it is therefore neglected. However, if not properly accounted for, it can significantly degrade the scanning performance of the array. A simple method to minimize the effect of radiation coupling is to introduce additional loading networks at the array edge elements, as proposed in Ispir (1996) and subsequently used in Georgiadis (2006) (Figure 4c).

As noted in the introduction, oscillating AIAs and arrays are used in transmitter configurations. Due to the limiting properties of the oscillators, amplitude modulation is not suitable for coupled oscillator systems, as they tend to eliminate large amplitude variations (Auckland, 1997; Kykkotis, 1998). However, constant envelope modulations such as continuous phase modulation (CPM) (Proakis, 2000) maybe employed. A simple way to introduce the modulation to the COA is by injection locking one or more elements to an external modulated source (Figure 4c).

Coupled Self-Oscillating Mixer Arrays (CSOMAs)

Frequency conversion coupled oscillator arrays have been used in retro-directive (RA) array implementations. RAs retransmit an interrogating signal back to its source without requiring a priori knowledge of its direction of arrival (DoA) or any signal processing (Figure 5). In the heterodyne mixing technique the incoming signal is mixed using a local oscillator of twice the RF frequency. One of the mixing products has the same frequency as the RF input and its phase reversed. As a result the transmitted signal with its phase reversed at each antenna is being transmitted back to the source (Pon, 1964).

The necessary LO signal for the mixing operation must have the same phase at each mixer. As a result a complicated corporate feed network is usually required. Alternatively, one may use an array of coupled self-oscillating mixers. The SOMs oscillate at twice the RF input frequency and are coupled together using a transmission line coupling network (Shiroma, 2003; Collado, 2006) (Figure 5). The use of SOMs provides a compact and low cost alternative to the use of a complicated LO feed network.

Alternatively, one may also implement upconverting (transmitting) and down-converting (receiving) arrays of SOMs. As it was shown, once the array elements are synchronized by the coupling network, their individual phases can be controlled by changing their free-running frequency through some control voltage of a tuning element such as a varactor diode. The beam-forming capabilities of such SOM arrays have been investigated in the literature (Nogi, 2005).

Constrained Beam-Forming

In addition to controlling the main beam direction, it is possible to generate more elaborate radiation patterns, by controlling the free-running frequency of all the array elements, rather than only the edge ones. In Heath (2001) for example, it was demonstrated that a difference pattern useful in tracking applications can be synthesized. A simple way to introduce nulls in the array factor is by perturbing the phases of the array elements from the constant phase difference values that set the direction of the main beam (Steyskal, 1983). This methodology was first demonstrated for 1D coupled oscillator arrays in Heath (2005).

In Steyskal (1983), the null constraint in the array factor is formulated as a convex optimization problem and solved analytically. In a convex optimization problem, both the optimization objective and the optimization constraints satisfy the property of convexity. There have been a great number of advances in this field over the last two decades in terms of developing powerful algorithms and extending the underlying theory. Once an optimization problem is formulated as a convex one, there exist many efficient algorithms to solve it, much like a linear system of equations (Boyd, 2004). One type of numerical algorithms for solving convex optimization problems is interior-point methods (Boyd, 2004; Nesterov, 1994; Sturm, 1999). Another branch of convex optimization algorithms is based on fixed point theory and set theoretic estimation (Combettes, 1993; Deutsch, 1998). Both of these families of algorithms have found numerous applications in communications and signal processing (Luo, 2006; Stark, 1998). Specifically, interior-point optimization techniques have been applied in antenna beam-forming (Lebret, 1997).

In Georgiadis (2007), the methodology of Heath (2005) was extended to include both amplitude and phase perturbations. Due to the nonlinear nature of the coupled oscillator array the element amplitudes vary according to the array dynamics, and it is more intuitive to allow for amplitude in addition to phase perturbations. Moreover, the problem of simultaneous beam forming and pattern nulling was formulated as a convex optimization problem that, in addition to the nulling constraints, included the array dynamics through (26) as a linear constraint.

Figure 5. Retro-directive array implementation using a coupled self-oscillating mixer (SOM) array

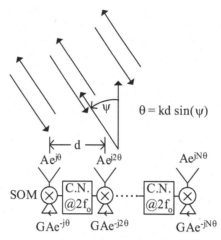

C.N. : Coupling Network

In other words, the beam forming and pattern nulling problem is solved by seeking among the amplitude and phase perturbations that only correspond to existing array steady state solutions. The stability of the solutions is subsequently examined through the perturbation equation (27). The optimization problem is defined as

$$\text{minimize } K(\Delta \mathbf{X}, \boldsymbol{\mu}) = \|\Delta \mathbf{X}\|^2 + \|\boldsymbol{\mu}\|^2 \tag{29a}$$

$$\text{subject to } \mathbf{f}_l \leq \mathbf{A}(\Delta \mathbf{X}) \leq \mathbf{f}_h \tag{29b}$$

$$\mathbf{H}_L(\mathbf{X}_u + \Delta \mathbf{X}, \mathbf{X}_{inj}, \boldsymbol{\mu}) = \mathbf{0} \tag{29c}$$

The pattern nulling constraints are included in (29b) (Georgiadis, 2007).

The radiation pattern of a thirteen element linear COA, optimized using (29) in order to steer the main beam at -10 deg from broadside, while accommodating two radiation nulls at 20 deg and 45 deg is shown in Figure 6.

CONCLUSION

The implementation of a true software radio (Mitola, 1995) that would ideally enable the coexistence of multiple wireless networks is becoming more and more feasible due to recent advances in digital technology, as well as signal processing and optimization theory and algorithms. In this context, intelligent multi-antenna systems employing smart antenna techniques are increasingly being used in modern communication systems. Due to their advantages over single antenna systems, they provide a capability for new applications that require large bandwidths while maintaining a high quality of service (QoS), and facilitate the coexistence of heterogeneous wireless networks.

Furthermore, novel analog front-ends are also being investigated in an attempt to maximize energy efficiency and minimize cost. Advances in simulation of nonlinear circuits have allowed for new applications and more accurate modelling and design of nonlinear AIAs and AIA arrays. The nonlinear properties of such arrays have demonstrated their potential for narrowband, smart antenna communication systems applications. As an example, adaptive beam-forming implementations of COA and SOM arrays have been proposed (Nogi, 2005;

Figure 6. Constrained beam-forming example of a thirteen element linear COA. The main beam is steered to -10 deg. Two additional nulls are imposed in the radiation pattern at 20 deg and 45 deg

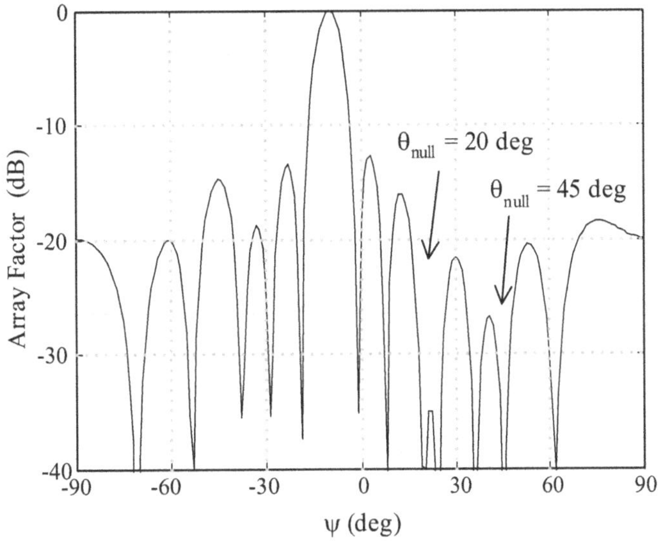

Ikuma, 2006), and communication systems based on retro-directive arrays in multi-path fading environments have been considered (Tuovinen, 2003).

ACKNOWLEDGMENT

The authors would like to thank Dr. Ana Pérez, Dr. Xavi Mestre and Dr. Christian Ibars for their contributions in the description of MIMO channels, and Dr. Ana Collado for providing insightful suggestions during the preparation of the manuscript.

REFERENCES

Adler, R. (1946). A study of locking phenomena in oscillators. *Proceedings IRE Waves and Electrons*, 34, 351–357.

Alexanian, A., Chang, H.C., & York, R.A. (1995). Enhanced scanning range in coupled oscillator arrays utilizing frequency multipliers. In IEEE, *Antennas and Progagation Symposium Digest*, (pp. 1308-1310). Newport Beach, CA: IEEE.

Appelbaum, S.P. (1976). Adaptive arrays, *IEEE Transactions on Antennas and Propagation*, 5, 585–598.

Auckland, D.T., Lilly, J., & York, R.A. (1997). Analysis of beam scanning and data rate transmission performance of a coupled oscillator phased array. In IEE, *Tenth International Conference on Antennas and Propagation, Conf. Publ. No. 436* (pp. 245-249). Edinburgh: IEE.

Balanis, C.A. (2005). *Antenna Theory: Analysis and Design*, 3rd Ed., New York NY: John Wiley and Sons.

Boyd, S., & Vandenberghe, L. (2004). *Convex Optimization*, New York NY: Cambridge University Press.

Capon, J., Greenfield, R. J., & Kolker, R. J. (1967), Multidimensional maximum-likelihood processing for a large aperture seismic array, *Proceedings IEEE*, 55, 192–211.

Chang, K., York, R.A., Hall, P.S., & Itoh, T. (2002). Active integrated antennas. *IEEE Transactions on Microwave Theory and Techniques*, 50(3), 937-944.

Collado, A., Georgiadis, A., & Suarez, A. (2006). Optimized Design of Retro-Directive Arrays Based on Self-Oscillating Mixers using Harmonic-Balance and Conversion-Matrix Techniques. In IEEE, *MTT-S International Microwave Symposium* (pp. 1125-1128), San Francisco, CA: IEEE.

Combettes, P.L. (1993). The foundations of set theoretic estimation. *Proceedins of the IEEE*, 81(2), 182-208.

Cox, H., Zeskind, R.M., & Owen, M.M. (1987). Robust adaptive beamforming, *IEEE Transactions on Acoustics, Speech, and Signal Processing*, 35(10), 1365–1376.

Deal, W.R., &, Itoh, T. (1997). An Active Phased Array With Optical Control And Beam-scanning Capability. In IEEE, *International Topical Meeting on Microwave Photonics (MWP)* (pp.175-178). Duisburg/Essen: IEEE.

Deutsch, F., & Yamada, I. (1998). Minimizing certain convex functions over the intersection of the fixed poit sets of nonexpansive mappings. *Numerical Functional Analysis and Optimization*, 19, 33-56.

Endo, T., & Mori, S. (1976). Mode analysis of a multimode ladder oscillator. *IEEE Transactions on Circuits and Systems*, 23(2), 100-113.

Feldman, D., & Griffiths, L.J. (1994). A projection approach for robust adaptive beamforming, *IEEE Transactions on Signal Processing*, 42(4), 867–876.

Feldman, D. (1996). An analysis of the projection method for robust adaptive beamforming, *IEEE Transactions on Antennas and Propagation*, 44(7), 1023–1030.

Fernández Prades, C. (2006). *Advanced Signal Processing Techniques for Global Navigation Satellite System Receivers*, doctoral dissertation, Universitat Politècnica de Catalunya (UPC), Barcelona, Spain.

Foschini, G.J., & Gans, M.J., (1998). On limits of wireless communications in a fading environment when using multiple antennas, *Wireless Personal Communications*, 6(3), 311-335, 1998.

Georgiadis, A. (2007). Design of Coupled Oscillator Arrays for Second Harmonic Radiation. In IEEE, *MTT-S International Microwave Symposium* (pp. 1727-1730), Honolulu, HI: IEEE.

Georgiadis, A., Collado, A. & Suarez, A. (2006). New Techniques for the analysis and design of coupled-oscillator systems. *IEEE Transactions on Microwave Theory and Techniques*, 54(11), 3864-3877.

Georgiadis, A., Collado, A. & Suarez, A. (2007). Pattern nulling in coupled oscillator antenna arrays. *IEEE Transactions on Antennas and Propagation,*55(5), 1267-1274.

Georgiadis, A., & Suarez, A. (2006). Nonlinear Synthesis of a Linear Active Oscillator Antenna Array Using Harmonic Balance and EM Simulation. In IEEE, *International Workshop on Integrated Nonlinear Microwave and Millimeter-Wave Circuits (INMMIC)* (pp. 176-179). Aveiro: IEEE.

Gershman, A.B. (2003, September). *Robust adaptive beamforming: an overview of recent trends and advances in the field*. Paper presented at the International Conference on Antenna Theory and Techniques, Sevastopol, Ukraine.

Giannini, F., & Leuzzi, G. (2004). *Nonlinear Microwave Circuit Design*, New York NY: John Wiley and Sons.

Haykin, S. (1996) *Adaptive Filter Theory*, Upper Saddle River, NJ: Prentice Hall.

Heath, T. (2001). Difference pattern beam steering of coupled, nonlinear oscillator arrays. *IEEE Microwave and Wireless Components Letters*, 11(8), 343-345.

Heath, T. (2004). Beam steering of nonlinear oscillator arrays through manipulation of coupling phases. *IEEE Transactions on Antennas and Propagation*, 52(7), 1833–1842.

Heath, T. (2005). Simulatneous beam steering and null formation with coupled, nonlinear oscillator arrays. *IEEE Transactions on Antennas and Propagation*, 53(6), 2031–2035.

Ikuma, T., Beex, A.A., Zeidler, J.R., & Meadows, B.K. (2006). Adaptive interference mitigation with a coupled nonlinear oscillator array beamformer. In IEEE, *Aerospace Conference* (pp. 13-26).

Ispir, R., Nogi, S., Sanagi, M., & Fukui, K. (1996). Transmission Line Coupled Active Microstrip Antennas for PhaseArrays. In IEEE, *MTT-S International Microwave Symposium* (pp. 931-934). San Francisco, CA: IEEE.

Jordan, D. W., & Smith, P. (1999). *Nonlinear Ordinary Differential Equations: an introduction to dynamical systems*, 3rd Ed., Oxford: Oxford University Press.

Lebret, H., & Boyd, S. (1997), Antenna array pattern synthesis via convex optimization. *IEEE Transactions on Signal Processing*, 45(3), 526-532.

Kurokawa, K. (1969). Some basic characteristics of broadband resistance oscillator circuits. *Bell System Technical Journal*, 1937-1955.

Kurokawa, K. (1973). Injection locking of microwave solid-state oscillators. *Proceedings of the IEEE*, 61(10), 1386- 1410.

Kundert, K.S., White, J.K., & Sangiovanni-Vincentelli, A.L. (1990). *Steady-state Methods for Simulating Analog and Microwave Circuits*. The Springer International Series in Engineering and Computer Science , Vol. 94, New York, NY: Springer.

Kykkotis, C., Hall, P.S., & Ghafouri-Shiraz, H. (1998). Performace of active antenna oscillator arrays under modulation for communication systems. *IEE Proceedings on Microwaves, Antennas and Propagation,* 142(4), 313–320.

Lagunas, M.A., & Pérez-Neira, A. (2006, November). *Antenna Arrays: What does it mean a good channel?* Paper presented at the first European Conference on Antennas and Propagation (EuCAP 2006), Nice, France.

Lai, X., & Roychowdhury, J. (2004). Capturing oscillator injection locking via nonlinear phase-domain macro-models. *IEEE Transactions on Microwave Theory and Techniques*, 52(9), 2251- 2261.

Lebret, H., & Boyd, S.P. (1997). Antenna array pattern synthesis via convex optimization, *IEEE Transactions on Signal Processing*, 45(3), 526–532.

Liao, P., & York, R.A. (1993). A new phase-shifterless beam-scanning technique using arrays of coupled oscillators. *IEEE Transactions on Microwave Theory and Techniques*, 41(10), 1810-1815.

Lin, J. & Itoh, T. (1994). Active integrated antennas. *IEEE Transactions on Microwave Theory and Techniques*, 42(12), 2186-2194.

Lynch, J.J. , & York, R.A., (2001). Synchronization of oscillators coupled through narrow-band networks. *IEEE Transactions on Microwave Theory and Techniques*, 49(2), 237-249.

Luo, Z.-Q., & Yu, W. (2006). An introduction to convex optimization for communications and signal processing. *IEEE Journal on Selected Areas in Communications*, 24(8), 1426-1438.

Lorenz, R.G., & Boyd, S.P. (2005). Robust minimum variance beamforming, *IEEE Transactions on Signal Processing*, 53(5), 1684–1696.

Mitola, J. (1995). The software radio architecture, *IEEE Communications Magazine*, 33(5), 26-38.

Monzingo, R.A., & Miller, T.W. (1980). *Introduction to Adaptive Arrays*, New York: John Wiley & Sons.

Navarro, J.A., & Chang, K. (1996). *Integrated Active Antennas and Spatial Power Combining*, New York NY: John Wiley and Sons.

Nesterov, Y., & Nemirovskii, A. (1994). *Interior Point Polynomial Methods in Convex Programming.* vol. 13, Studies in Applied Mathematics. Philadelphia, PA: SIAM.

Nogi, S., Lin, J., & Itoh, T. (1993). Mode analysis and stabilization of a spatial power combining array with strongly coupled oscillators. *IEEE Transactions on Microwave Theory and Techniques,* 41(10), 1827-1837.

Nogi, S., Sanagi, M., & Fujimori, K. (2005). Active integrated antenna techniques for beam control. *IEICE Transactions on Electronics*, E88-C(7), 1358-1367.

Nogi, S., Sanagi, M., & Fujimori, K. (2005). Beam control in unilaterally coupled active antennas with self-oscillating harmonic mixers. *IEICE Transactions on Electro*nics, E88-C(7), 1375-1381.

Pascual Iserte, A. (2005) *Channel State Information and Joint Transmitter-Receiver Design in Multi-Antenna Systems*, doctoral dissertation, Universitat Politècnica de Catalunya (UPC), Barcelona, Spain.

Pascual Iserte, A., Payaró, M., Pérez Neira, A.I., & Lagunas, M.A. (2006, July). *Impact of a line of sight component on the performance of a MIMO system designed under statistical channel knowledge.* Paper presented at the IEEE 7th International Workshop on Signal Processing Advances in Wireless Communications (SPAWC), Cannes, France.

Payaró, M., Pascual Iserte, A., Pérez Neira, A.I., & Lagunas, M.A. (2005, June). *Flexible MIMO Architectures: Guidelines in the design of MIMO parameters.* Paper presented at the IEEE 6th International Workshop on Signal Processing Advances in Wireless Communications (SPAWC), New York (USA).

Pogorzelski, R.J. (2001). On the dynamics of two-dimensional array beam scanning via perimeter detuning of coupled oscillator arrays. *IEEE Transactions on Antennas and Propagation,* 49(2), 234-242.

Pogorzelski, R.J. (2003). On the design of coupling networks for coupled oscillator arrays. *IEEE Transactions on Antennas and Propagation*, 51(4), 794-801.

Pon, C., (1964). Retrodirective array using the heterodyne technique. *IEEE Transactions on Antennas and Propagation*, 12(2), 176-180.

Proakis, J.G. (2000). *Digital Communications*, 4rd Ed., New York NY: McGraw Hill.

Qian, Y., & Itoh, T. (1998). Progress in active integrated antennas and their applications. *IEEE Transactions on Microwave Theory and Techniques*, 46(11), 1891-1900.

Rizzoli, V., Costanzo, A., Masotti, D., Lipparini, A., & Mastri, F. (2004). Computer-aided optimization of nonlinear microwave circuits with the aid of electromagnetic simulation. *IEEE Transactions on Microwave Theory and Techniques*, 52(1), 362-377.

Sanagi, M., Kano, K., Fujimori, K., & Nogi, S. (2006). Active phased array antenna radiating second harmonic output wave. *Electronics and Communications in Japan (Part II:Electronics),* 89(4), 39-50.

Seco, G., Fernández Rubio, J.A., & Fernández Prades, C. (2005). ML estimator and Hybrid Beamformer for multipath and interference mitigation in GNSS receivers. *IEEE Transactions on Signal Processing*, 53(3), 1194–1208.

Shahbazpanahi, S., Gershman, A.B, Luo, Z.Q., & Wong, K.M. (2003). Robust adaptive beamforming for general–rank signal models. *IEEE Transactions on Signal Processing*, 51(9), 2257–2269.

Shin, H. & Lee, J.H. (2003). Capacity of multiple-antenna fading channels: spatial fading correlation, double scattering and keyhole, *IEEE Transactions on Information Theory*, 49(10), 2636-2647.

Shiroma, G.S., Miyamoto, R.Y., & Shiroma, W.A. (2003). A 16-element two-dimensional active self-steering array using self-oscillating mixers. *IEEE Transactions on Microwave Theory and Techniques*, 51(12), 2476-2482.

Stark, H., & Yang, Y. (1998). *Vector Space Projections: A Numerical Approach to Signal and Image Processing, Neural Nets, and Optics*, New York NY: John Wiley and Sons.

Stephan, K.D. (1986). Inter-Injection-Locked Oscillators for Power Combining and Phased Arrays. *IEEE Transactions on Microwave Theory and Techniques,* 34(10), 1017-1025.

Steyskal, H. (1983). Simple method for pattern nulling by phase perturbation. *IEEE Transactions on Antennas and Propagation*, AP-31(1), 163-166.

Sturm, J.F. (1999). Using SeDuMi 1.02, a MATLAB toolbox for optimization over symmetric cones. *Optimization Methods and Software,* 11-12, 625-653.

Telatar, E. (1999). Capacity of Multi-antenna Gaussian Channels, *European Transactions on Telecommunications*, 10(6), 585-595.

Tuovinen, J., Shiroma, G.S., Forsyth, W.E., & Shiroma, W.A. (2003). Multipath communications using a phase-conjugate array. In IEEE, *MTT-S International Microwave Symposium* (pp. 1681-1684). Philadelphia, PA: IEEE.

York, R.A., Liao P., & Lynch, J.J. (1994). Oscillator array dynamics with broadband N-port coupling networks. *IEEE Transactions on Microwave Theory and Techniques*, 42(11), 2040–2042.

Van Trees, H.L. (2002) *Optimum Array Processing. Detection, Estimation and Modulation Theory, Part IV*, New York: Wiley Interscience.

Van Veen, B.D., & Buckley, K.M. (1988) Beamforming: A versatile approach to spatial filtering, *IEEE Signal Processing Magazine*, 5(2), 4–24.

Vanassche, P., Gielen, G.G.E., & Sansen, W. (2003). Behavioral modeling of (coupled) harmonic oscillators. *IEEE Transactions on Computer-Aided Design of Integrated Circuits and Systems*, 22(8), 1017-1026.

Viswanath, P., Tse, D.N.C., & Laroia, R. (2002). Opportunistic beamforming using dumb antennas. *IEEE Transactions on Information Theory*, 48(6), 1277-1294.

Vorobyov, S.A., Gershman, A.B., & Luo, Z.Q. (2003). Robust adaptive beamforming using worst–case performance optimization: A solution to the signal mismatch problem. *IEEE Transactions on Signal Processing*, 51(2), 313–324.

Wax, M., & Anu, Y. (1996) Performance analysis of the minimum variance beamformer, *IEEE Transactions on Signal Processing*, 44(4), 928–937.

Youn, W.S., & Un, C.K. (1994). Robust adaptive beamforming based on the eigenstructure method, *IEEE Transactions on Signal Processing*, 42(6), 1543–1547.

KEY TERMS

Active Integrated Antenna: An active integrated antenna (AIA) consists of a passive radiating element and an active circuit, integrated in the same substrate.

Beamforming: Beamforming with antenna arrays is a technique that consists of several antennas whose outputs are controlled in phase and gain, i.e., multiplied by complex weights, in order to achieve a gain pattern that can be manipulated electronically.

Channel Capacity: Amount of bits per second that can be transmitted in a reliable way by a communications channel.

Channel State Information: Knowledge about the communication channel matrix, which relates the transmitted and the received signals.

Coupled Oscillator Array: A nonlinear dynamical system formed by an array of oscillators coupled through a coupling network.

Multiple-Input Multiple-Output (MIMO) System: A system in which there are multiple antennas available simultaneously at the transmitter and the receiver.

Phased Array: An array of antennas in which the relative phases of the radiated signals are controlled in order to steer the main lobe of the radiation pattern towards a desired direction and minimize radiation towards undesired directions.

Retro-Directive Array: A retro-directive array is capable of re-transmitting an interrogating signal back to its source without requiring a priori knowledge of its direction of arrival (DoA) or any signal processing.

Self-Oscillating Mixer: A circuit that has the functionality of both a mixer and an oscillator. Usually, one first designs an oscillator and subsequently optimizes it to provide mixer conversion gain.

Spatial Diversity: Redundancy introduced in the system, generated by sampling the spatial domain using different antennas

Chapter XV
Simulation of Small–Scale Fading in Mobile Channel Models for Next–Generation Wireless Communications

Stelios A. Mitilineos
National Center for Scientific Research, "Demokritos," Greece

Christos N. Capsalis
National Technical University of Athens, Greece

Stelios C.A. Thomopoulos
National Center for Scientific Research, "Demokritos," Greece

ABSTRACT

Small-scale fading strongly affects the performance of a radio link; therefore radio channel simulation tools and models are broadly being used in order to evaluate the impact of fading. Furthermore, channel simulation tools and models are considered to be of utmost importance for efficient design and development of new products and services for Next Generation (Wireless) Networks (NGNs and NGWNs). In this chapter, a brief description of the most popular and broadly accepted mobile radio channel models and simulation techniques is given, mainly with respect to small-scale fading. In addition, certain research results on radio channel simulation are presented. The authors hope that the information provided herein will help researchers to acquire an insight to small-scale fading simulation techniques, which will be useful for a solid understanding of the underlying physical layer properties of NGWNs.

I. INTRODUCTION

According to the ITU definition [ITU, 2004], a Next Generation Network (NGN) is principally an heterogeneous network. NGNs are packet and IP-based networks, able of providing services (such as navigation or telecommunications services) using multiple broadband transport technologies, while service-related functions are independent from the underlying transport technologies. A user of a NGN enjoys different services from different providers

Copyright © 2009, IGI Global, distributing in print or electronic forms without written permission of IGI Global is prohibited.

seamlessly, anytime, anywhere (ubiquitous computing – ubiquitous communications). From a business-oriented point of view, NGNs will allow unrestricted access by users to different service providers; a specification that is expected to bring revolutionary effects to business models and functionality of all information and communication technology (ICT) enterprises. One of these effects is the already noticed unification of business sectors that were separated until now, like fixed and mobile telephony, internet and entertainment. From the user point of view, this means that she will be able of watching a streaming-video movie or placing a transatlantic call through a unique internet provider, or watching the weather forecast and hear her favourite songs from her mobile phone on the way to work. Furthermore, NGNs will naturally comply with all current and future regulatory requirements, regarding e.g. emergency communications (E-112 or E-911 for E.U. and U.S.A. respectively), or security and privacy/ethical issues, etc.

The heterogeneity of NGNs consists in services as well as physical networks. NGNs will offer a wide range of services, from relatively simple voice telephony and data transfer, to more demanding applications like streaming video, virtual private networks, public network computing or unified messaging. Furthermore, several futuristic services have been proposed like interactive and location-based gaming, distributed virtual reality, remote home/office management etc. The ultimate goal is nowadays considered to be the full integration of navigation and communications networks in order to provide exotic new services to end users [Ruggieri, 2006]. On the other hand, as long as physical networks are concerned, NGNs will comprise of lines ranging from simple PSTN to DSL broadband in wired cases, and from 2G to 4G cellular or WLAN, WiMAX, Wireless Sensor Networks, and other more exotic ones like interplanetary internet [Akan 2004], in wireless cases. This means that NGNs will be capable of seamlessly internetworking through legacy and broadband networks and will be characterized by generalized mobility. So far, the only means of achieving these goals is considered to be an all-IP approach, i.e. using the IP protocol in order to interconnect the most diverse devices and networks; therefore NGNs are often referred to all-IP networks as well, while the IPv6 protocol is expected to significantly contribute towards this direction (Dixit, 2006). At the same time, the most attractive physical layer means of implementing NGNs is via wireless infrastructure and/or ad-hoc networks (Next Generation Wireless Networks, NGWNs) in conjunction with gigabit-per-second order throughput wired infrastructures. Even in the case of wired NGNs, digital content is expected to be delivered to the end user via mobile handheld devices (mobile phones, palmtops, VoIP wireless phones etc.).

The critical finding regarding the wireless nature of NGNs is the main motivation for writing this chapter. It is more than evident that, since NGNs will basically consist of wireless and mobile networks, it is critical for engineers and researchers to obtain a solid understanding of the underlying wireless propagation medium of digital content delivery. Certainly, the wireless propagation channel is a very broad field of research, therefore we shall mainly hold back to small-scale fading attributes, which strongly affect the performance of a radio link. A presentation of the most popular and broadly accepted mobile radio channel models will be given, with respect to small-scale fading. On the other hand, it is also critical to be able to evaluate the performance of a telecommunications system under design or development. Analytic formulas for the calculation of critical channel characteristics are not available or are difficult to be extracted for state-of-the-art or beyond state-of-the-art radio channel models; therefore, simulation arises as the main tool for design and development. Therefore, the principles of small-scale fading simulation will be discussed and a number of simulation techniques and tools will be presented. Finally, certain research results regarding channel simulation will be illustrated. The authors hope that the information provided herein will help researchers to acquire an insight to small-scale fading simulation techniques, which will be useful for designing and developing NGWNs.

II. SIMULATION: DEFINITIONS AND CATEGORIZATION

Simulation may be defined as artificial reality, i.e. that research field whose intention is to mimic one or more attributes of reality (Jeruchim, 1992). The means of simulation, or simulation platform, is usually (and hereinafter) considered to be a computer system.

The complexity of communications and signal processing systems, as well as the increasing demand for telecommunications services, has led to significant efforts in order to accelerate *and* reduce the cost of the design and development of new products and services. Simulation is proposed as a useful approach which can allow the testing of brainstorming results and design proposals before a prototype is implemented or put to production line. Furthermore, simulation may offer a reference platform, which may be used in order to compare different techniques and algorithms, such as modulation techniques, smart antennas convergence algorithms, adaptive equalization algorithms, multiple access schemes, BER, diversity receivers, transmission strategies and other (Kotsopoulos, 2000; Karagiannidis, 2005; Sagias, 2005; Bithas 2007; Toumpakaris 2007). Another one of the advantages of using simulation is the large cutoff in resources spent in all stages of development. Therefore, it is not surprising that the simulation of telecommunications systems is widespread, and that the research and industry communities spend a large amount of time and money in order to develop efficient simulation tools.

The evaluation of a proposed solution may be accomplished via closed-form equations or numerical calculations, simulation, and implementation and measurement of a prototype. In practice, it usually comes out that an optimum combination of these three approaches must be followed. More specifically, closed-form equations may be used in order to assess a large number of candidate solutions during initial design stages. Of course, the assessment of complex systems and techniques is impossible by using equations and numerical calculations only. Therefore, during the middle design stages, simulation may be used in order to evaluate the most promising solutions. In these stages, simulation models are used that mimic the reality to the desired degree of complexity. In final stages, a prototype may be implemented and measured. Usually, a closed loop of simulation, prototype implementation and measurement, revision, re-calculation, re-implementation and so on is established until the desired outcome is reached.

In all cases, system designers' attention must be pointed out to the desired degree of detail in representing reality. In many applications, the exaggerated request for detailed representation will render the simulation time enormous without offering any advantages with respect to the simulation subject of research. Simulation time, which is the time needed in order to complete the simulation of a system, is the main criterion for evaluating a simulation tool – along with the accuracy of results of course!

The models and techniques for channel simulation are herein divided into three broad categories: in-situ measurements models, statistical and geometric models, and deterministic models. In the literature, there is an ambiguity with respect to statistical models (usually referred to as empirical models as well). Some authors consider that statistical modeling is the procedure of channel measurement for various transmitter-receiver placements and probability curve fitting to the experimental data. Others consider statistical modeling as arising from a geometric channel description which concludes to a statistical model. In fact, a statistical model that arises from a geometric description may be validated via measurements. On the other hand, a measurements campaign usually ends up with a statistical model, but this model does not correspond to a natural or geometric description or attribute of the channel, but rather is a best-curve fitting procedure. As an example, consider the Okumura-Hata model for the mean attenuation in macrocells (Okumura, 1968; Hata, 1980), or the Weibull PDF for the time interval between pulses time of arrival in wideband channel models (Yegani, 1991).

Herein, we adopt the assumption that channel measurements and curve fitting are categorized as in-situ measurements based modeling. On the other hand, we consider statistical modeling as either the direct utilization of PDFs for various channel attributes, such as Direction-of-Arrival (DoA), signal strength, Doppler spread and Doppler spectrum, etc., or the utilization of geometric channel models which are used in order to extract a desired channel attribute's PDF. Theoretical distributions often need to be validated via in-situ measurements, but this discrimination is used for clarity. Finally, there is another channel modeling category used, namely deterministic channel modeling (also referred to as site-specific propagation prediction). In this case, topographical maps or architectural plans of a specific site are used and conclusions are drawn up for the channel based on these data. Again, a deterministic model may be validated by in-situ measurements or a statistical model and so on. Finally, we consider that the objective of all types of modeling is the extraction of a statistical description of the radio channel with appropriate PDFs.

The discrimination among channel models to three broad categories is applied not only to mean attenuation but to small and large scale fading models as well, e.g., the mean attenuation may be calculated by in-situ measurements in a specific site. The experimental data may then be approximated by closed-form PDFs. For that reason, one of the available mean attenuation models may be utilized, e.g. Okumura-Hata models (Okumura, 1968; Hata, 1980), Lee models (Lee, 1986), etc. On the other hand, in-situ measurements may be avoided (with the respective impact to accuracy), and various statistical models be used instead. Finally, topographical maps and propagation prediction tools may also be used.

Similar procedures may be followed during large scale fading modeling. A possible statistical model in this case is that of Gudmundson (Gudmundson, 1991). However, as long as the deterministic modeling of large scale fading is concerned, this requires more detailed topographical data and larger resolution than in the mean attenuation case.

Finally, as long as small scale fading is concerned, various statistical properties may be calculated via in-situ measurements. These include Doppler, delay and angle spread, coherence time, bandwidth and distance, level crossing rate, average fade duration, etc. Also, it is possible to extract PDFs regarding the power and the complex envelope amplitude of the signal, the delay of arrivals, etc. Furthermore, it is possible to use geometric models or a priori PDFs in order to model fading. On the other hand, deterministic models have not yet been extensively used in order to model small scale fading, due to large detail depth and resolution of the digital representation of the actual environment that are required. Also, it is not easy to extract statistical conclusions regarding the effect of furniture, people moving around, etc., since the simulation time may become prohibitive for large and complex environments. Nevertheless, the ever growing computational power offers the possibility to present deterministic modeling solutions for small scale fading, as will be described later, but always under the constraint that the environment models are kept simple. In order for more complex environments, statistical analysis is proven more useful and is used more often in practical cases.

III. CHANNEL MEASUREMENTS

In-situ measurements may be performed in order to model a specific site. Depending on whether the signal measured is narrowband or wideband, mobile channel measurements deal with different channel and signal attributes. Narrowband signal measurements are usually related to frequency flat fading, while the ideal narrowband signal is an unmodulated carrier. To the contrary, wideband signal measurements usually refer to frequency selective fading, while the ideal wideband signal is a delta impulse function.

In narrowband signal measurements, it is usually the mean attenuation and power fluctuations that are of concern. Narrowband measurements and models do not offer information about the distribution of the delay of arrival or the power-delay profile, since it is considered that the respective delay differences are very small. They rather offer a statistical characterization of signal phase and Doppler shifts of the incoming signal components. As a result, they are used in order to calculate the attenuation factor β, the rms Doppler spread v_{RMS}, the PDF of the signal envelope, the level crossing rate and fade duration, etc. Then, the envelope's PDF may be used in order to calculate the Bit Error Rate (BER), Doppler spread may be used in order to calculate the level crossing rate, etc. Narrowband measurements are implemented by transmitting an unmodulated carrier and using appropriate measuring instruments, which have the capability of performing repetitive measurements with a high refresh rate (Pahlavan, 1995).

To the contrary, wideband measurements are mainly used in order to characterize the phenomenon of multipath fading itself. Using this type of measurements, we can calculate the number of different paths of the incoming signal components, the delay and mean power of each path (component), as well as the power PDF for each path. Thus, wideband measurements do rather simulate the delay distribution and power-delay profile, i.e. essentially the impulse response of the channel. The impulse response is measured either directly, by transmitting a very narrow pulse in the time domain (ideally a delta signal) and sounding the channel, or by measuring the frequency response of the channel for a large bandwidth and then calculating the impulse response via inverse Fourier transform (usually Inverse Fast Fourier Transform – IFFT). In any case, the achieved resolution is inversely proportional to the bandwidth of the transmitted signal.

An alternative method for measuring the impulse response is based on transmitting an inherently wideband pseudo-random sequence, such as a spread-spectrum sequence (e.g. direct-sequence spread spectrum), and then calculating the correlation of the received and transmitted signal. The result will be the channel impulse response. If the duration of each sequence chip (a "chip" is herein the "bit" of the pseudorandom signal modulating sequence) is sufficiently small in order to obtain the desired resolution, and at the same time the sequence period is sufficiently large in order to be able to detect large delays, such a system may replace the direct pulse sounding method. This method is considered to be preferable in the case of wide area networks (PCS, macrocells) because it offers stronger coverage than the direct pulse sounding method. On the contrary, the direct pulse sounding method is considered to offer better resolution, and thus it is preferred in small area networks (WLANs, micro- and pico-cells) (Pahlavan, 1995).

The interested reader may refer to the literature, where there have been reported interesting results regarding channel measurements and statistical modeling by various researchers, such as Alexander (Alexander, 1982), Saleh and Valenzuela (Saleh, 1987), Rappaport (Rappaport, 1989), Pahlavan et al. (Pahlavan, 1989), Hashemi and Tholl (Hashemi, 1994), Kim et al. (Kim, 1996), and other.

IV.   GEOMETRIC MODELS

Geometric models are based on abstract geometric characteristics of the propagation environment, which are common to mobile channels of the same type. In essence, they are a subset of the statistical channel models category, since they inevitably end up to specific distributions for the angle of arrival, the power to angle of arrival distribution, the signal envelope etc. However, geometric models are of special importance, since they are based on the channel's natural characteristics and offer an intuitive insight to the channel propagation mechanisms. Some of the most popular geometric models are presented herein.

Ossana's Model

Ossana's model assumes a flat power spectrum and the existence of a LOS component between transmitter and receiver (Ossana, 1964). Thus, Ossana's model is not useful for the majority of cellular systems, where there usually exist NLOS conditions.

Clarke's Model

A broadly accepted model for small-scale fading is Clarke's model (Clarke, 1968), which results to Rayleigh type fading (it is also reported in the literature as GBSBCM model (Liberti, 1999)).

This model assumes the existence of a dense ring of scatterers surrounding the mobile receiver, as well as a uniform distribution for the angle of arrival and phase of each incoming component. The amplitudes of all incoming components are equal to one another (isotropical scattering). This model is presented in Figure 1, where it is assumed that $d_1 > r$. It can be used in order to model macrocell channels, such as GSM and outdoor environment systems, where the transmitter is placed at a much greater height than the receiver. Therefore, all scatterers are densely distributed around the receiver, while there is none or very few scatterers around the transmitter.

The signal envelope in this case is shown to follow a Rayleigh distribution, having the classic Doppler spectrum given by (Liberti, 1999; Stuber, 2001)

$$S_{rr}(v) = \begin{cases} \dfrac{\Omega_p}{4\pi v_m} \dfrac{1}{\sqrt{1-[(v-f_c)/v_m]^2}} & ,|v-f_c| \le v_m \\ 0 & ,|v-f_c| \ge v_m \end{cases} \tag{1}$$

In the case of a Ricean type channel, the Doppler spectrum additionally includes a delta function with amplitude proportional to the K-factor, which function corresponds to the Doppler shift (and related to the angle of arrival) of the LOS component.

Furthermore, Figure 1 may be used in order to model the signal received by the Base Station (BS) (Jakes, 1994). In this case, the power to angle of arrival profile will be concentrated around the angle θ_1 (it is reminded that the principle of reciprocity should be carefully applied when it comes to the spatial characteristics of the wireless radio channel (Paulraj, 2003)).

Figure 1. Clarke's model for cellular systems

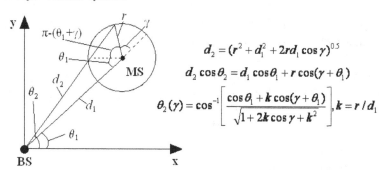

$$d_2 = (r^2 + d_1^2 + 2rd_1 \cos \gamma)^{0.5}$$

$$d_2 \cos \theta_2 = d_1 \cos \theta_1 + r \cos(\gamma + \theta_1)$$

$$\theta_2(\gamma) = \cos^{-1} \left[\frac{\cos \theta_1 + k \cos(\gamma + \theta_1)}{\sqrt{1 + 2k \cos \gamma + k^2}} \right], k = r / d_1$$

Elliptical Models

Elliptical models represent the radio channel by assuming that all scatterers are placed on one or more ellipses surrounding the transmitter and receiver, and that the foci of these ellipses coincide with the transmitter and receiver positions. A schematic representation of this category of models is shown in Figure 2. The elliptical models apply in cases where the transmitter and receiver have similar heights to one another, therefore the scatterers may be assumed to be placed densely around not only the receiver but the transmitter as well. These cases include micro- and pico-cell channels, such as indoor environment networks (e.g. WLANs etc.)

In the case of frequency flat fading, the differences among the delays of each signal component are negligible as long as the component's phase is *not* concerned. All scatterers may be modeled as being placed on an ellipse which surrounds both transmitter and receiver, as shown in Figure 2a. The main difference between this model and Jakes' model is that, despite the fact that the distribution of Angle-of-Departure (AoD) and power to AoD profile is uniform at the transmitter, the Angle-of-Arrival (AoA) and power to AoA distribution is not uniform at the receiver. Consequently, the Doppler spectrum is different than the one given by equation (1). Small differences in the scatterers placements on the ellipse result to large differences to the phase of the incoming component, therefore the phase of each component is still considered to be uniformly distributed.

In frequency selective channels, the scatterers are grouped to different ellipses, and the channel is modeled as the sum of multiple frequency flat channels, as shown in Figure 2b. In urban and suburban environments these ellipses may e.g. correspond to nearby scatterers like high buildings on the one hand, and faraway morphology characteristics like mountains etc. on the other hand. The ellipses are usually considered to be discrete, i.e. the model consists of a number of discrete ellipses, each of which corresponds to a different delay. This channel corresponds to a tapped delay line filter, as in Figure 3. This is due to the fact that all signals that are reflected from a particular ellipse arrive at the receiver having almost the same delay, no matter what the AoA or AoD are.

On the other hand, there are cases where a continuous ellipses assumption is more applicable, like in tropospheric scattering or some mobile channels. In this case, the model may also be represented by a tapped delay line filter, but the delays are now multiples of a differential delay as shown in Figure 4. In the case of digital systems with a sampling period of T_s, T_s being the symbol duration, it is usually suggested that $\Delta \tau = T_s$ (Stuber, 2001).

The GBSBEM Model

The GBSBEM model is an extension of the elliptical models, properly adapted for indoor environments (Liberti, 1996; Liberti, 1999). This model is characterized by the assumption of the existence of a large number of scatterers (in the ideal case there will be an infinite number of scatterers) which are uniformly distributed within an ellipse whose foci coincide with the transmitter and receiver positions, as shown in Figure 5. The size of the ellipse corresponds to the excess delay, which is the maximum delay observed in the channel. The scatterers are grouped to differential ellipses, which on the one hand are limited by the transmitter-receiver Line-Of-Sight (LOS) and

Figure 2. Elliptical geometric models configuration for frequency flat and frequency selective channels

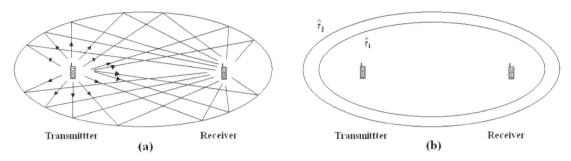

Transmittter   Receiver   Transmittter   Receiver

(a)   **(b)**

Figure 3. Discrete tapped delay line filter for the simulation of a frequency selective radio channel

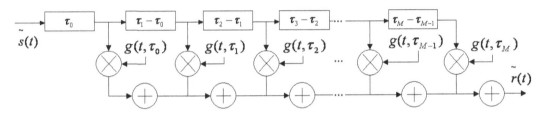

on the other hand are limited by the external boundary-ellipse. Furthermore, all incoming signal components are assumed to arise after *one* reflection only. For these reasons, this model is named GBSBEM (Geometrically Based Single Bounce Elliptical Model).

Referring to Figure 5, the normalized delay $r_i = \tau_i/\tau_0$ is defined as the ratio of the delay of an incoming component versus the delay corresponding to the LOS between transmitter and receiver. The maximum normalized delay is given by $r_m = \tau_m/\tau_0$. A way of calculating the maximum normalized delay is to set a threshold of the received power, e.g. TdB below the LOS component power, below which any received power may be considered to negligible. Then, the maximum normalized power is given by (Liberti, 1999)

$$r_m = 10^{\frac{T-L_r}{10n}}$$

(2)

where L_r represents the loss due to one scattering and n is the propagation attenuation factor.

Other Models

The following are cited some other popular geometric models. The interested reader may further refer to the informative works of Ertel et al. (Ertel, 1998), as well as Liberti-Rappaport (Liberti, 1999), but also to newer results included in the work by Sarkar et al. (Sarkar, 2002).

Lee's model is an extension of Clarke's model, where the scatterers are discrete and uniformly distributed around the mobile receiver (Lee, 1982). The main difference between this model and Clarke's model is that the scatterers have a discrete rather than a continuous distribution. Stapleton's model is a further extension of Lee's model, where it is additionally assumed that the scatterers have an angular velocity with respect to the receiver, while more than one ring of scatterers are considered (Stapleton, 1994; Stapleton, 1996). Another extension of Lee's model is Aszetly's model, where the scatterers occupy a sector rather than a whole ring. Also, Norklit's or Uniform Sector Distribution (USD) model should be mentioned, which is characterized by a uniform distribution of scatterers within a disc sector (Norklit, 1994).

Figure 5. A geometric representation of the GBSBEM model

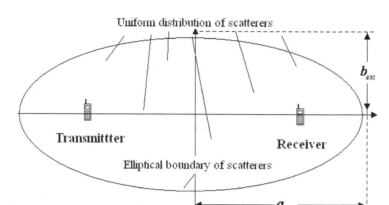

Figure 4. Continuous tapped delay line filter for the simulation of a frequency selective radio channel

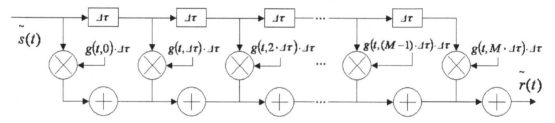

Furthermore, there are some popular models for cellular systems, namely the Typical Urban (TU) and Bad Urban (BU) models, as well as JTC and COST models (JTC, 1994; COST207, 1986). According to the TU model, a number of 120 scatterers are uniformly distributed within a circular disc of 1km radius centered at the Mobile Station (MS). The scatterers are assumed to be fixed as the MS moves for 5m, and then their relative positions to the MS are restored. In each 5m window, it is assumed that the incoming signal components are characterized by uniformly distributed phase and large scale fading with a standard deviation of 5-10dB. This model concludes to AoA distributions of the Gaussian type, like the GAA model cited (Ertel, 1998).

The BU model is similar to the TU, but there is an additional cluster of 120 scatterers, placed at an angle of 45° with respect to the main cluster and the BS]. The signal power corresponding to the secondary cluster of scatterers is 5dB below that of the main cluster. Due to this secondary cluster, the angle and delay spread are increased.

According to the Gaussian WSSUS (GWSSUS) model, the scatterers are grouped to cluster surrounding the receiver, while for each cluster the delay is considered to be constant (Zetterberg, 1995; Zetterberg, 1996). Each cluster consists of a large number of scatterers, therefore the Centrali Limit Theorem (CLT) can be applied. Another version of the GWSSUS model is the Gaussian Angle of Arrival (GAA) model, where only one cluster of scatterers is considered, while the angle of arrival is Gaussian distributed with mean value the angle of observation of the specific cluster.

Raleigh's model assumes that multipath fading is caused by a small number of dominant scatterers (Raleigh, 1995). Similar assumptions are made by the Polydorou-Capsalis model (Polydorou, 1997). However, the Raleigh model also takes into account the effect of large scale fading.

Klein and Mohr's model (Kein, 1996) is an extension of the tapped delay line filter model, where discrete AoAs are determined too, and therefore it offers information for the AoA of each incoming signal component too. The Lu-Lo-Litva model is an elliptical-type model, according to which the scatterers are clustered to elliptical rings surrounding the transmitter and receiver, while the number of scatterers of each cluster follows a Poisson distribution (Lu, 1997). The Lotter and van Rooyen model is a statistical model which is based to geometric assumptions as well as relative measurements found in the literature (Lotter, 1999), and can be applied to cellular DS-CDMA systems incorporating smart antennas. Other models for the impulse response of wideband radio channels are the Rappaport-Seidel model for indoor environments (Rappaport, 1991) and the Huang model for outdoor environments (Rappaport, 1993).

In order to model the slow-term variations due to shadow fading and also incorporate small scale fading, two basic approaches have been proposed. The first one has been presented by Suzuki (Suzuki, 1977) and Hansen and Meno (Hansen, 1977), and is based on a Rayleigh with a lognormal process. The second one has been presented by Loo and resembles a Ricean model with the additional property that the LOS component is lognormally distributed; this concludes to a model that adds a lognormal and a Rayleigh process (Loo, 1985). Loo's model has been further extended by Karadimas and Kotsopoulos by incorporating a sectored arrival of multipath energy and a 3-dimensional propagation model (Karadimas, 2007).

V. STATISTICAL MODELS – SIMULATION OF FREQUENCY FLAT FADING

The simulation of a narrowband mobile channel using statistical models may be performed by several proposed techniques. A popular technique consists in white noise filtering, thus creating the desired Doppler spectrum of the fading signal. Another widespread technique consists in summing multiple unmodulated carriers, each of which having an appropriate Doppler shift and phase distribution. The arising fading signal should have a prescribed envelope distribution, AoA distribution, power to angle of arrival profile, or Doppler spectrum. This means that these distributions are generated according to the prescribed channel specifications and do not necessarily correspond to the distributions that arise by the geometric models illustrated in Figures 1 and 2.

Simulation of Frequency Flat Fading Using Filtered White Noise

A popular technique for implementing flat fading simulators is by white noise filtering in order to generate the in-phase and quadrature phase components of the flat fading signal, and then vector summing these components. In order to implement a simulation tool of this type, it is required to create a white noise generator, which is used in order to generate two white noise signal samples having a phase difference of $\pi/2$ between each other. Each sample is then filtered by a bandpass filter with an appropriate frequency response, and then the two samples are vector summed. It must be preserved that the phase of the final signal is uniformly distributed within $[0,2\pi]$. In Figure 6 the block diagram of a white noise filtering channel simulator is illustrated.

In order to simulate a signal of prescribed Doppler spectrum, it is required to implement a filter having appropriate frequency response. In the case where the Doppler spectrum is given by equation (1), i.e. the Doppler spectrum corresponds to isotropical scattering (Rayleigh envelope), it is proposed that the frequency response of this filter be similar to the one illustrated in Figure 7 (Pahlavan, 1995). In order to implement a prescribed Level Crossing Rate (LCR), the rms bandwidth of the filter should be set equal to (Pahlavan, 1995)

$$B_{Do-rms} = 0.678 \cdot LCR \tag{3}$$

In the case where a dominant LOS component exists (Ricean channel), it is sufficient to add an unmodulated carrier of appropriate frequency to the vector summed output of the simulator.

A major disadvantage of the white noise filtering technique is that an applicable filter should be of great order, therefore the simulation time is encumbered. Nevertheless, this technique may be used without modifications in order to create multiple fading signals, under the only constraint that uncorrelated noise generators are used. The feature of creating multiple fading signals is very useful when e.g. simulating MIMO channels.

Simulation of frequency flat fading using vector summed sinusoidal carriers – The Jakes model.

With the vector summed carriers method, the channel response (also referred to as fading signal (Harada, 2002) is directly created by using

Figure 6. Implementation of a white noise filtering channel simulator

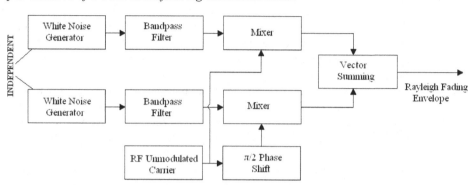

Figure 7. Frequency response of a filter required for the implementation of frequency flat small scale fading

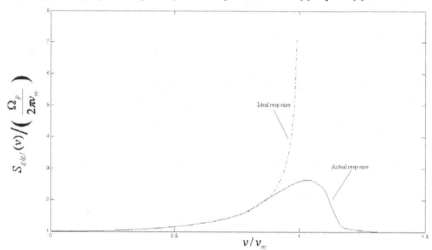

$$g(t,\tau) = \sum_{n=1}^{N} C_n(t) \exp(-j\varphi_n(t)) \delta(\tau - \hat{\tau}(t)) = g(t)\delta(\tau - \hat{\tau}(t)) \qquad (4)$$

$$\varphi_n(t) = 2\pi\{[f_c + v_{Do,n}(t)\tau_n(t)] - v_{Do,n}(t) \cdot t\} \qquad (5)$$

where $\delta(.)$ is the Delta function, $\phi_n(t)$, $C_n(t)$,$\tau_n(t)$ are the phase, amplitude and delay of arrival of the *n*-th incoming component, $v_{Do,n}(t)$ is the Doppler shift of the *n*-th component, and f_c is the carrier frequency. Furthermore, since flat fading is considered, it comes out that $\tau_i - \tau_j$ $T_s, \forall i \neq j$, T_s being the symbol period. Therefore, it can be considered that $\tau_n(t) \approx \hat{\tau}(t)$ (the approximation $\tau_n(t) \approx \hat{\tau}(t)$ may not be used when calculating the phase of the incoming components, due to the large carrier frequency, which results to large phase differences even from small delay differences).

Using a normal distribution generator for creating AoAs, the result will approach the Doppler spectrum of Figure 7. Also, by directly adding a dominant component at the output, a Ricean channel simulator is easily implemented. Furthermore, when using equation (5), any prescribed Doppler spectrum may be incorporated.

Certainly, the phase of each component must be appropriately selected in order that the final simulator output signal exhibits uniform phase distribution.

Aiming to keep the number of incoming components small, Jakes proposed a model which requires significantly fewer incoming components (Jakes, 1974; Jakes, 1994). According to Jakes model, the signal envelope is given by

$$g(t) = \frac{\Omega_p}{\sqrt{2N_0 + 1}} [g_c(t) + jg_s(t)] \tag{6}$$

where

$$g_c(t) = 2\sum_{n=1}^{N_0} \cos(\varphi_n)\cos(\omega_n t) + \sqrt{2}\cos(\varphi_N)\cos(\omega_m t) \tag{7}$$

$$g_s(t) = 2\sum_{n=1}^{N_0} \sin(\varphi_n)\cos(\omega_n t) + \sqrt{2}\sin(\varphi_N)\cos(\omega_m t) \tag{8}$$

In the previous equations $\omega_n = \omega_m \cos(2\pi n / N_0)$ and $\omega_m = 2\pi v_m$, where v_m is the maximum Doppler shift. Furthermore, ϕ_n is the bias phase of the n-th component while ϕ_N is the bias phase of the component corresponding to the maximum Doppler shift.

For the purposes of a laboratory experiment, a carrier of desired frequency may be modulated by the envelope $g(t)$ given by equation (6). Alternatively, in the case of computer aided simulation, the fading signal of equation (6) is directly applied to the equivalent complex bandpass information-bearing signal.

According to Jakes, it is sufficient to use $N_0 = 8$ components, which correspond to $N = 2(2N_0 + 1) = 34$ incoming signal components in equation (4) (Jakes, 1994). Nevertheless, equation (6) is not equivalent to equation (4). It has been proven that by using equations (7) and (8), the phases of the incoming signal components are correlated, which in turn implies that fading is not stationary (Pop, 1999; Pop, 2001). Evenmore, the envelope's autocorrelation when using Jakes model is significantly diverted from the theoretically predicted one for large time delays (Stuber, 2001). Pop and Beaulieu suggested an improved fading simulator based on Jakes model (Pop, 2001), however their simulation also generates second-order statistics that diverge to the theoretically predicted statistics. Moreover, it has been shown that this can not be corrected, not even in the case where $N_0 \rightarrow \infty$ (Chengshan, 2002). Pop and Beaulieu dealt with this issue and showed recently that the most efficient means of improving the statistical behavior of a fading simulator is to properly configure the output Doppler spectrum (Pop, 2002).

Simulation of frequency flat fading using vector summed sinusoidal carriers – Flat and Gaussian Doppler spectrum.

As already mentioned in the previous section, the Doppler spectrum may be given any desired shape. A case of special interest is the flat Doppler spectrum where,

$$S_{g_I g_I}(f) = 1 / 2\pi v_m, |v| \leq v_m \tag{9}$$

g_1 being the in-phase component of the channel response in equation (4).

Equation (9) corresponds to the case where the scatterers are placed with spherical symmetry around a constant velocity mobile receiver. The flat Doppler spectrum also applies to the case where the transmitter and receiver are fixed and there are scatterers moving around both of them in a stochastic manner, like in WLAN applications (Pahlavan, 1995).

In practical applications, the spectrum of equation (9) is implemented using either filtered white noise or by directly summing sinusoidal carriers like in equation (4). In the latter case, the sinusoidal carriers must have a Doppler shift that it uniformly distributed within the interval $[-v_m, v_m]$ rather than arising from the AoA distribution. This means the Doppler shift of each component is forced to follow a uniform distribution. Again, it is reminded that the components' phases in equation (4) must be appropriately selected in order that the output signal's phase is uniformly distributed.

Another case of Doppler spectrum shape with special interest is the Gaussian Doppler spectrum used in the COST207 model (COST207, 1986). In this model, the Gauss1 spectrum given by

$$S_{glgl}(f) = G(A, -0.8v_m, 0.05v_m) + G(A_1, 0.4v_m, 0.1v_m), |v| \leq v_m \tag{10}$$

as well as Gauss2 model given by

$$S_{glgl}(f) = G(B, 0.7v_m, 0.1v_m) + G(B_1, -0.4v_m, 0.15v_m), |v| \leq v_m \tag{11}$$

are used. In equations (10) and (11), $G(A, m, \sigma)$ is a Gaussian distribution with mean m, standard deviation σ and normalization factor A. Furthermore, $A_1 \big|_{dB} = A \big|_{dB} - 10dB$ and $B_1 \big|_{dB} = B \big|_{dB} - 15dB$. In practical cases, the Gaussian Doppler spectrum is implemented in a way similar to the flat Doppler spectrum described before.

Multiple Frequency Flat Fading Signals

A simulator is often required to be able to generate more than one fading signals, like in the case of simulating MIMO channels. The main objective in cases like this is to preserve that the multiple fading signals are uncorrelated to one another. Jakes proposed a modification to his technique, where a specific phase bias is added to each sinusoidal carrier, but this method can not deliver uncorrelated fading signals for time delays greater than zero (Stuber, 2001). An alternative solution is proposed by Dent et al, where it is suggested to use orthogonal Walsh-Hadamard codewords (Dent, 1993), which achieves a very low autocorrelation among the fading signals even for relatively large time delays.

Finally, in the case where it is desired to achieve a specific autocorrelation degree between two fading signals, it can be performed by a linear combination of two uncorrelated fading signals (Stuber, 2001).

VI. STATISTICAL MODELS—SIMULATION OF FREQUENCY SELECTIVE FADING

Frequency selective fading usually corresponds to wideband signals and channels. The simulation of frequency selective mobile channels using statistical models is based on the tapped delay line filters illustrated in Figures 3 and 4. The fading signal corresponding to each tap consists of a set of incoming components, is frequency flat and exhibits a specific envelope distribution, AoA distribution, power to AoA profile and Doppler spectrum. Furthermore, referring to Figure 8, we are also interested in determining the delay distribution of each incoming path as well as the distribution of the mean power with respect to the delay of arrival.

The time-variant nature of the radio channel should ideally be traced by sampling the impulse or frequency response of the channel with a rate equal or greater than two times the rms Doppler spread. (Pahlavan, 1995). In the case where the design of smart antennas or MIMO systems is of interest, then the distribution of the AoA of the main as well as subsequent paths, and the signal signature at the receiver should also be traced (Liberti, 1999), in order to evaluate whether or not a smart antenna would be able to trace successfully the time-variant characteristics of the radio channel.

Frequency selective fading modeling and simulation is performed either in the time or frequency domain, using the channel impulse response or frequency response respectively. Fourier theorem implies that these two techniques are equivalent to one another. In the following, some important aspects of time and frequency domain simulation are discussed.

Pulse Arrival Delay Distribution

A simple model for the time delay of incoming paths in wideband channels is the Poisson distribution, which is generally considered to be a good choice in the case where the scatterers are randomly placed around the receiver and transmitter (either for indoor or outdoor environments) (Pahlavan, 1995). Nevertheless, there are certain reports that the Poisson distribution does not sufficiently model the time delay of arriving paths (Turin, 1972; Suzuki, 1977; Yegani, 1991; Hashemi, 1993), which implies that the scatterers are not usually randomly placed around the receiver and transmitter. Ganesh and Pahlavan and Pahlavan and Levesque have dealt with this issue extensively in (Ganesh, 1989; Pahlavan, 1995).

Suzuki suggested an alternative time delay distribution (Suzuki, 1977), which was afterwards modified by Ganesh and Pahlavan for indoor environments (Ganesh, 1989), according to which the probability of a path incoming in a specific time window depends on whether a pulse arrived at the previous time window or not. It has been shown that this improved distribution approximates well enough the experimental data.

Furthermore, Saleh and Valenzuela suggested that all pulses in indoor environments arrive in clusters (Saleh, 1987). Each cluster's time delay is Poisson distributed, while the time delay of a specific pulse within a cluster also follows a Poisson distribution. This model also fits to the experimental data presented by Saleh and Valenzuela very well.

Furthermore, in a Poisson distribution the time intervals among the time delays of arrival are exponentially distributed. It has been suggested to replace the exponential distribution with other distributions, e.g. the Weibull distribution (Yegani, 1991); this approach may significantly improve the resulting accuracy of delay distribution estimation.

Pulse Amplitude Distribution for Each Path

It is broadly accepted that the pulse amplitude of each path suffers from flat fading, and more specifically follows the Rayleigh or Rice distribution, in the case where there exist NLOS or LOS conditions respectively. More specifically, it is considered that each path actually consists of more than one unresolvable paths. Thus, the wideband radio channel may be viewed as the sum of discrete narrowband radio channels with different time delays of arrival, as in Figure 2. The Doppler spectrum will be given by the appropriate equation, e.g. will be flat, Gaussian, Jakes or other.

Mean Path Power with Respect to Time Delay of Arrival

Ganesh suggested that the mean power of each path is exponentially distributed with respect to the time delay of arrival (Ganesh, 1991). This is a very important result, because it explicitly shows that the mean power of each path is exponentially declined with the time delay of arrival (of course, the instantaneous power still exhibits Rayleigh, Rice or other fading). More specifically, Ganesh calculated the mean power as the average within a small radius area rather than the average within a small time interval. It should herein be noted that this approach is correct only in the case where radio channel is homogeneous.

Models Given by Standards Committees

Standards committees suggest channel characteristics, which are then used as reference platforms in order to evaluate various methods and techniques, such as modulation schemes, adaptive filters and equalizers, link layer protocols, multiple access schemes etc. These standard characteristics usually include simulation models for large and small scale fading.

Referring to Figure 3, the suggested standards usually consist of tables in which the delays τ_i, as well as the mean values and PDFs of $g(t,\tau_i)$ are tabulated. Each table corresponds to a specific channel type. Certainly, the time delays are random and correlated, as well as time-variant. The same is valid for the amplitude and AoA of incoming components. Nevertheless, according to standards committees suggested models, all these character-

Figure 8. Impulse response snapshot for a wideband signal suffering from frequency selective fading

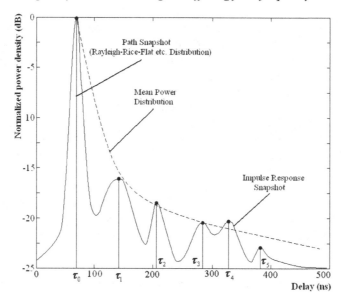

istics are considered to be time-invariant for simplicity and in order to configure a reference platform generally adopted.

The interested reader may refer to the GSM standard model (GSM, 1991), the JTC-PCS standard model (JTC, 1994), the COST207 standard model (COST207, 1986) etc.

Simulation Model of Wideband Channels in the Frequency Domain — Autoregressive Modeling

It is often desirable to simulate frequency selective fading in the frequency domain. The frequency response of the channel may be indirectly calculated via Fourier transformation of the impulse response or directly modeled using autoregressive models. Then, the impulse response of the channel may be indirectly calculated via inverse Fourier transformation.

An autoregressive process would use an all-pole finite filter in order to produce frequency response samples of the radio channel under study. More specifically, for a sample of frequency response measurements, the respective filter poles are calculated and then the statistics of the filter poles are determined. Then, in order to simulate the radio channel, the filter poles are randomly generated using their respective distributions, and the frequency response arises as the output of the generated filter (Pahlavan, 1995).

The frequency response for a specific frequency and time instance will depend on the frequency response at the same time instance and previous frequency values, as shown by

$$T(f_n, t) = \sum_{i=1}^{p} a_i T(f_{n-i}, t) + V(f_n) \tag{12}$$

where $V(f_n)$ is a white noise stochastic process with zero mean value, and a_i are the model's parameters. Using the z-transform operator in equation (12), it comes out that the frequency response $T(f_n, t)$ is the output of a linear filter given by

$$H(z) = \frac{1}{1 - \sum_{i=1}^{p} a_i z^{-1}} = \prod_{i=1}^{p} \frac{1}{(1 - p_i z^{-1})}.$$ (13)

Equation (13) corresponds to an all-pole filter. A frequency response sample consisting of, e.g., N frequency points, may be approximated using the p poles of equation (13), while usually it will be that $N > p$. It is noted that each sample generated by equation (12) also includes the impact of the white noise $V(f_n)$, and that the standard deviation of $V(f_n)$ is constant with frequency.

A critical attribute of autoregressive models is the model's order, i.e. the number of poles p. In relative reposts in the literature for indoor environments, the maximum selected order is five (Howard, 1991), but second-order filters are also reported to yield satisfactory results.

Comparison Between Simulation Techniques in Time Delay and Frequency Domain

Simulation in time delay domain is more popular and broadly accepted, mainly due to the fact that there is a one-to-one interpretation between model and natural channel characteristics (time delay and envelope amplitude distribution, Doppler spectrum etc.). Furthermore, all standards committees have developed extensive channel models in the time domain, thus offering a common reference platform.

On the other hand, it is difficult to implement automated algorithms in order to recognize and statistically classify time delays of arrival. Therefore, appropriate techniques must be developed in order to automatically recognize local maxima of the impulse response, the number of incoming paths, the amplitude distributions and time delay of arrival. However, some local maxima may arise due to noise rather than an incoming path.

As long as frequency domain simulation is concerned, there is not a direct interpretation of natural channel characteristics to model parameters. Furthermore, it is a common phenomenon that the impulse response calculated via inverse Fourier transform exhibits more local maxima than the corresponding impulse response which was directly calculated in the time domain. However, the classification and configuration of all-pole filters of autoregressive processes is much easier automated (Pahlavan, 1995).

VII. A STATISTICAL MODELS FADING SIMULATION TOOL

Introduction

A tool for the simulation of small scale fading in mobile channels using statistical models is presented next. The tool has been implemented in MATLAB and offers the ability of evaluating a radio channel's small scale fading characteristics via calculation of mean power, level crossing rate, average fade duration, BER etc (Mitilineos, 2004). It is based on user-defined PDFs for certain channel characteristics in order to evaluate a radio channel with respect to BER performance. For verification purposes, this tool has been applied to a Rayleigh radio channel, for which there exist analytic formulas as well as well-established tools for BER calculation. Then, it was applied to a GBSBEM radio channel for which no analytical formulas or other simulation reports exist. Furthermore, the tool's ability of simulating the case of directional or switched-beam arrays is also presented. The most interesting characteristic of the proposed simulator is the fact that it is based on an open architecture, allowing the implementation of any desired radio channel model.

Channel Simulation

Rayleigh channel simulation is based on vector summing of sinusoidal carriers, according to Figure 1 and equations (4), (5). The resulting received signal envelope is Rayleigh distributed. On the other hand, GBSBEM channel simulation could be implemented by using a tapped filter, like in Figure 3 and 4, but each tap does not suffer from Rayleigh fading. Rather, the AoA distribution for each tap will be biased towards the LOS between transmitter and receiver, and therefore the envelope of each tap is not Rayleigh distributed. For comparison purposes, it is selected herein to simulate a narrowband GBSBEM channel, i.e. a channel with one tap only (flat fading). This implies that it is assumed that $\tau_m - \tau_0 < T_b$, where τ_m is the maximum delay of arrival, corresponding to the boundary ellipse in Figure 5, τ_0 is the delay of arrival corresponding to the LOS, and T_b is the bit period. Incoming components are considered of equal power, while the phase of each incoming component is considered uniformly distributed in $[0,2\pi)$. The AoA of each component will be given by (Liberti, 1999)

$$f_\varphi(\varphi) = \frac{1}{2\pi\beta} \frac{\left(r_m^2 - 1\right)^2}{\left(r_m - \cos\varphi\right)^2}, -\pi \leq \varphi \leq \pi \tag{14}$$

Furthermore, the number of incoming components is selected to be equal to 50. An important detail is that the simulation procedure is executed for a time window, and then the scatterers' positions are re-arranged (i.e. the AoAs and phases of incoming components are re-initialized). As a result the fading signal is not constant during simulation time. Thus, the channel is assumed to be non-static (rather is semi-static), and the 50 simulated components are not constant during simulation. This strengthens the accuracy of simulation results.

In Figure 9, a block diagram of the proposed simulator is illustrated. Initially, a pseudorandom bit sequence is implemented, and then the baseband signal is constructed. Based on whether Rayleigh or GBSBEM channel model is to be simulated, $N=50$ incoming components are generated, having unitary amplitude and appropriate AoA distribution. The AoA distribution is either uniform or follows equation (14) for a Rayleigh or GBSBEM channel respectively. Thus, a frequency flat fading signal is generated. If the generation of frequency selective fading signals is desired, the same procedure is repeated with appropriately shifted delays as well as different normalized incoming signal amplitudes. Finally, white noise is added (Additive White Gaussian Noise – AWGN), taking into account the selected Signal to Noise Ratio (SNR), and the BER is calculated.

Numerical Results

The equivalent bandpass signal of a BPSK sequence with length equal to 65535 bits is generated, while the transmitting rate is set equal to 100kbps. The signal is 8 times oversampled, and root-Nyquist pulse shaping filters are assumed at both the transmitter and receiver. A fading signal is simulated via 50 uniform-phased incoming components. The Doppler shift of each component is calculated by the AoA and the mobile's velocity. All incoming components are summed and normalized in order that their mean power is unitary. The fading signal is multiplied with the transmitted signal and the fading-distorted signal is constructed. Then, the noise level is calculated via the assumed SNR level. The noise level is calculated in a way that discrete steps of E_b / N_0 values from 0 to 10dBs are simulated, where E_b is the mean bit energy and N_0 is the noise power spectral density. Based on the calculated noise level, AWGN samples are created and added to the fade-distorted signal. The final signal passes through the root-Nyquist receiver filter, and then a sampler and a comparator, where it is compared to a time delayed version of the initial generated sequence. Thus, the number of false received signals and BER are calculated. The procedure is repeated anew with a newly generated symbol sequence, new AoA values and incoming components phases, as well as new noise samples; the procedure is repeated 100 times for each E_b / N_0 ratio value. A maximum Doppler shift equal to $v_m = 16$Hz, which corresponds to a MS velocity of $u = 2$m/sec, which is a reasonable velocity for a pedestrian moving in indoor environment, is selected. The MS is assumed to move on the LOS line and draws away from the receiver. A block diagram of the simulated telecommunications system is shown in Figure 10.

The effect of a directional array may also be simulated. As an example, consider a perfect directional array pointing towards the transmitter's direction, with unitary radiation pattern at an angular interval of $\pm 20^o$ around the LOS line and zero elsewhere. Again, we assume 50 incoming components, but now many of them will be rejected by the directional array.

Figure 9. Block diagram of the proposed simulator

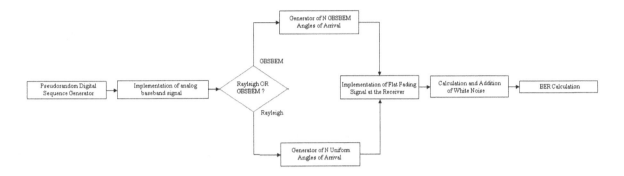

Figure 10. Block diagram of a simple telecommunications system

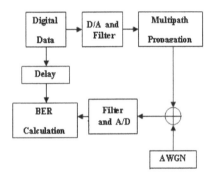

Figure 11. BER plots in the case of a BPSK system with Rayleigh flat fading

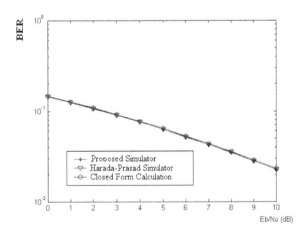

As long as the Rayleigh channel is concerned, there has been implemented a simulator by Harada-Prasad (Harada, 2002), but there is also a closed-form formula for BER calculation as given by

$$BER_{BPSK-FLAT-FADING} = \frac{1}{2}\left(1 - \left(\sqrt{1 + \frac{1}{E_b / N_o}}\right)^{-1}\right). \qquad (15)$$

In Figure 11 the respective numerical results for the proposed and the Harada simulator, as well as the analytic formula of equation (15) are illustrated. The results of the proposed simulator are in excellent agreement with the other two methods, forming an argument for the accuracy of the proposed simulator.

A similar procedure has been followed for the simulation of GBSBEM flat fading. The value of r_m is selected to be equal to 1.585, and arises from equation (2) with an attenuation factor of $n = 2$, loss factor L_r =6dB, and power threshold $T = 10$dB. The respective results for an omnidirectional and a directional receiver are illustrated in Figure 12. The directional receiver yields improved BER levels than the omnidirectional one as expected. However, the improvement is not much significant. A possible explanation for this is the fact that, despite the many incoming components discarded by the directional antenna, there are still many components arriving and contributing to flat fading.

Finally, in Figure 13 the more realistic case of a channel with a few incoming components is presented. In this case the Central Limit Theorem cannot be applied and the results of Gaussian PDF for the sum of incoming components are not valid (McPherson, 1990). In the literature, there are research results that handle the problem of the PDF of the sum of limited number of incoming components (Polydorou, 1997; Vellis, 2000). For the specific case, we assume 6 incoming components, which arrive at the receiver with GBSBEM AoA distribution. The maximum normalized delay is set equal to $r_m = 1585$. An omnidirectional and the perfect directional receiver described earlier are used. Due to the small number of components, the existence of a LOS component is forced to the simulator, i.e. if none of 6 generated components does not arrive from the LOS direction, we add another LOS component arbitrarily. As shown in Figure 13, there is a significant improvement to the resulted BER in the case where a directional receiver is used.

Resume

A simulation tool for the performance evaluation of telecommunications systems with respect to small scale fading is presented. The proposed tool allows for the simulation of any desired user-defined channel model, directional

Figure 12. BER plots in the case of a BPSK system with GBSBEM flat fading, omnidirectional and perfect directional receiver

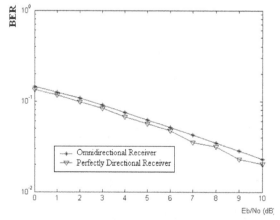

Figure 13. BER plots in the case of a BPSK system with GBSBEM flat fading, Low Multipath, omnidirectional and perfect directional receiver

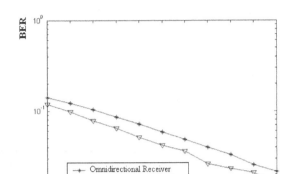

or omnidirectional antenna, E_b / N_0 ratio etc., due to its open architecture. It has been validated via simulation of the classical Rayleigh flat fading channel, and results for a GBSBEM channel are also presented.

VIII. DETERMINISTIC MODELS

Deterministic models calculate the mobile channel impulse response or the signal envelope distribution by using architectural or topographical plans of a specific site. Deterministic models are mainly used in mean attenuation and large scale fading modeling, but are not so broadly used for small scale fading simulation. One reason for this is that the finest possible resolution is needed in order to simulate small scale fading, which results to large or prohibitive computational cost and simulation time. Nevertheless, as the usage of architectural or topographical plans in electronic form is expanded, as well as computational power of modern units is leveraged, deterministic small scale fading modeling is becoming more and more popular.

Another argument that might be raised against deterministic modeling is that the results of deterministic models are valid for the specific site only. However, this is valid for on-site measurements too. Additionally, deterministic simulation of a large number of architectural or topographical plans may yield statistical models too, just like on-site measurements campaigns. On-site measurements are more accurate but also more costly than deterministic channel modeling, and one can choose between the two of them based on his needs and resources.

Deterministic models have been based on geometric optics or ray-tracing techniques. These techniques can be applied to simplified environment models and their execution time is not strongly affected by the dimensions of the environment under study. More complicated ray-tracing techniques include diffraction and scattering phenomena. A major advantage of these techniques is that they can model the AoA of incoming components.

Another approach, which has only recently been proposed due to the large computation cost related, is to solve Maxwell equations for a specific site, taking into account the boundary conditions on the objects and the bounds of the environment. This approach is mainly used for sites of small size. Some techniques used for this purpose are the Finite Differences in Time Domain (FDTD), Method of Moments (MoM), and other.

Ray-Tracing Algorithms

Ray-tracing algorithms simulate channel response using geometric optics techniques. They are simple, while at the same time offer the ability to calculate the power to AoA profile and AoA distribution, and can be applied to indoor as well as outdoor environments (Lebherz, 1989; Lebherz, 1992; Lawton, 1991; Lawton, 1992; Rappaport, 1992; Holt, 1992; Rossi, 1993; Yang, 1993a; Yang, 1993b).

Ray-tracing techniques may incorporate propagation mechanism in free space, as well as propagation via materials – refraction, reflection, diffraction, scattering, diffusion over rough surfaces etc. They may be three-dimensional or two-dimensional. Three-dimensional techniques offer the ability to model channels with antennas placed at different heights or, in the case where the antennas are placed at the same height, they offer the ability to model scatterers at various heights, such as roofs, floors, etc. Generally, they are more accurate but also much more complicated than two-dimensional techniques.

For refraction and reflection, a popular method of analysis is via image theory, where the images of transmitter and receiver are considered on the reflective surfaces, and thus the actual paths of propagation between transmitter and receiver are determined (McKown, 1991; Rustako, 1991). Using this technique, the problem solving procedure may become very computationally intensive, as the number of refractions/reflections taken into account increases. Another ray-tracing approach is the so-called ray-shooting technique (Deschamps, 1972; Ikegami, 1991). With this method, a virtual sphere around the transmitter is separated to solid angle intervals. Each interval corresponds to a ray propagating in space. The propagation is assumed to end in the case where the solid angle's surface reaches the receiver or in the case where the ray power falls below a threshold.

A more specialized and interesting problem is the multiple reflections and refractions within a flat surface with non-negligible thickness, where it can be shown that the multiple reflections and refractions may be modeled with a unique reflection and refraction factor (Burside, 1983). Furthermore, diffraction may arise in the case where the propagating wave is scattered by pins, tips and in general narrow and surfaces of oblique angles. In this case, the diffracted propagating wave is calculated using the Huygens principle and the diffraction coefficient determines the percentage of power which is diffracted towards the receiver. Finally, the phenomenon of diffusion arises in the case where the wave reflects from a rough surface, whose roughness is significant compared to the wavelength. In this case, the wave is not reflected, but rather diffused to all directions. Similarly to diffraction, this case may also be affronted by a point source placed at the point of incidence (Pahlavan, 1995). The diffusion factor is used in order to calculate the percentage of power which is diffused to the direction of the receiver.

In the literature, a number of research papers on ray-tracing algorithms can be found. Catedra et al. have presented a number of ray-tracing techniques, based on micro- and pico-cells applications (Catedra, 1998). Seidel and Rappaport suggested a ray-tracing model for PCS systems inside buildings (Seidel, 1994). Building modelling is performed using AutoCAD, while only large-sized objects with respect to the wavelength are incorporated. Smaller objects are neglected, mainly in order to cut off computational cost, but this poses some limitations on calculating the mean attenuation and large scale fading characteristics. Rizk et al. reported a ray-tracing technique for two-dimensional environments and micro-cells (Rizk, 1997), which is based on reflection and diffraction theory, as well as image theory. Yang et al. presented a ray-tracing technique, based in tetrahedral "ray-tubes" which are used in order to implement their method (Yang, 1998), while the respective application calculates multiple reflections and refractions of the propagated wave. Liang and Bertoni presented a novel ray-tracing technique, which significantly reduces the computational cost for outdoor environments and is based on the assumption that most scatterers in outdoor environments are vertically oriented wall surfaces (Liang, 1998). Fimally, Son and Myung reported a ray-tracing method for quasi-three-dimensional environments (Son, 1999). Their method is based on the "ray-tube tree" structure, while was further extended by Choi et al. in order to incorporate three-dimensional environments, as well as waves penetrating inside buildings (Choi, 2006).

Numerical Solution of Maxwell Equations—FDTD, MoM and UTD Methods

Another approach to deterministic simulation is by directly solving Maxwell equations for a specific environment. Numerical solution of Maxwell equations requires the construction of a grid of points on which differential equations will be numerically solved. The dimensions of the grid must be in the order of wavelength for accurate solution, which means that the computational intensity of the problem increases geometrically with frequency of the site's dimensions. Therefore, this approach demands the availability of extremely large computational power, which until recently was not easily available.

FDTD Method

Due to the evolution of computing systems, field equations solving has matured and attracts the interest of research community. A popular numerical method of Maxwell equations solving is the Finite Differences Time Domain (FDTD) method, where Maxwell equations are approached by finite differences in the time domain. The electric and magnetic field are solved in the time domain, therefore transient response is also calculated. In its first version, the FDTD method was proposed with orthogonal grid (Yee, 1966; Taflove, 1975), but since then it has been improved by utilization of various grid shapes, as well as other techniques for the speed-up of the solving procedure (Holland, 1983; Fusco, 1990; Harms, 1992; Lee, 1993; Yang, 1993a).

Compared to ray-tracing, FDTD techniques are much more demanding in time simulation and computational resources. It is not coincidental that research reports on FDTD channel modeling have been proposed only recently. Talbi presented a FDTD method for UHF wave propagation modeling in indoor environments, while utilizing the reciprocity principle in order to evaluate the effect of directional transmitter and receiver antennas (Talbi, 2001). Wallace and Jensen presented a model which evaluates MIMO systems by simulating wideband signals propagating into simplified two-dimensional indoor channel models (Wallace, 2003). Finally, Papamichael et al. reported the application of a FDTD method in indoor simulation at 434MHz (Papamichael, 2003).

Despite the requirements in computation power, the solution of the electromagnetic problem is much more accurate compared to ray-tracing results, but FDTD channel modeling is not always better than ray-tracing modeling (Pahlavan, 1995). An important reason is that, in fact, the true channel is much more complicated than any electromagnetic model used by FDTD or ray-tracing. Various small objects and details of the channel can never be exactly represented in a three-dimensional channel representation, and therefore the real channel is always different than the model. Therefore, ray-tracing as well as FDTD or other electromagnetic methods have an upper limit of accuracy. Nevertheless, as the channel representation model becomes more accurate, FDTD method will yield more accurate results than ray-tracing methods.

Hybrid UTD-MoM Method

Uniform Theory of Diffraction (UTD) techniques have been also proposed for channel modeling. This type of techniques is classified between ray-tracing and FDTD techniques with respect to computational power requirements. Zhang presented a simulation model based on UTD for wideband cellular systems (Zhang, 1997). Zhang's model is able of calculating mean attenuation values using UTD models, using a narrowband transfer function calculated by UTD, which takes into account refracted as well as reflected waves. O'Brien et al. presented an application where the UTD method is used together with analytic propagation formulas in order to model three-dimensional, indoor as well as outdoor environments (O'Brien, 2000). Finally, Oestges et al. presented a model based on a combined UTD and ray-tracing method (Oestges, 2002).

Recently, the possibility of using a hybrid MoM-UTD method for channel modeling has been presented in (Mitilineos, 2005; Varlamos, 2006). The UTD method is used alternatively to ray-tracing in order to model wave propagation and interaction with various dielectric materials, while the MoM method is used alternatively to FDTD in order to take into account the effect of metal and conductive surfaces (e.g. antennas and other surfaces). This hybrid method is classified as deterministic modeling, and more specifically as a electromagnetic field equations solving technique.

Comparison Between Statistical and Deterministic Models

Statistical models demand the minimum computational power among other model types but, in general, due to the fact that they are based on geometric assumptions of the natural channel characteristics, the corresponding simulation results are of least accuracy and are generally used as reference platforms for comparison purposes. The same is valid for statistical models that arise after measurements campaigns too. However, an advantage of these models is that they can be used as a good starting estimation.

Measurements based models are the most accurate and arise after measurements in a specific site but are valid for the specific site only. These models demand the least computational power, but have the disadvantage that for each specific site, a new set of measurements is required; a procedure which is time and money consuming, and sometimes not even applicable.

Finally, deterministic models demand the most computational power, and are more accurate than statistical and less accurate than measurements based models. Deterministic models, just like measurements campaigns, may be used in order to extract a statistical model. An advantage of deterministic models with respect to statistical models is that they are more applicable for selecting specific transmitter and receiver positions in a site.

Within the deterministic models class, ray-tracing techniques are characterized by strongly increasing complexity with the complexity of the environment model used. This means that it is not the size of the environment but the detail depth of the analysis, e.g. number of reflections, refractions etc. that are taken into account, the detail in objects and surfaces representation etc. On the contrary, FDTD techniques complexity increases strongly with an increase of the environment size or frequency, just like the hybrid MoM-UTD method.

IX. RESEARCH RESULTS—A SIMULATION TOOL FOR DETERMINISTIC MODELING OF INDOOR ENVIRONMENT

Introduction

A deterministic simulation tool for indoor mobile channel environments has been developed and presented in (Mitilineos, 2005). It is based on the hybrid MoM-UTD method and the SuperNEC application (Fourie, 2000), while it has been validated using indoor environments measurements results in the literature.

As aforementioned, small scale fading characterization is mainly implemented using statistical/geometric models, especially during early design stages. However, during final design stages, the initial assumptions need to be validated using on-site measurements, like in (Alexander 1982; Saleh, 1987; Rappaport, 1989; Hashemi, 1994; Kim, 1996) and other. Unfortunately, on-site measurements are extremely time and money consuming, or even non-applicable some times. Deterministic modeling is proposed to cover the gap between inexpensive, simple but low accuracy statistical models and expensive, resource draining, but high accuracy on-site measurements. It is a good choice only in the case where there is enough computational power available, and is mainly used in indoor environments.

The technique used herein is based on a hybrid MoM-UTD method. Simplified model of the site under simulation are used, while transmitter and receiver antennas are placed therein according to user requirements. Then, the frequency response is calculated, which is used in order to calculate the channel impulse response via Inverse Fast Fourier Transform (IFFT). The simulation procedure can be repeated for various neighbouring receiver positions, thus simulating receiver's moving. Having in hand the frequency and impulse response of the channel for multiple receiver positions, we are able to obtain information regarding its statistical characteristics, such as rms delay spread. As will follow, the numerical results obtained using our model are in excellent agreement to relative measurements in real environments (based on reports by Hashemi and Tholl (Hashemi, 1994) and Kim et al. (Kim, 1996)).

Model and Tool Description

Electromagnetic Model

The proposed deterministic simulation tool is able of offering accurate results regarding wave propagation using simplified representations of the propagating environment, in LOS as well as NLOS cases. A typical indoor environment shall include a floor and a roof, walls, furniture, office machinery, people etc., as well as a number of transmitting and receiving antennas.

The propagation environment model is created using SuperNEC, which incorporates the hybrid MoM-UTD method. UTD primitives (UTD is used for dielectric surfaces modeling) are two-dimensional rectangular surfaces with a desired thickness, as well as dielectric cylindrical surfaces. Typically, three reflections over dielectric materials and one reflection over conductive materials, one refraction and one combination of either refraction-reflection or reflection-refraction are taken into account; however the number of reflections and refractions taken into account may change according to user's requirements. The UTD method incorporated in SuperNEC yields credible results in the case where the dielectric surfaces are much larger compared to the wavelength. On the other hand, MoM segments are conductive, straight metallic pieces, with a cylindrical shape and a user-specifiable length (Fourie, 2000).

Roofs, floors, doors, walls and in general all dielectric materials are simulated by UTD, while antennas, reflectors, and in general all metallic materials are simulated by MoM. The necessary input data for dielectric materials include the dielectric permittivity ε_r, the magnetic permeability μ_r, the conductance *sigma* and the material's thickness, length and width. Naturally, all these parameters will correspond to actual measurements of real materials. On the other hand, for conductive materials the necessary input data include the conductance, the thickness, length and width, as well as the segment density per cm^2.

Mathematical Description of the Proposed Method

As mentioned before, the proposed application is based on the calculation of the channel's frequency response. The transmitting antenna is excited by sinusoidal carriers of unitary amplitude and zero phase. The antenna is excited over a large frequency range with constant frequency step. Let the frequency range be B, the frequency step be f_s; then N carriers are transmitted in total, where

$$N = \frac{B}{f_s} + 1. \tag{16}$$

The width and phase of the signal at the receiving antenna output are obtained by SuperNEC for each frequency tone, and thus the frequency response of the channel is recorded. Then, the channel's impulse response is calculated via IFFT. The resolution of the impulse response at the time delay dimension (delay step) is given by

$$\tau_{step} = \frac{1}{B} \tag{17}$$

while the impulse response has a period which is given by

$$T = \frac{1}{f_s}. \tag{18}$$

The detected incoming components are identified by the local maxima of the impulse response. A relative power threshold is specified, below which no local maxima are taken into account. The equivalent complex bandpass representation of the impulse response is given by,

$$h(t) = \sum_{i=1}^{L} \beta_i e^{j\varphi_i} \delta(t - \tau_i) \tag{19}$$

where L is the number of incoming components and β_i, ϕ_i, τ_i are the amplitude, phase and delay of the i-th component respectively (Pahlavan, 1995).

Setup Description for a Simplified Indoor Environment.

A simplified indoor office and NLOS environment is displayed in Figure 14, where propagation in the band 2.4-2.5GHz is studied. The room dimensions are 16m × 10m × 4m, while the brick wall in the middle of the room has a height of $h = 4$m and a width of $l = 8$m. The electrical characteristics of the inner and outer walls at the center frequency ($f = 2450$ MHz) are set to $\varepsilon_r = 4.5$, *sigma* = 0.027 s/m and $\mu_r = 1$ while for the roof and floor they are $\varepsilon_r = 8$, *sigma* = 0.095 s/m and $\mu_r = 1$, and are all selected in order to correspond to actual measurements of real materials (Yang, 1998). The walls thickness is set equal to 0.115m, while the roof and floor thickness are set equal to 0.1m.

Furthermore, the transmitting (TX) and receiving (RX) antennas are identical, vertically polarized dipoles. Their centers are placed at a height of 1.5m, while their length and radius are equal to 0.0555m and 0.001m respectively, thus resonating at 2.4GHz. The terminating (load) resistance at the receiver is set equal to 75Ω.

The channel behavior, as long as small scale fading is concerned, is recorded by measuring the frequency response for various receiver positions. The bandwidth is set equal to $B = 100$MXz, with upper and lower frequencies equal to $f_1 = 2400$ MHz and $f_2 = 2500$ MHz respectively. The frequency step is set equal to $f_s = 100$ kHz; thus for each receiver position we collect $N = 1001$ measurements of the voltage at the receiver's output. The receiver is assumed to move towards the transmitter with a low constant velocity of 1m/sec, and covers a distance of 1m orm 8.2λ, λ being the wavelength. The initial transmitter-receiver separation distance is equal to 9m, while the frequency response is collected every 2cm. This means that by the end of the procedure, there are 51 channel frequency responses available. Thus, via IFFT, we take 51 impulse responses, with step and period at the delay dimension equal to $\tau_{step} = \frac{1}{B} = 10$ns and $T = \frac{1}{f_s} = 10\mu$s respectively.

Numerical Results

Some channel impulse responses are presented in Figure 15. The frequency response of Figure 15b corresponds to a receiver position placed λ / 6 apart from the receiver position which corresponds to Figure 15a, while in Figure 15c the receiver is placed 2λ apart from Figure 15a. As can be seen in Figure 15c, there is an incoming component with delay 50ns, which is not visible in the other Figures. Furthermore, in Figure 5.15d the "average" impulse response, $h_{avg}(t)$, is displayed. The average impulse response is calculated by summing the impulse response at each receiver position and then dividing with the total number of positions, and reflects average channel behaviour.

Indicatively we mention that, on the average, we needed 1.84sec in order to calculate the frequency response at each receiver position and frequency tone. The overall simulation time may be calculated by multiplying 1.84sec times the number of frequency tones and receiver positions. Furthermore, in order to evaluate the simulation time in other environments, we modeled and simulated the building described in Kim et al. (Kim, 1996), where we needed on the average 3.89sec for each receiver position and frequency tone. All simulations are executed on a standard Pentium IV 2.4GHz PC, with 512MB of RAM.

The effect of multipath fading and the level of Intersymbol Interference (ISI) are determined by the rms delay spread, which is given by,

$$\tau_{rms} = \sqrt{E(\tau^2) - (E(\tau))^2} \tag{20}$$

where

$$E(\tau^n) = \frac{\sum_{i=1}^{L} \tau_i^n \beta_i^2}{\sum_{i=1}^{L} \beta_i^2} \tag{21}$$

while β_i, τ_i are the amplitude and delay of the i-th component respectively (Pahlavan, 1995).

For each receiver's position, the rms delay spread of the impulse response, $\tau_{rms,i}$, is calculated, and then the average and standard deviation of the rms delay spread, μ and respectively, are calculated using,

$$\mu = \frac{\sum_{i=1}^{N_s} \tau_{rms,i}}{N_s} \tag{22}$$

$$\sigma = \sqrt{\frac{1}{N_s - 1} \sum_{i=1}^{N_s} (\tau_{rms,i} - \mu)^2} \tag{23}$$

where $N_s = 51$ is the number of different receiver positions. The relative results are included in Table 1, together with respective results taken by measurements in two building types (A and B) which are included in (Hashemi, 1994). There are two threshold power values, below of which the multipath components are neglected. In the first case, $T_{threshold,1} = 20$dB, the average is equal to $\mu_1 = 15.53$ns and the standard deviation equal to $\sigma_1 = 3.78$ns, while in the second case, $T_{threshold,2} = 30$dB, the respective values are $\mu_2 = 17.70$ns and $\sigma_2 = 4.80$ns. The mean spread is larger in the second case, since more components take part into the calculation of the delay spread, and usually lower power components arise for longer time delays. All results are in good agreement with (Hashemi, 1994).

The "average" impulse response, $h_{avg}(t)$, offers an alternative means of channel characterization. For the two examined cases, $T_{threshold,1} = 20$dB $T_{threshold,2} = 30$dB, the average impulse responses are extracted and the rms delay spreads are calculated. In the first case, the result was $\tau_{rms,1}(h_{avg,1}) = 15.42$ns, while in the second case the result was $\tau_{rms,2}(h_{avg,2}) = 16.79$ns. Both these values are in good agreement with the average rms delay spread values given in Table 1.

Furthermore, the statistical behavior of the channel is examined deeper, by calculating the PDF of the rms delay spread. For this cause, Mean Square Error (MSE) tests are performed for all $N_s = 51$ impulse responses $\tau_{rms,i}$ which were collected during receiver movement. Then, MSE was calculated between the empirical distribution arising by simulation and three popular theoretical distributions. More specifically, Rayleigh, Normal (Gaussian) and Weibull distributions are examined. These distributions are given by,

$$f_{X,Rayleigh}(x) = \frac{x}{b_R^2} \exp\left(-\frac{x^2}{2b_R^2}\right) \tag{24}$$

$$f_{X,Normal}(x) = \frac{1}{\sigma_N \sqrt{2\pi}} \exp\left(-\frac{(x-\mu_N)^2}{2\sigma_N^2}\right) \tag{25}$$

$$f_{X,Weibull}(x) = a_W b_W x^{b_W-1} \exp\left(-a_W x^{b_W}\right) \tag{26}$$

respectively, where b_R, μ_N, σ_N, a_W, b_W are appropriate parameters for each distribution.

The MSE is calculated using

$$MSE = \frac{\sum_{i=1}^{N_{int}} (p_{D,j} - F_j)^2}{N_{int}} \tag{27}$$

where F_j is the empirical Cumulative Distribution Function (CDF), which is given by

$$F_j = prob\left(\tau_{rms} < \tau_j\right), j = 1,...,N_{int} \tag{28}$$

Table 1. Average and standard deviation of rms delay spread for the setup of Figure 14

Simulation Results				Building A (B) (Hashemi, 1994)		Building A (B) (Hashemi, 1994)	
$T_{threshold,1}$=20dB		$T_{threshold,2}$=30dB		$T_{threshold,1}$=20dB		$T_{threshold,2}$=30dB	
μ_1 (ns)	σ_1 (ns)	μ_2 (ns)	σ_2 (ns)	μ_1 (ns)	σ_1 (ns)	μ_2 (ns)	σ_2 (ns)
15.53	3.78	17.70	4.80	17.9 (18.4)	4.6 (4.8)	20.8 (20.7)	4.1 (4.4)

Figure 14. Representation of a simplified indoor environment

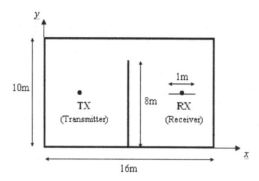

while $p_{D,j}$ is the the theoretical CDF which is given by

$$p_{D,j} = \int_0^{\tau_j} f_{X,D}(x)dx \qquad (29)$$

where the index D corresponds to the appropriate distribution (R for Rayleigh, N for Normal, W for Weibull). The parameter N_{int} corresponds to a desired number of calculation intervals between the minimum and maximum calculated τ_{rms}, while τ_j is the upper limit for each of the selected intervals. In the following, N_{int} is set equal to $N_{int} = 25$.

The theoretical PDF corresponding to the minimum MSE is selected. For each distribution, its parameters are calculated using the method of moments (not the electromagnetic MoM). More specifically, the first and second moment of the theoretical distributions are calculated as a function of its parameters, and then set equal to the corresponding parameters of the empirical distribution. The theoretical PDF parameters arise after solving the arising equations.

MSE tests results values for each distribution for both cases, $T_{threshold,1} = 20$dB and $T_{threshold,2} = 30$dB are tabulated in Table 2. It is concluded that the normal distribution is optimum and followed by Weibull and Rayleigh.

Finally, a comparison among the empirical and theoretical distributions is illustrated in Figures 16 and 17, for the assumed threshold values. It is worth to be noted that similar results regarding the normal distribution as optimally approximating empirical distributions of τ_{rms} are also reported in (Hashemi, 1994).

Resume

Using the proposed deterministic simulation tool, it is possible to extract valid results about the statistical behavior of a radio channel, without having to proceed to on-site measurements. The possibility of calculating statistical characteristics, such as the rms delay spread, but also characteristics such as frequency and impulse response, mean channel response and other are presented. It is worth noted that all results are in good agreement

Table 2. MSE tests results for Rayleigh, Normal and Weibull distributions

Theoretical Distribution of τ_{rms}	$T_{threshold}$=20dB MSE ($\times 10^{-3}$)	$T_{threshold}$=30dB MSE ($\times 10^{-3}$)
Rayleigh	35.188	17.535
Normal	**0.438**	**0.664**
Weibull	1.060	0.978

Figure 15. Channel impulse responses for the setup of Figure 14 and various receiver positions

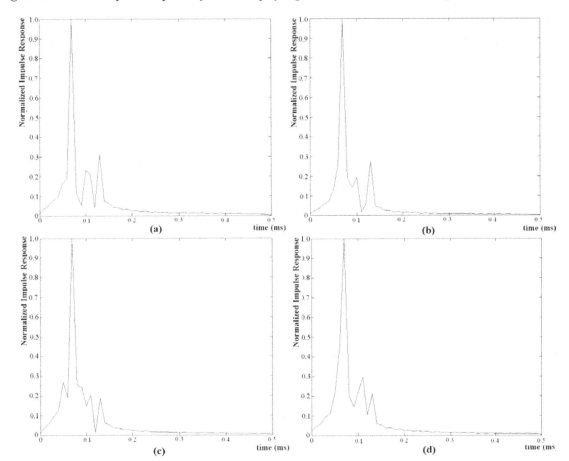

Figure 16. Comparison between empirical and theoretical distributions ($T_{threshold}$=20dB)

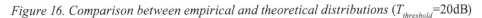
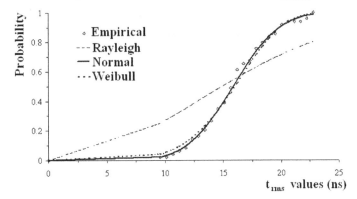

with corresponding measurements results to similar environments. As long as simulation time is concerned, it is not prohibitory, especially if the required spatial resolution is concerned, due to the fact that small scale fading study is required.

It is noted that with the proposed method, it is considered that wideband channel simulation is performed (frequency selective fading), while in the next section the case of narrowband channel simulation (frequency flat fading) is presented.

X. EXTENSION AND APPLICATION OF THE PROPOSED DETERMINISTIC SIMULATION TOOL

Introduction

Apart from drawing conclusions on the statistical attributes of fading in an indoor mobile channel, the proposed deterministic model can be used in a way to include smart antennas evaluation, as well as calculating BER (Varlamos, 2006). The case of use of Switched Parasitic Arrays (SPAs) is herein presented and comparative conclusions are drawn towards the improvement of the link in relation to the use of simple omnidirectional antennas, with respect to both mitigation of multipath fading and BER improvement. The proposed tool has been also used in order to evaluate a novel horizontally polarized switched-beam antenna in [Mit2006a], but this case will not be presented herein.

Rotation of a SPA's radiation pattern is achieved by entering the appropriate digital "word" to the control circuit, through high frequency switches. The ones, "1", of the digital word correspond to loaded elements while the zeros, "0", to short-circuited ones. All active elements are fed with voltage coefficients of equal amplitude and phase, but the amplitudes and phases of the corresponding currents, both in active and parasitic elements, are affected by electromagnetic coupling among all elements. SPAs have been extensively used to switched-beam applications (Preston, 1998; Schlub, 2000; Varlamos, 2003). Herein, the SPAs under examination are characterized by circular symmetry (Tillman, 1966; Sibille, 1997), while their behavior is studied from both the points of "smartness" evaluation as well as directivity alone.

Setup Description

The simulation setup is similar to the one described in Figure 14, but with a few important differences. The environment under study is pictured in Figure 18. The outer dimensions are again 16m x 10m x 4m while the inner wall is 4m high and 8m long. The operational frequency is chosen to be equal to $f = 1800$MHz. The roof,

Figure 17. Comparison between empirical and theoretical distributions ($T_{threshold}$=30dB)

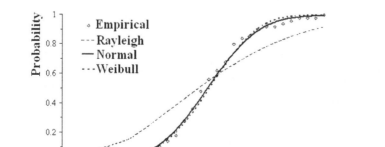

Table 3. Technical and performance characteristics of the SPCA antenna that was used during simulation

Dipoles' Length (λ)	Circle Radius (λ)	Dipoles' Radius (λ)	Gain (dBi)	RSLL (dB)	$\Delta\varphi_{3dB}$ (°)	Z_{in} (Ω)
0.486	0.534	0.001	7.59	-6.45	57.22	91.64+1.01*j*

Figure 18. Representation of the channel and antennas for SPA simulation. A magnified representation of the SPA receiver has been used for clarity purposes.

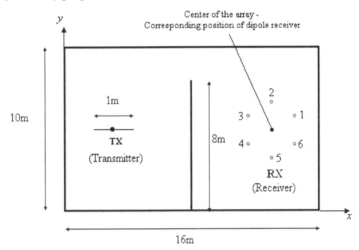

the floor and the inner/outer walls are simulated as UTD elements, with electric attributes for the walls $\varepsilon_r = 6$, $\sigma = 0.02s/m$ and $\mu_r = 1$, while for the roof and the floor $\varepsilon_r = 8$ $\sigma = 0.09s/m$, and $\mu_r = 1$ (Yang, 1998).

The antennas of the receiver and transmitter are vertically polarized and placed to 1.5m height. The transmission antenna is a dipole 0.46λ length and range 0.006λ, where λ the wavelength. The receiver antenna is either an identical dipole, when there is no simulation of the smart antenna, or a Switched Parasitic Circular Array (SPCA) when the use of the directional or switched beam array smart antenna is simulated.

The SPCA used has been proposed by Varlamos et al. (Varlamos, 2003). It consists of six vertically polarized identical dipoles, forming a uniform circular layout. The angle of the n-th dipole is $\varphi_n = (2n-1)\pi/6$, where $n = 1,...,6$.

The SPCA architecture is shown in Figure 18, where it is magnified for clarity purposes. By feeding the *n*-th dipole and short-circuiting the rest, the antenna is radiating towards the angle ϕ_n. The attributes of the SPCA are tabulated in Table 3. The termination resistance of the receiver is chosen in a way to maximize the power delivered to the load. Consequently in the case where the dipole is used as a receiver the termination resistance is 75Ω, while in the case where the SPA is used the termination resistance is 90Ω.

As a case study, consider transmitting a BPSK signal of power equal to 8.5dBm. A root-Nyquist filter is used at both the transmitter and receiver. A good approximation of the bandwidth necessary to transmit a BPSK signal is given by,

$$B_s = \frac{1.5}{T_b} = 1.5R \qquad (30)$$

where B_s is the bandwidth, T_b is the bit period, and R is the transmission rate. The environment of Figure 18 corresponds to an environment of the F-H type, according to the Pahlavan-Levesque guidelines (Pahlavan, 1995), and thus the maximum rms delay spread $\tau_{rms,max}$, is 0.1usec. Consequently, if a correlation factor of $\rho \geq 0.5$ is selected, then the coherence bandwidth is given by [Rap1999],

$$B_c(\rho \geq 0.5) = \frac{1}{5\tau_{rms}} = 2\text{MHz} \tag{31}$$

For simulation purposes, it is considered that $R=0.5\text{Mbps}$, with carrier frequency 1800MHz, so $B_s = 1.5R = 0.75\text{MHz} < B_c$. The important conclusion from this analysis is that the signal suffers from frequency flat fading. As it was mentioned in Section IX, it is herein attempted to simulate a narrowband signal with frequency flat fading, while it has already been proven the possibility of simulating wideband signals suffering from frequency selective fading.

Simulation Procedure

The transmitter is assumed to move along a straight section of 1m length while the receiver remains fixed. Every 2cm of the transmitter's displacement, measurements of the receiver's output take place at the frequency of $f = 1800$; totally, 51 measurements for different transmitter positions are collected.

If the receiver is desired to be the SPCA, the output of that radiation pattern providing the maximum power is recorded. Herein, the switching time is considered to be negligible, thus only the maximum power pattern is considered to be active. If the receiver is desired to be a directional antenna, the SPCA is again used, but only one pattern remains active as the transmitter moves. Finally, if the receiver is desired to be an omnidirectional antenna, a dipole identical to the transmitter is used.

BER Calculation

Considering the primary conclusion that the transmitted signal suffers from frequency flat fading, the BER calculation process can be analyzed as follows:

a. For each one of the transmitter's positions, i_p ($i_p = 1,...,N_p$) – obviously N_p 51-, the received power is calculated according to the formula

$$p_{r,i_p} = \left(|I_c|/\sqrt{2}\right)^2 R_L \tag{32}$$

where $|I_c|$ is the current amplitude induced to the central segment of the active receiver element, and R_L is the receiver termination resistance.

b. The mean value of the received power is calculated using the formula

$$\overline{p_r} = \left(1/N_p\right)\sum_{i_p=1}^{N_p} p_{r,i_p} \tag{33}$$

c. The appropriate mean noise power, σ_n^2, is calculated, so that the BER is calculated for the desired E_b/N_0, using the formula,

$$E_b/N_0 = \overline{p_r}/\sigma_n^2 \Rightarrow \sigma_n^2 = \frac{\overline{p_r}}{(E_b/N_0)} \tag{34}$$

By using the formula (34), the noise power is calculated for each E_b/N_0 value, which is considered to be constant during the movement of the transmitter.

d.   For each position of the transmitter the BER is calculated using,

$$\text{BER}_{i_p} = Q\left(\frac{p_{r,i_p}}{\sigma_n^2}\right) \tag{35}$$

where the equation $Q(.)$ depends on the modulation technique. For the specific case and based to the preceding analysis,

$$\text{BER}_{i_p} = \frac{1}{2}\text{erfc}\left(\sqrt{\frac{p_{r,i_p}}{\sigma_n^2}}\right). \tag{36}$$

e.   The mean BER is calculated using

$$\overline{\text{BER}} = \left(1/N_p\right)\sum_{i_p=1}^{N_p}\text{BER}_{i_p}. \tag{37}$$

Besides the proposed method, BER was also calculated using a Monte Carlo technique, where the power measurements to the output were used to develop the fading signal. The results were identical in both cases; therefore the proposed technique provides accurate calculations of BER without the large amount of resources needed for Monte Carlo simulation.

Numerical Simulation Results

For comparison purposes, simulations are conducted for the SPCA performing as SPA as well as a simple directional antenna. Furthermore, three different dipole receiver positions are also examined. The six directional patterns of the SPCA arise by appropriately selecting the element to be fed, while the three dipole positions are at the center of the SPCA, at the 3-rd SPCA element position, and at the 5-th SPCA element position. The mean BER was calculated for E_b/N_0 values from 0 to 12dB, with a step of 1dB.

Simulation results are illustrated in Table 4, where FD is used in order to denote Fade Depth, i.e. the maximum to minimum received power ratio. Furthermore, results for the mean received power as well as mean BER are presented for the case where $E_b/N_0 = 10$dB.

Table 4. Simulation results of SPA, directional and omnidirectional antennas

Receiver Type, RX	*FD* (dB)	Mean Received Power (dBm)	BER ($\times 10^{-2}$) (E_b/N_0=10dB)
SPCA - switched beam	6.84	-41.61	0.015
SPCA –Element 1 Active	32.40	-50.48	2.974
SPCA –Element 2 Active	11.75	-44.72	0.275
SPCA –Element 3 Active	16.84	-42.30	0.699
SPCA –Element 4 Active	22.28	-44.37	1.716
SPCA –Element 5 Active	9.55	-44.09	0.076
SPCA –Element 6 Active	26.92	-49.84	2.091
Dipole – SPCA Center	13.70	-42.78	0.354
Dipole – Position of SPCA 3rd Element	30.55	-46.18	1.435
Dipole – Position of SPCA 5th Element	19.65	-44.98	0.882

Figure 19. Comparison of received SPCA power to the directional SPCA having it 5th element active

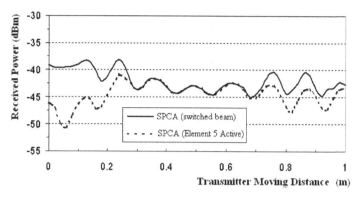

Figure 20. Comparison of the mean BER –SPCA, SPCA directional antenna having its 3rd element active, and SPCA directional antenna having its 5th element active

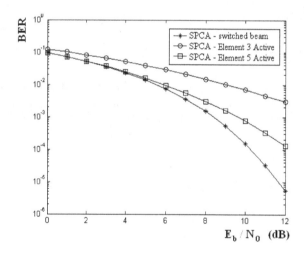

Figure 21. Comparison of received power of SPCA and the dipole placed at the center of the SPCA

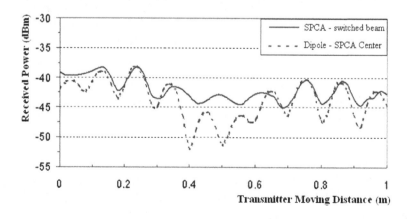

Figure 22. Comparison of the mean BER-SPCA, dipole at the center of the SPCA, dipole at the position of the 3rd element of SPCA, dipole at the position of the 5th element of the SPCA.

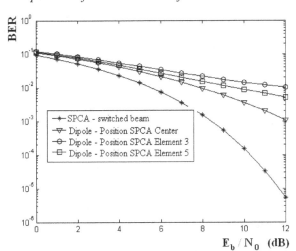

In Figure 19, the received power is depicted with respect to the position of the transmitter when the SPCA and the directional antenna with the 5th element active are used. In Figure 20 the BER plots for the SPA and the directional antennas with the 3rd or the 5th element active are depicted.

Similarly, in Figure 21 the compared received power is presented in the case where the SPCA or the omnidirectional dipole placed at the center of the SPA are used, while in Figure 22 the BER of the SPCA compared to three cases of different receiver positions is illustrated.

Evaluation of Results

From Table 4 and Figures 19-22, it is evident that the SPCA antenna exhibits superior performance in comparison to any other case of directional or omnidirectional antenna, with respect to the fade depth *FD*, the mean received power and the mean BER.

Furthermore, the directional antenna with the 3rd element active presents the maximum received power, as it is directed to the main arrival angle of the receiving signal, while the one with the 5th element active presents the minimum *FD*. Those two directional antennas exhibit enhanced performance compared to the respective cases of a dipole positioned at the positions of the corresponding active elements.

On the other hand, among directional antennas, the worst performance is exhibited by the antennas with their 1st or 6th element active. Maybe this is due to their orientation, since they aim to an angle opposite to that of the transmitter.

Returning to the SPCA, for BER = 10^{-4}, the cut to the transmitted power that can be achieved through its use is 2.25dB and 4.65dB, with respect to the use of the optimum directional or the optimum omnidirectional receiver respectively, as becomes evident from Figures 20 and 22. Finally, it is worth noting that the performance of the SPCA in Figures 19-22 is compared to the cases that the directional and omnidirectional receivers present the least favorable to the SPCA results. The improvement of the performance, in relation to the mean received power, the *FD* and the BER is more impressive if compared to other cases.

As a result, the proposed model has undertaken the necessary adjustments so that it is immediately employable for use in order to evaluate directional and switched-beam antennas, while it is evident that it is possible to simulate both frequency flat and selective fading.

XI. CONCLUSION

The de facto wireless nature of NGNs mandates the development of efficient radio channel simulation techniques in order to rapidly and cost-effectively design and develop NGWNs. Being motivated by this main conclusion, this chapter is focused on small scale fading and aims to present the most popular small scale fading modeling and simulation techniques for the mobile radio channel. Some popular simulation models are presented and classified, while a short discussion took place for each type of technique. Furthermore, two channel simulation tools (one statistical and one deterministic) are proposed and results are presented.

The authors hope that the information provided herein will help researchers to acquire an insight to small-scale fading simulation techniques, and will create a motivation in order to further study this exciting research field.

REFERENCES

Akan, O.B. (2004). *Advanced transport protocols for next generation heterogeneous wireless network architecture.* Unpublished Master thesis, Georgia Institute of Technology, Georgia, USA.

Alexander, S.E. (1982). Radio propagation within buildings at 900MHz, *IEE Electronics Letters*, Vol. 18, pp. 913-914.

Bithas, P., Mathiopoulos, T., and Kotsopoulos, S.A. (2007). Diversity Reception over Generalized-K (KG) Fading Channels, *IEEE Transactions on Wireless Communications*, to be published.

Burside, W.D., and Burgener, K.W. (1983). High frequency scattering of thin lossless dielectric slab, *IEEE Transactions on Antennas and Propagation*, Vol. AP-31, pp. 104-110.

Catedra, M.F., Perez, J., DeAbana, S.F., Gutierez, O. (1998). Efficient Ray-Tracing Techniques for Three-Dimensional Analyses of Propagation in Mobile Communications: Application to Picocell and Microcell Scenarios, *IEEE Antennas and Propagation Magazine*, Vol. 40, No. 22, pp. 437-440.

Chengshan, X., Zheng, Y.R., and Beaulieu, N.C. (2002). Second-order statistical properties of the WSS Jakes' fading channel simulator, *IEEE Transactions on Communications*, Vol. 50, No. 6, pp. 888-891.

Choi, M.S., Park, H.K., Heo, Y.H., Oh, S.H., and Myung, N.H. (2006). A 3-D propagation model considering building transmission loss for indoor wireless communications, *ETRI Journal*, Vol. 28, No. 2, pp. 247-249.

Clarke, R. (1968). A statistical theory of mobile radio reception, *Bell Systems Technical Journal*, Vol. 47, pp. 957-1000.

COST 207 TD(86) 51-REV 3 (WG1) (1986): "Proposal on channel transfer functions to be used in GSM tests late 1986", September 1986.

Dent, P., Bottomley, G.E., and Croft, T. (1993), Jakes fading model revisited, *IEE Electronics Letters*, Vol. 29, No. 13, pp. 1162-1163.

Deschamps, G.A. (1972). Ray techniques in electromagnetics, *Proceedings of the IEEE*, Vol. 60, pp. 1022-1035.

Dixit, S. (2006). On fixed-mobile network convergence, *Wireless Personal Communications*, Vol. 38, No. 1, pp. 55-65.

Ertel, R.B., Cartieri, P., Sowerby, K.W., Rappaport, T.S., and Reed, J.H. (1998). Overview of Spatial Channel Models for Antenna Array Communication Systems, *IEEE Personal Communications,* Vol. 5, No. 1, pp. 10-22.

Fourie, A., and Nitch, D. (2000). SuperNEC: antenna and indoor-propagation simulation program, *IEEE Antennas and Propagation Magazine*, Vol. 42, No. 3, 31-48.

Fusco, M. (1990). FDTD algorithm in curvilinear coordinates, *IEEE Transactions on Antennas and Propagation*, Vol. AP-38, pp. 76-88.

Ganesh, R., and Pahlavan, K. (1989). On arrival of paths in fading multipath indoor radio channels, *IEE Electronics Letters*, Vol. 25, No. 5, pp. 763-765.

Ganesh, R. (1991). *Time Domain Measurements, Modeling, and Simulation of the Indoor Radio Channel.* Ph.D. thesis, Worcester Polytechnic Institute.

GSM Recommendation 05.05 (1991). Radio transmission and reception, ETSI/PT, No. 12, January 1991.

Gudmundson, M. (1991). Correlation model for shadow fading in mobile radio systems, *Electronics Letters*, Vol. 27, No. 23, pp. 2145-2146.

Hansen, F., and Meno, F. I. (1977). Mobile fading – Rayleigh and lognormal superimposed, IEEE Transactions on Vehicular Technology, vol. VT-26, no. 4, pp. 332-335.

Harms, P.H., Lee, J.F., and Mittra, R. (1992). A study of the non-orthogonal FDTD method versus the conventional FDTD technique for computing resonant frequencies of cylindrical cavities, *IEEE Transactions on Microwave Theory and Techniques*, Vol. MTT-40, pp. 741-746.

Harada, H., and Prasad, R. (2002). *Simulation and Software Radio for Mobile Communications,* Artech House, Norwood, MA, USA.

Hashemi, H. (1993). Impulse response modeling of indoor radio propagation channels, *IEEE Journal on Selected Areas in Communications*, Vol. 11, pp. 967-978.

Hashemi, H., and Tholl, D. (1994). Statistical Modeling and Simulation of the RMS Delay Spread of Indoor Radio Propagation Channels, *IEEE Transaction on Vehicular Technology*, Vol. 43, No. 1, pp. 110-120.

Hata, M., and Nagatsu, T. (1980). Mobile location using signal strength measurements in cellular systems, *IEEE Transactions on Vehicular Technology*, Vol. 29, No. 2, pp. 245-251.

Holland, R. (1983). Finite difference solutions of Maxwell's equations in generalized non-orthogonal coordinates, *IEEE Transactions on Nuclear Science*, Vol. NS-30, No. 6, pp. 4589-4591.

Holt, T., Pahlavan, K., and Lee, J.F. (1992). A graphical indoor radio channel simulator using 2D ray tracing, *Proceedings of the PIMRC '92*, Boston, USA, pp. 411-416.

Howard, J.S., *Frequency Domain Characteristic and Autoregressive Modeling of the Indoor Radio Channel.* Ph.D. Thesis, Worcester Polytechnic Institute, Worcester MA.

Ikegami, F., Takeuchi, T., and Yoshida, S. (1991). Theoretical prediction of mean field strength for urban mobile radio, *IEEE Transactions on Antennas and Propagation*, Vol. 39, pp. 229-302.

International Telecommunication Union (ITU), "NGN Working Definition", available at http://www.itu.int/ITU-T/studygroups/com13/ngn2004/working_definition.html .

Jakes, W.C. (1974). *Microwave Mobile Communications.* Wiley, New York.

Jakes, W.C. (1994). *Microwave Mobile Communications.* IEEE Press.

Jeruchim, M.C., Balaban, P., and Shanmugan, K.S. (1992). *Simulation of Communication Systems.* Plenum Press, New York.

Joint Technical Committee of Committee T1 R1P1.4 and TIA TR46.3.3/TR45.4.4 on Wireless Access (1994). Final Report on RF Channel Characterization, No. JTC(AIR)/94.01.17-238R4, January 1994.

Karadimas, P., and Kotsopoulos, S.A. (2007). A modified Loo model with sectored and three dimensional multipath scattering, *World Wireless Congress 2007*, San Francisco, May 2007.

Karagiannidis, G.K., Zogas, D.A., Sagias, N.C., Kotsopoulos, S.A., and Tombras, G.S. (2005). Equal-gain and maximal-ratio combining over nonidentical Weibull fading channels, *IEEE Transactions on Wireless Communications*, Vol. 4, No. 3, pp. 841-846.

Kein, A., and Mohr, W. (1996). A statistical wideband mobile radio channel model including the direction of arrival, *IEEE 4th International Symposium on Spread Spectrum Techniques and Applications*, pp. 102-106.

Kim, S.C., Bertoni, H.L., Stern, M. (1996). Pulse Propagation Characteristics at 2.4GHz Inside Buildings, *IEEE Transactions on Vehicular Technology*, Vol. 45, No. 3, pp. 579-592.

Kotsopoulos, S.A., and Karagiannidis, G. (2000). Error Performance for Equal-gain Combiners over Rayleigh Fading Channels, *Journal of IEE Electronics Letters*, Vol.36, No. 10, pp. 892-894.

Lawton, M.C., Davies, R.L., and McGeehan, J.P. (1991). A ray launching method for the prediction of indoor radio channel characteristics, *PIMRC '91*, pp. 104-108, London, UK.

Lawton, M.C., and McGeehan, J.P. (1992). The application of GTD and ray launching techniques to channel modeling for cordless radio systems, *Proceedings of the 42nd IEEE Vehicular Technology Conference*, pp. 125-130, Denver, USA.

Lebherz, M., Wiesbeck, W., Blasberg, H.-J., and Krank, W. (1989). Calculation of broadcast coverage based on a digital terrain model, *Proceedings of the 1989 IEEE International Conference on Antennas and Propagation*, Vol. 2, pp. 355-359.

Lebherz, M., Wiesbeck, W., and Krank, W. (1992). A versatile wave propagation model for the VHF/UHF range considering three-dimensional terrain, *IEEE Transactions on Antennas and Propagation*, Vol. 40, pp. 1121-1131.

Lee, W.C.Y. (1982). *Mobile Communications Engineering*, McGraw Hill, New York.

Lee, W.C.Y. (1986). *Mobile Communications Design Fundamentals*, Sams, Indianapolis, IN.

Lee, J.F. (1993). Numerical solutions of TM scattering using an obliquely Cartesian finite difference time domain algorithm, *IEE Proceedings H: Microwaves, Antennas and Propagation*, Vol. 140, No. 1, pp. 23-28, February 1993.

Liang, G., Bertoni, H.K. (1998). A New Approach to 3-D Ray Tracing for Propagation Prediction in Cities, *IEEE Transactions on Antennas and Propagation*, Vol. 46, No. 6, pp. 853-863.

Liberti, J.C.Jr., and Rappaport, T.S. (1996). A geometrically based model for line-of-sight multipath radio channels, *Proceedings of the 46th IEEE Vehicular Technology Conference*, Vol. 2, pp. 844-848.

Liberti, J.C.Jr., and Rappaport, T.S. (1999). *Smart Antennas for Wireless Communications: IS-95 and Third Generation CDMA Applications*. Prentice Hall PTR, New Jersey.

Loo, C. (1985). A statistical model for a land mobile satellite link, IEEE Transactions on Vehicular Technology, vol. VT-34, no. 3, pp. 122-127.

Lotter, M.P., and van Rooyen, P. (1999). Cellular channel modeling and the performance of DS-CDMA systems with antenna arrays, *IEEE Journal on Selected Areas on Communications*, Vol. 17, No. 12, pp. 2181-2196.

Lu, M., Lo, T., and Litva, J. (1997). A physical spatio-temporal model of multipath propagation channels, *Proceedings of the 47th IEEE Vehicular Technology Conference*, pp. 180-184.

McKown, J.W., and Hamilton, R.L.Jr. (1991). Ray tracing as a design tool for radio networks, *IEEE Network Magazine*, Vol. 6, No. 6, pp. 27-30.

McPherson, G. (1990). *Statistics in Scientific Investigation*, Springer.

Mitilineos, S.A., Varlamos, P K., and Capsalis, C.N. (2004). A simulation method for bit error rate performance estimation for arbitrary angle of arrival channel models, *IEEE Antennas and Propagation Magazine*, Vol. 46, No. 2, pp. 158-163.

Mitilineos, S.A., Panagiotou, S.C., Varlamos, P.K., and Capsalis, C.N. (2005). Indoor environments propagation simulation using a hybrid MoM and UTD electromagnetic method, *Annals of Telecommunications*, Vol. 60, No. 9-10, pp.1231-1243.

Norklit, O., and Anderson, J.B. (1994). Mobile radio environments and adaptive arrays, *IEEE International Symposium on Personal, Indoor and Mobile Radio Communications (PIMRC)*, pp. 725-728.

O'Brien, W.M., Kenny, E.M., and Cullen, P.J. (2000). An Efficient Implementation of a Three-Dimensional Microcell Propagation Tool for Indoor and Outdoor Urban Environments, *IEEE Transactions on Vehicular Technology*, Vol. 49, No. 2, pp. 622-630.

Oestges, C., Clerck, B., Raynaud, L., and van Hoenacker, J.D. (2002). Deterministic Channel Modeling and Performance Simulation of Microcellular Wide-Band Communication Systems, *IEEE Transactions on Vehicular Technology*, Vol. 51, No. 6, pp. 1422-1430.

Okumura, Y., Ohmuri, E., Kawano, T., and Fukuda, K. (1968). Field strength and its variability in VHF and UHF land mobile radio service, *Rev. of the ECL*, Vol. 16, pp 825-873.

Ossana, J.Jr. (1964). A model for mobile radio fading due to building reflections: theoretical and experimental fading waveform power spectra, *Bell Systems Technical Journal*, Vol. 43, No. 6, pp. 2935-2971.

Pahlavan, K., Ganesh, R., and Hotaling, T. (1989). Multipath propagation measurements on manufacturing floors at 910MHz, *IEE Electronics Letters*, Vol. 25, No. 3, pp. 225-227.

Pahlavan, K., and Levesque, A.H. (1995). *Wireless Information Networks*. John Wiley & Sons, New York.

Papamichael, V., Soras, C., and Makios, V. (2003). FDTD Modeling and Characterization of the Indoor Radio Propagation Channel in the 434 MHz ISM Band, *ICECom 2003, 17th International Conference on Applied Electromagnetics and Communications*, pp. 217-220.

Paulraj, A., Nabar, R., and Gore, D. (2003). *Introduction to Space-Time Wireless Communications*. Cambridge University Press.

Polydorou, D.S., and Capsalis, C.N. (1997). A new theoretical model for the prediction of rapid fading variations in an indoor environment, *IEEE Transactions on Vehicular Technology*, Vol. 46, No. 3, pp. 748-754.

Pop, M.F., and Beaulieu, N.C. (1999). Statistical investigation of sum-of-sinusoids fading channel simulators, *GLOBECOM '99*, Vol. 1A, pp. 419-426, Rio de Janeiro, Brazil.

Pop, M.F., and Beaulieu, N.C. (2001). Limitations of sum-of-sinusoids fading channel simulators, *IEEE Transactions on Communications*, Vol. 49, No. 4, pp. 699-708.

Pop, M.F., and Beaulieu, N.C. (2002). Design of wide-sense stationary sum-of-sinusoids fading channel simulators, *Proceedings of th3 2002 IEEE International Conference on Communications*, Vol. 2, pp. 709-716.

Preston, S.L., Thiel, D.V., Smith, T.A, O'Keefe, S.G., and Lu, J.W. (1998). Base-station tracking in mobile communications using a switched parasitic antenna array, *IEEE Transactions on Antennas and Propagation*, Vol. 46, No. 6, pp. 841-844.

Raleigh, G.G., and Paulraj, A. (1995), "Time varying vector channel estimation for adaptive spatial equalization", *Proceedings of the 1995 IEEE GLOBECOM*, pp. 218-224.

Rappaport, T.S. (1989). Characterization of UHF multipath radio channels in factory building, *IEEE Transactions on Antennas and Propagation*, Vol. 37, No. 8, pp. 1058-1069.

Rappaport, T.S., Seidel, S.Y., and Takamizawa, K. (1991). Statistical channel impulse response models for factory and open plan building radio communication system design, *IEEE Transactions on Communications*, Vol. COM-39, No 5, pp. 794-806.

Rappaport, T.S., and Hawbaker, D.A. (1992). A ray tracing technique to predict path loss and delay spread inside buildings, *Proceedings of the 1992 IEEE GLOBECOM*, pp. 649-653.

Rappaport, T.S., Huang, W., and Feuerstein, M.J. (1993). Performance of decision feedback equalizers in simulated urban and indoor radio channels, *IEICE Transactions on Communications*, Vol. E76-B, No. 2.

Rizk, K., Wagen, J.F., Gardiol, F. (1997). Two-Dimensional Ray-Tracing Modeling for Propagation Prediction in Microcellular Environments, *IEEE Transactions on Vehicular Technology*, Vol. 46, No. 22, pp. 508-518.

Rossi, J.-P., and Levy, A.J. (1993). Propagation analysis in cellular environment with the help of models using ray theory and GTD, *Proceedings of the 43rd IEEE Vehicular Technology Conference*, pp. 253-256.

Ruggieri, M. (2006). Next generation of wired and wireless networks: the NavCom integration, *Wireless Personal Communications*, Vol. 38, No. 1, pp. 79-88.

Rustako, A.J., Amitay, N.Jr., Owens, G.J., and Roman, R.S. (1991). Radio propagation at microwave frequencies for line-of-sight microcellular mobile and personal communications, *IEEE Transactions on Vehicular Technology*, Vol. 40, pp. 203-210.

Sagias, N.C., Karagiannidis, G.K., Zogas, D.A., Tombras, G.S., and Kotsopoulos, S.A. (2005). Average output SINR of equal-gain diversity in correlated Nakagami-m fading with cochannel interference, *IEEE Transactions on Wireless Communications*, Vol. 4, No. 4, pp. 1407-1411.

Saleh, A.A.M., and Valenzuela, R.A. (1987). A statistical model for indoor multipath propagation, *IEEE Journal on Selected Areas in Communications*, Vol. SAC-5, No. 2, pp. 128-137.

Sarkar, T.K., Ji, Z., Kim, K., Medouri, Z., and Salazar-Palma, M. (2003). A survey of various propagation models for mobile communication, *IEEE Antennas and Propagation Magazine*, Vol. 45, No. 3, 51-82.

Schlub, R., Thiel, D.V., Lu, J.W., and O' Keefe, S.G. (2000). Dual-band switched parasitic wire antennas for communications and direction finding, *Proceedings of the 2000 IEEE Asia-Pacific Microwave Conference*, pp. 74-78, Sydney, Australia.

Seidel, S.Y., and Rappaport, T.S. (1994). Site-specific propagation prediction for wireless in-building personal communication system design, *IEEE Transactions on Vehicular Technology*, Vol. 43, No. 4, pp. 879-891.

Sibille, A., Roblin, C., and Poncelet, G. (1997). Circular switched monopole arrays for beam steering wireless communications," *Electronics Letters*, Vol. 33, No. 7, pp. 551-552.

Son, H.W., and Myung, N.H. (1999). A deterministic ray tube method for microcellular wave propagation prediction model, *IEEE Transactions on Antennas and Propagation*, Vol. 47, No. 8, pp. 1344-1350.

Stapleton, S.P., Carbo, X., and McKeen, T. (1994). Spatial channel simulator for phased arrays, *IEEE 44th Vehicular Technology Conference*, Vol. 3, pp. 1789-1792, Stockholm, Sweden.

Stapleton, S.P., Carbo, X., and McKeen, T. (1996). Tracking and diversity for a mobile communications base station array antenna", *IEEE 46th Vehicular Technology Conference*, Vol. 3, pp. 1695-1699, Atlanta, GA, USA.

Stuber, G.L. (2001). *Principles of Mobile Communication*. Kluwer Academic Publisher.

Suzuki, H. (1977). A statistical model for urban radio propagation: multipath characteristics in New York city, *IEEE Transactions on Communications*, Vol. 25, pp. 673-680.

Taflove, A., and Morris, M.E. (1975). Numerical solution of steady-state electromagnetic scattering problems using the time-dependent Maxwell's equations, *IEEE Transactions on Microwave Theory and Techniques*, Vol. MTT-23, pp. 623-630.

Talbi, L. (2001). Simulation of Indoor UHF Propagation Using Numerical Technique, *Canadian Conference on Electrical and Computer Engineering*, Vol. 2, pp. 1357-1362.

Tillman, J.D., Jr. (1966). *The Theory and Design of Circular Antenna Arrays*. University of Tennessee Engineering Experimental Station.

Toumbakaris, D., and Kotsopoulos, S.A. (2007). Delay-constrained transmission over flat fading channels in the low SNR range, *18th Annual IEEE International Symposium on Personal, Indoor and Mobile Radio Communications*, Athens, Greece, 3-7 September 2007, to be published.

Turin, G.L., Clapp, F.D., Johnston, T.L., Fine, S.B., and Lavry, D. (1972). A statistical model of urban multipath propagation, *IEEE Transactions on Vehicular Technology*, Vol. 21, No. 1, pp. 1-9.

Varlamos, P.K., and Capsalis, C.N. (2003). Design of a six-sector switched parasitic planar array using the method of genetic algorithms, *Wireless Personal Communications*, Vol. 26, No. 1, pp. 77-88.

Varlamos, P.K., Mitilineos, S.A., and Capsalis, C.N. (2006). Diversity performance of a switched parasitic circular array in an indoor multipath environment, *Proceedings of the European Microwave Association (EuMA)*, to be published, September 2006.

Vellis, F.E., and Capsalis, C.N. (2000). A model for the statistical characterization of fast fading in the presence of a user, *Wireless Personal Communications*, Vol. 15, pp. 207-219.

Wallace, J.W., and Jensen, M.A. (2003). Validation of Parametric Directional MIMO Channel Models from Wideband FDTD Simulations of a Simple Indoor Environment, *IEEE 2003 Antennas and Propagation Society International Symposium*, Vol. 2, pp. 535-538.

Yang, G., Li, S., Lee, J.F., and Pahlavan, K. (1993). "Computer simulation of indoor radio propagation, *IEEE 1993 International Symposium on Personal, Indoor and Mobile Radio Communication*, Yokohama, Japan.

Yang, G., Pahlavan, K., and Lee, J.F. (1993). A 3D propagation model with polarization characteristics in indoor radio channels, *Proceedings of the 1993 IEEE GLOBECOM*, Vol. 2, pp. 1252-1256, Houston, USA.

Yang, C.F., Wu, B.C., and Ko, C.J. (1998). A Ray-Tracing Method for Modeling Indoor Wave Propagation and Penetration, *IEEE Transactions on Antennas and Propagation*, Vol. 46, No. 6, pp. 907-919.

Yee, K.S. (1966). Numerical solution of initial boundary value problems involving Maxwell's equations in isotropic media, *IEEE Transactions on Antennas and Propagation*, Vol. AP-14, pp. 302-307.

Yegani, P., and McGillem, C.D. (1991). A statistical model for the factory radio channel, *IEEE Transactions on Communications*, Vol. 39, pp. 1445-1454.

Zetterberg, P. (1995). *Mobile Communication with Base Station Antenna Arrays: Propagation Modeling and System Capacity*. Master Thesis, Royal Institute of Technology, Stockholm, Sweden.

Zetterberg, P., Espensen, P.L., and Mogensen, P. (1996). Propagation, beamsteering and uplink combining algorithms for cellular systems, *Proceedings of the 1996 ACTS Mobile Communications Summit*, pp. 500-509, Granada, Spain.

Zhang, W. (1997). A Wide-Band Propagation Model Based on UTD for Cellular Mobile Radio Communications, *IEEE Transactions on Antennas and Propagation*, Vol. 45, No. 11, pp. 1669-1678.

KEY TERMS

Deterministic Channel Models: Channel models based on (usually digital) architectural plans or topographical maps of the propagation environment.

Empirical Channel Models: Channel models based on in-situ channel measurements.

Frequency Flat Fading: A type of small scale fading where all frequency signal components experience the same magnitude of fading; corresponds to the case where the signal bandwidth is smaller than the channel coherence bandwidth.

Frequency Selective Fading: A type of small scale fading where different frequency signal components therefore experience decorelated fading; corresponds to the case where the signal bandwidth is larger than the channel coherence bandwidth.

Geometric Channel Models: Channel models based on abstract geometric characteristics of the propagation environment.

Mobile Channel: A wireless communications propagation description, referring to mobile receivers and/or transmitters.

Simulation: Artificial Reality, i.e. the research field whose intention is to mimic one or more attributes of reality.

Smart Antennas: Antenna arrays that are capable of automatically controling each element's gain and phase, thus delivering optimal or sub-optimal radiation patterns with respect to a desired evaluation criterion.

Small Scale Fading: Severe signal strength fluctuations within distances in the order of wavelength.

Statistical Channel Models: Channel models based on given probability density functions of channel characteristics.

Chapter XVI
Stochastic Modeling of Narrowband Fading Channels with Three Dimensional Diffuse Scattering

Petros Karadimas
University of Patras, Greece

ABSTRACT

This chapter studies a composite stochastic model, in which the diffuse component arises from three dimensional (3-D) multipath scattering. That case occurs especially in dense scattering environments, in which the tall obstacles cause arrival of multipath power in the elevation plane, besides that arriving in the azimuth one. Also the multipath components are assumed to arrive at the mobile receiver in specific angular sectors at the azimuth receiver's plane. The last is physically justified by multipath power blocking due to the channel obstacles (shadow fading), or/and lack of scattering objects at specific angular directions, or/and directional antennas utilization. An extended Suzuki model, where the Rician process for the diffuse scattering component is multiplied by a lognormal one, is considered as an appropriate composite model. The most important metrics of the model are presented, according to its assumptions. More specifically, from the closed form autocorrelation function, the Doppler power spectral density (PSD) of the diffuse component can be analytically derived. Afterwards exact solutions for the envelope and phase probability density functions (PDF's) are presented. Exact solutions are also derived for the second order statistics, i.e. the level crossing rate (LCR) and the average duration of fades (ADF's). An efficient deterministic simulation scheme will be presented, which implements the analytical model on a digital computer. Finally a curve fitting of the LCR to real world data, drawn from channel measurements, will demonstrate the flexibility and usefulness of the extended Suzuki model.

I. INTRODUCTION

The transmission performance of wireless services is strongly influenced by the rapid amplitude and phase fluctuations of the received signal. Those fluctuations result from the constructive and destructive nature of the arriving multipath components at the receiver. In turn multipath components can arrive at the elevation plane, besides those arriving at the azimuth receiver's plane, due to 3-D electromagnetic wave propagation. Moreover an

Copyright © 2009, IGI Global, distributing in print or electronic forms without written permission of IGI Global is prohibited.

important contribution to the received signal variability arises from the shadowing mechanisms of the channel, causing time varying attenuation of the received signal mean value.

In order to model the slow term variations, due to shadow fading and incorporate them in the rapid short term variations, arising from multipath propagation, two basic models have been proposed. Each of them represents a different concept for the wireless mobile channel modeling. The first one was proposed by Suzuki (Suzuki, 1977) and Hansen and Meno (Hansen, 1977), the so called Suzuki process. This model is obtained by multiplying a Rayleigh process with a lognormal one. The second was proposed by Loo (Loo, 1985), (Loo, 1991). This model resembles a Rician model, with the additional property that the amplitude of the line of sight (LOS) component is no more constant, as this happens in the Rician model, but it is a random stochastic process following a lognormal PDF. Loo model arises by summing a lognormally distributed random phasor and a Rayleigh phasor. In international bibliography the term "modified" applies to the case where the inphase and quadrature Gaussian components generating the Rayleigh part are correlated, whereas the term "extended" refers to the case where a specular component of constant amplitude has been added to the diffuse one. Thus we obtain modified Suzuki processes (Krantzik, 1990), extended Suzuki processes, (Corazza, 1994; Patzold, 1998 A; Patzold, 1997; Li, 1996), (Patzold, pp. (157-208), 2002) and modified Loo models (Patzold, 1998 B), (Patzold, pp. (218-240), 2002). By adopting modified models we force the Doppler PSD of the diffuse scattering component to obtain an asymmetrical shape, in contrast to the classical symmetrical PSD, arising from two dimensional (2-D) propagation and given by Clarke (Clarke, 1968). Thus, it is a simple technique to model sectored arrival of multipath power. By adopting extended Suzuki processes we increase the flexibility and usefulness of the channel model, as this extension enables us to incorporate in it a LOS component, if a specific channel configuration implies its existence (e.g. an open environment). Apart from the already cited works, Suzuki models have been employed in several publications, in both single state (stationary) and multiple states (non-stationary) models. In (Vatalaro, 1995) and (Vatalaro, 2002) a generalized Rice-lognormal channel was studied, in which Suzuki model constitute a special case of it. In (Tjhung, 1999) the second order statistics of the Nakagami-lognormal channel were derived, whereas in (Xie, 2000) the received signal envelope and power PDF's of the Beckmann-lognormal model were investigated. Finally in (Lutz, 1991) a two states model was employed, where a Suzuki process occupies one state and a Rician the other one.

In order to account for multipath propagation in three dimensions, combined with shadow fading, we adopt in this chapter an extended Suzuki model, where the diffuse component arises from both 3-D scattering and partial arrival of multipath power (Karadimas, 2008 A). Apart from (Karadimas, 2008 A), where the PSD was analytically calculated, 3-D multipath scattering has been the topic of several publications. In (Aulin, 1979) a PDF for the elevation angles of arrival was considered, with the advantage of leading to an analytical expression for the PSD. In (Parsons, pp. (123-125), 2000) an alternative to (Aulin, 1979) PDF for the elevation angles of arrival was considered, but with the drawback of not leading to analytical expression for the PSD. In (Qu, 1999) a 3-D scattering model was proposed in which the PDF for the elevation angles of arrival was a family of functions with two parameters. Specific functions of that family led to analytical solutions for the Doppler PSD. In (Clarke, 1997) the PSD and autocorrelation function were calculated for isotropic scattering in both the azimuth and elevation plane. The models (Aulin, 1979), (Parsons, pp. (123-125), 2000), (Qu, 1999) and (Clarke, 1997) have in common that a uniform and continuous distribution for the angles of arrival in the azimuth plane has been considered. In (Karadimas, 2007) and (Karadimas, 2008 B) the diffuse component resulted from both 3-D scattering and partial arrival of multipath power. In (Ho, 2005) a generalized Doppler PSD was derived in closed form for arbitrary 3-D scattering environments. But this form, due to its high complexity, is only of mathematical value and cannot be easily adapted to practical problems for extracting real channel metrics, such as LCR or ADF's. The interested reader should only consider the algebraic manipulations the author made in (Ho, 2005), in order to generate from his model the classical U-shaped PSD proposed by Clarke (Clarke, 1968). In (Vatalaro, 1997) the Doppler spectrum for the mobile to mobile channel, in the presence of 3-D isotropic scattering at both the receiver and transmitter, was investigated and in (Ozdemir, 2004) a multiple input-multiple output (MIMO) channel with 3-D scattering was studied. Finally in (Pal, 2006) the second order moments of spatial fading were investigated, in the presence of 3-D scattering and sectored arrival of diffuse power.

The remaining of this chapter is organized as follows. Section II gives the analytical model for the extended Suzuki model with 3-D multipath scattering. More specifically the Doppler PSD of the diffuse component is analytically derived, after Fourier transforming the closed form autocorrelation function, which in turn arises by considering the azimuth and elevation angles of arrival distributions. Afterwards exact solutions for the PDF of the envelope and phase are derived, together with exact ones for the LCR and ADF's. In Section III we simulate the analytical model by applying an extended version of the deterministic simulation scheme, called method of exact Doppler spread (MEDS) (Patzold, 1996), (Patzold, pp. (128-133), 2002), presented in (Karadimas, 2008 B). In Section IV we demonstrate the flexibility and usefulness of the model by adapting the LCR to real world data, drawn from channel measurements. Finally Section V concludes this chapter with a synopsis of the main results and advantages of the model.

II. THE ANALYTICAL MODEL

The stochastic process $r(t)$ for modeling narrowband wireless channels arises by multiplying a Rice process $z(t)$ with a lognormal one $k(t)$, i.e. $r(t) = z(t) \cdot k(t)$, with t the time parameter. The Rice process comes from the modulus of a complex process $\mu_\rho(t)$ as $z(t) = |\mu_\rho(t)| = |\mu(t) + \rho \exp[j(2\pi f_\rho t + \theta_\rho)]|$, where $\mu(t) = \mu_1(t) + j\mu_2(t)$ and $\mu_1(t)$, $\mu_2(t)$ are real valued Gaussian processes with zero mean and equal variances. The process $\mu(t)$ characterizes the purely diffuse component (without the LOS), arising from 3-D multipath scattering. Moreover ρ is the amplitude of the LOS component and f_ρ and θ_ρ are its Doppler frequency and Doppler phase respectively. The lognormal process is generated by a third real valued Gaussian process $m(t)$ with zero mean and unit variance as $k(t) = \exp[lm(t) + n]$, where the parameters l and n are characteristic quantities of the specific shadowing environment. Thus the stochastic process describing the fading signal amplitude will be

$$r(t) = \sqrt{\mu_{\rho1}(t)^2 + \mu_{\rho2}(t)^2} \cdot \exp[lm(t) + n] \tag{1}$$

where $\mu_{\rho1}(t) = \mu_1(t) + \rho\cos(2\pi f_\rho t + \theta_\rho)$ and $\mu_{\rho2}(t) = \mu_2(t) + \rho\sin(2\pi f_\rho t + \theta_\rho)$. The fading signal phase process $\varphi(t)$ will be identical to the phase of $\mu_\rho(t)$ (Vatalaro, 1995). Thus,

$$\varphi(t) = \operatorname{atan}\left[\frac{\mu_{\rho2}(t)}{\mu_{\rho1}(t)}\right] \tag{2}$$

The stochastic process $r(t)$ is an appropriate one to describe narrowband wireless mobile fading channels in the complex baseband. Additionally by taking into account both 3-D scattering and sectored arrival of multipath power, we can find appropriate PSD shapes for modeling the channel frequency dispersion.

A. Autocorrelation functions and Doppler PSD's

The autocorrelation function of the purely diffuse component $\mu(t)$ will be derived according to the model assumptions. By using the notation in (Karadimas, 2008 A), we consider that the multipath components arrive at the XY azimuth receiver's plane in the angular sectors $a_1 \leq a \leq \pi - a_2$ and $-\pi + a_4 \leq a \leq -a_3$ with $0 \leq a_1, a_2, a_3, a_4 \leq \pi/2$ and the azimuth angle a counts from the value $a = -\pi$ in the negative Y axis returning to the same point in the clockwise direction. For the elevation angle of arrival β we use the same formulation as in (Aulin, eq. (25), 1979). In Figure 1 we depict the model geometry, with the definitions of the azimuth and elevation angles of arrival, together with the azimuth blocked sectors.

With the assumption that all the scattered multipath components are of identical amplitudes and following the standard procedure (Patzold, appendix (A), 2002) we end up to the following equation for the autocorrelation function $r_{\mu\mu}(\tau)$ of $\mu(t)$

$$r_{\mu\mu}(\tau) = \Omega \cdot E[\exp(j2\pi f\tau)] \qquad (3)$$

with τ the difference between two time instants, Ω the mean power of $\mu(t)$, $E[.]$ the expectation operator and f the Doppler frequency shifts, defined as

$$f = f_{max} \cos \beta \cos a. \qquad (4)$$

In (4) $f_{max} = vf_0 / c$ is the maximum Doppler frequency, with v the mobile unit speed, c the speed of light in free space and f_0 the carrier frequency. In order to proceed we should be aware of the PDF's $p_a(.)$, $p_\beta(.)$ of a and β respectively. A uniform distribution for a is assumed in the allowed (non-blocked) azimuth sectors (Karadimas, 2008 A), i.e.:

$$p_a(a) = \begin{cases} \dfrac{1}{2\pi - a_1 - a_2 - a_3 - a_4}, \\ a \in [-\pi + a_4, -a_3] \cup [a_1, \pi - a_2] \\ 0, otherwise \end{cases} \qquad (5)$$

Figure 1. Model geometry. a) Elevation angle of arrival. b) Azimuth angle of arrival and blocked sectors

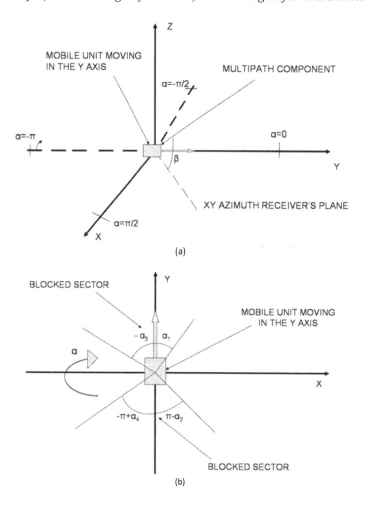

For the PDF of β we employ the following form (Aulin, eq. (25), 1979)

$$p_\beta(\beta) = \begin{cases} \dfrac{\cos\beta}{2\sin b_m}, |\beta| \le b_m \le \dfrac{\pi}{2} \\ 0, othewise \end{cases} \tag{6}$$

where $b_m \in [0, \pi/2]$ is the maximum elevation angle with respect to the azimuth plane, in which the receiver moves.

With the rational assumption of a and β being statistically independent, i.e. $p_{a\beta}(a, \beta) = p_a(a) p_\beta(\beta)$, with $p_{a\beta}(.,.)$ the joint PDF between a and β, using (4) in (3) and carrying out the expectation, with (5) and (6), we obtain

$$r_{\mu\mu}(\tau) = \frac{\Omega[I_1(\tau) + I_2(\tau)]}{(2\pi - a_1 - a_2 - a_3 - a_4)\sin b_m} \tag{7}$$

where

$$I_1(\tau) = \int_0^{b_m} \int_{a_1}^{\pi-a_2} \cos\beta \, e^{j2\pi f_{max}\tau\cos\beta\cos a} \, da \, d\beta \tag{8}$$

$$I_2(\tau) = \int_0^{b_m} \int_{a_3}^{\pi-a_4} \cos\beta \, e^{j2\pi f_{max}\tau\cos\beta\cos a} \, da \, d\beta \tag{9}$$

From (7)-(9) it is clear that the inphase and quadrature components of $\mu(t)$ are correlated. The autocorrelation function $r_{\mu_\rho\mu_\rho}(\tau)$ of $\mu_\rho(t)$ will be,

$$r_{\mu_\rho\mu_\rho}(\tau) = r_{\mu\mu}(\tau) + \rho^2 e^{j2\pi f_\rho\tau} \tag{10}$$

with $f_\rho = f_{max}\cos\beta_0\cos a_0$ being depended on the deterministic azimuth and elevation angles of arrival of the LOS component, a_0 and β_0 respectively.

By taking the Fourier transform of (7) we find the PSD $S_{\mu\mu}(f)$ of $\mu(t)$ as follows

$$S_{\mu\mu}(f) = \frac{\Omega\{F[I_1(\tau)] + F[I_2(\tau)]\}}{(2\pi - a_1 - a_2 - a_3 - a_4)\sin b_m} \tag{11}$$

with $F[.]$ the Fourier transform operator, where from (Karadimas, 2008 A)

$$F[I_2(\tau)] = F[I_1(\tau)]/_{a_1 \to a_3, a_2 \to a_4}. \tag{12}$$

$$F[I_1(\tau)] = \begin{cases} \dfrac{1}{2f_{max}}\left(\dfrac{\pi}{2} - \arcsin \dfrac{2\cos^2 b_m - 1 - \left(f/f_{max}\right)^2}{1 - \left(f/f_{max}\right)^2} \right), \\[4pt] \quad -f_{max}\cos a_2 \cos b_m \le f \le f_{max}\cos a_1 \cos b_m \\[6pt] \dfrac{1}{2f_{max}}\left(\dfrac{\pi}{2} - \arcsin \dfrac{f^2(\sin^2 a_1 + 1) - f_{max}{}^2 \cos^2 a_1}{(f_{max}{}^2 - f^2)\cos^2 a_1} \right), \\[4pt] \quad f_{max}\cos a_1 \cos b_m \le f \le f_{max}\cos a_1 \\[6pt] \dfrac{1}{2f_{max}}\left(\dfrac{\pi}{2} - \arcsin \dfrac{f^2(\sin^2 a_2 + 1) - f_{max}{}^2 \cos^2 a_2}{(f_{max}{}^2 - f^2)\cos^2 a_2} \right), \\[4pt] \quad -f_{max}\cos a_2 \le f \le -f_{max}\cos a_2 \cos b_m \\[6pt] 0, otherwise \end{cases} \tag{13}$$

For the special case $a_1 = a_2 = a_3 = a_4 = 0$ the PSD is similar to that presented in (Aulin, eq. (26), 1979). For $a_1 = a_3 = 0$ and $a_2 = a_4 = \pi/2$ we obtain the PSD for the diffuse component given in (Karadimas, 2007). For $b_m \to 0$, $a_1 = a_3 = 0$ and $a_2 = a_4$ the PSD becomes that in (Patzold, 1998 A) and (Patzold, pp. (157-161), 2002). For $b_m \to 0$, $a_1 = a_3$ and $a_2 = a_4$ the PSD becomes similar to that for the diffuse component as in (Patzold, pp. (218-225), 2002). Finally for $b_m \to 0$, $a_1 = a_3$ and $a_2 = a_4 = \pi/2$ our PSD gives the diffuse component PSD presented in (Patzold, 1998 B). From the aforementioned, the general form and flexibility of the derived PSD are easily concluded. The PSD of $\mu_\rho(t)$ can be obtained after Fourier transforming (10) as

$$S_{\mu_\rho \mu_\rho}(f) = S_{\mu\mu}(f) + \rho^2 \delta_d(f - f_\rho) \tag{14}$$

with $\delta_d(.)$ the Dirac delta function. The PSD of $\mu(t)$ [eq. (11)] is depicted graphically in Figure 2 for a parameter set defined as $f_{max} = 91 Hz$, $\Omega = 1$, $b_m = \pi/5$, $a_1 = \pi/6$, $a_2 = \pi/9$, $a_3 = \pi/3$ and $a_4 = \pi/3.5$. We can see that the PSD has an asymmetrical shape, which is strongly dependent on the angles a_i, $(i = 1, 2, 3, 4)$.

Figure 2. Doppler PSD of the process $\mu(t)$

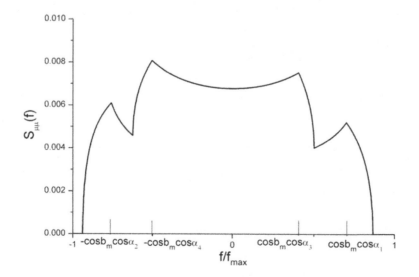

One more advantage of the proposed model is that we can construct both $\mu_1(t)$ and $\mu_2(t)$ from uncorrelated zero mean Gaussian process and create from them the already derived autocorrelation function [eq. (7)] and PSD [eq. (11)]. To do so we extend the scheme, presented in (Patzold, 1998 A), (Patzold, pp. (157-161), (218-225), 2002), for the inphase and quadrature components of $\mu(t)$, as follows (Karadimas 2008 B)

$$\mu_1(t) = v_1(t) + v_2(t) + v_3(t) + v_4(t) \tag{15}$$

$$\mu_2(t) = v_{1h}(t) - v_{2h}(t) + v_{3h}(t) - v_{4h}(t) \tag{16}$$

where $v_i(t)$, $(i = 1, 2, 3, 4)$ are statistically independent, real valued, zero mean Gaussian process and $v_{ih}(t)$ denotes the Hilbert transform of $v_i(t)$. An efficient deterministic simulation model can be created from the formulation [eqs. (15), (16)], based on the sum of sinusoids formulation. The last will be demonstrated in the next section, which concerns the implementation of the simulation model. It is clear from (15) and (16) that the processes $\mu_1(t)$ and $\mu_2(t)$ have equal variances $Var[\mu_1(t)]$ and $Var[\mu_2(t)]$ respectively, as required for a Rayleigh process, with $Var[.]$ the variance operator. More specifically

$$Var[\mu_1(t)] = Var[\mu_2(t)] = r_{\mu_1\mu_1}(0) = r_{\mu_2\mu_2}(0) \tag{17}$$

and

$$r_{\mu_1\mu_1}(\tau) = r_{\mu_2\mu_2}(\tau) = r_{v_{y_1}}(\tau) + r_{v_{y_2}}(\tau) + r_{v_{y_3}}(\tau) + r_{v_{y_4}}(\tau) \tag{18}$$

as the property $r_{v_{ih}v_{ih}}(\tau) = r_{v_{y_i}}(\tau)$ holds, with $r_{\mu_i\mu_i}(.)$, $(i = 1, 2)$ and $r_{v_{y_i}}(\tau)$, $r_{v_{ih}v_{ih}}(\tau)$, $(i = 1, 2, 3, 4)$, the autocorrelation functions of $\mu_i(t)$, $v_i(t)$ and $v_{ih}(t)$ respectively.

Each process $v_i(t)$ accounts for the blocking, represented by each angle a_i, $(i = 1, 2, 3, 4)$. In order the new formulation to give identical autocorrelation function $r_{\mu\mu}(\tau)$ and PSD $S_{\mu\mu}(f)$ with those of the initial model [eqs. (7) and (11)], we should define the autocorrelation functions $r_{v_{y_i}}(\tau)$ and PSD's $S_{v_{y_i}}(f)$ of $v_i(t)$ as in (7) and (11) respectively, by setting $a_1 = a_2 = a_3 = a_4 = a_i$. Thus we obtain after some manipulations (Karadimas, 2008 B)

$$S_{v_{y_i}}(f) = \begin{cases} \dfrac{\sigma_0^2}{8\sin b_m f_{max}}\left(\dfrac{\pi}{2} - asin\dfrac{2\cos^2 b_m - 1 - (f/f_{max})^2}{1 - (f/f_{max})^2}\right), \\ \quad |f| \le f_{max}\cos a_i \cos b_m \\[2mm] \dfrac{\sigma_0^2}{8\sin b_m f_{max}}\left(\dfrac{\pi}{2} - asin\dfrac{f^2(\sin^2 a_i + 1) - f_{max}^2\cos^2 a_i}{(f_{max}^2 - f^2)\cos^2 a_i}\right), \\ \quad f_{max}\cos a_i \cos b_m \le |f| \le f_{max}\cos a_i \\[2mm] 0, otherwise \end{cases} \tag{19}$$

$$r_{v_{y_i}}(\tau) = \frac{\sigma_0^2}{2\sin b_m}\int_0^{b_m}\int_{a_i}^{\pi/2} cos\beta\,\cos(2\pi f_{max}\tau\cos\beta\cos a)\,da\,d\beta \tag{20}$$

where the parameter σ_0 determines the mean power Ω_i of $v_i(t)$, $(i = 1, 2, 3, 4)$, as $\Omega_i = \sigma_0^2(\pi - 2a_i)/4$ and related to Ω as $\sigma_0^2 = \Omega/(2\pi - a_1 - a_2 - a_3 - a_4)$ (Karadimas, 2008 B). The alternative, but identical to (7), autocorrelation function will be

$$r_{\mu\mu}(\tau) = 2[r_{\mu_1\mu_1}(\tau) + jr_{\mu_1\mu_2}(\tau)] \tag{21}$$

with $r_{\mu_1\mu_2}(\tau)$ the cross correlation function between $\mu_1(t)$ and $\mu_2(t)$ defined as

$$r_{\mu_1\mu_2}(\tau) = -r_{\mu_2\mu_1}(\tau) = r_{v_1\nu_{1h}}(\tau) - r_{v_2\nu_{2h}}(\tau) + r_{v_3\nu_{3h}}(\tau) - r_{v_4\nu_{4h}}(\tau) \tag{22}$$

where $r_{v_i\nu_{ih}}(\tau)$ the cross correlation function between $v_i(t)$ and $v_{ih}(t)$, drawn from (20) as

$$r_{v_i\nu_{ih}}(\tau) = \frac{\sigma_0^{\,2}}{2\sin b_m} \int_0^{b_m} \int_{a_i}^{\pi/2} cos\beta \, \sin(2\pi f_{\max}\tau \cos\beta \cos a)\,da\,d\beta. \tag{23}$$

The alternative, but identical to (11), PSD will be given after Fourier transforming (21) and using (18) and (22) together with the property $F[r_{v_i\nu_{ih}}(\tau)] = -jsign(f)S_{v\nu_i}(f)$, with *sign* (.) the sign function. Thus we obtain

$$S_{\mu\mu}(f) = 2[1 + s\,i\,\mathrm{gn}(f)][S_{v\nu_1}(f) + S_{v\nu_3}(f)] + 2[1 - s\,i\,\mathrm{gn}(f)][S_{v\nu_2}(f) + S_{v\nu_4}(f)]. \tag{24}$$

From (24) it is clear that the processes $v_1(t)$ and $v_3(t)$ account for the positive Doppler frequencies, whereas $v_2(t)$ and $v_4(t)$ account for the negative ones.

Before we proceed it is pertinent to define the following parameter set, convenient for the rest of this chapter. More specifically we have

$$\psi_0 = r_{\mu_1\mu_1}(0) = r_{\mu_2\mu_2}(0) = r_{\mu\mu}(0)/2 \tag{25}$$

$$\varphi_{01} = r'_{\mu_1\mu_2}(0) = \mathrm{Im}[r'_{\mu\mu}(0)]/2 \tag{26}$$

$$\psi_{02} = r''_{\mu_1\mu_1}(0) = r''_{\mu_2\mu_2}(0) = r''_{\mu\mu}(0)/2 \tag{27}$$

where the primes denote derivatives with respect to the time difference τ and Im[.] the imaginary part of the bracketed term. By using (7), with (8) and (9), in (25)-(27) and after some algebraic manipulations we obtain

$$\psi 0 = \Omega/2 = \sigma_0^2(2\pi - a_1 - a_2 - a_3 - a_4)/2 \tag{28}$$

$$\varphi_{01} = \pi\sigma_0^{\,2} f_{\max}(\sin a_2 - \sin a_1 + \sin a_4 - \sin a_3)[\cos b_m + (b_m/\sin b_m)]/2 \tag{29}$$

$$\psi_{02} = \frac{\pi^2\sigma_0^{\,2} f_{\max}^{\,2}[\cos(2b_m) + 5]}{6} \times$$
$$[\sin(a_2 + a_1)\cos(a_2 - a_1) + \sin(a_4 + a_3)\cos(a_4 - a_3) - (2\pi - a_1 - a_2 - a_3 - a_4)]. \tag{30}$$

Moreover the parameters b and d should be defined as

$$b = -\psi_{02} - \frac{\varphi_{01}^{\,2}}{\psi_0} \tag{31}$$

$$d = \left(2\pi f_\rho - \frac{\varphi_{01}}{\psi_0}\right)\Big/\sqrt{2b}. \tag{32}$$

B. PDF of Amplitude and Phase, LCR and ADF's

The amplitude PDF $p_r(.)$ of $r(t)$ will follow the distribution of an extended Suzuki process (Patzold, eq. (6.56), 2002). Thus by setting in (Patzold, eq. (6.56), 2002) $1/y^2 = u$ and after some manipulations we take

$$p_r(z) = \frac{z}{\sqrt{2\pi}\Omega l} \int_0^\infty \exp\left[-\frac{z^2 u + \rho^2}{\Omega}\right] I_0\left(\frac{2z\rho\sqrt{u}}{\Omega}\right) \exp\left[-\frac{(\ln u + 2n)^2}{8l^2}\right] du, \, z \geq 0 \tag{33}$$

with $I_0(.)$ the modified Bessel function of zero order. The phase PDF $p_\varphi(.)$ will be given by the equation (Patzold, eq. (6.32), 2002)

$$p_\varphi(\varphi) = \frac{\exp[-\rho^2/\Omega]}{2\pi}\left\{1 + \sqrt{\frac{\pi}{\Omega}} \rho\cos(\varphi - 2 f\pi t - \theta_\rho) \times \right.$$

$$\left. \exp\left[\frac{\rho^2 \cos^2(\varphi - 2\pi f_\rho t - \theta_\rho)}{\Omega}\right]\left[1 + erf\left(\frac{\rho\cos(\varphi - 2 f\pi t - \theta_\rho)}{\sqrt{\Omega}}\right)\right]\right\}, \, -\pi \leq \varphi \leq \pi \tag{34}$$

where $erf(.)$ is the error function. As it can be seen from (33) and (34) the amplitude and phase PDF's are independent from b_m and a_i, ($i = 1, 2, 3, 4$). The amplitude PDF depends on l, n, Ω and ρ whereas the generally non-stationary phase process $\varphi(t)$, depends on Ω, ρ, f_ρ and θ_ρ. Only if $f_\rho = 0$ the phase process becomes strict sense stationary. If $\rho = 0$ (33) becomes the classical Suzuki (Rayleigh-lognormal) PDF [10, eq. (2.30), 2002], whereas (34) the uniform one. The amplitude and phase PDF's of the extended Suzuki model have been extensively studied in the literature (Patzold, 1998 A), (Patzold, 200), thus we will not reproduce here already derived figures and conclusions drawn from them. Otherwise the multipath angles of arrival affect the time selectivity, which in turn affects the channel second order statistics. Thus we will focus on depicting the impact of b_m and a_i, ($i = 1, 2, 3, 4$), on the LCR and ADF's.

The LCR $N_r(.)$, i.e. the average number of crossings per second at which $r(t)$ crosses a specified signal level z with positive slope, will be given by the well known equation

$$N_r(z) = \int_0^\infty y' p_{rr'}(z, y') dy' \tag{35}$$

with $p_{rr'}(.,.)$ being the joint PDF of $r(t)$ with its time derivative $r'(t)$ at the same time instant. The expression for the LCR is the one given in (Patzold, eq. (6.61), 2002). Thus

$$N_r(z) = \frac{z\sqrt{b}}{\pi^2 \psi_0 l} \int_0^\infty \frac{F(z,y)}{y^2} \exp\left(-\frac{(z/y)^2 + \rho^2}{2\psi_0}\right) \exp\left(-\frac{(\ln y - n)^2}{2l^2}\right) \int_0^{\pi/2} \cosh\left(\frac{z\rho\cos\theta}{\psi_0 y}\right) \times$$

$$\left\{\exp\left[-\left(\frac{d\rho\sin\theta}{F(z,y)}\right)^2\right] + \frac{\sqrt{\pi} d\rho\sin\theta}{F(z,y)} erf\left(\frac{d\rho\sin\theta}{F(z,y)}\right)\right\} d\theta dy, \, z \geq 0 \tag{36}$$

where

$$F(z,y) = \sqrt{1 + \frac{q}{b}\left(\frac{zl}{y}\right)^2} \tag{37}$$

and $q = r''_{mm}(0) = (2\pi\sigma_c)^2$, with σ_c a parameter characterizing the Gaussian PSD shape $S_{mm}(f)$ and autocorrelation function $r_{mm}(\tau)$ of $m(t)$, both defined as (Patzold, eqs. (6.43) and (6.44), 2002)

$$S_{mm}(f) = \frac{1}{\sqrt{2\pi}\sigma_c}\exp\left(-\frac{f^2}{2\sigma_c^2}\right) \tag{38}$$

$$r_{mm}(\tau) = \exp[-2(\pi\sigma_c\tau)^2]. \tag{39}$$

The ADF's, i.e. the mean value of the time intervals at which $r(t)$ remains below a specified signal level z is defined by the equation

$$T_r(z) = \frac{F_r(z)}{N_r(z)} \tag{40}$$

with $F_r(.)$ the cumulative distribution function (CDF) of the process $r(t)$, defined as

$$F_r(z) = \int_0^z p_r(x)dx. \tag{41}$$

For the special case $\rho = 0$, we obtain a similar expression for the LCR as that in (Krantzik, 1990), i.e. the LCR of modified Suzuki processes. If $b_m \to 0$, $a_1 = a_3 = 0$ and $a_2 = a_4$ we take the second order statistics derived in (Patzold, 1998 A) and (Patzold, pp. (174-176), 2002). In order to determine the impact of 3-D scattering and sectored arrival of multipath power we plot in figures 3 and 4 the normalized LCR $N_r(z)/f_{max}$ and normalized ADF's $T_r(z) \cdot f_{max}$ as a function of b_m and a_1, a_3 respectively. We define $l = 0.6$, $n = 0.3$, $\rho = 0$, $f_p = 0.15 f_{max}$ and $\sigma_c = 0$, whereas the remaining parameters are the same as in Figure 2 (apart from b_m in Figure 3 and a_1, a_3 in Figure 4). It is clear from Figure 3a that with increased elevation angle of arrival (b_m increases) the LCR decreases and fluctuations occur less frequently because the multipath propagation reduces its influence as being projected to the receiver's azimuth plane. From Figure 3b with increased elevation angle of arrival the ADF's increases, meaning more time the signal remains below small, medium and large levels, or equivalently fluctuates less frequently. Moreover from Figure 4a, with increased blocked multipath power (a_1, a_3 increase) the LCR decreases and fluctuations occur less frequently, because the multipath propagation reduces its influence, as being of more directional nature. Finally from Figure 4b, with increased blocked multipath power the ADF's increases, thus fluctuations occur less frequently.

III. THE DETERMINISTIC SIMULATION MODEL

The core of the analytical model is the separate Gaussian processes generating each stochastic process employed. More specifically the Gaussian processes $v_i(t)$, $i = 1, 2, 3, 4)$, together with their Hilbert transforms $v_{ih}(t)$, generate the Rice process $z(t)$ and the Gaussian process $m(t)$ generates the lognormal process $k(t)$. Thus our task is to

Figure 3. Second order statistics as a function of b_m. a) normalized LCR. b) normalized ADF's.

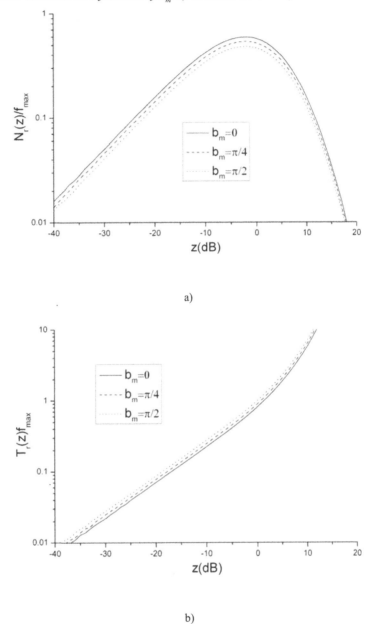

a)

b)

simulate the aforementioned nine processes in such a way that the first and second order statistics of both models (analytical and simulation models) are as close as possible (ideally identical).

We will simulate each process as a finite sum of sinusoids. A simulation formula based on sum of sinusoids can be either ergodic stochastic (deterministic) or non-ergodic stochastic. The deterministic simulation formula needs only one simulation run to generate its statistical properties, as it has constant parameters (gain, frequencies and phases) during the simulation. On the other hand the non-ergodic stochastic simulation formula has at least one parameter as a random variable and needs a large number of simulation runs and averaging the results

Figure 4. Second order statistics as a function of a_1, a_3. a) normalized LCR. b) normalized ADF's

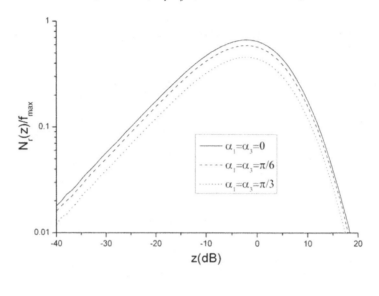

a)

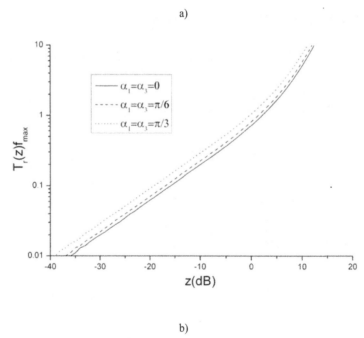

b)

in order to generate its statistical properties. Here we will not present in detail the sum of sinusoids simulation scheme, but the interested reader can see (Patzold, Ch. (5), 2002) for a detailed and well presented analysis of the main methods used in that scheme.

More specifically each Gaussian process is approximated by the sum of sinusoids as follows

$$v_{id}(t) = \sum_{j=1}^{N_i} c_{i,j} \cos(2\pi f_{i,j} t + \theta_{i,j}), \ (i = 1, 2, 3, 4) \tag{42}$$

$$v_{ihd}(t) = \sum_{j=1}^{N_i} c_{i,j} \sin(2\pi f_{i,j} t + \theta_{i,j}), \ (i = 1, 2, 3, 4) \tag{43}$$

$$m_d(t) = \sum_{j=1}^{N_m} c_{m,j} \cos(2\pi f_{m,j} t + \theta_{m,j}) \tag{44}$$

where $v_{id}(t)$, $v_{ihd}(t)$, $m_d(t)$ are the approximations for $v_i(t)$, $v_{ih}(t)$ and $m(t)$ respectively and N_i, $(i = 1, 2, 3, 4)$, N_m the numbers of sinusoids for each process. The parameters $c_{i,j}$-$c_{m,j}$, $f_{i,j}$-$f_{m,j}$ and $\theta_{i,j}$-$\theta_{m,j}$ are called Doppler coefficients, Doppler frequencies and Doppler phases respectively. For the computation of $c_{i,j}$ and $f_{i,j}$, $(i = 1, 2, 3, 4)$, we use an extended version of the MEDS, appropriate for 3-D scattering environments, presented in (Karadimas, 2008 B). For the remaining parameters of the simulation model we will employ already known formulas.

According to the extended MEDS (E-MEDS) the Doppler coefficients for $v_{id}(t)$ and $v_{ihd}(t)$, $(i = 1, 2, 3, 4)$ are calculated as follows

$$c_{i,j} = \frac{1}{N_i} \sqrt{\frac{2\Omega_i b_m}{\sin b_m} \sum_{p=1}^{N_i} \cos \beta_{i,p}}, j = 1, 2 ... N_i \tag{45}$$

where $\beta_{i,p}$ the discrete values of β defined as

$$\beta_{i,p} = \frac{(2p-1)b_m}{2N_i} \tag{46}$$

The Doppler frequencies are calculated as follows

$$f_{i,j} = f_{max} \sin a_{i,j} \ \mathrm{acos} \frac{\sum_{p=1}^{N_i} [\cos \beta_{i,p} \cos(\cos \beta_{i,p})]}{\sum_{p=1}^{N_i} (\cos \beta_{i,p})}, j = 1, 2 ... N_i \tag{47}$$

where $a_{i,j}$ the discrete values of a defined as

$$a_{i,j} = \frac{(2j-1)\pi}{4N_i'} \tag{48}$$

and N_i' the virtual number of harmonic functions of $v_{id}(t)$ and $v_{ihd}(t)$ which restricts the Doppler frequencies to the interval $[0, f_{max} \cos a_i]$, defined as (Patzold, pp. (179, 233), 2002)

$$N_i' = \frac{N_i \pi}{2 \arcsin(\cos a_i)} = \frac{N_i \pi}{\pi - 2a_i}. \tag{49}$$

If $b_m \to 0$ and $a_i = 0$, $(i = 1, 2, 3, 4)$, (45) and (47) become the Doppler coefficients and frequencies respectively of the MEDS for the 2-D scattering case, given in (Patzold, eqs. (5.73), (5.74), 2002). The Doppler phases $\theta_{i,j}$ are components of the Doppler phase vector $\theta_{i,j} = (\theta_{i,1}, \theta_{i,2}, ..., \theta_{i,N})$. Those components are the permuted elements of the phase vector $\Theta_i = [2\pi \cdot 1 / (N_i + 1), 2\pi \cdot 2 / (N_i + 1), ..., 2\pi \cdot N_i / (N_i + 1)]$ (Patzold, 1998 C), (Patzold, pp. (143-144), 2002). In order the deterministic processes $v_{id}(t)$, $(i = 1, 2, 3, 4)$, to be uncorrelated for any value of a_i, $(i = 1, 2, 3, 4)$, we should select N_i according to the criterion (Wang, ineq. (24), 2007), which allows at maximum one odd value for all N_i.

The calculation of the parameters $c_{m,j}, f_{m,j}$ and $\theta_{m,j}$ for $m_d(t)$ is carried out in a slightly different way, as the process $m(t)$ is zero mean Gaussian with unit variance, having the PSD shape defined in (38). Following the analysis in (Patzold, 1996) and (Patzold, pp. (131-132), 2002) the Doppler coefficients $c_{m,j}$ are calculated as

$$c_{m,j} = \sqrt{2/N_m}, j = 1, 2...N_m.$$

(50)

The Doppler frequencies $f_{m,j}$ are calculated via a slight modification of MEDS (Patzold, pp. (131), 2002) as

$$\frac{2j-1}{2N_m} - erf\left(\frac{f_{m,j}}{\sqrt{2}\sigma_c}\right) = 0, j = 1, 2...N_m - 1$$

(51)

and

$$f_{m,N_m} = \sqrt{\sigma_c^2 N_m - \sum_{j=1}^{N_m-1} f_{m,j}^2}.$$

(52)

The Doppler phases $\theta_{m,j}$ are again calculated by employing a similar scheme with that for $v_{id}(t)$ and $v_{ihd}(t)$.

From now on we can proceed in presenting the results of the deterministic model, as all of its parameters have been determined. The deterministic time function $r_d(t)$, which simulates the stochastic process $r(t)$, arises by substituting in $r(t)$ each Gaussian process $v_i(t)$, $v_{ih}(t)$, $(i = 1, 2, 3, 4)$ and $m(t)$ with its deterministic approximations $v_{id}(t)$ $v_{ihd}(t)$ and $m_d(t)$ respectively. Thus we obtain

$$r_d(t) = \sqrt{\mu_{\rho 1d}(t)^2 + \mu_{\rho 2d}(t)^2} \cdot \exp[lm_d(t) + n]$$

(53)

where

$$\mu_{\rho 1d}(t) = \mu_{1d}(t) + \rho \cos(2\pi f_\rho t + \theta_\rho)$$

(54)

$$\mu_{\rho 2d}(t) = \mu_{2d}(t) + \rho \sin(2\pi f_\rho t + \theta_\rho)$$

(55)

$$\mu_{1d}(t) = v_{1d}(t) + v_{2d}(t) + v_{3d}(t) + v_{4d}(t)$$

(56)

$$\mu_{2d}(t) = v_{1hd}(t) - v_{2hd}(t) + v_{3hd}(t) - v_{4hd}(t).$$

(57)

Similarly to (25)-(27) we can define the characteristic quantities of the deterministic model. Thus we obtain

$$\psi_{0d} = r_{\mu_1\mu_1d}(0) = r_{\mu_2\mu_2d}(0) = r_{v_1v_1d}(0) + r_{v_2v_2d}(0) + r_{v_3v_3d}(0) + r_{v_4v_4d}(0)$$

(58)

$$\varphi_{01d} = r'_{\mu_1\mu_2d}(0) = r'_{v_1v_1hd}(0) - r'_{v_2v_2hd}(0) + r'_{v_3v_3hd}(0) - r'_{v_4v_4hd}(0)$$

(59)

$$\psi_{02d} = r''_{\mu_1\mu_1d}(0) = r''_{\mu_2\mu_2d}(0) = r''_{v_1v_1d}(0) + r''_{v_2v_2d}(0) + r''_{v_3v_3d}(0) + r''_{v_4v_4d}(0)$$

(60)

where $r_{\mu_i\mu_id}(\tau)$ the autocorrelation functions of $\mu_{id}(t)$, $(i = 1, 2)$ and $r_{\mu_1\mu_2d}(\tau)$ the cross correlation function between $\mu_{1d}(t)$ and $\mu_{2d}(t)$. Moreover $r_{v_iv_id}(\tau)$ is the autocorrelation function of $v_{id}(t)$ and $r_{v_iv_ihd}(\tau)$ is the cross correlation function between $v_{id}(t)$ and $v_{ihd}(t)$, $(i = 1, 2, 3, 4)$, both defined as (Patzold, 2002)

$$r_{v y_{id}}(\tau) = \sum_{j=1}^{N_i} [c_{i,j}^{\;2} \cos(2\pi f_{i,j}\tau)/2] \tag{61}$$

$$r_{v y_{ihd}}(\tau) = \sum_{j=1}^{N_i} [c_{i,j}^{\;2} \sin(2\pi f_{i,j}\tau)/2]. \tag{62}$$

Using (61) and (62) in (58)-(60) and after some algebraic manipulations we obtain

$$\psi_{0d} = \sum_{j=1}^{N_1} \frac{c_{1,j}^{\;2}}{2} + \sum_{j=1}^{N_2} \frac{c_{2,j}^{\;2}}{2} + \sum_{j=1}^{N_3} \frac{c_{3,j}^{\;2}}{2} + \sum_{j=1}^{N_4} \frac{c_{4,j}^{\;2}}{2} \tag{63}$$

$$\varphi_{01d} = \pi \left[\sum_{j=1}^{N_1} (c_{1,j}^{\;2} f_{1,j}) - \sum_{j=1}^{N_2} (c_{2,j}^{\;2} f_{2,j}) + \sum_{j=1}^{N_3} (c_{3,j}^{\;2} f_{3,j}) - \sum_{j=1}^{N_4} (c_{4,j}^{\;2} f_{4,j}) \right] \tag{64}$$

$$\psi_{02d} = -2\pi^2 \left\{ \sum_{j=1}^{N_1} [(c_{1,j} f_{1,j})^2] + \sum_{j=1}^{N_2} [(c_{2,j} f_{2,j})^2] + \sum_{j=1}^{N_3} [(c_{3,j} f_{3,j})^2] + \sum_{j=1}^{N_4} [(c_{4,j} f_{4,j})^2] \right\}. \tag{65}$$

Moreover the parameters b_d and d_d should be defined as

$$b_d = -\psi_{02d} - \frac{\varphi_{01d}^{\;2}}{\psi_{0d}} \tag{66}$$

$$d_d = \left(2\pi f_\rho - \frac{\varphi_{01d}}{\psi_{0d}} \right) \bigg/ \sqrt{2b_d}. \tag{67}$$

In order to test the convergence behavior of the deterministic model we should not proceed in lengthy and time consuming simulations for the first and second order statistics of $r_d(t)$. Actually (33), (36) and (40) are still valid for them, provided that we substitute in each expression the characteristic quantities of the analytical model [eqs. (28)-(32)] with the respective of the simulation ones [eqs. (63)-(67)] (Patzold, pp. (176-181), 2002). Thus in order to test the convergence behavior of the deterministic model we plot in Figure 5 the characteristic quantities [eqs. (63)-(65)] as a function of the number M, which determines the number of sinusoids for each process. The last is done by parametrically defining N_i, in order to be compatible with the criterion (Wang, ineq. (24), 2007), as $N_1 = N_1(M) = M$, $N_2 = N_2(M) = M + 1$, $N_3 = N_3(M) = M + 2$, and $N_1 = N_1(M) = 4$, with M a positive even number. In the same graph we depict the characteristic quantities of the analytical model [eqs. (28)-(30)] for the shake of comparisons. The remaining parameters are the same as in Figure 2. It is clear from Figure 5 that the deterministic model converges almost perfectly to the analytical one, provided that $M \geq 10$, a result which has also been presented in (Patzold, Ch. (6), 2002).

IV. APPLICATIONS TO REAL WORLD CHANNELS

In this section we demonstrate the flexibility and usefulness of the extended Suzuki model by adapting the LCR to data drawn from measurements. More specifically we consider the measurements of the LCR in (Butterworth, 1983). The environments studied there were, the one a rural area with almost 35% tree cover (heavy shadowing) and the other an open area with almost no shadowing (light shadowing).

Figure 5. Characteristic quantities of the deterministic model. a) ψ_{0d} b) ϕ_{01d} c) ψ_{02d}

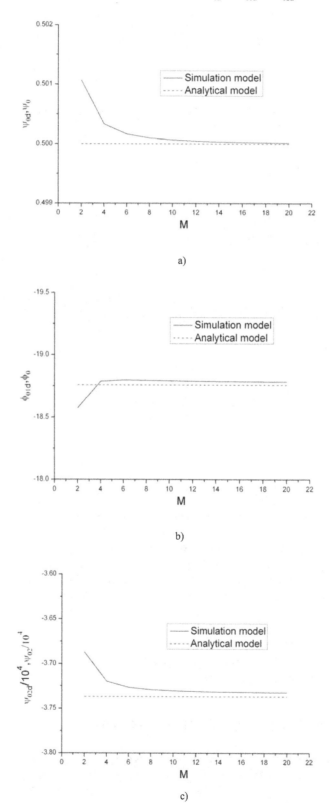

a)

b)

c)

Figure 6. Analytical and measured normalized LCR's. a) light shadowing environment. b) heavy shadowing environment

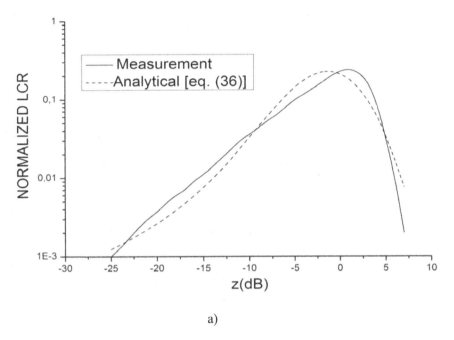

a)

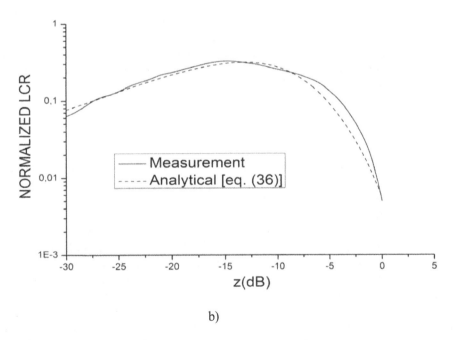

b)

Table I. Model parameters for light and heavy shadowing

SHADOWING	l	n	b_m	σ_0	ρ	a_1	a_2
LIGHT	0.269	-0.127	0	0.311	0.999	$\pi/2.534$	$\pi/3.335$
HEAVY	0.300	0.522	$\pi/2$	0.100	0.110	$\pi/2.685$	$\pi/3.927$

Our task is to find the proper values of the model parameters (l, n, b_m, σ_0, ρ, a_i, (i = 1, 2, 3, 4)), such that the absolute value of the difference between the analytical and measured LCR's is minimum. In order to do so we combine the model parameters to a multi-parametric function, seeking its minimum. That function is

$$g(l,n,b_m,\sigma_0,\rho,a_i) = \frac{1}{f_{max}}\left(\sum_{n=1}^{N}\left[\left(\frac{N_r(z_n)-N_p(z_n)}{N_p(z_n)}\right)^2\right]\right)^{1/2} \tag{68}$$

where $N_p(.)$ is the measured LCR and N the number of measured values. In order to simplify the minimization we set $a_1 = a_3$, $a_2 = a_4$ and, (i = 1, 2, 3, 4). We also set $\sigma_c = 0$, as in real world channels the lognormal process varies very slowly compared to the Rician one (Patzold, 1998 A), (Patzold, pp. (170), 2002), something which makes the assumption $\sigma_c \approx 0$ valid. The maximum Doppler frequency f_{max} is kept constant to 91Hz and is not optimized, as it does not constitute a channel parameter, being depended on the mobile unit speed and carrier frequency. Moreover the Doppler frequency f_ρ of the LOS component is kept constant to $f_\rho = 0$ and is not optimized, as it depends on the fixed azimuth and elevation angles of arrival of the LOS component, a_0 and β_0 respectively. Otherwise the experiments conducted in (Butterworth, 1983) allow us to approximately assume $\beta_0 \approx \pi / 2$ and $f_\rho \approx 0$. The minimization of (68) is carried out by applying any method of optimization inherent in mathematical software packets. By doing this, we find for the two cases (light and heavy shadowing) the parameter set given in table I. The resulting analytical and measured normalized LCR's are shown in Figure 6, from which a quite good agreement is revealed between the analytical model and the measured data.

We should notice how the parameter b_m characterizes each environment. In the heavy shadowing environment $b_m = \pi / 2$, which is a rational result, as most likely many multipath components will arrive at the receiver after having interacted with tall objects. Although such a big value of b_m is somehow unrealistic, we should keep in mind that this angle is of regulatory nature for the second order statistics, especially in small and medium levels (see Figure 3). This means that it does not affect the shape of the second order statistics, but slightly modifies them. On the contrary, for the light shadowing $b_m = 0$, which also seems rational, as lack of scattering objects close to the mobile receiver will make the diffuse scattering component to arrive mainly in the azimuth plane, in which the receiver moves.

CONCLUSION

An extended Suzuki model which combines shadowing with 3-D multipath scattering was presented. Moreover in the azimuth plane the multipath components are assumed to arrive at specific angular sectors. The analytically derived PSD became unsymmetrical, with that asymmetry being strongly dependent on the parameters of the azimuth angle of arrival PDF. It was shown that with increased elevation angle of arrival the received signal fluctuates less frequently. The last conclusion is also valid when diffuse scattering becomes more directional. It was also shown that the first order statistics (amplitude and phase PDF's) were unaffected from the parameters of both the azimuth and elevation angles of arrival distributions. The model derivation from a scheme employing uncorrelated Gaussian processes, with appropriate autocorrelation functions and PSD's, enabled us to proceed in the development of an efficient deterministic simulation model, based on the sum of sinusoids principle. The simulation model converges almost perfectly to the analytical one, provided that the parameter which characterizes the number of sinusoids for each of the uncorrelated Gaussian processes (parameter M) is chosen appropriately (i.e. $M \leq 10$). A curve fitting of the LCR to real word data, drawn from measurements, validated the usefulness and flexibility of the proposed model. In both the light and heavy shadowing environments the agreement between the proposed model and the measurements was quite good.

REFERENCES

Aulin, T. (1979). "A Modified Model for the Fading Signal at a Mobile Radio Channel," IEEE Trans. Veh. Technol., vol. 28, no. 3, pp. 182-203, Aug.

Butterworth, J. S. and Matt, E.E. (1983). "The Characterization of Propagation Effects for Land Mobile Satellite Services," Intern. Conf. Satellite Systems for Mobile Commun. Navigations, pp. 51-54, June.

Clarke, R. H. (1968). "A Statistical Theory of Mobile–Radio Reception," Bell Syst. Tech. J. vol. 47, pp. 957-1000, July/Aug.

Clarke, R. H. and Khoo, W. L. (1997). "3-D Mobile Radio Channel Statistics," IEEE Trans. Veh. Technol., vol. 46, no. 3, pp. 798-799, Aug.

Corazza, G. E. and Vatalaro, F. (1994). "A Statistical Model for Land Mobile Satellite Channels and its Application to Nongeostationary Orbit Systems," IEEE Trans. Veh. Technol., vol. 43, no. 3, pp. 738-742, Aug.

Hansen, F. and Meno, F. I. (1977)."Mobile Fading–Rayleigh and Lognormal Superimposed," IEEE Trans. Veh. Technol., vol. 26, no. 4, pp. 332-335, Nov.

Ho, J. T. Y. (2005). "A Generalized Doppler Power Spectrum for 3D Non-Isotropic Scattering Environments," Global Telecommunications Conference. GLOBECOM '05. IEEE, 28 Nov-2 Dec. pp. 1393-1396.

Karadimas, P. and Kotsopoulos, S. A. (Karadimas, 2007). "A Modified Loo Model with Sectored and Three Dimensional Multipath Scattering," Delson Group Inc. 8th World Wireless Congress-WWC, San Francisco, USA, pp. 25-30, May 2007

Karadimas, P. Vagenas, E. D. and Kotsopoulos, S. A. (2008 A). "A Small Scale Fading Model with Sectored and Three Dimensional Diffuse Scattering," IEEE 5th Cons. Commun. and Netw. Conf.-IEEE CCNC, Las Vegas, USA, pp. 943-947, Jan.

Karadimas, P. and Kotsopoulos, S. A. (2008). "A Modified Loo Model with Partially Blocked and Three Dimensional Multipath Scattering: Analysis, Simulation and Validation," under revision in Wireless Pers. Commun. Aug. 2008.

Krantzik, A. and Wolf, D. (1990). "Distribution of the Fading-Intervals of Modified Suzuki Processes," in *Signal Processing V: Theories and Applications*, L. Torres, E. Masgrau, and M. A. Lagunas, Eds. Amsterdam, The Netherlands: Elsevier, pp. 361-364.

Li, Y., Patzold, M., Killat U., and Laue, F. (1996). "An Efficient Deterministic Simulation Model for Land Mobile Satellite Channels," Proc. IEEE 46th Veh. Technol. Conf., VTC 96, Atlanta, Georgia, USA, pp. 1028-1032, Apr./May.

Loo, C. (1985). "A Statistical Model for a Land Mobile Satelite Link," IEEE Trans. Veh. Technol., vol. 34, no. 3, pp. 122-127, Aug. .

Loo, C. and Secord, N. (1991)."Computer Models for Fading Channels with Applications to Digital Transmissions," IEEE Trans. Veh. Technol., vol. 40, no. 4, pp. 700-707, Nov. .

Lutz, E. Cygan, D. Dippold, M. Dolainsky, F. and Papke, W. (1991). "The Land Mobile Satellite Communication Channel-Recording, Statistics and Channel Model," IEEE Trans. Veh. Technol., vol. 40, no. 2, pp. 375-386, May.

Ozdemir, M. K., Arslan, H. and Arvas, E. (2004). "A Narrowband MIMO Channel Model with 3-D Scattering," IEEE Intern. Conf. on Commun. ICC '04, vol. 5, pp. 2929-2933, June.

Pal, Beach, A. M. and Nix, A. (2006). "A Novel Quantification of 3D Directional Spread from Small-Scale Fading Analysis," IEEE Intern. Conf. on Commun. ICC '06, vol.4, pp.1699-1704, June.

Parsons, J. D. (2000). "The Mobile Radio Propagation Channel, Second Edition." Chichester, U.K.: Wiley.

Patzold, M. (2002). "Mobile Fading Channels." Chichester, U.K.: Wiley.

Patzold, M. Killat, U. and Laue,V. (1998). "An Extended Suzuki Model for Land Mobile Satellite Channels and its Statistical Properties," IEEE Trans. Veh. Technol., vol. 47, no. 2, pp. 617-630, May.

Patzold, M., Killat, U. Li, Y. and Laue, F. (1997). "Modeling, Analysis and Simulation of Nonfrequency-Selective Mobile Radio Channels with Asymmetrical Doppler Power Spectral Density Shapes," IEEE Trans. Veh. Technol., vol. 46, no. 2, pp. 494-507, May.

Patzold, U. Killat, F. Laue and Li, Y. (1996). "A New and Optimal Method for the Derivation of Deterministic Simulation Models for Mobile Radio Channels," Proc. IEEE 46th Veh. Technol. Conf., VTC 96, Atlanta, Georgia, USA, pp. 1423-1427, Apr./May.

Patzold,M., Killat, U., Laue, F. and Li, Y. (1998). "On the Statistical Properties of Deterministic Simulation Models for Mobile Fading Channels," IEEE Trans. Veh. Technol., vol. 47, no. 1, pp. 254-269, Feb.

Patzold, M. Li, Y. and Laue, F. (1998). "A Study of a Land Mobile Satellite Channel Model with Asymmetrical Doppler Power Spectrum and Lognormally Distributed Line of Sight Component," IEEE Trans. Veh. Technol., vol. 47, no. 1, pp. 297-310, Feb.

Qu, S. and Yeap, T. (1999)."A Three-Dimensional Scattering Model for Fading Channels in Land Mobile Environment," IEEE Trans. Veh. Technol., vol. 48, no. 3, pp. 765-781, May.

Suzuki, H. (1977). "A Statistical Model for Urban Radio Propagation," IEEE Trans. Commun., vol. 25, no. 7, pp. 673-680, July.

Tjhung, T. T. and Chai, C. C. (1999). "Fade Statistics in Nakagami-Lognormal Channels," IEEE Trans. Commun., vol. 47, no. 12, pp. 1769-1772, Dec.

Vatalaro, F. (1995). "Generalized Rice-Lognormal Channel Model for Wireless Communications," Elec. Letters., vol. 31, no. 22, pp. 1899-1900, Oct.

Vatalaro, F. and Forcella, A. (1997)."Doppler Spectrum in Mobile-to-Mobile Communications in the Presence of Three-Dimensional Multipath Scattering," IEEE Trans. Veh. Technol., vol. 46, no. 1, pp. 213-219, Feb.

Vatalaro, F., Mazzenga, F., De Maio, G. and Forcella, A. (2002). "The Generalized Rice Lognormal Channel Model-First and Second Order Statistical Characterization and Simulation," J. Wiley Int. Journal on Satell. Commun. , vol. 20, no. 1, pp. 29-45.

Wang, C-X., Patzold, M. and Yuan, D. (2007). "Accurate and Efficient Simulation of Multiple Uncorrelated Rayleigh Fading Waveforms," IEEE Trans. Wirel. Commun., vol. 6, no. 3, pp. 833-839, Mar.

Xie, Y. and Fang, Y. (2000). "A General Statistical Channel Model for Mobile Satellite Systems," IEEE Trans. Veh. Technol., vol. 49, no. 3, pp. 744-752, May.

KEY TERMS

Average Duration of Fades (ADF's): The mean value of the time intervals at which the stochastic process remains below a specified signal level.

Doppler Power Spectral Density (PSD): A mathematical function which characterizes the frequency dispersion of a narrowband fading channel.

Level Crossing Rate (LCR): The average number of crossings per second at which the stochastic process crosses a specified signal level with positive slope.

Line of Sight (LOS) Component: The component which directly arrives at the mobile receiver after no interaction with the channel scatterers.

Method of Exact Doppler Spread (MEDS): A deterministic simulation method based on the sum of sinusoids principle, for calculating the discrete amplitudes and frequencies of deterministic processes.

Probability Density Function (PDF): A mathematical function which characterizes the value distribution density of a random quantity.

Shadowing: The effect that the mean value of the received signal being time varying, for receiver movement to different local areas.

Suzuki Model: A composite distribution arising when multiplying a lognormal process with a Rayleigh one.

Three-Dimensional (3-D) Scattering: The effect multipath components arriving at the elevation plane, besides those arriving at the azimuth one, in which the receiver moves.

Chapter XVII
Channel Characterization and Modelling for Mobile Communications

Anastasios Papazafeiropoulos
University of Patras, Greece

ABSTRACT

As a consequence of the growing interest in wireless communications systems, much effort is being devoted to the channel characterization and modelling. This is obvious since the performance depends fundamentally on the channels under consideration, so a communication system design must be preceded by the study of channel characteristics. This chapter considers the propagation environment in which a wireless system operates. In other words, we are primarily interested in the characterization of radio links between the transmitter and the receiver antenna that will be modelled by randomly time-variant linear systems. Wireless communication channels are usually described by considering three separable phenomena, namely, path loss, shadowing, and multipath fading. In the following, we briefly overview various efforts to characterize such aspects of wireless communication channels. Firstly, in this chapter we address the estimation of signal decay due to propagation loss which is very important in the determination of the necessary transmission power and the coverage area. Although propagation loss models are sometimes quite accurate, they generally fail to predict signal fluctuations due to the effect of the terrain near the antenna. Such a phenomenon of signal fluctuations is usually called shadowing. However, the effect of multipath fading is generally more complex because it does not only change in time but also varies over frequency. As a result, this topic will also be presented in enough depth and a number of statistical models will be studied. Moreover, the various categories of fading will be discussed. Finally, a novel small-scale model derived by the author is presented in order to give a recent application of the theory.

INTRODUCTION

The mobile terminal operates in a dynamic, often hostile environment in which propagation conditions are constantly changing and have a significant impact on the achievable quality of service (QoS). The time-varying nature of the wireless mobile channel makes channel characterization and its analysis an important issue. In a mobile wireless scenario, the time-varying nature of the channel could be encountered in many different ways,

Copyright © 2009, IGI Global, distributing in print or electronic forms without written permission of IGI Global is prohibited.

e.g., a relative motion between the transmitter and the receiver, time variation in the structure of the medium, etc. All these scenarios make the channel characteristics random, and do not offer any easy analysis on the signals, transmitted through this channel. The strength of the received signal depends on the characteristics of the channel and on the distance between the transmitter and the receiver. In general, as an information signal propagates through the channel, the strength of this signal decreases as the distance between the transmitter and receiver increases.

In this chapter, at first we give mathematical representations of the transmitted and received signals. Then, the characterization of the variation in received signal power over distance due to path loss and shadowing follows. Path loss is caused by dissipation of the power radiated by the transmitter as well as effects of the propagation channel. Path loss models generally assume that path loss is the same at a given transmit-receive distance. We present the simplest model for signal propagation: free space path loss. A signal propagating between two points with no attenuation or reflection follows the free space propagation law. We also describe empirical models with parameters based on measurements for both indoor and outdoor channels. Shadowing is caused by obstacles between the transmitter and receiver that attenuate the signal power through absorption, reflection, scattering, and diffraction. In modern wireless communications, the effect of shadowing is usually compensated in the network layer by power control and/or rate adjustment. For the evaluation of such technologies, statistical description of the shadowing loss by a log-normal distribution provides useful insights and effective analytical channel models. The log-normal model based on a large number of shadowing objects is also given. When the attenuation is very strong, the signal is blocked. Variation due to path loss occurs over very large distances (100-1000 meters), whereas variation due to shadowing occurs over distances proportional to the length of the obstructing object (10-100 meters in outdoor environments and less in indoor environments). Since variations due to path loss and shadowing occur over relatively large distances, this variation is sometimes referred to as large-scale propagation effects. Also, we deal with the variation due to the constructive and destructive addition of multipath signal components. Variation due to multipath occurs over very short distances, on the order of the signal wavelength, so these variations are sometimes referred to as small-scale propagation effects. When the number of multipath components is large, or the geometry and dielectric properties of the propagation environment are unknown, statistical models must be used. The autocorrelation, cross correlation, and power spectral density of a received narrowband signal are presented and studied in depth. The case of uniform scattering is investigated. A thorough review of the most accepted statistical models proposed in the scientific literature is presented, considering small-scale fading. The level crossing rate (LCR) and the average duration of fades (AFD) are defined and given for the most basic models. Moreover, the wideband fading is presented and characterized by the equivalent lowpass time-varying channel impulse response and using it we can describe the channel in terms of certain parameters and define categories of the fading occurred. Finally, a novel small-scale model derived by the author is presented in order to give a recent application of the theory. In Figure 1 is illustrated the ratio of the received-to-transmit power in dB versus

Figure 1. Path loss, shadowing and multipath fading versus distance

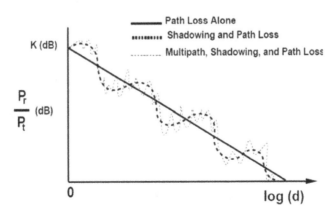

log-distance for the combined effects of path loss, shadowing, and multipath fading. We can observe clearly the very rapid variations due to multipath fading which change on the order of half the signal wavelength.

MATHEMATICAL REPRESENTATION OF SIGNAL MODELS

The contemporary wireless communications operate in the UHF and SHF bands, from 0.3-3 GHz and 3-30 GHz, respectively. The reasons are the small required antenna size and their advantageous propagation characteristics. As a result, our representation will focus on these bands of frequencies assuming that the range of transmission is small enough to neglect the earth's curvature.

The oscillators in use generate real sinusoids leading us to consider the transmitted and received signals as real that will correspond to the real parts of complex exponentials. In other words, the standard complex baseband representation for bandpass signals with bandwidth $B << f_c$, where f_c is the carrier frequency, will be used.

The mathematical representation of the transmitted signal is:

$$s(t) = \Re \left\{ u(t) e^{j 2\pi f_c t} \right\}$$
$$= \Re \left\{ u(t) \right\} \cos \left(2\pi f_c t \right) - \Im \left\{ u(t) \right\} \sin \left(2\pi f_c t \right) \tag{1}$$
$$= x(t) \cos \left(2\pi f_c t \right) - y(t) \sin \left(2\pi f_c t \right)$$

where $u(t) = x(t) + jy(t)$ is a complex baseband signal with in-phase component $x(t) = \Re\{u(t)\}$, quadrature component $y(t) = \Im\{u(t)\}$, bandwidth B, and power P. The signal $u(t)$ is called the complex envelope or complex lowpass equivalent signal of $s(t)$. This terminology is logically justifiable since the magnitude of $u(t)$ is the magnitude of $s(t)$ and the phase of $u(t)$ is the phase of $s(t)$. The power in the transmitted signal $s(t)$ is the half of $u(t)$, i.e., $P_s = P_u/2$.

Using a similar form for the received signal we have:

$$r(t) = \Re \left\{ v(t) e^{j 2\pi f_c t} \right\}, \tag{2}$$

where the complex baseband signal $v(t)$ will depend on the characteristics of the propagation channel. Assuming that a channel is time-invariant, then $v(t) = u(t) * c(t)$, where $c(t)$ is the equivalent lowpass impulse response of the channel. The received signal may have an apparent change in its frequency due to the relative motion of the mobile known as the Doppler shift and equal to $f_D = \upsilon \cos\theta/\lambda$, where θ is the arrival angle of the received signal relative to the direction of motion, υ is the receiver velocity towards the transmitter in the direction of motion, and $\lambda = c/f_c$ is the signal wavelength ($c = 3 \times 10^8$ m/s is the speed of light). Figure 2 depicts the geometry associated with the Doppler shift. The movement of the transmitter or receiver over a short time interval Δt corresponds to a slight change in distance $\Delta d = \Delta t \cos\theta$ resulting to a phase change equal to $\Delta\phi = 2\pi\upsilon\Delta t\cos\theta/\lambda$. The known relationship between signal frequency and phase is used to derive the desired Doppler frequency as:

$$f_D = \frac{1}{2\pi} \frac{\Delta\phi}{\Delta t} = \upsilon \cos\theta/\lambda. \tag{3}$$

The Doppler frequency may take positive or negative values according to the movement of the receiver in relation to the transmitter. More specifically, the Doppler frequency is positive when the receiver is moving towards the transmitter, while in the opposite case it is negative.

Assigning the power of $s(t)$ to P_s and the power of $r(t)$ to P_r, we can define the **linear path loss** of the channel as the ratio of transmit power to receive power:

$$P_L = \frac{P_t}{P_r}. \tag{4}$$

Accordingly, the dB value of the linear path loss is defined as **path loss**. It is a nonnegative number because of the attenuation of the signal caused by the channel and is expressed by:

Figure 2. Geometry associated with the Doppler shift

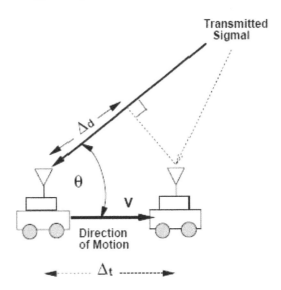

$$P_L \ dB = 10\log_{10}\frac{P_t}{P_r}dB. \tag{5}$$

Similarly, the dB **path gain** is defined as the negative of the dB path loss:

$$P_G = -P_L = 10\log_{10}\frac{P_r}{P_t}dB, \tag{6}$$

which is generally a negative number.

FREE-SPACE PATH LOSS

Assuming that there are no obstructions (free-space) during the transmission of a signal along a straight line from the transmitter to the receiver, the signal is constituted of a single or else line-of-sight (LOS) ray. In (Parsons, 1992) the received signal with a complex scale factor introduced by the free-space path is illustrated, i.e.,

$$r(t) = \Re\left\{\frac{\lambda\sqrt{G_l}e^{-j2\pi d/\lambda}}{4\pi d}u(t)e^{j2\pi f_c t}\right\}, \tag{7}$$

where $\sqrt{G_l}$ is the product of the transmit and receive antenna field radiation patterns in the LOS direction. The phase shift $e^{-j2\pi d/\lambda}$ is due to the distance d the wave travels, i.e., the distance between the transmitter and receiver.

The ratio of received to transmitted power results from (6) as:

$$\frac{P_r}{P_t} = \left[\frac{\sqrt{G_l}\lambda}{4\pi d}\right]^2. \tag{8}$$

From (7) it is clear that the received signal power is proportional to the square of the signal wavelength, so as the frequency increases, the received power decreases. Similarly, the received signal power falls off inversely proportional to the square of the distance d between the transmit and receive antennas. The expression of the received power in dBm is

$$P_r dBm = P_t dBm + 10\log_{10}(G_l) + 20\log_{10}(\lambda) - 20\log_{10}(4\pi) - 20\log_{10}(d).$$

Following the previous terminology, the Free-space path loss is defined as:

$$P_L \; dB = 10\log_{10}\frac{P_t}{P_r} = -10\log_{10}\frac{G_l\lambda^2}{(4\pi d)^2}, \tag{9}$$

while the **free-space path gain** is defined as:

$$P_G = -P_L \; dB = 10\log_{10}\frac{G_l\lambda^2}{(4\pi d)^2}. \tag{10}$$

EMPIRICAL PATH LOSS MODELS

The weakness of the free-space path loss to describe the complex propagation environments created the need for development of new path loss models. The majority of these models are derived in specific environmental conditions, frequency range and distance predicting the path loss in different wireless environments such as large urban macrocells, microcells, picocells, and inside buildings (Rappaport, 2001). Usually these models are applied to similar environments with those where the empirical measurements were made, which makes the accuracy of such empirically-based models applied to more general environments somewhat questionable.

The received power measurements are averaged over several wavelengths, in order to remove the multipath effects which are included in the measurements. The obtained path loss generally decreases with d due to free space path loss and signal obstructions. Usually other measurements are taken in multiple environments with similar characteristics. The path loss is averaged over all available measurements in the given environment. Our discussion will focus on common and known empirical models that describe different channel conditions.

The Okumura Model

This empirical model was derived using measurements of base station-to-mobile signal attenuation. The experiments took place in an irregular terrain in Tokyo. Its applicability is limited to frequencies between 150-1500 MHz, distances of 1-100 Km, i.e., it is used for signal prediction in large urban macrocells. The standard formula for empirical path loss under the Okumura model (Okumura et al., 1968) is:

$$P_L(d) \; dB = L(f_c, d) + A_{mu}(f_c, d) - G(h_t) - G(h_r) - G_{AREA}, \tag{11}$$

where $L(f_c, d)$ is free space path loss at distance d and carrier frequency f_c, $A_{mu}(f_c, d)$ is the median attenuation in addition to free space path loss across all environments, $G(h_t)$ is the base station antenna height gain factor, $G(h_r)$ is the mobile antenna height gain factor, and G_{AREA} is the gain due to the type of environment. The values of $A_{mu}(f_c, d)$ and G_{AREA} are obtained from Okumura's empirical plots (Okumura et al., 1968; Rappaport 2001). Okumura derived empirical formulas for $G(h_t)$ and $G(h_r)$ as:

$$G(h_t) = 20\log_{10}(h_t/200), \; 30m < h_t < 1000m, \tag{12}$$

$$G\left(h_r\right) = \begin{cases} 10\log_{10}\left(h_r/3\right), & h_r < 3m \\ 20\log_{10}\left(h_r/3\right), & 3m < h_r < 10m \end{cases} \tag{13}$$

It must be noted that the base station heights involved in these measurements were 30-100 m, the upper end of which is higher than the typical base stations today.

Hata Model

The Hata model (Hata, 1980) is one of the most common models for signal prediction in urban areas. Its applicability is valid in the range of frequencies between 150-1500 MHz and its advantage is its closed-form which simplifies enough the calculations of the path loss. Also, it is not based on empirical curves for the different parameters The empirical path loss formula of Hata model at distance d is:

$$P_{L,urban}\left(d\right) \ dB = 69.55 + 26.16\log_{10}\left(f_c\right) - 13.82\log_{10}\left(h_t\right) - a\left(h_r\right) + \left(44.9 - 6.55\log_{10}\left(h_t\right)\right)\log_{10}\left(d\right) \tag{14}$$

The parameter $a(h_r)$ is a correction factor for the mobile antenna height which is dependent on the size of the coverage area. So, for small to medium sized cities, this factor is given by (Hata, 1980; Rappaport 2001):

$$a(h_r) = (1.1\log_{10}(f_c) - 0.7)h_r - (1.56\log_{10}(fc) - 0.8)dB, \tag{15}$$

while for larger cities at frequencies $f_c > 300$ MHz, it is given by:

$$a(hr) = 3.2\log^2_{10}(11.75h_r) - 4.97dB. \tag{16}$$

The rest parameters in this model coincide with those of the Okumura model. The two models behave similarly for distances $d > 1$ Km, which is not the case of nowadays cellular systems with smaller cell sizes and higher frequencies.

In order to model suburban and rural environments, some corrections have been made to the urban case. The respective models are:

$$P_{L,suburban}(d) = P_{L,urban}(d) - 2\log^2_{10}(f_c/28) - 5.4 \tag{17}$$

and

$$P_{L,rural}(d) = P_{L,urban}(d) - 4.78\log^2_{10}(f_c) + 18.33\log_{10}(f_c) - K, \tag{18}$$

where K ranges from 35.94 (countryside) to 40.94 (desert).

COST 231 Extension to Hata Model

The European cooperative for scientific and technical research (EURO-COST 231, 1991) extended the Hata model for operation in 2 GHz as follows:

$$P_{L,urban}\left(d\right) \ dB = 46.3 + 33.9\log_{10}\left(f_c\right) - 13.82\log_{10}\left(h_t\right) - a\left(h_r\right) + \left(44.9 - 6.55\log_{10}\left(h_t\right)\right)\log_{10}\left(d\right) + C_M \tag{19}$$

where $a(h_r)$ is the same correction factor as before and C_M is 0 dB for medium sized cities and suburbs, and 3 dB for metropolitan areas. Its parameters belong to the ranges: $1.5GHz < f_c < 2GHz$, $30m < h_t < 200m$, $1m < h_r < 10m$, and $1Km < d < 20Km$.

SHADOW FADING

During the transmission of a signal may occur blockage from objects in the signal path and other changes in reflecting surfaces and scattering objects. As a consequence, the signal experiences a random variation, i.e., variation of its power, which can be characterized statistically (shadowing). In order to model these effects, the log-normal distribution is proposed whose validity has been confirmed in both outdoor and indoor radio propagation environments (see e.g. (Erceg et al., 1999; Ghassemzadeh et al., 2003).

More specifically, the ratio of transmit-to-receive power $\psi = P_t/P_r$ is assumed random and described by the log-normal distribution given by:

$$p(\psi) = \frac{\xi}{\sqrt{2\pi}\sigma_{\psi_{dB}}\psi} \exp\left[-\frac{\left(10\log_{10}\psi - \mu_{\psi_{dB}}\right)^2}{2\sigma_{\psi_{dB}}^2}\right], \ \psi > 0 \tag{20}$$

where $\xi = 10/\ln 10$, $\mu_{\psi_{dB}}$ is the mean of $\psi_{dB} = 10\log_{10}\psi$ in dB and $\sigma_{\psi_{dB}}$ is the standard deviation of ψ_{dB}, also in dB.

It can have also the form:

$$p(r) = \frac{1}{\sqrt{2\pi}\delta r} \exp\left[-\frac{\left(10\ln r - \mu\right)^2}{2\delta^2}\right], \tag{21}$$

where μ, and δ are the mean and standard deviation of the shadowed component $\ln r$.

Changing the variables in (20) we obtain the distribution of the dB value of ψ which is Gaussian with mean $\mu_{\psi_{dB}}$ and standard deviation $\sigma_{\psi_{dB}}$ as:

$$p(\psi_{dB}) = \frac{1}{\sqrt{2\pi}\sigma_{\psi_{dB}}} \exp\left[-\frac{\left(\psi_{dB} - \mu_{\psi_{dB}}\right)^2}{2\sigma_{\psi_{dB}}^2}\right] \tag{22}$$

It is clear that the log-normal distribution in (19) depends on two parameters: $\mu_{\psi_{dB}}$ and $\sigma_{\psi_{dB}}$. It takes values in the range $0 \leq \psi \leq \infty$. If $\psi = P_t/P_r < 1$, then $P_t > P_r$, which is physically impossible. Since this possibility is small when $\mu_{\psi_{dB}}$ is large and positive, the log-normal model offers a better description when $\mu_{\psi_{dB}} \gg 0$.

NARROWBAND FADING MODELS

The received signal can be written as the sum of the LOS path and all resolvable multipath components (Goldsmith, 2005):

$$r(t) = \Re\left\{\sum_{n=0}^{N(t)} a_n(t)v\left(t - \tau_n(t)\right)e^{j2\pi f_c\left(t-\tau_n(t)\right)+\varphi_{D_n}}\right\}, \tag{23}$$

where $n = 0$ corresponds to the LOS path. Letting

$$\varphi_n(t) = 2\pi f_c\tau_n(t) - \varphi_{D_n}.$$

then the received signal can be rewritten as:

$$r(t) = \Re\left\{\left[\sum_{n=0}^{N(t)} a_n(t)e^{-j\varphi_n(t)}v\left(t - \tau_n(t)\right)\right]e^{j2\pi f_c t}\right\}. \tag{24}$$

In the case that the delay spread T_m of a channel is small relative to the inverse signal bandwidth B of the transmitted signal, i.e., $T_m \ll B^{-1}$, then it is implied for the delay associated with the ith multipath component that $\tau_i \leq T_m \forall i$, so $v(t - \tau_i) \approx v(t) \, \forall i$. The received signal can be written as:

$$r(t) = \Re \left\{ v(t) e^{j 2\pi f_c t} \left(\sum_n a_n(t) e^{-j \varphi_n(t)} \right) \right\} \forall i \tag{25}$$

The characterization of the multipath can be obtained if $s(t)$ is written as an unmodulated carrier with random phase offset ϕ_0:

$$s(t) = \Re \left\{ e^{j(2\pi f_c t + \phi_0)} \right\} = \cos(2\pi f_c t + \phi_0) \tag{26}$$

which is narrowband for any T_m.

As a result, the received signal is expressed as:

$$r(t) = \Re \left\{ \left[\sum_{n=0}^{N(t)} a_n(t) e^{-j \varphi_n(t)} \right] e^{j 2\pi f_c t} \right\} = r_I(t) \cos(2\pi f_c t) + r_Q(t) \sin(2\pi f_c t), \tag{27}$$

where the in-phase and quadrature components are given by:

$$r_I(t) = \sum_{n=1}^{N(t)} a_n(t) \cos \varphi_n(t), \tag{28}$$

and

$$r_Q(t) = \sum_{n=1}^{N(t)} a_n(t) \sin \varphi_n(t), \tag{29}$$

where the phase term:

$$\varphi_n(t) = 2\pi f_c \tau_n(t) - \varphi_{D_n} - \phi_0 \tag{30}$$

now incorporates the phase offset ϕ_0 as well as the effects of delay and Doppler. The $r_I(t)$ and $r_Q(t)$ random processes can be approximated as jointly Gaussian if $a_n(t)$ and $\phi_n(t)$ are stationary and ergodic and $N(t)$ is large enough to apply the Central Limit Theorem. If $a_n(t)$ are Rayleigh distributed and $\phi_n(t)$ are uniformly distributed on $[-\pi, \pi]$, the Gaussian property is still valid for small N.

Autocorrelation, Cross Correlation, and Power Spectral Density

In this section, we present the autocorrelation and cross correlation of the in-phase and quadrature received signal components $r_I(t)$ and $r_Q(t)$. The formulas derived here are not valid when a dominant LOS component exists. It is assumed that each of the resolvable multipath components is associated with a single reflector. As a result, the amplitude $a_n(t)$, multipath delay $\tau n(t)$ and Doppler frequency $f_{D_n}(t)$ are changing slowly enough such that they are constant over the time intervals of interest: $a_n(t) \approx a_n$, $\tau_n(t) \approx \tau_n$, and $f_{D_n}(t) \approx f_{D_n}$. Also, both the Doppler phase shift and the phase of the nth multipath component become $\varphi_{D_n}(t) = \int 2\pi f_{D_n} dt = 2\pi f_{D_n} t$ and $\varphi_n(t) = 2\pi f_c \tau_n - 2\pi f_{D_n} t - \phi_0$, respectively. Since f_c is large, then for the nth multipath component the term $2\pi f_c \tau_n$ in $\phi_n(t)$ changes rapidly relative to all other phase terms in this expression and can go through a 360 degree rotation for a small change in multipath delay τ_n. So, $\phi_n(t)$ is uniformly distributed on $[-\pi, \pi]$ and in addition since a_n and ϕ_n are independent, we have:

$$E\left[r_I\left(t\right)\right]=E\left[\sum_n a_n \cos\varphi_n\left(t\right)\right]=\sum_n E\left[a_n\right]E\left[\cos\varphi_n\left(t\right)\right]=0 \tag{31}$$

The same holds for $r_Q(t)$, i.e., $\mathrm{E}[r_Q(t)] = 0$. As a consequence, the received signal has $\mathrm{E}[r(t)] = 0$, i.e., it is a zero-mean Gaussian process. If a dominant LOS component is present in the channel, the assumption of a random uniform phase no longer holds because the phase of the received signal is dominated by the phase of the LOS component. Also, the independence of a_n and ϕ_n, ϕ_n and ϕ_m ($n \neq m$), and the uniform distribution of ϕ_n lead to the following expression for the autocorrelation of the in-phase and quadrature components.

$$\begin{aligned}
E\left[r_I\left(t\right)r_Q\left(t\right)\right] &= E\left[\sum_n a_n \cos\varphi_n\left(t\right)\sum_m a_m \sin\varphi_m\left(t\right)\right]\\
&= \sum_n\sum_m E\left[a_n a_m\right]E\left[\cos\varphi_n\left(t\right)\sin\varphi_m\left(t\right)\right]\\
&= \sum_n E\left[a_n^2\right]E\left[\cos\varphi_n\left(t\right)\sin\varphi_n\left(t\right)\right]\\
&= 0
\end{aligned} \tag{32}$$

The fact that $r_I(t)$, $r_Q(t)$ are uncorrelated jointly Gaussian processes implies that they are also independent. Similarly, the autocorrelation of $r_I(t)$ is:

$$A_{r_I}\left(t,\tau\right)=E\left[r_I\left(t\right)r_I\left(t+\tau\right)\right]=\sum_n E\left[a_n^2\right]E\left[\cos\varphi_n\left(t\right)\cos\varphi_n\left(t+\tau\right)\right]. \tag{33}$$

If we make the substitutions $\varphi_n\left(t\right)=2\pi f_c\tau_n - 2\pi f_{D_n}t - \varphi_0$ and $\varphi_n\left(t+\tau\right)=2\pi f_c\tau_n - 2\pi f_{D_n}\left(t+\tau\right)-\varphi_0$ we have:

$$E\left[\cos\varphi_n\left(t\right)\cos\varphi_n\left(t+\tau\right)\right]=0.5E\left[\cos 2\pi f_{D_n}\tau\right]+0.5E\left[\cos\left(4\pi f_c\tau_n - 4\pi f_{D_n}t - 2\pi f_{D_n}\tau - 2\varphi_0\right)\right]. \tag{34}$$

The second expectation term in (39) goes to zero because $2\pi f_c\tau_n$ changes rapidly relative to all other phase terms and is uniformly distributed Also, it is assumed that $f_{D_n}=\upsilon\cos\theta_n/\lambda$ is fixed. So, we have:

$$A_{r_I}\left(t,\tau\right)=\sum_n E\left[a_n^2\right]E\left[\cos 2\pi f_{D_n}\tau\right]=0.5\sum_n E\left[a_n^2\right]\cos\left(2\pi\upsilon\tau\cos\theta_n/\lambda\right). \tag{35}$$

It is obvious that $A_{r_I}\left(t,\tau\right)=A_{r_I}\left(\tau\right)$, i.e., it depends only on τ. Following a similar procedure, the same result is obtained for the autocorrelation $A_{r_Q}\left(t,\tau\right)$, So, both $r_I(t)$ and $r_Q(t)$ are wide-sense stationary (WSS) random processes. The WSS property holds also for the cross correlation between the in-phase and quadrature components, i.e., the cross correlation depends only on τ. It is given by:

$$A_{r_I,r_Q}\left(t,\tau\right)=A_{r_I,r_Q}\left(\tau\right)=E\left[r_I\left(t\right)r_Q\left(t+\tau\right)\right]=-0.5\sum_n E\left[a_n^2\right]\sin\left(2\pi\upsilon\tau\cos\theta_n/\lambda\right)=-E\left[r_Q\left(t\right)r_I\left(t+\tau\right)\right] \tag{36}$$

The autocorrelation of the received signal $r(t) = r_I(t)\cos(2\pi f_c\tau) + r_Q(t)\sin(2\pi f_c\tau)$ can be shown that obeys the WSS property. It is given by:

$$A_r\left(\tau\right)=E\left[r\left(t\right)r\left(t+\tau\right)\right]=A_{r_I}\left(\tau\right)\cos\left(2\pi f_c\tau\right)+A_{r_I,r_Q}\left(\tau\right)\sin\left(2\pi f_c\tau\right). \tag{37}$$

This expression was obtained using the previous results. If now we make use of the **uniform scattering environment** introduced by Clarke (1968) and further developed by Jakes (1974.), then we have $\theta n = n\Delta\theta$, where $\Delta\theta = 2\pi/N$, since the channel consists of many scatterers densely packed with respect to angle. The parameter N is equal to the number of the multipath components. Moreover, it is assumed that each multipath component has the same received power, so $E[a_n^2] = 2P_r/N$, where P_r is the total received power. Making the substitution $N = 2\pi/\Delta\theta$, (35) becomes:

$$A_{r_I}(\tau) = \frac{P_r}{2\pi} \sum_{n=1}^{N} \cos(2\pi \upsilon\tau \cos n\Delta\theta/\lambda)\Delta\theta \tag{38}$$

If we assume uniform scattering from all directions, i.e., the number of scatterers grows to infinity, then $N \to \infty$, $\Delta\theta \to 0$, and the summation in (38) becomes an integral:

$$A_{r_I}(\tau) = \frac{P_r}{2\pi} \int \cos(2\pi \upsilon\tau \cos n\Delta\theta/\lambda)d\theta = P_r J_0(2\pi f_D\tau), \tag{39}$$

where $J_0(.)$ is the Bessel function of the $0th$ order. Following a similar procedure, we have:

$$A_{r_I,r_I}(\tau) = \frac{P_r}{2\pi} \int \sin(2\pi \upsilon\tau \cos n\Delta\theta/\lambda)d\theta = 0 \tag{40}$$

In the plot of $J_0(2\pi f_D\tau)$ is shown that the autocorrelation is zero for $f_D\tau \approx 0.4$ or equivalently, for $\upsilon\tau = 0.4\lambda$. In other words, assuming that θ_n is uniformly distributed, then the signal decorrelates over a distance of approximately one half wavelength. This result is very useful to determine many parameters of a system such as the antenna spacing in order to exploit the antenna diversity. It is also clear from the plot that the signal recorrelates after it becomes uncorrelated. This property does not allow a Markov model to be completely accurate for Rayleigh fading. Fortunately, in practical system analyses a correlation below 0.5 does not significantly degrade performance relative to uncorrelated fading (Simon, 2000). So, in these cases, when the separation distance is greater than a half wavelength, the signal remains decorrelated at all larger distances and the fading process can be modelled as Markov.

If we take the Fourier Transform of the autocorrelations $A_{r_I}(\tau)$ and $A_{r_Q}(\tau)$, then we obtain the respective power spectral densities (PSDs) $S_{r_I}(f)$ and $S_{r_Q}(f)$ of $r_I(t)$ and $r_Q(t)$. The equality of the autocorrelation functions entails the equality of the PSDs. So, we have:

$$S_{r_I}(f) = S_{r_Q}(f) = F[A_{r_I}(\tau)] = \begin{cases} \dfrac{P_r}{2\pi f_D} \dfrac{1}{\sqrt{1-(f/f_D)^2}} & |f| \le f_D \\ 0 & else \end{cases} \tag{41}$$

The PSD $S_r(f)$ of the received signal $r(t)$ under uniform scattering is obtained, if we use (37) with $A_{r_I,r_Q}(\tau)$, and (41) as

$$S_r(f) = F[A_r(\tau)] = 0.25[S_{r_I}(f-f_c) + S_{r_Q}(f+f_c)] = \begin{cases} \dfrac{P_r}{4\pi f_D} \dfrac{1}{\sqrt{1-(|f-f_c|/f_D)^2}} & |f-f_c| \le f_D \\ 0 & else \end{cases} \tag{42}$$

The PSD can be viewed as the distribution (pdf) of the random frequency due to Doppler associated with multipath since it models the power density associated with multipath components as a function of their Doppler frequency. The total received power P_r is obtained if we integrate the PSD. Since $S_{r_I}(f)$ goes to infinity at $f = \pm f_D$ as can be easily seen in Figure 4, then the $S_r(f)$ goes to infinity at $f = \pm f_C \pm f_D$. In practice, this does not happen because uniform scattering is just an approximation that can be valid for environments with dense scatterers. In this case, the PSD is maximized at frequencies close to the maximum Doppler frequency. The need for the description of nonuniform scattering occurred, in microcell and indoor environments, led to formulas that some of them can be found in (Jakes, 1974; Stuber, 2001). During simulations of fading processes, the use of PSD is very often. Usually, in order to simulate the envelope of a narrowband fading process we pass two independent white Gaussian noise sources with PSD $N_0/2$ through lowpass filters with frequency response $H(f)$ that satisfies:

$$S_{r_I}(f) = S_{r_Q}(f) = \frac{N_0}{2}|H(f)|^2 \tag{43}$$

The in-phase and quadrature components of the narrowband fading process with PSDs $S_{r_I}(f)$ and $S_{r_Q}(f)$ correspond to the filter outputs.

Statistical Models for Envelope and Power Distributions

Rayleigh Distribution

Assuming that $\phi_n(t)$ follow uniform distribution, then r_I and r_Q are both zero-mean Gaussian random variables as proved before. So, the signal envelope can be written as:

$$z(t) = |r(t)| = \sqrt{r_I^2(t) + r_Q^2(t)},$$
(44)

which is Rayleigh-distributed with distribution:

$$p_z(z) = \frac{2z}{P_r} \exp\left(-z^2/P_r\right) = \frac{z}{\sigma^2} \exp\left(-z^2/2\sigma^2\right),$$
(45)

if both the in-phase and quadrature components have also equal variance σ^2. The parameter $P_r = \sum_n E\left(a_n^2\right) = 2\sigma^2$ is the average received signal power of the signal, i.e., the received power based on path loss and shadowing.

Making the appropriate change of variables $z^2(t) = |r(t)|^2$ in (43) we obtain the power distribution:

$$p_{z^2}(x) = \frac{1}{P_r} e^{-x/P_r} = \frac{1}{2\sigma^2} e^{-x/(2\sigma^2)}, \ \ x \geq 0$$
(46)

which is exponentially distributed with mean $2\sigma^2$. Also, the phase $\theta = \arctan(r_Q(t)/r_I(t))$ can be shown to be uniformly distributed and independent of the envelope $|r(t)|$.

Rice Distribution

In rural and suburban environments, where there is a fixed LOS component, the corresponding channel is known as a Rician fading channel. In other words, the received signal is consisted by both a multipath and LOS components. In this case, the $r_I(t)$ and $r_Q(t)$ do not have zero-mean and the envelope of the signal has a Rician distribution (Rice, 1945), given by:

$$p_z(z) = \frac{z}{\sigma^2} \exp\left(-\frac{\left(z^2 + s^2\right)}{2\sigma^2}\right) I_0\left(\frac{zs}{\sigma^2}\right), \ \ z \geq 0,$$
(47)

where $2\sigma^2 = \sum_{n, n \neq 0} E\left(a_n^2\right)$ and $s^2 = a_0^2$ are the average power in the multipath components and the power in the LOS component, respectively. The function I_0 is the modified Bessel function of $0th$ order.

Another form of the Rician distribution follows using the fading parameter K, defined by:

$$K = \frac{s^2}{2\sigma^2}.$$
(48)

In this expression, K is equal to the ratio of the power in the LOS component to the power in the (non-LOS) multipath component and it takes values in the range $[0, \infty]$. If $K = 0$ we have Rayleigh fading, while in the case that $K = \infty$ we have no fading, i.e., a channel with no multipath and only a LOS component. Therefore the fading parameter K is a measure of the severity of the fading: a small K implies severe fading while a large K implies

Figure 3. Bessel Function versus $f_D\tau$

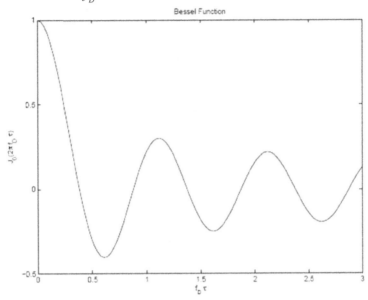

Figure 4. In-Phase and Quadrature PSD: $S_{r_I}(f) = S_{r_Q}(f)$

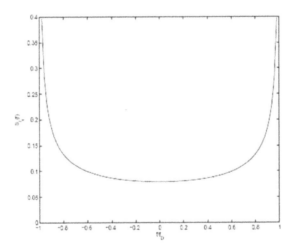

more mild fading. The Rice distribution can be rewritten in terms of K and P_r, if we make the substitutions $s^2 = KP/(K + 1)$ and $2\sigma^2 = P/(K + 1)$. Then we have:

$$p_Z(z) = \frac{2z(K+1)}{P_r}\exp\left(-K - \frac{(K+1)z^2}{P_r}\right)I_0\left(2z\sqrt{\frac{K(K+1)}{P_r}}\right), \quad z \geq 0$$

(49)

Nakagami-m Distribution

Nakagami distribution is selected to characterize the fading channel because it provides a closer match to some experimental data than either the Rayleigh or Rician distributions. The Nakagami fading distribution is given by:

$$p_Z(z) = \frac{2m^m z^{2m-1}}{\Gamma(m)P_r^m} \exp\left(-\frac{mz^2}{P_r}\right), \quad m \geq 0.5 \tag{50}$$

where P_r is the average received power and $\Gamma(\cdot)$ is the Gamma function. This distribution is a function of the parameters P_r and m. According to the values of the m parameter, we can obtain the Rayleigh distribution ($m = 1$) or approximately the Rice distribution ($m = (K+1)^2/(2K+1)$). Also, for $m = \infty$ there is no fading, and for $m = 0.5$ we obtain the One-Sided Gaussian distribution which describes the case that there is more severe fading than the Rayleigh. Following a similar procedure as before, the power distribution in Nakagami fading is given by:

$$p_{Z^2}(x) = \left(\frac{m}{P_r}\right)^m \frac{x^{m-1}}{\Gamma(m)} \exp\left(-\frac{mx}{P_r}\right). \tag{51}$$

Norton Distribution

The Norton distribution (Norton et al., 1955; Iskam, 1985; Martin, 1997) is a combination of the Rice and Nakagami distributions, in order to model small-scale fading. The pdf is:

$$p_{Norton}(z) = \frac{z^m m}{\sigma^2 s^{m-1}} \exp\left[-\frac{(z^2+s^2)}{2\sigma^2}m\right] I_{m-1}\left(\frac{zsm}{\sigma^2}\right) \tag{52}$$

where $s \geq 0$ is the direct component amplitude and $I_{m-1}(.)$ is the modified Bessel function of the first kind of order $m-1$, where $m \geq 1/2$ and σ^2 have a significance similar to that for the Rice and Nakagami distributions. It is able to produce better fitting than other distributions since it has three parameters. However, the additional complexity may not be justified in most situations.

Suzuki Distribution

The Suzuki pdf (1977) is widely accepted for urban terrestrial mobile channels and it is used to describe jointly large and small-scale fading, i.e., it is a composite pdf. It combines Rayleigh and lognormal statistics as follows:

$$p_{Suzuki}(z) = \frac{z}{\sqrt{2\pi}\delta} \int_0^\infty \frac{1}{\sigma^3} \exp\left[-\frac{1}{2}\left(\frac{z^2}{\sigma^2} + \frac{(\ln\sigma - \mu)^2}{\delta^2}\right)\right] d\sigma \tag{53}$$

where $2\sigma^2$ is the average received power for the Rayleigh process, and δ and μ are the standard deviation and the mean value of the normal variable associated with the lognormal distribution, as described in (20). Starting from the Suzuki pdf, many other models have been introduced that employ compositions of Rayleigh, Rice, and lognormal distributions to describe the peculiarities of satellite mobile channels.

Loo Distribution

The Loo model (1985) assumes that the received signal is affected by nonselective Rice fading with lognormal shadowing on the direct component only, while the diffuse scattered component has a constant average power level. It is suitable for rural environments, specifically accounting for shadowing due to roadside trees. The total complex fading coefficient g is the sum of the direct component contribution with lognormal envelope S and the diffuse component with Rayleigh envelope R:

$$g = Se^{j\varphi_0} + Re^{j\varphi} \tag{54}$$

where the phases ϕ_0 and ϕ are uniformly distributed. The resulting pdf conditioned to a certain S value is Rice distributed. In this case, the envelope pdf can be written as:

$$p_{Loo}(z) = \int_0^\infty p_{Rice}(z/S) p_{Lognormal}(S) dS \tag{55}$$

$$= \frac{z}{\sigma^2 \sqrt{2\pi}\delta} \int_0^\infty \frac{1}{S} \exp\left(-\frac{(\ln S - \mu)^2}{2\delta^2} - \frac{(z^2 + S^2)}{2\sigma^2}\right) I_0\left(\frac{zS}{\sigma^2}\right) dS$$

where $2\sigma_2^2$ is the average scattered power due to multipath, and δ and μ are the standard deviation and the mean value of the normal variate associated with the lognormal distribution. The pdf described by Loo corresponds to a lognormal distribution for large envelope values and to a Rayleigh distribution for small values (Loo, 1985):

$$p_{Loo}(z) = \begin{cases} p_{Lognormal}(z) & \text{for } z \gg \sigma \\ p_{Rayleigh}(z) & \text{for } z \ll \sigma \end{cases} \tag{56}$$

RLN Distribution

The Rice–lognormal (RLN) model (Corazza, 1994; Corazza et al., 1994) is a composition of Rice and lognormal statistics, with shadowing affecting both direct and diffuse components, and not only the direct path, as in the Loo model. As a matter of fact, the diffuse component power is no longer constant, since it suffers the same variations as the direct component. This is based on the observation that large-scale fading is caused by major obstacles that are likely to affect both direct and multipath components. The fading envelope is thus factored as the product of two independent variates, i.e.,

$$z = SR. \tag{57}$$

The shadowing S is lognormal distributed. The diffuse component R is a Rice process normalized in power (i.e., $E[R^2] = 1$) whose pdf can be expressed as a function of the Rice factor, K:

$$p_R(R) = 2R(K+1)\exp\left(-R^2(K+1) - K\right) I_0\left(2R\sqrt{K(K+1)}\right) \tag{58}$$

If $R = \frac{z}{S}$ then:

$$p(z/S) = 2(K+1)\frac{z}{S} \exp\left(-\left(\frac{z}{S}\right)^2 (K+1) - K\right) I_0\left(2\frac{z}{S}\sqrt{K(K+1)}\right) \tag{59}$$

it follows that:

$$p_z(z) = \int_0^\infty p(z/S) p_S(S) dS \tag{60}$$

Many of the previous nonselective statistical models can be derived as limiting cases of the RLN channel model for specific combinations of K, μ, and δ:

- if $K = 0$, r is described by a Rayleigh–lognormal pdf (Suzuki).
- if $K \to \infty$, the channel is lognormal since $p_R(R)$ tends to a Dirac pulse located at $R = 1$ and $p_z(z)$ tends to $p_s(r)$.
- if $\sigma_{\psi_{dB}} \to 0$, the channel is Rician because then $p_s(S)$ tends to $\delta(S - h\mu_{\psi_{dB}})$, which is a Dirac pulse located at its mean value and therefore, $p_Z(z) \to p(z/h\mu_{\psi_{dB}})$. In addition, if $K = 0$, the channel is Rayleigh.

The RLN model (Corazza, 1994) has been fitted and validated against experimental data collected by ESA (Sforza, 1993) in four different environments (rural tree-shadowed, urban, suburban, and open) and in a vast range of elevation angles α (20 to 80 degrees). This makes it also suitable for modelling the communication channel of a global satellite system adopting a nongeostationary orbit. In order to perform fitting, the optimum triplet (K, μ, δ) should be determined using the following polynomial empirical model:

$$K(a) = K_0 + K_1 a + K_2 a^2 + K_3 a^3 \tag{61}$$

$$\mu(a) = \mu_0 + \mu_1 a + \mu_2 a^2 + \mu_3 a^3 \tag{62}$$

$$\delta(a) = \delta_0 + \delta_1 a + \delta_2 a^2 + \delta_3 a^3 \tag{63}$$

These coefficients, i.e, K_i, μ_i, and δ_i ($i = 0, 1, 2, 3$), are provided for some environments. In other words, the RLN model can be characterized as a hybrid statistical-empirical model whose parameters for any elevation angle are obtained in an empirical manner.

Patzold et al. Distribution

Patzold et al. (1998) proposed an extended RLN model, where small-scale fading is modelled again through a Rice variate R, but with cross-correlated in-phase and quadrature components and a possible Doppler shift on the direct component:

$$R = \left| \rho e^{j\left(2\pi f_\rho t + \theta_\rho\right)} + R_p + jR_q \right|, \tag{64}$$

where ρ is the direct component amplitude, f_ρ is the direct component Doppler shift, θ_ρ is the direct component initial phase, and $R_p + jR_q$ is the complex diffuse component. The large-scale fading S is still lognormally distributed and multiplies the Rice variate, as in the RLN distribution. The two variables are statistically uncorrelated, and the corresponding envelope pdf is the same as that for the RLN model. The differences are visible in the second-order characterization.

GRLN Distribution

The generalized RLN (GRLN) model (Vatalaro, 1995) contains the RLN and Loo models as particular cases. The diffuse multipath component is subdivided into two parts, shadowed and unshadowed, respectively. The complex fading coefficient is written as:

$$g = ze^{j\theta} = x + jy = RSe^{j\phi} + x_1 + jy_1, \tag{65}$$

where the variate R is Rician with parameters s and σ^2 and is multiplied by the lognormal variable S with parameters μ and δ. The resulting product is added to the zero-mean complex Gaussian variate $x_1 + jy_1$, with Rayleigh envelope and variance $2\sigma_1^2$. S, x_1, and y_1 are mutually uncorrelated. Introducing the Rice factor, K, and the mean power ratio between the shadowed and unshadowed diffuse components, $\xi = \sigma^2 / 2\sigma_1^2$, the normalized envelope distribution conditioned on shadowing can be written as:

$$p(z/S) = \frac{2z\xi\,(K+1)}{1+\xi\,S^2}\exp\left(-\xi\,\frac{KS^2+(K+1)z^2}{1+\xi\,S^2}\right)I_0\left(2zS\,\frac{\xi\sqrt{K\,(K+1)}}{1+\xi\,S^2}\right). \tag{66}$$

This $p(z/S)$ expression must be substituted into Equation (60) to have the GRLN distribution. Note that for $\xi \to 0$ the GRLN tends to the Loo distribution, while for $\xi \to \infty$ the GRLN tends to the RLN distribution. The conditional phase pdf, $p(\theta/S)$, is given by:

$$
p(\theta/S) = \frac{1}{2\pi} \exp\left(-\frac{\xi KS^2}{1+\xi S^2} \right) + \sqrt{\frac{\xi KS^2}{\pi\left(1+\xi S^2\right)}} \cos\theta
$$

$$
\times \left[1 - \frac{1}{2} erfc\left(\sqrt{\frac{\xi KS^2}{\pi\left(1+\xi S^2\right)}} \cos\theta \right) \right] \exp\left(-\frac{\xi KS^2}{1+\xi S^2} \sin^2\theta \right) \tag{67}
$$

Xie and Fang Distribution

Xie and Fang (2000) derived another extension of the RLN model based on the propagation scattering theory. As before, the fading envelope is factored as the product of two independent variables related to large-scale and small-scale fading:

$$
z = RS, \tag{68}
$$

where S is lognormally distributed with parameters μ, and δ, and R is modelled through a generalization of the Rice distribution. The generalization allows the diffuse component to result from the composition of generic amplitude/phase scattering contributions. As a result, the real and imaginary small-scale fading components are still Gaussian but with a different mean and variance (a, σ_1^2, and β, σ_2^2, respectively). Therefore, we have:

$$
p_R(R) = \frac{R}{\sigma_1\sigma_2} \exp\left(-\frac{\sigma_1^2 R^2 + \sigma_2^2 a^2 + \sigma_1^2 \beta^2}{2\sigma_1^2\sigma_2^2} \right)
$$

$$
\times \frac{1}{2\pi} \int_0^{2\pi} \exp\left(\frac{2\sigma_2^2 aR\cos\theta + 2\sigma_1^2\beta R\sin\theta + \left(\sigma_1^2 - \sigma_2^2\right)R^2\cos^2\theta}{2\sigma_1^2\sigma_2^2} \right) d\theta \tag{69}
$$

The channel envelope pdf can be determined as the double integral:

$$
p_Z(z) = \int_0^\infty \frac{1}{S} p_R\left(\frac{R}{S}\right) p_S(S)\, dS. \tag{70}
$$

This model contains several particular cases. When $\delta = 0$, and $\sigma_1^2 = \sigma_2^2$, large-scale fading vanishes and (70) reduces to the Rice distribution. Furthermore, when $a = \beta = 0$, it reduces to the Rayleigh distribution. If $\sigma_{\psi_{dB}} \neq 0$, $\sigma_1^2 = \sigma_2^2$, and $a = \beta = 0$, (70) reduces to the Suzuki pdf. Finally, when $\sigma_1^2 = \sigma_2^2$ and $a^2 = \beta^2 = (2\sigma_1^4)/2$, (70) reduces to the RLN model.

Other Models

Hwang et al. (1997; Karaliopoulos, Pavlidou, 1999) proposed an extended Loo model where shadowing on the diffuse component is introduced. This is different from RLN because shadowing on the direct component is independent from shadowing on the diffuse component. The complex fading coefficient is therefore

$$
g = ze^{i\theta} = sS_1 e^{j\phi} + RS_2 e^{j(\varphi + \phi)} \tag{71}
$$

where s is the direct component amplitude, R is the Rayleigh-distributed diffuse component, and S_1 and S_2 are lognormally distributed with parameters μ_1, δ_1 and μ_2, δ_2, respectively. When $\delta_2 = 0$, the Hwang et al. model coincides with the Loo model.

Tjhung and Chai (1998; 1999) proposed a Nakagami–lognormal (NLN) statistical model to characterize multipath fading, shadowing, and path loss using the same formulation as the RLN model. The only difference stands in modelling the variate R with a Nakagami-m distribution in place of the Rice distribution.

Abdi et al. (2003) propose a model describing the direct component S through a Nakagami-m distribution and the diffuse component R by means of a Rayleigh distribution. The complex fading coefficient is expressed as:

$$g = Se^{j\varphi_0} + Re^{j\varphi},\tag{72}$$

where ϕ is uniformly distributed over $[0,2\pi)$ and ϕ_0 is the deterministic phase associated with the direct component. S and R are independent variates. Overall, this model can also be interpreted as a Rice distribution with Nakagami-distributed amplitude for the direct component.

Level Crossing Rate and Average Fade Duration

The LCR and AFD can be easily understood if we look carefully at Figure 5 and pay attention to the following definitions. The envelope LCR L_z is defined as the expected rate (crossings per second) at which the signal envelope crosses the level Z in the downward direction. In order to obtain L_z, the joint distribution of the signal envelope $z = |r|$ and its derivative with respect to time $\dot{z}$, $p(z,\dot{z})$, is required. The expected number of crossings of the envelope level Z per second, i.e., the LCR, is:

$$L_z = \int_{-\infty}^{0} \dot{z}\,p(Z,\dot{z})\,d\dot{z}.\tag{73}$$

Note that this is a general result that applies for any random process. The joint pdf of Z and $\dot{z}$ for Rician fading was derived in (Rice, 1945). Using this pdf in (73), the LCR for Rician fading can be found as:

$$L_z = \sqrt{2\pi(K+1)}\,f_D\rho e^{-K-(K+1)\rho^2}I_0\left(2\rho\sqrt{K(K+1)}\right),\tag{74}$$

where $\rho = Z/\sqrt{P_r}$. In the case of Rayleigh fading ($K = 0$) the LCR simplifies to:

$$L_z = \sqrt{2\pi}\,f_D\rho e^{-\rho^2},\tag{75}$$

where $\rho = Z/\sqrt{P_r}$.

The AFD is defined as the average time that the signal envelope stays below a given target level Z. Let t_i denote the duration of the ith fade below level Z over a time interval $[0, T]$. Thus t_i equals the length of time that the signal envelope stays below Z on its ith crossing. The stationarity and ergodicity of $z(t)$ in addition to the assumption that T is large enough offer the following expression.

$$p_Z\big(z(t)<Z\big)=\frac{1}{T}\sum_i t_i.\tag{76}$$

For T sufficiently large the AFD can be written as:

$$\bar{t}_z = \frac{1}{TL_z}\sum_{i=1}^{TL_z} t_i \approx \frac{p_Z\big(z(t)<Z\big)}{L_z}.\tag{77}$$

In the case of Rayleigh fading, the AFD can be expressed as:

$$\bar{t}_z = \frac{e^{\rho^2}-1}{\rho f_D \sqrt{2\pi}}, \tag{78}$$

with $\rho = Z/\sqrt{P_r}$. In other words, (78) expresses the AFD for the signal envelope (amplitude) level with z the target amplitude and $\sqrt{P_r}$ the average envelope level. It is a function of f_D and ρ. More specifically, the average fade duration decreases with Doppler frequency, because as the channel changes more quickly it remains below a given fade level for a shorter period of time, while it increases with ρ for $\rho \gg 1$ Because as the target level increases relative to the average, the signal is more likely to be below the target. In the case of Rician fading the AFD can be found in (Stuber, 2001)

The AFD is a useful measure which can indicate the number of bits or symbols affected by a deep fade. For example, in the case that the probability of bit error is high when $z < Z$ and considering an uncoded system with bit time T_b, then if $T_b \approx \bar{t}_z$, the system will likely experience single error events, where bits that are received in error have the previous and subsequent bits received correctly (since $z < Z$ for these bits). If $T_b \ll \bar{t}_z$ then many subsequent bits are received with $z < Z$, so large bursts of errors are likely while if $T_b \ll \bar{t}_z$ the fading is averaged out over a bit time in the demodulator, so it can be neglected.

WIDEBAND FADING MODELS

When the signal bandwidth is larger than the coherence bandwidth of the channel, frequency selectivity leads to wideband channels. The wideband channels are characterized by means of the equivalent lowpass time-varying channel impulse response $c(\tau, t)$ as a continuous function of τ and t (Goldsmith, 2005), which represent the impulse response associated with a given multipath delay, and time variations, respectively. It is assumed that $c(\tau, t)$ is a deterministic function. Taking the Fourier transform of $c(\tau, t)$ with respect to t, we obtain:

$$S_c(\tau,\rho) = \int_{-\infty}^{\infty} c(\tau,t) e^{-j2\pi\rho t} dt, \tag{79}$$

which is called the **deterministic scattering function** of the lowpass equivalent channel impulse response $c(\tau, t)$. In $S_c(\tau, \rho)$ the Doppler characteristics of the channel are found via the frequency parameter ρ since $S_c(\tau, \rho)$ is derived by means of the Fourier transform of $c(\tau, t)$ with respect to the time variation parameter t. The randomness of the parts of the multipath components, i.e., random amplitudes, phases, and delays of the random number of multipath components, lead to the need for a statistical description of $c(\tau, t)$. It can be assumed that $c(\tau, t)$ is a complex Gaussian process if the number of multipath components is large enough to use the Central Limit Theorem. As a result, the impulse response $c(\tau, t)$ can be described by the mean, autocorrelation, and cross-correlation of its in-phase and quadrature components. If the phase of each multipath component is uniformly distributed, then the in-phase and quadrature components of $c(\tau, t)$ are independent Gaussian processes with the same autocorrelation, a mean of zero, and a cross-correlation of zero.

Consequently, the equivalent channel impulse response $c(\tau, t)$ is determined by its **autocorrelation function**, given by:

$$A_c(\tau_1, \tau_2; t, \Delta t) = E(c^*(\tau_1, t) \, c(\tau_2, t + \Delta t)). \tag{80}$$

Since WSS processes are those whose joint statistics of the channel measured at two different times t and $t + \Delta t$ depends only on the time difference Δt, i.e., independent of t, then the autocorrelation of the corresponding bandpass channel $h(\tau, t) = \Re\left\{c(\tau, t) e^{j2\pi f_c t}\right\}$ can be obtained (Bello, 1963) from $A_c(\tau_1, \tau_2; t, \Delta t)$ as $A_h(\tau_1, \tau_2; t, \Delta t) = 0.5\Re\left\{A_c(\tau_1, \tau_2; t, \Delta t) e^{j2\pi f_c \Delta t}\right\}$. We will assume that our channel model is WSS, in which case the autocorrelation becomes:

$$A_c(\tau_1, \tau_2; \Delta t) = E(c^*(\tau_1, t) \, c(\tau_2, t + \Delta t)). \tag{81}$$

The case of uncorrelated scattering (US) occurs when the channel response associated with a given multipath component of delay τ_1 is uncorrelated with the response associated with a multipath component at a different delay $\tau_1 \neq \tau_2$, since the two components are caused by different scatterers. Channels that combine both the properties of WSS and US are called WSSUS channels.

$$E\left(c^*(\tau_1,t)c(\tau_2,t+\Delta t)\right)= A_c\left(\tau_1;\Delta t\right)\delta(\tau_1 - \tau_2) \triangleq A\left(\tau\Delta t\right) \tag{82}$$

In the case of random signals, the **scattering function** is defined as the Fourier transform of $A_c(\tau, \Delta t)$ with respect to the Δt parameter:

$$S_c(\tau,\rho)= \int_{-\infty}^{\infty} A_c(\tau,\Delta t)e^{-j2\pi\rho\Delta t}d\Delta t. \tag{83}$$

The scattering function is a function of the multipath delay τ and Doppler ρ, and describes the average output power associated with the channel. A typical scattering function is shown in Figure 6.

Parameters of Mobile Multipath Channel

A multipath channel is characterized by many important parameters. Among these parameters, delay spread and coherence bandwidth describe the time-dispersive nature of the channel in a local area. On the other hand, the Doppler spread and coherence bandwidth describe the time-varying nature of the channel in a small-scale region. Including these major parameters here, we will briefly discuss the channel parameters, which will provide a clear description of a mobile multipath channel.

Excess Delay

This is the relative delay of the ith multipath signal component, compared to the first arriving component and is given by τ_i.

Power Delay Profile

This is the average output signal power of the channel as a function of the excess time delay τ. In practice, it is measured by transmitting very narrow pulses, or equivalently a wideband signal, and cross-correlating the received signal with a delayed version of itself. It is also called the **multipath intensity profile** and is defined as the autocorrelation (80) with $\Delta t = 0$: $A_c(\tau) = A_c(\tau, 0)$. Using the power delay profile $A_c(\tau)$, we can define two new quantities, the average and rms delay spread as:

$$\mu_{T_m} = \frac{\int_0^{\infty} \tau A_c(\tau)d\tau}{\int_0^{\infty} A_c(\tau)d\tau} \tag{84}$$

Figure 5. LCR and AFD for a fading process

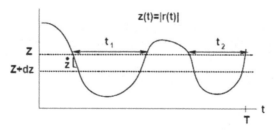

and

$$\sigma_{T_m} = \sqrt{\frac{\int_0^\infty \left(\tau - \mu_{T_m}\right)^2 A_c(\tau)\, d\tau}{\int_0^\infty A_c(\tau)\, d\tau}}. \tag{85}$$

Defining the pdf of p_{T_m} of the random delay spread T_m in terms of $A_c(\tau)$ as:

$$p_{T_m} = \frac{A_c(\tau)}{\int_0^\infty A_c(\tau)\, d\tau} \tag{86}$$

then μ_{T_m} and σ_{T_m} are basically the mean and rms values of T_m.

This delay spread equals the time delay between the arrival of the first received signal component (LOS or multipath) and the last received signal component associated with a single transmitted pulse and can be characterized by the time delay T where $A_c(\tau, 0)$ for $\tau \geq T$. If $T_s \ll \sigma_{T_m}$, where T_s is the symbol period of a linearly modulated signal, then the signal experiences significant ISI. On the other hand, if $T_s \gg \sigma_{T_m}$, then negligible ISI is experienced. In calculations, the above implie that $T_s < \sigma_{T_m}/10$ and $T_s > 10\sigma_{T_m}$, respectively. If T_s and σ_{T_m} have the same order of magnitude, then there will be some ISI experienced whose effect on performance, depends on the specific characteristics of the channel and system.

Coherence Bandwidth

The frequency band in which all the spectral components of the transmitted signal pass through a channel with equal gain and linear phase is known as coherence bandwidth of that channel. Over this bandwidth the channel remains invariant.

Taking the Fourier transform of $c(\tau, t)$ with respect to τ, we can characterize the time-varying multipath channel in the frequency domain defining the random process:

$$C(f;t) = \int_{-\infty}^\infty c(\tau;t) e^{-j2\pi f\tau}\, d\tau. \tag{87}$$

Figure 6. Scattering function

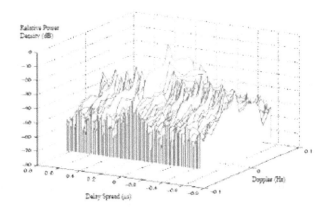

Since $c(\tau; t)$ is a complex zero-mean Gaussian random variable in respect to t, the Fourier transform just represents the sum of complex zero-mean Gaussian random processes, and therefore $C(f; t)$ is also a zero-mean Gaussian random process completely characterized by its autocorrelation. The autocorrelation of (88) is given by:

$$A_C(f_1, f_2; \Delta t) = E(C^*(f_1, t)\, C(f_2, t + \Delta t)). \tag{88}$$

Since $c(\tau; t)$ is a complex zero-mean Gaussian random process and WSS, then its integral $C(f; t)$ is also a complex zero-mean Gaussian random process and WSS. The $A_C(f_1, f_2; \Delta t)$ can be simplified as:

$$
\begin{aligned}
A_C(f_1, f_2; \Delta t) &= E\left[\int_{-\infty}^{\infty} c^*(\tau_1; t) e^{j2\pi f_1 \tau_1}\, d\tau_1 \int_{-\infty}^{\infty} c(\tau_2; t + \Delta t) e^{-j2\pi f_2 \tau_2}\, d\tau_2 \right] \\
&= \int_{-\infty}^{\infty}\int_{-\infty}^{\infty} E\left[c^*(\tau_1; t) c(\tau_2; t + \Delta t) \right] e^{j2\pi f_1 \tau_1} e^{-j2\pi f_2 \tau_2}\, d\tau_1 d\tau_2 \\
&= \int_{-\infty}^{\infty} A_c(\tau; \Delta t) e^{-j2\pi(f_2 - f_1)\tau}\, d\tau \\
&= A_C(\Delta f; \Delta t)
\end{aligned}
\tag{89}
$$

where $\Delta f = f_2 - f_1$. As a result, the autocorrelation of $C(f; t)$ in frequency depends only on the frequency difference Δf. Transmitting a pair of sinusoids separated in frequency by Δf through the channel and calculating their cross correlation at the receiver for the time separation Δt, we can measure the function $A_C(\Delta f; \Delta t)$ in practice. Defining $A_C(\Delta f) = A_C(\Delta f; 0)$ then from (87):

$$A_C(\Delta f) = \int_{-\infty}^{\infty} A_c(\tau) e^{-j2\pi\Delta f \tau}\, d\tau$$

$$\tag{90}$$

In other words, the $A_C(\Delta f)$ is the Fourier transform of the power delay profile. When $A_C(\Delta f) \approx 0$, then it is implied that the autocorrelation of the channel response is approximately independent at frequency separations Δf. The **coherence bandwidth** of the channel is called the frequency B_c where $A_C(\Delta f) \approx 0$ for all $\Delta f > B_c$. The frequency B_c is almost equal to the inverse rms delay spread σ_{T_m} of $A_c(\tau)$, i.e., $B_c \approx 1/\sigma_{T_m}$, but often $B_c \approx k/\sigma_{T_m}$ where k depends on the shape of $A_c(\tau)$ and the precise specification of coherence bandwidth.

In Figure 7 are depicted the $A_C(\Delta f)$ of both a narrowband signal with bandwidth much less than B_c and wideband signal with bandwidth much greater than B_c. The autocorrelation $A_C(\Delta f)$ is flat across the bandwidth of the narrowband signal, so this signal will experience flat fading or, equivalently, negligible ISI. On the other hand, within the bandwidth of the wideband signal, the autocorrelation $A_C(\Delta f)$ goes to zero, i.e., the fading will be independent across different parts of the signal bandwidth, so fading is frequency selective and a linearly modulated signal transmitted through this channel will experience significant ISI.

Doppler Power Spectrum and Channel Coherence Time

In order to characterize the Doppler effect (Doppler shift) caused by the motion of the transmitter or receiver, we take the Fourier transform of $A_C(\Delta f; \Delta \tau)$ relative to Δt, i.e.,

$$S_C(\Delta f, \rho) = \int_{-\infty}^{\infty} A_C(\Delta f, \Delta t) e^{-j2\pi\rho\Delta t}\, d\Delta t. \tag{91}$$

Setting Δf to zero and defining $S_C(\rho) \triangleq S_C(0, \rho)$, we achieve to characterize Doppler at any single frequency as:

$$S_C(\rho) = \int_{-\infty}^{\infty} A_C(\Delta t) e^{-j2\pi\rho\Delta t} d\Delta t, \tag{92}$$

where $A_C(\Delta t) \triangleq A_C(\Delta f = 0; \Delta t)$. Another useful parameter is the **channel coherence time** T_c defined as the range of values over which $A_c(\Delta t)$ is approximately nonzero. In other words, it expresses the time in seconds after which the channel in uncorrelated. In particular $A_c(\Delta t = T) = 0$ indicates that observations of the channel impulse response at times separated by T are uncorrelated and therefore independent, since the channel is a Gaussian random process. The **Doppler power spectrum** of the channel is described by the function $S_c(\rho)$. The maximum ρ value for which $|S_c(\rho)|$ is greater than zero is called the **Doppler spread** of the channel and is denoted by B_D. It expresses the spreading of the frequency spectrum of the transmitted signal resulting from the rate of change of the mobile radio channel. Since $A_c(\Delta t)$ and $S_c(\rho)$ are connected by a Fourier transform relationship, it holds that $B_D \approx 1/T_c$, but in general we have $B_D \approx k/T_c$ where k depends on the shape of $S_c(\rho)$. We illustrate the Doppler power spectrum $S_c(\rho)$ and its inverse Fourier transform $A_c(\Delta t)$ in Figure 8.

Transforms for Autocorrelation and Scattering Functions

From (91) we see that the scattering function $S_c(\tau; \rho)$ defined in (83) is the inverse Fourier transform of $S_c(\Delta f; \rho)$ in the Δf variable. Furthermore $S_c(\tau; \rho)$ and $A_c(\Delta f; \Delta \tau)$ are related by the double Fourier transform:

$$S_c(\tau;\rho) = \int_{-\infty}^{\infty}\int_{-\infty}^{\infty} A_C(\Delta f; \Delta t) e^{-j2\pi\rho\Delta t} e^{j2\pi\tau\Delta f} d\Delta t d\Delta f. \tag{93}$$

The relationships among the four functions $A_C(\Delta f; \Delta t)$, $A_C(\tau; \Delta t)$, $S_C(\Delta f; \rho)$, and $S_C(\tau; \rho)$ are shown in Figure 9.

Empirical measurements of the scattering function for a given channel are often used to approximate empirically the channel's delay spread, coherence bandwidth, Doppler spread, and coherence time.

Types of Small-Scale Fading

Small-scale fading is divided into two broad classes, which are based on the time delay spread and Doppler spread. The time delay spread-dependent class is divided into two categories, flat fading and frequency selective fading, while the Doppler spread-dependent class is categorized as fast and slow fading. It is important to note that fast and slow fading deal with the relationship between the time rate of change of the channel and the transmitted signal, and not with propagation path loss models.

Flat Fading

The received signal in a mobile radio environment experiences flat fading if the channel has a constant gain and linear phase response over a bandwidth that is greater than the bandwidth of the transmitted signal. The main characteristics of a flat fading channel follow:

- Symbol period of the transmitted signal is greater than the delay spread of the channel. As a rule of thumb it should be at least 10 times greater.
- Bandwidth of the channel is greater than the bandwidth of the transmitted signal. Since the bandwidth of the transmitted signal is narrower than the channel bandwidth, the flat fading channels are also known as narrowband channels.
- Typical flat fading channels result in deep fades, and this requires 20 to 30 dB more transmitter power to achieve low bit error rates (BERs) during times of deep fades, compared to systems operating over nonfading channels.

Frequency-Selective Fading

The received signal in a mobile radio environment experiences frequency-selective fading if the channel has a constant gain and linear phase response over a bandwidth that is smaller than the bandwidth of the transmitted signal. The main characteristics of a frequency-selective fading channel follow:

- Symbol period of the transmitted signal is smaller than the delay spread of the channel. As a rule of thumb it should be at least 10 times smaller.
- Bandwidth of the channel is smaller than the bandwidth of the transmitted signal. Since the bandwidth of the transmitted signal is wider than the channel bandwidth, the frequency-selective fading channels are also known as wideband channels.
- Frequency-selective channel results in intersymbol interference (ISI) for the received signal.
- This type of fading channels is difficult to model compared to the flat fading channels since each multipath signal needs to be modelled individually and the channel has to be considered as a linear filter.

Fast Fading

The received signal, in a mobile radio environment, experiences fast fading as a result of a rapidly changing channel impulse response within the symbol duration. The main characteristics of a fast fading channel follow:

- Coherence time of the channel is smaller than the symbol period of the transmitted signal. Thus this is also called time-selective fading.
- Doppler spread is greater than the transmitted signal bandwidth.
- Channel varies faster than the baseband signal variations.
- In fast-flat fading channels the amplitude of the received signal varies faster than the rate of change of the transmitted baseband signal.
- In fast-frequency-selective channels the amplitudes, phases, and time delays of the multipath components vary faster than the rate of change of the transmitted signal.

Slow Fading

The received signal, in a mobile radio environment, experiences slow fading as a result of a slowly varying channel impulse response within the symbol duration. The main characteristics of a slow fading channel follow:

- Coherence time of the channel is greater than the symbol period of the transmitted signal. In this case, the channel can be assumed to be static over one or several symbol durations.
- Doppler spread is smaller than the transmitted signal bandwidth.
- Channel varies slower than the baseband signal variations.

Figure 7. Power delay profile, RMS delay spread, and coherence bandwidth

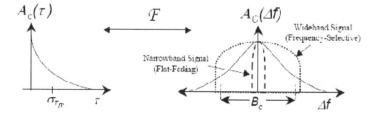

Figure 8. Doppler power spectrum, doppler spread, and coherence time

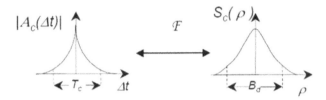

A SMALL SCALE MODEL FOR WIRELESS COMMUNICATIONS

In this section, a new general statistical model for wireless communications is proposed, which assembles many interesting concepts. The multipath component is a combination of the Weibull and Generalized Rice models combining the nonuniform with the nonlinear nature of the channel. So, the a parameter in the Weibull model declares the nonlinearity in terms of an exponent, while the in-phase and quadrature parts of the multipath are having different variances because of the nonuniform diffuse scattering. It is shown, that the nonlinearity affects not only the amplitude, but the phase too. The final result is an advanced physical representation of the channel outperforming in relation to the models presented previously. This proposed model can also be used as the basis of a multistate model. Numerical results show that the introduced general propagation model provides better fit to experimental data than other models available in the literature. The demonstration of its outperformance is shown in a variety of channel conditions (i.e., light and heavy shadowing).

General Statistical Modelling

In this section, the statistical properties of the analytical model are investigated. The description of the reference model and the derivation of the statistical properties are carried out here by using the (complex) baseband notation as usual. The Extended Generalized Rice model is comprised by both a direct and scattered component. This is described by a combination of the Generalized Rice and Weibull random processes.

Modellling and Analysis

The proposed model that describes the fast fading is given by the complex Gaussian process:

$$L(t) = \left(\rho e^{j\theta_0} + \mu_L(t)\right)^{2/a} = \left(\rho e^{j\theta_0} + x_L(t) + jy_L(t)\right)^{2/a} \tag{94}$$

where $L(t)$ is a combination of both the known Generalized Rice and Weibull random processes, as mentioned. This means that it is constituted by ρ, which is the LOS component, θ_0 is a phase shift of the LOS component offering an extra degree of freedom, and x_L, y_L are zero-mean Gaussian random processes with standard deviations σ_x, σ_y. The a parameter expresses the fading severity. When a increases the fading severity decreases, meaning strong specular components dominate in the channel. If $a = 2$, the Extended Generalized Rice process tends to the Generalized Rice one. The phase shift θ_0 entails the capability of having different mean values for the in-phase and quadrature components of the Gaussian process defined by (1). The absolute value of (1), i.e., the envelope $|L(t)|$ finally results in a new stochastic process $R(t)$ given as follows:

$$R(t) = \left([x_L + \rho\cos(\theta_0)]^2 + [y_L + \rho\sin(\theta_0)]^2\right)^{1/a} \tag{95}$$

Figure 9. Fourier transform relationships

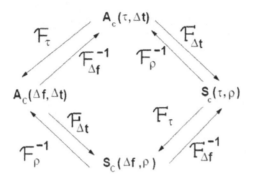

A starting point for the derivation of the statistical properties of the process $R(t)$ is given by the joint probability density function (JPDF) of the processes x_L, y_L, $\dot{x}_L$, and $\dot{y}_L$ at the same point within the time t. This JPDF will be denoted by $p_{x_L y_L \dot{x}_L \dot{y}_L}(x, y, \dot{x}, \dot{y})$ here. It should be noted, that since x_L, y_L are zero- mean Gaussian random processes with standard deviations σ_x, σ_y, then their time derivatives $\dot{x}_L$, $\dot{y}_L$ are also zero- mean Gaussian random processes with variances β_x, β_y. The quantities β_x, β_y represent the negative second derivatives of the autocorrelation functions of the processes x_L, y_L, respectively at the time $t = 0$, and are defined as $\beta_i = -\ddot{r}_{\mu_i \mu_i}(0) = 2(\pi \sigma_i f_{max_i})^2$ $(i =$ x, y), where f_{max_x}, f_{max_y} are the maximum frequencies of the corresponding Gaussian processes. In other words, we assume different maximum frequencies f_{max_x}, and f_{max_y}, for the Gaussian processes x_L, y_L, respectively. Although, the underlying assumption lacks of a clear physical basis, it allows to increase the flexibility of the model and enables therefore a better fitting to measurement data (Youssef et al., 2005). For a symmetrical Doppler power spectral density, where x_L, y_L, $\dot{x}_L$, and $\dot{y}_L$ are in pairs uncorrelated, it can be shown that:

$$p_{x_L y_L \dot{x}_L \dot{y}_L}(x, y, \dot{x}, \dot{y}) = \frac{1}{4\pi^2 \sigma_x \sigma_y \sqrt{\beta_x} \sqrt{\beta_y}} \exp\left(-\frac{1}{2}\left(\frac{x^2}{\sigma_x^2} + \frac{y^2}{\sigma_y^2} + \frac{\dot{x}^2}{\beta_x} + \frac{\dot{y}^2}{\beta_y}\right)\right) \tag{96}$$

Performing a transformation of the Cartesian coordinates (x_L, y_L) to polar coordinates (r, θ), the joint distribution $p_{R,\dot{R},\Theta,\dot{\Theta}}(r,\dot{r},\theta,\dot{\theta})$ is obtained. For that purpose, the following system of equations is considered:

$$r^a = x^2 + y^2 \tag{97}$$

$$\theta = \frac{2}{a}\tan^{-1}(y/x) \tag{98}$$

where $x = r^{\frac{a}{2}}\cos\frac{a\theta}{2} - \rho\cos\theta_0$ and $y = r^{\frac{a}{2}}\sin\frac{a\theta}{2} - \rho\sin\theta_0$ are the in-phase and quadrature components of the short term fading part of the signal.

Following the standard statistical procedure for the transformation of variates and after algebraic manipulations, the JPDF $p_{R,\dot{R},\Theta,\dot{\Theta}}(r,\dot{r},\theta,\dot{\theta})$ of the envelope, the phase, and their respective time derivatives, is obtained as:

$$p_{R,\dot{R},\Theta,\dot{\Theta}}(r,\dot{r},\theta,\dot{\theta}) = \frac{a^4 r^{2a-2}}{64\pi^2 \sigma_x \sigma_y \sqrt{\beta_x}\sqrt{\beta_y}} \exp\left(-\frac{1}{2}\left(\frac{\left(r^{\frac{a}{2}}\cos(\frac{a\theta}{2}) - \rho\cos(\theta_0)\right)^2}{\sigma_x^2} + \frac{\left(r^{\frac{a}{2}}\sin(\frac{a\theta}{2}) - \rho\sin(\theta_0)\right)^2}{\sigma_y^2} + \right.\right.$$

$$\left.\left. \frac{a^2\left(\dot{r}r^{\frac{a}{2}-1}\cos(\frac{a\theta}{2}) - r^{\frac{a}{2}}\dot{\theta}\sin(\frac{a\theta}{2})\right)^2}{4\beta_x} + \frac{a^2\left(\dot{r}r^{\frac{a}{2}-1}\sin(\frac{a\theta}{2}) + r^{\frac{a}{2}}\dot{\theta}\cos(\frac{a\theta}{2})\right)^2}{4\beta_y}\right)\right) \tag{99}$$

where $0 \le r < \infty$, $-\infty \le \dot{r} < \infty$, $0 \le \theta < 2\pi$, and $-\infty \le \dot{\theta} < \infty$.

Probability Density Function of the Envelope and the Phase

The PDF of $R(t)$, $p_R(r)$ is obtained from (5) according to the threefold integral:

$$p_R(r) = \int_0^{2\pi}\int_{-\infty}^{\infty}\int_{-\infty}^{\infty} p_{R,\dot{R},\Theta,\dot{\Theta}}(r,\dot{r},\theta,\dot{\theta})\,d\dot{r}\,d\dot{\theta}\,d\theta \tag{100}$$

Performing the suitable integrations and algebraic manipulations, the following expression for $p_R(r)$ is obtained as:

$$p_R(r) = \frac{a^3 r^{a-1}}{16\pi\sigma_x\sigma_y} exp[-\rho^2 h(\theta_0)]\int_0^{2\pi} Exp[-r^a h(\theta) + \rho r^{\frac{a}{2}} g(\theta_0,\theta)]d\theta \tag{101}$$

where $h(\theta) = \dfrac{\cos^2\dfrac{a\theta}{2}}{2\sigma_x^2} + \dfrac{\sin^2\dfrac{a\theta}{2}}{2\sigma_y^2}$, $\tag{102}$

Figure 10. The PDF $p_R(r)$ as a function of R ($\rho = 0.5$, $\sigma_x = 0.6$, $\sigma_y = 0.4$, and $\theta_0 = \pi/4$).

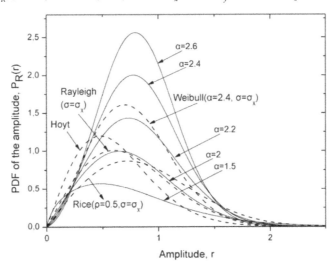

and
$$g(\theta_0,\theta) = \frac{\cos\frac{d\theta}{2}\cos\theta_0}{\sigma_x^2} + \frac{\sin\frac{d\theta}{2}\sin\theta_0}{\sigma_y^2} \qquad (103)$$

The complementary contribution distribution function (CCDF) is obtained through integration of the envelope's PDF:

$$P_{R+}(r_0) = \int_{r_0}^{\infty} p_R(v)dv \qquad (104)$$

Similarly, the PDF of the phase process θ(*t*), $p_\Theta(\theta)$, can he derived by evaluating the integrals over the JPDF $p_{R,\dot{R},\Theta,\dot{\Theta}}(r,\dot{r},\theta,\dot{\theta})$ according to:

$$p_\Theta(\theta) = \int_0^\infty \int_{-\infty}^\infty \int_{-\infty}^\infty p_{R,\dot{R},\Theta,\dot{\Theta}}(r,\dot{r},\theta,\dot{\theta})d\dot{r}d\dot{\theta}\,dr \qquad (105)$$

Once again, performing the appropriate integrations the result is:

$$p_\vartheta(\theta) = \frac{a\,exp\left[\rho^2\left(\frac{g^2(\theta_0,\theta)}{4h(\theta)} - h(\theta_0)\right)\right]}{8\pi\sigma_x\sigma_y h(\theta)}$$
$$\times \left[exp\left(-\left(\frac{\rho^2 g^2(\theta_0,\theta)}{4h(\theta)}\right) - \frac{\rho g(\theta_0,\theta)\sqrt{\pi}}{2\sqrt{h(\theta)}}\left(1 - \Phi\left(\frac{\rho g(\theta_0,\theta)}{2\sqrt{h(\theta)}}\right)\right)\right] \qquad (106)$$

where Φ(*x*) is the error function defined by $\Phi(x) = \frac{2}{\sqrt{\pi}}\int_0^x e^{-t^2}dt$.

The *a* parameter appears in the expression of the phase PDF, resulting a nonlinear expression. If *a* = 2, this expression is exactly the same as the respective one, derived in (Youssef et al., 2004).

Figure 11. The PDF $p_\Theta(\theta)$ as a function of θ (ρ – 0.5, σ_x – 0.6, σ_x – 0.4, and θ_0 – π/4)

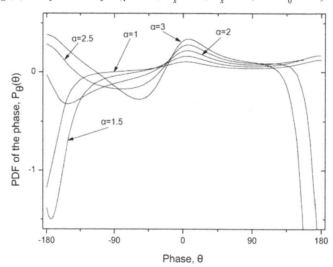

Level Crossing Rate and Average Duration of Fades

The rate of occurrence of fades, or LCR, and the AFD provide a dynamic characterization of the communication channel. As second-order statistical quantities, they complement the static probabilistic description of the fading signal (the first-order statistics), and have found several applications in the modelling and design of practical systems, such as estimation of the statistics of burst errors (Ohtani et al.,1981) and in velocity's estimation of mobile units (Tepedelenlioglu et al., 2001). The derivation of the LCR $N_R(r_0)$ of the process $R(t)$, i.e., the average number of crossings per second at which $R(t)$ crosses a specified signal level r_0 with positive slope, is performed by means of the fundamental relation (Rice, 1945):

$$N_R(r_0) = \int_0^\infty \dot{r} p_{R\dot{R}}(r_0, \dot{r}) d\dot{r} \tag{107}$$

where $p_{R\dot{R}}(r_0, \dot{r})$ denotes the JPDF of the process $R(t)$ and its corresponding time derivative $\dot{R}(t)$ at the same time. After appropriate manipulations, the following expression for the LCR of the envelope of the random process $R(t)$ is obtained as:

$$
\begin{aligned}
N_R(r_0) = \frac{a^2 r_0^{a/2}}{2^{7/2} \pi^{3/2} \sigma_x \sigma_y} \int_0^{2\pi} &\sqrt{\beta_x \cos^2 \frac{d\theta}{2} + \beta_y \sin^2 \frac{d\theta}{2}} \\
\times \exp &\left[-\frac{\left(r_0^{a/2} \cos \frac{d\theta}{2} - \rho \cos \theta_0 \right)^2}{2\sigma_x^2} - \frac{\left(r_0^{a/2} \sin \frac{d\theta}{2} - \rho \sin \theta_0 \right)^2}{2\sigma_y^2} \right] d\theta
\end{aligned}
\tag{108}
$$

Another statistical quantity that helps to quantify the characteristics of fading channels is the ADF. The ADF $T_R(r_0)$ is the expected value for the length of time intervals over which the process $R(t)$ is below a specified level r_0. In general, the ADF $T_R(r_0)$ is defined by (Jakes, 1993), as follows:

$$T_R(r_0) = \frac{P_{R-}(r_0)}{N_R(r_0)} = \frac{1 - P_{R+}(r_0)}{N_R(r_0)} \tag{109}$$

Because the AFD $T_R(r_0)$ depends on the quantities already studied, we will not consider its adaptation to measurement data.

Comparison with Other Fading Distributions

In this section, the relationship between the general model we have derived in the last section and the previously known models is investigated. We observe that the proposed model described in (1) contains many one-state models.

If $a = 2$, the result is Generalized Rice process and if also $\sigma_x = \sigma_y$, we lead to the famous Rice model. Moreover, if $\rho = 0$, the PDF $p_R(r)$ is equal to the Rayleigh. If $a = 2$, $\rho = 0$, and $\sigma_x \neq \sigma_y$, the Hoyt model is derived. On the other hand, if $a \neq 2$, $\rho = 0$, $\sigma_x = \sigma_y$, the Weibull PDF is obtained.

Table 1. Optimized parameters of the measurement data for the CCDF and the LCR

Shadowing	a	ρ	σ_x	σ_y	β_x	β_y	θ_0
Light	1.92	1.005	0.429	0.328	27922	182.8	1.571
Heavy	1.402	0.4	0.307	0.075	5601	83.845	2.606

Figure 12. CCDF $P_{R+}(r_0)$ for light and heavy shadowing

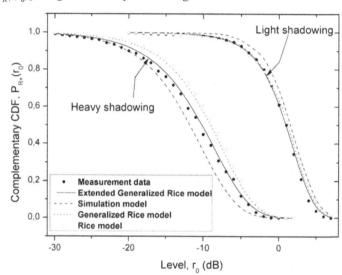

Figure 13. Normalized LCR $N_R(r_0)/f_{max}$ for light and heavy shadowing.

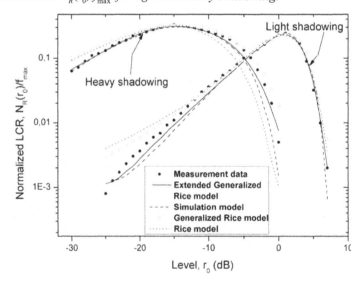

Simulation and Adaptation of the Generalized Rice Model To Measurement Data

In this section, some plots illustrate the formulations obtained in (7), (10), and (14). Some implications can be said concerning these figures. Figs. 1 and 2 depict the normalized PDF of the envelope and phase respectively for arbitrary values of the a parameter. To demonstrate the validation of this channel model for describing the statistics of real-world mobile fading channels, an adaptation of the CCDF and the LCR to measurement data is performed. The measurement data of the CCDF $P_{R+}(Ro)$ and the LCR $N_R(Ro)$ considered as object functions for the optimization of the parameters of the proposed channel model are adopted from (Butterworth, 1983). The environments studied there were, the one a rural area with almost 35% tree cover (heavy shadowing) and the other an open area with almost no shadowing (light shadowing). An appropriate error norm for our purpose which provide us with a measure of the difference between the analytical quantities and the measured ones is given by (34).

$$E(\Psi) = (\sum_{m=1}^{M} \{W_1(r_0)[P_{L+}(r_0) - P_{L+}^{*}(r_0)]\}^{1/2})^{1/2} + \frac{1}{f_{max}}(\sum_{m=1}^{M} \{W_2(r_0)[N_L(r_0) - N_L^{*}(r_0)]\}^{1/2})^{1/2} \tag{110}$$

where Ψ denotes the parameter vector $\Psi = \sigma_x, \sigma_y, \beta_x, \beta_y, \theta_0$, M is the number of measurement values, and $W_1(.)$, $W_2(.)$ are appropriate weighting functions which are defined here, for simplicity, by scaled versions of the reciprocal of $P_{R+}^{*}(\cdot)$ and $N_R^{*}(\cdot)$, respectively. The maximum Doppler frequency $f_{max} = f_{max_x}$ is kept constant and is not optimized, as it does not constitute a channel parameter, being depended on the mobile unit speed and carrier frequency. The results of the minimization of (109) are shown in Table I, where the optimized parameters of the proposed model are listed for the equivalent mobile satellite channel.

For further comparison, the fitted CCDFs and LCRs of the classic Rice and Generalized Rice models are also plotted. Thus, we can observe that the Extended Generalized Rice is in a better coincidence with measurement data than its simpler models. In addition, the validity of the proposed formulations is checked by comparing the theoretical curves against the simulation results. As it is observed, a good agreement has been achieved between the simulation results and the formulation proposed here. The results of the fitted, simulated, and measured CCDFs and LCRs are illustrated in figures 3, 4. It is obvious, that the analytical Extended Generalized Rice model is in good agreement with the measurement data and that it outperforms in relation to other simpler models.

CONCLUSION

In this chapter a primary interest in the characterization of radio links between the transmitter and the receiver antennae is given. We described the channel in terms of path loss, shadowing and multipath fading. More specifically, we presented the free-space model in order to study the path loss and we referred to empirical models that offer a better description of the path loss. The shadowing component was investigated by means of the famous lognormal distribution. Moreover, great attention was given at the description of multipath fading. We illustrated the various categories of fading channels using appropriate parameters which were also mentioned in this chapter. Narrowband and wideband fading channels are basically these categories and include other subcategories. In the case of narrowband fading, we quoted a significant number of statistical models. Finally, a new small-scale model is proposed and investigated in depth offering besides its novelty an application in order to achieve a better comprehension of the theory.

REFERENCES

Abdi, A., Lau, W.C., Alouini, M.S. and Kaveh, M. (2003). "A New Simple Model for Land Mobile Satellite Channels: First- and Second-Order Statistics," IEEE Trans. Wireless Commun., 2, 519–528.

Bello, P.A. (1963). "Characterization of randomly time-variant linear channels," IEEE Trans. Comm. Syst., pp. 360–393, Dec.

Clarke, R.H. (1968). "A statistical theory of mobile radio reception," Bell Syst. Tech. J., pp. 957-1000, July-Aug.

Corazza, G.E. and Vatalaro, F. (1994). "A Statistical Model for Land Mobile Satellite Channels and Its Application to Nongeostationary Orbit Systems," IEEE Trans. Vehicular Technol., 43, 738–742.

Corazza, G.E., Jahn, A. E. Lutz, and Vatalaro, F. (1994). "Channel Characterization for Mobile Satellite Communications," in Procedure of the First EuropeanWorkshop onMobile/Personal Satcoms, EMPS, pp. 225–262.

Erceg, V., Greenstein, L. J., Tjandra,S. Y., Parkoff, S. R., Gupta, A. Kulic, B., Julius, A. A. and Bianchi, R. (1999). "An empirically based path loss model for wireless channels in suburban environments," IEEE Journal on Selected Areas in Communications, pp. 1205–1211, July.

European Cooperative in the Field of Science and Technical Research EURO-COST 231 (1991). "Urban transmission loss models for mobile radio in the 900 and 1800 MHz bands," Revision 2, The Hague, Sept.

Ghassemzadeh,S.S., Greenstein, L.J. Kavcic, A. Sveinsson, T. Tarokh,V. (2003). "Indoor path loss model for residential and commercial buildings," Proc. Vehic. Technol. Conf., pp. 3115–3119, Oct.

Goldsmith, A. (2005). Wireless Communications, Cambridge University Press

Hata, M. (1980). "Empirical formula for propagation loss in land mobile radio services," IEEE Trans. Vehic. Technol., Vol VT-29, No. 3, pp. 317–325, Aug.

Hwang, S.H., Kim, K.J. Ahn, J.Y. and Whang, K.C. (1997). "A Channel Model for Nongeostationary Orbiting Satellite System," in IEEE Vehicular Technology Conference, May 4–7, pp. 41–45.

Iskam, V.Y. and Shaptsev, V.A. (1985). "Properties of the Nakagami-Rice Distribution as a Model for Signal Fading," Telecommun. Radio Eng., 2, 129–132.

Jakes, W.C. Jr., (1974). Microwave Mobile Communications. New York: Wiley.

Loo, C. (1985). "A Statistical Model for a Land Mobile Satellite Link," IEEE Trans. Vehicular Technol., 34, 122–127.

Martin, A.L. and Vu-Dinh, T. (1997). "A Statistical Characterization of Point-to-Point Microwave Links Using Biased Rayleigh Distributions," IEEE Trans. Antennas Propagation, 45, 806–821.

Norton, K.A., Vogler, L.E. Mansfield, W.V. and Short, P.J. (1955). "The Probability Distribution of the Amplitude of a Constant Vector Plus a RayleighDistributed Vector," Proc. IRE, 43, 1354–1361.

Ohtani, K., Daikoku, K., and Omori, H. (1981). "Burst error performance encountered in digital land mobile radio channel," IEEE Trans. Veh. Technol., vol. VT-23, no. 1, pp. 156–160.

Okumura, T., Ohmori, E. and Fukuda, K. (1968). "Field strength and its variability in VHF and UHF land mobile service," Review Electrical Communication Laboratory, Vol. 16, No. 9-10, pp. 825–873, Sept.-Oct.

Parsons, D. (1992). The Mobile Radio Propagation Channel. New York: Halsted Press (Division of Wiley).

Patzold, M., Killat, U., Laue, F., and Li, Y. (1998). "On the Statistical Properties of Deterministic Simulation Models for Mobile Fading Channels," IEEE Trans. Vehicular Technol., 47, 254–269.

Rappaport, T.S. (2001). Wireless Communications - Principles and Practice, 2nd Edition, Prentice Hall.

Rice, S.O. (1945). "Mathematical analysis of random noise," Bell System Tech. J., Vol. 23, No. 7, pp. 282–333, July 1944, and Vol. 24, No. 1, pp. 46–156, Jan.

Sforza, M. and Buonomo, S. (1993). "Characterization of the Propagation Channel for Nongeostationary LMS Systems at L- and S-Bands: Narrow Band Experimental Data and Channel Modelling," in Procedure XVII NAPEX Conference, Pasadena, CA, June 14–15.

Simon, M.K. and Alouini, M.-Sl. (2000). Digital Communication over Fading Channels, New York: Wiley.

Stuber, G.L. (2001). Principles of Mobile Communications, Kluwer Academic Publishers, 2nd Ed.

Suzuki, H. (1977). "A Statistical Model for Urban Radio Propagation," IEEE Trans. Commun., 25, 673–680.

Tepedelenlioglu, C., Abdi, A., Giannakis, G. B., and Kaveh, M. (2001). "Estimation of Doppler spread and signal stength in mobile communications with applications to handoff and adaptive transmission," Wirel. Commun. Mobile Comput., pp. 221–242.

Tjhung, T.T. and Chai, C.C. (1998). "Bit Error Rate Performance of π/4 DQPSK Nakagami-Lognormal Channels," IEEE Electron. Lett., 34, 625–627.

Tjhung, T.T. and Chai, C.C. (1999). "Fade Statistics in Nakagami-Lognormal Channels," IEEE Trans. Commun., 47, 1769–1772.

Vatalaro, F. (1995). "Generalized Rice-Lognormal Channel Model for Wireless Communications," IEEE Electron. Lett., 31, 1899–1900.

Xie, Y. and Fang, Y. (2000). "A General Statistical Channel Model for Mobile Satellite Systems," IEEE Trans. Vehicular Technol., 49, 744–752.

Youssef, Neji, Wang, Cheng-Xiang and Patzold, Matthias 2005). "A Study on the Second Order Statistics of Nakagami-Hoyt Mobile Fading Channels simulation models for mobile fading channels," IEEE Trans. Veh. Technol., vol. 54, no. 4, pp. 1259–1265.

Youssef, N., Wang, C. X., Patzold, M., Jaafar, I. and Tabbane, S. (2004). "On the Statistical Properties of Generalized Rice Multipath Fading Channels," Vehicular Technology Conference. VTC 2004-Spring. 2004 IEEE 59th.

KEY TERMS

AFD: Average Fade Duration

BER: Bit Error Rate

CCDF: Complementary Contribution Distribution Function

GRLN: Generalized Rice–Lognormal

ISI: Intersymbol Interference

JPDF: Joint Probability Density Function

LCR: Level Crossing Rate

LOS: Line-of-Sight

NLN: Nakagami–Lognormal

PSD: Power Spectral Density

RLN: Rice–Lognormal

QoS: Quality of Service

WSS: Wide-Sense Stationary

Section IV
Multiple Applications

Chapter XVIII
Innovation and E-Government:
An in Depth Overview on E-Services

Fotis C. Kitsios
Technical University of Crete, Greece

Spyros P. Angelopoulos
Technical University of Crete, Greece

John Zannetopoulos
Hellenic Ministry of the Interior, Greece

ABSTRACT

There is no doubt that e-government is a phenomenon of our era. E-business is becoming vital on the private sector as well as in the governmental institutions. The use of Information and Communication Technology (ICT) in order to change the structures and processes of government organizations in an attempt to allow the exchange of information with citizens, businesses and other arms of government, results to improved efficiency, convenience as well as better accessibility of public services. The three segments of e-government services are Government-to-Citizen (G2C), Government-to-Business (G2B) and Government-to-Government (G2G) in a correspondence to the business model segments. As many others aspects of science in their very beginning, e-government suffers from a definitional vagueness of its concept due to the fact that there is not a widely accepted definition among researchers. So, what exactly is e-government? Has anyone tried or managed to define its exact concept and meaning? Is it just an Internet-based government or are there any other non-internet technologies used in this context? How can next-generation heterogeneous networks, enhance its abilities on interconnectivity? These are all questions seeking for an answer in this paper. This study does not try to stand out either as a review or as a synthetic summary of the literature concerning e-government, rather, its main objective will be an in depth overview of the current status of e-government phenomenon. Future works need to give an answer to the dilemma whether e-government is really a tool for decentralization and democratization or the result of a sociotechnical process towards a new model of public administration. Finally, in an attempt to focus on the changes in business process that are needed inside governmental institutions in order e-government to be successfully implemented, a second recommendation for future work resides on the need for a holistic model which can embrace the back-office, the front-office as well as the real citizens' needs.

Copyright © 2009, IGI Global, distributing in print or electronic forms without written permission of IGI Global is prohibited.

INTRODUCTION

It is a common knowledge that Information and Communication Technologies (ICTs) contribute substantially to the acceleration of financial development and the elimination of poverty. This can be achieved by initially providing and continuously improving health and education. This, however, can only be implemented through the sharing of information and communication technology resources across governments and their citizens. Ample and uninhibited access to new technologies is essential for uniform and consistent diffusion of innovation.

The use of internet capabilities by governments all around the world has increased significantly over the last years. Among all the constituencies that are affected by the development of electronic government, businesses represent one constituency that may experience significant benefits (Thompson, Rust & Rhoda, 2005). Electronic government projects have a breadth of impact that extends far beyond the agency concerned and where benefits often expand beyond the agency owning the aforementioned project.

As many others aspects of science in their very beginning, e-government suffers from a definitional vagueness of its concept due to the fact that there is not a widely accepted definition among researchers. So, what exactly is e-government? Has anyone tried or managed to define its exact concept and meaning? Is it just an Internet-based government or are there any other non-internet technologies used in this context? How can next-generation heterogeneous networks, enhance its abilities on interconnectivity? These are all questions seeking for an answer in this study. However, this study does not try to stand out either as a review or as a synthetic summary of the literature concerning e-government, rather, its main objective will be an in depth overview of the current status of e-government phenomenon.

The rapidly changing business environment of the last years has created uncertainty in the market place and high risk for future decisions in the years to come. In order to survive in this demanding market place, service organizations have only one choice, to successfully develop new services. However the failure rate for new services projects is high, because the knowledge about how new services should be developed is limited (Kitsios, 2005). The success rate of new service projects is an average 58% (Griffin, 1997). In other words, four out of ten new service projects fail in the market place.

It is often argued that e-government research suffers from definitional vagueness of the e-government concept, oversimplification of the e-government development process within manifold institutional and political environments as well as various methodological limitations. In order to confront and resolve these issues, this study reviews the barriers in the e-government literature, and it suggests ways forward. In order to achieve these, this study provides an analysis of the development as well as various definitions of the e-government concept. After discussing the barriers of the concept, methodological and conceptual rectifications such as better studying and explaining the processes of e-government projects within complex political environments, addressing the problem of under-specification in the e-government literature by the production of more grounded, empirical studies that would create new theoretical arguments and provide new concepts and categories so as to enhance our understanding of e-government policy processes and actors, as well as attaching the subject of e-government strongly to mainstream public administration research are suggested in the final part of the analysis.

WHAT IS E-GOVERNMENT?

E-government is one of those concepts that mean a lot of different things to a lot of different groups (Grant & Chau, 2005). Electronic Government or e-government has emerged as a popular catch phrase in public administration (Yildiz, 2007). There is no e-government textbook and no e-government theory; knowledge comes from practice; excellence comes from best practices (Center for Democracy and Technology, 2002). Part of the problem that this article deals with arises from the vagueness of the e-government concept (Aldrich, Bertot & McClure, 2002; Hwang, Choi & Myeong, 1999). E-government can embrace a wide range of services. Services for citizens, for example, might include registration to government services such as health care, education or employment benefits. As regards businesses, e-government services can take the form of online alerts for public procurement or funding opportunities as well as information and support on applicable legislation in a given sector. E-government projects address the digital divide for citizens and businesses through multiple access channels and have been successful in creating a government without walls, doors and civil servant work shifts. E-government is also widely viewed as an opportunity for administrations to cut down on their costs, speed up their procedures and increase their efficiency and reactivity. Among the many promises of the digital revolution is its potential to strengthen democracy and make governments more responsive to the needs of their citizens (Center for Democracy and Technology, 2002).

Electronic government comprises the use of modern Information and Communication Technologies in order to deliver public services to citizens and businesses. It entails the transformation of public services available to citizens using new organizational processes as well as new technologies. The goal of e-government is to achieve in making government services more accessible, more citizen-focused, more relevant to citizens as well as more responsive to their needs and expectations. Furthermore, it is regarded as a player with a significant role in enabling greater citizen involvement in civic and democratic matters in the sense of direct democracy as the one practiced in the city-states of ancient Greece. E-government is also designed to facilitate a more integrated mode of government.

E-government encapsulates the relationships between governments, their customers and their suppliers by the use of electronic means (Means & Schneider, 2000). It is a model of government that is organized increasingly in terms of virtual agencies, cross agency and public-private networks whose structure and capacity depends on the Internet and Web.

However, e-government is not about the use of technology or technological innovation for its own sake. Technology is just a means to achieve e-government, which is a fundamental change in the way that governments do business with the stakeholders of government information and services. Certain technologies do not fundamentally define what e-government is and will be (Yildiz, 2007). Thompson, Rust & Rhoda (2005) propose that use of e-government is related to firms' ability to interact with government online. Ability has been extensively used to understand organizational and individual behavior in fields such as psychology (Ajzen & Fishbein, 1980), consumer behavior (MacInnis, Moorman & Jaworski, 1991), persuasion (Petty & Cacioppo, 1981) and organizational behavior (O'Reilly & Chatman, 1994). E-government is also perceived differently in connection with the theoretical frameworks, described by Garson (1999), within which it is conceptualized. The first framework involves the potential of IT in decentralization and democratization. The second normative / dystopian framework underlines the limitations and contradictions of technology. In the third framework, the sociotechnical systems approach emphasizes the continuous and two-way interaction between technology and the organizational - institutional environment. The fourth framework places e-government within theories of global integration.

Balutis (2001) classifies the development of e-government into four phases. These four phases include information dissemination, forms-only, end-to-end electronic transactions, and transforming government. According to his classification, information dissemination is the least-developed and fundamental phase, describing a stage in which information is simply provided online. In the second, forms-only phase, users can download forms electronically. The third, end-to-end electronic transactions involve allowing citizens begin their transaction digitally and ultimately ending their transaction in the same way. The transaction is hence characterized as being entirely executed digitally. The fourth phase in the development of e-government is the final goal of e-government, in which the government provides all services and information online. In this way, e-government acts as a stand-in for traditional forms of government services as citizens can simply log onto the Internet to meet their needs.

There is not any universally accepted definition of the e-government concept (Halchin, 2004). In order to cover the variety of uses and the nuances sufficiently, the most common definitions are presented as follows. E-government is defined as: "utilizing the internet and the world wide Web for delivering government information and services to citizens" (UN/ASPA, 2002). It may also include using other ICTs in addition to the Internet and the Web, such as "database, networking, discussion support, multimedia, automation, tracking and tracing, and personal identification technologies" (Jaeger, 2003). As quoted by Hernon in an interview with Duffy (2000), e-government is "simply using information technology to deliver government services directly to the customer 24/7. The customer can be a citizen, a business or even another government entity". Closely related to the change in e-government focus is the inherent incompatibility between a security-oriented perception of e-government and at least three of the original founding principles of the e-government phenomenon, namely fast and easy access to government information, open government, people's right to know, transparency and responsiveness (Doty & Erdelez, 2002).

E-government is the use of technology, especially Web-based applications to enhance access to and efficiently deliver government information and services (Brown & Brudney, 2001). According to the World Bank (2004), e-government refers to the use by government agencies of information technologies that have the ability to transform relations with citizens, businesses, and other arms of government. These technologies can serve a variety of different ends: better delivery of government services to citizens, improved interactions with business and industry, citizen empowerment through access to information, or more efficient government management. The resulting benefits can be less corruption, increased transparency, greater convenience, revenue growth, and/or cost reductions. Nations have traditionally relied on telephone networks to fulfill similar telecommunication functions (Atkin, Hallock & Lau, 2007; Atkin, Lau & Lin, 2006; Baldwin, McVoy & Steinfield, 1996; Bates, Albright & Washington, 2002; Singh, 1999), but information services are being increasingly migrated to Web-based modalities (Grant & Meadows, 2007; Lin & Atkin, 2007). Jaeger (2002), however, pointed out that extensive cooperation and information-sharing among agencies may endanger some constitutional principles such as the separation of powers and the distribution and balance of powers between the federal, state, and local governments (Doty & Erdelez, 2002). Last but not least, according to the Center for Democracy and Technology (2002), e-government is the use of information and communications technologies in order to transform government by making it more accessible, effective and accountable.

What is also lacking in the treatment of the subject is a more in-depth analysis of the political nature of the e-government development process, and a deeper recognition of complex political and institutional environments. However, e-government research up to date for the most part limited itself to the study of the outcomes and outputs of the e-government projects. Thus, understanding the political process behind e-government development is vital for overcoming both definitional and analytical limitations. Such an effort requires a historical understanding of the relationship between technology and administration (Yildiz, 2007).

FROM BRICKS TO CLICKS

Fundamental changes have occurred in the structure of most countries' economies since the Second World War, with services becoming the major sector of economic activity (OECD 2000). Technology was seen as a means to manage the limitations of bounded-rationality and provide the infrastructure for better decision making (Simon, 1976). In other words, until the introduction of the internet and widespread use of personal computers, the main objectives of technology use in government were enhancing the managerial effectiveness of public administrators while increasing government productivity (Yildiz, 2007). Until then, the main use of technology in government organizations was the automation of mass transactions such as financial transactions using mainframe computers (Schelin, 2003).

This was an era in which most government agencies are creating and operating their computer systems independent from each other, in 'stovepipe' fashion (Aldrich, Bertot & McClure, 2002). Technology was buffered from the core in order to manage the uncertainty. This was necessary since technology and environments were perceived to be the two basic sources of uncertainty that challenge rationality in organizational decision making (Thomson, 1967). In addition, since information technology was used for the automation of the backroom operations and improvement of the efficiency of clerical activities (Zuboff, 1988), government IT professionals were isolated from functional and executive oversights (Holden, 2003). Perrow (1967) differs by arguing that technology is an important determinant of the structure and the strategy of the organizations that use it.

The diffusion of personal computers in the early 80s provided each public administrator with a personal information technology system, and thus opened a new era of IT use in government. At this point, technology management began to be decentralized in government agencies. Along with decentralization came the realization that IT issues should be integrated to the core functions in government (Yildiz, 2007). Information and communication technologies were recognized to have tremendous administrative potential. For example it could help create a networked structure for interconnectivity (McClure, 2000), service delivery (Bekkers & Zouridis, 1999), efficiency and effectiveness (Heeks, 2001), interactivity (DiCaterino & Pardo, 1996), decentralization, transparency (La Porte, Jong & Demchak, 1999), as well as accountability (Ghere & Young, 1998).

By following the history of ICTs integration in the public sector and according to all the known attempts to define the concept of electronic government we can propose that e-government has been the application of Information and Communication technologies in the public sector all these decades, regardless being called e-government or not.

THE PRICE OF QUALITY IN E-SERVICES

In recent years, quality of service in the public sector has become an issue of great importance. Many governmental organizations and institutions, try to self-assess and measure the quality of service provided. Co instantaneously, significant progress has been made in the development of e-government services and e-participation systems. A variety of public services are now delivered online, with many benefits for e-citizens. All levels of government now provide a variety of online services to citizens as well as to businesses. Both G2B and G2C services involve opening up new distribution channels for traditional services, and the creation of new information-related, services. Although various initiatives investigate the application of quality management principles to the delivery of electronic public services, manifold problems related to quality of public e-services still exist (eGovernment Unit, 2004). Substantial direct benefits from G2C services may simply not be as tangible and identifiable for individual customers. In these early stages of e-government, Web portal navigation may be cumbersome and online services fragmented, uncustomized and generally difficult to use. In addition, the demand for G2C services will likely remain elastic as long as governments maintain other channels for citizens to conduct service transactions, for example, keeping open at least a few motor vehicle offices (Johnson, 2007).

Within the rapidly changing business environment there has been a resurgence of interest among marketing researchers regarding the role of innovation in gaining competitive advantage. However services innovation literature has grown significantly over the last decade, reflecting the increased contribution of service industries to the national economy (Kitsios & Zopounidis, 2007).

Although internationally there is a noticeable shift of governmental services provision from traditional channels to Web-based ones, restraints due to poor quality of service are apparent. We believe that in order to deliver a high quality of services we cannot draw close one of the two approaches disbounded one from the other. We need a more holistic view of the subject which embraces the back office, the front office and the customers' needs in a unified model. We believe that in order for an organization to deliver quality services, all the above must be taken into account and put effort and resources to it.

In most cases, e-government projects are developed and implemented directly by a government agency or by private vendors in cooperation or under contract with a government-sponsored governing committee or agency. The governing committee or agency is usually vested with the authority to make all policy and contracting decisions. There are two options for operating and administrating a state portal. The first option is a government agency which has been established for this purpose. The second option is a private vendor. It is customary practice that G2C and G2B services charges are under the authority of a governing board. The vendor proposes a fee structure for certain services that the governing board usually approves with no substantial changes. In either case, it does not appear that government officials are using an economic basis to derive portal charges. In most cases the convenience charge is established like other charges or fees in the budgetary process where the executive agency recommends a pricing structure and the legislature enacts it into law, sometimes with modification, without understanding the price elasticity of demand for the service and using such information to help determine price (Johnson, 2007). Managers in the public sector concentrate on the quality of services offered to citizens. A useful pricing strategy for maximizing consumer surplus for taxes and user prices is the inverse elasticity of Ramsey rule (Johnson, 2007). The Ramsey rule (Ramsey, 1927), states that in order to reduce total excess burden in taxation, the percent reduction in the quantity demanded of each good must be equal. This results in the inverse elasticity rule, where total excess burden is minimized where tax rates on goods are set inversely proportional to their price elasticities of demand (Sandmo, 1976). Governments may provide a convenience discount where the cost to the public is lower for services transacted online (Johnson, 2007).

Government officials often demonstrate reluctance in the imposition of additional charges for e-services. Nonetheless, said services should be considered because of the fact that carefully administered user charges may have several benefits. Firstly, they enable government to make people who benefit directly from the online service, pay for the online service. This improves equity because non-users are not forced to fully subsidize users. Secondly, they help officials gauge constituent preferences and estimate demand for an online service. This can enhance operational efficiency and improve internal resource allocation decisions because mandated services need only be provided online for users at the level they demand, and only non-mandated services for which there is a demand need be provided at all. In developing new e-services, governments should establish pricing approaches that are economically sound, equitable, and that help generate substantial social benefits. A step in this direction is for government officials to adopt G2C and G2B pricing structures that increase consumer surplus. To facilitate this strategy, government officials must understand the distinct demand structures for G2C and G2B services (Johnson, 2007).

BARRIERS IN IMPLEMENTATION OF E-GOVERNMENT

Meeting the challenges of an unstable and unsettled environment is not easy (Kitsios, 2006). Governments all around the world have been involved in a massive project with the objective of getting as many public services electronically enabled as possible during the first decade of the twenty-first century. E-government requires strong political leadership in order to succeed (Center for Democracy and Technology, 2002). Obviously, there are several economical and political reasons underpinning this move. It is believed that greater efficiencies can be achieved in public service delivery through the use of new information and communication technologies to which ever increasing proportions of the population now have access. In addition, online technologies are envisaged as playing a significant part in the re-engagement of politically alienated electorates in civic processes.

The utilization of Information and Communication technology in the government section and administration does not constitute a panacea. Its implementation can be impeded by many barriers such as the high cost or the low security. The integration of various IT applications and components inside and outside the organizational boundary remains costly and time consuming, due to the heterogeneity of the computing environments involved in public sector organizations (Themistocleous & Irani, 2002). Governments face a shortage of technical infrastructure and this unreliable IT infrastructure in public sector organizations will certainly degrade e-government performance (Bonham, Seifert & Thorson, 2001; Bourn, 2002; Dillon & Pelgrin, 2002; McClure, 2000; National Research Council, 2002). Said shortage presents a significant barrier to the development of government organizations' capabilities to provide online services and transactions.

The e-government concept is limited in four ways (Yildiz, 2007). The first limitation is that there is still no standard definition of the concept. In other words, it is difficult to define what exactly e-government is. This difficulty stems from a couple of reasons: First e-government is a concept defined by the objective of the activity, rather than by the specific technology used, provider of the service/information, or clear-cut activities of the related actors. Hence, many definitions of e-government are rather loose and gloss over the multiple meanings of e-government might have depending on the specific context, regulatory environment, dominance of a group of actors in a given situation, different priorities in government strategies etc. (Torres, Pina & Acerete, 2005).

A barrier frequently cited is the need to ensure adequate security and privacy in an e-government strategy (Daniels, 2002; James, 2000; Joshi & Ghafoor, 2001; Lambrinoudakis & Gritzalis, 2003; Layne & Lee, 2001). Bonham, Seifert & Thorson (2001) as well as Gefen & Pavlou (2002) agree that one of the most significant barriers for implementing e-government applications is computer security, privacy and confidentiality of personal data. Chen & Gant (2001), Heeks (2001), Ho (2002) and Moon (2002) identify the shortage of IT skills as another potential barrier that confronts some demanding challenges concerning a government's ability to provide the next generation of e-government services. Another barrier to the adoption of e-government is central government funding (Bonham, Seifert & Thorson, 2001; Heeks, 2001; Ho, 2002). Traditionally, the main financial resource for public sector organizations is coming from central government, which is hard to control, and sometimes comes and goes in cycles of "feast and famine" that make it difficult to plan sustainable IT initiative such as e-government (Heeks, 2001).

Organizational barriers relate to structural issues, such as fragmentation and poor relations and communication between functional departments, and an acceptance by senior management of the strategic benefits of new initiatives (Aichholzer & Schmutzer, 2000; Fletcher & Wright, 1995). It also relates to government business process, management strategy, and organizational culture (Lenk & Traunmuller, 2000; McClure, 2000). Moon (2002) concluded that to enhance the effectiveness of e-government practices, public sector organizations would need to move towards a higher level of e-government development, which will require a greater number of highly trained technical staff. Moreover, without fully developing staff capabilities, agencies stand to miss out on the potential customer service benefits presented by technology, so employees must have the training and tools they need to do their jobs.

CONCLUSION

This study does not try to stand out either as a review or as a synthetic summary of past literature concerning e-government, rather, its main objective has been an in depth overview of the current status of e-government phenomenon. E-government is considered to be one of the key contributors to the development of an information society. However, the application of information and communication technologies, and especially the use of heterogeneous next generation networks in e-government should not be considered as an end in itself.

It has already been clear that a competitive telecommunications market as well as an environment conducive for e-government will enable e-government to become an affordable channel for citizens and businesses to interact with government as long as legal frameworks provide the legitimacy and guarantees needed to secure and protect electronic transactions and data exchanges. In cases that telecommunications infrastructure is already available or affordable, as a result of competition, e-government applications are quickly embraced and its projects are more likely to lead to success. Governments all around the world have seen the rapid evolution of e-government when there is an integrated approach to planning and implementation of public sector reform.

As an addition to the current status of e-government, future works need to give an answer to the dilemma which derived from this study, whether e-government is really a tool for decentralization and democratization or the result of a sociotechnical process towards a new model of public administration. A scientifically documented answer will certainly boost the evolution of e-government. Finally, in an attempt to focus on the changes in business process that are needed inside governmental institutions in order e-government to be successfully implemented, a second recommendation for future work resides on the need for a holistic model which can embrace the back-office, the front-office as well as the real citizens' needs.

REFERENCES

Agnar, S. (1976). Optimal taxation: an introduction to the literature. Journal of Public Economics (6).

Aichholzer, G. & Schmutzer, R. (2000). Organisational challenges to the development of electronic government. IEEE Computer Society, London, paper presented at 11th International Workshop on Database and Expert Systems Applications.

Aldrich, J., Bertot, J.C. & McClure, C.R. (2002). E-government: initiatives, developments, and issues. Government Information Quarterly, 19, 349-355.

Ajzen, I. & Fishbein, M. (1980). Understanding attitudes and predicting social behaviour. Englewood Cliffs, N J: Prentice-Hall.

Assimakopoulos A.N., Angelopoulos P.S. & Riggas N.A. (2007). Development and analysis of a virtual enterprise that constructs wireless payment mechanisms using open source content management systems. Accepted for publication in International Journal of Applied Systemic Studies (IJASS) (http://www.inderscience.com/ijass).

Atkin, D., Hallock, J. & Lau, T.Y. (2007). Local and long distance telephony. In A. Grant, & J. Meadows (Eds.), Communication technology update, pp. 242–257. Boston: Focal Press.

Atkin, D., Lau, T.Y. & Lin, C. A. (2006). Still on hold: Assessing the impact of the Telecommunications Act of 1996 on its 10th year anniversary. Telecommunications Policy, 30, 413–433.

Baldwin, T.F., McVoy, D.S. & Steinfield, C. (1996). Convergence: Integrating media, information and communication. Thousand Oaks, CA: Sage.

Balutis, A. (2001). E-government 2001a, Part I: Understanding the challenge and evolving strategies. The public manager, Spring (p. 33).

Bates, B., Albright, K. & Washington, K. (2002). No your plain old telephone: New services and new impacts. In Lin C. and Atkin, D. (Eds.), Communication technology and society: Audience adoption and uses (pp. 65–90). Cresskill NJ: Hampton.

Bekkers, V.J.J.M. & Zouridis, S. (1999). Electronic service delivery in public administration: Some trends and issues. International Review of Administrative Sciences, 65 (2), 183-196.

Bonham, G.M., Seifert, J.W. & Thorson, S.J. (2001). The Transformational Potential of e-Government: The Role of Political Leadership. European Consortium for Political Research, which was held at the University of Kent at Canterbury, U.K.

Bourn, J. (2002). Better Public Services Through E-Government. The National Audit Office, London.

Brown, M.M. & Brudney, J.L. (2001). Achieving advanced electronic government services: An examination of obstacles and implications from an international perspective. Paper presented at the National Public Management Research Conference, Bloomington, IN.

Center for Democracy and Technology (2002). E-Government Handbook for Developing Countries. CDT POLICY POST, Vol. 8, No. 26.

Chaikalis, C. (2007) Efficient TTI for 3G Multimedia Applications. Advances in Multimedia, vol. 2007, Article ID 95474, 7 pages, 2007. doi:10.1155/2007/95474

Chaikalis, C. & Liolios, C. (2007). UMTS Turbo Decoder Dynamic Reconfiguration for Rural Outdoor Operating Environment. MOBIMEDIA 2007, 27-29 August 2007, Nafpaktos, Greece.

Chen, Y. & Gant, J. (2001). Transforming local e-government services: the use of application service providers. Government Information Quarterly, Vol. 18 No.4, pp. 343-55.

Craig, L. J. (2007). A framework for pricing government e-services. Electron. Comm. Res. Appl.

Daniels, M. (2002). E-Government Strategy: Simplified Delivery of Services to Citizens. Office of Management and Budget, Washington, DC.

DiCaterino, A. & Pardo, T.A. (1996). The world wide Web as a universal interface to government services. Available at: http://www.ctg.albany.edu/resources/abstract/itt96-2.html

Dillon, J. & Pelgrin, W. (2002). E-Government/Commerce in New York State. Office of Technology. New York, NY.

Dimitriadou, E., Ioannou, K., Panoutsopoulos, I., Garmpis, A. & Kotsopoulos, S. (2005). Priority to Low Moving Terminals in TETRA Networks. WSEAS Transactions on Communications, Issue 11, Volume 4, pp 1228-1236

Doty, P. & Erdelez, S. (2002). Information micro-practices in Texas rural courts: Methods and issues for E-government. Government Information Quarterly, 19, 369-387.

Duffy, D. (2000). Q&A: Balancing the role of e-government: Interview with Mike Hernon, vice president of e-government for New York City-based Gov Works. Available at: http://www.cnn.com/2000/TECH/computing/11/13/qna.egov.idg

eGovernment Unit, DG Information Society, European Commission, (2004). Top of the Web: user satisfaction and usage survey of egovernment services. Europe's Information Society Thematic Portal Web Site: http://europa. eu.int/information_society/activities/egovernment_research/doc/top_of_the_Web_report_2004.pdf

Fountain, J.E. (2001). Building the virtual state: Information technology and institutional change. Washington, DC: Brooking Institution Press.

Garson, G.D. (1999). Information systems, politics, and government: Leading theoretical perspectives. In G. D. Garson (Ed.), Handbook of public information systems (pp. 591-605). New York: Marcel Dekker.

Gefen, D. & Pavlou, P. (2002). Egovernment adoption. Paper presented at Americas Conference on Information Systems.

Ghere, R.K. & Young, B.A. (1998). The cyber-management environment: Where technology and ingenuity meet public purpose and accountability. Public Administration and Management: An interactive Journal, 3(1) Available at: http://www.pamij.com/gypaper.html

Grant, A. & Meadows, J. (2007). Communication technology update. Boston: Focal Press.

Grant, G. & Chau, D. (2005). Developing a generic framework for e-government. Journal of Global Information Management, 13 (1), 1-30.

Griffin, A., (1997). PDMA Research on new product development practices: updating trends and benchmarking best practices. Journal of Product Innovation Management, Vol. 14, No. 6, pp. 429-458.

Halchin, L.E. (2004). Electronic government: Government capability and terrorist resource. Government Information Quarterly, 21, 406-419.

Heeks, R (2001). Understanding e-governance for development. The University of Manchester, Institute for Development, Policy and Management Information Systems,, Technology and Government: Working Papers Series, Number 12/2001. Available at: http://idpm.man.ac.uk/idpm/igov11abs.htm

Ho, A.T-K. (2002). Reinventing local governments and the e-government initiative. Public Administration Review. Vol. 62, No.4, pp.434-44.

Holden, S.H. (2003). The evolution of information technology management at the federal level: Implications for public administration. In G.D Garson (Ed.). Public information technology: Policy and management issues (pp. 53-73). Hershey, PA: Idea Group Publishing.

Hwang, S.D., Choi, Y. & Myeong, S.H. (1999). Electronic government in South Korea: Conceptual problems. Government Information Quarterly, 16 (3), 277-285

IDABC/EIF (2004). European Interoperability Framework for Pan-European eGovernment Services, Office for Official Publications of the European Communities, Luxembourg, available at: http://europa.eu.int

Jaeger, P.T. (2002). Constitutional principles and e-government: An opinion about possible effects of federalism and separation of powers on e-government policies. Government Information Quarterly, 19, 357-368.

Jaeger, P.T. (2003). The endless wire: E-government as a global phenomenon. Government Information Quarterly, 20 (4), 323-331.

James, G. (2000). Empowering bureaucrats. MC Technology Marketing Intelligence, Vol. 20, No.12, pp.62-68.

Jasen, A. & S. Ines (2004). Quality assessment and benchmarking of Norwegian public Web sites. Proceeding from European Conference on e-government.

Johnson, C.L. (2007). A framework for pricing government e-services. Electronic Commerce Research and Applications, Vol. 6, No. 4, pp. 484-489.

Joshi, J. & Ghafoor, A. (2001), Digital government security infrastructure design challenges. IEEE Computer, Vol. 34, No.1, pp.66-72.

Ioannou, K., Dimitriadou, E., Ioannou, A., Panoutsopoulos I. & Kotsopoulos, S. (2006). Hierarchical Dynamic Channel Assignment Technique. WSEAS Transactions on Communications, Issue 1, Volume 5, pp 115-122

Ioannou, K., Panoutsopoulos, I. & Kotsopoulos, S. (2006). Optimizing the QoS of Ultra High and High Speed Moving Terminals in Satellite-aided cellular networks. Wireless Personal Communications, Volume 39, Number 3, pp307-319.

Kitsios, F. (2006). Services marketing in the hospitality economy: An exploratory study. 98th EAAE seminar, Marketing Dynamics within the Global Trading System: New Perspectives, Chania, Crete, Greece, 29 June – 02 July

Kitsios, F. & Skiadas C., (2001). Some Critical Issues Concerning Technological Change. 1st International Conference in Management of Change, Iasi, Romania, October

Kitsios, F. (2005). Innovation Management in New Service Development, PhD dissertation, Technical University of Crete.

Kitsios F. & Zopounidis, C. (2007). Services marketing in the hospitality economy: An exploratory study. The Southeuropean Review of Business Finance & Accounting, Vol. 5, No. 1

La Porte, T.M., De Jong, M. & Demchak, C.C. (1999). Public organizations on the world wide Web: Empirical correlates of administrative openness. Retrieved February 3, 2005, from University of Arizona Web site: http://www.cyprg.arizona.edu/publications/correlat.rtf

Lambrinoudakis, C. & Gritzalis, S. (2003). Security requirements for e-government services: a methodological approach for developing a common PKI-based security policy. Computer Communications, Vol. 26, No.16, pp. 1873-1883.

Layne, K. & Lee, J. (2001). Developing fully functional e-government: a four stage model. Government Information Quarterly, Vol. 18, No.2, pp.122-136.

Lenk, K. & Traunmuller, R. (2000). A framework for electronic government. IEEE Computer Society, London, paper presented at 11th International Workshop on Database and Expert Systems Applications.

Lin, C. & Atkin, D. (2007). Communication technology and social change. Mahwah, NJ: LEA.

Lin, C.S & Wu, S. (2002). Exploring the impact of Online Service Quality on Portal Site Usage. Proceeding of the 35th Hawaii International Conference on Systems Science, Hawaii, USA,

Macinnis, D.J., Moorman, C. & Jaworski, B.J. (1991). Enhancing and Measuring Consumers' Motivation. Opportunity, and Ability to Process Brand Information from Ads. Journal of Marketing, Vol. 55, No. 4, pp. 32-53.

McClure, D.L. (2000). Government online: Strategies and Challenges. Retrieved February 3, 2005, from The House of Representatives Web site: http://www.house.gov/reform/gmit/hearings/2000hearings/000522dm.htm

Means, G. & Schneider, D. (2000). Meta-capitalism: The e-business revolution and the design of 21st century companies and markets. New York: John Wiley & Sons Inc.

Moon, M.J. (2002). The evolution of e-government among municipalities: rhetoric or reality. Public Administration Review, Vol. 62 No.4, pp.424-33.

National Research Council (2002). Information Technology Research. Innovation, and E-Government. National Academy Press, Washington, DC.

OECD (2000). Annual Report 2000. Retrieved February 3, 2005, from OECD Web site: http://www.oecd.org/dataoecd/30/59/1842666.pdf

O'Reilly, C.A. & Chatman, J.A. (1994). Working smarter and harder: a longitudinal study of managerial success. Administrative Science Quarterly, Vol. 39, pp. 603-627.

Perrow, C. (1967). A framework for the comparative analysis of organizations. American Sociological Review, (32), 194-208.

Perrow, C. (1979). Complex organizations: A critical essay (2nd ed.). Dallas, TX: Scott, Foresman and Company.

Petty, R.E. & Cacioppo, J.T. (1981). Attitudes and persuasion: Classic and contemporary approaches. Dubuque, IA: Wm. C. Brown.

Ramboli Management (2004), Top of the Web: User Satisfaction and Usage Survey of E-government Services, prepared for the e-Government Unit, DG Information Society, European Commission, by Ramboli Management, Ramboli Management, Copenhagen, December.

Ramsey, P.F. (1927). A Contribution to the Theory of Taxation. Economic Journal (37).

Sandmo, A., (1976). Optimal taxation: An introduction to the literature. Journal of Public Economics, Vol. 6, No. 1-2, pp. 37-54.

Schelin, S.H. (2003). E-government: An overview. In G. David Garson (Ed.), Public Information Technology: Policy and management issues, pp. 120-137. Hershey, PA: Idea Group Publishing.

Simon, H.A. (1976). Administrative behaviour (3rd ed.). New York, NY: The Free Press.

Singh, J.P. (1999). Leapfrogging development? The political economy of telecommunications restructuring. New York: SUNY Press.

Sukasame, N. (2004). The development of e-service in Thai government. BU academic review, 3.

Themistocleous, M. & Irani, Z. (2002). Evaluating Enterprise Application Integration Technologies: A Novel Frame of References. European Journal of Operational Research, In Press.

Thomson, J.D. (1967). Organizations in action: Social science bases of administrative theory. New York: McGraw Hill.

Thompson, D.V., Rust, R.T. & Rhoda, J. (2005). The business value of e-government for small firms. International Journal of Service Industry Management, Vol. 16, No. 4, pp. 385 – 407.

Torres, L., Pina, V. & Acerete, B. (2005). E-government developments on delivering public services among EU cities. Government Information Quarterly, 22, 217-238.

United Nations & American Society for Public Administration (ASPA). (2002). Benchmarking e-government: A global perspective. New York, NY: U.N. Publications.

World Bank (2004), E *government: a definition of e-government. Retrieved February 3, 2005 from World Bank Web site: www.worldbank.org

Yang, Z., Chai, S., Zhou, Z. & Zhou, N., (2005). Development and validation of an instrument to measure user perceived service quality of information presenting Web portals. Information and Management, 42.

Yildiz, M. (2007). E-government Research: Reviewing the Literature, Limitations, and Ways Forward. Government Information Quarterly, Vol. 24, pp. 646-665.

Zuboff, S. (1988). In the age of the smart machine: The future of work and power. New York: Basic Books.

KEY TERMS

Computer Network: An interconnected group of computers. Networks may be classified by the network layer at which they operate according to basic reference models considered as standards in the industry. The majority of networks use the Internet Protocol Suite.

E-Government: The use of internet technology as a platform for exchanging information, providing services and transacting with citizens, businesses, and other arms of government.

Framework: A basic conceptual structure used to solve or address complex issues.

ICT (Information Communications Technology): An umbrella term that includes all technologies for the communication of information. It is apparently culminating to information communication with the help of personal computers networked through the Internet through information technology that can transfer information using satellite systems or intercontinental cables.

Internet: A worldwide, publicly accessible series of interconnected computer networks that transmit data by packet switching using the standard Internet Protocol.

QoS (Quality of Service): A defined measure of performance in a data communications system.

Web Portal: A site that provides a single function via a Web page or site. Web portals often function as a point of access to information on the World Wide Web. Portals present information from diverse sources in a unified way.

Chapter XIX
From E to U:
Towards an Innovative Digital Era

Spyros P. Angelopoulos
Technical University of Crete, Greece

Fotis C. Kitsios
Technical University of Crete, Greece

Eduard Babulak
Fairleigh Dickinson University, Canada

ABSTRACT

Telecommunications and Internet Technologies have evolved dramatically during the last decade, laying a solid foundation for the future generation of Ubiquitous Internet access, omnipresent Web technologies and ultimate automated information cyberspace. Ubiquitous computing has been investigated since 1993. As a result, current efforts in research and development in the areas of Next Generation Internet and Telecommunications Technologies promote the formation of inter-disciplinary international teams of experts, scientists, researchers and engineers to create a new generation of applications and technologies that will facilitate the fully-automated information cyberspace systems, such as Future House 2015. The authors discuss the current state-of-the-art in the world of Telecommunications and Internet Technologies, new technological trends in the Internet and Automation Industries, E-manufacturing, Ubiquity, Convergence, as well as the concept of the Fully-automated Future House 2015, the 2006 Web Report with the Microsoft project on Easy Living, while promoting research and development in the interdisciplinary projects conducted by multinational teams world-wide.

INTRODUCTION

The past century left us with the legacy of the global Internet, the final flight of Concord Air, CISCO monopoly in computer networking, etc., while large, medium and small corporations alike have discovered the need to adapt to the new technologies, or sink in the emerging global knowledge economy. There is no facet of life in the indus-

Copyright © 2009, IGI Global, distributing in print or electronic forms without written permission of IGI Global is prohibited.

trialized world that has not undergone some form of shift. The resultant new information economy has brought with it different approaches to work. The dawn of 21st Century has come up with new models of Economics, where global barriers are falling, economies are merging, communication is getting better and cheaper (Salvi & Sahai 2002) and "knowledge in the world" becomes more important (Dix et al., 2004). The current 21st century is perhaps one of the most interesting times in history to be alive. We are witnessing a phenomenal abundance of change in societies around the world in a very short period. The sources of most of this change are new technologies and the Internet. In the past decade we have seen every aspect of the lives of individuals and organizations go through many evolutions and uncertainties (Technology Advancements and Government Policies in Canada). There are plenty of publications on the subject of futuristic and ubiquitous computing for the 21st century presenting excellent discussion and possible scenarios in the subject area (Ubiquitous Security; Xerox Paul Alto Research; Course on Ubiquitous Computing; Mark Weiser's Vision; Bluetooth). History proved that one must look forward and accept the futuristic vision as possible scenarios of tomorrow's reality. Nowadays, technologies such as TV, Internet, Mobile Phone, Traffic lights, and cameras are essential part of daily life (AMR Research; Toyota; Military Agile Manufacturing Pilot Program; Convergence; Pervasive Computing; Distributed Systems Online). However, if one would suggest hundred years ago what would be the reality of 2005, surely he or she would be considered "with great caution" (Stajano, 2002; Weiser, 1996). In this chapter, we seek to contribute to the Ubiquitous Computing agenda (Tolmie et al., 2002).

PERVASIVE COMPUTING

Ubiquity postulates the omnipresence of networking. An unbounded and universal network. Omnipresence is the ability to be everywhere at a certain point in time. The widely used definition of ubiquitous computing is the method of enhancing computer use by making many computers available throughout the physical environment, but making them effectively invisible to the user (Wang, et. al., 2007). Ubiquitous computing is a post-desktop model of human-computer interaction in which information processing has been thoroughly integrated into everyday objects and activities. As opposed to the desktop paradigm, in which a single user consciously engages a single device for a specialized purpose, someone "using" ubiquitous computing engages many computational devices and systems simultaneously, in the course of ordinary activities, and may not necessarily even be aware that they are doing so.

Ubiquitous computing integrates computation into the environment, rather than having computers which are distinct objects. Ubiquitous activities are not so task-centric while the majority of usability techniques are. It is not at all clear how to apply task-centric techniques to informal everyday computing situations (Abowd & Mynat 2000). Other terms for ubiquitous computing include pervasive computing, calm technology, things that think and everyware. Promoters of this idea hope that embedding computation into the environment and everyday objects would enable people to interact with information-processing devices more naturally and casually than they currently do, and in whatever location or circumstance they find themselves (Ubiquitous Computing, 2007).

In the ubiquitous computing era, we can expect that computing systems become smaller and smaller, eventually invisible. They will be pervasive into our daily lives (Van de Kar, 2005). With the invention of new interaction devices and the requirements for ubiquitous access to application systems, user's interactions have moved beyond the desktop and evolved into a trend of ongoing development (Hong, Chiu & Shen, 2005). The purpose of ubiquitous computing is anywhere and anytime access to information within computing infrastructures that is blended into a background (Wang, et. al., 2007). The pervasive computing vision is increasingly enabled by the large success of wireless networks and devices. It seems then that routines are invisible in use for those who are involved in them. Contributing to the agenda set by Mark Weiser we wish to consider what it is about this unremarkable aspect of routines that could help us develop Ubiquitous Computing that is invisible in use and in its own way unremarkable (Tolmie et al., 2002).

In pervasive environments, heterogeneous software and hardware resources may be discovered and integrated transparently towards assisting the performance of users' daily tasks. An essential requirement towards the realization of such a vision is the availability of mechanisms enabling the discovery of resources that best fit the client applications' needs among the heterogeneous resources that populate the pervasive environment

(Mokhtar et al., 2007). At their core, all models of ubiquitous computing share a vision of small, inexpensive, robust networked processing devices, distributed at all scales throughout everyday life and generally turned to distinctly quotidian ends. Contemporary human-computer interaction models, whether command-line, menu-driven, or GUI-based, are inappropriate and inadequate to the ubiquitous case. This problem includes multiple machines per user, small devices attached to the network, and new services like location and context handling that are necessary for its applications. The environment is also highly dynamic, and includes mobile users and devices. Therefore, the system must enable adaptation (Ballesteros et al., 2006). This suggests that the "natural" interaction paradigm appropriate to a fully robust ubiquitous computing has yet to emerge - although there is also recognition in the field that in many ways we are already living in a "ubicomp world". Contemporary devices that lend some support to this latter idea include mobile phones, digital audio players, radio-frequency identification tags and interactive whiteboards. Resources and information in ubiquitous computing environments are shared by users, heterogeneous sensors and so on.

Security becomes vital in the environments since contextual information such as sensor locations and applications become an integral part of the system authorization. On the other hand, a variety of applications and users interaction with the pervasive environment poses new security challenges to the traditional user-password approach for computer security. The heterogeneous devices and mobile users in such dynamic pervasive computing environments make security management difficult, especially the access to authorized users since it is a basic security requirement for guaranteeing user's privacy, information confidentiality, integrity and availability (Wang et al., 2007).

Pervasive computing is considered roughly as the opposite of virtual reality. Where virtual reality puts people inside a computer-generated world, pervasive computing forces the computer to live out here in the world with people. Visualization and interaction of pervasive services can be implemented using context-aware augmented reality (Van de Kar, 2005). Thus, pervasive computing is considered a very difficult integration of human factors, computer science, engineering, and social sciences (Weiser, 1991). On the other hand, augmented reality (AR), another type of virtual reality, is considered as an excellent user interface for pervasive computing applications, because it allows intuitive information browsing of location-referenced information (Lee, Ju & Jeong, 2006; Schmalstieg & Reitmayr, 2005).

Pervasive information systems (PIS) constitute an emerging class of information systems (IS) where information technology (IT) is gradually embedded in the physical environment, capable of accommodating user needs and wants when desired. PIS differ from desktop information systems (DIS) in that they provide new means of interaction and can generate new experiences for their users (Kourouthanasis, Giaglis & Vrechopoulos, 2007). A new generation of information appliances has emerged (Roussos, 2003), differing from traditional general-purpose computers in what they do and in the much smaller learning overhead they impose on the user. This new class of IS has been called 'pervasive information systems' (PIS) (Birnbaum, 1997) and enables new interaction means beyond the traditional desktop paradigm. Ubiquitous embedded devices are the backbone of the pervasive computing world (Paar & Weimerskirch 2007). Embedded systems have become an integral part of our everyday life. Devices like vehicles, household appliances, and cell phones are already equipped with embedded microcontrollers. The networking of the myriads of embedded devices gives rise to the brave new world of pervasive computing.

Pervasive computing offers enormous advantages and opportunities for users and businesses through new applications, increased comfort, and cost reduction. One often overlooked aspect of pervasive computing, however, are new security threats (Paar & Weimerskirch 2007). Embedded controllers are said to have a market share of 98% or more of the global processor market, implying that less than 2% of all processors are employed in traditional computers (Estrin, Govindan & Heidemann, 2000). Different kinds of models are built for ubiquitous computing (Wang et al., 2007) and several papers have analysed the security requirements for ubiquitous computing (Seigneur & Jensen 2004; Sampemane, Naldurg & Campbell, 2002; Viswanathan, Gill & Campbell, 2001; Jai-muhtadi et al., 2002; Wang, Cao & Zhang, 2006). Research and development trends in the field of computing industry promote a vision of smart spaces, smart devices, clothing, fully automated houses etc., which create an environment where computers are everywhere and provide ultimate access to Internet.

Pervasive computing (Satyanarayanan, 2001) envisions the unobtrusive diffusion of computing and networking resources in physical environments, enabling users to access information and computational resources anytime and anywhere, and this in a user-centric way, i.e., where user interaction with the system is intuitive, pleasant and natural. Pervasive computing environments are populated with networked software and hardware resources providing various functionalities that are abstracted, thanks to the Service Oriented Architecture paradigm, as services. Within these environments, service discovery enabled by service discovery protocols (SDPs) is a critical functionality for establishing ad hoc associations between service providers and service requesters. Furthermore, the dynamics, the openness and the user-centric vision aimed at by the pervasive computing paradigm call for solutions that enable rich, semantic, context- and QoS-aware service discovery (Mokhtar et al., 2007).

The conventional approach to building pervasive environments relies on middleware to integrate different systems (Ballesteros et al., 2006). Systems that support ubiquitous computing are too abundant to be appropriately described here, however, some of them are: Plan 9 (Pike, et al., 1995), Plan B (Ballesteros et al., 2006), Odyssey (Noble, et al., 1997), Khazana (Carter, Ranganathan & Susarla, 1998), Semantic File system (Gifford, et. al., 1991), Gaia's Context File System (Hess & Campbell 2002), Globe (Kuz, van Steen & Sips, 2002), Speakeasy (Edwards et al., 2002), Ninja (Gribble et al., 2000), IWS (Johanson, Fox & Winograd, 2002), Gaia (Roman, et al., 2002), One.World (Grimm & Bershad, 2002) and WebOS (Vahdat et al., 1998). The problem they all address is how to provide a convenient operating system for a ubiquitous computing environment (Weiser, 1991). A recent computing paradigm particularly appropriate for pervasive systems is Service-Oriented Architectures (SOA) (Papazoglou & Georgakopoulos, 2003), however, in Zhu, Mutka & Ni (2005), a classification of academic and industry-supported SDPs, specifically for pervasive environments, is proposed.

A number of research efforts have been conducted in the area of matching semantic Web services based on their signatures. Signature matching deals with the identification of subsumption relationships between the concepts describing inputs and outputs of capabilities (Zaremski & Wing, 1995). A base algorithm for service signature matching has been proposed by Sycara et al. (2003), Paolucci et al. (2002). Other solutions based on the signature matching of semantic Web services have been proposed in the literature (Majithia, Walker & Gray, 2004; Trastour, Bartolini & Gonzalez-Castillo, 2001; Filho & van Sinderen, 2003). A more practical way to perform specification matching is to use query containment (Sirin, Parsia & Hendler, 2005; Sycara et al., 1999).

Pervasive computing environments provide many kinds of information and has become so popular for two main reasons. First, users desire natural interfaces that facilitate a richer variety of communication capabilities between humans and machines (Abowd & Mynat 2000). Second, the various contexts need a good representation model and a good reasoning model to enhance system and work efficiency by matching users' intentions (Hong, Chiu & Shen, 2005). Some of this information should be accessible only to a limited set of people. For example, a person's location is a sensitive piece of information, and releasing it to unauthorized entities might pose security and privacy risks. For instance, when walking home at night, a person will want to limit the risk of being robbed, and only people trusted by the person should be able to learn about his or her current location.

The access control requirements of information available in a pervasive computing environment have not been thoroughly studied. This information is inherently different from information such as files stored in a file system or objects stored in a database, whose access control requirements have been widely studied. The market is evolving from wired computing to pervasive computing, mobile and wireless, any time at any place. Many types of information available in a pervasive computing environment, such as people location information, should be accessible only to a limited set of people. Some properties of the information raise unique challenges for the design of an access control mechanism: Information can emanate from more than one source, it might change its nature or granularity before reaching its final receiver and it can flow through nodes administrated by different entities (Hengartner & Steenkiste, 2003). The emergence of ubiquitous computing brings context as part of implicit input, which effectively improves the interaction between human and computing devices (Hong, Chiu & Shen, 2005).

CONTEXT

What is context and why is it so important in ubiquitous environments and pervasive computing? Schilit, Adams & Want (1994) claimed that the three important aspects of context are: where you are, who you are with, and what resources are nearby. Chen, Li & Kotz (2000) redefine context as the set of environmental states and settings that either determines an application's behaviour or in which an application event occurs and is interesting to the user. Moreover, Dey, Abowd & Salber (2001) define it as any information that can be used to characterize the situation of entities (i.e., whether a person, place, or object) that are considered relevant to the interaction between a user and an application, including the user and the application themselves. A system is context-aware if it can extract, interpret, and use context information and adapt its functionality to the current context of use (Korkea-aho, 2000). In particular, context-awareness is also considered as one of the most important issues in pervasive computing, which is used to provide relevant services and information to users by exploiting contexts. By contexts, we mean information about locations, software agents, users, devices, and their relationships (Daftari, et. al., 2003; Wang, et. al., 2004). Recently, several researches have been in progress for developing flexible middlewares which can supply context-aware service infrastructure such as Context Toolkit (Dey & Abowd, 2000), Reconfigurable Context-Sensitive Middleware for Pervasive Computing (Yau, et. al., 2002), and SOCAM (Service-oriented Context-aware Middleware) (Gu, Pung, & Zhang, 2004), and GAIA (Biegel & Cahill, 2004).

There are three main reasons why context is important. First, context reduces the input cost. Second, context may provide an exciting user experience without much effort on the users' part. Third, users benefit through context sharing (Hong, Chiu & Shen, 2005). User preferences and security may vary depending on the device capabilities and other context conditions. Therefore, the context adaptability should provide for means to express conditions and reason them applicable to adaptable ubiquitous services (Gandon & Sadeh, 2004; Held, Buchholz, & Schill, 2002). One particular important issue is to combine context awareness with more natural and intuitive interfaces like augmented reality for providing more human-oriented visualization, interaction and collaboration of various pervasive services (Lee, Ju & Jeong, 2006). Further, in a dynamic heterogeneous environment, context adaptation for user-oriented services is a key concept to meet the varying requirements of different clients. In order to enable context-aware adaptation, context information must be gathered and eventually presented to the application performing the adaptation (Held, Buchholz, & Schill, 2002).

E-COMMERCE VIA UBIQUITOUS INTERNET

The most important benefit deriving from the deployment of pervasive retail systems is the creation of new shopping experiences and consequently, enthusiasm for the consumers. This is particularly important in the competitive retail sector where the provision of complimentary shopping schemes the advent of the Internet, and the urbanization of nowadays society have created the new consumer who is more knowledgeable about comparable product costs and price; more changeable in retail and brand preferences; showing little loyalty; self-sufficient, yet demanding more information; who holds high expectations of service and personal attention; and is driven by three new currencies: time, value, and information (Kourouthanassis, Giaglis & Vrechopoulos, 2007).

The manufacturing and automation technologies have crossed the frontiers from nanotechnology to Giga Networks Infrastructures that are essential in enabling the information flow between robots, powerful computing centres and manually controlled stations. Automated negotiations among multiple participants have been researched as one of the prominent fields in ecommerce (Kraus, 2001; Jennings et al., 2002). The current merger of current Computer Integrated Manufacturing Technologies and Data-Telecommunications Technologies present a new challenge to community of engineers and scientists in the manufacturing sector as well as, mathematics and computing science and engineering sector (Babulak, 2004; Babulak, 2005). The economic prospects, for the years to come, remain particularly hard to predict. Whilst the markets for Control and Power industry proved to be challenging for the companies, the Software and Automation industry have grown, particularly those businesses serving the oil, gas, power generation and auto markets (Babulak, 2004).

What gives rise to pressures in the market place are company drivers in conjunction with the industry drives. Globalization of the market with accelerating technological changes such as digital revolution and mobile technologies in conjunction with the customer demands represent main industrial drivers (Wohlwend, 2001). On the company site it is the cost efficiency combined with the new lines of products that give rise to business complexity. The major forces in industry today are e-commerce and e-manufacturing (AMR Research). E-manufacturing illustrated in Figures 1 and 2, has been well adopted in industry overseas and the next wave of the e-manufacturing is driven by customers utilizing full capacity of e-commerce (Toyota).

Figure 1. What is e-manufacturing (credit to Ivensys)

What Is E-Manufacturing

The complete electronic (computer systems) integration of all factory component using industry standards.

E-manufacturing extends from the Equipment to the Equipment Automation Systems to the MES (Manufacturing Execution Systems)/YMS (Yield Management System)/EEC (Equipment Engineering Capability) and to the ERP (Enterprise Resource Planning).

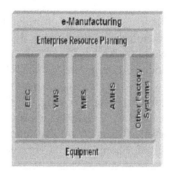

Figure. 2. E-manufacturing hierarchy (credit to Ivensys)

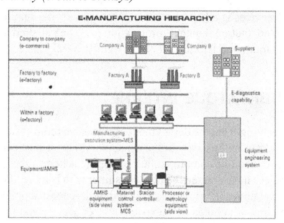

Toyota is one of many examples where e-manufacturing has become a major force for their productivity and business success. Future technological advancements open a new avenue for multidisciplinary development and research teams consisting of IT professionals, such as software developers, telecommunications engineers, production engineers and business managers to work closely with academics and industrial research teams on new e-manufacturing solutions. Sales marketing forces combined with the manufacturing and operation teams work together to plan the dynamics for future vision and the current reality, while facilitating the supply chain of products in response to customer chaotic orders.

A firm's ability to serve its customers needs determines its success. Initially, firms needed to meet face-to-face to meet most of their customer's needs; however, with the development of information technology, the requirement for face-to-face interaction has gradually declined. The Internet opened up a new channel for firm-customer interaction that has significantly changed the customer relationship equation. Now, cell phone networks are enabling m-commerce and further changes in the firm-customer dynamics (Watson, 2004). Traditionally, business has been biased by geography and located near rivers, roads, and other transport services so that the cost of being reached by or reaching customers is lowered. Now, business is increasingly using electronic networks (e.g., the Internet and mobile phone networks) to interact with customers. Thus in the next few years, it is likely that we will see the emergence of u-commerce, where u stands for ubiquitous, universal, unique, and unison.

Figure 3. What is ubiquity (credit to www.ubicom.org)

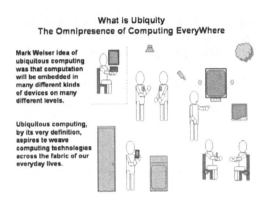

Figure 4. Convergence (credit to CISCO)

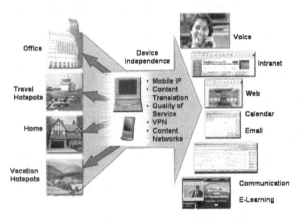

U-Commerce represents the use of ubiquitous networks to support personalized and uninterrupted communications and transactions between a firm and its various stakeholders to provide a level of value over, above, and beyond traditional commerce. Ubiquitous represents the concept of having (Watson, 2004) a network connection everywhere with all consumer devices, with the intelligence and information widely dispersed and always accessible, as well as smart entities including appliances, buildings, signs, street smart communities, etc. The main focus is to enable one global network that would be available 24 hours a day, seven days a week, whole year round and will provide best quality of services to anyone, anywhere and anytime (Figure 3).

There is a burgeoning population of 'effectively invisible' computers around us, embedded in the fabric of our homes, shops, vehicles, farms and some even in our bodies. They are invisible in that they are part of the environment and we can interact with them as we go about our normal activities. However they can range in size from large Plasma displays on the walls of buildings to microchips implanted in the human body. They help us command, control, communicate, do business, travel and entertain ourselves, and these "invisible" computers are far more numerous than their desktop counterparts.

The mobile telecommunications industry is searching for new services, not only to regain its investments in licenses but also to stay competitive in the future (Van de Kar, 2005). World's telecommunications providers are looking for ways to merge together all digital and analogue services (voice, video, data) on one common network, which would provide users with unlimited access to online information, business, entertainment, etc. Convergence's goal is to provide corporations with a highly secure and controllable solution that supports real-time collaborative applications (Convergence). In 2003, manufacturers were delivering the first network systems and terminals were making their appearance on the market. However, the new services that had to be delivered, were - and still are - in the development stage (Van de Kar, 2005). The current trends in communications technologies are driven by convergence and ubiquity, as shown in Figure 4.

FUTURE HOME 2015

The vision of pervasive computing consists of unobtrusively integrating computers with people's everyday lives at home and at work (Chen, Li & Kotz, 2007) and has inspired many researchers to work on new hardware, networking protocols, human-computer interactions, security and privacy, applications, and social implications (Weiser, 1991; Satyanarayanan, 2001). In the last decade, a number of researcher articles presented the vision and illustrated the scenarios of futuristic computing systems in the year 2005 (Babulak, 2005). Much of the research on Ubiquitous Computing has been dominated by a focus upon the office environment since when Mark Weiser articulated the notion of Ubiquitous Computing back in 1994, the office has been the default domain. However, today, we are in 2007 and much of the foreseen technology is already implemented and fully integrated in industry, military, businesses, education and home. Mark Weiser in his article which was written back in 1996 wrote about futuristic computer technologies applied in "Smart House in the year 2005" (Weiser, 1996). Mark Weiser's vision did indeed materialise and some of his concepts are currently part of ongoing research and implementation projects.

Ultimately the ubiquitous computer and Internet technologies should make everyday life more comfortable for all. As a distinguished Professor of Computer Science quite aptly once said: "Computer technology today has influenced almost every aspect of our lives, industry, business, and education. However, most unfortunately computer technology have mechanised the relationship between people due to e-mail and Internet technologies. It is important that the research, academic and industrial community work together to reverse that equation, whereby computer technology will be a tool that will improve human lives and mutual interaction." The authors encourage reader to reflect on that statement. In our current research we have been considering the notion of Ubiquitous Computing in the context of another domain – the home (Tolmie et al., 2002).

Let us imagine a scenario where a person lives in the "Smart House 2015". It is already 8:00 am and the alarm clock wakes Alice up while half opening the blinds to let the morning light enter her bedroom. The soundtrack of her favourite music station plays on the home cinema set while she takes her bath and a cup of fresh coffee waits for her at the kitchen. She dresses up and leaves home on time while pressing the button "exit" on the touch panel. The door closes behind her and immediately, all unnecessary lights as well as the toaster that she forgot switched on, turn off. The security alarm sets on and waits for Alice to get back. As soon as Alice arrives from work, she gets in her house using the fingerprint reader at the front door. At the very same time, the in-house lighting is set in the "welcome mode" and the air-conditioning system is set to suit her preferences. While she is entering the living room, TV switches on her favourite news station in order to inform her about the current affairs. She takes a look at the remote control, in order to check that everything is perfect and she initializes the multizone entertainment system. Her favourite music plays on the home cinema set and she is now ready to enjoy her bath, since the water is ready at the desired temperature. The ventilation works silently in order not to disturb the music listening, and it maximizes its power only when Alice gets out of the bathroom. She has not had the time to cook and the delivery boy rings the bell to deliver her favourite Chinese food. Immediately, the monitor that can be found closer to her location, shows the view of the man smiling at the front door and with the touch of a button, she opens the door and the front lighting to facilitate his entrance into the house.

We have provided an example that helps reveal what 'invisible in use' might mean but acknowledge that a great deal of research remains to be done in order to move from this to actual designs (Tolmie et al., 2002). Naturally,

Figure 5. Cyber home 2015

Cyber Home 2015

1. Home Information and Communications System
2. Home Business, Financing and Accounting
3. Home Education Centre
4. Home Food and Kitchen Centre
5. Home Security and Surveillance System
6. Home Medical Centre
7. Home Entertainment System
8. Home Car Surveillance and Maintenance Centre
9. Home Gardening Centre
10. Home Leisure and Sport Centre
11. Home Children Care Centre
12. Home Elderly Care Centre

there are issues related to the "House Automatic Positioning Systems" and "Security Systems", which will be carefully monitored and controlled remotely by the house owner or if necessary by the "Local Weather Centre". In case of natural disasters these systems will protect the house and its members while switching to contingency plan B. Figure 5 illustrates a simple set of some basic attributes for the Future Cyber Home 2015.

Pervasive computing will introduce new security threats, ranging from loss of privacy and financial damages, to bodily injuries. Some of the new security threats are well known from conventional IT systems, whereas others are unique to the pervasiveness of the devices. At the same time, strong security in pervasive applications, e.g., fee-based feature activation in products, offers new opportunities for businesses and users. Pervasive security is an emerging discipline and there is an active academic and industrial community working on strong security solutions (Paar & Weimerskirch 2007). Several approaches are developed to protect information for pervasive environments against malicious users. However, ad hoc mechanisms or protocols are typically added in the approaches by compromising disorganized policies or additional components to protect from unauthorized access (Wang et al., 2007).

All we need is to wait until 2015 and see if this vision will materialise. Fully automated environments will require sophisticated MIMO antenna systems and small smart devices that will be able to communicate within themselves all the time. These devices will have self healing capabilities to make sure that they are recharged regularly and will be operational without any interruption. In contrast to humans who have breakfast, lunch, dinner and snack on accession to make sure that they are able to do their job, and yet they sleep anywhere from 6 to 14 hours each day, the devices creating the fully automated space can not sleep, perhaps they may wait or be on pause mode, but as soldiers they must be in full operational readiness at any time and anywhere. The current efforts in Home automation and ubiquity are well on the way at many research centres and industries such Microsoft, Phillips, Sony, etc. Figure 6, illustrate some recent efforts and products that are available to public.

For a smart home, Easy Living (Brumitt et al., 2000; Shafer et al., 1998) is an intelligent system environment by Microsoft Research. It focuses on applications that can make computers easier to use and able to perform more tasks than traditional desktop computers. The system has information about the state of the world, such as locations of people, places, things, and other devices in space. The context, which could be interpreted by the system, helps users directly access all available devices, control some devices remotely, and control media players according to user preference. eHome or the Smart Home Usability and Living Experience project (Koskela & Väänänen-Vainio-Mattila, 2004) was carried out from May 2002 to March 2003 at the Institute of Software Systems at the Tampere University of Technology, Finland. The system supports users in controlling everyday "smart objects" such as moving curtains and status-aware pot plants through three user-interface devices: a personal computer, a media terminal (i.e., the TV), and a mobile phone. In the system, the PC acts as the central

Figure 6. Web report 2006

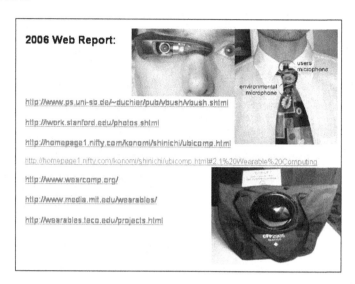

Figure 7. Easy living (credit Microsoft)

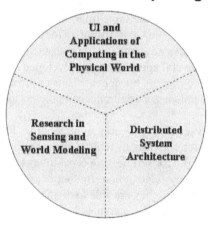

control unit. A mobile phone is a suitable remote controller when users are away from home. The Microsoft research group is working on the project of Easy Living while applying the cutting edge technology with the modern home environment and the home working. Figure 7, illustrates the basic elements of easy living, including user interface and applications of computing in the physical world with distributed system architecture and research in sensing and world modelling.

Figure 8. Working from home (credit to Microsoft)

Working from home example illustrated in Figure 8 facilitates:

- A person working from home engages in an augmented video- teleconference with a **(A)** colleague at the office.
- The various PCs, sensors, displays, and devices are integrated with the existing home environment.
- For example, **(B)** switch plates near the door of each room show the privacy-state of each room, and provide simple touch-screen interfaces to common room controls. **(C)** The room is aware of where people are and automatically switches to use the best video feed.

The advancement of current technologies in the fields of data and telecommunications, ubiquitous Internet access and sensor technologies combined with the new revolutionary explorations and concepts in biotechnology and nanotechnology, computer human interface-interaction, etc., present a great challenge for the research community not only as a result of mathematical complexity, but most of all as a result of the user's perception (Babulak, 2005).

CONCLUSION

Automation did inspire a number of outstanding scientists and engineers in the past centuries to find new solutions to make life easier for all mankind. The emergence and accessibility of advanced data and telecommunications technologies combined with the convergence of industry standards, as well as the convergence of data and telecommunications industries contribute towards the ubiquitous access to information resources via the Internet (Pervasive Computing; Distributed Systems Online). The automated environment and cyberspace systems for the 21st century entered a new era of innovation and technological advancements. The world's industry and commerce are becoming increasingly dependent on Web-based solutions, with regards to a global vision for the future. With increased benefits and improvements in overall information technology, the benefit-to-cost ratio has never been higher. It is essential to continue the development of industry standards and application of information technologies in order to increase the automation and ultimate success of modern logistics, the E-Commerce and E-manufacturing industries (Kropft, 2002; Shade 2001).

The authors present their own vision on future automated environment via information cyberspace for the year 2015. This chapter suggests the integration of automated environments and intelligent cyberspaces in light of applied robotics, logistics, smart devices, smart antennas and intelligent systems. The authors hope that this chapter will encourage the research and industrial community to invest their efforts in implementing fully automated environments via intelligent cyberspaces. Future efforts should be focused on designing a communication language and transmission media that will allow for instantaneous communication transfer and control between smart devices and humans.

REFERENCES

Abowd, G.D. & Mynatt, E.D. (2000). Charting past, present, and future research in ubiquitous computing. ACM Transactions on Computer-Human Interaction, 7(1): 29–58.

Assimakopoulos, A.N., Angelopoulos, P.S. & Riggas, N.A. (2007). Development and analysis of a virtual enterprise that constructs wireless payment mechanisms using open source content management systems. Accepted for publication in International Journal of Applied Systemic Studies (IJASS) (http://www.inderscience.com/ijass).

AMR Research: http://www.amrresearch.com/

Babulak, E. (2005). Automated Environment via Cyberspace. Proceedings of the International Conference on Applied Computing (IADIS), Algarve, Portugal.

Babulak, E. (2004). Manufacturing for the 21st Century, 1st International Conference on Manufacturing Management, Presov, Slovakia.

Babulak, E. (2005). Next Generation of Internet & Telecommunications Technologies for Fully Automated Cyberspace. Keynote Speech, the 7th International Conference on New Trends in Technology System Operation, Presov, Slovakia.

Babulak, E. (2005). Quality of Service Provision Assessment in the Healthcare Information and Telecommunications Infrastructures. Selected for publication in the International Journal of Medical Informatics, Elsevier Ireland Ltd.

Ballesteros, F.J., Guardiola, G., Leal, K. & Soriano, E. (2006). Omero: Ubiquitous user interfaces in the Plan B operating system, in: Proceedings of IEEE PerCom.

Ballesteros, F.J., Soriano, E., Leal, K. & Guardiola, G. (2006). Plan B: An operating system for ubiquitous computing environments, in: Proceedings of IEEE PerCom.

Birnbaum, J. (1997). Pervasive information systems. Communications of the ACM, 40(2), 40–41.

Bluetooth: http://www.bluetooth.com

Brumitt, B., Meyers, B., Krumm, J., Kern, A. & Shafer, S. (2000). Easyliving: Technologies for intelligent environments. In The Second International Symposium on Handheld and Ubiquitous Computing (HUC2000), pages 12–29, Bristol, UK. Springer-Verlag.

Carter, J., Ranganathan, A. & Susarla, S. (1998). Khazana. An infrastructure for building distributed services, in: Proceedings of ICDCS'98, IEEE, Amsterdam.

Chaikalis, C. (2007). Turbo decoder dynamic reconfiguration in urban/suburban outdoor operating environment for 3GPP. in Proceedings of IEEE International Symposium on Personal, Indoor and Mobile Radio Communications (PIMRC 2007), Athens, Greece.

Chaikalis, C. (2007). UMTS implementation issues. Chapter in book entitled: Progress in Wireless Communications Research, Editor: Alfred P. Martinhoff, Nova Science Publishers, New York, Invited, ISBN 1-60021-675-7.

Chen, G. & Kotz, D. (2000). A survey of context-aware mobile computing research. Technical Report TR2000-381, Department of Computer Science, Dartmouth College.

Chen, G., Li, M. & Kotz, D. (2007). Data-centric middleware for context-aware pervasive computing, Pervasive and Mobile Computing.

Convergence: http://www.telecommagazine.com

Course on Ubiquitous Computing: http://www.cs.albany.edu/~maniatty/teaching/ubicomp/index.html

Daftari, A., Mehta, N., Bakre, S. &. Sun, X.-H. (2003). On Design Framework of Context Aware Embedded Systems. Monterey Workshop, Chicago, Illinois, Available at: http://www.cs.uic.edu/~shatz/SEES/sun.paper.pdf.

Dey, A. K., Abowd, G.D. & Salber, D. (2001). A conceptual framework and a toolkit for supporting the rapid prototyping of context-aware applications. Human-Computer Interaction, 16:97–166.

Dickson K. Chiu, W. & Leung, H. (2005). Towards ubiquitous tourist service coordination and integration: a multi-agent and semantic Web approach. Proceedings of the 7th international conference on Electronic commerce ICEC '05. ACM Press

Distributed Systems Online: http://dsonline.computer.org/portal/site/dsonline/index.jsp

Dix, A., Finlay, J., Abowd G.D. & Beale, R. (2004). Human- Computer Interaction. Prentice Hall, Harlow, England, third edition.

Edwards, W., Newman, M.W., Sedivy, J., Smith, T. & Izadi, S. (2002). Challenge: Recombinant computing and the speakeasy approach, in: 8th ACM Mobicom.

Estrin, D., Govindan, R. & Heidemann, J. (2000). Embedding the Internet. Communications of the ACM;43(5):39–41.

Filho, J.G.P. & van Sinderen, M. (2003). Web service architectures – semantics and context-awareness issues in Web services platforms, Tech. rep., Telematica Instituut.

Garlan, D., Siewiorek, D., Smailagic, A. & Steenkiste, P. (2002). Project Aura: Towards Distraction-Free Pervasive Computing. IEEE Pervasive Computing, 1(2):22–31, April- June.

Gifford, D.K., Jouvelotl, P., Sheldon, M.A. & O'Toole Jr. J.W. (1991). Semantic file systems, in: Proceedings of 13th ACM Symposium on Operating Systems Principles, Association for Computing Machinery SIGOPS, pp. 16–25.

Gribble, S.D., Welsh, M., Behren, R., Brewer, E.A., Culler, D.E., Borisov, N., Czerwinski, S.E., Gummadi, R., Hill, J.R., Joseph, A.D., Katz, R.H., Z.M. Mao, Ross, S. & Zhao, B.Y. (2000). The ninja architecture for robust internetscale systems and services, in: Pervasive Computing, Computer Networks (35) (special issue).

Grimm, R. & Bershad B. (2002). Future directions: System support for pervasive applications, in: Proceedings of FuDiCo.

Held, A., Buchholz, S. & Schill, A. (2002). Modelling of context information for pervasive computing applications. In Proceedings of SCI2002/ISAS.

Hengartner, U. & Steenkiste, P. (2003). Protecting Access to People Location Information, Proceedings of the International Conference on Security in Pervasive Computing.

Hess, C.K. & Campbell, R.H. (2002). A context file system for ubiquitous computing environments, Technical Report No. UIUCDCS-R-2002-2285 UILU-ENG-2002-1729, July.

Hong, D., Chiu, D.K.W. & Shen V.Y. (2005). Requirements elicitation for the design of context-aware applications in a ubiquitous environment. Proceedings of the 7th international conference on Electronic commerce ICEC '05. ACM Press

Ioannou, K., Dimitriadou, E., Ioannou, A., Panoutsopoulos I. & Kotsopoulos, S. (2006). Hierarchical Dynamic Channel Assignment Technique. WSEAS Transactions on Communications, Issue 1, Volume 5, pp 115-122

Ioannou, K., Panoutsopoulos, I. & Kotsopoulos, S. (2006). Optimizing the QoS of Ultra High and High Speed Moving Terminals in Satellite-aided cellular networks. Wireless Personal Communications, Volume 39, Number 3, pp307-319.

Jai-muhtadi, J., Campbell, R., Kapadia, A., Mickunas, M. & Yi, S. (2002). Routing through the mist: Privacy preserving communication in ubiquitous computing environments, in: ICDCS '02: Proceedings of the 22nd International Conference on Distributed Computing Systems, ICDCS'02, IEEE Computer Society, Washington, DC, USA, p. 74.

Jennings, N.R., Faratin, P., Lomuscio, A.R., Parsons, S., Sierra, C. & Wooldridge, M. (2002). Automated negotiation: prospects, methods and challenges. International Journal of Group Decision and Negotiation 10 (2), 199–215.

Johanson, B., Fox, A. & Winograd, T. (2002). The interactive workspaces project: Experiences with Ubiquitous computing rooms, IEEE Pervasive Computing Magazine.

Kitsios, F. (2005). Innovation Management in New Service Development, PhD dissertation, Technical University of Crete.

Kitsios, F. (2006). Services marketing in the hospitality economy: An exploratory study. 98th EAAE seminar, Marketing Dynamics within the Global Trading System: New Perspectives, Chania, Crete, Greece, 29 June – 02 July

Kitsios, F. & Skiadas C. (2001). Some Critical Issues Concerning Technological Change. 1st International Conference in Management of Change, Iasi, Romania, October

Kitsios F. & Zopounidis, C. (2007). Services marketing in the hospitality economy: An exploratory study. The Southeuropean Review of Business Finance & Accounting, Vol. 5, No. 1

Korkea-aho, M. (2000). Context-aware application surveys. http://users.tkk.fi/~mkorkeaa/doc/context-aware.html

Koskela, T. & Väänänen-Vainio-Mattila, K. (2004). Evolution towards smart home environments: empirical evaluation of three user interfaces. Personal Ubiquitous Computing, 8:234–240, 2004.

Kourouthanassis, E.P., Giaglis, M.G. & Vrechopoulos, A.P. (2007). Enhancing user experience through pervasive information systems: The case of pervasive retailing, International Journal of Information Management 27, 319–335

Kraus, S. (2001). Strategic Negotiation in Multiagent Environments. The MIT Press, Cambridge, MA.

Kropft, P. (2002). What is Pervasive Computing. Series of Lecture notes.

Kuz, I., van Steen, M. & Sips, H. J. (2002). The globe infrastructure directory service. Computer Communications 25.

Lee, K.J. & Seo Y.H. (2006). A pervasive comparison shopping business model for integrating offline and online marketplace. Proceedings of the 8th international conference on Electronic commerce: The new e-commerce: innovations for conquering current barriers, obstacles and limitations to conducting successful business on the internet ICEC '06. ACM Press

Lee, K.J., Ju, J. & Jeong, J.M. (2006). Mobile and pervasive commerce track: A payment & receipt business model in U-commerce environment. Proceedings of the 8th international conference on Electronic commerce: The new e-commerce: innovations for conquering current barriers, obstacles and limitations to conducting successful business on the internet ICEC '06. ACM Press

Lukkari, J., Korhonen, J. & Ojala, T. (2004). SmartRestaurant: mobile payments in context-aware environment. Proceedings of the 6th international conference on Electronic commerce ICEC '04. ACM Press

Majithia, S., Walker, D.W. & Gray, W.A. (2004). A framework for automated service composition in service-oriented architecture. In: First European Semantic Web Symposium.

Mark Weiser's Vision: http://www.ubiq.com/hypertext/weiser/SciAmDraft3.html

Military Agile Manufacturing Pilot Program: http://www.darpa.mil/mto/solicitations/CBD/cbd_9431A.html

Mokhtar, S. B., Kaul, A., Georgantas, N. & Issarny V. (2007). EASY: Efficient Semantic Service Discovery in Pervasive Computing Environments. Springer Berlin.

Noble, B., Satyanarayanan, M., Narayanan, D., Tilton, T., Flinn, J. & Walker, K. (1997). Agile application-aware adaptation for mobility, in: Proceedings of the 16th ACM SOSP.

Norman, D.A. (1999). The Invisible Computer: Why Good Products Can Fail, the Personal Computer Is So Complex, and Information Appliances Are the Solution. The MIT Press.

Roman, M., Hess, C.K., Cerqueira, R., Ranganathan, A., Campbell, R.H., Narhstedt, K., Gaiaos. (2002). A middleware infrastructure to enable active spaces, IEEE Pervasive Computing Magazine.

Paar, C. & Weimerskirch, A. (2007). Embedded security in a pervasive world, Information Security Technical Report, (12) p. 155-161.

Paolucci, M., Kawamura, T., Payne, T.R. & Sycara, K. (2002). Semantic matching of Web services capabilities. Lecture Notes in Computer Science 2342, 333–347.

Papazoglou, M.P. & Georgakopoulos, D. (2003). Special section in Communications of the ACM, chap. In: Service-oriented computing. ACM Press.

Park, S. & Yang, S.-B. (2007). An efficient multilateral negotiation system for pervasive computing. Engineering Applications of Artificial Intelligence.

Pervasive Computing: http://www.computer.org/pervasive

Pike, R., Presotto, D., Dorward, S., Flandrena, B., Thompson, K., Trickey, H. & Winterbottom, P. (1995). Plan 9 from Bell Labs, Computing Systems 8 (3) 221–254.

Roman, M., Hess, C.K., Cerqueira, R., Ranganathan, A., Campbell, R.H., Narhstedt, K. & Gaiaos (2002). A middleware infrastructure to enable active spaces, IEEE Pervasive Computing Magazine.

Roussos, G. (2003). Appliance design for pervasive computing. IEEE Pervasive Computing, 2(4), 75–77.

Ruta, M., Noia, T.D., Sciascio, E.D., Piscitelli, G. & Scioscia, F. (2007). Session M5: e-business systems and applications: RFID meets bluetooth in a semantic based u-commerce environment Proceedings of the ninth international conference on Electronic commerce ICEC '07. ACM Press

Salvi, A.B. & Sahai, S. (2002). Dial m for money. Proceedings of the 2nd international workshop on Mobile commerce WMC '02. ACM Press

Sampemane, G., Naldurg, P. & Campbell, R. (2002). Access control for active spaces, in: ACSAC '02: Proceedings of the 18th Annual Computer Security Applications Conference, IEEE Computer Society, Washington, DC, USA, p. 343.

Satyanarayanan, M. (2001). Pervasive computing: Vision and challenges. IEEE Personal Communications, 8(4):10–17.

Schilit, B. N., Adams, N. & Want, R. (1994). Context-aware computing applications. In IEEE Workshop on Mobile Computing Systems and Applications, pages 85-90, Santa Cruz, CA, US.. IEEE.

Seigneur, J. & Jensen, C. (2004). Trust enhanced ubiquitous payment without too much privacy loss, in: SAC '04: Proceedings of the 2004 ACM Symposium on Applied Computing, ACM Press, New York, NY, USA, pp. 1593–1599.

Shade, B. (2001). Increased Productivity Through E-Manufacturing, by Cahners Business Information

Shafer, S., Krumm, J., Brumitt, B., Meyers, B., Czerwinski, M. & Robbins, D. (1998). The new easyliving project at microsoft research. In DARPA / NIST Smart Spaces Workshop, Gaithersburg, Maryland.

Shukla, S. & Nah F. F. (2005). Web browsing and spyware intrusion Communications of the ACM, Volume 48 Issue 8. ACM Press

Sirin, E., Parsia, B. & Hendler, J. (2005). Template-based composition of semantic Web services. In: AAAI Fall Symposium on Agents and the Semantic Web.

Stajano, F. (2002). Security for Ubiquitous Computing, Wiley press.

Sun, S., Su, C. & Ju, T. (2005). A study of consumer value-added services in mobile commerce: focusing on domestic cellular phone companies in Taiwan, China. Proceedings of the 7th international conference on Electronic commerce ICEC '05. ACM Press

Sycara, K., Lu, J., Klusch, M. & Widoff, S. (1999). Matchmaking among heterogeneous agents on the internet. In: Proceedings of the 1999 AAAI Spring Symposium on Intelligent Agents in Cyberspace.

Sycara, K., Paolucci, M., Ankolekar, A. & Srinivasan, N. (2003). Automated discovery, interaction and composition of semantic Web services, Web Semantics: Science, Services and Agents on the World Wide Web.

Technology Advancements and Government Policies in Canada: http://www.atirtf-geai.gc.ca/submissions/riley2001-05-30-f.html

Tolmie, P., Pycock, J., Diggins, T., MacLean A. & Karsenty, A. (2002). Unremarkable Computing, Xerox Research Centre Europe.

Toyota: http://www.toyota.com/

Trastour, D., Bartolini, C. & Gonzalez-Castillo, J. (2001). A semantic Web approach to service description for matchmaking of services. In: Proceedings of the First Semantic Web Working Symposium, (SWWS).

Ubicuitous Security: http://www.lce.eng.cam.ac.uk/~fms27/secubicomp/index.

Vahdat, A., Anderson, T., Dahlin, M., Culler, D., Belani, E., Eastham, P. & Yoshikawa, C. (1998). WebOS: Operating system services for wide area applications, in: Proceedings of the Seventh Symposium on High Performance Distributed Computing.

van de Kar, E. (2005). The design of a mobile information and entertainment service on a UMTS testbed. Proceedings of the 7th international conference on Electronic commerce ICEC '05. ACM Press

Viswanathan, P., Gill, B. & Campbell, R. (2001). Security architecture in Gaia, Tech. Rep., Champaign, IL, USA.

Vlachos, P. & Vrechopoulos, A. (2004). Emerging customer trends towards mobile music services. Proceedings of the 6th international conference on Electronic commerce ICEC '04. ACM Press

Wang, H., Cao, J. & Zhang, Y. (2006). Ubiquitous computing environments and its usage access control, in: Proceedings of the First International Conference on Scalable Information Systems, INFOSCALE, ACM Press, Hong Kong.

Wang, H. et. Al. (2007). Access control management for ubiquitous computing. Future Generation Computer Systems.

Wang, X.H., Zhang, D.Q., Gu, T. & Pung, H.K. (2004). Ontology Based Context Modeling and Reasoning using OWL. In Workshop Proceedings of the 2nd IEEE Conference on Pervasive Computing and Communications (PerCom2004) (Orlando, FL, USA, March 2004), pp. 18–22.

Wang, Y., van de Kar, E. & Meijer, G. (2005). Designing mobile solutions for mobile workers: lessons learned from a case study. Proceedings of the 7th international conference on Electronic commerce ICEC '05. ACM Press

Watson R.T. (2004). Data management: Databases and Organizations 4th edition, Willey press.

Watson, R.T. (2000). U-commerce: the ultimate. Ubiquity, Volume 1 Issue 33. ACM Press.

Watson, R.T. & Straub, D. W. (2007). Future IS research in net-enabled organizations. ACM SIGMIS Database, Volume 38 Issue 3. ACM Press.

Weimerskirch, A., Paar, C. & Wolf, M. (2005). Cryptographic component identification: enabler for secure vehicles. In: IEEE 62nd vehicular technology conference Dallas, USA.

Weiser, M. (1991). The computer for the 21st century. Scientific American, 265(3):66–75.

Weiser, M. (1993). Hot topics-ubiquitous computing, Computer 26 (10) 71–72.

Weiser, M. (1996). "Open House", Web magazine of the Interactive Telecommunications Program of New York University. Appeared in March, 1996 ITP, Review 2.0. http://www.itp.tsoa.nyu.edu/~review/

Weiser, M. (1993). Some computer science issues in ubiquitous computing. Communications of the ACM, 36(7):75–84.

Wohlwend, H. (2001). An E-Factory Vision. 2nd European Advanced Equipment Control/Advance Process Control Conf., April 18-20.

Wong, C.C. & Hiew, P.L. (2005). Correlations between factors affecting the diffusion of mobile entertainment in Malaysia. Proceedings of the 7th international conference on Electronic commerce ICEC '05. ACM Press

Xerox Paul Alto Research: http://www.ubiq.com

Yau, S., Karim, F., Wang, Y., Wang, B. & Gupta, S.K.S. (2002). Reconfigurable context-sensitive middleware for pervasive computing", IEEE Pervasive Computing, 1(3), July-September 2002, IEEE Computer Society Press, pp. 33-40.

Zaremski, A.M. & Wing, J.M. (1995). Signature matching: a tool for using software libraries. ACM Transactions on Software Engineering and Methodology 4 (2), 146–170.

Zhu, F., Mutka, M.W. & Ni, L.M. (2005). Service discovery in pervasive computing environments. Pervasive Computing, IEEE 4 (4), 81–90.

KEY TERMS

Cyberspace: Domain characterized by the use of electronics and the electromagnetic spectrum to store, modifies, and exchange data via networked systems and associated physical infrastructures.

E-Commerce: Buying and selling products or services over electronic systems such as the Internet and other computer networks.

Everyware: Computing that is everywhere yet is relatively hard to see, both literally and figuratively.

ICT (Information Communications Technology): An umbrella term that includes all technologies for the communication of information. It is apparently culminating to information communication with the help of personal computers networked through the Internet through information technology that can transfer information using satellite systems or intercontinental cables.

Innovation: The term innovation may refer to both radical and incremental changes in thinking, in things, in processes or in services. Invention that gets out in to the world is innovation.

Internet: A worldwide, publicly accessible series of interconnected computer networks that transmit data by packet switching using the standard Internet Protocol.

Ubiquitous Computing: A post-desktop model of human-computer interaction in which information processing has been thoroughly integrated into everyday objects and activities.

Chapter XX
Service Innovation Management:
New Service Development Strategies in the Telecommunication Industry Test Template for Data Mining Publications

Fotis C. Kitsios
Technical University of Crete, Greece

Panagiotis Tzortzatos
Technical University of Crete, Greece

Constantin Zopounidis
Technical University of Crete, Greece

ABSTRACT

Nowadays that the world depends more and more in services, there is no issue more fundamental for service organizations than understanding the factors that separate success from failure in new service development. The new service process is not so well studied and researched as new product development, and as a result the failure rate is high. However in order to survive in the market place, service organisations need to make the most of all of their resources in order to introduce new services to market ahead of the competition. The purpose of this exploratory study is to investigate the factors that have impact on success and failure in new service development (NSD) in the telecommunication (TLC) sector. The results of the exploratory study are summarized in a conceptual model for further research.

INTRODUCTION

In today's increasingly competitive climate, more and more senior managers are having to update themselves on the range of factors that determine service innovation success (F. Axel Johne and Patricia A. Snelson, 1988).The critical role of innovation has long been recognized in physical goods; however, the development of innovative services has received much less attention(de Brentani, 1989).

Copyright © 2009, IGI Global, distributing in print or electronic forms without written permission of IGI Global is prohibited.

The success rate for new service projects are on average 58 percent (Griffin, 1997), in other words four out of ten new services fail in the market place (Ottenbacher). Success factors for new services are in general similar to those for new product development, only the potency of the factors differ (Cooper and de Brentani, 1991). This can be explained by the nature of services, which are largely intangible, produced and consumed simultaneously, heterogeneous and perishable (Zeithaml and Bitner, 2000).

In studies of services management in general, quality has become a central concept. Many quality problems are recurrent and may to a great extent be seen as results of shortcomings in the development processes of new services (Edvardsson and Haglund, 1994; Mattsson, 1995).

BACKGROUND

The majority of NSD research has concentrated on the financial service sector, and one of the largest industries world-wide, the TLC industry, has not been specifically investigated. Drawing from the research stream of new service development in other industries, such as financial (Brentani, 1990; 1991; Edgett, 1993; 1994; Cooper and Brentani, 1991; Parkinson, 1994), hospitality (Ottenbacher), tourism (Kitsios, 2005) etc., and using a comparative methodology of analysing successes and failures, some answers could be suggested to may what drives success in developing new services. The whole idea is to make a parallelism for TLC industry by using results of similar researches and the knowledge of some expertise. Generally, the critical dimensions that influence new service performance can be categorised into four clusters: (1) product-related, (2) market-related, (3) company-related, and (4) process-related (de Brentani, 1999).

NATURE OF THE INDUSTRY

The telecommunications industry is at the forefront of the information age—delivering voice, data, graphics and video at ever increasing speeds and in an increasing number of ways. Whereas wire line telephone communication was once the primary service of the industry, wireless communication services and cable and satellite program distribution make up an increasing share of the industry.

During the late 1990s, the telecommunications industry experienced very rapid growth and massive investment in transmission capacity. Eventually this caused supply to significantly exceed demand, resulting in much lower prices for transmission capacity. The excess capacity and additional competition led to either declining revenues or slowing revenue growth, which has led to consolidation within the industry, as many companies merged or left the industry.

The largest sector of the telecommunications industry continues to be made up of wired telecommunications carriers. Establishments in this sector mainly provide telephone service via wires and cables that connect customers' premises to central offices maintained by telecommunications companies. The central offices contain switching equipment that routes content to its final destination or to another switching center that determines the most efficient route for the content to take. While voice used to be the main type of data transmitted over the wires, wired telecommunications service now includes the transmission of all types of graphic, video, and electronic data mainly over the Internet.

These new services have been made possible through the use of digital technologies that provide much more efficient use of the telecommunications networks. One major technology breaks digital signals into packets during transmission. Networks of computerized switching equipment, called packet switched networks, route the packets. Packets may take separate paths to their destination and may share the paths with packets from other users. At the destination, the packets are reassembled, and the transmission is complete. Because packet switching considers alternate routes, and allows multiple transmissions to share the same route, it results in a more efficient use of telecommunications capacity as packets are routed along less congested routes.

The transmission of voice signals requires relatively small amounts of capacity on telecommunications networks. By contrast, the transmission of data, video, and graphics requires much higher capacity. This transmission capacity is referred to as bandwidth. As the demand increases for high-capacity transmissions—especially with the rising volume of Internet data—telecommunications companies have been expanding and upgrading their networks to increase the amount of available bandwidth.

One way wired carriers are expanding their bandwidth is by replacing copper wires with fiber optic cable. Fiber optic cable, which transmits light signals along glass strands, permits faster, higher capacity transmissions than traditional copper wire lines. In some areas, carriers are extending fiber optic cable to residential customers, enabling them to offer cable television, video-on demand, high-speed Internet, and conventional telephone communications over a single line. However, the high cost of extending fiber to homes has slowed deployment. In most areas, wired carriers are instead leveraging existing copper lines that connect most residential customers with a central office, to provide digital subscriber lines (DSL) Internet service. Technologies in development will further boost the speeds available through a DSL connection.

Wireless telecommunications carriers, many of which are subsidiaries of the wired carriers, transmit voice, graphics, data, and Internet access through the transmission of signals over networks of radio towers. The signal is transmitted through an antenna into the wire line network. Other wireless services include beeper and paging services. Because wireless devices require no wire line connection, they are popular with customers who need to communicate as they travel, residents of areas with inadequate wire line service, and those who simply desire the convenience of portable communications. Increasing numbers of consumers are choosing to replace their home landlines with wireless phones.

Wireless telecommunications carriers are deploying several new technologies to allow faster data transmission and better Internet access that should make them competitive with wire line carriers. One technology is called third generation (3G) wireless access. With this technology, wireless carriers plan to sell music, videos, and other exclusive content that can be downloaded and played on phones designed for 3G technology. Wireless carriers are developing the next generation of technologies that will surpass 3G with even faster data transmission. Another technology is called "fixed wireless service," which involves connecting the telephone and/or Internet wiring system in a home or business to an antenna, instead of a telephone line. The replacement of landlines with cellular service should become increasingly common because advances in wireless systems will provide data transmission speeds comparable to broadband landline systems.

Cable and other program distribution is another sector of the telecommunications industry. Establishments in this sector provide television and other services on a subscription or fee basis. These establishments do not include cable networks. (Information on cable networks is included in the statement on broadcasting, which appears elsewhere in the *Career Guide*.) Distributors of pay television services transmit programming through two basic types of systems. Cable systems transmit programs over fiber optic and coaxial cables. Direct broadcasting satellite (DBS) operators constitute a growing segment of the pay television industry. DBS operators transmit programming from orbiting satellites to customers' receivers, known as mini-dishes.

Establishments in the cable and other program distribution industry generate revenue through subscriptions, special service fees—primarily installation—and advertising sales. They also charge fees for services, such as the transmission of specialty pay-per-view or video-on-demand programs; these often are popular movies or sporting events.

Some cable and satellite systems facilitate the transmission of digital television signals. Digital signals consist of simple electronic code that can carry more information than conventional television signals. Digital transmission creates higher resolution television images and improved sound quality. It also allows the transmission of a variety of other information. Digital television also uses compression technology to expand the number of channels.

Changes in technology and regulation now allow cable television providers to compete directly with telephone companies. An important change has been the rapid increase in two-way communications capacity. Conventional pay television services provided communications only from the distributor to the customer. These services could not provide effective communications from the customer back to other points in the system, due to signal interference and the limited capacity of conventional cable systems. As cable operators implement new technologies to reduce signal interference and increase the capacity of their distribution systems by installing fiber optic cables and improved data compression, some pay television systems now offer two-way telecommunications services, such as video-on-demand and high-speed Internet access. Cable companies are also increasing their share of the telephone communications market both through their network of conventional phone lines in some areas and their growing ability to use high-speed Internet access to provide VoIP (voice over Internet protocol).

VoIP is sometimes called Internet telephony, because it uses the Internet to transmit phone calls. While conventional phone networks use packet switching to break up a call onto multiple shared lines between central offices, VoIP extends this process to the phone. A VoIP phone will break the conversation into digital packets and transmit those packets over a high-speed Internet connection. Cable companies are using the technology to offer phone services without building a conventional phone network. Wire line providers' high-speed Internet connections also can be used for VoIP and cellular phones are being developed that use VoIP to make calls using local wireless Internet connections. All of the major sectors of the telecommunication industry are or will increasingly use VoIP.

Resellers of telecommunications services are another sector of the telecommunications industry. These resellers lease transmission facilities, such as telephone lines or space on a satellite, from existing telecommunications networks, and then resell the service to other customers. Other sectors in the industry include message communications services, such as e-mail and facsimile services, satellite telecommunications, and operators of other communication services, ranging from radar stations to radio networks used by taxicab companies.

The central question is what strategy should network operators follow? Introduce the next generation services 3G at once or gradually improve the previous 2G networks? Of course, this decision depends on the position of the network operator. The majority of the European network operators followed an incremental strategy. They upgraded the 2G networks and prepared for the big leap forward by investing in UMTS later on. There are few operators that began from scratch i.e. do not have a previous generation network in operation. This does not imply that new entry will not be a successful strategy. In the next section, we will discuss this intriguing question in more detail, we close this section with some remarks.

First, how to manage the risk of cannibalisation if 3G is introduced at once? The argument is that if 3G is competitively priced all potential demand for high quality mobile data services is attracted towards 3G. This potential demand consists of newly created demand and customers switching from 2G and 2.5 towards 3G. To decrease the size of the potential customer base non-3G operators apply all kind of lock-in costs: from SIM locks, to high costs for terminating the current (2G or 2.5G) contract before its expiry date. If these lock-in effects are substantial a new pure-play 3G operator gets a less significant first-mover advantage.

Thereinafter, we are going to present a methodology which mainly refers to multinational companies that gather the big shares in the TLC industry and that gives them the opportunity to be more flexible and innovative in order to increase their market shares.

ECONOMICAL SIZES OF MAINER TLC COMPANIES IN GREECE

Before presenting the methodology, we will present some evidence (*source: ICAP data*) which show the progress and the huge amounts of profit in TLC industry. In *Table 1* we are able to see the economical sizes of the four Mainer TLC companies, which are also entered to the Stock Market.

In Table 1 we can also see a comparison between these four companies, which have the largest market shares in Greece. These enterprises need to increase or maintain their market shares and the solution is NSD. As we can see from Table 1, TLC is a very profitable industry and apart from technology, new services are the next most important key of success. The TLC organizations must invest in NSD in order to keep prospering. Now it is time to see what the methodology is.

THE TLC CASE METHODOLOGY

The TLC segment represents one of the largest industries world-wide. Triad technologies of the Internet namely packet switching, Internet protocol and World Wide Web have fundamentally transformed the TLC industry (Christensen et al., 2001; Sherif, 2002; Trebing and Estabrooks, 1995). TLC segment had steady increased revenue from 1996 until 2002, whereas bankruptcy, debt and fraud are the major characteristics until nowadays (Fransman, 2001; Economist, 2003). Spurred on by rapidly changing information technology, new customer needs, deregulation, and ever-increasing competitive threats, TLC institutions are responding with a plethora of new services. The critical question is what distinguishes the successful new services from the failures? Johne and Storey (1998) argue that it is important to investigate if the findings in the financial service sector are applicable to other service sectors. The first step of the research was to get a better understanding of the underlying factors and dimensions that describe NSD in the TLC industry. This research must have two parts: the micro (with case studies) study and the macro (theoretical embedded ness, comparing NSD researches and induction of key themes). In our case, the first step refers to macro study which was committed through exploratory research (see Figure1) by interviewing five TLC managers, who are knowledgeable of NSD. The interviews were very enlightening for the way they perceive new service process. The five managers agreed to several basic principles in order to have better and more indicating results in our research below, which are summarized as follows:

- Sustaining the region's growth and development;
- Strengthening an open multilateral trading system directed towards forming a regional trading bloc;
- Recognizing the region's diversity during informal consultations where dialogue and consensus have equal respect for all views;

Table 1. Comparison of mainer companies of telecommunication

		OTE AE		COSMOTE AE		FORTHNET AE		LAN-NET AE	
		thousands €	Change	thousands €	Change	thousands €	Change	thousands €	Change
SALES	1-6/07	1.318.400	-4,3%	825.956	5,6%	54.312	17,2%	28.808	4,8%
	1-6/06	1.377.300		782.436		46.346		27.491	
PROFITS (DAMAGE) PRE TAXES	1-6/07	366.500	32,8%	212.311	-6,3%	-21.686		-2.316	
	1-6/06	275.900		226.475		-6.910		-3.002	
TOTAL OF ASSET	1-6/07	6.946.000	2,1%	3.665.489	-12,4%	228.116	-3,5%	159.567	2,1%
	31/12/06	6.801.400		4.185.773		236.271		156.315	
NET CONDITION	1-6/07	3.295.600	1,4%	793.936	-10,9%	135.835	-10,3%	66.292	-3,4%
	31/12/06	3.249.700		891.477		151.370		68.607	
LONG-TERM OBLIGATIONS	1-6/07	2.191.900	-0,5%	2.539.780	0,2%	6.677	47,3%	23.516	7,9%
	31/12/06	2.202.900		2.535.361		4.533		21.800	
SHORT-TERM BANKING OBLIGATIONS	1-6/07	17.500	8,7%	0	-100,0%	30.909	-9,1%	13.089	37,0%
	31/12/06	16.100		449.000		34.000		9.551	
TOTAL OBLIGATIONS	1-6/07	3.650.400	2,8%	2.871.553	-12,8%	92.281	8,7%	93.275	6,3%
	31/12/06	3.551.700		3.294.296		84.901		87.708	
MARGIN OF MIXED PROFIT	1-6/07	--		31,6%		*		39,5%	
	1-6/06	--		30,6%		20,3%		55,2%	
MARGIN OF NET PROFIT	1-6/07	27,8%		25,7%		*		*	
	1-6/06	20,0%		28,9%		*		*	
FOREIGNER/ PROPER FUNDS	1-6/07	1,1		3,6		0,7		1,4	
	31/12/06	1,1		3,7		0,6		1,3	

* Negative Indicator

- Focusing on economic matters rather than politics or security to advance common interests and foster constructive interdependence by encouraging the flow of goods, services, capital and technology;
- Complementing and drawing on existing regional organizations, and
- Assessing participation on the basis of economic linkages with the regions, extending participation by consensus.

As regards the micro study, it can be conducted in the future with an explanatory frame work after having taken the conceptual model from macro, and confirm the critical dimensions. Then the final results will indicate the relevance percentage between the service industries. Our cooperation with the TLC managers was very helpful, because without them it would have been impossible to compose the questionnaire.

RESULTS OF THE EXPLORATORY RESEARCH

The exploratory study in the TLC study showed that most NSD are improvements and revisions of existing services but there are also and many new ones'. TLC managers argued that having a mixture of the aforementioned sorts of services reflects a healthy and well-organized firm. That statement reflects that TLC managers are not so conservative in their NSD approaches and that they take more risk than managers in other industries. In that decision, the advent of new technologies-both hardware and software- plays an important role as they say. It emerged from the interviews that the development of "totally" new services comes from the sector of communications networks where technology "moves" so fast that allows the development of new service process. In contrary, the supply and demand sector tries to gain new clients by improving existing services like new packages of subscription. The interviews showed that commitment and the motivation of the staff towards the new service project, input from employees, training of staff, internal marketing and front-line expertise were significantly associated with the performance of new services. The contribution of salespeople in NSD efforts is very crucial. Financial measures, like profit and total sales are used as a primary evaluation of new services. Further, customer satisfaction and salespeople feedback are very important measures of success in the TLC sector.

CONCEPTUAL MODEL

There is no agreement in the NPD and NSD literature over the way in which success should be measured (Craig and Hart, 1992).Unfortunately, local policy makers tend to ignore telecommunications. As Graham and Marvin (1996, p 51) have pointed out, it is so bad that: *"many city planners and managers do not even know what the telecommunications infrastructure is in their cities; very few have the power, influence, or conceptual tools to reshape it so as to have desired impacts."* Moss (1987, p 535) states also that:

The telecommunications infrastructure—which includes the wires, ducts and channels that carry voice, data, and video signals—remains a mystery to most cities. In part, this is due to the fact that key components of the telecommunications infrastructure, such as underground cables and rooftop microwave transmitters, are not visible to the public. Unlike airports and garbage disposal plants, telecommunications facilities are not known for their negative side effects, and until recently, have not been the source of public disputes or controversy.

If there is any chance to make telecommunications and information technologies more central and useful to community life, we have to find a way to make them more vital parts of the existing local public policy agenda. At least, we must start thinking about the information infrastructure of local communities and sub-state regions in the same ways they have viewed the more conventional elements of their infrastructure—both hard and soft.

That is, they must begin to see the information technology and telecommunications capacities of communities and regions as key contributors to their vitality and essential to obtaining and sustaining the desirable qualities of life pursued within the community.

Figure 1. Overview of the research process

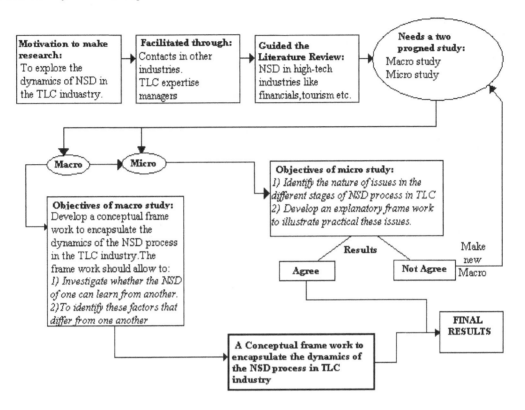

The evaluation of new services and products are most frequently based on financial measures of performance (Montoya-Weiss and Calantone, 1994; Griffin and Page, 1993). Nevertheless, using only financial measures is too limited, because it neglects several aspects of benefits of the company (Storey and Easingwood, 1999). The findings of success studies in NPD and NSD showed that success on one specific dimension of performance does not necessarily mean success on the other performance dimension (de Brentani, 1991). Therefore, this conceptual model includes 18 dimensions, including financial, customer satisfaction and other benefit aspects (see Figure 2). In relation to success factors, the model includes four product-related factors, *product advantage, technical quality, functional quality* and *innovative technology*. The importance of *product advantage* (Easingwood and Storey, 1991; 1993; Storey and Easingwood, 1993; 1996; 1998; Edgett, 1994; Edgett and Parkinson, 1994; Cooper *et al.*, 1994; de Brentani, 1991; 1993; Cooper and de Brentani, 1991; de Brentani and Cooper, 1992; Atuahene-Gima, 1996; de Brentani and Ragot, 1996), *technical quality* (Easingwood and Storey, 1991; 1993; Storey and Easingwood, 1993; 1996; 1998; Cooper *et al.*, 1994; de Brentani, 1991; 1993; Cooper and de Brentani, 1991; de Brentani and Cooper, 1992), *functional quality* (Edgett and Parkinson, 1994; Cooper *et al.*, 1994; de Brentani, 1989; 1991; 1993; Cooper and de Brentani, 1991; de Brentani and Cooper, 1992; Storey and Easingwood, 1993; 1996; 1998; de Brentani and Ragot, 1996; Easingwood and Storey, 1991; 1993) and *innovative technology* (Cooper *et al.*, 1994; Easingwood and Storey, 1991; Storey and Easingwood, 1993) have been recognised in several NSD studies.

Market features of the conceptual model are *market synergy, market attractiveness* and *competition*. Several empirical studies have outlined the importance of *market synergy* (Edgett, 1994; Edgett and Parkinson, 1994; de Brentani, 1991; 1993; Cooper and de Brentani, 1991; de Brentani and Cooper, 1992; Storey and Easingwood, 1996), *market attractiveness* (Cooper and de Brentani, 1991; de Brentani, 1991; de Brentani and Ragot, 1996; Edgett and Parkinson, 1994) and to a lower degree *competition* (Cooper and de Brentani, 1991; de Brentani and Cooper, 1992).

451

Figure 2. Overview of the conceptual model

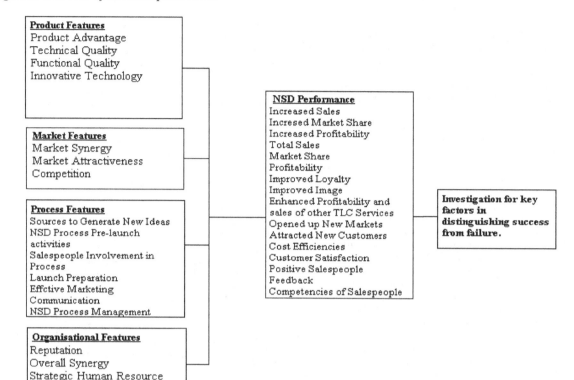

The process dimension includes six aspects: *sources that generate new ideas, pre-launch activities, salespeople involvement in the new service development process, launch preparation, effective marketing communication* and *NSD process management.* The importance of *pre-launch activities* of the development process has been stressed in NSD studies (Edgett, 1994; Edgett and Parkinson, 1994; Cooper *et al.*, 1994; de Brentani, 1991; 1993; Cooper and de Brentani, 1991; de Brentani and Cooper, 1992; Storey and Easingwood, 1996). Studies concerning the development process of new services suggested the *involvement of employees* (for example salespeople) in several development stages (Easingwood, 1986; Bowers, 1989; Scheuing and Johnson, 1989; de Brentani, 1989). The importance of launch preparation has been recognised in all NSD success studies on the project level (e.g. de Brentani, 1991). *Effective marketing communication* (Easingwood and Storey, 1991; 1993; Storey and Easingwood, 1993; 1996; Edgett, 1994; Edgett and Parkinson, 1994; Cooper *et al.*, 1994) and *NSD process management* (including *strategic finance management* over the projects) (Kitsios, 2005; Atuahene-Gima, 1996; de Brentani and Ragot, 1996; Edgett, 1994; de Brentani, 1991) has been linked to NSD success.

Reputation, overall synergy, strategic human resource management, selective staffing, training of salespeople, behaviour based evaluation, empowerment and *formalisation* represent the organisational dimension of the conceptual model. Several empirical studies showed that *reputation* (de Brentani, 1989; Storey and Easingwood, 1998) and *overall synergy* (Easingwood and Storey, 1991; 1993; Storey and Easingwood, 1993; 1996; Cooper *et*

Figure 3. Main categories of strategies for success

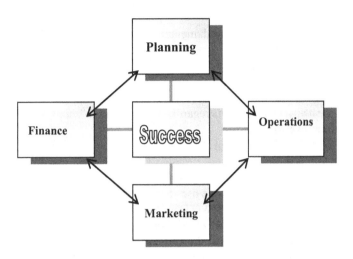

al., 1994; de Brentani, 1991; 1993; Cooper and de Brentani, 1991; de Brentani and Cooper, 1992; de Brentani and Ragot, 1996) have influence on the performance of NSD.

Most importantly service products include close interaction with customers, and this is the distinguishing aspect of service offerings (Johne and Storey, 1998). Therefore, service firms have to develop a service product, but also an appropriate nature for interaction with customers (Johne and Storey, 1998). The human element in services means that service quality heavily depends on human resource strategies (Zeithaml and Bitner, 2000). The attitudes and behaviours of service employees can significantly influence customers' perception of the service, and therefore, service organisations must find ways by which they can effectively manage their service employees attitudes and behaviours so that they deliver high quality service (Hartline *et al.*, 2000).

Organisational researchers have stressed that human resource planning is linked to strategic business planning (Schuler and Jackson, 1987) and organisations should view employees as a strategic resource (Huselid *et al.*, 1997), which has become known as *strategic human resource management*. A customer-oriented firm will in general produce better service quality and create more satisfied customers (Kelley, 1992). However, in service firms, employees who have customer contact are responsible for translating a customer-oriented strategy into service quality, because customers often judge a firm largely on the service received from front-line employees (Johne and Storey, 1998). Therefore, it is important to understand how managers can encourage front-line employees to perform a customer oriented strategy. Hartline *et al.* (2000) suggests three aspects that management can control, in order to support a customer-oriented strategy: *formalisation, empowerment and behaviour-based evaluation*.

However, some evidence suggests that there is considerable inertia in service organizations. Changes are needed in structures and strategy to facilitate new service development (Scheuing and Johnson, 1989).

THE FOUR PRIMARY DOMAINS OF SERVICE PROVIDER STRATEGIES

Figure 3 depicts the four primary categories of service provider (TLC companies) strategies. Within these categories there exist a lot of potential differentiation paths (many of these are shown in Figure 2) that are available to the service provider, in order to succeed. For each path, even before an initial market entry, and before each business planning development cycle, it is very important for TLC service providers to measure their current capabilities, the demands of the market, and the gap between them.

The strategic planning process within each of these domains should include at least the following actions so as to be well-taken:

- A statement of the enterprise's vision and fundamental values as it relates to the category of finance, planning, operations or marketing strategy.
- Measurement of the service provider's existing capabilities and estimation of these that is willing to reach.
- A critical assessment of the strengths and weaknesses relative to competitors.
- An assessment of the most attractive markets regarding their "growth", competitive dynamics and also the service provider's competitive strengths.
- A final estimation of the future development and direction of the selected markets in the previous step.

Strategic planning is far more accessible and effective when the process that is referred previously, includes tools like SWOT and PEST analysis. When someone uses SWOT analysis, he takes as a result the evaluation of strengths, weaknesses, opportunities and threats (SWOT) and the consideration of the political, economic, social and technological factors (PEST) that are valuable to develop the strategic overview. Using tools for strategic planning is effective, but planners need to balance the framework of a particular tool against the need of the process to be as much creative as it is possible. There are many tools that enable innovation, but some primarily increase operational efficiency. A strategic planning tool is most advantageous when it identifies three potential types of improvements, and which are: *Getting rid of unnecessary activities; Doing the existing activities more effectively; Finally identifying future opportunities that can not be* predicted *in everyday operations*. The truth is that strategic planning, tools and innovation in services can and will make the difference between success and failure in TLC industry.

Financial Strategies

Financial strategies are the most common between the four categories but the last years have also become very common in the TLC industry due to the fact that companies can gain competitive advantage and differentiation. The aim of these strategies is to maximize growth and profitability. Financial strategy demands considerable attention in order to be successful. Competitive markets will require a reassessment of financial goals and the development of new skills in management and differentiation. The paths to differentiation include business expansion, the use of innovative funding strategies, and cost leadership.

The options for business expansion include vertical or horizontal integration, mergers or start-ups to create new scale or scope of business, territorial expansion, or outside investment for the sake of diversification in a cyclical industry like TLC. The rapid pace of industry consolidation demonstrates what service providers believe and that is the benefits of huge scale, which offset the management and integration challenges that come. Investors demand growth and the criteria for those people are the success of a company's expansion mainly on its own growth and partly on its relative growth while the industry consolidates around them.

Funding strategies have changed as much as any other aspect of the deregulated market, but they still can be barely visible in favour of more attractive business processes. Nevertheless, the provider that creates innovative funding and financial management can outpace the provider with higher gross margins and casual fiscal practices.

Moreover, managing the revenue side of the income statement is popular for many reasons, especially in a booming economy, but some TLC service providers will succeed through their management of the cost side of the statement. Especially in a commodity marketplace, keeping costs as low as possible is a competitive advantage against the rest. The way to win a price war is to avoid having profit casualties.

Eventually each differentiation path combines both a business process and a plan of action. For example, the business modelling process assesses the market opportunities and the skills residing in or available to the TLC provider and develops a sustainable value proposition on which to define the business. The plan of action contains the results of the business process. In fact the main part of the modelling process is to decide which of the differentiation paths will have the priority for the business model, due to the fact that resources for R&D are always limited. Thus reducing the emphasis on selected differentiation paths without destroying the resulting business model is one of the challenges of the process.

Planning Strategies

The planning strategy encompasses a process where a set of decisions must be taken by the TLC provider so as to point out the probable way of success for the business. The process includes the business goals, investor and stakeholder requirements, human resources issues within the enterprise and also the environment surrounding the enterprise.

The pre-referred function includes business modelling, an objective assessment of core competencies, and organizational strategies. These differentiation paths are the most important decisions that a TLC service provider must make before venturing into a business or before transforming into a competitive enterprise. The decisions in this phase not only affect the following choices but are likely to require significant changes among management and employees. Business modelling involves the development of a corresponding concept. A proper business concept will attract those customers that seek the characteristics in which the TLC service provider shows strength. On the other hand, the concept must eliminate these services where the provider is weak and exclude those customers, who seek such characteristics.

When we talk about competencies, we mean the process in which the TLC service provider firmly reinforces its competitive advantages towards its opponents in the marketplace. This process needs a balance of resources because competencies demand investing in strategic differentiators requiring excellence, outsourcing or shaving down functions that require only adequacy, and eliminating those functions that are not profitable in the targeted markets.

In addition, organizational strategies refer to the enabling techniques of a company to ensure that it uses its resources with the most effective way in order to meet the organization's objectives. A TLC service provider can differentiate its services through its effective business processes, its efficient organizational structure, or its maximization of in-house talent.

Operational Strategies

Operations constitute, for a long time, a workhorse of the TLC services and nowadays operational excellence is becoming noteworthy as a distinct competitive strategy. Customer's lack of tolerance for much variation in the quality of TLC services creates a marketplace in which all service providers are trying to be good performers. If someone wants to achieve superior quality is quite difficult. What enterprises need, is a loyal customer base and premium prices. The differentiation paths of customer service, best in class performance and technology management represent opportunities within the operations domain.

Many TLC service providers have stated their missions to differentiate based on customer service. This is an obvious path to differentiation for incumbent local providers, because they are well aware that commodity markets compete through low cost. Most incumbents do not yet support the cost profiles to position themselves as the low-cost providers in their territories, so they are seeking opportunities to command higher prices for superior service. Incumbents also appear to believe that their reputations and infrastructures create a branding opportunity, and this is born out by customer survey data.

Many incumbent TLC service providers aspire to best in class performance because it melds well with their traditional corporate values. New entrants also view best in class performance as a potential differentiator in a crowded marketplace. This path to differentiators has many challenges, especially in the area of cost. While performance is undoubtedly important to customers, the standard is already too high and as a result prominence in the field is not easy. Furthermore, the areas, in which best of class performance is noticeable, generally require significant investment to participate competitively.

Another way to differentiate through operations is to provide network services of perceptible superiority, and several TLC service providers are already mobilizing to take this approach. To accomplish this, service providers will need to be particularly competent at technology management. Technology management can include proprietary innovations, but it can also differentiate through exceptional supplier management.

Marketing Strategies

Marketing is one of the most important success factors and because of that enterprises realise the necessity of differentiation with other competitors. The paths of this marketing differentiation address to competitive parity, distribution strategies, and pricing. Marketing is the weakest capability of many incumbent providers and has opened lately a gateway for new entrants to gain market share. The conventional marketing mix contains the elements of product, packaging, price, and distribution. In an industry like TLC, where both the product and the packaging continue to be relative commodities, the distribution strategy and the pricing offer the best potential for differentiation and success. These practices comprise a partial innovation, which also leads to success if it is well used.

Skills in managing competitive parity enable TLC service providers to maintain an acceptable level of profit and minimize the loss in customers, in an industry characterized by intense price competition and accelerating speed to market.

Competitive parity skills notify the TLC service providers when to take a significant market initiative. Sometimes it is appropriate to lead in the marketplace, and sometimes a competitor's action requires a competitive response. As TLC usage has proven to be elastic, lower prices result in more minutes of customer usage. Because customers are price-sensitive, a customer would be inclined to switch carriers if a matching decrease was not forthcoming from its current service provider.

Distribution strategies enable customers to locate the services they seek and enable TLC service providers to locate and serve customers. Distribution channels begin at the supplier, traverse the TLC provider, and continue outward through in-house sales channels, agents, resellers, brokers and retailers. The value of a given distribution channel depends on a variety of factors. These include the profitability of the participants within the channel, the proper choice to connect with the targeted segment, and the customer's access to product information and alternative channels.

Pricing innovation is essential in the TLC services market. First, the services are near commodities, making customers very price-sensitive. Second, even in view of an explosive demand, the short-term threat of overcapacity is real, putting downward pressure on prices. Technology products tend to fall in price, and rising usage is crucial to any service provider whose investors need to see continual revenue growth. Last, new TLC service providers need to find profitable pricing structures to overcome historical pricing anomalies, such as below-cost services, complex pricing equations, and settlements between cooperating providers.

CONCLUSION

For some years, a number of social, technological and economic trends have produced an environment which promotes the demand and distribution of mobile communication services. This causes a dramatic change of the mobile communications value chain. New actors (e.g. e-commerce firms, Internet portal providers) and new services (e.g. m-commerce, portal services) enlarge the value chain in both ways, functionally and institutionally. Mobile network operators can gain advantages out of the changed economic environment, through occupying the gatekeeper role. While their current revenue base, the transmission service, will shrink, they are well positioned to extend their revenue base to other segments of the value chain (e.g. advertising, revenue sharing with content providers). Activities like the grouping of different services, the access design via portals, the mediation of contents, pricing as well as billing for the different suppliers from other lines of business will be of essential importance for mobile network operators. Thus, based on their gatekeeper role, they have competitive advantages over other players (e.g. content provider like banks) so that they most likely will succeed.

Increasing global competition, advances in technology and dynamic markets obligates TLC and other services, to focus more on new services as both offensive and defensive weapons: new services to maintain the current portfolio competitive and new services to gain competitive advantage and exploit new market opportunities. NSD has not been widely researched (Martin and Horne, 1993) so there exists a need for further research in this field (Johne and Storey, 1998). In the last four years very few academic studies have concentrated on this area (e.g. Storey and Easingwood, 1998), which means that the knowledge of NSD has not advanced very far. Many firms have found that new service success does not come easily.

Telecommunications service is generally developed following several development stages: idea generation for new services, service development, service delivery, and life cycle management. For each development stage, a knowledge management system to check the likely success factors, learn from the specific cases but do not base on them exclusively, and propose possible risk management ideas would improve the quality of development process. Second, success cases can be incorporated and analyzed in addition to failure cases. The ultimate objective of the NSD process would be to include more success factors and eliminate failure factors in advance. Therefore, a study on the factors separating service success and failure would provide improve guidelines for the NSD process.

TLC organisations have to continuously develop new services in order to be successful and the results of this empirical research of the success factors in NSD and further investigations will be of potential value to TLC managers, as it will enable them to focus on NSD more strategically and professionally.

REFERENCES

Abhishek Gupta, Kulwant, Palie Smart, *"New product development in the pharmaceutical and telecommunication industries: A comparative study"* (2007)

Ottenbacher, M.,*"New service development in the hospitality industry: An exploratory study"*

Atuahene-Gima, K., *"Differential of factors affecting innovation performance in manufacturing and services firms in Australia"*. *Journal of Product Innovation Management* 13, (1996):35-52.

Bowers, M.R. "Developing new services: Improving the process makes it better." *Journal of Services Marketing* 3, no.1, (1989):15-20.

Cooper, R.G., & de Brentani, U. "New industrial services: What distinguishes the winners." *Journal of Product Innovation Management* 8, (1991).75-90.

Cooper, R.G., Easingwood, C.J., Edgett, S., Kleinschmidt, E.J., & Storey, C. "What distinguishes the top performing new products in financial services." *Journal of Product Innovation Management* 11, (1994):281-299.

Craig, A. & Hart, S. "Where to now in new product development research?" *European Journal of Marketing* 26, no.11, (1992):3-46.

de Brentani, U. "Success and failure in new industrial services." *Journal of Product Innovation Management* 6, (1989):239-258.

de Brentani, U. "Success factors in developing new business services." *European Journal of Marketing* 25, no.2, (1991):33-59.

de Brentani, U. "The new product process in financial services: Strategy for success." *International Journal of Bank Marketing* 11, no.3, (1993):15-22.

de Brentani, U. "An empirical analysis of the effect of product innovativeness on success and failure of new industrial services." Conference Proceedings: *ANZMAC 1999, University of New South Wales, Sydney, November/December (1999).*

de Brentani, U. & Cooper, R.G. "Developing successful new financial services for businesses." *Industrial Marketing Management* 21, no.3, (1992):231-242.

de Brentani, U. & Ragot, E. "Developing new business-to-business professional services: What factors impact performance." *Industrial Marketing Management* 25, (1996).517-530.

Dehoga (German Hotel and Restaurant Association). Online. Accessed 14.April 2000. http://www.dehoga. de/daten.

Easingwood, C.J. "New product development for service companies." *Journal of Product Innovation Management* 3, no.4 (1986):264-275.

Easingwood, C.J. & Storey, C. "Marketplace success factors for new financial services." *Journal of Services Marketing* 7, no.1, (1993).41-54.

Easingwood, C.J. & Storey, C. "Success factors for new consumer financial services." *International Journal of Bank Marketing* 9, no.1, (1991):3-10.

Edgett, S. "The traits of successful new service development." *Journal of Services Marketing* 8, no.3, (1994):40-49.

Edgett, S. & Parkinson, S. "The development of new financial services: Identifying determinants of success and failure." *International Journal of Service* 5, no.4, (1994):24-38.

Griffin, A. & Page, A.L. "An interim report on measuring product development success and failure." *Journal of Product Innovation Management* 10, (1993):291-308.

Griffin, A. "PDMA research on new product development practices: updating trends and benchmarking best practices." *Journal of Product Innovation Management* 14, no.6, (1997):429-458.

Hartline, M.D., Maxham J.G. & McKee, D.O. "Corridors of influence in the dissemination of customer-oriented strategy to customer contact employees." *Journal of Marketing* 64, (2000):35-50.

Huselid, M.A., Jackson, S.E., & Schuler, R.J. "Technical and strategic HRM effectiveness as determinants of firm performance." *Academy of Management Journal* 40, no.1, (1997):171-188.

Ioannou, K., E.Dimitriadou, A.Ioannou, I.Panoutsopoulos, A.Garmpis and S. Kotsopoulos, "Efficient Channel Assignment Technique providing Priority to Emergency Calls in Wireless Cellular Security Networks, WSEAS Transactions on Communications, Issue 1, Volume 5, January 2006, pp 84-91

Ioannou, K., Panoutsopoulos, I., Koubias S., and S. Kotsopoulos, "A new Dynamic Channel Management Scheme to increase the performance index of Cellular Networks", Electronics Letters, 10th June 2004, Vol.40, No 12, pp 744-746

Ioannou, K., I.Panoutsopoulos and S.Kotsopoulos, "Optimizing the QoS of Ultra High and High Speed Moving Terminals in Satellite-aided cellular networks", Wireless Personal Communications, Volume 39, Number 3, November 2006, pp307-319"

Johne, A. & Storey, C. "New service development: a review of literature and annotated bibliography." European Journal of Marketing 32, (1998):184-251.

Kitsios, F. and Zopounidis, C., (2007), "Services marketing in the hospitality economy: An exploratory study", The Southeuropean Review of Business Finance & Accounting, Vol. 5, No.1

Kitsios, F., "Services marketing in the hospitality economy: An exploratory study", 98th EAAE seminar, Marketing Dynamics within the Global Trading System: New Perspectives, Chania, Crete, Greece, 29 June – 02 July (2006)

Kitsios, F., Skiadas C., "Some Critical Issues Concerning Technological Change", 1st International Conference in Management of Change, Iasi, Romania, October (2001)

Kitsios, F., *"Innovation Management in New Service Development"*, *PhD dissertation, Technical University of Crete* (2005)

Kelley, S.W. "Developing customer orientation among service employees." *Journal of the Academy of Marketing Science* 20, (1992):27-36.

Kotler, P., Bowen, J. & Makens, J. *Marketing for Hospitality and Tourism.* 2nd ed. Upper Saddle River: Prentice Hall, Inc., 1999.

Martin, C. R. & Horne, D.A. "Services innovation: successful versus unsuccessful firms." *International Journal of Service Industry Management* 6, no.4, (1993):48-64.

Montoya-Weiss, M.M. & Calantone, R. "Determinants of new product performance: a review and meta-analysis." *Journal of Product Innovation Management* 11, (1994):397-417.

Scheuing, E.E. & Johnson, E.M. "A proposed model for new service development." *The Journal of Services Marketing* 3, no.2, (1989):25-34.

Schuler, R.S. & Jackson, S.E. "Linking competitive strategy with human resource management practices." *Academy of Management Executive* 1, no.3, (1987):207-219.

Storey, C. & Easingwood, C.J. "The impact of the new product development project on the success of financial services." *The Service Industries Journal* 13, no.3, (1993):40-54.

Storey; C. & Easingwood, C.J "Determinants of new product performance: a study in the financial service sector." *International Journal of Service Industry Management* 7, no.1, (1996).32-55.

Storey, C. & Easingwood, C.J. "The augmented service offering: a conceptualisation and study of its impact in new service success." *Journal of Product Innovation Management* 15, (1998):335-351.

Storey, C. & Easingwood, C.J. "Types of new product performance: evidence from the consumer financial services sector." *Journal of Business Research* 46, (1999):193- 203.

Strouce, Karen G. *"Strategies for success in the new telecommunications marketplace"*(2001),pp.115-125

Zeithaml, V.A. & Bitner, M.J. *Service marketing: Integrating customer focus across the firm.* Boston: McGraw-Hill Companies, 2000.Hong D. and Rappaport S.S.: "Traffic model and performance analysis for cellular mobile radio telephone systems with prioritized and non prioritized handover procedures" IEEE Trans. on Vehicular Technology, vol. VT-35, pp.77-91, 1985.

KEY TERMS

Critical Success Factors: Success factors, determinants of success

Service Innovation Management: New service development (NSD), innovation management in the service sector, new product development in the service sector, services management

Chapter XXI
The Expansion of E-Marketplace to M-Marketplace by Integrating Mobility and Auctions in a Location-Sensitive Environment:
Application in Procurement of Logistics Services

D. M. Emiris
University of Piraeus, Greece

C. A. Marentakis
University of Piraeus, Greece

ABSTRACT

Auctioning over Wireless Networks, constitutes an attractive emerging class for m-commerce applications and formulates a procurement negotiation tool supporting the announcement and execution of geographically focused auctions. This is feasible by using the Location-Based Services (LBS), which resulted from the unification of automatic position sensing (GPS) and wireless connectivity. The present article aims to analyse and match the properties of heterogeneous wireless networks (mobile, GPS) and to set a framework for the development of Reverse M-Auction based Marketplaces operating in a location sensitive context with application in freight services procurement. A location-sensitive, reverse, M-auction application in the freight transport market where potential suppliers (carriers) are able to place bids for Less-Than-Truckload (LTL) shipments or during empty trips while on the move aiming to gain from economies of scope, is the application examined in this chapter.

Copyright © 2009, IGI Global, distributing in print or electronic forms without written permission of IGI Global is prohibited.

INTRODUCTION

A decade ago companies used the Internet as dot com's to advertise their products. Later, by year 2000 many such companies used the connectivity properties of Internet to form e-Marketplaces not only supporting but also promoting business transactions over it, setting the basics for the transition to the e-economy. Recent developments in mobile communications formed a new business environment, independent of time and place, allowing the transition to m-Marketplaces or to m-economy. An e-Marketplace magnifies the market size and allows participants to apply revenue management techniques to allocate perishable items or services by retrieving proper information about market demand. Operation of enterprises in the "new economy" requires not only outsourcing activities but also the development of networks and collaborations and finally the creation of holonic enterprises where different enterprises participate in a self-motivated network, acting completed and organically and providing differentiated possibilities.

Bailey and Bakos (1997) predicted that electronic markets will rapidly increase as new public and private standards are established for information exchange and electronic commerce over the Internet. Also, during 1998, the Business Week magazine published an article entitled "Good-bye to fixed pricing?" (Cortese and Stepanek, 1998) focusing on the application of Internet in dynamic pricing via electronic auctions. An Internet-conducted auction has many properties: it breaks the limitations of time and space, has lower costs and increased overall efficiency. Typically an E-Marketplace enables the development and improvement of relationships between stakeholders, mostly those between sellers and buyers. The role of intermediaries (like store owners, wholesalers, physical infrastructure providers etc.) was critical in traditional (physical) markets. Many researchers argue that the role of intermediaries in e-Marketplaces will weaken and the value of the services they provide will decline. Examining some organizational issues of e-Marketplaces one could easily realize that this is not true yet; while some roles are diminished, new types of intermediaries, new services and of course new business opportunities will emerge. Actually, traditional forms and roles of intermediaries are transformed to new ones providing more non-physical value-added services.

Procurement via manual procedures was a time-consuming business function with complex transactions showing many errors concerning evaluation, ordering, pricing and payments. Transition to e-procurement allowed companies to speed-up the process, to eliminate errors and to support activities such as advertising tenders, electronic submission of orders, electronic ordering, sourcing via 3rd parties, electronic e-mailing, contract management, research into markets, integration between procurement, financial and inventory information systems, etc. (Hawking et al., 2004). E-Marketplaces are currently an ideal landscape for business transactions between companies and 3rd Party Logistics (3PL) service providers. The latter provide services related to the supply chain of the purchaser such as freight transport, warehousing, packaging, and provision of services like vehicle routing and fleet management, custom services and combinations of them.

Actually m-commerce is more than simply a mobile Internet or a desktop replacement. The true value of m-commerce can be realized when understanding the value of mobility in transactions between companies and/or consumers. Mobile Commerce is a continuously growing research discipline since 2000. The most recent literature review has been published by Ngai and Gunasekaran (2007). Barnes (2002) also describes and analyzes the m-commerce value chain consisting of processes related to content management and infrastructure/services. Obviously m-commerce provides business opportunities for a number of players as noticed by Buellingen and Woerter (2004). They also state that critical success factor for m-commerce operating in the Universal Mobile Telecommunications Systems (UMTS) are the transmission rate, reliability, user friendliness and interface between user and engine.

The purpose of the present article is to propose an e-auction marketplace for freight transport services trading and to expand so as to gain advantage of spatial attributes by deploying location-sensitive information retrieval and processing technology. The proposed marketplace will support both forward and reverse auction formats where the auction initiators are the carrier and shipper respectively. The proposed business model utilize wireless positioning in a two-directional way: (a) to automatically locate current users location and select which of them may act as potential bidders and (b) to identify which LBS are important for each user according to carriers' trucks current location, direction and speed. Operationally, it is designed to support all three mobility dimensions as described by Kakihara and Sørensen (2002), namely: (i) Spatiality (Where), (ii) Temporality (When), and (iii) Contextuality (What way, circumstance (e.g. available capacity), towards which actor(s)).

The operation of the proposed marketplace is based on the integration of Internet communication (wired), mobile communication (wireless) and GPS (satellite) networks. Finally, the present paper extends the marketplace proposed in Emiris et al., (2007) in a way to support: (i) initiation of trade either by carriers or by shippers, (ii) value-added spatial services (guide-me, find-me, get-together), and (iii) co-operation of small carriers.

This paper is organised as follows. In Section 2 a brief overview on auctions, auction-based electronic marketplaces and mobile trading is presented. Section 3 describes auctions and examines the case of auction-based electronic marketplaces by presenting their core system architecture. Section 4 focuses on the trading of logistics services via e-marketplaces and modifies the proposed architecture for this purpose. Section 5 extends the architecture for the formation of a mobile marketplace while Section 6 proposes an application for the freight transport case addressing important wireless-communication issues and applying location-sensing technologies. In Section 7 the main benefits of this survey are highlighted and further research guidelines are enumerated.

LITERATURE REVIEW

Auction theory is a generalized microeconomic approach to study the price formation problem. It models the strategic behaviour of auction participants facing information asymmetries. William Vickrey (1961) in his nobel-prize awarded seminal paper on auction theory, first studied questions concerning the bidding strategy and auction outcomes for different types of auctions. Extensive reviews on auction theory have been provided by Milgrom and Weber (1982), McAfee and McMillan (1987), Milgrom (1989), Feldman and Mehra (1993) and Wolfstetter (1996). An extensive review of early and recent research literature on auctions has been provided by Klemperer (1999).

Based on specific parameters related to trading items, participants and auction mechanism, a number of different auction formats may be developed. Depending on the number of trading items the auction may be characterized as a single-unit or multi-unit. A multi-unit auction where items are sold in bundles that impose positive complementarities is characterized as a combinatorial auction. Additionally depending on the way the available set of items is traded, the auction is distinguished as a simultaneous or a sequential. When the bid evaluation criterion is not only the price but also a set of item-related attributes, then the auction is characterized as multi-attribute. Auctions may also be distinguished between single-side and double-side auctions depending on the number of initiators and bidders simultaneously participating. Another parameter relates to the bid visibility to participants. When bids are visible to all participants, then the auction is characterized as an open (or outcry), otherwise is characterized as a sealed-bid auction. Finally depending on the auction progress and awarding price the auction evolves as an English or Dutch auction for the open case and as a k-th price for the sealed-bid case respectively where k denotes the awarding price rank. Specific combinations of visibility, progress and awarding price parameters are used for the development of the fundamental auction types:

- **English auctions:** The price offered is raised successively until only one bidder remains; this bidder is the winner and is awarded the object of the auction at the final price. It is by far the most common type.
- **Dutch auctions:** The auctioneer announces the highest desirable price; then the price decreases continuously or in discrete intervals until a bidder announces his willingness to pay the current price. This bidder is the winner and is awarded the object of the auction at the final price.
- **k-th price sealed bid auctions:** Each bidder submits independently a single sealed bid. The bidder that submitted the highest bid is awarded the object of the auction at the price corresponding to the k-th ranked bid. The case where k=1, is most commonly referred as first-price sealed-bid auction and is widely used in business procurement. The case where k=2, is most commonly referred as second-price sealed-bid auction or Vickrey auction.

Each basic auction type has specific properties while choosing a format is an empirical matter (Cramton, 1998) in terms of efficiency, revenue maximization, privacy, implementation, asymmetries levelling, risk aversion and collusion avoidance. In some cases it is useful to combine properties of two or more auction types, developing hybrid types. A brief overview of various simple and complex auction formats used in e-Marketplaces has been given by Anandalingam et al., (2005). Operationally the scope of the marketplace is to support all aspects of the trading process including participants' access, coordination of demand and supply, information exchange, price determination, allocation and payments. According to its scope an e-Marketplace may be managed by a seller or a buyer, and it may be horizontal, vertical or independent.

An electronic marketplace or electronic market system (from now on e-Marketplace) is an institution that allows the participating market members to exchange information about prices and offerings. An e-Marketplace is the basis for forming virtual markets via the development of virtual enterprises – temporary organizations of companies that come together to share costs and skills and to address temporal business opportunities that they could not undertake individually via a process of creation, operation, evolution and dissolution (Gou et al., 2003). An e-Marketplace generates value by lowering transaction costs, improving marketing functions, optimizing prices, strengthening customer relationships, increasing IT effectiveness and facilitating the backoffice. Stockdale and Standing (2004) summarize the benefits from the participation in e-Marketplaces in: magnification of markets range, potential for partnerships, administration and communication flexibility, convenience (24/7), information diffusion organizing, customer service improvement, information update, lower transaction costs, differentiation and customization of products and services, alleviation of barriers for small companies to join large companies supply chains. Prior to enter an e-Marketplace, a participant has to select the right one for his needs.

With all these characteristics, e-Marketplaces are able to support current and future commercial trends like differential, dynamic pricing especially in the area of Supply Chain Management by applying e-auctions (Bichler et al., 2002). Numerous approaches to sustainability, adoption and success factors of e-Marketplaces have been given by Brunn et al., (2002), Daniel et al., (2004), Albrecht et al., (2005), Fu et al., (2006), Hadaya (2006), Wang et al., (2006) while Ratnasingam (2007) identify four types of risks: economic, technological, implementation and relational.

E-commerce developments may vary between countries because their success depends on a set of factors analyzed by Javalgi and Ramsey (2001): IT infrastructure (hardware, software, and communications), social and culture infrastructure (language, education level, beliefs), commercial infrastructure (transport and energy capabilities, banking and financing institutions) and government and legal infrastructure (customer protections, security, taxation, liability). Being an important success factor related to transaction quality, workload of e-Marketplaces is a composition of sessions each of them corresponding to a specific sequence of functions by a single participant during a single entrance to the marketplace. The reliability of electronic transactions on the other hand depends heavily on the capacity of the infrastructure and the workload generated by the intended transactions (Menasce and Akula, 2003). The problem of workload control gets even more complex for business transactions executed over mobile networks as new constraints related to network bandwidth and device characteristics, etc., are present.

Auctions conducted electronically or over wireless networks have special requirements related to transmission bandwidth and range, topology changes and energy requirements for the devices used (mobile phones / PDA's). Chan et al., (2001) design an auction system able to support both Internet and mobile users. Of special interest is the implementation of mobile auctions when participants are moving in limited space (e.g. 300m²) using 433 MHz modems (Rodríguez-Hernández et al., 2002) or Bluetooth communications as proposed by Gonzáles-Castaño et al., (2005). They propose methods to overcome communication fairness and security issues.

Shih et al., (2005) propose a novel mobile Vickrey reverse auction system (MoRAAS) supporting bid privacy. Other mobile auction models have been provided by Tsai and Shen (2006) (Mobile Reverse Auction System – MRAS). A business decision view about m-commerce adoption is provided by Frolick and Chen (2004), while Pedersen et al., (2002) examine adoption enhancement considering users as technology users, consumers (or suppliers) and network members. An extensive analysis of benefits for participants was given by Kuo and Yu (2006). Mobile Commerce transactions have unique operational attributes as noted in (Ahluwalia and Varshney, 2003); these include: local (in single wireless or mobile networks) or end-to-end (over multiple heterogeneous networks), real-time or non-real-time, one-way, two-way or multiple-way, symmetric (same performance for all members) or asymmetric (different performance) etc. M-commerce critical success factors have been explored by Feng et al., (2006), while Ahluwalia and Varshney (2007) stated that measurement and management of QoS is becoming more complex for m-commerce transactions over multiple heterogeneous wireless networks or multicasting supported by rapidly evolving 3G and 4G networks with unique characteristics and differences

Figure 1. Location sensing technologies comparison

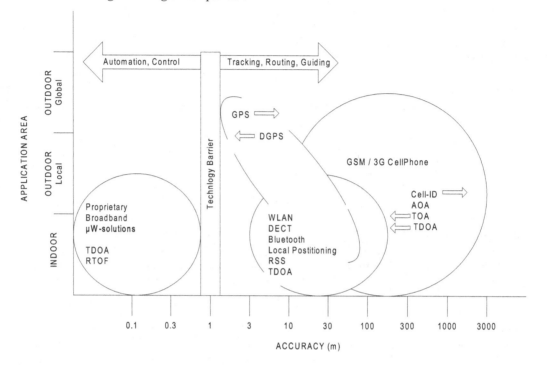

An e-marketplace may facilitate logistics operations in many ways. It may operate as a private, public or consortia-based market in a horizontal or vertical format and used by interested companies to collaborate, share demand, resources and information with each other. Rudberg et al., (2002) describe how an e-marketplace may support collaborative supply chain planning and propose a process for the case of transportation problem. In the continuous changing business environment supply-chain management (SCM) has shifted from engineering and improvement to the co-ordination of the activities of a dynamic supply chain network (Folinas et al., 2004). This is what they call "fourth SCM evolutionary type" in their extensive study on the evolution of SCM types. Park and Suresh (2005) investigate the effects of e-Marketplace development and adoption to supply chains, comparing the traditional supply chain of physical goods to the supply chain of auction-based e-Marketplace. They found that the e-Marketplace perform better on average mainly due its aggregation capabilities.

Location-Based Services (LBS) on the other hand, "open a new market for developers, cellular network providers, and service providers to develop and deploy value-added services" (Hand et al., 2006). It is predicted that global LBS market will reach $8 billion by 2010 (Kang et al., 2007). Although LBS is recognized as a "killer application", research articles are relatively limited, covering only 2% of the total of all research articles in M-Commerce and 10% of M-Commerce applications-related articles (Ngai and Gunasekaran, 2007).

LBS use two major data processing architectures; mobile device operates as a client sending location data to a back-end server for processing. Recent developments in CPUs and memory of mobile communications devices (handsets, PDA's), made back-end servers obsolete (Gilbertson et al., 2006). A general approach about value and revenue generation for partners has been given by Unni and Harmon (2003). Grajski and Kirk (2003) summarize Key Performance Indicators (KPI's) and Key Implementation Requirements (KIR's). Due to the number and heterogeneity of participants in LBS, the architecture should be based in self-organization: minimize user inputs, combine multiple location information sources, switch between indoor and outdoor operation seamlessly, support cooperation between neighbor clients to determine position or increase accuracy and support integration with future technologies. A typical example of a composable LBS is shown in (Ibach and Horbank, 2005).

A general modular LBS platform has been proposed by Xia et al., (2007). From a communication network provider's point of view a critical question is whether existing infrastructure is capable to support communication load added by LBS (Kuhn, 2004). He states three critical steps to estimate required network capacity: (i) Service definition and decomposition into elementary service activities, (ii) Network resources per type, access points and relevant attributes like coverage, bandwidth, costs, etc., and (iii) Traffic volume requirements per service based on data volume, frequency (periodic/ on demand), continuous data streams, number of potential users, etc.

An extensive analysis of mobile data management, requirements and techniques can be found in Madria et al., (2002). Various methods have been used to locate a mobile device's location; most important of them are in brief (Dao et al., (2002), (Adams et al., 2003), (Unni and Harmon, 2003), (Tayal, 2005), Gustafsson and Gunnarsson (2005). A comparison of the location technologies in terms of spatial characteristics and accuracy is shown in Figure 1 (Vossiek et al., 2003).

AUCTION-BASED ELECTRONIC MARKETPLACES

Overview

Developments in Information and Communication Technologies (ICT) in the areas of networking, continuous connectivity and data transmission realized by Internet and World Wide Web (WWW), set the infrastructure elements for conducting business electronically. In general, Internet is an excellent way to trade items and services with high information content; it creates new market forms and changes traditional models of business transactions by abolishing time and place limitations serving as a platform for conducting any type of auction; in this case the auction is characterized as electronic auction (e-auction). The evolution of Reverse Auctions (RA's) for procurement was dramatically strengthened with the evolution of Internet and related software applications. An extensive review of eRAs has been presented by Jap (2002) focusing on their differences from traditional (physical) auctions, application conditions, development and implementation methodologies and performance.

E-auctions are an emerging special auction category containing all types, forms and characteristics of classical auctions. Internet auctions first applied prior to the WWW based on newsgroups and e-mail discussion lists. Their development was rapid since 1995 when OnSale (5/1995) and eBay (9/1995) first appeared. E-auctions are beneficial for all participants (Halstead and Becherer, 2003); sellers may sell quickly, easily, with low cost and good prices via existing or new potential markets. On the other hand buyers may search and buy instantly, at any time, interactively, with low search costs. Advances on WWW and Information and Communication Technologies boosted the deployment of e-auctions covering almost any trading purpose offering numerous benefits. The main characteristics are:

- **Time-independency:** Internet offers 24-hour operation supporting continuous bidding.
- **Location-independency and accessibility:** Location is not an obstacle for participants; actually the only requirement is the availability of a WWW-connected computer while physical presence or gathering of bidders is not required. Consequently bidders do not face travel costs and auction conductors do not face costs related to invitation, lodging, etc.
- **Asynchronous operation:** Bidders are able to participate whenever they want during the auction process
- Complexity: The integration of WWW and computer applications may facilitate special complex auction formats (e.g. multi-dimensional auctions) and may provide tools supporting complex problems like the winner determination problem in combinatorial auctions.
- **Lifecycle shortening:** The lifecycle of e-auctions may be much shorter than physical auctions so they are able to support urgent procurement or liquidation needs and real-time transactions.
- **Market magnification:** Bidders can simultaneously participate in multiple auctions searching for best offers. From a seller's point of view, potential bidder base gets larger, competition is enhanced and expected prices rise.

- **Reinforcement of collaboration:** E-auction marketplaces can easily support special forms of collaboration by establishing connections to participants' extranets. In this way partners are able to form strong consortia in order to be able to participate an auction or to benefit from economies of scope / scale.
- **Pricing accuracy:** Bid and winning prices are easily identifiable and retrievable even in complex auction mechanisms by all participants; additionally, during the bidding process participants are confined to follow specific bidding rules.
- **Disintermediation and info-mediation:** E-Auctions eliminate the need of intermediaries (e.g. wholesalers) whose presence alters trading prices. On the other hand, e-Auctions generate opportunities for new type of intermediaries (usually called infomediaries) offering services like infrastructure, bidder screening, collecting, process safeguarding, etc.
- **Improvement of customer relations:** E-Auctions serve as common instances for users to interact equally and communicate with each other; moreover, the auction Web site supports exchange of information and messaging.
- **Data collection and reporting:** Participants are able to retrieve past auction historical data, information about other participants, and reports in order to make strategic and operational decisions. Data may be easily stored, managed and retrieved from the database server over which the e-Auction is conducted.

Weaknesses

Internet by nature has many weaknesses related to transaction security. Fraud treatment is an emerging research topic in the areas of economics and information technology. Core research questions focus on the design and application of secure mechanisms even when participants tend to violate rules. Internet's most important native weaknesses relates to user authentication and data transmission delay. Many auction Web sites provide various services to secure transactions, some of them being: (i) User eligibility check and rating feedback systems , (ii) Reputation management systems like Trusted Third Parties (TTP), (iii) Low-cost or free insurance and guarantee services, and (iv) Escrow services (intermediary who collects payment and delivers the item).

All the services described before have also many drawbacks; low-rated users can easily make a new register using untrue data; any user is free to rate any other user in an uncontrolled way; insurance services are obsolete when items are not accompanied with guarantee; last escrow services are not beneficial for low-value transactions. Another set of vulnerabilities of e-auctions relates to legal framework (Ba et al., 2003), firstly because law is unable to follow the rapid growth of e-transactions, secondly, because although e-auctions have global coverage, law has not global-wide influence, and thirdly because application of legal rules may be uneconomical especially for low-value transactions.

E-Auction Model and Data Flow

Kumar and Feldman (1998) present an e-auction application and study issues concerning mechanisms, security requirements, transactions before, during and after the auction, and propose a generic auction development architecture which may be integrated in ERP systems. The generic data flow architecture as shown in Figure 2 supports all standard functions which in brief are: Registration, Setup, Publicity, Bidding, Bid Evaluation and Closing and Settlement. The architecture of the platform utilizes several components, the most important of which are database tables and Web pages. Each of them serves specific purposes; internal data base tables store permanent customizing or transaction data for all auctions carried out. Structures (tables appended by blank arrows) contain temporal transaction data generated during each transaction session which are deleted after the end of the auction. Each database table is utilized in specific stages of the auction process to store or retrieve data via Web pages or forms by participants. For example, a seller uses a define or update form to determine in a formal manner the product wishing to sell or to change it – of course before the auction starts – storing this information in the Product table. A potential buyer is able to retrieve proper information concerning the auction item interested in using a search form providing access to the same Product table. Otherwise registered buyers may be automatically notified about the item set in auction via an alert message form. A number of structures are used to temporally store transaction data. For example a short_list structure is temporally filled with a selected set of auctions via the successive use of search and select forms with specific selection criteria. The contents of the structure are deleted each time a buyer executes the search or select forms or immediately after the log-off or session termination.

The application operates as a Web site with a solid page structure (Figure 3). In the following chapters, this architecture will be properly modified and extended to support the case of freight transport service procurement in a mobile context.

TRADING OF LOGISTICS SERVICES VIA E-AUCTIONS

Freight transport refers to the physical movement of goods from point to point within a specific time and cost. The transport business is diversified and fragmented over large geographical areas. A large section of economy depends on transportation of goods and the freight transport industry. The latter is extremely differentiated in terms of size (individual carriers, small and large international companies) operating in a very competitive market. New practices and marketplace platforms have been developed to match loads and capacity in cost-effective manner. A transportation marketplace attempts to match loads allowing shippers and carriers to post, search and negotiate their shipping and capacity utilization requirements via short-term transportation contracts. Aim of these markets is to lower search and transaction costs, increase convenience, and provide carriers and shippers access to larger markets. (Figliozzi et al., 2002) summarize the unique characteristics of freight business:

- Traded entity is a service which by nature is perishable and non-storable
- Freight service contracts contain terms relative to penalties for delay which are higher than the cost of transportation per se
- Demand and supply are geographically dispersed, uncertain over time and space
- Group effect (geographic closeness between loads)
- Network effect (value of shipment is related to current spatial and temporal state of the fleet)
- Economies of scope (complementarity, substitution)

Reverse auctioning is an emerging negotiation mechanism for the freight transport business area (conceptually defined as E-transportation) because they offer agility, optimal capacity allocation practices, flexibility, real-time negotiation (Nair, 2005). Obviously the benefits are the same for all participants for both auction types, either forward or reverse. As it is believed that small businesses constitute an important vehicle for development and growth (Tse and Soufani, 2003), one of the major benefits of the proposed system is that it enlarges the freight business market in a way that enables small and medium sized players to participate with low access cost; small carriers benefit by obtaining access to large markets, are able to act as subcontractors or collaborating with other small participants. On the other hand it gives small shippers the opportunity to collaborate by consolidating freight, supporting the creation of TL shipments.

The marketplace is also a source of revenue for many other stakeholders other than trading partners; Application Service Providers – ASP's (Software development and hosting), Purchasing consolidators (aggregation of buying power), Infomediaries (information providers, GPS), e-fulfillment companies (handle of LTL and e-commerce package transport) and many other. Common questions for bidders (carriers) are: participating or not, how to valuate the service, how to bundle various services and which bidding strategy to follow.

Model Generalization

The proposed freight service trading marketplace is developed within the context of the architecture described before with proper adaptations. From now on vocabulary adopted appears seems in Table 1.

Interestingly, for a number of reasons the initiators and their roles may be interchangeable: a carrier may want to consign his freight (if allowed) to another carrier for the end leg of his trip; a shipper may want to consolidate his shipment with other shippers' loads to fully utilize a hired truck. Describing buyer roles, Figliozzi et al., (2002) distinguish a number of initiators: a shipper wishing to transport a load, a carrier needing extra capacity

Table 1. Role-Based Auction Vocabulary

Initiator	Role	Bidder	Auction Format	Price
Carrier	Seller	Shippers	Forward	Ascending
Shipper	Buyer	Carriers	Reverse	Descending

Figure 2. A generic e-auction process data flow architecture (Kumar and Feldman, 1998)

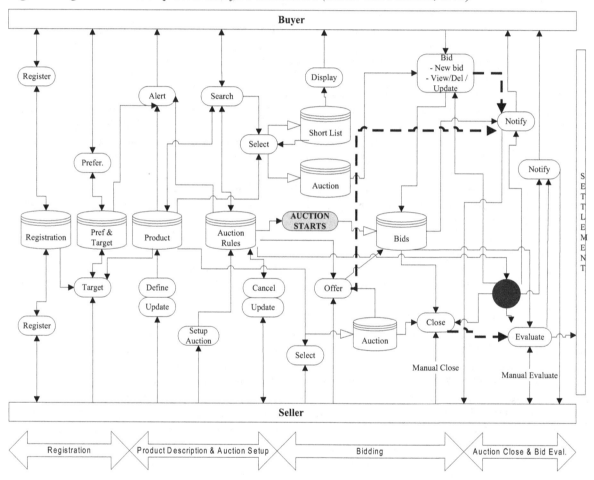

Squares (buyer, seller, settlement) produce or consume information. Cylinders are data base files, ovals are processes, solid arrows are information flow, dashed arrows show control and blank arrow show process generated - most times temporal information

by subcontracting or a third part wishing to resell this capacity. One of the innovative attributes of the proposed marketplace is that it can easily support role interchange via the use of "role_type" parameter database table from which the initiator has to choose from immediately after logging in.

For the typical reverse auction case for freight transport service procurement, buyers are shippers and sellers are carriers participating as bidders. Shippers announce randomly transportation needs and carriers compete for these. Each need is described by a pick-up location, a delivery location, time-windows for pick-up and delivery, truck type and license. The pair of pick-up and destination called a lane. Announcement of needs is real-time

Figure 3. E-auction Web-site structure (Kumar and Feldman, 1998)

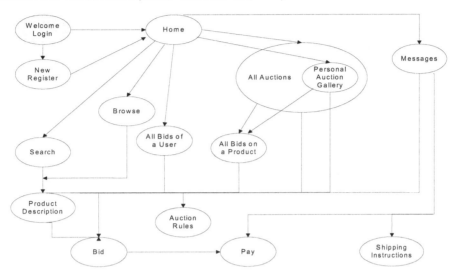

Figure 4. Model Modification: Reverse e-Auction for Freight Transport Procurement

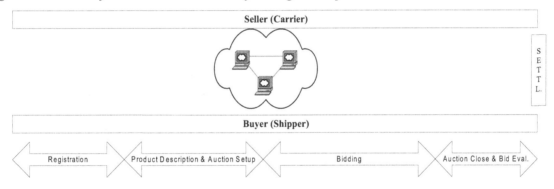

and the contract is allocated via an auction to the carrier with the lowest bid. When multiple transport needs are set, carriers may bid in multiple auctions simultaneously or in sequence.

Another option is to bid in combinations of transport jobs; the problem then becomes more complex for both carrier and shipper. Before the auction, interested carriers are screened via an eligibility check, referring basically to legal issues. Other carrier attributes and quality variables may also be used as evaluation criteria. The model supports this case by a simple interchange of roles in rectangles (Figure 4).

During the register process both shippers and carriers enter data related to their ID (e.g., name, address, business); shippers enter their preferences (freight data, warehouse locations, special transport needs) and carriers enter their available resources (trucks, capacity, equipment, licenses and specialties). During registration shippers should define their preferences and needs while carriers are able to define their abilities and targets. These data are used for a preliminary match between needs and offers aiming to promote partner relationships and eliminate unnecessary workload during the auction process. The shipper enters the attributes of the freight transport service she wants to procure via define or update process and customize an auction format defining

Figure 5. Database structure model

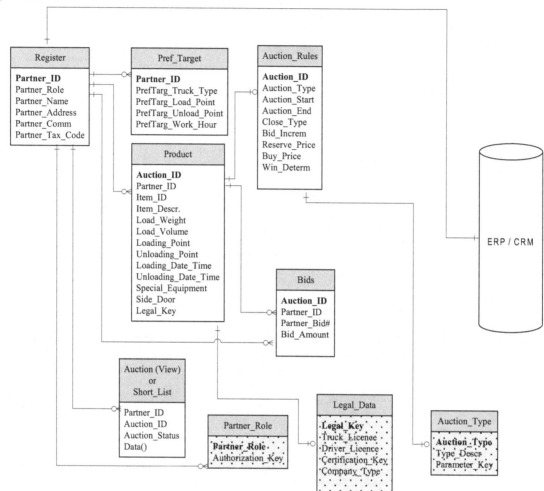

data like auction type, reserve price, duration via the setup auction process. Before the auction starts the shipper is able either to alter the auction format via the update process or to cancel it using the cancel process. Registered carriers are informed about the auction initiation or progress either by the alert process or using the search process by themselves. In case a carrier is interested in participating in more than one auction, she is able to create a private short list via the select process to access and monitoring them easily. Respectively a shipper is able to maintain his own auction short list using a select process. When auction starts, carriers submit their bids using the bid process and they are able to view, alter or withdraw them. If the price progress is imposed by the shipper during the auction (e.g. in Dutch or hybrid-Dutch auction types), then the shipper is able to define the ask price using the offer process. All participants stay continuously informed during the bidding process via the notify process. Once the auction closes (either automatically or manually) the system determines the winning carrier and price via the evaluate process, either automatically or manually. This information is communicated to all participants via a post-auction notify process. Finally evaluation data are transferred to a backend ERP system for trade settlement and reporting. Ideally the backend system includes a Customer Relationship Management (CRM) application which is updated by a pre-defined set of database tables updated during the auction.

Database Architecture and Parameterization

A specific relational database is developed for the Kumar and Feldman (1998) process model supporting the complete process – from the participant registration and auction set-up stages to final settlement and back-end information systems update. Access to each table via SQL-statements is done in a structured way in discrete stages of the process according to the system architecture safeguarding data coherence. Finally the proposed database utilizes relations between tables to avoid data redundancy and unnecessary data entry actions.

A primitive structure of the database is shown in Figure 5. Primary Keys are indicated in bold characters. This primitive form supports only single-dimension auction cases but it can easily be expanded. For example, multi-item auctions need the split of table Product to two relational tables, e.g. the Item_Table and the Auction_Table tied via an auction_ID field serving as primary key. For reasons described before the proposed database extends the proposed by Kumar and Feldman (1998) model, introducing a number of additional customizing tables presented as dashed boxes.

The database supports interchangeable buyer and seller roles for carriers and shippers. To avhieve this, an additional customizing table structure has been incorporated in the proposed database model, namely, the Partner_Role table. Immediately after the registration / log-on process, a partner has to select the role for the current session. According to his role he retrieves an Autorization_Key which defines a set of rules for transactions he is allowed to execute and transactions that are restricted for the current session. For example a partner who logs-in as a seller carrying out a forward auction is not allowed to modify a bid except from the case of the Dutch auction format where he is obliged to modify (descend) bids while bidders are not. The Autorization_Key remains constant during the whole auction lifecycle and cannot be changed in any way – otherwise auction fairness becomes weak.

This auction marketplace is able to support all four basic auction types and allows auction initiators to create custom auction formats creating single or multi-step mechanisms. This is facilitated by the introduction of

Figure 6. Auction customizing sequence

BASIC DATA	
Partner_Role	Buyer
Auction_Type	Vickrey
....	...

BUYER INPUT		
Parameter	**Optional / Mandatory**	**Visible to Bidders (Y/N)**
Duration	Mandatory	Y
Reserve_Price	Optional	Y/N
....	....	...

PREDEFINED PARAMETERS	
# Bids / Bidder	1
Winning_Bid	2nd lowest
Bid_Visibility (during auction)	N O
....	...

Figure 7. Auction customizing screen

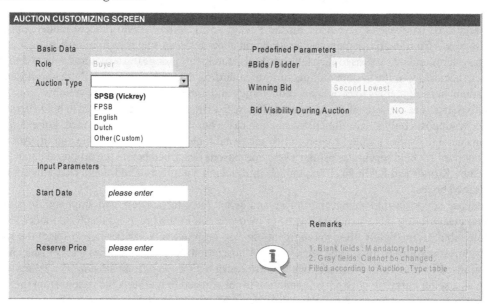

an additional customizing table structure, the Auction_Type table. This table contains a Parameter_Key which guides auction initiators to define specific parameters for the selected auction type and it also carries a set of predefined parameters. A typical example for the simple forward Vickrey auction type initiated by a Shipper acting as buyer is shown in Figure 6. The definition of the Parameter_Key becomes much more complex in case of hybrid auction types (single or multi-step combinations of basic auction types) and in cases of auction formats like multi-dimensional or combinatorial. Finally, the database uses a Legal_Data customizing table which contains a combination of rules and restrictions defined by law in a form of a Legal_Key composed by product (freight load) characteristics and requirements.

The corresponding input screen is shown in Figure 7.

Any registered participant may access specific services via a Web client as shown in corresponding Use-Case UML diagram (Figure 8).

Except of freight service trading via auctions, the proposed e-marketplace also serves as a platform where partners communicate, search, negotiate, retrieve information, etc. (Figure 9). For example, the marketplace may provide additional value-added services like: (i) Links to other Web sites of interest; (ii) A Search Engine to retrieve information related to freight and logistics services, (iii) a Chat Service for private communication between partners supporting for example direct trading or private negotiations, (iv) an E-mail account, (v) a Document Library serving as a knowledge base for participants, (vi) a Computer-Based Training service to strengthen participants' familiarity with marketplace operations, and (vii) Application Service Providers' (ASP) supporting participants to outsource their data processing operations.

MOBILE AUCTIONS (M-AUCTIONS) AND LOCATION BASED SERVICES

Mobility, Location Sensing and LBS for Freight Transport

Recent developments in mobile communications technology provide a scientific and business research area dealing with the transition from e-Commerce to Mobile Commerce (m-Commerce). Mobile Commerce in its

Figure 8. User access to services use-case model

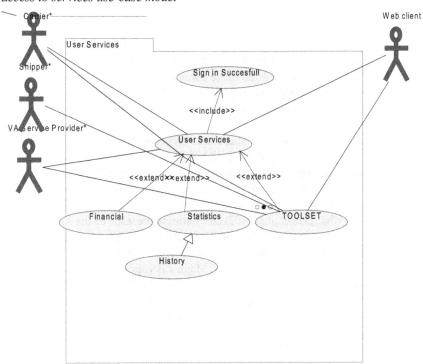

Figure 9. Service toolset use-case model

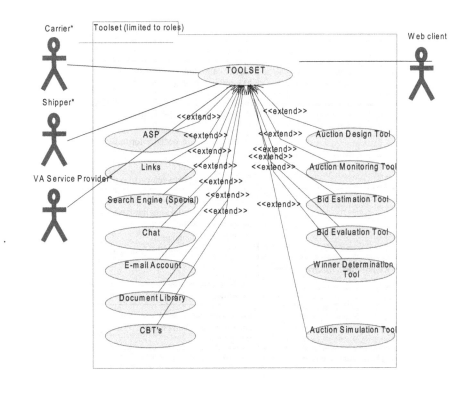

simplest form may be considered as an enhanced form of typical e-Commerce but with two additional critical properties – portability and mobility. A simple definition of mobile commerce has been proposed by Barnes (2002); m-commerce is any transaction with a monetary value – either direct or indirect – that is conducted over a wireless telecommunication network. Of special interest is the development of m-Commerce applications able to support mobile auctions (m-auctions) and mobile advertising (m-advertising) which demolish place restrictions and allow bidders to participate while on the move using their mobile communication devices (phones or PDA's), (Varhsney, 2001), (Varshney and Vetter, 2002). The combination of these two distinct classes provides a trading negotiation tool which takes into account participants' current location to announce and execute geographically-focused auctions.

In the current business environment, location information is becoming an important issue for a continuously growing number of cases ranging from simple navigation services to emergency occasions and from targeted advertising to complex business transactions. Location-Based Services (LBS) focus in providing location and context (situation) aware services for users while on the move based on their current and/or projected location. Application of mobile communications technology for supporting commercial transactions extends the e-commerce to location-based commerce or what Dao et al., (2002) call l-commerce. One of the simplest applications of LBS is geocasting, where one is able to send messages or communicate with mobiles in a specific geographical area by detecting the presence of mobiles in the geographical area of interest. A wireless communication enabled device is the only necessary equipment for a user to access LBS. Major LBS application categories include communication, fleet management, routing, safety, security and entertainment (D'Roza and Bilchev, 2003). Development of an LBS combines a number of disciplines and technologies such as mobile communications, GPS technologies, mobile devices, trading protocols, IT technologies, etc. To be able to provide context-aware services LBS should engage additional technologies like sensors.

The Less-Than-Truckload (LTL) freight business is a typical example of perishable good - sensitive to time and location; the available capacity of a truck has no value when it bypasses a loading point (e.g. logistics center); that is, the location of the truck is a critical issue for the value of the available (unused) capacity of the truck. Moreover a trucker's desire to gain revenue from this capacity increases while approaching the distribution center.

Table 2. Benefits for marketplace participants

Participant / role	Benefits
Auctioneer / Marketplace owner	Lower communication costs Magnification of subscriber base Lower transaction costs
Carrier	Revenue management / capacity utilization Co-operation opportunities New markets – especially for individuals Low participation costs LTL enhancement Subcontracting between carriers
Shipper / Logistics Center	Reduced freight rates (less than market price) Growth of potential supplier base Response to ad-hoc needs High procurement speed Better control on supply chain flows
Value-adding service providers (insurance, law, banking, collecting e.t.c.)	Market growth Business opportunities Advertising
Communication infrastructure providers	New source of revenue New service development Roaming
Other participants (IT, consulting e.t.c.)	Growth of business

It can be easily presumed that a moving carrier is expected to bid more aggressively for a shipment contract as he approaches the loading point. The fact of different carriers' valuations according to their distance from loading point, leads to low vulnerability because it is hard for bidders to collude due to temporality of valuation. Finally, a shipper knowing carriers' location is able to make rough estimations about their valuations. Integration of LBS to the freight procurement mobile auction offers many other benefits summarized in Table 2.

Requirements and Drawbacks

Essential communication requirements for the development and operation of m-auctions are Multicast, Location Management, Reliability and Roaming across multiple networks and operators. M-auctions are typical cases of group-oriented services which assume that besides real-time multicast, the system should support membership coordination, user inputs management, and application synchronization, continuous and stable connectivity for multi-stage processes, low delays (ideally real-time) and continuous connectivity (Varshney and Vetter, 2002), (Varshney, 2007), (Varshney, 2005). When communication quality from a provider is low, the user should be able to switch another network.

Although electronic auctions have been used widely for the last 10 years, use of mobile auctions is relatively limited especially in the area of B2B trading. Some critical parameters slowing down the mobile commerce adoption are: costly entry either for business or customers, lack of a globally-used standard (GSM, TDMA, CDMA, 3G), low bandwidth, instability of connections, device-specific applications and limited display capabilities. Such auctions have special requirements related to transmission bandwidth and range, topology changes and energy requirements for the devices used (mobile phones / PDA's). A strong shortcoming relies in the size of mobile devices. Due to recent trends mobile manufacturers make small-sized devices with proportionally small displays that limit the information that may be displayed. On the other hand wired internet does not have such limitations. Computer monitors support the display of large amount of information. Obviously transition from e-commerce to m-commerce is not very easy.

To relax such shortcomings recent technologies like voice recognition and audio feedback has been developed. Users' devices are heterogeneous in general, so a major problem for any LBS is to efficiently and equally well communicate with any of these devices and integrate them, so LBS technology should be compatible with any of the three major mobile Operation Systems (OS): PalmOS, PocketPC and Symbian OS. Communication cost is also another concern so communication over mobile telephone network should be eliminated. From a privacy regulation point-of-view, apart from known mobile malicious threats, it is critical for LBS to provide security mechanisms eliminating or abolish potential attacks aiming to gain access, steal or modify users' location data and identities. Finally mobile infrastructure should be "open" and scalable to cover future developments. Efficient integration between marketplace and LBS requires the presence of mobile communication technologies (GSM phones or PDA's) and location sensing equipment (GPS devices). Participants should not be required to commit to a specialized technology and information system infrastructure.

CASE ANALYSIS

A Generic Architecture

Information concerning vehicles' location is of special interest for freight business for many reasons: a shipper increases his information about carriers' value; he is also use this information to announce his transportation needs to a special geographically defined segment of carriers in order to reduce communication costs and computational complexity. On the forward type of auction carriers are able to offer their services to partners (e.g. shippers, load consolidators, other carriers e.t.c.) located in a certain geographical area. This chapter extends the e-Marketplace proposed in Section 5 to support the freight transport services trading via m-auctions and e-auctions as a multi-access system for mobile and static participants. The system proposed in this article aims to overcome static (spatial) nature of Web-based applications bridging the market opportunities gap between static and moving carriers by exploiting mobile communications and merging heterogeneous networks. It also attempts to combine the domains of m-commerce and LBS into an auction-based marketplace for the trade of freight transport services. As far as we know it is a novel application and business case.

This chapter describes in detail the proposed system for the reverse auction case. The innovative characteristic of the proposed marketplace is that it integrates an independent Location-Based Services (LBS) provider into it, to provide real-time information about carriers' current location before, during and after the auction process. In this marketplace a shipper (buyer) offers a tender to invited carriers (suppliers) who bid in a reverse auction to win the transportation contract at the lowest price in a very short time span of hours or minutes. The scenario examined in this paper refers to the simple case where a shipper invites multiple LTL carriers via mobile communications to submit a single sealed bid. Development of LBS requires extensive modeling of four types of entities (Jiang and Yao, 2006): users and their needs (types, devices, interests, behaviors), location (georeference system, World Geodetic System, symbolic models, address), context (location, environment, identity, and time) and geospatial data processing (visualization, query processing). The core idea of the proposed location-aware system is that it aims to locate potential participants (carriers) movement in a specific-interest geographical area, inform them via a message and continue to an auction with them. It may serve many freight transport trading situations simple or more complex as shown in Figure 10-12.

1.   Situation 1 - Carrier located in Logistics Center

Eligible carriers are only those having available capacity more than required capacity ($C_{avail} > C_{req}$). LBS does not apply here

2.   Situation 2 - Carriers on the move

Eligible carriers are only those having available capacity more than required capacity ($C_{avail} > C_{req}$). LBS is used to find carriers location, direction and speed. Eligible carriers are those within a certain distance from loading point and those heading for loading point following a route to unloading point with a minimum speed.

3.   Situation 3 - Carrier searching for subcontractors due to legal limitations (e.g. licence) and auctioning contract from a transhipment place.

Here carrier acts as a buyer. Eligible carriers are only those having available capacity more than required capacity ($C_{avail} > C_{req}$). Eligible carriers are those within a certain distance from transhipment location and those heading for transhipment location following a route to unloading point with a minimum speed.

Figure 10. Freight situation 1: Carriers located in logistics center

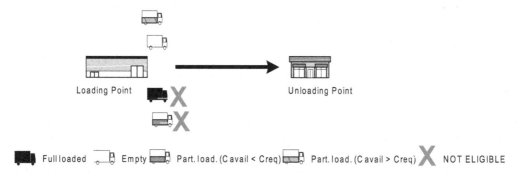

Figure 11. Freight situation 2: Carriers on-the-move

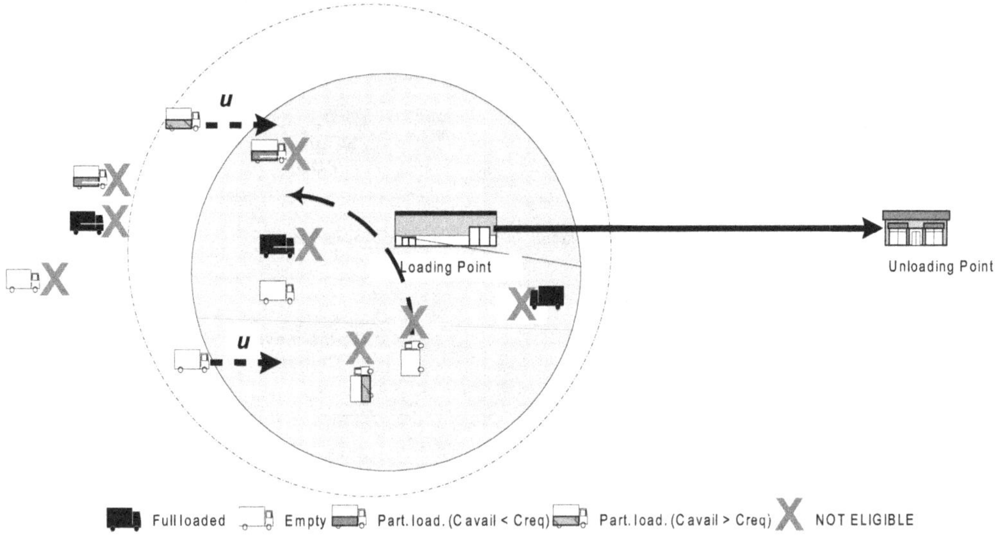

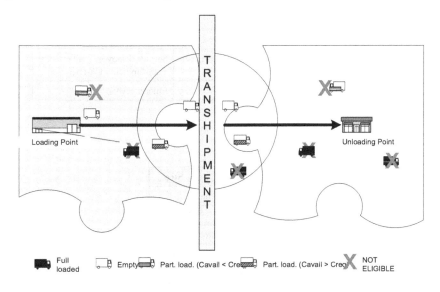

Figure 12. Freight Situation 3: Carriers Acting as subcontractors

Additionally, proposed technology offers a range of possible non trade-related applications for carriers, depending on the architecture used (Table 3).

Communication Flow and Volume

The generic architecture of the marketplace is shown in Figure 13. The marketplace utilizes LBS before the auction execution to locate potential carriers' spatial state (location, direction and speed). Based on these dimensions the

Figure 13. Marketplace architecture overview

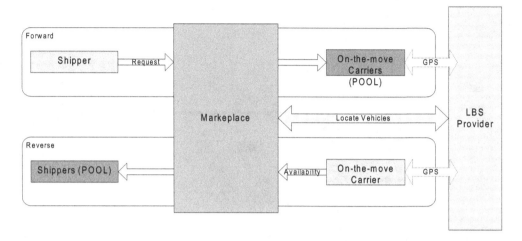

Table 3. Other services (non-tradeable)

Service	User	Application
Where am I now	Carrier	Positioning
Following	Shipper	Tracking
How can I get there	Carrier	Routing
Where is nearest logistics center	Carrier	Business offer discovery
Where are nearest LTL trucks	Carrier / Shipper	Service discovery / advertising Transhipment / Co-operation
Call 112	Carrier	Emergency case

Table 4. Mobile auction session model

Session	Steps
Connection Session	1-5
Call Session	6-11
Designation Session	12-13
Auction Session	14-15
Evaluation Session	16-18
Conclusion Session	19-21

system announces the auction to subscribed trucks located within an area defined by an arc and trucks moving towards the boundary of the arc with a minimum speed.

The software-centric presentation of the complete auction process is based on the Session Auction Model proposed by Shih et al, (2005). The system employs three agent types (buyer, auctioneer, seller) and six transactional sessions (Table. 4) which here are: Connection Session (buyer send message to auctioneer requesting

Figure 14. LBS-based mobile auction UML sequence model

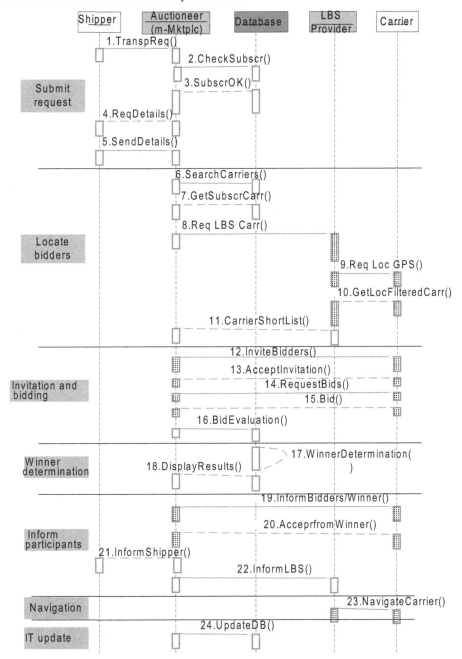

auction and describing the item and it's attributes), Call Session (buyer agent send multicast message to discover sellers able to offer desired item), Designation Session (buyer selects sellers' agents to negotiate with), Auction (a copy of seller's agent is sent to buyer agent to execute the auction process), Evaluation (decision making for winner determination, allocation and payment) and Conclusion (end of process).

Figure 15. Model modification: LBS-based reverse m-auction for freight transport procurement

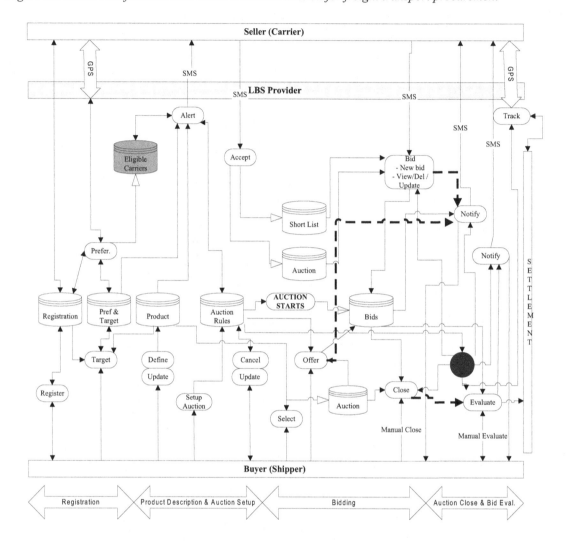

Efficient integration between marketplace and LBS requires the presence of mobile communication devices (e.g. mobile phone) and location sensing equipment (for the case studied here, GPS). Minimum requirements consist of simultaneous data transmission, continuous connectivity, user interface generic design for most devices' display size and type, identification and authentication. The design of the LBS should take into account the following factors (Varshney, 2003): (i) location accuracy, (ii) response time and priority, (iii) network coverage, (iv) number of devices involved, (v) wireless dependability and reliability, (vi) type of communications, (vii) number of location queries per transaction, and (viii) frequency and duration of transactions. A detailed data workflow model has been developed as a UML sequence diagram to control the overall process and estimate the data volume (Figure 14).

Based on this workflow model, Emiris et al., (2007) estimated the expected communication requirements for a given usual transport scenario showing that the required bandwidth for the overall process is commercially efficient and viable.

Figure 16. Incorporation of communication agents

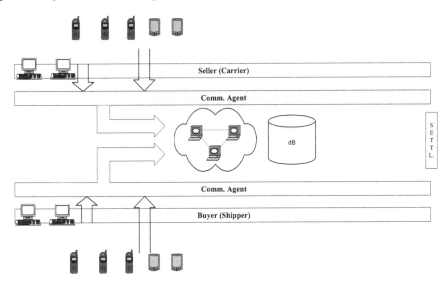

Table 5. Auction mechanism parameters

Parameter	Value
Auction type	Second-price sealed-bid (Vickrey)
Auction format	Reverse
Duration	Predefined
Reserve price	Winning bid <= market price
Number of bidders	• Subscribed • f(distance, heading, velocity) + tolerance
Entry fee	0
Cost of bidding	• # SMS (€) • Participation Acceptance, bid, contract acceptance (winner only)
Immediate sell option	Yes in market price
Bidder subsidizing	SMS cost for weak bidders (e.g. individuals)
Evaluation Criterion	Price
Winner determination and announcement	Instantly

Model Modifications

The proposed model (Figure 15) incorporates a new entity – that of the LBS provider that collects and transmits registered carriers' spatial information to interested shipper. The auction initiator (shipper) search for carriers then filters the set of potential carriers and selects a subset of carriers satisfying specific spatial attributes. Then the system sends SMS to this subset of carriers asking for participation. Interested bidders data are temporary stored in a Short List which checks eligibility during the bidding process and after that. After the auction ends, winner and losers are notified via an SMS. During the transport a shipper is able to monitor her freight using a relevant LBS service. The system then sends this tracking data to the Settlement System for billing and future reference (eligibility checks).

In a combined use of m- and e- trade, mobile users compared to wired users are not competitive enough due to mobile communications' native characteristics (bandwidth, latency, connection stability e.t.c.). These characteristics create multicast-related asymmetries and affect fairness negatively. Yet, equality between m-users is insecure for the same reasons. To overcome this problem the proposed system incorporates a set of two mobile communicating agents – one for each trading side - which collects and stores the information sent by participants during the auction and transfers it to Web-servers (Figure 16) and vice-versa.

The two proposed models (e- and LBS m-) may be easily merged to support both mobile and Web- users, being TL, LTL, loading-point based (e.g. Logistics Center) or On-the-move.

Auction Mechanics and Bandwidth Consumption

As an example, the proposed auction mechanism parameters are enumerated in Table 5.

The auction type proposed in the current article is the second-price sealed-bid (Vickrey auction) auction type for two reasons related to operational and efficiency properties: (i) bids submitted by mobile devices are sealed, and (ii) being an one-shot auction type it has predefined duration, it may be short in time, and winner determination is relatively easy.

Concerning efficiency, in the Vickrey auction the winner is the carrier who submitted the lowest bid and her revenue equals the second losing bid (reverse type). In his seminal paper Vickrey (1961) showed that bidders' optimal strategy in 2nd price sealed-bid auctions is to bid their actual cost. If the bid exceeds bidder's marginal cost the probability of winning will decrease without affecting the payment because the 2nd price does not depend on the winner. It is obvious that a bidder loses if the bid is lower than his marginal cost. As a result, it is strategy-proof and allocates items optimally. It makes untruthful bidding meaningless and allocates the load to the (rational) carrier with lower cost regardless if her belief of other carriers cost. Since it provides incentives for truthful bidding there is no need for much iteration, complex strategies and enhanced security parameters (Table 6).

For the case described here bidding behavior depends heavily on a set of special parameters which affect intensity and aggressiveness (Table 7).

Table 6. Auction type comparison

Auction type	Communication Complexity	Dominant Strategy	Optimal Allocation
English	Multi-round	Yes	Yes
Dutch	Multi-round	No	No
First-price sealed-bid	One round	No	No
Second-price sealed-bid (Vickrey)	One round	Yes	Yes

Table 7. Carriers' bidding behavior

Bidding behavior parameter	Trend	Effect on intensity and aggressiveness
Available Capacity	▲	▲
Distance	▼	▲
Auction Closing Time	▼	▲
Cost	▲	▼

Table 8. Auction communication load parameters

Parameter	Value	Multiplier
Auction Type	Vickrey (2nd price, sealed bid)	
Number of Shippers	1	
Number of Carrier (Individuals)	#	C_i
Number of Carrier (Companies)	#	$C_n (=f(C_i))$
Number of Bidding Rounds	#	BR_n
Number of Location Requests	#	$LR_n = BR_n$
Number of bid dimensions	#	1

By default, a Vickrey auction has a predefined closing time. For the case studied here, actual closing time is depends on each truck location; when a truck passes by the loading point, the auction closes for it. So actual duration is subjective and different for each bidder, depends on location and velocity and it may be less than the announced auction duration. Obviously a sealed-bid auction has the minimum number of bids – one from each bidder. Emiris et al., (2007) have estimated the expected communication load for the case described before when mobile communications are done via SMS. They show that with a minimum number of 8 SMS for each shipper – carrier transaction the m-marketplace is commercially viable. The auction parameters used are shown in Table 8.

The Initial Communication Traffic (ICT) can be calculated as follows:

$$ICT = (N_{carriers} \times DropOff\% \times Particip\%) \times LocPosReqfreq \times MessageSize \times NumbOfMessages$$

For the case studied herein, location search and update frequency is a critical issue as trucks outside the pre-specified area may enter the geographic area of interest in some minutes (see Figure 11), so frequency depends on velocity and heading of the truck. So the question is how to give quick response to query related to potential participants' location (e.g. which subscribers are located in a radius of 70 Km from the Distribution Center and are moving to the South?). A novel query solution method has ben proposed by Wu et al., (2005). For an overview of spatial queries see Brimicombe and Li (2006). Adopting Choi and Tekinay's (2003) formulation, the optimal frequency for updates is:

$$LocPosReqfreq = TruckSpeed / Size of Area$$

Typically the mobile velocity of a vehicle is not constant but for simplicity one may accept the road's speed limit. Of course, with the use of technologies like GPS the average speed can easily be estimated. Any auction mechanism should ensure fairness; In a Vickrey auction, auctioneer has to announce second price (winner has no doubt about the amount she has to pay) and keep private losers; bids. In the proposed system auctioneer informs all bidders about their bid status immediately after the winner determination.

CONCLUSION AND GUIDELINES FOR FUTURE RESEARCH

The present chapter combines the properties of different communication networks (internet, mobile and GPS) developing a marketplace model where geographically static and moving members are able to make trade transactions via auctions. More specifically, it modifies a previously proposed Internet auction model to support mobile auctions and conduct them on the basis of location-sensitive information. The model integrates location-awareness technology (e.g. GPS) to advertise auction, pre-select market members and monitor after-sales service. The spatial attributes of the marketplace, makes it an ideal platform supporting geographically-dispersed markets of moving traders like the freight transport market. Given that participation via Internet or mobile devices is inexpensive depending only on wireless communication, the marketplace is accessible to carriers of almost any size, with numerous benefits:

- Cost-effective accessibility to small carriers
- Reduction of empty miles (deadheading) and better capacity utilization
- Generation of collaboration or subcontracting opportunities especially for individual carriers to offer adjacent long-haul services independently of their license, or to increase their capacity to win large shipments

Due to their nature freight transport services cannot benefit from economies of scale but they may benefit from economies of scope and economies of speed. Such economies may be supported via multi-dimensional auctions. For example, a freight service offer may have other evaluation parameters except from the price, like pick-up times, delivery time window and so on. In this case (multi-attribute) the bid consists from a price and a number of other data. Another case is the simultaneous auctioning of a number of lines where carriers bid on bundles of complementary lines creating times more value (combinatorial auctions). Such auction mechanisms bear three important difficulties: (a) they impose additional data volume exchange in the trading process; (b) bidding process becomes more complex especially via mobile devices and (c) the winner determination problem becomes more complex therefore Operations Research methodologies and algorithms and IT support are indispensable. Extension of the proposed system to support such auctions is an area for future research.

Having in mind that speech is the elementary and most efficient means of communication it is believed that voice interfaces development will be beneficial for any electronic service. Voice interface does not have the limitations of a typical mobile device: small screen size, slow typing speed and inconvenient keyboard. From a service provider's point-of-view it offers 24/7 operation with the use of automatic voice technology. Of course voice enabled services are still not mature: first, voice recognition is not always successful and second, they are not multi-lingual. Such problems can be confronted with the use of standard messages after language selection by the user. Although hard to design and implement, it offers some critical advantages: hands-free operation and user participation while driving, less time and effort for bid submission especially for complex auction formats like multi-attribute and combinatorial.

REFERENCES

Adams, P., Ashwell, G. W. B., Baxter, R. (2003). Location-Based Services - An Overview of the Standards. BT Technology Journal 21(1), 34-43.

Ahluwalia, P., Varshney, U. (2003,). A Link and Network Layer Approach to Support Mobile Commerce Transactions. Paper presented at the Vehicular Technology Conference, 2003. VTC 2003-Fall. 2003 IEEE 58th

Ahluwalia, P., Varshney, U. (2007). Managing End-to-End Quality of Service in Multiple Heterogeneous Wireless Networks. International Journal of Network Management, 17(3), 243-260.

Albrecht, C., Dean, D. L., Hansen, J. V. (2005). Marketplace and Technology Standards for B2B E-commerce: Progress, Challenges and the State of the Art. Information & Management, 42(6), 865-875.

Anandalingam, G., Day, R. W., Raghavan, S. (2005). The Landscape of Electronic Market Design. Management Science, 51(3), 316-327.

Ba, S., Whinston, A. B., Zhang, H. (2003). Building trust in online auction markets through an economic incentive mechanism. Decision Support Systems, 35(3), 273-286.

Bailey, J., Bakos, Y. (1997). An Exploratory Study of the Emerging Role of Electronic Intermediaries. International Journal of Electronic Commerce, 1(3), 7-20.

Barnes, S. (2002). The Mobile Commerce Value Chain: Analysis and Future Developments. International Journal of Information Management, 22, 91-108.

Bichler, M., Kalagnanam, J., Katircioglu, K., King, A. J., Lawrence, R. D., Lee, H. S., Lin, G. Y., Lu, Y. (2002). Applications of flexible pricing in business-to-business electronic commerce. IBM Systems Journal, 41(2), 287-302.

Brimicombe, A., Li, Y. (2006). Mobile Space-Time Envelopes for Location-Based Services. Transactions in GIS, 10(1), 5-23.

Brunn, P., Jensen, M., Skovgaard, J. (2002). e-Marketplaces: Crafting a Winning Strategy. European Management Journal, 20(3), 286-298.

Buellingen, F., Woerter, M. (2004). Development Perspectives, Firm Strategies and Applications in Mobile Commerce. Journal of Business Research, 57(12), 1402-1408.

Chan, H., Ho, I. S. K., Lee, R. S. T. (2001). Design and Implementation of a Mobile Agent-Based Auction System. Paper presented at the IEEE PACRIM'2001, Victoria, BC, Canada.

Choi, W., Tekinay, S. (2003). Location-Based Service Provisioning for Next Generation Wireless Networks. International Journal of Wireless Information Networks, 10(3), 127-139.

Cortese, A. E. & Stepanek, M. (1998). Good-Bye to Fixed Pricing? Business Week, May 4, 70-84.

Cramton, P. (1998). Ascending auctions. European Economic Review, 42(3-5), pp. 745-756.

D'Roza, T., Bilchev, G. (2003). An Overview of Location-Based Services. BT Technology Journal, 21(1), 20-27.

Daniel, E., Hoxmeier, J., White, A., Smart, A. (2004). A framework for the sustainability of e-marketplaces. Business Process Management Journal, 10(3), 277-290.

Dao, D., Rizos, C., Wang, J. (2002). Location-Based Services: Technical and Business Issues. GPS Solutions, 6(3), 169-178.

Emiris, D., Marentakis, C., Laimos, P. (2007). Towards an Integrated LBS-Enabled, Mobile Auctions Marketplace for Logistics Services. Paper presented at the 18th Annual IEEE International Symposium on Personal, Indoor and Mobile Radio Communications (PIMRC'07), Athens, 2007.

Feldman R. A., Mehra, R. (1993). Auctions: Theory and applications. International Monetary Fund. Staff Papers, 40(3), 485-511.

Feng, H., Hoegler, T., Stucky, W. (2006,). Exploring the Critical Success Factors for Mobile Commerce. Paper presented at the International Conference on Mobile Business (ICMB'06).

Figliozzi, M., Mahmassani, H. S., Jaillet, P. (2002,). A Framework for the Study of Carrier Strategies in an Auction Based Transportation Marketplace. Paper presented at the 82nd Annual Meeting of the Transportation Research Board (TRB2003).

Folinas, D., Manthou, V., Sigala, M., Vlachopoulou, M. (2004). E-volution of a Supply Chain: Cases and best Practices. Internet Research, 14(4), 274-283.

Frolick, M., Chen, L.D. (2004). Assessing M-Commerce Opportunities. Information Systems Management, 21(2), 53-61.

Fu, H., Ho, Y.C., Chen, R. C. Y., Chang, T. H., Chien, P. H. (2006). Factors Affecting the Adoption of Electronic Marketplaces. International Journal of Operations & Production Management, 26(12), 1301-1324.

Gilbertson, P., Edwards, R., Coulton, P. (2006,). Reducing Processing Time for Real-Time Mobile Hosted Location Based Services. Paper presented at the The 17th Annual IEEE International Symposium on Personal, Indoor and Mobile Radio Communications (PIMRC'06).

González-Castaño, F., Gil-Castiñeira, F. J., García-Reinoso, J. (2005,). Bluetooth Real-Time Mobile Auctions. Paper presented at the IEEE 16th International Symposium on Personal, Indoor and Mobile Radio Communications (PIMRC'07).

Gou, H., Huang, B., Liu, W., Li, X. (2003). A Framework for Virtual Enterprise Operation Management. Computers in Industry, 50(3), 333-352.

Grajski, K., Kirk, E. (2003). Towards a Mobile Multimedia Age - Location-Based Services: A Case Study. Wireless Personal Communications, 26(2/3) 105-116.

Gustafsson, F., Gunnarsson, F. (2005). Mobile Positioning Using Wireless Networks. IEEE Signal Processing Magazine, 22(4), 41-53.

Hadaya, P. (2006). Determinants of the Future Level of Use of Electronic Mareketplaces: The Case of Canadian Firms. Electronic Commerce Research, 6(2), 173-185.

Halstead, D., Becherer, R. C. (2003). Internet Auction Sellers: Does Size Really Matters? Internet Research: Electronic Networking Applications and Policy, 13(3), 183-194.

Hand, A., Cardiff, J., Magee, P., Doody, J. (2006). An Architecture and Development Methodology for Location-Based Services. Electronic Commerce Research and Applications, 5(3), 201-208.

Hawking, P., Stein, A., Wyld, D. C., Foster, S. (2004). E-procurement: is the ugly duckling actually a swan down under? Asia Pacific Journal of Marketing and Logistics, 16(1), 3-26.

Ibach, P., Horbank, M. (2005). Highly Available Location-Based Services in Mobile Environments. Paper presented at the International Service Availability Symposium (ISAS 2004).

Jap, S. (2002). Online Reverse Auctions: Issues, Themes, and Prospects for the Future. Academy of Marketing Science, Journal, 30(4), 506-525.

Javalgi, R., Ramsey, R. (2001). Strategic issues of e-commerce as an alternative global distribution system. International Marketing Review, 18(4), 376-391.

Jiang, B., Yao, X. (2006). Location-Based Services and GIS in Perspective. Computers, Environment and Urban Systems, 30(6), 712-725.

Kakihara, M., Sørensen, C. (2002,). Mobility: An Extended Perspective. Paper presented at the 35th Hawaii International Conference on System Sciences.

Kang, S., Kim, T. J., Jang, S. G. (2007). Location-Based Services: Enabling Technologies and a Concierge Service Model. In Miller, H. (Ed.), Societies and Cities in the Age of Instant Access (pp. 227-239). GeoJournal Library , Vol. 88, Springer-Verlag.

Klemperer, P. (1999). Auction Theory: A Guide to the Literature, Journal of Economic Survey, 13(3), pp. 227-286.

Kuhn, P. (2004). Location-Based Services in Mobile Communication Infrastructures. International Journal of Electronic Communications, 58, 159-164.

Kumar, M., Feldman, S. I. (1998). Internet Auctions. Paper presented at the 3rd USENIX Workshop on Electronic Commerce, Boston, Massachusetts.

Kuo, Y., Yu, C. W. (2006). 3G Telecommunication Operators' Challenges and Roles: A Perspective of Mobile Commerce Value Chain. Technovation, 26(12), 1347-1356.

Madria, S., Mohania, M., Bhowmick, S. S., Bhargava, B. (2002). Mobile Data and Transaction Management. Information Sciences, 141, 279-309.

McAfee, R., McMillan, J. (1987). Auctions and bidding. Journal of Economic Literature 25(2), 699-738.

Menasce, D., Akula, V. (2003,). Towards Workload Characterization of Auction Sites. Paper presented at the Sixth IEEE Workshop on Workload Characterization (WWC-6), Austin, TX.

Milgrom, P. (1989). Auctions and Bidding: A Primer. The Journal ofEconomic Perspectives, 3(3), 3-22.

Milgrom, P., Weber, R. J. (1982). A Theory of Auctions and Competitive Bidding. Econometrica, 50(5), 1089-1122.

Nair, A. (2005). Emerging Internet-Enabled Auction Mechanisms in Supply Chain. Supply Chain Management: An International Journal, 10(3), 162-168.

Ngai, E., Gunasekaran, A. (2007). A Review for Mobile Commerce Research and Applications. Decision Support Systems, 43(1), 3-15.

Park, S., Suresh, N. C. (2005,). An Investigation of the Roles of Elecgtronic Marketplace in the Supply Chain. Paper presented at the 38th Hawaii International Conference on System Sciences.

Pedersen, P., Methlie, L. B., Thorbjørnsen, H. (2002,). Understanding Mobile Commerce End-User Adoption: A Triangulation Perspective and Suggestions for an Exploratory Service Evaluation Framework. Paper presented at the 35th Hawaii International Conference on System Sciences.

Ratnasingam, P. (2007). A Risk-Control Framework for the E-Marketplace Participation: The Findings of Seven Cases. Information Management & Computer Security, 15(2), 149-166.

Rodríguez-Hernández, P., González-Castaño, F. J., Pousada-Carballo, J. M., Fernández-Iglesias, M. J., García-Reinoso, J. (2002). Cellular Network for Real-Time Mobile Auction. Wireless Personal Communications, 22(1), 23-40.

Rudberg, M., Klingenberg, N., Kronhamn, K. (2002). Collaborative Supply Chain Planning Using Electronic Marketplaces. Integrated Manufacturing Systems, 13(8), 596-610.

Shih, D., Huang, S. Y., Yen, D. C. (2005). A New Reverse Auction Agent System for M-Commerce Using Mobile Agents. Computers Standards & Interfaces, 27(4), 383-395.

Stockdale, R., Standing, C. (2004). Benefits and barriers of electronic marketplace participation: an SME perspective. The Journal of Enterprise Information Management, 17(4), 301-311.

Tayal, M. (2005,). Location Services in the GSM and UMTS Networks. Paper presented at the ICPWC'05. New Delhi.

Tsai, C., Shen, B. F. (2006,). Online Reverse Auctions via Wireless Instant Message Networks. Paper presented at the 6th International Conference on ITS Telecommunications.

Tse, T., Soufani, K. (2003). Business strategies for small firms in the new economy. Journal of Small Business and Enterprise Development, 10(3), 306-320.

Unni, R., Harmon, R. (2003,). Location-Based Services: Models for Strategy Development in M-Commerce. Paper presented at the World. Portland International Conference on Technology Management for Reshaping (PICMET '03).

Varshney, U. (2001,). Location Management Support for Mobile Commerce Applications. Paper presented at the WMC'01, Rome, Italy.

Varshney, U. (2003). Location Management for Mobile Commerce Applications in Wireless Internet Environment, ACM Transactions on Internet Technology, 3(3), pp. 236-255

Varshney, U., Vetter, R. (2002). Mobile Commerce: Framework, Applications and Networking Support. Mobile Networks and Applications, 7(3), 185-198.

Varshney, U. (2005). Performance Evaluation of Protocols for Group-Oriented Mobile Services. Mobile Networks and Applications, 10(4), 465-474.

Varshney, U. (2007). Supporting Dependable Group-Oriented Mobile Transactions: Redundancy-Based Architecture and Performance. International Journal of Network Management ,17(3), 219-229.

Vickrey, W. (1961). Counterspeculation, Auctions and Competitive Sealed Tenders. The Journal of Finance 16(1), 8-37.

Vossiek, M., Wiebking, L., Gulden, P., Wieghardt, J., Hoffmann, C., Heide, P. (2003). Wireless Local Positioning. IEEE Microwave Magazine, 4(4), 77-86.

Wang, S., Archer, N. P., Zheng, W. (2006). An Exploratory Study of Electronic Marketplace Adoption: A Multiple Perspective View. Electronic Markets, 16(4), 337-348.

Wolfstetter, E. (1996). Auctions: An Introduction. Journal of Economic Surveys, 10(4), 367-420.

Wu, K., Chen, S.K., Yu, P. S. (2005). Efficient Processing of Continual Range Queries for Location-Aware Mobile Services. Information Systems Frontiers, 7(4/5), 435-448.

Xia, Y., Bae, H. Y, (2007). General Platform of Location Based Services in Ubiquitous Environment, Paper presented at the International Conference on Multimedia and Ubiquitous Engineering (MUE'07).

KEY TERMS

E-Marketplace: It is an Internet-based environment that brings together buyers, sellers and intermediaries so that they can trade more efficiently online.

Enterprise Resource Planning System (ERP): It is an integrated information system that serves all departments within an enterprise. It can support manufacturing, order entry, accounting, purchasing, warehousing, transportation and human resources functions.

Global Positioning System (GPS): A worldwide system of a constellation of 24 satellites in orbit and user receiving devices used to computer positions on the Earth. It uses transmitted signals and mathematical triangulation to pinpoint location.

Less-Than-Truckload Shipment (LTL): Transportation of relatively small fright collected from various shippers. It is consolidated and delivered with various other shipments and is usually not delivered directly to a destination as full truckloads are. Opposite: Full Truckload (FTL).

Location-Based Services (LBS): Information services utilizing the ability to make use of the location of the mobile device. They employ real-time positioning technologies and networked resources.

M-Commerce: Trading of goods and services through wireless handheld devices such as cellular phones and PDA's.

Supply Chain Management (SCM): It is the planning and management of all activities involved in sourcing, procurement, conversion, and logistics management activities. It also includes coordination and collaboration with channel partners, which can be suppliers, intermediaries, third-party service providers, and customers.

Unified Modeling Language (UML): It is an ISO (International Standards Organization) specification language for modeling objects. It's a refinement of earlier Object Oriented Design (OOD) and Object Oriented Analysis (OOA) methodologies. It is considered to be a useful language when designing large applications involving many classes and objects.

Chapter XXII
Deploying Ubiquitous Computing Applications on Heterogeneous Next Generation Networks

Achilles D. Kameas

Hellenic Open University and Computer Technology Institute / DAISy group, Greece

ABSTRACT

This chapter describes a human centric approach for designing and deploying ubiquitous computing applications. These are considered as activity spheres consisting of tasks which must be executed using the resources available in an Ambient Intelligence space. Such resources include objects augmented with embedded ICT components and software modules. An architectural approach and a corresponding middleware are described, which enable the management of activity spheres. Then, the communication requirements are presented and the role of heterogeneous next generation networks in supporting this architecture is discussed.

INTRODUCTION

Ubiquitous computing constitutes a novel computational paradigm, which will pervade all aspects of everyday life in the coming decades. From a technology perspective, ubiquitous computing composes distributed systems, miniaturized hardware and wireless networks and builds on the achievements of these and other research and engineering disciplines. At the same time, it is expected to have a strong societal impact, as it will transform the way everyday and emergency human activity is carried out. This is because ubiquitous computing technology is inherently deployable on every object, task or process in people's immediate environment or activity. Moreover, tasks supported by this technology will eventually be easily accessible, safety enhancing and intuitive to use, thus realizing Mark Weiser's vision of calm technology (Weiser, 1991) or ISTAG's vision of Ambient Intelligence (ISTAG).

The vision of Ambient Intelligence (AmI) implies a seamless environment of computing, advanced networking technology and specific interfaces. An important characteristic of AmI environments is the merging of physical

Copyright © 2009, IGI Global, distributing in print or electronic forms without written permission of IGI Global is prohibited.

and digital space (i.e. tangible objects and physical environments are acquiring a digital representation). Still, people's interaction with their environment will not cease to be task-centric: we are still interested to carry out our tasks, using the skills, tools and information available in our heads or in the environment.

Every new technology is manifested with objects that realize it. These objects may be new or improved versions of existing objects, which by using the new technology, allow people to carry out new tasks or old tasks in new and better ways. Up to now, the ways that an object could be used and the tasks it could be used for have always been determining and depending on its shape. As the computer disappears in the environments surrounding our activities, the objects therein become augmented with Information and Communication Technology (ICT) components (i.e. sensors, actuators, processor, memory, wireless communication modules) and can receive, store, process and transmit information; in the following, we shall use the term "artifacts" for this type of augmented objects.

In the forthcoming AmI environments, artifacts will have a dual self: they are objects with physical properties and they have a digital counterpart accessible through a network. Thus, (a) people will realize their tasks using the available artifacts and the services they offer, (b) some of these artifacts will be public and some will be private, (c) knowledge will exist both in people's heads (in the form of upgraded skills) and in the environment (in the knowledge bases of the artifacts) and (d) successful execution of tasks will depend on the quality of interactions among artifacts and among people and artifacts.

It is the latter point (d) which provides the rationale for this chapter, as interaction entails communication, which requires a networking layer. Before dealing with it, we shall describe our task-centric approach in modeling ubiquitous computing applications in the next section. Then in section 3, we shall present a generic architecture of ubiquitous computing applications. Section 4 discusses GAS-OS, the middleware we have developed to support our world model. The discussion places emphasis on the communication aspects of GAS-OS, so that in the next section we introduce the requirements that our approach imposes on the networking layer and discuss why and how Next Generation Networks are expected to meet them.

AMI ARTIFACTS, ENVIRONMENTS AND ACTIVITY SPHERES

The AmI environment can be considered to host several ubiquitous computing applications, which make use of the infrastructure provided by the environment and the services provided by the artifacts therein (Zaharakis, 2008). A ubiquitous computing application is considered as an orchestration of services that are accessible via the AmI environment. Usually, AmI artifacts act as service bearers; therefore, a ubiquitous computing application is manifested by a set of co-operating artifacts (Zaharakis, 2006).

AmI Artifacts

AmI artifacts differ from traditional objects in a number of properties and abilities:

- **Information processing:** The information that an artifact processes can be descriptions of the context of use, data to be used for a task, guidelines on how to perform a new task (i.e. a program), messages to be sent or that have been received from other objects. The result of information processing is a set of services, that is, a set of abilities that appear in the digital space and relate to information; an artifact may offer or request services
- **Interaction with environment:** Artifacts can perceive properties of their context of use (via their embedded sensors, or by communicating with other artifacts) and can also produce responses to these stimuli (via their actuators)
- **Autonomy:** The operation of artifacts depends on electrical power; thus their autonomy depends on the availability of electrical power (which most of the times depends on the capacity of their battery)
- **Collaboration:** Artifacts can exchange messages via (usually wireless) communication channels; the content of these messages may range from plain data to complex structures, including programs, database parts etc.

Norman (1988) states that affordances "refer to the perceived and actual properties of the thing, primarily those fundamental properties that determine just how the thing could possibly be used". The affordances of an ordinary object are a direct consequence of the anticipated uses that object designers "embed" into the object's physical properties. This association is in fact bi-directional: the objects have been designed to be suitable for certain tasks, but it is also their physical properties that constrain the tasks people use them for. The "digital self" of artifacts includes their properties (what the object is), capabilities (what the object knows to do) and services (what the object can offer to others). At the same time, they acquire extra capabilities, which during the formation of ubiquitous computing applications can be combined with capabilities of other artifacts or adapted to the context of operation. Thus, artifacts offer two new affordances to their users:

- **Composeability:** Artifacts can be used as building blocks of larger and more complex systems. Composeability is perceived by users through the presentation -via the object's digital self- of the object's connectable capabilities, and thus by providing users the possibility to achieve connections and compose applications of two or more objects. This in implementation terms is achieved via a communication unit that artifacts possess, which requires universal descriptions of tasks and services.
- **Changeability:** Artifacts that possess or have access to digital storage can change the digital services they offer. In other words, the tangible object can be partially disassociated from the artifact's digital services, as they are based on the manipulation of information. Changeability is offered as an affordance to users by the mere observation of the disassociation of the software and the digital self of objects.

Both these affordances are a result of the ability to produce descriptions of properties, capabilities and services, which carry information about the artifact in the digital space. This ability improves an artifact's object/service independence, as an artifact that acts as a service consumer may seek a service producer based only on a service description. In order to be consistent with the physical world, functional autonomy of artifacts must also be preserved; thus, they must be capable to function without any dependencies from other objects or infrastructure.

AmI Environment

Nowadays, an increasing number of artifacts (that is, objects having embedded ICT components) are continuously being made commercially available, whereas more advanced prototypes are being designed by research groups. The mobile phone is the artifact exhibiting the greatest popularity among everyday users; however, digital cameras, music players, and other entertainment devices have been turned into information appliances and have acquired the ability to share content. This ability has longtime been available in PDAs, laptops and their peripherals, which undergo significant change in their form and affordances. Not very surprisingly, objects very intimate, such as clothes, or very common, such as cars, are being gradually turned into artifacts.

In addition to objects, spaces also undergo a change towards becoming smart and eventually AmI spaces. An AmI space is to a physical space the same as to that what an artifact is to an object. To be more precise, an AmI space embeds sensing, actuating, processing and networking infrastructure in a physical (usually closed) space and offers a set of services in the digital space. Examples of existing (still primitive) AmI spaces are:

- The AmInOffice (DAISy group CTI, Greece), a one-roomed fully operational workplace equipped with the usual office furniture (PC, desk, table, chairs, couch, bookshelves, etc) as well as with several devices ranging from simple sensors and RFID tags to complicated sensors/actuators supporting the information perception/diffusion in the AmI space. AmInOffice participants may configure the available artifacts (via special user-friendly editors) according to their habits. In addition, the AmInOffice enables users to protect their privacy and to manage how they present themselves to their social network by providing the means to maintain awareness of the activities and the situation of each other.
- The iSpace Living Lab (Univ. of Essex, UK) (Hagras, 2007) integrates ubiquitous networked sensors and actuators, the infrastructure for which is accommodated within the specially constructed walls, so that the heterogeneous networking infrastructure is hidden from view. Designed to provide a flexible test-bed for research into intelligent buildings and adaptive environments within a pervasive and ubiquitous computing

context the iSpace offers the possibility for examining the deployment of embedded agents and sophisticated user interfaces within the intelligent environments of tomorrow.

An AmI environment is considered as an abstraction over AmI spaces; it integrates or defines AmI spaces as container objects offering computation and communication services to the contained artifacts. In this context, a contained artifact is any artifact that relates to an AmI space having the main role of a service consumer. Thus, a mobile phone is contained within a GPRS cell, a temperature sensor is contained within a smart room, etc. The seams between adjacent AmI spaces may or may not be perceptible; current technological solutions in most cases provide seamful integration of AmI spaces, but aim at providing seamless service continuation between spaces. In the following we shall base our discussion on AmI environments, considering that any AmI space "inherits" their properties.

Activity Spheres

With the proliferation of networks, information appliances and artifacts, a large volume of data is being collected, exchanged and processed in AmI environment, generating knowledge about patterns and context of human activity, which they aim to improve. As a side-effect of the availability of new technologies, the nature of the human activities eventually assisted by artefacts is rapidly changing. People have to (consent to) build new task models or adapt the ones they have already been using. Execution of new tasks will be even harder due to the inherent systemic complexity of ubiquitous computing applications, which, among others, results from device incompatibility, and huge number of interactions among visible and non-visible actors. Humans, with their "analog" way of thinking and acting, have difficulties in using digital systems, because the latter demand precision, cannot tolerate misuse and are unable to adapt to changes in operating environment (Norman, 1998).

In order to model the way everyday activities are carried out within an AmI environment, we introduce the notion of "activity sphere". An activity sphere is intentionally created by an actor (human or agent) in order to support a specific activity. The sphere is deployed over an AmI environment and uses its resources (artifacts, networks, services etc). An activity usually consists of a set of interrelated tasks; the sphere contains models of these tasks and their interaction. These models can be considered as the counterparts of programs, only that they are not explicitly programmed, but are usually learnt by the system through observation of task execution. The sphere can also form and use a model of its context of deployment (the AmI environment), in the sense that it discovers the services offered by the infrastructure and the contained objects. The sphere instantiates the task models within the specific context composed by the capabilities and services of the container AmI environment and its contained objects. In this way, it supports the realization of concrete tasks.

Thus, a sphere is considered as a distributed yet integrated system that is formed on demand to support people's activities. An activity sphere is realized as a composition of configurations between the artifacts and the provided services into the AmI space. People inhabit in the AmI space and intentionally form spheres by using the artifacts and the provided services. An activity sphere continuously observes people interactions with artifacts in different contexts, can learn their interests and habits and can exhibit cognitive functions, such as goal-directed behavior, adaptation, learning, etc. Thus, the end-user cohabits with spheres, and this allows us to model them as another basic building block that generates events and changes the environment.

An activity sphere has the following properties:

- **Intention and identity:** As we said before, an activity sphere is formed intentionally, in order to facilitate a specific set of tasks; these tasks usually determine the sphere identity
- **Transient nature:** A sphere is active only as long as the activity it supports is ongoing. Once the activity is terminated, the sphere relinquishes all the resources it used; traces of activity services may be maintained by the participating artifacts
- **Specific boundaries:** An activity sphere is a finite construct, which makes its boundaries visible. Boundaries are dynamic; in fact they are a negotiation zone, wherein the sphere borders are set depending on context (for example, other spheres may be perceived as a sphere's context). In addition, boundaries have a controlled degree of permeability, that is, the sphere can regulate its data exchange with the AmI environment

- **Self-* properties:** these are properties that determine the degree of sphere autonomy. Spheres can be considered as autonomic systems, as they (a) manage locally the resources of the AmI environment, (b) include models of self and environment, (c) exhibit goal-directed functionality, and (d) can adapt its functionality to changes in itself or the environment.

The configuration of a sphere could be realized in two ways, explicit and tacit. In the former mode, people configure spheres by explicitly composing artifact affordances, based on the visualized descriptions of the artifact properties, capabilities and services. To operate this mode, people must form explicit task models and translate them into artifact affordances; then they must somehow select or indicate the artifacts that bear these affordances. The independence between object and service is maintained, although there do not exist clear guidelines regarding the degree of visibility (of system properties and seams) that a sphere should offer to people.

The tacit mode operates completely transparently to the user and is based on the system observing user's interactions and actions within the sphere. In an ideal AmI space, people will still use the objects in their environment to carry out their tasks. Because objects and space are artifacts, they can monitor user actions and record, store and process information about them. Then, they can deduce user goals or habits and pro-actively support people's activities within the sphere (i.e. by making the required services available, by optimizing use of resources, etc). The sphere can learn user preferences and adapt to them, as it can adapt to the configuration of any new AmI space that the user enters. To achieve this, the encoding of task- and context-related metadata is required, as well as of the adaptation policies, which will be used by the task realization mechanisms.

Role of Ontology

An ontology is usually defined as "a formal, explicit specification of a shared conceptualization" (Gruber, 1993). A "conceptualization" refers to an abstract model of some phenomenon in the world, which identifies the relevant concepts of that phenomenon. "Explicit" means that the type of concepts used and the constraints on their use are explicitly defined. "Formal" refers to the fact that the ontology should be machine readable. "Shared" reflects the notion that an ontology captures consensual knowledge, that is, it is not private of some individual, but accepted by a group. Thus, an ontology is a structure of knowledge, used as a means of knowledge sharing within a community of heterogeneous entities.

In the case of activity spheres, there are multiple causes of heterogeneity:

- Artifacts and other engineered sphere components, each of which has a proprietary, usually closed, model of itself and the world
- AmI spaces, public or private, which have their own models of their resources and services
- Task models, expressed in various domain-dependent notations, as well as dialogue states and interfaces
- Multimedia objects, which usually adhere to the metadata of multimedia standards; the sane holds for other types of "intelligent" content
- Networking protocols and, in general, communication schemes, which require specific descriptions of artifacts and services and usually have a restricted closed world model
- People, who have their own individual profiles and ways of perceiving, understanding and accepting technology

To deal with the semantically-rich annotations attached to the artifacts, devices, software and other resources of activity spheres, we need several layers of independent ontologies. For example, each artifact is expected to carry proprietary descriptions of its services; the same will probably happen with networking protocols, while people will have to use these descriptions in the composition of activity spheres.

When realising ambient spheres, one faces three kinds of research questions:

- To develop a commonly accepted high level ontology for pervasive and adaptive services and verify its wide applicability over various contexts, and

- To develop mechanisms for interfacing the heterogeneous and possibly inaccurate third-party ontologies of the ambient sphere components
- To represent state changes and different versions of the sphere ontology

Regarding the first issue, currently, there are two major standardisation efforts in the ontology domain, carried out by IEEE and the World Wide Web Consortium. The former is concerned with a standard for upper ontology, and due to its general approach is likely to have only a limited impact. The proposal of W3C and its ontology task group (W3C) concerns the ontology language OWL (Web Ontology Language) (Wang, 2004), which is the evolution of DAML+OIL. The OWL language provides support for merging of ontologies, through the use of language features which enable importing other ontologies and enable expression of conceptual equivalence and disjunction. This encourages separate ontology development, refinement and re-use.

The second issue is even more complex. Although common ontologies can serve as the means to achieve efficient communication between heterogeneous artifacts, it seems that they are not always effective (i.e. using a common ontology is not possible in the case where artifacts use closed proprietary ontologies). A different ontology-based mechanism is required, which will make the ontologies of the interacting artifacts semantically interoperable. Current techniques for ontology matching require access to the internal structure of constituent ontologies, which must be verified for consistency, and result in static solutions (a set of mappings or a new ontology), which in addition have to be stored somewhere. But an activity sphere is a transitory, dynamically evolving entity, composed of heterogeneous, independent, usually third-party components. That is why we are applying the ontology alignment technique, which describes a process of discovering similarities between two black-box source ontologies, resulting in the specification of the correspondences between the ontologies.

For the representation of the state changes of an activity sphere, the techniques of ontology mapping or ontology merging are employed. With ontology mapping, the correspondences between the two ontologies are stored separately from the ontologies and thus are not part of the ontologies themselves. The correspondences can be used, for example, for querying heterogeneous knowledge bases using a common interface or transforming data between different representations. When performing ontology merging, a new ontology is created, which is the union of the source ontologies. The new ontology, in general, replaces the original source ontologies. There are two distinct approaches in ontology merging. In the first approach, the input of the merging process is a collection of ontologies and the outcome is a new, merged ontology, which captures the original ontologies. In the second approach, the original ontologies are not replaced, but rather a "view", called bridge ontology, is created which imports the original ontologies and specifies the correspondences using bridge axioms. The merged ontology captures all the knowledge from the original ones. The challenge in ontology merging is to ensure that all correspondences and differences between the ontologies are reflected in the merged ontology.

GAS

We have designed the Gadgetware Architectural Style (GAS) as a generic architectural style for activity spheres. GAS constitutes a generic framework, shared by users and designers, for consistently describing, using, reasoning about ubiquitous computing applications deployed within an AmI environment (Kameas, 2004). GAS provides:

- A vocabulary that can be used to describe the sphere as an artifact collection, which appears intuitive to people, as it builds upon notions already used in similar contexts;
- A framework for the interpretation of the sphere operation (that is, for assigning meaning to the vocabulary). Such a framework is implemented as a layered ontology and ontology management components;
- Rules that define the application of task decomposition and artifact interaction schemes, as well as policies to ensure correctness, privacy and other social properties of the sphere.

GAS adopts the principles of software component technology and service oriented architectures and applies these to the domain of ubiquitous computing, in order to describe the process whereby people configure and use complex collections of interacting artifacts (Kameas, 2003). Thus, a component in the ubiquitous computing domain is an artifact, physical or digital, which is independently built and delivered as an autonomous functional unit that offers interfaces by which it can be connected with other components to compose a larger system, without compromising its shape or functionality. The aforementioned definition emphasizes the fact that any sphere component provides its functionality in the form of well-defined services; these are accessible via interfaces. Ubiquitous computing application components are treated as black-boxes encapsulating implementation details. Components collaborate by exchanging messages with other components; these trigger local component computations which in turn affect the state of the application.

An interface is a description of a set of operations related to the external specification of a component. An interface consists of the artifact properties and capabilities, a set of operations that a component needs to access in its surrounding environment (required interface) and a set of operations that the surrounding environment can access on the given component (provided interface). An operation is a unit of functionality implemented by a component, which may map to a method, a function or a procedure.

The adoption of the component paradigm has various benefits: it increases the degree of abstraction during sphere programming, provides proven (error-free) solutions for certain aspects of the application domain, increases productivity, and facilitates maintenance and evolution of software systems. A correct representation of context is also required to make such a system usable.

Components of GAS

GAS defines the logical elements necessary to support a variety of ubiquitous computing applications (**Figure 1**). The basic definitions encapsulated in GAS are:

- **eEntity:** It is the digital counterpart of an entity (i.e. a person, object, software process etc). An eEntity constitutes the basic component of a sphere. 'e' stands here for extrovert and is used to denote the acquired through technology competence of an entity to interact with other entities in an augmented way for the purpose of supporting the users' everyday activities meaningfully. This interaction is mainly related with either the provision or consumption of context and services between the participating entities.
- **Artifacts:** An artifact is a tangible object which bears digitally expressed properties. An artifact is an eEntity. Examples of artifacts are furniture, clothes, devices, sensors, a digital clock, etc.
- **Services:** These are treated as resources provided by an eEntity. Their functionality is encapsulated in the provider eEntity and they contribute in realizing tasks by requester eEntities.
- **Ambient ecology:** The services of two or more eEntities can be combined in a ubiquitous computing application; then these eEntities form an Ambient Ecology. Since the same eEntity may participate in many Ambient Ecologies the whole-part relationship is not exclusive.
- **Plugs:** They are the interface of an eEntity and provide to the other eEntities its properties, capabilities and services. Plugs are characterized by their direction and data type. Plugs may be output (O) in case they manifest their corresponding property (e.g. as a provided service), input (I) in case they associate their property with data from other artifacts (e.g. as service consumers), or I/O when both happens. Plugs also have a certain data type, which can be either a semantically primitive one (e.g. integer, boolean, etc.), or a semantically rich one (e.g. image, sound etc.).
- **Synapses:** They are associations between two compatible plugs. When a property of a source entity changes, the new value is propagated through the synapse to the target entity. The initial change of value caused by a state transition of the source entity causes finally a state transition to the target entity. In that way, synapses are a realization of the functional context of the entity.
- **Spheres:** An activity sphere is an Ambient Ecology deployed over an AmI space having a specific purpose.

GAS acts as a consistent conceptual and technical referent among artifact designers and application designers. It allows the former to provide the building blocks and rules for the latter to compose functional applications. It also serves as conveyor of design semantics from design experts to application designers. Design options and compositional constraints can be embedded in artifacts in the form of configuration rules which guide and inform the composition and use of applications. For the end-user, this model can serve as a high level task interface; for the developer, it can serve as a domain model and a methodology. In both cases, it can be used as a communication medium, which people can understand, and by using it they can manipulate the "disappearing computers" within their environment. GAS plays the role of a vehicle for transforming people from passive consumers to creative shapers of their environment, by enabling them to create new and emerging functionalities out of artifacts pre-fabricated by application designers.

Conceptualizing Activity Spheres

As is the usual case, in order to carry everyday activities, people will look for services or objects they can use. Using the GAS approach, people will be able to carry out their activities using artifact combinations. A prerequisite to this step is the decomposition of activities into tasks and the selection of services that can support them. As we discussed earlier, this can be done either explicitly by the user or tacitly by the system.

In GAS terms, this means that the system or the user has to look for the artifacts that have properties matching the task requirements, select the most appropriate ones and combine the respective plugs into functioning synapses, which they can manually adapt in order to optimize the collective functionality. The establishment of a synapse is only possible between plugs that are compatible. Two levels of plug compatibility exist: Direction and data type compatibility. According to direction compatibility output or I/O plugs can only be connected to input or I/O plugs. According to Data type compatibility, plugs must have the same data type to be connected via a synapse.

No other limitation exists in making a synapse. Although this may mean that meaningless synapses are allowed, it has the advantage of letting the user create associations and cause the emergence of new collective sphere behaviors that the artifact manufacturer may have never thought of. Because the composition of artifacts is regarded as a high-level programming task, "run-time" errors may appear causing artifact compositions not to function properly as expected. Optimization is a trial-and-error process: people use the activity sphere and adapt the synapses and the mappings in order to achieve the desired functionality.

The development of activity spheres as ubiquitous computing applications requires a powerful programming paradigm. Traditional software programs have followed the procedure call paradigm, where the procedure is the central abstraction called by a client to accomplish a specific service. Programming in this paradigm requires that the client has detailed knowledge about the procedures (services) provided by the server. However, this kind of knowledge is not possible in the context of an Ami space, because it usually contains artifacts that were separately developed possibly by different vendors. Synapse-based application development follows the principles of service based application composition. Synapses represent the glue that binds together interfaces of different artifacts.

The idea of building ubiquitous computing applications out of components is possible only in the context of a supporting component framework that acts as a middleware. The kernel of such a middleware is designed to support basic functionality such as accepting and dispatching messages, managing local hardware resources (sensors/actuators), the plug/synapse interoperability and a semantic service discovery protocol. In the next section, we shall describe GAS-OS, the middleware that implements the GAS concepts.

Figure 1. The concepts of artifact, plug and synapse

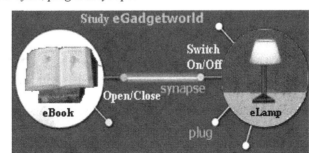

Figure 2. The layers of GAS architectural framework

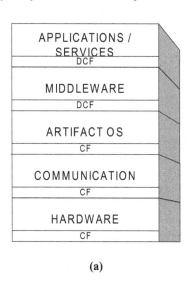

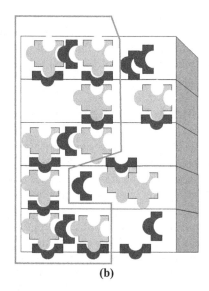

(a)   (b)

The Abstract Sphere Layered Architecture

At a high level GAS contains five layers (**Figure 2a**); each layer regards the immediately lower layer as a virtual machine that it can use, and serves as a virtual machine to the immediately higher layer. Each layer is not treated as a closed stack of protocols and software, but as a repository of interoperable components (**Figure 2b**). This model, which may be corresponded to the ISO/OSI network model, is generic enough to encompass current approaches to distributed systems architectures.. A few examples of such system architectures could be J2EE and JINI. J2EE is a set of coordinated specifications and practices that together enable solutions for developing, deploying, and managing multi-tier server-centric applications. JINI is a recent distributed system technology that is language-centric, based on Java.

The J2EE application model divides enterprise applications into three fundamental parts: components, containers, and connectors. Thus J2EE simplifies enterprise applications by basing them on standardized, modular components, by providing a complete set of services to those components, and by handling many details of application behavior automatically, without complex programming. A significant issue of J2EE standard is that it includes complete specifications and compliance tests to ensure portability of applications across the wide range of existing enterprise systems capable of supporting J2EE. Some other key aspects are that it provides scalability and can support various types of communication with respect to the communication components that are selected.

JINI is a well-established distributed system architecture and it can correspond to the middleware layer of the framework offering a distributed computing environment in which services can be dynamically discovered and invoked in a fault-tolerant manner. In the JINI architecture the artifacts are by definition mobile entities but asynchronous communication among these artifacts is not possible. Finally JINI is language-centric since it assumes Java as the implementation language.

The bottom layer groups the artifact (object or space) hardware components. They are expected to be "black boxes" of functionality, which have to be managed by the middleware as local artifact resources. Nevertheless, this layer "grounds" the sphere in the real world, as all activity tasks will have to be realized using the services and properties of the hardware. Thus, if any of these components comes with an ontology, it would describe categories of tangible things.

The communication layer contains the protocols used for actual exchange of messages between artifacts. GAS requires the establishment of synapses, which are virtual communication channels between artifacts; implementation of synapses is based on the components of this layer.

The local artifact OS is responsible for managing the artifact resources (i.e. hardware components, power source, communication, etc).

The middleware layer contains the components that realize a distributed component framework capable of managing processes and resources at the sphere level. An example of such middleware, GAS-OS, will be described in the next section.

The application layer contains descriptions of activity tasks, which are realized by the middleware. It also contains models of services emerging at the sphere level; mappings of these services can be stored in artifacts that participate in the sphere, using ontology alignment mechanisms.

Levels of Abstraction

The use of high-level abstractions for expressing artifact associations allows the flexible configuration and reconfiguration of ubiquitous computing applications. This is where the new affordances (composeability and changeability) of artifacts come to play. GAS supports three abstraction levels:

- **Network independence:** The Plug/Synapse model is independent of the underlying protocols, needed for example to route messages or to discover resources in realization of an application.
- **Physical independence:** The services offered by an artifact are independent of the artifact itself; this does not hold for its physical characteristics. Thus the creation of artifact compositions does not require the continuous presence of an artifact (provided they do not involve physical characteristics)
- **Semantic independence:** The description of artifact compositions or applications is based only on the types of the participating plugs and is independent of the way the plugs are realized in each artifact

Example

Let's take a look at the life of Patricia, a 27-year old single woman, who lives in a small apartment near the city centre and studies Spanish literature at the Open University. A few days ago she passed by this store, where she saw an advertisement about these new augmented artifacts, the "extrovert Gadgets". Pat decided to enter. Half an hour later she had given herself a very unusual present: a few furniture pieces and other devices that would turn her apartment into a smart one: Pat had what it took to compose a Study Sphere. Pat had asked the store employee to pre-configure some of the e-Gadgets, so that she could create a smart studying corner in her living room. Her idea was simple (she felt a little silly when she spoke to the employee about it): when she sat on the chair and she would draw it near the desk and then open a book on it, then the study lamp would be switched on automatically. If she would close the book or stand up, then the light would go off (she hadn't thought of any use of the carpet, but she liked the colors).

The GAS approach can be illustrated with this very simple scenario, which contains the following artifacts: eBook, eChair, eDeskLamp and eDesk. The eDesk can sense light intensity, temperature, weight on it, and proximity of a chair. The eChair can tell whether someone was sitting on it. The eDeskLamps can remotely be turned on and off. The eBook can tell whether it is open or closed and determine the amount of light that falls on it. Collective artifact operation is accomplished by establishing three synapses between the constituent artifacts. For example, the ReadingActivity property, associated with the eDesk artifact, depends on the input properties defined as BookOnTop and ChairInFront; the later have been derived as relational properties between eDesk and the pair of eBook and eChair artifacts respectively. In the case of the synapse between eDesk.ReadingActivity and eDeskLamp.Light plugs, a data type compatibility issue arises, and one has to define mappings that will make the two plugs collaborate (**Figure 3**).

The collective function of this application can be described as:

When this CHAIR is NEAR the DESK
AND
ANY BOOK is ON the DESK,
AND

SOMEONE is sitting on the CHAIR
AND
The BOOK is OPEN
THEN
TURN the LAMP ON.

In order to achieve the collective functionality required by Pat, the employee in the store had to create a set of Synapses among the e-Gadgets' Plugs (**Figure 4**). This type of functionality and component structure is created, inspected and modified through GAS compatible end-user tools (i.e. the Editor). For example, Pat can subsequently define the intensity of the eLamp when it's being automatically switched on; thus the light won't blind her. Or, if an intelligent agent is used, it could adjust each time the light intensity based on the overall amount of light in the room, as it is recorded by luminosity sensors distributed on objects in the room.

We assume that a process for turning an object into artifact has been followed (Kameas, 2004). Broadly it will consist of two phases: a) embedding the hardware modules into the object and b) installing the software modules that will determine its functionality. Then, the scenario that is implemented is as follows: when the particular chair is near the desk and someone is sitting on it and any book is on the desk and the book is open then the system infers that reading activity is taking place and the lamp intensity is adjusted according to the book luminosity. An actual implementation of this ecology is shown in **Figure 5**.

In the following we shall explain how the proposed middleware supports collective sphere functionality.

GAS-OS MIDDLEWARE

The GAS-OS middleware provides ubiquitous computing application designers and developers with a runtime environment that can execute the activity task models, as they are instantiated on the artifacts that exist in a specific AmI space. Artifacts have to run GAS-OS in order to establish context-based communication, and enable

Figure 3. Visualization of study sphere with the help of the editor

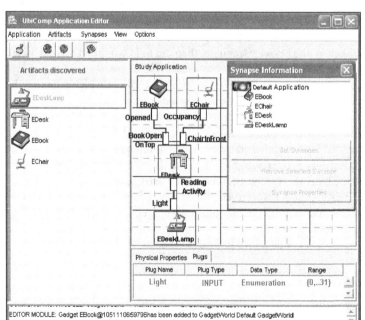

people to access their services, properties and capabilities in a uniform way. In order to execute GAS-OS on an artifact, the following software modules need to be installed:

- **Operating system:** Any operating system supporting the Personal Java is adequate.
- **Local drivers:** Provide the necessary communication protocol between the control circuitry of the artifact hardware modules and the middleware.
- **Artifact software:** The specific software that defines the behavior of the artifact, using the interaction model provided by the middleware. Behavior here means the manifestation of its hardware changes in the digital space and vice versa as well as the services it will provide or consume.
- **GAS-OS middleware:** Provides the necessary communication layer as well as the abstraction layer (interaction model) that enables an artifact to collaborate with other artifacts and take part in activity sphere applications.

The architecture of GAS-OS is shown in **Figure 6** (adopted from (Drossos, 2007), where it is presented in more detail).

The GAS-OS kernel is designed to provide support for accepting and dispatching messages, managing local hardware resources (sensors/actuators), and implementing the plug/synapse interaction mechanism. The kernel is also capable of managing service and artifact discovery messages in order to facilitate the formation of the proper synapses.

The GAS-OS kernel encompasses a P2P Communication Module, a Process Manager, a State Variable Manager, and a Property Evaluator module. The P2P Communication Module is responsible for application-level communication between the various GAS-OS nodes (Kameas, 2002). The Process Manager is the coordinator module of GAS-OS. The main function of this module is to monitor and execute the rules that define how and when the infrastructure should react to changes in the environment. Furthermore, it is responsible for handling the memory resources of an artifact and caching information of other artifacts to improve communication performance when service discovery is required. The State Variable Manager handles the runtime storage of artifact's state variable values, reflecting both the hardware environment (sensors/actuators) at each particular moment and properties that are evaluated based on sensory data and P2P communicated data. The Property Evaluator is responsible for the evaluation of artifact's composite properties and is based on a set of rules that govern artifact transition from one state to another.

Extending the functionality of the GAS-OS kernel can be achieved through plug-ins, which can be easily incorporated to an artifact running GAS-OS, via the plug-in manager. Using ontologies, for example, and the ontology manager plug-in all artifacts can use a commonly understood vocabulary of services and capabilities, in order to mask heterogeneity in context understanding and real-world models (Christopoulou, 2005). In that

Figure 4. Schematic representations of the connections between appliances, in the above scenario

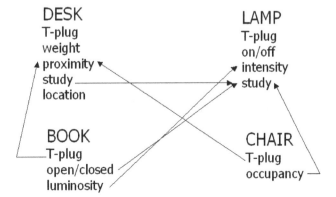

Figure 5. Realization of the study sphere using artifacts

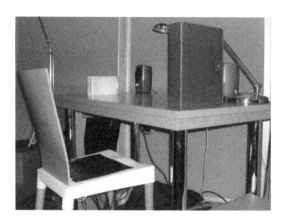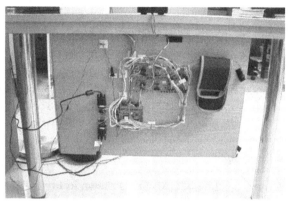

way, high-level descriptions of services and resources independent of the context of a specific application are possible, facilitating the exchange of information between heterogeneous artifacts as well as the discovery of services. The security manager plug-in on the other hand, when developed, will be responsible for realizing the security policies of each artifact. These policies will be encoded as rules in the ontology, thus becoming directly available to the Process Manager. The security manager will mediate information exchange via synapses in order to ensure that security policies are respected.

The current version of GAS-OS has been implemented in the Java Personal Edition (PE) that is fully compatible with the Java Standard Edition 1.1.8. So far, GAS-OS has been tested in laptops, IPAQs and finally in the EJC (Embedded Java Controller) board. The proliferation of systems besides classical computers capable of executing Java, make Java a suitable underlying layer providing a uniform abstraction for our middleware. The use of Java as the underlying platform of the middleware decouples GAS-OS from typical operations like memory management, networking, etc. Furthermore, it facilitates the deployment on a wide range of devices from mobile phones and PDAs to specialized Java processors.

In the following, we shall present implementation details concerning two basic services provided by GAS-OS that support the formation of activity spheres. First, synapse management, a mechanism that handles the process of establishing synapses among artifacts, and then inter-artifact communication, a mechanism that supports the formation and operation of synapses at the network layer by establishing peer-to-peer connections over the physical layer.

Synapse Management

The management of synapses is performed by the Process Manager module. The Process Manager collaborates with the Communication Module and the State Variable Manager (**Figure 7**), and sets up an event based internal messaging system that combines input from sensors and actuators with input received from other artifacts, via the network.

As an example, let's consider the synapsing process among the ReadingActivity plug of the eDesk and the Light plug of the eLamp:

- **Synapse Request:** Synapse request occurs after the one artifact has discovered the other, thus property schemas of each artifact are available to each other. The eDesk sends a "Connection Request" message to the eLamp. The message contains information concerning the eDesk and its ReadingActivity plug as well as the name of the Light plug.

Figure 6. GAS-OS architecture

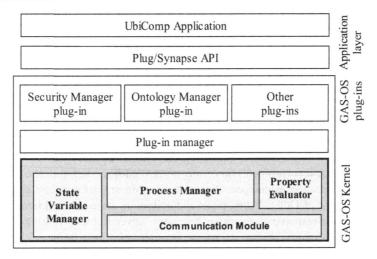

Figure 7. Synapse establishment between plugs Reading and Light_Switch

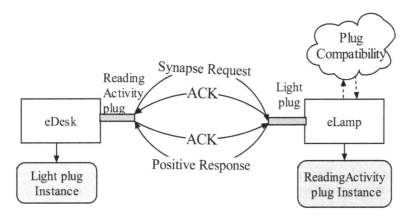

- **Synapse Response:** When the eLamp receives the message it first checks the plug compatibility of the ReadingActivity and Light plugs. In the example the Reading plug is output and the Light plug is input, so the direction compatibility test is passed. Data type incompatibility does not hapt the synapsing process, however it needs to be dealt via the use of mappings. Following, an instance of the ReadingActivity plug is created in the eLamp (as a local reference) and a positive response is sent back to the eDesk. The instance of the ReadingActivity plug is notified for changes by its remote counterpart plug and this interaction serves as an intermediary communication channel. In case of a negative plug compatibility test, a negative response message is sent to the eDesk, while no instance of the ReadingActivity plug is created. When the eDesk receives a positive response, it also creates an instance of the Light plug, and the connection is established.
- **Synapse Activation:** After connection has been established, the two plugs are capable of exchanging data. Output plugs (ReadingActivity) use specific objects, called shared objects (SO), to encapsulate the plug data to send, while input plugs (Light) use specific event-based mechanisms, called shared object listeners (SOL), to become aware of incoming plug data. When the value of the shared object of the ReadingActiv-

ity plug changes the instance of the Light plug in the eDesk is notified and a synapse activation message is sent to the eLamp. The eLamp receives the message and changes the shared object of its ReadingActivity plug instance. This, in turn, notifies the target Light plug, which reacts as specified.

- **Synapse Disconnection:** Finally, if one of the two connected plugs breaks the synapse, a synapse disconnection message is sent to the remote plug in order to also terminate the other end of the synapse. Synapse disconnection can be either initiated explicitly by the user, or indirectly if one of the two artifacts becomes unavailable (e.g. goes out of range, its battery fails etc.).

Inter—Artifact Communication

The Communication Module is responsible for effecting the communication between different artifacts. This module, implements application-level protocols for connectionless ad-hoc communication as well as mechanisms for internal diffusion of information exchanged. Peer-to-peer communication is implemented by adopting the basic principles and definitions of JXTA. Peers, pipes and endpoints are combined into a layered architecture. Peers implement protocols for resource and service discovery, advertisement, routing as well as the queuing mechanisms to support asynchronous message exchange. In order to avoid large messages and as a consequence traffic congestion in the network, XML-based messages are used to wrap the information required for each protocol. Pipes correspond to the session and presentation layers of the ISO-OSI reference model, implementing protocols for connection establishment between two peers, supporting multicast communication for service and artifact discovery, while at the same time guaranteeing reliable delivery of messages. In cases where reliable network protocols are used in the transport layer (e.g. TCP/IP), pipes are reduced to acknowledging application-level resource availability (e.g. sending synapse request message to an incompatible plug will return a NACK message). Endpoints are considered as the fundamental networking units and are associated to specific network resources (e.g. a TCP port). According to the transport layer chosen we can have many different endpoints (e.g. IP-based, Bluetooth, IrDA, etc.), which can also serve as a bridge for different networks. **Figure 8** shows the p2p communication between the eDesk and eLamp artifacts described in the example. Both the eDesk and the eLamp are considered to own a communication module with an IP-based (dynamically determined) Endpoint. Plug/Synapse interactions (e.g. synapse establishment) are translated to XML messages by the communication module and delivered to the remote peer at the specified IP address.

The Communication Module is implemented as a decentralized messaging based system (i.e. the CM requires no fixed infrastructure or the support of any other entity except computing peers) abstracting the underlying network and communication protocol and providing services through a well-defined interface. All communication between peers, even within the platform layers, take place via asynchronous XML based messages.

Figure 8. From plug/synapse interactions to p2p communication

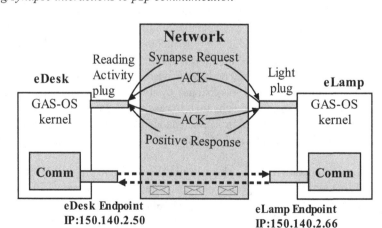

The main communication protocols of the GAS-OS Communication Module are (**Figure 9**):

- **Gadget Discovery Protocol (GDP).** This protocol is used to discover artifacts in the network using resources as criteria. Resources are represented as advertisements, and are usually information about a remote artifact (i.e. ID, Services, Relay, etc.). This information can then be used to establish a p2p communication. An artifact creates a discovery message that is sent to all listening artifacts through a Multicast Endpoint. There are two kinds of discovery messages, the simple ones, where a specific artifact ID is requested and the complex ones, where either a specific service from an unknown artifact is requested.
- **Gadget Advertisement Protocol (GAP).** This protocol is used to advertise one or more attributes of an artifact. An advertisement message is usually a response to a discovery message, thus formed according to the requested information.
- **Gadget Information Protocol (GIP).** This protocol is used for exchange of data between two artifacts. It uses a single unicast pipe to send the information to a specific peer. Each data message is folded inside an envelope that contains the recipient's identification.
- **Message Acknowledging Protocol (MAP).** This underlying protocol is responsible for the robustness of the communication system. Its main task is to provide acknowledgements (ACK) for each arrived message to the sender and NACK receipts for each lost message. Furthermore if a message is lost the MAP protocol is responsible for resending the message to the target artifact.

SPHERE DEPLOYMENT

In this section, we shall discuss the available technologies for deployment of GAS compatible activity spheres.

Commercially Available Solutions

During the design process of GAS-OS several existing solutions for the Communication Module as well as for middleware/operating systems were studied in terms of suitability to our concept and requirements. Different

Figure 9. The communication process between artifacts A and B

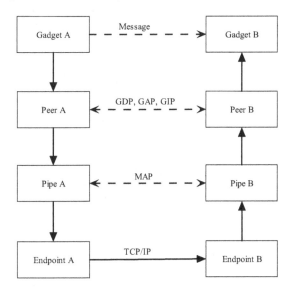

middleware systems like CORBA, Java RMI, Jini, and DCOM have been developed to produce interoperable applications based on distributed objects. However, on the one hand, most of them are language (RMI, Jini) or system (DCOM) dependent, and on the other hand, they try to provide as much functionality as possible, which leads to very complex and resource consuming systems, unsuitable for small devices. Furthermore, conventional middleware systems are designed mostly for stable network environments, in which service unavailability is a rare event and can be treated as an error.

An attractive approach is represented by SOAP, a lightweight protocol for exchange of information in a decentralized, distributed environment that provides an XML messaging system for the communication scheme. Nevertheless, the specification given for creating tags for the message envelopes, encoding rules and RPC representation are rather complex and create large messages, which may reduce the network performance when scalability issues occur.

Universal Plug and Play (UPnP) is a framework that offers IP address allocation and DNS name assignment for mobile devices. It is designed to bring easy to use, flexible, standards based connectivity to ad-hoc or unmanaged networks whether in the home, car, public spaces, or attached to the Internet. Moreover, UPnP is a distributed, open networking architecture that leverages TCP/IP and the Web technologies to enable seamless proximity networking in addition to control and data transfer among networked devices in the home, office and public spaces. UPnP's Simple Service Discovery Protocol (SSDP) supports registration and discovery of devices. This may involve dedicated directory services but does not rely on them.

Requirements for Sphere Deployment

In order to deploy and manage activity spheres in AmI spaces, there exists a set of important requirements that the underlying infrastructure must meet. Some of these are:

- **Advertisement of services:** The networking layer should provide an efficient mechanism for artifacts to advertise their services, so that the activity sphere management software can discover them
- **Discovery of available services within an AmI space:** GAS supports the instantiation of spheres on an AmI sphere by exploiting the services available therein. An efficient, non centralized mechanism is required to support service discovery
- **Efficient management of the dynamic topology of the network:** As artifacts move in and out of spheres, and the availability of services changes dynamically, a flexible mechanism to maintain the current state of the sphere is required
- **Unobtrusive handover:** as spheres may be deployed over different AmI spaces, the networking layer must ensure that the user disturbance from moving from one AmI space to the other is kept at a minimum
- **End-to-end user support:** People do not need to be aware of the exchanges between the various GAS layers when creating or using activity spheres
- **Support for content:** Several everyday activities entail the use of multimedia content. Multimedia files are large and pose severe performance requirements of the networking layer
- **Privacy support:** Although currently this aspect is handled at the middleware layer, it must be supported by all the layers in the architecture
- **Management transparency:** Referring to the layered GAS architecture, each layer manages its resources transparently to the layers above it. Thus, the management of network resources should be made locally in the communication layer
- **Scalability:** One important drawback of existing approaches is that they do not scale well to support spheres having hundreds or thousands of artifacts. However this is expected to be the size of the average sphere
- **Heterogeneity management:** At least two dimensions of heterogeneity affect the networking layer: the one is due to the heterogeneous artifacts and the other is due to the fact that several activity spheres will have to be instantiated in the same AmI space

The Role of Next Generation Networks

Next Generation Networks (NGN) are packet based networks that exploit recent advances in telecommunications to provide advanced communication services. The main feature of NGN is the separation of the network services from the transport layer, which allows the two layers to evolve independently. Thus, the provision of services can be supported seamlessly by different access networks, resulting in flexible and dynamic network architecture (Knightson, 2005).

In order to improve the user experience, AmI spaces must be developed as environments of integrated services, which enable the reuse of the user information between services, the ability to integrate easily new services and the service continuity whatever is the access medium and the access device. An AmI space must provide service elements like identity management, community management and availability management, and should also be able to integrate third party services. Communication services should not be conceived anymore independently from this environment of integrated service and should be accessible seamlessly in a user centric way.

By separating the service layer from the transport layer, NGN can meet the requirements of management transparency, scalability, flexibility and management of heterogeneity. The management of the network is delegated to control services operating either at the transport layer or the service layers, thus increasing flexibility. Ensuring compatibility between these two layers increases management transparency. The ability to access different transport protocols in a seamless way increases scalability and contributes to the management of heterogeneity, because this problem is now solved at the networking layer of the architecture.

The management architecture of NGN can meet the other requirements. It consists of four layers: business process, functional, informational and physical. Each of these makes available several functions to support the related layer management activities. For example, functions in the physical layer support the communication between "real" sphere components, such artifacts and software processes, while functions in the informational layer are mostly concerned with managing the resources of the sphere (which are abstractions of physical elements). The functional layer can support the advertisement and discovery requirements of AmI space components, while the business layer can provide management functions for higher level activities, such as privacy, handling of content and quality of service.

CONCLUSION

In this chapter, we have described a novel user centric approach to the design of future ubiquitous computing applications. This approach uses the resources of an AmI space to deploy activity spheres. An activity sphere uses the available resources to support user tasks. Spheres are considered as compositions of services offered by artifacts in the AmI space; an artifact is an object augmented with ICT components. Then, a composition can happen between compatible services and can be initiated either by the user or the system.

A layered architecture was presented that supports this concept. In this architecture, all communication support components have been included in the networking layer, while the middleware layer is used to provide higher level support to the management of spheres. A specific middleware system, GAS-OS, was described; this system supports the definition and management of spheres, but also provides support for many lower level functions, due to the lack of appropriate technology.

With the advent of NGN, it is expected that all communication management functions will be delegated to the networking layer, thus enhancing performance and privacy. NGN, by separating transport from service, will also contribute to managing heterogeneity and to increasing transparency, thus leading to the efficient development of spheres capable of supporting large scale human activities.

REFERENCES

Christopoulou, E., and Kameas, A. (2005). GAS Ontology: an ontology for collaboration among ubiquitous computing devices. *International Journal of Human-Computer Studies, 62*(5), 664-685.

Drossos, N., Goumopoulos, C., and Kameas, A. (2007). A conceptual model and the supporting middleware for composing ubiquitous computing applications. *Journal of Ubiquitous Computing and Intelligence*, American Scientific Publishers(ASP), 1(2), 1-13.

Gruber, T. (1993). A translation approach to portable ontologies. *Knowledge Acquisition 5*(2), 199-220.

Hagras, H., Doctor, F., Lopez, A., Callaghan, V. (2007). An Incremental Adaptive Life Long Learning Approach for Type-2 Fuzzy Embedded Agents in Ambient Intelligent Environments. *IEEE Transactions on Fuzzy Systems, 15*(1), 41-55.

ISTAG in FP6: Working Group 1, IST Research Content, Final Report (2006). Last retrieved on 11/22/2006 from http://www.cordis.lu/ist/istag.htm

Kameas, A., Bellis, S., Mavrommati, I., Delaney, K., Colley, M., and Pounds-Cornish, A. (2003). An Architecture that Treats Everyday Objects as Communicating Tangible Components. In *Proc. 1st IEEE International Conference on Pervasive Computing and Communications (PerCom03)*, Fort Worth, USA.

Kameas, A., Mavrommati, I. and Markopoulos, P. (2004). Computing in tangible: using artifacts as components of Ambient Intelligent Environments. In Riva, G., Vatalaro, F., Davide, F. and Alcaniz, M. (eds) *Ambient Intelligence*, IOS Press, 121-142.

Kameas, A., Ringas, D., Mavrommati, I and Wason, P. (2002). eComP: an Architecture that Supports P2P Networking Among Ubiquitous Computing Devices. In *Proc. IEEE P2P 2002 Conference*, Linkoping, Sweden..

Knightson, K., Morita, N. and Towle, T. (2005). NGN architecture: generic principles, functional architecture and implementation. *IEEE Communications, 43*(10), 49-56.

Norman, D.A. (1998). *The Invisible Computer.* MIT press

Norman, D.A. (1988). *The Psychology of Everyday Things*. New York, Basic books.

Wang, X. H., Zhang, D. Q., Gu, T., and Pung, H. K. (2004). Ontology based context modeling and reasoning using OWL. In *Proc. of the Second IEEE Annual Conference on Pervasive Computing and Communications Workshops,* IEEE Computer Society, 18.

Weiser, M. (1991). The computer for the 21st century. *Scientific American, 265*(3), 94-104.

Zaharakis, I. D. and Kameas A. (2006). Emergent Phenomena in AmI Spaces. *The EASST (European Association of Software Science and Technology) Newsletter, 2006-12* 82-96.

Zaharakis I. D. and Kameas A. (2008). Engineering Emergent Ecologies of Interacting Artefacts". In Lumsden, J. (Ed.) *Handbook of Research on User Interface Design and Evaluation for Mobile Technology*, IGI Global.

KEY TERMS

Activity Sphere: A schema describing all the resources required in order to achieve a specific goal of an actor (human or agent) within an AmI space.

Ambient Intelligence (AmI): The vision of Ambient Intelligence implies a seamless environment of computing, advanced networking technology and specific interfaces.

Ambient Intelligence Space (AmI space): A physical space augmented with ubiquitous computing technology. An AmI space is considered to contain sensors, actuators, networking, processing and storage capacity and offers connectivity services, location-based services, discovery services etc.

Artifact: An everyday object augmented with sensing, actuating, storage, processing, and networking capabilities. An artifact is considered to have a dual presence, both in the physical (because it is an object of the real world) and digital worlds (by publishing its services and properties on the network).

Middleware: Special purpose software, which masks the complexity and distribution of the nodes of a distributed system. Middleware makes available the collective capabilities of the underlying distributed system as services, which are accessible in a unified manner, regardless of the location or availability of the system nodes.

Ontology: A formal specification of a shared conceptualization. In other words, everything we know about a subject. An ontology is usually expressed as a network of classes, each of which represents a conceptual entity (i.e. a category) of the subject. Classes are connected with semantically rich relationships, while constraints may also be applied.

Ubiquitous Computing: A novel computing paradigm, which integrates among others distributed systems, embedded systems, ad-hoc (wireless) networks, middleware and user interface design. It comprises the set of computer and network based technologies used to achieve the vision of AmI.

Chapter XXIII

Channel Management Schemes to Support Services in Ubiquitous Communications Infrastructures for Future Transportation Technologies

Eduard Babulak
Fairleigh Dickinson University, Canada

Konstantinos G. Ioannou
University of Patras, Greece

Athanasios Ioannou
Hellenic Organization of Telecommunications SA, Patras, Greece

ABSTRACT

Transportation and Internet Technologies have evolved dramatically during the last decade, laying solid foundation for the future generation of the Ubiquitous Internet access, omnipresent Web technologies and ultimate automated information cyberspace. As a result, the current efforts in the research and development in the areas of Future Transportation and Next Generation of Internet Technologies promotes formation of inter-disciplinary international teams of experts, scientists, researchers and engineers to create a new generation of applications and technologies that will facilitate the future transportation system. The authors present a dynamic channel management scheme for a Mobile Communication System, that supports services in Ubiquitous Communications Infrastructures for Future Transportation Technologies (DCMS-FTT). The performance is improved as it can be seen from the simulation results.

I. INTRODUCTION

The motor industry faces a time of change. Increasing competition, globalization and newly developing markets are challenges to all businesses involved in the industry. How they respond may determine the way future generations around the world live their lives.

Copyright © 2009, IGI Global, distributing in print or electronic forms without written permission of IGI Global is prohibited.

The past 20th century left us with legacy of the US highways, UK and German motorways, final flight of Concord Air, global Internet and CISCO monopoly in computer networking, etc. The current 21st century is perhaps one of the most interesting times in history to be alive. We are witnessing a phenomenal abundance of change in societies around the world in a very short period. Large, medium and small corporations alike have discovered the need to adapt to the new technologies, or sink in the emerging global knowledge economy.

There is no facet of life in the industrialized world that has not undergone some form of shift. The resultant new information economy has brought with it different approaches to work. In the past decade we have seen every aspect of the lives of individuals and organizations go through many evolutions and uncertainties. There are plenty of publications on the subject of futuristic and ubiquitous computing for the 21st century presenting excellent discussion and possible scenarios in the subject area. History proved that one must look forward and accept the futuristic vision as possible scenarios of tomorrow's reality. Nowadays, modern transportation technologies, controlled traffic, ubiquitous Internet access via mobile phones, road surveillance cameras are essential part of daily life Transportation technology will continue be present and essential for everyone. After introduction section, the in second section author discusses issues related to future transportation. In the third and forth sections author discusses future computing and ubiquitous communications infrastructures. Section five presents conclusions.

II. FUTURE TRANSPORTATION

The global economy and mobility of people inspires the various authors to plan for the future transportation that will be environmentally friendly, most economical and available on command at any time, anywhere for anyone.

You leave home, step into your car, turn the seat around and start working your way through your e-mail inbox, as the car drives you to work. Or you use whatever comes to be your mobile phone to summon one of a swarm of automatic buses.

Don't fancy stepping out into the rain? Then perhaps Telepresencing is how you'll win friends and influence people. It's the three-dimensional visual conference call of the future. These are all visions of Britain in 2055 from the heavyweight government Foresight report into how we'll travel in the next five decades. Futurology often goes too far. There aren't many of the mono-rails or flying cars predicted 50 years ago. But this report claims not to be a prediction of the future, but a set of alternative futures.

You don't have to steer, obviously. But your car will also talk to others to find out where all the traffic is and avoid it. Communications are mobile, instantaneous, and constant, 24/7. One scenario has been given the name "Perpetual Motion". It assumes personal transport continues to be the norm, but everything future technology has to offer is used to make getting around easier.

Figure 1. Perpetual motion by Tom Symonds

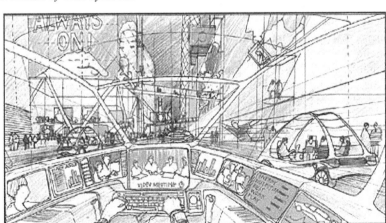

Figure 2. Good intentions: When green issues are the top priority by Tom Symonds

Figure 3. Suzuki car on narrow street

England is known for its narrow streets and very busy traffic. Car industry has adapted their strategy to manufacture smaller vehicles that could be used en the city centres as well as on the major motorways. Figure 3 illustrates example of the Suzuki vehicle.

The future transport will require complex computing and communications infrastructures to facilitate control and synchronization of traffic throughout the country. Figures 5 and 6 illustrate possible improvements in transport control and communication vehicle technology.

Future enhancements may include integration of adaptive cruise control functions to adjust speed based on the shape of the road, obtained via a map database and navigation system. Ideally, there will be infrastructure enhancements to communicate with in-vehicle sensors in detecting surface conditions as well.

In next two sections, author discusses the future trend in Computing and Communications Technologies that may be used in support of future transportation.

III. FUTURE COMPUTING

Research and development trends in the filed of computing industry promote a vision of smart spaces, smart devices, clothing, fully automated houses etc., which creates an environment where computers are everywhere and provide ultimate access to Internet. Future computing environments, such as the ones studied in CMU's Aura

Figure 5. Intelligent transportation system

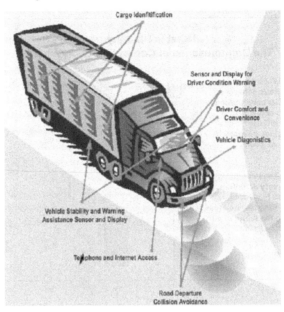

Figure 4. Intelligent transportation system

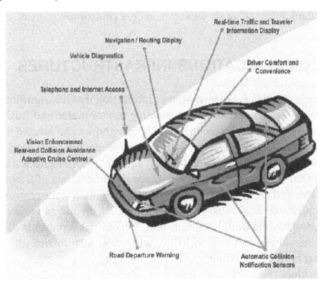

project, provide many kinds of information. Some of this information should be accessible only by a limited set of people. For example, a person's location is a sensitive piece of information, and releasing it to unauthorized entities might pose security and privacy risks. For instance, when walking home at night, a person will want to limit the risk of being robbed, and only people trusted by the person should be able to learn about her current location. The access control requirements of information available in a pervasive computing environment have not been thoroughly studied. The market is evolving from wired computing to pervasive computing, mobile and wireless, anytime at anyplace. Many types of information available in a pervasive computing environment,

Figure 6. What is ubiquity (Credit to www.ubicom.org)

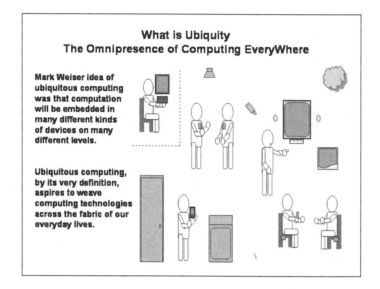

such as people location information, should be accessible only by a limited set of people. Some properties of the information raise unique challenges for the design of an access control mechanism.

IV. UBIQUITOUS COMMUNICATIONS INFRASTRUCTURES

The Internet opened up a new channel for firm-customer interaction that has significantly changed the customer relationship equation. Now, cell phone networks are enabling m-commerce and further change in the firm-customer dynamics. Traditionally, transport has been biased by geography and located near rivers, roads, and other transport services so that the cost of being reached by travellers or reaching travellers is lowered. Now, transport is increasingly using electronic networks (e.g., the Internet and mobile phone networks) to interact with customers. Thus in the next few years, it is likely that we will see the emergence of u-transport, where u stands for ubiquitous, universal, unique, and unison. U-Transport is the use of ubiquitous networks to support personalized and uninterrupted communications and transportation between a firm and its various stakeholders to provide a level of value over, above, and beyond traditional transport. Ubiquitous represents concept of having a networks everywhere with all consumer durable devices, with the intelligence and information widely dispersed and always accessible, as well as smart entities including appliances, buildings, signs, street smart communities, etc. The main focus is to enable one global network that would be available 24 hours a day, seven days a week, whole year round and will provide best quality of services to anyone, anywhere and anytime (Figure 6).

There is burgeoning population of 'effectively invisible' computers around us, embedded in the fabric of our homes, shops, vehicles, farms and some even in our bodies. They are invisible in that they are part of the environment and we can interact with them as we go about our normal activities. However they can range in size from large Plasma displays on the walls of buildings to microchips implanted in the human body. They help us command, control, communicate, do business, travel and entertain ourselves, and these 'invisible'computers are far more numerous than their desktop cousins.

World's telecommunications providers are looking for the ways to merge together all digital and analogue services (voice, video, data) on one common network, which would provide users with unlimited access to online information, business, entertainment, etc. Convergence's goal is to provide corporations with a highly secure

Figure 7. Convergence (Credit to CISCO)

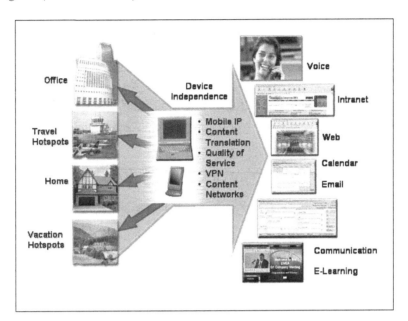

and controllable solution that supports real-time collaborative applications. The current trend in communications technologies are driven by convergence and ubiquity, as shown in Figure 7.

V. CHANNEL MANAGEMENT SCHEME

The proposed channel management scheme is based on a multi-layer cellular architecture. The proposed multilayer architecture is introduced in order to dedicate different types of services according to their type of call (Voice Calls - VC, Data Calls - DC) in the same geographical area.

The Proposed Dynamic Channel Management Scheme (DCMS) is based both on a One-Layer Cellular Architecture as described and on a Two-Layer Architecture, as TLCA described in. The number of layers (one or two) that is used depends on which architecture gives better optimization to the cellular system proposed to the offered traffic load. Let n be the number of microcells that consist the microcellular layer. The total offered load in the system is:

$$T_{off}^{tot} = \sum_{i=1}^{n} T_{off}(i) \tag{1}$$

Let C_s is the total number of channels in the system. In the microcellular layer, priority is given to handoff attempts by assigning guard channels $C_h(i)$ exclusively for handoff calls of Data Calls (DC) among the $C(i)$ channels in microcell i. The remaining $(C(i)-C_h(i))$ channels are shared by both new calls of Data Calls (DC) and Voice Calls (VC) and handoff calls of VC [25] and [26]. Let C_u be the channels assigned to umbrella cell to serve only handoff calls of DC. Hence:

$$C_S = \sum_{i}^{n} C(i) + C_u \tag{2}$$

Figure 8. State transition diagram for:(a) microcell (i) and (b) umbrella cell of DCMS-FTT

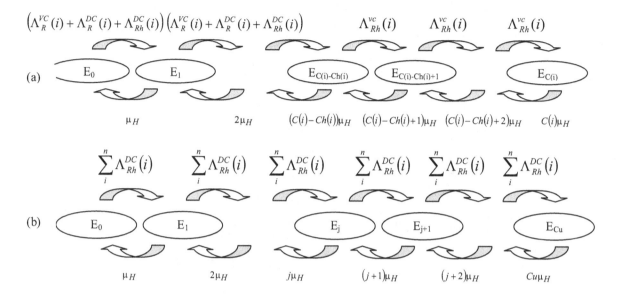

The mean rate of generation of handoff calls of DC is $\Lambda_{Rh}^{DC}(i)$ for cell i, so the mean rate generated in the umbrella is

$$\sum_{i}^{n}\Lambda_{Rh}^{DC}(i)$$

The proposed scheme investigates both the handoff and new call blocking probability in microcells and in the umbrella cell. It is applicable in areas with random offered traffic load. The number of the allocated channels to every microcell and umbrella cell is regulated by a micro-controller located in the Master Switching Center (MSC). The regulation is based upon the level of the occurred call blocking probability (handoff and new call) and tends to reduce it. More specifically, channels from cells with low call blocking probabilities are removed and assigned to cells with higher call blocking probability. A reduction to a high call blocking probability is of major importance than an increase to a low call blocking probability. Also, in the proposed scheme, the optimal number of channels is assigned to umbrella cell and microcellular layer, in order to improve the performance of handover calls of DC, as in TLCA scheme. In very low offered traffic load the application of OLCA presents better performance compared to the TLCA Consequently, in the DCMS – FTT, the ratios C(i)/Cs for i=1:n and C_u/C_S are regulated dynamically in the time period, with the criterion of decreasing the blocking probabilities in microcells and umbrella cell, contributing to the improvement of performance blocking probability of moving terminals. In very low offered traffic load tha architecture of the cellular system is based on a One-Layer Cellular Architecture

The steady state probabilities that j channels are busy in microcell (i) can be derived from Figure 8a

$$P_j^m(i) = \begin{cases} \dfrac{\left(\Lambda_R^{DC}(i) + \Lambda_R^{VC}(i) + \Lambda_{Rh}^{VC}(i)\right)}{j!\mu_H^{\ j}} P_0^m & j = 1,2,...,C(i) - C_h(i) \\[20pt] \dfrac{\left(\Lambda_R^{DC}(i) + \Lambda_R^{VC}(i) + \Lambda_{Rh}^{VC}(i)\right)^{C(i)-C_h(i)} \Lambda_{Rh}^{VC}(i)^{j-(C(i)-C_h(i))}}{j!\mu_H^{\ j}} P_0^m & j = C(i) - C_h(i) + 1,...,C(i) \end{cases} \tag{3}$$

Where $P_0^m(i) = \left[\displaystyle\sum_{k=0}^{C(i)-C_k(i)} \frac{\left(\Lambda_R^{DC}(i) + \Lambda_R^{VC}(i) + \Lambda_{Rh}^{VC}(i)\right)}{k!\mu_H k} + \displaystyle\sum_{k=C(i)-C_k(i)+1}^{C(i)} \frac{\left(\Lambda_R^{DC}(i) + \Lambda_R^{VC}(i) + \Lambda_{Rh}^{VC}(i)\right)^{C(i)-C_k(i)} \Lambda_{Rh}^{VC}(i)^{k-(C(i)-C_k(i))}}{k!\mu_H k} \right]^{-1}$ (8)

The blocking probability for a new call (either for DC or VC) in microcell (i) is the sum of probabilities that the state number of the microcell is $\geq C(i)-C_h(i)$. Hence:

$$P_B^m(i) = \sum_{j=C(i)-Ch(i)}^{C(i)} P_j^m(i) \tag{4}$$

The probability of handoff attempt failure $P_{fh}^m(i)$ is the probability that the state number of the microcell is equal to $C(i)$.

Thus: $p_{fh}^m(i) = p_C^m(i)$ (5)

For the umbrella cell, the steady state probabilities that j channels are busy can be derived from Figure 8b:

$$P_j^u = \frac{\left(\displaystyle\sum_{i=1}^n \Lambda_{Rh}^{DC}(i)\right)^j}{j!\mu_H^{\ j}} P_0^u \text{ for } j = 1,2,...,C_u \text{ (11) where } P_0^u = \left[\sum_{k=0}^{C_u} \frac{\left(\displaystyle\sum_{i=1}^n \Lambda_{Rh}^{VC}(i)\right)^k}{k!\mu_H^{\ k}} \right]^{-1} \tag{6}$$

The probability that a handoff call will be blocked in the umbrella cell is $P_{fh}^m(i)$ and is the probability that state number of the cell is equal to C_u. Thus: $P_{fh}^m(i) = (P_C^m\ i)$ (13). The mean call blocking probability (P_{nl}^m) for the microcellular layer (n microcells), considering new calls of VC and DC and handoff calls of VC is defined as:

Table 1. Relative mobilities and Offered traffic load in microcells

	1st microcell	2nd microcell	3nd microcell
α_L	0.41	0.38	0.46
α_H	0.46	0.41	0.48
α_{HL}	0.43	0.38	0.47
T_{off}/T_{off}^{Tot}	0.55	0.3	0.15

Figure 10. Handoff blocking probability of DC against total offered traffic load in the system

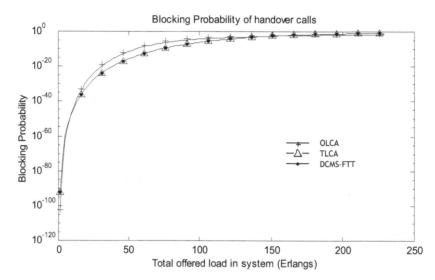

Figure 11. Mean call blocking probability of the microcellular layer (Pnl), against total offered traffic load in the system

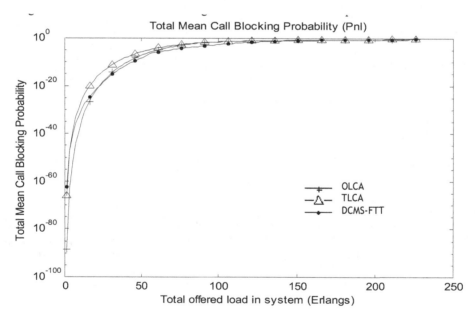

$$P_{nl}^m = \frac{\sum_{i=1}^{n}\left(\left(\Lambda_R^{DC}(i) + \Lambda_R^{VC}(i)\right)\cdot P_B^m(i) + \Lambda_{Rh}^{VC}(i)\cdot P_{fh}^m(i)\right)}{\sum_{i=1}^{n}\left(\Lambda_R^{H}(i) + \Lambda_{Rh}^{L}(i) + \Lambda_R^{L}(i)\right)} \tag{7}$$

RESULTS: Figure 10 shows the handoff blocking probability of DC against T_{off}^{Tot}. Figure 11 shows the mean call blocking probability of the microcellular layer P_{nl} as a function of T_{off}^{Tot}. In both figures is represented the performance of a One-Layer Cellular Architecture (OLCA) [1]. Also is shown the performance of a Two-Layer Cellular Architecture (TLCA). Lastly, is represented the performance of the DCMS–FTT. In the performed simulation, the number of microcells is considered to be n=3, C_s=180 without affecting the generality of the model. The following parameters are also considered: $C_h(i)$=0.1C(i) for i=1:n, T_H=80s. Figure 9 represents the relative mobilities and the ratio of the offered traffic load in microcells to the total offered traffic load in system.

Curves of Figures 10 and 11 show that the DCMS–FTT has the same results with TLCA, concerning the hand-off call blocking probability of DC, but improves the mean call blocking probability of the microcellular layer and has better performance comparing with TCS. Applying the DCMS–FTT to a cellular network we manage to decrease the P_{nl} comparing to TLCA. Comparing the DCMS – FTT with the TCA there is a decrease in P_{nl} for traffic load over 30 erl. For offered traffic load less than 30 erl the umbrella layer is removed and the channels that were assigned to that layer are assigned to the microcells

VI. CONCLUSION

Transportation industry inspired number of outstanding scientists and engineers in the past centuries to find new solution to ease lives for all mankind. The emergence and accessibility of advanced data and telecommunications technologies combined with convergence of industry standards, as well as the convergence of data and telecommunications industries contribute towards the ubiquitous access to information resources via Internet. The future transportation environment and Next Internet for the 21st century entered a new era of innovation and technological advancements. Transport industry is becoming more and more computerized. Current uses include industrial application and public transportation. Gradually, over time, the uses of the intelligent vehicle will be incorporated into the "light" vehicles based on stability of technology, optimization of algorithms, and public support. This is, however, not something that might happen for another ten to twenty years.

It is essential to continue in the developments of transport industry standards and communications technologies. Author presents his own vision on future transportation via ubiquitous communications infrastructures. Paper suggests the integration of transport environment and intelligent communications infrastructures in light of smart devices, smart antennas and intelligent transport systems. Author hopes that this paper will encourage the research and industrial community to invest their efforts in implementing future intelligent transport technologies via ubiquitous communications. Future efforts should be focused on designing intelligent transport and communication infrastructures especially in channel management schemes, that will allow for optimal and instantaneous control.

ACKNOWLEDGMENT

This work has been partially funded by grant UC3M-TEC-05-056 of the Program to Support the Creation and Consolidation of Universidad Carlos III in Madrid Research Groups. The authors are grateful for the support and encouragement received during the course of this work from his colleagues at Universidad Carlos III in Madrid and the University of Patras.

REFERENCES

Babulak, Eduard (2005). Automated Environment via Cyberspace. *Proceedings of the International Conference on Applied Computing (IADIS)* 2005, February, Algarve, Portugal.

Babulak, Eduard (2005) Next Generation of Internet & Telecommunications Technologies for Fully Automated Cyberspace. Keynote Speech, *the 7th International Conference on New Trends in Technology System Operation*, Presov, Slovakia, October 2005.

Garlan, D., Siewiorek, D., Smailagic, A., and Steenkiste, P. (April- June 2002). Project Aura: Towards Distraction-Free Pervasive Computing. *IEEE Pervasive Computing, 1*(2), 22–31.

Hengartner, U. and Steenkiste, P., (2003). Protecting Access to People Location Information. *Proceedings of the International Conference on Security in Pervasive Computing (SPC 2003)*, March 2003.

Hong D. and Rappaport, S. S. (1986). Traffic model and performance analysis for cellular mobile radio telephone systems with prioritized and non prioritized handoff procedures. IEEE Trans., VT-35, pp 77-92.

Ioannou K., Louvros, S., Panoutsopoulos, I., Kotsopoulos, S. and Karagiannidis, G. K. (October 2002). Member IEEE, Optimizing the Handover Call Blocking Probability in Cellular Networks with High Speed Moving Terminals. *IEEE Communications Letters, 6*(10).

Ioannou, K., I.Panoutsopoulos, Koubias, S. and Kotsopoulos, S. (June 2004) "A new Dynamic Channel Management Scheme to increase the performance index of Cellular Networks", *Electronics Letters, 10th, 40*(12), 744-746

Kitsios, F. and Zopounidis, C., (2007), Services marketing in the hospitality economy: An exploratory study. *The Southeuropean Review of Business Finance & Accounting, 5*(1)

Kropft, P (2002). *What is Pervasive Computing*. Series of Lecture notes.

Muncy, Mark (2003). The future of Transportation. *California Engineer, 81*(13), 15-19.

Stajano, F (2002). *Security for Ubiquitous Computing*. Wiley press.

Rappaport, T. S. (July 1999). *Wireless Communications*, pp. 112-121.

Compilation of References

3GPP TR 25.944 V3.5.0. (2001). *Channel coding and multiplexing examples*, Release 1999.

3GPP, TR 25.913. *Requirements for Evolved UTRA and Evolved UTRAN*. www.3gpp.org.

3GPP TS 25.201 V3.3.0. (2002). *Physical layer-General description*, Release 1999.

3GPP TS 25.212 V3.9.0. (2002). *Multiplexing and channel coding (FDD)*, Release 1999.

3GPP, (2005). Technical Specification Group Services and System Aspects; 3GPP System to Wireless Local Area Networks (WLAN) Interworking; System Description (Release 6), 3GPP TS 23.234 v.6.6.0.

3rd Generation Partnership Project. (2002, September). Network Architecture (Release 1999). TS 23.002.

3rd Generation Partnership Project. (2003, December). Network Architecture (Release 6). TS 23.002.

3rd Generation Partnership Project. (2003, June). Network Architecture (Release 4). TS 23.002.

Aatique, M. (1997). *Evaluation of TDOA techniques for position location in CDMA systems*. Unpublished master's thesis, Faculty of the Virginia Polytechnic Institute and State University, Virginia.

Abdi, A., Lau, W.C., Alouini, M.S. and Kaveh, M. (2003). "A New Simple Model for Land Mobile Satellite Channels: First- and Second-Order Statistics," IEEE Trans. Wireless Commun., 2, 519–528.

Abhishek Gupta, Kulwant, Palie Smart, *"New product development in the pharmaceutical and telecommunication industries: A comparative study"* (2007)

Aboba and D. Somin (1999). PPP EAP TLS Authentication Protocol, IETF RFC 2716.

Abowd, G.D. & Mynatt, E.D. (2000). Charting past, present, and future research in ubiquitous computing. ACM Transactions on Computer-Human Interaction, 7(1): 29–58.

Abrardo, A., Benelli, G., & Sennati, D. (2001). Centralized radio resource management strategies with heterogeneous traffics in HAPS WCDMA cellular systems. *IEEE Vehicular Technology Conference, 2*, 640-644

Ackerman, E. I., & Cox, C. H. (2001). RF Fiber-Optic Link Performance. *IEEE Microwave*, December 2001, 50-58.

Adams, P., Ashwell, G. W. B., Baxter, R. (2003). Location-Based Services - An Overview of the Standards. BT Technology Journal 21(1), 34-43.

Adel Al-Hezmi (2003). 'Design and Implementation of an OSA/Parlaycompliant Interactive Multimedia Response Unit for Mobile All-IP Networks', Thesis, Technische Universität Berlin.

Adler, R. (1946). A study of locking phenomena in oscillators. *Proceedings IRE Waves and Electrons*, 34, 351–357.

Agnar, S. (1976). Optimal taxation: an introduction to the literature. Journal of Public Economics (6).

Agrawal G. P. (1997). *Fiber Optic communication systems*. NY. Wiley.

Agrawal, A., Subramanian, V., & Berry, R. (2007). Joint scheduling and resource allocation in CDMA systems.

Copyright © 2009, IGI Global, distributing in print or electronic forms without written permission of IGI Global is prohibited.

Retrieved September 8, 2007, from http://www.ece.northwestern.edu/~rberry/opt.pdf

Agrawal, P., Chuah, M. C., & Zander, J. (2004). Multimedia Multicast/Broadcast Services in 3G/4G Networks. *IEEE Communications Magazine*, February 2004.

Ahluwalia, P., Varshney, U. (2003,). A Link and Network Layer Approach to Support Mobile Commerce Transactions. Paper presented at the Vehicular Technology Conference, 2003. VTC 2003-Fall. 2003 IEEE 58th

Ahluwalia, P., Varshney, U. (2007). Managing End-to-End Quality of Service in Multiple Heterogeneous Wireless Networks. International Journal of Network Management, 17(3), 243-260.

Agrawal, R., Berry, R., Huang, J., & Subramanian, V. (2006). Optimal scheduling for OFDMA systems. In *Fortieth Asilomar Conference on Signals, Systems and Computers* (pp. 1347-1351). IEEE.

Aichholzer, G. & Schmutzer, R. (2000). Organisational challenges to the development of electronic government. IEEE Computer Society, London, paper presented at 11th International Workshop on Database and Expert Systems Applications.

Ajzen, I. & Fishbein, M. (1980). Understanding attitudes and predicting social behaviour. Englewood Cliffs, N J: Prentice-Hall.

Akan, O.B. (2004). *Advanced transport protocols for next generation heterogeneous wireless network architecture.* Unpublished Master thesis, Georgia Institute of Technology, Georgia, USA.

Akram, M. N., Silfvenious, C., Kjeborn, O., and Schatz, R. (2004). Design optimization of InGaAsP-InGaAlAs 1.55 strain-compensated MQW lasers for direct modulation applications. *Semicond. Sci. Technol.*, 19, 615-625.

Albrecht, C., Dean, D. L., Hansen, J. V. (2005). Marketplace and Technology Standards for B2B E-commerce: Progress, Challenges and the State of the Art. Information & Management, 42(6), 865-875.

Aldrich, J., Bertot, J.C. & McClure, C.R. (2002). E-government: initiatives, developments, and issues. Government Information Quarterly, 19, 349-355.

Alexander, S.E. (1982). Radio propagation within buildings at 900MHz, *IEE Electronics Letters*, Vol. 18, pp. 913-914.

Alexanian, A., Chang, H.C., & York, R.A. (1995). Enhanced scanning range in coupled oscillator arrays utilizing frequency multipliers. In IEEE, *Antennas and Progagation Symposium Digest*, (pp. 1308-1310). Newport Beach, CA: IEEE.

Alfredsson, S., Brunstrom, A., & Sternad, M. (2006). Transport Protocol Performance over 4G Links: Emulator Methodology and Results. *International Symposium on Wireless Communication Systems ISWCS*, Valencia, Spain.

Alocci, I., Berioli, M., Celandroni, N., Giambene, G., & Karapantazis, S. (2007). Proposal of a reliable multicast protocol in a HAP-satellite architecture. *IEEE Vehicular Technology Conference*, 1380-1384.

Al-Raweshidy, H. & Komaki, S. (2002). *Radio over Fiber Technologies for Mobile Communications Networks.* Artech House.

AMR Research: http://www.amrresearch.com/

Anandalingam, G., Day, R. W., Raghavan, S. (2005). The Landscape of Electronic Market Design. Management Science, 51(3), 316-327.

Andrews, M. (2005). A survey of scheduling theory in wireless data networks. In *Proc. of the 2005 IMA summer workshop on wireless communications.*

Appelbaum, S.P. (1976). Adaptive arrays, *IEEE Transactions on Antennas and Propagation*, 5, 585–598.

Arroyo-Fernandez B., Fernandes, J., & Prasad R. (2003). Composite Reconfigurable Wireless Networks: The EU R&D Path Toward 4G. *IEEE Communications Magazine*, July 2003, Part I.

Arroyo-Fernandez, B., Fernandes, J. & Prasad R. (2004). Composite Reconfigurable Wireless Networks: The EU R&D Path Toward 4G. *IEEE Communications Magazine*, May 2004, Part II.

Assimakopoulos A.N., Angelopoulos P.S. & Riggas N.A. (2007). Development and analysis of a virtual enterprise that constructs wireless payment mechanisms using open source content management systems. Accepted for publication in International Journal of Applied Systemic Studies (IJASS) (http://www.inderscience.com/ijass).

Assimakopoulos, A.N., Angelopoulos, P.S. & Riggas, N.A. (2007). Development and analysis of a virtual enterprise that constructs wireless payment mechanisms using open source content management systems. Accepted for publication in International Journal of Applied Systemic Studies (IJASS) (http://www.inderscience.com/ijass).

Atkin, D., Hallock, J. & Lau, T.Y. (2007). Local and long distance telephony. In A. Grant, & J. Meadows (Eds.), Communication technology update, pp. 242–257. Boston: Focal Press.

Atkin, D., Lau, T.Y. & Lin, C. A. (2006). Still on hold: Assessing the impact of the Telecommunications Act of 1996 on its 10th year anniversary. Telecommunications Policy, 30, 413–433.

Atuahene-Gima, K., *"Differential of factors affecting innovation performance in manufacturing and services firms in Australia".* Journal of Product Innovation Management 13, (1996):35-52.

Auckland, D.T., Lilly, J., & York, R.A. (1997). Analysis of beam scanning and data rate transmission performance of a coupled oscillator phased array. In IEE, *Tenth International Conference on Antennas and Propagation, Conf. Publ. No. 436* (pp. 245-249). Edinburgh: IEE.

Aulin, T. (1979). "A Modified Model for the Fading Signal at a Mobile Radio Channel," IEEE Trans. Veh. Technol., vol. 28, no. 3, pp. 182-203, Aug.

Aune, F. (2004). Cross-Layer Design Tutorial. *Norwegian University of Science and Technology, Dept. of Electronics and Telecommunications*: Trondheim, Norway.

Austin, A. (1967). *Decision-Feedback Equalisation for Digital Communication over Dispersive Channels,* M.I.T. Res. Lab Electron., Tech. Rep. 461.

Avangina, D., Dovis, F., Ghiglione, A., & Mulassano, P., (2002). Wireless networks based on high-altitude platforms for the provision of integrated navigation/com-munication services. *IEEE Communications Magazine, 40*(2), 119-125.

Ba, S., Whinston, A. B., Zhang, H. (2003). Building trust in online auction markets through an economic incentive mechanism. Decision Support Systems, 35(3), 273-286.

Babulak, E. (2004). Manufacturing for the 21st Century, 1st International Conference on Manufacturing Management, Presov, Slovakia.

Babulak, E. (2005). Automated Environment via Cyber-space. Proceedings of the International Conference on Applied Computing (IADIS), Algarve, Portugal.

Babulak, E. (2005). Next Generation of Internet & Telecommunications Technologies for Fully Automated Cyberspace. Keynote Speech, the 7th International Conference on New Trends in Technology System Operation, Presov, Slovakia.

Babulak, E. (2005). Quality of Service Provision Assessment in the Healthcare Information and Telecommunications Infrastructures. Selected for publication in the International Journal of Medical Informatics, Elsevier Ireland Ltd.

Babulak, Eduard (2005) Next Generation of Internet & Telecommunications Technologies for Fully Automated Cyberspace. Keynote Speech, *the 7th International Conference on New Trends in Technology System Operation*, Presov, Slovakia, October 2005.

Babulak, Eduard (2005). Automated Environment via Cyberspace. *Proceedings of the International Conference on Applied Computing (IADIS)* 2005, February, Algarve, Portugal.

Bachrach, J., & Taylor, C. (2005). Localization in sensor networks. In I. Stojmenović (Ed.), *Handbook of sensor networks: algorithms and architectures* (pp. 277-310). New Jersey, Hoboken: John Wiley & Sons, Inc.

Bailey, J., Bakos, Y. (1997). An Exploratory Study of the Emerging Role of Electronic Intermediaries. International Journal of Electronic Commerce, 1(3), 7-20.

Bakaul, M. (2006). *Technologies for DWDM Millimetre-Wave Fibre-Radio Networks*. Doctoral Dissertation, University of Melbourne, Australia.

Bakker John-Luc, McGoogan Judith R., Opdyke William F., and Panken Frans (July–September 2000). 'Rapid Development and Delivery of Converged Services Using APIs', Bell Labs Technical Journal.

Balakrishnan, H., Padmanabhan, V. N., Seshan, S., & Katz, R. H. (1997). A comparison of mechanisms for improving TCP performance over wireless links. *IEEE/ACM Transactions on Networking*, 5(6), 756 – 769.

Balanis, C.A. (2005). *Antenna Theory: Analysis and Design*, 3rd Ed., New York NY: John Wiley and Sons.

Baldwin, T.F., McVoy, D.S. & Steinfield, C. (1996). Convergence: Integrating media, information and communication. Thousand Oaks, CA: Sage.

Ballesteros, F.J., Guardiola, G., Leal, K. & Soriano, E. (2006). Omero: Ubiquitous user interfaces in the Plan B operating system, in: Proceedings of IEEE PerCom.

Ballesteros, F.J., Soriano, E., Leal, K. & Guardiola, G. (2006). Plan B: An operating system for ubiquitous computing environments, in: Proceedings of IEEE PerCom.

Balutis, A. (2001). E-government 2001a, Part I: Understanding the challenge and evolving strategies. The public manager, Spring (p. 33).

Bandyopadhyay, S., Coyle, E. J. (April, 2003). An Energy Efficient Hierarchical Clustering Algorithm for Wireless Sensor Networks. *IEEE Infocom 2003*.

Bangolea, S., Bell, C., Qi, E. (2006). Performance Study of Fast BSS Transition using IEEE 802.11r. *International Conference on Communications and Mobile Computing 2006*, (pp. 737-742), Vancouver, British Columbia, Canada.

Bannister, J., Wiley InterScience (Online Service), & John Wiley & Sons (2004). *Convergence Technologies for 3G Networks IP, UMTS, EGPRS and ATM*. (1st ed ed.) Chichester: John Wiley Sons Ltd.

Barnes, S. (2002). The Mobile Commerce Value Chain: Analysis and Future Developments. International Journal of Information Management, 22 , 91-108.

Barney, J.B. (1991). Firm resources and sustained competitive advantage. *Journal of Management*, 17:99-120.

Barney, J.B. (1996). The resource-based theory of the firm. *Organizational Science*, 7:469.

Bates, B., Albright, K. & Washington, K. (2002). No your plain old telephone: New services and new impacts. In Lin C. and Atkin, D. (Eds.), Communication technology and society: Audience adoption and uses (pp. 65–90). Cresskill NJ: Hampton.

Bates, K.A., & Flynn, J.E. (1995). Innovation history and competitive advantage: A resource-based view analysis of manufacturing technology innovations. *Academy of Management Best Papers Proceedings*: 235-239.

Bekkers, V.J.J.M. & Zouridis, S. (1999). Electronic service delivery in public administration: Some trends and issues. International Review of Administrative Sciences, 65 (2), 183-196.

Bello, P.A. (1963). "Characterization of randomly time-variant linear channels," IEEE Trans. Comm. Syst., pp. 360–393, Dec.

Bello, P.A. (1963). *Characterization of Randomly Time-Variant Linear Channels*, IEEE Transactions on Communication Systems, Vol. CS-11.

Berrou, C., & Glavieux, A. (1996). *Near optimum error correcting coding and decoding: Turbo codes*. IEEE Transactions on Communications, Vol. 44, No. 10, 1261-1271.

Berry, R. A., & Gallager, R. G. (2002). Communication over fading channels with delay constraints, *IEEE Transactions on Information Theory*, 48(5), 1135-1149.

Berry, R. A., & Yeh , E. M. (2004). Cross-layer wireless resource allocation, *IEEE Signal Processing Magazine*, 21(5), 59-68.

Bersani, F. and Tschofenig, H. (2007), "The EAP-PSK Protocol: A Pre-Shared Key Extensible Authentication Protocol (EAP) Method", IETF RFC 4764.

Bichler, M., Kalagnanam, J., Katircioglu, K., King, A. J., Lawrence, R. D., Lee, H. S., Lin, G. Y., Lu, Y. (2002). Applications of flexible pricing in business-to-business electronic commerce. IBM Systems Journal, 41(2), 287-302.

Bih, J. (2005) Deploy XML-based network management approach, Potentials IEEE, Volume 24, Issue 4, Oct.-Nov. 2005 Pages: 26 – 31.

Bikram, S., Bakshi, B., Krishna, P., Vaidya, N. H., & Pradhan, D. K. (1997). Improving Performance of TCP over Wireless Networks. *International Conference on Distributed Computing Systems.*

Birkos, K., & Kotsopoulos, S. (2007, May). On the intrinsic quality of service performance issues of a new proposed multiple-HAPs based system architecture. *Paper presented at the World Wireless Congress*, San Francisco, CA.

Birkos, K., Chrysikos, T., & Kotsopoulos, S. (2007). An inter-HAP handover scheme over a worst case fading scenario. *Proceedings of the 7th European Conference of young research and science workers (TRANSCOM 2007), 3*, 19-22.

Birnbaum, J. (1997). Pervasive information systems. Communications of the ACM, 40(2), 40–41.

Bisio, I., & Marchese, M., (2006). Study and performance evaluation of bandwidth controls over high altitude platforms. *11ᵗʰ IEEE Symposium on Computers and Communications.*

Bithas, P., Mathiopoulos, T., and Kotsopoulos, S.A. (2007). Diversity Reception over Generalized-K (KG) Fading Channels, *IEEE Transactions on Wireless Communications*, to be published.

Black, J.A., & Boal, K.B. (1994). Strategic resources: Traits configurations and paths to sustainable competitive

advantage. *Strategic Management Journal*, 15 (Summer Special Issue):131-148.

Bluetooth: http://www.bluetooth.com

Bonham, G.M., Seifert, J.W. & Thorson, S.J. (2001). The Transformational Potential of e-Government: The Role of Political Leadership. European Consortium for Political Research, which was held at the University of Kent at Canterbury, U.K.

Borkowski, J., & Lempiäinen, J. (2006). Practical network-based techniques for mobile positioning in UMTS. *EURASIP Journal on Applied Signal Processing*, doi:10.1155/ASP/2006/12930, 1-15.

Bourn, J. (2002). Better Public Services Through E-Government. The National Audit Office, London.

Bouzouki, S., Kotsopoulos, S., Karagiannidis, G., Hasomeris, K., & Lymberopoulos, D. (2001). *On optimal cell planning case study for a DCS 1800 System*, International Journal of Communication Systems. Vol. 14, No. 9, 857-870.

Bowers, M.R. "Developing new services: Improving the process makes it better." *Journal of Services Marketing* 3, no.1, (1989):15-20.

Box, G. E. P., & Draper, N. R. (1987). *Empirical Model Building and Response Surfaces.* New York, NY, USA: John Wiley & Sons, Inc.

Box, G., & Wilson, K. (1951). On The Experimental Attainment of Optimum Conditions. *Journal of Royal Statistical Society*, 13(1), 1-38.

Boyd, S., & Vandenberghe, L. (2004). *Convex Optimization*, New York NY: Cambridge University Press.

Braden, R., Clark, D., & Shenker, S. (1994). Integrated Services in the Internet Architecture: an Overview. *RFC 1633.*

Brida, P., Cepel, P., & Duha, J. (2006). A novel adaptive algorithm for RSS positioning in GSM networks. In *CSNDSP 2006 PROCEEDINGS*: (pp. 748-751). Greece: University of Patras.

Brida, P., Cepel, P., Duha, J. & Vestenicky, M. (under review). An experimental evaluation of AGA algorithm performance for RSS positioning in GSM networks. Manuscript submitted for publication.

Brida, P., Duha, J., & Krasnovsky, M. (2007). On the accuracy of weighted proximity based localization in wireless sensor networks. In *Proccedings of the 12th IFIP Internacional Conference on Personal Wireless Communications*: (pp. 423-432). Czech Republic: Prague.

Brimicombe, A., Li, Y. (2006). Mobile Space-Time Envelopes for Location-Based Services. Transactions in GIS, 10(1), 5-23.

Brown, M.M. & Brudney, J.L. (2001). Achieving advanced electronic government services: An examination of obstacles and implications from an international perspective. Paper presented at the National Public Management Research Conference, Bloomington, IN.

Brumitt, B., Meyers, B., Krumm, J., Kern, A. & Shafer, S. (2000). Easyliving: Technologies for intelligent environments. In The Second International Symposium on Handheld and Ubiquitous Computing (HUC2000), pages 12–29, Bristol, UK. Springer-Verlag.

Brunato, M., & Battiti, R. (2005). Statistical learning theory for location fingerprinting in wireless LANs. *Computer Networks and ISDN Systems*, 47(6), 825-845.

Brunn, P., Jensen, M., Skovgaard, J. (2002). e-Marketplaces: Crafting a Winning Strategy. European Management Journal, 20(3), 286-298.

Buellingen, F., Woerter, M. (2004). Development Perspectives, Firm Strategies and Applications in Mobile Commerce. Journal of Business Research, 57(12), 1402-1408.

Bulusu, N., Heidemann, J., & Estrin, D. (2000). GPS-less low cost outdoor localization for very small devices. *IEEE Personal Communications*, 7(5), 28-34.

Burside, W.D., and Burgener, K.W. (1983). High frequency scattering of thin lossless dielectric slab, *IEEE Transactions on Antennas and Propagation*, Vol. AP-31, pp. 104-110.

Butterworth, J. S. and Matt, E.E. (1983). "The Characterization of Propagation Effects for Land Mobile Satellite Services," Intern. Conf. Satellite Systems for Mobile Commun. Navigations, pp. 51-54, June.

C. Rigney, A. C. Rubens, W. A. Simpson and S. Willens (2000). Remote Authentication for Dial In User Service (RADIUS), IETF RFC2865.

C.-C. Tseng, L.-H. Yen, H.-H. Chang, & K.-C. Hsu, (2005). Topology-aided cross-layer fast handoff designs for IEEE 802.11/mobile IP environments. *IEEE Communications Magazine*, 43(12), 156 – 163.

Caffery, J. J., Jr. (2000). *Wireless location in CDMA cellular radio systems* (1st ed.). Massachusetts: Kluwer Academic Publishers.

Cain, B., Deering, S., Kouvelas, I., Fenner, B. and Thyagarajan, A. (2002). Internet Group Managemet Protocol, Version 3, IETF RFC2236.

Camarillo, G. & Garcia-Martin, M. A. (2006). The 3G IP multimedia subsystem (IMS) merging the Internet and the cellular worlds. (2nd ed ed.) Chichester: Wiley.

Camarillo, G., Kauppinen, T., Kuparinen, M. and Ivars, I. M. (2007, March). Towards an Innovation Oriented IP Multimedia Subsystem, IEEE Communications Magazine.

Capon, J., Greenfield, R. J., & Kolker, R. J. (1967), Multidimensional maximum-likelihood processing for a large aperture seismic array, *Proceedings IEEE*, 55, 192–211.

Carlsson C., et al. (2001). High Performance Microwave Link Using a Multimode VCSEL and a High-Bandwidth Multimode Fiber. *IEEE International Topical Meeting on Microwave Photonics (pp. 81-84)*. IEEE

Carlsson, C., Larsson, A., & Alping, A. (2004). RF Transmission Over Multimode Fibers Using VCSELs - Comparing Standard and High-Bandwidth Multimode Fibers. *IEEE J. Lightwave Technology.*, 22, 1694-1702.

Carter, J., Ranganathan, A. & Susarla, S. (1998). Khazana. An infrastructure for building distributed services, in: Proceedings of ICDCS'98, IEEE, Amsterdam.

Cast, Mathew (1999). 802.11 Wireless Networks, The definitive Guide, O'reilly.

Castanias, R.P., & Helfat, C.E. (1991). Managerial resources and rents. *Journal of Management*, 17:155-171.

Catedra, M.F., Perez, J., DeAbana, S.F., Gutierez, O. (1998). Efficient Ray-Tracing Techniques for Three-Dimensional Analyses of Propagation in Mobile Communications: Application to Picocell and Microcell Scenarios, *IEEE Antennas and Propagation Magazine*, Vol. 40, No. 22, pp. 437-440.

Catovic, A. & Sahinoglu, Z. (2004). Hybrid TOA/RSS and TDOA/RSS location estimation schemes for short-range wireless networks. *Bechtel Telecommunication Technical Journal*, 2(2), 77-84.

Center for Democracy and Technology (2002). E-Government Handbook for Developing Countries. CDT POLICY POST, Vol. 8, No. 26.

Chaikalis, C. & Liolios, C. (2007). UMTS Turbo Decoder Dynamic Reconfiguration for Rural Outdoor Operating Environment. MOBIMEDIA 2007, 27-29 August 2007, Nafpaktos, Greece.

Chaikalis, C. (2003). *Reconfigurable structures for turbo codes in 3G mobile radio transceivers*, PhD thesis, School of Engineering Design and Technology, University of Bradford, UK.

Chaikalis, C. (2007) Efficient TTI for 3G Multimedia Applications. Advances in Multimedia, vol. 2007, Article ID 95474, 7 pages, 2007. doi:10.1155/2007/95474

Chaikalis, C. (2007). Turbo decoder dynamic reconfiguration in urban/suburban outdoor operating environment for 3GPP. in Proceedings of IEEE International Symposium on Personal, Indoor and Mobile Radio Communications (PIMRC 2007), Athens, Greece.

Chaikalis, C. (2007). UMTS implementation issues. Chapter in book entitled: Progress in Wireless Communications Research, Editor: Alfred P. Martinhoff,

Nova Science Publishers, New York, Invited, ISBN 1-60021-675-7.

Chaikalis, C. (in press). *Implementation of a reconfigurable turbo decoder in 3GPP for flat Rayleigh fading.* Elsevier Digital Signal Processing Journal.

Chaikalis, C., & Noras, J. M. (2004). *Reconfigurable turbo decoding for 3G applications.* Elsevier Signal Processing Journal, Vol. 84, No. 10, 1957-1972.

Chakraborty, S., Peisa, J., Frankkila, T. and P. Synnergren. (2007). IMS Multimedia Telephony over Cellular Systems, JohnWiley & Sons.

Chan, H., Ho, I. S. K., Lee, R. S. T. (2001). Design and Implementation of a Mobile Agent-Based Auction System. Paper presented at the IEEE PACRIM'2001, Victoria, BC, Canada.

Chan, M. C., & Ramjee, R. (2002). TCP/IP performance over 3G wireless links with rate and delay variation. *ACM International Conference on Mobile Computing and Networking*, 71 – 82.

Chang, G.-K., Yu, J., & Jia, Z. (2007). Architectures and Enabling Technologies for Super-Broadband Radio-over-Fiber Optical Wireless Access Networks. *IEEE International Topical Meeting on Microwave Photonics (pp. 24-28).* IEEE.

Chang, K., York, R.A., Hall, P.S., & Itoh, T. (2002). Active integrated antennas. *IEEE Transactions on Microwave Theory and Techniques*, 50(3), 937-944.

Chang, Z., Gaydadjiev, G. N., & Vassiliadis, S. (2007). Infrastructure for Cross-Layer Designs Interaction. *The 16th IEEE International Conference on Computer Communications and Networks (IC3N)*, Honolulu, Hawaii USA.

Chen, G. & Kotz, D. (2000). A survey of context-aware mobile computing research. Technical Report TR2000-381, Department of Computer Science, Dartmouth College.

Chen, G., Li, M. & Kotz, D. (2007). Data-centric middleware for context-aware pervasive computing, Pervasive and Mobile Computing.

Chen, J., Lv, T., & Zheng, H. (2004). Cross-layer design for QoS wireless communications. *Proceedings of the 2004 International Symposium on Circuits and Systems (ISCAS)*, 217 – 220.

Chen, K., Shah, S. H., & Nahrstedt, K. (2002). Cross-Layer Design for Data Accessibility in Mobile Ad hoc Networks. *Wireless Personal Communications, Special Issue on Multimedia Network Protocols and Enabling Radio Technologies*, 21, 49-75, Kluwer Academic Publishers.

Chen, L., Low, S.H., & Doyle, J.C. (2005). Joint Congestion Control and Media Access Control Design for Ad Hoc Wireless Networks. *Proc. INFOCOM 2005*.

Chen, W., Neely M. J., & Mittra, U. (2007). Energy Efficient Scheduling with Individual Packet Delay Constraints: Offline and Online Results, In *Proc. IEEE INFOCOM 2003. Twenty-Sixth Annual Joint Conference of the IEEE Computer and Communications Societies: Vol. 1.* (pp. 1136-1144), IEEE.

Chen, Y. & Gant, J. (2001). Transforming local e-government services: the use of application service providers. Government Information Quarterly, Vol. 18 No.4, pp. 343-55.

Chengshan, X., Zheng, Y.R., and Beaulieu, N.C. (2002). Second-order statistical properties of the WSS Jakes' fading channel simulator, *IEEE Transactions on Communications*, Vol. 50, No. 6, pp. 888-891.

Chiang, M., Low, S. H., Calderbank, A. R., & Doyle, J. C. (2007). Layering as Optimization Decomposition: A Mathematical Theory of Network Architectures. *Proceedings of the IEEE*, 95(1), 255 – 312.

Chiang, M., Low, S. H., Calderbank, A. R., & Doyle, J. C., Layering as optimization decomposition: a mathematical theory of network architectures, *Proceedings of the IEEE*, 95(1), 255-312.

Choi, M.S., Park, H.K., Heo, Y.H., Oh, S.H., and Myung, N.H. (2006). A 3-D propagation model considering building transmission loss for indoor wireless communications, *ETRI Journal*, Vol. 28, No. 2, pp. 247-249.

Choi, W., Tekinay, S. (2003). Location-Based Service Provisioning for Next Generation Wireless Networks. International Journal of Wireless Information Networks, 10(3), 127-139.

Chon, B.S., Choi, J.H., Barnett, G.A., Danowski, J.A., & Joo, S.H. (2003). A structural analysis of media convergence: cross industry mergers and acquisitions in the information industries. *Journal of Media Economics* 16(3): 141-157.

Christopoulou, E., and Kameas, A. (2005). GAS Ontology: an ontology for collaboration among ubiquitous computing devices. *International Journal of Human-Computer Studies, 62*(5), 664-685.

Chrostowski, L., Zhao, X., Chang-Hasnain, C., Shau, R., & Amann, M. (2004). Very high resonance frequency (>40 GHz) optical injection-locked 1.55 μm VCSELs. *IEEE International Topical Meeting on Microwave Photonics (pp. 255–258)*. IEEE.

Chung, H. S., Chang, S. H., Park, J. D., Chu, M.-J. & Kwangjoon, K. (2007). Transmission of Multiple HD-TV Signals Over a Wired/Wireless Line Millimeter Wave Link With 60 GHz. *IEEE J. Lightwave Technology, 25*(11).

Ci, S., Turner, S. W., & Sharif, H. (2003). An energy-efficient TCP quick timeout scheme for wireless LANs. *IEEE International Performance, Computing, and Communications Conference*, 193 – 197.

Cianca, E., De Luise, A., De Sanctis, M., Ruggieri, M., & Prasad, R. (2004). TCP/IP performance over satellite and HAP integrated systems. *Proceedings of IEEE Aerospace Conference*, 2, 1209-1216.

Cianca, E., Prasad, R., De Sanctis, M., De Luise, A., Antonini, M., Teotino, D. et al. (2005). Integrated satellite-HAP systems. *IEEE Communications Magazine*, 43(12), 33-39.

Cimini, L.J. (1985). *Analysis and Simulation of a Digital Mobile Channel Using Orthogonal Frequency Division Multiplexing*. IEEE Transactions on Communications, Vol. COM-33, No. 7.

Clarke, R. (1968). A statistical theory of mobile radio reception, *Bell Systems Technical Journal*, Vol. 47, pp. 957-1000.

Clarke, R. H. (1968). "A Statistical Theory of Mobile–Radio Reception," Bell Syst. Tech. J. vol. 47, pp. 957-1000, July/Aug.

Clarke, R. H. and Khoo, W. L. (1997). "3-D Mobile Radio Channel Statistics," IEEE Trans. Veh. Technol., vol. 46, no. 3, pp. 798-799, Aug.

Clarke, R.H. (1968). "A statistical theory of mobile radio reception," Bell Syst. Tech. J., pp. 957-1000, July-Aug.

Clemm, A., (2007). Network Management Fundamentals: A guide to understanding how network management technology really works, Cisco Press, 2007.

Collado, A., Georgiadis, A., & Suarez, A. (2006). Optimized Design of Retro-Directive Arrays Based on Self-Oscillating Mixers using Harmonic-Balance and Conversion-Matrix Techniques. In IEEE, *MTT-S International Microwave Symposium* (pp. 1125-1128), San Francisco, CA: IEEE.

Combettes, P.L. (1993). The foundations of set theoretic estimation. *Proceedins of the IEEE*, 81(2), 182-208.

Conner, K.R. (1991). A historical comparison of resource-based theory and five schools of thought within industrial organization economics. Do we have a new theory of the firm? *Journal of Management*, 17: 121-154.

Conta, A., & Deering, S. (1998). *Internet Control Message Protocol (ICMPv6) for the Internet Protocol Version 6 (IPv6) Specification*. RFC 2463.

Convergence: http://www.telecommagazine.com

Cooper, R.G., & de Brentani, U. "New industrial services: What distinguishes the winners." *Journal of Product Innovation Management* 8, (1991).75-90.

Cooper, R.G., Easingwood, C.J., Edgett, S., Kleinschmidt, E.J., & Storey, C. "What distinguishes the top performing new products in financial services." *Journal of Product Innovation Management* 11, (1994):281-299.

Corazza, G. E. and Vatalaro, F. (1994). "A Statistical Model for Land Mobile Satellite Channels and its Application to Nongeostationary Orbit Systems," IEEE Trans. Veh. Technol., vol. 43, no. 3, pp. 738-742, Aug.

Corazza, G.E. and Vatalaro, F. (1994). "A Statistical Model for Land Mobile Satellite Channels and Its Application to Nongeostationary Orbit Systems," IEEE Trans. Vehicular Technol., 43, 738–742.

Corazza, G.E., Jahn, A. E. Lutz, and Vatalaro, F. (1994). "Channel Characterization for Mobile Satellite Communications," in Procedure of the First European Workshop on Mobile/Personal Satcoms, EMPS, pp. 225–262.

Cortese, A. E. & Stepanek, M. (1998). Good-Bye to Fixed Pricing? Business Week, May 4, 70-84.

COST 207 TD(86) 51-REV 3 (WG1) (1986): "Proposal on channel transfer functions to be used in GSM tests late 1986", September 1986.

Course on Ubiquitous Computing: http://www.cs.albany.edu/~maniatty/teaching/ubicomp/index.html

Cox, C. H. III, Ackerman, E. I., Betts, G. E., & Prince, J. L. (2006). Limits on the Performance of RF-Over-Fiber Links and Their Impact on Device Design. *IEEE Trans. Microwave Theory Techniques.* 54, 906- 920.

Cox, C., Ackerman, E., Helkey, R., & Betts, G. E. (1997). Techniques and performance of intensity-modulation direct-detection analogue optical links. *IEEE Trans. Microwave Theory Techniques.* 45(8), 1375–1383.

Cox, H., Zeskind, R.M., & Owen, M.M. (1987). Robust adaptive beamforming, *IEEE Transactions on Acoustics, Speech, and Signal Processing*, 35(10), 1365–1376.

Craig, A. & Hart, S. "Where to now in new product development research?" *European Journal of Marketing* 26, no.11, (1992):3-46.

Craig, L. J. (2007). A framework for pricing government e-services. Electron. Comm. Res. Appl.

Cramton, P. (1998). Ascending auctions. European Economic Review, 42(3-5), pp. 745-756.

Crimi, J.C. (2000) *Next Generation Network (NGN) Services*. A White Paper. Telcordia Technologies.

Crisp, J., Li, S., Watts, A., Penty, R.V., & White H. Ian. (2007). Uplink and Downlink Coverage Improvements of 802.11g Signals Using a Distributed Antenna Network. *IEEE J. Lightwave Technology,* 25(11).

Cvijetic, N., Wilson, S. G., & Zarubica, R. (2007). Performance Evaluation of a Novel Converged Architecture for Digital-Video Transmission Over Optical Wireless Channels. . *IEEE J. Lightwave Technology,* 25(11).

D. Estrin, D. Farinacci, A. Helmy, D. Thaler, S. Deering, M. Handley, V. Jacobson, C. Liu, P. Sharma and L. Wei (1998). Protocol Independent Multicast-Sparse Mode (PIM-SM): Protocol Specifications, IETF RFC 2362.

D'Roza, T., Bilchev, G. (2003). An Overview of Location-Based Services. BT Technology Journal, 21(1), 20-27.

Daftari, A., Mehta, N., Bakre, S. &. Sun, X.-H. (2003). On Design Framework of Context Aware Embedded Systems. Monterey Workshop, Chicago, Illinois, Available at: http://www.cs.uic.edu/~shatz/SEES/sun.paper.pdf.

Dan Harkins and Dave Carrel (1998). The Internet Key Exchange (IKE), IETF RFC 2409.

Dang, B. L., & Niemegeers, I. (2005). Analysis of IEEE 802.11 in radio over fiber home networks. *Proc. 30th IEEE Conf. LCN*, pp. 744–747.

Daniel, E., Hoxmeier, J., White, A., Smart, A. (2004). A framework for the sustainability of e-marketplaces. Business Process Management Journal, 10(3), 277-290.

Daniels, M. (2002). E-Government Strategy: Simplified Delivery of Services to Citizens. Office of Management and Budget, Washington, DC.

Danowski, J.A., & Choi, J.H. (1998). Convergence in the information industries: Telecommunications, broadcasting and data processing 1981-1996, in H. Sawhney &

Danzeisen, M., Rodellar, D., Braun, T., Winiker, S. (Oct., 2003). Heterogeneous Networking Establishment assisted by cellular operators. *The 5th IFIP TC6 International Conference on MWCN 2003*, Singapore.

Dao, D., Rizos, C., Wang, J. (2002). Location-Based Services: Technical and Business Issues. GPS Solutions, 6(3), 169-178.

Darcie, T. E., & Driessen, P. F. (2006). Class-AB Techniques for High-Dynamic-Range Microwave-Photonic Links. *IEEE Photon. Technol. Let.* 18(8), 929-931.

Das, A., Mjeku, M., Nkansah, A., & Gomes, N. J. (2007). Effects on IEEE 802.11 MAC Throughput in Wireless LAN Over Fiber Systems. *IEEE J. Lightwave Technology,* 25(11), 3321-3328.

Das, A., Nkansah, A., Gomes, N. J., Garcia, I. J., Batchelor, J., & Wake, D. (2006). Design of low-cost multimode fiber fed indoor wireless networks. *IEEE Trans. Microw. Theory Tech.*, 54(8), 3426–3432.

de Brentani, U. & Cooper, R.G. "Developing successful new financial services for businesses." *Industrial Marketing Management* 21, no.3, (1992):231-242.

de Brentani, U. & Ragot, E. "Developing new business-to-business professional services: What factors impact performance." *Industrial Marketing Management* 25, (1996).517-530.

de Brentani, U. "An empirical analysis of the effect of product innovativeness on success and failure of new industrial services." Conference Proceedings: *ANZMAC 1999, University of New South Wales, Sydney, November/December (1999)*.

de Brentani, U. "Success and failure in new industrial services." *Journal of Product Innovation Management* 6, (1989):239-258.

de Brentani, U. "Success factors in developing new business services." *European Journal of Marketing* 25, no.2, (1991):33-59.

de Brentani, U. "The new product process in financial services: Strategy for success." *International Journal of Bank Marketing* 11, no.3, (1993):15-22.

De Nardis, L., & Di Benedetto, M.-G. (2007). Overview of the IEEE 802.15.4/4a standards for low data rate Wireless Personal Data Networks. *4th Workshop on Positioning, Navigation and Communication*, 285 – 289.

Deal, W.R., &, Itoh, T. (1997). An Active Phased Array With Optical Control And Beam-scanning Capability. In IEEE, *International Topical Meeting on Microwave Photonics (MWP)* (pp.175-178). Duisburg/Essen: IEEE.

Deering, S., & Hinden, R. (1998). *Internet Protocol, Version 6 (IPv6) Specification*. RFC 2460.

Deguang Le, Xiaoming Fu, & Hogref, D. (2006). A review of mobility support paradigms for the internet. *IEEE Communications Surveys & Tutorials*, 8(1), 38 – 51.

Dehoga (German Hotel and Restaurant Association). Online. Accessed 14.April 2000. http://www.dehoga.de/daten.

Deligiannis, N. & Kotsopoulos, S. (2007). Mobile positioning based on existing signalling messaging in GSM Networks. In Proceedings of 3rd International Mobile Multimedia Communications Conference (MSAN). 27-29 August 2007, Greece: Nafpaktos.

Dent, P., Bottomley, G.E., and Croft, T. (1993), Jakes fading model revisited, *IEE Electronics Letters*, Vol. 29, No. 13, pp. 1162-1163.

Deschamps, G.A. (1972). Ray techniques in electromagnetics, *Proceedings of the IEEE*, Vol. 60, pp. 1022-1035.

Deutsch, F., & Yamada, I. (1998). Minimizing certain convex functions over the intersection of the fixed poit sets of nonexpansive mappings. *Numerical Functional Analysis and Optimization*, 19, 33-56.

Devetsikiotis, M., & Townsend, J. K. (1993). Statistical Optimization of Dynamic Importance Sampling Parameters for Efficient Simulation of Communication Networks. *IEEE/ACM Transactions on Networking*, 1(3), 293 – 305.

Dey, A. K., Abowd, G.D. & Salber, D. (2001). A conceptual framework and a toolkit for supporting the rapid prototyping of context-aware applications. Human-Computer Interaction, 16:97–166.

DiCaterino, A. & Pardo, T.A. (1996). The world wide Web as a universal interface to government services.

Available at: http://www.ctg.albany.edu/resources/abstract/itt96-2.html

Dickson K. Chiu, W. & Leung, H. (2005). Towards ubiquitous tourist service coordination and integration: a multi-agent and semantic Web approach. Proceedings of the 7th international conference on Electronic commerce ICEC '05. ACM Press

Dillon, J. & Pelgrin, W. (2002). E-Government/Commerce in New York State. Office of Technology. New York, NY.

Dimitriadou, E., Ioannou, K., Panoutsopoulos, I., Garmpis, A. & Kotsopoulos, S. (2005). Priority to Low Moving Terminals in TETRA Networks. WSEAS Transactions on Communications, Issue 11, Volume 4, pp 1228-1236

Distributed Systems Online: http://dsonline.computer.org/portal/site/dsonline/index.jsp

Dix, A., Finlay, J., Abowd G.D. & Beale, R. (2004). Human- Computer Interaction. Prentice Hall, Harlow, England, third edition.

Dixit, S. (2006). On fixed-mobile network convergence, *Wireless Personal Communications*, Vol. 38, No. 1, pp. 55-65.

Djuknic, G., Freidenfelds, J., & Okunev, Y. (1997). Establishing wireless communications services via high-altitude aeronautical platforms: a concept whose time has come?. *IEEE Communications Magazine*, 35(9), 128-135.

Doherty, L., Pister, K. S. J., & El Ghaoui, L. (2001). Convex position estimation in wireless sensor networks. In *Proceedings IEEE of Infocom 2001, Vol. 3*, (pp. 1655-1663). USA: Anchorage.

Dong, Y, & Yau, D. K. Y., (2005). Adaptive Sleep Scheduling for Energy-efficient Movement-predicted Wireless Communication. *Proceedings of the 13TH IEEE International Conference on Network Protocols (ICNP)*, 391 – 400.

Donohue, J., Houck, E., & Myers, R. (1995). Simulation Designs for the Estimation of Response Surface Gradients in the Presenced of Model Misspecification. *Management Science*, 41(2), 244-262.

Doty, P. & Erdelez, S. (2002). Information micro-practices in Texas rural courts: Methods and issues for E-government. Government Information Quarterly, 19, 369-387.

Dovis, F., Lo Presti, L., & Mulassano, P. (2005). Support infrastructures based on high altitude platforms for navigation satellite systems. *IEEE Wireless Communications Magazine*, 12(5), 106-112.

Drane, C. (1998). Positioning GSM telephones. *IEEE Communications Magazine*, 36(4), 46-59.

Drossos, N., Goumopoulos, C., and Kameas, A. (2007). A conceptual model and the supporting middleware for composing ubiquitous computing applications. *Journal of Ubiquitous Computing and Intelligence*, American Scientific Publishers(ASP), 1(2), 1-13.

Duca, E., Carrozzo, V., & Roseti, C. (2007). Performance evaluation of a hybrid satellite network based on high-altitude-platforms. *IEEE Aerospace Conference*, 1-12.

Duffy, D. (2000). Q&A: Balancing the role of e-government: Interview with Mike Hernon, vice president of e-government for New York City-based Gov Works. Available at: http://www.cnn.com/2000/TECH/computing/11/13/qna.egov.idg

E. Yeh and A. Cohen, (2004) "Information theory, queuing, and resource allocation in multi-user fading communications," in *Proc. Conf. Information Sciences and Systems*, Princeton, NJ, 2004, pp. 1396–1401.

Easingwood, C.J. & Storey, C. "Marketplace success factors for new financial services." *Journal of Services Marketing* 7, no.1, (1993).41-54.

Easingwood, C.J. & Storey, C. "Success factors for new consumer financial services." *International Journal of Bank Marketing* 9, no.1, (1991):3-10.

Easingwood, C.J. "New product development for service companies." *Journal of Product Innovation Management* 3, no.4 (1986):264-275.

Eberle, W., Bougard, B., Pollin, S., & Catthoor, F. (2005). From myth to methodology: cross-layer design for energy-efficient wireless communication. *Design Automation Conference*.

Eddy, W. M. (2006). At What Layer Does Mobility Belong? *IEEE Communications Magazine,* 42(10), 155-159.

Edgett, S. "The traits of successful new service development." *Journal of Services Marketing* 8, no.3, (1994):40-49.

Edgett, S. & Parkinson, S. "The development of new financial services: Identifying determinants of success and failure." *International Journal of Service* 5, no.4, (1994):24-38.

Edwards, W., Newman, M.W., Sedivy, J., Smith, T. & Izadi, S. (2002). Challenge: Recombinant computing and the speakeasy approach, in: 8th ACM Mobicom.

eGovernment Unit, DG Information Society, European Commission, (2004). Top of the Web: user satisfaction and usage survey of egovernment services. Europe's Information Society Thematic Portal Web Site: http://europa.eu.int/information_society/activities/egovernment_research/doc/top_of_the_Web_report_2004.pdf

El Defrawy, K. M., El Zarki, M. S., & Khairy, M. M. (2006). Proposal for a cross-layer coordination framework for next generation wireless systems. *ACM International Conference On Communications And Mobile Computing*, 141 – 146.

El Malki, K., (2007). Low-Latency Handoffs in Mobile IPv4. RFC 4881.

El-Jabu, B., & Steele, R. (2001). Cellular communications using aerial platforms. *IEEE Transactions on Vehicular Technology*, 50(3), 686-700.

Emiris, D., Marentakis, C., Laimos, P. (2007). Towards an Integrated LBS-Enabled, Mobile Auctions Marketplace for Logistics Services. Paper presented at the 18th Annual IEEE International Symposium on Personal, Indoor and Mobile Radio Communications (PIMRC'07), Athens, 2007.

Endo, T., & Mori, S. (1976). Mode analysis of a multimode ladder oscillator. *IEEE Transactions on Circuits and Systems*, 23(2), 100-113.

Erceg, V., Greenstein, L. J., Tjandra,S. Y., Parkoff, S. R., Gupta, A. Kulic, B., Julius, A. A. and Bianchi, R. (1999). "An empirically based path loss model for wireless channels in suburban environments," IEEE Journal on Selected Areas in Communications, pp. 1205–1211, July.

Ericsson. (2005, April). Evolution towards converged services and networks, White Paper.

Ericsson. (2007, March). Introduction to IMS, White Paper.

Erl, T. (2004). Service-Oriented Architecture: A Field Guide to Integrating XML and Web Services, Prentice Hall, 2004.

Erl, T., (2006). Service-Oriented Architecture: Concepts, Technology, and Design, Prentice Hall, 2006.

Ertel, R.B., Cartieri, P., Sowerby, K.W., Rappaport, T.S., and Reed, J.H. (1998). Overview of Spatial Channel Models for Antenna Array Communication Systems, *IEEE Personal Communications,* Vol. 5, No. 1, pp. 10-22.

Estrin, D., Govindan, R. & Heidemann, J. (2000). Embedding the Internet. Communications of the ACM;43(5):39–41.

ETSI (2002). TS 101 528: *Location Services (LCS); Broadcast network assistance for Enhanced Observed Time Difference (E-OTD) and Global Positioning System (GPS) positioning methods*; version 8.4.1.

ETSI (2002). TS 101 529: *Location Services (LCS); Serving Mobile Location Centre - Serving Mobile Location Centre (SMLC - SMLC)*; version 8.1.1.

ETSI (2002). TS 101 724: *Location Services (LCS); Functional description*, 3GPP TS 03.71, version 8.7.0.

ETSI (2006). TS 125 302: *Universal Mobile Telecommunications System (UMTS);* Services provided by the physical layer (3GPP TS 25.302 version 7.1.0).

ETSI EN300-744 v1.2.1, Digital Video Broadcasting (DVB): Framing Structure, channel coding and modulation for digital terrestrial television, ETSI 1999-01.

European Cooperative in the Field of Science and Technical Research EURO-COST 231 (1991). "Urban transmission loss models for mobile radio in the 900 and 1800 MHz bands," Revision 2, The Hague, Sept.

Fahy, J. (1996). Competitive advantage in international services: A resource-based view. *International Studies in Management and Organization*, 26 (2):24-37

Falconer, D., Ariyavisitakul, S., Benyamin-Seeyar, A., & Eldson, B. (2002). *Frequency-Domain Equalisation for Single-Carrier Broadband Wireless Systems*. IEEE Communications Magazine, Vol. 2002, No. 4.

Falletti, E., Laddomada, M., Mondin, M., & Sellone, F. (2006). Integrated services from high-altitude platforms: a flexible communication system. *IEEE Communications Magazine,* 44(2), 85-94.

Feeney, L. M., & Nilsson, M. (2001). Investigating the energy consumption of a wireless network interface in an ad hoc networking environment. *Twentieth Annual Joint Conference of the IEEE Computer and Communications Societies (INFOCOM)*, 3, 1548 – 1557.

Feldman R. A., Mehra, R. (1993). Auctions: Theory and applications. International Monetary Fund. Staff Papers, 40(3), 485-511.

Feldman, D. (1996). An analysis of the projection method for robust adaptive beamforming, *IEEE Transactions on Antennas and Propagation*, 44(7), 1023–1030.

Feldman, D., & Griffiths, L.J. (1994). A projection approach for robust adaptive beamforming, *IEEE Transactions on Signal Processing*, 42(4), 867–876.

Feng, H., Hoegler, T., Stucky, W. (2006,). Exploring the Critical Success Factors for Mobile Commerce. Paper presented at the International Conference on Mobile Business (ICMB'06).

Fernández Prades, C. (2006). *Advanced Signal Processing Techniques for Global Navigation Satellite System Receivers*, doctoral dissertation, Universitat Politècnica de Catalunya (UPC), Barcelona, Spain.

Fernando, X. (2006). Improved Expression for Intensity Noise in Multimedia over Fiber Networks. *International Conference on Industrial and Information Systems ICIIS 2006 (pp. 425-429). IEEE.*

Fernando, X., (2006). Radio over Fiber in Multimedia Access Networks. *International Conference on Access Networks (AccessNets'06). ACM.*

Fidler, R. (1997). *Mediamorphosis: Understanding New Media.* Thousand Oaks, CA: Pine Forge Press.

Figliozzi, M., Mahmassani, H. S., Jaillet, P. (2002,). A Framework for the Study of Carrier Strategies in an Auction Based Transportation Marketplace. Paper presented at the 82nd Annual Meeting of the Transportation Research Board (TRB2003).

Filho, J.G.P. & van Sinderen, M. (2003). Web service architectures – semantics and context-awareness issues in Web services platforms, Tech. rep., Telematica Instituut.

Finkenzeller, K. (2003). *RFID handbook: Fundamentals and applications in contactless smart cards and identification* (2nd ed.). West Sussex: John Wiley & Sons, Ltd.

Fiol, C.M. (1991). Managing culture as a competitive resource: An identity-based view of sustainable competitive advantage. *Journal of Management*, 17: 191-211.

Firoiu, V., Le Boudec, J.-Y., Towsley, D., & Zhang, Z.-L. (2002). Theories and models for Internet quality of service. *IEEE Proceedings*, 90(9), 1565 – 1591.

Fixed-Mobile Convergence Alliance (2006). 'FMCA Convergence Application Scenarios', Release 1.0.

Flood, P.C., Smith, K.A., & Derfus, P. (1996). Guest Editors' introduction –*Top management teams: A neglected topic in strategic human resource management.* Ibar, 17: 1-17.

Fock, L., Kwan, A., & Tucker R. S. (1992). Reduction of semiconductor laser intensity noise by feedforward compensation: experiment and theory. *IEEE J. Lightwave Technology*, 10, 1919–1925.

Folinas, D., Manthou, V., Sigala, M., Vlachopoulou, M. (2004). E-volution of a Supply Chain: Cases and best Practices. Internet Research, 14(4), 274-283.

Fontana, R. J. (2004). Recent System Applications of Short-Pulse Ultra-Wideband (UWB) Technology (In-vited Paper). *IEEE Microwave Theory & Tech.*, 52(9), 2087-2104.

Foo, Y. C., & Lim, W. L. (2005). Speed and direction adaptive call admission control for high altitude platform station (HAPS) UMTS. *IEEE Military Communications Conference*, 4, 2182-2188.

Foo, Y. C., Lim, W. L., & Tafazolli, R. (2002). Centralized downlink call admission control for high altitude platform station UMTS with onboard power resource sharing. *IEEE Vehicular Technology Conference*, 1, 549-553.

Forney, G.D. (1973). *The Viterbi algorithm.* Proceedings of the IEEE Vol. 61, No. 3.

Forrester Research. June (2006), *European Mobile Landscape*

Foschini, G.J., & Gans, M.J., (1998). On limits of wireless communications in a fading environment when using multiple antennas, *Wireless Personal Communications*, 6(3), 311-335, 1998.

Fountain, J.E. (2001). Building the virtual state: Information technology and institutional change. Washington, DC: Brooking Institution Press.

Fourie, A., and Nitch, D. (2000). SuperNEC: antenna and indoor-propagation simulation program, *IEEE Antennas and Propagation Magazine*, Vol. 42, No. 3, 31-48.

Fraleigh, C., Moon, S., Lyles, B., Cotton, C., Khan, M., Moll, D., Rockell, R., Seely, T., & Diot, S.C. (2003). Packet-level traffic measurements from the Sprint IP backbone. *IEEE Network*, 17(6), 6 – 16.

Frolick, M., Chen, L.D. (2004). Assessing M-Commerce Opportunities. Information Systems Management, 21(2), 53-61.

Fu, H., Ho, Y.C., Chen, R. C. Y., Chang, T. H., Chien, P. H. (2006). Factors Affecting the Adoption of Electronic Marketplaces. International Journal of Operations & Production Management, 26(12), 1301-1324.

Fudenberg, D., & Tirole, J. (1991). *Game Theory*, The MIT Press.

Fusco, M. (1990). FDTD algorithm in curvilinear coordinates, *IEEE Transactions on Antennas and Propagation*, Vol. AP-38, pp. 76-88.

G. P. Agrawal, Fiber-Optic Communication Systems, 3rd , Wiley, New York, 2002.

G.A. Barnett (Eds), *Progress in Communication Sciences* (Vol 15: 125-150) Stamford, CT: Ablex.

Gallager, R. G. (1985). A perspective on multiaccess channels, *IEEE Transactions on Information Theory,* 31(2), 124-142.

Ganesh, R. (1991). *Time Domain Measurements, Modeling, and Simulation of the Indoor Radio Channel.* Ph.D. thesis, Worcester Polytechnic Institute.

Ganesh, R., and Pahlavan, K. (1989). On arrival of paths in fading multipath indoor radio channels, *IEE Electronics Letters*, Vol. 25, No. 5, pp. 763-765.

Garlan, D., Siewiorek, D., Smailagic, A. & Steenkiste, P. (2002). Project Aura: Towards Distraction-Free Pervasive Computing. IEEE Pervasive Computing, 1(2):22–31, April- June.

Garlan, D., Siewiorek, D., Smailagic, A., and Steenkiste, P. (April- June 2002). Project Aura: Towards Distraction-Free Pervasive Computing. *IEEE Pervasive Computing, 1*(2), 22–31.

Garson, G.D. (1999). Information systems, politics, and government: Leading theoretical perspectives. In G. D. Garson (Ed.), Handbook of public information systems (pp. 591-605). New York: Marcel Dekker.

Gefen, D. & Pavlou, P. (2002). Egovernment adoption. Paper presented at Americas Conference on Information Systems.

Georgiadis, A. (2007). Design of Coupled Oscillator Arrays for Second Harmonic Radiation. In IEEE, *MTT-S International Microwave Symposium* (pp. 1727-1730), Honolulu, HI: IEEE.

Georgiadis, A., & Suarez, A. (2006). Nonlinear Synthesis of a Linear Active Oscillator Antenna Array Using Harmonic Balance and EM Simulation. In IEEE, *Inter-national Workshop on Integrated Nonlinear Microwave and Millimeter-Wave Circuits (INMMIC)* (pp. 176-179). Aveiro: IEEE.

Georgiadis, A., Collado, A. & Suarez, A. (2006). New Techniques for the analysis and design of coupled-oscillator systems. *IEEE Transactions on Microwave Theory and Techniques*, 54(11), 3864-3877.

Georgiadis, A., Collado, A. & Suarez, A. (2007). Pattern nulling in coupled oscillator antenna arrays. *IEEE Transactions on Antennas and Propagation,*55(5), 1267-1274.

Georgiadis, L., Neely, M. J., & Tassiulas, L. (2006). *Resource allocation and cross-layer control in wireless networks.* Now.

Gershman, A.B. (2003, September). *Robust adaptive beamforming: an overview of recent trends and advances in the field.* Paper presented at the International Conference on Antenna Theory and Techniques, Sevastopol, Ukraine.

Ghassemzadeh,S.S., Greenstein, L.J. Kavcic, A. Sveinsson, T. Tarokh,V. (2003). "Indoor path loss model for residential and commercial buildings," Proc. Vehic. Technol. Conf., pp. 3115–3119, Oct.

Ghere, R.K. & Young, B.A. (1998). The cyber-management environment: Where technology and ingenuity meet public purpose and accountability. Public Administration and Management: An interactive Journal, 3(1) Available at: http://www.pamij.com/gypaper.html

Giannini, F., & Leuzzi, G. (2004). *Nonlinear Microwave Circuit Design*, New York NY: John Wiley and Sons.

Giddens, A. (1991) *Modernity and Self-Identity: Self and Society in the Late Modern Age.* Stanford University Press: California.

Gifford, D.K., Jouvelotl, P., Sheldon, M.A. & O'Toole Jr. J.W. (1991). Semantic file systems, in: Proceedings of 13th ACM Symposium on Operating Systems Principles, Association for Computing Machinery SIGOPS, pp. 16–25.

Gilbertson, P., Edwards, R., Coulton, P. (2006,). Reducing Processing Time for Real-Time Mobile Hosted Location Based Services. Paper presented at the The 17th Annual IEEE International Symposium on Personal, Indoor and Mobile Radio Communications (PIMRC'06).

Gliese, U., Norskov, T., Norskov, S., & Sturkjaer, T. E. (1998). Multifunctional fiber-optic microwave links based on remote-heterodyne detection. *IEEE Trans. Microw. Theory Tech.*, 46, 458- 468.

Gloge, D., & Marcatili, E. A. J. (1973). Multimode theory of graded-core fibers. *Bell Systems Tech. J.*, Nov. 1973, 1563-1578.

Goldsmith, A. (2005). Wireless Communications, Cambridge University Press

Goldsmith, A., & Varaiya, P (1997). Capacity of fading channels with channel side information, *IEEE Transactions on Information Theory*, 43(6), 1986-1992.

González-Castaño, F., Gil-Castiñeira, F. J., García-Reinoso, J. (2005,). Bluetooth Real-Time Mobile Auctions. Paper presented at the IEEE 16th International Symposium on Personal, Indoor and Mobile Radio Communications (PIMRC'07).

Gottschalk, K., Graham, S., Kreger, H., Snell, J. (2002). Introduction to Web Services Architecture, IBM Systems Journal, Vol41, No2, 2002.

Gou, H., Huang, B., Liu, W., Li, X. (2003). A Framework for Virtual Enterprise Operation Management. Computers in Industry, 50(3), 333-352.

Goud, P., Sesay, A., & Fattouche, M. (1991). A spread spectrum radiolocation technique and its application to cellular radio. In *IEEE Pacific Rim Conference on Communications, Computers and Signal Processing: Vol. 2.* (pp. 661-664). Canada: Victoria.

Goyal, M., Kumar, A., & Sharma, V. (2003). Power constrained and delay optimal policies for scheduling transmission over a fading channel. In *Proc. IEEE INFOCOM 2003. Twenty-Second Annual Joint Conference of the IEEE Computer and Communications Societies: Vol. 1.* (pp. 311-320), IEEE.

Grace, D., Capstick, M. H., Mohorcic, M., Horwath, J., Bobbio, M., & Fitch, M. (2005). Integrating users into the wider broadband network via high altitude platforms. *IEEE Wireless Communications*, 12(5), 98-105.

Grace, D., Thornton, J., Chen, G., White, G. P., & Tozer, T. C. (2005). Improving the system capacity of broadband services using multiple high-altitude platforms. *IEEE Transactions on Wireless Communications*, 4(2), 700-709.

Grajski, K., Kirk, E. (2003). Towards a Mobile Multimedia Age - Location-Based Services: A Case Study. Wireless Personal Communications, 26(2/3) 105-116.

Granelli, F., Kliazovich, D., & da Fonseca, N. L. S. (2005). Performance Limitations of IEEE 802.11 Networks and Potential Enhancements. In Yang Xiao (ed) & Yi Pan (ed), *Wireless LANs and Bluetooth*, Hardbound: Nova Science Publishers.

Granelli, F., Kliazovich, D., Hui, J., & Devetsikiotis, M. (2007). Performance Optimization of Single-Cell Voice over WiFi Communications Using Quantitative Cross-Layering Analysis. *In Proceedings of ITC 20*, Ottawa, Canada.

Grant, A. & Meadows, J. (2007). Communication technology update. Boston: Focal Press.

Grant, G. & Chau, D. (2005). Developing a generic framework for e-government. Journal of Global Information Management, 13 (1), 1-30.

Grant, R.M. (1996). Prospering in dynamically-competitive environments: Organizational capability as knowledge integration. *Organizational Science*, 7:375-387.

Green Paper 1997, *On the Convergence of the Telecommunications, Media and Information Technology Sectors, and the Implications for Regulation.*

Gribble, S.D., Welsh, M., Behren, R., Brewer, E.A., Culler, D.E., Borisov, N., Czerwinski, S.E., Gummadi, R., Hill, J.R., Joseph, A.D., Katz, R.H., Z.M. Mao, Ross, S. & Zhao, B.Y. (2000). The ninja architecture for robust internetscale systems and services, in: Pervasive Computing, Computer Networks (35) (special issue).

Griffin, A. & Page, A.L. "An interim report on measuring product development success and failure." *Journal of Product Innovation Management* 10, (1993):291-308.

Griffin, A. "PDMA research on new product development practices: updating trends and benchmarking best practices." *Journal of Product Innovation Management* 14, no.6, (1997):429-458.

Griffin, A., (1997). PDMA Research on new product development practices: updating trends and benchmarking best practices. Journal of Product Innovation Management, Vol. 14, No. 6, pp. 429-458.

Grimm, R. & Bershad B. (2002). Future directions: System support for pervasive applications, in: Proceedings of FuDiCo.

Gruber, T. (1993). A translation approach to portable ontologies. *Knowledge Acquisition 5*(2), 199-220.

GSM Recommendation 05.05 (1991). Radio transmission and reception, ETSI/PT, No. 12, January 1991.

Gudmundson, M. (1991). Correlation model for shadow fading in mobile radio systems, *Electronics Letters*, Vol. 27, No. 23, pp. 2145-2146.

Gustafsson, F., Gunnarsson, F. (2005). Mobile Positioning Using Wireless Networks. IEEE Signal Processing Magazine, 22(4), 41-53.

H. Harney, U. Meth, A. Colegrove and G. Gross (2006). GSAKMP: Group secure Association Key Management Protocol", IETF RFC 4535.

H. Krawczyk (1996). SKEME: A versatile secure key exchange mechanism for Internet, in the Proceedings of the 1996 IEEE Symposium on Network and Distributed Systems Security, pages: 114-127.

H. Ueno, H. Suzuki, N. Ishikawa and O. Takahashi (2005). A Receiver Authentication and Group Key Delivery Protocol for Secure Multicast, IEICE Transaction on Communications, Volume E88-B, number 3, pages: 1139-1148.

Hadaya, P. (2006). Determinants of the Future Level of Use of Electronic Mareketplaces: The Case of Canadian Firms. Electronic Commerce Research, 6(2), 173-185.

Hagenauer, J., & Hoher, P. (1989). *A Viterbi algorithm with soft outputs and its applications*, IEEE GLOBECOM '89, Dallas, USA, 1680-1686.

Hagras, H., Doctor, F., Lopez, A., Callaghan, V. (2007). An Incremental Adaptive Life Long Learning Approach for Type-2 Fuzzy Embedded Agents in Ambient Intelligent Environments. *IEEE Transactions on Fuzzy Systems, 15*(1), 41-55.

Halchin, L.E. (2004). Electronic government: Government capability and terrorist resource. Government Information Quarterly, 21, 406-419.

Hall, E., & Wilson, S. (1998). *Design and analysis of turbo codes on Rayleigh fading channels*. IEEE Journal on Selected Areas in Communications, Vol. 16, No. 2, 160-174.

Halstead, D., Becherer, R. C. (2003). Internet Auction Sellers: Does Size Really Matters? Internet Research: Electronic Networking Applications and Policy, 13(3), 183-194.

Han, Z., Himsoon, T., Siriwongpairat, W. P., Liu, K. J. R. Power Control with Cooperative Diversity over Multisuser OFDM Networks: Who helps whom and how to cooperate, *White papers,* University of Maryland.

Han, Z., Liu, K. J. R. (2002) Adaptive coding for joint power control and beamforming over wireless networks, *SPIE Advanced Signal Processing Algorithms, Architectures and Implementations XII,* Dec.

Hand, A., Cardiff, J., Magee, P., Doody, J. (2006). An Architecture and Development Methodology for Location-Based Services. Electronic Commerce Research and Applications, 5(3), 201-208.

Hanrahan, H. (2007). Network Convergence: Services, Applications, Transport and Operation Support, Willey & Sons, ltd, 2007.

Hansen, F. and Meno, F. I. (1977)."Mobile Fading–Rayleigh and Lognormal Superimposed," IEEE Trans. Veh. Technol., vol. 26, no. 4, pp. 332-335, Nov.

Hansen, F., and Meno, F. I. (1977). Mobile fading – Rayleigh and lognormal superimposed, IEEE Transactions on Vehicular Technology, vol. VT-26, no. 4, pp. 332-335.

Harada, H., and Prasad, R. (2002). *Simulation and Software Radio for Mobile Communications,* Artech House, Norwood, MA, USA.

Harms, P.H., Lee, J.F., and Mittra, R. (1992). A study of the non-orthogonal FDTD method versus the conventional FDTD technique for computing resonant frequencies of cylindrical cavities, *IEEE Transactions on Microwave Theory and Techniques,* Vol. MTT-40, pp. 741-746.

Harper, N. (2006). Using Assisted-GNSS to locate handsets in wireless networks. *Coordinates,* 2(12), 24-27.

Harper, N., Nicholson, P., Mumford, P., & Poon, E. (2004). Process for improving GPS acquisition assistance data and server-side location determination for cellular networks. *Journal of Global Positioning Systems,* 3(1-2), 133-142.

Hartline, M.D., Maxham J.G. & McKee, D.O. "Corridors of influence in the dissemination of customer-oriented strategy to customer contact employees." *Journal of Marketing* 64, (2000):35-50.

Hartmann, P., Penty, R.V., White, I.H., Seeds, A.J., (2004). Dual Service Wireless LAN antenna-remoting system using uncooled directly modulated DFB Laser diodes. *CLEO 2004.*

Hartmann, P., Qian, X., Penty, R. V., & White, I. H. (2004). Broadband multimode fibre (MMF) based IEEE 802.11a/b/g WLAN distribution system. *IEEE Int. Top. Meeting Microw. Photon. (pp. 173–176)*, IEEE.

Hashemi, H. (1993). Impulse response modeling of indoor radio propagation channels, *IEEE Journal on Selected Areas in Communications,* Vol. 11, pp. 967-978.

Hashemi, H., and Tholl, D. (1994). Statistical Modeling and Simulation of the RMS Delay Spread of Indoor Radio Propagation Channels, *IEEE Transaction on Vehicular Technology,* Vol. 43, No. 1, pp. 110-120.

Hata, M. (1980). "Empirical formula for propagation loss in land mobile radio services," IEEE Trans. Vehic. Technol., Vol VT-29, No. 3, pp. 317–325, Aug.

Hata, M., and Nagatsu, T. (1980). Mobile location using signal strength measurements in cellular systems, *IEEE Transactions on Vehicular Technology,* Vol. 29, No. 2, pp. 245-251.

Hata, M., & Nagatsu, T. (1980). Mobile location using signal strength measurements in a cellular system. *IEEE Transaction on Vehicular Technology,* 29(2), 245-252.

Hawking, P., Stein, A., Wyld, D. C., Foster, S. (2004). E-procurement: is the ugly duckling actually a swan down under? Asia Pacific Journal of Marketing and Logistics, 16(1), 3-26.

Haykin, S. (1996) *Adaptive Filter Theory,* Upper Saddle River, NJ: Prentice Hall.

Haykin, S. (1996). *Adaptive Filter Theory, 3rd Edition,* Prentice Hall, Upper Saddle River (US).

He, T., Huang, C., Blum, B. M., Stankovic, J. A., & Abdelzaher, T. (2003). Range-free localization schemes in large scale sensor networks. In *Proceedings of the 9th Annual International Conference on Mobile Computing and Networking (Mobicom)*: (pp. 81-95). USA: San Diego.

Hearst, M. A. (1998). Support Vector Machines. *IEEE Intelligent Systems,* 13(4), 18-28.

Heath, T. (2001). Difference pattern beam steering of coupled, nonlinear oscillator arrays. *IEEE Microwave and Wireless Components Letters,* 11(8), 343-345.

Heath, T. (2004). Beam steering of nonlinear oscillator arrays through manipulation of coupling phases. *IEEE Transactions on Antennas and Propagation,* 52(7), 1833–1842.

Heath, T. (2005). Simulatneous beam steering and null formation with coupled, nonlinear oscillator arrays. *IEEE Transactions on Antennas and Propagation,* 53(6), 2031–2035.

Hecht, J. (2002). *Understanding Fiber Optics.* Prentice Hall.

Heeks, R (2001). Understanding e-governance for development. The University of Manchester, Institute for Development, Policy and Management Information Systems,, Technology and Government: Working Papers

Series, Number 12/2001. Available at: http://idpm.man.ac.uk/idpm/igov11abs.htm

Hegering, HG, Abeck, S., Neumair, B. (1999). Integrated Management of Networked Systems: Concepts, Architectures, and Their Operational Application. Morgan Kaufmann, 1999.

Heidelberger, P., (1995). Fast simulation of rare events in queuing and reliability models. *ACM Transactions on Modeling and Computer Simulation (TOMACS)*, 5(1), 43 – 85.

Held, A., Buchholz, S. & Schill, A. (2002). Modelling of context information for pervasive computing applications. In Proceedings of SCI2002/ISAS.

Henderson, T. R. (2003). Host Mobility for IP Networks: A Comparison, *IEEE Network*, Nov. 2003, pp. 18–26

Hengartner, U. & Steenkiste, P. (2003). Protecting Access to People Location Information, Proceedings of the International Conference on Security in Pervasive Computing.

Hengartner, U. and Steenkiste, P., (2003). Protecting Access to People Location Information. *Proceedings of the International Conference on Security in Pervasive Computing (SPC 2003)*, March 2003.

Hess, C.K. & Campbell, R.H. (2002). A context file system for ubiquitous computing environments, Technical Report No. UIUCDCS-R-2002-2285 UILU-ENG-2002-1729, July.

Hirata, A., Harada, M., & Nagatsuma, T. (2003). 120-GHz Wireless Link Using Photonic Techniques for Generation, Modulation, and Emission of Millimeter-Wave Signals. *IEEE J. Lightwave Technology*, 21(10), 2145-2153.

Hirata, A., Minotani, T., & Nagatsuma, T. (2002) .Millimeter-Wave Photonics for 10 Gbit/s Wireless Links. *LEOS 2002, vol.2, (pp. 477 – 478)*. LEOS.

Ho, A.T-K. (2002). Reinventing local governments and the e-government initiative. Public Administration Review. Vol. 62, No.4, pp.434-44.

Ho, J. T. Y. (2005). "A Generalized Doppler Power Spectrum for 3D Non-Isotropic Scattering Environments,"

Global Telecommunications Conference. GLOBECOM '05. IEEE, 28 Nov-2 Dec. pp. 1393-1396.

Holden, S.H. (2003). The evolution of information technology management at the federal level: Implications for public administration. In G.D Garson (Ed.). Public information technology: Policy and management issues (pp. 53-73). Hershey, PA: Idea Group Publishing.

Holland, R. (1983). Finite difference solutions of Maxwell's equations in generalized non-orthogonal coordinates, *IEEE Transactions on Nuclear Science*, Vol. NS-30, No. 6, pp. 4589-4591.

Holma, H., & Toskala, A. (2000). *WCDMA for UMTS: Radio Access for Third Generation Mobile Communications*, J.Wiley.

Holt, T., Pahlavan, K., and Lee, J.F. (1992). A graphical indoor radio channel simulator using 2D ray tracing, *Proceedings of the PIMRC '92*, Boston, USA, pp. 411-416.

Home Gateway Initiative (2006). 'Home Gateway Technical Requirements: Release 1', Version 1.0.

Hong D. and Rappaport, S. S. (1986). Traffic model and performance analysis for cellular mobile radio telephone systems with prioritized and non prioritized handoff procedures. IEEE Trans., VT-35, pp 77-92.

Hong, D., Chiu, D.K.W. & Shen V.Y. (2005). Requirements elicitation for the design of context-aware applications in a ubiquitous environment. Proceedings of the 7th international conference on Electronic commerce ICEC '05. ACM Press

Hong, T. C., Ku, B. J., Park, J. M., Ahn, D., & Jang, Y. (2005). Capacity of the WCDMA system using high altitude platform stations. *International Journal of Wireless Information Networks*, 13(1), 5-17.

Hooli K., Juntti M., Heikkilä M.J., Komulainen P., Latva-aho M., & Lilleberg J. (2002). *Chip-Level Channel Equalisation in WCDMA Downlink*. Eurasip Journal on Applied Signal Processing, Vol. 2002, No. 8.

Howard, J.S., *Frequency Domain Characteristic and Autoregressive Modeling of the Indoor Radio Channel*. Ph.D. Thesis, Worcester Polytechnic Institute, Worcester MA.

Hsieh, R., Zhou, Z. G., & Seneviratne, A. (2003). S-MIP: a seamless handoff architecture for mobile IP. *Twenty-Second Annual Joint Conference of the IEEE Computer and Communications Societies*, 3, 1774 – 1784.

Hsu, C.-C., & Devetsikiotis, M. (in press). An Adaptive Approach to Accelerated Evaluation of Highly Reliable Systems. *ACM Transactions on Modeling and Computer Simulation*.

Hsu, C-C., & Devetsikiotis, M. (2007). A Framework for Automatic Software Performance Evaluation and Optimization Using Response Surface Methodology and Importance Sampling. *In Proceedings of the 40th Annual Simulation Symposium*, Norfolk.

Huang, W. L., & Letaief, K. B. (2007). Cross-Layer Scheduling and Power Control Combined With Adaptive Modulation for Wireless Ad Hoc Networks. *IEEE Transactions on Communications*, 55(4), 728 – 739.

Hui, J. & Devetsikiotis, M. (2006). Metamodeling of Wi-Fi Performance. *Proc. IEEE ICC 2006*: Istanbul, Turkey.

Hui, J., & Devetsikiotis, M. (in press). A Metamodeling Framework for Wi-Fi Performance Evaluation. *IEEE Transactions on Wireless Communications*.

Hui, R., Zhu, B., Huang, R., Allen, C.T. , Demarest, K.R., & Richards, D. (2002). Subcarrier multiplexing for high-speed optical transmission. *IEEE J. Lightwave Technol*ogy., 20, 417–427.

Hung, V. W., Mc Garvey B., et al. (2007). Red VCSEL Transceivers for Gigabit Data Transmission over Plastic Optical Fibre. *16th international conference on plastic optical fibers, Italy, 2007*.

Huselid, M.A., Jackson, S.E., & Schuler, R.J. "Technical and strategic HRM effectiveness as determinants of firm performance." *Academy of Management Journal* 40, no.1, (1997):171-188.

Hwang, S.D., Choi, Y. & Myeong, S.H. (1999). Electronic government in South Korea: Conceptual problems. Government Information Quarterly, 16 (3), 277-285

Hwang, S.H., Kim, K.J. Ahn, J.Y. and Whang, K.C. (1997). "A Channel Model for Nongeostationary Orbit-

ing Satellite System," in IEEE Vehicular Technology Conference, May 4–7, pp. 41–45.

I. P. Kaminow and, T. Li, Eds., Optical Fiber Telecommunications, Vols. III-A, III-B (1997), IV-A and IV-B (2002), Academic Press, San Diego.

Ibach, P., Horbank, M. (2005). Highly Available Location-Based Services in Mobile Environments. Paper presented at the International Service Availability Symposium (ISAS 2004).

IDABC/EIF (2004). European Interoperability Framework for Pan-European eGovernment Services, Office for Official Publications of the European Communities, Luxembourg, available at: http://europa.eu.int

IEEE 802.11, (Aug., 1999). Wireless LAN Medium Access Control (MAC) and Physical Layer (PHY) specifications", IEEE Standard, .

IEEE 802.11e, (July, 2005). Wireless LAN Medium Access Control (MAC) and Physical Layer (PHY) specifications: Medium Access Control (MAC) Enhancements for Quality of Service (QoS), IEEE 802.11e Workgroup.

IEEE 802.11i, (July, 2004). Wireless LAN Medium Access Control (MAC) and Physical Layer (PHY) specifications: Medium Access Control (MAC) Security Enhancements, IEEE 802.11i Workgroup, .

IEEE 802.11k/D7.0, (2003). Wireless LAN Medium Access Control (MAC) and Physical Layer (PHY) specifications: Specification for Radio Resource Measurement. IEEE 802.11k Workgroup

IEEE 802.11r/D6.0, (2004). Wireless LAN Medium Access Control (MAC) and Physical Layer (PHY) specifications: Fast Roaming/Fast BSS Transition, IEEE 802.11r Workgroup.

IEEE 802.16.2. (2004). Recommended Practice for Local and metropolitan area networks. Coexistence of Fixed Broadband Wireless Access Systems. *IEEE Computer Society & IEEE Microwave Theory and Techniques Society*, March 2004.

IEEE 802.16e, (Feb., 2006). Air Interface for Fixed and Mobile Broadband Wireless Access Systems – Amendments for Physical and Medium Access Control Layers for Combined Fixed and Mobile Operation in Licensed Bands, IEEE Standard.

IEEE 802.21, (May, 2005). Handover and interoperability between heterogeneous network types including both 802 and non 802 networks.

IEEE Std 802.11a-1999. (1999). Part 11: Wireless LAN Medium Access Control (MAC) and Physical Layer (PHY) specifications: High Speed Physical Layer in the 5GHz Band. *IEEE.*

IEEE Std. 802.11 (1999). IEEE Standards for Information Technology -- Telecommunications and Information Exchange between Systems -- Local and Metropolitan Area Network -- Specific Requirements - Part 11: Wireless LAN Medium Access Control (MAC) and Physical Layer (PHY) Specifications. *IEEE Press.*

IEEE Std. 802.11e (2005). *Local and metropolitan area networks - Specific requirements Part 11: Wireless LAN Medium Access Control (MAC) and Physical Layer (PHY) specifications Amendment 8: Medium Access Control (MAC) Quality of Service Enhancements*, IEEE Press.

IEEE Std. 802.16 (2001). IEEE Standard for Local and Metropolitan Area Networks, part 16, Air Interface for Fixed Broadband Wireless Access Systems. *IEEE Press.*

IEEE Std. 802.1X, (2004). IEEE Standard for Port-Based Network Access Control.

IEEE, (2007). Special Section on Convergence of Optical and Wireless Access Networks. *IEEE J. Lightwave Technology,* 25(11).

Ikegami, F., Takeuchi, T., and Yoshida, S. (1991). Theoretical prediction of mean field strength for urban mobile radio, *IEEE Transactions on Antennas and Propagation*, Vol. 39, pp. 229-302.

Ikuma, T., Beex, A.A., Zeidler, J.R., & Meadows, B.K. (2006). Adaptive interference mitigation with a coupled nonlinear oscillator array beamformer. In IEEE, *Aerospace Conference* (pp. 13-26).

International Telecommunication Union (ITU), "NGN Working Definition", available at http://www.itu.int/ITU-T/studygroups/com13/ngn2004/working_definition.html .

Ioannou K., Louvros, S., Panoutsopoulos, I., Kotsopoulos, S. and Karagiannidis, G. K. (October 2002). Member IEEE, Optimizing the Handover Call Blocking Probability in Cellular Networks with High Speed Moving Terminals. *IEEE Communications Letters,* 6(10).

Ioannou, K., Dimitriadou, E., Ioannou, A., Panoutsopoulos I. & Kotsopoulos, S. (2006). Hierarchical Dynamic Channel Assignment Technique. WSEAS Transactions on Communications, Issue 1, Volume 5, pp 115-122

Ioannou, K., Dimitriadou, E., Ioannou, A., Panoutsopoulos I. & Kotsopoulos, S. (2006). Hierarchical Dynamic Channel Assignment Technique. WSEAS Transactions on Communications, Issue 1, Volume 5, pp 115-122

Ioannou, K., E. Dimitriadou, A. Ioannou, I. Panoutsopoulos, A. Garmpis and S. Kotsopoulos, "Efficient Channel Assignment Technique providing Priority to Emergency Calls in Wireless Cellular Security Networks, WSEAS Transactions on Communications, Issue 1, Volume 5, January 2006, pp 84-91

Ioannou, K., Panoutsopoulos, I. and S.Kotsopoulos, "Optimizing the QoS of Ultra High and High Speed Moving Terminals in Satellite-aided cellular networks", Wireless Personal Communications, Volume 39, Number 3, November 2006, pp307-319"

Ioannou, K., Panoutsopoulos, I., Koubias, S. and Kotsopoulos, S. (June 2004) "A new Dynamic Channel Management Scheme to increase the performance index of Cellular Networks", *Electronics Letters, 10th, 40*(12), 744-746

Ioannou, K., Panoutsopoulos, I. & Kotsopoulos, S. (2006). Optimizing the QoS of Ultra High and High Speed Moving Terminals in Satellite-aided cellular networks. Wireless Personal Communications, Volume 39, Number 3, pp307-319.

Ioannou, K., Panoutsopoulos, I. & Kotsopoulos, S. (2006). Optimizing the QoS of Ultra High and High

Speed Moving Terminals in Satellite-aided cellular networks. Wireless Personal Communications, Volume 39, Number 3, pp307-319.

Ioannou, K., Panoutsopoulos, I., Koubias S., and S. Kotsopoulos, "A new Dynamic Channel Management Scheme to increase the performance index of Cellular Networks", Electronics Letters, 10th June 2004, Vol.40, No 12, pp 744-746

Ioannou, K., Panoutsopoulos, I., Koubias, S., & Kotsopoulos, S. (2004). *A new Dynamic Channel Management Scheme to Increase the Performance Index of Cellular Networks*. IEE Electronics Letters, Vol. 40, No. 12, 744-746.

Ishigure T., Koike Y., & Fleming J. W. (2000). Optimum Index Profile of the Perfluorinated Polymer-Based GI Polymer Optical Fiber and Its Dispersion Properties. *IEEE J. Lightwave Technology*, 18, 178-184.

Iskam, V.Y. and Shaptsev, V.A. (1985). "Properties of the Nakagami-Rice Distribution as a Model for Signal Fading," Telecommun. Radio Eng., 2, 129–132.

Ismail, T., Liu, C. P., & Seeds, A. J. (2004). Uncooled directly modulated high dynamic range source for IEEE802.11a wireless over fibre LAN applications. *Optical Fibre Communications 2004 (OFC 2004)*.

Ispir, R., Nogi, S., Sanagi, M., & Fukui, K. (1996). Transmission Line Coupled Active Microstrip Antennas for Phase Arrays. In IEEE, *MTT-S International Microwave Symposium* (pp. 931-934). San Francisco, CA: IEEE.

ISTAG in FP6: Working Group 1, IST Research Content, Final Report (2006). Last retrieved on 11/22/2006 from http://www.cordis.lu/ist/istag.htm

ITU, *NGN* (2004). *Project Description*, version 3, February 2004.

ITU Recommendation M.3010, (2000). Principles for a telecommunications management network, Feb. 2000.

ITU, World Telecommunication Development Report 2002: Reinventing Telecoms, March 2002 (available online:http://www.itu.int/itud/ict/publications/).

ITU-T G.711, (1998). Pulse Code Modulation (PCM) of voice parameters.

ITU-T Recommendation M.3050.1 (2007). Enhance Telecom Operations Map: The Business Process Framework (eTOM), March 2007.

ITU-T Recommendation M.3016.0. (2005). Security for the management plane: Overview, May 2005.

ITU-T Recommendation M.3060/Y.2401, (2006). Principles for the Management of Next Generation Networks, March 2006.

ITU-T Recommendation M.3100. (2005). Generic network information model, April 2005.

ITU-T Recommendation M.3400, (2000). Telecommunications management network: TMN management functions, Feb. 2000.

ITU-T Recommendation X.805, (2003). Security architecture for systems providing end-to-end communications, Oct. 2003.

ITU-T Recommendation Y.120/Annex A (Feb 1999.). 'Global information infrastructure scenario methodology – Example of use'.

ITU-T Recommendation Y.2001 (Dec., 2004) 'General overview of NGN'.

ITU-T Recommendation Y.2001, (2004). General overview of NGN, Dec. 2004.

ITU-T Recommendation Y.2011 (Oct., 2004). 'General principles and reference model for NGNs'.

ITU-T Recommendation Y.2011, (2004). General principles and reference model for Next Generation Networks, Oct. 2004.

ITU-T Recommendation Y.2012 (Sept., 2006). 'Functional requirements and architecture of the NGNs of Release-1', .

ITU-T Recommendation Y.2013 (Dec., 2006). 'Converged services framework functional requirements and architecture'.

J. Arkko, E. Carrara, F. Lindholm, M. Naslund and K. Norrman (2004). MIKEY: Multimedia Internet Keying, IETF RFC3830.

Jaeger, P.T. (2002). Constitutional principles and e-government: An opinion about possible effects of federalism and separation of powers on e-government policies. Government Information Quarterly, 19, 357-368.

Jaeger, P.T. (2003). The endless wire: E-government as a global phenomenon. Government Information Quarterly, 20 (4), 323-331.

Jai-muhtadi, J., Campbell, R., Kapadia, A., Mickunas, M. & Yi, S. (2002). Routing through the mist: Privacy preserving communication in ubiquitous computing environments, in: ICDCS '02: Proceedings of the 22nd International Conference on Distributed Computing Systems, ICDCS'02, IEEE Computer Society, Washington, DC, USA, p. 74.

Jain, B., & Agrawala, A. (1993). *Open Systems Interconnection*. New York: McGraw-Hill.

Jakes, W. C. (1974). *Microwave Mobile Communications*, J. Wiley & Sons, New York.

Jakes, W.C. (1974). *Microwave Mobile Communications*. Wiley, New York.

Jakes, W.C. (1994). *Microwave Mobile Communications*. IEEE Press.

Jakes, W.C. Jr., (1974). Microwave Mobile Communications. New York: Wiley.

Jakobsson, A., Swindlehurst, A. L., & Stoica, P. (1998). Subspace-based estimation of time delays and doppler shifts. *IEEE Transactions on Acoustics, Speech and Signal Processing*, 46(9), 2472-2483.

James, G. (2000). Empowering bureaucrats. MC Technology Marketing Intelligence, Vol. 20, No.12, pp.62-68.

Janevski, T. (2003). *Traffic analysis and design of wireless IP networks*. Boston: Artech House

Jap, S. (2002). Online Reverse Auctions: Issues, Themes, and Prospects for the Future. Academy of Marketing Science, Journal, 30(4), 506-525.

Jasen, A. & S. Ines (2004). Quality assessment and benchmarking of Norwegian public Web sites. Proceeding from European Conference on e-government.

Javalgi, R., Ramsey, R. (2001). Strategic issues of e-commerce as an alternative global distribution system. International Marketing Review, 18(4), 376-391.

Jayashree, L. S., Arumugam, S., Anusha, M., & Hariny, A. B. (2006). On the accuracy of centroid based multilateration procedure for location discovery in wireless sensor networks, In *Proceedings of Wireless and Optical Communications Networks*. 11-13 April 2006, India: Bangalore.

Jennings, N.R., Faratin, P., Lomuscio, A.R., Parsons, S., Sierra, C. & Wooldridge, M. (2002). Automated negotiation: prospects, methods and challenges. International Journal of Group Decision and Negotiation 10 (2), 199–215.

Jeruchim, M.C., Balaban, P., and Shanmugan, K.S. (1992). *Simulation of Communication Systems*. Plenum Press, New York.

Jia, Z., Yu, J., Chowdhury, A., Ellinas, G., & Chang, G.-K. (2007). Simultaneous Generation of Independent Wired and Wireless Services Using a Single Modulator in Millimeter-Wave-Band Radio-Over-Fiber Systems. *IEEE Photonics Technology Letters*. 19(20), 1691-1693.

Jiang, B., Yao, X. (2006). Location-Based Services and GIS in Perspective. Computers, Environment and Urban Systems, 30(6), 712-725.

Jiang, H., Zhuang, W., & Shen, X., (2005). Cross-layer design for resource allocation in 3G wireless networks and beyond. *IEEE Communications Magazine*, 43(12), 120 -126.

Johanson, B., Fox, A. & Winograd, T. (2002). The interactive workspaces project: Experiences with Ubiquitous computing rooms, IEEE Pervasive Computing Magazine.

Johne, A. & Storey, C. "New service development: a review of literature and annotated bibliography." European Journal of Marketing 32, (1998):184-251.

Johnson, C.L. (2007). A framework for pricing government e-services. Electronic Commerce Research and Applications, Vol. 6, No. 4, pp. 484-489.

Joint Technical Committee of Committee T1 R1P1.4 and TIA TR46.3.3/TR45.4.4 on Wireless Access (1994). Final Report on RF Channel Characterization, No. JTC(AIR)/94.01.17-238R4, January 1994.

Jordan, D. W., & Smith, P. (1999). *Nonlinear Ordinary Differential Equations: an introduction to dynamical systems*, 3rd Ed., Oxford: Oxford University Press.

Joshi, J. & Ghafoor, A. (2001), Digital government security infrastructure design challenges. IEEE Computer, Vol. 34, No.1, pp.66-72.

Judge, P., and Ammar, M. (2002). Gothic: A Group Access Control Architecture for Secure Multicast and Anycast, in the proceedings of IEEE 21st Annual Joint Conference of the IEEE Computer and Communications Societies, INFOCOM 2002, Volume: 3, pages: 1547-1556.

Jun Zheng, Hussein T. Mouftah, Optical WDM Networks: Concepts and Design Principles, Wiley-IEEE Press, 2004.

Kaino T., Fujiki M., & Jinguji K., (1984). Preparation of plastic optical fibers. *Rev. Electron. Commun. Lab.*, 32, 478–488.

Kakihara, M., Sørensen, C. (2002,). Mobility: An Extended Perspective. Paper presented at the 35th Hawaii International Conference on System Sciences.

Kameas, A., Bellis, S., Mavrommati, I., Delaney, K., Colley, M., and Pounds-Cornish, A. (2003). An Architecture that Treats Everyday Objects as Communicating Tangible Components. In *Proc. 1st IEEE International Conference on Pervasive Computing and Communications (PerCom03)*, Fort Worth, USA.

Kameas, A., Mavrommati, I. and Markopoulos, P. (2004). Computing in tangible: using artifacts as components of Ambient Intelligent Environments. In Riva, G., Vatalaro, F., Davide, F. and Alcaniz, M. (eds) *Ambient Intelligence*, IOS Press, 121-142.

Kameas, A., Ringas, D., Mavrommati, I and Wason, P. (2002). eComP: an Architecture that Supports P2P Networking Among Ubiquitous Computing Devices. In *Proc. IEEE P2P 2002 Conference*, Linkoping, Sweden..

Kandus, G., Svigelj, A., & Mohorcic, M. (2005). Telecommunication network over high altitude platforms. *7th International Conference on Telecommunications in Modern Satellite, Cable and Broadcasting Services*, 2, 344-347.

Kang, N. & Johansson, S. (2000) Cross-border mergers and acquisitions: Their role in industrial globalisation. *STI Working Papers No 2000/1*.

Kang, S., Kim, T. J., Jang, S. G. (2007). Location-Based Services: Enabling Technologies and a Concierge Service Model. In Miller, H. (Ed.), Societies and Cities in the Age of Instant Access (pp. 227-239). GeoJournal Library , Vol. 88, Springer-Verlag.

Karadimas, P. and Kotsopoulos, S. A. (2008). "A Modified Loo Model with Partially Blocked and Three Dimensional Multipath Scattering: Analysis, Simulation and Validation," under revision in Wireless Pers. Commun. Aug. 2008.

Karadimas, P. and Kotsopoulos, S. A. (2007). "A Modified Loo Model with Sectored and Three Dimensional Multipath Scattering," Delson Group Inc. 8th World Wireless Congress-WWC, San Francisco, USA, pp. 25-30, May 2007

Karadimas, P., and Kotsopoulos, S.A. (2007). A modified Loo model with sectored and three dimensional multipath scattering, *World Wireless Congress 2007*, San Francisco, May 2007.

Karadimas, P. Vagenas, E. D. and Kotsopoulos, S. A. (2008 A). "A Small Scale Fading Model with Sectored and Three Dimensional Diffuse Scattering," IEEE 5th Cons. Commun. and Netw. Conf.-IEEE CCNC, Las Vegas, USA, pp. 943-947, Jan.

Karagiannidis, G.K., Zogas, D.A., Sagias, N.C., Kotsopoulos, S.A., and Tombras, G.S. (2005). Equal-gain and maximal-ratio combining over nonidentical Weibull fading channels, *IEEE Transactions on Wireless Communications*, Vol. 4, No. 3, pp. 841-846.

Kawada, V., & Kumar, P. R. (2005). A Cautionary Perspective on Cross-Layer Design. *IEEE Wireless Communications*, 12(1), 3-11.

Kawadia, V., Kumar, P. R. (2003). Power Control and Clustering in Ad Hoc Networks. *IEEE Infocom 2003*, April.

Kein, A., and Mohr, W. (1996). A statistical wideband mobile radio channel model including the direction of arrival, *IEEE 4ᵗʰ International Symposium on Spread Spectrum Techniques and Applications*, pp. 102-106.

Kelley, S.W. "Developing customer orientation among service employees." *Journal of the Academy of Marketing Science* 20, (1992):27-36.

Kilkki, K. (1999). *Differentiated Services for the Internet*. Indianapolis, IN, USA: Macmillan Technical Publishing.

Kim, B.-J. (2001). A network service providing wireless channel information for adaptive mobile applications: I: Proposal. *IEEE International Conference on Communications (ICC)*, 1345 – 1351.

Kim, S.C., Bertoni, H.L., Stern, M. (1996). Pulse Propagation Characteristics at 2.4GHz Inside Buildings, *IEEE Transactions on Vehicular Technology*, Vol. 45, No. 3, pp. 579-592.

Kim, Y., Jeong, B. J., Chung, J., Hwang, C-S., Ryu, J. S., Kim, K-H., & Kim Y. K., (2003). Beyond 3G: Vision, Requirements, and Enabling Technologies. *IEEE Communications Magazine*, March, pp. 120 – 124.

Kitayama, K. (2000). Architectural Considerations of Fiber-Radio Millimeter-Wave Wireless Access Systems. *Fiber and Integrated Optics*, 19(2), 167-186.

Kitayama, K., Kuri, T., Onohara, K., Kamisaka, T., & Murashima, K. (2002). Dispersion effects of FBG filter and optical SSB filtering in DWDM millimeter-wave fiber-radio systems. *IEEE J. Lightwave Technology.*, 20(8), 1397–1407.

Kitsios F. & Zopounidis, C. (2007). Services marketing in the hospitality economy: An exploratory study. The Southeuropean Review of Business Finance & Accounting, Vol. 5, No. 1

Kitsios F. & Zopounidis, C. (2007). Services marketing in the hospitality economy: An exploratory study. The Southeuropean Review of Business Finance & Accounting, Vol. 5, No. 1

Kitsios, F. & Skiadas C. (2001). Some Critical Issues Concerning Technological Change. 1st International Conference in Management of Change, Iasi, Romania, October

Kitsios, F., (2005), *Innovation Management in New Service Development*, PhD dissertation, Technical University of Crete.

Kitsios, F. (2006). Services marketing in the hospitality economy: An exploratory study. 98th EAAE seminar, Marketing Dynamics within the Global Trading System: New Perspectives, Chania, Crete, Greece, 29 June – 02 July

Kitsios, F., Skiadas C., "Some Critical Issues Concerning Technological Change", 1st International Conference in Management of Change, Iasi, Romania, October (2001)

Kitsios, F. and Zopounidis, C., (2007), Services marketing in the hospitality economy: An exploratory study. *The Southeuropean Review of Business Finance & Accounting,* 5(1)

Kleijnen, J. P. C., (1998). *Experimental design for sensitivity analysis, optimization, and validation of simulation models.*

Klemperer, P. (1999). Auction Theory: A Guide to the Literature, Journal of Economic Survey, 13(3), pp. 227-286.

Kliazovich, D., Ben Halima, N., & Granelli, F., (2007). Cross-Layer Error Recovery Optimization in WiFi Networks. *Tyrrhenian International Workshop on Digital Communication (TIWDC)*, Ischia island, Naples, Italy.

Kliazovich, D., Granelli, F., Redana, S., & Riato, N. (2007). Cross-Layer Error Control Optimization in 3G LTE. *IEEE Global Communications Conference (GLOBECOM)*, Washington, DC, U.S.A.

Klukas, R. (1997). *A superresolution based cellular positioning system using GPS time synchronization*. Unpublished doctoral dissertation, University of Calgary, Calgary, Alberta, Canada.

Knapp, C. H., & Carter, G. C. (1976). The generalized correlation method for estimation of time delay. *IEEE Transactions on Acoustics, Speech and Signal Processing*, 24(4), 320-327.

Knightson, K., Morita, N. and Towle, T. (2005). NGN architecture: generic principles, functional architecture and implementation. *IEEE Communications, 43*(10), 49-56.

Koike Y. & Ishigure T., (1997). *Progress of low-loss GI polymer optical fiber from visible to 1.5-mm wavelength.* 23rd European Conf. Opt. Commun. (ECOC), vol. 1, Edinburgh, Scotland. pp. 59–62.

Koonen, A. M. J., Ng'oma A., et al., (2007). *In-house broadband wireless service delivery using radio over fibre.* 16th international conference on plastic optical fibers, Italy, 2007.

Koonen, T. (2006). Fiber to the home/fiber to the premises: What, where and when?" *Proc. IEEE*, 94(5), 911–934.

Korkea-aho, M. (2000). Context-aware application surveys. http://users.tkk.fi/~mkorkeaa/doc/context-aware.html

Koskela, T. & Väänänen-Vainio-Mattila, K. (2004). Evolution towards smart home environments: empirical evaluation of three user interfaces. Personal Ubiquitous Computing, 8:234–240, 2004.

Kotler, P., Bowen, J. & Makens, J. *Marketing for Hospitality and Tourism*. 2nd ed. Upper Saddle River: Prentice Hall, Inc., 1999.

Kotsopoulos, S., & Lymberopoulos, D. (1991). *A new Medical Data Management Concept in a Hybrid Cellular Mobile Radio Communication Network*, IEEE GLOBECOM'91, Phoenix, USA, 674-680.

Kotsopoulos, S., & Lymberopoulos, D. (1992). *Communication protocols and on-board processor for a new national scale private mobile radio service*, IEEE International Conference on Selected Topics in Wireless Communications, Vancouver, Canada.

Kotsopoulos, S.A., and Karagiannidis, G. (2000). Error Performance for Equal-gain Combiners over Rayleigh Fading Channels, *Journal of IEE Electronics Letters*, Vol.36, No. 10, pp. 892-894.

Koukal, M., Bestak, R. (2006, June). Architecture of IP Multimedia Subsystem. IEEE, 48th International Symposium ELMAR, Zadar, Croatia

Kourouthanassis, E.P., Giaglis, M.G. & Vrechopoulos, A.P. (2007). Enhancing user experience through pervasive information systems: The case of pervasive retailing, International Journal of Information Management 27, 319–335

Koutsopoulos, I., & Tassiulas, L. (2006). Cross-layer adaptive techniques for throughput enhancement in wireless OFDM-based networks, *IEEE/ACM Transactions on Networking*, 14(5), 1056-2006.

Kozat, U. C., Koutsopoulos, I., & Tassiulas, L. (2006). Cross-Layer Design for Power Efficiency and QoS Provisioning in Multi-Hop Wireless Networks. *IEEE Transactions on Wireless Communications*, 5(11), 3306 – 3315.

Krantzik, A. and Wolf, D. (1990). "Distribution of the Fading-Intervals of Modified Suzuki Processes," in *Signal Processing V: Theories and Applications*, L. Torres, E. Masgrau, and M. A. Lagunas, Eds. Amsterdam, The Netherlands: Elsevier, pp. 361-364.

Kraus, S. (2001). Strategic Negotiation in Multiagent Environments. The MIT Press, Cambridge, MA.

Kreger, H. (2001). Web Services Conceptual Architecture (WSCA 1.0), IBM Software Group, May 2001.

Kreger, H. et al. (2005). Management Using Web Services: A Proposed Architecture and Roadmap, tech report, IBM, Hewlett-Packard, and Computers Assoc., June 2005.

Krievs, R. (2002). Using fading to improve accuracy of

Cell ID based mobile positioning algorithms: Analysis of special cases. In *Scientific Proceedings of Baltic Electronic Conference (BEC)*. Estonia: Tallinn.

Kropft, P (2002). *What is Pervasive Computing*. Series of Lecture notes.

Kropft, P. (2002). What is Pervasive Computing. Series of Lecture notes.

Ku, B. J., Ahn, D. S., Lee, S. P., Shishlov, A. V., Reutov, A. S., Ganin, S. A. et al. (2002). Radiation pattern of multibeam array antenna with digital beamforming for stratospheric communication **system:** statistical simulation. *ETRI Journal*, 24(3), 197-204.

Kuhn, P. (2004). Location-Based Services in Mobile Communication Infrastructures. International Journal of Electronic Communications, 58, 159-164.

Kumar, M., Feldman, S. I. (1998). Internet Auctions. Paper presented at the 3rd USENIX Workshop on Electronic Commerce, Boston, Massachusetts.

Kundert, K.S., White, J.K., & Sangiovanni-Vincentelli, A.L. (1990). *Steady-state Methods for Simulating Analog and Microwave Circuits*. The Springer International Series in Engineering and Computer Science , Vol. 94, New York, NY: Springer.

Kuo, Y., Yu, C. W. (2006). 3G Telecommunication Operators' Challenges and Roles: A Perspective of Mobile Commerce Value Chain. Technovation, 26(12), 1347-1356.

Kurniawan, T., Nirmalathas, A., Lim, C., Novak, D., & Waterhouse, R. (2006). Performance analysis of optimized millimeter-wave fiber radio system, *IEEE Transactions on Microwave Theory and Technique*, 54. 921-928.

Kurokawa, K. (1969). Some basic characteristics of broadband resistance oscillator circuits. *Bell System Technical Journal,* 1937-1955.

Kurokawa, K. (1973). Injection locking of microwave solid-state oscillators. *Proceedings of the IEEE*, 61(10), 1386- 1410.

Kurt, T., Abbas Yongacoglu, A., & Chouinard, J-Y. (2006). OFDM and Externally Modulated Multi-mode Fibers in Radio over Fiber Systems. *IEEE Trans. On Wireless Communications*, 5(10), 2669-2674.

Kuz, I., van Steen, M. & Sips, H. J. (2002). The globe infrastructure directory service. Computer Communications 25.

Kykkotis, C., Hall, P.S., & Ghafouri-Shiraz, H. (1998). Performace of active antenna oscillator arrays under modulation for communication systems. *IEE Proceedings on Microwaves, Antennas and Propagation,* 142(4), 313–320.

La Porte, T.M., De Jong, M. & Demchak, C.C. (1999). Public organizations on the world wide Web: Empirical correlates of administrative openness. Retrieved February 3, 2005, from University of Arizona Web site: http://www.cyprg.arizona.edu/publications/correlat.rtf

Lado, A.A., & Wilson, M.C. (1994). Human Resource Systems and sustained competitive advantage: a competency-based perspective. *Academy of Managment Review*, 19:699-727.

Lagunas, M.A., & Pérez-Neira, A. (2006, November). *Antenna Arrays: What does it mean a good channel?* Paper presented at the first European Conference on Antennas and Propagation (EuCAP 2006), Nice, France.

Lai, X., & Roychowdhury, J. (2004). Capturing oscillator injection locking via nonlinear phase-domain macro-models. *IEEE Transactions on Microwave Theory and Techniques*, 52(9), 2251- 2261.

Laitinen, H., Ahonen, S., Kyriazakos, S., Lähteenmäki, J., Menolascino, R., & Parkkila, S. (2001, November). *Cellular Location Technology* (Project: Cellular network optimisation based on mobile location). Cello Consortium.

Lambrinoudakis, C. & Gritzalis, S. (2003). Security requirements for e-government services: a methodological approach for developing a common PKI-based security policy. Computer Communications, Vol. 26, No.16, pp. 1873-1883.

Lannoo, B., Colle, D., Pickavet, M., & Demeester, P. (2007). Radio-over-Fiber-Based Solution to Provide Broadband Internet Access to Train Passengers. *IEEE Communications Magazine*, February 2007, 56-62.

Larrodé M. G., Koonen, A. M. J. & Vegas Olmos, J. J. (2006). Overcoming Modal Bandwidth Limitation in Radio-over-Multimode Fiber Links. *IEEE Photonics Technology Letters*. 18(22), pp. 2428-2430.

Lau, K. Y., & Blauvelt, H. (1988). Effect of low-frequency intensity noise on high frequency direct modulation of semiconductor injection lasers. *Appl. Phys. Lett.*, 52, 694-696.

Lawton, M.C., and McGeehan, J.P. (1992). The application of GTD and ray launching techniques to channel modeling for cordless radio systems, *Proceedings of the 42nd IEEE Vehicular Technology Conference*, pp. 125-130, Denver, USA.

Lawton, M.C., Davies, R.L., and McGeehan, J.P. (1991). A ray launching method for the prediction of indoor radio channel characteristics, *PIMRC '91*, pp. 104-108, London, UK.

Layne, K. & Lee, J. (2001). Developing fully functional e-government: a four stage model. Government Information Quarterly, Vol. 18, No.2, pp.122-136.

Lebherz, M., Wiesbeck, W., and Krank, W. (1992). A versatile wave propagation model for the VHF/UHF range considering three-dimensional terrain, *IEEE Transactions on Antennas and Propagation*, Vol. 40, pp. 1121-1131.

Lebherz, M., Wiesbeck, W., Blasberg, H.-J., and Krank, W. (1989). Calculation of broadcast coverage based on a digital terrain model, *Proceedings of the 1989 IEEE International Conference on Antennas and Propagation*, Vol. 2, pp. 355-359.

Lebret, H., & Boyd, S. (1997), Antenna array pattern synthesis via convex optimization. *IEEE Transactions on Signal Processing*, 45(3), 526-532.

Lebret, H., & Boyd, S.P. (1997). Antenna array pattern synthesis via convex optimization, *IEEE Transactions on Signal Processing*, 45(3), 526–532.

Lee, Chi H. (Ed.). (2007). *Microwave Photonics*. CRC Press.

Lee, J.F. (1993). Numerical solutions of TM scattering using an obliquely Cartesian finite difference time domain algorithm, *IEE Proceedings H: Microwaves, Antennas and Propagation*, Vol. 140, No. 1, pp. 23-28, February 1993.

Lee, K.J. & Seo Y.H. (2006). A pervasive comparison shopping business model for integrating offline and online marketplace. Proceedings of the 8th international conference on Electronic commerce: The new e-commerce: innovations for conquering current barriers, obstacles and limitations to conducting successful business on the internet ICEC '06. ACM Press

Lee, K.J., Ju, J. & Jeong, J.M. (2006). Mobile and pervasive commerce track: A payment & receipt business model in U-commerce environment. Proceedings of the 8th international conference on Electronic commerce: The new e-commerce: innovations for conquering current barriers, obstacles and limitations to conducting successful business on the internet ICEC '06. ACM Press

Lee, S. H., & Kang, J. M. (2006). Linearization of DFB Laser Diode by External Light-Injected Cross-Gain Modulation for Radio-Over-Fiber Link. *IEEE Photon. Technol. Let.*, 18(14), 1545-1547.

Lee, W.C.Y. (1986). *Mobile Communications Design Fundamentals*, Sams, Indianapolis, IN.

Lee, W.C.Y. (1982). *Mobile Communications Engineering*, McGraw Hill, New York.

Lee, W. C. Y. (2005). Wireless and Cellular Communications. 3 edition, McGraw-Hill Professional.

Lenk, K. & Traunmuller, R. (2000). A framework for electronic government. IEEE Computer Society, London, paper presented at 11th International Workshop on Database and Expert Systems Applications.

Li, Y., Patzold, M., Killat U., and Laue, F. (1996). "An Efficient Deterministic Simulation Model for Land Mobile Satellite Channels," Proc. IEEE 46th Veh. Technol. Conf., VTC 96, Atlanta, Georgia, USA, pp. 1028-1032, Apr./May.

Li, Y., Wei, X., Cruickshank, D.G.M. & McLaughlin, S. (2006). *Hybrid DFE with variable length feedback filter.* IEE Proceedings, Vol. 154, No. 1.

Liang, G., Bertoni, H.K. (1998). A New Approach to 3-D Ray Tracing for Propagation Prediction in Cities, *IEEE Transactions on Antennas and Propagation*, Vol. 46, No. 6, pp. 853-863.

Liao, P., & York, R.A. (1993). A new phase-shifterless beam-scanning technique using arrays of coupled oscillators. *IEEE Transactions on Microwave Theory and Techniques*, 41(10), 1810-1815.

Liberti, J.C.Jr., and Rappaport, T.S. (1996). A geometrically based model for line-of-sight multipath radio channels, *Proceedings of the 46th IEEE Vehicular Technology Conference*, Vol. 2, pp. 844-848.

Liberti, J.C.Jr., and Rappaport, T.S. (1999). *Smart Antennas for Wireless Communications: IS-95 and Third Generation CDMA Applications.* Prentice Hall PTR, New Jersey.

Lim, W. L., Foo, Y. C., & Tafazolli, R. (2002). Adaptive softer handover algorithm for high altitude platform station UMTS with onboard power resource sharing. *5th International Symposium on Wireless Personal Multimedia Communications*, 1, 52-56.

Lim, W. L., Foo, Y. C., & Tafazolli, R. (2005). Inter-system handover algorithms for HAPS and tower–based overlay UMTS. *5th International Conference on Information, Communications and Signal Processing*, 419-424.

Lin, C. & Atkin, D. (2007). Communication technology and social change. Mahwah, NJ: LEA.

Lin, C.S & Wu, S. (2002). Exploring the impact of Online Service Quality on Portal Site Usage. Proceeding of the 35th Hawaii International Conference on Systems Science, Hawaii, USA,

Lin, J. & Itoh, T. (1994). Active integrated antennas. *IEEE Transactions on Microwave Theory and Techniques*, 42(12), 2186-2194.

Lin, Wen-Piao. (2005). Wavelength Division Multiplexed Millimeter Waveband Radio-on-Fiber System Using Continuum Light Source. *IEEE J. Lightwave Technology*, 23(9), 2610–2621.

Lin, X., & Shroff, N.B. (2005). The Impact of Imperfect Scheduling on Cross Layer Rate Control in Wireless Networks. *Proc. INFOCOM 2005*.

Lin, X., Shroff, N. B., & Srikant, R. (2006). A tutorial on cross-layer optimization in wireless networks, *IEEE Journal on Selected Areas in Communications*, 24(8), 1452-1463.

Lin, Y. B. & Ebooks Corporation (2005). *Wireless and Mobile All-IP Networks.* Hoboken: John Wiley & Sons, Inc.

Liu, C. P., Ismail, T., & Seeds, A. J. (2006). Broadband access using wireless-over-fibre technologies. *BT Technology Journal*, 24(3), 130-143.

Llyod, B. and Simpson, W. A. (1992). PPP Authentication Protocol, IETF RFC 1334

Loo, C. (1985). "A Statistical Model for a Land Mobile Satelite Link," IEEE Trans. Veh. Technol., vol. 34, no. 3, pp. 122-127, Aug. .

Loo, C. (1985). "A Statistical Model for a Land Mobile Satellite Link," IEEE Trans. Vehicular Technol., 34, 122–127.

Loo, C. (1985). A statistical model for a land mobile satellite link, IEEE Transactions on Vehicular Technology, vol. VT-34, no. 3, pp. 122-127.

Loo, C. and Secord, N. (1991)."Computer Models for Fading Channels with Applications to Digital Transmissions," IEEE Trans. Veh. Technol., vol. 40, no. 4, pp. 700-707, Nov. .

Lorenz, R.G., & Boyd, S.P. (2005). Robust minimum variance beamforming, *IEEE Transactions on Signal Processing*, 53(5), 1684–1696.

Lotter, M.P., and van Rooyen, P. (1999). Cellular channel modeling and the performance of DS-CDMA systems with antenna arrays, *IEEE Journal on Selected Areas on Communications*, Vol. 17, No. 12, pp. 2181-2196.

Lu, H., Makino, T., & Li, G. P., (1995). Dynamic properties of partly gain-coupled 1.55-μm DFB lasers. *IEEE J. Quant. Electron.*, 31, 1443-1450.

Lu, M., Lo, T., and Litva, J. (1997). A physical spatio-temporal model of multipath propagation channels, *Proceedings of the 47ᵗʰ IEEE Vehicular Technology Conference*, pp. 180-184.

Lu, X., Su, C. B., Lauer, R. B., Meslener, G. J., & Ulbricht L. W. (1996). Analysis of relative intensity noise in semiconductor lasers and its effect on subcarrier multiplexed Lightwave systems. *IEEE J. Lightwave Technology*, 12, 1159-1165.

Lucky, R.W. (1965). *Automatic Equalisation for Digital Communication*. The Bell System Technical Journal, Vol. 44, No. 4.

Lukkari, J., Korhonen, J. & Ojala, T. (2004). SmartRestaurant: mobile payments in context-aware environment. Proceedings of the 6th international conference on Electronic commerce ICEC '04. ACM Press

Luo, Z.-Q., & Yu, W. (2006). An introduction to convex optimization for communications and signal processing. *IEEE Journal on Selected Areas in Communications*, 24(8), 1426-1438.

Lutz, E. Cygan, D. Dippold, M. Dolainsky, F. and Papke, W. (1991). "The Land Mobile Satellite Communication Channel-Recording, Statistics and Channel Model," IEEE Trans. Veh. Technol., vol. 40, no. 2, pp. 375-386, May.

Lynch, J.J. , & York, R.A., (2001). Synchronization of oscillators coupled through narrow-band networks. *IEEE Transactions on Microwave Theory and Techniques*, 49(2), 237-249.

M. Baugher, B. Weis, T. Hardjono, H. Harney (2003). The Group Domain of Interpretation, IETF RFC3547.

M. Baugher, R. Canetti, L. R. Dondeti, F. Lindholm, "Multicast Security (MSEC) Group Key Management Architecture", IETF RFC4046, April 2005.

M. Gast (2005). 802.11 Wireless Networks: The Definitive Guide, O-Reilly Publishing.

M. Vanderveen and H. Soliman (2006), "Extensible Authentication Protocol method for Shared secret Authentication and Key Establishment (EAP-SAKE)", IETF RFC 4763

Maack D., (1999). Reliability of lithium niobate Mach Zehnder modulators for digital optical fiber telecommunication systems. *SPIE Crit. Rev.*, vol. CR 73, 197–230.

Macinnis, D.J., Moorman, C. & Jaworski, B.J. (1991). Enhancing and Measuring Consumers' Motivation. Opportunity, and Ability to Process Brand Information from Ads. Journal of Marketing, Vol. 55, No. 4, pp. 32-53.

Madria, S., Mohania, M., Bhowmick, S. S., Bhargava, B. (2002). Mobile Data and Transaction Management. Information Sciences, 141, 279-309.

Maeda, M., Nakatogawa, T., & Oyamada, K. (2005) Optical fiber transmission technologies for digital terrestrial broadcasting signals. *IEICE Trans. Commun*, E88-B(5), 1853–1860.

Majithia, S., Walker, D.W. & Gray, W.A. (2004). A framework for automated service composition in service-oriented architecture. In: First European Semantic Web Symposium.

Marino, K.E. (1996). Developing consensus on firm competencies and capabilities. *Academy of Management Executive*: 10(3):40-51.

Mark Weiser's Vision: http://www.ubiq.com/hypertext/weiser/SciAmDraft3.html

Marshall, P., Barrabee, L., & Griffin, K. (2004). *Divergent Approach to Fixed/Mobile Convergence*. The Yankee Group.

Martin, A.L. and Vu-Dinh, T. (1997). "A Statistical Characterization of Point-to-Point Microwave Links Using Biased Rayleigh Distributions," IEEE Trans. Antennas Propagation, 45, 806–821.

Martin, C. R. & Horne, D.A. "Services innovation: successful versus unsuccessful firms." *International Journal of Service Industry Management* 6, no.4, (1993):48-64.

Martin, R.K., & Johnson, C.R. (2005). *Adaptive Equalisation: Transitioning from Single-carrier to Multicarrier Systems*. IEEE Signal Processing Magazine.

Mata, F.J., Fuerst, W.L., & Barney, J.B. (1995). Information technology and sustained competitive advantage: A resource-based analysis. *MIS Quarterly*, 19:487-505.

May, P. (2005). Application Services in an IP Multimedia Subsystem (IMS) Network, Data Connection Limited, White Paper.

McAfee, R., McMillan, J. (1987). Auctions and bidding. Journal of Economic Literature 25(2), 699-738.

McClure, D.L. (2000). Government online: Strategies and Challenges. Retrieved February 3, 2005, from The House of Representatives Web site: http://www.house.gov/reform/gmit/hearings/2000hearings/000522dm.htm

McDermott-Wells, P. (2005). What is Bluetooth? *IEEE Potentials*, 23(5), 33- 35.

McGahan, A. (2004) How Industries Change, *Harvard Business Review*, 82(10):98-106.

McKown, J.W., and Hamilton, R.L.Jr. (1991). Ray tracing as a design tool for radio networks, *IEEE Network Magazine*, Vol. 6, No. 6, pp. 27-30.

McPherson, G. (1990). *Statistics in Scientific Investigation*, Springer.

Means, G. & Schneider, D. (2000). Meta-capitalism: The e-business revolution and the design of 21st century companies and markets. New York: John Wiley & Sons Inc.

Menasce, D., Akula, V. (2003,). Towards Workload Characterization of Auction Sites. Paper presented at the Sixth IEEE Workshop on Workload Characterization (WWC-6), Austin, TX.

Michalisn, M.D., Smith, R.D., & Kline, D.M. (1997). In search of strategic assets. *International Journal of Organizational Analysis*, 5:360-387.

Mikroulis, S., Karabetsos, S., Pikasis, E. & Nassiopoulos A. (2008). Performance Evaluation of a Radio over Fiber (RoF) System Subject to the Transmitter's Limitations for Application in Broadband Networks. IEEE Transactions on Consumer Electronics, 54(2), 437 - 443.

Milgrom, P. (1989). Auctions and Bidding: A Primer. The Journal of Economic Perspectives, 3(3), 3-22.

Milgrom, P., Weber, R. J. (1982). A Theory of Auctions and Competitive Bidding. Econometrica, 50(5), 1089-1122.

Military Agile Manufacturing Pilot Program: http://www.darpa.mil/mto/solicitations/CBD/cbd_9431A.html

Miller, G. J., Thompson, K., & Wilder, R. (1997). Wide-area Internet traffic patterns and characteristics. *IEEE Network*, 11(6), 10 – 23.

Mishra, M. Shin, W. Arbaugh, (2003). An empirical analysis of the IEEE 802.11 MAC layer Handoff Process, *ACM SIGCOMM Computer Communications Review*, vol. 33, no. 2, (pp. 93-102).

Mitchell J. E., (2004). Performance of OFDM at 5.8 GHz using radio over fibre link. *Electronics Letters*, 40(21).

Mitchell, T. (1997). *Machine learning* (1st ed.). USA: McGraw-Hill Higher Education.

Mitilineos, S.A., Panagiotou, S.C., Varlamos, P.K., and Capsalis, C.N. (2005). Indoor environments propagation simulation using a hybrid MoM and UTD electromagnetic method, *Annals of Telecommunications*, Vol. 60, No. 9-10, pp.1231-1243.

Mitilineos, S.A., Varlamos, P K., and Capsalis, C.N. (2004). A simulation method for bit error rate performance estimation for arbitrary angle of arrival channel models, *IEEE Antennas and Propagation Magazine*, Vol. 46, No. 2, pp. 158-163.

Mitola, J. (1995). The software radio architecture, *IEEE Communications Magazine*, 33(5), 26-38.

Mizusawa, G. A. (1996). *Performance of hyperbolic position location techniques for code division multiple access*. Unpublished master's thesis, Faculty of the Virginia Polytechnic Institute and State University, Blacksburg, Virginia.

Mokhtar, S. B., Kaul, A., Georgantas, N. & Issarny V. (2007). EASY: Efficient Semantic Service Discovery in Pervasive Computing Environments. Springer Berlin.

Montoya-Weiss, M.M. & Calantone, R. "Determinants of new product performance: a review and meta-analysis." *Journal of Product Innovation Management* 11, (1994):397-417.

Monzingo, R.A., & Miller, T.W. (1980). *Introduction to Adaptive Arrays*, New York: John Wiley & Sons.

Moon, H., & Sedaghat R. (2006). FPGA-Based adaptive digital predistortion for radio-over-fiber links. *Microprocessors and Microsystems*, 30, 145–154.

Moon, M.J. (2002). The evolution of e-government among municipalities: rhetoric or reality. Public Administration Review, Vol. 62 No.4, pp.424-33.

Morita, N., Imanaka, H. (2007). Introduction to the Functional Architecture of NGN. IEICE Trans. Commun., VOL.E90-B, no.5, May 2007.

Muncy, Mark (2003). The future of Transportation. *California Engineer, 81*(13), 15-19.

Murhammer, M. W. & Murphy, E. (1998). *TCP/IP: Tutorial and Technical Overview.* Upper Saddle River, NJ: Prentice-Hall.

Nagpal, R., Shrobe, H., & Bachrach, J. (2003). Organizing a global coordinate system from local information on an ad hoc sensor network. In *Proceedings of the 2nd International Workshop on Information Processing In Sensor Networks*. April, 2003, USA: Palo Alto.

Nair, A. (2005). Emerging Internet-Enabled Auction Mechanisms in Supply Chain. Supply Chain Management: An International Journal, 10(3), 162-168.

Najar, M., & Vidal, J. (2001). Kalman tracking based on TDOA for UMTS mobile location. In *Proceedings of IEEE PIMRC, Vol. 1.* (pp. 45-49). USA: San Diego.

Nakasyotani, T., Toda, H., Kuri, & Kitayama, K. (2006). Wavelength Division Multiplexed Millimeter Waveband Radio-on-Fiber System Using Continuum Light Source. *IEEE J. Lightwave Technology.*, 24(1), 404–410.

Nana, P., Mohapi, S. and Hanrahan, H., (2001). 'An API based representation of TINA's Service Session Manager (SSM) for use in Next Generation Networks (NGNs).' Proceedings of SATNAC.

Nana P., Mohapi S. and Hanrahan H (2002). 'Re-usable service components based on the Parlay API and TINA for the Next Generation Network', Proceedings of SATNAC.

Narula-Tam, A., Macdonald, T., Modiano, E., & Servi, L. (2004). A dynamic resource allocation strategy for satellite communications. *IEEE Military Communications Conference (MILCOM)*, 1415 – 1421.

National Research Council (2002). Information Technology Research. Innovation, and E-Government. National Academy Press, Washington, DC.

Navarro, J.A., & Chang, K. (1996). *Integrated Active Antennas and Spatial Power Combining*, New York NY: John Wiley and Sons.

Nesterov, Y., & Nemirovskii, A. (1994). *Interior Point Polynomial Methods in Convex Programming.* vol. 13, Studies in Applied Mathematics. Philadelphia, PA: SIAM.

Newman, P. (2004). In search of the all-IP mobile network. *IEEE Communications Magazine*, 42(12), s3- s8.

Nexus Telecom, Neeser, F. (2005, May). Testing Media Gateways to Enable Convergence, White Paper.

Ng'oma, A. (2005). *Radio-over-Fibre Technology for Broadband Wireless Communication Systems.* Doctoral Dissertation, Eindhoven University of Technology, Netherlands.

Ngai, E., Gunasekaran, A. (2007). A Review for Mobile Commerce Research and Applications. Decision Support Systems, 43(1), 3-15.

Niculescu, D., & Nath, B. (2001). Ad hoc positioning system (APS). In *Proceedings of IEEE GLOBECOM 2001: Vol. 5.* (pp. 2926–2931). USA: San Antonio.

Niculescu, D., & Nath, B. (2003a). Ad hoc positioning system (APS) using AoA. In *Proceedings of IEEE INFOCOM 2003: Vol. 3.* (pp. 1734-1743). USA: San Francisco.

Niculescu, D., & Nath, B. (2003b). DV based positioning in ad hoc networks. *Telecommunication Systems,* 22(1-4), 267–280.

Niiho, T., Nakaso, M., Masuda, K., Sasai, H., Utsumi, K., & Masaru, Fuse M. (2006). Transmission Performance of Multichannel Wireless LAN System Based on Radio Over-Fiber Techniques. *IEEE Transactions on Microwave Theory and Techniques*, 54(2), 980-989.

Noble, B., Satyanarayanan, M., Narayanan, D., Tilton, T., Flinn, J. & Walker, K. (1997). Agile application-aware adaptation for mobility, in: Proceedings of the 16th ACM SOSP.

Noel, L., Wake, D., Moodie, D. G., Marcenac, D. D., Westbrook, L. D., & Nesset D. (1997). Novel techniques for high capacity 60-GHz fiber-radio transmission system. *IEEE Trans. Microwave Theory and Techniques*, 45(8), 1416–1423.

Nogi, S., Lin, J., & Itoh, T. (1993). Mode analysis and stabilization of a spatial power combining array with strongly coupled oscillators. *IEEE Transactions on Microwave Theory and Techniques,* 41(10), 1827-1837.

Nogi, S., Sanagi, M., & Fujimori, K. (2005). Active integrated antenna techniques for beam control. *IEICE Transactions on Electronics*, E88-C(7), 1358-1367.

Nogi, S., Sanagi, M., & Fujimori, K. (2005). Beam control in unilaterally coupled active antennas with self-oscillating harmonic mixers. *IEICE Transactions on Electronics*, E88-C(7), 1375-1381.

Nokia, Oyj (April 30, 2003). Presence Application Development Guide, Version 1.0, Forum Nokia.

Norklit, O., and Anderson, J.B. (1994). Mobile radio environments and adaptive arrays, *IEEE International Symposium on Personal, Indoor and Mobile Radio Communications (PIMRC)*, pp. 725-728.

Norman, D.A. (1988). *The Psychology of Everyday Things*. New York, Basic books.

Norman, D.A. (1998). *The Invisible Computer*. MIT press

Norman, D.A. (1999). The Invisible Computer: Why Good Products Can Fail, the Personal Computer Is So Complex, and Information Appliances Are the Solution. The MIT Press.

Norton, K.A., Vogler, L.E. Mansfield, W.V. and Short, P.J. (1955). "The Probability Distribution of the Amplitude of a Constant Vector Plus a Rayleigh Distributed Vector," Proc. IRE, 43, 1354–1361.

Novak, D., Nirmalathas, A., Lim, C., Waterhouse, R., Bakaul, M., & Kurniawan, T. (2007). Hybrid Fiber Radio – Concepts and Prospects. In Chi H. Lee (Ed.), *Microwave Photonics (pp. 157-183)*. CRC Press.

O'Brien, W.M., Kenny, E.M., and Cullen, P.J. (2000). An Efficient Implementation of a Three-Dimensional Microcell Propagation Tool for Indoor and Outdoor Urban Environments, *IEEE Transactions on Vehicular Technology*, Vol. 49, No. 2, pp. 622-630.

O'Reilly, C.A. & Chatman, J.A. (1994). Working smarter and harder: a longitudinal study of managerial success. Administrative Science Quarterly, Vol. 39, pp. 603-627.

OASIS, (2004). Introduction to UDDI: Important features and Functional Concepts, Organization for the Advancement of Structured Information Standards (OASIS), White Paper, Oct. 2004.

OECD (2000). Annual Report 2000. Retrieved February 3, 2005, from OECD Web site: http://www.oecd.org/dataoecd/30/59/1842666.pdf

OECD (1998). *Content as a new growth industry*

OECD (2005). Directory for Science, Technology, and Industry, Working Party on Telecommunication and Information Services Policies, *Next Generation Network Development in OECD Countries*, January.

Oestges, C., Clerck, B., Raynaud, L., and van Hoenacker, J.D. (2002). Deterministic Channel Modeling and Performance Simulation of Microcellular Wide-Band Communication Systems, *IEEE Transactions on Vehicular Technology*, Vol. 51, No. 6, pp. 1422-1430.

Office of the Director of Telecommunications Regulation (ODTR) (2001). 'Next Generation Networks', Odtr01/88, Irish Life Centre, Dublin.

Ogawa, H., Polifko, D., & Banba S. (1992). Millimeter-wave fiber optics systems for personal radio communication. *IEEE Trans. Microwave Theory and Techniques,* 40, 2285–2292.

Ohtani, K., Daikoku, K., and Omori, H. (1981). "Burst error performance encountered in digital land mobile radio channel," IEEE Trans. Veh. Technol., vol. VT-23, no. 1, pp. 156–160.

OKI, 'Next Generation Solutions.' Retrieved from http://www.oki.com/en/NGN/#difference

Okumura, T., Ohmori, E. and Fukuda, K. (1968). "Field strength and its variability in VHF and UHF land mobile service," Review Electrical Communication Laboratory, Vol. 16, No. 9-10, pp. 825–873, Sept.-Oct.

Okumura, Y., Ohmuri, E., Kawano, T., and Fukuda, K. (1968). Field strength and its variability in VHF and UHF land mobile radio service, *Rev. of the ECL,* Vol. 16, pp 825-873.

Olesen, H. & Jacobsen, G. (1982). A theoretical and experimental analysis of laser fields and power spectra. *IEEE J. Quant. Electron.,* 18, 2069- 2080.

Ossana, J.Jr. (1964). A model for mobile radio fading due to building reflections: theoretical and experimental fading waveform power spectra, *Bell Systems Technical Journal,* Vol. 43, No. 6, pp. 2935-2971.

Ottenbacher, M.,*"New service development in the hospitality industry: An exploratory study"*

Owen, G.M.W. (1991) Competing for the Global Telecommunications Market. *Long Range Planning,* 54(21):52-56.

Ozdemir, M. K., Arslan, H. and Arvas, E. (2004). "A Narrowband MIMO Channel Model with 3-D Scattering," IEEE Intern. Conf. on Commun. ICC '04, vol. 5, pp. 2929-2933, June.

P. Eronen, T. Hiller and G. Zorn (2005). Diameter Extensible Authentication Protocol (EAP) Application, IETF RFC 4072.

P. Pillai and Y. F. Hu (2007). An AAA Framework for commercial deployment of IP Multicast, submitted to IEEE Communications Magazine.

P. R. Calhoun, J. Loughney, J. Arkko, E. Guttman and G. Zorn (2002). Diameter Base Protocol", IETF RFC 3588.

P. Savola (2005). Multicast: is it ever going to take off?, 22nd NORDUnet Networking Conference, Svalbard. http://www. nordunet2005.no/index.html.

Paar, C. & Weimerskirch, A. (2007). Embedded security in a pervasive world, Information Security Technical Report, (12) p. 155-161.

Pace, P., & Aloi, G. (2007). Multilayered architecture supporting efficient HAP-satellite routing. *IEEE Vehicular Technology Conference,* 1360-1364.

Pack, S., Choi, J., Kwon, T. and Choi, Y. (2007). Fast Handoff Support in IEEE 802.11 Wireless, *appeared in IEEE Communication Surveys and Tutorials.* (S.Pack, 2007).

Pahlavan, K., and Levesque, A.H. (1995). *Wireless Information Networks.* John Wiley & Sons, New York.

Pahlavan, K., Ganesh, R., and Hotaling, T. (1989). Multipath propagation measurements on manufacturing floors at 910MHz, *IEE Electronics Letters,* Vol. 25, No. 3, pp. 225-227.

Pal, Beach, A. M. and Nix, A. (2006). "A Novel Quantification of 3D Directional Spread from Small-Scale Fading Analysis," IEEE Intern. Conf. on Commun. ICC '06, vol.4, pp.1699-1704, June.

Panoutsopoulos, I., Kotsopoulos, S. and Tountopoulos, V. (2002, July). Handover and New Call Admission Policy Optimization in G3G Systems", Journal on Wireless Networks, Vol.8, No.4, pp.381-389.

Paolucci, M., Kawamura, T., Payne, T.R. & Sycara, K. (2002). Semantic matching of Web services capabilities. Lecture Notes in Computer Science 2342, 333–347.

Papamichael, V., Soras, C., and Makios, V. (2003). FDTD Modeling and Characterization of the Indoor Radio Propagation Channel in the 434 MHz ISM Band, *ICECom 2003, 17th International Conference on Applied Electromagnetics and Communications,* pp. 217-220.

Papazoglou, M.P. & Georgakopoulos, D. (2003). Special section in Communications of the ACM, chap. In: Service-oriented computing. ACM Press.

Park, S. & Yang, S.-B. (2007). An efficient multilateral negotiation system for pervasive computing. Engineering Applications of Artificial Intelligence.

Park, S., Suresh, N. C. (2005,). An Investigation of the Roles of Elecgtronic Marketplace in the Supply Chain. Paper presented at the 38th Hawaii International Conference on System Sciences.

Park, Y.-H., Okada, M., & Komaki, S. (2000). The Performance of Fiber-Radio Road Vehicle Communication System with Macro-Diversity. *Wireless Personal Communications*, 14, 125-132.

Parlay Group, 'Parlay and Next Generation Networks.' White Paper, May 2005.

Parsons, D. (1992). The Mobile Radio Propagation Channel. New York: Halsted Press (Division of Wiley).

Parsons, J. D. (2000). "The Mobile Radio Propagation Channel, Second Edition." Chichester, U.K.: Wiley.

Paschos, G.S. Papapanagiotou, I., Argyropoulos C.G., and Kotsopoulos, S.A. (September, 2006). A Heuristic Strategy for IEEE 802.16 WiMAX scheduler for Quality of Service. *FITCE 2006*. Athens, Greece.

Pascual Iserte, A. (2005) *Channel State Information and Joint Transmitter-Receiver Design in Multi-Antenna Systems*, doctoral dissertation, Universitat Politècnica de Catalunya (UPC), Barcelona, Spain.

Pascual Iserte, A., Payaró, M., Pérez Neira, A.I., & Lagunas, M.A. (2006, July). *Impact of a line of sight component on the performance of a MIMO system designed under statistical channel knowledge.* Paper presented at the IEEE 7th International Workshop on Signal Processing Advances in Wireless Communications (SPAWC), Cannes, France.

Patwari, N., & Alfred O. Hero III (2003). Using proximity and quantized RSS for sensor localization in wireless networks. In *Proceedings of WSNA'03*, (pp. 20-29). USA: San Diego.

Patzold, M. (2002). "Mobile Fading Channels." Chichester, U.K.: Wiley.

Patzold, U. Killat, F. Laue and Li, Y. (1996). "A New and Optimal Method for the Derivation of Deterministic Simulation Models for Mobile Radio Channels," Proc. IEEE 46th Veh. Technol. Conf., VTC 96, Atlanta, Georgia, USA, pp. 1423-1427, Apr./May.

Patzold, M. Killat, U. and Laue,V. (1998). "An Extended Suzuki Model for Land Mobile Satellite Channels and its Statistical Properties," IEEE Trans. Veh. Technol., vol. 47, no. 2, pp. 617-630, May.

Patzold, M. Li, Y. and Laue, F. (1998). "A Study of a Land Mobile Satellite Channel Model with Asymmetrical Doppler Power Spectrum and Lognormally Distributed Line of Sight Component," IEEE Trans. Veh. Technol., vol. 47, no. 1, pp. 297-310, Feb.

Patzold, M., Killat, U. Li, Y. and Laue, F. (1997). "Modeling, Analysis and Simulation of Nonfrequency-Selective Mobile Radio Channels with Asymmetrical Doppler Power Spectral Density Shapes," IEEE Trans. Veh. Technol., vol. 46, no. 2, pp. 494-507, May.

Patzold, M., Killat, U., Laue, F., & Li, Y. (1998). *On the statistical properties of deterministic simulation models for mobile fading channels.* IEEE Transactions on Vehicular Technology, Vol. 47, No. 1, 254-269.

Patzold,M., Killat, U., Laue, F. and Li, Y. (1998). "On the Statistical Properties of Deterministic Simulation Models for Mobile Fading Channels," IEEE Trans. Veh. Technol., vol. 47, no. 1, pp. 254-269, Feb.

Paulraj, A., Nabar, R., and Gore, D. (2003). *Introduction to Space-Time Wireless Communications.* Cambridge University Press.

Pavlik, J.V. (1998) *New Media Technology: Cultural and Commercial Perspectives.* Boston: Allyn & Bacon.

Pawsey, C. (2004) *FMC: Explaining CTP and UMA*, Ovum.

Pawsey, C. (2006) *BT Fusion - The FMC Story so far*, Ovum.

Payaró, M., Pascual Iserte, A., Pérez Neira, A.I., & Lagunas, M.A. (2005, June). *Flexible MIMO Architectures: Guidelines in the design of MIMO parameters.* Paper presented at the IEEE 6th International Workshop on Signal Processing Advances in Wireless Communications (SPAWC), New York (USA).

Pearce, D. A., & Grace, D. (2003). Optimizing the downlink capacity of broadband fixed wireless access systems for packet-based communications. *IEEE International Conference on Communications,* 3, 2149-2153.

Pedersen, P., Methlie, L. B., Thorbjørnsen, H. (2002,). Understanding Mobile Commerce End-User Adoption: A Triangulation Perspective and Suggestions for an Exploratory Service Evaluation Framework. Paper presented at the 35th Hawaii International Conference on System Sciences.

Pentikousis, K. (2000). TCP in Wired-Cum-Wireless Environments. *IEEE Communications Surveys*, 3(4), 2-14.

Perez-Costa, X. and Camps-Mur, D. (2006). AU-APSD: Adaptive IEEE 802.11e Unscheduled Automatic Power Save Deliver. *IEEE International Conference (ICC) 2006*, Vol.5. (pp. 2020-2027). Istanbul, Turkey.

Perez-Costa, X., Camps-Mur, D., Palau, J. Rebolleda, D. and Akbarzadeh, S. (April, 2007). Overlapping Aware Scheduled Automatic Power Save Delivery Algorithm. *European Wireless,* Paris, France.

Perrow, C. (1967). A framework for the comparative analysis of organizations. American Sociological Review, (32), 194-208.

Perrow, C. (1979). Complex organizations: A critical essay (2nd ed.). Dallas, TX: Scott, Foresman and Company.

Pervasive Computing: http://www.computer.org/pervasive

Petty, R.E. & Cacioppo, J.T. (1981). Attitudes and persuasion: Classic and contemporary approaches. Dubuque, IA: Wm. C. Brown.

Pietrobon, S. (1998). *Implementation and performance of a turbo/MAP decoder.* International Journal of Satellite Communications, Vol. 16, No. 1, 23-46.

Pike, R., Presotto, D., Dorward, S., Flandrena, B., Thompson, K., Trickey, H. & Winterbottom, P. (1995). Plan 9 from Bell Labs, Computing Systems 8 (3) 221–254.

Pinter, Z. S., & Fernando, N. X. (2005). Fiber-Wireless Solution for Broadband Multimedia Access. *IEEE Canadian Review*, First Quarter 2005, 6-9.

Pogorzelski, R.J. (2001). On the dynamics of two-dimensional array beam scanning via perimeter detuning of coupled oscillator arrays. *IEEE Transactions on Antennas and Propagation,* 49(2), 234-242.

Pogorzelski, R.J. (2003). On the design of coupling networks for coupled oscillator arrays. *IEEE Transactions on Antennas and Propagation*, 51(4), 794-801.

Pollin, S., Bougard, B., & Lenoir, G. (2003). Cross-Layer Exploration of Link Adaptation in Wireless LANs with TCP Traffic. *Proc. IEEE Benelux Chapter on Communications and Vehicular Technology.*

Polydorou, D.S., and Capsalis, C.N. (1997). A new theoretical model for the prediction of rapid fading variations in an indoor environment, *IEEE Transactions on Vehicular Technology*, Vol. 46, No. 3, pp. 748-754.

Pon, C., (1964). Retrodirective array using the heterodyne technique. *IEEE Transactions on Antennas and Propagation*, 12(2), 176-180.

Pop, M.F., and Beaulieu, N.C. (1999). Statistical investigation of sum-of-sinusoids fading channel simulators, *GLOBECOM '99*, Vol. 1A, pp. 419-426, Rio de Janeiro, Brazil.

Pop, M.F., and Beaulieu, N.C. (2001). Limitations of sum-of-sinusoids fading channel simulators, *IEEE Transactions on Communications*, Vol. 49, No. 4, pp. 699-708.

Pop, M.F., and Beaulieu, N.C. (2002). Design of wide-sense stationary sum-of-sinusoids fading channel simulators, *Proceedings of th3 2002 IEEE International Conference on Communications*, Vol. 2, pp. 709-716.

Portio Market Research (2007). Worldwide Mobile Market Statistics 2007. *Portio Market Research.*

Postel, J. (1981). *Internet Control Message Protocol.* RFC 792.

Powell, T.C. (1992). Strategic Planning as competitive advantage. *Strategic Management Journal*, 13: 551-558.

Powell, T.C. (1997). Information technology as competitive advantage: The role of human, business and technology resources. *Strategic Management Journal*, 18:375-405.

Preston, S.L., Thiel, D.V., Smith, T.A, O'Keefe, S.G., and Lu, J.W. (1998). Base-station tracking in mobile communications using a switched parasitic antenna array, *IEEE Transactions on Antennas and Propagation*, Vol. 46, No. 6, pp. 841-844.

Proakis, J.G. (1995). *Digital Communications, 3rd Edition*, McGraw-Hill, New York (US).

Proakis, J.G. (2000). *Digital Communications, 4rd Ed.*, New York NY: McGraw Hill.

Qian, Y., & Itoh, T. (1998). Progress in active integrated antennas and their applications. *IEEE Transactions on Microwave Theory and Techniques*, 46(11), 1891-1900.

Qu, S. and Yeap, T. (1999)."A Three-Dimensional Scattering Model for Fading Channels in Land Mobile Environment," IEEE Trans. Veh. Technol., vol. 48, no. 3, pp. 765-781, May.

Qureshi, S.U.H. (1985). *Adaptive Equalisation*, Proceedings of the IEEE, Vol. 73, No. 9.

R. Ramaswamiand, K. N. Sivarajan, Optical Networks, 2nd, Morgan Kaufmann, San Francisco, 2002.

Radziunas M., Glitzky, A., Bandelow, U., Wolfrum, M., Troppenz, U., Kreissl, J., Rehbein, W. (2007). Improving the modulation bandwidth in semiconductor lasers by passive feedback. *IEEE J. Selected Topics in Quantum Electronics*, 13(1), 136-142.

Raisinghani, V. T., & Iyer, S. (2006). Cross Layer Feedback Architecture for Mobile Device Protocol Stacks. *IEEE Communications Magazine*, 44(1), 85 – 92.

Raleigh, G.G., and Paulraj, A. (1995), "Time varying vector channel estimation for adaptive spatial equalization", *Proceedings of the 1995 IEEE GLOBECOM*, pp. 218-224.

Ramakrishnan, K., Floyd, S., & Black, D. (2001). The Addition of Explicit Congestion Notification (ECN) to IP. *RFC 3168.*

Raman, G. L., (1999). Fundamentals of Telecommunications Network Management, IEEE Press, 1999.

Ramboli Management (2004), Top of the Web: User Satisfaction and Usage Survey of E-government Services, prepared for the e-Government Unit, DG Information Society, European Commission, by Ramboli Management, Ramboli Management, Copenhagen, December.

Ramsey, P.F. (1927). A Contribution to the Theory of Taxation. Economic Journal (37).

Rappaport, T. S. (July 1999). *Wireless Communications*, pp. 112-121.

Rappaport, T.S. (1989). Characterization of UHF multipath radio channels in factory building, *IEEE Transactions on Antennas and Propagation*, Vol. 37, No. 8, pp. 1058-1069.

Rappaport, T.S. (1996). *Wireless Communications Principles and Practice*, Prentice Hall, Upper Saddle River (US).

Rappaport, T.S. (2001). Wireless Communications - Principles and Practice, 2nd Edition, Prentice Hall.

Rappaport, T.S., and Hawbaker, D.A. (1992). A ray tracing technique to predict path loss and delay spread inside buildings, *Proceedings of the 1992 IEEE GLOBECOM*, pp. 649-653.

Rappaport, T.S., Huang, W., and Feuerstein, M.J. (1993). Performance of decision feedback equalizers in simulated urban and indoor radio channels, *IEICE Transactions on Communications*, Vol. E76-B, No. 2.

Rappaport, T.S., Seidel, S.Y., and Takamizawa, K. (1991). Statistical channel impulse response models for factory and open plan building radio communication system design, *IEEE Transactions on Communications*, Vol. COM-39, No 5, pp. 794-806.

Rappaport, T. S., Reed, J., & Woerner, B. (1996). Position location using wireless communications on highways of the future. *IEEE Communication Magazine*, 34(10), 33-41.

Ratnasingam, P. (2007). A Risk-Control Framework for the E-Marketplace Participation: The Findings of Seven Cases. Information Management & Computer Security, 15(2), 149-166.

Redl, S., Weber, M. K., Oliphant, M. (1995). An Introduction to GSM. Artech House, Mar.

RFC 791 (1981). Internet Protocol.

Rice, S.O. (1945). "Mathematical analysis of random noise," Bell System Tech. J., Vol. 23, No. 7, pp. 282–333, July 1944, and Vol. 24, No. 1, pp. 46–156, Jan.

Riera-Palou, F. (2002). *Reconfigurable structures for Direct Equalisation in Mobile Receivers*, PhD thesis, University of Bradford. Available on-line at http://dmi.uib.es/~friera/phdthesis .

Riera-Palou, F., Noras J.M., & Cruickshank, D.G.M. (2001). *Linear equalisers with dynamic and automatic length selection*. IEE Electronics Letters, Vol. 37, No. 25.

Rizk, K., Wagen, J.F., Gardiol, F. (1997). Two-Dimensional Ray-Tracing Modeling for Propagation Prediction in Microcellular Environments, *IEEE Transactions on Vehicular Technology*, Vol. 46, No. 22, pp. 508-518.

Rizzoli, V., Costanzo, A., Masotti, D., Lipparini, A., & Mastri, F. (2004). Computer-aided optimization of non-linear microwave circuits with the aid of electromagnetic simulation. *IEEE Transactions on Microwave Theory and Techniques*, 52(1), 362-377.

Robertson, P., Villebrun, E., & Hoeher, P. (1995). *A comparison of optimal and sub-optimal MAP decoding algorithms operating in the log domain*, IEEE ICC'95, Seattle, USA, 1009-1013.

Rodríguez-Hernández, P., González-Castaño, F. J., Pousada-Carballo, J. M., Fernández-Iglesias, M. J., García-Reinoso, J. (2002). Cellular Network for Real-Time Mobile Auction. Wireless Personal Communications, 22(1), 23-40.

Roman, M., Hess, C.K., Cerqueira, R., Ranganathan, A., Campbell, R.H., Narhstedt, K., Gaiaos. (2002). A middleware infrastructure to enable active spaces, IEEE Pervasive Computing Magazine.

Roman, M., Hess, C.K., Cerqueira, R., Ranganathan, A., Campbell, R.H., Narhstedt, K. & Gaiaos (2002). A middleware infrastructure to enable active spaces, IEEE Pervasive Computing Magazine.

Roselli, L., Borgioni ,V., Zepparelli, F., Ambrosi, F., Comez, M., Faccin, P., & Casini A. (2003). Analog Laser Predistortion for Multiservice Radio-Over-Fiber Systems. *IEEE J. Lightwave Technology*, 21(5).

Rossi, J.-P., and Levy, A.J. (1993). Propagation analysis in cellular environment with the help of models using ray theory and GTD, *Proceedings of the 43rd IEEE Vehicular Technology Conference*, pp. 253-256.

Roussos, G. (2003). Appliance design for pervasive computing. IEEE Pervasive Computing, 2(4), 75–77.

Rubinstein, R. Y., & Melamed, B. (1998). *Modern Simulation and Modeling*. New York, NY, USA: John Wiley & Sons, Inc.

Rudberg, M., Klingenberg, N., Kronhamn, K. (2002). Collaborative Supply Chain Planning Using Electronic Marketplaces. Integrated Manufacturing Systems, 13(8), 596-610.

Ruggieri, M. (2006). Next generation of wired and wireless networks: the NavCom integration, *Wireless Personal Communications*, Vol. 38, No. 1, pp. 79-88.

Rustako, A.J., Amitay, N.Jr., Owens, G.J., and Roman, R.S. (1991). Radio propagation at microwave frequencies for line-of-sight microcellular mobile and personal communications, *IEEE Transactions on Vehicular Technology*, Vol. 40, pp. 203-210.

Ruta, M., Noia, T.D., Sciascio, E.D., Piscitelli, G. & Scioscia, F. (2007). Session M5: e-business systems and applications: RFID meets bluetooth in a semantic based u-commerce environment Proceedings of the ninth international conference on Electronic commerce ICEC '07. ACM Press

Sagias, N.C., Karagiannidis, G.K., Zogas, D.A., Tombras, G.S., and Kotsopoulos, S.A. (2005). Average output SINR of equal-gain diversity in correlated Nakagami-m fading with cochannel interference, *IEEE Transactions on Wireless Communications*, Vol. 4, No. 4, pp. 1407-1411.

Saleh, A.A.M., and Valenzuela, R.A. (1987). A statistical model for indoor multipath propagation, *IEEE Journal on Selected Areas in Communications*, Vol. SAC-5, No. 2, pp. 128-137.

Salinas, Arturo (2006). 'Advantages and disadvantages of using presence service', Helsinki University of Technology, TKK T-110.5190 Seminar on Internetworking, -05-4/5.

Salkintzis, A.K. and Chamaz, C. , (1998). An in-band power saving protocol for mobile data networks, *IEEE Transactions on Communications*, vol. 46, (pp. 1194-1205).

Salvi, A.B. & Sahai, S. (2002). Dial m for money. Proceedings of the 2nd international workshop on Mobile commerce WMC '02. ACM Press

Sampemane, G., Naldurg, P. & Campbell, R. (2002). Access control for active spaces, in: ACSAC '02: Proceedings of the 18th Annual Computer Security Applications Conference, IEEE Computer Society, Washington, DC, USA, p. 343.

Sanagi, M., Kano, K., Fujimori, K., & Nogi, S. (2006). Active phased array antenna radiating second harmonic output wave. *Electronics and Communications in Japan (Part II:Electronics),* 89(4), 39-50.

Sandmo, A., (1976). Optimal taxation: An introduction to the literature. Journal of Public Economics, Vol. 6, No. 1-2, pp. 37-54.

Sarkar, T.K., Ji, Z., Kim, K., Medouri, Z., and Salazar-Palma, M. (2003). A survey of various propagation models for mobile communication, *IEEE Antennas and Propagation Magazine*, Vol. 45, No. 3, 51-82.

Sarolahti, P., & Floyd, S. (2007). *Cross-layer Indications for Transport Protocols*. Internet draft draft-sarolahti-tsvwg-crosslayer-00.txt.

Sarolahti, P., Allman, M., & Floyd, S. (2007). Determining an Appropriate Sending Rate Over an Underutilized Network Path. *Computer Networks Special Issue on Protocols for Fast, Long-Distance Networks*, 51(7).

Sato, K., Fujise, M., Shimizu, S. & Nishi, S. (2005). Millimeter-Wave High-Speed Spot Communication System Using Radio-over-Fiber Technology. *IEICE Trans. Electron.*, E88-C(10), 1932-1938.

Satyanarayanan, M. (2001). Pervasive computing: Vision and challenges. IEEE Personal Communications, 8(4):10–17.

Savarese, C. Rabay, J., & Langendoen, K. (2002). Robust positioning algorithms for distributed ad-hoc wireless sensor networks. In *Proceedings of the USENIX Technical Annual Conference*, (pp. 317-328). California: Monterey.

Savvides, A., & Srivastava, M. B. (2004). Location discovery. In S. Basagni, M. Conti, S. Giordano & I. Stojmenović (Eds.), *Mobile ad hoc networking* (pp. 231-254). Hoboken, New Jersey: IEEE Press and John Wiley & Sons, Inc.

Schelin, S.H. (2003). E-government: An overview. In G. David Garson (Ed.), Public Information Technology: Policy and management issues, pp. 120-137. Hershey, PA: Idea Group Publishing.

Scheuing, E.E. & Johnson, E.M. "A proposed model for new service development." *The Journal of Services Marketing* 3, no.2, (1989):25-34.

Schilit, B. N., Adams, N. & Want, R. (1994). Context-aware computing applications. In IEEE Workshop on Mobile Computing Systems and Applications, pages 85-90, Santa Cruz, CA, US.. IEEE.

Schlub, R., Thiel, D.V., Lu, J.W., and O' Keefe, S.G. (2000). Dual-band switched parasitic wire antennas for communications and direction finding, *Proceedings of the 2000 IEEE Asia-Pacific Microwave Conference*, pp. 74-78, Sydney, Australia.

Schuler, R.S. & Jackson, S.E. "Linking competitive strategy with human resource management practices."

Academy of Management Executive 1, no.3, (1987):207-219.

Seco, G., Fernández Rubio, J.A., & Fernández Prades, C. (2005). ML estimator and Hybrid Beamformer for multipath and interference mitigation in GNSS receivers. *IEEE Transactions on Signal Processing*, 53(3), 1194–1208.

Seeds, A. J. & Williams K. J. (2006). Microwave Photonics. *IEEE J. Lightwave Technology*, 24(12), 4628 – 4641.

Seidel, S.Y., and Rappaport, T.S. (1994). Site-specific propagation prediction for wireless in-building personal communication system design, *IEEE Transactions on Vehicular Technology*, Vol. 43, No. 4, pp. 879-891.

Seigneur, J. & Jensen, C. (2004). Trust enhanced ubiquitous payment without too much privacy loss, in: SAC '04: Proceedings of the 2004 ACM Symposium on Applied Computing, ACM Press, New York, NY, USA, pp. 1593–1599.

Seong, K., Narasimhan, R., & Cioffi, J. M. (2006). Queue proportional scheduling via geometric programming in fading broadcast channels, *IEEE Journal on Selected Areas in Communications*, 24(8), 1593-1602.

Sforza, M. and Buonomo, S. (1993). "Characterization of the Propagation Channel for Nongeostationary LMS Systems at L- and S-Bands: Narrow Band Experimental Data and Channel Modelling," in Procedure XVII NAPEX Conference, Pasadena, CA, June 14–15.

Shade, B. (2001). Increased Productivity Through E-Manufacturing, by Cahners Business Information

Shafer, S., Krumm, J., Brumitt, B., Meyers, B., Czerwinski, M. & Robbins, D. (1998). The new easyliving project at microsoft research. In DARPA / NIST Smart Spaces Workshop, Gaithersburg, Maryland.

Shahbazpanahi, S., Gershman, A.B, Luo, Z.Q., & Wong, K.M. (2003). Robust adaptive beamforming for general–rank signal models. *IEEE Transactions on Signal Processing*, 51(9), 2257–2269.

Shen, G., Tucker, R. S., & Chae, C.-J. (2007). Fixed Mobile Convergence Architectures for Broadband Access: Integration of EPON and WiMAX. *IEEE Communications Magazine*, August 2007. 44-50.

Shenker, S. (1995). Fundamental Design Issues for the Future Internet. *IEEE Journal of Selected Areas in Communication*, 13(7), 1176-1188.

Sherer, P.D., Rogovsky, N., & Wright, N. (1998). What drives employment relationships in taxicab organizations? Linking agency to firm capabilities and strategic opportunities. *Organizational Science*, 9:34-48.

Shih, D., Huang, S. Y., Yen, D. C. (2005). A New Reverse Auction Agent System for M-Commerce Using Mobile Agents. Computers Standards & Interfaces, 27(4), 383-395.

Shin, H. & Lee, J.H. (2003). Capacity of multiple-antenna fading channels: spatial fading correlation, double scattering and keyhole, *IEEE Transactions on Information Theory*, 49(10), 2636-2647.

Shiroma, G.S., Miyamoto, R.Y., & Shiroma, W.A. (2003). A 16-element two-dimensional active self-steering array using self-oscillating mixers. *IEEE Transactions on Microwave Theory and Techniques*, 51(12), 2476-2482.

Shukla, S. & Nah F. F. (2005). Web browsing and spyware intrusion Communications of the ACM, Volume 48 Issue 8. ACM Press

Sibille, A., Roblin, C., and Poncelet, G. (1997). Circular switched monopole arrays for beam steering wireless communications," *Electronics Letters*, Vol. 33, No. 7, pp. 551-552.

Siemens. (2006, April). Fixed Mobile Convergence (FMC) Based on IMS. For Mobile Network Operators.

Silventoinen, M. I., & Rantalainen, T. (1996). Mobile station emergency locating in GSM. In *Proceedings of IEEE ICPWC '96,* (pp. 232-238). India: New Delhi.

Simon, H.A. (1976). Administrative behaviour (3rd ed.). New York, NY: The Free Press.

Simon, M.K. and Alouini, M.-Sl. (2000). Digital Communication over Fading Channels, New York: Wiley.

Singh, J.P. (1999). Leapfrogging development? The political economy of telecommunications restructuring. New York: SUNY Press.

Singh, S., Woo, M., & Raghavendra, C. S. (1998). Power-aware routing in mobile ad hoc networks. *Proceedings of the 4th annual ACM/IEEE international conference on Mobile computing and networking*, 181 – 190.

Sirin, E., Parsia, B. & Hendler, J. (2005). Template-based composition of semantic Web services. In: AAAI Fall Symposium on Agents and the Semantic Web.

Sklar, B. (2001). *Digital Communications: Fundamentals and Applications, 2nd Edition*, Prentice Hall PTR, Upper Saddle River (NJ, US).

Smyth, F., Kaszubowska, A., Barry, L.P. (2004). Overcoming laser diode nonlinearity issues in multi-channel radio-over-fiber systems. *Optics Communications*, 217–225.

SnapTrack (2003). SnapTrack's Wireless Assisted GPS™ (A-GPS) Solution Provides the Industry's Best Location System. Whitepaper from *SnapTrack, A QUALCOMM Company.*

Son, H.W., and Myung, N.H. (1999). A deterministic ray tube method for microcellular wave propagation prediction model, *IEEE Transactions on Antennas and Propagation*, Vol. 47, No. 8, pp. 1344-1350.

Spirito, M. A., & Mattiolli, A. G. (1999). Preliminary experimental results of a GSM mobile phones positioning system based on timing advance. In *Proceedings of the 50th IEEE Vehicular Technology Conference, Vol. 4.* (pp. 2072-2076). The Netherlands: Amsterdam.

Srivastava, V., & Motani, M. (2005). Cross-layer design: a survey and the road ahead. *IEEE Communications Magazine*, 43(12), 112 – 119.

Srivastava, V., Neel, J., MacKenzie, A. B.. Menon, R., DaSilva, L.A., Hicks, J.E., Reed, J.H., Gilles, R.P. (2005). Using Game Theory to Analyze Wireless Ad Hoc Networks. *IEEE Communications Surveys & Tutorials*, 7(4), 46-56.

Stajano, F (2002). *Security for Ubiquitous Computing.* Wiley press.

Stamatios V. Kartalopoulos DWDM: Networks, Devices, and Technology, Wiley-IEEE Press, 2002.

Stapleton, S.P., Carbo, X., and McKeen, T. (1994). Spatial channel simulator for phased arrays, *IEEE 44th Vehicular Technology Conference*, Vol. 3, pp. 1789-1792, Stockholm, Sweden.

Stapleton, S.P., Carbo, X., and McKeen, T. (1996). Tracking and diversity for a mobile communications base station array antenna", *IEEE 46th Vehicular Technology Conference*, Vol. 3, pp. 1695-1699, Atlanta, GA, USA.

Stark, H., & Yang, Y. (1998). *Vector Space Projections: A Numerical Approach to Signal and Image Processing, Neural Nets, and Optics*, New York NY: John Wiley and Sons.

Stephan, K.D. (1986). Inter-Injection-Locked Oscillators for Power Combining and Phased Arrays. *IEEE Transactions on Microwave Theory and Techniques,* 34(10), 1017-1025.

Stephens, W. E. & Joseph T. R. (1987). System characteristics of direct modulated and externally modulated RF fiberoptic links. *IEEE J. Lightwave Technology,* LT-5, 380- 387.

Steyskal, H. (1983). Simple method for pattern nulling by phase perturbation. *IEEE Transactions on Antennas and Propagation*, AP-31(1), 163-166.

Stine, J. A. (2006). Cross-Layer Design of MANETs: The Only Option. *Military Communications Conference*, 1-7.

Stockdale, R., Standing, C. (2004). Benefits and barriers of electronic marketplace participation: an SME perspective. The Journal of Enterprise Information Management, 17(4), 301-311.

Storey, C. & Easingwood, C.J. "The augmented service offering: a conceptualisation and study of its impact in new service success." *Journal of Product Innovation Management* 15, (1998):335-351.

Storey, C. & Easingwood, C.J. "The impact of the new product development project on the success of financial services." *The Service Industries Journal* 13, no.3, (1993):40-54.

Storey, C. & Easingwood, C.J. "Types of new product performance: evidence from the consumer financial services sector." *Journal of Business Research* 46, (1999):193- 203.

Storey; C. & Easingwood, C.J "Determinants of new product performance: a study in the financial service sector." *International Journal of Service Industry Management* 7, no.1, (1996).32-55.

Strouce, Karen G. "*Strategies for success in the new telecommunications marketplace*"(2001),pp.115-125

Stuber, G.L. (2001). *Principles of Mobile Communication*. Kluwer Academic Publisher.

Stuber, G.L. (2001). Principles of Mobile Communications, Kluwer Academic Publishers, 2nd Ed.

Sturm, J.F. (1999). Using SeDuMi 1.02, a MATLAB toolbox for optimization over symmetric cones. *Optimization Methods and Software*, 11-12, 625-653.

Sukasame, N. (2004). The development of e-service in Thai government. BU academic review, 3.

Sun, S., Su, C. & Ju, T. (2005). A study of consumer value-added services in mobile commerce: focusing on domestic cellular phone companies in Taiwan, China. Proceedings of the 7th international conference on Electronic commerce ICEC '05. ACM Press

Sundaram, N., & Ramanathan, P. (2002). Connectivity based location estimation scheme for wireless ad hoc networks. In *Proceedings of IEEE Globecom 2002, Vol. 1*, (pp. 143-147). Taiwan: Taipei.

Suzuki, H. (1977). "A Statistical Model for Urban Radio Propagation," IEEE Trans. Commun., vol. 25, no. 7, pp. 673-680, July.

Suzuki, H. (1977). "A Statistical Model for Urban Radio Propagation," IEEE Trans. Commun., 25, 673–680.

Suzuki, H. (1977). A statistical model for urban radio propagation: multipath characteristics in New York city, *IEEE Transactions on Communications*, Vol. 25, pp. 673-680.

Sycara, K., Lu, J., Klusch, M. & Widoff, S. (1999). Matchmaking among heterogeneous agents on the internet. In: Proceedings of the 1999 AAAI Spring Symposium on Intelligent Agents in Cyberspace.

Sycara, K., Paolucci, M., Ankolekar, A. & Srinivasan, N. (2003). Automated discovery, interaction and composition of semantic Web services, Web Semantics: Science, Services and Agents on the World Wide Web.

T. C. Clancy and H. Tschofenig (2007). EAP Generalised Pre-Shared Key (EAP-GPSK), work in progress, draft-ietf-emu-eap-gpsk-02.txt.

T. C. Clancy and W. Arbaugh (2006). Extensible Authentication Protocol (EAP) Password Authenticated Exchange, IETF RFC 4746.

T. Dierks and C. Allen (1999). The TLS Protocol: Version 1.0, IETF RFC 2246.

T. Hardjono and B. Weis (2004). The Multicast Group Security Architecture, IETF RFC3740.

T. Hayashi, A. Tanabe, D. Andou, K. Izutsu, H. Satou, H. He and W. Tawbi (2004). IGAP: Secure group management protocol for multicast content delivery network, in the proceedings of the 2004 Joint Conference of the 10th Asia Pacific Conference on Communications and the 5th International Symposium on Multi-Dimensional Mobile Communications, Volume 2, pages: 626-630.

T. Hayashi, D. Andou, H. He, W. Tawbi, and T. Niki (2003). Internet Group Membership Authentication Protocol, Internet Draft (expired), draft-hayashi-igap-03.txt.

T. Otto (2005). The EAP SKL Protocol, work in progress, draft-otto-eap-skl-0.2.txt.

Taflove, A., and Morris, M.E. (1975). Numerical solution of steady-state electromagnetic scattering problems using the time-dependent Maxwell's equations, *IEEE Transactions on Microwave Theory and Techniques*, Vol. MTT-23, pp. 623-630.

Talbi, L. (2001). Simulation of Indoor UHF Propagation Using Numerical Technique, *Canadian Conference on Electrical and Computer Engineering*, Vol. 2, pp. 1357-1362.

Tang, P. K., Ling Chuen Ong, Alphones A., Luo, B., & Fujise, M. (2004). PER and EVM Measurements of a Radio-Over-Fiber Network for Cellular and WLAN System Applications. *IEEE J. Lightwave Technology,* 22(11), 2370-2376.

Tassiulas, L., & Ephremides, A. (1993). Dynamic server allocation to parallel queues with randomly varying connectivity, *IEEE Transactions on Information Theory*, 39(2), 466-478.

Tayal, M. (2005,). Location Services in the GSM and UMTS Networks. Paper presented at the ICPWC'05. New Delhi.

Technology Advancements and Government Policies in Canada: http://www.atirtf-geai.gc.ca/submissions/riley2001-05-30-f.html

Tektronix. (2002, June). UMTS Technology Seminars, June 2002

Telatar, E. (1999). Capacity of Multi-antenna Gaussian Channels, *European Transactions on Telecommunications*, 10(6), 585-595.

Telatar, I. E., & Gallager, R. G. (1995). Combining queuing theory with information theory for multi-access, *IEEE Journal on Selected Areas in Communications* ,13(6), 963-969.

Tepedelenlioglu, C., Abdi, A., Giannakis, G. B., and Kaveh, M. (2001). "Estimation of Doppler spread and signal stength in mobile communications with applications to handoff and adaptive transmission," Wirel. Commun. Mobile Comput., pp. 221–242.

Themistocleous, M. & Irani, Z. (2002). Evaluating Enterprise Application Integration Technologies: A Novel Frame of References. European Journal of Operational Research, In Press.

Thompson, D.V., Rust, R.T. & Rhoda, J. (2005). The business value of e-government for small firms. International Journal of Service Industry Management, Vol. 16, No. 4, pp. 385 – 407.

Thomson, J.D. (1967). Organizations in action: Social science bases of administrative theory. New York: McGraw Hill.

Thornton, J. (2004). A low sidelobe asymmetric beam antenna for high altitude platform communications. *IEEE Microwave and Wireless Components Letters*, 14(2), 59-61.

Thornton, J., Grace, D., Capstick, M. H., & Tozer, T. C. (2003). Optimizing an array of antennas for cellular coverage from a high altitude platform. *IEEE Transactions on Wireless Communications*, 2(3), 484-492.

Thornton, J., Grace, D., Spillard, C., Konefal, T., & Tozer, T. C. (2001). Broadband communications from a high-altitude platform: the European HeliNet program. *Electronics and Communication Engineering Journal*, 13(3), 138-144.

Tian, H., Bose, S. K., Law, C. L., & Xiao, W. (2005). CLA-QOS: A Cross-Layer QoS Provisioning Approach for Mobile Ad-hoc Networks. *TENCON*, 1 – 6.

Tillman, J.D., Jr. (1966). *The Theory and Design of Circular Antenna Arrays*. University of Tennessee Engineering Experimental Station.

Tjhung, T. T. and Chai, C. C. (1999). "Fade Statistics in Nakagami-Lognormal Channels," IEEE Trans. Commun., vol. 47, no. 12, pp. 1769-1772, Dec.

Tjhung, T.T. and Chai, C.C. (1998). "Bit Error Rate Performance of π/4 DQPSK Nakagami-Lognormal Channels," IEEE Electron. Lett., 34, 625–627.

Tjhung, T.T. and Chai, C.C. (1999). "Fade Statistics in Nakagami-Lognormal Channels," IEEE Trans. Commun., 47, 1769–1772.

Tolmie, P., Pycock, J., Diggins, T., MacLean A. & Karsenty, A. (2002). Unremarkable Computing, Xerox Research Centre Europe.

Tonguz, O. K., & Jung H. (1996). Personal communication access networks using subcarrier multiplexed optical links. *IEEE J. Lightwave Technology*, 14, 1400-1409.

Torres, L., Pina, V. & Acerete, B. (2005). E-government developments on delivering public services among EU cities. Government Information Quarterly, 22, 217-238.

Toumbakaris, D., and Kotsopoulos, S.A. (2007). Delay-constrained transmission over flat fading channels in the low SNR range, *18th Annual IEEE International Symposium on Personal, Indoor and Mobile Radio Communications*, Athens, Greece, 3-7 September 2007, to be published.

Toumpis, S., & Goldsmith, A. J., (2003). Capacity Regions for Wireless Ad Hoc Networks. *IEEE Transactions on Wireless Communications*, 2(4), 746-748.

Tourki, K., Gesbert, D., Deneire, L. (2007). Cooperative Diversity using per-user Power Control in the multiuser MAC channel, *IEEE International Symposium on Information Theory,* Nice, France, Jun.

Toyota: http://www.toyota.com/

Tozer, T. C. (2000). High altitude platforms: The future for communications?, http://www.skylarc.com/HAPsmainpres2000/HAPSmainpres.pdf.

Tozer, T. C., & Grace, D. (2001). High-altitude platforms for wireless communications. *Electronics and Communication Engineering Journal*, 13(3), 127-137.

Trastour, D., Bartolini, C. & Gonzalez-Castillo, J. (2001). A semantic Web approach to service description for matchmaking of services. In: Proceedings of the First Semantic Web Working Symposium, (SWWS).

Troppenz, U., Kreissl J., Rehbein W., Bornholdt C., Gaertner T., Radziunas M., Glitzky A., Bandelow U., Wolfrum M. (2006). '*40 Gb/s directly modulated InGaAsP passive feedback DFB laser*', European Conference on Optical Communications (ECOC) Proc. Ser., paper Th 4.5.5.

Tsai, C., Shen, B. F. (2006,). Online Reverse Auctions via Wireless Instant Message Networks. Paper presented at the 6th International Conference on ITS Telecommunications.

Tsatsanis, M., Zhang, R., & Banerjee, S. (2000). Network-assisted diversity for random access wireless networks. *IEEE Transactions on Signal Processing*, 48(3), 702–711.

Tse, D., & Hanly, S. (1998). Multi-access fading channels: Part I and Part II, *IEEE Transactions on Information Theory*, 44(7), 2796–2831.

Tse, D., & Viswanath, P (2005). *Fundamentals of wireless communication*, Cambridge University Press.

Tse, T., Soufani, K. (2003). Business strategies for small firms in the new economy. Journal of Small Business and Enterprise Development, 10(3), 306-320.

Tseng, Y. C., Huang, C. F., & Kuo, S. P. (2005). Positioning and Location Tracking in Wireless Sensor Networks. In M. Ilyas & I. Mahgoub (Eds.), *Handbook of sensor networks: compact wireless and wired sensing systems.* Florida, Boca Raton: CRC Press LLC.

Tuovinen, J., Shiroma, G.S., Forsyth, W.E., & Shiroma, W.A. (2003). Multipath communications using a phase-conjugate array. In IEEE, *MTT-S International Microwave Symposium* (pp. 1681-1684). Philadelphia, PA: IEEE.

Turin, G.L., Clapp, F.D., Johnston, T.L., Fine, S.B., and Lavry, D. (1972). A statistical model of urban multipath propagation, *IEEE Transactions on Vehicular Technology*, Vol. 21, No. 1, pp. 1-9.

Tzeng, S.-J. (2006). CATV/Radio-on-Fiber transport system based on direct modulation. *Optics Communications*, 259, 127-132.

Ubicuitous Security: http://www.lce.eng.cam.ac.uk/~fms27/secubicomp/index.

United Nations & American Society for Public Administration (ASPA). (2002). Benchmarking e-government: A global perspective. New York, NY: U.N. Publications.

Unni, R., Harmon, R. (2003,). Location-Based Services: Models for Strategy Development in M-Commerce. Paper presented at the World. Portland International Conference on Technology Management for Reshaping (PICMET '03).

Uysal-Biyikoglu, E., El-Gamal, A., & Prabhakar, B. (2002). Adaptive transmission of variable-rate data over a fading channel for energy efficiency. In *Proc. Global Telecommunications Conference (GLOBECOM): Vol. 1.* (pp. 97-101), IEEE.

Vadde, K. K., & Syrotiuk, V. R. (2004). Factor Interaction on Service Delivery in Mobile Ad Hoc Networks. *IEEE Journal on Selected Areas In Communications (JSAC)*, 22(7), 1335-1346.

Vahdat, A., Anderson, T., Dahlin, M., Culler, D., Belani, E., Eastham, P. & Yoshikawa, C. (1998). WebOS: Operating system services for wide area applications, in: Proceedings of the Seventh Symposium on High Performance Distributed Computing.

van de Kar, E. (2005). The design of a mobile information and entertainment service on a UMTS testbed. Proceedings of the 7th international conference on Electronic commerce ICEC '05. ACM Press

Van Trees, H.L. (2002) *Optimum Array Processing. Detection, Estimation and Modulation Theory, Part IV*, New York: Wiley Interscience.

Van Veen, B.D., & Buckley, K.M. (1988) Beamforming: A versatile approach to spatial filtering, *IEEE Signal Processing Magazine*, 5(2), 4–24.

Van Trees, H. L. (2001). *Detection estimation and modulation theory, Part 1* (republished in paperback). NY: John Wiley & Sons, Inc.

Vanassche, P., Gielen, G.G.E., & Sansen, W. (2003). Behavioral modeling of (coupled) harmonic oscillators. *IEEE Transactions on Computer-Aided Design of Integrated Circuits and Systems*, 22(8), 1017-1026.

Varlamos, P.K., and Capsalis, C.N. (2003). Design of a six-sector switched parasitic planar array using the method of genetic algorithms, *Wireless Personal Communications*, Vol. 26, No. 1, pp. 77-88.

Varlamos, P.K., Mitilineos, S.A., and Capsalis, C.N. (2006). Diversity performance of a switched parasitic circular array in an indoor multipath environment, *Proceedings of the European Microwave Association (EuMA)*, to be published, September 2006.

Varshney, U. (2001,). Location Management Support for Mobile Commerce Applications. Paper presented at the WMC'01, Rome, Italy.

Varshney, U. (2003). Location Management for Mobile Commerce Applications in Wireless Internet Environment, ACM Transactions on Internet Technology, 3(3), pp. 236-255

Varshney, U. (2005). Performance Evaluation of Protocols for Group-Oriented Mobile Services. Mobile Networks and Applications, 10(4), 465-474.

Varshney, U. (2007). Supporting Dependable Group-Oriented Mobile Transactions: Redundancy-Based Architecture and Performance. International Journal of Network Management ,17(3), 219-229.

Varshney, U., Vetter, R. (2002). Mobile Commerce: Framework, Applications and Networking Support. Mobile Networks and Applications, 7(3), 185-198.

Vatalaro, F. (1995). "Generalized Rice-Lognormal Channel Model for Wireless Communications," Elec. Letters., vol. 31, no. 22, pp. 1899-1900, Oct.

Vatalaro, F. (1995). "Generalized Rice-Lognormal Channel Model for Wireless Communications," IEEE Electron. Lett., 31, 1899–1900.

Vatalaro, F. and Forcella, A. (1997)."Doppler Spectrum in Mobile-to-Mobile Communications in the Presence of Three-Dimensional Multipath Scattering," IEEE Trans. Veh. Technol., vol. 46, no. 1, pp. 213-219, Feb.

Vatalaro, F., Mazzenga, F., De Maio, G. and Forcella, A. (2002). "The Generalized Rice Lognormal Channel Model-First and Second Order Statistical Characterization and Simulation," J. Wiley Int. Journal on Satell. Commun. , vol. 20, no. 1, pp. 29-45.

Vellis, F.E., and Capsalis, C.N. (2000). A model for the statistical characterization of fast fading in the presence of a user, *Wireless Personal Communications*, Vol. 15, pp. 207-219.

Venkatraman, S., Caffery, J. Jr., & Heung-Ryeol, Y. (2004). A novel ToA location algorithm using LoS range estimation for NLoS environments. *IEEE Transactions on Vehicular Technology*, 53(5), 1515-1524.

Vickrey, W. (1961). Counterspeculation, Auctions and Competitive Sealed Tenders. The Journal of Finance 16(1), 8-37.

Vilhar, A., & Novak, R. (2005). Home agent placement optimization for HAP-based network mobility. *2nd International Symposium on Wireless Communication Systems*, 873-877.

Viswanath, P., Tse, D.N.C., & Laroia, R. (2002). Opportunistic beamforming using dumb antennas. *IEEE Transactions on Information Theory*, 48(6), 1277-1294.

Viswanathan, H., & Kumaran, K. (2005). Rate scheduling in multiple antenna downlink wireless systems, IEEE Transactions on Communications, 53(4), 645-655.

Viswanathan, P., Gill, B. & Campbell, R. (2001). Security architecture in Gaia, Tech. Rep., Champaign, IL, USA.

Vlachos, P. & Vrechopoulos, A. (2004). Emerging customer trends towards mobile music services. Proceedings of the 6th international conference on Electronic commerce ICEC '04. ACM Press

Vorobyov, S.A., Gershman, A.B., & Luo, Z.Q. (2003). Robust adaptive beamforming using worst–case performance optimization: A solution to the signal mismatch problem. *IEEE Transactions on Signal Processing*, 51(2), 313–324.

Vossiek, M., Wiebking, L., Gulden, P., Wieghardt, J., Hoffmann, C., Heide, P. (2003). Wireless Local Positioning. IEEE Microwave Magazine, 4(4), 77-86.

Vrdoljak, M., Vrdoljak, S. I. and Skugor, G. (2000, February). Fixed-Mobile Convergence Strategy: Technologies and Market Opportunities, IEEE Communications Magazine.

W. Daum, J. Krauser, P. Zamzow, O. Ziemann, Polymer optical fibers for data communication, Springer-Verlag Berlin Heidelberg 2002.

Wake D., Webster M., Wimpenny G., Beacham K.and Crawford L. (2004). *Radio over fiber for mobile communications*. IEEE Conference on Microwave Photonics, invited paper.

Wallace, J.W., and Jensen, M.A. (2003). Validation of Parametric Directional MIMO Channel Models from Wideband FDTD Simulations of a Simple Indoor Environment, *IEEE 2003 Antennas and Propagation Society International Symposium*, Vol. 2, pp. 535-538.

Wang, C-X., Patzold, M. and Yuan, D. (2007). "Accurate and Efficient Simulation of Multiple Uncorrelated Rayleigh Fading Waveforms," IEEE Trans. Wirel. Commun., vol. 6, no. 3, pp. 833-839, Mar.

Wang, H. et. Al. (2007). Access control management for ubiquitous computing. Future Generation Computer Systems.

Wang, H., Cao, J. & Zhang, Y. (2006). Ubiquitous computing environments and its usage access control, in: Proceedings of the First International Conference on Scalable Information Systems, INFOSCALE, ACM Press, Hong Kong.

Wang, L.-C., & Lee, C.-H. (2005). A TCP-physical cross-layer congestion control mechanism for the multirate WCDMA system using explicit rate change notification. *International Conference on Advanced Information Networking and Applications*, 2, 449 – 452.

Wang, Q., & Abu-Rgheff, M. A. (2003). Cross-layer signaling for next-generation wireless systems. *IEEE Wireless Communications and Networking (WCNC)*, 1084 – 1089.

Wang, S., Archer, N. P., Zheng, W. (2006). An Exploratory Study of Electronic Marketplace Adoption: A Multiple Perspective View. Electronic Markets, 16(4), 337-348.

Wang, X. H., Zhang, D. Q., Gu, T., and Pung, H. K. (2004). Ontology based context modeling and reasoning using OWL. In *Proc. of the Second IEEE Annual Conference on Pervasive Computing and Communications Workshops*, IEEE Computer Society, 18.

Wang, X.H., Zhang, D.Q., Gu, T. & Pung, H.K. (2004). Ontology Based Context Modeling and Reasoning using OWL. In Workshop Proceedings of the 2nd IEEE Conference on Pervasive Computing and Communications (PerCom2004) (Orlando, FL, USA, March 2004), pp. 18–22.

Wang, Y., van de Kar, E. & Meijer, G. (2005). Designing mobile solutions for mobile workers: lessons learned from a case study. Proceedings of the 7th international conference on Electronic commerce ICEC '05. ACM Press

Wang, X., Wang, Z., & O'Dea, B. (2003). A TOA-based location algorithm reducing the errors due to non-line-of-sight (NLOS) propagation. *IEEE Transactions on Vehicular Technology,* 52(1), 112 - 116.

Watanabe, H., Aoyagi, T., Takemoto, A., Omura, B. (1996). 1.3-μm strained MQW-DFB Lasers with extremely low intermodulation distortion for high-speed analog transmission. *IEEE J. Quant. Electron*, 32(6), 1015-1023.

Watson R.T. (2004). Data management: Databases and Organizations 4th edition, Willey press.

Watson, R.T. & Straub, D. W. (2007). Future IS research in net-enabled organizations. ACM SIGMIS Database, Volume 38 Issue 3. ACM Press.

Watson, R.T. (2000). U-commerce: the ultimate. Ubiquity, Volume 1 Issue 33. ACM Press.

Wax, M., & Anu, Y. (1996) Performance analysis of the minimum variance beamformer, *IEEE Transactions on Signal Processing*, 44(4), 928–937.

Way, W. I. (1993). Optical fiber-based microcellular systems: An overview. *IEICE Trans. Commun.*, E76–B(9), 1091–1102.

Wei, X., Cruickshank, D.G.M., Mulgrey, B., & Riera-Palou, F. (2007). *A Unified Approach to Dynamic Length Algorithms for Adaptive Equalisers.* IEEE Transactions on Signal Processing, Vol. 55, No. 3.

Weimerskirch, A., Paar, C. & Wolf, M. (2005). Cryptographic component identification: enabler for secure vehicles. In: IEEE 62nd vehicular technology conference Dallas, USA.

Weingarten, H., Steinberg, Y., & Shamai, S (2006). The capacity region of the Gaussian Multiple-Input Multiple-Output Broadcast Channel, *IEEE Transactions on Information Theory,* 52(9), 3936-3964.

Weis, B. Gross, G. and Ingjatic, D. (2006). Multicast Extensions to the Security Architecture for the Internet

Protocol, work in progress, draft-ietf-msec-IPSec-extensions-04.txt.

Weiser, M. (1991). The computer for the 21st century. Scientific American, 265(3):66–75.

Weiser, M. (1991). The computer for the 21st century. *Scientific American, 265*(3), 94-104.

Weiser, M. (1993). Hot topics-ubiquitous computing, Computer 26 (10) 71–72.

Weiser, M. (1993). Some computer science issues in ubiquitous computing. Communications of the ACM, 36(7):75–84.

Weiser, M. (1996). "Open House", Web magazine of the Interactive Telecommunications Program of New York University. Appeared in March, 1996 ITP, Review 2.0. http://www.itp.tsoa.nyu.edu/~review/

White, G. P., & Zakharov, Y. V. (2007). Data communications to trains from high-altitude platforms. *IEEE Transactions on Vehicular Technology*, 56(4), 2253-2266.

Widrow, B., & Hoff, M.E. (1960). *Adaptive Switching Circuits*, IRE WESCON Convention Record, Pt. 4.

Wi-Fi Alliance. Retrieved from www.wi-fi.com

Willassen, S. Y. (1998). A method for implementing Mobile Station Location in GSM. Retrieved September 16, 2005, from http://www.willassen.no/msl/node1.html.

Wilson, S.K., & Cioffi, J.M. (1993). *Equalisation Techniques for Direct Sequence Code-Division Multiple Access Systems in Multipath Channels*, IEEE International Symposium on Information Theory, San Antonio (US).

WINNER project. Information available at https://www.ist-winner.org/

Winter, R., Schiller, J. H., Nikaein, N., & Bonnet, C. (2006). CrossTalk: cross-layer decision support based on global knowledge. *IEEE Communications Magazine*, 44(1), 93 – 99.

Wireless World Research Forum (2003). 'I-centric Communications – Basic Terminology', Version 1.0, Working

Group 2: Service Architectures for the Wireless World, Whitepaper.

Wohlwend, H. (2001). An E-Factory Vision. 2nd European Advanced Equipment Control/Advance Process Control Conf., April 18-20.

Wolfstetter, E. (1996). Auctions: An Introduction. Journal of Economic Surveys, 10(4), 367-420.

Wong, C.C. & Hiew, P.L. (2005). Correlations between factors affecting the diffusion of mobile entertainment in Malaysia. Proceedings of the 7th international conference on Electronic commerce ICEC '05. ACM Press

Woodard, J., & Hanzo, L. (2000). *Comparative study of turbo decoding techniques: An overview.* IEEE Transactions on Vehicular Technology, Vol. 49, No. 6, 2208-2233.

World Bank (2004), E *government: a definition of e-government. Retrieved February 3, 2005 from World Bank Web site: www.worldbank.org

World Wide Web Consortium Recommendation (W3C), (2001). Web Service Description Language (WSDL) 1.1, March. 2001. http://www.w3.org/TR/wsdl

World Wide Web Consortium Recommendation (W3C), (2006). Extensible Markup Language (XML) 1.0 (fourth edition), Sep. 2006. http://www.w3.org/TR/REC-xml

World Wide Web Consortium Recommendation (W3C), (2007). Simple Object Access Protocol (SOAP) version 1.2 Part 1: Messaging Framework (Second Edition), April 2007. http://www.w3.org/TR/soap12-part1/

Wu, J. C.-S., Cheng, C.-W., Huang, N.-F., & Ma, G.-K. (2001). Intelligent Handoff for Mobile Wireless Internet. *ACM/Kluwer Mobile Networks and Applications (MONET)*, 6(1), 69 – 79.

Wu, K., Chen, S.K., Yu, P. S. (2005). Efficient Processing of Continual Range Queries for Location-Aware Mobile Services. Information Systems Frontiers, 7(4/5), 435-448.

Xerox Paul Alto Research: http://www.ubiq.com

Xia, Y., Bae, H. Y, (2007). General Platform of Location Based Services in Ubiquitous Environment, Paper presented at the International Conference on Multimedia and Ubiquitous Engineering (MUE'07).

Xiao, Y. (2005). Energy Saving Mechanism in the IEEE 802.16e Wireless MAN", *IEEE Communication Letters*, Vol. 9, No. 7.

Xie, Y. and Fang, Y. (2000). "A General Statistical Channel Model for Mobile Satellite Systems," IEEE Trans. Veh. Technol., vol. 49, no. 3, pp. 744-752, May.

Xie, Y. and Fang, Y. (2000). "A General Statistical Channel Model for Mobile Satellite Systems," IEEE Trans. Vehicular Technol., 49, 744–752.

Xylomenos, G., Polyzos, G. C., Mahonen, P., & Saaranen, M. (2001). TCP performance issues over wireless links. *IEEE Communications Magazine*, 39(4), 52 – 58.

Yang, C.F., Wu, B.C., and Ko, C.J. (1998). A Ray-Tracing Method for Modeling Indoor Wave Propagation and Penetration, *IEEE Transactions on Antennas and Propagation*, Vol. 46, No. 6, pp. 907-919.

Yang, G., Li, S., Lee, J.F., and Pahlavan, K. (1993). "Computer simulation of indoor radio propagation, *IEEE 1993 International Symposium on Personal, Indoor and Mobile Radio Communication*, Yokohama, Japan.

Yang, G., Pahlavan, K., and Lee, J.F. (1993). A 3D propagation model with polarization characteristics in indoor radio channels, *Proceedings of the 1993 IEEE GLOBECOM*, Vol. 2, pp. 1252-1256, Houston, USA.

Yang, Z., Chai, S., Zhou, Z. & Zhou, N., (2005). Development and validation of an instrument to measure user perceived service quality of information presenting Web portals. Information and Management, 42.

Yau, S., Karim, F., Wang, Y., Wang, B. & Gupta, S.K.S. (2002). Reconfigurable context-sensitive middleware for pervasive computing", IEEE Pervasive Computing, 1(3), July-September 2002, IEEE Computer Society Press, pp. 33-40.

Yee, K.S. (1966). Numerical solution of initial boundary value problems involving Maxwell's equations in isotropic media, *IEEE Transactions on Antennas and Propagation*, Vol. AP-14, pp. 302-307.

Yee, M. L., Luo, B., Ong, L. C., Zhou, M. T., Shao, Z., Fujise, M. (2006). *Performance and noise analysis of VCSEL RoF using spherical ended multimode fiber coupling.* 6th international conference on ITS telecommunications.

Yegani, P., and McGillem, C.D. (1991). A statistical model for the factory radio channel, *IEEE Transactions on Communications*, Vol. 39, pp. 1445-1454.

Yeh, E. M., & Berry, R (2005). Throughput optimal control of cooperative relay networks. In Proc. *International Symposium on Information Theory (ISIT).* pp.1206-1210. IEEE.

Yeh, E. M., & Cohen, S. A. (2003). "Throughput and delay optimal resource allocation in multiaccess fading channels," in *Proc. Int. Symp. Information Theory*, Yokohama, Japan, 2003, p. 245.

Yildiz, M. (2007). E-government Research: Reviewing the Literature, Limitations, and Ways Forward. Government Information Quarterly, Vol. 24, pp. 646-665.

York, R.A., Liao P., & Lynch, J.J. (1994). Oscillator array dynamics with broadband N-port coupling networks. *IEEE Transactions on Microwave Theory and Techniques*, 42(11), 2040–2042.

Yoshihara N. (1998). *Low-loss, high-bandwidth fluorinated POF for visible to 1.3-mm wavelength.* Optic. Fiber Commun. Conf. (OFC'98), San Jose, CA, Feb. 1998, Paper ThM4.

Youn, W.S., & Un, C.K. (1994). Robust adaptive beamforming based on the eigenstructure method, *IEEE Transactions on Signal Processing*, 42(6), 1543–1547.

Youssef, N., Wang, C. X., Patzold, M., Jaafar, I. and Tabbane, S. (2004). "On the Statistical Properties of Generalized Rice Multipath Fading Channels," Vehicular Technology Conference. VTC 2004-Spring. 2004 IEEE 59th.

Youssef, Neji, Wang, Cheng-Xiang and Patzold, Matthias 2005). "A Study on the Second Order Statistics of Nakagami-Hoyt Mobile Fading Channels simulation models for mobile fading channels," IEEE Trans. Veh. Technol., vol. 54, no. 4, pp. 1259–1265.

Yuen, R., & Fernando, X. N., (2005). Analysis of Sub-Carrier Multiplexed Radio Over Fiber Link for the Simultaneous Support of WLAN and WCDMA Systems. *Wireless Personal Communications.* 33,1-20.

Zaharakis I. D. and Kameas A. (2008). Engineering Emergent Ecologies of Interacting Artefacts". In Lumsden, J. (Ed.) *Handbook of Research on User Interface Design and Evaluation for Mobile Technology*, IGI Global.

Zaharakis, I. D. and Kameas A. (2006). Emergent Phenomena in AmI Spaces. *The EASST (European Association of Software Science and Technology) Newsletter, 2006-12* 82-96.

Zaremski, A.M. & Wing, J.M. (1995). Signature matching: a tool for using software libraries. ACM Transactions on Software Engineering and Methodology 4 (2), 146–170.

Zeithaml, V.A. & Bitner, M.J. *Service marketing: Integrating customer focus across the firm.* Boston: McGraw-Hill Companies, 2000.Hong D. and Rappaport S.S.: "Traffic model and performance analysis for cellular mobile radio telephone systems with prioritized and non prioritized handover procedures" IEEE Trans. on Vehicular Technology, vol. VT-35, pp.77-91, 1985.

Zetterberg, P. (1995). *Mobile Communication with Base Station Antenna Arrays: Propagation Modeling and System Capacity.* Master Thesis, Royal Institute of Technology, Stockholm, Sweden.

Zetterberg, P., Espensen, P.L., and Mogensen, P. (1996). Propagation, beamsteering and uplink combining algorithms for cellular systems, *Proceedings of the 1996 ACTS Mobile Communications Summit*, pp. 500-509, Granada, Spain.

Zhang, B., Huang, C., & Devetsikiotis, M. (2006). Simulated Annealing Based Bandwidth Reservation for QoS Routing. *In proceedings of IEEE ICC 2006*, Istanbul.

Zhang, W. (1997). A Wide-Band Propagation Model Based on UTD for Cellular Mobile Radio Communications, *IEEE Transactions on Antennas and Propagation*, Vol. 45, No. 11, pp. 1669-1678.

Zhang, Y., Qui, X., Meng, L. (2006). A Web services-based dynamically cooperative network management architecture. IEEE Conference in Communications and Networking, Oct. 2006.

Zhou, Z., McKinley, P. K., & Sadjadi, S. M. (2004). On quality-of-service and energy consumption tradeoffs in FEC-encoded audio streaming. *IEEE International Workshop on Quality of Service*, 161 – 170.

Zhu, F., Mutka, M.W. & Ni, L.M. (2005). Service discovery in pervasive computing environments. Pervasive Computing, IEEE 4 (4), 81–90.

Zhu, H., Li, M., Chlamtac, I., & Prabhakaran, B. (2004). A survey of quality of service in IEEE 802.11 networks. *IEEE Wireless Communications*, 11(4), 6 – 14.

Zhu, L., & Zhu, J. (2000). Signal-strength-based cellular location using dynamic window-width and double-averaging algorithm. In *Proceedings of the 52nd IEEE Vehicular Technology Conference, Vol. 6*, (pp. 2992-2997). USA: Boston.

Zorzi, M., & Rao, R. R. (2001). Energy efficiency of TCP in a local wireless environment. *Mobile Networks and Applications*, 6(3), 265 – 278.

Zuboff, S. (1988). In the age of the smart machine: The future of work and power. New York: Basic Books.

About the Contributors

Stavros A. Kotsopoulos was born in Argos-Argolidos (Greece) in the year 1952. He received his B.Sc. in Physics in the year 1975 from the Aristotle University of Thessaloniki.(Greece), and in the year 1984 got his Diploma in Electrical and Computer Engineering from the University of Patras (Greece). He did his postgraduate studies in the University of Bradford (United Kingdom), and he is an M.Phil and Ph.D. holder since 1978 and 1985 correspondingly. He is a member of the academic staff of the Department of Electrical and Computer Engineering of the University of Patras and holds the position of Professor. Since 2004, is the Director of the Wireless Telecommunications Laboratory (WTL) and develops his professional life teaching and doing research in the scientific area of Telecommunications, with interest in cellular mobile communications, Wireless Network Technologies, interference, satellite communications, telematics applications, communication services and antennae design. Moreover he is the (co)author of the book titled "mobile telephony". He has offered consultant services to various Telecom Organizations and Bodies in Greece and he is member of various Technical Committees. The research activity is documented by more than 200 publications in scientific journals and proceedings of International Conferences. Professor Kotsopoulos has been the leader of several European and many National research projects. Finally, he is member of the Greek Physicists Society and member of the Technical Chamber of Greece.

Konstantinos G. Ioannou. Dr. Konstantinos G. Ioannou was born in Patras, Greece, in 1975. He received the Diploma and the PhD in Electrical and Computer Engineering in 1998 and 2004, respectively, from the Polytechnic School of the University of Patras. His dissertation, elaborated at the Wireless Telecommunications Laboratory of the Department of Electrical and Computer Engineers, dealt with Channel Assignment Techniques, Handover Procedures, Traffic Modeling and Call Admission Policies in 2G, 3G Mobile Systems and Security Mobile Systems. During his Postgraduate Studies, he participated in many European and National Research Projects. Since the September of 2006, he is working as Network Engineer in Ministry of Interior of Greece and as a Post Doctor in Wireless Telecommunication Laboratory in Department of Electrical and Computer Engineering in University of Patras. During the last 2 years, he belonged also to the Technical Consultants Team of the Ministry of Public Order, regarding the C4I Olympic Security System, involved, among others, with TETRA and AVL subsystems. His scientific interests include Mobile and Satellite Communications, Wired and Wireless Networks, Handover and Channel Assignment Techniques and Communication Services. A lot of publications in scientific journals and conference proceedings - 27 and 41, respectively – and 3 chapters in books, document his research activity. Konstantinos Ioannou is a member of the Technical Chamber of Greece (TEE).

* * *

Spyros Angelopoulos was born in 1981 at the Heraklio of Crete in Greece. He graduated from the Department of Production Engineering and Management of the Technical University of Crete. He followed this by a master's in business administration in the same University. His work during his studies dealt with marketing as well as data analysis and forecasting. In general, his research allowed for a series of journal and conference publications while in parallel he enriched his professional skills by working as a Web programmer. His work now concentrates on e-governmet. He has general research interests that deal with e-business, e-democracy, as well as the semantic Web.

Copyright © 2009, IGI Global, distributing in print or electronic forms without written permission of IGI Global is prohibited.

Eduard Babulak. Professor Eduard Babulak is international scholar, researcher, consultant, educator, professional engineer and polyglot with more than twenty five years of teaching experience and industrial experience as a professional engineer and consultant. He currently holds visiting professorships in information technology in Vancouver, BC, Canada and works as expert-evaluator for the European Commission in Brussels. He is registered Panelist with the American Society for Engineering Education Engineering (ASEE) for the National Science Foundation (NSF) Graduate Research Fellowship Program (GRFP), the National Defense Science and Engineering Graduate (NDSEG) Program, and the Science, Mathematics, and Research for Transformation Defense Scholarship for Service (SMART) Program.Prof. Babulak worked as full professor and head of MIS Department in Cyprus, Visiting professor in Telematics Engineering, Informatics and Computing at the Universities in Spain, Czech Republic and Rimouski, Quebec, Canada. In the past, he worked as senior lecturer of computing in UK, associate professor of computer science in California and lecturer of computer engineering in Pennsylvania, USA. He also worked as university lecture of mathematics, teaching assistant electrical and computer engineering and computing science in Canada, Germany, Austria as well as, college instructor in Czechoslovakia. Prof. Babulak successfully completed his postdoctoral habilitation work in the Czech Republic. His academic and engineering work was recognized internationally by the Engineering Council in UK, European Federation of Engineers and credited by the Ontario Society of Professional Engineers in Canada. His research interests are in future networks and ubiquitous computing and qos, e-health, it, mis, applied informatics in transportation, e-manufacturing, human centric computing, e-learning, automation and applied mathematics. Professor Babulak speaks 14 languages, was nominated fellow of the British Computer Society (BCS) and the Association of Computer Machinery (ACM). He is a senior member of IEEE and ACM, corporate member of the Institution of Engineering Technology, Professional member of British Computer Society (BCS), ACM, American Society for Engineering Education (ASEE), American Mathematical Association (AMA) and Mathematical Society of America (AMS). Professor Babulak's biography was selected for citation in the *Cambridge Blue Book* 2005, the *Cambridge Index of Biographies* 2004-2005, the *Dictionary of International Biography* 2004, published by the *Cambridge Centre of International Biographies*, *Who's Who in the Science and Engineering* 2003, 2005-2006, 2008-2009, *Who's is Who in the Industry and Finance* 2004-2005, 2006-2007 and in the *Who's, Who in the World* 2003, 2004, 2006-2007, 2008-2009, Who's Who in America 2008.

Konstantinos Birkos was born in Athens, Greece, in 1982. He received his engineering diploma from the Department of Electrical and Computer Engineering of the University of Patras in 2006. He is currently working towards his PhD in the Wireless Telecommunication Laboratory of the same institution. His main research interests include high altitude stratospheric platforms, teletraffic analysis and QoS of wireless IP networks, 3G and beyond and IP convergence.

Peter Brida was born in Bojnice, Slovakia, in 1979. He received the Ing. degree in telecommunications and the PhD degree in mobile radio communications from the University of Zilina, Slovakia, in 2002 and 2006, respectively. His doctoral work was in the area of the mobile positioning. He currently works in Department of Telecommunications at the University of Zilina. His research interests include wireless positioning in cellular, ad hoc networks and satellite navigation systems. **Christos N. Capsalis** was born in Nafplion, Greece, in 1956. He received the Diploma in Electrical and Mechanical Engineering from the NTUA in 1979 and the Diploma in Economics from the University of Athens in 1983. He obtained the PhD. degree in Electrical Engineering from NTUA in 1985. He is currently a Professor with the ECE department of NTUA. His current scientific activity concerns satellite and mobile communications, antenna theory and design, and electromagnetic compatibility.

Peter Cepel was born in Martin, Slovakia, in 1979. He received the Ing. degree in telecommunications and the PhD. degree in mobile radio communications from the University of Zilina, Slovakia in 2003 and 2007, respectively. His doctoral work was in the area of MIMO systems and smart antennas. His research interests include proposal of the hybrid adaptive antenna system. He is currently working for Siemens Program and System Engineering s.r.o. in Zilina, Slovakia.

Costas Chaikalis was born in Athens, Greece, on March 1973. He received the BSc. degree in electrical engineering in 1995 from Technological Educational Institute of Lamia, Greece. He also received the MSc and PhD. degrees from Department of Electronics and Telecommunications, University of Bradford, Bradford, UK in 1999 and 2003, respectively. During his doctoral studies he worked as a research assistant for Mobile Virtual Center of Excellence (Mobile VCE), Terminals Group, UK. His research interests are in all areas of mobile communications but especially in forward error correction coding, reconfigurable (software radio) architectures, cross layer architectures and DSP applications.

Michael Devetsikiotis received the diploma degree in electrical engineering from the Aristotle University of Thessaloniki, Greece, in 1988, and the MSc and PhD degrees in electrical engineering from North Carolina State University, Raleigh, in 1990 and 1993, respectively. In October 1993 he joined the Broadband Networks Laboratory at Carleton University, Ottawa, Canada, as a research associate. He became an adjunct professor in the Systems and Computer Engineering Department, Carleton University, in 1995, an assistant professor in 1996 and an associate professor in 1998. Since November 2000 he has been with the Department of Electrical and Computer Engineering, North Carolina State University, Raleigh, where he has been a Professor since 2006. His research work has been in the areas of telecommunication systems modeling, performance evaluation, and efficient simulation; traffic characterization and management; and optimization techniques applied to the analysis and design of communication systems. His present focus is on the performance of information networks as they become larger in size, and more complex in topology and workload.

Jan Duha was born in Slovakia, in 1940. He received the Ing. degree in electrical engineering from Moscow Electrical Institute for Communications, Russia and the PhD degree in telecommunications from the University of Zilina, Slovakia, in 1963 and 1982, respectively. From 1987 he is the associate professors at the Department Telecommunications in University of Zilina. His research interest includes mobile networks, radio relay networks and television technology.

Dimitrios M. Emiris. Dr. Dimitrios M. Emiris (emiris@unipi.gr) is an assistant professor at the Department of Industrial Management and Technology, University of Piraeus, Greece. He was born in Athens in 1965. He obtained the Diploma in electrical engineering from the National Technical University of Athens, in 1987. He obtained the MSc and the PhD, in 1988 and 1991, respectively, from the Department of Electrical Engineering, University of Rochester. From 1997 to 2001 he served as an Assistant Professor of the Production Systems Division at the Department of Production Engineering and Management, of the Technical University of Crete. He has published over 100 articles in international journals and conferences. He is the author of two books in robotics and he has first translated and published the *Guide to the Project Management Body of Knowledge of the Project Management Institute*, in Greek. He has taught over 80 graduate and undergraduate semester courses in robotics, project management and ERP. His research interests lie in the areas of robotics and computational intelligence, as well as project and production management.

Apostolos Georgiadis was born in Thessaloniki, Greece. He received the BS degree in physics and the MS degree in telecommunications from the Aristotle University of Thessaloniki, Greece, in 1993 and 1996, respectively. He received the PhD degree in electrical engineering from the University of Massachusetts, Amherst, in 2002.

Dr. Georgiadis is a senior research associate at the Centre Tecnològic de Telecomunicacions de Catalunya (CTTC), Barcelona, Spain, in the area of communication subsystems. His research interests include nonlinear microwave circuit design, active antenna arrays and wireless systems.

Fabrizio Granelli received the Laurea (MSc) degree in electronic engineering, in 1997, with a thesis on video coding, awarded with the TELECOM Italy prize, and the PhD. in telecommunications, in 2001, both from the University of Genoa, Italy. Since 2000 he is carrying on his teaching activity as assistant professor in telecommunications at the Department of Information and Communication Technology – University of Trento (Italy), where he coordinates the research and didactic activities in networking. He is author or co-author of more than 70 papers published in international journals, books and conferences. Dr. Granelli is guest-editor of *ACM/Springer*

Journal on Mobile Networks and Applications, special issues on "WLAN Optimization at the MAC and Network Levels" and "Ultra Wide Band for Sensor Networks". Dr. Granelli was chair or co-chair of several international events, including CAMAD'04, CAMAD'06, Globecom 2007 Symposium on "Performance Modeling, QoS and Reliability" and Globecom 2008 Symposium on "Communications QoS, Reliability and Performance Modeling". He is currently senior member of IEEE and vice-chair of the IEEE ComSoc Technical Committee on Communication Systems Integration and Modeling (CSIM).

Y. Fun Hu is professor of wireless communications engineering in the School of Engineering, Design and Technology (EDT) at the University of Bradford, where she leads the Mobile and Wireless Technologies Group of the Mobile and Satellite Communications Research Centre (MSCRC). Prof. Hu has extensive experience in the development of mobile and wireless communications, including wireless sensor networks and technologies, through participation in projects funded by the EC, ESA, EPSRC, DTI, the local council and industries. She was UK delegate of the EU COST 253, COST 256, and COST 272 Actions. She was an executive member of the IEE Electronics and Communications Divisions Professional Network Group on Satellite Systems and Applications (2000-2002) and has been a member of the Technical Advisory Panel of the same Professional Network Group since 2002. In November 2007, Prof. Hu was appointed as the Yorkshire Forward Chair in Wireless Communications Engineering, sponsored by the regional development agency.

Anthony Ioannidis. Dr. Anthony Ioannidis is an assistant professor of management at the Department of Business Administration, Athens University of Economics and Business, Greece. He has previously taught at the University of Patras, Greece, University of La Verne California, Athens Campus, and Baruch College, The City University of New York. He holds a BS from the University of Athens, Greece, and, an MBA, an MPhil, and a PhD from Baruch College, The City University of New York. He also possesses working experience as management consultant with leading consultancy firms in the United States and Greece, in the areas telecommunications, media and technology. His current research interests include strategy formation, organizational design, entrepreneurship, and public-private partnerships.

Athanasios Ioannou. Dr. Athanasios G. Ioannou was born in K. Vasiliki - Nafpaktias (Greece) in the year 1969. He received his B.Sc. in Physics in the year 1991 from the University of Patras. He is a MSc and PhD holder since 1999 and 1996 correspondingly. He did his postgraduate studies in the University of Patras in Greece. Currently he is Telecom Engineer in Hellenic Organization of Telecommunications SA. He develops his professional life working as telecom engineer in OTE, teaching in TEI of Mesologgi and doing research at the Laboratory of Wireless Telecommunications (Univ. Of Patras), with interest in mobile communications, and communication services. The research activity is documented by more than 48 publications in scientific journals and proceedings of conferences. Dr. Athanasios Ioannou has been scientific member of several international and many national research projects. Finally, he is member of the Greek Physicists Society.

Achilles D. Kameas received his engineering diploma (1989) and his PhD (1995, in human-computer interaction) from the Department of Computer Engineering and Informatics, Univ. of Patras, Hellas. Since 2003, he is an Assistant Professor with the Hellenic Open University, where he teaches software design and engineering. He is also R&D manager with Research Academic Computer Technology Institute (CTI), where he is the head of Research Unit 3 (Applied Information Systems) and the founder of DAISy group (http://daisy.cti.gr). His research interests focus around the design of ubiquitous computing and ambient intelligence systems, Interaction models and the uses of ontologies. He is a member of ACM, IEEE CS and Hellenic AI Society.

Sotiris Karabetsos received the BS degree in Electrical and computer engineering from the National Technical University of Athens (NTUA), in 2004 and the MS degree in data communications from Brunel University of London, in 2003. He has also received the BS degree in electronic engineering from the Technological and Educational Institution of Athens (TEI of Athens), in 1999. He is currently working towards the PhD. degree in the area of speech processing and especially in speech synthesis at the National Technical University of Athens (NTUA). From 2003, he is with the Institute for Language and Speech Processing (ILSP). He is also with the

Technological and Educational Institution of Athens (TEI of Athens), Department of Electronics, as a teaching assistant in laboratory courses. He is author and co-author of papers in peer reviewed conferences in the areas of speech processing and communication.

Petros Karadimas was born in Tripolis Greece in 1977. He received the diploma of electrical and computer engineering from University of Patras-Greece in the year 2002. He is currently with the Wireless Telecommunications Laboratory of University of Patras-Greece completing his PhD His research interests concern among others statistical characterization of wireless channels, RF propagation, modeling of scattering mechanisms in wireless channels and microwave communications. He has participated in research projects concerning field measurements in the VHF and UHF frequency bands and as technical consultant during the design of "Athens Antenna Park" with the task of characterizing the wireless radio propagation environment and the design of antenna systems.

Panagiotis Kasimatis was born in Athens, Greece in 1976. He received his diploma in electrical and computer engineering, Polytechnic School of University of Patras, Greece in the Division of Telecommunications and Information Technology. After several years in the R&D of Mobile Switching Core in Siemens Networks AG, Munich, Germany, he is now working as a senior consultant for IBM Network Services & Solutions GmbH in System Verification SGSN, currently in Nokia Siemens Networks GmbH, Munich, Germany. His main interests are Mobile and Fixed Networks, as well as telecommunication implementations in further systems than the classic telecom ones.

Fotis Kitsios graduated from the Technical University of Crete with a diploma in Production and Management Engineering Department, he went on with a master's degree on organization and management and he did a PhD on innovation management with a specialization in services. He has worked as a consultant in several SME's in the field of marketing, management, in adopting innovation techniques and financing. He is also a certified auditor in quality management systems. He has been involved in the implementation and coordination of national and European research projects including: RKMnet, ISTOS, MetaForesight, Innoregio, Leonardo da Vinci, Ecos Ouverture, Adapt, Youthstart, Fair. He has lectured on marketing, management, market research, strategic planning, total quality management, production management, design technologies, data analysis and technological forecasting at Technical University of Crete, University of Macedonia and University of Central Greece, as adjunct professor and he has jointly supervised numerous masters and diploma theses. He also teaches in various public and private vocational training centers and institutions. His scientific research interests mainly focus on new service and product development, innovation measurement, marketing management and decision making.

Dzmitry Kliazovich received his master's degree from Belarusian State University of Informatics and Radio-electronics in 2002, and PhD degree from University of Trento, Italy, in 2006 both in telecommunication science. In 2005/2006 he was a visiting researcher at the Computer Science Department of the University of California at Los Angeles. Currently he is a research fellow at the University of Trento, Italy. He is an author of more than 20 research papers and active member of Technical Program Committee for ICC, GLOBECOM, and CAMAD conferences. His main research activities are in the field of networking with a focus on cross-layer design and next-generation networking.

Konstantinos S. Kotsopoulos received his MSc degree in mobile and satellite communications from School of Engineering, Design and Technology (EDT) at the University of Bradford in 2006. He is currently a researcher at the Mobile and Satellite Communications Research Centre (MSCRC) at the University of Bradford working towards his PhD in the field of network management. He holds an EPSRC PhD studentship. His main research interest areas include network management, distributed systems, SOA, Web services, performance monitoring of satellite communications.

Jiorgis Kritsotakis. Dr. Jiorgis Kritsotakis is an assistant professor of strategy and organization at the Hellenic American University. Jiorgis has previously lectured full time on strategy and organizational change at the Management School of the University of St Andrews, UK. As a visiting faculty, Jiorgis has also taught at the

University of Dundee and at the Athens University of Economics and business. Jiorgis' research focuses on the process of strategy formation in dynamic industries and the management of innovation and organizational transformation. Before joining the Hellenic American University, Jiorgis Kritsotakis was a senior strategy consultant at the London office of a global consultancy firm, specializing in the converging communications and high tech industries. Jiorgis' work was focused on enabling client organizations to achieve higher performance through the design and management of enterprise-wide organizational change. Jiorgis holds a BSc (marketing management), an MBA (innovation and new venture management) and a PhD in Strategic Management.

Jungwon Lee received his BS degree in electrical engineering from Seoul National University in 1999, and his MS and PhD degrees in electrical engineering from Stanford University in 2001 and 2005, respectively. From 2000 to 2003, he worked as an intern for National Semiconductor, Telcordia Technologies, and AT&T Shannon Labs Research and as a consultant for Ikanos Communications. Since 2003, he has worked for Marvell Semiconductor Inc., Santa Clara, California, where he is now a principal design engineer. His specific research interests are in wireless and wireline communication theory with emphasis on system design, transmission optimization, resource allocation, and estimation.

Pouwan Lei. Dr. Pouwan Lei is currently a lecturer in the school of Engineering, Design and Technology at the University of Bradford, United Kingdom. Previously she was a lecturer of business information systems at the University of Macao, China. She had several years working experience as system and network administrator with the responsibilities of formulating IT strategy, security and network management. Her research interests are service-oriented architecture based applications, semantic Web and intelligent agents. She holds a doctor of philosophy degree from the University of Sussex, United Kingdom.

Dimitris K. Lymberopoulos (M'95) was born in Tripolis, Greece, in 1956. He received the electrical engineering diploma and the PhD. degree from the University of Patras, Patras, Greece, in 1980 and 1988, respectively. He is currently an assistant professor in the Department of Electrical and Computer Engineering, University of Patras, where he lectures on digital communication systems, multimedia communications, and telemedicine services. Since 1982, he has been involved as a technical supervisor in various research programs funded by the Greek Government, European Union, Greek Telecommunications Organization, and major Greek telecommunication industries. He has authored or co-authored over 100 papers in international journals and conferences and over 100 technical papers and reports. His research interests include telephony, data transmission, ISDN networks, ATM transmission and switching technologies, broad-band communications, multimedia services, telemedicine applications, data management in medical applications, teleworking (telemedicine) development platforms, medical communication networks, cellular mobile radio communication systems, and radio interference problems. Prof. Lymberopoulos is a member of Technical Chamber of Greece and the Greek Society of Electrical and Mechanical Engineers.

Charis Marentakis (chmarent@unipi.gr) is a PhD candidate in the Department of Industrial Management & Technology of University of Piraeus, Greece. He was born in 1973 in Chania, Crete. He obtained a Diploma in Production Management Engineering from Technical University of Crete in 1996 and in 1997 received a Best Diploma Thesis Award from Technical Chamber of Greece. Since 1997 he worked as a senior logistics and ERP consultant for many consulting companies. He is currently working for an express logistics company as head of long-haul transportation and sorting network. He is an ERP instructor in the area of production planning in the logistics management MSc program at the University of Pireaus. He has published many articles in the area of logistics management. His current research interests include auction theory, e-commerce, Location-based services, logistics management and ERP systems.

Nikos Merlemis. Dr Nikos Merlemis, born in 1971, studied physics at the University of Patras, in Greece. Upon graduation in 1993 he obtained in 1995 an MSc in atomic and molecular Physics at the University of Crete and he started his doctorate research at the University of Crete, where he received his doctoral degree in 2002, writing his dissertation on a subject in the field of laser physics. In 1995, he was also employed by the Science and

Technology Park of Crete as a network administrator, IT consultant and project manager in several EU programs and he was a co-founder and R&D manager of DPS Ltd since 1999. Since 2003 he is an adjunct assistant professor at the general department of physics, chemistry and materials of the Technological Education Institute of Athens and an Instructor of the "Broadband & Wireless Networks" course for the MSc program "E-commerce" at the Technological Education Institute of Piraeus and he is also a researcher in the field of laser physics at the department of Physics of the University of Patras since 2004.

Spiros Mikroulis was born in Corfu, Greece, in 1973. He received the BS degree in physics in 1998, the MS degree in optoelectronics/microelectronics in 2001, from University of Crete, Greece and the PhD in optical communications in 2007 from the University of Athens. He worked in the Institute of Electronic Structure and Laser (IESL), Foundation of Research and Technology Hellas (FORTH) from 1999 to 2001 in growth and characterization of III-V compound semiconductors for optoelectronic applications. He was awarded for the best research work of post-graduate student in the 1st conference of Microelectronics Microsystems and Nanotechnology in Greece (MMN 2000) organized by the National Center for Scientific Research, Demokritos, (NCFSR-Demokritos). Currently, he is working as a research associate in the Optical Communications group, Department of Informatics and Telecommunications, University of Athens, a teaching associate in the Electronics department, Technological Educational Institute (TEI) of Athens and a research associate in RDTL. He is the author of about 25 papers in selected journals and conferences and he has been 38 times cited. His present research interests are semiconductor microring devices for all-optical signal processing, microring lasers for application in WDM networks, angular velocity sensors, and radio over fiber (RoF) systems for applications in broadband communication services.

Stelios A. Mitilineos was born in Athens, Greece, in 1977. He received the diploma in electrical and computer engineering (ECE) from the National Technical University of Athens, Greece, (NTUA) in October 2001, and the PhD degree in ECE from the same university in December 2006. His research interests are in the areas of antennas and propagation, smart antennas and mobile communications, microwave components and position location.

Athanase Nassiopoulos received the BS degree in Physics from the University of Athens, Greece in 1976 and the MS and PhD degrees from the University of Paris XI, Orsay, France, in 1977 and 1979, respectively.

He was a research engineer with Thomson - CSF, Paris France, until 1984. From 1984 to 1986, he was R&D Manager of the company CSEE, Paris, and Technical Director of TALCO Hellas Electronics, Athens, from 1987 to 1992. He then moved to M&S Hourdakis Electronics SA, Greece as R&D and product manager. Since 1997 he is a professor in the Department of Electronics of the Technological Educational Institute (TEI) of Athens and Head of the Research and Development Telecommunications Laboratory (RDTL). He is an author or coauthor of several publications in journals, reviews and conference proceedings and also an author of 3 books. He coordinates an important number of EU-funded and national projects.

Tzortzatos Panagiotis is currently an undergraduate student of the Technical University of Crete. From the very first years of his studies, he has been interested in new service development as well as innovation. This had lead him to take advantage of the opportunity offered by the university he is studying in, to be involved in projects concentrated in his favorite subjects and contribute to research.

Ioannis Papapanagiotou has graduated from the Electrical and Computer Engineering School of University of Patras, Greece. He is now enrolled in the ECE Department of North Carolina State University (NCSU). He is currently working on energy consumption, quality of service (QoS), and mobility in ad hoc and mesh networks based on the WiFi (IEEE 802.11) and WiMAX (IEEE 802.16) standards.

Anastasios Papazafeiropoulos received his BSc in physics in 2003 and MSc in electronics and computer science in 2005 both from University of Patras, Patras, Greece. He is currently working as a PhD student in the field of characterization and statistical modelling of the propagation channel. He also works as a professor in high school. Previously he worked as a research assistant at Intracom where he made his master thesis. His current research interests include narrowband fading, diversity techniques and MIMO channels.

Georgios Stavrou Paschos (IEEE m99) was born in Athens, Greece, in 1978. He received his diploma in electrical and computer engineering, Polytechnic School of Aristotle University of Thessaloniki (2002) and the PhD. degree in quality of service in wireless networks in the School of Electrical and Computer Engineering in the University of Patras (2006), both in Greece. He is a researcher in the National Research Institute of Finland, VTT, under an ERCIM fellowship for postdoctoral studies. His main interests are Performance Analysis of Wireless Networks and Network Information Theory.

Prashant Pillai. Dr Prashant Pillai received his BSc in electronics in 2000 and MSc in Informatics in 2002 both from University of Delhi, Delhi, India and his PhD in the field of network security at University of Bradford, Bradford, United Kingdom in 2007. He is currently working as a lecturer in electrical and electronic engineering in the School of Engineering, Design and Technology at the University of Bradford. He takes lectures in the areas of network security, multicast communication, object oriented programming and wireless sensor networks. Previously he worked as a research assistant at the University of Bradford from 2002 to 2007 and was involved in several projects like the WirelessCabin Project funded under the EU FP5 IST framework, the SatNEx project funded under the Network of Excellence mechanism in the EU FP6 IST Framework. His current research interests include AAA and security protocols, VoIP, DVB based systems and wireless sensor networks. Dr Pillai is a member of IET and IEEE.

Carles Fernández Prades (Barcelona, 1976) received the MS and PhD (cum-laude) in electrical engineering from the Universitat Politècnica de Catalunya (UPC) in 2001 and 2006 respectively. In 2001 he joined the Department of Signal Theory and Communication at UPC as a research assistant. He was Teaching Assistant of Analog and Digital Communications (2001-2005).

In May 2006 he joined the Centre Tecnològic de Telecomunicacions de Catalunya (CTTC), where he currently holds a position as a Research Associate and the direction of the communications subsystems area. His primary areas of interest include signal processing, estimation theory, navigation systems and RF front-ends.

Felip Riera-Palou received the MS degree in computer engineering from the University of the Balearic Islands (UIB), (Palma, Mallorca, Spain) in 1997, the MSc and PhD degrees in communication engineering from the University of Bradford (UK) in 1998 and 2002, respectively, and the MSc degree in statistics from the University of Sheffield (UK) in 2006. From May 2002 to March 2005, he was with Philips Research Laboratories (Eindhoven, The Netherlands) first as a postdoctoral fellow (Marie Curie program, European Union) and later as a member of technical staff. In April 2005 he became a research associate (Ramon y Cajal program, Spanish Government) in the Mobile Communications Group of the Department of Mathematics and Informatics at UIB where he is researching techniques suitable for future wireless systems.

Stelios C. A. Thomopoulos received the diploma in electrical and mechanical engineering from NTUA in July 1978, and the MSc and PhD degrees in electrical engineering from the State University of New York, in 1981 in 1983 respectively. He was with the faculty of EE at Penn State Univ. (1989-1996) and SIU (1983-1989). He served as president & CEO of Intelnet Inc. (1994-1999). He was elected and served as director of the Institute of Informatics and Telecommunications, National Center of Scientific Research "Demokritos", Greece (IIT-NCSR) (1998-2003), where he is currently director of research at the Integrated Systems Laboratory. Since 2006 he is serving as director with the IIT, NCSR, Greece. His main research interests lie within the areas of decision theory, data fusion, data networks, location based systems, biometrics and nonlinear and adaptive signal processing. Dr. Thomopoulos holds U.S. Patent No. **5,978,495**.

Dimitris Toumpakaris received his diploma in electrical and computer engineering from the National Technical University of Athens, Greece in 1997, and his MS and PhD degrees in Electrical Engineering from Stanford University in 1999 and 2003, respectively. He was a senior design engineer in Marvell Semiconductor Inc., Santa Clara, California from 2003 to 2006. He has also worked as an intern for Bell-Labs, CERN and France Télécom, and as a consultant for Ikanos Communications and Marvell Semiconductor Inc. He is currently an assistant professor in the Wireless Telecommunications Laboratory, Department of Electrical & Computer Engineering,

University of Patras, Greece. Dr. Toumpakaris research interests include information theory with emphasis on multi-user communications systems, digital communication, synchronization and estimation, and cross-layer optimization. He is a member of the IEEE and of the Technical Chamber of Greece.

Dimitra Varla was born in Sparta, Greece in 1981. She received her diploma in electrical and computer engineering in National Technical University of Athens (NTUA) in 2004. She worked for three years as a software engineer in the R&D department of Mobile Switching Core Network in Siemens AE, in Munich, Germany, and in Athens, Greece. She is now working as experienced system engineer in the Customer Support section of Ericsson Services for Greece, Cyprus, Albania and Malta. She is working in the GPRS core network; she is mainly interested in packet-switched telecom networks and also in the evolution of the traditional networks towards an all-IP convergence, in terms of development, analysis and deployment.

John Zannetopoulos, born at Rhodes 1947, married with two children. Studies : (a) degree in civil engineering (1971, National Technical University of Athens), (b) degree in informatics (1980, Universite des Sceances Sociales, Grenoble, France). Currently head of the General Directorate of Development Projects of the Hellenic Ministry of the Interior. Former head of the directorate of informatics (1987-2007)in the same ministry. Between 1980 and 1987 I served as an analyst programmer at the directorate of Elections of the same ministry. I have been a trainer in IT issues for the National Education Centre of Public Administration (NCPA). During the last 27 years I participated in many steering committees and task forces for many major governmental projects in the field of IT (i.e, one stop shops, national registration scheme, residence cards for third countries nationals, IT projects for local governments, national electoral rolls, etc). Also I participated as an expert / national representative in committees of the Council of Europe (e-voting, e-democracy) and the European Union.

Dimitrios Zevgolis. Dr Dimitrios Zevgolis was born in Athens in 1951. He studied physics at the Aristotle University of Thessaloniki (Greece) and received his doctoral degree in 1981 (Kaiserslautern, Germany). He was assistant professor at the University of Crete, visiting professor at the Technical University of Zurich (ETH), and associate professor at the University of Patras. Since 2006 he is Professor at the Hellenic Open University. His scientific interests are focused on the field of laser physics and optical technologies.

Constantin Zopounidis is professor of financial management and operations research, at the Department of Production Engineering and Management at Technical University of Crete (Greece). He is editor-in-chief in the following journals: *Operational Research: An International Journal* (Springer), *The Journal of Financial Decision Making* (Klidarithmos) and *The Journal of Computation Optimization in Economics and Finance* (Nova Publishers). He is also associate editor in *New Mathematics and Natural Computation* (World Scientific, Optimization Letters (Springer), *International Journal of Banking, Accounting and Finance* (Inderscience) και *European Journal of Operational Research* (Elsevier). In recognition of his scientific work, his research has been awarded and among all he has been attributed in 1996, the Gold Medal and diploma of social and human sciences from the MOISIL International Foundation, for his research in multicriteria intelligent decision support systems and their application to the scientific world of financial management and credit risk assessment, and in 2000, the Best Interdisciplinary Research Paper Award, from the Decision Sciences Institute. He has published 50 books in international publishing companies and more than 400 papers are appearing in international scientific journals on finance, accounting and operations research, fields that his research interests fall into. He has accomplished many lectures as visiting professor in many European universities.

Index

Copyright © 2009, IGI Global, distributing in print or electronic forms without written permission of IGI Global is prohibited.

U

ubiquitous computing 428, 434, 438, 439, 440, 442, 444, 508, 509, 520, 526, 529, 532, 544, 546, 561
unified modeling language (UML) 489
unified modelling language (UML) 144, 150
universal description discovery and integration (UDDI) 173
universal mobile telecommunications system (UMTS) 151, 221, 249, 272, 533
universal personal number (UPN) 151
unlicensed mobile access (UMA) 261, 269
uplink (UL) 98, 196, 199, 220, 530
user datagram protocol (UDP) 221
user network interface (UNI) 138, 150

V

very high speed digital subscriber line (VDSL) 151
video on demand (VoD) 140, 151
virtual private network (VPN) 151
visitor location register (VLR) 222
voice over IP (VOIP) 177, 196, 222
voice over WLAN (VoWLAN) 196

W

wavelength division multiplexing 68, 79, 103, 151
wavelength division multiplexing (WDM) 68, 79, 103, 151
web portal 426
weighted proximity positioning (WEP) 252
wide-sense stationary (WSS) 413
wire equivalent protocol (WEP) 196
wireless application protocol (WAP) 151
wireless communication 19, 20, 24, 101, 129, 522, 531, 552, 566
wireless fidelity (Wi-Fi) 196, 222
wireless local area network (WLAN) 4, 8, 66, 196, 222
wireless word research forum (WWRF) 145, 151
worldwide interoperability of microwave access (WiMax) 151
World Wide Web Consortium (W3C) 151